THE MIGHTY EIGHTH WAR DIARY

ROGER A. FREEMAN
WITH ALAN CROUCHMAN AND VIC MASLEN

ARMS AND
ARMOUR

RESEARCH SOURCES

8th AF Daily Intops Summaries, Maxwell AFB, Alabama, USA
8th AF Operational Folders: Public Record Office, London
USTTAF Weekly Intelligence Summaries: PRO, London
8th AF individual Squadron, Group, Wing, Division and HQ records: Maxwell AFB
Luftwaffe Quartermaster-General Returns: Imperial War Museum, London
British ROC (Royal Observer Corps), Police, Civil Defence and Lifeboat Service records

SELECT BIBLIOGRAPHY

Army Air Forces in World War II: Caven & Cate
The Air Plan That Defeated Hitler: Major Gen Haywood Hansell
Combat Squadrons of the Air Force: Maurer Maurer
Confound and Destroy: Martin Streetly
Unofficial histories of various groups
Stars and Stripes: London edition
Nostalgic Notes: 94BG Association journal
The Buzz, West Drayton base paper, 1956: *He Gave Them Rules To Live By*: Col J. F. Watters
Richmond News Reader, 11 May 1943: *The General Goes Flying*

First published in the United Kingdom in 1981 by Jane's Publishing Company Limited. This revised edition published in 1990 by Arms and Armour Press, Villiers House, 41/47 Strand, London WC2N 5JE.

British Library Cataloguing in Publication Data
Freeman, Roger A. (Roger Anthony) *1928–*
The mighty eighth war diary. – 2nd rev. ed.
1. World War 2. Air operations by United States. Army Air Force. Air Force, 8th
I. Title
940.544973
ISBN 1-85409-071-2

Printed and bound in Great Britain by The Bath Press, Avon.

ACKNOWLEDGEMENTS

The compilation of this miscellany of 8th Air Force operations owes much to those who supplied me with information and material. While most of the mission details were drawn from official records it was discovered, not for the first time, that these were frequently incomplete, sometimes misleading and even inaccurate, particularly in respect of losses. As it is, there are periods where extensive enquiries have failed to locate the required data for some specialised operations. The daily statistics required a prodigious research effort and the basic work of putting this into an acceptable form was performed by Alan Crouchman (to April 1944) and Vic Maslen (from May 1944). My grateful thanks go to both for the very many hours toil on this formidable undertaking.

Special acknowledgement for spending considerable time in assisting the author must go to Stewart Evans, Michael Gibson, Patricia Keen, Ian Mactaggart and Douglas Underwood. Authorities and enthusiasts, most generous with help in checking details and providing information, some more than others, will I hope, accept this my acknowledgement of gratitude to John Archer, Roley Andrews, Mike Bailey, Serge Blandin, Cliff Bishop, Stan Bishop, Patrick Burgess, Ron Buxton, Dana Bell, Quinton Bland, Allan Blue, David Crowe, Ken Everitt, John Foreman, Pat Carty, Charlie Gallagher, Mick Gibson, Werner Girbig, Chris Gotts, Steve Gotts, Cliff Hall, Peter Harris, Mike Harvey, Ken Harbour, Ian Hawkins, Harry Holmes, Roy Humphreys, Ron Mackay, Ian Maclachlan, Danny Morris, Tony North, Malcolm Osborn, Norman Ottaway, John Page, Keith Paul, Ken Ranson, Kenn Rust, Andy Saunders, Geoff Ward and Gerrit Zwanenburg.

To the veterans of the 8th Air Force who supplied information often vital to the narratives I express my sincere thanks, trusting that no offence is caused by listing them alphabetically without rank or other distinction: James Aicardi, John Blyth, Clinton Ball, Paul Burnett, Franklin Colby, Paul Chryst, Urban Drew, William Duane, Ira Eaker, Dick Eselgroth, John Ford, Walter Flagg, Art Frankel, Frank Gyidik, Sol Greenberg, Cliff Hatcher, Ed Huntzinger, Frank Halm, Carroll Henry, Leonard Herman, Gordon Hunsberger, Don V. Jones, Joe F. Jones, Paul King, Immanuel Klette, John Latham, George Lawson, Joe Milliken, Claude Murray, Don Olds, Merle Olmsted, Ted Parker, George Parks, John Parsons, James Patterson, Nicholas Perkins, Robert Randall, William Robertie, Denny Scanlan, Fran Schuster, Roy Stahl, Aaron Schultz, Glen Tessmer, Tommy Thompson, William Thorns, Henry Terry, Gordon Thorup, Doug Underwood, Frank Valesh, Robert Vickers, Robert Vincent, Bill Whitlow, John Woolnough, John Watters, Tom Welch, Harold Wildrick, John Driscoll, Glen Duncan and Russell Zorn.

Two ladies, Mrs Winifred Castle Milliken and Mrs Lorraine Ingles, were of great assistance in the preparation of the accounts on their respective distinguished brothers (General Castle and Colonel Righetti).

Major General John W. Huston, Chief USAF Office of History (himself one of the very last USAF General Officers who flew combat with the 8th Air Force in England) and his staffs at Maxwell AFB and the Arlington Photographic Depository responded helpfully to my request and provided material, as did the Imperial War Museum and Public Record Office in London, and the National Archives at Washington.

On the production side, Julia Brown, Jean Freeman and Fiona Hyde produced the typed copy. John Archer ran a professional eye over the galleys and Bruce Robertson advised on editorial matters. Usually the publisher's editor goes unsung, but it would be amiss not to acknowledge the patience and consciencious-ness of Alex Vanags-Baginskis in guiding this complicated production. Likewise the Printer's Reader, Alan Baker, who was particularly helpful. Finally, whilst appreciating that it is but a poor excuse, I apologise if I have overlooked the names of others who rightfully deserve mention. To all I express my sincere thanks.

CONTENTS

Awesome herald of a wartime morn. A 466BG Liberator, main gear retracting, climbs away past Mousewood after leaving Attlebridge's runway 22; September 1944. Each launch of an ordnance and fuel overladen bomber was a critical event: a drama repeated nearly three-quarters of a million times in eastern England. If an engine failed disaster and possibly death were but seconds away. (C. Gotts)

ERRATA AND ADDENDUM TO THE 1990 EDITION

In the first printing of this book a number of typographical and factual errors appeared. Corrections are noted in the following listing by page number (in bold). Included with the corrections are additional items of pertinent information that have come to light since the original study.

Page 6 *Claims.*Inadvertently omitted last sentence: – Credits for fighter groups given under *Remarks* for individual operations are based on USAF Historical Study No. 85 which was a final post-war reassessment.

Page 8 Third caption: Col. Claude Duncan not Asa.

Page 10 B-17E 19021 had no nickname at this date.

Page 16 7 Sept 42 A B/d 97BG B-17 Cat E base.

Page 19 9 Oct 42 WIA total 13 not 10.

Page 25 18 Nov 42 2 91BG B-17s collided during assembly but landed safely.

Page 34 21 Jan 43 A 93BG B-24 attempted Moling mission.

Page 35 26 Jan 43 A 93BG B-24 attempted Moling mission.

Page 36 29 Jan 43 A 93BG B-24 attempted Moling mission.

Page 39 16 Feb 43 Caption. Ashcraft not Ashcroft.

Page 48 25 Mar 43 A 93BG B-24 attempted Moling mission.

Page 50 31 Mar 43 303BG B-17s crashed at Mears Ashby.

Page 51 5 Apr 43 VIIIBC50. 936 persons killed and 1,342 injured in Antwerp district.

Page 53 8 Apr 43 78FG sent 4 not 12 P-47s.
10 Apr 43 2 Spitfires despatched not 1 P-47.

Page 64 29 May 43 VIIIBC 61: The 379BG B-17 c/l near Little Staughton. Caption DeRussy not de Russey.

Page 65 11 Jne 43 VIIIBC 62: B/d 379BG B-17 Cat E Coltishall.

Page 66 13 Jne 43 VIIIBC 63: B/d 96BG B-17 Cat E base – 4BW E total 2.

Page 71 26 Jne 43 No F-5 MIA. Triqueville A/F not Tricqueville.

Page 72 28 Jne 43 2 95BG B-17s ditched off Newlyn, Devon.

Page 79 26 Jly 43 A fourth B-17 (95BG) ditched off Norfolk coast, crew rescued. The 306BG c/l in The Wash; crew rescued. 96BG B-17 m/f after t/o and c/l Little Snoring.

Page 80 28 Jly 43 306BG B-17 c/l Framlingham A/F not SW Oxford.

Page 82 29 Jly 43 B/d 305BG B-17 Cat E Oulton A/F not base. 56FG P-47 c/l base – Cat E.

Page 83 30 Jly 43 VIIIBC 80. Additional 379BG B-17 c/l near Alconbury – 1BW E total 6.

Page 88 15 Aug 43 A 92BG B-17 cr on t/o.

Page 90 17 Aug 43 Caption incorrect. Photograph taken by Sgt Arnold Anderson north of Liège. Me 110 shot down by P-47s of 56FG.

Page 97 19 Aug 43 VIIIFC FO 108. Withdrawal and penetration forces reversed.

Page 105 3 Sep 43 VIIIBC 90. A 100BG B-17 ditched; crew rescued.

Page 110 11 Sep 43 Only 2 fatal casualties resulting from B-26 crash.

Page 111 15 Sep 43 VIIIBC 95. The 351BG B-17 c/l at Lutton.

Page 112 15 Sep 43 VIIIFC 132. Only 1 353FG P-47 MIA. Other a/c cr. Week St. Mary, Cornwall, pilot baled.

Page 115 23 Sep 43 VIIIBC 100. The 92BG B-17 exploding at Deeping St. Nicholas. 1BD Dam total 51 not 41.

Page 118 23 Sep 43 VIIIFC FO 147. The 353FG P-47 c/l at Ludham A/F.

Page 120 2 Oct 43 VIIIBC 106. Details incorrect re 303BG B-17 under REMARKS.

Page 122 4 Oct 43 VIIIFC FO 150. The 355FG P-47 c/l at Monkton, Kent.

Page 124 9 Oct 43 VIIIBC 113. B/d 306BG B-17 c/l Matlask A/F. B/d 306BG B-17 Cat E base. Gdynia Force E total 3 not 1.

Page 125 10 Oct 43 VIIIBG 114. B/d 384BG B-17 c/l Desford.

Page 126 14 Oct 43 VIIIBG 115. 384BG B-17s cr Baydon not Blaydon and Riseley not Roseley. 2 92BG B-17s c/l Winkfield and Shiplake on return. E total 8.

Page 127 14 Oct 43 Photo of Me 410 attacking 94BG B-17 taken 12 May 1944 not 14 Oct 43.

Page 131 20 Oct 43 MIA 95BG B-17 ditched off Gt. Yarmouth, crew rescued.

Page 134 5 Nov 43 VIIIBC 121. B/d 381BG f/l West Malling, 7 of crew baled France.

Page 138 13 Nov 43 VIIIBC 130. During assembly 2 306BG B-17 cr at Gt. Haseley (10k) and Princes Risborough (1k). 92BG B-17 cr Fenny Compton (10k) before Group abandoned mission. No 305BG B-17 cr. E total 8. MIA 96BG B-17 collided over target.

Page 141 25 Nov 43 The 20FG P-38 c/l Felstead.

Page 142 26 Nov 43 B/d 384BG B-17 c/l Leiston A/F. B/d 303BG B-17 c/l Attlebridge.

Page 145 30 Nov 43 VIIIBC 143: B-17 c/l Little Staughton not Cat E.

Page 146 1 Dec 43 VIIIFC FO 194 56FG P-47 c/l Manston. Cat E.

Page 149 11 Dec 43 VIIIFC FO 198: The 355FG P-47 cr nr Hastings on return, not after t/o.

Page 151 13 Dec 43 VIIIFC FO 199: 355FG in sea hit tree on t/o.

Page 152 16 Dec 43 VIIIFC FO 203: 355FG P-47 c/l Rackheath A/F on return.

Page 155 21 Dec 43 VIIIFC FO 206: The 359FG P-47 cr. Manston.

Page 158 Caption: Col Bowman on right not left of photo.

Page 159 30 Dec 43 VIIIBC 169. 91BG B-17 c/l Old Windsor on 31 Dec not 30 Dec. 91BG B-17 c/l Steeple Morden after t/o.

Page 161 31 Dec 43 VIIIBC 171: 91BG B-17 c/l Old Windsor. B/d 379BG B-17 Cat E Rattlesden A/F. E Total 17. 93BG B-24 ditched off Start Point, 4 rescued.

Page 162 5 Jan 44 8AF 176: Effective total 215 not 225. 92BG Cat E base after t/o accident.

Page 164 7 Jan 44 8AF 178: The 351BG B-17 cr Moulton, Lincs.

Page 165 11 Jan 44 8AF 182: b/d 303BG B-17 Cat E Metfield. B/d 306BG B-17 c/l Andrewsfield. Cat E total – 4. VIIIFC FO 216. One 359FG P-47 cr Rednal, Shrops, not Wales. The 355FG P-47 cr near base after t/o, pilot baled.

Page 168 21 Jan 44 VIIIFC FO 221. First e/a ground strafing claims by 356FG not 56FG.

Page 175 4 Feb 44 8AF 208: b/d 381BG B-17 c/l base. 96BG B-17 c/l Shropham after t/o. 445BG B-24 cr base.

Page 176 6 Feb 44 8AF 212: b/d 381BG B-17 Cat E Dunkeswell 96BG B-17 lost collided with FW 190.

Page 177 8 Feb 44 8AF 214: The B-17 (384BG) down nr Brighton was repaired.

Page 178 10 Feb 44 VIIIFC FO 239: The 20FG P-38 cr. Friday Bridge not Sutton Bridge.

Page 183 20 Feb 44 8AF 226: b/d 392BG B-24 cr. Manston, 10k 303BG B-17 c/l Bozeat on return. B/d 305BG B-17 c/l Redhill. Cat E total 7.

Page 195 6 Mar 44 8AF 250: The b/d 452BG B-17 c/l Metfield A/F on return. 91BG B-17 c/l Steeple Morden after t/o. B/d 306BG B-17 Cat E base. Cat E total 8. VIIIFC FO 262: The 359FG P-47 cr at base.

Page 197 9 Mar 44 8AF 253: Effective total 489 not 490. 92BG B-17 cr t/o, all k.

Page 201 16 Mar 44 8AF 262: The b/d 44BG B-24 cr Woodchurch not Friston, 6k.

Page 203 18 Mar 44 8AF 264: b/d 100BG at Raydon, incorrect date, see 19 Mar.

Page 204 19 Mar 44 8AF 266: b/d 100BG B-17 Cat E. Raydon A/F.

Page 205 22 Mar 44 8AF 273: b/d B-17 c/l Horsey was 306BG.

Page 206 22 Mar 44 8AF 273: Incorrect caption to second photo. Shows 92BG B-17 on 1 Dec 43 mission. A/c survived.

Page 212 30 Mar 44 FO 67W 14: 359FG P-47 c/l base on return. Cat E.

Page 214 8 Apr 44 7PG despatched 4 Spitfires and 2 F-5s Germany and France.

Page 215 9 Apr 44 8AF 293: 303BG B-17 cr. North Walsham.

Page 216 10 Apr 44 7PG despatched 5 Spitfires and 8 F-5s to France, Low Countries and Germany.

Page 217 11 Apr 44 8AF 298: 96BG PFF B-17 shot down by intruder at Gt. Glemham prior to mission. 7PG despatched 5 Spitfires and 15 F-5s to France and Germany.

Page 219 12 Apr 44 7PG despatched 19 F-5s and 3 Spitfires to Continent: 2 F-5s MIA.

Page 219 13 Apr 44 VIIIFC FO 298: 354FG should read 364FG under losses. 7PG despatched 2 Spitfires to Germany.

Page 220 15 Apr 44 VIIIFC FO 299: e/a credits should read 55FG – 2, 56FG – 5.

Page 220 17 Apr 44 7PG despatched 1 Spitfire to France.

Page 221 18 Apr 44 7PG despatched 4 F-5s and 3 Spitfires to France, Low Countries and Germany.

Page 222 19 Apr 44 7PG despatched 6 Spitfires and 20 F-5s to Continent. 1 F-5 cr UK.

Page 223 20 Apr 44 7PG despatched 1 Spitfire and 3 F-5s to Holland and France.

Page 224 21 Apr 44 7PG despatched 5 Spitfires and 23 F-5s to France, Holland and Germany. 1 F-5 MIA.

Page 224 22 Apr 44 7PG despatched 12 F-5s to France.

Page 225 23 Apr 44 7PG despatched 2 Spitfires and 38 F-5s to France and Low Countries.

Page 226 24 Apr 44 8AF 315: Bomb tonnage on Oberpfaffenhofen 175.0 lB. VIIIFC FO 312. Total claims should read 57-0-36(G) and 70-6-2 B-17 in photo nicknamed *Booby Trap*. 7PG despatched 15 F-5s and 1 Spitfire to France and Germany.

Page 227 25 Apr 44 Nancy/Essey a/f not Nancy/Essay. Metz/Frescaty a/f not Metz/Frascaty. 7PG despatched 7 F-5s and 3 Spitfires to France and Germany.

Page 228 26 Apr 44 7PG despatched 2 Spitfires and 19 F-5s to France.

Page 230 27 Apr 44 8AF 323: Bomb tonnage on Ostend 35.7 lB. 7PG despatched 29 F-5s and 4 Spitfires to France, Belgium and Germany.

Page 232 28 Apr 44 7PG despatched 16 F-5s and 3 Spitfires to France.

Page 233 29 Apr 44 VIIIFC FO 320: The 359FG P-47 Cat E c/l Framlingham A/F on return. 7PG despatched 1 F-5 and 1 Spitfire to France.

Page 234 30 Apr 44 VIIIFC FO 321: 359FG P-47 c/l base on return. 7PG despatched 25 F-5s and 5 Spitfires to France and Germany.

Page 235 1 May 44 8AF 333: B-17s effective Metz 43 not 42. 7PG despatched 12 F-5s and 5 Spitfires to France and Low Countries.

Page 235 1/2 May 44 8AF 334: First H2X Mosquito mission by 482BG.

Page 235 2 May 44 8AF 335: B-24 c/l near Hoxne. 7PG despatched 3 F-5s to France.

Page 236 3 May 44 7PG despatched 6 F-5s and 2 Spitfires to Belgium and France.

Page 236 4 May 44 8AF 338: The 356FG P-47 c/l base. 7PG despatched 4 F-5s and 3 Spitfires to France and Germany.

Page 237 5 May 44 7PG despatched 1 Spitfire to France and Belgium.

Page 237 6 May 44 7PG despatched 1 F-5 to France.

Page 238 7 May 44 7PG despatched 5 F-5s to France.

Page 239 8 May 44 8AF 345: 482BG H2X Mosquito on night operation. 7PG despatched 28 F-5s to France and Germany. 2 F-5s MIA.

Page 240 9 May 44 8AF 347. Effective total 800 not 802. 7PG despatched 30 F-5s to France and Low Countries and 8 Spitfires to Germany.

Page 241 10 May 44 7PG despatched 11 F-5s and 2 Spitfires to France and Germany.

Page 242 11 May 44 7PG despatched 21 F-5s and 3 Spitfires to France, Belgium and Germany.

Page 242 12 May 44 7PG despatched 25 F-5s and 8 Spitfires to France, Low Countries and Germany.

Page 243 12/13 May 44 482BG H2X Mosquito c/l base on return.

Page 243 13 May 44 8AF 355: Osnabruck bomb tonnage 1834 not 1833.5. 7PG despatched 14 F-5s and 2 Spitfires to Continent.

Page 244 15 May 44 7PG despatched 2 F-5s to France.

Page 245 15/16 May 44 1 482 BG B-17 H2X sortie Holland.

Page 245 17 May 44 7PG despatched 2 F-5s to France.

Page 245 19 May 44 VIIIFC FO 342: Despatched total 700. Damaged P-47 3 not 4. 7PG despatched 1 Spitfire to Germany.

Page 246 20 May 44 8AF 359: a/c damaged total 94 not 114. 96BG B-17 c/l landing base. 7PG despatched 1 Spitfire and 6 F-5s to the Continent.

Page 246 21 May 44 VIIIFC FO 344: b/d 353FG P-47 c/l base. Cat E total 4.

Page 247 22 May 44 VIIIFC FO 346: Only 1 56FG P-47 Cat E – c/l nr Leiston. 7PG despatched 11 F-5s to France, Low Countries and Germany.

Page 248 23 May 44 7PG despatched 15 F-5s and 6 Spitfires to France, Low Countries and Germany.

Page 249 Tonnerre m/y not Tonnere.

Page 249 24 May 44 7PG despatched 19 F-5s and 1 Spitfire to Continent.

Page 250 25 May 44 8AF 370: Totals for Despatched, Effective and Bomb tonnage should read 1033, 859 and 2167-8 respectively.

Page 251 27 May 44 8AF 373: 4 not 3 96BG B-17s lost through collisions over e/t.

Page 253 29 May 44 8AF 379. Bomb Tonnage total 2134.5 not 2054.5.

Page 254 30 May 44 VIIIFC FO 354. The Cat E 359FG P-51 cr landing base.

Page 255 30 May 44 8AF 381: Creil force should read 1 P-38 and 12 P-47s despatched and effective. Additional force of 9 P-38s bombed Hoboken S/Y (P) with 9 tons.

Page 258 Massy-Palaiseau R/B, not Massey-Palaiseau. Romorantin/Pruniers A/F not Romorantin/Prunieres A/F.

Page 259 6 Jne 44 56FG flew 7 not 11 missions.

Page 261 7 Jne 44 B/d 56FG P-47 c/l base – Cat E.

Page 262 8 Jne 44 VIII FO 377. The B/d 355FG P-51 cr. Eyeworth, pilot k. Touquet-Paris-Plage not Toucquet-Paris-Plage. Wimereux not Wimereau.

Page 263 10 Jne 44 B/d 356FG P-47 c/l south coast airstrip. B/d 56FG P-47 c/l on return.

Page 263 11 Jne 44 VIIIFC FO 382. B/d 359FG cr Maltot, Fr., pilot k. Montfort Bridge not Montford Bridge.

Page 265 13 Jne 44 VIIIFC FO 386 & 387: Despatched total 788 not 675. Going out 339FG P-51 cr. Thornham, pilot baled. B/d 353FG P-47 c/l Normandy beachhead A/S and 2 359FG P-51 became first 8AF fighters to land on Normandy A/S.

Page 266 Denain Prouvy not Denain Drousey.

Page 267 Peronne R/B not Peccone. Etampes/Mondesire not Etampes/Modesir.

Page 271 19 Jne 44 VIIIFC FO 400. MIA a/c should read 4 P-38s and 12 P-51s. Claims 1-0-1; MIA casualties total 16.

Page 273 20 Jne 44 8AF 425. MIA 389BG B-24 PFF lead for 448BG landed intact in enemy territory.

Page 273 21 Jne 44 8AF 428: 38D casualties – 1 KIA, 9 WIA, 80 MIA. VIIIFC escorts 3BD Ruhland and 1BD had no a/c losses. Fighter Group credits; 352FG – 10 not 8.

Page 274 21/22 Jne 44 47 not 44 B-17s destroyed and 24 not 26 damaged at Poltava.

Page 275 22 Jne 44 8AF 431. Sug (P) tonnage 99.3. A/c damage total 495 not 478. P-47s despatched for 2BD 36 not 46. 457BG B-17 c/l base on return. The 2 56FG P-47 crashing collided near base. Abandoned b/d 34BG B-24 cr. Sherfield. Lieusant R/R not Lieusant. Saumur BR not Samur.

Page 277 24 Jne 44 VIIIFC: 82 P-51s despatched on B-24 escort. Total effective 700 not 726.

Page 279 27 Jne 44 VIIIFC Despatched, effective and bomb tonnage totals should read 591, 509 and 109.4 respectively.

Page 281 28 Jne 44 8AF 445: Addition – 3BD B-24, 129 despatched, 0 effective. Bomb tonnage 1556 not 1554.

Page 282 29 Jne 44 8AF 447: 8 not 18 B-17 effective Wittenberg.

Page 283 30 Jne 44 VIIIFC: Effective total 473 not 305. Bomb tonnage 92.2 not 75.8.

Page 284 4 Jly 44 8AF 451: Effective total 254 not 364.

Page 286 5 Jly 44 VIIIFC: Effective total 658 not 668. P-51 MIA casualties 2.

Page 291 11 Jly 44 8AF 466: MIA 453BG B-24 ditched east Clacton, 8 rescued. The 355FG P-51 down over UK was returning from radio-relay mission.

Page 291 12 Jly 44 8AF 469: MIA casualties total 222 not 216.

Page 294 16 Jly 44 VIIIFC: only one force of 85 P-38s on 2BD escort.

Page 296 17 Jly 44 8AF 478: The 100BG B-17 cr Friston during assembly; crew baled.

Page 298 19 Jly 44 8AF 482: 98 2BD B-24s despatched with 3BD B-24s. Effective total 1100 not 1082. Schweinfurt bomb tonnage 411.5. Total tonnage 2825.7 not 2780.4. Total damaged a/c 367 not 347. The 388BG B-17 collided with 96BG B-17 during assembly and cr. Thurston; 96BG a/c landed. One man escaped from shot down 398BG B-17 illustrated on page 299.

Page 300 20 Jly 44 8AF 484: Effective total 1075 not 1077.

Page 301 21 Jly 44 8AF 486: B/d 96BG B-17 c/l Bentwaters. 361FG P-51 cr. Ickleton. The abandoned 359FG cr. Wingham. Cat E totals 4 bombers and 4 fighters.

Page 305 28 Jly 44 8AF 501: On return 2 100BG B-17s c/l base.

Page 306 29 Jly 44 8AF 503: B/d 96BG B-17 cr. near base, 3k.

Page 312 2 Aug 44 VIIIFC: No 355FG P-51 Cat E – a/c in sea after pilot baled – included in MIA.

Page 313 3 Aug 44 VIIIFC: Additional 52 P-51s despatched as escort for 2BD and 3BD 8AF 512.

Page 313 and 314 4 Aug 44 8AF 514: Cat E total 9 not 15. MIA casualties for 1BD 30 not 40 and total 133 not 120. VIIIFC: The 30-0-5 for P-47s at Plantlunne A/F are ground claims. Total claims were 38-1-5 and 43-0-5(G) not 68-1-10 and 13-0-5(G). The 381BG B-17 crashing during assembly had 1k, not entire crew.

Page 315 5 Aug 44 8AF 519: Effective total 1113 not 583, WIA and MIA casualties 18 and 107, not 10 and 79. B/d 96BG B-17 c/l Hardwick A/F – Cat E.

Page 316 6 Aug 44 8AF 524. Despatched. Effective and Tonnage totals 1182, 926 and 2526. 4 respectively, not 1186, 929 and 2373.6. Hamburg/Deutsche (P) Tonnage 155.8. VIIIFC: Effective total 649 not 713.

Page 323 12 Aug 44 VIIIFC: Effective total 1092 not 109.

Page 324 13 Aug 44 8AF 548: Effective and tonnage totals 1210 and 3365.4 not 1209 and 3265.4. VIIIFC: B/d 353FG P-47 c/l base. 359FG cr on return, pilot baled. MIA 356 FG P-47 shot down British AA.

Page 326 15 Aug 44 8AF 554: Bomb tonnage 2173.9 not 2171.4. Damaged 101 not 156. 3BD MIA casualties 9.

Page 327 16 Aug 44 8AF 556: Bomb tonnage 2381.7 not 1473.

Page 329 18 Aug 44 VIIIFC: Despatched 908 not 858. Effective 699 not 611. P-38 force 59 despatched, 50 effective. P-38 46-0-15 claims ground not air. Total claims 10-1-5 and 46-0-18(G), not 56-1-20 and 2-0-3(G). 355FG losses 3 not 2 and 2 pilots rescued, one from sea the other by a P-51 landing in e/t.

Page 330 and 331 24 Aug 44 8AF 568. 2BD MIA, E and Damage figures 5, 1, 183 repeated, also Freital target data.

Page 332 25 Aug 44 8AF 570: Bomb tonnage 2931.2 not 2911.2 and MIA casualties for 2BD 50 not 64.

Page 334 26 Aug 44 8AF 575: 93BG not operating. 25BG despatched Mosquitoes not 35BG.

Page 335 28 Aug 44 VIIIFC: B/d 355FG P-51 c/l Manston. MIA 356FG P-47 in sea, pilot rescued.

Page 336 30 Aug 44 8AF 590: Effective total 828 not 823. 20CBW commence Trucking supplies to French A/Fs.

Page 338 5 Sep 44 BAF 605: MIA casualties total 76 not 54.

Page 341 8 Sep 44 8AF 611: WIA casualties 27 not 18. VIIIFC: 355FG P-51 cr on t/o.

Page 343 10 Sep 44 8AF 619 and 620: Despatched, effective and tonnage totals should read 1146, 1064 and 2804.4. B/d 100BG B-17 c/l Belgium.

Page 344 11 Sep 44 8AF 623: Tonnage and MIA totals 2538.8 and 39, not 2438.8 and 40. The b/d 100BG B-17 c/l at Joigny, Fr. The 100BG B-17 cr Eastchurch not b/d. VIIIFC: Despatched and effective totals 715 and 663, not 440 and 411.

Page 345 12 Sep 44 8AF 626: WIA and MIA casualties 21 and 317, not 22 and 307. VIIIFC: 359FG P-51 c/l base.

Page 346 16 Sep 44 8AF 635: 353FG P-47 c/l Southend – Cat E.

Page 349 18 Sep 44 8AF 639. The Cat E 359FG P-51 c/l Fersfield. B/d 356FG P-47 c/l Netherlands, pilot evades.

Page 350 19 Sep 44 8AF 642: Damaged total 279 not 345. VIIIFC: Despatched total 529 not 528. 55 P-51s effective on Frantic escort.

Page 351 21 Sep 44 8AF 644. The 93BG B-24 cr. Ingelmunster, Bel. after collision going out.

Page 354 27 Sep 44 8AF 650: VIIIFC: 158 not 58 P-51s despatched on 2BD escort. Damaged total 8 not 6.

Page 355 28 Sep 44 8AF 652: MIA casualties 310 not 309.

Page 358 3 Oct 44 8AF 662: Tonnage total 2523.2 not 2522.7. VIIIFC: 140 P-51s on 2BD escort. 355FG P-51 lost in landing attempt to rescue downed pilot.

Page 361 7 Oct 44 8AF 669: Magdeburg/Rothensee tonnage of 65 duplicated. Total tonnage 3253.7 not 3188.2. Effective total 1311 not 1401.

Page 363 12 Oct 44 8AF 674: 353FG P-47 cr landing base – Cat E.

Page 364 14 Oct 44 8AF 676: Effective total 722 not 732.

Page 365 15 Oct 44 8AF 678: Despatched, effective, tonnage and damaged totals 1241, 1112, 3069.3 and 629, not 787, 722, 1983.8 and 629. VIIIFC: 359FG P-51 c/l base.

Page 367 17 Oct 44 8AF 681: tonnage total 2918.2 not 2917.2. The b/d 453BG B-24 cr nr Malmédy and 398BG B-17 at Linsmeau.

Page 368 18 Oct 44 8AF 682: 339FG P-51 cr. Belgium, pilot inj.

Page 369 22 Oct 44 8AF 685: The 355FG P-51 did not cr continent but was destroyed in taxi accident on return, pilot k. 359FG P-51 c/l t/o, pilot safe.

Page 370 25 Oct 44 8AF 688: tonnage total 2818.5 not 1195.9.

Page 371 26 Oct 44 8AF 689: Effective total 1128 not 1104. 1 7PG RCM P-38 MIA. INCIDENT: The B-25 cr. Mourmelon le Grande A/F after being hit by AA near Trier.

Page 373 Sentence omitted after 'spun' in eighth line from end of INCIDENT – 'Element leader Lt Gail Jacobson also got into a spin and hurtled down.' This incident occurred 30 Oct not the last day of month as stated.

Page 374 1 Nov 44 8AF 696: 359 FG P-51 m/f, cr. NE Norwich, pilot baled.

Page 377 5 Nov 44 8AF 702: 2BD MIA casualties 0 not 112. 359FG P-51 c/l base on return.

Page 382 16 Nov 44 8AF 715: 357FG P-51 cr Shotesham, Norfolk on return, pilot k.

Page 283 20 Nov 44 8AF 718: Effective total 536 not 322.

Page 384 21 Nov 44 8AF 720: A lost 356FG P-51 c/l Haro, Spain, pilot safe.

Page 385 23 Nov 44 8AF 722: Despatched total 168 not 188.

Page 386 26 Nov 44 8AF 725: 732 not 132 fighters despatched. The 355FG P-51 lost collided with another over sea.

Page 387 27 Nov 44 8AF 727: 356FG P-51 c/l t/o, 356FG P-51 abandoned over Belgium, pilot baled. Object of mission to engage e/a. Only occasion bomber effort subordinate to fighters.

Page 388 29 Nov 44 8AF 729: b/d 355FG P-51 c/l base.

Page 388 30 Nov 44 8AF 731 not 8AF 212. KIA and MIA casualties totals 25 and 262 not 24 and 304. Fighters despatched total 975 not 972.

Page 390 4 Dec 44 8AF 736: 212 B-17 effective Kassel.

Page 393 10 Dec 44 8AF 745: 359FG P-51 cr t/o.

Page 394 11 Dec 44 8AF 746: 2 56FG P-47s cr. France, pilots baled. 355FG P-51 c/l base.

Page 394 12 Dec 44 8AF 748: Bombers despatched, effective and tonnage totals 1275, 1217 and 2365, not 895, 858 and 1310.8.

Page 395 15 Dec 44 8AF 750: Fighters despatched total 576 not 434.

Page 397 19 Dec 44 8AF 756: The 93BG B-24 cr after t/o not during assembly.

Page 398 23 Dec 44 8AF 757: 355FG P-51 cr t/o – Cat E.

Page 399 and 400 24 Dec 44 8AF 760: Bomber damaged total 596 not 487. Fighter claims total 74-1-20. B/d 95BG B-17 c/l near Sarrable, Fr. MIA 359FG P-51 pilot safe Allied territory.

Page 406 27 Dec 44 8AF 764: Tonnage total 1575.5 not 1578.2 2 446 BG B-24s cr. Belgium, crews baled – 6 in e/t. The MIA 359FG P-51s collided over Thames when returning from France where landed after 26 Dec ops. Fighter MIA total 3 not 5.

Page 407 28 Dec 44 8AF 766: 34 1BD B-17s effective at Rheinbach m/y (P) dropping 98 tons (printing omission). 355FG P-51 c/l Continent.

Page 408 29 Dec 44 8AF 769: MIA casualties total 27 not 17. 81 P-47s and 47 P-51 despatched in fighter sweep and 107 effective. 353FG P-51 cr t/o.

Page 411 31 Dec 44 8AF 772: Tonnage 3519.3 not 3524.3. 1 MIA 388BG B-17 had 96BG crew. B/d 100BG B-17 c/l base.

Page 415 3 Jan 45 8AF 778: Bomber despatched total 1163 not 1168. 355FG P-51 cr. Charleville, Fr. pilot baled. 355FG P-51 c/l base on return.

Page 416 5 Jan 45 8AF 781: B/d 390BG B-17 c/l Steanay, Fr.

Page 417 6 Jan 45 8AF 783: Bomber effective total 777 not 778. B/d 96BG B-17 c/l Couvron, Fr.

Page 418 7 Jan 45 8AF 785: 96BG B-17 cr landing base.

Page 420 10 Jan 45 8AF 789: Tonnage 2199.5 not 2196.5.

Page 422 13 Jan 45 8AF 791: The 353FG P-51 cr Lindsey not base. 359FG P-51 c/l base on return.

Page 423 14 Jan 45 8AF 792: 357FG e/a credits 55½ not 48½.

Page 425 16 Jan 45 8AF 796: 93BG B-24 cr t/o base. B/d 466BG B-24 c/l nr Strassburg, Fr. 3 355FG P-51 cr UK, pilots baled. 359FG P-51 c/l nr Merville, Fr. pilot safe. 2 356FG P-51 c/l continent.

Page 425 17 Jan 45 8AF 798: Bomber MIA casualties 92 not 72. B/d 93BG B-24 c/l SE England. 356FG P-51 cr t/o Beauvais/Tille for mission, pilot k.

Page 426 21 Jan 45 8AF 803: Bomber despatched total 913 not 912.

Page 430 28 Jan 45 8AF 809: 1AD casualties KIA 0, WIA 4, MIA 35. B/d 96BG B-17 cr Belgium, 9k. 359FG P-51 c/l on return.

Page 430 and 431 29 Jan 45 8AF 811: Kassel m/y tonnage 444.3 not 44.3. 96BG B-17s collided assembling not on return. The 359FG P-51 cr France, Pilot k was shot down by US AA. Another 359FG P-51 cr France, pilot baled. Third 359FG P-51 cr near Exeter on return, pilot baled.

Page 433 3 Feb 45 8AF 817: B/d 381BG B-17 c/l base. B/d 356FG P-51 cr France, pilot baled. 353FG P-51 c/l Continent.

Page 435 6 Feb 45 8AF 821: B/d 96BG B-17 c/l Belgium. The 339FG P-51 cr at Puckpool, Isle of Wight. 55FG P-51 cr Capel, Surrey.

Page 436 9 Feb 45 8AF 824: 1 303BG B-17 in collision c/l near Ghent, Belgium. B/d 355FG P-51 cr Liège, Bel, pilot k.

Page 438 11 Feb 45 8AF 827: Tonnage total 338.8 not 335.8.

Page 439 14 Feb 45 8AF 830: B/d 355FG P-51 cr Belgium, pilot k.

Page 440 15 Feb 45 8AF 832: M/f 359FG P-51 cr South Beveland Isle, pilot baled.

Page 443 20 Feb 45 8AF 836: No MIA losses for 78FG and 339FG. Fighter MIA total 10 not 13. The 339FG P-51s collided and cr over France not Germany. 2 78FG P-51s collided on return and cr nr Cambrai, Fr.

Page 447 23 Feb 45 8AF 843: 359FG pilot killed in crash UK not Continent.

Page 449 25 Feb 45 8AF 847: 3AD Munich m/y tonnage 898.6 not 989.6. 356FG P-51 c/l near Nancy, Fr., pilot inj. B/d 359FG P-51 cr nr Kalterberg, pilot baled.

Page 452 1 Mar 45 8AF 857: 3AD effective Ulm 420 not 449. Effective total 1180 not 1209. On return 44BG B-24 cr nr St. Quentin, Fr. Crew baled.

Page 454 2 Mar 45 8AF 859: 6 B-24 of Screening Force effective. Total bomb tonnage 2609.2 not 2589.2.

Page 457 7/8 Mar 45 8AF 871: B-24s dropped 50 tons not 150.

Page 459 9 Mar 45 8AF 875: 359FG P-51 cr nr base on return, pilot baled.

Page 460 10 Mar 45 8AF 877: 359FG P-51 c/l Continent – hit US AA.

Page 464 15 Mar 45 8AF 889: the b/d 453BG B-24 on continent shot up over Soviet held territory, crew baled – 2 k 2b/d 355FG P-51s c/l behind Russian lines.

Page 465 17 Mar 45 8AF 892: 359FG P-51 c/l on return.

Page 466 18 Mar 45 8AF 894: total effective 1264 not 1184.

Page 468 20 Mar 45 8AF 898: 359FG P-51 c/l base on return.

Page 469 21 Mar 45 8AF 901 & 8AF 904: Totals for both should read 1500 despatched, 1443 effective, 3309.5 tonnage and 249 damaged.

Page 470 22 Mar 45 8AF 906: B/d 355FG P-51 c/l base.

Page 472 24 Mar 45 8AF 911: B/d 389BG B-24 on continent cr near Venlo, Neth. Abandoned 448BG B-24 cr in sea.

Page 478 3 Apr 45 8AF 924: PR escort effective 4 not 44.

Page 480 5 Apr 45 8AF 928: Bomb tonnage 2809 not 2815.3. The MIA 355FG P-51 shot down flak after t/o Neth., pilot k.

Page 483 8 Apr 45 8AF 932: 1AD despatched 399 not 339 and grand total 1233 not 1173.

Page 484 9 Apr 45 8AF 935: 381BG B-17 c/l Lympne during assembly. B/d 359FG P-51 cr west Mannheim, pilot safe.

Page 485 10 Apr 45 8AF 938: Fighters despatched total 908 not 905.

Page 488 14 Apr 45 8AF 948: the abandoned 388BG B-17 cr Leon, nr Royan, not Lyon.

Page 490 16 Apr 45 8AF 945: The b/d Cat E 361FG P-51 cr on a Dutch island, pilot safe. 353FG P-51 c/l Florennes A/F. B/d 355FG P-51 c/l Germany, pilot WIA.

Page 490 17 Apr 45 8AF 957: 2AD escort's 53-0-29 are ground claims.

Page 502 7 May 45 8AF 985: Escort provided by 356FG, last fighter operation.

INTRODUCTION

This book is basically a detailed chronology of operations conducted by units of the US 8th Air Force during the Second World War. The 8th Air Force was the largest air striking force ever committed to battle and a definitive study of just one full-strength operation would more than fill a book of this size. The only practical way to embrace the significant facts of the many hundreds of operations carried out in 34 months of hostilities is to present them in statistical form. Even so, it has been necessary to reduce the scope of data covering 1944–45 missions when many hundreds of sorties were flown daily.

As the Group was the basic operational unit of the 8th Air Force, statistics given are concentrated at this level and, even for the peak operational period, the participation of individual groups is acknowledged. Accompanying each statistical summary are brief notes on points of interest arising from the missions. Additionally, throughout the book, there are accounts of incidents and activities on specific occasions that relate to various aspects of 8th Air Force operations. Mostly these involve combatants and in the case of notable personalities they have been developed into biographies. The illustrations, covering all spheres of 8th Air Force operational activities, are identified to the date on which the photographs were taken; they are not merely representative views. As far as can be ascertained, this has not previously been possible on such a scale in a published work of this nature. The majority of photographs have not been published before, and where 'oldies' are included it is to reveal facts not previously expressed in captions.

MIGHTY EIGHTH WAR DIARY is intended as a browsing book for the intrigued, and a reference work for the enthusiast. It is hoped that the narrative accounts and illustrations will provide a further insight into 8th Air Force activities quite apart from the recorded facts and figures. While complementary and a companion volume to the narrative history in THE MIGHTY EIGHTH, this is a completely self-contained volume, in no way dependent on the earlier work. This will also apply to a third book, MIGHTY EIGHTH MISCELLANY covering operational techniques, aircraft and equipment, special projects and commanders.

MIGHTY EIGHTH WAR DIARY is not a repetitive venture to squeeze more out of a popular subject. It was planned for inclusion as part of THE MIGHTY EIGHTH, to provide an operational diary, but was omitted because of space considerations. It has since been expanded to give a more comprehensive cover. The basic source material has been taken from official USAF archives, but nowhere was there to be found a consistent record covering the information now presented in this book. Many hundreds of hours were spent searching documents for the relevant details. The majority of facts in captions and the narrative were researched in a vast variety of sources other than official archives. Some six thousand hours were involved in the preparation of this volume with the overall object to provide an accurate and informative record of the 8th Air Force in the Second World War.

THE STRATEGIC BOMBING OFFENSIVE

Such was the sophistication and range of military equipment used in the Second World War that, for the first time in man's turbulent history of conflict, the machine dominated the scene. The diverse military hardware produced by vast industrial complexes, in turn supported by basic industries, involved the major part of national economies. No longer were hostilities confined to combatants; the whole populace supported the war effort as never before. With military dependence upon machines came the counter of destroying an adversary's war industry, only given real credence with the development of aircraft capable of ranging beyond the enemy's fleet and battle lines. Thus was born the concept of strategic bombing, a planned campaign to destroy a nation's industrial capacity. Initially, such employment of the bombing aeroplane was chiefly nurtured by senior officers in the Royal Air Force and the air service of the US Army, but not until the development of true long-ranged and heavy load carrying bombers in the late 1930s did this extension of warfare become a practical proposition. Theoretically, a well executed campaign of strategic bombing would, through near total destruction of industry and fuel supplies, deny an enemy the means of effectively continuing combat. Strategic bombing alone could bring defeat.

The Plan

In the summer of 1941 the United States Army Air Forces' recently formed Air War Plans Division produced an ambitious design for air operations when – as seemed inevitable – the United States became involved in the European war. Known as AWPD-1, the plan was formulated by a team consisting of Lt.Col Harold L. George, Lt.Col Kenneth Walker, Maj Lawrence S. Kuter and Maj Haywood S. Hansell Jr. The latter two ultimately played a part in the execution of its major objective, the creation of a strategic bombing force. Although sensitive to the dominant view in the US War Department that air power should be primarily used in support of land forces, a strategic bombing campaign was presented as a necessary pre-requisite to any invasion and land operations in continental Europe. A total force of 4,000 bomber aircraft would be required to decimate Germany's industrial power in a six month period, this force to be in place 21 months after America's mobilisation. Initially, current production heavy bombers, the B-17 Fortress and B-24 Liberator, were to be employed from bases in England, and when available the extra heavy B-29 and B-32 types from Northern Ireland and Egyptian bases. Medium range bombers, the B-25 and B-26, were also to be used from the United Kingdom but replaced by additional heavy bombers as soon as production allowed. Additionally a giant intercontinental ranged bomber, the B-36, was to be developed in case the UK and Middle East bases were lost. For the whole war effort a production of more than 60,000 aircraft of all types and well over 2 million men was the stated requirement.

To cripple German war economy, AWPD-1 proposed three primary objectives:– the electrical power system, transportation (road, rail and canals) and the petroleum industry. A necessary intermediate objective was the neutralisation of the German fighter defences through attacks on aircraft manufacturing and associated industries.

The German electrical power network was one of the most advanced in Europe and a very large proportion of manufacturing industry was dependent upon it. The fuelled power stations and hydro-electric plants were many, small targets and difficult to destroy, but repair and replacement would be a long and difficult process. A successful bombing campaign against 50 targets would, it was calculated, have far-reaching repercussions on industry.

The railway system featured prominently in an attack on transportation as an estimated 72 per cent of tonnage was moved by rail through a complex system of marshalling yards. Destroying these yards could create chaos. A well developed canal system, handling over 25 per cent of goods, appeared particularly vulnerable to air attack at aqueduct and elevated sections. AWPD-1 identified 47 targets for the transportation campaign.

Petroleum products were essential to the machinery of a modern military and naval power. Effective disruption of oil refineries in synthetic plant production would keep U-boats in port, bring armoured vehicles to a standstill and ground aircraft. At the time AWPD-1 was prepared it was believed the synthetic plants were primarily concerned with high grade aviation fuels and producing somewhat over half the Luftwaffe's requirements. The bulk of natural oil was drawn from the Romanian fields. The inflammable nature of the product made oil a particularly inviting target system with 27 installations listed for attack.

To allow the strategic bombers to go about their work, AWPD-1 acknowledged that the German fighter force would have to be suppressed or defeated. It would be necessary first to direct bombers to attack sources of aircraft production, air depots and airfields. US fighters would be assigned to England to give support within the limits of their range and defend the bomber bases, but the mass fire power of the bomber formations would hopefully keep losses to an acceptable level while they devastated the German aviation industry.

With the Japanese attack on Pearl Harbor and the United States' entry into the war, AWPD-1 became the basic consultative document on which the USAAF's strategic bombing offensive was based. In the light of the changing war scene new considerations arose and the basic plan was subject to some, if minor, revision. In August 1942 as a result of a Presidential request for an updated assessment of aviation production to meet US and Allied plans, the opportunity was taken to prepare another study embracing force requirements and potential targets. Known as AWPD-42, and based on the earlier plan, it was formulated principally by Col. Haywood Hansell Jr (a member of the AWPD-1 team), Col Harris Hull, senior Intelligence Officer with the USAAF in England, and Group Capt A.C.H. Sharpe, a prominent RAF strategist. Adhering to the 'beat Germany first' policy, the major portion of US air units were to be deployed in Europe with increased numbers of heavy bombers for the United Kingdom. The target plan showed notable changes, the most significant being anti-submarine objectives as a first priority after the intermediate priority of the German air force. This introduction came as a direct result of the heavy losses incurred by Allied shipping during the first half of 1942 when U-boats were sinking a greater tonnage per month than the combined British and American shipyards could replace. Bombing bases and construction facilities was deemed to be essential in reducing U-boat activity. AWPD-42 also transposed the priorities of electricity and transportation, the latter being assessed as more vulnerable to high altitude bombing. An additional target system was rubber, of which nearly half Germany's supply was believed to come from two synthetic plants. At the time of the preparation of AWPD-42, US heavy bombers had begun initial operations from England, suffering few losses and apparently well able to ward off enemy fighter attacks. This influenced the authors to express a confidence in the day bombers to survive in combat. The new plan revised the numbers of aircraft to be deployed in the United Kingdom to over 7,000, of which 2,000 were to be heavy bombers of the B-17 and B-24 types. It was now evident that the B-29 and B-32 would be delayed and the intercontinental B-36 would not be developed in time. While AWPD-42 was to be the basic design for 1943, it too would be quickly revised to meet new assesments.

The USAAF agency chosen to engage in strategic bombardment from England and follow the aims outlined in AWPD-42 and its predecessor, was known as the 8th Air Force. In practice its Bomber Command was more influenced by the British Air Ministry than the consultative plans in its selection of targets, primarily because the RAF supplied the intelligence data. The early exploratory missions involved fairly shallow penetrations of hostile airspace and targets attacked were rail centres, airfields and shipyards, which broadly related to the brief of dominating the German air force and disrupting transportation. With such small forces these early attacks were a little more than nuisance to the enemy. In October 1942 the campaign against the U-boat installations began with long-range missions to the French Atlantic coast and, in the following year, to the German North Sea ports. The direction of bombers to hit U-boats was a deflection from the real aim of strategic bombing in that it was basically a defensive measure. The anti-submarine campaign continued until the summer of 1943, in the main directed at five construction yards and seven ports; at times causing considerable damage to facilities, it rarely brought destruction to the U-boats themselves due to the substantial concrete bunkers that protected them when in port.

Railway marshalling yards predominated as the alternative target during this period while there were occasional strikes at airfields and industrial sites. Not until mid-1943 did VIII Bomber Command possess a substantial force of bombers to engage in telling blows. The creation of the 12th Air Force for despatch to North Africa in support of the TORCH invasion depleted the 8th Air Force of much men and material including its most experienced heavy bomber and longest ranged fighter groups. During the following months build-up was hampered by a continual diversion of units, originally earmarked for the United Kingdom, to North Africa.

Following the Casablanca Conference of January 1943, Allied leaders called for a Combined Bomber Offensive (CBO) against Germany, and a plan which would form the basis of a new target directive. A combined US-British team prepared the document which was principally designed as a plan to destroy the German air force prior to the cross Channel invasion in the spring of 1944. Whereas AWPD-1 and AWPD-42 specified US air requirements on a world-wide basis, the CBO plan dealt exclusively with a bombing campaign against Germany.

In December 1942 General Arnold had set up a Committee of Operations Analysts to study and prepare a list of potential targets which, if destroyed, would cause maximum hurt to the German war economy. Their findings were used by the CBO team. They were broadly in line with the target systems listed in AWPD-42 but the Committee went to some lengths to identify items vital to war production and located in a few sites. Paramount in their conclusions was the anti-friction bearing industry with only four main centres of production. The destruction of these plants would have a far reaching effect on all German aircraft, vehicle and vessel construction. Thus ball bearings were given the first priority after the intermediate objectives of the German air force and submarine facilities which remained at the top as in AWPD-42. Transportation was moved from third to sixth priority and confined to military transport, while electric power was no longer among the major priorities at all.

Apparently the Committee of Operations Analysis had concluded that the extent and diversity of the German electricity system put its destruction beyond the capabilities of the bomber force available. Similarly the requirements of a successful campaign against all forms of transportation were beyond the scope of available forces. While adopting the Committee's recommendations, the CBO team had some reservations about the low priorities given to the latter and in particular the practical elimination of electric power. The CBO plan with its six major priorities involved only 76 selected targets, nearly 100 less than the suggested programme in AWPD-42. The US force to accomplish the task was to build up to 2,700 heavy bombers in 51 groups by the spring of 1944. In the earlier plans the full US bomber complement was to be on hand by the autumn of 1943, although the overall number was now substantially increased.

The Major Campaign

The Combined Bomber Offensive commenced officially in June 1943 with the issue of a directive code named POINT BLANK. The 8th Air Force now turned its attention more to attacks against the German aircraft and associated industries together with operational airfields in occupied countries. This was in line with the overriding priority expressed in POINTBLANK and the previous plans to neutralise the Luftwaffe. Deeper strikes occurred during the summer months against important aircraft factories and occasionally against component industries. The especially vulnerable rubber and ball-bearing plants were also attacked.

Weather conditions and fighter opposition both proved more formidable than originally anticipated. In the autumn of 1943 radar 'blind bombing' devices were introduced to permit operations in cloud, while the development of suitable long-range fighter escort was hurried to challenge the Luftwaffe. The slow build-up of the UK bomber force was further hampered by a USAAF Headquarters decision to form another strategic bombing force in the Mediterranean area to conduct operations from southern Italy. Over 1,000 heavy bombers (15 groups) scheduled for the 8th Air Force were to be diverted to the new Air Force, the 15th. During the winter of 1943–44 the V-weapon sites being constructed in the French coastal regions became additional targets on which considerable effort was directed, albeit usually when weather did not allow long-range missions to priority targets. Such operations were also of a defensive nature and mitigated against the strategic application of the force. During the winter and following early spring of 1944 the number of 8th Air Force heavy bombers had doubled and the maximum planned strength of 2,000 operational aircraft (40 groups) was finally realised on 6 June 1944, the day of the cross-Channel invasion. The Combined Bomber Offensive had officially terminated on 1 May when by previous agreement the 8th Air Force and RAF Bomber Command came under the control of the Supreme Allied Commander and were thereafter primarily directed to operations in support of the forthcoming invasion. The neutralisation of the German fighter force had been achieved through a concentrated series of attacks against aviation manufacturing plants in February and March 1944, but chiefly by the US long-range fighters being allowed to take the offensive and gaining air superiority in combat.

German aircraft production eventually recovered and the Luftwaffe was not seriously short of fighter aircraft despite combat attrition. However, it would never again achieve dominance in those areas where the 8th's bombers operated. While some two thirds of bombing effort during the immediate pre and post invasion periods was directed principally at communications targets in occupied countries, the heavy bombers were still able to press attacks on strategic objectives. In May 1944 the first missions were flown against oil plants and this campaign continued until March the following year. The success of these attacks quickly made oil products a critical item for the German forces and by the autumn of 1944 the supply had been reduced to a fifth of that prior to the campaign. The position was so serious that enemy operations were often limited by lack of fuels.

Released from regular tactical operations in support of the ground forces, the 8th Air Force conducted a number of missions against German military vehicle plants and depots during the late summer of 1944. This was aimed at restricting the replacement of transport lost during the German retreat from France. A series of attacks on rail centres followed, aimed at delaying reinforcements for the Western Front. Bad weather during the winter of 1944–1945 curtailed operations and with the final German land offensive of the war tactical targets again predominated involving three-quarters of the sorties flown. In February the strategic assault was pursued against communications in Germany on a larger scale than ever, although the distinction between strategic and tactical targets had then become blurred. During the final weeks of the war the devastation caused by the heavy bombers had a profound effect upon the tottering German war economy, but by this time the German army was defeated in the field by superior Allied forces and thus the true achievement of the strategic attacks was difficult to assess in such complex circumstances.

In the war against Nazi Germany even the most fervent advocates of strategic bombing did not see it achieving the enemy's collapse in isolation. They did, however, initially expect it to play the major part in his downfall. In the event, a major part would be a fair evaluation of the contribution of the British and American bombers, although many historians and latter day commentators would consider this too generous an assessment. That air power generally played a decisive part in the Allied victory in Europe is fact. That the strategic bombing offensive did not win positive acclaim can be attributed to two main factors: the emotive issue of the slaughter of enemy civilians, and the failure of the campaign to show any significant signs of success – other than achieving air superiority – in advance of the cross-Channel invasion of the continent.

However much civilian casualties might be deplored, they were and are an inevitable part of the greater involvement of a whole nation in modern warfare. While the leaders of RAF Bomber Command accepted this – and indeed had little option in the furtherance of their type of bombing – the USAAF command leaders were more sensitive to the old morality, as they could be when precision bombardment was the practice of their forces. While the day bombing usually caused fewer civilian casualties, spillage and incorrect target identification were not infrequent occurrences. The use of radar in bombing through overcast also brought an increase in civilian casualties.

The failure of the strategic bomber to live up to the beliefs of its adherents was due primarily to the slow build-up of forces and the diversion of those available to other operations. Both RAF and USAAF bombers did not achieve planned strength until the eve of the cross-Channel invasion. America with her unsurpassed industrial capability could have provided a sizeable contingent by the spring of 1943 had it not been for the demands of the Pacific and Mediterranean war theatres and anti-submarine requirements. The assembly of a sizeable bombing force in the United Kingdom was interrupted on a number of occasions and, despite damaging attacks on German industry carried out both day and night during 1943, the campaign was never sufficiently sustained to cause a critical situation for the enemy. During the final year of hostilities the strategic bombers were frequently committed to what were tactical targets in support of the invasion of western Europe. Even so, they were able to press attacks at the target systems which were of a strategic nature with outstanding success. A true campaign of strategic bombing against Germany with a sizeable force never occurred in isolation as some 46 per cent of the bombing effort by the 'heavies' was diverted to supporting the ground armies or to meet some defensive emergency. The potential was better realised in the bombing of Japan, but even there unfulfilled when eclipsed by the atomic weapons and the revised strategy of destruction that they introduced.

NOTES FOR OPERATIONAL DIARY

Between the first mission on 4 July 1942 and the cessation of hostilities in Europe on 8 May 1945, 8th Air Force crews were despatched on well over half a million operational flights – 619,454 to be precise. These were made in the course of carrying out more than a thousand separate missions but predominantly on 459 days when bombing raids were launched. Such were the scale and complexity of just one major mission that a fully detailed account can more than fill a book; a definitive work on all 8th Air Force operations would take many volumes. Thus the following summaries of daily operations are perforce concise and largely in statistical form as this is the only way to provide the maximum information within the confines of this book.

The data used are based primarily on the 8th Air Force daily Narrative of Operations with additional information from the USSTAF Daily and Weekly Intelligence Summaries. Other details are drawn from group or divisional records and European sources. The figures given may sometimes be at variance with those in other published works. Even 8th Air Force records covering the same operation often have different sets of statistics. This can be due to error in the original compilation, revised information not incorporated in all documents, or varying interpretations and assessments at different command levels. Although there were fairly firm guidelines for intelligence officers, inevitably borderline cases would arise.

The definitions and abbreviations used here are predominantly those that appeared in the wartime summaries, when the 8th Air Force adopted similar terminology and methods of reporting to the RAF.

It has not been possible to locate data on individual operations conducted by 7th Photo Group between 2 April and 23 May 1944, the Air/Sea Rescue spotter squadron prior to 1 August 1944 and *Carpetbagger* units prior to 1 April 1944. There are also certain periods for both bomber and fighter operations where certain details are not available.

Date: The date form day-month-year is used as this was the form stipulated for wartime reports. A double date separated by an oblique stroke indicates night operations.

Mission Number: The major bomber and fighter operations are distinguished by the Mission or Field Order numbers of the appropriate command. When VIII Bomber Command Hq. became 8th Air Force Hq. in January 1944, the mission numbering system was perpetuated, applicable to major 8th Air Force operations and usually embracing fighter participation. Until 19 August 1942, VIII Fighter Command only had administrative control of assigned fighter groups. Although thereafter it exercised operational control, the few combat units available were still despatched on operations planned and co-ordinated by RAF Fighter Command. The early P-47 missions were also in conjunction with RAF operations but in April 1943 VIII Fighter Command commenced issuing its own directives as Field Orders. FO numbers came into general use in May 1943. Individual fighter wings also issued their own Field Orders in conjunction with those of VIII Fighter Command, and also for special operations planned at fighter wing level. When fighter groups were passed from VIII Fighter Command to Bomb Division control in the autumn of 1944, Field Order numbers were those of either the controlling fighter wing or the 8th Air Force.

Despatched: An aircraft departing from friendly territory on an operation against the enemy. It should be noted that aircraft 'despatched' was often not the number requested by high command or the number prepared for despatch by a group. Sometimes it was not possible to meet the command requirement due to shortage of serviceable aircraft, or mechanical difficulties or other problems might arise before take-off. The greater proportion of mission abortives (scheduled aircraft failing to participate because of mechanical, crew or equipment failure) occurred during the engine start, take-off and formation assembly periods.

Units involved in a mission are given under *Despatched*. The basic operational unit, the group, is used wherever possible during the 1942–1943 period but thereafter the size of mission forces often precludes such detail in the columns and groups participating are listed under *Remarks*. From late 1943 combat wings often flew two separate formations on a mission, distinguished as 'A' or 'B'. The regular groups of a combat wing would often have contingents in both 'A' and 'B' formations. Unit abbreviations used are:–

AD	– Air Division
BD	– Bomb Division
BG	– Bomb Group
BS	– Bomb Squadron
BW	– Bomb Wing
CW	– Combat Wing
ERS	– Emergency Rescue Squadron
FG	– Fighter Group
FS	– Fighter Squadron
FW	– Fighter Wing
NLS	– Night Leaflet Squadron
PG	– Photographic Group
PS	– Photographic Squadron
RCM	– Radio Counter-Measures Squadron
RG	– Reconnaissance Group
RS	– Reconnaissance Squadron
RW	– Reconnaissance Wing

Effective: An aircraft which carries out the purpose of the mission. For bombers this means bombing a target. It can also apply to the dropping of leaflets or anti-radar foil, photography, weather flights, fighter escort or strafing. A lost aircraft was considered effective unless definitely known to have gone down without reaching its objective. 'Effective' is not the same as a 'credit sortie', which only acknowledged that an aircraft had entered hostile airspace. For the years 1944–1945 unit details are more often given for aircraft effective than for despatched.

Target: The place name of target location followed by detail of type of target and its priority for the mission. The time of attack (first and last formation) is also given for early missions. The type of target is generally indicated by an abbreviation:–

A/D	– Air Depot	N/B	– Naval Base
A/F	– Airfield	O/D	– Oil Dump
AFV/V	– Armoured Fighting Vehicle Industry	O/I	– Oil Industry
		O/P	– Oil Plant
A/I	– Aviation Industry	O/R	– Oil Refinery
A/S	– Air Strip	P/A	– Port Area
BI	– Bearings Industry	P/S	– Power Station
BR	– Bridge	R/B	– Rail Bridge
C/B	– Coastal Battery	R/I	– Rail Industry
C/C	– Communications Centre	R/J	– Rail Junction
		R/R	– Railway
C/D	– Coastal Defences	R/S	– Rail Stwtion
C/O	– Coke Ovens	R/V	– Rail Viaduct
C/P	– Choke Points	S/D	– Signals Depot
D/B	– Dive Bombing	S/I	– Steel Industry
E/S	– Electrical Switching Station (Transformers)	SR/I	– Synthetic Rubber Industry
F/B	– Fighter-Bombing	S/Y	– Ship Yard
F/D	– Fuel Dump	TAC/T	– Tactical Targets
G/B	– Gun Batteries	T/T	– Transportation Targets
H/B	– Highway Bridge		
I/A	– Industrial Area	U/B	– U-boat Base
L/G	– Landing Ground	U/Y	– U-boat Yard
M/D	– Munitions Dump	V/S	– V-weapon site
M/I	– Munitions Industry	W/V	– Water Viaduct
MT/I	– Motor Transport Industry	W/W	– Waterway (Canal)
M/Y	– Marshalling Yard		

Abbreviations for target priority:– (P) – Primary, (S) – Secondary, (O) – Target of Opportunity, and (L) Last resort target.

Bombs/Tonnage: As dropped on targets (but not necessarily hitting them). For 1942–1943 missions the number and type of bombs dropped (pounds weight each) delivered by a task force are given with the tonnage of same in the totals. On later missions only tonnage is given.
Abbreviations:– IB – Incendiary Bombs, GP – General Purpose (High Explosive), FRAG – Fragmentation Bombs, IC – Incendiary Cluster.
Claims: Claims of enemy aircraft destroyed by air gunners or fighter pilots (in appropriate columns). Enemy aircraft destroyed on the ground by strafing or bombing are indicated by (G) following the figures. The form of claims report used is that adopted during World War II: the first figure is aircraft considered destroyed, the second those probably destroyed, and the third damaged. Gun camera film evidence was essential for allowing ground claims. Bomber crew claims were in general highly exaggerated due to the confused nature of an air battle where several gunners might be firing at the same enemy aircraft. On average, air gunners' claims were six or seven times greater than the true destroyed figure. They do, however, give an indication of the intensity of the air fighting. On the other hand, fighter pilot claims – which were usually backed by gun camera film – were much nearer true Luftwaffe losses. Claims were continually revised and adjusted in the light of new evidence and different interpretations. The figures given here are the original allowed claims in daily reports.
Losses: These are Missing In Action losses and cover aircraft known lost in enemy territory or at sea, whether through enemy action or accident. For example, an aircraft crashing into the sea just off the English coast at the start of a mission and an aircraft seen shot down over the target would both be classified MIA. Damaged aircraft sometimes sought sanctuary in neutral Sweden or Switzerland and these, originally entered as MIA, were later reassessed in some documents. The losses made public during wartime were the MIA figures. E – Category E indicates an aircraft damaged beyond economical repair while engaged in performing an operational mission. This covers crashes in the UK or friendly territory as well as aircraft that managed to return to friendly territory but were so badly damaged as to be beyond economical repair. The classification was based on an initial inspection by engineering personnel but it often happened that a badly damaged aircraft originally considered repairable was later reassessed as Category E and declared salvage. In these circumstances mission records were unlikely to be amended. There are also instances where aircraft originally classified as Category E were repaired. Where possible individual group category E losses are identified under *Remarks*. Up to the end of 1943, individual bomber group MIA losses are given under that heading in the tables, whereas individual fighter group MIA losses are given under *Remarks*. From 1 January 1944, all individual group losses are given under *Remarks*. It should be noted that the figures given are MIA losses and that Category E losses, where identified, are additional to the MIA figures.
Damaged: All aircraft damaged during the course of an operational mission which were considered repairable. Apart from Category E there were three other damage classifications: Category A covered damage that could be repaired by a combat unit within 36 hours, Category AC was for damage requiring 36 or more hours work, and Category B for badly damaged aircraft which required major repair work by a specialised engineering unit. In the following summaries all classifications of repairable damage are given as a single figure. Near the end of hostilities many aircraft classified AC or B were not repaired and eventually written off as Category E.
Casualties: KIA – Killed in Action: airmen known killed in the performance of a combat mission including fatalities and dead crewmen in returned bombers. WIA – Wounded In Action: also includes crewmen injured in operational accidents. MIA – Missing In Action: personnel in MIA aircraft. Many of these were unharmed and taken prisoner and some evaded capture.
Remarks: Notable events or facts pertaining to a mission. The location of crashes in the UK are given in some instances. Unless specified these relate to the Category E write-offs. Aircraft crash-landing that were repaired are, generally, not listed. Neither are non-operational crashes covered. Abbreviations used under *Remarks*: a/c – aircraft; b/d – battle damage; c/l crash landing; cr. – crashed; e/a – enemy aircraft; e/t – enemy territory; f/l – force landed; inj – injured; k – killed; m/f – mechanical failure; mls – miles; PR – photographic reconnaissance; r/v – rendezvous; s/d – shot down; t/o –take off; WR – weather reconnaissance.
Code Words: The 8th Air Force continued the practice of the RAF in using special words to denote a particular type of operational activity. In 1942 and early 1943 VIII Fighter Command units were frequently despatched on one or more of the following:–
Circus – Heavy fighter escort of a small force of bombers designed to provoke enemy fighter activity.
Ramrod – The escort of bombers to or from a target.
Rhubarb – A small number of aircraft engaging in attacking ground targets, usually in poor weather conditions.
Roadstead – Fighter escort for a shipping strike.
Rodeo – A fighter sweep for the purpose of destroying enemy fighters.
Other operations were:–
Duck – A North Sea diversion.
Nickeling – Dropping leaflets over enemy held territory.
Moling – Bad weather operations by single a/c designed to alert the enemy's air raid warning system.
Spoof – A small number of a/c attempting to deceive the enemy into believing a major offensive operation was under way.
To these the 8th Air Force added code words for its own specialised operations:–
Aphrodite – Overall code name for 8AF experimental operations with radio and television-controlled aircraft and bombs.
Azon – Operations using Azon bombs (bombs controllable in azimuth by radio).
Batty – Experimental missions using radio directed bombs.
Blue Stocking – Weather reconnaissance mission.
Carpetbagger – Clandestine night operations in support of underground forces in occupied lands.
Castor – One-way mission involving radio/television-controlled explosive-laden heavy bombers.
Chattanooga – Fighter strafing missions against German railways.
Chowhound – Food dropping missions to Dutch civilians in early May 1945.
Dilly – Night flash-bomb aided photographic reconnaissance of V-weapon sites.
Disney – Missions using rocket-boosted concrete piercing bombs.
Frantic – Shuttle missions by heavy bombers and fighters to the Soviet Union and Italy.
Jackpot – Fighter strafing attacks on airfields in assigned areas of Germany.
Joker – Night photographic mission using flash bombs.
Noball – Code name for V-weapon sites but commonly used for operations against these targets.
Revival – The return of POWs by air to friendly territory after VE-Day.
Skywave – Special navigational flights – the calibration of *Loran* equipment.
Trolley – Carrying of ground personnel on sight-seeing missions over Germany after hostilities ceased.
Trucking – Carrying supplies in heavy bombers to continental airfields.

OPERATIONAL DIARY

29 JUNE 1942

No 2 GROUP, RAF.

Despatched		Effective	Target	
15BS	1	1	HAZEBROUCK M/Y	No loss or casualties.

REMARKS: Capt Charles Kegelman and crew flew one of 12 Bostons of RAF 226 Sqn to become the first USAAF crew to bomb occupied Europe.

4 JULY 1942

VIII BC

				Bombs		Losses			Casualties		
Despatched		Effective	Target	Tonnage	E/A	MIA	E	Dam	KIA	WIA	MIA
15BS	6	6	4 DUTCH A/Fs		0	2	1	1	0	0	6

REMARKS: Accompanied 6 a/c of 226 Sqn RAF in aircraft borrowed from that sqn. First 8AF operation. Two US crewed aircraft to De Koog (one MIA), one to Bergen/Alkamaar (MIA), one to Haanstede and two to Valkenberg.

Left. Early type steel helmets and gas mask haversacks were the parade order on 11 July when Charles C. Kegelman became the first member of the 8th Air Force to receive the Distinguished Service Cross. The award was made for bringing home a badly damaged Boston from the first USAAF bombing operation. This picture was taken just after Maj-Gen Spaatz had pinned the medal to the newly promoted Major's uniform. Kegelman was killed in the Pacific theatre in 1944 when commanding a B-25 group.

Right. The other members of Kegelman's Independence Day crew received the DFC from General Eaker at the same ceremony at Molesworth. Seen here posing with Kegelman in front of a borrowed RAF Boston are, left to right, Sgts Cunningham and Golay and Lt Dorton. The two sergeants also flew with Kegelman on the first bomber sortie made by an 8th AF crew, 29 June.

12 JULY 1942

VIII BC

				Bombs		Losses			Casualties		
Despatched		Effective	Target	Tonnage	E/A	MIA	E	Dam	KIA	WIA	MIA
15BS	6	6	ABBEVILLE/DRUCAT A/F		0	0	0	2	0		0

REMARKS: Aircraft borrowed from RAF. 15BS temporarily stood down after this raid to make ready their own aircraft, which were also ex RAF machines.

26 JULY 1942

				Losses			Casualties		
Despatched		Groups	E/A	MIA	E	Dam	KIA	WIA	MIA
Spitfire	6	31FG	0	1		0	0	0	1

REMARKS: First fighter operation. Accompanied RAF Spitfires from Biggin Hill on sweep over Gravelines, St. Omer and Abbeville area. Lt Col Clark baled out and made POW.

INCIDENT

During the period of the 8th Air Force's stay in the United Kingdom accident accounted for more than one in six of the total heavy bomber losses – which were in excess of 6,500 B-17s and B-24s. While this toll could be attributed to many factors the major cause was human error with machines that allowed little margin for error, particularly when operating fully loaded. There had to be a first time and this occurred at Grafton Underwood on the afternoon of 1 August 1942 involving Lt Lawrence when landing B-17E 41-9024, alias *King Kondor*, after a local flight. Near the end of the landing run the brakes failed to operate and the bomber sped on, crashing through a boundary hedge and into a civilian lorry on the public road beyond. The driver was badly injured, dying later that day. With a smashed nose and no parts available for making repairs, *King Kondor* marked up another first in becoming a 'hangar queen', providing spares for other Fortresses because new ones had not arrived from the United States.

In the last week of July Lockheed P-38Fs of the elite 1FG arrived at Goxhill after a ferry flight via Greenland and Iceland. This one was flown by Col Ben Kelsey. Radio modifications delayed the fighter's introduction on cross-Channel operations where P-38 units had no opportunity to engage in combat before being withdrawn for service in North Africa.

Three of the P-38s in 1FG's movement to England were piloted by VIII Fighter Command staff officers. Col Ben Kelsey, who made the first P-38 test flight, is on the extreme left of this group at Goxhill on 29 July. He would eventually head the important USAAF air technical organisation in the UK. Next to Kelsey is Col John Gerhart who, after service at 8AF Hq was given command of the 95BG and subsequently a heavy bomber combat wing. Second from the right is Maj Cass Hough, another technical expert who would play a major part in extending the range of 8AF fighters. In the centre is Maj John Zahn, Air Executive of 1FG (with the unit's Intelligence Officer behind him). 1FG CO, Col John Stone, stands on the extreme right.

The top brass came to Bovingdon on 2 August to inspect the Eighth's only heavy bomber group. By coincidence they chose to pose for photographers beneath the nose of B-17E 41-2578 which fifteen days later would become the very first of 30,000 8AF heavy bombers to penetrate enemy airspace during 32 months of hostilities. From left to right: Brig.-Gen Robert Candee (CG VIII GASC), Brig.-Gen Frank Hunter (CG VIII FC), Col Asa Duncan (Chief of Staff, VIII BC), Maj.-Gen Walter Frank (CG VIII AFSC), Lt-Gen Dwight Eisenhower (CG US Forces Europe), Maj.-Gen Carl Spaatz (CG 8AF) and Brig.-Gen Ira Eaker (CG VIII BC). (USAAF).

5 AUGUST 1942

VIII FC

					Losses			Casualties		
Despatched		**Groups**	**E/A**		**MIA**	**E**	**Dam**	**KIA**	**WIA**	**MIA**
Spitfire	11	31FG	0		0	0	0	0	0	0

REMARKS: Despatched on a practice *Rodeo*.

6 AUGUST 1942

VIII FC

					Losses			Casualties		
Despatched		**Groups**	**E/A**		**MIA**	**E**	**Dam**	**KIA**	**WIA**	**MIA**
Spitfire	11	31FG	0		0	0	0	0	0	0

REMARKS: Sent on a practice *Rodeo*.

9 AUGUST 1942

VIII FC

Despatched		Groups	E/A	Losses MIA	E	Dam	Casualties KIA	WIA	MIA
Spitfire	2	31FG	0–0–1	0	0	0	0	0	0

REMARKS: Despatched on a defensive patrol.

Spitfire	11	31FG		0					

REMARKS: As top cover on a feint *Rodeo* to Dieppe.

11 AUGUST 1942

VIII FC

Despatched		Groups	E/A	Losses MIA	E	Dam	Casualties KIA	WIA	MIA
Spitfire	12	31FG	0	0	0	0	0	0	0

REMARKS: Despatched on a feint *Rodeo*.

12 AUGUST 1942

VIII FC

Despatched		Groups	E/A	Losses MIA	E	Dam	Casualties KIA	WIA	MIA
Spitfire	13	31FG	0	0	0	0	0	0	0

REMARKS: Sent on a feint *Rodeo* – Clacton/Dunkirk/Calais/Dover.

15 AUGUST 1942

VIII FC

Despatched		Groups	E/A	Losses MIA	E	Dam	Casualties KIA	WIA	MIA
Spitfire	2	31FG	0	0	0	0	0	0	0

REMARKS: Sent on convoy patrol.

Spitfire	12	31FG	0	0					

REMARKS: Sent on a feint sweep of Dieppe/Etretat area.

17 AUGUST 1942

VIII BC 1

	Despatched		Effective	Target	Bombs Tonnage	E/A	Losses MIA	E	Dam	Casualties KIA	WIA	MIA
				ROUEN/SOTTEVILLE (P)	45 × 600GP							
B-17	97BG	12	12	M/Y 1739–1746 hrs	9 × 1100GP	0–0–1	0	0	2	0	0	0
B-17	97BG	6	–	DIVERSION								

REMARKS: First VIII BC and 97BG heavy bomber mission.

INCIDENT

Despite the worst fears, the 12 B-17Es that flew the 8th Air Force's first heavy bomber raid returned with only superficial damage to two aircraft. Its leaders believed the formations might not have been so fortunate had everything gone according to plan. For the attack the two squadrons had flown one behind the other, bombing by three-plane flights on each flight leader – the aircraft flew approximately 150 yards apart. Col Armstrong, who was in *Butcher Shop* in the first squadron, arranged with Capt Flack flying in *Yankee Doodle*, the lead of the second, to radio a message when his unit had bombed, at which Armstrong would turn his squadron to the right allowing the second squadron to join to make a large single formation for better defence against possible fighter interception. Having bombed, Armstrong continued to fly straight ahead, waiting for the radio signal. No signal came. Then Major Paul Tibbetts, Armstrong's pilot, spotted Flack's formation out to the right. At that moment a number of anti-aircraft shells burst between the two squadrons, in a position to where it was estimated the lead squadron would have turned had it received Flack's 'Bombs Away' signal.

Return from Rouen. US and British officers on Grafton Underwood control tower watching the Fortresses approach. Gen Spaatz stands just to the left of the ladder. Beirne Lay is behind the guy-rope, Fred Castle at the near corner, and most of the other officers who formed the nucleus of VIII Bomber Command are present. (USAAF)

While the last three-plane element passes overhead, *Yankee Doodle* makes its approach to Grafton's runway 24. (USAAF)

Fortresses and aircraft commanders that flew Mission No.1.

Tail Number	*Nickname*	*Squadron*	*Pilot*
12578	*Butcher Shop*	340 BS	Col Frank A. Armstrong & Maj Paul W. Tibbets
19125	*Prowler*	342 BS	Lt Alexander Blair Jr.
19026	*Baby Doll*	342 BS	Lt James M. Sammons
19042	*The Berlin Sleeper*	342 BS	Lt George D. Burgess
19043	*Peggy D*	342 BS	Capt William B. Musselwhite
19017	*Heidi Ho*	342 BS	Lt Walter F. Kelly
19023	*Yankee Doodle*	414 BS	Lt John P. Dowswell
19089	*Johnny Reb*	414 BS	Lt Richard S. Starks
19103	*Dixie Demo*	414 BS	Lt Clarence L. Thacker
19021	*The Big Bitch*	414 BS	Lt Claire M. Smartt
19030	*Big Punk*	414 BS	Lt William P. Saunders
19100	*Birmingham Blitzkrieg*	414 BS	Lt Thomas H. Borders

While Col Armstrong is listed as pilot in 97th BG records, Tibbetts claims to have been the pilot and he was certainly the more experienced of the two at the controls of a B-17. Armstrong's scratch crew were mostly members of Lt Glen Leland's and the B-17 was that assigned to Lt Butcher. Of the 111 men who flew to Rouen, 31 were later missing or killed during hostilities. The co-pilot of *Johnny Reb* was killed four days later and the pilot wounded; the rest of the crew were missing over Lorient on 21 October. Lt William Tingle, co-pilot of *Baby Doll*, and Lt Harry Erickson, bombardier on *Peggy D*, were also missing on the same Lorient raid. All nine men who had flown *Birmingham Blitzkrieg* were MIA over Tunisia in December 1942. The crew of *Prowler* – except bombardier Lt William Lewis who was not present – went down over Sicily in April 1943. The bombardier on *Big Punk*, Lt George Ludolph; navigator of *Dixie Demo*, Lt Jim Watson; and the tail gunner on *Yankee Doodle*, Sgt Ray Lewis, were also lost over Sicily flying with other crews. Sgt Robert Nichols, waist gunner on *The Big Bitch*, went down with another crew over Italy in August 1943. George Burgess, pilot of *The Berlin Sleeper*, completed his tour and returned for a second as squadron commander in another group in Italy only to be killed in a crash. The Fortresses that participated were, along with other B-17Es, transferred to the 92nd BG on 25 August 1942 for use in operational training. In the spring of 1943 the B-17Es were dispersed among other training units and operational B-17 groups where they served for target towing and transport duties. Those that survived to the end of hostilities were broken up at base air depots in the UK.

First Fortress to land taxies in carrying Gen Eaker, VIII BC CG. Lt John Dowswell surveys the waiting dignitaries from the pilot's window. A grinning Carl Schultz peers over the top of his bombsight which he has covered with a canvas to hide its secrets from cameramen.

The very first of the many. Back on Grafton, the B-17E known as *Butcher Shop*, in which Col Armstrong and Maj Tibbets led the Rouen formations. The rest of the crew have an elated discussion in front of the bomber and oblige a cameraman. Left to right: Lt Frank Beadle (bombardier), Sgt Chester Love (tail gunner), Sgt Richard Williams (ball gunner), Lt Levon Ray (navigator), Lt Glen Leland (a pilot who acted as observer and waist gunner), Sgt Fran Rebello (engineer-gunner), Sgt Joseph Cummings (waist gunner) and Sgt Zane Gemill (radio operator).

18 AUGUST 1942

VIII FC

Despatched		Groups	E/A	Losses MIA	E	Dam	Casualties KIA	WIA	MIA
Spitfire	13	31FG	0	0	0	0	0	0	0
REMARKS: Sent on *Circus 9*.									
Spitfire	12	31FG	0	0	0	0	0	0	0
REMARKS: Sent to patrol French coast.									
Spitfire	11	31FG	0	0	0	0	0	0	0
REMARKS: Despatched to sweep Dieppe/Etretat area.									

19 AUGUST 1942

VIII BC 2

	Despatched		Effective	Target	Bombs Tonnage	E/A	Losses MIA	E	Dam	Casualties KIA	WIA	MIA
B-17	97BG	24	22	ABBEVILLE/DRUCAT A/F 1032–1040 hrs	108 × 600GP 41 × 250IB	0–0–0	0	0	3	0	0	0
1BW				DIVERSIONS								
B-17	97BG	6	–			0–0–0	0	0	0	0	2	0

VIII FC

Despatched		Groups	E/A	Losses MIA	E	Dam	Casualties KIA	WIA	MIA
Spitfire	123	31FG	1–1–5	8	0	0	0	0	4
REMARKS: On eleven missions in support of the Dieppe landings. Fighter e/a credits:– 31FG – 2.									
Spitfire	4	52FG	0	0					
REMARKS: Sent on defensive patrol to intercept e/a reported off Northern Ireland. First operational sorties for 52FG. First operations by VIII FC units under VIII FC operational control.									

20 AUGUST 1942

VIII BC 3

	Despatched		Effective	Target	Bombs Tonnage	E/A	Losses MIA	E	Dam	Casualties KIA	WIA	MIA
1BW				AMIENS/LONGEAU	40 × 1100GP							
B-17	97BG	12	11	M/Y (P) 1801 hrs	8 × 250IB	0	0	0	0	0	0	0

VIII FC

Despatched		Groups	E/A	Losses MIA	E	Dam	Casualties KIA	WIA	MIA
Spitfire	12	31FG	0	0	0	0	0	0	0

REMARKS: As escort for B-17s.

Spitfire	12	31FG	0	0	0	0	0	0	0

REMARKS: Sent on a diversion with RAF Defiants.

Spitfire	12	31FG	0	0	0	0	0	0	0

REMARKS: Despatched on a diversion sweep.

Spitfire	11	31FG	0	0	0	0	0	0	0

REMARKS: Used on a diversion.

Spitfire	2	31FG	0	0	0	0	0	0	0

REMARKS: As escort to RAF Lysander on ASR duties.

21 AUGUST 1942

VIII BC 4

	Despatched		Effective	Target	Bombs Tonnage	E/A	Losses MIA	E	Dam	Casualties KIA	WIA	MIA
1BW												
B-17	97BG	12	0	ROTTERDAM S/Y	0	2–5–6	0	0	1	1	5	0

REMARKS: Bombers were 16 minutes late for rendezvous with fighter escort, which could only stay until half way to target. 20–25 e/a attacked as fighters turned for home. Bombers recalled at French coast.

VIII FC

Despatched		Groups	E/A	Losses MIA	E	Dam	Casualties KIA	WIA	MIA
Spitfire	11	31FG	0	0	0	0	0	0	0

REMARKS: As a diversion to B-17s.

Spitfire	11	31FG	0	0	0	0	0	0	0

REMARKS: Despatched on an ASR mission.

Spitfire	11	31FG	0	0	0	0	0	0	0

REMARKS: Sent out on patrol.

24 AUGUST 1942

VIII BC 5

	Despatched		Effective	Target	Bombs Tonnage	E/A	Losses MIA	E	Dam	Casualties KIA	WIA	MIA
1BW				LE TRAIT S/Y (P)								
B-17	97BG	12	12	1616–1623 hrs	48 × 1000GP	0	0	0	3	0	5	0

VIII FC

Despatched		Groups	E/A	Losses MIA	E	Dam	Casualties KIA	WIA	MIA
Spitfire	12	31FG	0	0	0	0	0	0	0
Spitfire	6	31FG	0	0	0	0	0	0	0

REMARKS: Sent to intercept enemy raider.

27 AUGUST 1942

VIII BC 6

	Despatched		Effective	Target	Bombs Tonnage	E/A	Losses MIA	E	Dam	Casualties KIA	WIA	MIA
1BW				ROTTERDAM S/Y (P)	28 × 500GP							
B-17	97BG	9	7	1740 hrs	12 × 1000GP	0	0	0	3	0	1	0

VIII FC

Despatched		Groups	E/A	Losses MIA	E	Dam	Casualties KIA	WIA	MIA
Spitfire	12	31FG	0	0	0	0	0	0	0
REMARKS: As cover for ASR launches.									
Spitfire	4	31FG	0	0	0	0	0	0	0
REMARKS: To patrol over Beachy Head.									
Spitfire	6	31FG	0	0	0	0	0	0	0
REMARKS: Sent to patrol coast line off Shoreham.									
Spitfire	12	31FG	0	0	0	0	0	0	0
REMARKS: Sent to protect ASR Walrus a/c.									
Spitfire	2	31FG	0	0	0	0	0	0	0
REMARKS: Sent out on patrol.									
Spitfire	6	31FG	0	0	0	0	0	0	0
REMARKS: As escort on a rescue mission.									

28 AUGUST 1942

VIII BC 7

	Despatched		Effective	Target	Bombs Tonnage	E/A	Losses MIA	E	Dam	Casualties KIA	WIA	MIA
1BW				MEAULTE A/I (P)	72 × 500GP							
B-17	97BG	14	11	1337–1344 hrs	12 × 1100GP	0	0	0	3	1	0	0

VIII FC

Despatched		Groups	E/A	Losses MIA	E	Dam	Casualties KIA	WIA	MIA
Spitfire	12	31FG	0	0					
REMARKS: Carried out sweep, as a diversion to B-17s.									
Spitfire	12	31FG	0	0					
REMARKS: Carried out fighter sweep.									
Spitfire	12	31FG	0	0					
REMARKS: As top cover to RAF Tangmere Wing.									
Spitfire	2	31FG	0	0					
REMARKS: Patrol over Selsey Bill.									

29 AUGUST 1942

VIII BC 8

	Despatched		Effective	Target	Bombs Tonnage	E/A	Losses MIA	E	Dam	Casualties KIA	WIA	MIA
1BW				COURTRAI A/F (P)	91 × 300GP	0–1–1	0	0	3	0	0	0
B-17	97BG	13	11	1131–1136 hrs	58 × 500GP							
			1	STEENE A/F (O)								
				1137 hrs	4 × 500GP							
TOTALS:			12		22.95	0–1–1	0		3	0	0	0

VIII FC

Despatched		Groups	E/A	Losses MIA	E	Dam	Casualties KIA	WIA	MIA
Spitfire	36	31FG	0	0	0	0	0	0	0
REMARKS: Sent to patrol off enemy coast. First mission for 31FG as a group. Individual squadrons flying since 5 August 1942.									
P-38	2	1FG	0	0	0	0	0	0	0
REMARKS: Scrambled to intercept enemy raiders.									
P-38	2	1FG	0	0	0	0	0	0	0
REMARKS: Scrambled to intercept enemy raiders.									

1 SEPTEMBER 1942

VIII FC

Despatched		Groups	E/A	Losses MIA	E	Dam	Casualties KIA	WIA	MIA
P-38	32	1FG	0	0	0	0	0	0	0

REMARKS: Sent on a fighter sweep.

Despatched		Groups	E/A	Losses MIA	E	Dam	Casualties KIA	WIA	MIA
Spitfire	12	52FG	0	0	0	0	0	0	0

REMARKS: Sent on a practice *Rodeo*.

2 SEPTEMBER 1942

VIII FC

Despatched		Groups	E/A	Losses MIA	E	Dam	Casualties KIA	WIA	MIA
Spitfire	12	52FG	0	0	0	0	0	0	0

REMARKS: Sent out to patrol Le Touquet–Boulogne area.

Despatched		Groups	E/A	Losses MIA	E	Dam	Casualties KIA	WIA	MIA
Spitfire	13	52FG	0	0	0	0	0	0	0

REMARKS: Carried out a sweep of the enemy coastline, Le Touquet–Gris Nez area.

Despatched		Groups	E/A	Losses MIA	E	Dam	Casualties KIA	WIA	MIA
Spitfire	2	31FG	0	0	0	0	0	0	0

REMARKS: Sent out to patrol St. Catherines Point.

Despatched		Groups	E/A	Losses MIA	E	Dam	Casualties KIA	WIA	MIA
Spitfire	12	52FG	0	0	0	0	0	0	0

REMARKS: Sent out to patrol the Channel between Manston and Calais.

4 SEPTEMBER 1942

VIII FC

Despatched		Groups	E/A	Losses MIA	E	Dam	Casualties KIA	WIA	MIA
P-38	2	1FG	0	0	0	0	0	0	0

REMARKS: Scrambled to patrol off Ibsley.

Despatched		Groups	E/A	Losses MIA	E	Dam	Casualties KIA	WIA	MIA
Spitfire	2	31FG	0	0	0	0	0	0	0

REMARKS: Sent on patrol off Selsey Bill.

Johnny Reb, the Fortress in which 8AF sustained its first heavy bomber combat fatality on 21 August, lifts off from Bovingdon on a training flight, 4 September. The co-pilot has braked the main wheels which are just starting to retract. Along with the other B-17E models of the 97BG this aircraft was transferred to the Combat Crew Replacement Centre in late August.

5 SEPTEMBER 1942

VIII BC 9

	Despatched		Effective	Target	Bombs Tonnage	E/A	Losses MIA	E	Dam	Casualties KIA	WIA	MIA
1BW				LE HAVRE P/A								
DB-7	15BS	12	11	0932 hrs	44 × 500GP							
1BW				ROUEN/SOTTEVILLE								
B-17	97BG	25	31	M/Y (P)	32 × 1100GP							
	301BG	12		1030–1035 hrs	43 × 1000GP							
					123 × 500GP							
					16 × 250 IB							
TOTALS:		49	42		82.85	0	0		0	0	0	0

REMARKS: First mission for 301BG.

VIII FC

Despatched		Groups	E/A	Losses MIA	E	Dam	Casualties KIA	WIA	MIA
Spitfire	24	31FG	0	0	0	0	0	0	0

REMARKS: As escort for DB-7s attacking Le Havre.

P-38	2	1FG	0	0	0	0	0	0	0

REMARKS: Scrambled on a coastal patrol.

P-38	2	1FG	0	0	0	0	0	0	0

REMARKS: Despatched to intercept e/a.

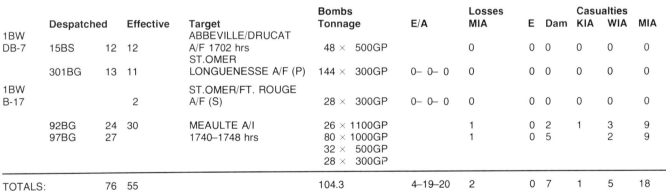

The crew of 15BS's Boston *Texas* – left to right Lt Terrell (navigator/bombardier), Sgt Evans (gunner), Lt Jackson (pilot) and Sgt Spellman (gunner) do not look particularly enthusiastic about the 'cup of tea' provided by the YMCA ladies from their new US-donated mobile snack bar. Most GIs soon became 'acclimatised' to British tea and coffee and the YMCA vehicles were a welcome sight at airfield dispersal points. The Boston, AL445, recently repainted in USAAF olive drab, was one of the aircraft that took part in attack on Abbeville on the day of the photograph, 6 September.

6 SEPTEMBER 1942

VIII BC 10

	Despatched		Effective	Target	Bombs Tonnage	E/A	Losses MIA	E	Dam	Casualties KIA	WIA	MIA
1BW				ABBEVILLE/DRUCAT								
DB-7	15BS	12	12	A/F 1702 hrs	48 × 500GP		0	0	0	0	0	0
				ST.OMER								
	301BG	13	11	LONGUENESSE A/F (P)	144 × 300GP	0–0–0	0	0	0	0	0	0
1BW				ST.OMER/FT. ROUGE								
B-17			2	A/F (S)	28 × 300GP	0–0–0	0	0	0	0	0	0
	92BG	24	30	MEAULTE A/I	26 × 1100GP		1	0	2	1	3	9
	97BG	27		1740–1748 hrs	80 × 1000GP		1	0	5		2	9
					32 × 500GP							
					28 × 300GP							
TOTALS:		76	55		104.3	4–19–20	2	0	7	1	5	18

REMARKS: First heavy bomber losses for the VIII BC. First mission for 92BG.

VIII FC

Despatched		Groups	E/A	Losses MIA	E	Dam	Casualties KIA	WIA	MIA
Spitfire	37	31FG	0	0	0	0	0	0	0

REMARKS: 31FG as escort to 15BS DB-7s.

P-38	2	1FG	0	0	0	0	0	0	0

REMARKS: Sent to intercept e/a.

7 SEPTEMBER 1942

VIII BC 11

	Despatched		Effective	Target	Bombs Tonnage	E/A	Losses MIA	E	Dam	Casualties KIA	WIA	MIA
1BW				ROTTERDAM S/Y (P)								
B-17	97BG	15	4	7 a/c 1015–1030 hrs	35 × 1000GP (P)	8– 4– 7	0	0	4	1	3	0
				UTRECHT								
	301BG	14	5	2 a/c 1011 hrs	10 × 1000GP (O)	4– 6– 5	0	0	1	0	1	0
TOTALS:		29	9		22.5	12-10-12	0	0	5	1	4	0

VIII FC

Despatched		Groups	E/A	Losses MIA	E	Dam	Casualties KIA	WIA	MIA
P-38	2	1FG	0	0	0	0	0	0	0

REMARKS: Scrambled on a defensive mission.

Despatched		Groups	E/A	Losses MIA	E	Dam	Casualties KIA	WIA	MIA
Spitfire	11	52FG	0	0	0	0	0	0	0

REMARKS: Carried out sweep along French coast between Berck and Calais.

8 SEPTEMBER 1942

VIII FC

Despatched		Groups	E/A	Losses MIA	E	Dam	Casualties KIA	WIA	MIA
P-38		1FG	0	0	0	0	0	0	0

REMARKS: Sent on a practice sweep with RAF.

Despatched		Groups	E/A	Losses MIA	E	Dam	Casualties KIA	WIA	MIA
P-38		1FG	0	0	0	0	0	0	0

REMARKS: Sent on a sweep of enemy territory with RAF.

Despatched		Groups	E/A	Losses MIA	E	Dam	Casualties KIA	WIA	MIA
P-38	2	1FG	0	0	0	0	0	0	0

REMARKS: Scrambled to intercept e/a.

10 SEPTEMBER 1942

VIII FC

Despatched		Groups	E/A	Losses MIA	E	Dam	Casualties KIA	WIA	MIA
Spitfire	11	52FG	0	0	0	0	0	0	0

REMARKS: Carried out sweep of enemy territory.

16 SEPTEMBER 1942

VIII FC

Despatched		Groups	E/A	Losses MIA	E	Dam	Casualties KIA	WIA	MIA
P-38	24	1FG	0	0	0	0	0	0	0

REMARKS: Sent on a sweep of the French coastline between Dieppe and Le Touquet.

17 SEPTEMBER 1942

VIII FC

Despatched		Groups	E/A	Losses MIA	E	Dam	Casualties KIA	WIA	MIA
P-38	24	1FG	0	0	0	0	0	0	0

REMARKS: Carried out sweep.

Maj Harrison Thyng commanded 309FS at Westhampnett and on 22 September (the date of this photo) was one of two pilots who intercepted a Ju88 over the Channel. Here Thyng talks to 1/Lt Ivor Williby, 31FG Intelligence Officer. In November Thyng took his unit to North Africa where he shot down five enemy aircraft. In the Korean War he was credited with five MiG victories. Note the crowbar in Spitfire V hatch panel; for use in forcing a way out of the cockpit if the canopy jammed in an emergency.

Nearly as numerous as the B-17 and P-38 by the late summer of 1942, Douglas C-47 transports were on hand to carry troops and supplies to North Africa once Operation Torch was launched. The 8AF 'produced' the 12AF for this invasion campaign and in mid-September the 120 C-47s were transferred to the offspring. On the 23rd of that month the 60 men of 2 Battalion, 503 US Parachute Infantry Regiment were making practice jumps from C-47s of the 60 Troop Carrier Group. Here paratroopers are checking each other's harness prior to boarding Skytrains lined up on Aldermaston. These men and aircraft flew from England to Oran on the night of 7/8 November.

22 SEPTEMBER 1942

VIII FC

Despatched		Groups	E/A	Losses MIA	E	Dam	Casualties KIA	WIA	MIA
Spitfire	2	31FG	1–0–0	0	0	0	0	0	0

REMARKS: Scrambled to intercept e/a off Selsey Bill.

26 SEPTEMBER 1942

VIII BC 12

	Despatched		Effective	Target	Bombs Tonnage	E/A	Losses MIA	E	Dam	Casualties KIA	WIA	MIA
1BW	92BG	17	7	DIVERSION	–							
B-17	301BG	26	0	CHERBOURG/ MAUPERTUS A/F	0							
	97BG	19	0	MORLAIX/POUJEAN A/F	0							
	92BG	13	9	DIVERSION	–	0						
TOTALS:		75	16		0	0	0		0	0	0	0

REMARKS: 301BG recalled because escort fighters not seen. Cloud prevented 97BG bombing; they had miscalculated a tail wind and finally turned for home over the Bay of Biscay.

VIII FC

Despatched		Groups	E/A	Losses MIA	E	Dam	Casualties KIA	WIA	MIA
P-38	36	1FG	0	0	0	0	0	0	0

REMARKS: 1 FG recalled shortly after take-off for heavy bomber escort. 133 Sqn RAF about to be absorbed by 4FG, lost 11 Spitfire IXs during bomber support. 1 'Eagle Squadron' pilot credited with an e/a destroyed.

Spitfire	37	31FG	0	0	0	0	0	0	0

REMARKS: Sent on a diversionary *Circus*.

30 SEPTEMBER 1942

VIII FC

Despatched		Groups	E/A	Losses MIA	E	Dam	Casualties KIA	WIA	MIA
Spitfire	42		0	0	0	0	0	0	0

REMARKS: Sent on a practice sweep.

Back from the mission to Meaulte on 2 October a B-17F of the Eighth's second heavy bomber group, the 301st, taxies along the Chelveston perimeter track. Easier manoeuvring of the 20-ton bomber was achieved by shutting off the two inboard engines (Nos 2 and 3).

2 OCTOBER 1942

VIII BC 13

	Despatched		Effective	Target	Bombs Tonnage	E/A	Losses MIA	E	Dam	Casualties KIA	WIA	MIA
1BW	97BG	18	32	MEAULTE A/I	240 × 500GP	1– 4–4	0	0	0	0	0	0
B-17	301BG	25			70 × 250 IB	3– 5–1	0		6	0	3	0
	97BG	6	6	ST.OMER/ LONGUENESSE A/F 1517–1518 hrs	50 × 500GP	5– 4–4	0	0	0	0	0	0
1BW DB-7	15BS	12	11	LE HAVRE (SHIP IN DOCK) 1431 hrs	44 × 500GP		0	0	0	0	0	0
TOTALS:		61	49		92.25	9–13–9	0		6	0	3	0

REMARKS: 1 301BG B-17 c/l at Gatwick with 3 WIA.

VIII FC

	Despatched		Groups	E/A	Losses MIA	E	Dam	Casualties KIA	WIA	MIA
	P-38	31	1FG	0	1					
	Spitfire	23	4FG	4–0–1	0					
TOTALS:		54		4–0–1	1	0	0	0	0	0

REMARKS: P-38s as escort to main force attacking Meaulte. Spitfires of 4FG on first mission as escort to diversionary force attacking St. Omer. Fighter group e/a credits:– 4FG – 4.

				E/A	Losses MIA	E	Dam	KIA	WIA	MIA
	Spitfire	7		0	0	0	0	0	0	0
	Spitfire	34		0	0	0	0	0	0	0
	P-38	19		0	0	0	0	0	0	0
TOTALS:		60		0	0	0	0	0	0	0

REMARKS: Sent on practice sweeps and defensive sorties.

				E/A	Losses MIA	E	Dam	KIA	WIA	MIA
	Spitfire	36	31FG	0	0	0	0	0	0	0

REMARKS: As escort for RAF Bostons.

6 OCTOBER 1942

VIII FC

Despatched		Groups	E/A	Losses MIA	E	Dam	Casualties KIA	WIA	MIA
Spitfire	18	52FG	0	0	0	0	0	0	0

REMARKS: Despatched on shipping patrol.

9 OCTOBER 1942

VIII BC 14

	Despatched		Effective	Target		Bombs Tonnage	E/A	Losses MIA	E	Dam	Casualties KIA	WIA	MIA
1BW													
B-24	93BG	24	10	LILLE I/A	(P)	100 × 500GP		1	1		0	2	10
B-17	97BG	22	16	LILLE I/A	(P)	130 × 500GP		0	0		0	0	0
	306BG	24	19	LILLE I/A	(P)	159 × 500GP		1	1		0	1	9
			2	COURTRAI A/F	(S)	20 × 500GP							
	301BG	23	21	LILLE I/A	(P)	179 × 500GP		1	0		0	4	0
			2	ROUBAIX	(O)	10 × 500GP							
	92BG	15	3	LILLE I/A	(P)	24 × 500GP							
			6	ST. OMER/ LONGUENESSE A/F	(L)	48 × 500GP		1	0		0	6	10
TOTALS:		108	79			167.5	25–38–44	4	2	46	0	10	29
1BW				DIVERSION									
B-17	92BG	7				0							

REMARKS: 1 92BG and 1 301BG B-17 down in sea, one crew rescued. First mission for 93BG and first VIII BC B-24 mission and loss. First mission for 306BG. Last mission for 92BG until 14 May 1943. B/d 93BG B-24 c/l upon return at Northolt. 2 92BG B-17s collided 20 miles west of Dunkirk but returned. B/d 306BG B-17 c/l Manston A/F, crew safe.

VIII FC

Despatched		Groups	E/A	Losses MIA	E	Dam	Casualties KIA	WIA	MIA
P-38	36	1FG	0	0	0	1	0	0	0
Spitfire	36	4FG	0	0	0	0	0	0	0
TOTALS:	72		0	0	0	1	0	0	0

REMARKS: P-38s sent as second target support to *Circus 224*. Spitfires sent as third diversion on *Circus 224* in conjunction with 92BG B-17s. P-38 f/l on a cliff top near Beachy Head through fuel shortage, flown off later. Last mission for 1FG prior to transferring to 12AF.

INCIDENT

The Liberators did not have such an easy combat initiation as the Fortresses some two months earlier. Determined enemy opposition encountered on the Lille raid resulted in the loss of one B-24 and damage to several. Lt Joe Tate's *Ball Of Fire* provided the first narrow-escape story for a Liberator crew. An FW 190 firing 20 mm cannon shells scored three hits; one smashing the tail, one hitting the bomb bay and the third exploding under the pilot's seat. Shrapnel severed oxygen lines in the cockpit forcing Tate to use emergency bottles passed to him by the co-pilot. Both men in the nose compartment were also deprived of oxygen and had to use auxiliary units. Once clear of the enemy coast, tail gunner T/Sgt Aaron Moses came forward and on entering the bomb bay found it drenched with gasoline. Realising a fuel line had been damaged by a shell fragment he endeavoured to trace the leak. Removing a glove he felt for the fracture and stopped the flow with his fingers but not before being liberally sprayed with fuel in eyes and face. By the time other crew members arrived to help Moses' hand was badly frozen. Tate made a successful emergency landing on the small grass surfaced airfield at Northolt.

INCIDENT

The large close formations that were an essential part of the 8th Air Force's mode of operations presented a constant danger – collisions. During the course of nearly a thousand days of operations there were to be over a hundred collisions involving heavy bombers; the first occurred on the Lille raid. The 92nd Group's B-17Es were over the Channel some 20 miles west of Dunkirk on the way out when 41-9020, piloted by Lt Dempsy, manoeuvring for position, rose and his vertical tail struck the right wing and two engines of Lt Wiley's 41-9051. Dempsy's aircraft lost its entire rudder and part of the fin, but miraculously gunner Sgt Kirk escaped injury although his compartment was badly damaged. The impact caused the Fortress to fall away in a dive, but the pilots managed to regain control and fly the crippled bomber back for a safe landing at home base. The other Fortress had two engines disabled and a fuel tank ruptured but after jettisoning its bombs managed to make an emergency landing at Detling.

INCIDENT

Four hundred and fifty 8th Air Force heavy bombers are known to have made forced landings on water – ditchings – during hostilities. Of the 4,370 men involved 1,547 were rescued. The first successful heavy bomber ditching was by a 301st Group B-17F on the 9 October 1942 Lille mission. Hit by enemy fighter fire and with loss of power causing a 1,500 ft a minute descent, 1/Lt Donald Swenson was aware he would have to come down in the sea. With the intercom inoperative, he told the co-pilot to take the controls while he went to the various crew positions and instructed all men to go to the radio room. The sea, running 15 to 20 ft high waves, thwarted Swenson's effort to accomplish a smooth touch-down. The impact caught most of the crew off guard. One was pitched into the bomb bay and another was cut on the head by a Very pistol he had in his lap. The pilots extricated themselves through the cockpit windows while the rest of the crew went out of the radio room gun hatch – having jettisoned the gun while still in flight. Only one of the rubber life rafts would inflate properly, the others having been riddled by shell fragments.

The Fortress sank after about a minute and a half by which time all ten men were out and afloat. It appeared the Mae West life-savers would not support their weights, so they assisted each other in struggling out of their heavy sheepskin flying clothes. Swenson ordered three of the gunners on to the raft while two men held on to its edge and the rest of the crew clung to the side of a half inflated one. The water was very cold and although they were quite near to land – only about a mile off North Foreland – the prospects of survival were not good. However the bomber's emergency calls, sent by the radio operator prior to ditching, had been heard and an RAF Air-Sea Rescue launch vectored to the position. The launch captain had seen the Fortress coming down and was on the spot within 15 minutes, just in time as one man had drifted away from the rest. Because of the rough sea, picking up the men proved difficult although this was successfully accomplished. One of the rescued, M/Sgt Glenn Doerr, was a ground crew man who had persuaded the pilot to take him on the raid without obtaining official permission. Doerr was of great assistance during the ditching and this probably influenced the authorities in taking a lenient view of the breach of regulations.

14 OCTOBER 1942

VIII FC

Despatched		Groups	E/A	Losses MIA	E	Dam	Casualties KIA	WIA	MIA
Spitfire	11	4FG	0	0	0	0	0	0	0

REMARKS: Sent out on a shipping strike off Holland.

15 OCTOBER 1942

VIII FC

Despatched		Groups	E/A	Losses MIA	E	Dam	Casualties KIA	WIA	MIA
Spitfire	36	4FG	0	0	0	0	0	0	0

REMARKS: As escort to RAF Bostons.

P-38	24	14FG	0	0	0	0	0	0	0

REMARKS: Despatched on *Circus 227* to Le Havre.

A magazine of 20 mm cannon shells being passed to an armourer for installation on a Spitfire V of 2FS, 52FG at Goxhill. The unit never had an opportunity to test the Spitfire's armament in combat while in the UK, for a week after this picture was taken, on 19 October, all personnel were aboard a ship bound for the Mediterranean. The photo also shows that, despite official admonitions, in practice there was often a casual attitude to smoking in close proximity to aircraft. (USAAF)

20 OCTOBER 1942

VIII FC

Despatched		Groups	E/A	Losses MIA	E	Dam	Casualties KIA	WIA	MIA
Spitfire	10	4FG	0	1	0	0	0	0	0

REMARKS: Carried out defensive sorties of 2 a/c on convoy patrol, 1 exploded in mid-air 10 miles off Harwich.

21 OCTOBER 1942

VIII BC 15

	Despatched		Effective	Target	Bombs Tonnage	E/A	Losses MIA	E	Dam	Casualties KIA	WIA	MIA
1BW				LORIENT U/B (P)								
B-17	97BG	21	15	1306 hrs	30 × 2000GP		3	0	6	0	5	30
	301BG	25	0				0	0	0	0	0	0
	306BG	20	0				0	0	0	0	0	0
B-24	93BG	24	0	LORIENT U/B	0		0	0	0	0	0	0
B-17	11CCRC	17	8	CHERBOURG A/F 1213 hrs	161 × 100GP	10–4–3	0	0	0	0	0	0
TOTALS:		107	23		38.05	10–4–3	3		6	0	5	30

REMARKS: Cloud prevented most bombing. Last mission for 97BG prior to transferring to 12AF.

VIII FC

Despatched		Groups	E/A	Losses MIA	E	Dam	Casualties KIA	WIA	MIA
P-38	24	14FG	0	0	0	0	0	0	0

Men assemble to watch Fortresses of the 306th Group land at Thurleigh after the abortive mission of 21 October. Trucks in the foreground are ready to pick up crews from aircraft dispersal points. Station Headquarters buildings (with ventilation towers) are beyond the hangar on the right.

22 OCTOBER 1942

VIII FC

				Losses			Casualties		
Despatched		**Groups**	**E/A**	**MIA**	**E**	**Dam**	**KIA**	**WIA**	**MIA**
Spitfire	2	4FG	0	0	0	0	0	0	0

REMARKS: Sent on a weather recce.

23 OCTOBER 1942

VIII FC

				Losses			Casualties		
Despatched		**Groups**	**E/A**	**MIA**	**E**	**Dam**	**KIA**	**WIA**	**MIA**
Spitfire	14	4FG	0	0	0	0	0	0	0

REMARKS: Carried out defensive sorties.

24 OCTOBER 1942

VIII FC

				Losses			Casualties		
Despatched		**Groups**	**E/A**	**MIA**	**E**	**Dam**	**KIA**	**WIA**	**MIA**
Spitfire	22	4FG	0	0	0	0	0	0	0

REMARKS: Carried out defensive sorties.

25 OCTOBER 1942

VIII FC

				Losses			Casualties		
Despatched		**Groups**	**E/A**	**MIA**	**E**	**Dam**	**KIA**	**WIA**	**MIA**
Spitfire	35	4FG							
P-38	24	14FG							
TOTALS:	59		0	0	0	0	0	0	0

REMARKS: Spitfires sent to escort *Circus 232*, P-38 carried out rear support. 4FG returned early because of weather. Last mission for 14FG prior to transferring to 12AF.

29 OCTOBER 1942

VIII FC

			Losses			Casualties		
Despatched	**Groups**	**E/A**	**MIA**	**E**	**Dam**	**KIA**	**WIA**	**MIA**
Spitfire 2	4FG	0	0	0	0	0	0	0

REMARKS: Sent to attack enemy shipping, 2 barges damaged. First USAAF *Rhubarb*.

31 OCTOBER 1942

VIII FC

			Losses			Casualties		
Despatched	**Groups**	**E/A**	**MIA**	**E**	**Dam**	**KIA**	**WIA**	**MIA**
Spitfire 2	4FG	0	0	0	0	0	0	0

REMARKS: Carried out a *Rhubarb*, one locomotive damaged.

6 NOVEMBER 1942

VIII FC

			Losses			Casualties		
Despatched	**Groups**	**E/A**	**MIA**	**E**	**Dam**	**KIA**	**WIA**	**MIA**
Spitfire 21	4FG	0	0	0	0	0	0	0

REMARKS: Sent on a *Ramrod*, with RAF Bostons to Caen A/F.

7 NOVEMBER 1942

VIII BC 16

					Bombs		Losses			Casualties		
	Despatched		**Effective**	**Target**	**Tonnage**	**E/A**	**MIA**	**E**	**Dam**	**KIA**	**WIA**	**MIA**
1BW				BREST U/B (P)								
B-17	306BG	24	15	1230–1239 hrs	75 × 1000GP	1–2–5	0	0	0	0	0	0
	91BG	14	8		80 × 500GP	1–1–0	0	0	11	0	0	0
	301BG	18	0			0–0–0	0	0	0	0	0	0
B-24	93BG	12	11		44 × 1000GP	2–0–2	0	1	1	0	2	0
TOTALS:		68	34		79.5	4–3–7	0	1	12	0	3	0
2BW				DIVERSION								
B-24	44BG	7	–									

REMARKS: On return 93BG B-24 c/l at Exeter, crew safe. First mission for 91BG and 44BG.

8 NOVEMBER 1942

VIII BC 17

					Bombs		Losses			Casualties		
	Despatched		**Effective**	**Target**	**Tonnage**	**E/A**	**MIA**	**E**	**Dam**	**KIA**	**WIA**	**MIA**
				ABBEVILLE/DRUCAT								
	91BG	15	11	A/F (P) 1158 hrs	110 × 500GP	1–2– 1	0	0	5	0	5	0
1BW												
B-17	301BG	18	17	LILLE I/A (P)	293 × 500GP	2–1– 6	0	0	4	0	1	0
	306BG	20	14	1210–1215hrs		8–3– 7	1	0	4	0	2	11
TOTALS:		53	42		100.75	11–6–14	1	0	13	0	8	11

REMARKS: Last mission for 301BG, prior to transferring to 12AF.

VIII FC

			Losses			Casualties		
Despatched	**Groups**	**E/A**	**MIA**	**E**	**Dam**	**KIA**	**WIA**	**MIA**
Spitfire 36	4FG	0	0	0	0	0	0	0

REMARKS: Sent as withdrawal support for bombers attacking Lille.

Man O'War was a famous pre-war American racehorse and stud. Its namesake was not a winner, being one of three 306BG aircraft lost while bombing St.Nazaire from 7,500 feet on 9 November. Three days earlier the ground crew were putting the finishing touches to the flamboyant insignia. *Man O'War* flew its first mission 9 October – see single bomb symbol.

9 NOVEMBER 1942

VIII BC 18

	Despatched		Effective	Target	Bombs Tonnage	E/A	Losses MIA	E	Dam	Casualties KIA	WIA	MIA
1BW				ST.NAZAIRE U/B (P)								
B-17	91BG	14	13	1405 hrs			0	0	10	0	11	0
	306BG	19	18	1440–1441 hrs			3	0	12	1	0	32
B-24	93BG	9	7	1402 hrs	137 × 1000GP		0	0	1	0	0	0
2BW												
B-24	44BG	5	5	1408 hrs	180 × 500GP		0	0	0	0	0	0
TOTALS:		47	43		113.5	0–0–0	3	0	23	1	11	32

REMARKS: 91BG B-17 c/l on return, Cab AC.

VIII FC

Despatched		Groups	E/A	Losses MIA	E	Dam	Casualties KIA	WIA	MIA
Spitfire	36	4FG	0	0	0	0	0	0	0

REMARKS: As escort to RAF Bostons attacking Le Havre area.

10 NOVEMBER 1942

VIII FC

Despatched		Groups	E/A	Losses MIA	E	Dam	Casualties KIA	WIA	MIA
Spitfire	36	4FG	0	0	0	0	0	0	0

REMARKS: As rear support to RAF Bostons.

On 13 November King George VI paid his first visit to VIII BC installations. At Chelveston Col Ronald Walker, CO of 301BG, showed him *Holey Joe* which had flown on five of the Group's eight missions. At this date the 301st was non-operational and together with the 97BG would soon leave the Eighth and England for North Africa.

11 NOVEMBER 1942

VIII FC

Despatched		Groups	E/A	Losses MIA	E	Dam	Casualties KIA	WIA	MIA
Spitfire	2	4FG	0	0	0	0	0	0	0

REMARKS: Sent on a shipping recce.

Despatched		Groups	E/A	Losses MIA	E	Dam	Casualties KIA	WIA	MIA
Spitfire	23	4FG	0	0	0	0	0	0	0

REMARKS: Sent on offensive sorties.

14 NOVEMBER 1942

VIII BC 19

	Despatched		Effective	Target	Bombs Tonnage	E/A	Losses MIA	E	Dam	Casualties KIA	WIA	MIA
1BW				ST.NAZAIRE P/A (S)								
B-17	91BG	14	9	1340 hrs	30 × 2000GP		0	0	0	0	0	0
	306BG	7	6	1337 hrs			0	0	0	0	0	0
B-24	93BG	13	9	1340 hrs	108 × 500GP	0–0–0	0	0	1	0	0	0
TOTALS:		34	24		57.0	0–0–0	0	0	1	0	0	0
2BW												
B-24	44BG	6	–	DIVERSION		0–0–0	0	0	0	0	0	0

REMARKS: Primary, La Pallice, covered by 10/10 cloud.

VIII FC

Despatched		Groups	E/A	Losses MIA	E	Dam	Casualties KIA	WIA	MIA
Spitfire	6	4FG	0	0	0	0	0	0	0

REMARKS: Sent on a shipping recce.

16 NOVEMBER 1942

VIII FC

Despatched		Groups	E/A	Losses MIA	E	Dam	Casualties KIA	WIA	MIA
Spitfire	4	4FG	0	0	0	0	0	0	0

REMARKS: Sent on a ground strafing mission of French coast. One a/c hit a tree at Brachy, France, severely damaged.

17 NOVEMBER 1942

VIII BC 20

	Despatched		Effective	Target	Bombs Tonnage	E/A	Losses MIA	E	Dam	Casualties KIA	WIA	MIA
1BW				ST.NAZAIRE U/B (P)								
B-17	91BG	20	14	1121 hrs	140 × 500GP	5–7–1	0	0	6	0	0	0
	303BG	16	0			0–0–0	0	0	0	0	0	0
	306BG	13	9	1124 hrs	90 × 500GP	1–1–1	0	0	3	1	3	0
B-24	93BG	14	12	1125 hrs	144 × 500GP	0–0–0	0	0	7	0	0	0
TOTALS:		63	35		93.5	6–8–2	0	0	16	1	3	0
2BW				CHERBOURG/								
B-24	44BG	6	0	MAUPERTUS A/F (P)	0	0–0–0	0	0	0	0	0	0
1BW												
B-17	305BG	10	–	DIVERSION			0					

REMARKS: 44BG found their target covered by 10/10 cloud. First mission for 305BG and 303BG. 303BG unable to locate target.

VIII FC

Despatched		Groups	E/A	Losses MIA	E	Dam	Casualties KIA	WIA	MIA
Spitfire	6	4FG	0	0	0	0	0	0	0

REMARKS: Sent on shipping recce.

Orbiting Alconbury after return from the 18 November operation, 93BG's *Katy Bug* had 2 motors fail. The pilot attempted to belly-land in a field. Unfortunately the B-24D ended up along a hedgerow ditch which ripped out the bottom of the fuselage, killing four men and injuring six. The shoulder wing design of the Liberator did not lend itself to hard crash-landings as the fuselage would often crumble. Extracting mangled bodies from the twisted wreckage was a difficult and grisly task . . . but someone had to do it. (H. Coleman)

18 NOVEMBER 1942

VIII BC 21

					Bombs		Losses			Casualties		
	Despatched		Effective	Target	Tonnage	E/A	MIA	E	Dam	KIA	WIA	MIA
1BW				LORIENT								
B-24	93BG	13	13	1203 hrs	156 × 500GP		0	1	3	5	8	0
				ST.NAZAIRE (O)								
B-17	303BG	21	19	1222 hrs	190 × 500GP		0	0	15	0	3	0
				LA PALLICE U/B (P)								
	91BG	17	8	1254	128 × 500GP		0	0	0	0	0	0
	306BG	14	13	1258 hrs			1	0	9	1	3	0
TOTALS:		65	53		118.5	5–3–1	1	1	27	6	14	0
B-17	305BG	20	–	DIVERSION								
2BW												
B-24	44BG	6	–	DIVERSION								
TOTALS:		26	–									

REMARKS: 1 93BG B-24 crashed near base, after two engines had failed. 303BG mistook St.Nazaire as briefed target La Pallice, although it was 100 miles away.

VIII FC

				Losses			Casualties		
Despatched		Groups	E/A	MIA	E	Dam	KIA	WIA	MIA
Spitfire	2	4FG	0	0	0	0	0	0	0

REMARKS: Despatched on a strafing mission, 1 loco blown up.

19 NOVEMBER 1942

VIII FC

				Losses			Casualties		
Despatched		Groups	E/A	MIA	E	Dam	KIA	WIA	MIA
Spitfire	8	4FG	1–0–0	0	0	0	0	0	0

REMARKS: Despatched on a shipping patrol.

INCIDENT

The early missions of the 44th Bomb Group left combat officers in no doubt as to the vulnerability of the crew of a B-24 due to a lack of armour protection. This was particularly so in the vital nose section and Group Engineering personnel were quick to innovate. On 19 November the staff at 2nd Bomb Wing Headquarters received notice that one Shipdham Liberator had the floor of the nose compartment paved with boiler plate obtained from a local source. Not only did this afford protection to the bombardier and navigator but, it was claimed, gave better balance to the aircraft. A request was made for official permission to fit out other B-24Ds in this fashion and also to add a slab of boiler plate to the side of the fuselage to protect the two pilots from bullets and shell fragments. Sanction was eventually forthcoming for some of this steel work and by the spring of 1943 more than forty modifications were made to Liberators arriving from the US, chiefly in connection with armour and armament.

20 NOVEMBER 1942

VIII FC

Despatched		Groups	E/A	Losses MIA	E	Dam	Casualties KIA	WIA	MIA
Spitfire	2	4FG	1–0–0	1	0	0	0	0	0

REMARKS: Carried out *Rhubarb*, 1 Spitfire down in sea, pilot safe – paddled ashore near Foulness.

22 NOVEMBER 1942

VIII BC 22

	Despatched		Effective	Target	Bombs Tonnage	E/A	Losses MIA	E	Dam	Casualties KIA	WIA	MIA
1BW				LORIENT U/B (P)								
B-17	91BG	18	0	1410 hrs	22 × 2000GP							
	303BG	18	11									
	305BG	23	0									
	306BG	9	0									
B-24	93BG	8	0									
TOTALS:		76	11		22.0	0–0–0	0	0	0	0	0	0

REMARKS: 303BG managed to find a gap in the 10/10 cloud cover. First bombing mission for 305BG, although bombs were returned.

INCIDENT

There were many people in the London borough of Walthamstow who on the afternoon of 22 November 1942 turned their heads skywards at the sound of a discordant aero-engine. They saw a Spitfire, flames streaming back along the fuselage, descending rapidly. The expectation was for the pilot to leave the stricken aircraft and take to his parachute, but this did not happen and soon insufficient height remained for a successful bale out. The Spitfire, its engine engulfed in flame, lifted over the roof tops. The pilot was obviously making for the one piece of open ground in the vicinity, a football field. But the attempted belly-landing failed and the fighter ended up as a broken blazing wreck, the pilot being killed. It was plain that rather than bale out and let his burning Spitfire crash into the built-up area, with probable civilian casualties, 2/Lt Harvey Johnson had chosen to remain in the cockpit and try for the only field he could see. For this action he was posthumously awarded the first Distinguished Service Cross (second highest US award for bravery) to go to an 8th Air Force fighter pilot. This incident was mentioned in the House of Commons a few days later, Harvey Johnson being the only individual American airman to be singled out for such special acknowledgement and a standing salute by Members of Parliament. Johnson had been in the USAAF only a month at the time of his death, following transfer from the RCAF.

23 NOVEMBER 1942

VIII BC 23

	Despatched		Effective	Target	Bombs Tonnage	E/A	Losses MIA	E	Dam	Casualties KIA	WIA	MIA
1BW				ST.NAZAIRE U/B (P)								
B-17	91BG	10	0		23 × 2000GP	4–1–0	2	1	2	3	11	22
	303BG	12	11	1330 hrs	16 × 2000GP	2–1–0	1	0	9	0	2	11
	305BG	20	14	1345 hrs	23 × 1000GP	0–0–0	0	0	1	0	0	0
	306BG	8	3	1330 hrs	6 × 2000GP	9–0–0	1	0	4	0	0	10
B-24	93BG	8	8	1340 hrs	22 × 2000GP	1–0–1	0	0	1	0	3	0
TOTALS:		58	36		78.5	16–2–1	4	1	17	3	16	43

REMARKS: On return 91BG B-17 c/l Leavesden, Herts., 2 k, 8 injured.

INCIDENT

Despite careful analysis of bomber gunners' claims of enemy aircraft shot down the credits were, on average, treble those of actual enemy losses. The criteria for assessing claims for destruction were that the enemy pilot must be seen to abandon his aircraft in the air, or the aircraft must have been observed to crash, or have been seen to explode and come to pieces in the air. While several gunners unwittingly claiming the destruction of the same aircraft was an obvious reason for inflated credits, the sheer pace of air combat, and the failure of an individual under battle stress to recall accurately what he saw, was probably the major cause. Undoubtedly the high claims for enemy fighters allowed proved a helpful morale factor with bomber crews when their own losses began to mount. At this time both participants and Command believed heavy attrition was being caused in Luftwaffe fighter units.

An incident where it is possible to isolate a bomber crew's claims and compare this with Luftwaffe records, occurred on 23 November 1942 when the 306th BG was leaving St.Nazaire. Eight FW 190s of JG2 attacked the trailing Fortress, 1/Lt William Casey's *Banshee*. The interrogation report ran as follows: '13.28 hrs – Enemy aircraft attacked from below. As he passed, tail gunner fired, hitting the tail and as the FW 190 turned, he got a spray of bullets in the nose. Heavy black smoke came out and the plane disintegrated. One wheel seen to fly through air and pilot to bale out. 13.34: E/a came in from below. Right-waist gunner fired steadily from medium range. At 200 yds the FW 190 fell out of control. It was seen to hit the sea. 13.35: FW 190 attacked from the rear, coming up from below. Ball-turret gunner fired first, hitting the e/a at 100 yds. At 50 yds, bullets entered the motor and the fighter burst into flame and broke to pieces. Crew doubts if pilot could have baled out. 13.36: E/a came in from above, attacking from 1 o'clock. Top-turret gunner fired hitting the e/a at long range. At 200 yds the plane peeled off in smoke and flames, then broke into pieces after tracer bullets were seen to enter the engine. 13.38: FW 190 came in from 1 o'clock high, out of sun. Right-waist gunner fired at medium range. At 200 yds the plane was hit in the nose, began smoking heavily and pilot baled out. 13.39: E/a attacked from below, zooming up at the ball-gunner, who fired, seeing tracers go into the engine and through cockpit. The aircraft disintegrated and was seen to fall into the water. 13.40: E/a came in from 1 o'clock high. As it came over, left-waist gunner fired, hitting plane as it dived away. E/a fell out of control at about 1,000 yds and was seen by ball-turret gunner to hit the sea.' This total of seven FW 190 shot down in 12 minutes stood as a record for a single B-17 crew until the following April. In addition to the Casey crew's seven, two other FW 190s were credited to other gunners in the 306th formation on 23 November. The actual losses of the German unit involved were a single FW 190A-4 and pilot of III/JG2 into the sea at approximately 13.30 hrs.

'Wild Bill' Casey and crew were involved in a number of combats with enemy fighters, mostly when lending support to damaged B-17s. On 17 April 1943 their own aircraft was shot down near Bremen, Casey finishing the war in a POW camp.

26 NOVEMBER 1942

VIII FC

Despatched		Groups	E/A	Losses MIA	E	Dam	Casualties KIA	WIA	MIA
Spitfire	2	4FG	0	0	0	0	0	0	0

REMARKS: Carried out a *Rhubarb* against canals and roads NE of Dunkirk.

28 NOVEMBER 1942

VIII FC

Despatched		Groups	E/A	Losses MIA	E	Dam	Casualties KIA	WIA	MIA
Spitfire	2	4FG	0	0	0	0	0	0	0

REMARKS: Sent on a shipping recce.

29 NOVEMBER 1942

VIII FC

Despatched		Groups	E/A	Losses MIA	E	Dam	Casualties KIA	WIA	MIA
Spitfire	2	4FG	0	0	0	0	0	0	0

REMARKS: Sent on a shipping recce.

30 NOVEMBER 1942

VIII FC

Despatched		Groups	E/A	Losses MIA	E	Dam	Casualties KIA	WIA	MIA
Spitfire	2	4FG	0	0	0	0	0	0	0

REMARKS: Sent on offensive sorties.

Spitfire	2	4FG	0	0	0	0	0	0	0

REMARKS: Sent on patrol.

1 DECEMBER 1942

VIII FC

Despatched		Groups	E/A	Losses MIA	E	Dam	Casualties KIA	WIA	MIA
Spitfire	8		0	0	0	0	0	0	0

REMARKS: Sent on patrols.

4 DECEMBER 1942

VIII FC

Despatched		Groups	E/A	Losses MIA	E	Dam	Casualties KIA	WIA	MIA
Spitfire	35	4FG	0	0	0	0	0	0	0

REMARKS: Sent out as rear support on a *Rodeo*.

5 DECEMBER 1942

VIII FC

Despatched		Groups	E/A	Losses MIA	E	Dam	Casualties KIA	WIA	MIA
Spitfire	2	4FG	0	0	0	0	0	0	0

REMARKS: Carried out convoy patrol.

6 DECEMBER 1942

VIII BC 24

	Despatched		Effective	Target	Bombs Tonnage	E/A	Losses MIA	E	Dam	Casualties KIA	WIA	MIA
2BW				ABBEVILLE/DRUCAT								
B-24	44BG	19	6	A/F 1124 hrs	111 × 100GP	0–3–1	1		1	0	3	10
1BW				LILLE I/A								
B-17	91BG	22	18	1208–1210 hrs	20 × 1000GP	2–3–1	0		6	1	2	0
	303BG	20	15		320 × 500GP	1–1–1	0		3	0	0	0
	305BG	24	4			1–1–3	1		0	0	0	10
TOTALS:		85	43		95.55	5–8–6	2	0	10	1	5	20
1BW	11CCRC	6	–	DIVERSION								
B-17	306BG	16	–	MOCK DIVERSION								
TOTALS:		22	–									

REMARKS: B-24s recalled by fighters; one sqdn did not hear the recall and carried on. 11CCRC recalled whilst over their base.

VIII FC

Despatched		Groups	E/A	Losses MIA	E	Dam	Casualties KIA	WIA	MIA
Spitfire	36	4FG	0–0–1	0	0	0	0	0	0

REMARKS: As support to RAF Bostons.

Despatched		Groups	E/A	Losses MIA	E	Dam	Casualties KIA	WIA	MIA
Spitfire	8	4FG	0	0	0	0	0	0	0

REMARKS: Despatched on convoy patrols.

Displaying recently applied squadron code letters and flying the stagger formation which it was developing, the 305BG returns from Lille 6 December. Designed to obtain the maximum defensive capability by allowing a good field of fire while minimising the danger of shooting into other bombers, the six or seven plane squadrons that usually composed a flying group 'box' flew a tilted wedge. *Wham Bam* (extreme right) heads the lead squadron. Four aircraft of the high squadron are to be seen middle left, and five of the low squadron in the foreground. B-17 nearest the camera (sixth aircraft of the squadron) is *SNAFU* (later renamed *We The People*) which endured in the 305th longer than any other B-17 in the photo.

8 DECEMBER 1942

VIII FC

Despatched		Groups	E/A	Losses MIA	E	Dam	Casualties KIA	WIA	MIA
Spitfire	2	4FG	0	0	0	0	0	0	0

REMARKS: Sent on a strafing mission of French coast.

Spitfire	4	4FG	0	0	0	0	0	0	0

REMARKS: Despatched on convoy patrols.

9 DECEMBER 1942

VIII FC

Despatched		Groups	E/A	Losses MIA	E	Dam	Casualties KIA	WIA	MIA
Spitfire	4	4FG	0	0	0	0	0	0	0

REMARKS: Sent out on patrols.

10 DECEMBER 1942

VIII FC

Despatched		Groups	E/A	Losses MIA	E	Dam	Casualties KIA	WIA	MIA
Spitfire	2	4FG	0	0	0	0	0	0	0

REMARKS: Offensive mission, but returned before reaching the French coast through transmitter failure.

11 DECEMBER 1942

VIII FC

Despatched		Groups	E/A	Losses MIA	E	Dam	Casualties KIA	WIA	MIA
Spitfire	2	4FG	0–0–1	0	0	0	0	0	0

REMARKS: Sent out on offensive mission, ground targets shot up.

Spitfire	10	4FG	0	0	0	0	0	0	0

REMARKS: Despatched on patrol.

12 DECEMBER 1942

VIII BC 25

	Despatched		Effective	Target	Bombs Tonnage	E/A	Losses MIA	E	Dam	Casualties KIA	WIA	MIA
1BW												
B-17	91BG	19	4	ROUEN/SOTTEVILLE		3–2–0	0	0	1	0	1	0
	303BG	20	7	M/Y (L)		2–2–1	2	0	3	0	3	20
	305BG	21	0	1239–1241 hrs		0–1–1	0	0	1	0	4	0
	306BG	18	6			14–3–0	0	0	6	0	4	0
TOTALS:		78	17		35. HE 5. IB	19–8–2	2	0	11	0	8	20
2BW				ABBEVILLE/DRUCAT								
B-24	44BG	12	0	A/F		0–0–0	0	0		0	0	0
1BW	11CCRC	6	0	FEINT		0–0–0	0	0		0	0	0
B-17												

REMARKS: 305BG could not bomb because of cloud. Primary was Romilly A/D

VIII FC

Despatched		Groups	E/A	Losses MIA	E	Dam	Casualties KIA	WIA	MIA
Spitfire	41	4FG	0	0	0	0	0	0	0

REMARKS: 6 of the Spitfires performed an offensive shipping strike.

Spitfire	4	4FG	0	0	0	0	0	0	0

REMARKS: Sent on defensive patrols.

Spitfire	6	4FG	0	0	0	0	0	0	0

REMARKS: Despatched on convoy patrols.

13 DECEMBER 1942

VIII FC

Despatched		Groups	E/A	Losses MIA	E	Dam	Casualties KIA	WIA	MIA
Spitfire	2	4FG	0	0	0	0	0	0	0

REMARKS: Sent on a defensive patrol.

14 DECEMBER 1942

VIII FC

Despatched		Groups	E/A	Losses MIA	E	Dam	Casualties KIA	WIA	MIA
Spitfire	6	4FG	0	0	0	0	0	0	0

REMARKS: Sent on patrol.

15 DECEMBER 1942

VIII FC

Despatched		Groups	E/A	Losses MIA	E	Dam	Casualties KIA	WIA	MIA
Spitfire	2	4FG	0–1–0	0	0	1	0	0	0

REMARKS: Sent to attack barges in the Bruges/Ghent canal, 1 Ju52 chased into its own Flak. 1 Spitfire Cat B damage – Flak.

20 DECEMBER 1942

VIII BC 26

	Despatched		Effective	Target	Bombs Tonnage	E/A	Losses MIA	E	Dam	Casualties KIA	WIA	MIA
1BW				ROMILLY-SUR-SEINE A/D (P)								
B-17	91BG	17	13	1241 hrs	612 × 500GP	24– 1–2	2	1	11	0	5	19
	303BG	21	14	1246 hrs	100 × 250IB	14 –5–3	1	0	5	0	1	10
	305BG	23	18	1245 hrs		1 –2–3	0	0	1	0	0	0
	306BG	19	15	1240 hrs		12 –5–0	3	0	12	1	4	29
2BW												
B-24	44BG	21	12	1245 hrs		2– 0–0	0	0	1	1	2	0
TOTALS:		101	72		153.0HE 12.5IB	53–13–8	6	1	30	2	12	58

REMARKS: 1 91BG B-17 c/l at Fletching, crew safe. 1 303BG c/l at Bovingdon (Cat B), 8 of crew baled out over Maidstone but were picked up safely.

VIII FC

Despatched		Groups	E/A	Losses MIA	E	Dam	Casualties KIA	WIA	MIA
Spitfire	36	4FG	0	0	0	0	0	0	0

REMARKS: Sent out as third diversion on *Circus 244*.

INCIDENT

In the first few months of the 8th Air Force operations decorations were awarded far more liberally than during the following two years of hostilities. The Distinguished Service Cross, second highest standing decoration for bravery, was given for actions that in later days would have brought lesser awards, or none. Even the recipients were sometimes surprised. When Maj Algene Key was informed that he was to receive the DSC his reaction was one of astonishment: 'I don't see that I did anything special', he said. Piloting a 44th Bomb Group B-24 during the 20 December raid on Romilly-sur-Seine he took evasive action when facing a head-on attack by FW 190s. Despite these manoeuvres, enemy fire struck the rear fuselage mortally wounding the right waist gunner, severing cables and making control difficult. Key continued to the target and safely back to base although the damaged bomber was difficult to fly. Similar action would soon be an every mission occurrence. Key, however, was undoubtedly deserving of some high decoration for, apart from his participation in early B-24 operations from England, he had previously flown combat with the 7th Bomb Group in Java where his B-17E was shot up by Japanese fighters. Al Key, with his brother Fred, had earned fame in 1953 by setting a world endurance record of 653 hours, 34 minutes using a modified Curtiss Robin.

INCIDENT

In the early days of VIII Bomber Command operations there were several occasions when a pilot had pulled his bomber out of formation in order to aid a damaged and trailing comrade with additional firepower. Eventually such individual action was forbidden as it weakened the formation integrity. From the beginning it had been frowned upon, but at first condoned as there were instances where it appeared stragglers had been saved. Sometimes the protector suffered more grievously than the protected. On the Romilly-sur-Seine mission of 20 December 1942, the B-17s met the most determined opposition so far. Lead bomber of one 91st Bomb Group squadron was *Rose O'Day*, piloted by Capt Ken Wallick. A near flak burst caused damage to the landing gear controls causing the main wheels to extend. The drag was such that *Rose O'Day* began to drop behind the main formation. Seeing Wallick's predicament 1/Lt Bruce Barton, flying *Chief Sly* in the same flight, reduced power and kept position with *Rose O'Day* to provide extra firepower for defence. Enemy fighters soon directed attacks against the straggling pair but now concentrated on *Chief Sly*. In a series of attacks hits were obtained on the tail, fuselage and wings, disabling two engines and jamming up the right aileron. The navigator, 2/Lt Paul Burnett, was seriously wounded by a bullet strike in the upper thigh. Shortly thereafter enemy fighter activity ceased and both aircraft regained the English coast. Weather had deteriorated and the two bombers separated to avoid collision when they penetrated the undercast. Wallick, with a propeller missing from his peppered Fortress, managed to reach Bassingbourn and land safely. The ailing *Chief Sly* emerged from the clouds at 500 ft and, unable to maintain height, Barton had no option but to make a crash-landing on the first likely site. He successfully 'bellied' on sheep pasture at Fletching, Sussex, reducing a flock by two before coming to rest in a ploughed field. Canadian troops stationed near by were quickly on the scene with an ambulance for the wounded navigator.

As a result of the air fighting gunners on *Rose O'Day* claimed five FW 190s destroyed and those on *Chief Sly* seven – which was double the Luftwaffe total loss in contesting the whole mission. *Rose O'Day* would fly and fight again but the damage to her protector was such that *Chief Sly* was fit only for spare parts.

21 DECEMBER 1942

VIII FC

Despatched		Groups	E/A	Losses MIA	E	Dam	Casualties KIA	WIA	MIA
Spitfire	2	4FG	0	0	0	0	0	0	0
REMARKS: Despatched on a *Rhubarb* to Le Touquet.									
Spitfire	4	4FG	0	0	0	0	0	0	0

22 DECEMBER 1942

Despatched		Groups	E/A	Losses MIA	E	Dam	Casualties KIA	WIA	MIA
Spitfire	8	4FG	0	0	0	0	0	0	0

REMARKS: Sent on a shipping patrol.

23 DECEMBER 1942

VIII FC

Despatched		Groups	E/A	Losses MIA	E	Dam	Casualties KIA	WIA	MIA
Spitfire	2	4FG	0	0	0	0	0	0	0

REMARKS: Sent on a defensive patrol.

29 DECEMBER 1942

Despatched		Groups	E/A	Losses MIA	E	Dam	Casualties KIA	WIA	MIA
Spitfire	6	4FG	0	0	0	0	0	0	0
REMARKS: Sent on a strafing mission.									
Spitfire	12	4FG	0	0					
REMARKS: Sent out on patrols.									

30 DECEMBER 1942

VIII BC 27

	Despatched		Effective	Target	Bombs Tonnage	E/A	Losses MIA	E	Dam	Casualties KIA	WIA	MIA
1BW				LORIENT U/B (P)								
B-17	91BG	19	16	1138–1142 hrs	32 × 2000GP	19–5–0	1	0	13	1	7	10
	303BG	16	10		20 × 2000GP	4–1–0	0	0	4	0	0	0
	305BG	24	13		26 × 2000GP	6–1–3	1	0	5	1	10	10
	306BG	18	1		2 × 1600AP	0–0–0	1	0	0	0	0	10
TOTALS:		77	40		79.6	29–7–3	3	0	22	2	17	30

REMARKS: Most 306BG aircraft returned before mission start point.

30 DECEMBER 1942 *(contd.)*

VIII FC

Despatched		Groups	E/A	Losses MIA	E	Dam	Casualties KIA	WIA	MIA
Spitfire	2	4FG	0	0	0	0	0	0	0

REMARKS: Sent on a strafing attack at Cappelle.

31 DECEMBER 1942

VIII FC

Despatched		Groups	E/A	Losses MIA	E	Dam	Casualties KIA	WIA	MIA
Spitfire	12	4FG	0	0	0	0	0	0	0

REMARKS: Sent out on patrols.

2 JANUARY 1943

VIII FC

Despatched		Groups	E/A	Losses MIA	E	Dam	Casualties KIA	WIA	MIA
Spitfire	20	4FG	0	0	0	0	0	0	0

REMARKS: Despatched on fighter patrols.

VIII BC 27A

	Despatched		Effective	Target	Bombs Tonnage	E/A	Losses MIA	E	Dam	Casualties KIA	WIA	MIA
93BG	B-24	4										

REMARKS: *Moling* operation – abandoned due to improving weather over North Sea.

3 JANUARY 1943

VIII BC 28

	Despatched		Effective	Target	Bombs Tonnage	E/A	Losses MIA	E	Dam	Casualties KIA	WIA	MIA
1BW				ST.NAZAIRE U/B (P)								
B-17	91BG	16	12	1130 hrs	57 × 1000GP	6–12–1	1	0	11	2	6	10
	303BG	17	10	1130 hrs	50 × 1000GP	6– 5–2	4	0	8	0	0	40
	305BG	22	21	1134 hrs	105 × 1000GP	2– 1–1	0	0	16	0	3	0
	306BG	17	17	1140 hrs	83 × 1000GP	0– 0–0	2	0	9	0	3	20
2BW				ST.NAZAIRE U/B (P)								
B-24	44BG	13	8	1135 hrs	47 × 1000GP	0– 0–0	0	3	3	3	17	0
TOTALS:		85	68		171.0	14–18–4	7	3	47	5	29	70

REMARKS: 44BG casualties in 3 a/c c/l due to fuel shortage on return, at Dale and Talbenny A/F, Wales.
305BG using stagger formation.

VIII FC

Despatched		Groups	E/A	Losses MIA	E	Dam	Casualties KIA	WIA	MIA
Spitfire	16	4FG	0	0	0	0	0	0	0

REMARKS: Sent on ship protection patrols.

4 JANUARY 1943

VIII FC

Despatched		Groups	E/A	Losses MIA	E	Dam	Casualties KIA	WIA	MIA
Spitfire	20	4FG	0	0	0	0	0	0	0

REMARKS: Sent on ship protection patrols.

8 JANUARY 1943

VIII FC

Despatched		Groups	E/A	Losses MIA	E	Dam	Casualties KIA	WIA	MIA
Spitfire	12	4FG	0	0	0	0	0	0	0

REMARKS: Carried out defensive patrols.

9 JANUARY 1943

VIII FC

Despatched		Groups	E/A	Losses MIA	E	Dam	Casualties KIA	WIA	MIA
Spitfire	6	4FG	0	0	0	0	0	0	0

REMARKS: Despatched to patrol coast line.

11 JANUARY 1943

VIII FC

Despatched		Groups	E/A	Losses MIA	E	Dam	Casualties KIA	WIA	MIA
Spitfire	2	4FG	0	0	0	0	0	0	0

REMARKS: Sent on ship protection patrols.

12 JANUARY 1943

VIII FC

Despatched		Groups	E/A	Losses MIA	E	Dam	Casualties KIA	WIA	MIA
Spitfire	2	4FG	0	0	0	0	0	0	0

REMARKS: Used on a fighter patrol.

13 JANUARY 1943

VIII BC 29

	Despatched		Effective	Target	Bombs Tonnage	E/A	Losses MIA	E	Dam	Casualties KIA	WIA	MIA
1BW				LILLE I/A								
B-17	91BG	13	10	1427–1430 hrs	100 × 500GP	0–1–0	0	0	3	0	3	0
	303BG	19	18		90 × 1000GP	1–0–0	0	0	1	1	0	0
	305BG	23	22		219 × 500GP	2–3–5	1	0	10	1	6	10
	306BG	17	14		2 × 1100GP 68 × 1000GP	0–0–0	2	0	1	0	0	20
TOTALS:		72	64		125	3–4–5	3	0	15	2	9	30
2BW												
B-24	44BG	16	–	DIVERSION								

REMARKS: 2 306BG B-17s collided after bombing.

VIII FC

Despatched		Groups	E/A	Losses MIA	E	Dam	Casualties KIA	WIA	MIA
Spitfire	69	4FG	3–4–5	1	0	0	0	0	0

REMARKS: Escort for VIII BC 29 and two raids by RAF Bostons against St.Omer. 1 Spitfire forced down Tangmere A/F due to engine failure, Cat B.

Spitfire	2		0	0	0	0	0	0	0

REMARKS: Sent on a fighter patrol.

14 JANUARY 1943

VIII FC

Despatched		Groups	E/A	Losses MIA	E	Dam	Casualties KIA	WIA	MIA
Spitfire	8	4FG	2–0–0	0	0	2	0	0	0

REMARKS: Carried out three *Rhubarbs*. FW 190s engaged W. of Ostend. 1 Spitfire f/l Bradwell Bay A/F with Flak damage.

15 JANUARY 1943

VIII FC

Despatched		Groups	E/A	Losses MIA	E	Dam	Casualties KIA	WIA	MIA
Spitfire	12	4FG	0	0	0	0	0	0	0

REMARKS: Despatched on fighter patrols.

17 JANUARY 1943

VIII FC

Despatched		Groups	E/A	Losses MIA	E	Dam	Casualties KIA	WIA	MIA
Spitfire	4	4FG	0	0	0	0	0	0	0

REMARKS: Carried out ship protection patrols.

20 JANUARY 1943

VIII FC

Despatched		Groups	E/A	Losses MIA	E	Dam	Casualties KIA	WIA	MIA
Spitfire	22	4FG	0	0	1	0	0	0	0

REMARKS: Sent on a *Rhubarb* (2 a/c), interception (14 a/c) and defensive patrols (6 a/c). 3 locomotives attacked at Calais.

21 JANUARY 1943

VIII FC

Despatched		Groups	E/A	Losses MIA	E	Dam	Casualties KIA	WIA	MIA
Spitfire	26	4FG	0	0	0	0	0	0	0

REMARKS: As escort to RAF Venturas attacking Caen/Carpiquet.

Despatched		Groups	E/A	Losses MIA	E	Dam	Casualties KIA	WIA	MIA
Spitfire	23	4FG	0	0	0	0	0	0	0

REMARKS: In support of *Circus* to Caen later in the day.

22 JANUARY 1943

VIII FC

Despatched		Groups	E/A	Losses MIA	E	Dam	Casualties KIA	WIA	MIA
Spitfire	25	4FG	4–0–0	1	1	1	0	0	1

REMARKS: Despatched to support Boston bombers. Enemy aircraft credits: 4FG – 4. 1 Spitfire c/l Penhurst on return.

23 JANUARY 1943

VIII BC 30

	Despatched		Effective	Target	Bombs Tonnage	E/A	Losses MIA	E	Dam	Casualties KIA	WIA	MIA
1BW				LORIENT P/A (P)								
B-17	306BG	17	14	1348–1351 hrs	92 × 1000GP	0–1–0	0	0		0	0	0
	91BG	13	8		160 × 500GP	0–1–0	0	1		1	5	0
	303BG	21	14*			7–5–4	5	1		1	19	50
				BREST U/B (S)	45 × 1000GP							
	305BG	22	18	1413 hrs	91 × 500GP	0–0–1	0	0		0	2	0
TOTALS:		73	54		131.25	7–7–5	5	2	30	2	26	50
2BW												
B-24	44BG	17	0	DIVERSION	–	0–0–0	0	0	0	0	0	0

REMARKS: Lead group – 305BG – bombed Brest as attack on Lorient frustrated by condensation on bombsight of lead a/c. At Brest bomb pierced tunnel joining arsenal to port. *1 303BG B-17 attacked Brest. On return 91BG B-17 c/l at Little Horwood and 303BG B-17 c/l Lulsgate Bottom A/F, crews safe.

VIII FC

Despatched		Groups	E/A	Losses MIA	E	Dam	Casualties KIA	WIA	MIA
Spitfire	4	4FG	0	0	0	0	0	0	0

REMARKS: Sent out on ship protection patrols.

Although showing little sign of battle damage, 303BG's *Thumper* had the hydraulic system and two engines damaged by cannon shells and bullets near Lorient on 23 January. Lt John Castle and his co-pilot overshot, putting the B-17F down at Lulsgate Bottom. The crew had previously baled out, one being killed when his parachute failed to open. The bomber would never fly again as the rear fuselage twisted when the ball turret suspension frame was forced up through the spine, aft of radio room hatch. This was the usual result with Fortresses in belly landings unless the ball turret had previously been jettisoned.

25 JANUARY 1943

VIII FC CIRCUS 255

Despatched		Groups	E/A	Losses MIA	E	Dam	Casualties KIA	WIA	MIA
Spitfire	17	4FG	0	0	0	0	0	0	0

REMARKS: As escort to Boston bombers on *Circus 255*.

26 JANUARY 1943

VIII FC CIRCUS 256

Despatched		Groups	E/A	Losses MIA	E	Dam	Casualties KIA	WIA	MIA
Spitfire	22	4FG	0	1	0	0	0	0	0

REMARKS: To escort 12 Venturas on *Circus 256*. 1 Spitfire down in sea, not due to enemy action, pilot rescued.

27 JANUARY 1943

VIII BC 31

	Despatched		Effective	Target	Bombs Tonnage	E/A	Losses MIA	E	Dam	Casualties KIA	WIA	MIA
1BW				WILHELMSHAVEN NAVAL BASE (P)								
B-17	91BG	19	16	1110 hrs	70 × 1000GP	3–3–0	0	0	16	0	0	0
	303BG	11	8	1113 hrs	40 × 1000GP	1–0–1	0	0	1	0	1	0
	305BG	18	17	1112 hrs	85 × 1000GP	6–3–6	1	0	4	0	0	10
	306BG	16	14	1110 hrs	70 × 1000GP	0–0–0	0	0	11	0	0	0
2BW	44BG	20	0	WILHELMSHAVEN		9–5–4	2	0	9	2	2	20
B-24	93BG	7	0			3–3–2	0	0	2	0	0	0
TOTALS:		91	55		137.5	22–14–13	3	0	43	2	3	30

REMARKS: B-24s unable to locate target due to weather and poor navigation. First VIII BC raid on Germany. 2 91BG B-17s attacked Emden as T/O at 1135 (carried in Effective and Tonnage totals).

VIII FC

Despatched		Groups	E/A	Losses MIA	E	Dam	Casualties KIA	WIA	MIA
Spitfire	7	4FG	0	0	0	0	0	0	0

REMARKS: Despatched on fighter patrols.

29 JANUARY 1943

VIII FC

Despatched		Groups	E/A	Losses MIA	E	Dam	Casualties KIA	WIA	MIA
Spitfire	6	4FG	0	0	0	0	0	0	0

REMARKS: Sent out on a defensive patrol.

William Wyler, director of such famous Hollywood movies as *Mrs Miniver*, was asked to make a motion picture that would explain 8AF operations to the US public. During the winter of 1942–43 he and his team took a considerable colour footage of activities at Bassingbourn and Chelveston and also on combat flights. 91BG Fortress *The Bad Penny* was used for some of the air photography with 16 mm cameras in the nose, tail, waist and radio hatch positions. Prior to a local flight on 1 February, Maj Wyler (centre) chats with British war correspondent Cavo Chin (left). The result of Wyler's work was *The Memphis Belle*, the best wartime documentary about the B-17 operations.

1 FEBRUARY 1943

VIII FC

Despatched		Groups	E/A	Losses MIA	E	Dam	Casualties KIA	WIA	MIA
Spitfire	20	4FG	0	0	0	0	0	0	0

REMARKS: Sent on defensive and fighter patrols.

2 FEBRUARY 1943

VIII BC 32

REMARKS: 83 a/c (61 B-17 and 22 B-24) sent to Hamm M/Y but returned after finding weather conditions bad over North Sea. All six VIII BC groups involved.

VIII FC CIRCUS 257

Despatched		Groups	E/A	Losses MIA	E	Dam	Casualties KIA	WIA	MIA
Spitfire	25	4FG	0	0	0	0	0	0	0

REMARKS: In support of 12 RAF Venturas on *Circus 257*.

Spitfire	9	4FG	0	0	0	0	0	0	0

REMARKS: Sent out on ship patrol.

3 FEBRUARY 1943

VIII FC CIRCUS 258

Despatched		Groups	E/A	Losses MIA	E	Dam	Casualties KIA	WIA	MIA
Spitfire	22	4FG	0	0	0	0	0	0	0

REMARKS: Sent to escort 12 RAF Venturas on *Circus 258*.

Spitfire	25	4FG	0	0	0	0	0	0	0

REMARKS: On offensive missions.

4 FEBRUARY 1943

VIII BC 23

	Despatched		Effective	Target	Bombs Tonnage	E/A	Losses MIA	E	Dam	Casualties KIA	WIA	MIA
1BW				EMDEN I/A (L)								
B-17	91BG	17	16	1200 hrs	151 × 500GP	5–2–0	2	0	0	0		20
	303BG	13	6	1215 hrs	60 × 500GP	8–1–2	1	0	0	0		10
	305BG	18	0	–	–	7–3–4	2	0	0	0		20
	306BG	17	17	1200 hrs	170 × 500GP	5–2–0	0	0	0	0		0
TOTALS:		65	39		92.25	25–8–6	5	0	0	0	17	50
2BW	44BG	15	0	HAMM M/Y		0–0–0	0	0	0	0	0	0
B-24	93BG	6	0			0–0–0	0	0	0	0	0	0
TOTALS:		21	0		0	0–0–0	0	0	0	0	0	0

REMARKS: 1 91BG B-17 and 44BG B-24 which aborted dropped 22 × 500GP on a convoy. 44 & 93BGs turned back before Dutch coast due to extreme cold, below −40°C (the limit of the thermometers). 305BG B-17 lost in collision with FW 190. Twin engined fighters attacked bombers for the first time. Heavy cloud covered briefed target, Hamm M/Y.

VIII FC

Despatched		Groups	E/A	Losses MIA	E	Dam	Casualties KIA	WIA	MIA
Spitfire	21	4FG	0	0	0	0	0	0	0

REMARKS: Carried out fighter patrols and ASR search – nothing seen.

INCIDENT

The 4 February 1943 Emden operation was the 11th and final mission for Lt William J. Crumm and the men of the 91st Group Fortress *Jack the Ripper*. They were to be the first VIII Bomber Command crew sent home, having been selected for their combat experience to co-operate in the preparation of an aircrew combat manual. Leaving their regular bomber at Bassingbourn, they collected a B-17 incorporating all the modifications devised for the type in the Command to fly to the United States. (In another war, 24 years later, Maj.Gen Crumm was killed in a collision between two B-52s returning to Guam after operations over Vietnam, 7 July 1967.)

5 FEBRUARY 1943

VIII FC

Despatched		Groups	E/A	Losses MIA	E	Dam	Casualties KIA	WIA	MIA
Spitfire	2	4FG	0	0	0	0	0	0	0

REMARKS: Despatched on patrols.

Spitfire	6	4FG	0	1	0	0	0	0	0

REMARKS: Sent out to strafe an enemy shipping convoy. 2 corvettes and 1 merchant ship damaged. Spitfire of 335FS hit by Flak, pilot MIA.

6 FEBRUARY 1943

VIII FC

Despatched		Groups	E/A	Losses MIA	E	Dam	Casualties KIA	WIA	MIA
Spitfire	6	4FG	0	0	0	0	0	0	0

REMARKS: Sent out on shipping patrols.

10 FEBRUARY 1943

VIII FC

Despatched		Groups	E/A	Losses MIA	E	Dam	Casualties KIA	WIA	MIA
Spitfire	2	4FG	0	0	0	0	0	0	0

REMARKS: Sent out on shipping patrol.

12 FEBRUARY 1943

VIII FC

Despatched		Groups	E/A	Losses MIA	E	Dam	Casualties KIA	WIA	MIA
Spitfire	16	4FG	0	0	0	0	0	0	0

REMARKS: Sent out on shipping patrols.

Despatched		Groups	E/A	Losses MIA	E	Dam	Casualties KIA	WIA	MIA
Spitfire	2	4FG	0	0	0	0	0	0	0

REMARKS: Carried out a defensive patrol.

13 FEBRUARY 1943

VIII FC

Despatched		Groups	E/A	Losses MIA	E	Dam	Casualties KIA	WIA	MIA
Spitfire	24	4FG	0	1	0	0	0	0	0

REMARKS: Carried out shipping patrols. MIA pilot baled out off Harwich, lost.

14 FEBRUARY 1943

VIII BC 34

	Despatched		Effective	Target	Bombs Tonnage	E/A	Losses MIA	E	Dam	Casualties KIA	WIA	MIA
1BW				HAMM M/Y								
B-17	91BG	20	0			0	0	0	0	0	0	0
	303BG	17	0			1–0–0	0	0	0	0	0	0
	305BG	17	0			0	0	0	1	0	0	0
	306BG	20	0			0	0	0	0	0	0	0
TOTALS:		74	0			1–0–0	0	0	1	0	0	0

REMARKS: Abandoned because of weather 1045–1100 hrs. Recalled between coast and Dokkum.

VIII FC

Despatched		Groups	E/A	Losses MIA	E	Dam	Casualties KIA	WIA	MIA
Spitfire	18	4FG	0	0	0	0	0	0	0

REMARKS: Sent out on shipping patrols.

15 FEBRUARY 1943

VIII BC 35

	Despatched		Effective	Target	Bombs Tonnage	E/A	Losses MIA	E	Dam	Casualties KIA	WIA	MIA
2BW				DUNKIRK P/A &								
B-24	44BG	17	16	MERCHANT VESSELS	188 × 500GP	2–1–0	2	1	5	1	0	24
	93BG	6	5	1540 hrs	60 × 500GP	1–0–0	0	0	2	0	0	0
TOTALS:		23	21		62	3–1–0	2	1	7	1	0	24

REMARKS: B-24 of 44BG c/l Sandwich Flats, Kent, after Flak and e/a damage.

VIII FC

Despatched		Groups	E/A	Losses MIA	E	Dam	Casualties KIA	WIA	MIA
Spitfire	30	4FG	0	0	0	0	0	0	0

REMARKS: Sent on shipping patrols.

16 FEBRUARY 1943

VIII BC 36

	Despatched		Effective	Target	Bombs Tonnage	E/A	Losses MIA	E	Dam	Casualties KIA	WIA	MIA
1BW				ST.NAZAIRE P/A (P)	62 × 1000GP							
B-17	91BG	18	13	1054 hrs	102 × 500GP	5– 1–0	0	0	6	1	0	0
	303BG	15	13	1055 hrs	10 × 1000GP	4– 1–1	2	0	5	0	0	20
					10 × 500GP							
	305BG	18	15	1053 hrs	70 × 1000GP	4– 5–0	2	0	11	0	2	21
	306BG	20	18	1052 hrs	89 × 1000GP	3– 3–1	2	0	6	0	5	20
2BW												
B-24	44BG	12	6	1053 hrs	33 × 1000GP	4– 2–0	2	0	2	0	0	20
	93BG	6	0			0– 0–0	0	0	0	0	0	0
TOTALS:		89	65		160.0	20–12–2	8	0	30	1	7	81

REMARKS: 2 44BG B-24s collided over the Channel off Selsey, Sussex.

VIII FC

Despatched		Groups	E/A	Losses MIA	E	Dam	Casualties KIA	WIA	MIA
Spitfire	34	4FG	0	0	0	0	0	0	0

REMARKS: Sent out on fighter patrols.

INCIDENT

Near St.Nazaire on 16 February 1943 crews of the 91st Group observed a pair of FW 190s dive on two B-17s and release a cluster of bomb-like objects. The enemy aircraft came from the rear and were an estimated 150 ft above the Fortresses when the release was made. The clusters burst about 60 ft behind the two bombers at about the same level. Crews described seeing about 50 bursts of red and white smoke, each of about the same size as made by a 20 mm cannon shell burst. These were some of the first Luftwaffe experiments in attempts to drop time-fused fragmentation bombs into the US bomber formations.

Southern Comfort was a 305BG Fortress that was damaged by flak and fighters' cannon fire on seven occasions during her brief career. Her regular pilot, Hugh Ashcroft gives the okay sign while the bomber is in the hangar for repair after the 4 February raid. Her record in painted symbols showed four bombing missions, one diversion (the duck) and one enemy fighter destroyed claim (swastika). The wolf head insignia was derived from the official badge of 364BS and carried by most of the unit's original B-17Fs.

17 FEBRUARY 1943

VIII FC

Despatched		Groups	E/A	Losses MIA	E	Dam	Casualties KIA	WIA	MIA
Spitfire	38	4FG	0	0	0	0	0	0	0

REMARKS: Sent out on patrols during the day.

18 FEBRUARY 1943

VIII FC

Despatched		Groups	E/A	Losses MIA	E	Dam	Casualties KIA	WIA	MIA
Spitfire	26	4FG	0	0	0	0	0	0	0

REMARKS: Despatched on shipping and defensive patrol duty.

19 FEBRUARY 1943

VIII FC

Despatched		Groups	E/A	Losses MIA	E	Dam	Casualties KIA	WIA	MIA
Spitfire	2	4FG	0	0	0	0	0	0	0

REMARKS: Sent out on a defensive patrol.

Despatched		Groups	E/A	Losses MIA	E	Dam	Casualties KIA	WIA	MIA
Spitfire	24	4FG	0	0	0	0	0	0	0

REMARKS: Sent out on an offensive sweep of St.Omer area.

20 FEBRUARY 1943

VIII FC

Despatched		Groups	E/A	Losses MIA	E	Dam	Casualties KIA	WIA	MIA
Spitfire	2	4FG	0	0	0	0	0	0	0

REMARKS: Used on an ASR patrol.

24 FEBRUARY 1943

VIII FC

Despatched		Groups	E/A	Losses MIA	E	Dam	Casualties KIA	WIA	MIA
Spitfire	14	4FG	0	0	0	0	0	0	0

REMARKS: Despatched on shipping patrols during the day.

26 FEBRUARY 1943

VIII BC 37

	Despatched		Effective	Target	Bombs Tonnage	E/A	Losses MIA	E	Dam	Casualties KIA	WIA	MIA
1BW				WILHELMSHAVEN								
B-17	91BG	20	17	U/Y (O) 1125 hrs	656 × 500GP	2–0–0	2	0				
	303BG	19	12	1123 hrs		2–0–1	0	0				
	305BG	20	17	1125 hrs		7–1–2	3	0				
	306BG	17	13	1123 hrs		1–1–0	0					
2BW				WILHELMSHAVEN								
B-24	44BG	11	3	U/Y (O) 1124 hrs		6–1–0	2	0				
	93BG	6	3	1124 hrs		3–6–2	0	1				
TOTALS:		93	65		164.25	21–9–5	7	1		0	14	73

REMARKS: 93BG B-24 c/l at Ludham. Briefed target Bremen obscured by cloud. Bomb tonnage includes 1 × 500GP dropped on a convoy.

VIII FC

Despatched		Groups	E/A	Losses MIA	E	Dam	Casualties KIA	WIA	MIA
Spitfire	6	4FG	0	0	0	0	0	0	0

REMARKS: Despatched on shipping patrols.

Despatched		Groups	E/A	Losses MIA	E	Dam	Casualties KIA	WIA	MIA
Spitfire	76	4FG	0	0	0	0	0	0	0

REMARKS: 26 a/c, 26 a/c and 24 a/c as escort for 3 out of 5 raids by RAF Venturas attacking Dunkirk.

INCIDENT

To afford some protection to aircrew from low velocity shrapnel the wearing of infantry type steel helmets was advised. The helmet was heavy and uncomfortable and many airmen were sceptical of its value. At Chelveston, after 26 February 1943, views changed rapidly. Near Wilhelmshaven that day, 2/Lt James Moberly, navigator on *Southern Comfort*, was busily firing a side gun at oncoming enemy fighters when a 20 mm cannon shell ripped into the nose and exploded about an inch above his head. The blast drove Moberly's head forward and down with such force that the steel helmet he was wearing cracked the wood navigation table. The navigator felt decidedly woozey for a little while but was otherwise unhurt. A gaping 18 by 10 inch hole in the top of the compartment was another result of the explosion. Later, when Moberly examined his helmet he found seven dents made by shell fragments. He realised he owed his life to that 'tin hat'.

INCIDENT

There had been many requests from the news media in the United States to let their correspondents fly on a combat mission. Eventually 8th Air Force approved such requests, accepting eight reporters but first insisting that they go through a high altitude flight and survival course at the Bovingdon CCRC. On 26 February 1943 six of these men were allowed to fly their first mission. Five went with B-17 units but Robert B. Post of the *New York Times* chose to ride with the B-24s of the 44th Bomb Group. The 44th dubbed itself the *Flying Eight Balls*, a hard luck outfit. The newsmen believed it when they learned that Post had gone down with one of the two 44th Liberators missing that day.

FDR's Potato Peeler Kids five miles above the Atlantic pounded Brest peninsula on 27 February. Bombs dropped short of the target. (IWM)

27 FEBRUARY 1943

VIII BC 38

	Despatched		Effective	Target	Bombs Tonnage	E/A	Losses MIA	E	Dam	Casualties KIA	WIA	MIA
1BW				BREST U/B (P)								
B-17	91BG	18	15	1456 hrs	71 × 1000GP		0	0	0	0	0	0
	303BG	16	15	1500 hrs	75 × 1000GP							
	305BG	12	0	–	0		0	0	0	0	0	0
	306BG	17	16	1455 hrs	80 × 1000GP		0	0	0	0	0	0
2BW												
B-24	44BG	10	9	1458 hrs	54 × 1000GP		0	0	2	0	0	0
	93BG	5	5	1500 hrs	30 × 1000GP		0	0	0	0	0	0
TOTALS:		78	60		155.0	0–0–0	0	0	2	0	0	0

REMARKS: 305BG turned whilst in sight of the target after a bogus recall message was received.

VIII FC

Despatched		Groups	E/A	Losses MIA	E	Dam	Casualties KIA	WIA	MIA
Spitfire	16	4FG	0	0	0	0	0	0	0

REMARKS: Sent on shipping patrols.

Despatched		Groups	E/A	Losses MIA	E	Dam	Casualties KIA	WIA	MIA
Spitfire	24	4FG	0	0	0	0	0	0	0

REMARKS: As part of escort for RAF Venturas bombing Dunkirk.

28 FEBRUARY 1943

VIII FC

Despatched		Groups	E/A	Losses MIA	E	Dam	Casualties KIA	WIA	MIA
Spitfire	12	4FG	0	0	0	0	0	0	0

REMARKS: Sent out on patrols.

1 MARCH 1943

VIII FC

Despatched		Groups	E/A	Losses MIA	E	Dam	Casualties KIA	WIA	MIA
Spitfire	24	4FG	0	0	0	0	0	0	0

REMARKS: Sent out on patrols during the day.

2 MARCH 1943

VIII FC

Despatched		Groups	E/A	Losses MIA	E	Dam	Casualties KIA	WIA	MIA
Spitfire	12	4FG	0	0	0	0	0	0	0

REMARKS: Sent on shipping and defensive patrols.

3 MARCH 1943

VIII FC

Despatched		Groups	E/A	Losses MIA	E	Dam	Casualties KIA	WIA	MIA
Spitfire	28	4FG	0	0	0	0	0	0	0

REMARKS: Sent out on patrols during the day.

INCIDENT

The destructive power of a .50-calibre bullet was considerable. Within short range its velocity was such that a single strike could shatter a human body. Evidence of this was, unfortunately, occasionally available through mishaps, not least by gunners accidentally swinging their fire into other bombers in a formation during the heat of battle. With no mission on 3 March 1943 the 305th Group ran target practice flights for air gunners over The Wash range. Maj Henry Macdonald, CO of 364th Bomb Squadron, flew a Douglas Boston converted to target towing, the technique being to fly parallel and slightly below the B-17s with cable fully extended so that gunners could safely fire at the drogue sleeve without endangering the towing aircraft. Unfortunately, one gunner continued to fire when the tow-plane had passed ahead of his B-17. A bullet penetrated the Boston's fuselage, hit Macdonald in the shoulder and departed through the side of the cockpit windshield. The pilot's shoulder blade and collarbone were shattered but fighting against loss of consciousness he was able to land at Polebrook where the holding party on this unoccupied airfield rushed him to Lilford Hospital. Doctors operated and opined that Macdonald would probably have a permanently crippled right arm which would prohibit a return to operational flying.

A few days after this accident Macdonald learned that his brother, a squadron commander in the 44th Bomb Group, had been killed in a raid on Dunkirk. From then on Macdonald's determination to recover became primed by a desire to return to combat and avenge his brother's death. With this in mind he refused repatriation to the US. Although he could not lift his arm after the wound had healed, he engaged in rigorous exercise in the attempt to regain full use. Games and work-outs became his obsession and within six months he could play tennis with powerful strokes; by sheer determination he regained 60 per cent use of his shoulder muscles and was given a physical waiver to fly. Rejoining the 305th he resumed operations and eventually was promoted to command of the Group, remaining until it was run down in Germany in 1946. He was the only combat officer in the 305th to serve throughout its wartime existence.

Taken on the day of the incident, this photograph shows the hole in the A-20 windshield made by the .50 calibre bullet. (DeRussy)

Henry G. Macdonald: a picture when he had just returned from leading the Gdynia mission, 9 October 1943.

4 MARCH 1943

VIII BC 39

	Despatched		Effective	Target	Bombs Tonnage	E/A	Losses MIA	E	Dam	Casualties KIA	WIA	MIA
1BW				HAMM M/Y (P) ROTTERDAM (L)								
B-17	91BG	20	16	1043 hrs	80 × 1000GP	13–3–4	4	0	9	1	7	33
	303BG	18	16	1020 hrs	140 × 1000GP	0–0–0	0	0	1	0	0	0
	305BG	12	12	1021 hrs		2–0–0	0	0	8	0	0	0
	306BG	21	0	–		1–0–0	1	0	6	0	0	9
TOTALS:		71	44		110.0	16–3–4	5	0	24	1	7	42
2BW				DIVERSION								
B-24	44BG	9										
	93BG	5										
TOTALS:		14	–			0–0–0	0			0	0	0

REMARKS: 7 men picked up by ASR from ditched 91BG B-17. 91BG became separated from the main force whilst on instruments and found clear weather over Germany. First attack on Ruhr. 91BG received DUC for action this day. B-24s looking for any shipping whilst on the diversion. Some B-24s damaged by empty .50 cartridges from preceding a/c.

VIII FC

Despatched		Groups	E/A	Losses MIA	E	Dam	Casualties KIA	WIA	MIA
Spitfire	24	4FG	0	0	0	0	0	0	0

REMARKS: Despatched on fighter patrols.

Despatched		Groups	E/A	Losses MIA	E	Dam	Casualties KIA	WIA	MIA
Spitfire	2	4FG	0	0	0	0	0	0	0

REMARKS: Carried out offensive patrols over Ostend/Dunkirk area.

5 MARCH 1943

VIII FC

Despatched		Groups	E/A	Losses MIA	E	Dam	Casualties KIA	WIA	MIA
Spitfire	4	4FG	0	0	0	0	0	0	0

REMARKS: Despatched on patrols.

6 MARCH 1943

VIII BC 40

	Despatched		Effective	Target	Bombs Tonnage	E/A	Losses MIA	E	Dam	Casualties KIA	WIA	MIA
				LORIENT U/B (P)								
1BW	91BG	14	13	1441–1445 hrs	325 × 1000GP	1–0–0	0	0	0	0	0	0
B-17	303BG	18	17			0–0–0	1	0	1	0	0	10
	305BG	18	14			0–0–0	0	0	1	0	0	0
	306BG	21	21			6–2–1	2	0	6	0	0	20
TOTALS:		71	65		162.5	7–2–1	3	0	8	0	0	30
2BW				BREST U/B								
B-24	44BG	10	10	1416–1417 hrs	89 × 1000GP	1–0–0	0	0	1	0	0	0
	93BG	5	5			1–0–2	0	0	2	0	0	0
TOTALS:		15	15		44.5	2–0–2	0	0	3	0	0	0

REMARKS: B-24s sent out on a diversionary raid.

VIII FC

Despatched		Groups	E/A	Losses MIA	E	Dam	Casualties KIA	WIA	MIA
Spitfire	14	4FG	0	0	0	0	0	0	0

REMARKS: Sent on defensive patrols.

7 MARCH 1943

VIII FC

Despatched		Groups	E/A	Losses MIA	E	Dam	Casualties KIA	WIA	MIA
Spitfire	2	4FG	0	0	0	0	0	0	0

REMARKS: Sent out on a defensive patrol.

8 MARCH 1943

VIII FC 41

	Despatched		Effective	Target	Bombs Tonnage	E/A	Losses MIA	E	Dam	Casualties KIA	WIA	MIA
1BW				RENNES M/Y (P)								
B-17	91BG	14	12	1430 hrs	539 × 500GP	4–1–0	0	0	0	0	0	0
	303BG	19	12			4–0–1	0	1	1	0	0	0
	305BG	16	15			3–0–3	1	0	4	0	7	10
	306BG	18	15			3–0–1	1	0	4	0	1	10
TOTALS:		67	54		134.75	14–1–5	2	1	9	0	8	20
2BW				ROUEN M/Y								
B-24	44BG	10	7	1402–1403 hrs	156 × 500GP	11–2–3	2	0	1	5	0	17
	93BG	6	6			3–1–0	0	1	2	0	3	0
TOTALS:		16	13		39.0	14–3–3	2	1	3	5	3	17

REMARKS: Loss of lead B-24 resulted in confusion and scattered bombing. 303BG B-17 c/l on return. 93BG B-24 crashed at Bredhurst.

VIII FC

Despatched		Groups	E/A	Losses MIA	E	Dam	Casualties KIA	WIA	MIA
Spitfire	25	4FG	0	0	0	0	0	0	0

REMARKS: 4FG provided cover, along with RAF sqdns.

Spitfire	8	4FG	0	0	0	0	0	0	0

REMARKS: Carried out shipping patrols.

9 MARCH 1943

VIII FC

Despatched		Groups	E/A	Losses MIA	E	Dam	Casualties KIA	WIA	MIA
Spitfire	24	4FG	0	0	0	0	0	0	0

REMARKS: Sent out in support of offensive operations against Boulogne.

Spitfire	26	4FG	0	0	0	0	0	0	0

REMARKS: Despatched on shipping patrols during the day.

10 MARCH 1943

VIII FC

Despatched		Groups	E/A	Losses MIA	E	Dam	Casualties KIA	WIA	MIA
Spitfire	12	4FG	0	0					
P-47	14	4FG	0	0					
TOTALS: 26			0	0	0	0	0	0	0

REMARKS: Sent out on offensive patrols. First operation for P-47s.

Spitfire	6	4FG	0	0	0	0	0	0	0

REMARKS: Despatched on a patrol.

11 MARCH 1943

VIII FC

Despatched		Groups	E/A	Losses MIA	E	Dam	Casualties KIA	WIA	MIA
Spitfire	18	4FG	0	0	0	0	0	0	0

REMARKS: Sent out on patrols during the day.

12 MARCH 1943

VIII BC 42

	Despatched		Effective	Target	Bombs Tonnage	E/A	Losses MIA	E	Dam	Casualties KIA	WIA	MIA
1BW				ROUEN/SOTTEVILLE								
B-17	91BG	18	18	M/Y (P) 1241–1244 hrs	208 × 1000GP							
	303BG	18	12		210 × 500GP							
	305BG	17	14									
	306BG	19	19									
TOTALS:		72	63		156.5	0–0–0	0			0	0	0
2BW				DIVERSION								
B-24	44BG	6										
	93BG	12										
TOTALS:		18	–			0–0–0	0			0	0	0

VIII FC

Despatched		Groups	E/A	Losses MIA	E	Dam	Casualties KIA	WIA	MIA
Spitfire	41	4FG	0–0–1	1			0	0	1

REMARKS: Sent on fighter sweeps. Lost Spitfire shot down by e/a; pilot seen to bale out nr St.Omer.

Despatched		Groups	E/A	Losses MIA	E	Dam	Casualties KIA	WIA	MIA
Spitfire	2	4FG	0	0	0	0	0	0	0

REMARKS: Sent on shipping patrol.

13 MARCH 1943

VIII BC 43

	Despatched		Effective	Target	Bombs Tonnage	E/A	Losses MIA	E	Dam	Casualties KIA	WIA	MIA
1BW				AMIENS/LONGEAU								
B-17	91BG	21	19	M/Y 44 a/c	258 × 1000GP				0	0	0	0
	303BG	20	19	1515–1517 hrs	10 × 500GP				0	0	0	0
	305BG	19	17	31 a/c on T/O	184 × 1000GP				11	0	6	0
	306BG	20	20			2–0–2			0	0	0	0
TOTALS:		80	75		223.5	2–0–2	0	0	11	0	6	0
2BW B-24		16	–	DIVERSION	0	0–0–0	0			0	0	0

REMARKS: 12 91BG and 19 306BG a/c attacked T/Os – 21 a/c bombed Romescamps R/R, 8 Abbeville/Drucat A/F and 2 other T/Os.

VIII FC

Despatched		Groups	E/A	Losses MIA	E	Dam	Casualties KIA	WIA	MIA
Spitfire	27	4FG	0	0	0	0	0	0	0

REMARKS: Sent on an offensive mission but failed to r/v with bombers.

Despatched		Groups	E/A	Losses MIA	E	Dam	Casualties KIA	WIA	MIA
Spitfire	6	4FG	0	0	0	0	0	0	0

REMARKS: Despatched on shipping patrols.

14 MARCH 1943

VIII FC

Despatched		Groups	E/A	Losses MIA	E	Dam	Casualties KIA	WIA	MIA
Spitfire	35	4FG	0	0	0	0	0	0	0

REMARKS: Despatched on patrols.

Despatched		Groups	E/A	Losses MIA	E	Dam	Casualties KIA	WIA	MIA
Spitfire	2	4FG	0	0	0	0	0	0	0

REMARKS: Scrambled to intercept 2 FW 190s in Felixstowe area.

15 MARCH 1943

VIII FC

Despatched		Groups	E/A	Losses MIA	E	Dam	Casualties KIA	WIA	MIA
Spitfire	24	4FG	0	0	0	0	0	0	0

REMARKS: Despatched on fighter patrols.

16 MARCH 1943

VIII FC

Despatched		Groups	E/A	Losses MIA	E	Dam	Casualties KIA	WIA	MIA
Spitfire	14	4FG	0	0	0	0	0	0	0

REMARKS: Sent out on defensive patrols.

17 MARCH 1943

VIII BC 44

REMARKS: Bad weather prevented fighters taking off and caused subsequent recall of 78 B-17s, bound for Rouen-Sotteville M/Y, before they had left England.

27 of a force of 28 B-24 carried out a diversionary sweep over the North Sea, the other B-24 returned early due to a fuel leak. Rest of formation recalled before carrying out further sweeps.

18 MARCH 1943

VIII BC 45

	Despatched		Effective	Target	Bombs Tonnage	E/A	Losses MIA	E	Dam	Casualties KIA	WIA	MIA
1BW				VEGESACK U/Y (P)								
B-17	91BG	18	16	1531–1535 hrs	536 × 1000GP	13– 1– 1	0	0				0
	303BG	20	20			6½–1– 2	1	1	9	1	8	10
	305BG	18	17			7½–1– 1	0	0				0
	306BG	20	20			7– 0– 0	0	0				0
2BW												
B-24	44BG	9	9			13– 6– 8	0	0	14	0	8	0
	93BG	18	15			5–11–11	1	0		0		10
TOTALS:		103	97		268	52–20–23	2	1	23	1	16	20

REMARKS: The 303BG B-17 lost was manned by a 92BG crew. 303BG crew member Lt Jack W. Mathis posthumously awarded MOH for action this day. 303BG B-17 made an emergency landing at Matlask, 3 wounded. B/d 303BG B-17 c/l near base.

VIII FC

Despatched		Groups	E/A	Losses MIA	E	Dam	Casualties KIA	WIA	MIA
Spitfire	16	4FG	0	0	0	0	0	0	0

REMARKS: Sent on defensive and convoy patrols.

INCIDENT

The Vegesack mission was the first into Germany for the 93rd Bomb Group; a painful initiation with frequent fighter attacks during the hour and three-quarters that the formation was in hostile airspace. The pilot of *Shoot Luke*, Capt John Murphy, saw that the B-24 commanded by his former co-pilot, Frank Lown, had an engine disabled and other damage causing it to lag behind the formation. Enemy fighters having turned away, Murphy and crew elected to drop back and afford some protection to the ailing B-24 should any more fighters arrive. A lone FW 190 did appear to make a single pass, its pilot selecting *Shoot Luke* rather than the cripple. The attack was made from below, the enemy fire raking the length of *Shoot Luke*'s fuselage. Two cannon shells and several small calibre rounds penetrated the nose and rear fuselage wounding seven of the ten man crew. One shell slammed into the rear gunner's seat, exploding under his left buttock. The force of the explosion hurled the gunner, S/Sgt Paul Slankard, through the turret plexiglass so that the upper part of his body was outside the aircraft. Had not his left foot caught in the gun controls, he might have been blasted fully out of the turret. His wounds were terrible; the force of the explosion had embedded coins and the contents of a trouser pocket deep into his left hip. Unable to fight against the force of the slipstream, Slankard remained pinned partly out of the turret until T/Sgt Floyd Mabee, realising what had happened, pulled him down. Despite his own injuries – he had a painful eye wound – Mabee managed to get Slankard back into the waist and put an auxiliary oxygen mask on him. Informed of the tail gunner's wounds, the bombardier, Lt Ed Janic, who also had head wounds, came back to administer first aid. It appeared that Slankard's left leg was nearly severed but the major problem

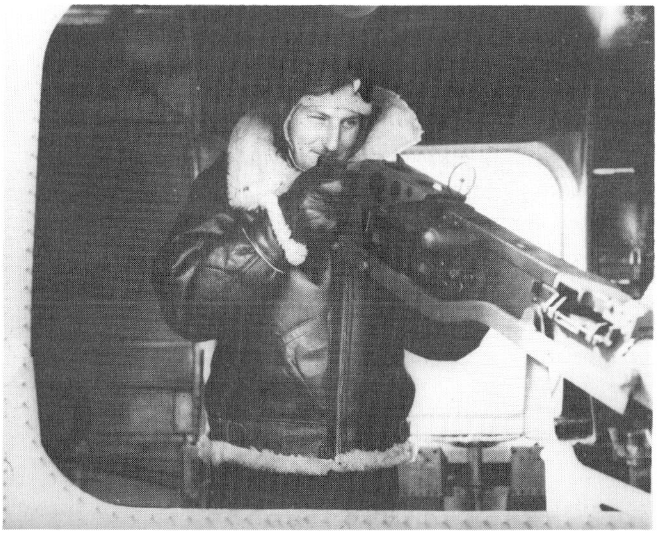

Sgt Paul Slankard at the waist gun of a B-24. (F. Mabee)

was to stop him bleeding to death from the gaping wound. Sulphonamide powder was applied, but the extent of the wound was such that blood loss was the immediate problem. Janic and Mabee hit on the idea of exposing the pulped mass to the freezing blast of air coming through the hole made by a cannon shell in the fuselage skin. This proved successful in sealing severed veins. Attempts to ease the gunner's pain were frustrated by frozen hypodermic needles despite Janic's efforts to thaw them in his mouth. Two hours and forty-five minutes elapsed before *Shoot Luke* landed, and to the medics it looked doubtful if Slankard would live for long. However, the doctors found that his leg and hip could be saved and after surgery Slankard made a remarkable recovery, one of the few men who survived a 20 mm shell explosion in his body without amputation or major disability.

19 MARCH 1943

VIII FC

Despatched		Groups	E/A	Losses MIA	E	Dam	Casualties KIA	WIA	MIA
Spitfire	6	4FG	0	0	0	0	0	0	0

REMARKS: Sent out on a defensive and convoy patrol.

20 MARCH 1943

VIII FC

Despatched		Groups	E/A	Losses MIA	E	Dam	Casualties KIA	WIA	MIA
Spitfire	2	4FG	0	0	0	0	0	0	0

REMARKS: Sent out on shipping patrols.

22 MARCH 1943

VIII BC 46

	Despatched		Effective	Target	Bombs Tonnage	E/A	Losses MIA	E	Dam	Casualties KIA	WIA	MIA
1BW				WILHELMSHAVEN								
B-17	91BG	21	18	U/Y (P)	448 × 1000GP	5–1–1	1	0	12	1	7	10
	303BG	18	15	1501–1510 hrs		2–0–2	0	0				
	305BG	18	17			2–0–0	0	0				
	306BG	19	19			2–1–0	0	0				
2BW				WILHELMSHAVEN								
B-24	44BG	12	10	U/Y (P)		10–6–0	2	0	10	0	11	22
	93BG	14	5	1501–1510 hrs		7–1–6	0	0				
TOTALS:		102	84		224.0	28–9–9	3	0	22	1	18	32

VIII FC

Despatched		Groups	E/A	Losses MIA	E	Dam	Casualties KIA	WIA	MIA
Spitfire	4	4FG	0	0	0	0	0	0	0

REMARKS: Despatched on fighter patrols.

Above. Damage to No.4 engine of *Wheel and Deal* and failure of the feathering mechanism brought a 'runaway' propeller. Friction in the over-speeding hub eventually caused the whole propeller assembly to part company with the engine – fortunately without striking another part of the aircraft. Maj Wallick brought the bomber down safely at base.

Right. On 22 March mission some 91BG Fortresses were still using the .300 rifle calibre machine gun that could be transferred to any one of three ball sockets set in the plexiglass nosepiece. *Delta Rebel* also had a .50 installation in the nose on an improvised mount designed to absorb the considerable 'kick'. The .300 gun was going out of use as it was considered of little value in countering frontal attacks.

23 MARCH 1943

VIII FC

Despatched		Groups	E/A	Losses MIA	E	Dam	Casualties KIA	WIA	MIA
Spitfire	8	4FG	0	0	0	0	0	0	0

REMARKS: Sent out on fighter patrols.

24 MARCH 1943

VIII FC

Despatched		Groups	E/A	Losses MIA	E	Dam	Casualties KIA	WIA	MIA
Spitfire	26	4FG	0	0	0	0	0	0	0

REMARKS: Despatched on fighter patrols.

25 MARCH 1943

VIII FC

Despatched		Groups	E/A	Losses MIA	E	Dam	Casualties KIA	WIA	MIA
Spitfire	12	4FG	0	0	0	0	0	0	0

REMARKS: Sent out on defensive and convoy patrols.

26 MARCH 1943

VIII FC

Despatched		Groups	E/A	Losses MIA	E	Dam	Casualties KIA	WIA	MIA
Spitfire	8	4FG	0	0	0	0	0	0	0

REMARKS: Despatched on fighter patrols.

28 MARCH 1943

VIII BC 47

	Despatched		Effective	Target	Bombs Tonnage	E/A	Losses MIA	E	Dam	Casualties KIA	WIA	MIA
1BW				ROUEN/SOTTEVILLE								
B-17	91BG	22	15	M/Y	418 × 500GP	2–1–0	1	0	6	0	1	10
	303BG	18	17	1248–1250 hrs	209 × 1000GP	0–0–0	0	0	0	0	0	0
	305BG	19	18			2–2–1	0	0	1	0	0	0
	306BG	20	20			1–1–0	0	0	2	0	1	0
2BW												
B-24	44BG	11	0									
	93BG	13	0									
TOTALS:		103	70		209	5–4–1	1	0	9	0	2	10

REMARKS: 2BW a/c recalled at 1245 hrs because of poor weather.

VIII FC

Despatched		Groups	E/A	Losses MIA	E	Dam	Casualties KIA	WIA	MIA
Spitfire	33	4FG	0	0	0	0	0	0	0

REMARKS: Sent on shipping and defensive patrols.

An F-5A of 13 PS Sqdn on first 8AF photo reconnaissance sortie over Dieppe.

INCIDENT

Photographic coverage of both prospective and bombed targets was provided by the RAF during the first nine months of 8th Air Force operations and predominantly so for a further similar period. 'PR' was a new art for the USAAF whose own establishment engaged in this form of intelligence gathering was based on the highly successful methods evolved by the British. The Lockheed P-38 Lightning was the best aircraft available to adapt to the task of fast high altitude sorties, the spacious nose-gun bay housing cameras. Under the designation F-5A, a dozen of these camera-equipped Lightnings were delivered to Mount Farm for the 13th Photo Squadron beginning January 1943 and by late March the unit was ready to go to work. Maj James G. Hall, 45-year-old commander of the squadron, undertook sortie number 1 on 28 March with the port of Dieppe as the objective. He was gone ninety minutes and back in time for lunch at Mount Farm. Clouds hid Dieppe so he set the cameras in motion to photograph a strip of the enemy coast that was in the clear to the east of his original objective as far as Ault. The developed film revealed Le Treport marshalling yard with a larger than usual concentration of goods wagons, information leading to an RAF attack the following day. This was the first of 4,593 sorties despatched by Mount Farm units during hostilities. In June 1943 Hall was called to Washington to oversee all USAAF photographic reconnaissance activities.

James Hall, who initiated 8AF's photographic reconnaissance operations.

29 MARCH 1943

VIII FC

				Losses			Casualties		
Despatched		Groups	E/A	MIA	E	Dam	KIA	WIA	MIA
Spitfire	18	4FG	0	0	0	0	0	0	0

REMARKS: Despatched on shipping patrols during the day.

30 MARCH 1943

VIII FC

				Losses			Casualties		
Despatched		Groups	E/A	MIA	E	Dam	KIA	WIA	MIA
Spitfire	28	4FG	0	0			0	0	0

REMARKS: Sent out to make shipping patrols.

Lt.-Col Chesley Peterson, CO 4FG, was probably the most experienced US fighter pilot in England in the spring of 1943. An early American volunteer for RAF service, he joined the first Eagle squadron in November 1940 and had amassed some 400 hours operational flying in Hurricanes and Spitfires. In late March he and some of his pilots featured in a press photographic session at Debden where 4FG Spitfires were also prominent. At this date the Spits had been taken off offensive ops while the Group converted to the new P-47 Thunderbolt. While giving genuine cover of a US fighter unit, the press photos were also aimed at making enemy intelligence believe US Spitfires were still in business.

31 MARCH 1943

VIII BC 48

	Despatched		Effective	Target	Bombs Tonnage	E/A	Losses MIA	E	Dam	Casualties KIA	WIA	MIA
1BW				ROTTERDAM S/Y								
B-17	91BG	20	0	1225 hrs	198 × 1000GP	0–0–0	0	0	1	0	0	0
	303BG	20	17			0–0–0	2	2	0	15	3	0
	305BG	19	16			1–0–0	1	1	1	1	4	0
	306BG	19	0			0–1–0	0	0	2	0	0	0
2BW				ROTTERDAM S/Y								
B-24	44BG	12	0			0–0–0	0	0	0	0	3	0
	93BG	12	0			0–0–2	1	0	1	0	0	10
TOTALS:		102	33		99.0	1–1–2	4	3	5	16	10	10

REMARKS: Most failed to bomb because of clouds. 2 303BG B-17s collided during assembly near Wellingborough; 15 killed. 305BG B-17 with battle damage crashed near Wickham Bishops after crew baled out. Missing B-24 last seen with one engine on fire heading for England.

VIII FC

Despatched		Groups	E/A	Losses MIA	E	Dam	Casualties KIA	WIA	MIA
Spitfire	31	4FG	0	0	0	0	0	0	0

REMARKS: Despatched on fighter patrols during the day.

1 APRIL 1943

VIII FC

Despatched		Groups	E/A	Losses MIA	E	Dam	Casualties KIA	WIA	MIA
Spitfire	14	4FG	0	0	0	0	0	0	0

REMARKS: Sent out on a shipping patrol. Last Spitfire operation by VIII FC.

3 APRIL 1943

3 photographic sorties by F-5s of 13PS to French coast.

4 APRIL 1943

VIII BC 49

	Despatched		Effective	Target	Bombs Tonnage	E/A	Losses MIA	E	Dam	Casualties KIA	WIA	MIA
1BW				PARIS RENAULT WKS								
B-17	91BG	26	20	(at Billancourt) (P)	502 × 1000GP	11– 4–0	0			0	0	0
	303BG	23	20	1414–1417 hrs		4– 2–1	1			0	0	9
	305BG	18	18			25– 6–5	3			0	5	30
	306BG	30	27			7– 1–0	0			0	1	0
TOTALS:		97	85		251	47–13–6	4	0	16	0	6	39

REMARKS: 25 2BW B-24s carried out diversionary sweeps over the N.Sea. 305BG received DUC for this mission. 305BG B-17 with wounded crew down at Dunsfold.

13PS flew 3 F-5 sorties to Belgium and France. 1 F-5 MIA near Antwerp.

5 APRIL 1943

VIII BC 50

	Despatched		Effective	Target	Bombs Tonnage	E/A	Losses MIA	E	Dam	Casualties KIA	WIA	MIA
1BW				ANTWERP I/A (P)								
B-17	91BG	20	16	1530 hrs	383 × 1000GP	6–1–1	0	0	3	0	1	0
	303BG	21	17			3–1–0	0	0	3	0	0	0
	305BG	18	15			0–1–0	0	0	0	0	0	0
	306BG	20	16			5–2–3	4	0	6	0	2	40

continued on facing page

2BW				ANTWERP I/A								
B-24	44BG	14	11	1534–1537 hrs	216 × 500GP	7–3–0	0	0	1	0	0	0
	93BG	11	7			2–0–0	0	0	0	0	0	0
TOTALS:		104	82		245.5	23–8–4	4	0	13	0	3	40

REMARKS: Belgian Ambassador to the USA protested about the inaccurate bombing that resulted in many civilian casualties. On this day 306BG crew member T/Sgt Roscovitch became first man in 8AF to complete a tour of 25 operations.

13PS despatched 5 F-5s to French coast ports.

'Army'

Generals were not encouraged to participate in combat operations: Command experience was too valuable to chance in the costly missions VIII Bomber Command undertook. There was also the risk that if such senior officers were shot down and captured the enemy might be able to trick or force valuable information from such important prisoners. Nevertheless, the generals commanding the Eighth's Bombardment Wings did make occasional flights as observers to better understand the problems facing their bomber crews. On 5 April 1943, Brig.Gen Frank A. Armstrong, who headed the 101st Provisional Combat Wing, went to Thurleigh to fly with the 306th Group which he had recently commanded. He rode on the flight deck of the lead Fortress piloted by Lt.Col James Wilson and Capt John Regan. Armstrong's main reason for going along was to see how the pilots performed as leaders of a combat wing formation. What happened that day is recorded in the notes he made during the mission as time and opportunity allowed:–

'Stood behind pilot while we took off . . . Moved to navigator-bombardier compartment and rode with them until we gained considerable altitude, when I returned to a position behind the pilot and co-pilot . . . Adjusted oxygen mask and arranged parachute so top turret mechanism would not knock it down . . . Placed pilot's parachute in a better position for him to get it if an emergency arose. Made sign language to pilot to be on alert for enemy attackers through this overcast in early stages of the attack . . . Pointed out two smoke trails coming out of France high to our left. Checked time of turn as we left the English coast. Checked on the formation by looking through the side window. Looked at Belgium as we crossed the coast line, wondering how the people were doing down there. Cursed a FW 190 as it came into our right. Watched the first enemy attack develop ahead of the formation. Pointed out the attackers to the pilot as they became more ferocious and concentrated. Pressed the control column forward as a FW 190 met us head-on. Back seat driving, and I was sorry about it. FW 190 rolled under wing, missed a collision by a few feet. Watched fire from cannons as Germans increased their attack. (Only one cannon was firing from a few of the enemy aircraft – out of ammunition, maybe.) Flinched as shell exploded the oxygen and hydraulic system. Looked at the pilot and co-pilot to see how badly they were wounded. Began to feel queer . . . checked oxygen supply – pressure down to 100. Tried to attach oxygen lead to emergency supply bottle. Couldn't get it to fasten, so tore up mask. Co-pilot reached for emergency oxygen bottle. Gave it to him. Asked for a whiff and he gave it to me. Pilot told me that Capt Robert J. Salitrnik, navigator, had been hit and wanted some assistance. Got another whiff of oxygen from co-pilot and started to forward compartment. Crawled through hydraulic fluid on hands and knees to navigator. The navigator had received a severe shrapnel wound in the leg and was bleeding badly. Used oxygen mask connecting hose as tourniquet on navigator's leg. Helped to take navigator's parachute off and stretch him out. Re-arranged tourniquet and gave to bombardier to hold (had my own thumb on it). Took navigator's data out of navigator's pocket and tried to locate our position on the map. Couldn't get maps straight. Crawled back to pilot's compartment to give him compass course on the paper . . . lost information on the floor and crawled back for it. Rearranged tourniquet and continued to nose of aircraft. Put on throat mike and headset. Called pilot to inform him he would be forced to land at the first RAF station because the navigator was seriously wounded . . . gave pilot course to fly. Could not locate any field on the ground. Crawled over to navigator and slapped his face. Looked at his eyes. Requested pilot to get down as rapidly as possible as all oxygen for navigator had been used. Sat by navigator feeling his head. Rearranged tourniquet. Held navigator's arm while bombardier tried to give him a hypo. (Fluid ran out before needle got in.) Sat down. Pilot called to report a fire had started in the cockpit. Remained seated. Just sat until lower altitude was reached. Crawled back to pilot's compartment and notified him I would stand by rear door with fire extinguisher ready. Sat behind ammunition box for crash-landing. Opened door and ran around to front of airplane after it had stopped – no fire. Placed $400 in the back seat of an automobile and walked away and left it. Forgot what driver's name was. Tried to get the pilot to go over for a cup of coffee. Drank coffee and ate doughnuts. Began to function normally.' What Armstrong did not mention was that for 25 minutes following the departure of the Spitfire escort near Ghent, Luftwaffe fighters made an estimated 25 head-on passes in an effort to destroy the lead Fortress which sustained several hits and severe damage. The Luftwaffe came very close that day to claiming the 8th Air Force's most knowledgeable bomber leader, a man whose experience would become the basis for an outstanding post-war motion picture.

'Army' in pensive mood listens to Lt.-Col Fargo at Chelveston on 18 June. He wears the British DFC ribbon and was the first USAAF officer in England to receive this award – made for his leadership of the inaugural heavy bomber mission.

Frank Armstrong was one of the six officers that Ira Eaker had brought to England in February 1942. His first knowledge of this assignment came on 24 January that year when General Eaker walked into his office – Armstrong was Assistant Chief of Operations at USAAF Hq. Washington – and announced without explanation that he, Armstrong, would be going to England with him. The background to this selection was Eaker's respect for Armstrong's abilities gained during the controversial carrying of mail by Army aircraft during 1934. At that time Capt Eaker had the task of handling the treacherous western routes. Lt Armstrong volunteered to fly the trickiest route of all which entailed flying through a canyon. Impressed with the way his duties were performed, Eaker made Armstrong his chief pilot at the Salt Lake City, Utah base. The enterprise displayed in planning and conducting these flights over difficult terrain and in bad weather was something Eaker did not forget. Another qualification for accompanying his superior to England was that in November 1940 Armstrong had gone to the UK to study RAF methods and knew the situation and conditions in which the American bomber force would have to be established. This earlier visit had some bearing on Armstrong's attitude to the war. He had experienced the London Blitz and what he saw left him with a desire to contribute to any future aerial retribution.

Like many of the more senior USAAF pilots, Armstrong wanted a flying post when the US entered hostilities but found desk jobs were the lot of age and experience – he was in his fortieth year when he arrived in England to help establish VIII Bomber Command. As Operations Officer he was involved in developing procedural methods for bombing missions, and setting up the various operations departments to sustain such an offensive. Although Armstrong had a great liking and respect for his boss he also stood slightly in awe of him and was often apprehensive when summoned to Eaker's office. Such was the case when late in July he was called before the head of VIII Bomber Command to be told that he was to replace the CO of 97th Group, complete its training and take it into combat. Armstrong could hardly suppress his elation at having been given the 8th's first heavy bomber formation. His task was not easy; many 97th men had received little training in the duties they would have to perform. He was given two weeks to get the Group operational and flew with them at every opportunity, evaluating climb power settings and formation procedures, trying to establish the optimums. The basic concepts of high altitude precision bombing had been established back in the US but putting them into practice in Europe involved much trial and error.

The Group was first alerted for combat on 12 August 1942 but this and two further Field Orders were cancelled. The initiation finally came on 17 August when Armstrong flew in the leading Fortress of a 12-plane formation to bomb marshalling yards at Rouen. On return Armstrong, delighted, quipped: 'We ruined Rouen', which was more a comment on the overall success of the flight than a serious statement on bombing results. Over the next few weeks he led the 97th on five more missions and on the last witnessed the shooting down of the first B-17 lost by his group and the 8th Air Force. Much of the operational technique evolved through these early raids was due to Armstrong's work and ideas. He had expected to be allowed to continue with his combat command only to be dismayed when told that the 97th would be taking part in the invasion of North Africa and he would not be going with them. While General Eaker could do nothing to retain his most experienced bomber group he was determined to see that he did not lose his most able commander and in late September Armstrong found himself back in VIII Bomber Command behind a desk. On New Year's Day, 1943, when he had all but come to accept his destiny as a staff officer, General Eaker summoned 'Army' – his nickname for Armstrong – to his office and informed him he was being recommended for promotion to Brigadier General and was to take over the 306th Group at Thurleigh.

Eaker had been concerned about the performance of the 306th; its losses were high, air discipline was poor and on the last mission most of its aircraft had abandoned the mission before the start point, weakening the force despatched. He found the group had a despondent, defeatist attitude and that the CO was something of a father figure who had become so involved with the misfortunes of his men that he seemed more anxious to defend than improve their poor performance. The general standard of military order at Thurleigh he also considered very lax. Armstrong's job once again was that of troubleshooter and circus master; but this time it was different, with a morale problem and a lingering allegiance to the commander replaced.

Armstrong took command on 4 January 1943. An indication of the problems he faced was the casual attitude of the gate guard when he arrived. No disciplinarian, Armstrong was nevertheless aware that a firm hand was required and the 306th was made quickly aware that his rule would be tough. There was a wall of resentment which was not easily broken down. Armstrong made changes and continually emphasised training whenever the Group was not on operations. It was an exhausting task for a man with his sensitive nature. On 27 January he flew in the lead B-17 to Wilhelmshaven for the first 8th Air Force raid on Germany. On return, pleased at the way things went, he commented, 'I could go out and dance all night'. Slowly, the 306th came to accept their mentor and improve their bombing. With his promotion confirmed Armstrong became the only General to hold command of an 8th Air Force bomb group, albeit briefly. Having upgraded the 306th's performance to Eaker's satisfaction, a younger man was given command of the Group. 'Army' was then made commander of the newly-formed 101st Provisional Combat Wing, with tactical control over the Thurleigh and Bassingbourn groups. The mission of 5 April to Antwerp was his second in this capacity and his ministrations to the wounded navigator, recorded earlier, undoubtedly ensured the man reaching England alive although sadly, after making a seemingly good recovery, he died a few weeks later.

For his actions that day Armstrong received the DSC. There is no doubt he was a courageous man and the more so in that he knew and acknowledged the grip of fear. He had been one of the few Army fliers to be awarded a DFC in peacetime: this in 1936 for landing a crippled amphibian after an aerial explosion. To his compatriots he was a personable, soft-spoken genial man with a sense of humour, enthusiastic and firm in his duties. What many did not sense or see was that he was a very sentimental man, particularly with regard to a longing to be reunited with his wife and young son. Surprisingly for such an adventurous and eager man he was secretly extremely superstitious. On the Rouen mission he had entered the Fortress by the rear fuselage door and lugged his equipment up to the flight deck across the narrow bomb-bay catwalk. Although later deciding entry through the nose hatch would be less tedious, in all his combat missions he continued to enter through the rear door for fear of breaking his chain of luck. Armstrong also never went on a mission unless carrying his son's baby shoes. These had been in his possession for over 13 years and were so fragile that they were kept in a special pocket-case.

In June 1943 Armstrong was elevated to head 1st Bomb Wing which controlled all the veteran B-17 groups and their provisional combat wings. It was a trying period for VIII Bomber Command and the responsibilities of command began to tire him. Injuries sustained during a fire in his quarters at Brampton during July did not help, and later that month Eaker decided to send 'Army' back to the States where his expertise would be invaluable in the training of new units. Armstrong relinquished command of 1st Wing to his old friend and colleague Bob Williams at the beginning of August. Subsequently he was to command and fly with a special wing of Superfortresses that devastated the Japanese oil industry, and to have a distinguished post-war career.

Frank Armstrong's service with the 8th Air Force was to be highlighted in an usual way. At the end of hostilities, Maj Sy Bartlett, who had worked with Armstrong in England, proposed to another colleague, Col Beirne Lay, that they write a novel based on Armstrong's task of rejuvenating the 306th Bomb Group. Both men were involved in screen writing for the Hollywood film industry and from their novel came the brilliant film *'Twelve O'Clock High'*. The central character was General Frank Savage, a composite of several real group commanders both authors had known, but primarily based on Frank Armstrong. Perhaps Gregory Peck's portrayal of the burdened commander was not truly akin to the character of Frank Armstrong, but the film is unmistakably a tribute to this fine leader.

While Cpl John Murray makes some necessary perforations, Sgt Lewis Simpson adds the 22nd mission completed symbol to the score board on *Delta Rebel No.2*. The previous day, 5 April, Lt 'Red' Cliburn and crew had taken the bomber to Antwerp. At this time the 'Rebel' was a favourite for the first Fortress to reach a quarter century in missions completed, but a few days later it sustained damage that put it out of the running. Fourteen fighter destroyed symbols indicate several fierce air battles, but the Luftwaffe finally got the 'Rebel' on the first Schweinfurt raid.

8 APRIL 1943

VIII FC

Despatched		Groups	E/A	Losses MIA	E	Dam	Casualties KIA	WIA	MIA
P-47	23	4FG, 56FG, 78FG	0	0	0	0	0	0	0

REMARKS: Sent out on a *Rodeo* between Dunkirk and Sangatte, a/c from each group made up the individual flights. Flown from Debden with 56FG and 78FG providing 4 and 12 a/c respectively.

13PS despatched 1 F-5 over NW France.

10 APRIL 1943

VIII FC

Despatched		Groups	E/A	Losses MIA	E	Dam	Casualties KIA	WIA	MIA
P-47	1	4FG	0	0	0	0	0	0	0

REMARKS: Sent out on an offensive patrol.

11 APRIL 1943

VIII FC RODEO 200

Despatched		Groups	E/A	Losses MIA	E	Dam	Casualties KIA	WIA	MIA
P-47	6	4FG	0	0	0	0	0	0	0

REMARKS: Despatched on a *Rodeo* to Calais.

12 APRIL 1943

13PS despatched 1 F-5 to NW France.

13 April 1943

VIII FC

Despatched		Groups	E/A	Losses MIA	E	Dam	Casualties KIA	WIA	MIA
P-47	36	4FG, 56FG, 78FG	0	1	0	0	0	0	0

REMARKS: Sent out on a diversion to *Ramrod 50*, combined formation with 4FG. Recorded as first 78FG mission. 56FG contributed 4 a/c flying from Debden and 78FG despatched 12 from Duxford. A 78FG pilot baled out over Channel when P-47 had engine failure, rescued by ASR.

P-47	40	4FG, 56FG, 78FG	0	0	1	0	0	0	0

REMARKS: Sent on *Rodeo 202*. 56FG despatched 4 a/c from Debden and 8 from Horsham St.Faith. 78FG despatched 12 a/c from Duxford. A 56FG P-47 had engine failure but pilot managed to glide to make a belly landing near Deal. First 56FG mission.

13PS despatched 4 F-5 sorties to NW France.

15 APRIL 1943

VIII FC RODEO 204

Despatched		Groups	E/A	Losses MIA	E	Dam	Casualties KIA	WIA	MIA
P-47	59	4FG, 56FG, 78FG	3–0–1	3	0	1	0	0	2

REMARKS: Carried out sweeps of Furnes/St.Omer area. A MIA 4FG pilot rescued from sea. Fighter group losses:– 4FG – 3: Fighter group e/a credits:– 4FG – 3.

13PS despatched 4 F-5 sorties to NW France. 1 F-5 MIA.

16 APRIL 1943

VIII BC 51

	Despatched		Effective	Target	Bombs Tonnage	E/A	Losses MIA	E	Dam	Casualties KIA	WIA	MIA
1BW				LORIENT U/B(P)								
B-17	91BG	21	13	1412–1414 hrs	294 × 1000GP	0–0–0	0	0	0	0	1	0
	303BG	21	16			2–3–1	0	0	1	0	0	0
	305BG	21	18			4–1–1	1	0	5	0	3	10
	306BG	20	12			3–0–0	0	0	2	0	3	0
TOTALS:		83	59		147.0	9–4–2	1	0	8	0	7	10
2BW				BREST U/B(P)								
B-24	44BG	12	11	1337–1338 hrs	208 × 500GP	0–0–0	0	0	8	0	0	0
	93BG	13	8			2–3–1	3	1	1	0	3	31
TOTALS:		25	19		52.0	2–3–1	3	1	9	0	3	31

REMARKS: Attack on Brest hindered by an effective smoke screen. B/d 93BG B-24 c/l St. Eval A/F.
13PS despatched 1 F-5 on the unit's first damage assessment photo mission to Lorient, unsuccessful due to cloud.

17 APRIL 1943

VIII BC 52

	Despatched		Effective	Target	Bombs Tonnage	E/A	Losses MIA	E	Dam	Casualties KIA	WIA	MIA
1BW				BREMEN A/I (P)								
B-17	91BG	32	28	1259–1303 hrs	531× 1000GP	24– 9–10	6	0		1	0	60
	303BG	29	29		(107 a/c)	11– 3– 1	0	0		0	0	0
	305BG	28	28			20– 3– 5	0	0		0	3	0
	306BG	26	22			8– 0– 1	10	0		1	1	99
TOTALS:		115	107		265.5	63–15–17	16	0	39	2	4	159

REMARKS: One a/c bombed a T/O and another dropped part of load on primary and a T/O. Crews reported that this was the heaviest opposition to date.

VIII FC

Despatched		Groups	E/A	Losses MIA	E	Dam	Casualties KIA	WIA	MIA
P-47	81	4FG, 56FG, 78FG	0	0	0	0	0	0	0

REMARKS: Sent on sweeps covering Blankenberghe/Bruges/Flushing areas, as part of *Rodeo 205*.

P-47	59	4FG, 78FG	0	0	0	0	0	0	0

REMARKS: Despatched on a diversion, on *Circus 285*.

13PS despatched 1 F-5 on damage assessment photo sortie.

INCIDENT

The Bremen mission of 17 April 1943 witnessed the most successful Luftwaffe fighter opposition so far to the heavy bombers with well co-ordinated waves of FW 190s causing the loss of 15 B-17s in the leading combat wing. The total loss for the day was double that for any previous mission and disturbed the faith of those VIII Bomber Command officers who believed in the ability of the B-17s to more than hold their own in conflict with interceptors. There were other reactions too. At Bassingbourn a large party had been arranged for that evening with an expectation of 150 service and civilian guests in addition to some 200 base officers. The 91st Group had lost 6 crews – five from its 401st Squadron – and several of the missing officers had invited guests, a situation causing some concern to the organisers. The shadow the day's mission cast over proceedings was further emphasised by the activities of some of the surviving combatants who drank heavily and engaged in riotous behaviour as the night wore on. The Group historian recorded his disapproval in moderate terms: 'Some little excitement occurred during the later stages of the party when several of the combat crew members indulged too freely as a reaction against their experiences during the day. By and large, this party did not induce the same carefree participation which has been usual in the past.'

18 APRIL 1943

VIII FC

Despatched		Groups	E/A	Losses MIA	E	Dam	Casualties KIA	WIA	MIA
P-47	16	4FG	0	0	0	0	0	0	0

REMARKS: Sent on a sweep of Nieuport/Dunkirk/Hazebrouck/Sangatte area.

20 APRIL 1943

13PS despatched 4 F-5 to NW France.

21 APRIL 1943

VIII FC RODEO 208

Despatched		Groups	E/A	Losses MIA	E	Dam	Casualties KIA	WIA	MIA
P-47	82	4FG, 56FG, 78FG	0	0	0	0	0	0	0

REMARKS: Carried out high altitude sweeps over enemy territory (Westhoofd, Noordwijk and The Hague area).

13PS despatched 1 F-5 to NW France.

On 26 April the recently introduced Thunderbolt escort fighters were displayed before the press at Horsham St.Faith. It was a non-operational day for 56FG, still very much an untried organisation that had yet to encounter the Luftwaffe. These 61FS aircraft have the national markings enlarged and painted under both wings as an extra identification feature.

The firepower of the P-47 was in keeping with the fighter's size. Eight .50 guns delivered a concentrated torrent of 'half inch' bullets that were considered more destructive than 20 mm shells. The staggered position of these guns and the case ejector slots under the wings show well on LM-S, personal aircraft of 62FS CO Maj Dave Schilling, borrowed on this occasion by the Group CO – Lt Col Hubert Zemke. Both men would soon become famous.

28 APRIL 1943

13PS despatched 2 F-5 to NW France.

29 APRIL 1943

VIII FC RODEO 211

Despatched		Groups	E/A	Losses MIA	E	Dam	Casualties KIA	WIA	MIA
P-47	112	4FG, 56FG, 78FG	0	2	0	2	0	0	2

REMARKS: Carried out a high altitude sweep of Pas de Calais/Hague area. 56FG had first encounters with e/a this day. Fighter group losses:– 56FG – 2.

1 MAY 1943

VIII BC 53

	Despatched		Effective	Target	Bombs Tonnage	E/A	Losses MIA	E	Dam	Casualties KIA	WIA	MIA
1BW				ST.NAZAIRE U/B (P)								
B-17	91BG	20	2	1125–1131 hrs	57 × 2000GP	3–0–0	1	0	3	0	4	10
	303BG	19	10			5–6–6	2	0	8	2	0	20
	305BG	21	5			2–0–2	1	0	3	0	1	10
	306BG	18	12			8–0–0	3	2	6	1	12	33
TOTALS:		78	29		57.0	18–6–8	7	2	20	3	17	73
2BW				DIVERSION								
B-24	44BG	18		BRITTANY COAST								
	93BG	6										
TOTALS:		24	–		0	0–0–0	0		0	0	0	0

REMARKS: Poor weather prevented most bombing. 306BG crew member Sgt Maynard Smith received MOH for action this day. The B-17 in which he was flying landed at Predannack with severe battle damage and was salvaged.

13PS despatched 2 F-5 to photograph French ports.

INCIDENT

Throughout 8th Air Force operations there were numerous instances of navigational error precipitating disaster. Constant vigilance was demanded to fly a briefed course across undercasts and through weather fronts that so often hindered the heavy bombers. In such conditions it was very easy for navigation to go astray. On May Day, 1943, heavy cloud frustrated a mission to St.Nazaire. Turning for home the bombers were supposed to take a north-westerly course to ensure they skirted the Brest peninsula by 60 miles. The leading 306th Group somehow miscalculated and made a turn to the north and England too early. Losing altitude the Group was suddenly made aware of its wandering by flak from the Brest area, an error which cost three B-17s. The trailing 91st Group saw what was happening and made a sharp turn left. This manoeuvre dispersed the formation and enemy fighters then arrived to take advantage of the situation. Such happenings, coupled with the inability to successfully bomb a target, had a particularly damping effect on aircrew morale.

3 MAY 1943

VIII FC FO 8

Despatched		Groups	E/A	Losses MIA	E	Dam	Casualties KIA	WIA	MIA
P-47	118	4FG, 56FG, 78FG	0	0	0	0	0	0	0

REMARKS: Despatched to sweep Walcheren Island/Knokke/Ostend/Nieuport areas.

4 MAY 1943

VIII BC 54

	Despatched		Effective	Target	Bombs Tonnage	E/A	Losses MIA	E	Dam	Casualties KIA	WIA	MIA
1BW				ANTWERP I/A (P)								
B-17	91BG	25	19	1839–1843 hrs	323 × 1000GP	2–0–1	0	0	2	0	0	0
	303BG	27	21			4–0–1	0	0	5	0	2	0
	305BG	27	25			4–0–0	0	0	9	0	1	0
TOTALS:		79	65		161.5	10–0–2	0	0	16	0	3	0
1BW				DIVERSION								
B-17	306BG	20					0	0	0	0	0	0
2BW												
B-24	44BG	13					0	0	0	0	0	0
TOTALS:		33	–			0–0–0	0	0	0	0	0	0

VIII FC FO 10

Despatched		Groups	E/A	Losses MIA	E	Dam	Casualties KIA	WIA	MIA
P-47	117	4FG, 56FG, 78FG	1–0–0	1	0	0	0	0	1

REMARKS: P-47 lost through engine failure, pilot in sea MIA. Fighter group losses: 4FG – 1.

13PS despatched 3 F-5 sorties to NW France.

Camera work in front of *Knock-Out Dropper* (the 303BG B-17F that became the first in the 8AF to complete both 50 and 75 missions) attracts unusual attention – Hollywood's most celebrated male star, Clark Gable, arrived in England with the 351BG during April 1943. The 42-year-old Captain headed a team of six former motion picture employees given the task of making a film about 8AF combat gunnery for use in training establishments. While the 351st was undergoing theatre indoctrination and preparing for combat, Gable and his cameraman chose to begin combat filming with a seasoned B-17 group. On 4 May he went to the neighbouring 303BG at Molesworth and flew as an observer in the leadplane, *Eight Ball II* on a mission to Antwerp. When enemy fighters made a pass and slightly damaged the bomber, Gable manned the radio room gun. Gable flew a mission in each of the following four months and the B-17s in which he flew came under fighter attack on three of these. His great personal fear was that he might be captured and exhibited in a cage by Hitler.

7 MAY 1943

VIII FC FO 12

				Losses			Casualties		
Despatched		Groups	E/A	MIA	E	Dam	KIA	WIA	MIA
P-47	104	4FG, 56FG, 78FG	0	0	0	0	0	0	0

REMARKS: Despatched to sweep Flushing/Ostend/Knokke area.

13PS despatched 2 F-5 sorties to NW France.

11 MAY 1943

VIII FC FO 16

				Losses			Casualties		
Despatched		Groups	E/A	MIA	E	Dam	KIA	WIA	MIA
P-47	128	4FG, 56FG, 78FG	0	0	0	0	0	0	0

REMARKS: Sweep Dunkirk/Knokke. Cancelled shortly after t/o – bad weather.

13PS despatched 5 F-5 sorties to France.

13 MAY 1943

VIII BC 55

					Bombs		Losses			Casualties		
	Despatched		Effective	Target	Tonnage	E/A	MIA	E	Dam	KIA	WIA	MIA
1BW				MEAULTE A/F (P)								
B-17	91BG	25	24	1628–1630 hrs	863 × 500GP	3–2–0	2	0		0	0	21
	303BG	21	21		16 × 300GP	2–0–0	0	0		0	1	0
	305BG	27	22			6–1–1	1	0		0	0	10
	306BG	24	21			0–0–0	0	0		0	0	0
TOTALS:		97	88		218.15	11–3–1	3	0	11	0	1	31
4BW				ST.OMER/ LONGUENESSE A/F (P)								
B-17	94BG	19	16	1637-1638 hrs	489 × 300GP		0	0				
	95BG	19	15				0	0				
	96BG	20	0				1	1		1	2	0
1BW				ST.OMER/FT.ROUGE								
B-17	351BG	14	0	A/F	0	0–0–0	0	0	0	0	0	0
TOTALS:		72	31		73.35	0–0–0	1	1	0	1	2	0

REMARKS: 96BG B-17 crashed in The Wash at start of mission. St.Omer/Ft.Rouge not attacked due to a misunderstanding in the formation leaders and a straggling formation of 351BG which abandoned mission at mid-Channel. First mission for 4BW units (94BG, 95BG and 96BG) and 351BG.

VIII FC FO 17

Despatched		Groups	E/A	Losses MIA	E	Dam	Casualties KIA	WIA	MIA
P-47	124	4FG, 56FG, 78FG	0	0	0	0	0	0	0

REMARKS: Fighters in support of one HB formation only.

13PS despatched 2 F-5 sorties to France.

INCIDENT

On 13 May 1943 VIII Bomber Command's operational strength doubled in one go as the 4th Provisional Wing groups flew their first mission. It was not an auspicious debut for when the leadship of the second combat wing had to abort due to an oxygen leak in the ball turret, the whole formation (96th and 351st Groups) became disorganised and returned to base. One bomber was lost through an unusual accident. Shortly after take-off from Grafton Underwood 96th Group B-17F 42-29752 was critically damaged by a run-away machine gun. The weapon was in the left waist, internally stowed and was being checked by the gunner when accidentally discharged. Bullets went through the side of the fuselage and shot away half the right horizontal stabiliser and severed the control cables on that side of the bomber. The waist gunner was injured and the tail gunner seriously wounded by the burst. Pilot, Capt Derrol Rogers, managed to keep control but found he could only fly the aircraft in a gradual turn. Coming back to the vicinity of the base the wounded tail gunner and the other five men in the rear of the bomber were ordered to bale out, after which Rogers continued in a wide circle towards the Wash where the bombs were jettisoned. Believing that the damage to the aircraft would make a safe landing impossible, Rogers had the bombardier and navigator parachute and when the orbit brought the bomber back over the Wash he and the co-pilot followed. It was an hour and a half before 2/Lt Norville Gorse, the co-pilot, by then suffering from exposure, was found and rescued from the water. The search continued in the Wash for Rogers and when eventually located he was found to be dead. This tragic accident brought a directive that in future guns were not to be adjusted or primed while in the stowed position.

14 MAY 1943

VIII BC 56

	Despatched		Effective	Target	Bombs Tonnage	E/A	Losses MIA	E	Dam	Casualties KIA	WIA	MIA
1BW				KIEL S/Y (P)								
B-17	91BG	27	26	1200–1203 hrs	244 × 1000GP	5– 0– 1	1	0		0	0	10
	92BG	7	5		569 × 500GP	1– 0– 0	1	0		0	0	10
	303BG	27	25			13– 4–12	1	0		2	3	10
	305BG	28	27			11– 6–10	0	0		0	1	0
	306BG	26	26			11– 1– 3	0	0		0	1	0
2BW				KIEL S/Y (P)	202 × 100 IB							
B-24	44BG	21	17	1200–1203 hrs	67 × 500 IB	21–13– 1	5	1	9	1	12	51
TOTALS:		136	126		291.1	62–24–27	8	1	36	3	17	81

REMARKS: First mission for 92BG since 9 Oct 1942. 44BG received DUC for this day's operation. A b/d B-24 abandoned nr base, cr in sea off Sheringham. Enemy parachute bombs reported at Kiel. 1 91BG B-17 in totals bombed Süderoog Island (L).

	Despatched		Effective	Target	Bombs Tonnage	E/A	Losses MIA	E	Dam	Casualties KIA	WIA	MIA
4BW				ANTWERP I/A (P)								
B-17	94BG	21	17	1320 hrs	346 × 500GP	3–0–0	1			0	2	0
	95BG	21	21			2–1–4	1			0	1	10
TOTALS:		42	38		86.5	5–1–4	1		15	0	3	10
4BW				COURTRAI A/D								
B-17	96BG	21	21		291 × 300GP	0–0–0	0			0	0	0
1BW												
B-17	351BG	18	13		127 × 500GP	0–0–1	2			0	0	20
TOTALS:		39	34		75.4	0–0–1	2		10	0	0	20
3BW				IJMUIDEN P/S (P)								
B-26	322BG	12	11	1100hrs	43 × 500GP	0–0–0	0	1	9	1	7	0

REMARKS: First mission for 322BG and first use of B-26 in ETO. B/d B-26 crashed on return near base, 5 of crew parachuted, pilot killed.

VIII FC FO 18

Despatched		Groups	E/A	Losses MIA	E	Dam	Casualties KIA	WIA	MIA
P-47	118	4FG 56FG 78FG	4–6–11	3	0	1	0	0	3

REMARKS: Fighters flew support for Antwerp mission only. 78FG P-47 came down in sea. Fighter Group losses:– 78FG – 3. Fighter group e/a credits:– 4FG – 2, 78FG – 3.

13PS despatched 8 F-5 on PR over France.

A section of 83FS Thunderbolts tuck wheels away as they clear the perimeter at Duxford. They were part of the 78th FG force sent on a sweep over Holland on 15 May.

15 MAY 1943

VIII BC 57

	Despatched		Effective	Target	Bombs Tonnage	E/A	Losses MIA	E	Dam	Casualties KIA	WIA	MIA
1BW				T/Os (HELIGOLAND								
B-17	91BG	25	24	DÜNE &	744 × 500GP	8– 3– 6	0	0		0	0	0
	92BG	10	9	WANGEROOGE ISLE)		1– 0– 2	1	0		0	0	10
	303BG	24	7	1050–1055 hrs (L)		3– 1– 3	1	0		0	0	10
	305BG	30	17			11– 2– 8	0	1		1	7	0
	306BG	24	19			6–14–11	3	0		0	0	31
TOTALS:		113	76		186.0	29–20–30	5	1	26	1	7	51
1BW				EMDEN								
B-17	351BG	19	18			3– 0– 0	1			0	0	10
4BW				EMDEN								
B-17	94BG	26	15	1056–1103 hrs	202 × 500 IC	2– 0– 1	0			0	0	0
	95BG	12	7		346 × 500GP	3– 2– 0	0			0	0	0
	96BG	23	19			6– 1– 0	0			0	0	0
TOTALS:		80	59		137.0	14– 3– 1	1	0	9	0	0	10

REMARKS: 303BG and 305BG formed a composite group. A bombardier in 94BG did not fully understand ballistics of M50 and M45 IBs; thought bombs not going to drop as aircraft appeared to be passing target; moved sight controls to rectify matters and bombs fell short. B/d 305BG B-17 Cat E base. 1BW primary was Wilhelmshaven.

VIII FC FO 19

Despatched		Groups	E/A	Losses MIA	E	Dam	Casualties KIA	WIA	MIA
P-47	116	4FG, 56FG, 78FG	0–0–2	1	0	0	0	0	1

REMARKS: Carried out high altitude sweeps of Amsterdam/Rotterdam area prior to bombing raid by VIII BC. 78FG P-47 abandoned over sea due to engine trouble. 16 P-47 despatched on an ASR search during the day.

13PS despatched 2 F-5 on PR over France.

16 MAY 1943

VIII FC FO 20

Despatched		Groups	E/A	Losses MIA	E	Dam	Casualties KIA	WIA	MIA
P-47	114	4FG, 56FG, 78FG	2–2–3	1	0	0	0	0	1

REMARKS: Carried out sweep of Walcheren/Bruges/Dunkirk area. Fighter group losses:– 78FG – 1. Fighter Group e/a credits:– 78FG – 3.

P-47	113	4FG, 56FG, 78FG	0	0	0	0	0	0	0

REMARKS: Carried out a diversionary fighter sweep in Cayeux/Abbeville/Gravelines area.

13PS despatched 5 F-5 on PR over France. 1 F-5 MIA on Paris sortie.

After a low altitude flight over the Atlantic B-24s of 44BG and 93BG climbed to 22,000 ft to perform some accurate bombing at Bordeaux port. Extensive damage was done to lock gates and other facilities. Inevitably some bombs fell wide, the early drops churning up mud outside in the estuary.

17 MAY 1943

VIII BC 58

	Despatched		Effective	Target	Bombs Tonnage	E/A	Losses MIA	E	Dam	Casualties KIA	WIA	MIA
1BW				LORIENT U/B (P)								
B-17	91BG	24	19	1213–1215 hrs	395 × 1000GP	6–0– 2	0			0	0	0
	92BG	10	8			2–0– 1	0			0	0	0
	303BG	21	18			8–2– 6	0			0	0	0
	305BG	21	14			9–4– 7	4			1	4	36
	306BG	24	21			2–0– 0	0			0	3	0
4BW				LORIENT P/S (P)								
B-17	94BG	21	16	1215–1217 hrs	368 × 500GP	4–1– 3	1	0		0	1	10
	95BG	18	10			10–1– 7	0	1		0	0	0
	96BG	20	12			6–0– 3	1	0		0	0	11
TOTALS:		159	118		289.5	47–8–29	6	1	27	1	8	57
2BW				BORDEAUX U/B (P)								
B-24	44BG	21	20	1238–1244 hrs	342 × 500GP	0–0– 0	1	0		0	2	11
	93BG	18	14			0–1– 0	0	0		0	0	0
TOTALS:		39	34		85.5	0–1– 0	1	0	1	0	2	11
3BW				IJMUIDEN P/S								
B-26	322BG	11	0	& HAARLEM P/S	0	0	10	0	0	0	0	58

REMARKS: 305BG B-17 down in sea on way back, 5 rescued. 44BG B-24 developed engine trouble and crash-landed in Gijon, Spain. One B-26 aborted, the rest were lost. Lead B-26 shot down by Flak, 2 collided shortly thereafter and the explosion brought down another. 2 survivors from 1 B-26 picked up 2 days later by British destroyer. B/d 95BG B-17 c/l Exeter A/F.

VIII FC FO 22

Despatched		Groups	E/A	Losses MIA	E	Dam	Casualties KIA	WIA	MIA
P-47	113	4FG, 56FG, 78FG	0	0	0	0	0	0	0

REMARKS: Sent on an uneventful sweep of the Brest/Cherbourg area.

13PS despatched 6 F-5 on PR to France.

18 MAY 1943

VIII FC FO 23

Despatched		Groups	E/A	Losses MIA	E	Dam	Casualties KIA	WIA	MIA
P-47	100	4FG, 56FG, 78FG	1–0–0	1	0	0	0	0	0

REMARKS: Sent on fighter sweeps of Knokke/Blankenberghe/Nieuport area. 1 4FG pilot shot down into sea. Fighter group e/a credits:– 4FG – 2. 2 P-47 despatched on a defensive patrol.

13PS despatched 6 F-5 on PR over France, Holland and Heligoland.

Brig.-Gen Fred Anderson – who would eventually become the number two man in US Strategic Air Forces Europe – flew in turn with each of the three groups that made up 4th Wing when that organisation began operations in May 1943. At Bassingbourn on the 15th he posed with a 94BG crew before the Emden mission: (left to right) Sgts Polk, Herndon, McNemar, Gen Anderson, Col 'Dinty' Moore (Group CO), Cpt 'Bucky' Steele (pilot), Cpt Watters (Group bombardier) 1/Lt Schaefer (navigator). In the front row, Sgts Porath, Asiala, Lewis and Lt Stanford (bombardier).

19 MAY 1943

VIII BC 59

		Despatched	Effective	Target	Bombs Tonnage	E/A	Losses MIA	E	Dam	Casualties KIA	WIA	MIA
1BW				KIEL U/Y (P)								
B-17	91BG	19	16	1329–1333 hrs	699 × 500GP	4–0– 0	1			0	0	10
	92BG	10	9		156 × 500 IB	9–0– 0	0	0		0	0	0
	303BG	27	22		464 × 100 IB	14–1–10	0	0		0	2	0
	305BG	22	19			11–5– 7	4	0		0	2	40
	306BG	24	21			3–0– 1	0	0		0	1	0
	351BG	21	16*			7–1– 3	1	0		1	2	10
TOTALS:		123	103		236.95	48–7–21	6	0	28	1	7	60
4BW				FLENSBURG U/Y (P)								
B-17	94BG	26	25	1325–1328 hrs	536 × 500GP	6–0– 4		0		2	0	0
	95BG	15	11			3–2– 6		0		0	4	0
	96BG	23	19			3–2– 4		0		0	0	0
TOTALS:		64	55		134.0	12–4–14	0	0	9	2	4	0
1BW				DIVERSION								
B-17	379BG		24			0–0– 0	0	0	0	0	0	0

REMARKS: 1 British civilian (news correspondent) was killed on the 91BG a/c MIA. *1 351BG a/c attacked Flensburg (S) and another Kriegmarinewerft dock yards (L) with 10 × 500GP each – included in the totals for Kiel.

VIII FC FO 24

Despatched		Groups	E/A	Losses MIA	E	Dam	Casualties KIA	WIA	MIA
P-47	117	4FG, 56FG, 78FG	0	0	0	0	0	0	0

REMARKS: Escort for 379BG on diversion.

6 P-47 despatched on coastal patrol.

13PS despatched 4 F-5 on PR to France and Germany. Sortie to Kiel was first 8AF PR over Germany.

20 MAY 1943

VIII FC FO 25

Despatched		Groups	E/A	Losses MIA	E	Dam	Casualties KIA	WIA	MIA
P-47	115	4FG, 56FG, 78FG	0	1	0	0	0	0	1

REMARKS: Carried out sweeps over Holland. 78FG P-47 abandoned over Channel, pilot lost.

6 P-47 sent on coastal patrol during day.

21 MAY 1943

VIII BC 60

	Despatched		Effective	Target	Bombs Tonnage	E/A	Losses MIA	E	Dam	Casualties KIA	WIA	MIA
1BW				WILHELMSHAVEN U/Y(P)								
B-17	91BG	21	18	1244–1245 hrs	772 × 500GP	17–1– 9	4	0		0	6	40
	303BG	19	18			8–2– 1	0	0		0	0	0
	305BG	18	15			4–1– 0	0	0		0	0	0
	306BG	21	14			12–1– 3	3	0		0	3	20
	351BG	19	12			6–0– 4	0	0		1	0	0
TOTALS:		98	77		193.0	47–5–17	7	0	24	1	9	60
4BW	92BG	6	0	EMDEN U/Y (P)		0–0– 0	0	0		0	0	0
B-17	94BG	20	18		444 × 500GP	11–2– 0	3	1		2	1	30
	95BG	15	6	1244–1246 hrs		5–0– 1	1	0		0	0	10
	96BG	22	22			15–4– 5	1	1		0	4	10
TOTALS:		63	46		111.0	31–6– 6	5	2	9	2	5	50

REMARKS: 306BG B-17 down in sea, crew saved. 94BG B-17 c/l at North Weald. 4BW B-17 ditched by itself after the crew had abandoned it. 1 96BG a/c attacked Wilhelmshaven U/Y (L) – bomb tonnage only included in totals. B/d 96BG B-17 c/l on return.

VIII FC FO 26

Despatched		Groups	E/A	Losses MIA	E	Dam	Casualties KIA	WIA	MIA
P-47	105	4FG, 56FG, 78FG	0–0–1	3	0	0	0	0	3

REMARKS: Sent on a fighter sweep of Ostend/Ghent area. Fighter group losses:– 4FG – 3. Fighter group e/a credits:– 4FG – 1.

6 P-47 despatched on coastal patrols.

A section taken from 306BG's salvaged *Sweet Pea* ready for installation on *Eight Ball*, 14 June. Material hanging from nose is insulation material.

INCIDENT

The early operations of 4th Wing were notable for the number of mission failures that could be attributed to the inexperience and inadequate training of crews, and also the quick and positive action of their commander, Brig.Gen Fred Anderson, in putting matters to rights. No bombs found the target on the Wing's second mission to Emden. In one of the two combat wings this was through an unfortunate accident. As the lead Fortress of the 94th Group was on its run from the Initial Point to the target, enemy fighters made head-on attacks. The lead bombardier had time to fire his gun at the oncoming fighters but when he pressed the trigger the mechanism jammed and the gun 'ran away'. The force of this continuous firing threw the bombardier backwards as the gun tore from its mount, the rear end smashing against the bomb sight. As the bombardier picked himself up he saw to his horror that the controls on the sight had moved and salvoed the bomb load. Seeing the lead plane's bombs release, all the other 94th aircraft and those of the trailing 95th Group unloaded too. Thereafter bombardiers were forbidden to fire the nose gun from the IP to the target.

INCIDENT

An all too frequent and significant hazard in the operation of B-17s and B-24s at high altitude was 'windmilling' propellers, when failure of the feathering mechanism could lead to excessive vibration and threaten the safety of the whole aircraft. During climb-out over the North Sea for the mission of 21 May 1943, there had been a minor problem with the propeller governor on No.2 engine of the 351st Group Fortress *Eight Ball*. After passing 20,000 ft the engine 'ran away' and defied the efforts of Lt Carl Wilson and his co-pilot to feather it, causing them to abort. As the aircraft's speed built up on the descent, vibration became so bad that it seemed as if the troubled engine would shake loose from the wing. To minimise this vibration the pilots had to periodically pull the B-17 up into a semi-stall position, to reduce forward speed to 125 mph. At first there were some fears that the B-17 might have to be ditched, but when the English coast was

reached near The Wash there appeared a good chance of making their Polebrook base. A new crisis arose when Lt Carl Stackhouse, the navigator, from his vantage point in the nose reported that the propeller shaft had apparently sheared. This was evident when the aircraft's flight attitude was changed from slightly nose up to nose down and vice versa as the windmilling propeller would move in and out from the cowling. Notwithstanding this condition, *Eight Ball* was brought in for a landing. When about 200 yards down the landing run the No.2 propeller finally flew off, smashing the left hand nose gun and doing extensive damage to surrounding skin and structure before being run over by the still speeding bomber. *Eight Ball* was in need of major repair and that to the nose was effected by cutting away the damaged area and substituting a similar but sound section taken from the salvaged remains of the 306th Group's *Sweet Pea*; a very intricate piece of metal surgery. When restored, and before return to combat, the bomber was given a new nickname: *No Balls At All.*

Back on the line with the ground crew and a change of name. Dark symbol indicates the abortive mission.

22 MAY 1943

VIII FC

6 P-47 despatched on coastal patrols.

23 MAY 1943

VIII FC

6 P-47 despatched on coastal patrols.

13PS despatched 1 F-5 on PR to Belgium (Florennes area). A/c returned due to weather.

25 MAY 1943

VIII FC FO 28

				Losses			Casualties		
Despatched		Groups	E/A	MIA	E	Dam	KIA	WIA	MIA
P-47	116	4FG, 56FG, 78FG	0	0	0	0	0	0	0

REMARKS: Carried out a high altitude sweep in Mardyck/Ypres/Knokke area.

26 MAY 1943

VIII FC FO 29

				Losses			Casualties		
Despatched		Groups	E/A	MIA	E	Dam	KIA	WIA	MIA
P-47	122	4FG, 56FG, 78FG	0	0	0	0	0	0	0

REMARKS: Carried out sweeps in Egmond/Amsterdam/Hague area.

27 MAY 1943

VIII FC FO 30

				Losses			Casualties		
Despatched		Groups	E/A	MIA	E	Dam	KIA	WIA	MIA
P-47	111	4FG, 56FG, 78FG	0	0	0	0	0	0	0

REMARKS: Sent out on a fighter sweep of Knokke/Roulers/Gravelines area.

28 MAY 1943

VIII FC FO 32

				Losses			Casualties		
Despatched		Groups	E/A	MIA	E	Dam	KIA	WIA	MIA
P-47	120	4FG, 56FG, 78FG	0	0	0	0	0	0	0

REMARKS: Carried out a *Rodeo* in Walcheren/Eekloo/Dixmude/Dunkirk areas.

13PS despatched 5 F-5 on PR to Germany and France.

29 MAY 1943

VIII BC 61

		Despatched	Effective	Target	Bombs Tonnage	E/A	Losses MIA	E	Dam	Casualties KIA	WIA	MIA
1BW				ST.NAZAIRE U/B								
B-17	91BG	23	21	1706–1711 hrs	277 × 2000GP	0–0–0	0	0		0	1	0
	92BG	22	19			0–0–0	0	0		0	0	0
	303BG	30	28			3–0–1	1	0		0	0	10
	305BG	25	21			0–0–0	3	0		0	9	21
	306BG	24	21			0–0–0	0	0		0	0	0
	351BG	21	16			1–0–0	1	0		0	0	10
	379BG	24	21			2–0–0	3	1		0	0	30
TOTALS:		169	147		277.0	6–0–1	8	1	58	0	10	71
2BW				LA PALLICE U/B								
B-24	44BG	21	20		99 × 2000GP							
	93BG	17	14									
TOTALS:		38	34		99.0	0–0–0	0	0	0	0	0	0
4BW				RENNES NAVAL								
B-17	94BG	18	16	STORAGE DEPOT	530 × 500GP	5–1–3	3	1		1	2	32
	95BG	18	18	1601–1605 hrs		6–0–5	2	0		0	1	22
	96BG	20	20			8–4–6	1	0		0	7	10
	Comp. of 94BG 95BG 96BG	16	3			0–0–0	0	0		0	0	0
TOTALS:		72	57		132.5	19–5–14	6	1	30	1	10	64

REMARKS: 7 a/c of 92BG and 1 of 305BG totals were YB-40s, first use of this type. Composite group comprised 4 94BG, 2 95BG and 10 96BG a/c. First mission for 379BG. 379BG B-17 c/l on return. Last mission for 44BG prior to going to N.Africa. 4BW navigators did not use DR but tried pin-pointing formation, became lost and did not make effective run-up on target. B/d 94BG B-17 c/l Northolt A/F. 305 BG B-17 ditched off Start Point, 9 saved.

VIII FC FO 33

Despatched		Groups	E/A	Losses MIA	E	Dam	Casualties KIA	WIA	MIA
P-47	131	4FG, 56FG, 78FG	0–1–0	0	0	0	0	0	0

REMARKS: Support for bomber operations.

13PS despatched 1 F-5 on PR to Holland.

31 MAY 1943

VIII FC FO 34

Despatched		Groups	E/A	Losses MIA	E	Dam	Casualties KIA	WIA	MIA
P-47	110	4FG, 56FG, 78FG	0	1	0	0	0	0	1

REMARKS: Sent out on fighter sweeps over France – Knokke/Courtrai/Dunkirk area. 56FG P-47 rolled over into vertical dive and continued into clouds, thought to have been oxygen failure, pilot MIA.

2 JUNE 1943

VIII FC

4 P-47 despatched on coastal patrol.

3 JUNE 1943

13PS despatched 2 F-5 on PR to French ports.

4 JUNE 1943

VIII FC

6 P-47 sent on fighter patrol.

5 JUNE 1943

13PS despatched 1 F-5 on PR to a French port.

Lt.-Col John de Russey was one of 305BG's most distinguished personnel. Here recuperating in the base hospital, 2 June, scars show on his neck where he was hit and severely wounded during frontal attacks by enemy fighters on the Kiel raid of 21 May. Despite his wounds he instructed the pilot to continue to the target. That day 305BG became separated from other groups owing to confusion caused by another group firing the same flare colours during assembly.

7 JUNE 1943

VIII FC FO 38

Despatched		Groups	E/A	Losses MIA	E	Dam	Casualties KIA	WIA	MIA
P-47	143	4FG, 56FG, 78FG	0	0	0	0	0	0	0

REMARKS: Sent out with RAF Spitfires to engage enemy fighters in the Pas de Calais area.

10 JUNE 1943

VIII FC FO 40

Despatched		Groups	E/A	Losses MIA	E	Dam	Casualties KIA	WIA	MIA
P-47	92	56FG, 78FG	0	0	0	0	0	0	0

REMARKS: Sent out to sweep the Dutch Islands in conjunction with a mission by 6 Mitchell bombers.

13PS despatched 2 F-5 on a PR of French coast.

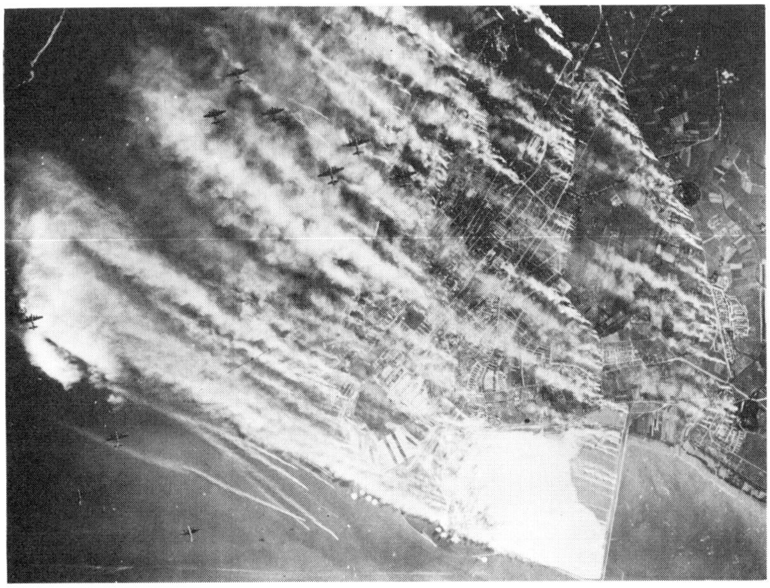

The Germans made effective use of smoke screens at many targets and made bombardiers' work more difficult. At Wilhelmshaven on 11 June, the use of smoke buoys put an almost complete blanket over the harbour where bombs from B-17s can be seen exploding.

11 JUNE 1943

VIII BC 62

	Despatched		Effective	Target	Bombs Tonnage	E/A	Losses MIA	E	Dam	Casualties KIA	WIA	MIA
1BW				WILHELMSHAVEN								
B-17	91BG	21	18	U/Y 168 a/c	560 × 500GP	10–0–0	0			0	0	0
	92BG	14	12	CUXHAVEN P/A	327 × 1000GP	6–1–0	0			0	0	0
	303BG	25	19	30 a/c – 4BW	150 × 1000GP	9–5–2	1			0	3	10
	305BG	24	19	T/Os	11 × 1000GP	13–2–3	0			0	0	0
	306BG	27	24	20 a/c	170 × 500GP	7–1–0	0			0	0	0
	351BG	24	18			18–3–1	0			2	4	0
	379BG	31	29			13–8–5	6			1	13	60
4BW												
B-17	94BG	29	25			1–0–1	0			0	0	0
	95BG	29	27			5–0–8	1			0	0	10
	96BG	28	27			3–0–4	0			0	0	0
TOTALS:		252	218		426.5	85–20–24	8	0	62	3	20	80

REMARKS: 4 a/c of 1BW despatched total were spares and returned as planned. 303BG a/c lost in collision with FW 190. Lead 303BG B-17 had two engines knocked out on bomb run which caused formation to scatter, a/c being unable to close formation until on return over the sea.

VIII FC FO 37

Despatched		Groups	E/A	Losses MIA	E	Dam	Casualties KIA	WIA	MIA
P-47	136	4FG, 56FG, 78FG	0	0	0	0	0	0	0

REMARKS: Despatched on a high altitude sweep of Ostend/Eekloo area.

FO 41

P-47	139	4 FG, 56FG, 78FG	0	0	0	0	0	0	0

REMARKS: Sent on a sweep of Gravelines/Hazebrouck/Courtrai/Ostend area.

13PS despatched 2 F-5 on PR to France and Germany.

12 JUNE 1943

VIII FC FO 43

	Despatched		Groups	E/A	Losses MIA	E	Dam	Casualties KIA	WIA	MIA
	P-47	96	4FG, 56FG	1–0–0	0	0	0	0	0	0

REMARKS: Despatched to make high altitude sweeps in Blankenberghe/Calais area. Fighter group e/a credits: 56FG – 1.

FO 42

	Despatched		Groups	E/A	Losses MIA	E	Dam	Casualties KIA	WIA	MIA
	P-47	44	78FG	0–2–0	2	0	0	0	0	0

REMARKS: Sent out to sweep Calais/St.Pol/Abbeville/Cayeux area.

At the end of May the Liberators were taken off high altitude bombing missions and practised formation flying at very low altitudes. Although there was much speculation as to the special operation they were obviously going to undertake, few could have guessed it would be from North Africa. Half the B-24Ds in this picture – taken as the 93BG swept over Hardwick at 1600 hours on 13 June – would not survive the epic low-level mission to Ploesti on 1 August. The three nearest the camera would – *Jerks' Natural*, *Bomberang* and *Jersey Bounce*, in that order; *Bomberang* to become the first 8AF B-24 to complete 50 missions, the others to be lost over Germany.

13 JUNE 1943

VIII BC 63

	Despatched		Effective	Target	Bombs Tonnage	E/A	Losses MIA	E	Dam	Casualties KIA	WIA	MIA
1BW				BREMEN U/Y (P)								
B-17	91BG	21	17	(102 a/c)	1015 × 500GP	0–0– 1	0			0	1	0
	92BG	17	16		(P)	1–0– 0	0			0	2	0
	303BG	27	24	T/Os	202 × 500GP	0–0– 0	0			0	0	0
	305BG	24	15	(20 a/c)	(T/O)	0–0– 0	1			0	2	10
	306BG	28	28			0–1– 0	1			0	3	10
	351BG	21	12			1–1– 0	2			0	0	12
	379BG	13	10			0–0– 0	0			0	0	0
TOTALS:		151	122		304.25	2–2– 1	4	0	31	0	8	32
4BW				KIEL U/Y (P)								
B-17	94BG	26	22	(44 a/c)	399 × 500GP (P)	8–2– 3	9	0		1	9	80
	95BG	26	24	T/O – KIEL P/A	79 × 500GP	16–3– 4	10	1		0	2	103
	96BG	24	14	(16 a/c)	(T/O)	15–0– 7	3	0		2	9	30
TOTALS:		76	60		119.5	39–5–14	22	1	23	3	20	213

REMARKS: 1BW a/c bombed both P and T/O. Crew rescued from 94BG a/c down in the sea. 95BG B-17 with 2 WIA crashed at Rackheath on return from mission. 351BG B-17 came down in sea, 2 lost 8 rescued. 95BG B-17 hit by e/a crashed into another causing the loss of both. Brig.Gen N. B. Forrest MIA with 95BG a/c whilst riding as an observer.

VIII FC FO 44

	Despatched		Groups	E/A	Losses MIA	E	Dam	Casualties KIA	WIA	MIA
	P-47	96	4FG, 56FG	3–0–2	0	0	0	0	0	0

REMARKS: Carried out sweep of Gravelines/Bailleul/Knokke area. Fighter group e/a credits:– 56FG – 3.

FO 45

	Despatched		Groups	E/A	Losses MIA	E	Dam	Casualties KIA	WIA	MIA
	P-47	44	78FG	2–0–2	2	0	0	0	0	0

REMARKS: Carried out *Rodeo* Ypres–St.Pol area.

13PS despatched 4 F-5 on PR to France and Germany.

14 JUNE 1943

13PS despatched 1 F-5 on PR to France.

15 JUNE 1943

VIII BC 64

REMARKS: 155 B-17 despatched, but were recalled before reaching the French coast. 2 91BG a/c attacked by e/a, no claims or casualties.

VIII FC FO 46

REMARKS: Only part of P-47 force for escort of HB mission were airborne when operation cancelled. 4FG P-47 MIA crashed into Channel after m/f, pilot rescued.

17 JUNE 1943

VIII FC FO 47

Despatched		Groups	E/A	Losses MIA	E	Dam	Casualties KIA	WIA	MIA
P-47	137	4FG, 56FG, 78FG	0	0	1	0	0	0	0

REMARKS: Sent out on a sweep of Westhoofd/Goes/Eekloo/Ypres/Gravelines area in support of a bombing attack on Flushing. 4FG P-47 c/l nr. North Weald due to engine trouble.

Maj Eliza LeDoux in the cockpit of a 509BS Fortress on 20 June. His unit produced the extraordinary record of not losing a single bomber or crew over enemy territory between 13 June 1943 and 11 January 1944 in 52 missions flown with the parent 351BG. This was during a period when 8AF heavy bomber losses were averaging over five per cent of sorties flown.

20 JUNE 1943

VIII FC FO 49

Despatched		Groups	E/A	Losses MIA	E	Dam	Casualties KIA	WIA	MIA
P-47	80	4FG, 78FG	0	0	0	0	0	0	0

REMARKS: Sent on sweep of Le Touquet/St.Omer/Calais area.

FO 50

P-47	47	56FG	0	0	0	0	0	0	0

REMARKS: Sent on sweep of Hague/Rotterdam area.

13PS despatched 5 F-5 on PR to France and Germany 1 F-5 MIA on Bremen sortie.

Many an English mansion became an 8AF Headquarters. Sunninghill Park near Windsor served VIII Air Support Command. Officially handed over by the RAF on 22 June, a B-26 fly-by concluded the ceremony. The building later became the first UK home of 9th Air Force.

22 JUNE 1943

VIII BC 65

					Bombs		Losses			Casualties		
	Despatched		Effective	Target	Tonnage	E/A	MIA	E	Dam	KIA	WIA	MIA
1BW				HÜLS R/I (P)								
B-17	91BG	22	16		1202 × 500GP	9– 2– 4	5			1	5	41
	92BG	29	25			0– 1– 1	1			0	1	10
	303BG	15	14		243 × 1000GP	0– 0– 1	1			0	1	10
	305BG	25	18			0– 1– 0	1			0	0	10
	306BG	24	16			4– 0– 0	1			0	0	10
	351BG	21	15			17– 1–12	1			1	0	10
	379BG	16	14			2– 3– 5	1			0	2	10
	Comp. of 303BG 379BG	20	16			0– 1– 1	0			0	0	0
4BW				HÜLS R/I (P)								
B-17	94BG	16	9			5– 2– 2	2			0	7	20
	95BG	17	16			5– 5– 3	1			0	0	10
	96BG	30	24			4– 5– 6	2			0	0	20
TOTALS:		235	183		422.0	46–21–35	16	0	75	2	16	151
1BW				ANTWERP								
B-17	381BG	22	19	I/A (S)	191 × 1000GP	0–1–7	2	1		1	0	20
	384BG	20	20			1–1–2	2	0		0	3	20
TOTALS:		42	39		95.5	1–2–9	4	1	17	1	3	40
4BW				DIVERSION								
B-17	100BG	21	–		0	0–0–0	0	0	0	0	0	0

REMARKS: 92BG totals include 11 YB-40s, 1 of which was MIA to Flak. On the Hüls mission 1 a/c bombed Vlieland and another bombed Dortmund. Composite group made up of 13 303BG a/c and 7 379BG. 100BG diversion was sent too late to confuse enemy. First missions for 100BG, 381BG and 384BG. B/d 381BG B-17 c/l Kent, near North Foreland, 6 injured.

VIII FC FO 52

Despatched		Groups	E/A	Losses MIA	E	Dam	Casualties KIA	WIA	MIA
P-47	136	4FG, 56FG, 78FG	7–0–0	0	0	0	0	0	0

REMARKS: Escort for 1BW Antwerp mission only. Fighter group e/a credits:– 4FG – 4, 78FG – 3.

13PS despatched 2 F-5 on PR to France.

INCIDENT

Ejected .50-calibre cases were an additional and constant hazard in bomber formations under attack. Broken and cracked plexiglass often resulted from striking falling cases and sometimes serious damage occurred that could cause the loss of an aircraft. On the Hüls raid the lead aircraft of the 94th Group was 14 minutes from the Initial Point when an engine overheated and had to be shut down. The cause was a .50 case from a preceding, higher group lodged in the oil cooler. The pilots, Maj 'Buck' Steele and Capt Kee Harrison, found they could not maintain sufficient speed to keep *Mr Five By Five* up with the other Fortresses so, after six minutes, they passed the lead to the deputy and headed for home. A single B-17 at altitude over Germany was in a perilous position and soon after turning back *Mr Five By Five* came under fighter attack. Splinters from a cannon shell that detonated in the nose hit navigator Lt Robert Scheefer's knee and cut Group bombardier Capt John Watters above the left eye. To evade the fighters the pilots elected to dive to hedge-hopping height where the bomber would be difficult to track. As *Mr Five By Five* skimmed over Holland Capt Watters, fearing they might soon have to crash-land, destroyed the bombsight as per operational instructions by firing three revolver shots into the delicate mechanism. However, the Fortress was able to return safely to base, where the Group bombardier was kidded unmercifully about his destruction of the tool of his trade.

An acrid cloud of black smoke climbs high above the burning synthetic rubber plant at Huls on VIII BC's first major attack in the Ruhr. The damage was caused by less than 100 of the 1,445 bombs aimed at the plant from five miles above. An estimated three months' production was lost through the attack although the plant was working again within a month. The photo was taken from a 96BG Fortress.

23 JUNE 1943

VIII BC 66

	Despatched
91BG	13
92BG	14+8 YB-40
303BG	22
305BG	21
306BG	22
351BG	20
379BG	20
381BG	22
384BG	18
TOTALS:	172+8 YB-40

REMARKS: 140 a/c sent to Villacoublay and 40 a/c to Bernay St.Martin, all aircraft recalled due to weather.
381BG B-17 blew up whilst being prepared for mission damaging another parked near by. 22 men killed plus 1 British civilian.

Debden was still the show place of US fighter stations in the early summer of 1943 and many VIPs were visitors. On 15 June Ambassador Winant – here being shown a P-47 cockpit by 'Monk' Hunter, the dashing CG of VIII FC – and Lt.-Gen Devers, CG US Forces in Europe, were present. On 25 June the Duchess of Kent had Col Edward Anderson, 4FG CO and Gen Hunter in attendance. (Note improved mirror attachment on P-47 windshield.) The Duchess was there to present the original RAF Eagle Squadron badges to the three American successor units. Thus 334FS, 335FS and 336FS became the only USAAF squadrons to have royal crests, although this was something Washington would never officially sanction.

Fly pasts were staged on each occasion. A section of 334th P-47 Thunderbolts pass in front of the control tower on the 24th. Mr Ketley's much photographed farm is on the far side of the airfiled.

24 JUNE 1943

VIII FC FO 55

				Losses			Casualties		
Despatched		Groups	E/A	MIA	E	Dam	KIA	WIA	MIA
P-47	48	4FG	0	0	0	0	0	0	0

REMARKS: Sent on fighter sweep of Hesdin/Boulogne/Doullens area.

FO 54

				Losses			Casualties		
Despatched		Groups	E/A	MIA	E	Dam	KIA	WIA	MIA
P-47	80	56FG, 78FG	1–0–1	0	0	0	0	0	0

REMARKS: Sent on fighter sweep in Hague and St.Omer areas. Fighter group e/a credits:– 78FG – 1.

13PS and 22PS despatched 5 F-5 on PR to France. First 22PS operation.

25 JUNE 1943

VIII BC 67

		Despatched	Effective	Target	Bombs Tonnage	E/A	Losses MIA	E	Dam	Casualties KIA	WIA	MIA
1BW				2 a/c on CONVOY (L)								
B-17	91BG	18	15	0820 hrs (off	18 × 500GP	1–0– 1	0	0		0	0	0
	92BG	23	19	WANGEROOGE ISLAND)	(L)	4–1– 4	0	0		0	0	0
	303BG	25	18	T/Os 0824–0905 hrs		14–2– 8	3	1		1	2	21
	305BG	25	19		1436 × 500GP	3–1– 3	1	0		1	1	11
	306BG	23	20		(T/Os)	3–1– 3	1	0		0	0	10
	351BG	20	17			1–0– 3	0	0		0	2	0
	379BG	20	19			17–3–12	6	0		0	5	60
	381BG	24	17			3–0– 1	1	0		1	1	10
	384BG	19	5			0–0– 2	3	0		0	0	30
TOTALS:		197	149		363.5	46–8–37	15	1	39	3	11	142
4BW				CONVOY (off								
B-17	94BG	15	0	JUIST ISLAND) (L)	180 × 500GP	0–0– 0	0			0	0	0
	95BG	18	16			6–1– 1	0			0	0	0
	96BG	26	0			10–2– 0	0			0	3	0
	100BG	19	2			0–0– 2	3			0	0	30
TOTALS:		78	18		45.0	16–3– 3	3		22	0	3	30

REMARKS: 92BG despatched totals include 7 YB-40, 3 of which were abortive. 303BG B-17 abandoned near Caister and crashed in The Wash. Clouds and heavy contrails made formation flying very difficult. First combat mission for 100BG. MIA 303BG B-17 ditched, 10 rescued.

VIII FC FO 56

Despatched		Groups	E/A	Losses MIA	E	Dam	Casualties KIA	WIA	MIA
P-47	130	4FG, 56FG, 78FG	0	0	0	0	0	0	0

REMARKS: Escort and support for heavy bombers. Fighters returned early.

13PS despatched 4 F-5 on PR to France.

INCIDENT

In many bombers that were lost over enemy territory it is probable that courageous and selfless acts by crew members went unrecorded because all perished. There were survivors to tell of the bravery of pilot 1/Lt George Riches who died on his first mission, and the facts were revealed in an unusual way. S/Sgt Ralph Lavoie was seriously injured when baling out of the stricken 384th Group B-17 *Yankee Powerhouse* on the Hamburg raid of 25 June 1943. His next few months were spent in German prison hospitals until late the following year he was involved in a POW exchange and repatriated to the United States. One of Lavoie's first actions was to write to the CO of the 384th: 'I was ball turret gunner on an original crew of the 384th and was shot down on the Group's second mission. Four of my crew were killed and six taken prisoner. The story I really want to tell you is about my pilot, who was killed saving six lives. The co-pilot was hit by flak and killed. Lt Riches' right arm was almost shot off which made it impossible for him to work the automatic pilot. Our ship was on fire. He used his good arm to fly the plane and ordered the rest of us out. The ship blew up before he had a chance to get out himself. Lt Riches died saving our lives.'

As a result of this letter the Silver Star, third ranking decoration for gallantry, was posthumously awarded to Riches. The survivors of his crew thought him worthy of the Medal of Honor.

Britain's Foreign Secretary, Anthony Eden, visited Shipdham on 25 June where a photographer caught him at the controls of 44BG's *Bewitching Witch*. Such VIP visits served two purposes; they helped morale at combat bases and it hopefully influenced influential British as to the value of VIII BC operations.

The inexperienced 56FG took a severe hammering from the Luftwaffe on 26 June. The Group lost four pilots, five aircraft and four more aircraft were badly damaged. P-47C 41-6620 was hit by five 20 mm cannon shells. The damage caused put the fighter into a series of spins from which pilot, 2/Lt Justus Foster, was only able to make recovery after losing some 20,000 feet of altitude. He managed to belly the Thunderbolt in at Hawkinge where this photo was taken after it had been raised onto its undercarriage. Foster's adversary in an FW 190 of JG 2 claimed the P-47 as destroyed.

26 JUNE 1943

VIII BC 68

	Despatched		Effective	Target	Bombs Tonnage	E/A	Losses MIA	E	Dam	Casualties KIA	WIA	MIA
1BW				VILLACOUBLAY A/D (P)								
B-17	91BG	14	0	(12 a/c)	112 × 500GP	0–0–0	0					
	92BG	18	5	1829–1833 hrs	(P)	3–1–4	0			0	0	0
	303BG	20	0	POISSY A/F (S)	49 × 500GP	1–0–0	0			0	0	0
	351BG	21	0	(6 a/c)	(S)	1–0–5	0			0	0	0
	379BG	13	12			3–1–0	0			0	0	0
	381BG	19	0			1–0–0	0			0	0	0
	384BG	18	0			4–1–1	5			0	0	50
1BW				TRICQUEVILLE A/F								
B-17	305BG	21	20	1746 hrs	601 × 300GP	0–0–0				0	0	0
	306BG	21	19			4–2–0				1	3	1
TOTALS:		165	56		130.4	17–5–10	5	0	14	1	3	51
4BW				LE MANS A/F								
B-17	94BG	19										
	95BG	18										
	96BG	21										
	100BG	23										
TOTALS:		81	0		0	0–0 0	0		0	0	0	0

REMARKS: 1 B-17 dropped 2 bombs on Villacoublay and 3 on Poissy. 92BG despatched totals include 5 YB-40s, all of which were abortive. 4BW aircraft turned back before target.

VIII FC FO 57

Despatched		Groups	E/A	Losses MIA	E	Dam	Casualties KIA	WIA	MIA
P-47	130	4FG, 56FG, 78FG	3–3–2	5	1	5	0	1	4

REMARKS: 56FG P-47 came down in sea off Scratby, pilot saved – only one wheel would come down so returned to coast to abandon aircraft. Fighter group losses:– 56FG – 5. Fighter group e/a credits:– 4FG – 2, 56FG – 2. B/d 56FG P-47 c/l Hawkinge.

13PS and 22PS despatched 9 F-5 on PR to NW France. 1 F-5 MIA.

27 JUNE 1943

13PS despatched 3 F-5 on PR over France.

28 JUNE 1943

VIII BC 69

		Despatched	Effective	Target	Bombs Tonnage	E/A	Losses MIA	E	Dam	Casualties KIA	WIA	MIA
1BW				ST.NAZAIRE LOCK								
B-17	91BG	20	18	GATES & P/A	300 × 2000GP	7–0–0	1			0	4	10
	92BG	16	13	1655–1700 hrs		1–1–1	0			1	1	0
	305BG	21	18			2–1–0	0			0	0	0
	306BG	21	19			3–0–0	0			1	0	0
	351BG	20	19			10–3–2	4			1	2	40
	381BG	22	17			5–1–5	0			0	2	0
4BW				ST.NAZAIRE LOCK								
B-17	94BG	13	7	GATES & P/A			0			0	1	0
	95BG	21	18	1711–1713 hrs			3			0	1	0
	96BG	16	11				0			0	2	0
	100BG	21	18				0			0	1	0
TOTALS:		191	158		300.0	28–6–8	8	0	57	3	14	50
1BW				BEAUMONT LE								
B-17	303BG	18	17	ROGER A/F	688 × 300GP							
	379BG	14	13	1736–1740 hrs								
	384BG	18	13									
TOTALS:		50	43		103.2	0–0–0	0		6	0	0	0

REMARKS: 92BG totals include 6 YB-40s. 3 95BG crews saved by ASR. 4BW used B-17s with long range tanks: their first operational use.

VIII FC FO 58

Despatched		Groups	E/A	Losses MIA	E	Dam	Casualties KIA	WIA	MIA
P-47	130	4FG, 56FG, 78FG	0	0	3		0	0	0

REMARKS: P-47s escorted 1BW part way to St.Nazaire. No escort for 4BW. RAF escorted Beaumont le Roger force. 3 4FG P-47s involved in crash-landings.

13PS despatched 3 F-5 on PR over France.

29 JUNE 1943

VIII BC 70

		Despatched	Effective	Target	Bombs Tonnage	E/A	Losses MIA	E	Dam	Casualties KIA	WIA	MIA
1BW				VILLACOUBLAY A/D								
B-17	92BG	14		(P)		0–1–2						
	303BG	19				0–0–0						
	305BG	20				0–0–0						
	306BG	21				0–2–1						
	379BG	16				0–0–0						
	384BG	18				0–0–0						
1BW				TRICQUEVILLE A/F								
B-17	91BG	19		(P)								
	351BG	7										
	381BG	14										
TOTALS:		148	0		0	0–3–3	0	0	14	0	0	0
4BW				LE MANS A/I (P)								
B-17	94BG	21	16	1959–2003 hrs	726 × 500GP							
	95BG	21	21		(P)							
	96BG	21	20	LE MANS M/Y								
	100BG	21	19	(T/O) 2 a/c								
TOTALS:		84	76		181.5	0–0–0	0	0	0	0	0	0

REMARKS: 92BG despatched total includes 2 YB-40s. Both 1BW forces found 10/10 cloud cover.

VIII FC FO 59

Despatched		Groups	E/A	Losses MIA	E	Dam	Casualties KIA	WIA	MIA
P-47	126	4FG, 56FG, 78FG	2–0–0	0	0	0	0	0	0

REMARKS: Fighter group e/a credits:– 78FG – 2.

13PS despatched 2 F-5 on PR to St.Nazaire, 2 F-5 MIA.

Rigor Mortis sets out from Chelveston for Villacoublay on 29 June. Despite the danger of being swept backwards by the slip stream there were some B-17 gunners who found it exhilarating to ride take-off sitting on the edge of the radio hatch.

Many a local farmer gained additional hay for his cattle by offering to cut the grass that flourished around aircraft dispersals. Having given permission the authorities then found they had created a fire risk and to expedite its departure the military provided labour and transport. On the evening of 29 June three men from a quartermaster unit at Chelveston were pitching while the farmer stamped down the hay. In the background stands *Centaur* which in late September had the unfortunate distinction of becoming the first of two Fortresses lost on night bombing raids with the RAF.

The decorations on this 305BG B-17F tell its record and show that the engines had girls' names (*Betty* on No.3). It was also common for crew members to embellish their stations with wives' or girl friends' names (*Ann* on top turret; *Dot* on D/F cover). *Target for Tonite* became a leaflet dropper in October 1943 and was sent back to the US in April 1944 after 74 missions.

The Chelveston ordnance section unloading 500 lb bombs from a truck, 29 June, in the usual way – rolling them off to fall on the ground. Accepted as safe and common at all bases until an occasion where the high explosive was not stable.

1 JULY 1943

VIII FC FO 60

Despatched		Groups	E/A	Losses MIA	E	Dam	Casualties KIA	WIA	MIA
P-47	129	4FG, 56FG, 78FG	4–1–5	1	0	3	0	0	1

REMARKS: Carried out fighter sweeps, 78FG the only group to meet e/a. Fighter group losses:– 78FG – 1. Fighter group e/a credits:– 78FG – 3.

13PS despatched 1 F-5 on PR to France.

2 JULY 1943

VIII FC FO 62

Despatched		Groups	E/A	Losses MIA	E	Dam	Casualties KIA	WIA	MIA
P-47	80	56FG, 78FG	0	0	0	0	0	0	0

REMARKS: Despatched on fighter sweeps in Le Touquet area.

3 JULY 1943

13PS despatched 2 F-5 on PR to France.

4 JULY 1943

VIII BC 71

	Despatched		Effective	Target	Bombs Tonnage	E/A	Losses MIA	E	Dam	Casualties KIA	WIA	MIA
1BW				LE MANS A/I (P)								
B-17	91BG	19	16	1240–1243 hrs	1038 × 500GP	2– 0– 0	0	0	6	0	1	0
	303BG	24	20			6– 2– 2	1	0	5	1	0	10
	351BG	18	17			3– 0– 0	0	0	3	0	0	0
	379BG	20	17			7– 1– 5	0	0	3	0	1	0
	381BG	21	19			3– 0– 2	1	0	5	0	0	10
	384BG	19	16			3– 2– 6	2	0	7	0	0	20
1BW				NANTES A/I (P)								
B-17	92BG	19	18	1246–1249 hrs	580 × 500GP	10– 4– 1	1	1	11	0	3	10
	305BG	25	21			11– 3– 3	2	0	11	0	4	20
	306BG	27	22			7– 2– 3	0	0	12	0	0	0
TOTALS:		192	166		404.5	52–14–22	7	1	53	1	9	70
4BW				LA PALLICE (P)								
B-17	94BG	18	12	LOCK GATES	275 × 1000GP	0– 0– 0	0		0	0	0	0
	95BG	23	18	1201–1204 hrs		0– 0– 0	0		0	0	0	0
	96BG	16	16			0– 0– 0	0		0	0	0	0
	100BG	26	25			0– 1– 0	1		1	0	0	10
TOTALS:		83	71		137.5	0– 1– 0	1		1	0	0	10

REMARKS: 92BG totals include 3 YB-40s. 2 303BG a/c dropped 20 × 500GP on (S), Le Mans M/Y, included in totals. B/d 92BG B-17 c/l Portreath A/F.

VIII FC FP 64

Despatched		Groups	E/A	Losses MIA	E	Dam	Casualties KIA	WIA	MIA
P-47	93	4FG, 78FG	0	0	0	0	0	0	0

REMARKS: P-47s despatched as withdrawal cover. P-47 cover recalled due to weather.

13PS despatched 4 F-5 on PR to France.

INCIDENT

Brig.Gen Orvil Anderson, air power zealot and Chairman of the Combined Operational Planning Committee, had his first experience of a bombing mission with the 8th Air Force on Independence Day 1943. Flying in *Muggs*, the lead Fortress of a 100th Group formation, he witnessed a narrow escape drama en route to the target. Maj John Egan, the pilot, looked over his shoulder to catch sight of a pair of flying boot clad feet hanging limply above the top-turret platform. Suspecting the gunner had suffered an oxygen failure, he left his seat and went back to investigate. He found T/Sgt John Shay's supply hose disconnected and the gunner collapsed forward, head between turret side and gunsight and hands still grasping the controls; another case where a man had been overcome by anoxia without realising he was no longer breathing sufficient life-sustaining oxygen. Having left his own supply, Egan risked unconsciousness himself, but some men were less quick to succumb to anoxia than others. He climbed up into the turret and fixed Shay's oxygen line; unfortunately, before he could get down again the reviving gunner touched the turret controls and sent the turret spinning. Egan narrowly escaped being jammed in the mechanism as he and Shay were banged against the sides of the whirling turret. Egan made frantic efforts to pull Shay from the controls and stop the movement but not before the gunner suffered a chip fracture of the hip bone and the Major had the clothes down to his shirt torn from one arm. 'I had visions of being ground up into one great meat ball', Egan later reflected, 'but I'm going to miss that shirt . . . it was my Sunday best.'

6 JULY 1943

VIII FC FO 65

Despatched		Groups	E/A	Losses MIA	E	Dam	Casualties KIA	WIA	MIA
P-47	124	4FG, 56FG, 78FG	0	0	0	0	0	0	0

REMARKS: Sent on fighter sweeps in Rotterdam area.

8 JULY 1943

7PG despatched 3 F-5 on PR to France.

Installing the heavy K-24 cameras under the nose hood of an F-5A was a tricky job. The twin 24-inch focal length models made 9 by 9-inch negatives. *Dim View* was one of the original Lightnings received by 13PS and had seven sorties over Europe to its credit at this date – 8 July.

9 JULY 1943

VIII FC FO 67

Despatched		Groups	E/A	Losses MIA	E	Dam	Casualties KIA	WIA	MIA
P-47	128	4FG, 56FG, 78FG	0	0	0	0	0	0	0

REMARKS: Sent on fighter sweeps in Ghent area.

13PS despatched 1 F-5 on PR over France.

10 JULY 1943

VIII BC 72

	Despatched		Effective	Target	Bombs Tonnage	E/A	Losses MIA	E	Dam	Casualties KIA	WIA	MIA
1BW				CAEN A/F								
B-17	91BG	21	0	0832 hrs	496 × 300GP	10–5–3	1		13	0	0	10
	92BG	14	3			0–0–1	0		1	0	0	0
	305BG	20	16			0–0–0	0		1	0	0	0
	306BG	25	15			0–0–0	0		2	0	0	0
	351BG	19	0			6–1–1	0		7	0	1	0
	381BG	22	0			1–1–1	0		5	0	0	0
1BW				ABBEVILLE A/F								
B-17	303BG	26	3	0729–0735 hrs	399 × 100GP	0–0–0	0		4	0	0	0
	379BG	20	19		295 × 300GP	0–0–0	0		0	0	0	0
	384BG	18	14			0–0–0	0		0	0	0	0
TOTALS:		185	70		138.6	17–7–6	1	0	33	0	1	10
4BW				LE BOURGET A/F								
B-17	94BG	20				2–0–2	0		2	1	1	0
	95BG	27				7–1–2	1		2	0	0	10
	96BG	28				11–4–1	0		3	0	0	0
	100BG	26				4–3–2	1		9	0	2	10
TOTALS:		101	0		0	24–8–7	2	0	16	1	3	20

REMARKS: 92BG despatched totals include 5 YB-40s, 2 of which were abortive. Cloud caused 4BW mission to be abandoned over France.

VIII FC FO 68

Despatched		Groups	E/A	Losses MIA	E	Dam	Casualties KIA	WIA	MIA
P-47	128	4FG, 56FG, 78FG	0	0	0	0	0	0	0

REMARKS: Escort for heavy bombers.

13PS despatched 2 F-5 on PR to France.

The two commanders of the Anglo-American bomber offensive from Britain: Maj.Gen Ira Eaker and Air Vice Marshal Arthur Harris. The head of RAF Bomber Command seen leaving Daws Hill House after lunching with the CG BAF and Henry Stimson, US Secretary of War. AVM Leigh-Mallory, C in C RAF Fighter Command (background) was also a guest.

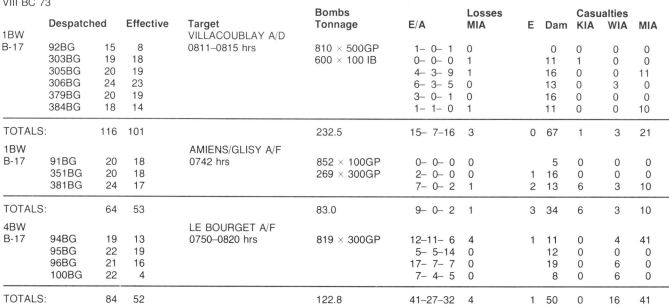

13 JULY 1943

13PS despatched 3 F-5 on PR to France.

14 JULY 1943

VIII BC 73

	Despatched		Effective	Target	Bombs Tonnage	E/A	Losses MIA	E	Dam	Casualties KIA	WIA	MIA
1BW				VILLACOUBLAY A/D								
B-17	92BG	15	8	0811–0815 hrs	810 × 500GP	1– 0– 1	0		0	0	0	0
	303BG	19	18		600 × 100 IB	0– 0– 0	1		11	1	0	0
	305BG	20	19			4– 3– 9	1		16	0	0	11
	306BG	24	23			6– 3– 5	0		13	0	3	0
	379BG	20	19			3– 0– 1	0		16	0	0	0
	384BG	18	14			1– 1– 0	1		11	0	0	10
TOTALS:		116	101		232.5	15– 7–16	3	0	67	1	3	21
1BW				AMIENS/GLISY A/F								
B-17	91BG	20	18	0742 hrs	852 × 100GP	0– 0– 0	0		5	0	0	0
	351BG	20	18		269 × 300GP	2– 0– 0	0	1	16	0	0	0
	381BG	24	17			7– 0– 2	1	2	13	6	3	10
TOTALS:		64	53		83.0	9– 0– 2	1	3	34	6	3	10
4BW				LE BOURGET A/F								
B-17	94BG	19	13	0750–0820 hrs	819 × 300GP	12–11– 6	4	1	11	0	4	41
	95BG	22	19			5– 5–14	0		12	0	0	0
	96BG	21	16			17– 7– 7	0		19	0	6	0
	100BG	22	4			7– 4– 5	0		8	0	6	0
TOTALS:		84	52		122.8	41–27–32	4	1	50	0	16	41

REMARKS: 92BG totals include 5 YB-40s. 381BG B-17 exploded during assembly, cr near Rattesden, 6 killed. 381BG B-17 collided with FW 190, but managed to return and c/l Manston A/F, crew safe. 351BG B-17 c/l southern England. 94BG B-17 abandoned over UK on return. 303BG B-17 ditched 30 miles off Shoreham, crew rescued.

VIII FC FO 71

Despatched		Groups	E/A	Losses MIA	E	Dam	Casualties KIA	WIA	MIA
P-47	128	4FG, 56FG, 78FG	3–0–3	3	1	1		0	2

REMARKS: Fighters escorted Amiens Glisy force only. 1 battle damaged 78FG P-47 abandoned off Newhaven, pilot saved. Fighter group losses:– 4FG – 1, 78FG – 2. Fighter group e/a credits:– 78FG – 1. 67RG Pilot flying with RAF, Capt J.R. Walker, MIA in Spitfire IX over France –first loss of unit.

13PS despatched 2 F-5 on PR to France.

15 JULY 1943

13PS despatched 2 F-5 on PR to France.

The hazards of formation flying in turbulence are well illustrated by this gaping hole caused by contact with the propeller blades of a higher 306BG B-17 on the 14 July mission.

The first presentation of a Congressional Medal of Honor (top US decoration for gallantry) was made by the US Secretary of War during a visit at Thurleigh on 15 July. The recipient, S/Sgt Maynard Smith (who extinguished a fire in a badly shot-up B-17) stands between Henry Stimson and 306BG CO, Lt.Col George Robinson. Behind to the right are Generals Devers, Eaker and Anderson. Vantage point for cameramen is one of the famous B-17s on the Group, *Wahoo II*, subsequently transferred to the 384BG and abandoned over Suffolk following the first Munster mission.

The most colourful commander of the early bomber organisations was Col Stanley Wray, who moved from the 91BG to 103 Combat Wing in the spring of 1943. When a photographer asked him to pose at Molesworthy on 15 July, Col Wray obliged with the Rigid Digit salute, a gesture that caused considerable mirth to those in the know. A great humourist, Stan Wray devised an unofficial award for those members of the 91st guilty of some supreme folly. Many US airmen had been amused by the RAFs vulgar condemnation for ineptitude whereby the erring individual was described as having his finger implanted in his rear end. Stan Wray adopted the sign indicative of this state of laxity and the motto 'My God, Am I Right?' for the specially struck medals produced by a Bedford silversmith and funded out of the Colonel's own pocket. Dubbed the *Order of the Rigid Digit* it was to be awarded with a suitable citation of condemnation at a ceremony in the Officers Mess. However, by skilful treachery some officers at Bassingbourn contrived to have the first award made to its unsuspecting originator. Latei some very senior officers in VIII Bomber Command were also recipients. The Rigid Digit salute became well known throughout the Eighth as a humorous symbol of alertness.

16 JULY 1943

VIII ASC 1

		Despatched	Effective	Target	Bombs Tonnage	E/A	Losses MIA	E	Dam	Casualties KIA	WIA	MIA
3BW				ABBEVILLE M/Y								
B-26	323BG	16	14	2000 hrs	16.75	0	0		10	0	2	0

REMARKS: First VIII ASC operation and use of B-26s at medium altitude. First mission for 323BG.

VIII FC FO 72

Despatched		Groups	E/A	Losses MIA	E	Dam	Casualties KIA	WIA	MIA
P-47	127	4FG, 56FG, 78FG	0	0	0	0	0	0	0

REMARKS: Fighters sent out in support of a diversionary raid in Dunkirk/Calais/Ostend/St.Omer area.

13PS despatched 1 F-5 on a Met flight to France.

17 JULY 1943

VIII BC 74

		Despatched	Effective	Target	Bombs Tonnage	E/A	Losses MIA	E	Dam	Casualties KIA	WIA	MIA
1BW				T/Os								
B-17	91BG	25	4		290 × 500GP	1–0– 0	0	1	7	0	2	0
	303BG	27	0		64 × 250 IB	1–1– 0	0		2	0	0	0
	351BG	28	15			17–3– 0	1		11	1	1	0
	381BG	30	14			5–1– 3	0		10	0	0	0
	92BG	18	0			5–2– 0	0		11	0	5	1
	305BG	26	0			0–0– 0	0		1	0	0	0
	306BG	28	0			3–0– 0	0		6	0	1	0
	379BG	25	0			0–0– 0	0		2	0	0	2
TOTALS:		207	33		80.5	32–7– 3	1	2	50	1	9	3
4BW				CONVOY (L)								
B-17	94BG	18	0		10 × 500GP	9–8–15	1	0	14	0	1	10
	95BG	23	0			3–1– 6	0	0	7	1	0	0
	96BG	21	1			11–0– 7	0	0	5	0	0	4
	100BG	22	0			5–0– 5	0	1	4	0	2	0
4BW				AMSTERDAM A/I								
B-17	385BG	21	5		206 × 500GP	0–0– 0	0	0	7	0	0	0
	388BG	20	16			0–0– 0	0	0	4	0	0	0
TOTALS:		125	22		54.0	28–9–33	1	1	41	1	3	14

REMARKS: 1BW sent to Hannover R/I and 4BW to Hamburg A/I, both missions recalled due to weather at 0955 hrs. 92BG despatched total includes 2 YB-40s. 351BG B-17 hit by e/a after leaving enemy coast and ditched, crew safe. Attempts to hit the Fokker plant at Amsterdam hindered by cloud and target missed, killing 150 cilivians. First mission for 385BG and 388BG. 2 379BG men baled out over Holland. B/d 91BG B-17 f/l Tempsford A/F after 7 baled.

VIII FC FO 74

Despatched		Groups	E/A	Losses MIA	E	Dam	Casualties KIA	WIA	MIA
P-47	126	4FG, 56FG, 78FG	0	0	0	0	0	0	0

REMARKS: P-47s provided escort for 385BG and 388BG, rest of fighters recalled.

VIII ASC 2

3BW B-26 DIVERSION, Cayeux area.

13PS despatched 6 F-5 on PR to France. 1 F-5 MIA.

23 JULY 1943

7PG despatched 1 F-5 on Met. flight to Rouen.

24 JULY 1943

VIII BC 75

					Bombs		Losses			Casualties		
	Despatched		Effective	Target	Tonnage	E/A	MIA	E	Dam	KIA	WIA	MIA
1BW				HEROYA I/A (P)								
B-17	91BG	22	14	1317–1414 hrs	1657 × 500GP	0–0–0	0		1	0	0	0
	92BG	15	15			4–0–0	0		10	0	0	0
	303BG	20	19			0–0–0	0		9	0	0	0
	305BG	19	18			2–0–0	0		3	0	0	0
	306BG	21	20			3–2–0	0		6	0	3	0
	351BG	21	21			0–0–0	0		2	0	0	0
	379BG	21	21			0–0–0	0		3	0	0	0
	381BG	21	20			0–0–0	1		10	0	0	10
	384BG	20	19			0–0–0	0		9	0	0	0
TOTALS:		180	167		414.25	9–2–0	1	0	53	0	3	10
4BW				TRONDHEIM P/A								
B-17	95BG	21	21		324 × 500GP	2–2–3	0	0		0	1	0
	100BG	24	20			2–0–0	0	1		0	2	0
TOTALS:		45	41		81.0	4–2–3	0	1	9	0	3	0
4BW				BERGEN P/A								
B-17	94BG	21							0			
	96BG	21							0			
	385BG	21							2			
	388BG	21							0			
TOTALS:		84	0		0	0–0–0	0	0	2	0	0	0

REMARKS: First 8AF attack on Norwegian targets. 92BG totals include 1 YB-40. Second 4BW force found 10/10 cloud cover so brought bombs back. All 4BW a/c had long-range tanks, and flew at low altitude until just off Norwegian coast so as to conserve fuel. 381BG B-17 MIA c/l in Sweden, crew interned. B/d 100BG B-17 cr. landing Fraserburgh A/F.

7PG despatched 1 F-5 on Met. flight to Rouen.

25 JULY 1943

VIII BC 76

					Bombs		Losses			Casualties		
	Despatched		Effective	Target	Tonnage	E/A	MIA	E	Dam	KIA	WIA	MIA
1BW				HAMBURG S/Y (S)								
B-17	91BG	18	17	and T/Os	540 × 500GP	1–0– 0	1		13	0	0	10
	303BG	20	20	1630–1645 hrs	176 × 250 IB	6–1– 8	1		9	0	2	10
	351BG	20	17		680 × 100 IB	4–2– 1	1		13	0	0	10
	379BG	21	21			15–2– 4	2		15	1	0	20
	381BG	23	14			2–0– 1	3		7	0	1	30
	384BG	21	11			10–1–13	7		10	0	2	70
TOTALS:		123	100		195.9	38–6–27	15	0	67	1	5	150
1BW				MISSION								
B-17	92BG	18	0	ABANDONED								
	305BG	20	0									
	306BG	21	0									
TOTALS:		59	0			0	0	0	0	0	0	0
4BW				KIEL S/Y (O)								
B-17	94BG	20	19	1630–1700 hrs	861 × 500GP	2–0– 0	1	0	9	0	0	10
	95BG	27	25	AND T/Os	212 × 250 IB	1–0– 0	1	0	7	1	2	10
	96BG	21	16		847 × 100 IB	3–0– 0	0	1	5	0	0	0
	100BG	24	15			0–0– 0	1	0	11	0	1	10
	385BG	28	25			0–0– 0	0	0	8	0	0	0
	388BG	21	18			0–0– 0	1	0	10	0	0	10
TOTALS:		141	118		522.2	6–0– 0	4	1	50	1	3	40

REMARKS: Most Formations encountered extensive cloud over primaries. 1BW Hamburg Force briefed to attack diesel engine works. 1BW secondary Force briefed for Kiel S/Y but unable to assemble formation due to weather. 4BW primary was Warnemünde A/I. Included in totals are: 14 381BG B-17s dropped 140 × 500GP on Heide as a T/O and 18 other 1BW a/c dropped on various T/Os: 18 388BG B-17s dropped 179 × 500GP on Rerik/West A/F at 1637 hrs as a T/O; 33 other 4BW a/c dropped 220 × 500GP, 96 × 100IB on various T/Os. 94BG B-17 ditched, crew rescued. 96BG B-17 c/l Little Snoring, crew safe.

VIII ASC 3
3BW

	Despatched		Effective	Target	Bombs Tonnage	E/A	Losses MIA	E	Dam	Casualties KIA	WIA	MIA
B-26	323BG	18	13	GHENT COKE OVENS 1458 hrs	16.0	0	0	0	6	0	0	0

REMARKS: Escorted by RAF Spitfires.

VIII FC FO 78

Despatched		Groups	E/A	Losses MIA	E	Dam	Casualties KIA	WIA	MIA
P-47	112	4FG, 56FG, 78FG	0	0	0	0	0	0	0

REMARKS: Carried out uneventful sweep of Belgian–Dutch coast in support of B-26s.

FO 79

P-47	34	56FG	0	0	0	0	0	0	0

REMARKS: Carried out uneventful sweep in support of RAF Bostons.

7PG despatched 2 F-5 on PR to France.

26 JULY 1943

VIII BC 77

	Despatched		Effective	Target	Bombs Tonnage	E/A	Losses MIA	E	Dam	Casualties KIA	WIA	MIA
1BW				HANNOVER R/I (P)								
B-17	92BG	19	17	1200–1243 hrs	160 × 1000GP	5–0– 3	3			2	2	11
	305BG	20	14		393 × 500GP	9–1– 3	1	0		2	1	10
	306BG	21	21		224 × 250 IB	4–0– 0	2	1		0	11	20
4BW				HANNOVER R/I (P)								
B-17	95BG	22	17	1200–1243 hrs	152 × 100 IB	14–6–10	4			0	4	40
	96BG	18	12			1–0– 6	1			0	1	5
	388BG	21	15			7–2– 6	5			0	3	40
TOTALS:		121	96		133.85	40–9–28	16	1		4	22	126
4BW				CONVOY and others								
B-17	100BG	20	16	T/Os	80 × 1000GP	0–1– 1	0			0	1	0
	94BG	20	18		18 × 500GP	10–0– 5	3			1	1	20
	385BG	21	15		12 × 100 IB	5–0– 1	3			0	1	31
					272 × 250 IB							
TOTALS:		61	49		79.1	15–1– 7	6			1	3	51
1BW				HAMBURG U/Y (P)								
B-17	91BG	20	9	1159–1200 hrs	388 × 500GP	0–0– 1	2			0	1	20
	303BG	20	15		234 × 250 IB	4–0– 0	0			0	0	0
	351BG	24	15			0–0– 0	0			0	1	0
	379BG	19	0			0–0– 0	0			0	0	0
	381BG	18	15			1–0– 0	0			1	1	0
	384BG	20	0			0–0– 0	0			0	0	0
TOTALS:		121	54		126.25	5–0– 1	2	3*	86*	1	3	20

REMARKS: 1BW Hannover force attacked the Nordhafen rubber plant and 4BW the Continental Gummiwerke. 3 B-17s from groups attacking Hannover dropped total 15,000 lb bombs on T/Os – 1 306BG and 2 95BG a/c. 49 other 4BW B-17s bombed T/Os:– 18 94BG attacked Wilhelmshaven, 15 385BG attacked Wesermünde and 16 100BG bombed a convoy between 1115 hrs and 1132 hrs. 92BG despatched 2 YB-40s, 1 of which was abortive. 3 B-17s ditched on return, crews rescued – 1 92BG off Sheringham, 1 388BG off Overstrand, and a 94BG 125 miles from Cromer. 306BG B-17 c/l near The Wash on return. F/O John C. Morgan awarded MOH for exploits this day.
* Totals for all missions.

26 JULY 1943 *(contd.)*

VIII FC FO 80

Despatched		Groups	E/A	Losses MIA	E	Dam	Casualties KIA	WIA	MIA
P-47	129	4FG, 56FG, 78FG	0–1–0	0	0	0	0	0	0

REMARKS: Flew diversionary sweeps in Rotterdam area, prior to raid of heavies.

FO 81

Despatched		Groups	E/A	Losses MIA	E	Dam	Casualties KIA	WIA	MIA
P-47	128	4FG, 56FG, 78FG	0	0	0	0	0	0	0

REMARKS: Carried out uneventful sweep in Lille/Dunkirk/Cayeux area later in the day.

VIII ASC 4

	Despatched		Effective	Target	Bombs Tonnage	E/A	Losses MIA	E	Dam	Casualties KIA	WIA	MIA
3BW				ST.OMER/ LONGUENESSE A/F (O)								
B-26	323BG	18	15	1112 hrs	14.8	0	0	0	4	0	0	0

REMARKS: Primary was St.Omer/Ft.Rouge A/D.

7PG despatched 5 F-5 on PR of French coast.

27 JULY 1943

VIII ASC 5

	Despatched		Effective	Target	Bombs Tonnage	E/A	Losses MIA	E	Dam	Casualties KIA	WIA	MIA
3BW				TRICQUEVILLE A/F								
B-26	323BG	18	17	1825 hrs	18.0	0	0	0	0	0	0	0

VIII FC FO 82

Despatched		Groups	E/A	Losses MIA	E	Dam	Casualties KIA	WIA	MIA
P-47	119	4FG, 56FG, 78FG	0	0	0	0	0	0	0

REMARKS: Fighters sent to escort B-26s and carry out sweep in the Rouen area.

7PG despatched 1 F-5 on PR to French coast.

28 JULY 1943

VIII BC 78

	Despatched		Effective	Target	Bombs Tonnage	E/A	Losses MIA	E	Dam	Casualties KIA	WIA	MIA
1BW				KASSEL A/I (P)								
B-17	91BG	20	0	(FIESELER WKS)	340 × 500GP	0– 0– 0	0	0	1	0	0	0
	92BG	17	14	1027–1054 hrs	160 × 250 IB	3– 1– 0	2	0	8	0	1	20
	303BG	20	4	T/Os	80 × 100 IB	0– 0– 0	0	0	0	0	0	0
	305BG	21	20		49a/c (P)	5– 0– 2	1	0	18	0	2	10
	306BG	24	16			10– 2– 4	2	3	11	0	6	20
	351BG	21	0			0– 0– 0	0	0	0	0	0	0
	379BG	19	0			8– 2– 7	1	1	13	0	6	10
	381BG	20	0			0– 0– 0	0	0	0	0	0	0
	384BG	20	4			1–10– 9	1	0	3	0	0	11
TOTALS:		182	58		109.0 (P)	27–15–22	7	4	54	0	15	71
4BW				OSCHERSLEBEN A/I (P)								
B-17	94BG	18	11	& T/Os	238 × 500GP	12– 2– 4	0	0	12	0	2	0
	95BG	20	11		24 × 500 IB	22– 8–11	3	1	10	0	4	33
	96BG	21	4		48 × 100 IB	7– 7–14	7	0	14	0	3	71
	100BG	21	0		28 a/c (P)	2– 1– 4	0	0	1	0	1	0
	385BG	26	2			6– 1– 6	4	0	8	0	0	20
	388BG	14	9			7– 0– 2	1	0	19	0	1	10
TOTALS:		120	37		67.9 (P)	56–19–41	15	1	64	0	11	134

REMARKS: 4 1BW a/c dropped on T/Os (Wetrup – 2 a/c, Beeststorzwagg – 1 a/c and U/I T/O – 1 a/c). 14 other aircraft on T/Os. 155 a/c abandoned mission because of weather. Only 28 4BW a/c dropped on (P); 8 a/c of 95BG attacked Alsleben by mistake – incorrect target identification through gap in clouds. B/d 379BG B-17 c/l at Foulsham, 4 WIA. B/d 95BG B-17 c/l Framlingham, 3 of crew baled in target area, rest safe. 3 306BG B-17 c/l on return (1 SW Oxford, 1 at Sudbourne and 1 at Hawkinge nr Dover; crews safe).

VIII FC FO 83

Despatched		Groups	E/A	Losses MIA	E	Dam	Casualties KIA	WIA	MIA
P-47	123	4FG, 56FG, 78FG	9–1–6	1	0	1	0	0	1

REMARKS: 4FG engaged 45 e/a attacking bombers over Holland and was also first 8AF fighter group to penetrate German airspace. P-47s provided withdrawal support. 4FG use jettisonable fuel tanks giving an extra 30 mile radius of action. Fighter group losses:– 4FG – 1, Fighter group e/a credits:– 4FG – 9.

INCIDENT

The first known success of Luftwaffe air launched rockets against a Fortress formation occurred on 28 July 1943. An aircraft of the 385th Group received a direct hit from one of these missiles and broke up, crashing into two other B-17s in the formation. All three aircraft went down, a heart-rending sight for other airmen of this unit that had only recently entered combat. The rocket was an adaptation of an infantry weapon, the Wfr.Gr.42 spr. Carried in a cumbersome launch tube suspended beneath the wings of FW 190s and Me 110s, each missile weighed a little under 250 lb of which the warhead accounted for some 21 lb. Time-fused to detonate at a pre-set range of up to 1,200 yards, the great advantage of the weapon was that it could be launched from outside the effective range of the B-17s' defensive armament. Although difficult to aim with accuracy a direct hit usually destroyed a bomber.

For most of the 4th Wing force despatched to Oschersleben on 28 July the operation was a disaster. Off the north German coast layers of high cloud caused formations to become separated and spread, a situation the Luftwaffe was quick to exploit. 95BG came under attack from FW 190s of JG 1 which made frontal attacks. In the first photo a pair of 190s can be seen making their pass from 1 o'clock: in the second, one is Split-Essing (rollover and curve away in dive) to escape B-17 defensive fire. The smoke-trailing Focke Wulf in the third frame was probably claimed as destroyed by bomber gunners. However, it is more likely that it is unharmed and that the smoke comes from engine exhaust after the pilot had opened up the throttle. The low grade fuels used in German fighters caused poor combustion.

VIII ASC 6 & 7

	Despatched		Effective	Target	Bombs Tonnage	E/A	Losses MIA	E	Dam	Casualties KIA	WIA	MIA
3BW				ZEEBRUGGE COKE								
B-26	323BG	18	17	OVENS 1105 hrs	33 × 1000GP				3			
	323BG	18	0	TRICQUEVILLE A/F	0				0			
TOTALS:		36	17		16.5	0	0		3	0	0	0

REMARKS: The aircraft despatched to Triqueville were recalled because r/v with fighters was not accomplished.

VIII FC FO 84

Despatched		Groups	E/A	Losses MIA	E	Dam	Casualties KIA	WIA	MIA
P-47	119	4FG, 56FG, 78FG	0	0	0	0	0	0	0

REMARKS: Sent out as escort, escort cover and top cover to B-26s on diversionary raid. 2 B-26 diversions flown this day; in the morning 322BG feinted to Holland, whilst that of the afternoon, by 386BG, was towards Abbeville.

7PG despatched 8 F-5 on PR over France.

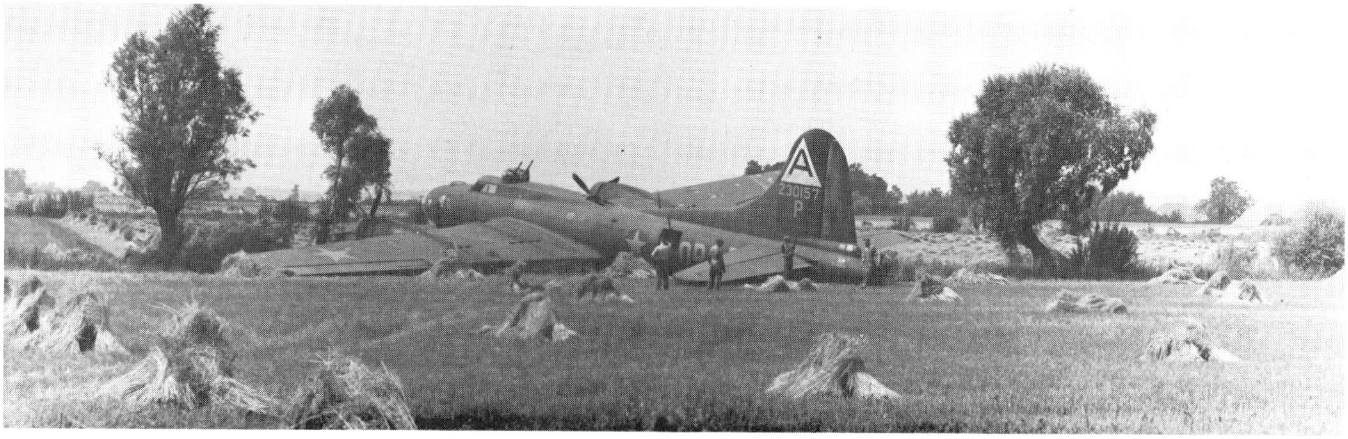

Farming near the end of a runway was difficult as crops were frequently run down by aeroplanes and the men and vehicles that came to retrieve them. A shot out hydraulic system left *Hell's Belles* with no brakes when it landed at Bassingbourn on 28 July. The Fortress did not stop until it had thundered over a field of traved oats and met a rather deep ditch.

29 JULY 1943

VIII BC 79

		Despatched	Effective	Target	Bombs Tonnage	E/A	Losses MIA	E	Dam	Casualties KIA	WIA	MIA
1BW				KIEL S/Y (P)								
B-17	91BG	18	16	0901 hrs	596 × 500GP	1–0– 1	0	0	6	0	1	0
	92BG	14	12	(91 a/c) & T/Os	332 × 250 IB	5–0– 2	0	0	11	0	0	0
	305BG	19	18		348 × 100M47A1	8–0– 1	0	1	11	1	2	1
	306BG	18	13			6–0– 4	4	0	4	0	0	40
	351BG	19	18			8–1–13	0	0	16	1	3	0
	381BG	24	18			7–1– 8	0	1	7	0	2	0
1BW				T/Os (L)								
B-17	303BG	20	20		261 × 500GP	5–1– 0	0	0	2	0	0	0
	379BG	19	12		336 × 250 IB	0–1– 1	1	0	0	0	0	10
	384BG	17	12			8–2– 3	1	0	5	0	0	10
TOTALS:		168	139		315.15	48–6– 33	6	2	62	2	8	61
4BW				WARNEMÜNDE A/I (P)								
B-17	94BG	15	11	(HEINKEL WKS)	420 × 500GP	0–0– 0	1			0	0	10
	95BG	8	4	0922–0924 hrs	192 × 250 IB	0–0– 0	0			0	0	0
	96BG	11	9			0–0– 0	1			0	0	10
	100BG	21	14			0–1– 0	0			0	0	0
	385BG	16	10			0–1– 0	1			0	0	10
	388BG	10	6			0–0– 0	1			0	0	10
TOTALS:		81	54		129.0	0–2– 0	4	0	7	0	0	40

REMARKS: Cloud caused 44 a/c of 103CW sent to Kiel to attack last resort targets. 91BG, 305BG, 306BG and 351BG each had 1 B-17 bomb a T/O. 92BG totals include 1 YB-40. 2 B-17s (96BG and 388BG) collided near coast (Sea Palling), crews lost. B/d 305BG B-17 Cat E base. Aborting 385BG B-17 ditched, crew rescued. 767,000 leaflets also dropped by 1BW at Kiel. B/d 381BG B-17 c/l near Thetford, crew safe.

VIII ASC 8 & 9

		Despatched	Effective	Target	Bombs Tonnage	E/A	Losses MIA	E	Dam	Casualties KIA	WIA	MIA
3BW				AMSTERDAM/SCHIPOL								
B-26	323BG	18	0	A/F ST. OMER	56 × 300GP		0		0	0	0	0
	323BG	21	19	FT.ROUGE A/F 1828 hrs	201 × 100GP		0		8	0	0	0
TOTALS:		39	19		18.45		0	0	8	0	0	0

REMARKS: Escorted by 12 Sqdns of RAF Spitfires.

VIII FC FO 85

Despatched		Groups	E/A	Losses MIA	E	Dam	Casualties KIA	WIA	MIA
P-47	118	4FG, 56FG, 78FG	0–1–0	1		1			1

REMARKS: Sent on sweeps over Belgium and Holland. 56FG a/c MIA, pilot seen in the Channel.

FO 86

Despatched		Effective	Target	Bombs Tonnage	E/A	Losses MIA	E	Dam	Casualties KIA	WIA	MIA
P-47	128		4FG, 56FG, 78FG		0–0–1	0	0	1	0	0	0

REMARKS: Escorted 20 B-26s of 386BG on a diversionary raid, for 323BG attacking St.Omer.

7PG despatched 4 F-5 on PR over France.

Above. Alice From Dallas, an original B-17F of 100BG wings its way across the cloud shrouded North Sea on route to Warnemunde, 29 July. 4th Wing groups went to the most distant targets during the late July Blitz Week as all their B-17s were new long-range models with extra wing tanks which increased the fuel load from 1,730 to 2,810 US gallons. However, the additional 9,000 lb weight demanded slower climbs to altitude to avoid engine overstrain – 200 feet per minute at 150 mps IAS.

Right. The Heinkel assembly plant on the Warnemünde peninsula was in the clear when the combined 96BG and 388BG formation arrived at the head of the 4th Wing force. The aim of bombardier Lt Tom Hines was right on the mark.

30 July 1943

VIII BC 80

	Despatched		Effective	Target	Bombs Tonnage	E/A	Losses MIA	E	Dam	Casualties KIA	WIA	MIA
1BW				KASSEL A/I (P)								
B-17	91BG	20	17	(BETTENHAUSEN	680 × 500GP	3–1– 5	2	1	15	0	0	20
	303BG	23	19	FIESELER WKS)	378 × 250 IB	4–2– 8	1	0	9	1	4	0
	351BG	21	16	0910–0917 hrs		8–0– 4	0	2	12	0	4	0
	379BG	24	13			17–1– 6	2	1	9	10	1	22
	381BG	18	18			2–3– 3	1	0	17	0	1	10
	384BG	13	11			6–0– 3	0	1	2	0	0	0
TOTALS:		119	94		217.25	40–7–29	6	5	64	11	10	52
4BW				KASSEL A/I (P)								
B-17	94BG	15	10	(WALDAU FIESELER	260 × 500GP	0–0– 0	0		2	0	0	0
	95BG	6	3	WKS)	146 × 250 IB	2–1– 1	1		3	0	0	5
	96BG	10	4	0925–0928 hrs	(37 a/c)	3–3– 1	2		3	0	0	10
	100BG	17	14			0–1– 1	0		5	0	0	0
	365BG	7	2			2–0– 0	0		0	0	0	0
	388BG	12	7			1–1– 0	3		5	0	1	30
TOTALS:		67	40		90.25	8–6– 3	6	0	18	0	1	45

REMARKS: 1 94BG B-17 and 2 100BG B-17s dropped 16 × 250 IB and 20 × 500GP on T/Os. 3 B-17s, one each from 95BG, 96BG and 303BG, ditched on return, crews rescued but 5 men from the 95BG a/c baled out over Holland. On return 2 351BG B-17s c/l, one at Leiston A/F and the other on Woodbridge A/F. 379BG B-17 cr Framlingham, crew killed. B/d 384BG B-17 with 6 men WIA landed Boxted A/F – Cat E. 91BG B-17 cr. landing base.

VIII FC FO 87

Despatched		Groups	E/A	Losses MIA	E	Dam	Casualties KIA	WIA	MIA
P-47	107	4FG, 56FG, 78FG	25–4–8	7	1	0	0	0	6

REMARKS: Escort and support for heavy bombers. Second use of drop tanks by P-47s. 78FG pilot Maj Roberts scored first 8AF 'triple kill'. Lt Q.L. Brown, 78FG, carried out first strafing attack with a P-47. Fighter group e/a credits:– 4FG – 5, 56FG – 3, 78FG – 16. Fighter group losses:– 4FG – 1, 56FG – 2, 78FG – 4. 78FG pilot in sea saved by ASR. 78FG P-47 c/l West Wickham.

A German soldier stands guard on the burnt out wreck of a 532BS Fortress which crash-landed in Holland during the mission of 30 July.

30 JULY 1943 *(contd.)*

VIII ASC 10A & 10B

	Despatched		Effective	Target	Bombs Tonnage	E/A	Losses MIA	E	Dam	Casualties KIA	WIA	MIA
3BW B-26	386BG	24	11	WOENSDRECHT A/F 0657 hrs	88 × 300GP		1	1	5	0	7	6
	323BG	24	0	COURTRAI/WEVELGHEM A/F	0		0	0	0	0	0	0
TOTALS:		48	11		13.2	6–5–1	1	1	5	0	7	6

REMARKS: First mission for 386BG and first e/a attacks on B-26s at medium altitude. 386BG B-26 crashed on t/o Boxted. 323BG mission recalled due to escort being fog bound.

7PG despatched 4 F-5 on PR over France.

2 US crews of 153 RS, 67RG flying with 107 Sqn RAF in an attack on Schipol A/F. 1 MIA in North Sea.

31 JULY 1943

VIII ASC 11A 11B 11C & 11D

	Despatched		Effective	Target	Bombs Tonnage	E/A	Losses MIA	E	Dam	Casualties KIA	WIA	MIA
3BW B-26	323BG	21	20	MERVILLE A/F 1120 hrs	155 × 300GP 56 × 300GP		0		2	0	0	0
	323BG	21	19	POIX/NORD A/F 1122 hrs	260 × 100GP		1		5	0	0	7
	386BG	21	21	ABBEVILLE/DRUCAT A/F 1617 hrs	72 × 300GP 209 × 100GP		0					
	322BG	21	18	TRICQUEVILLE A/F 1623 hrs	56 × 300GP 1172 × 100GP	0–1–0	0		5	0	0	0
TOTALS:		84	78		79.7	0–1–0	1	0	12	0	0	7

REMARKS: 387BG carried out a diversion (ASC 11E). First occasion that bombers sent on two missions in one day. First mission for 322BG since 17 May.

VIII FC FO 88

Despatched		Groups	E/A	Losses MIA	E	Dam	Casualties KIA	WIA	MIA
P-47	128	4FG, 56FG, 78FG	0	0	0		0	0	0

REMARKS: Fighters sent in support of B-26 diversion by 387BG north of Dunkirk.

7PG despatched 1 F-5 to France.

INCIDENT

One of the B-24 airmen killed in the spectacular low-level raid on Ploesti on 1 August was S/Sgt Albert H. Oser of the 93rd Group, a gunner credited with six enemy aircraft destroyed. This ranked the highest score for 8th Air Force Liberator gunners and was only equalled by two 44th Group men, T/Sgt John Pitcovich and Lt William G. Morton. In fact, only five gunners achieved the unofficial accolade of becoming an 'ace' through shooting down five or more enemy aircraft while flying in Liberators from England or on detachment in North Africa. In addition to the top scorers, T/Sgt Willard W. Scott was credited with 5½ and T/Sgt Ravelle A. Bennett with five; both were top-turret gunners and also served with the 44th Group.

2 AUGUST 1943

VIII ASC 12A & 12B

	Despatched		Effective	Target	Bombs Tonnage	E/A	Losses MIA	E	Dam	Casualties KIA	WIA	MIA
3BW B-26	323BG	34	31	MERVILLE A/F 0810 hrs	245 × 300GP			1	15			
	386BG	21	18	ST.OMER/FT.ROUGE A/F 0900 hrs	64 × 300GP 137 × 100GP			0	13			
TOTALS:		55	49		54.40	0	0	1	28	0	6	0

REMARKS: VIII ASC 13A, an attack on Woensdrecht A/F by 322BG, cancelled. 387BG flew a diversion (13B). 323BG B-26 had to make a f/l at Manston on return.

VIII FC FO 91

Despatched		Groups	E/A	Losses MIA	E	Dam	Casualties KIA	WIA	MIA
P-47	128	4FG, 56FG, 78FG		0	0	0	0	0	0

REMARKS: Escort for 387BG B-26s flying diversion followed by sweep; latter cancelled.

4 AUGUST 1943

VIII ASC 14

	Despatched		Effective	Target	Bombs Tonnage	E/A	Losses MIA	E	Dam	Casualties KIA	WIA	MIA
3BW				LE TRAIT S/Y								
B-26	322BG	36	33	1926 hrs	40.0	0	0	0	0	0	0	0

8 AUGUST 1943

VIII ASC 15

	Despatched		Effective	Target	Bombs Tonnage	E/A	Losses MIA	E	Dam	Casualties KIA	WIA	MIA
3BW				POIX/NORD A/F								
B-26	323BG	36	0		0	0	0	0	0	0	0	0

REMARKS: Formation turned back due to weather.

7PG despatched 4 F-5 on PR over France.

A photographer in *Margie* took this view of *Seductive Susie* and other 386BG Marauders crossing the French coast on 9 August as cloud is encountered. Soon the ground was completely hidden from view and the bombers had to return with bomb loads undelivered at St.Omer.

9 AUGUST 1943

VIII ASC 16A & 16B

	Despatched		Effective	Target	Bombs Tonnage	E/A	Losses MIA	E	Dam	Casualties KIA	WIA	MIA
3BW				ST.OMER/FT.ROUGE								
B-26	386BG	36	0	A/F 1904 hrs	5 × 500GP				4	0		0
	322BG	36	1						7	0		0
TOTALS:		72	1		1.25	0	0	0	11	0	6	0

REMARKS: Clouds prevented bombing.

VIII FC FO 95

Despatched		Groups	E/A	Losses MIA	E	Dam	Casualties KIA	WIA	MIA
P-47	139	4FG, 56FG, 78FG 353FG	0	0	0	0	0	0	0

REMARKS: Sent on fighter sweeps of Abbeville/Poix area. First mission for squadrons of 353FG.

On a non-operational day, 11 August, a photographer at Snetterton Heath captured a selection of the nicknames and decorations that distinguished individual Fortresses. These would later reflect the loss rate of 96BG – second highest in the Eighth. *Flak Happy* was lost to fighter attack going to Bremen on 8 October. Capt Walter Flagg was the original pilot of *Wabbit-Twacks III* but was not along when the bomber went down at Schweinfurt, 14 October, *Ole Puss* and *Holy Mackerel* were lost in two separate collisions while under fighter attack on 16 December: *The Klap Trap II* (with D/F antenna housing used as clothes rack) did not return from Ludwigshafen on 7 January 1944; likewise *Big Dick* from Regensburg on 25 February, and *Mischief Maker II* on the Berlin mission of 4 March. The latter was originally Capt Vernon Iverson's lead plane. Some of these bombers were the second with the same nickname and resulted from the replacement of the original B-17s with long-range models.

12 AUGUST 1943

VIII BC 81

		Despatched	Effective	Target	Bombs Tonnage	E/A	Losses MIA	Casualties E	Dam	KIA	WIA	MIA
1BW				BOCHUM								
B-17	91BG	22	10	GELSENKIRCHEN	836 × 500GP	0–1– 0	4	0	6	2	5	40
	92BG	19	12	RECKLINGHAUSEN	784 × 250IB	3–0– 4	4	0	11	2	7	41
	303BG	20	19	& other T/Os		6–1– 1	1	0	14	0	0	10
	305BG	20	16	0845–0925hrs		2–0– 2	1	0	15	0	11	10
	306BG	20	16			1–2– 1	1	0	15	0	3	10
	351BG	21	14			4–0– 2	0	1	11	1	7	0
	379BG	21	19			6–1– 1	4	1	13	0	6	41
	381BG	20	16			3–0– 0	3	0	13	0	0	30
	384BG	20	11			0–0– 0	5	0	5	0	10	50
TOTALS:		183	133		307.0	25–5–11	23	2	103	5	49	232
4BW				BONN								
B-17	94BG	21	17	& other T/Os	2 × 2000GP	0–0– 2	0	0	15	1	4	0
	95BG	21	9	0850–0858 hrs	743 × 500GP	3–2– 0	2	0	9	0	2	21
	96BG	21	16		523 × 250IB	1–0– 0	0	0	7	0	0	0
	100BG	21	20			0–0– 0	0	0	4	0	0	0
	385BG	21	11			0–0– 0	0	0	15	0	0	0
	388BG	21	18			0–0– 0	0	0	16	0	0	0
	390BG	21	19			0–0– 0	0	1	3	0	1	0
TOTALS:		147	110		253.1	4–2– 2	2	1	69	1	7	21

REMARKS: 1BW became separated on the bomb run and bombed various T/Os. 16 4BW aircraft dropped on leader when e/a forced him to jettison on the bomb run. First mission for 390BG. 390BG B-17 c/l due to failure of right main gear at base. 351BG B-17 c/l at Leiston a/d. 4 4BW a/c dropped 40 × 500GP bombs on other T/Os, the rest of Force in Bonn area. B/d 379BG B-17 c/l Bury St.Edmunds A/F.

VIII FC FO 98

Despatched		Groups	E/A	Losses MIA	Casualties E	Dam	KIA	WIA	MIA
P-47	131	4FG, 56FG, 78FG	2–1–4	0	0	0	0	0	0

REMARKS: First use of pressurised belly tanks by fighters. Fighter group e/a credits:– 4FG – 4.

VIII FC FO 99

Despatched		Groups	E/A	Losses MIA	Casualties E	Dam	KIA	WIA	MIA
P-47	27	353FG	0	0	0	0	0	0	0

REMARKS: Sent on high altitude sweep over Westhoffd/Eekloo/Ostend area. First group mission for 353FG.

VIII ASC 17 & 18

	Despatched		Effective	Target	Bombs Tonnage	E/A	Losses MIA	E	Dam	Casualties KIA	WIA	MIA
3BW				POIX/NORD A/F	161 × 500GP		0		13	0	0	0
B-26	322BG	36	34	1052 hrs			0		0	0	0	0
	323BG	35	0				0		0	0	0	0
TOTALS:		71	34		40.25	0	0	0	13	0	0	0

REMARKS: 323BG recalled by fighter escort over Channel. 7PG despatched 3 F-5 on PR to France. 14PS flew first sortie.

Waist gunners, standing at their posts, had little protection from armour and superstructure and in consequence suffered the highest injury rate among B-17 crewmen. S/Sgt Jayson C Smart was luckier than 10 other men of 305BG who were wounded in the air fight on 12 August. A small splinter nicked his head and back at base he was able to walk away from Fortress *Big Bust*. The blood streaks across his nose and face were made by the oxygen mask.

Despite Britain's strict quarantine rules concerning the importance of animals, several pets arrived unannounced by air at new bomber stations. The mascot of 569BS was *Roscoe Ann*, a bear cub acquired shortly before the unit flew to England. This animal – seen reposing on boxes of 50 calibre, 13 August – brought delight to village children and consternation to farmers on its occasional unaccompanied forays at Parham. Eventually the local constabulary brought pressure to bear on 390BG command, pointing out that there was a limit to which Suffolk county could be turned into the Wild West. In any case, by the winter *Roscoe Ann* was developing fast and becoming something of a hazard around the base, so it was decreed that she would have to be executed.

14 AUGUST 1943

VIII FC FO 102

Despatched		Groups	E/A	Losses MIA	E	Dam	Casualties KIA	WIA	MIA
P-47	88	56FG, 353FG	0	0	0	0	0	0	0

REMARKS: Sent on a diversionary sweep, in support of bombers, on a diversionary raid.

The ingenuity of 8AF personnel was remarkable. One of the most notable attempts to improve B-17F forward defensive firepower was the unofficially sanctioned installation of a 20 mm cannon by the 385BG. Early in August a weapon obtained from British sources was installed in *Roundtrip Jack*. CWO Nugent Thompson masterminded the installation which involved prefabricating several parts and strengthening the nose gun supports. The length of the weapon made manipulation difficult and a range flight was conducted on 13 August which showed that the recoil kick vibrated cockpit instruments. The small sighting glass panel over the gun barrel cracked (it can be seen in the exterior photo taken the following day). *Roundtrip Jack* took part in the mission to Vitry en Artois on 15 August with Thompson as cannoneer but no enemy fighters were encountered. It was to be the only operational use as higher authority had received word of the installation and immediately condemned it as unsafe: the B-17's nose was not suitably stressed.

First B-17 missing in action from 390BG went down through a collision. Minus the complete rear fuselage and tail it tumbles down past 385BG's *Shack Bunny*, just south-east of Dunkirk on 15 August.

15 AUGUST 1943

VIII BC 82

		Despatched	Effective	Target	Bombs Tonnage	E/A	Losses		Casualties			
							MIA	E	Dam	KIA	WIA	MIA
1BW				FLUSHING								
B-17	91BG	20	19	(VLISSINGEN)	1434 × 300GP				18	0	3	0
	351BG	19	18	A/F (91 a/c) (S)					6	0	0	0
	381BG	23	0	1926–1930 hrs					0	0	0	0
	92BG	18	18	AMIENS	550 × 100GP				5	0	0	0
	305BG	19	16	1928–1931 hrs	478 × 120Frag				5	0	0	0
	306BG	20	20	POIX A/F (O)	257 × 100GP				0	0	0	0
	303BG	20	18						1	0	0	0
	379BG	21	21						10	0	0	0
	384BG	20	17						3	0	0	0
TOTALS:		180	147		284.1	0–0–0	0	0	48	0	3	0
4BW				MERVILLE A/F &								
B-17	94BG	21	21	LILLE/VENDEVILLE	926 × 100GP	1–0–0	0		0	0	0	0
	385BG	21	20	A/F (82 a/c)	1036 × 100GP	4–0–0	1		1	0	2	10
	390BG	21	20	1925–1933 hrs		1–0–0	1		1	0	0	10
	95BG	21	21	VITRY EN ARTOIS	1364 × 100GP	1–0–0	0		3	0	0	0
	96BG	21	19	A/F (61a/c)	2 × 2000GP	0–0–1	0		3	0	1	0
	100BG	21	21	1929–1931 hrs		2–0–0	0		2	1	0	0
	388BG	21	21			0–0–0	0		1	0	0	0
TOTAL:		147	143		168.3	9–0–1	2	0	11	1	3	20

REMARKS: 1BW – 91BG 92BG 305BG 306BG 351BG bombed (S) – 56 a/c attacked Amiens, and 14 a/c of these also attacked Poix. 4BW – 82 a/c dropped half their load on Merville and half on Lille/Vendeville. 390BG lost 1 a/c in a collision, other a/c involved returned to base. 1 badly damaged 385BG B-17 landed at RAF field.

VIII FC FO 104

	Despatched	Groups	E/A	Losses		Casualties			
				MIA	E	Dam	KIA	WIA	MIA
P-47	187	4FG, 56FG, 78FG 353FG	0	0	1		1	0	0

REMARKS: 56FG were 30 minutes early at rendezvous and so unable to give any support to bombers. 78FG P-47 crash landed at Duxford, pilot killed.

VIII FC FO 103

	Despatched	Groups	E/A	Losses		Casualties			
				MIA	E	Dam	KIA	WIA	MIA
P-47	176	4FG, 56FG, 78FG, 353FG	0	0	0	0	0	0	0

REMARKS: Carried out sweeps of Knokke/Bruges/Lille/St.Omer area.

VIII ASC 19A 19B & 20

	Despatched	Effective	Target	Bombs Tonnage	E/A	Losses		Casualties			
						MIA	E	Dam	KIA	WIA	MIA
			ST.OMER/FT.ROUGE								
387BG	36	31	A/F 0959 hrs	231 × 300GP				18	0	0	0
			WOENSDRECHT A/F								
386BG	36	0	ABBEVILLE M/Y					0	0	0	0
323BG	21	19	1933 hrs	54 × 1000GP				9	0	1	0
TOTALS:	93	50		61.7	0	0	0	27	0	1	0

REMARKS: First bombing mission for 387BG. VIII ASC 20 was 323BG mission. 386BG turned back at Dutch coast. 323BG accidentally dropped a 1000GP bomb 'safe' in field 2 miles S. of Redhill.

7PG despatched 5 F-5 on PR to France.

16 AUGUST 1943

VIII BC 83

		Despatched	Effective	Target	Bombs Tonnage	E/A	Losses MIA	E	Dam	Casualties KIA	WIA	MIA
1BW				LE BOURGET A/F								
B-17	91BG	21	19	0929–0937 hrs	2649 × 300GP	1–0– 0	1		2	0	1	0
	92BG	17	17			3–0– 0	0		12	0	0	0
	303BG	20	20			4–1– 2	0		6	0	0	0
	305BG	20	18			0–0– 0	0		4	0	0	0
	306BG	20	19			1–0– 0	0		2	0	0	0
	351BG	21	21			0–0– 0	0		3	0	0	0
	379BG	21	19			9–0– 4	2		10	0	0	21
	381BG	20	19			1–0– 0	0		1	0	0	0
	384BG	20	19			10–2– 5	1		6	1	3	10
TOTALS:		180	171		397.35	29–3–11	4	0	46	1	4	31
4BW				POIX A/F (65 a/c)								
B-17	94BG	21	21	& ABBEVILLE A/F (64 a/c)	786 × 100GP				5	0	0	0
	96BG	24	24		8 × 300GP				21	0	0	0
	388BG	21	21	0911–0923 hrs	763 × 100GP				12	0	0	0
TOTALS:		66	66		78.65	0–0– 0	0	0	38	0	0	0

REMARKS: 4BW a/c dropped half their load on each target. 91BG B-17 down in sea, crew rescued. 92BG figures included 1YB-40, the last regular operation of this type.

VIII FC FO 105

Despatched		Groups	E/A	Losses MIA	E	Dam	Casualties KIA	WIA	MIA
P-47	180	4FG, 56FG, 78FG, 353FG	18–2–7	3	2		0	0	3

REMARKS: Escort and support for B-17s. Fighter group losses:– 4FG – 1 56FG – 1 353FG – 1.

Fighter group e/a credits:– 4FG – 18. On return 4FG P-47 c/l New Romney and 353FG P-47 c/l Lewes, pilots safe.

VIII ASC 21 & 22A

		Despatched	Effective	Target	Bombs Tonnage	E/A	Losses MIA	E	Dam	Casualties KIA	WIA	MIA
3BW				BERNAY ST.MARTIN (P)								
B-26	387BG	36	31	A/F 1117 hrs	248 × 300GP				2	0	0	0
				BEAUMONT LE ROGER (P)								
	322BG	36	29	A/F 1700 hrs	226 × 300GP				3	0	0	0
				CONCHES A/F (O)								
			3	1703 hrs	24 × 300GP							
TOTALS:		72	63		74.7	0	0		5	0	0	0

REMARKS: VIII ASC 22B was a diversion by 323BG.

7PG despatched 11 F-5 on PR to France.

The first battle of Schweinfurt. Smoke envelops the target as 379BG turns for home.

17 AUGUST 1943

VIII BC 84

		Despatched	Effective	Target	Bombs Tonnage	E/A	Losses MIA	E	Dam	Casualties KIA	WIA	MIA
1BW				SCHWEINFURT B/I (P)								
B-17	91BG	24	9	1459–1511 hrs	1017 × 250IB	13– 1– 3	10	1	10	1	1	97
	92BG	22	21		719 × 500GP	17– 3– 1	2	0	14	0	1	20
	303BG	29	27		235 × 1000GP	20– 7– 9	0	1	23	1	4	0
	305BG	29	27		(183 a/c)	17– 1– 4	2	0	14	1	1	24
	306BG	30	30			16– 1– 3	0	0	14	0	0	0
	351BG	28	26			25– 2–21	2	0	15	0	0	20
	379BG	24	18			11– 3– 2	4	0	9	0	1	40
	381BG	26	18			21– 0–14	11	0	12	0	1	101
	384BG	18	12			8–0– 6	5	1	7	0	3	50
TOTALS:		230	188		424.3	148–18–63	36	3	118	3	12	352

17 AUGUST 1943 *(contd.)*

4BW				REGENSBURG A/I (P)								
B-17	94BG	21	20	1148–1207 hrs	971 × 500GP	13– 1– 5	1	1	12	0	1	10
	95BG	21	14		448 × 250IB	25– 1– 8	4	0	5	0	0	40
	96BG	21	19		(126 a/c)	5– 1– 0	0	0	6	0	0	0
	100BG	21	14			36–10– 7	9	0	3	1	2	90
	385BG	21	19			48– 4– 4	3	0	5	2	1	20
	388BG	21	21			7– 0– 4	1	0	7	0	3	0
	390BG	20	20			6– 2– 8	6	0	12	1	2	40
TOTALS:		146	127		298.75	140–19–36	24	1	50	4	9	200

REMARKS: 1BW – 4 a/c bombed T/Os and 1 Frankfurt. 4BW – 1 390BG B-17 bombed T/O. 4BW continued on to bases in North Africa. 2 1BW B-17s crashed in sea (1 91BG, 1 381BG), crews rescued. 8 4BW B-17s came down in the Mediterranean. 2 damaged 4BW B-17 crash-landed in Switzerland (390BG & 100BG). All 4BW groups received DUC for this mission. B/d 384BG B-17 c/l at base. B/d 303BG B-17 c/l Woolbridge A/F, crew safe. B/d 91BG B-17 cr. Manston after 7 baled.

VIII FC FO 106

Despatched		Groups	E/A	Losses MIA	E	Dam	Casualties KIA	WIA	MIA
P-47	240	4FG, 56FG, 78FG, 353FG	19–3–4	3	0	0	0	0	3

REMARKS: Fighters despatched on bomber penetration, although 56FG and 353FG flew a second formation as withdrawal support. Fighter group losses: 56FG – 3. Fighter group e/a credits:– 56FG – 17, 78FG – 2, 353FG – 1.

VIII ASC 23 & 24

	Despatched		Effective	Target	Bombs Tonnage	E/A	Losses MIA	E	Dam	Casualties KIA	WIA	MIA
3BW				BRYAS SUD A/F								
B-26	386BG	36	29	1051 hrs	232 × 300GP				2	0	0	
	387BG	36	0	POIX/NORD A/F					0	0	0	
	323BG	36	35	1552 hrs	279 × 300GP				20	0	1	0
TOTALS:		108	64		76.65	0	0	0	22	0	1	0

REMARKS: RAF Spitfire escort recalled 387BG.

7PG despatched 5 F-5 on PR to France.

The censor painted in a false waterway to mask the location in this view of two pieces of burning wreckage – part of an Me 110 – falling past 305BG Fortresses on 17 August.

INCIDENT

Leader of the high, composite group at the head of the Schweinfurt air task force was the 351st Group's Maj Clinton Ball, flying with Capt Harry Morse and crew. As Command Pilot, Ball was responsible for seeing that the composite group adhered to the briefed plan, and for making on the spot decisions to meet any contingencies that might arise during the course of the mission. This control could be exercised through directions to the pilot and, if necessary, over the appropriate radio channel to other aircraft in the formation. It was usual for the Command Pilot to take the co-pilot's seat while the co-pilot removed to the tail position where he could observe and report on the following bombers. But the Command Pilot was free to decide what position he would take in the aircraft and some chose to sit on a jump-seat behind the regular pilots; others to move to different locations as they saw fit.

On this occasion the leader had definite plans as he later recounted: 'I had decided that somewhere in World War II Clint Ball was going to shoot a 50-calibre machine gun at the enemy.' He picked the Schweinfurt mission to do so. 'After assembly of the lead wing I moved down to the nose compartment to join Lt Blair (bombardier) and Lt Shaw (navigator), and to man the right nose gun. The regular co-pilot had been assigned as tail gunner and he moved back up to the pilot's compartment. Now we were ready to shoot down the entire Luftwaffe! Anyhow, Morse led the group beautifully to the target and back. Fighter attacks were light on our formation out, but on the way back the enemy consolidated and was waiting. Line abreast, the German FWs hit us head-on. Empty cartridge cases three-to-four inches deep covered the floor of the nose. Glancing back during one attack, I stared into Shaw's startled, wide open eyes above his oxygen mask. He grabbed his groin and sank to the floor, grovelling through the shell cases. I thought he had been hit bad. Then would you believe it, Shaw got back to his feet, holding his navigator's chronograph (watch). What had happened was that Blair's front nose gun had jammed. He had lifted the base plate to clear the weapon, but forgot about the recoil spring which had flown rearward through the cabin, hitting Shaw hard in the privates and causing him to drop his chronograph. From the look on Shaw's face I thought Blair was about to become a casualty. We all got a laugh and went back to our guns.'

The original commander of the 511th Bomb Squadron, Clint Ball had the unique distinction in the USAAF of not only having his name embodied in the Squadron's official insignia – a ball device – but throughout the war new B-17s assigned to the unit were given nicknames featuring the word 'ball', e.g. *Fireball*, *Cannon Ball*, *High Ball*, *Belle of the Ball*, and so on, from a list of some 250.

During an air battle en route to Schweinfurt a photographer on 384BG's *Lucky Thirteen* took this graphic picture of a B-17 in its death throes with an FW 190 closing in on the victim.

A SIGHT THAT SURPASSED FICTION

The most graphic description of an air battle between a Fortress formation and Luftwaffe fighters is that prepared by Lt.Col Beirne Lay after his return from the *Shuttle* mission to Africa. It has appeared in abridged form in other publications, but it is given here in its entirety. Lay, a member of the VIII Bomber Command nucleus that General Eaker brought to the UK in February 1942, flew to Regensburg as an observer for 8th Air Force headquarters. His experiences on this and other missions are reflected in the epic film *Twelve O'Clock High* (1949) for which he wrote the screenplay with another former 8th Air Force Hq. officer, Sy Bartlett.

SUBJECT: Personal report on the REGENSBURG mission, 17 August 1943.
TO: Commanding Officer, 100th Bombardment Group (H).

1. This report does not attempt to render a complete summary of the mission. It is merely an eyewitness account of what was seen by the undersigned, together with certain recommendations pertinent thereto, during an ordeal in which the 100th Group fought its way to the target through fierce and prolonged enemy fighter attacks and accurately bombed a vital target.
2. When the 100th Group crossed the coast of Holland south of the Hague at 1008 hours at our base altitude of 17,000 ft, I was well situated to watch the proceedings, being co-pilot in the lead ship of the last element of the high squadron. The Group had all of its 21 B-17Fs tucked in tightly and was within handy supporting distance of the 95th Group, ahead of us at 18,000 ft. We were the last and lowest of the seven groups of a long, loose-linked chain in the bright sunlight – too long, it seemed. Wide gaps separated the three combat wings. As I sat there in the tail-end element of that many miles long procession, gauging the distance to the lead group, I had the lonesome foreboding that might come to the last man about to run a gauntlet lined with spiked clubs. The premonition was well founded.

At 1017 hrs, near Woensdrecht, I saw the first flak blossom out in our vicinity, light and inaccurate. A few minutes later, approximately 1025 hrs, two FW 190s appeared at 1 o'clock level and whizzed through the formation ahead of us in a frontal attack, nicking two B-17s of the 95th Group in the wings and breaking away beneath us in half-rolls. Smoke immediately trailed from both B-17s but they held their stations. As the fighters passed us

Survivors of the 100BG cross the Alps after bombing Regensburg. The nearest Fortress is Lt Robert Wulff's *Wolf Pack* with life raft door open, raft gone and a large dent in left tailplane where raft hit. Gash in fin was caused by 20 mm shell. The highest B-17 is *Laden Maiden* piloted by 'Cowboy' Roane which endured with 100BG for 31 missions. (Thorpe Abbotts Tower Assoc.)

Out of fuel a Fortress briefly floats in the 'Med' after a successful ditching. Picture taken from 385BG's *Yank*.

OA-10 42-109024 amphibian rescuing the crew of a Regensburg Fortress. Crewman on wing had secured a line to one raft to guide it to the hull. Supporting RAF search plane took the photo.

at a high rate of closure, the guns of our group went into action. The pungent smell of burnt powder filled our cockpit, and the B-17 trembled to the recoil of nose and ball-turret guns. I saw pieces fly off the wing of one of the fighters before they passed from view.

Here was early action. The members of the crew sensed trouble. There was something desperate about the way those two fighters came fast right out of their climb without any preliminaries. For a few seconds the interphone was busy with admonitions: 'Lead 'em more' . . . 'short bursts' . . . 'don't throw rounds away' . . . 'there'll be more along in a minute'.

Three minutes later, the gunners reported fighters climbing up from all around the clock, singly and in pairs, both FW 190s and Me 109Gs. This was only my fourth raid, but from what I could see on my side, it looked like too many fighters for sound health. A co-ordinated attack followed, with the head-on fighters coming in from slightly above, the 9 and 3 o'clock attackers approaching from about level, and the rear attackers from slightly below. Every gun from every B-17 in our Group and the 95th was firing, criss-crossing our patch of the sky with tracers to match the time-fuse cannon shell puffs that squirted from the wings of the Jerry single-seaters. I would estimate that 75 per cent of our fire was inaccurate, falling astern of the target – particularly the fire from hand-held guns. Nevertheless, both sides got hurt in this clash, with two B-17s from our low squadron and one from the 95th Group falling out of formation on fire with crews baling out, and several fighters heading for the deck in flames or with their pilots lingering behind under dirty yellow parachutes. Our group leader, Major John Kidd, pulled us nearer to the 95th Group for mutual support.

I knew that we were already in a lively fight. What I didn't know was that the real fight, the *Anschluss* of Luftwaffe 20 mm cannon shells, hadn't really begun. A few minutes later we absorbed the first wave of a hailstorm of individual fighter attacks that were to engulf us clear to the target. The ensuing action was so rapid and varied that I cannot give a chronological account of it. Instead, I will attempt a fragmentary report of salient details that even now give me a dry mouth and an unpleasant sensation in the stomach to recall. The sight was fantastic and surpassed fiction.

It was at 1041 hrs, over Eupen, that I looked out of my co-pilot's window after a short lull and saw two whole squadrons, 12 Me 109s and 11 FW 190s, climbing parallel to us. The first squadron had reached our level and was pulling ahead to turn into us and the second was not far behind. Several thousand feet below us were many more fighters, with their noses cocked at maximum climb. Over the interphone came reports of an equal number of enemy aircraft deploying on the other side. For the first time, I noticed an Me 110 sitting out of range on our right. He was to stay with us all the way to the target, apparently reporting our position to fresh squadrons waiting for us down the road. At the sight of all these fighters, I had the distinct feeling of being trapped – that the Hun was tipped off, or at least had guessed our destination and was waiting for us. No P-47s were visible. The life expectancy of the 100th Group suddenly seemed very short, since it had already appeared that the fighters were passing up the preceding groups, with the exception of the 95th, in order to take a cut at us.

Swinging their yellow noses around in a wide U-turn, the 12-ship squadron of Me 109s came in from 12 to 2 o'clock in pairs and in fours and the main event was on.

A shining silver object sailed past over our right wing. I recognised it as a main exit door. Seconds later a dark object came hurtling through the formation, barely missing several props. It was a man, clasping his knees to his head, revolving like a diver in a triple somersault. I didn't see his 'chute open.

A B-17 turned gradually out of the formation to the right, maintaining altitude. In a split second, the B-17 completely disappeared in a brilliant explosion, from which the only remains were four small balls of fire, the fuel tanks, which were quickly consumed as they fell earthward.

Our airplane was endangered by various debris. Emergency hatches, exit doors, prematurely opened parachutes, bodies, and assorted fragments of B-17s and Hun fighters breezed past us in the slip-stream.

I watched two fighters explode not far beneath, disappearing in sheets of orange flame, B-17s dropping out in every stage of distress, from engines on fire to control surfaces shot away, friendly and enemy parachutes floating down, and, on the green carpet far behind us, numerous funeral pyres of smoke from fallen fighters, marking our trail.

On we flew through the strewn wake of a desperate air battle, where disintegrating aircraft were commonplace and 60 'chutes in the air at one time were hardly worth a second look.

I watched a B-17 turn slowly out to the right with its cockpit a mass of flames. The co-pilot crawled out of his window, held on with one hand, reached back for his 'chute, buckled it on, let go and was whisked back into the horizontal stabiliser. I believe the impact killed him. His 'chute didn't open.

Ten minutes, twenty minutes, thirty minutes, and still no let-up in the attacks. The fighters queued up like a breadline and let us have it. Each second of time had a cannon shell in it. The strain of being a clay duck in the wrong end of that aerial shooting gallery became almost intolerable as the minutes accumulated toward the first hour.

Our B-17 shook steadily with the fire of its .50s and the air inside was heavy with smoke. It was cold in the cockpit, but when I looked across at Lt Thomas Murphy, the pilot, and a good one, sweat was pouring off his forehead and over his oxygen mask. He turned the controls over to me for a while. It was a blessed relief to concentrate on holding station in formation instead of watching those everlasting fighters boring in. It was possible to forget the fighters. Then the top-turret gunner's twin muzzles would pound away a foot above my head, giving a realistic imitation of cannon-shells exploding in the cockpit, while I gave an even better imitation of a man jumping six inches out of his seat.

A B-17 of the 95th Group, with its right Tokyo tanks* on fire, dropped back to about 200 ft above our right wing and stayed there while seven of the crew successively baled out. Four went out the bomb-bay and executed delayed jumps, one baled from

* The popular name for the additional long-range fuel tanks installed in the outer wing sections of the B-17.

The 385BG's *Sly Fox* reached North Africa safely only to run a main wheel off the PSP track while taxiing and lose its tail fin and rudder in the resulting swing into another aircraft. Note carburettor air filter box under No.4 engine. This was a special fitment on Shuttle aircraft to cope with blowing sand.

the nose, opened his chute prematurely and nearly fouled the tail. Another went out the left waist-gun opening, delaying his 'chute opening for a safe interval. The tail gunner dropped out of his hatch, apparently pulling the ripcord before he was clear of the ship. His 'chute opened instantaneously, barely missing the tail, and jerked him so hard that both his shoes came off. He hung limp in the harness, whereas the others had showed immediate signs of life after their 'chutes opened, shifting around in the harness. The B-17 then dropped back in a medium spiral and I did not see the pilots leave. I saw it just before it passed from view, several thousand feet below us, with its right wing a solid sheet of yellow flame.

After we had been under constant attack for a solid hour, it appeared certain that the 100th Group was faced with annihilation. Seven of our group had been shot down, the sky was still mottled with rising fighters and it was only 1120 hours, with target-time still 35 minutes away. I doubt if a man in the group visualised the possibility of our getting much further without 100 per cent loss. I knew that I had long since mentally accepted the fact of death, and that it was simply a question of the next second or the next minute. I learned first-hand that a man can resign himself to the certainty of death without becoming panicky. Our group fire power was reduced 33 per cent, ammunition was running low. Our tail-guns had to be replenished from another gun station. Gunners were becoming exhausted and nerve-tortured from the prolonged strain, and there was an awareness on everybody's part that something must have gone wrong. We had been the aiming point for what seemed like most of the Luftwaffe and we fully expected to find the rest of it primed for us at the target.

Fighter tactics were running fairly true to form. Frontal attackers hit the low squadron and lead squadron, while rear attackers went for the high. The manner of their attacks showed that some pilots were old-timers, some amateurs, and that all knew pretty definitely where we were going and were inspired with a fanatical determination to stop us before we got there. The old-timers came in on frontal attacks with a noticeably slower rate of closure, apparently throttled back, obtaining greater accuracy than those that bolted and in many cases seemed able to time their thrusts so as to catch the top and ball turret gunners engaged with rear and side attacks. Less experienced pilots were pressing attacks home to 250 yds and less to get hits, offering point-blank targets on the break-away, firing long bursts of 20 seconds, and, in some cases, actually pulling up instead of going down and out. Several FW pilots pulled off some first rate deflection shooting on side attacks against the high group, then raked the low group on the break-away out of a side-slip, keeping the nose cocked up in the turn to prolong the period the formation was in their sights.

I observed what I believe was an attempt at air-to-air bombing, although I didn't see the bombs dropped. A patch of 75 to 100 grey-white bursts, smaller than flak bursts, appeared simultaneously at our level, off to one side.

One B-17 dropped out on fire and put its wheels down while the crew baled out. Three Me 109s circled it closely, but held their fire, apparently ensuring that no one stayed in the ship to try for home. I saw Hun fighters hold their fire even when being shot at by a B-17 from which the crew was baling out.

Near the IP, at 1150 hrs, one hour and a half after the first of at least 200 individual fighter attacks, the pressure eased off, although hostiles were still in the vicinity. We turned at the IP at 1154 hrs with 14 B-17s left in the group, two of which were badly crippled. They dropped out soon after bombing the target and headed for Switzerland, one of them '042', carrying Col William Kennedy as tail-gunner. No.4 engine was on fire, but not out of control. Major William Veal, leader of the high squadron, received a cannon shell in his No.3 engine just before the start of the bombing run and went into the target with the prop feathered.

Weather over the target, as on the entire trip, was ideal. Flak was negligible. The group got its bombs away promptly on the leader. As we turned and headed for the Alps, I got a grim satisfaction out of seeing a rectangular column of smoke rising straight up from the Me 109 shops, with only one burst over in the town of Regensburg.

The rest of the trip was a marked anti-climax. A few more fighters pecked at us on the way to the Alps. A town in the Brenner pass tossed up a lone burst of futile flak. Col LeMay, who had taken excellent care of us all the way, circled the air division over Lake Garda long enough to give the cripples a chance to join the family, and we were on our way toward the Mediterranean in a gradual descent. About 25 fighters on the ground at Verona stayed on the ground. The prospect of ditching as we approached Bone, short of fuel, and the sight of other B-17s falling into the drink, seemed trivial matters after the vicious nightmare of the long trip across southern Germany. We felt the reaction of men who had not expected to see another sunset.

At 1815 hrs, with red lights showing on all our fuel tanks in my ship, the seven B-17s of the group who were still in formation circled over Bertoux and landed in the dust. Our crew was unscratched. Sole damage to the airplane: a bit of ventilation around the tail from flak and 20 mm shells. We slept on the hard ground under the wings of our B-17, but the good earth felt softer than a silk pillow.

3. Recommendations:

a. That combat wings always comprise three groups, spaced close enough for mutual support, on deep penetrations and that the interval between combat wings be as close as is flyable in order to cut down the over-all distance from the head to the tail of the column. This should result in a more even distribution of fighter attacks with lower average loss per group. Enemy *Staffeln* near their fuel limits did not try to catch preceding groups but concentrated on the tail of the long column we presented on the Regensburg mission.

b. That fighter escorts give particular attention to protection of rear groups on deep penetrations. I would judge that 17,000 ft,

A 20 mm cannon shell from an FW 190 clipped the wing tip of 390BG's *Devil's Daughter* during the air battle for Regensburg.

Diversions to support the major heavy bomber mission on 17 August came from RAF and US medium bombers. *Utah Gamecock*, seen rising from Earls Colne, was one of 323BG's Marauders sent to bomb Poix fighter base. VIII ASC's B-26s carried out regular attacks on enemy airfields within their range during the high summer of 1943. Much of the heavy armament of five fixed and seven flexible guns shows in this view.

our base altitude, was too low – an awkward altitude for P-47s – even if fighter escort had covered us, which it didn't.

c. That emphasis on deflection shooting on the part of our gunners be continued and intensified. A B-17 group can put out tremendous fire power, and the 100th Group did some accurate shooting, but too many of the gunners were firing on targets that had just left.

d. That groups expecting to operate on the return trip from North African airdromes carry with them engine, gun and radio compartment covers for protection against dust and mud.

e. That continued thought be given to further protective measures in the formation for the low squadron, which in our group, at least, was the AP for frontal attacks.

f. That better exchange of information be provided between air divisions. Even several days after a mission, groups in the 4th Air Division have little knowledge of what happened to the 1st Air Division, except through hearsay.

g. That 30 combat missions be reduced to 25 for crews that have engaged in deep penetrations. It takes a rugged constitution to stand up to missions like Regensburg and even the toughest crew members were badly shaken by nearly two hours under persistent attack. The less phlegmatic were already potential candidates for the rest home when we landed in Africa. My four previous missions, in one of which our bombardier was killed, were pieces of cake in comparison to the 11 hour Regensburg show, and I doubt if 20 such normal missions would take the same amount out of a man as one stint to Regensburg.

4. *Awards:* The following suggested awards are recommended to the attention of the Group Commander.

a. DISTINGUISHED FLYING CROSS: To every combat crew member of the 100th Group who participated in the Regensburg mission, for courage and achievement in enabling the group to reach and successfully bomb a vital target against odds that could easily have resulted in 100 per cent loss had it not been for the outstanding air discipline of the group as a whole. A tight formation was held, in spite of reshuffling of the group from consecutive losses, and cool judgement and self-control were exercised by individual crews under prolonged strain.

b. DISTINGUISHED SERVICE CROSS:

Maj John Kidd, group leader, for heroism and skill in his leadership of the group to target and final destination. This 24-year-old officer carried out superbly an assignment above and beyond the call of duty for an officer of his age and experience. He had had only three previous missions.

Maj William Veal, leader of the high squadron, for heroic and skillful leadership of his squadron. Just before turning in to the bombing run, a cannon shell hit his No.3 engine, setting it on fire, and oxygen failure occurred. Instead of turning toward the safety of the Swiss border, approximately 65 miles distant, Major Veal feathered his No.3 prop, a sure tip-off to the fighters in the vicinity, in order to regain position in the formation. He successfully bombed the target, extinguished the engine fire, crossed the Alps and several hundred miles of Mediterranean and reached base in North Africa, all on three engines.

c. Lt Wolff, a wing man in the lead squadron. The under-signed did not have an opportunity to interview Lt Wolff or his crew, but observed his ship hobbling along with the formation all the way to North Africa in spite of what looked like the worst battle damage of any airplane in the group. Appropriate investigation and award is recommended.

d. CONGRESSIONAL MEDAL OF HONOR:

Major Gale W. Cleven, leader of the low squadron. Throughout approximately two hours of constant fighter attack, Major Cleven's squadron was the principal focal point of the enemy's fire. Early in the encounter, south of Antwerp, he lost his entire second element of three B-17s, yet maintained his vulnerable and exposed position in the formation rigidly in order to keep his guns uncovered.

Approximately 30 minutes before reaching the target his airplane received the following battle damage. A 20 mm cannon shell penetrated the right side of the airplane and exploded beneath the pilot, damaging the electrical system and injuring the top turret gunner in the leg. A second 20 mm shell entered the radio compartment, killing the radio operator, who bled to death with his legs severed above the knees. A third 20 mm shell entered the left side of the nose, tearing out a section of plexiglass about two feet square, tore away the right hand nose-gun installation and injured the bombardier in the head and shoulder. A fourth 20 mm shell penetrated the right wing into the fuselage and shattered the hydraulic system, releasing fluid all around the cockpit. A fifth 20 mm shell entered the cabin roof and severed the rudder cables to one side of the rudder. A sixth 20 mm cannon shell exploded in the No.3 engine, destroying all engine controls. The engine caught fire and lost its power, but the fire eventually died out.

Winching a 500 lb HE bomb into the bay of a 386BG B-26 in preparation for the 17 August mission. Bomb shackle fitted to lugs on top of bomb will be attached to vertical rack on central walkway. Bay was as large as a B-17's.

Confronted with structural damage, partial loss of control, fire in the air and serious injuries to personnel, and faced with fresh waves of fighters still rising to the attack, Major Cleven had every justification for abandoning ship. His crew, some of them comparatively inexperienced youngsters, were preparing to bale out, since no other course appeared open. The co-pilot pleaded repeatedly with Major Cleven to abandon ship. Major Cleven's reply at this critical juncture was blunt. His strong words were heard over the interphone and had a magical effect on the crew. They stuck to their guns. The airplane continued to the target, bombed it and reached base in North Africa.

Sgt Ferroggiaro, left waist gunner and veteran of the war in China in 1932 and of 7 months at the front in Spain in 1938, voiced the opinion of the crew to the under-signed when he stated that the completion of the mission was solely due to the extraordinary heroism and inspired determination of Major Cleven. The under-signed believes that under the circumstances which obtained, Major Cleven's actions were far above and beyond the call of duty, and that the skill, courage and strength of will displayed by him as airplane and squadron commander in the face of hopeless odds have seldom, if ever, been surpassed in the annals of the Army Air Forces.

5. It is requested that should any portion of this report be used for public relations purposes, the name of the under-signed be strictly withheld and that reference be made only to 'an officer'.

Beirne Lay, Jr.
Lt. Colonel, A.D.

There were so many examples of bravery among 8th Air Force combat men at this time that Lay's specific recommendations were not upheld; but Maj Cleven did receive a DSC for his actions.

18 AUGUST 1943

VIII ASC 25A & 25B

	Despatched		Effective	Target	Bombs Tonnage	E/A	Losses MIA	E	Dam	Casualties KIA	WIA	MIA
3BW				YPRES/VLAMERTINGHE								
B-26	322BG	36	22	A/F 1016 hrs (O)	206 × 300GP				23	0	0	0
				WOENSDRECHT (P)								
	386BG	36	32	A/F 1032 hrs	250 × 300GP				8	0	0	0
TOTALS:		72	54		76.5	0	0	0	31	0	0	0

REMARKS: Boxted A/F bombed by e/a at night. 322BG briefed to attack Lille/Vendeville.

VIII ASC 26

	Despatched		Effective	Target	Bombs Tonnage	E/A	Losses MIA	E	Dam	Casualties KIA	WIA	MIA
3BW				LANNION/BREST			0	0	0	0	0	0
A-20	67RG	2	2	PENN. (PHOTO RECON)								

REMARKS: Escorted by RAF Spitfires of 610 Sqn. First mission for 67RG units.

VIII FC FO 107

Despatched		Groups	E/A	Losses MIA	E	Dam	Casualties KIA	WIA	MIA
P-47	40	353FG	0	0	0	0	0	0	0

REMARKS: Carried out sweeps in Westhoofd, Woensdrecht and Knokke area.

7PG despatched 4 F-5 on PR to France but one broke up over coast going out, pilot baled.

INCIDENT

The only Lockheed Lightnings on combat operations from England during the summer of 1943 were the 7th Photo Group's F-5 models. The lone, unarmed photographic sorties incurred a relatively high loss ratio although not always through enemy action. One such loss occurred on 18 August and involved a new F-5A-10 and F/O Malcolm 'Doc' Hughes.

'I took off from base at 0720 hours to photograph my target near Lille, France. After gaining altitude I passed over base at 15,000 ft and continued to climb to 35,000 ft. The mission was not deep into enemy territory, so I carried no extra fuel tanks. I headed

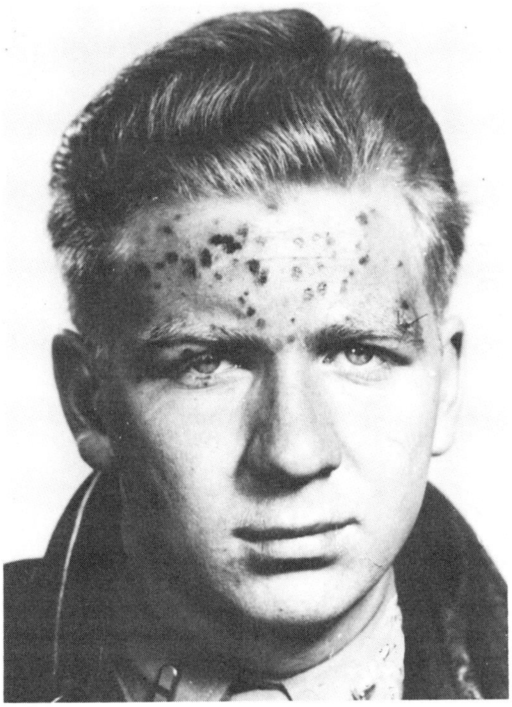

Doc Hughes exhibiting the results of hail stone damage.

south and east directly towards my target, over 10/10ths cloud.

At 35,000 ft I felt my aircraft surge once or twice and noticed light hail on the windscreen. The storm didn't seem unusually severe. Then with a shudder, the altimeter started up and climbed rapidly to about 40,000 ft where it suddenly stopped and started down with another shudder. I had not moved the controls.

I looked behind, and to my amazement saw the tail assembly gone. The aircraft was out of my control. My first thought was to bale out, and I jettisoned the hood. But by now what remained of my kite was in a spin and the airspeed was mounting rapidly. I couldn't move; centrifugal force pinned me to the cockpit. The air speed indicator registered 450 mph. My nose was bleeding.

I was finally able to roll down the left window, and using the rear view mirror for a brace, pulled myself out. The strong wind carried me off the wing, pulling the mask off my face. I felt my leg strike the boom. Then I felt a stinging sensation about my face but thought it was the wind. I started falling, tumbling over and over again, but there was really no sensation of falling – just the rush of air and fog against me.

The moment before I left the cockpit I again checked the altimeter, which indicated 25,000 ft and having no bale-out oxygen bottle, decided to delay the opening of the 'chute until I was closer to earth.

As I tumbled over and over several times I thought it time to pull the rip-cord and in fact started to pull it, but then decided to wait longer, as I originally planned. After falling for some time I decided I must pull the rip-cord now, when suddenly I broke through the clouds and could see the ground about 5,000 ft below me. I jerked the cord and found myself hanging by my left leg head downward. I managed after a struggle to untangle my leg from the shrouds and righted myself, floating to the ground. I found myself in a beet field.

This was the first time I had seen the ground since I took off from my airdrome. My parachute had opened over water but I drifted a half mile inland – but in what country? I didn't know. I landed facing into the wind and had some difficulty spilling my 'chute, and it dragged me. I kept looking about to see what I could recognise. Nothing seemed familiar. Three military trucks were parked in the distance but I couldn't recognise the style. My first thought was that I must be in enemy territory and I began to make plans of escape when I saw two people on the other side of the field rushing towards me and I knew concealment and escape was undoubtedly hopeless.

The two people turned out to be English girls and I was never so overjoyed in my life at seeing English girls – I knew I had landed in England.'

Subsequent examination of the tail wreckage established that a trim tab control rod had broken allowing elevator flutter to develop and precipitating the aircraft's break-up. As a result modifications were made to all Lightnings, and the 7th Group's were grounded for two weeks.

19 AUGUST 1943

VIII BC 85

		Despatched	Effective	Target	Bombs Tonnage	E/A	Losses MIA	E	Dam	Casualties KIA	WIA	MIA
1BW				GILZE–RIJEN A/F								
B-17	91BG	8	8	38 a/c 1802–1814 hrs	519 × 100GP	2–0–0	0		2	0	0	0
	92BG	19	17	& FLUSHING A/F	222 × 20 Frag	0–0–0	0		4	0	1	0
	303BG	20	10	55 a/c 1756 hrs		21–1–2	2		14	0	6	21
	305BG	19	18		880 × 300GP	0–0–0	1		18	0	2	10
	306BG	20	20			0–0–0	0		0	0	0	0
	351BG	9	7			5–0–0	0		1	0	0	0
	379BG	16	8			0–0–0	0		1	0	0	0
	381BG	7	5			1–0–0	1		2	0	0	10
	384BG	7	0			0–0–0	0		0	0	0	0
TOTALS:		125	93		180.2	29–1–2	4	0	42	0	9	41

		Despatched	Effective	Target	Bombs Tonnage	E/A	Losses MIA	E	Dam	KIA	WIA	MIA
4BW				WOENSDRECHT A/F								
B-17	94BG	3				0–0–0	0	0	1	0	0	0
	95BG	7				0–0–0	0	0	2	0	0	0
	96BG	8				0–0–0	0	1	0	0	0	0
	100BG	7				0–0–0	0	0	1	0	0	0
	385BG	6				0–1–0	0	0	0	0	0	0
	388BG	7				0–0–0	1	0	0	0	0	10
	390BG	7				1–0–2	0	0	4	0	0	0
TOTALS:		45	0			1–1–2	1	1	8	0	0	10

REMARKS: Weather prevented 4BW bombing. During assembly a 96BG B-17 caught fire, c/l Wolferton Sands.

VIII FC FO 108

Despatched		Groups	E/A	Losses MIA	E	Dam	Casualties KIA	WIA	MIA
P-47	175	4FG, 56FG, 78FG, 353FG	9–2–4	1	0	0	0	0	1

REMARKS: Bombers made two orbits in target area before turning for home, causing fighters to stay much longer than planned. 4FG and 78FG as penetration support, 56FG and 353FG as withdrawal. Fighter group losses: 56FG – 1. Fighter group e/a credits:– 56FG – 9, 78FG – 1.

VIII ASC 27A, 27B & 28

	Despatched		Effective	Target	Bombs Tonnage	E/A	Losses MIA	E	Dam	Casualties KIA	WIA	MIA
3BW				AMIENS/GLISY A/F								
B-26	323BG	36	36	1129 hrs POIX/	351 × 300GP	1–0–2		1	9	0	2	0
	387BG	36	35	NORD A/F 1218 hrs	350 × 300GP	0–0–0		0	1	0	0	0
	322BG	36	0	BRYAS SUD A/F	0	0–0–0		0	9	0	0	0
TOTALS:		108	71		105.15	1–0–2	0	1	19	0	2	0

REMARKS: 322BG found target obscured by cloud. 323BG B-26 c/l base on return.

VIII ASC 29

	Despatched		Effective	Target	Bombs Tonnage	E/A	Losses MIA	E	Dam	Casualties KIA	WIA	MIA
3BW				PHOTO RECON								
A-20	67RG	2	2	LANNION/BREST	–	0	0	0	0	0	0	0

REMARKS: Escort of RAF Spitfires, 610 Sqn.

7PG despatched 7 F-5 on PR to France.

INCIDENT

During the latter half of 1943 an increasing number of B-17s were destroyed by fires originating in the top turret. The cause was an electrical short, resulting from the revolving action of the turret fraying cables and oxygen lines where they passed through the central spigot. One instance occurred on 19 August when the 96th Group despatched eight Fortresses to head an attack on Woensdrecht airfield. At the front was *Black Heart Jr* in which Col James Travis, 403rd Wing executive officer, was flying as air commander. As this Fortress led the formation over Norfolk at 13,000 ft its engineer reported a turret fire. Shortly afterwards an oxygen bottle exploded and flames swept through the flight deck. Fearing a further explosion, the pilot, 2/Lt Attaway, manoeuvred *Black Heart Jr* out of formation nearly colliding with another B-17, *Dry Run III*. He then gave the bale out alarm, opened the side window so that the slipstream swept flames and fumes to the rear, set the automatic pilot to direct the bomber out to sea, and joined Travis and four other crew members in the nose.

As the men started to bale out a second explosion occurred, ripping away part of the nose near the entrance hatch, miraculously without causing serious injury to anyone. The co-pilot, 2/Lt Matthew Vinson, then made the horrifying discovery that his parachute was missing, probably due to the explosion. By this time only bombardier John Miller remained with Vinson, and informed of the co-pilot's predicament he suggested they cling to one another and jump together. Vinson thought this suicidal, refused and persuaded Miller to leave. There was the possibility of a spare parachute in the rear of the aircraft. Climbing back through the smouldering flight deck Vinson tried to open the door leading to the bomb-bay, but the handle was too hot to hold and the door wouldn't budge. He then realised his only hope of survival was to try and crash-land the burning aircraft. Going back to the cockpit, he found that air streaming in through a fracture in the windshield was clearing fire and fumes. The pilots' seats had been badly burned and after releasing the auto-pilot he had to balance over the control wheel in a crouching position. Amazingly, despite the fire damage, the bomber still responded to the controls. Vinson's anxiety was such that he hardly noticed the searing pain from his face and hands. The windshield was blackened by smoke and he could only see out through the open side windows. He caught a glimpse of the coast below; the B-17 was down to about 2,000 ft. Gently he flew towards the water, aiming for a sand bank. As the aircraft touched and skidded along, the propeller from No.1 engine came off and slashed into the nose. Immediately *Black Heart Jr* came to a stop Vinson squeezed out of the cockpit window and ran, only to trip and fall after a few yards. Civilians who had seen the crash came to his aid and helped the shocked, exhausted and blackened pilot to safety. The heavy flying clothes he was wearing had protected him from much of the flames but he was badly burned about the face and hands. Meanwhile the fire had taken a firm hold in the Fortress and fifteen minutes after coming down the bomb load exploded, scattering wreckage in The Wash off Wolferton. This extraordinary feat of survival earned Vinson a DSC.

The first men to return from the North African shuttle mission were high rank officers and those combat crews whose bombers were beyond economical repair. Some 100BG personnel arrived back at Thorpe Abbotts on 22 August and included John Egan, 418BS CO. Raconteur and humourist, Egan relates his experiences in the Interrogation Room while wearing a souvenir fez adorned with his Major's insignia. One of 100BG's most illustrious pilots he was lost leading the notorious Münster mission which brought 100BG its epithet The Bloody Hundredth. He survived as a POW.

22 AUGUST 1943

VIII ASC 30A & 30B

	Despatched		Effective	Target	Bombs Tonnage	E/A	Losses MIA	E	Dam	Casualties KIA	WIA	MIA
3BW				BEAUMONT LE ROGER A/F								
B-26	386BG	36	35	2110 hrs	344 × 300GP	3–0–0	1		8	0	1	6
	322BG	36	0	POIX/NORD A/F	0		0		0	0	0	0
TOTALS:		72	35		51.6	3–0–0	1	0	8	0	1	6

REMARKS: 322BG returned early as they were unable to contact RAF Spitfire escort.

23 AUGUST 1943

VIII ASC 31A & 31B

	Despatched		Effective	Target	Bombs Tonnage	E/A	Losses MIA	E	Dam	Casualties KIA	WIA	MIA
3BW				GOSNAY P/S								
B-26	322BG	21	0	POIX/NORD A/F								
	386BG	36	0									
TOTALS:		57	0		0	0	0	0	0	0	0	0

REMARKS: Cloud covered targets.

VIII ASC 32

	Despatched		Effective	Target	Bombs Tonnage	E/A	Losses MIA	E	Dam	Casualties KIA	WIA	MIA
				PHOTO RECON	–	0	0	0	0	0	0	0
A-20	67RG	2	2	ST.MICHEL								

VIII FC FO 111

Despatched		Groups	E/A	Losses MIA	E	Dam	Casualties KIA	WIA	MIA
P-47	158	4FG, 56FG, 78FG, 353FG	0	0	0	0	0	0	0

REMARKS: Sent on fighter sweeps of Bruges/Woensdrecht/Schipol area, with 353FG simulating bombers.

24 AUGUST 1943

VIII BC 86 PART I

	Despatched		Effective	Target	Bombs Tonnage	E/A	Losses MIA	E	Dam	Casualties KIA	WIA	MIA
1BW				VILLACOUBLAY A/D								
B-17	91BG	14	0	1800–1805 hrs	1029 × 500GP				5	0	0	0
	92BG	19	17						14	0	2	0
	305BG	18	17			1–0–1			6	0	4	0
	306BG	18	18						17	0	4	0
	351BG	22	16						9	0	0	0
	379BG	12	12						5	0	0	0
	381BG	7	6						8	0	0	0
TOTALS:		110	86		257.2	1–0–1	0	0	64	0	10	0
1BW				DIVERSION								
B-17	303BG	18	18									
	379BG	6	6									
	384BG	12	11									
TOTALS:		36	35			0–0–0	0	0	0	0	0	0
4BW				CONCHES A/F								
B-17	94BG	6	0	& EVREUX/	496 clusters				0	0	0	0
	95BG	7	6	FAUVILLE A/F	6 × 20 lb Frag				7	0	3	0
	96BG	3	3	1844–1858 hrs					0	0	0	0
	100BG	7	7						2	0	2	0
	385BG	6	0						0	0	0	0
	388BG	6	0						0	0	0	0
	390BG	7	6			0–0–2	1		6	1	4	0
TOTALS:		42	22		29.7	0–0–2	1	0	15	1	9	0

REMARKS: Weather prevented rest of 4BW a/c bombing. B/d 390BG B-17 ditched on return, 1 man lost, rest of crew rescued.

The 305BG setting out for the target on 24 August. The Fortress marked KY-G is one of 305BG's original complement of 36 still surviving. It would return from this its 36th mission and others to finally escape the war by limping into Switzerland in September 1943.

VIII FC FO 112

Despatched		Groups	E/A	Losses MIA	E	Dam	Casualties KIA	WIA	MIA
P-47	166	4FG, 56FG, 78FG, 353FG	6–1–6	0			0	0	0

REMARKS: Escort for B-17s. Fighter group e/a credits:– 56FG – 3, 78FG – 2, 353FG – 1.

VIII BC 86 PART II

	Despatched		Effective	Target	Bombs Tonnage	E/A	Losses MIA	E	Dam	Casualties KIA	WIA	MIA
4BW				BORDEAUX/MERIGNAC								
B-17	94BG	17	12	A/F	567 × 500GP	0–0– 2	1	0		0	0	10
	95BG	8	3	1157–1200 hrs		1–0– 4	0	0		0	0	0
	96BG	15	14			0–0– 0	0	0		0	0	0
	100BG	6	5			0–0– 0	0	0		0	0	0
	385BG	13	0			0–1– 0	2	0		0	0	20
	388BG	16	15			0–1– 1	0	2		0	0	0
	390BG	10	9			2–1– 3	0	0		0	0	0
TOTALS:		85	58		141.75	3–3–10	3	2	40	0	0	30

REMARKS: Attacked Bordeaux/Merignac A/F en route to England from North Africa. 9 a/c in difficulties returned to North Africa. 385BG B-17 came down in sea off Lands End, 8 of crew saved. 388BG B-17 Cat E in Africa. Another 388BG B-17 c/l at Stanton, Suffolk.

VIII ASC 33A & 33B

B-26s flew 2 diversions for heavy bombers.

25 AUGUST 1943

VIII ASC 34A & 34B

	Despatched		Effective	Target	Bombs Tonnage	E/A	Losses MIA	E	Dam	Casualties KIA	WIA	MIA
3BW				ROUEN P/S								
B-26	387BG	21	21	1832 hrs	63 × 1000GP	0–0–0			2	0	0	0
	322BG	36	31	TRICQUEVILLE A/F								
				1834 hrs	295 × 300GP	1–8–5			2	0	0	0
TOTALS:		57	52		75.75	1–8–5	0	0	4	0	0	0

VIII FC FO 114

Despatched		Groups	E/A	Losses MIA	E	Dam	Casualties KIA	WIA	MIA
P-47	90	56FG, 353FG	0	0	0	0	0	0	0

REMARKS: Carried out sweeps in Dunkirk/Lille/Le Touquet area.

26 AUGUST 1943

VIII ASC 35

	Despatched		Effective	Target	Bombs Tonnage	E/A	Losses MIA	E	Dam	Casualties KIA	WIA	MIA
3BW				CAEN/CARPIQUET								
B-26	323BG	36	36	A/F 1846 hrs	47.5	0	0	1	0	0	0	0

REMARKS: 323BG B-26 overshot Shoreham and crash landed 1 mile east of airfield, crew safe.

27 AUGUST 1943

VIII BC 87

	Despatched		Effective	Target	Bombs Tonnage	E/A	Losses MIA	E	Dam	Casualties KIA	WIA	MIA
1BW				WATTEN V/S								
B-17	91BG	13	11	1846–1941 hrs	368 × 2000GP	1–0–2	0	0	9	0	0	1
	92BG	19	16			0–0–0	1	1	13	1	4	0
	303BG	20	19			0–0–0	1	0	15	0	4	10
	305BG	18	17			0–0–0	1	0	5	0	1	11
	306BG	18	9			0–0–0	0	0	10	0	2	0
	351BG	22	20			5–0–1	1	0	12	0	1	10
	379BG	21	21			1–0–2	0	0	5	0	3	0
	381BG	10	10			0–0–0	0	0	9	0	0	0
	384BG	18	1			0–0–1	0	0	5	0	3	0
4BW				WATTEN V/S								
B-17	94BG	11	11	1846–1941 hrs		0–0–0	0	0	5	0	0	0
	95BG	7	7			0–0–0	0	0	1	0	0	0
	96BG	9	9			0–0–0	0	0	0	0	0	0
	100BG	7	7			0–0–0	0	0	1	0	0	0
	385BG	12	10			0–0–0	0	0	3	0	0	0
	388BG	12	12			0–0–0	0	0	5	0	0	0
	390BG	7	7			0–0–0	0	0	0	0	0	0
TOTALS:		224	187		368.0	7–0–6	4	1	98	1	18	32

REMARKS: First 8AF attack on V-weapon sites. 92BG B-17 came down in sea, crew rescued. 1 B-17 dropped 2 × 2000GP on a T/O. B/d 92BG B-17 c/l base.

VIII FC FO 116

Despatched		Groups	E/A	Losses MIA	E	Dam	Casualties KIA	WIA	MIA
P-47	173	4FG, 56FG, 78FG, 353FG	8–1–2	1	0	0	0	0	1

REMARKS: Escort and support for B-17s. One flight from 56FG was bounced by Spitfires, resulting in damage to one aircraft. Fighter group losses:– 353FG – 1.

On the line; Molesworth: 27 August. Work around *Walleroo*. To aid bombardiers of other aircraft in a formation, the leadplane's bombs were usually painted in bright colours to make them more easily seen after release. These 500 pounders are painted red and white.

On the line; Molesworth: 27 August. Work around *Miss Bea Haven*. Another engine change under threatening skies. It took a day to make the complete change and on average 40 engines were changed a week at a bomber base. In the background stands the *Duchess*, the Fortress in which 8AF's first Medal of Honor was earned.

On the line; Molesworth: 27 August. Work around *The 8 Ball Mk II*. While the crew chief runs up engines, ordnance men fix arming wires on 100 lb demolition bombs.

The 303BG contingent takes off from Molesworth's runway 27 for the first 8AF attack on a V-weapon site, 27 August. An aircraft became airborne every minute. Bringing up the rear is *Yankee Doodle Dandy*.

VIII ASC 36A & 36B

	Despatched		Effective	Target	Bombs Tonnage	E/A	Losses MIA	E	Dam	Casualties KIA	WIA	MIA
3BW				POIX NORD A/F		0	0	0		0	0	0
B-26	386BG	36	35	0826 hrs	349 × 300GP							
	322BG	21	0	ROUEN P/S	0	1–8–5	1	0		0	2	6
TOTALS:		57	35		52.35	1–8–5	1	0	6	0	2	6

REMARKS: 322BG unable to bomb because of cloud cover.

VIII ASC 37

	Despatched		Effective	Target	Bombs Tonnage	E/A	Losses MIA	E	Dam	Casualties KIA	WIA	MIA
3BW				PHOTO RECON								
A-20	67RG	2	2	NW FRANCE		0	0	0	0	0	0	0

30 AUGUST 1943

VIII ASC 38

	Despatched		Effective	Target	Bombs Tonnage	E/A	Losses MIA	E	Dam	Casualties KIA	WIA	MIA
3BW				EPERLECQUES M/D								
B-26	323BG	36	33	1859 hrs	48.75	0	0	0	14	0	3	0

31 AUGUST 1943

VIII BC 88

	Despatched		Effective	Target	Bombs Tonnage	E/A	Losses MIA	E	Dam	Casualties KIA	WIA	MIA
1BW				AMIENS/GLISY A/F (L)								
B-17	91BG	16	7	1807–1824 hrs	1240 × 500GP	0–0–0	2	1	3	5	3	22
	92BG	19	18			0–0–0	0	0	1	0	0	0
	303BG	20	9			0–0–0	1	0	3	0	0	11
	305BG	18	17			3–0–3	0	0	9	0	4	0
	306BG	18	0			0–0–0	0	0	10	0	0	0
	351BG	21	19			1–0–0	0	0	6	0	0	0
	379BG	21	16			1–1–0	0	0	1	0	1	0
	381BG	19	19			0–0–0	0	0	2	0	0	0
	384BG	18	0			0–0–0	0	0	0	0	0	0
TOTAL:		170	105		310.0	5–1–3	3	1	35	5	8	33
4BW												
B-17	94BG	21	0					0	0	0	0	0
	95BG	22	1		12 × 500GP			0	0	0	0	0
	96BG	21	0					0	2	0	0	0
	100BG	19	0					0	0	0	0	0
	385BG	21	0					0	0	0	0	0
	388BG	22	0					0	2	0	0	0
	390BG	23	0					0	15	0	1	0
TOTALS:		149	1		3.0	0–0–0	0	0	19	0	1	0

REMARKS: 4BW primary Meulan aircraft plant cloud covered. Only 1 95BG a/c bombed a T/O – railway NE of Rouen. Going out 2 91BG B-17s collided off English coast and fell into sea, debris damaging another 91BG B-17 which cr. at Polegate. 1BW primary was Romilly A/D.

31 AUGUST 1943 *(contd.)*

VIII FC FO 119

Despatched		Groups	E/A	Losses MIA	E	Dam	Casualties KIA	WIA	MIA
P-47	160	4FG, 56FG, 78FG, 353FG	2–1–1	2	0	0	0	0	2

REMARKS: Escort and support for B-17s. 2 353FG P-47s collided south of St.Omer.

VIII ASC 39A, 39B & 39B & 40

	Despatched		Effective	Target	Bombs Tonnage	E/A	Losses MIA	E	Dam	Casualties KIA	WIA	MIA
3BW				MAZINGARBE P/S								
B-26	322BG	36	33	0718 hrs	96 × 1000GP		0	0	1	0	0	0
	387BG	36	36	LILLE/VENDEVILLE A/F 0721 hrs	359 × 300GP		1	0	11	0	2	6
	322BG	36	0	HESDIN			0	0	0	0	0	0
	386BG	36	0				0	0	0	0	0	0
TOTALS:		144	69		101.85	0	1	0	12	0	2	6

REMARKS: 10/10 cloud prevented 323BG and 386BG bombing.

INCIDENT

Col William Gross, the 'Boss' of 101st Combat Wing, advocated the use of VHF radio in aiding assembly and control of formations during a mission. From the outset of operations VIII Bomber Command had adopted the RAF's law of radio silence to avoid giving the German listening service intelligence. Gross argued that prudent use of bomber communications could add little to the enemy's knowledge as once the B-17s were at radar detection altitude the enemy would be well aware of an impending raid, and such was the size of the formations he was unlikely to lose track of them over his own territory. There was some scepticism as to the value of VHF control among his command but Gross proved his point by airborne radio direction of a large formation in a trial over a Cambridge–Ely–Thetford circuit. An opportunity to show how VHF command could benefit the outcome of a combat mission came on 31 August 1943 when Gross flew as air commander to attack Romilly-sur-Seine airfield. When his leading formation reached the target area they found it obscured by clouds. Gross immediately radioed the situation to following combat wings saving them needless miles over enemy territory. On the route in Gross had observed Amiens/Glisy airfield, another important Luftwaffe base. He now announced that his Wing would attack it on the way back if a visual sighting could be made. He also radioed the Initial Point to be used, directions for attack and re-forming the combat wing afterwards. The mission stood as the first where VHF was used to accomplish an improvised and controlled attack on a target.

2 SEPTEMBER 1943

VIII BC 89

	Despatched		Effective	Target	Bombs Tonnage	E/A	Losses MIA	E	Dam	Casualties KIA	WIA	MIA
1BW				AIRFIELDS IN								
	92BG 305BG 306BG	55	0	NW FRANCE	0	0	0		0			
	91BG 351BG 381BG	57	0		0	0	0		0			
	303BG 379BG 384BG	55	0		0	0	0		0			
TOTALS:		167	0		0	0	0	0	0	0	0	0
4BW				AIRFIELDS IN								
B-17	95BG 100BG 390BG	66	0	NW FRANCE	0	0	0		0	0	0	0
	94BG	21	0	MARDYCK A/F (O)	216 × 500GP				0	0	0	0
	385BG	21	0	1922 hrs	188 × 500GP				0	0	0	0
	96BG	21	18	DENAIN/PROUVY A/F (O)					7	0	0	0
	388BG	23	16	1905 hrs			0		2	0	2	0
TOTALS:		152	34		101.0	0–0–0	0	0	9	0	2	0

REMARKS: Mission recalled and abandoned at French coast due to heavy cloud. 2 388BG men WIA. Only 96BG and 388BG bombed T/Os.

VIII FC FO 120

Despatched		Groups	E/A	Losses MIA	E	Dam	Casualties KIA	WIA	MIA
P-47	182	4FG, 56FG, 78FG, 353FG	0	3	1	4	0	0	3

REMARKS: Intended escort for heavy bombers but carried out fighter sweeps. 56FG P-47 down in sea near Dutch Islands. Fighter group losses: 4FG – 1, 56FG – 2. B/d 56FG P-47 c/l Eastchurch A/F pilot safe.

VIII ASC 41 & 42

	Despatched		Effective	Target	Bombs Tonnage	E/A	Losses MIA	E	Dam	Casualties KIA	WIA	MIA
3BW												
B-26	386BG	36	0	ROUEN P/S			0		0	0	0	0
	387BG	36	0	POIX/NORD A/F			0		0	0	0	0
	322BG	36	36	HESDIN F/D			0		0	0	0	0
	323BG	36	33	HESDIN F/D			0		0	0	0	0
	387BG	36	0	LILLE/NORD A/F			1		13	0	5	6
	386BG	36	35	MAZINGARBE P(S			0		0	0	0	0
TOTALS		216	104		149.80	0	1	0	13	0	5	6

REMARKS: Cloud prevented bombing at some targets.

INCIDENT

A simple but effective aid to better pilot view to the rear of a Thunderbolt arose as a result of Lt John W. Voght's experiences on 2 September 1943. On this day the 56th Group was 'jumped' by Luftwaffe fighters while escorting an abortive B-17 raid. The enemy used high cloud to advantage and without loss shot down two P-47s and damaged those flown by Col Zemke and Lt Voght. FW 190s of II/JG26 dived and approached low from the rear without being seen. Voght's combat report stated, 'I broke into the first attack but a deflection shot from one enemy aircraft hit me (20 mm) and my airducts were punctured enabling me to pull only 35 inches boost at 20,000 ft. The same hit also caused my guns to become inoperative and blew away my elevator and trim tab controls. Several attacks were made in rapid succession upon me, causing me to break several times more – always into the attacks which this time were coming from all directions. I finally half rolled to the deck, with one FW 190 right behind me. He fired all the way down and because of insufficient manifold pressure in my aircraft, kept with me easily. I evaded by violent sliding and slipping. I hedge-hopped from the point where I hit the deck (approximately 10 miles south-east of Ghent) to just north of Dunkirk with the 190 about 100 yards behind me all the way. I managed to evade his 20 mm until his supply was exhausted. He then continued to fire the .30-cals which did no serious damage when they did hit. The enemy aircraft broke off the engagement and I crossed the French coast. Some fragments from one of his 20 mms embedded themselves in my leg, but were removed at a hospital near Eastchurch airdrome where I finally set down. Landing was made after sunset (approx 2005 hrs) with no flaps (hydraulic system shot out) and with wheels down. The ship nosed up at the end of the field.' The FW 190 pilot, Lt Kehl, claimed the P-47 as destroyed.

John Voght returned to Halesworth following this narrow escape convinced his squadron would not have been jumped if pilots could have had a better view to the rear. The original rear-view mirrors attached to the top of the cockpit windshield had been replaced by the British panoramic mirrors, similar to those used on Spitfires. While these gave a much wider cover of the rear the P-47's large fuselage tended to limit this to 180 degrees over the tailplane. Voght aired his grievance to his crew chief, S/Sgt Frank Gyidik, who proposed fitting one of the discarded, original, P-47 mirrors to either side of the fuselage just forward of the cockpit. With Voght sitting in the P-47, Gyidik positioned the mirrors until his pilot felt they were in the best location and then fixed them to the fuselage skin. A test flight revealed that Voght now had much improved rear vision. At a later date Capt Walker Mahurin, destined to be one of the great aces of the Group, used Voght's *Lucky Little Devil* on a mission and was so taken with the additional mirrors that on return he requested that Gyidik make a similar installation on his aircraft. Other pilots were also attracted to the innovation and Gyidik's brain-child eventually appeared on P-47s in other groups.

3 SEPTEMBER 1943

VIII BC 90

	Despatched		Effective	Target	Bombs Tonnage	E/A	Losses MIA	E	Dam	Casualties KIA	WIA	MIA
1BW				ROMILLY SUR SEINE (P)								
B-17	91BG	14	10	A/D 0903–0911 hrs	1177 × 500GP	1–0– 0	0		10	0	0	0
	351BG	19	16	100 a/c		3–0– 3	0		3	0	0	0
	381BG	22	19			2–0– 4	1		6	0	2	10
				ST.ANDRÉ DE L'EURE								
	92BG	19	16	(S)	325 × 500GP	1–0– 2	1		5	0	0	10
	305BG	18	16	A/F 0947–0949 hrs		1–0– 0	0		0	0	0	0
	306BG	18	16	28 a/c		1–1– 0	0		9	0	0	0
	303BG	19	15	EVREUX/FAUVILLE (L)	138 × 500GP	1–0– 0	0		6	0	0	0
	379BG	21	20	A/F 0955 hrs		0–0– 0	1		16	0	0	10
	384BG	18	12	12 a/c		1–0– 1	1		0	0	0	10
TOTALS:		168	140		410.0	11–1–10	4	0	55	0	2	40

3 SEPTEMBER 1943 *(contd.)*

4BW				DUMMY A/F								
B-17	94BG	21	18	NR.DIEPPE (O)	216 × 500GP				0	0	0	0
				MEULAN LES								
	96BG	21	19	MUREAUX A/F (P)					0	0	0	0
	388BG	23	19	0843–0844 hrs	454 × 500GP				2	0	0	0
TOTALS:		65	56		167.5	0–0– 0	0	0	2	0	0	0

Paris lies below in the morning sun as *San Antonio Rose* (lower left) and other 95BG Fortresses turn off target on 3 September, the only unit able to attack the Renault works before clouds hid it.

The 'Big Chief', General 'Hap' Arnold, head of the USAAF, paid his first visits to 8AF installations in early September 1943. On the 3rd he visited Bury St.Edmunds where he talked to 94BG crews just returned from a mission to France. What he did not learn was that they had bombed an airfield as a target of opportunity while not recognising it as a dummy. Behind Arnold are Curtis LeMay (CG 4BW), Fred Anderson (CG VIII BC) and Fred Castle (CO 94BG).

				Target	Bombs Tonnage	E/A	Losses MIA	E	Dam	KIA	WIA	MIA
4BW				CAUDRON-RENAULT								
B-17	95BG	22	20	(PARIS) I/A 0845 hrs	240 × 500GP	9–0–1	0		8	0	2	0
	100BG	21	17	U/I A/F 0925 hrs	204 × 500GP	6–4–7	5		10	0	2	40
	390BG	22	0			0–0–0	0		0	0	0	0
TOTALS:		65	37		111.0	15–4–8	5	0	18	0	4	40

REMARKS: 390BG unable to locate other formations. 385BG B-17 blew up after catching fire at engine start, mission cancelled.

VIII FC FO 121

Despatched		Groups	E/A	Losses MIA	E	Dam	Casualties KIA	WIA	MIA
P-47	160	4FG, 56FG, 78FG, 353FG	4–1–0	1	0	2	0	0	0

REMARKS: Escort for heavy bombers. Fighter group losses: 56FG – 1. Fighter group e/a credits: 56FG – 4.

VIII FC FO 122

Despatched		Groups	E/A	Losses MIA	E	Dam	Casualties KIA	WIA	MIA
P-47	95	56FG, 78FG	0	0	0	0	0	0	0

REMARKS: Carried out fighter sweeps in Dunkirk area.

VIII ASC 44

	Despatched		Effective	Target	Bombs Tonnage	E/A	Losses MIA	E	Dam	Casualties KIA	WIA	MIA
3BW				BEAUMONT LE ROGER								
B-26	323BG	36	31	A/F 1007 hrs								
				BEAUVAIS/TILLE								
	322BG	36	36	A/F 0907 hrs								
				LILLE/NORD								
	387BG	36	31	A/F 0828 hrs								
	386BG	33	0									
TOTALS		141	98		145.65		0		20	0	1	0

REMARKS: 7PG despatched 4 F-5s to Northern and Western France.

VIII ASC 43

	Despatched		Effective	Target	Bombs Tonnage	E/A	Losses MIA	E	Dam	Casualties KIA	WIA	MIA
A-20	67RG	1	1	PHOTO RECON LERUN and KERGAL areas of BRITTANY		0	0	0	0	0	0	0

VIII ASC 46

	Despatched		Effective	Target	Bombs Tonnage	E/A	Losses MIA	E	Dam	Casualties KIA	WIA	MIA
A-20	67RG	1	1	PR ST.MICHEL EN GRAVE to KERALIE		0	0	0	0	0	0	0

(VIII ASC 45 was cancelled mission to Hazebrouck M/Y and Lille/Nord A/F.)

4 SEPTEMBER 1943

VIII ASC 47

	Despatched		Effective	Target	Bombs Tonnage	E/A	Losses MIA	E	Dam	Casualties KIA	WIA	MIA
3BW				COURTRAI								
B-26	387BG	36	33	1756 hrs								
				LILLE/								
				DELIVERANCE								
	386BG	36	33	M/Y 1756 hrs								
				HAZEBROUCK M/Y								
	323BG	36	34	1831 hrs								
	322BG	36	23	ST.POL M/Y								
				1833 hrs								
TOTALS:		144	123		195.5		0		22	0	3	0

4 SEPTEMBER 1943 (*contd.*)

VIII FC FO 124

Despatched		Groups	E/A	Losses MIA	E	Dam	Casualties KIA	WIA	MIA
P-47	95	56FG, 78FG	0	0	0	0	0	0	0

REMARKS: Despatched on fighter sweeps in Antwerp area.

7PG despatched 6 F-5 to France and Holland.

5 SEPTEMBER 1943

VIII ASC 48

	Despatched		Effective	Target	Bombs Tonnage	E/A	Losses MIA	E	Dam	Casualties KIA	WIA	MIA
3BW				GHENT M/Y								
B-26	323BG	36	31	0827 hrs								
	322BG	36	32	0831 hrs								
	386BG	36	0	COURTRAI M/Y								
TOTALS:		108	63		93.5		0	0	38	0	4	0

REMARKS: 323BG B-26 c/l RAF airfield, crew safe. Cat AC.

VIII ASC 49

	Despatched		Effective	Target	Bombs Tonnage	E/A	Losses MIA	E	Dam	Casualties KIA	WIA	MIA
A-20	67RG	2	2	PR of ST.POL DE LEON		0	0	0	0	0	0	0

6 SEPTEMBER 1943

VIII BC 91

	Despatched		Effective	Target	Bombs Tonnage	E/A	Losses MIA	E	Dam	Casualties KIA	WIA	MIA
3BD				STUTTGART &								
B-17	95BG	23	13	VARIOUS T/Os	1198 × 500GP	14– 3– 3	4		8	0	1	40
	100BG	21	10	0940–1229 hrs	145 × 1000GP	9– 1– 6	3		3	0	1	30
	390BG	24	18		156 × 250 IB	13– 1– 1	0		16	0	0	0
	94BG	21	16			0– 0– 1	0		13	1	2	0
	96BG	21	20			6– 1– 8	0		14	0	1	0
	385BG	23	14			12– 4– 4	0		7	0	1	0
	388BG	24	20			12– 4– 6	11		8	1	7	110
TOTALS:		157	111		391.5	66–14–29	18	1	69	2	13	180
1BD				VARIOUS T/Os								
B-17	91BG	16	12	0951–1017 hrs	980 × 500GP	3– 0– 2	3	1	7	0	0	13
	92BG	21	17		2078 × 100 IB	5– 1– 1	7	1	6	0	3	30
	303BG	19	16			2– 4– 3	1	2	5	0	0	0
	305BG	20	11			2– 0– 1	5	0	4	0	1	40
	306BG	21	20			3– 0– 0	2	2	11	0	3	20
	351BG	23	19			1– 0– 0	2	1	1	0	3	0
	379BG	19	17			9– 1–12	2	1	8	0	4	0
	381BG	21	19			1– 0– 0	0	1	3	0	0	0
	384BG	21	20			6– 0– 2	5	0	2	0	0	50
TOTALS:		181	151		348.9	32– 6–21	27	9	47	0	14	153

The 6 September mission to Stuttgart proved to be one of the most costly fiascos in 8AF history. Clouds frustrated attacks on briefed objectives and formations became separated, a situation enemy defences exploited to the full. To cap it all many of the short-range B-17s of 1st Wing ran out of fuel on return with 20 having to ditch or crash-land. One was 303BG's *Winning Run* which, having had No.2 engine put out of action over France (see feathered prop'), had to 'belly in' with fuel tanks dry just short of West Malling airfield. A forlorn crew member watches a more fortunate B-17 go in for a landing.

Leading 303BG was Major Lewis Lyle, veteran B-17 pilot. Ultimately, he flew 69 missions in the ETO.

2BD				DIVERSION								
B-24	44BG	18	15									
	93BG	18	14									
	389BG	15	13									
	392BG	18	18									
TOTALS:		69	60		0	0– 0– 0	0	0	0	0	0	0

REMARKS: Briefed target was Stuttgart I/A. Extensive cloud prevented all but a few a/c from attacking primary. Formations became separated and disorganised and attacked T/Os over a wide area. 4 B-17s landed in Switzerland (2 – 305BG, 1 – 306BG, 1 – 388BG) and 1 100BG B-17 crashed in Swiss lake. Several 1BD B-17s short of fuel on return and came down in sea or c/l in southern England. Of 12 B-17 in sea all crews rescued (118 men) by ASR. B-17s crash-landing:– 1 91BG at Winchelsea, 1 92BG at Penhurst, 1 303BG at and 1 303BG near West Malling, 1 306BG at Deanland, 1 306BG and 1 351BG near New Romney and 1 381BG near Ashford. A 379BG landing at Gatwick taxied into a Halifax. First mission of B-24s since return from Africa.

VIII FC FO 125

Despatched		Groups	E/A	Losses MIA	E	Dam	Casualties KIA	WIA	MIA
P-47	176	4FG, 56FG, 78FG, 353FG	1–0–0	1	0	0	0	0	0

REMARKS: Escort and support for HB. Fighter group losses:– 353FG – 1. Fighter group e/a credits:– 4FG – 1.

VIII ASC 50 & 51

	Despatched		Effective	Target	Bombs Tonnage	E/A	Losses MIA	E	Dam	Casualties KIA	WIA	MIA
3BW				ROUEN M/Y								
B-26	387BG	36	34	0738 hrs					0	0	0	0
	386BG	36	32	GHENT M/Y					0	0	0	0
	322BG	36	0	0739 hrs					3	0	1	0
	323BG	36	0						0	0	0	0
				AMIENS M/Y								
	323BG	36	33	1755 hrs					0	0	0	0
	322BG	36	33	1756 hrs					0	0	0	0
				SERQUEUX M/Y								
	386BG	36	36	1755 hrs					0	0	0	0
	387BG	36	34	1757 hrs					3	0	0	0
TOTALS:		288	202		298.	0	0	0	6	0	1	0

REMARKS: 7PG despatched 8 F-5s to France and Holland.

7 SEPTEMBER 1943

VIII BC 92

	Despatched		Effective	Target	Bombs Tonnage	E/A	Losses MIA	E	Dam	Casualties KIA	WIA	MIA
1BD				BRUSSELS/EVERE								
B-17	303BG	14	13	A/F(P) 0849–0852 hrs	1243 × 500GP			0	3			
	384BG	14	11					0	1			
	379BG	14	14					0	1			
	306BG	12	11					0	0			
	305BG	12	11					0	0			
	92BG	12	12					0	0			
	351BG	19	18					1	2			
	381BG	17	15					0	3			
TOTALS:		114	105		315.0	0–0–0	0	1	10	0	0	0
2BD				BERGEN/ALKMAAR								
B-24	44BG	13	10	A/F(P) 3 a/c 0857 hrs	36 × 500GP (P)							
				CONVOY OFF TEXEL (O)	1140 × 20Frag (O)							
	389BG	16	12	19 a/c	102 × 500GP							
TOTALS:		29	22		45.9	0–0–0	0	0	0	0	0	0
3BD				WATTEN V/S (P)								
B-17	385BG	21	0	0820–0854 hrs	116 × 2000GP				0		0	0
	94BG	21	0						0		0	0
	95BG	21	21						11		0	0
	100BG	18	18						0		2	0
	390BG	26	3						7		0	0
	388BG	18	0						11		0	0
	96BG	22	16						10		5	0
TOTALS:		147	58		116.0	0–0–0	0	0	39	0	7	0

REMARKS: 1 92BG a/c attacked T/O. 351BG B-17 c/l at base. Weather prevented most 3BD a/c from bombing

7 SEPTEMBER 1943 *(contd.)*

VIII FC FO 126

Despatched		Groups	E/A	Losses MIA	E	Dam	Casualties KIA	WIA	MIA
P-47	178	4FG, 56FG, 78FG, 353FG	3–0–2	1	1	1	0	0	1

REMARKS: Escort for 1BD and 2BD only, RAF escorted 3BD. 353FG P-47 c/l at Westleton. Fighter group losses: 4FG – 1. Fighter group e/a credits: 56FG – 2.

VIII ASC 52

	Despatched		Effective	Target		Bombs Tonnage	E/A	Losses MIA	E	Dam	Casualties KIA	WIA	MIA
3BW													
B-26	386BG	36	0	LILLE M/Y	(P)					2			
				ST.POL M/Y	(O)								
	387BG	36	12	0857 hrs						0			
				ST.POL M/Y	(P)								
	322BG	36	35	0854 hrs						0			
	323BG	36	34	0858 hrs						0			
TOTALS:		144	81			121.0	0–0–1	0	0	2	0	0	0

REMARKS: Confusion at rendezvous point resulted in 386BG and most of 387BG a/c abandoning mission. 12 387BG a/c joined 322BG.

7PG despatched 5 F-5s to France and Belgium.

8 SEPTEMBER 1943

VIII ASC 53 & 54

	Despatched		Effective	Target	Bombs Tonnage	E/A	Losses MIA	E	Dam	Casualties KIA	WIA	MIA
3BW				LILLE/NORD A/F								
B-26	323BG	35	33	0922 hrs			0	0	0	0		0
	387BG	36	35	0922 hrs			0	0	3	0		0
				LILLE/VENDEVILLE A/F								
	322BG	36	32	1011 hrs			0	0	18	0		0
	386BG	36	36	1013 hrs			1	1	3	0		1
				BOULOGNE C/D								
	387BG	18	18	1756 hrs			0	0	2	0		0
	322BG	18	14	1758 hrs			0	0	6	0		0
	386BG	18	18	1805 hrs			0	0	11	0		0
	323BG	18	18	1818 hrs			0	0	7	0		0
TOTALS:		215	204		298.40		1	1	50	0	7	1

REMARKS: 386BG a/c ditched in sea near Goodwin Sands, 5 of crew rescued. First ASR for UK based B-26. B/d 386BG a/c c/l base.

VIII FC FO 127

Despatched		Groups	E/A	Losses MIA	E	Dam	Casualties KIA	WIA	MIA
P-47	93	56FG, 78FG	0	0	0	0	0	0	0

REMARKS: Flew sweeps in the Courtrai/Ghent/Haamstede area.

7PG despatched 3 F-5s to Holland and France.

VIII BC 93 NIGHT ATTACK – BOULOGNE AREA (WITH RAF)

	Despatched		Effective	Target	Bombs Tonnage	E/A	Losses MIA	E	Dam	Casualties KIA	WIA	MIA
1BD				BOULOGNE AREA								
B-17	422BS	5	5	2210–2216 hrs	43 × 500GP 5 × Photoflash		0	0	0	0	0	0

9 SEPTEMBER 1943

VIII BC 94

		Despatched	Effective	Target	Bombs Tonnage	E/A	Losses MIA	E	Dam	Casualties KIA	WIA	MIA
3BD				PARIS I/A 20 a/c (P)								
	95BG	23	17	0903 hrs	232 × 500GP	5–2–6	0		1	0	0	0
	96BG	20	18	BEAUMONT SUR OISE	557 × 500GP	1–0–0	1		0	0	1	10
	388BG	21	13	A/F 48 a/c (S)		4–0–1	1		14	0	1	11
	390BG	23	20	0855–0916 hrs		6–0–2	0		6	0	1	0
TOTALS:		87	68		197.25	16–2–9	2	0	21	0	3	21
3BD				BEAUVAIS/TILLE								
B-17	94BG	21	21	A/F 0816–0819 hrs	8490 × 20Frag				4	0	0	0
	100BG	21	19						0	0	0	0
	385BG	21	19						2	0	0	0
TOTALS:		63	59		84.9	0–0–0	0	0	6	0	0	0
1BD				LILLE/NORD A/F								
B-17	351BG	19	19	0830–0833 hrs	5256 × 20Frag				0	0	0	0
	381BG	18	18						10	0	2	0
TOTALS:		37	37		52.5	0–0–0	0	0	10	0	2	0
1BD				LILLE/VENDEVILLE								
B-17	92BG	19	18	A/F 0830–0840 hrs	7452 × 20Frag				0	0	0	0
	305BG	19	17						0	0	0	0
	306BG	18	17						7	0	0	0
TOTALS:		56	52		74.5	0–0–0	0	0	7	0	0	0
1BD				VITRY-EN-ARTOIS								
B-17	303BG	18	18	A/F 0837–0840 hrs	7518 × 20Frag							
	379BG	20	18									
	384BG	18	15									
TOTALS:		56	51		75.2	0–0–0	0	0	0	0	0	0
2BD				ST.OMER/FT.ROUGE								
B-24	93BG	20	14	A/F ST.OMER/	436 × 300GP				0	0	0	0
	389BG	18	14	LONGUENESSE A/F					3	0	1	0
TOTALS:		38	28		65.4	0–0–0	0	0	3	0	1	0
2BD				ABBEVILLE/DRUCAT								
B-24	44BG	19	17	A/F	288 × 300GP							
	392BG	21	18		1980 × 20Frag							
TOTALS:		40	35		63.0	0–0–0	0	0	0	0	0	0

REMARKS: First mission for 392BG.

VIII FC FO 128

Despatched		Groups	E/A	Losses MIA	E	Dam	Casualties KIA	WIA	MIA
P-47	215	4FG, 56FG, 78FG, 352FG, 353FG	1–0–0	2	0	0	0	0	1

REMARKS: Escort for all formations except 2BD attacking Abbeville/Drucat A/F. The 352FG flew first mission, a patrol over the English coast to cover the landings of the 56FG and 353FG. A second fighter mission was planned for later in the day, but was abortive because of weather. 355FG carried out a practice sweep under FO 129. Fighter group losses:– 4FG – 2. 4FG pilot rescued from Channel 11 Sep. Fighter group e/a credits:– 56FG – 1.

VIII ASC 55

		Despatched	Effective	Target	Bombs Tonnage	E/A	Losses MIA	E	Dam	Casualties KIA	WIA	MIA
3BW				BOULOGNE C/D (P)								
B-26	322BG	54	51	0745–0800			1	0	21	0	0	7
	323BG	54	50	0800–0815			0	0	0	6	0	0
	386BG	55	53	0829–0846			1	0	3	0	0	6
	387BG	54	48	0845–0915			1	2	0	5	8	6
TOTALS:		217	202		334.65	0	3	2	24	11	8	19

REMARKS: 387BG B-26 crashed on t/o in early morning fog. 387BG B-26 c/l on return, 1 injured.

7PG despatched 6 F-5s to Northern and Western France.

11 SEPTEMBER 1943

VIII ASC 56

	Despatched		Effective	Target	Bombs Tonnage	E/A	Losses MIA	E	Dam	Casualties KIA	WIA	MIA
3BW				LE TRAIT S/Y (S)								
B-26	322BG	20	19	1704 hrs				0	14	0	1	0
				BEAUMONT LE ROGER								
	323BG	35	32	A/F 1756 hrs				1	0	4	0	0
TOTALS:		55	51		67.05	0	0	1	14	4	1	0

REMARKS: 323BG B-26 with engine trouble cr. trying to land Bury St.Edmunds A/F on return, crew killed.

7PG despatched 1 F-5 to Cherbourg area.

Capt Gerald Johnson received acclaim as the first 56FG 'ace' and second Thunderbolt pilot to be credited with five air victories. Johnson maintained much of his success was due to the men who kept his fighter in peak performance. Pausing in their work, for the photographer, on 14 September, they are left to right: Cpl Jack Kazanjian (assistant crew chief) Pvt Albert Asplint (armourer), S/Sgt Howard Buchner (radio mechanic) and S/Sgt George Baltimore (crew chief).

14 SEPTEMBER 1943

VIII ASC 57

	Despatched		Effective	Target	Bombs Tonnage	E/A	Losses MIA	E	Dam	Casualties KIA	WIA	MIA
3BW				WOENSDRECHT A/F								
B-26	322BG	36	0						0	0	0	0
	386BG	36	0	LILLE/NORD A/F					11	0		0
	387BG	36	0									
TOTALS:		108	0		0	0	0		18	0	3	0

REMARKS: Formations recalled because of weather.

VIII FC FO 130

Despatched		Groups	E/A	Losses MIA	E	Dam	Casualties KIA	WIA	MIA
P-47	176	4FG, 56FG, 352FG, 355FG	0	0	1	0	0	0	0

REMARKS: Carried out sweep of Dunkirk and Dutch Islands. First mission for 355FG. 355FG P-47 hit tree and c/l after t/o, pilot safe.

VIII FC FO 131

Despatched		Groups	E/A	Losses MIA	E	Dam	Casualties KIA	WIA	MIA
P-47	83	352FG, 355FG	0	1	0	0	0	0	0

REMARKS: Carried out sweep of the Knokke/Calais area. 352FG P-47 down in sea.

15 SEPTEMBER 1943

VIII BC 95

	Despatched		Effective	Target	Bombs Tonnage	E/A	Losses MIA	E	Dam	Casualties KIA	WIA	MIA
1BD				ROMILLY-SUR-SEINE								
B-17	91BG	19	18	A/D(O) 1848–1850 hrs	828 × 500GP			0		0	0	0
	305BG	18	18		57 × 1000GP			1		0	0	0
	306BG	18	17		641 × 100 IB			0		0	0	0
	351BG	19	17					1		0	3	0
	381BG	19	17					0		0	0	0
TOTALS:		93	87		267.55	0–0–0	0	2	7	0	3	0

3BD					CAUDRON-RENAULT								
					I/A (PARIS)								
B-17	95BG	23	21		(40 a/c) 1855 hrs	475 × 500GP	1–0–0	1			0	0	10
					BILLANCOURT-								
	100BG	20	19		RENAULT Wks	252 × 500GP	3–0–0	1			0	1	10
	390BG	23	21		(21 a/c) 1854 hrs		1–0–0	0			0	0	0
3BD					HISPANO-SUIZA								
B-17	94BG	21	20		A/I (PARIS)	916 × 500GP	0–0–0	0			0	0	0
	96BG	23	19				0–2–2	3			0	1	31
	385BG	22	21				2–0–1	0			0	0	0
	388BG	20	18				5–0–1	0			0	0	0
TOTALS:		152	139			410.75	12–2–4	5	0	33	0	2	51
2BD					CHARTRES A/F								
B-24	44BG	22	12		1904–1911 hrs	564 × 500GP	0–0–0	0		0	0	0	0
	93BG	21	18				0–0–0	1		0	0	0	10
	389BG	20	17				3–0–0	0		0	0	0	0
TOTALS:		63	47			141.0	3–0–0	1	0	0	0	0	10

REMARKS: Some 1BD a/c carried 1000 lb bombs on external racks. On return 305BG B-17 c/l Hawkinge and 351BG B-17 c/l near base. Last mission for B-24s prior to returning to N. Africa.

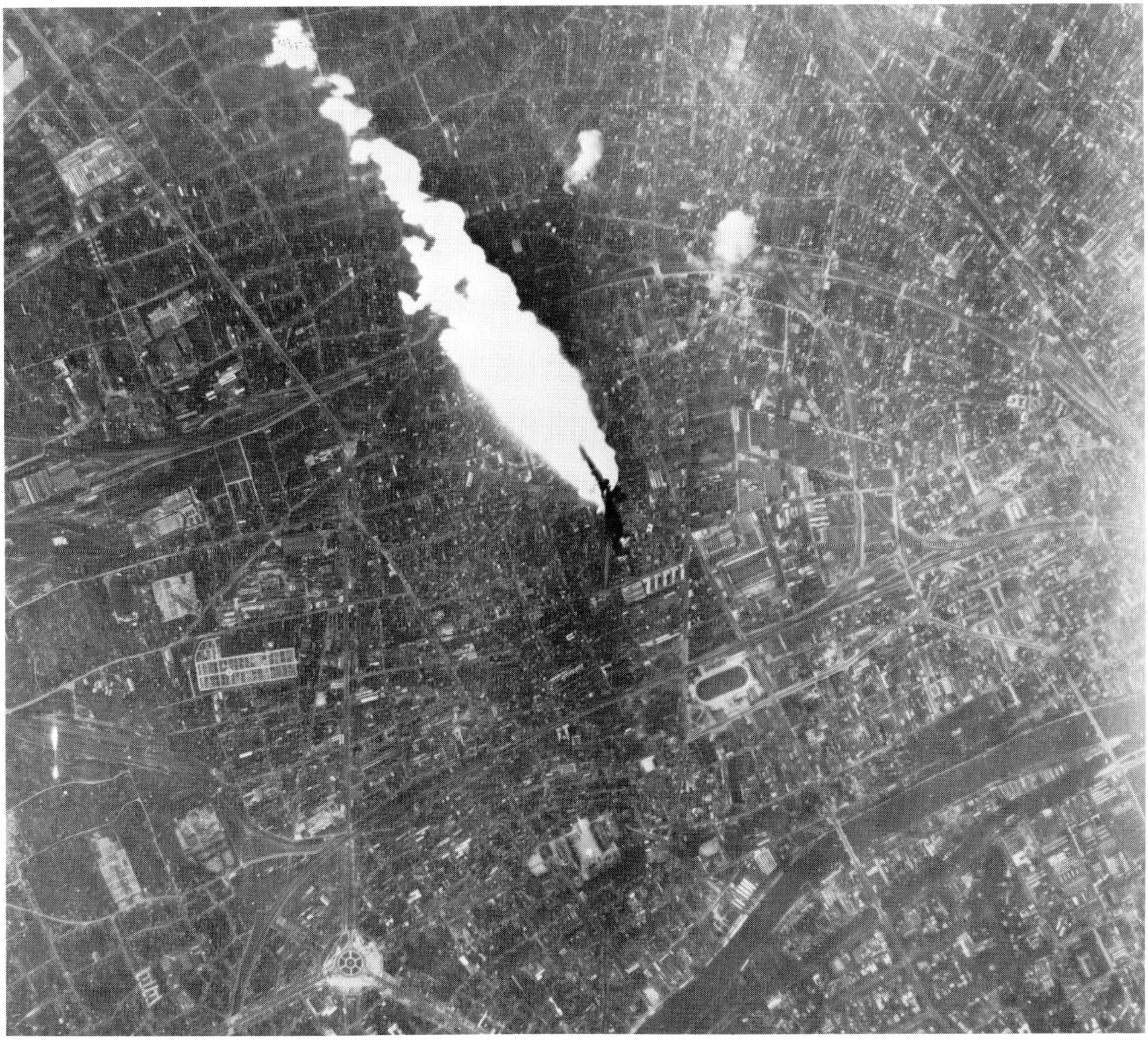

A direct flak hit on the right wing of 96BG B-17F 42-30607 flown by 1/Lt K.E. Murphy and crew sent it flaming into the centre of Paris on 15 September. Arc de Triomphe can be seen lower left.

15 SEPTEMBER 1943 *(contd.)*

VIII FC FO 132

Despatched		Groups	E/A	Losses MIA	E	Dam	Casualties KIA	WIA	MIA
P-47	201	4FG, 56FG, 78FG, 352FG, 353FG	0–0–1	2	0	0	0	0	0

REMARKS: 353FG P-47 down in sea, pilot lost. Fighter group losses: 353FG – 2.

VIII ASC 58

	Despatched		Effective	Target	Bombs Tonnage	E/A	Losses MIA	E	Dam	Casualties KIA	WIA	MIA
3BW				LILLE/NORD A/F								
B-26	322BG	36	0						0	0	0	0
	323BG	36	0						0	0	0	0
				MERVILLE A/F								
	387BG	36	34	1745 hrs						0		0
	386BG	36	34	1748 hrs						0		0
TOTALS:		144	68		100.05		0		27	0	2	0

7PG despatched 6 F-5s to French coast (Calais to Cherbourg).

15/16 SEPTEMBER 1943

VIII BC 96 NIGHT ATTACK – MONTLUCON I/A (WITH RAF)

	Despatched		Effective	Target	Bombs Tonnage	E/A	Losses MIA	E	Dam	Casualties KIA	WIA	MIA
1BD				MONTLUCON I/A								
B-17	422BS	5	5	2337 to 2351	22 × 1000GP		0	0	0	0	0	0

16 SEPTEMBER 1943

VIII BC 97

	Despatched		Effective	Target	Bombs Tonnage	E/A	Losses MIA	E	Dam	Casualties KIA	WIA	MIA
1BD	91BG	18	15	NANTES P/A	1540 × 500GP	2–0–0	1	0	11	0	2	10
B-17	303BG	19	19	1502–1512 hrs		5–1–1	0	0	6	0	0	0
	305BG	16	16	(79 a/c)		0–0–0	0	0	2	0	0	0
	306BG	18	18	NANTES/CHATEAU –		0–0–0	0	1	2	0	0	0
	351BG	19	19	BOUGON A/F		0–0–0	0	0	5	0	1	0
	379BG	19	14	1509–1512 hrs		7–0–2	4	0	8	0	0	40
	381BG	20	18	(51 a/c)		2–0–0	0	0	12	0	4	0
	384BG	18	12			6–1–2	2	0	1	0	2	10
TOTALS:		147	131		385.0	22–2–5	7	1	47	0	9	60
3BD	95BG	24	20	LA PALLICE P/A	717 × 500GP	0–0–0	1	0	2	0	0	10
B-17	96BG	20	19	1755–1758 hrs		10–0–4	0	0	4	0	3	0
	100BG	19	17	LAROCHELLE/LALEAU		0–0–0	1	0	0	0	0	10
	388BG	18	16	A/F 1755–1758 hrs		0–1–0	1	3	4	24	6	0
	390BG	24	0	COGNAC/	210 × 500GP	0–0–0	1	1	0	10	0	10
	94BG	21	21	CHATEAUBERNARD		2–1–1	0	0	1	0	0	0
	385BG	22	0	A/F 1731 hrs		10–1–3	0	1	6	10	0	0
TOTALS:		148	93		231.75	22–3–8	4	5	17	44	9	30

REMARKS: 3BD returned at dusk and encountered weather front. B-17s lost on return: 388BG cr. near South Molton (2k), 388BG cr. into a hill nr Rhayader, 10 k. 388BG with radio failure ditched off Northumberland coast (2k), 390BG cr. into hill near Abergavenny (10k), 385BG cr. Rickinghall Superior (10k) after colliding in dark with a 95BG B-17 which landed safely. 384BG B-17 cr. in sea off South coast, crew rescued. 1 1BD B-17 dropped 12 × 500GP on convoy off French coast with no hits. 2 MIA 379BG B-17s lost to aerial bombs released by e/a. 306BG B-17 c/l on return.

VIII FC FO 133

Despatched		Groups	E/A	Losses MIA	E	Dam	Casualties KIA	WIA	MIA
P-47	79	56FG, 353FG	2–0–1	0	0	0	0	0	0

REMARKS: Escort provided for 1BD only. Fighter group e/a credits: 56FG – 2.

VIII ASC 59

	Despatched		Effective	Target	Bombs Tonnage	E/A	Losses MIA	E	Dam	Casualties KIA	WIA	MIA
3BW				BEAUMONT LE ROGER								
B-26	322BG	36	34	A/F 1735 hrs						0	0	0
				TRICOUEVILLE								
	323BG	36	33	A/F 1735 hrs						0	0	0
TOTALS:		72	67		92	0	0	0	2	0	0	0

7PG despatched 11 F-5s to France and Belgium.

16/17 SEPTEMBER 1943

VIII BC 98 NIGHT ATTACK – MODANE M/Y (WITH RAF)

	Despatched		Effective	Target	Bombs Tonnage	E/A	Losses MIA	E	Dam	Casualties KIA	WIA	MIA
1BD				MODANE M/Y								
B-17	422BS	5	5	0029 to 0044	35 × 500GP		0	0	0	0	0	0

17 SEPTEMBER 1943

VIII ASC 60

	Despatched		Effective	Target	Bombs Tonnage	E/A	Losses MIA	E	Dam	Casualties KIA	WIA	MIA
A-20	67RG	1	1	PR BREST PENINSULA						0	0	0

18 SEPTEMBER 1943

VIII ASC 61 & 62

	Despatched		Effective	Target	Bombs Tonnage	E/A	Losses MIA	E	Dam	Casualties KIA	WIA	MIA
3BW	386BG	36	0	BEAUVAIS/TILLE					7	0	0	0
B-26	387BG	36	25	A/F					5	0	0	0
	322BG	18	0	ROUEN M/Y					0	0	0	0
	323BG	36	0	BEAUMONT LE					0	0	0	0
	387BG	36	0	ROGER A/F					0	0	0	0
TOTALS:		162	25		36.9	0	0	0	12	0	0	0

REMARKS: Fighters recalled Beaumont le Roger force 10 miles from the French coast because of weather.

7PG despatched 2 F-5s to Cherbourg area.

19 SEPTEMBER 1943

VIII ASC 63 & 64

	Despatched		Effective	Target	Bombs Tonnage	E/A	Losses MIA	E	Dam	Casualties KIA	WIA	MIA
3BW				LILLE/NORD								
B-26	386BG	36	18	1139 hrs A/F					0	0	0	0
	387BG	36	0						10	0	4	0
	322BG	36	0	MERVILLE					0	0	0	0
	323BG	36	0	A/F					0	0	0	0
TOTALS:		144	18		25.65	0	0	0	10	0	4	0

REMARKS: Clouds prevented three groups from bombing.

7PG despatched 2 F-5s to Northern and Western France.

Donald Crossley in the tail gun position, a picture taken after his 23rd mission.

INCIDENT

Highest scoring gunner 'ace' to emerge from the great daylight air battles of 1943 was S/Sgt Donald W. Crossley, a 25-year-old B-17 tail gunner in the 95th Group. In his 25 missions he received credit for the destruction of 12 enemy aircraft, the only 8th Air Force gunner to run his victory score into double figures. Much of Crossley's success can be attributed to his great interest in marksmanship and skill developed through shooting as a hobby. Before enlisting, when he worked for a steel company in Follansbee, Virginia, his passion for shooting was pursued through membership of three different rifle clubs.

With the original 95th Group combat complement arriving in the UK in April 1943, Don Crossley was tail gunner on 1/Lt John W. Johnson's crew. His first two victories were credited the following month and his third on 11 June. On this date the Johnson crew were flying the B-17 *Little Lady* when attacked by fighters over the target. A mechanical problem developed in Crossley's tail guns rendering them inoperative. At about the same time one of the nose guns used by the navigator was hit by enemy fire and damaged. Hearing this over the interphone, Crossley went to the nose, removed part of the mechanism from the damaged gun, and was able to use this in getting his guns back into operation. Shortly afterwards when another fighter attack developed he was able to obtain fatal strikes on an FW 190. Two days later, on the hotly contested Kiel raid, the Johnson crew was flying B-17 *Easy Aces*, an appropriate nickname in view of Crossley claiming his fourth and fifth enemy fighters to become one of the first gunner aces in the Group.

After this mission the crew received a new long-range B-17F which was named *The Brass Rail* after a well known American restaurant chain. Over the next few weeks Crossley flew on most of the major raids and his score mounted steadily. On another mission to Kiel, 25 July 1943, *The Brass Rail* came under fighter attack and although Crossley was able to claim one of the enemy the bomber was badly shot up, a cannon shell exploding in the cockpit mortally wounding 'Johnny' Johnson. The co-pilot flew the bomber home and in subsequent operations became the new crew captain. Over the Ruhr on 12 August, *The Brass Rail* was again under attack and Crossley claimed another double to raise his score to 11. His 12th and final victory was achieved on his 22nd mission in September 1943, following which he received the simultaneous awards of the DFC and cluster. The 3rd Division planned to use Crossley as a lecturer and instructor in the zone sighting method of firing once he had completed his tour, so that other bomber gunners might benefit from his expertise.

21 SEPTEMBER 1943

VIII ASC 65

	Despatched		Effective	Target	Bombs Tonnage	E/A	Losses MIA	E	Dam	Casualties KIA	WIA	MIA
3BW				BEAUVAIS/TILLE A/F (P)								
B-26	387BG	37	34	0937 hrs		0	1	1	11	1	1	7
	322BG	36	10	0938 hrs		1–0–0	0	0	1	1	3	0
TOTALS:		73	44		65.1	1–0–0	1	1	12	2	4	7

7PG despatched 1 F-5 to Nantes area.

22 SEPTEMBER 1943

VIII ASC 66

	Despatched		Effective	Target	Bombs Tonnage	E/A	Losses MIA	E	Dam	Casualties KIA	WIA	MIA
3BW				BEAUVAIS/TILLE								
B-26	322BG	36	0	A/F								
	387BG	36	0									
				EVREUX/FAUVILLE A/F								
	323BG	36	35	1612 hrs								
	386BG	36	35	1614 hrs								
TOTALS:		144	70		105.15	0	0	0	0	0	0	0

REMARKS: 322BG and 387BG recalled by escort due to weather.

VIII FC FO 138

Despatched		Groups	E/A	Losses MIA	E	Dam	Casualties KIA	WIA	MIA
P-47	240	4FG, 56FG, 78FG, 352FG, 353FG, 355FG	2–0–0	1	1	0	0	0	1

REMARKS: Carried out sweeps of Calais/Egmond area. Fighter group losses: 78FG – 1, 355FG – 1 (Cat E).

VIII FC FO 139

Despatched		Groups	E/A	Losses MIA	E	Dam	Casualties KIA	WIA	MIA
P-47	155	56FG, 352FG, 353FG, 355FG	0	0	0	0	0	0	0

REMARKS: Carried out sweeps of Furnes/Lille/Ghent/Flushing area.

7PG despatched F-5 on Met. flight mid-Channel.

22/23 SEPTEMBER 1943

VIII BC 99 NIGHT ATTACK – HANNOVER (WITH RAF)

	Despatched		Effective	Target	Bombs Tonnage	E/A	Losses MIA	E	Dam	Casualties KIA	WIA	MIA
1BD				HANNOVER								
B-17	422BS	5	5	2143–2209 hrs	60 × 500GP	0	0	0	0	0	0	0

23 SEPTEMBER 1943

VIII BC 100

	Despatched		Effective	Target	Bombs Tonnage	E/A	Losses MIA	E	Dam	Casualties KIA	WIA	MIA
1BD				NANTES P/A (P)								
B-17	91BG	21	15	0813–0818 hrs	537 × 500GP	7–0–2	0	0	14	0	2	0
	92BG	19	0			0–0–0	0	1	0	3	7	0
	305BG	18	7			3–0–0	0	1	4	10	0	0
	306BG	18	0			0–0–0	0	0	0	0	0	0
	351BG	19	13			4–0–1	0	0	16	0	2	0
	381BG	22	11			8–1–0	0	0	17	0	0	0
TOTALS:		117	46		134.25	22–1–3	0	2	41	13	11	0
3BD				VANNES/MEUCON								
B-17	95BG	22	18	A/F(P) 0825–0826 hrs	660 × 500GP		0		1	0	0	0
	100BG	23	16				0		0	0	0	0
	390BG	22	21				0		6	0	0	0
TOTALS:		67	55		165.0	0–0–0	0	0	7	0	0	0
3BD				KERLIN/BASTARD								
B-17	94BG	21	21	A/F (P) 0814–0818 hrs	621 × 500GP	2–0–0	0		3	0	0	0
	96BG	20	12			0–0–0	1		2	0	0	10
	385BG	22	20			0–0–0	0		5	0	0	0
TOTALS:		63	53		155.25	2–0–0	1	0	10	0	0	10

REMARKS: Many 1BD a/c had difficulty locating formations in bad weather. 92BG B-17 exploding during assembly and cr. near Crowland (3 k). On return 305BG B-17 cr. base (10 k) after collision.

VIII FC FO 140

Despatched		Groups	E/A	Losses MIA	E	Dam	Casualties KIA	WIA	MIA
P-47	158	4FG, 56FG, 78FG, 353FG	4–0–1	1	0	2	0	0	1

REMARKS: Fighter group losses:– 353FG – 1. Fighter group e/a credits:– 353FG – 7. Thorney Island used as forward base.

VIII ASC 67 & 68

	Despatched		Effective	Target	Bombs Tonnage	E/A	Losses MIA	E	Dam	Casualties KIA	WIA	MIA
3BW												
B-26	322BG	36	35	CONCHES A/F (P)						0	0	0
	387BG	36	35	0907 hrs						0	0	0
	323BG	36	34	BEAUVAIS/TILLE						0	0	0
	386BG	36	35	A/F (P) 1544–1546 hrs						0	0	0
TOTALS:		144	139		198.15	0	0	0	20	0	0	0

VIII FC FO 141

Despatched		Groups	E/A	Losses MIA	E	Dam	Casualties KIA	WIA	MIA
P-47	74	352FG, 355FG	0	0	0	0	0	0	0

REMARKS: P-47s sent as a diversionary force for B-26s attacking Beauvais.

23 SEPTEMBER 1943 *(contd.)*

VIII BC 101

	Despatched		Effective	Target	Bombs Tonnage	E/A	Losses MIA	E	Dam	Casualties KIA	WIA	MIA
1BD				NANTES P/A (P)								
B-17	92BG	17	15	1810–1815 hrs	696 × 500GP		0	0	7	0	0	0
	303BG	19	15	(61 a/c)			0	0	0	0	0	0
	306BG	18	14	RENNES/ST.JACQUES			0	1	7	0	10	0
	379BG	19	19	A/F (O) 1834 hrs	228 × 500GP		1	0	10	0	2	10
	384BG	18	17	(19 a/c)			1	0	2	0	0	10
TOTALS:		91	80		231.0	0–0–0	2	12	6	0	12	20
2BD				DIVERSION								
B-24	392BG	26	0		0	0–0–0	0	0	0	0	0	0

REMARKS: First occasion two HB missions flown on one day. Bombers returned at dusk. B/d 306BG B-17 cr. near Wing A/F.

VIII FC FO 142

Despatched		Groups	E/A	Losses MIA	E	Dam	Casualties KIA	WIA	MIA
P-47	109	4FG, 56FG, 353FG	0–0–0	0	0	0	0	0	0

REMARKS: Penetration support for heavy bombers. Thorney Island used as forward base.

7PG despatched 9 F-5s to France.

23/24 SEPTEMBER 1943

VIII BC 102 NIGHT ATTACK – MANNHEIM (WITH RAF)

	Despatched		Effective	Target	Bombs Tonnage	E/A	Losses MIA	E	Dam	Casualties KIA	WIA	MIA
1BD				MANNHEIM								
B-17	422BS	5	4	2211–2222 hrs	28 × 500GP	0	0	0	1	0	0	0

24 SEPTEMBER 1943

VIII ASC 69 & 70

	Despatched		Effective	Target	Bombs Tonnage	E/A	Losses MIA	E	Dam	Casualties KIA	WIA	MIA
3BW				EVREUX/FAUVILLE								
B-26	386BG	36	36	A/F (P) 1149 hrs		0–0–0			0	0		0
	387BG	36	35	1150 hrs		0–1–0			4	0		0
				BEAUVAIS/TILLE								
	323BG	36	30	A/F 1602 hrs		0–0–0			10	0		0
	322BG	36	36	1603 hrs		1–0–0			7	0		0
TOTALS:		144	137		171.40	1–1–0	0	0	21	0	1	0

VIII FC 143

Despatched		Groups	E/A	Losses MIA	E	Dam	Casualties KIA	WIA	MIA
P-47	128	78FG, 352FG, 355FG	0	0	0	0	0	0	0

REMARKS: Fighters carried out sweeps in Sangatte/Lille/Ghent/Blankenberghe area.

7PG despatched 8 F-5s to France. 1 a/c forced to return due to e/a interception.

NOTE: Heavy bomber mission to Stuttgart scrubbed. A practice mission by 3BD B-17s to test PFF equipment and technique was intercepted by e/a over North Sea. 1 100BG B-17 was shot down. The 3BD staff B-17 (with special bare metal finish) was attacked but escaped into clouds.

25 SEPTEMBER 1943

VIII ASC 71

	Despatched		Effective	Target	Bombs Tonnage	E/A	Losses MIA	E	Dam	Casualties KIA	WIA	MIA
3BW				ST.OMER/ LONGUENESSE								
B-26	322BG	36	35	A/F (P) 1717 hrs					2	0	0	0
	387BG	36	33	1718 hrs					2	0	0	0
TOTALS:		72	68		100.25	0	0	0	4	0	0	0

On 26 September, 3BD groups carried two 1,000 lb bombs on external wing racks to short range targets. Cloud obscured the target for these 94BG bombers which had to return without bombing. The additional drag and weight had such a detrimental effect on range and high altitude performance that thereafter external loads were only carried on specialised operations. The C2 identification on *Ramrod Ramsbottom* indicates the second 'C-Charlie' in 94BG, a marking system used during the late summer and autumn of 1943.

26 SEPTEMBER 1943

VIII BC 103

	Despatched		Effective	Target	Bombs Tonnage	E/A	Losses MIA	E	Dam	Casualties KIA	WIA	MIA
1BD				ABANDONED								
B-17	91BG	19	0					1	2	0	0	0
	381BG	18	0					0	6	0	0	0
	351BG	18	0					0	0	0	0	0
TOTALS:		55	0		0	0–0–0	0	1	8	0	0	0
3BD				REIMS/CHAMPAGNE								
B-17	94BG	18	0	A/F 1751–1752 hrs	228 × 500GP			0	0	0	0	0
	96BG	22	19	REIMS/CHAMPAGNE	38 × 1000GP			0	7	0	0	0
	385BG	23	0	A/F 1751–1752 hrs	840 × 100 IB			2	0	20	0	0
	388BG	21	21					0	14	0	0	0
TOTALS:		84	40		118.0	0–0–0	0	2	21	20	0	0
3BD				ABANDONED								
B-17	95BG	21	0						0	1	0	0
	100BG	21	0						0	0	0	0
	390BG	21	0						0	1	0	0
TOTALS:		63	0		0	0–0–0	0	0	0	2	0	0
2BD				DIVERSION								
B-24	44BG	3	0									
	392BG	34	0									
TOTALS:		37	0		0	0–0–0	0	0	0	0	0	0

REMARKS: Primary targets in Paris area not attacked due to weather. 1BD abandoned mission shortly after crossing enemy coast. Cloud also prevented 5 3BD groups from bombing Meulon Les Mureaux and Citroën. 1 91BG B-17 crashed near Medstead A/F, crew safe. 2 385BG B-17s collided on return over East Hornden, crashing at Brentwood and Tillingham, 1 gunner surviving.

VIII FC FO 145

Despatched		Groups	E/A	Losses MIA	E	Dam	Casualties KIA	WIA	MIA
P-47	243	4FG, 56FG, 78FG, 352FG, 353FG, 355FG							

REMARKS: Heavy bomber escort and support. Recalled.

VIII ASC 72

	Despatched		Effective	Target	Bombs Tonnage	E/A	Losses MIA	E	Dam	Casualties KIA	WIA	MIA
3BW				CONCHES A/F (P)								
B-26	323BG	36	0									
	386BG	36	0									
TOTALS:		72	0		0	0	0	0	0	0	0	0

REMARKS: B-26s recalled due to weather.

7PG despatched 1 F-5 to Nantes and Rennes area.

27 SEPTEMBER 1943

VIII BC 104

		Despatched	Effective	Target	Bombs Tonnage	E/A	Losses MIA	E	Dam	Casualties KIA	WIA	MIA
3BD				EMDEN I/A (P)								
	94BG	19	6	0958–1008 hrs	1707 × 500GP	4–0– 5	3	0	2	0	0	31
	95BG	22	21	& T/Os	22 × 1000GP	0–0– 0	0	0	2	0	0	0
	96BG	21	19		1356 × 100 IB	4–4– 7	1	1	14	0	8	10
	100BG	20	17		(178 a/c) (P)	0–0– 0	0	0	0	0	0	0
	385BG	18	18			0–0– 0	0	0	5	0	0	0
	388BG	20	16			9–2– 2	0	0	8	0	0	0
	390BG	21	20			0–0– 0	0	0	0	0	0	0
1BD												
B-17				EMDEN I/A (P)								
	91BG	19	14	0958–1008 hrs	277 × 500GP	3–0– 1	3	0	8	1	5	30
	92BG	16	16	& T/Os	57 × 1000GP	0–0– 0	0	0	0	0	0	0
	303BG	19	6		1657 × 100IB	0–0– 0	0	0	8	0	1	0
	305BG	18	2		(68 a/c) (T/O)	0–0– 0	0	0	3	0	0	0
	306BG	18	18			0–0– 0	0	0	1	0	0	0
	351BG	18	17			0–0– 1	0	0	2	0	0	0
	379BG	19	18			7–0– 3	0	0	10	0	0	0
	381BG	19	18			4–1– 5	0	0	11	0	4	0
	384BG	18	18			1–0– 0	0	0	2	0	0	0
			PFF									
	482BG	3	2	AS ABOVE		0–0– 0	0	0	2	0	0	0
TOTALS:		308	246		686.15	32–7–24	7	1	78	1	18	71
2BD				DIVERSION								
B-24	44BG	2	0									
	392BG	22	0									
TOTALS:		24	0		0	0–0–0	0		0	0	0	0

REMARKS: First Pathfinder (PFF) mission led by H2S equipped B-17s of 482BG. B/d 96BG B-17 c/l Ludham A/F.

VIII FC FO 147

Despatched		Groups	E/A	Losses MIA	E	Dam	Casualties KIA	WIA	MIA
P-47	262	4FG, 56FG, 78FG, 352FG, 353FG, 355FG	21–2–6	1	1	1	0	0	1

REMARKS: Escort for heavy bombers. Fighter group losses: 56FG – 1. Fighter group e/a credits: 4FG – 1, 56FG – 5, 78FG – 10, 353FG – 8. 353FG P-47 c/l on return, pilot safe. 4FG and 78FG used Hardwick and Hethel as forward bases. First use of 108 US gal drop tanks.

VIII ASC 73 & 74

		Despatched	Effective	Target	Bombs Tonnage	E/A	Losses MIA	E	Dam	Casualties KIA	WIA	MIA
3BW				BEAUVAIS/TILLE								
B-26	322BG	36	29	A/F (P) 1044 hrs		2–5–3	0	0	11	0		0
	387BG	36	36	1045 hrs		2–1–1	0	1	12	0		4
				CONCHES								
	323BG	36	33	A/F (P) 1729 hrs			0	0	1	0		0
	386BG	36	35	1729 hrs			1	0	3	0		6
TOTALS:		144	133		175.9	4–6–4	1	1	27	0	5	10

REMARKS: 1 387BG B-26 c/l base with b/d. 4 gunners from this group parachuted over enemy territory from damaged a/c.

7PG despatched 3 F-5s to France and NW Germany.

INCIDENT

During September 1943 the four Marauder groups of VIII ASC were regularly pounding airfields in France and the Low Countries, causing the Luftwaffe difficulties in maintaining fighter bases. Although the Marauders were usually screened by substantial numbers of RAF Spitfires, FW 190s and Me 109s would occasionally evade the escort. Five minutes after leaving the target at Beauvais/Tille on 27 September, 387th Group was intercepted by a *Staffel* of FW 190s. A B-26 named *Wuneach*, at the rear of the box formation, hit in the fuselage and right engine, dropped away from the rest. This aircraft's nickname was derived from the proviso 'one each' when the crew were issued with personal equipment for overseas movement. Seeing an engine aflame and fearing the bomber to be out of control, its gunners in the rear prepared to abandon ship. The waist gunner in baling out inadvertently caught and opened the parachute of the following man, S/Sgt Laverne Stein. Before Stein could do anything to prevent it, his canopy had billowed and was whipped by the slipstream out through the hatch. Stein's legs followed and his boots were ripped off his feet when part of the parachute harness snagged on some structure in the fuselage. The force exerted on

Taxiing in at Chipping Ongar after mission 13. (Byron Smith)

During 94BG's bomb run at Emden on 27 September, *Elusive Elcy*, flown by Lt Harley Roberts and crew, was seen with engines on fire. As the aircraft peeled out of formation an explosion tore off the wing, an instant captured in this picture. Two 'chutes were reported as the Fortress spun down. The mission was significant in that it was the first led by H2S pathfinders and with P-47s using larger drop-tanks permitting cover at the target. Some of these fighters (contrails) can be seen orbiting above the bombers.

Stein's body by the parachute trailing outside the aircraft could have caused him serious injury but for the quick action of the top turret gunner, Sgt Ed Kovalchik, who cut the harness with his escape knife. Meantime pilot Lt George Snyder had regained full control of *Wuneach*, the engine fire had been extinguished – as had others in the radio compartment and bomb bay by co-pilot 2/Lt Thornton Stark. The damaged Marauder was flown back to home base at Chipping Ongar where, due to the loss of under-carriage hydraulic power, Snyder accomplished a smooth belly landing.

EVENT

The inauguration of missions led by Pathfinder Force (PFF) on 27 September 1943 was encouraging, although they indicated the unreliable nature of the early equipment. Four B-17Fs with H2S radars (a British device) were despatched from Alconbury to the bases of the group with which they were to fly to Emden next day; two aircraft to Bassingbourn for the 1st Division, and one each to Knettishall and Thorpe Abbotts for the 3rd Division. Brig.Gen Gross, CO 1st Wing, flew as 1st Division force commander in *Finger R-Roger* with Maj Clement Bird, CO 813th Bomb Squadron (the unit equipped with the H2S Fortresses) at the controls to lead the 91st Group and the VIII Bomber Command to Emden. Before *R-Roger* departed the English coast the radar operator discovered his equipment was not working and the lead position was taken by the back-up pathfinder *Finger N-Nan*, piloted by Lt K.W. Gurney with Maj Alford of 91st Group riding as deputy Division commander. General Gross's aircraft continued with the formation only to have flak fragments damage the already defunct radar equipment while crossing the Dutch coast. The H2S equipment of the Knettishall pathfinder, *Finger M-Mike*, was found faulty before take-off so this Fortress – first in the 8th Air Force to have H2S fitted – did not go on the mission. *Finger S-Sugar* flying from Thorpe Abbotts performed satisfactorily for the 3rd Division and formations released bombs into the clouds below the pathfinder's marker flares. Some bombs found the docks at Emden but most fell far and wide around the general area of the city.

INCIDENT

With increasing losses on daylight raids, 8th Air Force gave serious consideration to engaging in night operations during the late summer of 1943. In September the 95th, 96th and 385th Groups in 3rd Division were instructed to begin training and the modification of 30 aircraft at each station was put in hand. Gun flash eliminators, resin lights, flame dampers and black-out curtains were installed and a programme of local night flights arranged. On 27 September the 96th and 385th Groups each despatched a B-17 for a first participation in one of the RAF's 'Bulls Eye' practice night bombings. For another 385th Group crew out that night, one of the dangers of operating in darkness was illustrated all too clearly. On a training sortie, 1/Lt Don Jones found flying conditions poor and after an uncomfortable few minutes in the vicinity of some barrage balloons, set course for home base at a higher altitude. At the precise moment when Jones pushed the control column forward to reduce altitude again 'the whole sky lit up around us'. Instantly aware that there was an enemy intruder shooting at his bomber, Jones cut all recognition lights and engaged in some evasive manoeuvres lest the assailant was still in contact. After a few minutes the B-17 arrived over the blacked-out home base and Jones radioed the tower for landing instructions. It was arranged for the Fortress to fly the circuit and make an approach whereupon runway illumination would be provided. Jones complied and as he brought the bomber in the runway lights were switched on and then off again giving just enough time for the B-17 to touch down. Extinguishing the lights again proved a wise action for as the Fortress continued its blind roll up the runway the intruder, probably a Ju 88, passed low overhead, unable to see its quarry. On inspection only a few bullet holes were to be found in the fin of the B-17, Jones having been fortunate in making his descent just as the enemy chose to attack.

27/28 SEPTEMBER 1943

VIII BC 105 NIGHT ATTACK – HANNOVER (WITH RAF)

	Despatched	Effective	Target	Bombs Tonnage	E/A	Losses MIA	E	Dam	Casualties KIA	WIA	MIA
1BD			HANNOVER	40 × 500GP							
B-17	422BS 5	4	2208–2217 hrs	4 × Photoflash		1	0	0	0	0	10

Howard 'Deacon' Hively was at 28 one of the older pilots of 4FG. An ex-RAF Eagle Squadron flier, he endured at Debden until January 1945 and rose through squadron command of 334FS to acting Group CO. Here Duke, an ex-police Alsatian, seems to have taken exception to the pilot's gloves.

2 OCTOBER 1943

VIII BC 106

		Despatched	Effective	Target	Bombs Tonnage	E/A	Losses MIA	E	Dam	Casualties KIA	WIA	MIA
3BD				EMDEN I/A (P)								
B-17	94BG	23	22	1557–1603 hrs	2795 × 500GP	0–0–0	0		2	0	0	0
	95BG	22	22		93 × 1000GP	6–1–2	0		3	0	0	0
	96BG	42	39		4160 × 100GP	0–0–0	0		1	0	0	0
	100BG	26	26			3–3–2	0		0	0	0	0
	385BG	25	23			0–0–0	0		0	0	0	0
	388BB	21	21			0–0–0	1		0	0	0	10
	390BG	27	27			4–2–4	0		5	0	0	0
1BD				EMDEN I/A (P)								
B-17	91BG	16	15	1557–1603 hrs		0–0–2	0		7	0	1	0
	92BG	19	17			0–0–0	0		0	0	0	0
	303BG	19	19			1–0–1	1		6	0	1	11
	305BG	17	16			0–0–0	0		1	0	0	0
	306BG	18	18			0–0–0	0		0	0	0	0
	351BG	19	19			1–0–0	0		4	0	0	0
	379BG	17	17			0–0–1	0		3	0	0	0
	381BG	19	19			0–0–0	0		1	0	0	0
	384BG	17	17			0–0–0	0		0	0	0	0
	PFF			As above								
	482BG	2	2			0–0–0	0		1	0	0	0
TOTALS:		349	339		953.25	15–6–12	2	0	34	0	2	21
2BD				WOENSDRECHT A/F								
B-24	392BG	21	0			0–0–0	0	0	0	0	0	0

REMARKS: 392BG target obscured by cloud. 303BG B-17 ditched off Essex coast on return after all crew except pilot had baled out over land. Pilot rescued.

VIII FC FO 148

Despatched		Groups	E/A	Losses MIA	E	Dam	Casualties KIA	WIA	MIA
P-47	227	4FG, 56FG, 78FG, 353FG, 355FG	5–3–1	0	0	1	0	0	0

REMARKS: Heavy bomber escort. Group credits: 4FG – 2, 56FG – 3, 353FG – 1.

VIII ASC 75

		Despatched	Effective	Target	Bombs Tonnage	E/A	Losses MIA	E	Dam	Casualties KIA	WIA	MIA
3BW				ST.OMER/								
B-26	322BG	36	6	LONGUENESSE			0		11	1	3	0
	387BG	36	0	A/F (P) 1715 hrs					1	0	1	0
TOTALS:		72	6		9.0	0	0	0	12	1	4	0

7PG despatched 1 F-5 to Emden area.

2/3 OCTOBER 1943

VIII BC 107 NIGHT ATTACK – MUNICH (WITH RAF)

		Despatched	Effective	Target	Bombs Tonnage	E/A	Losses MIA	E	Dam	Casualties KIA	WIA	MIA
1BD				MUNICH								
B-17	422BS	2	2	2245–2258 hrs	20 × 500GP	0	0	0	0	0	0	0

3 OCTOBER 1943

VIII ASC 76, 77 & 78

		Despatched	Effective	Target	Bombs Tonnage	E/A	Losses MIA	E	Dam	Casualties KIA	WIA	MIA
3BW				LILLE/VENDEVILLE								
B-26	323BG	18	0	A/F				0	0			
	386BG	18	0					0	0			
				AMSTERDAM/								
	323BG	36	35	SCHIPHOL				0	29			
	322BG	36	36	A/F 1120–1121 hrs				0	9			
	387BG	36	29	WOENSDRECHT A/F (P)				0	9			
	386BG	36	31	1121–1125 hrs (34 a/c)				0	0			
				HAAMSTEDE A/F (S)								
				1128–1136 hrs (26 a/c)								
	387BG	18	13	BEAUVAIS/TILLE (P)				0	2			
	322BG	18	16	A/F 1724–1727 hrs				0	5			
	323BG	18	16					0	3			
	386BG	18	18					1	17			
TOTALS:		252	194		288.85		0	1	74	0	5	0

REMARKS: On ASC 77 mission, 387BG and 386BG formations attacked both targets. 386 BG B-26 cr. landing base after Beauvais mission.

VIII FC FO 65

Despatched		Groups	E/A	Losses MIA	E	Dam	Casualties KIA	WIA	MIA
P-47	70	4FG, 353FG	0	0	0	0	0	0	0

REMARKS: P-47s sent out on fighter sweeps. 7PG despatched 3 F-5 to Northern France.

4 OCTOBER 1943

VIII BC 108

		Despatched	Effective	Target	Bombs Tonnage	E/A	Losses MIA	E	Dam	Casualties KIA	WIA	MIA
1BD				FRANKFURT I/A 77 a/c								
B-17	306BG	16	14	& WIESBADEN I/A	180 × 1000GP	5–0– 3	0	15 a/c	13	1	2	0
	92BG	17	17	15 a/c (P)	372 × 500GP	1–0– 3	1		3	0	2	10
	305BG	17	15	1059–1105 hrs	666 × 100IB	2–0– 4	1		9	0	1	10
	303BG	19	15		(77 a/c)	7–1– 1	1		7	0	2	10
	379BG	18	16		90 × 1000GP	2–2– 1	1		11	0	0	10
	384BG	17	16		(15 a/c)	2–0– 3	1		2	1	1	0
TOTALS:		104	93		261.3	19–3–15	5	0	45	2	8	40
1BD				FRANKFURT CITY (P)								
B-17	381BG	17	12	1110–1111 hrs	143 × 500GP	5–1– 4	0		11	0	0	0
	351BG	17	14		1050 × 100IB	10–6–11	2		13	0	1	20
	91BG	17	11			3–1– 7	1		11	1	1	10
TOTALS:		51	37		88.25	18–8–22	3		35	1	2	30
3BD				SAARLAUTERN I/A 67 a/c								
B-17	95BG	21	19	ST.DIZIER/	216 × 1000GP	5–1– 1	1	1	1	0	1	9
	100BG	25	23	ROBINSON A/F 38 a/c (L)	1215 × 100IB	9–1– 0	1	0	2	0	0	10
	390BG	25	25	1136–1145 hrs	(67 a/c)	5–2– 2	0	0	2	0	1	0
	385BG	20	17		82 × 1000GP	5–1– 1	1	0	2	0	1	0
	94BG	24	21		885 × 100IB	13–2– 3	1	1	12	0	3	10
					(38 a/c)							
TOTALS:		115	105		254.0	37–7– 7	4	2	19	0	6	29
3BD				SARREGUEMINES &								
B-17	96BG	35	32	SAARBRÜCKEN M/Ys (L)	192 × 500GP	0–0– 0	0		2	0	0	0
	388BG	18	15	1133–1139 hrs	1095 × 100IB	0–0– 0	0		0	0	0	0
TOTALS:		53	47		102.75	0–0– 0	0	0	2	0	0	0
2BD				DIVERSION								
B-24	392BG	32	–			12–5– 3	3		16	0	6	31
	44BG	6	–			1–1– 0	1		3	0	5	12
TOTALS:		38	–			13–6– 3	4	0	19	0	11	43

REMARKS: Leaders of mission 100 miles off course. Crews of 100BG & 384BG B-17s down in sea, rescued. 385BG with b/d abandoned over Southwold on return, crashed in sea, crew safe. 94BG B-17 c/l near Margate on return. 95BG B-17 c/l Earls Colne A/F, m/f, crew safe. Me 109 fighter collided with MIA 44BG B-24.

4 OCTOBER 1943 *(contd.)*

VIII FC FO 150

Despatched		Groups	E/A	Losses MIA	E	Dam	Casualties KIA	WIA	MIA
P-47	223	4FG, 56FG, 78FG, 353FG, 355FG	19–1–2		1	15	1	0	0

REMARKS: Escort and support for heavy bombers. Fighter group e/a credits: 56FG – 16, 353FG – 1, 355FG –1. 355FG P-47 damaged by e/a c/l, pilot k. First use of drop tanks by 355FG.

VIII ASC 79

	Despatched		Effective	Target	Bombs Tonnage	E/A	Losses MIA	E	Dam	Casualties KIA	WIA	MIA
3BW				BEAUVAIS/								
B-26	386BG	17	0	NIVILLIERS A/F								
	323BG	8	0	EVREUX/FAUVILLE A/F								
TOTALS		25	0		0		0	0	0	0	0	0

4/5 OCTOBER 1943

VIII BC 109 NIGHT ATTACK – FRANKFURT-AM-MAIN (WITH RAF)

	Despatched		Effective	Target		Bombs Tonnage	E/A	Losses MIA	E	Dam	Casualties KIA	WIA	MIA
1BD				FRANKFURT-AM-MAIN									
B-17	422BS	3	2	2145 hrs	(P)	10 × 500GP		1	0	0	0	0	10
				WIESBADEN	(O)								

7/8 OCTOBER 1943

VIII BC 110 NIGHT LEAFLET OPERATION – FRANCE

	Despatched		Effective	Locality	No. of leaflets	Losses
1BD				PARIS		
B-17	422BS	4	4	2257–2307 hrs	240,352	0

Above. Smoke pot flares strung out along a major road provided a patchy cloak over Bremen on 8 October as 388BG Fortresses attack. By this date 22 enemy ports were known to have smoke screen facilities.

Right. S/Sgt Louis Kiss was credited with the destruction of three enemy fighters during the air battle on 8 October when 390BG's *Phyllis Marie* was under attack for five minutes. The tail gunner used his name to pointed effect to decorate his location.

Leaving a huge pall of smoke over Marienburg, *House Of Lords* and other 94BG B-17s face a long flight back to base. The destruction wrought at the aircraft plant on 9 October was an extraordinarily successful example of daylight precision bombing. Despite a 1,500 mile round trip and nearly 10 hours in the air, good weather and little opposition made this a red letter day and allowed the B-17s to attack from altitudes as low as 12,000 feet. At a time when VIII BC campaign was at a critical stage full advantage was taken of photographs such as this, released and carried in most US and British newspapers aimed at maintaining public and official confidence in this form of strategic bombing.

8 OCTOBER 1943

VIII BC III

	Despatched		Effective	Target	Bombs Tonnage	E/A	Losses MIA	E	Dam	Casualties KIA	WIA	MIA
1BD				BREMEN S/Y (P)								
B-17	91BG	16	15	1505–1513 hrs	520 × 500GP	3– 1– 6	1		15	0	9	10
	381BG	21	18	AND T/OS	(44 a/c) (P)	19– 1– 8	7		11	2	3	70
	351BG	19	14			2– 0– 6	0		5	0	1	0
	379BG	21	20			4– 0– 1	1		20	0	3	10
	384BG	21	18			14– 0– 7	0		3	0	2	0
	303BG	20	20			0– 0– 0	0		7	0	0	0
TOTALS:		118	105		130.0 (P)	42– 2–28	9	0	61	2	18	90
1BD				BREMEN I/A (P)								
B-17	305BG	17	15	1512–1513 hrs	180 × 500GP	6– 1– 5	1		15	0	4	10
	306BG	20	20	AND T/OS	720 × 100IB	15– 5–10	3		17	1	6	31
	92BG	19	18		(33 a/c) (P)	3– 1– 2	0		12	0	2	0
TOTALS:		56	53		81.0 (P)	24– 7–17	4	0	44	1	12	41
2BD				VEGESACK U/Y (P)								
B-24	389BG	18	13	1622–1624 hrs	342 × 500GP	10– 1– 2	1		4	0	1	10
	93BG	19	17		(P)	4– 0– 3	0		8	0	3	0
	392BG	18	13			3– 0– 2	2		9	1	1	20
TOTALS:		55	43		85.5 (P)	17– 1– 7	3	0	21	1	5	30
3BD				BREMEN CITY (P)								
B-17	388BG	21	21	1505–1527 hrs	993 × 500GP	1– 0– 2	0		17	0	0	0
	94BG	21	19	AND T/OS	(197 a/c)*	4– 2– 1	0		19	0	3	0
	96BG	42	40			6– 3–17	3		32	0	3	30
	385BG	22	18			4– 2– 0	1	0	0	0	0	10
	100BG	22	19			13– 0– 3	7	1	9	0	13	70
	390BG	21	20			32– 3– 5	3	0	17	0	1	30
	95BG	21	19			24– 2– 5	0	1	16	0	1	0
TOTALS:		170	156		248.25	84–12–33	14	2	110	0	21	140

REMARKS: Cloud caused several formations to attack T/Os. 19 1BD B-17s dropped 228 × 500GP on Vegesack at 1505–1517 hrs. 18 1BD B-17 dropped 676 × 100IB on Oldenburg at 1512 hrs. 3 1BD B-17 dropped 12 × 500GP and 72 × 100IB on Meppen at 1512–1517 hrs. 1 93BG B-24 dropped 12 × 500GP on Emden at 1625 hrs and 13 392BG dropped 512 × 100IB on T/Os.* Bremen city bomb totals include 1BW drops as T/O. First mission of 93BG and 389BG since returning from Africa. 381BG awarded a DUC for action this day. B/d 95BG B-17 c/l Rackheath A/F. B/d 100BG B-17 cr. landing Ludham A/F.

VIII FC FO 151

Despatched		Groups	E/A	Losses MIA	E	Dam	Casualties KIA	WIA	MIA
P-47	274	4FG, 56FG, 78FG, 352FG 353FG 355FG	12-2-4	3	0	5	0	2	3

REMARKS: Escort for 1BD and 3BD only. Fighter group losses: 4FG – 2, 56FG – 1. Fighter group e/a credits: 4FG – 6, 56FG – 5, 353FG – 2.

VIII ASC 80

	Despatched		Effective	Target	Bombs Tonnage	E/A	Losses MIA	E	Dam	Casualties KIA	WIA	MIA
3BW				LILLE/VENDEVILLE								
B-26	323BG	36	0	A/F								
	386BG	36	0	CHIEVRES A/F								
	322BG	36	0									
	387BG	36	0									
TOTALS:		144	0		0	0	0	0	4	0	0	0

REMARKS: Abandoned due to weather. Last missions with VIII ASC for 322 and 386 Groups, prior to transferring to 9AF.

7PG despatched 4 F-5 to France and Holland.

8/9 OCTOBER 1943

VIII BC 112 NIGHT LEAFLET OPERATION – FRANCE

	Despatched		Effective	Locality	No. of Leaflets	Losses
1BD				RENNES		
B-17	422BS	2	2	0005–0011 hrs	266,336	0

9 OCTOBER 1943

VIII BC

	Despatched		Effective	Target	Bombs Tonnage	E/A	Losses MIA	Casualties E	Dam	KIA	WIA	MIA
1BD				ANKLAM I/A (P)								
B-17	303BG	20	18	1142–1146 hrs	318 × 1000GP	2– 2– 6	1	0	7	0	0	10
	379BG	20	20		530 × 100IB	9– 2– 4	2	1	7	0	10	20
	384BG	21	19			9– 1– 2	2	0	2	0	0	20
	351BG	21	20			26– 2–18	5	0	16	0	5	51
	91BG	17	13			6– 5– 7	5	0	8	0	4	50
	381BG	16	16			13– 7–10	3	0	11	0	6	34
TOTALS:		115	106		185.5	65–19–47	18	1	51	0	25	185
3BD				MARIENBURG I/A (P)								
	385BG	22	21	1253–1302 hrs	598 × 500GP	2– 0– 0	1		1	0	2	11
	94BG	18	18		1368 × 100IB	0– 1– 0	0		5	0	0	0
	390BG	21	21			2– 1– 0	0		4	0	0	0
	100BG	16	13			0– 0– 0	0		0	0	0	0
	95BG	23	23			5– 0– 0	1		3	0	1	10
TOTALS:		100	96		217.9	9– 2– 0	2	0	13	0	3	21
2BD				DANZIG U/Y (P)								
B-24	93BG	17	13	1305 hrs	201 × 500GP	0– 0– 0	2	0	7	0	1	21
	389BG	12	10			2– 0– 0	0	1	1	0	0	0
	44BG	8	8	GDYNIA P/A (S)	144 × 500GP	3– 3– 0	0	0	2	0	0	0
	392BG	14	10			2– 0– 4	0	0	9	0	0	0
TOTALS:		51	41		86.25	7– 3– 4	2	1	19	0	1	21
3BD				GDYNIA P/A (P)								
B-17	96BG	28	28	1304–1324 hrs	544 × 1000GP	13– 3– 4	2	0	17	0	4	20
	388BG	24	23			17– 1– 2	2	1	20	0	2	20
1BD				GDYNIA P/A (P)								
B-17	305BG	18	17	1304–1324 hrs		2– 0– 0	0	0	8	0	0	0
	92BG	21	21			7– 0– 0	1	0	13	0	0	10
	306BG	21	20			2– 1– 4	1	0	4	0	0	10
TOTALS:		112	109		272.0	41– 5–10	6	1	62	0	6	60

REMARKS: Excellent bombing by 3BD. First bombing mission of 44BG since returning from Africa. 351BG awarded DUC for action this day. 1 96BG B-17 and 2 93BG B-24s interned in Sweden. 385BG B-17 with mechanical trouble c/l in Denmark. 388BG B-17 out of fuel c/l at Lt. Barningham. B/d 389BG B-24 c/l at Choseley. B/d 379BG B-17 c/l near base out of fuel.

VIII FC FO 152

Despatched		Groups	E/A	Losses MIA	Casualties E	Dam	KIA	WIA	MIA
P-47	153	78FG, 352FG, 353FG, 355FG	0	0	0	0	0	0	0

REMARKS: Fighters swept Leeuwarden area prior to joining bombers.

VIII ASC 81

	Despatched		Effective	Target	Bombs Tonnage	E/A	Losses MIA	Casualties E	Dam	KIA	WIA	MIA
3BW				WOENSDRECHT A/F (P)								
B-26	323BG	36	34	1516–1526 hrs	203 × 500GP				10	0	0	0
	387BG	36	32		316 × 300GP				16	0	0	0
TOTALS:		72	66		98.15	0	0	0	26	0	0	0

REMARKS: Final VIII ASC B-26 operation prior to transfer to 9AF.

7PG despatched 8 F-5 sorties to France and Holland.

One of the most concentrated air battles to date saw the three groups of 13CBW lose 25 B-17s at Münster on 10 October. Badly damaged, one of these, 95BG's *Herky Jerky II* (circled), Capt Snow and crew, managed to make it back across the North Sea to an emergency landing at Beccles.

Son of the US Ambassador to Britain, Lt John Winant was pilot of a 390BG Fortress that went down on the Münster raid. The 21-year-old pilot baled out and was taken prisoner. Photo taken in August a few days after completing his first combat sortie.

10 OCTOBER 1943

VIII BC 114

	Despatched		Effective	Target	Bombs Tonnage	E/A	Losses MIA	E	Dam	Casualties KIA	WIA	MIA
3BD				MÜNSTER R/R								
B-17	94BG	21	18	& W/W (P)	41 × 1000GP	10– 0– 2	0	0	9	0	1	0
	95BG	20	17	1503–1518 hrs	804 × 500GP	41– 5–19	5	0	10	0	5	51
	96BG	21	20		4050 × 100IB	16– 2– 6	1	0	4	0	0	10
	100BG	14	12			2– 1– 1	12	1	1	0	2	120
	385BG	19	17		(P)	34– 3– 5	2	0	6	0	0	20
	388BG	19	18			14– 3– 8	1	0	17	0	3	10
	390BG	19	17			60– 6– 8	8	0	9	1	3	85
1BD				MÜNSTER R/R (P)								
B-17	91BG	10	6	& W/W		1– 0– 0	1	0	6	0	0	10
	351BG	17	8			3– 1– 2	0	1	2	0	3	0
	381BG	6	5			0– 0– 0	0	0	5	0	1	0
	92BG	19	15	COESFELD (O)	396 × 500GP	0– 0– 0	0	0	12	1	0	0
	306BG	18	18		34 × 1000GP	0– 0– 0	0	0	16	0	0	0
	303BG	20	20		1428 × 100IB	0– 0– 0	0	0	2	0	0	0
	384BG	18	15		173 × 500GP	0– 0– 0	0	1	0	0	0	0
	305BG	16	15	ENSCHEDE A/F (O)	30 × 1000GP	2– 0– 0	0	0	0	0	0	0
	379 BG	17	15		620 × 100IB on T/O	0– 0– 0	0	0	3	0	0	0
2BD				DIVERSION								
B-24	44BG	19	0					0	0	0	0	0
	93BG	9	0					0	0	0	0	0
	389BG	11	0					0	0	0	0	0
TOTALS:		313	236		700.65	183–21–51	30	3	102	2	18	306

REMARKS: Strong fighter opposition to 3BD. 390BG claims were an all-time record for e/a destroyed by a bomber group on one operation. 95BG received a DUC for action this day. 30 305BG and 379BG B-17s dropped on Enschede A/F, Holland as a T/O but town hit killing 155 civilians. Only 1 100BG B-17 returned to base, the other surviving 100BG B-17 c/l Wattisham due to b/d. Two B-17s with b/d abandoned by crews on return – 384BG a/c cr. near Eye and a 351BG a/c cr. in sea off Covehithe. 91BG B-17 c/l Tannington out of fuel but later repaired.

VIII FC FO 153

Despatched		Groups	E/A	Losses MIA	E	Dam	Casualties KIA	WIA	MIA
P-47	216	4FG, 56FG, 78FG, 352FG, 353FG	19–0–0	1	2	1	0	0	1

REMARKS: Escort and support for heavy bombers. Fighter group losses: 352FG – 1. Fighter group e/a credits: 56FG – 10, 78FG – 5, 353FG – 5. 352FG P-47 cr. base, pilot injured. 56FG P-47 collided with vehicle at Boreham A/F.

An escort fighter with the range to accompany B-17s and B-24s to their most distant targets, the P-38 Lightning was scheduled for operations from Britain in the late summer. Two groups arrived but shortage of P-38s and technical problems delayed the introduction. Although 20FG moved into Kingscliffe in August it did not have sufficient aircraft to allow it to become fully operational until the end of the year. These examples taxiing past the control tower on 13 October lacked radio modifications and were only used for training.

14 OCTOBER 1943

VIII BC 115

		Despatched	Effective	Target	Bombs Tonnage	E/A	Losses MIA	E	Dam	Casualties KIA	WIA	MIA
1BD				SCHWEINFURT I/A (P)								
B-17	91BG	11	7	1439–1445 hrs	459 × 1000GP	3– 0– 0	1	0	6	0	2	10
	92BG	19	13		663 × 500GP	26– 5– 8	6	1	3	1	4	60
	303BG	19	18		1751 × 100IB	20– 4–13	1	1	15	0	5	11
	305BG	16	3			1– 0– 1	13	0	2	0	3	130
	306BG	18	5			4– 1– 6	10	0	6	0	2	100
	351BG	16	10			4– 1– 7	1	0	9	0	5	10
	379BG	17	17			17– 4– 9	6	0	9	0	3	60
	381BG	17	15			11– 0– 7	1	0	12	0	3	10
	384BG	16	13			5– 1– 2	6	3	1	0	2	60
3BD				SCHWEINFURT I/A (P)								
B-17	94BG	21	21	1451–1457 hrs		21– 2– 9	6	0	14	1	2	50
	95BG	18	16			18– 1– 1	1	0	5	0	0	13
	96BG	41	32			11– 1–12	7	0	12	2	5	70
	100BG	8	8			7– 0– 0	0	0	1	0	0	0
	385BG	21	20			18– 2– 9	0	1*	14	1	2	0
	388BG	18	16			6– 2– 3	0	1	15	0	1	0
	390BG	15	15			14– 3– 2	1	0	14	0	1	10
2BD				DIVERSION (O)								
B-24	93BG	15	0			0– 0– 0	0	0	0	0	0	0
	392BG	14	0			0– 0– 0	0	0	0	0	0	0
TOTALS:		320	229		482.8	186–27–89	60	7	138	5	40	594

REMARKS: Of 60 B-24s scheduled, only 29 able to make formation in poor weather. This force abandoned mission and carried out diversion towards Emden. 1 303BG B-17 dropped 3 × 1000GP and 5 × 100IB on T/O. 390BG awarded DUC for action this day.

1 94BG B-17 MIA manned by 96BG crew. 1 388BG B-17 cr. on t/o, crew safe. 1 305BG B-17 interned in Switzerland. On return 3 b/d 384BG B-17s abandoned over England – one cr. Wakerley, one cr. Blaydon, the third at Chetwode. 1 303BG B-17 cr. near Roseley after crew baled out. 1 92BG B-17 c/l at Aldermaston. *1 385BG B-17 flown by 96BG crew c/l near Bovingdon – out of fuel.

VIII FC FO 156

Despatched		Groups	E/A	Losses MIA	E	Dam	Casualties KIA	WIA	MIA
P-47	196	4FG, 56FG, 352FG, 353FG	13-1-5	1	4	2	1	0	1

REMARKS: Cloud caused difficulties for Fighters. 352FG escorted B-24s. 4FG unable to locate bombers and recalled at enemy coast. 78FG and 355FG restricted by weather. 56FG and 353FG gave penetration support for heavy bombers. Fighter group losses: 353FG – 1. Fighter group e/a credits: 56FG – 3, 353FG – 10. B/d 355FG P-47 c/l base, pilot safe. On return 353FG P-47 cr. Herongate, pilot killed; 56FG P-47 c/l Breznett and 56FG P-47 c/l Doddington, Kent, pilots safe.

INCIDENT

In view of the deep penetration of enemy defences and the mauling suffered by the Fortresses on the August mission, staff and combatants alike expected fierce opposition to the second Schweinfurt raid. For this reason and the importance of the target, commanders were on hand at briefing to give special encouragement. At Great Ashfield Lt.Col Vandevanter concluded the tense briefing session for aircrew with: 'This is a tough job and I know you can do it. Good luck, good bombing and good hunting.' To which a gunner at the back of the room added in a loud voice: 'And good-bye!' The tension was broken by loud guffaws. The apprehensive gunner and all 385th Group bombers returned safely.

INCIDENT

Luftwaffe fighters were chiefly responsible for the punishing assault on the Fortresses during the second Schweinfurt mission. Nevertheless, flak claimed at least two of the bombers and damaged others. The leadplane of the 3rd Division force nearly fell to flak and the story of its survival is one of the most dramatic incidents of the raid. The importance of the target called for an expert team to lead. Assembled to fly in the 96th Bomb Group's *Fertile Myrtle III* that morning were Capt Tom Kenny, Operations Officer of 338th Bomb Squadron, as pilot and Col Archie Olds, CO of 45th Combat Wing, the Task Force commander as co-pilot. The Group navigator, Maj Robert Hodson, with Capt Bill Jones, another lead navigator, were to ensure there was no deviation on route, and Capt John Latham, Group Bombardier of the 96th, would sight on target. Although the formation was under attack by

Capt John Latham pointing out a target. Picture made 26 August.

Strike photo from 96BG's *Fertile Myrtle III*. Flak positions circled.

An Me 410 coming in on 94BG during approach to Schweinfurt.

fighters for one-and-a-half hours the lead Fortress did not take any hurt until the bomb run when a flak shell exploded close to the nose. Fragments hit bombardier Latham in the head and legs and he was knocked from the bombsight. Righting himself, he returned to the instrument to complete his task, resulting in an accurate strike on the bearing factories.

Fertile Myrtle III avoided further opposition until passing Reims where a railway flak battery suddenly opened fire. One burst hit the nose blasting Maj Hodson's back and killing him instantly. The same shell drove fragments into Latham's upper left thigh, peppered Capt Jones, shattered plexiglass into Kenny's legs and blew Olds out of his seat. Numbers 2 and 3 engines took fire but the flames disappeared when the propellers were feathered. The Fortress, at 20,000 ft, went into a dive from which the pilots made a recovery around 11,000 ft. A flight of Me 110s then appeared alongside and to the crew the chances of the crippled B-17 enduring much longer seemed slim. Gunners Roy Bayford and Bill Thorns claimed hits on two of the Messerschmitts before Kenny managed to seek sanctuary in clouds. As the fighters turned away, it seems probable that their ammunition was exhausted. The bomber, still losing height and down to 3,500 ft, was only just above stalling speed as it reached the Channel. The pilots restarted one of the damaged engines to try and gain height only to have to feather it again when it showed signs of catching fire. The emergency procedure of the crew dumping guns and loose equipment overboard was ordered in an effort to avoid ditching. To their relief the cliffs of Dover at last appeared ahead. Low over Kent, down to a few hundred feet, a landing place was becoming imperative when the grass airfield at Gravesend came into view. Kenny, a brilliant pilot, brought the bomber in safely even though forced into a down-wind approach. The crew's relief that the ordeal was over was subdued by the harrowing sight of the Group Navigator's mutilated body being removed from the Fortress. As Col Olds dropped to the ground from the nose hatch he said to Kenny, 'Save me a pew in church on Sunday.'

Some members would receive awards for their conduct, Latham his country's second highest award for bravery. Something of a reluctant hero he later protested – one suspects tongue-in-cheek – that the aftermath was his greater ordeal. His account reveals a delightful sense of humour:

'An ambulance came and took me and Jones to the infirmary, and the rest of them went to the Officers' Mess to have a drink. A medic dressed a slight wound Archie had received. Bill Jones and I wanted to go to the Mess and have a few also, but they refused. When we got to the infirmary there was no one there but an orderly. The orderly asked us if we would like a drink and we eagerly responded in the affirmative. He returned after several minutes and gave us each a cup of tea, which was not what we wanted at all. Another long wait and a doctor arrived and told us to strip so he could examine us. Bill was wearing Long Johns with a white top and red legs. We had told the doctor we had been shot in the legs and when Bill dropped his breeches the Long Johns had just enough blood on them to look like his legs were due to fall off at any moment. We really got some action then . . . the doctor started screaming at orderlies and everybody was tearing around. The doctor ended up putting about fifty band aids on Bill's legs. He put a few on mine but said I would have to go to the hospital as I had some holes in my thigh and hip that he could not fix. Bill had to go with me for X-rays. So we got back in the ambulance and headed for hospital. On the way we conned the driver to go by the Officers' Mess so we could tell the fellows where we were going. We hobbled in and had three quick ones before the orderlies dragged us out. Then came the most terrifying incident of the Schweinfurt mission. When we got to hospital we went in the Emergency Entrance and two nurses took us to a dressing room where they told us to strip to the buff. We refused to do it unless they left the room. We were very pure young Americans and in our hospitals male orderlies always helped us. A big argument ensued and finally a Sister and two more nurses arrived and stripped us forthwith. We were then X-rayed and they put me on an operating table and carried me to an operating room in which two boys were standing. They said they were surgeons. When I asked their age one said 19 and the other said 20. I requested immediate removal to an American hospital, but they just gave me a shot. When I awoke I was in a big ward and Bill was in the bed next to me. When he saw I was awake he leaned over and said: "Lathe, you ain't going to get no breakfast in the morning." Although I really wasn't interested in breakfast at that moment I had to ask why. Bill said, "Because you weren't here to order it." Well, Bill was right.

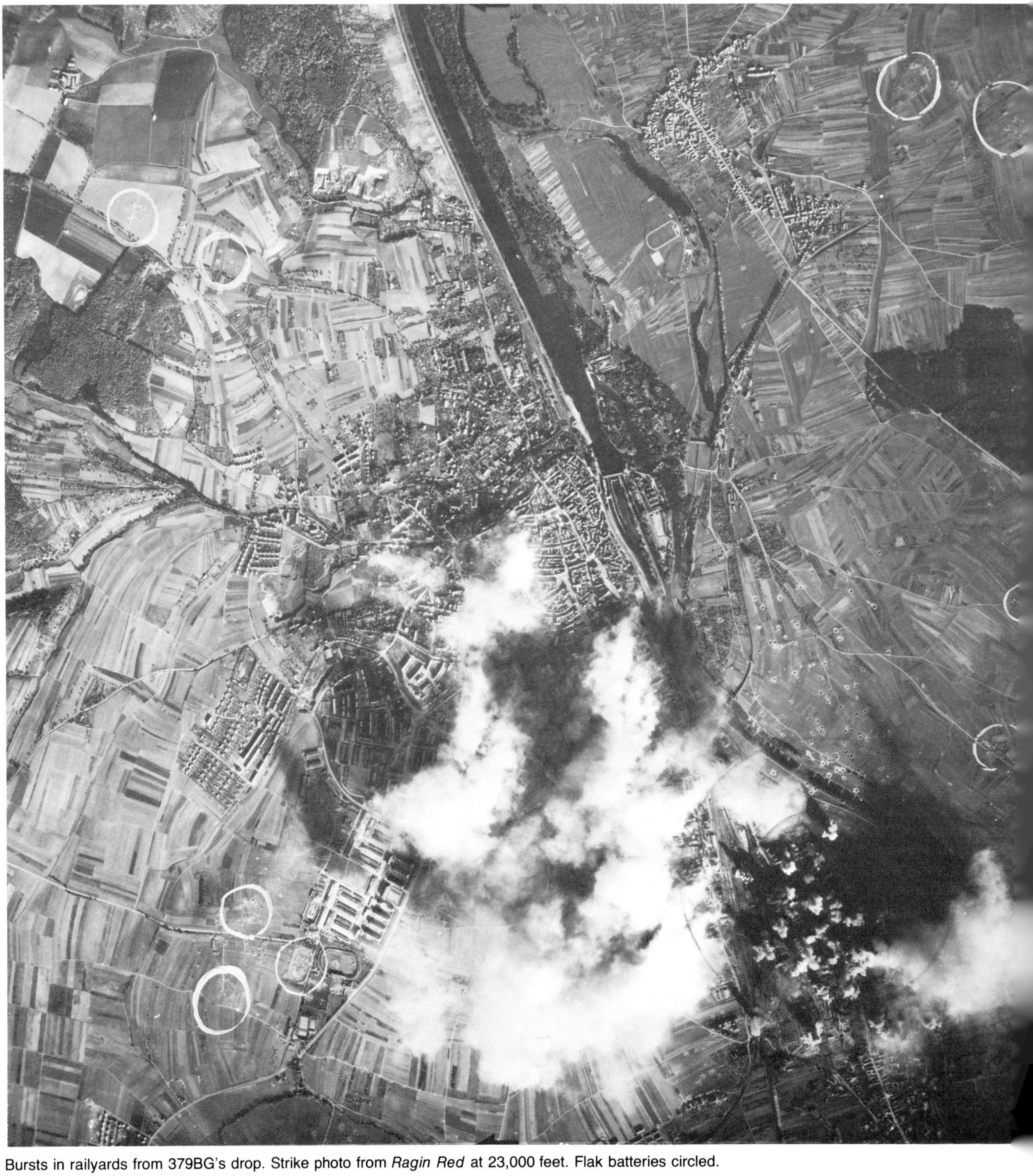

Bursts in railyards from 379BG's drop. Strike photo from *Ragin Red* at 23,000 feet. Flak batteries circled.

The next day some fellows from the 96th came and got Bill, but I remained. It was an interesting experience and an enjoyable one. It seems that I was the first "Yank" the folks in the ward and their relatives had ever seen. A few of them had had sons trained in the States and they could not do enough for me. I tried to refuse all the cakes and cookies because I knew it might mean their whole month's rations, but they would not take no for an answer. They were wonderful people. I held out going to the bathroom for a couple of days as I did not want a nurse to give me a bedpan. Tried to make it to the bathroom a couple of times on my own but fell flat on my face. They fed me so damn many prunes that I ended up with no choice in the matter. I also got used to being bathed by a Red Cross and St. John lady. Unfortunately my boots had been blown off in the raid and my feet were frostbitten. The good lady just thought I had dirty feet (they were black at the bottom) and she scrubbed them hard for three days before I could see them and explain to Sister what the problem was. The lady used rubbing alcohol on my feet. I should add that this is my most painful memory of the Schweinfurt raid as I cannot abide cold weather, or rather my feet cannot.

At night I was terrified in the hospital. The Germans seemed to drop bombs on Gravesend all the time and the hospital shook like it was in an earthquake. I had never been in bombing raids from this end. The gentleman in the bed next to me was a victim of one of these raids. He said he had been blown clean through his house, and that it was the third time that he had been bombed out. From the standpoint of survival, he was most comforting. A pretty little nurse would also come and hold my hand when the raids were going on as I would start yelling when I heard the air raid siren. So much for being a hero. My days were spent in trying to convince the other 39 people in the ward that I was not a "Yank" but a "Johnny Reb" (Southerner). I never succeeded, and they called me "Yank" until the day Kenny came to get me and carry me to our base hospital.'

SCHWEINFURT

Schweinfurt became the most infamous of 8th Air Force target names through the exceptionally high losses incurred in the execution of the first two missions. The second was the culmination of a series of high-loss operations by unescorted bombers and brought temporary curtailment of very deep penetrations until more long-range fighters were available. The following account of his experiences on 14 October was written shortly afterwards by Capt Edwin Millson, lead bombardier of the 379th Bomb Group.

'At 0330 the Charge of Quarters awakened me with the order to report to operations. I walked along the moonlit road to the operations block wondering what the target for the day would be and feeling an odd excitement. Checking the operations board I saw that our crew was scheduled to lead a combat wing of Fortresses on the day's mission with Lt.Col Louis Rohr as our pilot. In the map room I found Navigator, Capt Joe Wall, drawing up his flight plan. 'You sure picked a nice one for your thirteenth!' he said with a laugh and pointed to his map where a long zig-zagging line snaked its way into the heart of Germany and stopped at a medium sized town. . . . Schweinfurt. Again came the surge of excitement and as I settled down to another two hours of study and preparation of bombing data I knew that it would be rough – for this target was the one we had been studying so diligently for several weeks.

After a hasty breakfast and an exhaustive check of our ship – *Ragin' Red* – and her equipment, we took off at 1030 hrs into a sky already dotted with other formations. We circled the field and gained altitude while the rest of our group slipped into position and then moved off on course. At 1238 hrs the tail gunner reported the high and low groups in position, just as the English coast slipped by below us.

Overhead waves of P-47s appeared – beneath was the icy Channel – and ahead lay the long route yet to be covered. Light inaccurate flak to our right as we passed over the enemy coast indicated that Joe Wall had the wing directly on course. The crew, alert and watchful, called out the presence of friendly fighters and we were mighty happy to have our little friends around. Their range at this stage of the war was limited and shortly after we entered enemy territory they had to depart for home.

'Their departure spelled trouble, because soon afterwards we observed enemy "Bandits" climbing up to make things interesting. Little black dots grew into formations of FW 190s and Me 109s which began sweeping attacks into our formations. Attacking from eleven o'clock to one o'clock they would come in fast, rolling as they fired and "split S-ing" down out of range. The interphone crackled with terse statements – "fighters at one o'clock" – "I smoked that one" – "Fort down, six chutes".

Koblenz and Frankfurt were passed as we wove our way through rather spotty enemy opposition. Joe was successfully evading flak areas and then we reached the IP and started the bomb run. I took control and turned my attention to finding our aiming point. One glance took in checkpoints we had spent so many hours studying, and up ahead lay our target – Schweinfurt. After opening the bomb-bay doors and checking the switches for the umpteenth time, I bent over the Norden bombsight to find our aiming point on one of the three important ball-bearing factories. Flak was uncomfortably close – one burst blotting my view of the target for a brief second and a rattle like hail on a tin roof announcing another close call. I had the target lined up in the sight and I noticed smoke from hits on one of the other factories by the preceding wing was beginning to roll over our aiming point. Just as another burst of flak hailed against the side of the ship I called, "Bombs away, doors closing – let's get the hell out of here!"

Colonel Rohr took the ship again and began the turn off of the target. As he turned, a formation of FW 190s ripped in out of the sun in an unannounced, vicious fighter attack. Before anyone could open their mouth I heard the sharp crack of a bursting 20 mm shell right in back of me. Half expecting to find Joe badly injured, I whirled around to find him laughing and pointing to an object on the floor. There was my chest chute, which I had placed right next to my right hip, ripped and torn from the direct burst of the shell. I was left without a chute but it had saved both of us from possible serious injury. Looking around and checking the group, we found that the bandits had knocked down three ships on that one pass – later we found that one had been rammed by one of the attacking fighters!!

From then on Jerry started concentrated fighter attacks. I think that they had every possible available plan within range of our route in the air that day. In fact the Hun had vectored squadrons from long distances which arrived in time to give us hell somewhere along the route home. They began pressing home with rocket attacks and up ahead in the other wing I saw three Forts explode in mid-air from rocket hits. Jerry was attacking from all around the clock and we saw several obsolete types of German aircraft, one of which was a two-engine Dornier 217. They seemed determined to wipe us out.

Forts in other groups glided out of formation with feathered props or other tell-tale damage and once clear of the formation, chutes would spill out. Our formations were so split and weakened that both wings combined to make one for mutual support. Frequently the dark chutes of German fighter pilots could be seen intermingled with the white ones of our bomber crew men.

All along the route home we could see the smoking, flaming wreckage of ships that had gone down during the aerial battle. For awhile one could actually follow the path of the battle by looking at the wreckage on the ground. After what seemed an eternity of bucking strong head winds which the Germans were utilising for head-on attacks, our friendly fighter escort showed up and swept in on our attackers, dispersing them and shooting several down. As they circled around us one of the gunners was heard to utter a fervent "Thank God", voicing the sentiments of the entire formation. After another interval Joe announced that we had reached the cloud covered "tight little isle" – England.

At 1840 our wheels hit the runway, we had been in the air for eight hours and ten minutes, we had the worst fighter attacks anyone had ever seen and the flak had been rough as hell. I knew that our losses had been heavy but I felt that results were worth the cost in men and planes.

'After interrogation my first thought was about the strike photos. I hurried over to the photo lab, where the technicians were rushing the processing of the film. 1/Lt Ted Rohr, the group photo interpreter, was examining the wet prints. He answered my unasked question, "You hit, brother, you plastered hell out of the place!"

Later as he plotted the bomb hits we knew that our group and the groups that had preceded us had had excellent success. This somewhat alleviated the shock of our heavy losses – for sixty Forts had gone down on this one mission.'

15 OCTOBER 1943

VIII FC FO 157

Despatched		Groups	E/A	Losses MIA	E	Dam	Casualties KIA	WIA	MIA
P-38	36	55FG	0	0		1	0	0	0
P-47	34	356FG	0	0		0	0	0	0
TOTALS:	70		0	0		1	0	0	0

REMARKS: Fighters carried out sweeps over the Dutch Islands. First missions for both groups, and first time that P-38s had operated from England in over a year.

16 OCTOBER 1943

VIII FC FO 159

Despatched		Groups	E/A	Losses MIA	E	Dam	Casualties KIA	WIA	MIA
P-38	39	55FG	0	0					
P-47	132	352FG, 355FG, 356FG	0	0					
TOTALS:	171		0	0	0	0	0	0	0

REMARKS: Fighters performed sweeps over the Dutch Islands. 55FG also carried out a practice sweep with B-24s under FO 158.

7PG despatched 1 F-5 on Met flight to Amsterdam/Schipol.

17 OCTOBER 1943

VIII FC FO 161

Despatched		Groups	E/A	Losses MIA	E	Dam	Casualties KIA	WIA	MIA
P-38	35	55FG	0	0					
P-47	28	356FG	0	0					
TOTALS:	63		0	0	0	0	0	0	0

REMARKS: Carried out fighter sweeps over Northern France. Heavy bomber mission to Düren recalled and abandoned when leading elements – 3BD – over North Sea. 1 96BG B-17 caught fire and cr. in sea after crew baled out off Cromer. 10 men missing.

18 OCTOBER 1943

VIII FC FO 162

Despatched		Groups	E/A	Losses MIA	E	Dam	Casualties KIA	WIA	MIA
P-38	33	55FG	0	1		0	0	0	1
P-47	296	4FG, 56FG, 78FG, 352FG, 353FG, 355FG, 356FG	1–0–0	2		0	0	0	2
TOTALS:	329		1–0–0	3	0	0	0	0	3

REMARKS: Despatched on bomber escort but weather prevented rendezvous. Fighter group e/a credits: 56FG – 1. Fighter group losses: 55FG – 1, 78FG – 1, 355FG – 1.

Heavy bomber mission to Düren recalled over North Sea – weather deteriorated. B-24s carried out diversion feint. 94BG B-17 cr. near Dover, crew safe. 390BG B-17 abandoned by crew during assembly and cr. Icklesham.

19 OCTOBER 1943

VIII FC 66FW FO 20

Despatched		Groups	E/A	Losses MIA	E	Dam	Casualties KIA	WIA	MIA
P-38	37	55FG	0	0	0	0	0	0	0

REMARKS: Sweeps over Northern France.

20 OCTOBER 1943

VIII BC 116

	Despatched		Effective	Target	Bombs Tonnage	E/A	Losses MIA	E	Dam	Casualties KIA	WIA	MIA
3BD				DÜREN I/A (P)								
B-17	94BG	17	15	1413–1416 hrs	509 × 500GP	0–0–0	2	0	4	0	0	20
	95BG	16	16		1635 × 100IB	0–0–0	1	0	0	0	0	0
	96BG	21	19			0–0–0	2	1	0	0	0	20
	100BG	8	8			0–0–0	0	0	1	0	0	0
	385BG	17	11*			2–0–0	1	0	0	3	1	10
	388BG	16	16			0–0–0	0	0	0	0	0	0
	390BG	14	12			0–0–0	1	0	4	0	1	14
1BD				DÜREN I/A (P)								
B-17	91BG	3	0			0–0–0	0	0	0	0	0	0
	92BG	14	0			0–0–0	0	0	0	0	0	0
	303BG	19	0			2–1–1	2	0	1	0	0	21
	305BG	7	0			0–0–0	0	0	0	0	0	0
	306BG	11	0			0–0–0	0	0	0	0	0	0
	351BG	7	0			0–0–0	0	0	0	0	0	0
	379BG	17	17	WOENSDRECHT A/F (O)	10 × 500GP	0–0–0	0	0	0	1	0	0
	381BG	7	0	T/Os	156 × 500GP	0–0–0	0	0	0	0	0	0
	384BG	18	0	1430 hrs		0–0–0	0	0	0	0	0	0
2BD				DIVERSION								
B-24	44BG	18	0			0–0–0	0	0	0	0	0	0
	93BG	17	0			0–0–0	0	0	0	0	0	0
	389BG	18	0			0–0–0	0	0	0	0	0	0
	392BG	17	0			0–0–0	0	0	0	0	0	
TOTALS:		282	114		252.4	4–1–1	9	1	10	4	2	85

REMARKS: First use of Oboe PFF. Failure of this equipment in 1BD lead cause of return without bombing by most formations. As cloud tops were at 29,500ft 3BD bombed from 30,000ft. 3 gunners in a 385BG B-17 died through failure of oxygen equipment. On return 96BG B-17 cr. Beddingham, crew baled. The *11 B-17s of 385BG dropped 38 × 100IB on Aachen as a T/O; bombs not included in tables.

VIII FC FO 163

Despatched		Groups	E/A	Losses MIA	E	Dam	Casualties KIA	WIA	MIA
P-38	39	55FG	0–0–0	0	0	0	0	0	0
P-47	321	4FG, 56FG, 78FG, 352FG, 353FG, 355FG, 356FG	6–0–5	0	0	2	0	0	0
TOTALS:	360		6–0–5	0	0	2	0	0	0

REMARKS: Escort for heavy bombers. Fighter group e/a credits: 56FG – 2, 78FG – 1, 355FG – 1.

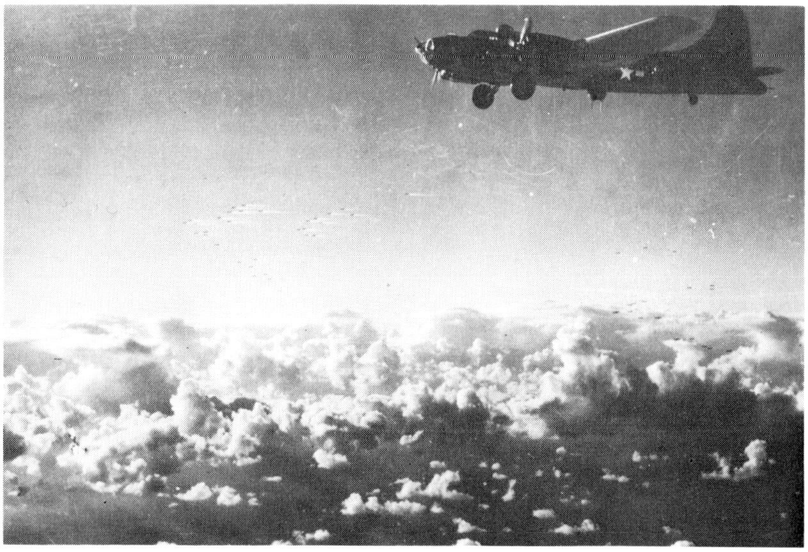

Wheels down was an 'I am aborting' signal to other aircraft in a formation. A fuel leak forced 388BG's *Iza Angel* to abandon the Düren mission of 20 October while at 22,000 ft over Essex. Other group formations can be seen in the distance. (via S. Evans)

20/21 OCTOBER 1943

VIII BC 117 NIGHT LEAFLET OPERATION – FRANCE

	Despatched		Effective	Locality	No. of Leaflets	Losses
1BD	422BS	5	5	ROUEN, PARIS	876,960	0
B-17				2211–2217 hrs		

22 OCTOBER 1943

VIII FC FO 165

Despatched		Groups	E/A	Losses MIA	E	Dam	Casualties KIA	WIA	MIA
P-38	42	55FG	0	0	0	1	0	0	0
P-47	349	4FG, 56FG, 78FG, 352FG, 353FG, 355FG, 356FG	0	2	1	8	0	0	2
TOTALS:	391		0	2	1	9	0	0	2

REMARKS: Despatched in support of 9AF B-26s. Fighter group losses: 353FG – 2. 355FG P-47 Cat E in c/l.

24 OCTOBER 1943

VIII FC FO 166

Despatched		Groups	E/A	Losses MIA	E	Dam	Casualties KIA	WIA	MIA
P-38	48	55FG	0	0	0	0	0	0	0
P-47	205	56FG, 78FG, 353FG, 356FG	1–1–0	0	0	1	0	0	0
TOTALS:	253		1–1–0	0	0	1	0	0	0

REMARKS: Sent out in support of 9AF B-26s. Fighter group e/a credits: 78FG – 1. A locomotive also claimed damaged by strafing.

7PG despatched 8 F-5s to Northern and Western France.

It was claimed that Rusty, pet spaniel of 1/Lt Robert C. Peterson, had flown on the low level Ploesti mission after being smuggled from England to Africa. Back at Shipdham on 24 October dog and master posed in veteran B-24 *Avenger*. The score board includes an Italian among the 19 fighter claims, while Ploesti is indicated by the horizontal bomb symbol.

Back from an escort on 24 October, Major Eugene Roberts partakes of the almost ritual after-mission Coffee and Doughnuts in company with Capt Charles London and war correspondent Randolf Hearst Jr, son of the US newspaper magnate. Four days earlier Roberts had shot down his ninth enemy fighter to become leading 8AF fighter ace, a position he would not retain for long. London had been the first to gain this unofficial accolade.

Duxford airfield had a grass surface which when ground conditions were favourable allowed four P-47s to take off simultaneously and thus save time and fuel in assembling a formation. Preparing for such a launch on 24 October 16 aircraft of 82FS are assembled at the north end of the 'Duckpond' awaiting the 'go' signal. Each has a 75 gallon drop tank slung under the fuselage.

24/25 OCTOBER 1943

VIII BC 118 NIGHT LEAFLET OPERATION – FRANCE

	Despatched		Effective	Locality	No. of Leaflets	Losses
1BD				CAEN, ROUEN, PARIS		
B-17	422BS	4	4	0005–0009 hrs	779,500	0

27 OCTOBER 1943

7PG despatched 2 F-5s to France.

30 OCTOBER 1943

Heavy bomber mission abandoned after take-off.

7PG despatched 4 F-5s to Northern France.

The dedication of the crew chiefs to their charges was impressive. Many would forgo meals and sleep to ensure a bomber was in tip-top condition. M/Sgt Herbert Hastings had care of 93BG's *The Duchess* which had 22 missions without a mechanical failure when this picture was taken 3 November. *The Duchess* would eventually fly 54 before being lost in the Furth raid. Hastings' first B-24 *Hot Freight* had been lost after 12 missions.

3 NOVEMBER 1943

VIII BC 119

	Despatched		Effective	Target	Bombs Tonnage	E/A	Losses MIA	E	Dam	Casualties KIA	WIA	MIA
1BD				WILHELMSHAVEN P/A(P)								
B-17	91BG	24	23	1307–1334 hrs	2640 × 500GP	11–0–13	3		14	0	4	30
	92BG	25	25			0–0– 0	0		1	0	0	0
	303BG	23	22			0–2– 1	0		0	0	0	0
	305BG	20	20			0–0– 0	0		0	0	0	0
	306BG	25	23			0–0– 0	2		3	0	0	20
	351BG	25	24			7–1– 6	1		8	0	4	10
	379BG	24	24			1–0– 0	0		2	0	0	0
	381BG	27	26			0–0– 1	0		1	0	1	0
	384BG	24	24			1–0– 2	0		2	0	2	0
3BD				WILHELMSHAVEN P/A(P)								
B-17	94BG	33	32	1307–1334 hrs	9594 × 100 IB	1–0– 1	1		4	0	0	10
	95BG	27	27			0–0– 0	0		0	0	0	0
	96BG	50	48			0–0– 0	0		3	0	0	0
	100BG	26	23			0–0– 0	0		0	0	0	0
	385BG	27	26			0–0– 0	0		3	0	1	0
	388BG	30	28			0–0– 0	0		1	0	0	0
	390BG	28	28			0–0– 0	0		0	0	0	0
2BD				WILHELMSHAVEN P/A(P)								
B-24	44BG	28	22	1330–1335 hrs	413 × 1000GP	0–0– 0	0		1	0	0	0
	93BG	28	26		2039 × 100 IB	0–0– 0	0		0	0	0	0
	389BG	33	30			0–0– 0	0		1	0	0	0
	392BG	28	27			0–0– 0	0		3	0	0	0
PATHFINDER												
	482BG	11	11	As above		0–0– 0	0		0	0	0	0
TOTALS:		566	539		1448.15	21–3–24	7	2	47	0	12	70

REMARKS: First use of H2X radar by PFF a/c. 1 B-24 dropped 4 × 1000GP at the IP. 96BG first group to fly A, B and C formations – double strength group. 2 B-17s collided near Farnborough during assembly. 2 306BG B-17s collided before reaching target.

VIII FC FO 168

Despatched		Groups	E/A	Losses MIA	E	Dam	Casualties KIA	WIA	MIA
P-38	45	55FG	3–5–5		0	0	0	0	0
P-47	333	4FG, 56FG, 78FG, 352FG, 353FG, 355FG, 356FG	11–0–2	2	1	5	0	1	2
TOTALS:	378		14–5–7	2	1	5	0	1	2

REMARKS: Escort and support for heavy bombers. A sqdn of 20FG (79FS) flew as part of 55FG. Fighter group e/a credits:– 4FG – 1, 55FG – 4, 56FG – 4, 78FG – 1, 353FG – 5. Fighter group losses:– 4FG – 2, 4FG P-47 cr. after t/o Halesworth, pilot inj.

7PG despatched 1 Spitfire and 7 F-5 on PR over France, Belgium and Holland. First use of Spitfire XI by 7PG.

3/4 NOVEMBER 1943

VIII BC 120 NIGHT LEAFLET OPERATION – BELGIUM AND HOLLAND

	Despatched		Effective	Locality	No of Leaflets	Losses MIA	E
1BD				ANTWERP			
B-17	422BS	2	2	1915 hrs	1,592,000	0	0
				ROTTERDAM			
				2008 hrs			

With the left wing trailing edge heavily serrated by flak, a 94BG Fortress heads home from Gelsenkirchen, 5 November.

5 NOVEMBER 1943

VIII BC 121

	Despatched		Effective	Target		Bombs Tonnage	E/A	Losses MIA	E	Dam	Casualties KIA	WIA	MIA
3BD				GELSENKIRCHEN	(P)								
B-17	94BG	29	24	M/Y & O/R		1570 × 500GP	0–0– 0	1	0	17	0	0	10
	95BG	25	9	1313–1350 hrs		6936 × 100 IB	0–0– 0	0	0	7	0	1	0
	96BG	43	37				0–0– 0	0	0	19	1	3	0
	100BG	25	21				0–0– 0	1	1	7	1	0	18
	385BG	24	22				0–0– 0	0	0	17	0	0	0
	388BG	25	23				0–0– 0	2	1	20	0	4	20
	390BG	23	19				0–0– 0	1	0	18	0	1	0
1BD				GELSENKIRCHEN	(P)								
B-17	91BG	18	14	M/Y 1313–1350 hrs			0–0– 0	0	0	11	0	1	0
	92BG	22	20				0–0– 0	1	0	14	0	4	10
	303BG	19	19				0–0– 0	1	0	13	0	0	10
	305BG	19	18				0–0– 0	0	0	12	0	0	0
	306BG	21	18				0–0– 0	0	0	6	0	0	0
	351BG	18	17				0–0– 0	0	1	16	2	4	0
	379BG	21	20				0–0– 0	0	0	19	0	5	0
	381BG	22	22				2–0– 0	1	0	20	0	8	16
	384BG	20	20				3–1– 3	0	0	0	0	0	0
TOTALS:		374	323			739.3	5–1– 3	8	3	216	4	31	84
2BD				MÜNSTER M/Y	(P)								
B-24	44BG	32	26	1349–1358 hrs		16 × 100GP	0–0– 0	0	0	11	0	7	0
	93BG	26	25			657 × 500 IB	10–3– 3	0	1	7	7	8	0
	389BG	30	28			680 × 100 IB	8–1– 1	0	0	12	0	2	0
	392BG	30	25			340 × 500GP	3–0– 3	3	0	13	0	5	31
TOTALS:		118	104			284.05	21–4– 7	3	1	43	7	22	31
PATHFINDER													
	482BG	11	9	AS ABOVE			1–0– 1	0		7	0	4	0
TOTALS FOR DAY:		503	436			1023.35	27–5–11	11	4	266	11	57	115

REMARKS: 1 and 3BD a/c and bombs totals include 5 482BG PFF B-17. 2BD a/c and bombs totals include 4 482BG PFF B-17. 1 B-24 dropped 12 × 500 M50 IB on Coesfeld (O). 1 B-24 dropped 8 × 500GP and 16 × 100 IB on Haltern (O). B/d 351BG B-17 c/l Ipswich A/F on return. B/d 388BG B-17 cr. South Elmham St.Cross after crew baled out. 100BG B-17 c/l Leiston due to engine trouble. 390BG B-17 down in sea due to engine trouble on way out.

VIII FC FO 170

	Despatched		Groups	E/A	Losses MIA	E	Dam	Casualties KIA	WIA	MIA
	P-38	47	55FG	5–2–2	0	0	0	0	0	0
	P-47	336	4FG, 56FG, 78FG, 352FG, 353FG, 355FG, 356FG	13–4–1	4	1	0	0	0	4
TOTALS:		383		18–6–3	4	1	0	0	0	4

REMARKS: Escort for 1BD and 3BD only. Fighter group e/a credits:– 4FG – 1, 55FG – 5, 56FG – 6, 353FG – 5, 355FG – 2. Fighter group losses:– 353FG – 3, 355FG – 1. 352FG P-47 c/l near base, pilot safe.

7PG despatched 5 F-5 on PR over France and Holland.

It was supposed to be a young man's war and because of this 48-year-old S/Sgt David J. Cole was grounded following his participation in the 5 November mission as a tail gunner. Next day the former taxi driver and First World War veteran appeared happy enough as he had yet to hear of the decision by 385BG Hq. This picture also gives a clear view of the perforated barrel protectors and the flash eliminators on .50-calibre guns.

5/6 NOVEMBER 1943

VIII BC 122 NIGHT LEAFLET OPERATION – FRANCE

	Despatched		Effective	Locality	No of Leaflets	Losses MIA	E
1BD				PARIS, AMIENS, ROUEN, CAEN			
B-17	422BS	5	5	1917–2005 hrs	1,004,000	0	0

6/7 NOVEMBER 1943

VIII BC 123 NIGHT LEAFLET OPERATION – FRANCE

	Despatched		Effective	Locality	No of Leaflets	Losses MIA	E
1BD				PARIS			
B-17	422BS	2	2	0241–0250 hrs	440,000	0	0

7 NOVEMBER 1943

VIII BC 124

	Despatched		Effective	Target	Bombs Tonnage	E/A	Losses MIA	E	Dam	Casualties KIA	WIA	MIA
1BD				WESEL I/A (P)								
B-17	91BG	18	14	1124–1125 hrs	343 × 500GP				4	1	0	0
	351BG	20	19		784 × 100 IB					0	0	0
	381BG	21	20							0	2	0
TOTALS:		59	53		124.95	0–0–0	0	0	4	1	2	0
3BD				DÜREN I/A (P)								
B-17	390BG	20	18	37 a/c 1114 hrs	186 × 500GP (P)				1	0	0	0
	100BG	23	23		752 × 100 IB				0	0	0	0
				RANDERATH (S)								
	95BG	17	16	20 a/c	160 × 500GP (S)				1	0	0	0
				1114–1125 hrs	160 × 100 IB							
TOTALS:		60	57		132.1	0–0–0	0	0	2	0	0	0
PATHFINDER												
	482BG	3	2	As above		0–0–0	0	0	0	0	0	0
TOTALS FOR DAY:		122	112		257.05	0–0–0	0	0	6	1	2	0

REMARKS: Poor weather restricted operations. Oboe PFF failure resulted in wide scatter of bomb loads.

VIII FC FO 172

Despatched		Groups	E/A	Losses MIA	E	Dam	Casualties KIA	WIA	MIA
P-47	283	56FG, 78FG, 352FG, 353FG 355FG 356FG	1–0–0	6	0	0	0	0	6

REMARKS: Escort and support for B-17s. 78FG flew first fighter double-group mission with 'A' and 'B' formations. Fighter group e/a credits:– 355FG – 1. Fighter group losses:– 56FG – 1, 355FG – 5.

INCIDENT

A Fortress nicknamed *Hard Luck* with a serial number ending 13, that had arrived at Thorpe Abbotts on Friday the 13 August 1943 and was assigned to the 'hard luck' 100th Group, was not an inviting war chariot for the superstitious. It didn't cause misgivings to 1/Lt John Mitchell and his crew who had brought her into Thorpe Abbotts and flew her regularly. They did, however, wonder if they were chancing things when mission number 13 had to be flown and they found *Hard Luck* was parked on hardstand number 13! However, the trip to Düren on 7 November proved to be a 'milk run'.

7 NOVEMBER 1943 *(contd.)*

VIII FC FO 173

Despatched		Groups	E/A	Losses MIA	E	Dam	Casualties KIA	WIA	MIA
P-38	54	55FG	0	2	0	0	0	0	2
P-47	49	4FG	0	0	0	0	0	0	0
TOTALS:	103		0	2	0	0	0	0	2

REMARKS: Despatched in support of 9AF B-26s. Sweeps in Ostend/Lille/Lens/Calais area. 8 P-38s of 20FG (79FS) flew as part of 55FG and two failed to return – one seen in sea. Fighter group losses:– 20FG – 2.

7/8 NOVEMBER 1943

VIII BC 125 NIGHT LEAFLET OPERATION – FRANCE

	Despatched		Effective	Locality	No of Leaflets	Losses MIA	E
1BD				PARIS			
B-17	422BS	2	2	0038–0041 hrs	312,000	0	0

10 NOVEMBER 1943

VIII FC FO 175

Despatched		Groups	E/A	Losses MIA	E	Dam	Casualties KIA	WIA	MIA
P-38	58	55FG	0	0	0	0	0	0	0
P-47	208	4FG, 78FG, 355FG, 356FG	0	0	0	0	0	0	0
TOTALS:	266		0–0–0	0	0	0	0	0	0

REMARKS: Despatched in support of 9AF B-26s. 79FS/20FG accompanied the 55FG.

10/11 NOVEMBER 1943

VIII BC 126 NIGHT LEAFLET OPERATION – FRANCE

	Despatched		Effective	Locality	No of Leaflets	Losses MIA	E
1BD				PARIS, RENNES, LE MANS, ROUEN			
B-17	422BS	5	5	2020–2051 hrs	1,000,000	0	0

Following a conference at Great Ashfield on 10 November, Brig.Gen LeMay enjoys his pipe and chats with two of his group commanders, Lt.Col Vandevanter and Col Castle. Vandevanter flew B-17s in the Philippines when the Japanese attacked and his conduct earned him command of the 385BG which he trained and brought to England.

Transportation to aircraft dispersals was limited and full use was made of Dodge 'Command Cars'. The normal carrying capacity could be trebled – as in this case – although the driver's lot was not easy. One of these 55FG pilots, off on the 11 November escort, has RAF fleece lined leggings over his flying shoes – cold was a major problem for P-38 fliers. Also note escape knives and maps tucked in boots and pilots' names on various pieces of personal equipment.

Taxiing along the muddy Nuthamstead perimeter track prior to the 11 November escort, these 55FG P-38Hs carry two 150 gallon drop tanks each to give ample endurance for the flight to the Ruhr. In the background 20FG aircraft wait to leave dispersal points to form a fourth squadron for the operation.

11 NOVEMBER 1943

VIII BC 127

	Despatched		Effective	Target	Bombs Tonnage	E/A	Losses MIA	E	Dam	Casualties KIA	WIA	MIA
3BD				MÜNSTER M/Y (P)								
B-17	94BG	21	19	1408 hrs	204 × 500GP	10–0–2	3		11	0	2	30
	95BG	20	0		1422 × 100 IB	0–0–0	0		0	0	0	0
	96BG	42	0			0–0–0	0		0	0	0	0
	100BG	20	0			0–0–0	0		0	0	0	0
	385BG	20	19			0–0–0	1		6	0	2	10
	388BG	23	0			0–0–0	0		0	0	0	0
	390BG	21	20			0–0–0	0		10	0	0	0
1BD				WESEL (P) (MISSION ABANDONED)								
B-17	91BG	18	0			0–0–0	0		0	0	0	0
	92BG	20	0			0–0–0	0		0	0	0	0
	303BG	20	0			0–0–0	0		0	0	0	0
	305BG	19	0			0–0–0	0		0	0	0	0
	306BG	21	0			0–0–0	0		0	0	0	0
	351BG	18	0			0–0–0	0		0	0	0	0
	379BG	21	0			0–0–0	0		0	0	0	0
	381BG	17	0			0–0–0	0		0	0	0	0
	384BG	21	0			0–0–0	0		1	0	0	0
PATHFINDER												
	482BG	5	1			0–0–0	0		0	0	0	0
TOTALS:		347	59		122.1	10–0–2	4	0	28	0	4	40

REMARKS: Adverse weather conditions caused 1BD to abandon mission. Due to failure of PFF a/c the 95BG, 96BG, 100BG and 388BG turned back before enemy coast. Second 96BG fomation of 21 a/c turned back after fire in lead B-17 caused pilot to drift off course and lose altitude, the rest of formation following. 1 3BD B-17 dropped 40 × 100 IB on Cleve (O).

VIII FC FO 177

	Despatched		Groups	E/A	Losses MIA	E	Dam	Casualties KIA	WIA	MIA
	P-38	59	55FG	0	0	0	0	0	0	0
	P-47	342	4FG, 56FG, 78FG, 352FG, 353FG, 355FG, 356FG	8–1–2	2	0	1	0	0	2
TOTALS:		401		8–1–2	2	0	1	0	0	2

REMARKS: Escort and support for bombers. 79FS of 20FG accompanied 55FG. Fighter group e/a credits:– 56FG – 6, 353FG – 3. Fighter group losses:– 56FG – 1, 356FG – 1.

11/12 NOVEMBER 1943

VIII BC 128 SPECIAL NIGHT OPERATION – EMMERICH (P)

	Despatched		Effective	Locality	Bombs Tonnage	Losses MIA	E
1BD				REES (O)	2 × 2000GP		
B-17	482BG	1	1	2057 hrs	1 × Photoflash	0	0

REMARKS: Oboe test.

12/13 NOVEMBER 1943

VIII BC 129 SPECIAL NIGHT OPERATION – EMMERICH

	Despatched		Effective	Locality	Bombs Tonnage	Losses MIA	E
1BD				EMMERICH	2 × 2000GP		
B-17	482BG	1	1	2115 hrs	1 × Photoflash	0	0

REMARKS: Oboe test.

13 NOVEMBER 1943

VIII BC 130

	Despatched		Effective	Target	Bombs Tonnage	E/A	Losses MIA	E	Dam	Casualties KIA	WIA	MIA
3BD				BREMEN P/A (P)								
B-17	94BG	16	11	1120–1145 hrs	18 × 500GP	2– 0– 0	0	0	0	0	0	0
	385BG	17	9	AND T/Os	576 × 500 IB	2– 2– 1	2	0	1	0	2	20
	95BG	21	1		2270 × 100 IB	1– 1– 2	0	0	1	0	1	0
	100BG	18	0			0– 2– 2	0	0	0	0	1	0
	390BG	21	7			0– 0– 2	0	0	0	0	0	0
	96BG	40	31			3– 1– 3	1	0	8	0	0	10
	388BG	21	18		142 × 500 IB	1– 0– 1	0	1	0	0	0	0
1BD	305BG	2	1		636 × 100 IB	0– 1– 0	0	1	0	8	0	0
B-17	306BG	2	1		(T/O)	0– 0– 0	0	0	2	0	0	0
	381BG	1	0			0– 0– 0	0	0	0	0	0	0
2BD	93BG	25	8			2– 3– 0	5	1	0	0	0	52
B-24	389BG	27	20			6– 1– 0	2	0	3	0	1	20
	44BG	33	19			1– 2– 0	2	2	1	2	21	20
	392BG	24	14			2– 1– 2	4	0	6	0	0	40
PATHFINDER												
	482BG	4	3	As above		0– 0– 0	0	0	0	0	0	0
TOTALS:		272	143			20–14–13	16	6*	22	21	26	162

REMARKS: PFF attack. Bad weather caused part of 1BD Force to abandon mission during assembly. 95BG, 385BG, and 390BG attacked T/Os. 8 a/c of 93BG made visual attack on Heligoland as a T/O. 520,000 leaflets released over Bremen. B-24s flew 12 a/c section formations for first time.* During assembly 384BG B-17 cr. Wargrave, 9 killed. 305BG B-17 cr. Shiplake Bend, 8 killed. 388BG B-17 abandoned near East Wretham on fire. 2 385BG B-17s collided on route, 1 cr. in sea, 1 ditched, crew rescued. 2 389BG B-24s collided on bomb run. On return, 44BG B-24 cr. Northrepps; 93BG B-24 cr. landing Lympne A/F; 44BG B-24 c/l near base, Garveston.

VIII FC FO 180

Despatched		Groups	E/A	Losses MIA	E	Dam	Casualties KIA	WIA	MIA
P-38	45	55FG	7–3–5	7	2	5	0	0	7
P-47	345	4FG, 56FG, 78FG, 352FG, 353FG, 355FG, 356FG	3–0–1	3	0	2	0	0	2
TOTALS:	390		10–3–6	10	2	7	0	0	9

REMARKS: Escort and support for bombers. Fighter group e/a credits:– 55FG – 6, 355FG – 3. Fighter group losses:– 55FG – 7, 355FG – 2, 356FG – 1. On return, 2 P-38 c/l, pilots safe, 1 at East Wretham A/F, 1 at Debden A/F. Severe winds limited range of fighters.

16 NOVEMBER 1943

VIII BC 131

	Despatched		Effective	Target	Bombs Tonnage	E/A	Losses MIA	E	Dam	Casualties KIA	WIA	MIA
1BD				KNABEN I/A (P)								
B-17	384BG	21	19	1133–1238 hrs	1252 × 500GP	0–0–0	0		0	0	0	0
	303BG	20	0			0–0–0	0		0	0	0	0
	379BG	22	19			0–0–0	0		0	0	0	0
	351BG	20	17			0–0–0	0		0	0	0	0
	91BG	20	0			2–0–4	0		4	0	0	0
	381BG	22	22			0–0–0	0		2	0	1	0
	305BG	23	21			0–0–0	0		0	0	0	0
	92BG	21	13			0–0–0	1		0	0	0	10
	306BG	20	19			0–0–0	0		1	0	0	0
TOTALS:		189	130		313.0	2–0–4	1	0	7	0	1	10

Viewed through the nose plexiglass of a 303BG B-17 other aircraft of the Group wing their way to Norway on 16 November. Nearest aircraft is the famous *Duchess* which had flown on its and the Group's first mission a year before: 17 November 1942.

3BD				RJÜKAN I/A (P)								
B-17	385BG	20	19	1143–1145 hrs	711 × 1000GP	0–0–0	0	0	0	0	0	0
	94BG	20	19			0–0–0	0	0	0	0	0	0
	388BG	19	17			2–0–0	0	0	3	0	0	0
	96BG	40	36			0–0–0	0	0	0	0	0	0
	95BG	20	18			0–0–0	0	0	0	0	0	0
	100BG	21	20			0–0–0	0	0	0	0	0	0
	390BG	20	18			0–0–0	1	1	0	2	0	10
2BD				RJÜKAN I/A (P)								
B-24	93BG	14	10	1204–1212 hrs	295 × 500GP	0–0–0	0	0	0	0	0	0
	389BG	4	4			0–0–0	0	0	0	0	0	0
	44BG	3	2			0–0–0	0	0	0	0	0	0
	392BG	18	13			0–0–0	0	0	0	0	0	0
TOTALS:		199	176		429.25	2–0–0	1	1	3	2	0	10
TOTALS FOR DAY:		388	306		742.25	4–0–4	2	1	10	2	1	20

REMARKS: 4 3BD B-17s dropped 20 × 1000GP on Knaben (O). 2 1BD B-17s dropped 24 × 500GP on Rjükan I/A (O). 303BG B-17 'Knock-out Dropper' became first 8AF heavy bomber to complete 50 missions. 390BG B-17 caught fire and cr. in sea near Norway. 390BG B-17 cr. Tannington after t/o, 2 k.

7PG despatched 1 F-5 to Martinvast, France.

18 NOVEMBER 1943

VIII BC 132

	Despatched		Effective	Target	Bombs Tonnage	E/A	Losses MIA	E	Dam	Casualties KIA	WIA	MIA
2BD				OSLO – KJELLER								
B-24	44BG	34	24	A/F	838 × 500GP	4–3–1	5	1		2	8	50
	93BG	20	15			0–0–2	1	0		0	0	10
	389BG	26	22			5–0–2	1	0		0	1	11
	392BG	22	21			1–4–0	2	2		0	0	20
TOTALS:		102	82		209.5	10–7–5	9	3	10	2	9	91

REMARKS: 4 B-24s dropped 44 × 500GP on Rygge A/D (O). 3 a/c landed in Sweden (44BG, 93BG and 392BG). B/d 44BG B-24 c/l base.

7PG despatched 1 Spitfire to Wesel and Hüls area.

18/19 NOVEMBER 1943

VIII BC 133 NIGHT LEAFLET OPERATION – FRANCE

	Despatched		Effective	Locality	No. of Leaflets	Losses
1BD				PARIS, ORLEANS, CHARTRES, RENNES, LE MANS		
B-17	422BS	5	5	2015 to 2041	980,000	0

19 NOVEMBER 1943

VIII BC 134

	Despatched		Effective	Target	Bombs Tonnage	E/A	Losses MIA	E	Dam	Casualties KIA	WIA	MIA
3BD				T/Os GERMAN –								
B-17	95BG	17	16	HOLLAND BORDER	544 × 500GP			1		10		
	100BG	21	15	(1241–1251 hrs)	2906 × 100 IB			0		0		
	390BG	23	22					0		0		
	388BG	19	16					0		0		
	96BG	42	41					0		0		
	94BG	18	0					0		0		
	385BG	21	17					0		0		
	PATHFINDER											
	482BG	6	3					0		0		
TOTALS:		167	130		281.3	0–0–0	0	1	0	10	0	0

REMARKS: 95BG B-17 cr. after t/o at Redlingfield, 10 k. Primary was Gelsenkirchen, but adverse weather and PFF malfunction caused mission failure.

VIII FC FO 184

Despatched		Groups	E/A	Losses MIA	E	Dam	Casualties KIA	WIA	MIA
P-47	288	56FG, 78FG, 352FG, 353FG, 355FG, 356FG	0–0–0	0	0	0	0	0	0

REMARKS: Escort for heavy bombers. 55FG also scheduled but were prevented by bad weather.

INCIDENT

The mission to Gelsenkirchen on 19 November 1943 was abandoned because of the failure of the pathfinder force. The 130 bombers reaching the target area searching for gaps in the clouds, scattered bombs far and wide. Six Oboe equipped B-17s of 482nd Group were assigned to lead formations of 3rd Division over an undercast, but none of the Pathfinders were able to receive the beamed signals from England upon which this technique depended. The reason for the failure was not clear, but range and altitude were suspected of being too great for the prevailing conditions. Thereafter VIII Bomber Command put its faith primarily in H2S and H2X – the aircraft-carried radar ground scanner – for blind bombing missions, apart from experimental sorties to test Oboe Mk II. Disenchantment finally resulted in the decision to hand Oboe, plus the many technicians versed in its ways, over to the 9th Air Force whose lower altitude medium bombing missions seemed more suited to Oboe application. Indeed, B-26 Marauders used it with great success until the cessation of hostilities.

19/20 NOVEMBER 1943

VIII BC 135 NIGHT LEAFLET OPERATION – HOLLAND, BELGIUM AND FRANCE

	Despatched		Effective	Locality	No. of Leaflets	Losses
1BD				AMIENS, REIMS, BRUSSELS, GHENT, AMSTERDAM, THE HAGUE		
B-17	422BS	6	6	1915–2011 hrs	2,316,000	0

A damp chilly scene far removed from the action on a sweltering Rumanian summer day that led to this parade. Officers and men of 44BG in front of the Shipdham control tower for Col Leon Johnson to receive Medal of Honor from Gen Devers on 22 November. Devers reads the citation with senior 8AF commanders behind him (Eaker at right-hand end of row). Photographers and newsmen jostle for position in the foreground. The airfield identification letters on the tower square, and the Flying Eightball symbol of 44BG painted on the nose of unnamed Ploesti veteran (41-23813 V) have been masked with white material for site security reasons.

Leon Johnson after the ceremony (Medal of Honor fastened around the neck). Former CO of 44BG and one of the most distinguished 8AF Liberator pilots, he commanded a Bombardment Wing for the rest of hostilities.

23 NOVEMBER 1943

7PG despatched 4 F-5s to France and Belgium.

24 NOVEMBER 1943

7PG despatched 2 F-5s to France and Belgium.

24/25 NOVEMBER 1943

VIII BC 136 NIGHT LEAFLET OPERATION – BELGIUM AND FRANCE

	Despatched	Effective	Locality	No. of Leaflets	Losses
1BD			LILLE, BRUSSELS ANTWERP, CHARLEROI/ GOSSELIES GHENT		
B-17	422BS 7	7	2026–2111 hrs	2,400,000	0

25 NOVEMBER 1943

VIII FC FO 190

Despatched		Groups	E/A	Losses MIA	E	Dam	Casualties KIA	WIA	MIA
P-38	55	55FG	3–3–4	2	2	7	0	0	2
P-47	276	56FG, 78FG, 352FG, 353FG, 356FG	0–0–0	1	0	16	0	1	1
TOTALS:	331		3–3–4	3	2	23	0	1	3

REMARKS: First use of P-47s as dive bombers in an attack on St.Omer A/F. A B-24 was used as sighter for 56FG and 353FG. Other groups carried out a sweep in the Lille area. 77FS/20FG flew as part of the 55FG. Fighter group e/a credits:– 55FG – 4. Fighter group losses:– 55FG – 2, 353FG – 1. 55FG P-38 c/l Duxford and 20FG P-38 c/l near Bishops Stortford, pilots safe.

7PG despatched 4 Spitfire and 6 F-5 to France and Belgium.

25/26 NOVEMBER 1943

VIII BC 137 NIGHT LEAFLET OPERATION – FRANCE

	Despatched	Effective	Locality	No. of Leaflets	Losses
1BD			REIMS, PARIS ROUEN, AMIENS, CHARTRES, EVREUX		
B-17	422BS 7	7	2010–2015	1,176,000	0

It came as something of a surprise to most combat fliers at Molesworth to learn that the pilot with the most flying time on the base was the lady who ran the Red Cross Aeroclub. Lucille Parker had amassed 1,619 hours time in light aircraft back in the US and as a member of Howard May's flying circus had made 189 parachute jumps. Her experience in the latter art was put to good use in that she was able to give regular talks to 303BG crews on what for most was an unknown experience. Lucille also engaged in a few demonstrations as when snapped entering a B-17 on 20 November.

An elated Capt Walker Mahurin after three Me 110 victories on 26 November. He was destined to become one of the great aces of the 56FG and 8AF.

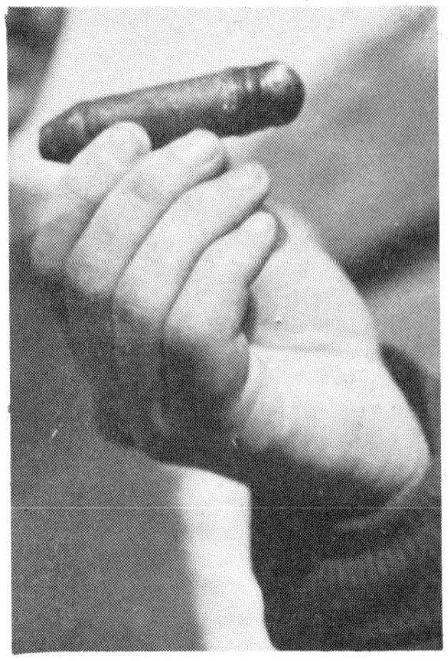

On 26 November the up and coming 56FG was credited with 23 enemy fighters destroyed, a new 8AF record for one mission. Major Francis Gabreski got two Me 110s and also collected this unexploded 20 mm cannon shell found in his P-47's engine compartment after returning to base.

26 NOVEMBER 1943

VIII BC 138

		Despatched	Effective	Target	Bombs Tonnage	E/A	Losses MIA	E	Dam	Casualties KIA	WIA	MIA
1BD				BREMEN CITY (P)								
B-17	91BG	29	19	1145–1228 hrs	3311 × 500GP	0–0– 0	1	0	10	0	0	0
	92BG	23	19		7541 × 100 IB	2–0– 1	2	0	7	1	3	20
	303BG	35	32			1–0– 0	2	0	19	0	0	10
	305BG	22	22			4–3– 1	5	0	6	6	3	50
	306BG	29	28			0–0– 2	1	0	5	0	0	20
	351BG	38	37			0–0– 0	2	1	12	0	2	1
	379BG	37	37			2–0– 1	2	0	18	0	2	20
	381BG	29	23			0–0– 0	0	0	5	0	17	0
	384BG	21	20			3–0– 5	4	0	3	1	3	32
	401BG	20	16			0–0– 0	0	1	11	1	1	0
3BD	95BG	6	6			0–0– 0	0	0	0	0	0	0
B-17	96BG	43	37			0–0– 0	1	0	12	0	0	10
	100BG	9	8			0–0– 0	0	1	1	0	0	0
	388BG	43	41			0–0– 0	2	0	30	0	0	21
	390BG	6	5			0–0– 0	0	0	0	0	0	0
2BD	44BG	26	21			4–0– 0	1	1	8	1	2	10
B-24	93BG	25	17			0–0– 0	0	0	2	0	0	0
	389BG	26	23			0–0– 0	1	0	5	0	2	10
	392BG	24	16			0–0– 0	1	0	4	0	0	11
PATHFINDER												
	482BG	14	13			0–0– 0	0	0	7	0	0	0
TOTALS:		505	440		1204.8	16–3–10	25	4	165	10	35	215
3BD	385BG	22	0	PARIS B/I		2–0– 1	0	0	1	0	1	0
B-17	94BG	42	0			5–2– 1	3	0	10	0	0	30
	390BG	21	0			0–0– 0	0	0	2	0	0	0
	100BG	21	0			1–0– 1	1	0	3	0	2	10
	95BG	22	0			0–0– 0	0	0	2	0	0	0
TOTALS:		128	0			8–2– 3	4	0	18	0	3	40
TOTALS FOR DAY:		633	440		1204.8	24–5–13	29	4	183	10	38	255

REMARKS: 13 B-17 and 5 B-24 dropped 159 × 500GP and 345 × 100 IB on T/Os. First mission of 401BG. 100BG B-17 cr. after t/o at Dickleburgh. 2 B-17 (401BG and 388BG) collided over enemy territory; the 401BG a/c returning to Detling (Cat E) minus ball gunner; the 388BG a/c was lost. B/d 351BG B-17 cr. on approach at Marham, crew safe – 1 man baled over e/t. 94BG B-17 collided with Me 109 and lost. 388BG high sqdn lead a/c hit by incendiaries from 96BG and lost. 4 B-17s ditched – 2 351BG crews, 1 91BG crew and 7 men from a 384BG a/c rescued. 44BG B-24 Cat E through damage in collision.

VIII FC FO 191

Despatched		Groups	E/A	Losses MIA	E	Dam	Casualties KIA	WIA	MIA
P-38	28	55FG	0	0	0	0	0	0	0
P-47	353	4FG, 56FG, 78FG, 352FG, 353FG, 355FG, 356FG	36–3–9	4	3	7	0	0	4
TOTALS:	381		36–3–9	4	3	7	0	0	4

REMARKS: Escort and support for heavy bombers. 77FS of 20FG flew as part of 55FG formation. Fighter group e/a credits:– 4FG – 1, 20FG – 1, 55FG – 2, 56FG – 23, 78FG – 4, 352FG – 3. Fighter group losses:– 56FG – 1, 78FG – 3. On return 3 78FG P-47s c/l at A/F near SE coast – low on fuel.

7PG despatched 4 F-5 and 2 Spitfire to Germany, Holland, Belgium and France.

28/29 NOVEMBER 1943

VIII BC 139 NIGHT LEAFLET OPERATION – BELGIUM AND HOLLAND

	Despatched		Effective	Locality	No. of Leaflets	Losses
1BD B-17	422BS	7	7	GOSSELIES, GHENT, LIEGE, BRUSSELS, ANTWERP, ROTTERDAM 2101–2118 hrs	1,640,000	0

29 NOVEMBER 1943

VIII BC 140

	Despatched		Effective	Target	Bombs Tonnage	E/A	Losses MIA	E	Dam	Casualties KIA	WIA	MIA
3BD				BREMEN (P)								
B-17	94BG	40	29	1429–1450 hrs	1112 × 500GP	1– 2– 1	1	0	4	0	1	10
	95BG	20	16	& T/Os	2643 × 100 IB	0– 0– 0	1	0	1	0	0	10
	96BG	41	27		(137 a/c)	7– 8– 4	4	0	22	0	6	40
	100BG	20	19		126 × 500GP	0– 0– 1	0	0	0	0	0	0
	385BG	20	12		307 × 100 IB	1– 0– 2	2	0	3	0	4	20
	388BG	20	1		(17 a/c – T/Os)	0– 0– 0	1	1	2	1	2	10
	390BG	21	0			0– 0– 0	0	0	0	0	0	0
1BD	91BG	21	0			0– 0– 0	0	0	0	0	0	0
	92BG	18	0			0– 0– 0	0	0	0	0	0	0
	303BG	20	15			3– 1– 2	2	0	5	0	0	21
	305BG	9	0			0– 0– 0	0	0	0	0	0	0
	306BG	27	0			0– 0– 0	0	1	0	0	0	0
	351BG	19	0			0– 0– 0	0	0	0	0	0	0
	379BG	19	18			2– 0– 0	2	0	5	0	0	20
	381BG	22	0			0– 0– 0	0	0	0	0	0	0
	384BG	18	14			1– 0– 0	0	0	1	1	0	0
	482BG	5	3			0– 0– 0	0	1	0	0	0	0
TOTALS:		360	154		457.0	15–11–10	13	3	43	2	13	131

REMARKS: Cloud tops to over 29,000 ft in places. 17 B-17s in total attacked T/Os dropping 126 × 500GP and 307 × 100 IB. On return, 1 388BG B-17 ditched, 3 saved; 385BG B-17 c/l Beccles A/F; 306BG B-17 c/l Little Stoughton A/F.

VIII FC FO 192

Despatched		Groups	E/A	Losses MIA	E	Dam	Casualties KIA	WIA	MIA
P-38	38	55FG	2-0-2	7	0	0	0	0	7
P-47	314	4FG, 56FG, 78FG, 352FG, 353FG, 355FG, 356FG	13-4-4	9	1	1	0	1	9
TOTALS:	352		15-4-6	16	1	1	0	1	16

REMARKS: Escort and support for bombers. High winds caused fuel shortages. 77FS of 20FG flew as part of 55FG formation. Fighter groups e/a credits:– 55FG – 2, 56FG – 5, 355FG – 1, 356FG – 5. Fighter group losses: 55FG – 7, 56FG – 1, 355FG – 3, 356FG – 5.

7PG despatched 3 F-5 and 3 Spitfire XIs to France and Germany.

Flight Surgeon George Hornig hands out coffee to 56FG pilots during post-mission interrogation at Halesworth on 29 November. This gave him a good opportunity to observe signs of nervous stress 'combat fatigue'. In the front row (first and fourth from right) are two of the most notable fighter pilots produced by the Group, Gabreski and Schilling.

Extremely low temperatures made it difficult for bombers to maintain close formation on 29 November. This 95BG B-17 on the bomb run at Bremen attracted the attentions of a lone FW 190. The contrails left by both aircraft appear dark. B-17 formation in the distance is also well spread.

INCIDENT

The onset of the north-west European winter, with high air humidity and extremely low temperatures at the altitudes used in 8th Air Force operations, put increased strain on both men and aircraft. Enemy opposition aside, the dangers of stratospheric flight were considerable as the crew of the 94th BG Fortress *Wolverine II* discovered on their third raid, 29 November 1943. High cloud formations had forced a climb to 30,000 ft approaching the German coast. In the rear of the bomber a dangerous situation had arisen due to failure of the left side oxygen system. There was no response over the interphone from the man in the tail, Sgt George Hommes, so at the direction of the pilot, right waist gunner Harold Luttrell took a walk-around oxygen bottle and went back to investigate: 'Hommes had his mask off, his hands and face frozen and swelled up. I tried to reach his oxygen connection but there just wasn't room enough back there. By this time my oxygen bottle was almost empty so I went back to the waist for another. Coming back the second time I managed to pull him up to the tail wheel. I had taken my flak suit off and this made it a little easier. By the time I had him to the tail wheel though, I was out of oxygen again and had to go back for another bottle.

'The third trip I got him up in the waist and strapped a high pressure bottle on him. He was so frozen and swollen up from the cold and lack of oxygen that he couldn't have helped himself even if he were conscious. Just then, the radio operator, coming back to give me a hand and on an emergency bottle too, passed out. The left waist gunner trying to help the radio operator pulled loose his own oxygen connection and passed out right on top of the radio man. By this time the tail gunner was OK again. I had to take the top one of the new pile that had passed out. So first I got the left waist gunner back on his own system, then I dragged the radio gunner over to my position and plugged him in on my line. I was taking whiffs of the high pressure bottle on Hommes and feeling pretty dizzy by this time. After the radio gunner came around, I sent him back to his own position and plugged in my own system again. I was so weak I felt as if I couldn't support myself at all. Boy, that steady supply of oxygen sure felt good.'

Movement in the narrow tail section of a Fortress fuselage was difficult enough in heavy flying clothes; to pull a similarly clad man from the tail turret was an exceptional feat in the circumstances described. Sgt Luttrell's action undoubtedly saved Hommes' life and probably that of the other two gunners.

Meanwhile another crisis had arisen. Over the Frisian Islands the pilot, 2/Lt Robert Randall, noticed the oil pressure on No.3 engine had suddenly dropped. A few seconds later he was alarmed to see the manifold pressure on No.2 engine fail. The power demands of lifting some 35 tons through cold thin air had been too much for them – the outside temperature gauge was indicating 46 degrees below zero centigrade. No.3 engine finally failed and the propeller could not be feathered. No.2 was successfully feathered but with *Wolverine II* lagging behind the formation, and easy prey for enemy fighters, Randall decided to abandon the mission and head for home.

Vibration caused by the windmilling blades of No.2 propeller reached such a pitch that the radio operator could not write in his log. Randall was only able to contain the shaking by reducing air speed to 135 mph. The bomb load was hastily salvoed and the bomber descended through the undercast. Turbulence caused it to go out of control, and by the time the pilots made recovery the speed had built up to 250 mph. Concerned that the windmilling propeller would eventually fly off and cut into the nose, Randall sent the navigator, bombardier and co-pilot back into the rear of the aircraft. Visibility was hindered by ice formation on the windshield and Randall had to rely on instruments but some of these were not functioning correctly. Finally the Fortress broke out of the clouds at less than a thousand feet above the sea where Randall was relieved to find he could at last maintain height. He had opened his side window for better visibility and off to his left could see one of the Frisian Islands. Over the interphone he told his radio man to send an SOS and alerted the crew to prepare for ditching:

'In a few minutes the cheerful face of my engineer was looking over my shoulder with "How 're we doing sir?" and asking if he could help. I told him to throw everything overboard we didn't need – guns, ammunition, flak suits, clothing – the more the merrier. He kept everyone busy the next few minutes on this job. My navigator was so zealous he threw one of the coils for our liaison radio set out. My bombardier pleased me when he came up and turned the top turret guns around so I could get out in case we ditched. For almost two hours we fought a headwind and rain squalls, not more than 300 feet off the white caps. My radio operator was doing a marvellous job keeping us in touch with a station in England and getting position reports every few minutes. It made us feel a lot better to know that if we went down now, Air-Sea Rescue would know where to look for us. About half way home, for some inexplicable reason, No.2 engined unfeathered itself. I managed to get it running at about third power, which helped a lot. When we finally saw the breakers off the English coast we knew we could probably make it.'

Crossing the coast and struggling to gain enough height to avoid a balloon barrage, Randall finally brought the Fortress in for a safe landing at the first airfield seen, Tibenham. As *Wolverine II* rolled down the runway No.3 engine suddenly disintegrated, the propeller and gearing falling onto the concrete and small fragments peppering the fuselage.

29/30 NOVEMBER 1943

VIII BC 141 NIGHT LEAFLET OPERATION – FRANCE

		Despatched	Effective	Locality	No. of Leaflets	Losses
1BD				PARIS, REIMS, LE MANS, ORLEANS, CHARTRES, AMIENS, ROUEN		
B-17	422BS	8	8		1,600,000	0

29/30 NOVEMBER 1943

VIII BC 142 SPECIAL NIGHT OPERATION – EMMERICH

		Despatched	Effective	Locality	Bombs Tonnage	Losses
1BD				EMMERICH	2 × 2000GP	
B-17	482BG	1	1	2108 hrs	1 × Photoflash	0

30 NOVEMBER 1943

VIII BC 143

		Despatched	Effective	Target	Bombs Tonnage	E/A	Losses MIA	E	Dam	Casualties KIA	WIA	MIA
1BD				SOLINGEN I/A (P)								
B-17	91BG	24	0	1155–1158 hrs	580 × 500GP	0–0–0	0		0	0	0	0
	92BG	20	0		1527 × 100 IB	0–0–0	0	1	0	9	0	1
	303BG	20	1			0–0–0	0		0	0	0	0
	305BG	16	0			0–0–0	0		0	0	0	0
	306BG	22	0			0–0–0	0		0	0	0	0
	351BG	34	0			0–0–0	0		0	0	0	0
	379BG	22	0			0–0–0	0		0	0	0	0
	381BG	22	0			0–0–0	0		0	0	0	0
	384BG	20	0			0–0–0	0		0	0	0	0
	401BG	21	0			0–0–0	0		3	0	0	0
3BD	94BG	32	7			0–0–0	0		0	0	0	0
B-17	95BG	20	17			0–0–0	1		1	0	5	10
	96BG	14	12			0–0–0	0		2	0	0	0
	100BG	18	11			1–0–0	0		2	0	2	0
	385BG	13	2			0–0–0	1	1	0	2	0	2
	388BG	12	10			0–0–0	0		1	0	3	0
	390BG	19	19			0–0–0	1		0	0	0	10
2BD	44BG	24	0			0–0–0	0		0	0	10	0
B-24	389BG	5	0			0–0–0	0		0	0	0	0
	PFF											
	482BG	3	1			0–0–0	0		0	0	0	0
TOTALS:		381	80		224.35	1–0–0	3	3	9	11	20	23

REMARKS: Cloud prevented 1st and 2nd BD from continuing to the target. 1 a/c dropped 8 × 500GP and 20 × 100 IB on Wermelskirchen (O). 92BG B-17 blew up over Helmdon during assembly, all killed. 385BG B-17 caught fire whilst assembling, aircraft abandoned and cr. Chappel. B-17 c/l Little Stoughton A/F, Cat E.

VIII FC FO 193

Despatched		Groups	E/A	Losses MIA	E	Dam	Casualties KIA	WIA	MIA
P-38	20	55FG	0–0–0	1	0	1	0	0	1
P-47	327	4FG, 56FG, 78FG, 352FG, 353FG, 355FG, 356FG	0–2–1	5	0	1	0	0	5
TOTALS:	347		0–2–1	6	0	2	0	0	6

REMARKS: Escort and support for bombers. 77FS of 20FG flew as part of 55FG formation. Fighter group e/a credits: 78FG – 1. Fighter group losses:– 55FG – 1, 56FG – 1, 78FG – 1, 352FG – 3.

7FG despatched 4 F-5 and 1 Spitfire to Belgium and France.

30 NOVEMBER/1 DECEMBER 1943

VIII BC 144 NIGHT LEAFLET OPERATION – FRANCE AND GERMANY

		Despatched	Effective	Locality	No. of Leaflets	Losses
1BD				PARIS, ROUEN, TOURS, KREFELD,		
B-17	422BS	6	6	OPLADEN	1,407,500	0

1 DECEMBER 1943

VIII BC 145

		Despatched	Effective	Target	Bombs Tonnage	E/A	Losses MIA	E	Dam	Casualties KIA	WIA	MIA
1BD				SOLINGEN I/A (P) &								
B-17	91BG	27	25	LEVERKUSEN I/A (P)	1530 × 500GP	0–0–1	5	0		0	0	50
	92BG	18	17	1159–1212 hrs	6399 × 100IB	0–0–0	1	0		0	1	10
	303BG	17	17			0–0–0	2	0		0	0	10
	305BG	16	15			0–0–1	0	0		0	2	0
	306BG	22	22			1–0–0	0	1		1	0	1
	351BG	36	34			1–0–1	2	0		2	2	20
	379BG	20	20			0–0–0	1	0		0	1	10
	381BG	25	23			0–0–0	4	1		0	9	40
	384BG	19	18			0–0–0	4	0		0	0	30
	401BG	15	15			1–0–0	0	0		0	2	6

continued on next page

1 DECEMBER 1943 *(contd.)*

2BD				SOLINGEN I/A (P)								
B-24	44BG	18	18	1159–1212 hrs		0–0–0	1	0		0	0	10
	93BG	21	17			1–3–0	2	0		0	5	20
	389BG	24	22			0–2–2	2	1		9	1	20
	392BG	15	12			0–0–0	0	0		0	0	0
PATHFINDER				As above								
	482BG	6	6			0–0–0	0	0		1	0	0
TOTALS:		299	281		702.45	4–5–5	24	3	85	13	23	227

REMARKS: 3BD mission abandoned due to weather. 1BD units briefed for Leverkusen dropped on Solingen as PFF secondary. Sieburg, Rossbach and other T/Os received a total of 440 × 100IB and 151 × 500GP (additional to above tonnage). A 389BG B-24 broke up in air nr Manston, 9 k. During assembly 306BG B-17 cr. near Lasham, crew baled, 1 k. B/d 381BG B-17 cr. Allhallows, Kent, 3 injured.

VII FC FO 194

				Losses			Casualties		
Despatched		Groups	E/A	MIA	E	Dam	KIA	WIA	MIA
P-38	42	55FG	0–0–0	2	1	0	0	0	2
P-47	374	4FG, 56FG, 78FG, 352FG, 353FG, 355FG, 356FG	20–4–7	5	1	3	0	0	5
TOTALS:	416		20–4–7	7	2	3	0	0	7

REMARKS: Escort and support for Mission 145. Fighter group e/a credits:– 4FG – 1, 56FG – 3, 78FG – 2, 352FG – 2, 353FG – 3, 356FG – 1. Fighter group losses:– 55FG – 2, 56FG – 3, 355FG – 2. 55FG P-38 cr. Gillingham, pilot safe. 353FG P-47 c/l nr. Metfield killing 2 horses, pilot safe. Introductory sweep flown by P-51s of 354FG, under VIII FC control.

7PG despatched 2 F-5 on PR over France.

2/3 DECEMBER 1943

VIII BC 146 SPECIAL NIGHT OPERATION – GERMANY

	Despatched		Effective	Locality	Bombs Tonnage	Losses
1BD				HÜLS		
B-17	482BG	1	1	2139 hrs	2 × 2000GP 1 × Photoflash	0

REMARKS: Oboe test.

NIGHT LEAFLET OPERATION – GERMANY

	Despatched		Effective	Locality	No. of Leaflets	Losses
1BD				BREMEN, OLDEN-		
B-17	422BS	4	4	BURG, HAMBURG	2,090,000	0

3/4 DECEMBER 1943

VIII BC 147 NIGHT LEAFLET OPERATION – FRANCE

	Despatched		Effective	Locality	No. of Leaflets	Losses
1BD				ROUEN, LILLE, PARIS		
B-17	422BS	4	4	0222–0330 hrs	800,000	0

4 DECEMBER 1943

VIII FC FO 195

				Losses			Casualties		
Despatched		Groups	E/A	MIA	E	Dam	KIA	WIA	MIA
P-47	140	56FG, 352FG, 353FG	3–0–0	0	0	0	0	0	0

REMARKS: 16 P-47 of 353FG dive-bombed Gilze–Rijen A/F with other 353FG and 56FG a/c as escort. 352FG carried out sweep. Fighter group e/a credits:– 352FG – 3.

7PG despatched 2 Spitfire and 1 F-5 on PR over France and Germany.

4/5 DECEMBER 1943

VIII BC 148 NIGHT LEAFLET OPERATION – FRANCE

		Despatched	Effective	Locality	No. of Leaflets	Losses
1BD				LE MANS, ORLEANS,		
B-17	422BS	4	4	TOURS, LAVAL	800,000	0
				2037–2125 hrs		

On take-off for the mission of 5 November, 401BG's *Zenobia* crashed into buildings in the village of Deenethorpe. Miraculously all the crew managed to escape from the wreck and warn villagers before the bomb-load exploded leaving this aftermath. Regularly flown with over-load weights of fuel and bombs there was little safety margin if a bomber lost power on take-off.

5 DECEMBER 1943

VIII BC 149

		Despatched	Effective	Target	Bombs Tonnage	E/A	Losses MIA	E	Dam	Casualties KIA	WIA	MIA
1BD				LA ROCHELLE – (P)				0	0			
B-17	91BG	10	0	LALEU				0	0			
	92BG	19	0	ST.JEAN D'ANGELY (P)				0	0			
	303BG	20	0	PARIS – IVRY (P)				0	0			
	305BG	20	0	PARIS – BOIS				0	0			
	306BG	21	0	D'COLOMBES (P)				0	1			
	351BG	35	0	A/Fs				0	0			
	379BG	21	0					0	0			
	381BG	30	0					0	0			
	384BG	20	0					0	0			
	401BG	20	0					1	0			
TOTALS:		216	0		0	0–0–0	0	1	1	0	0	0
2BD				COGNAC –								
B-24	44BG	26	0	CHATEAUBERNARD			0		0	0	1	0
	93BG	24	0	A/F (P)	80 × 100IB		0		0	0	0	0
	389BG	23	2	ST.NAZAIRE (O)	(T/O)		1		5	0	1	10
	392BG	23	0				0		2	0	0	0
TOTALS:		96	2		4.0	0–0–0	1	0	7	0	2	10
3BD				BORDEAUX –								
B-17	94BG	42	0	MERIGNAC A/D (P)		11–4–4	3		8	0	3	20
	95BG	24	0		1 × 500GP	0–0–0	0		0	0	0	0
	96BG	41	1		(T/O)	0–0–0	0		2	0	0	0
	100BG	22	0			0–0–0	0		0	0	0	0
	385BG	21	0			0–0–0	2		0	0	0	20
	388BG	46	0			1–1–1	2		9	0	1	10
	390BG	40	0			0–0–0	1		0	1	0	0
TOTALS:		236	1		0.25	12–5–5	8	0	19	1	4	50
TOTALS FOR DAY:		548	3		4.25	12–5–5	9	2	27	1	6	60

REMARKS: Weather disrupted mission. Only aircraft bombing were 2 389BG B-24s on St.Nazaire (O) and 1 96BG B-17 in vicinity of target. 401BG B-17 cr. on take-off in Deenethorpe village and exploded, no casualties. 385BG B-17 down in sea off Portugal. B/d 388BG B-17 abandoned over Cornwall, crew parachuted; a/c crashed in sea. 390BG B-17 in sea off Kent coast – out of fuel.

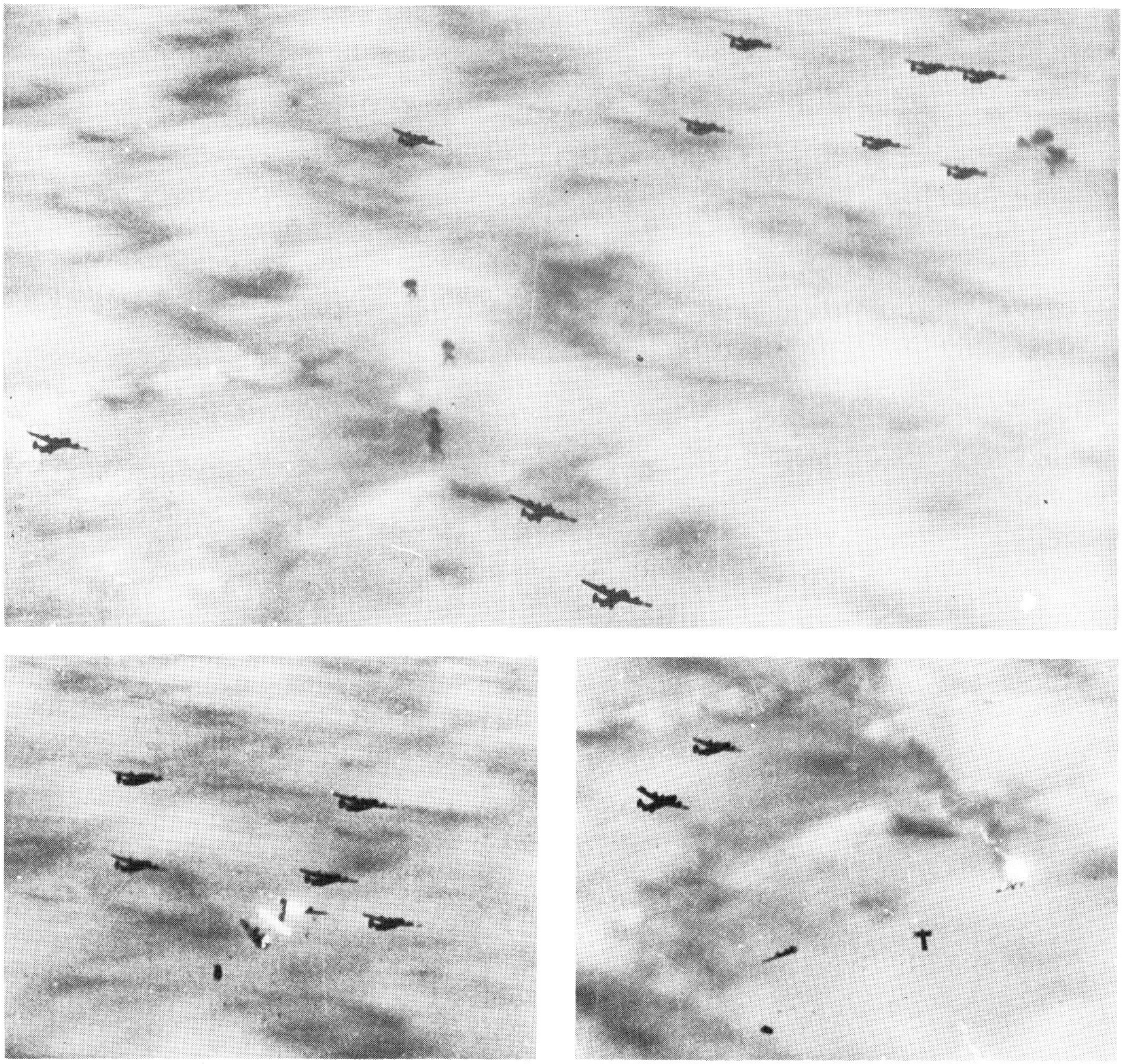

On 5 December the 389BG was sent to attack an airfield at Cognac used by Luftwaffe long-range bombers to harry Allied shipping skirting the Bay of Biscay. 'A 'solid' overcast extended across much of south-eastern France and the Group was ordered to bring bombs home. The return trip should not have been fraught with danger if the formation had kept well out to sea. Unfortunately it veered east and its proximity to St.Nazaire was unappreciated until flak suddenly bracketed the Liberators. A photographer in the high squadron clicked his shutter as the first salvo blossomed. An instant later *The Oklahoman*, flying right wing to the leader, took a direct hit in the bomb bay. The camera's next frame caught the result of the explosion as nose, rear fuselage and each wing fell separated. A third frame shows the four major items of wreckage as they tumbled towards the clouds – one wing burning fiercely. Lt Mason and his crew were all Ploesti veterans and well on the way to completing their tour.

VIII FC FO 196

				Losses			Casualties		
Despatched		Groups	E/A	MIA	E	Dam	KIA	WIA	MIA
P-38	34	55FG		0	0	0	0	0	0
P-47	266	4FG, 56FG, 78FG, 352FG, 353FG, 355FG, 356FG		1	0	0	0	0	1
P-51	36	354FG (IXFC)		0	0	0	0	0	0
TOTALS:	336		0–0–0	0	0	0	0	0	1

REMARKS: First bomber support mission for P-51 – 354FG under VIII FC control. 55FS of 20FG flew as part of 55FG. Fighter group losses:– 56FG – 1.

7PG despatched 1 F-5 on Met. flight to Abbeville and Poix.

10/11 DECEMBER 1943

VIII BC 150 SPECIAL NIGHT OPERATION – KNAPSACK

	Despatched		Effective	
1BD				
B-17	482BG	1	0	Turned back due to oxygen leak. 2 × 2000lb GP and 1 Photoflash jettisoned 1 min off French coast.

NIGHT LEAFLET OPERATION – FRANCE AND BELGIUM

	Despatched		Effective	Locality	No. of Leaflets	Losses
1BD				ROUEN, PARIS,		
B-17	422BS	6	6	CAEN, AMIENS, GHENT – 2026–2102 hrs	1,200,000	0

11 DECEMBER 1943

VIII BC 151

	Despatched		Effective	Target	Bombs Tonnage	E/A	Losses MIA	E	Dam	Casualties KIA	WIA	MIA
1BD				EMDEN I/A (P)								
B-17	91BG	24	22	1220–1312 hrs	660 × 1000GP	0– 0– 0	0	0	14	0	0	0
	92BG	18	15		2356 × 500GP	0– 0– 0	0	0	6	0	0	0
	303BG	20	20		9758 × 100IB	0– 0– 0	0	0	2	0	0	0
	305BG	21	21			0– 0– 0	0	0	7	0	0	0
	306BG	20	20			0– 0– 0	1	0	16	0	0	10
	351BG	40	34			1– 0– 0	0	0	6	0	1	0
	379BG	21	18			1– 0– 0	0	0	14	0	0	0
	381BG	28	27			0– 0– 0	0	0	7	0	0	0
	384BG	24	21			0– 0– 0	0	0	0	0	0	0
	401BG	22	21			0– 0– 0	0	0	16	0	0	8
2BD				EMDEN I/A (P)								
B-24	44BG	26	25	1220–1312 hrs		14– 2– 1	1	0	6	0	8	11
	93BG	24	20			0– 0– 0	0	0	2	0	0	0
	389BG	22	21			6– 1– 0	0	0	1	0	1	0
	392BG	21	20			4– 0– 0	1	0	9	0	0	10
3BD				EMDEN I/A (P)								
B-17	94BG	41	30	1220–1312 hrs		13– 4– 6	2	1	8	0	2	21
	95BG	40	33			9– 2– 1	2	0	1	1	0	20
	96BG	44	41			3– 2– 1	0	0	7	0	0	0
	100BG	22	22			5– 0– 0	1	0	0	0	0	10
	385BG	22	20			14– 8– 4	3	0	3	0	0	30
	388BG	42	32			5– 0– 2	1	0	5	0	1	10
	390BG	41	40			11– 3– 8	5	0	8	1	7	55
TOTALS:		583	523		1406.9	86–22–23	17	1	138	2	20	185

REMARKS: B/d 401BG B-17 landed Lindholme after 8 of crew baled out over Holland. A B-24 damaged by cable trailed into a formation by an FW 190.

VIII FC FO 198

Despatched		Groups	E/A	Losses MIA	E	Dam	Casualties KIA	WIA	MIA
P-38	31	55FG	0	0	0	0	0	0	0
P-47	313	4FG, 56FG, 78FG, 352FG, 353FG, 355FG, 356FG	21–0–7	3	1	3	1	0	3
P-51	44	354FG (IXFC)	0	1	1	0	0	0	1
TOTALS:	388		21–0–7	4	2	3	1	0	4

REMARKS: Escort and support for VIII BC 151. 2 56FG P-47s collided when preparing to attack e/a. 55FG failed to rendezvous with bombers. 55FS of 20FG flew as part of 55FG formation. 355FG P-47 cr. base after t/o – engine trouble, pilot killed. Fighter group e/a credits:– 4FG – 1, 56FG – 17, 78FG – 1, 352FG – 1. Fighter group losses:– 56FG 2, 355FG – 1, 354FG – 1.

7PG despatched 4 F-5 to France, Holland and Germany.

REMARKS: 1 F-5 returned due to being intercepted, another cr. near Didcot just before reaching base – pilot killed.

11/12 DECEMBER 1943

VIII BC 152 NIGHT LEAFLET OPERATION – FRANCE

	Despatched		Effective	Locality	No. of Leaflets	Losses
1BD				LAVAL, RENNES,		
B-17	422BS	4	4	LE MANS, NANTES 2026–2039 hrs	800,000	0

12 DECEMBER 1943

7PG despatched 2 F-5 on Met. flights to Boulogne and Frankfurt.

12/13 DECEMBER 1943

VIII BC 153 NIGHT LEAFLET OPERATION – FRANCE

	Despatched		Effective	Locality	No. of Leaflets	Losses
1BD				PARIS, AMIENS,		
B-17	422BS	4	4	ORLEANS	800,000	0
				2033–2044 hrs		

13 DECEMBER 1943

VIII BC 154

	Despatched		Effective	Target	Bombs Tonnage	E/A	Losses MIA	E	Dam	Casualties KIA	WIA	MIA
1BD				BREMEN P/A (P)								
B-17	91BG	31	31	1159–1206 hrs	915 × 500GP	0–0– 0	0	0	12	0	2	0
	303BG	40	37		4567 × 100IB	0–0– 0	0	0	4	1	0	0
	379BG	43	41		includes	0–0– 0	0	0	2	0	0	0
	381BG	30	29		4 PFF a/c	0–0– 0	0	0	12	0	1	0
	384BG	38	33			0–0– 0	0	1	0	0	0	0
TOTALS:		182	171		457.1	0–0– 0	0	1	30	1	3	0
1BD				KIEL P/A (P)								
B-17	92BG	28	26	1245–1247 hrs		0–0– 0	0	0	8	0	0	0
	305BG	27	24			0–0– 0	0	0	4	0	0	0
	306BG	22	20			0–0– 1	1	0	11	0	0	10
	351BG	21	18			0–0– 0	0	0	7	0	0	0
	401BG	21	18			0–0– 0	0	0	4	0	0	0
2BD				KIEL P/A (P)								
B-24	44BG	24	23	1310 hrs	1620 × 500GP	0–0– 0	0	0	1	0	0	0
	93BG	27	22		4670 × 100IB	1–0– 0	0	0	0	0	0	0
	389BG	22	19		973 × 500IB	0–0– 0	0	0	0	0	0	0
	392BG	25	24		includes	0–0– 0	1	0	1	0	0	10
	445BG	15	11		6 PFF a/c	0–0– 0	0	0	2	0	0	0
3BD				KIEL P/A (P)								
B-17	94BG	41	38	1306–1317 hrs		4–3– 5	0	0	22	0	3	0
	100BG	19	17			0–0– 0	0	0	2	0	1	0
	385BG	21	19			2–0– 3	0	0	3	0	0	0
	388BG	40	38			0–0– 3	0	0	40	1	0	0
Comp.	385BG & 94BG	21	18			0–0– 2	1	0	*	0	0	10
Comp.	390BG & 100BG	19	17			0–0– 0	0	0	*	0	0	0
				HAMBURG (O)								
	95BG	43	42	1300–1305 hrs	771 × 500GP	0–0– 1	0	0	3	0	2	0
	96BG	38	36		1442 × 100IB	0–0– 1	2	1	25	0	2	20
Comp.	388BG & 96BG	21	17		includes 2 PFF a/c	0–0– 0	0	0	*	3	8	0
	390BG	21	19			0–0– 0	0	0	7	0	0	0
TOTALS:		516	466		1146.6	7–3–17	5	1	140	4	16	50
PATHFINDER	482BG	12	12	As above		0–0– 1	0			0	0	0
TOTALS FOR DAY:		710	649		1603.7	7–3–18	5	2	170	5	19	50

REMARKS: Part of 3BD Force attacked targets of opportunity in the Hamburg area when heavy frosting and poor visibility disrupted Formations. 5 other B-17s dropped 22 × 500GP and 124 × 100IB on T/Os. First mission of 445BG. B/d 384BG B-17 cr. base, landing 2 inj. 96BG B-17 c/l East Harling, 3 k, 7 inj.

* – incl. in main formation data.

The Henslin crew are all smiles, 13 December, despite *Tinker Toy* 'losing' No.2 engine (feathered propeller). There were mixed emotions at Ridgewell about this bomber whose record of death and misfortunes caused it to be viewed as a 'jinx ship' on one hand and as the epitome of the Group's resilience on the other. A week later, 20 December, *Tinker Toy* was lost in a spectacular collision with an enemy fighter at the same target.

The expenditure of .50 calibre ammunition was averaging 180,000 rounds per mission for bombers in the autumn of 1943. Re-setting the link trace was a time-consuming job. These ordnance men at Rougham (Bury St.Edmunds) on 13 December are making up trace with one incendiary round (silver tip) to every nine armour piercing rounds (black tip).

VIII FC FO 199

				Losses			Casualties		
Despatched		**Groups**	**E/A**	**MIA**	**E**	**Dam**	**KIA**	**WIA**	**MIA**
P-38	31	55FG	1–0–1	0	1	1	0	1	0
P-47	322	56FG, 78FG, 352FG, 353FG, 355FG, 356FG,	0	1	1	0	0	1	0
P-51	41	354FG (IXFC)	0	1	0	0	0	0	1
TOTALS:	394		1–0–1	2	2	1	0	2	1

REMARKS: Support for VIII BC 154. Fighter Group e/a credits:– 55FG – 1. Fighter Group losses:– 355FG – 1. 55FG P-38 cr. Ludham village, pilot injured. 355FG P-47 in sea off Sizewell, pilot baled over land – injured.

VIII FC FO 200

				Losses			Casualties		
Despatched		**Groups**	**E/A**	**MIA**	**E**	**Dam**	**KIA**	**WIA**	**MIA**
P-47	36	359FG	0	0	0	0	0	0	0

REMARKS: Carried out a sweep in the Pas de Calais area. First mission for 359FG.

13/14 DECEMBER 1943

VIII BC 155 NIGHT LEAFLET OPERATION – FRANCE

	Despatched		Effective	Locality	No. of Leaflets	Losses
1BD				LE MANS, RENNES,		
B-17	422BS	5	5	TOURS, NANTES,	1,000,000	0
				CHARTRES		
				2138–2155 hrs		

16 DECEMBER 1943

VIII BC 156

	Despatched		Effective	Target	Bombs Tonnage	E/A	Losses MIA	E	Dam	Casualties KIA	WIA	MIA
3BD				BREMEN P/A (P)								
B-17	94BG	39	34	1309–1322 hrs	4023 × 500GP	0– 0– 0	0	0	21	0	0	0
	95BG	40	38		10,044 × 100IB	11– 3– 4	1	0	4	0	3	10
	96BG	36	33			5– 2– 3	7	1	10	0	2	70
	100BG	24	23			0– 0– 1	0	0	1	0	0	0
	385BG	21	18			0– 0– 0	0	0	8	0	0	0
	388BG	39	36			1– 6– 3	0	0	18	0	0	0
	390BG	40	37			0– 0– 0	1	0	5	0	0	10
2BD												
B-24	44BG	22	22			0– 0– 0	0	0	6	6	0	4
	93BG	26	24			0– 0– 0	0	0	2	0	3	0
	389BG	28	27			0– 0– 0	0	0	0	0	0	0
	392BG	17	16			0– 0– 0	0	0	2	0	0	0
	445BG	24	24			0– 0– 0	0	0	11	0	0	0
	446BG	24	20			0– 0– 0	0	2	1	0	0	0
1BD												
B-17	91BG	27	26			0– 0– 0	0	0	9	0	0	0
	92BG	20	17			0– 0– 0	1	0	8	0	0	10
	303BG	19	19			0– 0– 0	0	0	16	0	0	0
	305BG	23	21			0– 0– 0	0	0	8	0	0	0
	306BG	20	18			0– 0– 0	0	0	1	0	0	0
	351BG	35	0			0– 0– 0	0	0	0	0	0	0
	379BG	23	22			0– 0– 0	0	0	9	0	0	0
	381BG	31	31			1– 0– 0	0	0	7	0	0	0
	384BG	22	19			0– 0– 0	0	1	3	0	0	0
	401BG	20	0			0– 0– 0	0	0	0	0	0	0
PATHFINDER												
	482BG	11	10	As above		0– 0– 0	0	0	5	0	0	0
TOTALS:		631	535		1507.95	18–11–11	10	4	155	6	8	104

REMARKS: 5 B-17s and 2 B-24s in total dropped 56 × 500GP and 132 × 100IB (not in totals) on T/Os. First mission for 446BG. 4 of the 96BG B-17s lost collided in two separate incidents. On return 2 446BG B-24s c/l on and near base. 384BG B-17 overshot Coltishall, Cat E. B/d 96BG B-17 abandoned by crew on return and cr. Taverham.

VIII FC FO 203

	Despatched		Groups	E/A	Losses MIA	E	Dam	Casualties KIA	WIA	MIA
	P-38	31	55FG		0	1	1	1	0	0
	P-47	131	4FG, 355FG, 356FG		1	0	0	0	0	1
	P-51	39	354FG (IXFC)		0	0	0	0	0	0
TOTALS:		201		2–0–0	1	1	1	1	0	1

REMARKS: Escort and support for VIII BC 156. 55FG did not make appointed rendezvous owing to bombers being late. Fighter group e/a credits:– 4FG – 1, 354FG 1. Fighter group losses:– 356FG – 1. 356FG P-47 went into sea on way out. 55FG P-38 went out of control in cloud on return and cr. Wakerley, pilot killed.

INCIDENT

Individual bombers that became famous did so through surviving an exceptional number of sorties, the exploits of their crews, or participation in a notable event. A few aircraft that came into these categories were apparently overlooked by the Public Relations men. One such was a B-17F of the 96th Group about which its flight engineer, Sgt William Thorns, wrote in his diary on the night of 16 December 1943: 'My plane *Fertile Myrtle III* was badly shot up with all control surfaces damaged and several cables severed, the fin slashed nearly in two plus holes in wings and fuselage. The crew got her back over England but as the aircraft was too unstable to land, they baled out after setting the auto-pilot on a heading towards the sea.' Shortly after the last man jumped the Fortress went out of control and crashed on Silver Fox Farm, Taverham, near Norwich.

Assigned originally to Capt Tom Kenny and crew on 18 July 1943, the then new Fortress had long range tanks and the latest in bombing and navigational equipment qualifying it as a 'lead-ship'. The Kenny crew first operated *Fertile Myrtle III* on 28 July, bound for Oschersleben, and next to the Ruhr on 12 August, although during this period they were being groomed for a very special mission. This came on 17 August when *Fertile Myrtle III* left Snetterton Heath bound for Regensburg and North Africa with Kenny in the pilot's seat, Maj J.E. Hayes as co-pilot and Col Curtis LeMay, the Task Force commander. *Myrtle* spearheaded the Group and the whole Regensburg force. Kenny's lead crew only flew every fourth mission and sometimes other crews took *Myrtle* out but on 14 October they were together again to lead the whole Division to Schweinfurt. On this occasion she carried a Colonel, two Majors and two Captains together with other members of her normal crew. The Group navigator was killed and the bombardier later received the second highest standing US decoration for bravery. *Myrtle* was fairly well battered when she put down at Gravesend on return and it took some weeks for the installation of a new nose and two engines to get her back into service. When finally wrecked her tally of missions was small but significantly included leadership in two of the most famous 8th Air Force missions of the war where highly effective bombing was performed.

16/17 DECEMBER 1943

VIII BC 157 NIGHT LEAFLET OPERATION – GERMANY, FRANCE & BELGIUM

	Despatched		Effective	Locality	No. of Leaflets	Losses
1BD B-17	422BS	4	4	HANNOVER, BRUSSELS, LILLE 1903–1943 hrs	1,952,000	0

18 DECEMBER 1943

7PG despatched 2 F-5s on Met. flights to Hannover.

19/20 DECEMBER 1943

VIII BC 158 NIGHT LEAFLET OPERATION – FRANCE

	Despatched		Effective	Locality	No. of Leaflets	Losses
1BD B-17	422BS	5	5	PARIS, AMIENS, CHARTRES (O) 49°51′N–00°48′E 2059–2135 hrs	1,000,000	0

20 DECEMBER 1943

VIII BC 159

	Despatched		Effective	Target	Bombs Tonnage	E/A	Losses MIA	E	Dam	Casualties KIA	WIA	MIA
1BD				BREMEN P/A (P)								
B-17	91BG	27	24	1142–1214 hrs	1954 × 500GP	0– 0– 0	0	1	21	1	1	0
	92BG	19	16		12,221 × 100IB	0– 0– 1	1	0	12	1	0	10
	303BG	20	18			2– 2– 3	3	0	14	0	7	20
	305BG	22	18			1– 2– 0	2	0	17	0	3	20
	306BG	18	16			0– 0– 0	1	0	7	1	0	10
	351BG	33	26			0– 1– 0	0	0	7	0	1	2
	379BG	17	16			0– 0– 1	1	0	13	3	4	11
	381BG	28	28			3– 0– 1	4	0	15	1	1	40
	384BG	22	20			0– 0– 0	1	0	2	0	1	10
	401BG	19	15			0– 0– 0	0	0	14	0	1	0
3BD												
B-17	94BG	19	16			0– 0– 0	0	0	9	0	0	0
	95BG	27	26			3– 1– 5	1	0	6	0	3	10
	96BG	31	18			0– 0– 1	2	0	13	0	0	20
	100BG	22	21			0– 0– 0	0	0	6	0	0	0
	385BG	18	15			0– 1– 0	0	0	0	0	0	0
	390BG	35	34			10– 6– 9	3	0	20	0	7	35
	388BG	30	30			0– 0– 0	1	0	26	0	3	11
2BD												
B-24	44BG	28	19			0– 1– 1	1	0	3	0	0	10
	93BG	27	23			1– 0– 0	2	1	4	1	0	18
	389BG	24	18			0– 0– 0	1	0	2	0	2	11
	392BG	22	21			0– 0– 0	1	1	10	1	3	11
	445BG	25	22			0– 0– 1	1	0	15	0	2	11
	446BG	1	0			0– 0– 0	1	0	0	0	0	10
PATHFINDER												
	482BG	12	12	As above		1– 0– 0	0	0	11	0	2	0
TOTALS:		546	472		1099.55	21–14–23	27	3	247	9	41	270

REMARKS: 5 B-17s and 2 B-24s dropped 48 × 500GP and 116 × 100IB on T/Os. 2 men rescued from 303BG B-17 in sea off Cromer, one, T/Sgt Vosler, awarded MOH for actions this day. 381BG B-17 lost in collision with e/a. One B-24 lost collided with P-47. 91BG B-17 c/l Cambridge A/F on return. 392BG B-24 c/l base on return, and 93BG B-24 cr. Mendham.

An Me 410 rolls through a section of 305BG Fortresses at Bremen, 20 December.

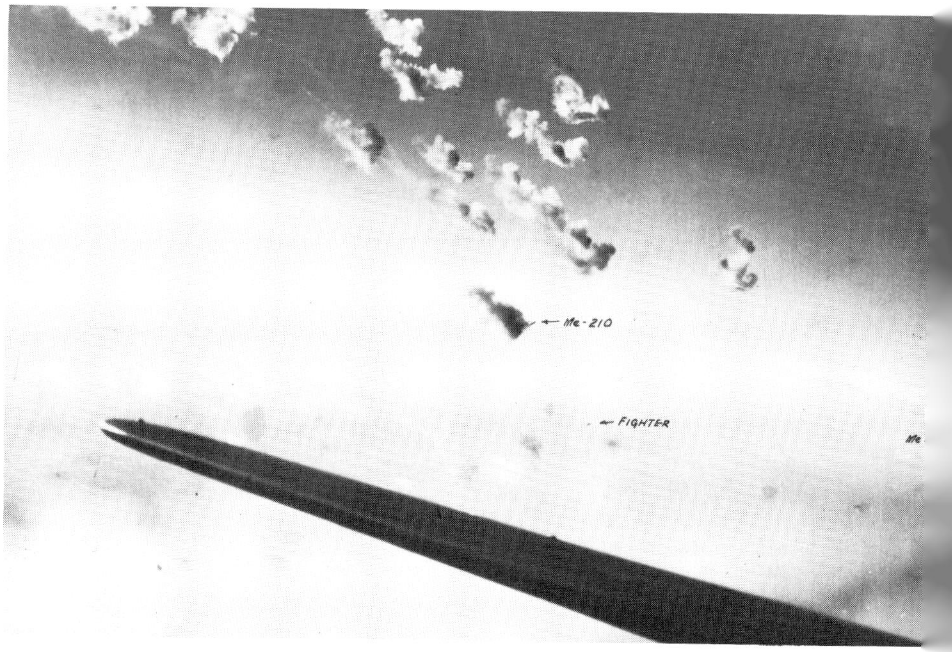

Twin-engine Me 410s coming in to attack 390BG B-17s with rockets on 20 December. A previous pass by other Me 410s resulted in the time-fused missiles bursting clear of the bombers.

The 392BG ran into intense flak at Bremen. One B-24 had a propeller separate which, like a giant scimitar, slashed through the right rudder and then severed the tail turret (with the unfortunate gunner) of *El Lobo*.

VIII FC FO 204

Despatched		Groups	E/A	Losses			Casualties		
				MIA	E	Dam	KIA	WIA	MIA
P-38	26	55FG		0	0	0		0	0
P-47	418	4FG, 56FG, 78FG, 352FG, 353FG, 356FG, 358FG, 359FG		2	1	5		1	2
P-51	47	354FG (IXFC)		4	0	0		0	3
TOTALS:	491		19–3–6	6	1	5		1	5

REMARKS: Escort and support for heavy bombers. First mission of 358FG. Fighter group e/a credits:– 4FG – 1, 56FG – 5, 78FG – 1, 5,353FG – 4, 352FG – 4, 354FG – 3. Fighter group losses:– 56FG – 1, 356FG – 1, 354FG – 4. 356FG P-47 collided with B-24, both lost. 56FG P-47 c/l near Southwold, pilot injured. 356FG P-47 c/l Bromeswell, pilot safe.

7PG despatched 13 F-5s and Spitfires to France, Germany and Holland.

20/21 DECEMBER 1943

VIII BC 160 NIGHT LEAFLET OPERATION – FRANCE & BELGIUM

	Despatched		Effective	Locality	No. of Leaflets	Losses
1BD B-17	422BS	5	5	LILLE, LENS, GHENT, BRUSSELS 2005–2015 hrs	1,000,000	0

21 DECEMBER 1943

VIII FC FO 206

Despatched		Groups	E/A	Losses MIA	E	Dam	Casualties KIA	WIA	MIA
P-47	208	78FG, 356FG, 358FG, 359FG	4–1–2	0	1	0	0	0	0

REMARKS: Sent in support of 9AF B-26s. Fighter group e/a credits:– 78FG – 4. 359FG P-47 cr., pilot safe.

22 DECEMBER 1943

VIII BC 161

	Despatched		Effective	Target	Bombs Tonnage	E/A	Losses MIA	E	Dam	Casualties KIA	WIA	MIA
1BD				OSNABRÜCK C/C (P)								
B-17	91BG	28	28	1356–1405 hrs	1441 × 500GP	2–0–2	1	0	8	0	2	10
	92BG	22	21		1369 × 250IB	2–0–0	1	0	4	0	0	10
	303BG	20	0		includes	0–0–0	0	0	0	0	0	0
	305BG	19	18		2 PFF a/c	0–0–0	0	0	0	0	0	0
	306BG	21	21			6–1–1	1	0	5	0	5	10
	351BG	31	0			0–0–0	1	0	2	3	0	2
	379BG	21	21			0–0–0	1	1	0	2	0	10
	381BG	22	19			2–1–0	0	0	1	0	1	0
	384BG	20	19			0–0–0	0	0	1	0	0	0
	401BG	21	0			0–0–0	0	1	0	0	0	0
2BD				OSNABRÜCK C/C (P)								
B-24	93BG	18	12	1405–1434 hrs		1–0–1	5	0	2	0	0	45
	389BG	26	22			2–4–1	1	0	1	0	1	10
	445BG	26	21			2–1–1	2	1	3	1	3	22
	446BG	25	20			1–0–0	2	0	2	0	0	20
	448BG	26	12			0–1–0	2	0	3	0	1	21
TOTALS:		346	234		531.4	18–8–6	17	3	32	6	13	160
3BD				MÜNSTER C/C (P)								
B-17	94BG	20	18	1353–1417 hrs	572 × 500GP	0–0–0	0	0	0	0	0	0
	95BG	30	26		1338 × 100IB	0–0–0	1	1	0	0	0	10
	96BG	27	26		1156 × 250IB	0–0–0	0	0	4	0	0	0
	100BG	30	29		includes	0–0–0	1	0	1	0	0	10
	385BG	20	18		3 PFF a/c	0–0–0	0	0	0	0	0	0
	388BG	31	29			0–0–0	1	0	20	0	1	10
	390BG	19	18			0–0–0	0	0	4	0	0	0
2BD				MÜNSTER C/C (P)								
B-24	44BG	23	19			0–0–0	2	0	0	0	0	20
	392BG	20	11	1353–1417 hrs		0–0–0	0	0	0	0	0	0
TOTALS:		220	194		354.4	0–0–0	5	1	29	0	1	50
PATHFINDER	482BG	8	6	As above		4–0–0	0	0	2	0	0	0
TOTALS FOR DAY:		574	434		885.8	22–8–6	22	4	63	6	14	210

REMARKS: Heavy cloud disrupted formations. 5 B-17 of 390BG 'A' Group followed 1BD and dropped 80 × 250IB on Osnabrück. 20 B-17s and B-24s dropped 265 × 500GP on T/Os. 3 groups failed to bomb – 303BG due to another formation passing underneath; 351BG through lead plane malfunction; and 401BG due to PFF breakdown. 2 3BD B-17s lost to accident; 448BG B-24 lost to bomb strike. 401BG B-17 suffered bomb strike and abandoned on return, cr. Washingley. 379BG B-17 cr. Ubbeston, 2 k. 95BG B-17 c/l Potter Heigham. B/d 445BG B-24 c/l Manston. 448BG flew first mission.

22 DECEMBER 1943 (*contd.*)

VIII FC FO 207

Despatched		Groups	E/A	Losses MIA	E	Dam	Casualties KIA	WIA	MIA
P-38	40	55FG		2	0	0	0	0	2
P-47	448	4FG, 56FG, 78FG, 352FG, 353FG, 355FG, 356FG, 358FG, 359FG		2	0	1	0	0	2
P-51	28	354FG (IXFC)		0	0	0	0	0	0
TOTALS:	516		15–1–6	4	0	1	0	0	4

REMARKS: Escort and support for VIII BC 161. Fighter group e/a credits:– 4FG – 3, 56FG – 4, 78FG – 1, 352FG – 6, 353FG – 1. Fighter group losses:– 55FG – 2, 352FG – 1, 353FG – 1.

7PG despatched 8 F-5s to France, Holland and Germany.

A man who reached his 25th mission and completed his tour was a symbol of hope to others. There was no lack of well wishers to greet the lucky guy – in this case T/Sgt Edward Fee. The 30-year-old top-turret gunner on the 91BG's *Black Swan* finished his 'ops' on 22 December and enjoys an exchange of suggestions as to how he will celebrate.

At first sight 95BG's *Impatient Virgin* does not appear to have sustained irreparable damage in this crash-landing. However, the distortion of the rear fuselage was sufficient to have the aircraft declared salvage. Dismantling and haulage from the site took about a week, usable components going to Honington depot for the repair of other aircraft, unusable to the old airship station at Pulham St.Mary where they would eventually be despatched by rail to smelting works. This veteran of the 95th's summer battles was damaged on the 22 December mission and was attempting to land at Ludham airfield near Potter Heigham when loss of power forced the pilot to bring it down in a pasture at Repps. The sky blue fuselage identity letters were unique to this squadron.

INCIDENT

One of the most unusual and possibly unique awards of the Distinguished Service Cross was that posthumously to 2nd/Lt Arthur E. Barks, killed on 22 December 1943. The 445th Group was on its fourth mission and 2/Lt.Glen Jorgensen's crew, in which Barks was navigator, were on their third flying a 'borrowed' Ford-built B-24H called *Lizzie*. As the formation levelled out at 22,000 ft over Germany, en route to the target at Osnabrück, No.2 engine lost power. Even with the manifold pressure on the other engines increased to maximum, the heavily loaded bomber began to slip back from its position in the low element of the lead squadron. Jorgensen attempted to gain power from the ailing No.2 by manipulating the supercharger controls back and forth but by the time the target was reached *Lizzie* was trailing the formation, and continued to do so in the withdrawal across Holland.

The fear that stragglers attracted attention from enemy fighters was soon realised. The crew watched helplessly as another lagging Liberator was attacked and sent spinning into the undercast. Then the fighters turned on *Lizzie*. By taking evasive action Jorgensen managed to escape the first assaults from the rear. A flight of Me 110s appeared and in a climbing pass put cannon shells into No.1 engine and holed a fuel tank – fortunately without igniting it. Another pass brought hits in the bomb-bay and waist, slightly wounding both gunners. One 20 mm shell, penetrating the nose, detonated against Barks' side where the flak jacket was open, literally blasting him from his position into bombardier 2/Lt Roy Stahl. The explosion also drove fragments into Stahl's legs and ignited something in the compartment, filling it with smoke. Stahl picked himself up and groped for an extinguisher, but the smoke began to clear. Barks had somehow returned to his table, re-connected his interphone and was giving the pilot a heading when he collapsed. Stahl tried to administer aid to Barks, quickly realising that his wounds were mortal and that there was little he could do to help his friend. The bombardier's oxygen lines had been disconnected when the navigator's body had struck him and he then reconnected them to receive the much needed oxygen. Meanwhile top turret gunner T/Sgt Charles Jones had despatched one of the antagonists and the other Messerschmitts withdrew, apparently low on fuel. Jorgensen and co-pilot Charlie Mathews were left to coax *Lizzie* 300 miles to England on the two functioning engines.

Losing altitude rapidly the Liberator plunged through the undercast finally emerging when over the sea. Every item of equipment that could be spared was pushed overboard to lighten the bomber in the hope of checking the descent taking it nearer and nearer to the waves. Stahl called up Jorgensen on the interphone and asked if the body of the dead navigator should be dropped out. Jorgenson pondered the question and answered in the affirmative; it was the most agonising decision he had ever had to make. Barks was a well-built youngster, 170 pounds plus flight clothing, weight that might make the difference as to whether or not nine other men returned safely. For Stahl it was a particularly heart-rending task to push the body of his friend and training classmate out of the escape hatch with the help of the nose turret gunner. Altitude still diminished but now less rapidly and 25 minutes later the crew of *Lizzie* were relieved to cross the white cliffs of the Kent coast – although by less than a thousand feet. Very soon the runway at Manston came into view and the undercarriage was lowered for a straight-in approach. Only the right main wheel extended and then would not retract. The pilots had little option other than to continue the landing run, which Jorgensen did, balancing the bomber on the one main and the nose wheel for about three quarters of the length of the runway before loss of flying speed caused the left wing to dip and spin *Lizzie* round to a violent stop, but without harm to the crew.

While there were no criteria for the bestowal of the DSC in such circumstances, and the citation for Arthur Barks makes no mention of the sacrifice of his dead body to better the chance of survival of his comrades, it was in this respect that the posthumous award of this high decoration was made. It was also the only DSC to go to a member of the 445th Group during hostilities.

A complete undercast greeted B-24s at Münster on 22 December and bombing had to be carried out on markers dropped by PFF B-17s.

Rarely were pursuer and pursued caught in a single picture as in this gun camera frame. Major Everitt Stewart was firing at an Me 110 (note strikes on left wing) when, unaware of this, Lt Coleman, a member of the same 352FG flight, cut in front. Stewart had to cease fire and let Coleman despatch the enemy. The combat took place near Zwolle at 14,000 feet on 22 December.

(IWM)

22/23 DECEMBER 1943

VIII BC 162 NIGHT LEAFLET OPERATION – FRANCE

	Despatched	Effective	Locality	No. of Leaflets	Losses
1BD			PARIS, AMIENS,		
B-17	422BS 6	6	CHARTRES,	1,212,000	0
			ORLEANS, RENNES		
			1942–2018 hrs		

VIII BC 163 SPECIAL NIGHT OPERATION – KNAPSACK (P)

	Despatched	Effective	Locality	No. of Leaflets	Losses
1BD			COLOGNE (O)	2 × 2000GP	
B-17	482BG 1	1	2020 hrs	1 × Photoflash	0

REMARKS: Oboe test.

23 DECEMBER 1943

65FW FO 81 & 66FW FO 37

Despatched		Groups		Losses			Casualties		
			E/A	MIA	E	Dam	KIA	WIA	MIA
P-47	92	56FG, 353FG	0	0	0	0	0	0	0

REMARKS: 353FG dive-bombed Gilze-Rijen A/F, 56FG as escort.

7PG despatched 3 Spitfires to NW Germany. 1 Spitfire MIA.

REMARKS: 1 Spitfire XI belly-landed upon return.

24 DECEMBER 1943

VIII BC 164

	Despatched		Effective	Target	Bombs Tonnage	E/A	Losses MIA	E	Dam	Casualties KIA	WIA	MIA
1BD				PAS DE CALAIS (P)								
B-17	91BG	33	23	V/S	7084 × 300GP				25	0	3	0
	92BG	20	20	1330–1510 hrs	2451 × 500GP				0	0	0	0
	303BG	27	10		450 × 250GP				0	0	0	0
	305BG	28	27		26 × 1000GP				0	0	0	0
	306BG	25	25						0	0	0	0
	351BG	34	34						0	0	0	0
	379BG	37	37						19	0	0	0
	381BG	26	25						0	0	1	0
	384BG	27	27						0	0	0	0
	401BG	20	20						0	0	0	0
2BD												
B-24	44BG	24	24						0	0	0	0
	93BG	25	24						0	0	0	0
	389BG	30	30						0	0	0	0
	392BG	28	28						0	0	0	0
	445BG	35	35						0	0	0	0
	446BG	27	26						0	0	0	0
	448BG	27	25					2	0	0	0	0
3BD												
B-17	94BG	36	24						0	0	0	0
	95BG	42	42						0	0	0	0
	96BH	36	35						1	0	0	0
	100BG	21	21						0	0	0	0
	385BG	18	18						16	0	0	0
	388BG	37	37						7	0	0	0
	390BG	41	41						0	0	0	0
	447BG	18	12						17	0	0	0
TOTALS:		722	670		1744.6	0–0–0	0	2	85	0	4	0

REMARKS: First mission for 447BG. 2 448BG B-24s c/l base on return after collision damage over target.

VIII FC FO 209

Despatched		Groups	E/A	Losses MIA	E	Dam	Casualties KIA	WIA	MIA
P-38	40	55FG		0	0	0			
P-47	459	4FG, 56FG, 78FG, 352FG, 353FG, 355FG, 356FG, 358FG, 359FG		0	2	0			
P-51	42	354FG (IXFC)		0	0	2			
TOTALS:	541		0–0–0	0	2	2			

REMARKS: General area support for heavy bombers. 359FG P-47 crashed near Reigate, pilot safe. 352FG P-47 crashed at Tandridge, pilot safe.

7PG despatched 4 F-5 to Northern French coast.

The 'Old Man' (the invariable epithet for the Group CO whatever his age) watches his boys come home. Col Harold Bowman (left) was a staff officer in Washington before bringing the 401BG to England and led it to turn in one of the best operational records for a B-17 group. He was later General Spaatz's 'right-hand man' in the United States Strategic Air Forces (USSTAF) which controlled both 8th and 15th AFs. Seen with him on the Deenethorpe tower on Christmas Eve is his Executive Officer, Lt.Col Allison Brooks, who went on to lead the 1st Scouting Force after completing his tour in B-17s.

27/28 DECEMBER 1943

VIII BC 165 NIGHT LEAFLET OPERATION – FRANCE

	Despatched		Effective	Locality	No. of Leaflets	Losses
1BD				PARIS, LILLE,		
B-17	422BS	7	7	EVREUX, ROUEN, CAEN 1735–1812 hrs	1,392,000	0

VIII BC 166 SPECIAL NIGHT OPERATION – QUADRATH (P)

	Despatched		Effective	Locality	Bombs Tonnage	Losses
1BD				Unknown (L)	2 × 2000GP	
B-17	482BG	1	1		1 × Photoflash	0

28 DECEMBER 1943

67FW FO

			Losses		Casualties		
Despatched	Groups	E/A	MIA	E Dam	KIA	WIA	MIA
P-38 36	20FG	0	0	0 0	0	0	0

REMARKS: Carried out sweep along Dutch coast. First group mission for 20FG, although individual squadrons had been acting as a fourth squadron to the 55FG since 3 November.

29/30 DECEMBER 1943

VIII BC 167 SPECIAL NIGHT OPERATION – QUADRATH (P)

	Despatched	Effective	Locality		Bombs Tonnage	Losses
1BD			DÜSSELDORF	(O)	2 × 2000GP	
B-17	482BG 1	1			1 × Photoflash	0

REMARKS: Oboe test.

VIII BC 168 NIGHT LEAFLET OPERATION – GERMANY, FRANCE & HOLLAND

	Despatched	Effective	Locality	No. of Leaflets	Losses
1BD			HANNOVER, OSNA-		
B-17	422BS 6	6	BRÜCK, HILDESHEIM, ZWOLLE, AMIENS 1950–2027 hrs	2,840,000	0

30 DECEMBER 1943

VIII BC 169

	Despatched		Effective	Target	Bombs Tonnage	E/A	Losses MIA	E	Dam	Casualties KIA	WIA	MIA
1BD				LUDWIGSHAFEN (P)								
B-17	91BG	26	26	P/A & O/R	16,395 × 100IB	0–1–0	0	1	11	0	0	0
	92BG	26	26	1156–1300 hrs	2017 × 500GP	0–0–0	0	0	6	0	0	0
	303BG	33	29		560 × 250IB	0–0–0	1	0	11	0	0	10
	305BG	29	29			0–0–1	0	0	7	0	1	0
	306BG	27	25			0–0–0	0	0	1	0	1	0
	351BG	36	35			0–0–0	1	1	0	4	1	10
	379BG	38	37			2–0–1	1	0	5	0	2	10
	381BG	28	28			0–0–1	0	0	6	1	2	0
	384BG	25	21			0–0–0	1	0	4	0	0	1
	401BG	21	20			0–0–0	1	0	0	0	0	10
2BD												
B-24	93BG	21	16			0–0–0	0	0	0	0	0	0
	446BG	28	25			0–0–0	0	0	0	0	0	0
	448BG	25	21			0–0–0	3	0	1	0	0	30
3BD												
B-17	94BG	38	37			0–0–0	0	1	10	1	4	0
	95BG	38	32			0–0–0	1	0	5	0	1	10
	96BG	31	30			0–0–0	0	0	0	0	0	0
	100BG	19	19			1–2–2	2	1	6	1	4	20
	385BG	20	19			0–1–2	2	0	5	0	1	20
	388BG	36	33			0–0–0	2	0	8	0	0	10
	390BG	40	38			4–0–0	1	0	8	0	0	10
	447BG	19	18			0–0–0	1	0	10	0	0	10
2BD												
B-24	44BG	24	22			0–0–0	1	1	3	0	2	10
	389BG	22	19			3–0–1	2	0	2	0	0	19
	392BG	25	23			0–0–0	1	0	2	0	0	10
	445BG	23	19			1–0–0	2	0	3	4	0	10
PATHFINDER												
	482BG	12	11	As above		1–0–1	0	0	3	0	0	0
TOTALS:		710	658		1394.0	12–4–9	23	5	117	11	19	200

REMARKS: 5 B-17s dropped 210 × 100IB on T/Os. 91BG B-17 c/l Steeple Morden following t/o engine fire. 445BG B-24 ditched off Beachy Head, 6 saved – one of first successful B-24 ditchings. 388BG B-17 ditched off I. of Wight, 4 saved. 384BG B-17 ditched off Newhaven – 9 saved. On return 351BG B-17 c/l New Romney, 4 crew killed when baling out too low. B/d 100BG B-17 c/l nr. Harleston, 3WIA. 94BG B-17 c/l St. Marys-in-the-Marsh. B/d 44BG B-24 c/l nr. Manston. 91BG B-17 c/l Old Windsor, crew safe.

30 DECEMBER 1943 *(contd.)*

VIII FC FO 210

Despatched		Groups	E/A	Losses MIA	E	Dam	Casualties KIA	WIA	MIA
P-38	79	20FG, 55FG		0	0	0		0	0
P-47	463	4FG, 56FG, 78FG, 352FG, 353FG, 355FG, 356FG, 358FG, 359FG		11	1	5		0	10
P-51	41	354FG (IXFC)		2	0	0		0	2
TOTALS:	583		8–3–6	13	1	5		0	12

REMARKS:
Escort and support for VIII BC 169. Fighter group e/a credits:– 56FG – 1, 78FG – 4, 353FG – 2. Fighter group losses:– 78FG – 1, 352FG – 3, 353FG – 2, 355FG – 3, 356FG – 2, 354FG – 2. The 2 356FG P-47s MIA, collided over France, pilots killed. The 2 354FG P-51s also lost in a collision. Some fighters short of fuel. 78FG P-47 cr. in sea off Beachy Head after pilot had baled over land. 352FG P-47 c/l Beachy Head, pilot safe.

7PG despatched 9 F-5 and Spitfires to France and Germany.

30/31 DECEMBER 1943

VIII BC 170 NIGHT LEAFLET OPERATION – FRANCE & BELGIUM

	Despatched		Effective	Locality	No. of Leaflets	Losses
1BD B-17	422BS	5	5	ANTWERP, GHENT, BRUSSELS, LENS, CAMBRAI 2319–2340 hrs	1,000,000	0

31 DECEMBER 1943

VIII BC 171

	Despatched		Effective	Target	Bombs Tonnage	E/A	Losses MIA	E	Dam	Casualties KIA	WIA	MIA
1BD				BORDEAUX –								
B-17	91BG	32	28	MERIGNAC A/F (P)	2247 × 500GP	1– 0– 1	2	0	24	0	1	20
	92BG	20	12	COGNAC–	1462 × 100IB	2– 3– 2	3	0	4	0	3	30
	305BG	21	0	CHATEAUBERNARD A/F (S)	190 × 500GP (O)	0– 0– 0	0	1	1	4	6	0
	306BG	23	23	1211–1315 hrs		1– 0– 0	0	1	4	4	9	0
	351BG	31	31			2– 0– 1	7	2	12	0	7	70
	381BG	26	25			0– 0– 2	1	1	12	0	0	10
	401BG	22	20			3– 1– 7	2	2	10	0	3	20
3BD				COGNAC–								
B-17	94BG	21	21	CHATEAUBERNARD (P)		3– 3– 5	2	1	16	0	1	21
	385BG	20	20	A/F 1211–1315 hrs		0– 0– 0	0	0	4	0	0	0
	447BG	20	20			5– 6– 9	1	0	16	1	4	10
2BD				COGNAC –								
B-24	93BG	17	16	CHATEAUBERNARD (S)		0– 0– 0	1	0	0	0	0	10
	446BG	25	24	A/F 1211–1313 hrs		0– 0– 0	2	1	0	0	0	20
	448BG	18	17	& LANDES BUSSAC (O)		0– 0– 0	2	1	5	0	2	20
TOTALS:		296	257		682.35	17–13–27	23	10	108	9	36	231
1BD				BLOCKADE RUNNER								
B-17	303BG	20	0	AT GIRONDE (P)		0– 0– 0	0	0	1	0	0	0
	379BG	21	0			0– 0– 0	0	0	2	1	5	0
	384BG	16	0			0– 0– 0	0	1	0	1	0	0
TOTALS:		57	0		0	0– 0– 0	0	1	3	2	5	0
2BD				ST.JEAN								
B-24	44BG	20	20	D'ANGELY A/F (P)	549 × 500GP	2– 0– 0	0	0	2	0	0	0
	389BG	25	24	1211–1235 hrs	892 × 100IB	6– 1– 0	0	2	0	0	0	0
	392BG	27	22			0– 0– 0	1	0	0	0	0	10
	445BG	22	21			1– 0– 1	0	1	3	0	0	0
TOTALS:		94	87		181.85	9– 1– 1	1	3	5	0	0	10

3BD				PARIS – IVRY I/A (P)								
B-17	95BG	21	21	BOIS – COLOMBES I/A(P) 1397 × 500GP	0– 0– 0	0	0	0	0	0	0	
	96BG	32	30	1207–1227 hrs	0– 0– 0	1	0	18	0	0	10	
	100BG	21	21		0– 0– 0	0	0	0	0	0	0	
	388BG	29	26		0– 0– 0	0	1	21	0	0	0	
	390BG	22	22		0– 0– 0	0	0	10	0	2	0	
TOTALS:		125	120	349.25	0– 0– 0	1	1	49	0	2	10	
TOTALS FOR DAY:		572	464	1213.45	26–14–28	25	15	165	11	43	251	

VIII BC 171

REMARKS: 20CBW B-24s attacked Cognac A/F and a T/O instead of their primary, La Rochelle A/F. Some 1BD Formations also bombed Cognac A/F as a secondary. 306BG B-17 cr. on railway nr. Stevenage on return, 4k, 6 inj. Bad weather and fuel shortages caused several losses and 6 bombers are known to have come down in the sea. On return 384BG B-17 cr. Whittlesey, 1 killed. 2 401BG B-17s abandoned due to fuel shortage, cr. nr. Ware and Kimbolton. 351BG B-17 c/l Burnham-on-Sea. 351BG B-17 abandoned nr. Cambridge and cr. Whitwell. 381BG B-17 c/l Sywell A/F. 388BG B-17 c/l Dymchurch. 448BG B-24 c/l Portreath, 445BG B-24 c/l Gosfield A/F. 2 389BG B-24s c/l Kent, nr. Ash and Bexhill. B/d 94BG B-17 c/l nr. Manston. 305BG B-17 c/l near Oxford, 4 k, 6 inj. MIA 384BG B-17 abandoned over Sussex, crew safe, a/c cr. in sea.

VIII FC FO 211

Despatched		Groups	E/A	Losses MIA	E	Dam	Casualties KIA	WIA	MIA
P-38	74	20FG, 55FG	3–0–1	1	1	1	0	0	0
P-47	441	4FG, 56FG, 78FG, 352FG, 353FG, 355FG, 356FG, 358FG, 359FG	4–1–0	2	6	0	0	3	1
P-51	33	354FG (IXFC)	2–0–0	1	0	0	0	0	1
TOTALS:	548		9–1–1	4	7	1	0	3	2

REMARKS: Escort and support for VIII BC 171. Fighter group e/a credits:– 55FG – 3, 56FG – 2, 78FG – 2, 354FG – 2. Fighter group losses:– 55FG – 1, 56FG – 1, 354FG – 1. MIA 55FG P-38 ditched, pilot saved by ASR. 358FG very low on fuel on return and 6 P-47s c/l in Kent (at Tenterden, Hythe, Bexhill, Dungeness and 2 at Gravesend), 3 pilots seriously injured. 20FG P-38 c/l Isle of Wight, pilot safe.

7PG despatched 14 F-5s and Spitfires to Germany, Belgium and France.

2 JANUARY 1944

7PG despatched 2 F-5s to Holland and Belgium.

2/3 JANUARY 1944

8AF 172 NIGHT LEAFLET OPERATION – FRANCE AND GERMANY

	Despatched		Effective	Locality	No. of Leaflets	Losses
1BD				BREMEN, RENNES, NANTES, PARIS, BREST		
B-17	422BS	5	5	2053–2128 hrs	1,200,000	0

3/4 JANUARY 1944

8AF SPECIAL NIGHT OPERATION – GERMANY

	Despatched		Effective	
1BD				
B-17	482BG	1	0	Turned back at 0600 hrs due to oxygen failure in tail gun position.

REMARKS: Oboe test.

4 JANUARY 1944

8AF 174

	Despatched		Effective	Target	Bombs Tonnage	E/A	Losses MIA	E	Dam	Casualties KIA	WIA	MIA
1BD	B-17	263	205	KIEL P/A (P)			6	2	82	14	34	51
3BD	B-17	176	166	& T/Os			5	0	29	1	6	60
2BD	B-24	130	115				6	3	16	7	13	59
TOTALS:		569	486		1069.0	4–12–4	17	5	127	22	53	170

REMARKS: Groups participating: 1BD – 91BG, 92BG, 303BG, 305BG, 306BG, 351BG, 379BG, 381BG, 384BG, 401BG. 3BD – 94BG, 95BG, 100BG, 385BG, 390BG, 447BG. 2BD – 44BG, 93BG, 389BG, 392BG, 445BG, 446BG, 448BG. 7 1BD B-17s and 34 2BD B-24s dropped on T/Os. Bomb group losses:– 92BG – 2, 93BG – 1, 94BG – 1, 96BG – 1, 303BG – 1, 306BG – 1, 384BG – 1, 385BG – 1, 390BG – 2, 392BG – 5, 401BG – 1.

95BG B-17 ditched off Bawdsey, crew rescued. 381BG B-17 crashed after take off near Sible Hedingham, Essex. MIA 379BG B-17 and 392BG B-24 interned in Sweden. B/d 401BG and 95BG B-17s ditched, crews rescued. On return, 44BG B-24 c/l Shipdham, crew safe; 392BG B-24 cr. nr. Sheringham, 4 k, 6 injured. 381BG B-17 c/l Cawston. 445BG B-24 c/l Birch.

VIII FC FO 212

Despatched		Groups	E/A	Losses MIA	E	Dam	Casualties KIA	WIA	MIA
P-38	70	20FG, 55FG	0–0–1	1	1	0	0	1	1
P-51	42	354FG (IX FC)	1–1–3	1	0	0	0	0	1
TOTALS:	112		1–1–4	2	1	0	0	1	2

REMARKS: Fighter support, Kiel bombers. Fighter group losses:– 20FG – 1, 354FG – 1. A 55FG P-38 that developed engine trouble after t/o, cr. into a vehicle while trying to land at base; pilot slightly injured.

8AF 174

	Despatched		Effective	Target	Bombs Tonnage	E/A	Losses MIA	E	Dam	Casualties KIA	WIA	MIA
3BD	B-17	75	68	MÜNSTER CITY (P)	192.0	0–0–0	2	1	35	0	1	20

REMARKS: Groups participating: 3BD – 96BG, 388BG. Bomb group losses: 96BG – 2, collided near the IP. 388BG B-17 c/l Eastchurch A/F, crew safe.

VIII FC FO 212

Despatched		Groups	E/A	Losses MIA	E	Dam	Casualties KIA	WIA	MIA
P-47	430	4FG, 56FG, 78FG, 352FG, 353FG, 355FG, 356FG, 358FG, 359FG	7–0–2	0	0	1	0	0	0

REMARKS: Fighter support for Münster bombers. 78FG strafed a locomotive in Germany. Fighter group e/a credits: 56FG – 1, 78FG – 6. First use of paddle blade propellers by P-47s of 56FG.

7PG despatched 10 F-5s and 2 Spitfires to France, Germany and Belgium.

REMARKS: 3 a/c returned with engine trouble, another with radio trouble.

4/5 JANUARY 1944

8AF 175 NIGHT LEAFLET OPERATION – FRANCE

	Despatched		Effective	Locality	No. of Leaflets	Losses
1BD				ORLEANS, LORIENT, ROUEN, TOURS		
B-17	422BS	4	4	2005–2021 hrs	800,000	0

REMARKS: First *Carpetbagger* op from Tempsford on this night.

5 JANUARY 1944

8AF 176

	Despatched		Effective	Target	Bombs Tonnage	E/A	Losses MIA	E	Dam	Casualties KIA	WIA	MIA
1BD	B-17	131	119	KIEL S/Y & I/A (P)	215.8HE		5	3	61	33	5	50
2BD	B-24	114	96	& T/Os	386.8IB		5	1	15	3	0	50
TOTALS:		245	225		602.6	41–6–13	10	4	76	36	5	100

REMARKS: Groups participating: 1BD – 92BG, 303BG, 305BG, 306BG, 379BG, 384BG, 482BG. 2BD – 44BG, 93BG, 389BG, 392BG, 445BG, 446BG, 448BG. 10 a/c dropped on T/Os (included in total). Types of bomb used: 100IB, 500IB and 500GP. Bomb group losses:– 305BG – 1, 306BG – 1, 379BG – 1, 384BG – 2, 445BG – 1, 448BG – 4. 2 B-17s collided during assembly near Catworth (1 303BG and 1 379BG); 10 k. 379BG B-17 crashed after t/o Covington, 7 k, 3 inj. 445BG B-24 cr. Fritton during assembly, 3 k. 93BG conducts first test of GH equipment.

VIII FC FO 213

Despatched		Groups	E/A	Losses MIA	E	Dam	Casualties KIA	WIA	MIA
P-38	70	20FG, 55FG	6–1–3	7	0	0	0	0	7
P-51	41	354FG (IX FC)	16–0–5	0	0	0	0	0	0
TOTALS:	111		22–1–8	7	0	0	0	0	7

REMARKS: Fighter support for Kiel bombers. Fighter group e/a credits: 55FG – 5, 354FG – 15. Fighter group losses:– 20FG – 3, 55FG – 4.

8AF 176

	Despatched		Effective	Target	Bombs Tonnage	E/A	Losses MIA	E	Dam	Casualties KIA	WIA	MIA
3BD	B-17	117	112	BORDEAUX/MERIGNAC A/F (P)	266.2HE	50–10–9	11	2	49	11	21	110

REMARKS: Groups participating: 3BD – 94BG, 96BG, 385BG, 388BG, 447BG. Types of bomb used: 300GP and 500GP. Lead bombardier fatally wounded on bomb run, lead handed over to low group. Bomb group losses: 94BG – 4, 96BG – 5, 388BG – 1, 447BG – 1. 96BG B-17 cr. Larling after t/o, 9 killed.

VIII FC FO 213

Despatched		Groups	E/A	Losses MIA	E	Dam	Casualties KIA	WIA	MIA
P-47	76	78FG A & B	2–0–1	5	1	1	0	0	5

REMARKS: Fighter support for Bordeaux/Merignac bombers. Fighter group e/a credits:– 78FG – 2. Fighter group losses: 78FG – 5. B/d 78FG P-47 c/l, Ford A/F, pilot safe.

8AF 176

	Despatched		Effective	Target	Bombs Tonnage	E/A	Losses MIA	E	Dam	Casualties KIA	WIA	MIA
1BD	B-17	79	78	TOURS A/F (P)	176.8HE	2–0–0	1	0	10	0	0	10

REMARKS: Groups participating: 1BD – 91BG, 351BG, 381BG, 401BG. Bomb group losses: 381BG – 1. 91BG flew 100th mission, first 8AF group to do so.

VIII FC FO 213

Despatched		Groups	E/A	Losses MIA	E	Dam	Casualties KIA	WIA	MIA
P-47	149	4FG, 352FG	3–0–1	0	1	1	0	0	0

REMARKS: Fighter support for Tours bombers. Fighter group e/a credits:– 4FG – 2, 352FG – 1.

8AF 176

	Despatched		Effective	Target	Bombs Tonnage	E/A	Losses MIA	E	Dam	Casualties KIA	WIA	MIA
3BD	B-17	78	73	NEUSS (O)	66.0	2–5–2	2	1	22	0	2	20
				GEILENKIRCHEN AREA (O)	60.0							
				DÜSSELDORF (O)	50.0							
				WASSENBURG (O)	18.0							
					194.0HE							

REMARKS: Groups participating: 3BD – 95BG, 100BG, 390BG. Primary was ball-bearing plants at Elberfeld. Bomb group losses:– 95BG – 2. On return 100BG B-17 c/l Tarrant Rushton A/F.

VIII FC FO 213

Despatched		Groups	E/A	Losses MIA	E	Dam	Casualties KIA	WIA	MIA
P-47	243	56FG, 353FG, 358FG, 359FG	6–1–0	0	0	1	0	0	0

REMARKS: Fighter support for Elberfeld bombers. Fighter group e/a credits:– 56FG – 4, 353FG – 1.

7PG despatched 7 F-5s and 4 Spitfires to France and Germany.

6 JANUARY 1944

7PG despatched 15 F-5s and 3 Spitfires to France.

REMARKS: 2 a/c had engine trouble, 1 had radio trouble, another lost its canopy and one pilot became ill. One other returned due to e/a interception.

6/7 JANUARY 1944

8AF 177 NIGHT LEAFLET OPERATION – FRANCE

	Despatched		Effective	Locality	No. of Leaflets	Losses
1BD				AMIENS, LILLE, VALENCIENNES,		
B-17	422BS	5	5	CAMBRAI, REIMS	984,000	0

Carpetbagger operation.

7 JANUARY 1944

8AF 178

	Despatched		Effective	Target	Bombs Tonnage	E/A	Losses MIA	E	Dam	Casualties KIA	WIA	MIA
3BD	B-17	172	167	LUDWIGSHAFEN	540.0HE		2	1	18	1	1	20
1BD	B-17	210	184	I/A & T/Os	461.0IB		3	1	86	9	7	30
2BD	B-24	120	69				7	2	18	4	5	71
TOTALS:		502	420		1001.0	30–6–17	12	4	122	14	13	121

REMARKS: Groups participating: 3BD – 94BG, 95BG, 96BG, 100BG, 385BG, 388BG, 390BG, 447BG. 1BD – 91BG, 92BG, 303BG, 305BG, 306BG, 351BG, 379BG, 381BG, 384BG, 401BG. 2BD – 93BG, 389BG, 392BG, 445BG, 446BG. 2 1BD B-17s and 1 B-24, shown in totals, dropped on T/Os. 44BG and 448BG abandoned the mission at the Dutch coast, as they were unable to reach the planned altitude, and were being outdistanced. Bomb types used: 100IB, 250IB, 500IB, 500GP, 1000GP.

Bomb group losses:– 93BG – 3, 94BG – 1, 96BG – 1, 305BG – 1, 381BG – 1, 384BG – 1, 389BG – 4. 93BG B-24 interned in Switzerland. After t/o 95BG B-17 crashed at Wilby. On return 351BG B-17 cr. at Sutton Bridge, 9 k, 1 injured; 445BG B-24 cr. at Wetheringsett, 4 k, 6 injured; 392BG B-24 c/l at Wendling, crew safe.

VIII FC FO 215

Despatched		Groups	E/A	Losses MIA	E	Dam	Casualties KIA	WIA	MIA
P-38	71	20FG, 55FG	1–0–2	1	0	0	0	0	1
P-47	463	4FG, 56FG, 78FG, 352FG, 353FG, 355FG, 356FG, 358FG, 359FG	6–0–1	5	0	1	0	0	5
P-51	37	354FG (IX FC)	0–0–0	0	0	0	0	0	0
TOTALS:	571		7–0–3	6	0	1	0	0	6

REMARKS: Fighter support, 8AF 178. Fighter group e/a credits: 4FG – 3, 20FG – 1, 353FG – 3. Fighter group losses:– 55FG – 1, 356FG – 1, 358FG – 4.

7PG despatched 14 F-5s and 2 Spitfires to France.

REMARKS: 1 F-5 was MIA. 5 a/c had engine trouble. 2 were intercepted by e/a so returned early.

Bomb-bay on fire, a 389BG Liberator goes down after fighter attack during the return from Ludwigshafen, 7 January. Air Commander of a sister group, 445BG, that day was Maj James Stewart – the film star.

7/8 JANUARY 1944

8AF 179 NIGHT LEAFLET OPERATION – FRANCE

	Despatched	Effective	Locality	No. of Leaflets	Losses
1BD B-17	422BS 5	5	PARIS, CHARTRES, CAEN, EVREUX	1,080,000	0

8 JANUARY 1944

7PG despatched 1 F-5 to Le MANS–LAVAL area.

8/9 JANUARY 1944

8AF 180 NIGHT LEAFLET OPERATION – FRANCE and BELGIUM

	Despatched	Effective	Locality	No. of Leaflets	Losses
1BD B-17	422BS 5	5	ANTWERP, BRUSSELS, RENNES, BREST, NANTES	2,292,000	0

REMARKS: 1 a/c c/l on return due to landing gear failure, no casualties.

10/11 JANUARY 1944

8AF 181 NIGHT LEAFLET OPERATION – FRANCE

	Despatched	Effective	Locality	No. of Leaflets	Losses
1BD B-17	422BS 5	5	ORLEANS, CHATEAUROUX, ROUEN, LE MANS, TOURS	4,800,000	0

11 JANUARY 1944

8AF 182

	Despatched		Effective	Target		Bombs Tonnage	E/A	Losses MIA	E	Dam	Casualties KIA	WIA	MIA
1BD	B-17	177	139	OSCHERSLEBEN A/I	(P)	455.5HE	174–32–63	34	2	83	9	11	349
			20	T/Os									
1BD	B-17	114	52	HALBERSTADT A/I	(P)	142.7IB	35–11–19	8	1	42	1	18	81
			55	T/Os									
TOTALS:		291	266			598.2	209–43–82	42	3	125	10	29	430

REMARKS: Groups participating: 1BD (Oschersleben) – 91BG, 92BG, 303BG, 351BG, 379BG, 381BG, 401BG. 1BD (Halberstadt) – 305BG, 306BG, 384BG, 482BG. The heaviest enemy opposition met since the Schweinfurt mission of 14 Oct 1943. Bomb types used: 500GP, 100IB. Bomb group losses:– 91BG – 5, 92BG – 2, 303BG – 11, 306BG – 4, 351BG – 6, 379BG – 1, 381BG – 8, 401BG – 4, 482BG – 1. 2 306BG B-17s collided during e/a attack. 401BG B-17 c/l at Ludham A/F on return. Collision damaged 305BG B-17 Cat E.

VIII FC FO 216

Despatched		Groups	E/A	Losses MIA	E	Dam	Casualties KIA	WIA	MIA
P-47	177	4FG, 56FG, 356FG, 359FG	14– 4– 5	2	3	4	2	0	2
P-51	44	354FG (IXFC)	15– 7– 9	0	0	1	0	0	0
TOTALS:	221		29–11–14	2	3	5	2	0	2

REMARKS: Fighter support, 8AF 182 (Oschersleben and Halberstadt). Col James H. Howard (354FG, 9AF) awarded MOH for his exploits in alone protecting a B-17 wing. Fighter group e/a credits: 56FG – 10, 356FG – 1, 354FG – 16. Fighter group losses: 359FG – 2. 2 359FG P-47s cr. Wales and near Chipping Warden, both pilots k. B/d 355FG P-47 abandoned over UK, pilot safe.

INCIDENT

In the great 1943–44 air battles between the Luftwaffe and the Fortresses there was one air leader who time and again was fated to be in the van. The resilience of Theodore 'Ross' Milton was remarkable in view of oft repeated harrowing experiences and the strain of leadership under adverse circumstances. The 11 January 1944 episode was traumatic by any standard, and did not go unrecognised by the historian of 1st Bomb Wing who wrote: 'Oschersleben was quite a yarn in itself. It came to be known as "Milton's Kampf". Lt.Col Ross Milton, formerly of Polebrook and now of the 91st, was allergic to tough rides. It seemed every time he led the Wing, he would inevitably wind up in the front position, whether the mission was so laid out or not, and the mission would meet violent opposition. Oschersleben was no exception. Leading the combat wing formation, he found himself in front and, for the most part, without fighter escort almost throughout the trip. Over an hour before reaching the target, the Wing was jumped by a large number of Jerry fighters. The lead aircraft was badly hit. An engine was lost, several cannon shells exploded in the cockpit, and Col Milton and Capt Everett, the pilot, were both painfully wounded. The Wing nevertheless ploughed through and bombed the target, although 13 aircraft were lost in the attack. The 91st Group's bombs went astray due to structural damage to the lead ship which affected the mounting of the bombsight, but the 381st's bombs fell true and straight on the MPI, and these bombs and those of the wings that followed did a complete demolition job on an important aircraft factory.' This was by no means the end of Col Milton's allergy.

8AF 182

	Despatched		Effective	Target	Bombs Tonnage	E/A	Losses MIA	E	Dam	Casualties KIA	WIA	MIA
3BD	B-17	234	47	BRUNSWICK A/I (P)	82.5HE 21.4IB		16	1	47	0	5	156
			114	OSNABRÜCK (O)	203.75HE 46.4IB							
			25	BIELEFELD (O)	70.0HE							
			22	PEINE (O)	2.5HE 39.8IB							
			10	HERFORD (O)	19.5IB							
			1	NIENBURG (O)	1.9IB							
2BD	B-24	138	0	BRUNSWICK A/I (P)			2	1	7	0	0	20
			58	MEPPEN (O)	154.25HE							
			1	LINGEN (O)	3.0HE							
			7	T/Os	21.0HE							
TOTALS:		372	285		666.0	19–17–16	18	2	54	0	5	176

REMARKS: Groups participating: 3BD – 94BG, 95BG, 96BG, 100BG, 385BG, 388BG, 390BG, 447BG. 2BD – 44BG, 93BG, 389BG, 392BG, 445BG, 446BG, 448BG. Formations were recalled, but leading 4 CBW was then near target so attacked. The others turned and sought T/Os. First use of B-24 H2S-equipped aircraft. Bomb types used: 500GP, 100IB. Bomb group losses:– 94BG – 8, 95BG – 1, 96BG – 1, 388BG – 2, 390BG – 1, 447BG – 3, 448BG – 2. 96BG B-17 ditched in flames, crew rescued. 392BG B-24 c/l at Wendling due to b/d, crew safe. B/d 94BG B-17 Cat E base.

VIII FC FC 216

Despatched		Groups	E/A	Losses MIA	E	Dam	Casualties KIA	WIA	MIA
P-38	49	20FG, 55FG	0–0–1	1	0	0	0	0	1
P-47	322	56FG, 78FG, 352FG, 353FG, 355FG, 356FG, 358FG	2–1–1	2	0	1	0	0	0
TOTALS:	371		2–1–2	3	0	1	0	0	1

REMARKS: Fighter support for Brunswick bombers. Second mission for 56FG and 356FG. Fighter group e/a credits: 356FG – 2. Fighter group losses: 55FG – 1, 353FG – 1, 356FG – 1.

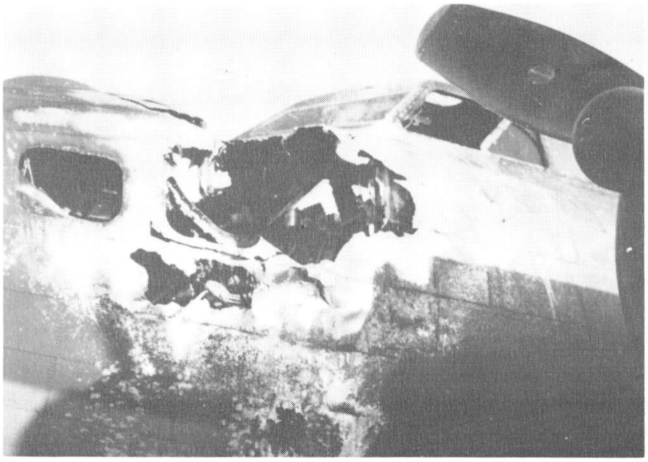

Daylight can be seen through the other side of the cockpit where fire burnt away the instrument panel of *Belle of Maryland*.

INCIDENT

When deteriorating weather on 11 January 1944 brought a recall signal to the 3rd Division, the leading combat wing was only some 25 miles from its objective and with a good chance of being able to make a visual attack, the leader, Lt.Col Thorup, elected to go on. His group, the 94th, circled in the target area to obtain a good run and was rewarded with an excellent strike on the Waggum plant. They also became the major attraction for enemy fighters and in the ensuing battle seven B-17s went down and others were badly damaged.

The *Belle of Maryland* started the mission in the second element of the high squadron, but after three B-17s had been shot out of this formation it ended up on the left wing of the leader. 2/Lt Cliff Hatcher, co-pilot, was flying the bomber from the left seat when an enemy fighter, attacking from 11 o'clock and aiming for the cockpit area, scored 20 mm hits on the lower side of the nose. Miraculously neither the bombardier, Kenton Trimble, nor the navigator, Truman Ball, were injured although the hits ignited electrical equipment between them and the pilot's instrument panel. The men in the nose immediately tried to deal with the smouldering wiring but without much success. Fearing the fire would spread to the oxygen system, they asked the pilots to take the B-17 down out of oxygen-use altitudes as soon as the formation was clear of the enemy coast. Every now and then Trimble and Ball would go back past the flight deck to collect more extinguishers; even so, they only just managed to keep the fires from spreading. Occasionally Hatcher and pilot George Kacsuta would see flames licking back on either side of the nose. Acrid smoke was swept back through the fuselage by the force of air coming through the skin holes blasted by cannon shells. To add to their predicament, No.1 engine with battle damage resisted efforts to feather its propeller and near home base began emitting flames and smoke. A successful landing was made, but the moment the *Belle of Maryland* was brought to a stop the nose erupted in flames. The crew vacated in great haste and the fire trucks put out the blaze – although not before damage to nose and cockpit had placed this Fortress beyond economical repair.

14 JANUARY 1944

8AF 183

	Despatched		Effective	Target	Bombs Tonnage	E/A	Losses MIA	E	Dam	Casualties KIA	WIA	MIA
1BD	B-17	176	169	PAS DE CALAIS		0–0–0	2	0	64	1	10	21
3BD	B-17	198	187	V/S (P) & T/O		0–0–0	0	0	2	0	0	0
2BD	B-24	178	175			8–0–1	1	1	9	0	1	10
TOTALS:		552	531		1553.0HE	8–0–1	3	1	75	1	11	31

REMARKS: Groups participating: 1BD – 91BG, 92BG, 303BG, 305BG, 306BG, 351BG, 379BG, 384BG, 401BG. 2BD – 44BG, 93BG, 389BG, 392BG, 445BG, 446BG, 448BG. 3BD – 94BG, 95BG, 96BG, 100BG, 385BG, 388BG, 390BG, 447BG. 19 B-24s attacked T/Os. Bomb types used: 500GP. 20 out of 21 V-weapon sites briefed were attacked with varying results. Bomb group losses: 44BG – 1, 303BG – 1, 384BG – 1. 392BG B-24 c/l at base due to b/d, crew safe.

VIII FC FO 217

	Despatched		Groups	E/A	Losses MIA	E	Dam	Casualties KIA	WIA	MIA
	P-38	98	20FG, 55FG	0–0–0	1	0	0		0	1
	P-47	504	4FG, 56FG, 78FG, 352FG, 353FG, 355FG, 356FG, 358FG, 359FG	13–1–0	1	1	9		0	1
	P-51	43	354FG (IX FC)	1–0–0	1	0	1		0	1
TOTALS:		645		14–1–0	3	1	10		0	3

REMARKS: Fighter support 8AF 183. Fighter group e/a credits: 4FG – 10, 20FG – 2, 354FG – 1. Fighter group losses: 20FG – 1, 356FG – 1, 354FG – 1. 359FG P-47 c/l upon return at Wormingford.

7PG despatched 5 F-5s and 5 Spitfires to France.

REMARKS: 1 a/c was recalled due to weather, whilst another experienced oxygen failure.

INCIDENT

Bomber aircrew had mixed feelings about the *No Ball* missions – code name for attacks on V-weapon sites in the Pas de Calais area of France. Although fairly substantial flak had to be faced *No Ball* raids entailing a comparatively short period in hostile airspace were therefore considered safer than the long hauls into Germany. On the other hand, more dedicated individuals saw these attacks as a diversion from the strategic bombing objectives which would hasten victory. While this was true, 8th Air Force attempted to schedule attacks on the V-sites when weather over Germany was suspect or other factors prevented visits to strategic targets. Such an occasion was 14 January 1944 when weather was questionable and all three divisions went to the Pas de Calais. The 446th Group was on its second *No Ball* operation and cloud frustrated attempts to attack the briefed site. One squadron of five B-24s turned to look for a target of opportunity. South of Amiens near Poix, 1/Lt Frank Jordan, bombardier in the leading aircraft, spotted a viaduct on the Rouen–Amiens rail line with a freight train heading towards it. Informing his pilot, a run was set up; Jordan's work with the bombsight was so precise that one of the first 500 lb bombs released made a direct hit on the track at a centre arch of the viaduct. It appears that by some quick braking action the locomotive crew just managed to stop short of the breach, but the destruction stopped all traffic on this line for several days.

14/15 JANUARY 1944

8AF 184 NIGHT LEAFLET OPERATION – FRANCE

	Despatched		Effective	Locality	No. of Leaflets	Losses
1BD B-17	422BS	4	4	AMIENS, LILLE, CAMBRAI, ST.OMER	840,000	0

8AF 185 NIGHT TEST OBOE MK II

	Despatched		Effective	Locality	Bombs Tonnage	Losses
B-17	482BG	2	1	WESEL	2.0HE	0

REMARKS: One aircraft abandoned mission as signals were not received during the bomb run.

20 JANUARY 1944

7PG despatched 2 F-5 on PR over Cherbourg.

20/21 JANUARY 1944

8AF 186 NIGHT LEAFLET OPERATION – FRANCE

	Despatched		Effective	Locality	No. of Leaflets	Losses
1BD				LILLE, BREST,		
B-17	422BS	5	4	CAEN, CHARTRES	960,000	0

21 JANUARY 1944

8AF 187

	Despatched		Effective	Target	Bombs Tonnage	E/A	Losses MIA	E	Dam	Casualties KIA	WIA	MIA
1BD	B-17	306	156	PAS DE CALAIS &			0	0	74	0	8	0
2BD	B-24	198	77	CHERBOURG V/S			5	3	41	2	16	58
3BD	B-17	291	161	(P) & (O)			1	0	29	0	7	16
TOTALS:		795	394		1141.0HE	5–1–2	6	3	144	2	31	74

REMARKS: Groups participating: 1BD – 91BG, 92BG, 303BG, 305BG, 306BG, 351BG, 379BG, 381BG, 384BG, 401BG. 2BD – 44BG, 93BG, 389BG, 392BG, 445BG, 446BG, 448BG. 3BD – 94BG, 95BG, 96BG, 100BG, 385BG, 388BG, 390BG, 447BG. 36 V-weapon sites assigned, 34 in the Pas de Calais and 2 in Cherbourg, of which 24 attacked. 10 1BD a/c, 9 2BD a/c and 5 3BD a/c attacked T/Os which were 2 further V-weapon sites and 3 airfields. 401BG abandoned the mission because of weather. Some groups stayed in target area too long identifying targets, and fighters becoming low on fuel had to leave as enemy fighters attacked, resulting in the loss of 5 B-24s. 1 target required 10 runs before it was finally attacked. Going to target 4 men baled out of lead 448BG a/c, thinking aircraft was on fire, when smoke marker ignited in bay – lost in Channel. Bomb types used: 1000GP, 500GP. Bomb group losses:– 44BG – 5, 390BG – 1. 44BG B-24 ditched off Cape Gris Nez, crew lost. On return 44BG B-24 c/l near Manston and 448BG B-24 c/l Hawkinge A/F, crew safe. B/d 446BG B-24 c/l near Dover.

VIII FC FO 221

	Despatched		Groups	E/A	Losses MIA	E	Dam	Casualties KIA	WIA	MIA
	P-38	49	20FG, 55FG	0–0–0	0	0	0	0	0	0
	P-47	531	4FG, 56FG, 78FG, 352FG, 353FG, 355FG, 356FG, 358FG, 359FG, 361FG	6–0–4	1	1	5	0	0	1
	P-51	48	354FG (IX FC)	0–0–0	0	0	0	0	0	0
TOTALS:		628		6–0–4 2–2–0 (G)	1	1	5	0	0	1

REMARKS: Fighter support 8AF 187. P-38s provided support in the Cherbourg area, all other aircraft in Pas de Calais area. First mission for 361FG. Fighter group e/a credits: 4FG – 1, 353FG – 3, 355FG – 2, 356FG – 1. Fighter group losses: 56FG – 1. 56FG P-47 c/l Manston A/F on return. 56FG made first e/a ground strafing claims.

7PG despatched 6 F-5 on PR over France, Belgium and Holland.

21/22 JANUARY 1944

8AF 188 NIGHT LEAFLET OPERATION – FRANCE

	Despatched		Effective	Locality	No. of Leaflets	Losses
1BD				REIMS, NANTES, LE MANS, TOURS,		
B-17	422BS	5	5	ORLEANS	1,200,000	0

23 JANUARY 1944

VIII FC FO 65FW 82

Despatched		Groups	E/A	Losses MIA	E	Dam	Casualties KIA	WIA	MIA
P-47	57	356FG	0	0	0	0	0	0	0

REMARKS: Sent on a fighter bomber mission against enemy airfield, no bombs dropped.

23/24 JANUARY 1944

8AF 189 NIGHT LEAFLET OPERATION – FRANCE

	Despatched		Effective	Locality	No. of Leaflets	Losses
1BD				ROUEN, AMIENS, LILLE, CAMBRAI,		
B-17	422BS	5	5	VALENCIENNES	1,200,000	0

23/24 JANUARY 1944

8AF 190 NIGHT TEST OBOE MK II

	Despatched		Effective	Locality	Bombs Tonnage	Losses
B-17	482BG	2	1	DÜREN	2.0HE	0

REMARKS:
One aircraft turned back due to 'Gee' failure, the other dropped on ETA due to special equipment failure.

24 JANUARY 1944

	Despatched		Effective	Target		Bombs Tonnage	E/A	Losses MIA	E	Dam	Casualties KIA	WIA	MIA
3BD	B-17	272	56	ZUKUNFT P/S (ESCHWEILER)	(T/O)	101.0HE 42.0IB		2	1	5	1	0	21
1BD	B-17	291	2					0	1	0	4	0	0
2BD	B-24	0	0					0	0	0	0	0	0
TOTALS:		563	58			143.0	1–0–3	2	2	5	5	0	21

REMARKS: Participating groups: 3BD – 94BG, 95BG, 96BG, 100BG, 388BG, 390BG, 447BG. 1BD – 91BG, 351BG, 381BG. Primaries were aviation industry plants and marshalling yards at Frankfurt. Most bombers had trouble forming up in bad weather and only 563 out of 857 airborne were despatched. 2BD recalled before being despatched. Because of worsening weather all groups were recalled at 1020 hrs. All did so except lead CW of 3BD (Included 2 1BD a/c which had joined the formation) who were at the German border and elected to seek a T/O. Bomb group losses: 95BG – 2. 100BG B-17 cr. after t/o Shelfanger, 1 k. 91BG B-17 cr. after t/o Ickleton, 4 k.

VIII FC FO 222

Despatched		Groups	E/A	Losses MIA	E	Dam	Casualties KIA	WIA	MIA
P-38	101	20FG, 55FG	2–2–1	4	0	0	0	0	4
P-47	535	4FG, 56FG, 78FG, 352FG, 353FG, 355FG, 356FG, 358FG, 359FG, 361FG	17–1–6	3	0	6	0	0	3
P-51	42	354FG (IX FC)	0–1–2	2	0	0	0	0	2
TOTALS:	678		19–4–9	9	0	6	0	0	9

REMARKS: Fighter support, 8AF 191. For the first time the escorting fighters were assigned area patrol, protecting all bombers as they passed through their designated areas. However, this was abandoned when the bombers were recalled, and continuous support provided. Fighter group e/a credits: 20FG – 1, 78FG – 2, 353FG – 6, 356FG – 10, 354FG – 1. Fighter group losses:– 20FG – 3, 55FG – 1, 78FG – 2, 355FG – 1, 354FG – 2.

INCIDENT

During assembly for the Frankfurt mission on 24 January, the 91st Group Fortress piloted by Lt Marco DeMara suffered a top turret fire that could not be put out. DeMara ordered the crew to bale out, the men in the rear section obeying and T/Sgt Jack Webb, the top turret gunner suffering from burns, was pushed out of the nose hatch by the co-pilot. The latter, together with the bombardier and navigator, elected to remain with DeMara who announced he would try to belly-land the bomber, rather than abandon it over England with the risk of killing civilians. The attempt – in a field at Ickleton, Cambridgeshire – failed and the four men remaining were killed in the crash. (DeMara was awarded a posthumous DSC – his Squadron, the 324th, eventually had more DSC awards than any other bomber unit in the 8th Air Force.) As parachuting Sgt Webb neared the ground he saw he would probably land in a meadow where a horse was grazing. His attention was then diverted to electricity cables crossing the spot and some sharp pulls on his canopy shrouds were needed in order to deflect his descent away from these. Looking down again he saw he was about to drop on the still peacefully munching horse. His shouts did not alert the animal before landing astride its back with a thump. Webb dismounted as quickly as he arrived, the horse rearing in alarm and bolting across the field.

25 JANUARY 1944

VIII FC FO 66FW 40

Despatched		Groups	E/A	Losses MIA	E	Dam	Casualties KIA	WIA	MIA
P-47	218	78FG, 352FG, 353FG, 358FG, 359FG	0	0	0	0	0	0	0

REMARKS: Dive bombing mission. Only Leeuwarden A/F attacked by the 353FG (44 × 500GP). 359FG carried out weather recce in area.

7PG despatched 6 F-5 to France, Belgium and Holland. 1 a/c had engine trouble and pilot baled out – a/c cr. Linchmere.

25/26 JANUARY 1944

8AF 192 NIGHT LEAFLET OPERATION – FRANCE

	Despatched		Effective	Locality	No. of Leaflets	Losses
1BD				CAEN, REIMS, CHARTRES, CHATEAUROUX,		
B-17	422BS	5	5	BREST	1,200,000	0

8AF 193 NIGHT TEST OBOE MK II

	Despatched		Effective	Locality	Bombs Tonnage	Losses
1BD 482BG	B-17	1	1	AACHEN	2.0HE	0

REMARKS: Special equipment failed 3 minutes before target, so a/c dropped on ETA. Aircraft slightly damaged by Flak.

26 JANUARY 1944

7PG despatched 1 F-5 on PR over Germany.

27/28 JANUARY 1944

8AF 194 NIGHT LEAFLET OPERATION – FRANCE

	Despatched		Effective	Locality	No. of Leaflets	Losses
1BD				PARIS, RENNES,		
B-17	422BS	5	5	LE MANS, ORLEANS	1,440,000	0

28 JANUARY 1944

8AF 195

	Despatched		Effective	Target	Bombs Tonnage	E/A	Losses MIA	E	Dam	Casualties KIA	WIA	MIA
2BD	B-24	54	31	BONNIERES V/S (P) & (S)	90.5HE							
			12	T/O	32.0HE		0	0	1	0	0	0
TOTALS:		54	43		122.5HE	0–0–0	0	0	1			

REMARKS: Groups participating: 2BD-93BG, 446BG. 2 GH equipped PFF a/c led each group, the first such use of this type of equipment. Due to technical difficulties the second formation (446BG) was ordered to follow lead and bomb same target as a secondary. 4 minutes before the target the leader of one section accidentally released and the following 11 a/c did likewise. 1 a/c damaged when it was struck by a PFF marker. Bomb types used: 2000GP, 500GP.

VIII FC FO 225

Despatched		Groups	E/A	Losses MIA	E	Dam	Casualties KIA	WIA	MIA
P-47	122	78FG, 361FG	0–0–0	0	0	0	0	0	0

REMARKS: Support for bombers.

VIII FC FO 67FW 8

Despatched		Groups	E/A	Losses MIA	E	Dam	Casualties KIA	WIA	MIA
P-47	158	352FG, 359FG	0	0	0	0	0	0	0

REMARKS: Sent to dive-bomb Leeuwarden A/F in Holland. 352FG to provide area support. Failed to rendezvous.

28/29 JANUARY 1944

8AF 196 NIGHT LEAFLET OPERATION – FRANCE

	Despatched		Effective	Locality	No. of Leaflets	Losses
1BD				AMIENS, ROUEN, CAMBRAI, REIMS,		
B-17	422BS	5	5	CAEN	1,360,000	0

8AF 197 NIGHT TEST OBOE MK II

	Despatched		Effective	Locality	Bombs Tonnage	Losses
B-17	482BG	1	1	EMMERICH	2.0HE	0

29 JANUARY 1944

8AF 198

	Despatched		Effective	Target	Bombs Tonnage	E/A	Losses MIA	E	Dam	Casualties KIA	WIA	MIA
3BD	B-17	309	291	FRANKFURT (P)	1248.75HE		13	1	34	7	6	132
1BD	B-17	366	345	& T/Os	646.8IB		11	1	82	4	12	110
2BD	B-24	188	170				5	3	19	11	14	57
TOTALS:		863	806		1895.55	75–27–48	29	5	135	22	32	299

REMARKS: Groups participating: 3BD – 94BG, 95BG, 96BG, 100BG, 385BG, 388BG, 390BG, 447BG. 1BD – 91BG, 92BG, 303BG, 305BG, 306BG, 351BG, 379BG, 381BG, 384BG, 401BG, 482BG. 2BD – 44BG, 93BG, 389BG, 392BG, 445BG, 446BG, 448BG. One 3BD formation bombed Ludwigshafen after a navigational error; this formation lost 11 a/c, as it lacked the fighter protection of the main force. One group failed to see PFF flares and dropped 11 minutes late. 3 1BD a/c dropped on a T/O. 2,600,000 leaflets released by 1BD. Bomb types used: 500GP, 500IB, 100IB. Bomb group losses:– 44BG – 2, 92BG – 1, 95BG – 2, 96BG – 5, 303BG – 1, 379BG – 3, 381BG – 2, 385BG – 3, 388BG – 1, 389BG – 2, 390BG – 1, 392BG – 1, 401BG – 3, 447BG – 1. 2 B-17s ditched in North Sea, crews lost. 392BG B-24 collided with a 482BG PFF B-24 during assembly, and cr. Gissing, only 3 survivors (482BG). 446BG B-24 c/l at Detling on return. B/d 91BG B-17 c/l Sittingbourne. 100BG B-17 cr. t/o at Diss, 7 k.

VIII FC FO 226

	Despatched	Groups	E/A	Losses MIA	E	Dam	Casualties KIA	WIA	MIA
P-38	89	20FG, 55FG	10–1– 1	5	1	3	0	0	5
P-47	503	4FG, 56FG, 78FG, 352FG, 353FG, 355FG, 356FG, 358FG, 359FG, 361FG	32–4– 9	10	0	1	0	0	9
P-51	40	354FG (IX FC)	5–1– 4	0	0	0	0	0	0
TOTALS:	632		47–6–14	15	1	4	0	0	14

REMARKS: Fighter support, 8AF 198. Fighter group e/a credits: 4FG – 9, 20FG – 12, 55FG – 1, 56FG – 6, 78FG – 3, 352FG – 6, 356FG – 1, 358FG – 2, 359FG – 1, 354FG – 4. Fighter group losses: 4FG – 1, 20FG – 5, 56FG – 1, 78FG – 1, 352FG – 1, 355FG – 4, 356FG – 1, 361FG – 1. 1 352FG P-47 abandoned over Channel, pilot rescued by ASR. A b/d 20FG P-38 c/l Bury St.Edmunds A/F. B/d 4FG P-47 c/l Lashenden A/F.

7PG despatched 4 F-5 and 2 Spitfires on PR over France. 1 a/c on a shuttle to Naples, after mapping Lyon area.

Although operational since early September 1943, 352FG at Bodney saw few combats during the next three months. Thereafter the situation began to change. Among P-47 pilots claiming victories on 29 January were Capt George Preddy (left) and Lt William Whisner (centre), comparative unknowns who would later become among the most famous aces in the 8AF. The Group was led that day by its CO, Col Joe Mason (right), soon recognised as one of the ablest leaders in VIII FC.

29/30 JANUARY 1944

8AF 199 NIGHT LEAFLET OPERATION – FRANCE

	Despatched		Effective	Locality	No. of Leaflets	Losses
1BD				LILLE, TOURS, LORIENT, NANTES,		
B-17	422BS	5	5	VALENCIENNES	1,200,000	0

30 JANUARY 1944

8AF 200

	Despatched		Effective	Target	Bombs Tonnage	E/A	Losses MIA	E	Dam	Casualties KIA	WIA	MIA
1BD	B-17	349	333	BRUNSWICK CITY (S)	1235.5HE		15	3	95	1	14	156
3BD	B-17	274	266	& T/Os	511.6IB		3	0	9	1	0	30
2BD	B-24	154	104	HANNOVER (T/O)			2	0	11	2	0	20
			39									
TOTALS:		777	742		1747.1	51–7–27	20	3	115	4	14	206

REMARKS: Groups participating: 1BD – 91BG, 92BG, 303BG, 305BG, 306BG, 351BG, 379BG, 381BG, 384BG, 401BG, 482BG. 3BD – 94BG, 95BG, 96BG, 100BG, 385BG, 388BG, 390BG, 447BG. 2BD – 93BG, 389BG, 392BG, 445BG, 446BG, 448BG. Primaries were aviation industry plants in Brunswick but cloud cover prevented visual bombing. 1CW of B-24s found such dense smoke and contrails over the secondary that rather than risk the formation being split-up, they attacked Hannover as a T/O. 2 1BD B-17s and 2 2BD B-24s attacked other T/Os (totals included in figures in chart). Bomb types used: 500GP, 500IB, 100IB. Bomb group losses: 92BG – 2, 93BG – 1, 305BG – 1, 351BG – 1, 379BG – 4, 381BG – 3, 384BG – 3, 385BG – 1, 388BG – 1, 401BG – 1, 445BG – 1, 447BG – 1. MIA 92BG B-17s collided. 351BG B-17 c/l at Polebrook on return. 379BG B-17 c/l Ash, Kent. 384BG B-17 c/l base on return.

VIII FC FO 227

	Despatched	Groups	E/A	Losses MIA	E	Dam	Casualties KIA	WIA	MIA
	P-38	20FG, 55FG	4– 0– 1	2	0	2	0	1	2
	P-47	4FG, 56FG, 78FG, 352FG, 353FG, 355FG, 356FG, 358FG, 359FG, 361FG	36–13–20	2	0	3	0	0	2
	P-51	354FG (IX FC)	5– 2–10	0	0	2	0	0	0
TOTALS:	635		45–15–31	4	0	7	0	1	4

REMARKS: Fighter support 8AF 200. Last mission for 358FG whilst assigned to VIII FC – 358FG exchanged for 357FG of IX FC on 1 Feb. Fighter group e/a credits: 4FG – 1, 20FG – 4, 56FG – 16, 78FG – 2, 352FG – 7, 353FG – 5, 358FG – 2, 359FG – 2, 361FG – 4, 354FG – 5. Fighter group losses: 4FG – 1, 20FG – 2, 361FG – 1.

7PG despatched 4 F-5s and 2 Spitfires to France.

Aircrew not flying and ground men often gathered to watch bombers return to base. A member of the crew of this B-24H lurching along the Shipdham perimeter can be seen looking out of the hatch forward of the top turret. He was posted to watch for obstructions and warn the pilot whose view of the wing tips was obstructed by the engines. 30 January 1944.

30/31 JANUARY 1944

8AF 201 NIGHT LEAFLET OPERATION – FRANCE

	Despatched		Effective	Locality	No. of Leaflets	Losses
1BD				CHATEAUROUX, BREST, CHARTRES,		
B-17	422BS	5	5	LE MANS, CAEN	1,200,000	0

8AF 202 NIGHT TEST OBOE MK II

	Despatched		Effective	Locality	Bombs Tonnage	Losses
B-17	482BG	1	1	DÜREN	2.0HE	0

31 JANUARY 1944

8AF 203

				Bombs		Losses			Casualties		
	Despatched	Effective	Target	Tonnage	E/A	MIA	E	Dam	KIA	WIA	MIA
2BD			ST.POL/SIRACOURT (P)								
	B-24 74	74	V/S	216.8	0–0–0	0	2	0	0	0	0

REMARKS: Groups participating: 2BD – 93BG, 389BG, 392BG, 446BG. One group turned back whilst near London; this group was late in taking off due to a blocked runway. This group PFF a/c joined the third formation, giving them two PFF a/c. 446BG B-24 c/l Detling A/F. 445FG B-24 cr. landing base.

VIII FC FO 229

			Losses			Casualties		
Despatched	Groups	E/A	MIA	E	Dam	KIA	WIA	MIA
P-47 114	56FG, 356FG	0–0–0	0	0	0	0	0	0

REMARKS: Fighter support, 8AF 203.

7PG despatched 1 F-5 on PR over Dijon area.

8AF 204 FIGHTER BOMBING – GILZE-RIJEN A/F

				Losses			Casualties		
Despatched		Groups	E/A	MIA	E	Dam	KIA	WIA	MIA
P-38	47	55FG	7–0–1	6	1	0	0	1	6
P-47	162	4FG, 78FG, 355FG	6–1–1	0	0	2	0	0	0
TOTALS:	209		13–1–1	6	1	2		1	6

REMARKS: 75 P-47s with 500GP bombs (4FG – 21 a/c, 78FG – 35 a/c, 355FG – 19 a/c) were despatched and escorted by a/c of their own groups, of which 70 attacked the target dropping 170 tons of bombs (4 4FG and 1 355FG a/c failed to attack) 55FG carried out sweeps in the Eindhoven/Venlo/Arnhem area. Fighter group e/a credits:– 4FG – 6, 55FG – 7. Fighter group losses:– 55FG – 6. 55FG P-38 c/l base.

7PG despatched 1 F-5 to the Dijon area.

When 390BG's *Pickle Dropper* made a belly landing near Wimy, France on 30 December it had sustained so little major damage that the Luftwaffe considered it worth careful salvage. Over the next few weeks it was dismantled and taken to Orly airfield where attempts at reassembly were apparently abandoned after Allied air attack on the airfield. These pictures of components loaded and parked on a road prior to the journey to Orly were secretly snapped by a Frenchman during field harrowing work. (R. Anthoine)

INCIDENT

The lot of the 55th Fighter Group pilots during the winter of 1943–44 was not a happy one. For much of this period, the only P-38 group on escort duties, the 55th, were plagued by mechanical difficulties, chilled in inadequately heated cockpits and placed persistently at a disadvantage in combat with an enemy frequently holding the tactical advantages of numbers and altitude. The Lightning had a creditable performance at lower level, but at the altitudes it was forced to operate to protect the bombers it had shortcomings. The 55th generally got the worst of its early combats with the Luftwaffe, although its contribution towards protecting the bombers was considerable. The Group's record for the last day of January reflects these difficult days: 'This was blue Monday for the 55th, one of the bluest. Weather didn't permit large operations, but the Wing scheduled us for a fighter sweep. We penetrated to the border of Germany with 47 P-38s and headed north, where we encountered a gaggle of 13 Me 109s about 5,000 feet above us. As the Group was climbing to engage, the Me's broke, made a pass and zoomed back up, and made another pass, at all times keeping four to five of their planes above us to knock off our tail-end Charlies in case we turned around and headed for the deck. One P-38 was seen to smoke and go down in a 30 degree dive, but the other five losses cannot be accounted for. We did destroy seven enemy aircraft, which although compensating somewhat for our loss, doesn't conclude the story. With renewed vigor every pilot of the Fighting 55th really resolved to determinedly hunt out the Hun and annihilate him.'

The claims were later reduced to five and then subsequently elevated to seven again when one of the missing pilots returned – via an escape organisation in the Low Countries. 2/Lt Leroy Hodkinson reported that after the initial fight near Venlo he and his element leader had become separated from the main formations and set course for base at low level. Near Eindhoven they were intercepted by a staffel of Me 109s. Outnumbered, the two P-38 pilots flew tight defensive orbits. A diving pass by an Me 109 ignited the leader's P-38 and this went down in flames. Hodkinson broke his turn and went after the Me 109 concerned, firing until he believed it crashed. Another Me 109 attacked head-on and both hit each other in the exchange of fire, the Me 109 crash-landing – later confirmed by the Belgians – and Hodkinson, baling out at about 2,000 ft, successfully evaded capture. The actual losses of the German unit involved with the 55th Group, III/JG 1, were one aircraft and one pilot killed. Their claims, seven P-38s. The true statistics of air combat were always difficult to establish.

2 FEBRUARY 1944

8AF 205

	Despatched		Effective	Target	Bombs Tonnage	E/A	Losses MIA	E	Dam	Casualties KIA	WIA	MIA
2BD	B-24	110	95	ST.POL/SIRACOURT & WATTEN V/Ss (P)	314.5 HE	0–0–0	2	1	2	10	0	19

REMARKS: Groups participating: 2BD – 44BG, 93BG, 389BG, 392BG, 445BG. Lead group of Watten force had to make a second run because the second group turned inside them at IP and approached the target on a collision course. Bomb types used: 2000GP, 500GP, 100GP. Bomb group losses:– 392BG – 1, 445BG – 1. 44BG B-24 cr. upon return at Willingdon, 10 k.

VIII FC FO 231

Despatched		Groups	E/A	Losses MIA	E	Dam	Casualties KIA	WIA	MIA
P-47	183	4FG, 355FG, 356FG, 361FG	0–0–0	0	0	0	0	0	0

REMARKS: Fighter support for 8AF 205.

VIII FC 323

	Despatched		Groups	E/A	Losses MIA	E	Dam	Casualties KIA	WIA	MIA
	P-38	34	20FG	0	0	0	0	0	0	0
	P-47	44	359FG	0	0	0	0	0	0	0
TOTALS:		78		0	0	0	0	0	0	0

REMARKS: Sent in support of IX BC B-26 attacking Tricqueville A/F. 359FG late in taking off and failed to make rendezvous.

3 FEBRUARY 1944

8AF 206

	Despatched		Effective	Target		Bombs Tonnage	E/A	Losses MIA	E	Dam	Casualties KIA	WIA	MIA
3BD	B-17	323	247	WILHELMSHAVEN P/A	(P)			2	0	20	2	2	20
			56	EMDEN AREA	(O)	996.25HE							
1BD	B-17	348	306	WILHELMSHAVEN P/A	(P)	418.45HE		2	0	27	0	7	22
2BD	B-24	53	0	EMDEN P/A	(P)			0	1	0	0	0	0
TOTALS:		724	609			1414.7	0–1–0	4	1	47	2	9	42

REMARKS: Groups participating: 3BD – 94BG, 95BG, 96BG, 100BG, 385BG, 388BG, 390BG, 447BG. 1BD – 91BG, 92BG, 303BG, 305BG, 306BG, 351BG, 379BG, 381BG, 384BG, 401BG, 482BG. 2BD – 445BG, 448BG. 1 B-17 of 1BD dropped on Oldenburg as T/O. 1,800,000 leaflets also dropped by 1BD. Only 53 B-24s despatched out of a total of 193 airborne; these 53 a/c abandoned the mission over the Zuider Zee due to high cloud. Lead CW of 3BD turned too sharply at IP, due to PFF and navigational error, so bombed Emden area as T/O. Bomb types used: 500GP, 100IB. Bomb group losses:–303BG – 1, 306BG – 1, 385BG – 2. MIA 385BG a/c collided going out 20m E. of Gt. Yarmouth. The other two B-17s lost, forced to ditch. 93BG B-24 cr. at Hempnall after t/o.

VC FC FO 233

	Despatched		Groups	E/A	Losses MIA	E	Dam	Casualties KIA	WIA	MIA
	P-38	74	20FG, 55FG	0–0–0	0	0	0	0	0	0
	P-47	508	4FG, 56FG, 78FG, 352FG, 353FG 355FG, 356FG, 358FG (IX FC), 359FG, 361FG	8–0–3	8	3	13	0	0	8
	P-51	50	354FG (IX FC)	0–0–0	1	0	0	0	0	1
TOTALS:		632		8–0–3	9	3	13	0	0	9

REMARKS: Fighter support 8AF 206. Includes 48 P-47 and 50 P-51 of IX FC under VIII FC control. Severe head winds caused fuel shortages. Fighter group e/a credits:– 56FG – 2, 352FG – 1, 353FG – 1, 359FG – 1. Fighter group losses:– 4FG – 1, 56FG – 1, 352FG – 2, 353FG – 3, 359FG – 1, 354FG – 1. 2 353FG P-47 collided during combat, 1 lost. Another 353FG P-47 and pilot lost in North Sea on return as a result of engine failure. 56FG P-47 abandoned off Norfolk coast, pilot lost. 354FG P-51 in sea 14m off Southwold, pilot lost. 2 56FG P-47s crash landed due to fuel shortages at Mutford and Bulcamp. 352FG P-47 c/l Wootton Park, pilot safe.

3/4 FEBRUARY 1944

8AF 207 NIGHT LEAFLET OPERATION – FRANCE

	Despatched		Effective	Locality	No. of Leaflets	Losses
1BD				PARIS, ROUEN, AMIENS, REIMS, ORLEANS, RENNES		
B-17	422BS	7	7	2110–2146 hrs	420 bundles	0

4 FEBRUARY 1944

8AF 208

		Despatched	Effective	Target	Bombs Tonnage	E/A	Losses MIA	E	Dam	Casualties KIA	WIA	MIA
1BD	B-17	287	183	FRANKFURT/MAIN M/Y (S)			8	1		5	16	83
			73	T/Os	1284.75HE							
3BD	B-17	302	163	FRANKFURT/MAIN M/Y (S)	699.2IB		10	1		0	4	100
			124	T/Os								
2BD	B-24	159	27	FRANKFURT/MAIN M/Y (S)			2	1		2	0	20
			63	T/Os								
TOTALS:		748	633		1983.95	4–0–1	20	3	359	7	20	203

REMARKS: Groups participating: 1BD – 91BG, 92BG, 305BG, 306BG, 351BG, 379BG, 381BG, 384BG, 401BG, 482BG. 3BD – 94BG, 95BG, 96BG, 100BG, 385BG, 388BG, 390BG, 447BG. 2BD – 93BG, 389BG, 446BG, 448BG. 14 CBW failed to join Division and abandoned mission because PFF a/c had failed to take-off. T/Os included: Giessen 122 B-17 a/c, Wiesbaden 51 B-17 a/c, Trier area 17 B-24 a/c, Arloff area 15 B-24 a/c, Rüsselheim area 2 B-24 a/c, Grafenhausen 1 B-24 a/c, Darmstadt 1 B-24 a/c and Koblenz 1 B-17 and 1 B-24 a/c, plus 26 B-24 and 23 B-17 on unknown T/Os. Bomb types used: 500GP, 500IB, 100IB. Bomb group losses:– 91BG – 2, 92BG – 2, 93BG – 1, 94BG – 1, 96BG – 1, 100BG – 3, 306BG – 2, 385BG – 2, 388BG – 1, 390BG – 1, 401BG – 1, 446BG – 1, 482BG – 2. 385BG B-17 c/l near Gt. Ashfield. 92BG B-17 c/l at Matching due to engine failure, 5 k. 44BG B-24 c/l near Eastbourne.

VIII FC FO 234

Despatched		Groups	E/A	Losses MIA	E	Dam	Casualties KIA	WIA	MIA
P-38	56	20FG, 55FG	0–0–0	1	0	5	0	0	1
P-47	537	4FG, 56FG, 78FG, 352FG, 353FG, 355FG, 356FG, 358FG (IX FC), 359FG, 361FG,	8–0–4	0	1	4	0	0	0
P-51	44	354FG (IX FC)	0–0–0	0	0		0	0	0
TOTALS:	637		8–0–4	1	1	9	0	0	1

REMARKS: Fighter support, 8AF 208. Includes 48 P-47 and 44 P-51 of IX FC under VIII FC control. Fighter group e/a credits: 56FG – 4, 352FG – 4. Fighter group losses:– 20FG – 1. 352FG P-47 c/l at Manston, pilot safe.

7PG despatched 6 F-5 and 2 Spitfires to France.

4/5 FEBRUARY 1944

8AF 209 NIGHT LEAFLET OPERATION – FRANCE & BELGIUM

	Despatched		Effective	Locality	No. of Leaflets	Losses
1BD				LORIENT, TOURS, NANTES, RAISMES, LILLE, CAMBRAI, ANTWERP		
B-17	422BS	7	7	2102–2132 hrs	319 bundles	0

5 FEBRUARY 1944

8AF 210

		Despatched	Effective	Target		Bombs Tonnage	E/A	Losses MIA	E	Dam	Casualties KIA	WIA	MIA
1BD				CHATEAUROUX/									
	B-17	103	50	MARTINERIE A/F	(P)	147.75HE		0	1	11	1	10	0
			50	AVORD A/F	(P)	147.75HE		0	0	1	0	0	0
1BD	B-17	121	61	CHATEAUDUN A/F	(P)	183.0HE		0	0	0	0	0	0
			60	ORLEANS/BRICY A/F	(P)	159.0HE							
						10.0IB		0	0	1	0	0	0
2BD				TOURS/PARCAY									
	B-24	103	90	MESLAY A/F	(P)	261.25HE		2	1	14	0	4	20
			8	CHATEAUDUN	(L)	24.0HE		0	0	17	0	0	0
3BD	B-17	182	133	VILLACOUBLAY	(S)	332.5HE							
						47.5IB		0	2	26	0	1	2
TOTALS:		509	452			1312.75	5–0–5	2	4	70	1	15	22

REMARKS: Groups participating: 1BD (Chateauroux and Avord) – 91BG, 351BG, 381BG, 401BG. 1BD (Chateaudun and Orleans) – 92BG, 303BG, 305BG, 306BG, 379BG, 384BG. 2BD – 44BG, 93BG, 392BG, 445BG, 446BG, 448BG, 453BG. 3BD – 94BG, 95BG, 96BG, 100BG, 385BG, 388BG, 390BG, 447BG, 452BG. Primary for 3BD was Romilly-sur-Seine A/D. 1 1BD a/c, of Chateauroux force, attacked Villacoublay as last resort, a/c joined 3BD formation. 1 3BD a/c attacked Darbert A/F – as T/O. 447BG was late and abandoned mission whilst over France. A section of one B-24 group released on Chateaudun after leader's bombs hung-up over Tours. First missions for 452BG and 453BG. Bomb types used: 500GP and 500IB. Bomb group losses:– 44BG – 1, 93BG – 1. 390BG B-17 abandoned during assembly and cr. Salehurst, 1 injured. A b/d 96BG B-17 abandoned over coast and cr. on Dymchurch Police Station, 2 of crew missing, 2 civilians k. 401BG B-17 c/l near coast due to b/d. A 93BG B-24 cr. at Old Buckenham, during assembly.

5 FEBRUARY 1944 *(contd.)*

VIII FC FO 235

Despatched		Groups	E/A	Losses MIA	E	Dam	Casualties KIA	WIA	MIA
P-38	92	20FG, 55FG	2–0–0	0	1	1	0	0	0
P-47	496	4FG, 56FG, 78FG, 352FG, 353FG, 355FG, 356FG, 358FG (IX FC), 359FG, 361FG,	4–0–3	2	1	1	0	0	2
P-51	46	354FG (IX FC)	0–0–1	0	0	0	0	0	0
TOTALS:	634		6–0–4	2	2	2	0	0	2

REMARKS: Fighter support for 8AF 210. Includes 48 P-47 and 46 P-51 of IX FC under VIII FC control. Fighter group e/a credits:– 20FG – 2, 55FG – 1, 353FG – 1, 355FG – 2. Fighter group losses:– 56FG – 1, 353FG – 1. 20FG P-38 c/l, pilot safe. 361FG P-47 Cat E.

7PG despatched 5 F-5 and 1 Spitfire to Holland, Germany and France.

REMARKS: 1 F-5 had engine cut out near target; upon return, he overshot runway and crashed in river Thames, Pilot and photos safe.

5/6 FEBRUARY 1944

8AF 211 NIGHT LEAFLET OPERATION – BELGIUM

	Despatched		Effective	Locality	No. of Leaflets	Losses
1BD				GHENT, MONCEAU-SUR-SAMBRE, ANTWERP, BRUSSELS		
B-17	422BS	5	5	2026–2037 hrs	300 bundles	0

Carpetbagger operation.

Nine Yanks And A Rebel in trouble again! This 379BG B-17F had a reputation for taking some hard knocks. Having only recently been repaired after losing a tail stabiliser it came home from France on 6 February less a propeller. The cause was not uncommon – failure of the feathering mechanism with the over-speeding 'fan' finally 'melting' the shaft and flying off. Such damage always brought an audience.

When the 56FG ace set out on the 6 February mission, Crew Chief Ralph Stafford and his men had not had time to complete the painting of victory symbols for 'Gabby' Gabreski's aircraft destroyed credits obtained a week before.

6 FEBRUARY 1944

8AF 212

	Despatched		Effective	Target	Bombs Tonnage	E/A	Losses MIA	E	Dam	Casualties KIA	WIA	MIA
3BD	B-17	189	60	ST.ANDRÉ DE L'EURE A/F (O)	178.0HE		3	1	30	0	0	30
			40	EVREUX/FAUVILLE A/F (O)	142.0HE							
1BD	B-17	303	60	CAEN/CARPIQUET A/F (O)	166.5HE		1	0	13	0	0	13
2BD	B-24	150	37	CHATEAUDUN A/F (O)	93.0HE							
			9	ECLIMEUX V/S (O)	25.25HE		0	1	7	7	3	0
TOTALS:		642	206		604.75	3–3–0	4	2	50	7	3	43

REMARKS: Groups participating: 3BD – 94BG, 95BG, 96BG, 100BG, 385BG, 388BG, 390BG, 452BG. 1BD – 91BG, 92BG, 303BG, 305BG, 306BG, 351BG, 379BG, 381BG, 384BG, 401BG. 2BD – 44BG, 389BG, 392BG, 445BG, 446BG, 448BG, 453BG. Primaries were: for 3BD – Romilly-sur-Seine A/D, for 1BD – Nancy/Essay A/F and Dijon/Longvic A/F and for 2BD – St.Pol/Siracourt V/S. Because of cloud cover formations split up to seek T/Os. 1 group from 1BD released early after a short circuit in leader's a/c caused bombs to drop. 1 448BG B-24 accidentally released 1 bomb over England, which did not explode. Bomb types used: 500GP. Bomb group losses:– 95BG – 1, 96BG – 1, 303BG – 1, 447BG – 1. 453BG B-24 exploded after t/o, 7 k. 452BG B-17 cr. on t/o, crew safe.

VIII FC FO 236

Despatched		Groups	E/A	Losses MIA	E	Dam	Casualties KIA	WIA	MIA
P-38	85	20FG, 55FG	0–0–0	3	1	1	0	0	3
P-47	506	4FG, 56FG, 78FG,	11–2–3						
		352FG, 353FG,	2–0–7(G)	1	2	1	0	2	1
		355FG, 356FG,							
		358FG (IX FC)							
		359FG, 361FG							
P-51	47	354FG (IX FC)	0–0–0	0	0	0	0	0	0
TOTALS:	638		11–2–3 2–0–7 (G)	4	3	2	0	2	4

REMARKS: Fighter support, 8AF 212. Includes 48 P-47 and 47 P-51 of IX FC, under VIII FC control. First ground credits for e/a. Fighter group e/a credits: 4FG – 3, 56FG – 5, 78FG – 3, 356FG – 1, 358FG – 1. Fighter group losses:– 4FG – 1, 20FG – 1, 55FG – 2. 2 55FG P-38 collided, one MIA, the other c/l upon return. 356FG P-47 Cat E – c/l Manston, pilot inj. 56FG P-47 c/l, pilot inj.

7PG despatched 6 F-5 and 5 Spitfires to Holland, Germany and France.

7/8 FEBRUARY

8AF 213 NIGHT LEAFLET OPERATION – BELGIUM

	Despatched		Effective	Locality	No. of Leaflets	Losses
1BD				BRUSSELS, ANTWERP, GHENT, LIEGE, MONCEAU-SUR-SAMBRE		
B-17	422BS	6	6	2202–2225 hrs	363 bundles	0

Carpetbagger operation

8 FEBRUARY 1944

8AF 214

	Despatched		Effective	Target		Bombs Tonnage	E/A	Losses MIA	E	Dam	Casualties KIA	WIA	MIA
2BD	B-24	54	53	SIRACOURT V/S	(P)			0	0	9	0	2	0
		73	57	WATTEN V/S	(P)			0	0	32	0	8	0
TOTALS:		127	110			363.5HE	0–0–0	0	0	41	0	10	0

REMARKS: Groups participating: 2BD – 44BG, 93BG, 392BG, 445BG, 446BG. Bomb types used: 500GP, 1000GP, 2000GP.

VIII FC FO 237

Despatched		Groups	E/A	Losses MIA	E	Dam	Casualties KIA	WIA	MIA
P-47	89	359FG, 362FG (IX FC)	0–0–0	0	0	0	0	0	0

REMARKS: Fighter support, 8AF 214 (V-weapon sites). 362FG IX FC flew under VIII FC control (41 a/c).

8AF 214

	Despatched		Effective	Target	Bombs Tonnage	E/A	Losses MIA	E	Dam	Casualties KIA	WIA	MIA
1BD	B-17	120	51	FRANKFURT M/Y (P)	352.5HE		9	1	78	0	4	90
			39	T/Os								
3BD	B-17	116	37	FRANKFURT M/Y (P)	132.6IB		4	1	30	11	0	40
			68	T/Os								
TOTALS:		236	195		485.1	1–3–0	13	2	108	11	4	130

REMARKS: Groups participating: 1BD – 92BG, 303BG, 305BG, 306BG, 379BG, 384BG, 482BG. 3BD – 94BG, 96BG, 385BG, 388BG, 447BG, 452BG. Lead a/c of high group, second CW (92BG) indicated it was turning back, but rest of group followed. It was immediately attacked by e/a and 3 a/c were lost. Group eventually reformed and returned to base. 452BG, whose leader was forced to leave formation due to engine failure, became temporarily disorganised and three a/c which descended into the cloud cover failed to return. The fourth CW which had only 1PFF a/c (the other failed to take-off due to a taxi-ing accident) released in the Wiesbaden area due to problems with equipment. Bomb types used: 500GP, 500IB, 100IB. Bomb group losses:– 92BG – 3, 305BG – 1, 306BG – 1, 379BG – 2, 384BG – 1, 385BG – 1, 452BG – 3, 482BG – 1. 452BG B-17 cr. at Morley St.Peter on t/o, 11 k. On return, B-17 c/l near Brighton, crew safe.

8 FEBRUARY 1944 (*contd.*)

VIII FC FO 238

	Despatched		Groups	E/A	Losses MIA	E	Dam	Casualties KIA	WIA	MIA
	P-38	77	20FG, 55FG	4–0–0	2	0	0	0	0	2
	P-47	435	4FG, 56FG, 78FG, 352FG, 353FG, 355FG, 356FG, 361FG, 358FG (IX FC)	12–1–7	3	1	4	0	0	3
	P-51	41	354FG (IX FC)	0–0–1	4	0	0	0	0	4
TOTALS:		553		16–1–8	9	1	4	0	0	9

REMARKS: Fighter support for 8AF 214 (Frankfurt). Includes 41 P-51 and 48 P-47 of IX FC under VIII FC control. 7 locomotives were destroyed, 1 by 20FG and 6 by 354FG. Fighter group e/a credits:– 20FG – 4, 56FG – 1, 78FG – 1, 353FG – 7, 358FG – 2. Fighter group losses:– 20FG – 2, 352FG – 3, 354FG – 4. B/d 56FG P-47 c/l Manston A/F on return.

7PG despatched 6 F-5s and 5 Spitfires to France, Holland and Germany on PR.

8/9 FEBRUARY 1944

8AF 215 NIGHT LEAFLET OPERATION – FRANCE

	Despatched		Effective	Locality	No. of Leaflets	Losses
1BD				CAEN, ROUEN, PARIS RENNES, AMIENS		
B-17	422BS	6	6	2106–2136 hrs	360 bundles	0

Carpetbagger operation.

9 FEBRUARY 1944

7PG despatched 5 F-5s to France, Holland and Germany.

10 FEBRUARY 1944

8AF 216

	Despatched		Effective	Target	Bombs Tonnage	E/A	Losses MIA	E	Dam	Casualties KIA	WIA	MIA
3BD				BRUNSWICK I/A								
	B-17	169	143	& T/Os	355.1	42–30–61	29	1	52	2	3	295

REMARKS: Groups participating: 3BD – 94BG, 95BG, 96BG, 100BG, 385BG, 388BG, 390BG, 447BG, 452BG; 482BG. 2 B-17s dropped on T/Os. Bomb group losses:– 94BG – 5, 95BG – 7, 96BG – 3, 100BG – 2, 388BG – 3, 390BG – 2, 447BG – 2, 452BG – 5. MIA 388BG B-17 ditched, crew lost.

VIII FC FO 239

	Despatched		Groups	E/A	Losses MIA	E	Dam	Casualties KIA	WIA	MIA
	P-38	64	20FG, 55FG	11–0–8	5	1	0	1	0	5
	P-47	357	4FG, 56FG, 78FG, 352FG, 353FG, 356FG, 359FG, 362FG (IX FC)	37–0–15	4	0	6	0	1	4
	P-51	45	354FG (IX FC)	8–1–17	0	1	0	0	0	0
TOTALS:		466		56–1–40 0–0–2 (G)	9	2	6	1	1	9

REMARKS: Fighter support for 8AF 216 (Brunswick). 2 P-47 groups unable to take-off because of weather (one for penetration, one on withdrawal). On withdrawal 1 group was 14 minutes late whilst two others were so late as to be ineffective in support. Fighter group e/a credits:– 4FG – 5, 20FG – 6, 55FG – 5, 78FG – 9, 352FG – 2, 353FG – 2, 356FG – 10, 359FG – 7, 354FG – 10, 362FG – 1. Fighter group losses:– 20FG – 4, 55FG – 1, 78FG – 2, 356FG – 1, 362FG – 1. On return, 354FG P-51 cr. Ardleigh, pilot baled. 20FG P-38 cr. Sutton Bridge, pilot K.

8AF 216

	Despatched		Effective	Target	Bombs Tonnage	E/A	Losses MIA	E	Dam	Casualties KIA	WIA	MIA
2BD	B-24	81	27	GILZE-RIJEN A/F (P)	71.0	0–0–0	0	4	0	26	14	0

REMARKS: Groups participating: 2BD – 93BG, 389BG, 445BG, 446BG, 448BG, 453BG. Dense contrails and frost prevented most a/c from attacking. During assembly 389BG B-24 cr. Taverham, 10 k. P-47 and 448BG B-24 collided near Tibenham, B-24 cr. 9 k, 1 safe. 448BG caught fire and blew up during assembly, cr. Badingham, 7 k, 2 baled. 453BG B-24 c/l Hilgay on return, crew safe.

VIII FC FO 239

Despatched		Groups	E/A	Losses MIA	E	Dam	Casualties KIA	WIA	MIA
P-47	91	355FG, 361FG	0–0–0	0	0	0	0	0	0

REMARKS: Fighter support for 8AF 216 (Gilze-Rijen).

7PG despatched 1 Spitfire to the Poix area of France.

INCIDENT

As the accident statistics reveal, flying in heavily loaded B-17s and B-24s presented an element of danger apart from enemy action. These bombers would perform the job they were designed to do but their limitations were soon reached, particularly in adverse flying conditions. Built-in safety margins were few; the aircraft were utility and expendable. The cause of every accident was investigated with the object of preventing similar occurrences. Sometimes, however, the cause remained a mystery. The mission of 10 February 1944 was launched in bleak winter weather with extensive cloud and snow flurries. Assembly was difficult. In 448th Group Liberator 42-52115, bombardier 2/Lt Richard Nardi was looking out of his nose window at 15,000 ft when he was suddenly enveloped in a flash of flame. For a fleeting moment he was aware of the aircraft disintegrating and then that he had plunged through the nose hatch. He fell no further; a cable had snagged his parachute pack and he hung suspended, trying desperately to free himself as the bomber plummeted earthward. For several precious seconds his efforts were in vain, until he grasped the sides of the hatch, pulling himself up sufficiently to clear the cable at last to drop free. Nardi was only a few hundred feet above the fields when his parachute opened. His landing was heavy and he lay there winded, shocked and hurt. Explosions followed by flame and a cloud of smoke marked the spot where the B-24 had crashed at Badingham, Suffolk, a few fields away. Only Nardi and a gunner in the rear of the aircraft escaped. It was a traumatic experience that was to haunt the young bombardier for many weeks. In a letter to a friend at the manufacturing plant where he had worked before enlisting Nardi wrote . . . 'The shock of the loss of those wonderful companions in our crew, I can't get out of my mind. Their screams still ring in my ears . . .'

The reason for the sudden disintegration of the Liberator was never ascertained. The accident investigators proposed three alternatives; that it had been in collision with another unknown aircraft, that structural failure had occurred, or an explosion taken place. The latter seems the most likely as wreckage was scattered over a wide area and was consistent with an explosion. A complete tail fin landed in a hedgerow three miles from the crash site and remained there for 24 years, a winter shelter for pheasants, until removed to a museum as a war relic.

10/11 FEBRUARY 1944

8AF 217 NIGHT LEAFLET OPERATION – FRANCE & BELGIUM

	Despatched		Effective	Locality	No. of Leaflets	Losses
1BD				RENNES, ANTWERP, CAEN, ROUEN, AMIENS		
B-17	422BS	5	5	2111–2145 hrs	260 bundles	0

Carpetbagger operation.

379BG Fortress *Carol Dawn* had a tyre burst while landing from the 11 February mission, causing a change of runway while a service team struggled to change the wheel. A photographer caught the tired crew lugging parachutes and personal equipment down the runway to meet motor transportation.

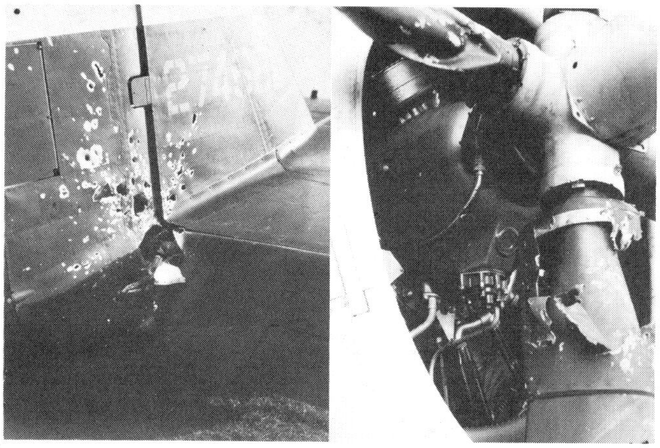

On 11 February 355 FG's Lt Duffy suffered an oxygen blackout at 27,000 feet, recovered at 4,000 feet and came home 'on the deck'. Near Antwerp his P-47, WR:Y, was hit by ground fire, four 20 mm shells hitting propeller, fuselage, wing and tail.

The name game. Naming a bomber in honour of the WACs (Women's Army Corps) was a special public relations idea. A 392BG B-24H was adorned with the WAC insignia plus appropriate names and on the afternoon of 11 February a few WACs from 2nd Division Hq arrived at Wendling to pose for photographers. Here PFC Emma Utter pretends a little artistry while Group personnel look on. The pictures obtained were widely displayed in the USA as part of a WAC recruitment drive.

11 FEBRUARY 1944

8AF 218

	Despatched		Effective	Target		Bombs Tonnage	E/A	Losses MIA	E	Dam	Casualties KIA	WIA	MIA
2BD	B-24	201	94	SIRACOURT V/S	(P)	274.0	0–0–0	1	1	17	1	1	10

REMARKS: Groups participating: 2BD – 44BG, 93BG, 389BG, 392BG, 445BG, 446BG, 448BG, 453BG. 4 groups attacked Siracourt with PFF equipment, whilst the other 4 groups, which were assigned individual targets without PFF, failed to bomb. Bomb group losses:– 93BG – 1. 392BG B-24 c/l due to b/d.

VIII FC FO 240

Despatched		Groups	E/A	Losses MIA	E	Dam	Casualties KIA	WIA	MIA
P-47	85	356FG, 362FG (IX FC)	0	0	0	0	0	0	0
P-51	41	357FG	0	0	0	0	0	0	0
TOTALS:	126		0–0–0	0	0	0	0	0	0

REMARKS: Fighter support for 8AF 218 (V-weapon site). 362FG IX FC flew under VIII FC control. First mission for 357FG, an area sweep in the Rouen area.

8AF 218

	Despatched		Effective	Target		Bombs Tonnage	E/A	Losses MIA	E	Dam	Casualties KIA	WIA	MIA
1BD	B-17	223	157	FRANKFURT M/Y	(P)	388.0							
			32	LUDWIGSHAFEN	(O)	98.0							
			19	SAARBRÜCKEN	(O)	39.0							
			4	T/Os		10.2							
TOTALS:		223	212			535.2	3–0–2	5	3	124	1	26	51

REMARKS: Groups participating: 1BD – 91BG, 303BG, 305BG, 306BG, 351BG, 379BG, 381BG, 384BG, 401BG, 482BG. Bomb types used: 500GP, 100IB. Bomb group losses:– 306BG – 1, 351BG – 1, 381BG – 1, 384BG – 2. 351BG B-17 c/l upon return at Southend and caught fire. 1 303BG B-17 overshot Shoreham, Cat E, crew safe. 303BG B-17 c/l West Malling, 1 K.

VIII FC FO 240

Despatched		Groups	E/A	Losses MIA	E	Dam	Casualties KIA	WIA	MIA
P-38	82	20FG, 55FG	2–2– 4	8	0	2	0	0	8
P-47	486	4FG, 56FG, 78FG, 352FG, 353FG, 355FG, 356FG, 359FG, 361FG & 358FG (IX FC)	14–0–14	4	2	4	0	0	4
P-51	38	354FG (IX FC)	14–0–10	2	1	0	0	0	2
TOTALS:	606		30–2–28 2–1– 4 (G)	14	3	6		0	14

REMARKS: Fighter support for 8AF 218 (Frankfurt). 2 P-47 groups failed to locate bombers on withdrawal. Fighter group e/a credits:– 20FG – 2, 56FG – 5, 78FG – 4, 355FG – 3, 356FG – 4 and IX FC 354FG – 13, 358FG – 1. Fighter group losses:– 20FG – 8, 78FG – 2, 355FG – 1, 356FG – 1 and IX FC 354FG – 2. Aborting 78FG P-47 c/l Nuthampstead, 359FG P-47 cr. on t/o, pilots safe. 354FG P-51 c/l I. of Wight.

11/12 FEBRUARY 1944

8AF 219 NIGHT LEAFLET OPERATION – BELGIUM

	Despatched		Effective	Locality	No. of Leaflets	Losses
1BD				GHENT, BRUSSELS, ANTWERP		
B-17	422BS	5	5	2118–2146 hrs	250 bundles	0

12 FEBRUARY 1944

8AF 220

	Despatched		Effective	Target	Bombs Tonnage	E/A	Losses MIA	E	Dam	Casualties KIA	WIA	MIA
2BD				ST.POL/								
	B-24	99	97	SIRACOURT V/S (P)	279.0	0–0–0	0	0	29	0	0	0

REMARKS: Groups participating: 2BD – 44BG, 93BG, 389BG, 392BG. Bomb types used: 2000GP, 500GP. Each group led by a 93BG GH equipped B-24.

VIII FC FO 241

	Despatched		Groups	E/A	Losses MIA	E	Dam	Casualties KIA	WIA	MIA
	P-47	84	4FG, 362FG (IX FC)	0	0	0	0	0	0	0
	P-51	41	357FG	0	0	0	0	0	0	0
TOTALS:		125		0–0–0	0	0	0	0	0	0

REMARKS: Fighter support, 8AF 220. 362FG (IX FC) flew under VIII FC control. P-47 groups as close escort; P-51s swept the area.

13 FEBRUARY 1944

8AF 221

	Despatched		Effective	Target		Bombs Tonnage	E/A	Losses MIA	E	Dam	Casualties KIA	WIA	MIA
2BD				5 PAS DE CALAIS V/S (P)									
	B-24	192	138	MARIES MINE	(O)	404.0		0	2	57			
			12	BUILDINGS		33.0							
3BD				12 PAS DE CALAIS									
	B-17	277	266	V/S (P)		734.0		4	2	74			
TOTALS:		469	416			1171.0	0–1–0	4	4	131	7	23	24

REMARKS: Groups participating: 2BD – 44BG, 93BG, 389BG, 392BG, 445BG, 446BG, 448BG, 453BG. 3BD – 94BG, 95BG, 96BG, 100BG, 385BG, 388BG, 390BG, 447BG, 452BG. Bomb types used: 2000GP, 500GP. Bomb group losses:– 94BG – 1, 385BG – 1, 447BG – 2. 385BG B-17 ditched 18m SW of Dungeness – 7 rescued. 94BG B-17 came down in sea, 9 rescued. 389BG B-24 c/l base. 385BG c/l Detling A/F, crew safe. B/d 96BG B-17 c/l West Malling A/F, B/d 445BG B-24 c/l near Dover.

VIII FC FO 242

	Despatched		Groups	E/A	Losses MIA	E	Dam	Casualties KIA	WIA	MIA
	P-47	189	78FG, 352FG, 353FG, 356FG	6–1–4	0	0	4	0	0	0
	P-51	43	357FG	0–0–0	1	0	0	0	0	0
TOTALS:		232		6–1–4 0–0–4 (G)	1	0	4	0	0	0

REMARKS: Fighter support, 8AF 221. Fighter group e/a credits:– 356FG – 6. Fighter group losses:– 357FG – 1; this a/c came down in the sea off Clacton, pilot rescued.

7PG despatched 6 F-5s and 2 Spitfires to Germany, Holland and France.

14 FEBRUARY 1944

8AF 222/VIII FC 243

	Despatched		Groups	E/A	Losses MIA	E	Dam	Casualties KIA	WIA	MIA
	P-47	48	353FG	0	0	0	0	0	0	0

REMARKS: Dive-bombing: Gilze-Rijen A/F(S) attacked by 46 a/c with 23 × 500lb HE. (P) was Eindhoven A/F but obscured by cloud.

15 FEBRUARY 1944

8AF 223

	Despatched		Effective	Target	Bombs Tonnage	E/A	Losses MIA	E	Dam	Casualties KIA	WIA	MIA
2BD				ST.POL								
	B-24	54	52	SIRACOURT V/S (P)	149.5	0	0	0	29	0	0	0

REMARKS: Groups participating: 93BG, 389BG, 445BG, 453BG. Bomb types used: 100IB, 500GP, 2000GP.

8AF 224

Despatched		Groups	E/A	Losses MIA	E	Dam	Casualties KIA	WIA	MIA
P-47	95	4FG, 356FG	0	0	0	1	0	0	0

REMARKS: Sent to dive bomb two airfields in France, but both groups recalled. Whilst returning 356FG sighted airfield thought to have been Coxyde and 34 a/c dropped 8.5 tons of bombs.

7PG despatched 2 F-5 to France; 1 F-5 MIA.

15/16 FEBRUARY 1944

8AF 225 NIGHT LEAFLET OPERATION – FRANCE

	Despatched		Effective	Locality	No. of Leaflets	Losses
1BD				ORLEANS, CHARTRES, CAMBRAI, LE MANS, LILLE, REIMS		
B-17	422BS	6	6	2124–2155 hrs	300 bundles	0

16 FEBRUARY 1944

7PG despatched 1 F-5 to Bordeaux area.

The name game. During the winter of 1943–44 the British public raised large sums of savings in so-called Wings for Victory Weeks. The much blitzed London borough of Bermondsey raised £800,000 and was invited to 'buy' four B-17s (£55,000 each). These were nicknamed *London Avenger*, *Bermondsey Battler*, *Rotherhithe's Revenge* and *Bermondsey* here lined up at Kimbolton on 15 February for a suitable ceremony involving the dignitaries of Bermondsey.
London Avenger flew 108 missions before having to belly land on 20 January 1945. *Bermondsey Battler* was MIA on 22 February 1944 and *Bermondsey* was retired in the summer of 1944.

The name game. A new B-17G only recently received by 381BG was named *Rotherhithe's Revenge*. Using an empty ammunition box as a stand, Councillor E.J. Gibson, Chairman of Bermondsey's War Savings Committee, conducted the christening by smashing a bottle filled with Thames River water on a gun barrel. The bomber proved a good investment for she was to survive the war with 122 combat missions.

The cold job of guard is helped by a little warm breath on the hands. German war correspondent Schwarz took the photograph of a soldier and 20FG P-38 *Jack* on its belly in a Dutch field. Capt Carl Jackson had claimed 2 FW 190s destroyed during air fights on 20 February but an engine then failed and on the way home the second began to show signs of strain. Knowing that he would have little chance of surviving if forced to bale out into the icy North Sea he chose to 'belly in' on a field in the Low Countries. Allison engines could not withstand the low temperatures and moisture laden atmosphere encountered over Europe which were the root cause of more than half the P-38 losses during the winter of 1943–44.

A dramatic moment as 351BG's Col Romig and Maj LeDoux in the trailing B-17F radio landing instructions to the engineer and navigator flying damaged B-17G over Polebrook, 20 February. The co-pilot had been killed and the pilot wounded during fighter attacks on route to Leipzig and Lt Walter Truemper and Sgt Archie Mathies managed to fly the Fortress, *Ten Horsepower*, back to base. After other crew members had baled out they elected to try and land in an effort to save the life of the badly wounded pilot. On a fourth attempt they crashed in a field near the A1 highway and were killed. Their sacrifice brought both posthumous Medal of Honor awards.

20 FEBRUARY 1944

8AF 226	Despatched		Effective	Target	Bombs Tonnage	E/A	Losses MIA	E	Dam	Casualties KIA	WIA	MIA
3BD				TUTOW A/F (P)								
	B-17	314	105	& AREA (O)	506.0HE							
			76	ROSTOCK (O)	202.0IB							
			115	T/Os								
TOTALS:		314	296		708.0	15–15–10	6	1	37	3	0	60

REMARKS: Groups participating: 3BD – 94BG, 95BG, 96BG, 100BG, 385BG, 388BG, 390BG, 447BG, 452BG; 482BG. A PFF a/c failed to t/o so Tutow Force dropped on ETA in vicinity of Tutow, Greifswald and Stralsund. Targets at Posen and Kreising were assigned as primaries for the rest of the formation, but leaders decided that clouds would prevent bombing so they turned on Rostock and other T/Os. Bomb types used: 500GP, 100IB. Bomb group losses:– 100BG – 2, 385BG – 1, 388BG – 2, 390BG – 1, 452BG – 1. 100BG B-17 interned in Sweden. 385BG B-17 cr. at Tuttington during assembly, 3 k.

8AF 226	Despatched		Effective	Target	Bombs Tonnage	E/A	Losses MIA	E	Dam	Casualties KIA	WIA	MIA
1BD												
	B-17	417	239	LEIPZIG/MOCKAU A/F (P)	655.0HE	14– 5– 6	7	1	161	7	17	72
				HEITERBLICK A/I (P)	188.0IB							
				ABTNAUNDORF A/I (P)								
			37	BERNBURG A/I (P)								
			44	OSCHERSLEBEN (O)								
			20	T/Os								
2BD				BRUNSWICK								
	B-24	272	76	WILHELMTOR & (P)	507.0HE	36–13–13	8	3	37	10	10	77
				NEUPETRITOR A/Is	160.0IB							
			87	GOTHA A/I (P)								
			13	OSCHERSLEBEN (L)								
			58	HELMSTEDT (L)								
			10	T/Os								
TOTALS:		689	584		1510.0	50–18–19	15	4	198	17	27	149

REMARKS: Groups participating: 1BD – 91BG, 92BG, 303BG, 305BG, 306BG, 351BG, 379BG, 381BG, 384BG, 401BG, 482BG. 2BD – 44BG, 93BG, 389BG, 392BG, 445BG; 446BG, 448BG, 453BG. B-24 primary at Halberstadt obscured by cloud and PFF equipment failed, so Oschersleben and Helmstedt bombed as last resort. 2 B-17 CWs bombed T/Os, one mistook Oschersleben for its primary at Aschersleben, the other bombed in the Helmstedt area as they were unable to set up on the primary in time. MOHs awarded to 1st Lt William R. Lawley Jr, 305BG, and, posthumously, to 2nd Lt Walter E. Truemper and S/Sgt Archibald Mathies, both of the 351BG, for their actions this day. Bomb types used: 500GP, 500IB, 100IB. Bomb group losses:– 44BG – 2, 91BG – 1, 92BG – 1, 305BG – 2, 306BG – 1, 381BG – 1, 384BG – 1. 389BG – 2, 401BG – 1, 445BG – 3, 453BG – 1. 351BG B-17 cr. at Glatton due to b/d. 44BG B-24 c/l at Holbrook, after running out of fuel, crew safe. B/d 392BG B-24s c/l at Paglesham, 1 injured, and Tibenham A/F, 2 injured.

20 FEBRUARY 1944 *(contd.)*

VIII FC FO 245

Despatched		Groups	E/A	Losses MIA	E	Dam	Casualties KIA	WIA	MIA
P-38	94	20FG, 55FG		1	0		0	0	1
P-47	668	4FG, 56FG, 78FG, 352FG, 353FG, 355FG, 356FG, 359FG, 361FG, 358FG (IX FC), 362FG (IX FC)		2	2		0	0	2
P-51	73	357FG, 354FG (IX FC)		1	0		0	0	1
TOTALS:	835		61–7–37	4	2	4	0	0	4

REMARKS: Fighter support, 8AF 226 (Leipzig and Brunswick). 55FG, 356FG, 361FG and IX FC 362FG flew two missions in support of this operation. 20FG unable to make contact with bombers due to e/a encounters. Fighter group e/a credits:– 4FG – 6, 20FG – 7, 56FG – 14, 78FG – 3, 352FG – 11, 355FG – 2, 357FG – 2, 354FG – 16. Fighter group losses:– 4FG – 1, 20FG – 1, 357FG – 1, 358FG – 1. 358FG P-47 MIA after being sent out to escort crippled B-17. B/d 4FG P-47 c/l Eastchurch, 356FG P-47 c/l near base, pilots safe.

7PG despatched 2 F-5s to Germany and Holland.

20/21 FEBRUARY 1944

8AF 227 NIGHT LEAFLET OPERATION – FRANCE

	Despatched		Effective	Locality	No. of Leaflets	Losses
1BD				TOURS, NANTES, BREST, LORIENT		
B-17	422BS	5	4	2123–2200 hrs	200 bundles	0

Returning from Brunswick on 21 February 100BG Fortress 42-37796 was seen straggling behind the formation with one engine feathered and another smoking. Over the VHF radio the pilot, Lt W.H. Fletcher, announced that he could not make it across the Channel and was going to crash-land. This was successfully accomplished north-east of Spaarndam in the Netherlands. Efforts by the crew to set fire to the aircraft were not entirely successful before they attempted escape into the countryside. A Dutch resistance fighter took this picture.

21 FEBRUARY 1944

8AF 228

	Despatched		Effective	Target		Bombs Tonnage	E/A	Losses MIA	E	Dam	Casualties KIA	WIA	MIA
3BD	B-17	281	175	DIEPHOLZ A/F	(P)								
				BRUNSWICK CITY	(P)	549.0HE	2– 5– 2	5	3	36	20	4	57
			88	HANNOVER	(O)	74.0IB							
				ALHORN A/F	(O)								
				VERDEN A/F	(O)								
1BD	B-17	336	285	ACHMER A/F	(O)	752.0HE	12– 5– 8	8	3	63	4	13	75
				HOPSTEN A/F	(O)	54.0IB							
				RHEINE A/F	(O)								
				COEVORDEN M/Y	(O)								
				DIEPHOLZ A/F	(O)								
				QUAKENBRÜCK A/F	(O)								
				BRAMSCHE A/F	(O)								
				LINGEN M/Y	(O)								
2BD	B-24	244	11	ACHMER A/F	(P)	549.0HE	5– 6– 4	3	1	6	0	3	31
			203	DIEPHOLZ A/F	(O)								
				VERDEN A/F	(O)								
				HESEPE A/F	(O)								
				LINGEN	(O)								
TOTALS:		861	762			1978.0	19–16–14	16	7	105	24	20	163

REMARKS: Groups participating:– 3BD – 94BG, 95BG, 96BG, 100BG, 385BG, 388BG, 390BG, 447BG, 452BG. 1BD – 91BG, 92BG, 303BG, 305BG, 306BG, 351BG, 379BG, 381BG, 384BG, 401BG, 457BG, 482BG. 2BD – 44BG, 93BG, 389BG, 392BG, 445BG, 446BG, 448BG, 453BG. Primaries for 1BD were Gütersloh A/F, Lippstadt A/F and Werl A/F. Primaries for 2BD were Achmer A/F and Handorf A/F. 3BD was only Force with PFF a/c so, due to weather, most other formations had to seek T/Os. First mission for 457BG. Bomb types used:– 500GP, 100IB. Bomb group losses:– 91BG – 4, 92BG – 2, 95BG – 2, 96BG – 1, 100BG – 1, 351BG – 1, 392BG – 1, 448BG – 2, 457BG – 1, 482BG – 1. 351BG B-17 cr. on t/o at Barnwell. 351BG B-17 ditched 30 m from Lowestoft, 7 rescued. On return a 94BG B-17 c/l at Debach A/F; 2 385BG B-17s collided over Reedham both crews killed. B/d 305BG B-17 c/l coastal A/F on return; B/d 457BG B-17 Cat E base, B/d 448BG B-24 Cat E base.

VIII FC FO 246

Despatched		Groups	E/A	Losses MIA	E	Dam	Casualties KIA	WIA	MIA
P-38	69	20FG, 55FG	0–1– 0	0	1	0	0	0	0
P-47	542	4FG, 56FG, 78FG, 352FG, 353FG, 355FG, 356FG, 359FG, 361FG, 358FG (IX FC), 362FG (IX FC)	19–3–14	2	2	3	0	0	2
P-51	68	357FG, 354FG (IX FC)	14–1– 4	3	0	0	0	0	3
TOTALS:	679		33–5–18	5	3	3	0	0	5

REMARKS: Fighter support, 8AF 228. Fighter group e/a credits: 4FG – 2, 56FG – 12, 355FG – 3, 356FG – 1, 357FG – 1, 354FG – 9. Fighter group losses:– 356FG – 1, 357FG – 1, 361FG – 1, 354FG – 2. 361FG P-47 aborted mission and failed to return. On return 4FG P-47 c/l at Pulham, pilot safe. 352FG P-47 cr. Attlebridge, pilot safe. 55FG P-38 c/l base.

7PG despatched 1 F-5 and 1 Spitfire to the Poix area of France.

21/22 FEBRUARY 1944

8AF 229 NIGHT LEAFLET OPERATION – FRANCE

	Despatched		Effective	Locality	No. of Leaflets	Losses
1BD				ROUEN, CAEN, PARIS, AMIENS		
B-17	422BS	5	5	2215–2327 hrs	250 bundles	0

After conducting the first strafing of enemy airfields by his group, Lt.Col Glenn Duncan, 353FG, was hedge-hopping home when: 'I saw a single engine aircraft coming across in front of me at about 500 feet and passing from right to left. I let him pass then fell in behind him and closed up to about 50 to 75 yards. It was a FW 190 and he never knew that I was behind him. My gun sight burned out but I was so close that I just squeezed the trigger without sighting. He lit up slowly and his wheels came down as he slid off on his left wing and crashed near a small town. The crash left a line of blazing parts where he disintegrated. I claim 1 FW' (verbatim; encounter report).

22 FEBRUARY 1944

8AF 230

	Despatched		Effective	Target		Bombs Tonnage	E/A	Losses MIA	E	Dam	Casualties KIA	WIA	MIA
1BD	B-17	289	34	ASCHERSLEBEN A/I	(P)	361.0HE	32–18–17	38	4	141	35	30	367
			47	BERNBURG A/I	(P)	65.0Frag							
			18	HALBERSTADT A/I	(P)	33.0IB							
			32	BÜNDE	(O)								
			19	WERNEGERODE	(O)								
			15	MAGDEBURG	(O)								
			9	MARBURG	(O)								
			7	T/Os									
3BD	B-17	333	0	SCHWEINFURT I/A				0	0	2	0	0	0
2BD	B-24	177	74	ENSCHEDE	(O)	201.0HE	2– 0– 0	3	0	3	0	0	30
				ARNHEM	(O)	7.0IB							
				NIJMEGEN	(O)								
				DEVENTER	(O)								
TOTALS:		799	255			667.0	34–18–17	41	4	146	35	30	397

REMARKS: Groups participating:– 1BD – 91BG, 92BG, 303BG, 305BG, 306BG, 351BG, 379BG, 381BG, 384BG, 401BG, 457BG, 482BG. 2BD – 93BG, 389BG, 392BG, 445BG, 446BG, 448BG, 453BG. Severe weather prevented 3BD a/c from forming properly, and they were forced to abandon mission prior to the enemy coast. 2BD was recalled when 100 miles inland, and since they were over Germany they sought T/Os; however, strong winds caused the formation to drift over Holland and four targets were bombed unintentionally. 92BG detailed to attack Aalburg West A/F but clouds covered the target, so bombs were not released to avoid harming Danish civilians. 1 bomb accidentally dropped on Tibenham A/F by returning a/c, 3 killed. Bomb types used:– 500GP, 100GP, 100IB, 20 Frag. Bomb group losses:– 44BG – 2, 91BG – 5, 92BG – 2, 303BG – 4, 305BG – 1, 306BG – 7, 351BG – 2, 379BG – 5, 381BG – 6, 384BG – 4, 401BG – 2, 453BG – 1, During assembly 303BG B-17 and 384BG B-17 collided near Irthlingborough, 18 killed. On return a 351BG B-17 abandoned over UK, cr. in sea off Cromer; b/d 351BG B-17 c/l at Framlingham; 305BG B-17 crashed at Sheffield on return. 91BG B-17 ditched, 9 rescued.

22 FEBRUARY 1944 *(contd.)*

VIII FC FO 247

Despatched		Groups	E/A	Losses MIA	E	Dam	Casualties KIA	WIA	MIA
P-38	67	20FG, 55FG	1–0–0	0	1	6		0	0
P-47	535	4FG, 56FG, 78FG, 352FG, 353FG, 355FG, 356FG, 359FG, 361FG, 358FG (IX FC), 362FG (IX FC), 368FG (IX FC)	39–6–15	8	0	12		0	8
P-51	57	357FG, 354FG (IX FC)	19–1–10	3	0	3		0	3
TOTALS:	659		59–7–25	11	1	21		0	11

REMARKS: Fighter support, 8AF 230. Fighter group e/a credits:– 4FG – 3, 56FG – 15, 78FG – 8, 353FG – 2, 357FG – 7, 359FG – 3, 361FG – 3, 354FG – 13. Fighter group losses:– 78FG – 1, 353FG – 5, 357FG – 2, 361FG – 354FG – 1, 362FG – 1. 1 of 353FGs P-47s MIA was being flown by the leading ace in the ETO, Major Beckham.

7PG despatched 13 F-5s and 5 Spitfires to Germany, France and Holland.

23 FEBRUARY 1944

8AF 231/VIII FC FO 249

Despatched		Groups	E/A	Losses MIA	E	Dam	Casualties KIA	WIA	MIA
P-38	40	20FG	0	0	0	0	0	0	0

REMARKS: Sent on a high altitude sweep for familiarisation of coastal areas of Holland, Belgium and France.

7PG despatched 9 F-5s and 2 Spitfires to Germany, Holland, Belgium and France.

23/24 FEBRUARY 1944

8AF 232 NIGHT LEAFLET OPERATION – FRANCE

	Despatched		Effective	Locality	No. of Leaflets	Losses
1BD				RENNES, LE MANS, CHARTRES, LILLE, ORLEANS		
B-17	422BS	5	5	2136–2232 hrs	250 bundles	0

For S/Sgt Joe Roundhill, Schweinfurt was every bit as bad as its reputation when he paid a visit with 379BG on 24 February. Flying as right waist gunner on his second mission he saw the other waist gunner, Sgt Noonan, killed by a flak fragment through the heart. 'A 'runaway prop' on No.3 caused the B-17 to head for England on its own, luckily escaping attentions of enemy fighters. Back at Kimbolton after 7½ hours in the air, Roundhill (in front of star insignia) tells Doc Agnew what happened as medics prepare to lift the dead gunner's body into an ambulance. Note flak splinter hole near star insignia. Roundhill was unusual in that he enlisted in the 8AF in England. He was born in the US of English parents who returned with their son to England prior to the war.

24 FEBRUARY 1944

8AF 233

	Despatched		Effective	Target	Bombs Tonnage	E/A	Losses MIA	E	Dam	Casualties KIA	WIA	MIA
3BD				ROSTOCK &								
	B-17	304	295	UNIDENTIFIED T/Os	685.0	23–11–15	5	0	60	0	8	50

REMARKS: Groups participating:– 3BD – 94BG, 95BG, 96BG, 100BG, 385BG, 388BG, 390BG, 447BG, 452BG. 61 a/c released on Pathfinders accidental release, shortly before target. Primaries were aviation industry plants at Tutow, Posen and Kreising. Bomb types used: 500GP, 500IB, 100IB. Bomb group losses:– 95BG – 1, 385BG – 2, 388BG – 1, 452BG – 1. MIA 388BG B-17 landed Sweden.

8AF 233

	Despatched		Effective	Target		Bombs Tonnage	E/A	Losses MIA	E	Dam	Casualties KIA	WIA	MIA
1BD	B-17	266	238	SCHWEINFURT I/A	(P)	401.0HE 172.0IB	10– 1– 7	11	1	160	2	5	110
2BD	B-24	239	169	GOTHA A/I	(P)	372.0HE	50–10–20	33	1	28	3	6	324
			44	EISENACH	(O)	116.0IB							
TOTALS:		505	451			1061.0	60–11–27	44	2	188	5	11	434

REMARKS: Groups participating: 1BD – 91BG, 92BG, 303BG, 305BG, 306BG, 351BG, 379BG, 381BG, 384BG, 401BG, 457BG, 482BG. 2BD – 44BG, 93BG, 389BG, 392BG, 445BG, 446BG, 448BG, 453BG. Lead bombardier of 2BD suffering from anoxia, due to a faulty oxygen mask, mistook Eisenach as primary and 43 a/c released on him. Others realised the mistake and attacked primary. 458BG flew a diversion for this mission. Bomb types used: 1000GP, 500GP, 100GP, 100IB, 100Frag. 1BD also dropped 3,976,000 leaflets. Bomb group losses:– 44BG – 2, 92BG – 3, 93BG – 1, 303BG – 2, 305BG – 1, 306BG – 2, 351BG – 2, 389BG – 7, 392BG – 7, 445BG – 13, 446BG – 2, 448BG – 1, 457BG – 1. 305BG B-17 crashed on t/o Chelveston. On return 446BG B-24 crashed at Sternfield, crew baled out, pilot k.

VIII FC FO 250

Despatched		Groups	E/A	Losses MIA	E	Dam	Casualties KIA	WIA	MIA
P-38	70	20FG, 55FG	1–0– 0	4	0	0		0	4
P-47	609	4FG, 56FG, 78FG, 352FG, 353FG, 355FG, 356FG, 359FG, 361FG, 362FG (IX FC), 365FG (IX FC)	31–0–13	4	0	11		1	4
P-51	88	357FG, 354FG (IX FC), 363FG (IX FC)	6–1– 1	2	0	0		0	2
TOTALS:	767		38–1–14	10	0	11	0	1	10

REMARKS: Fighter support, 8AF 233 (Schweinfurt and Gotha). 359FG and 365FG (IX FC) flew two missions for this operation. 361FG P-47 abandoned, pilot lost, after Flak hit from an E-boat which 361FG attacked 55 miles E. of Southend. Fighter group e/a credits:– 20FG – 1, 55FG – 1, 56FG – 8, 78FG – 7, 352FG – 2, 353FG – 6, 357FG – 6, 359FG – 4, 361FG – 3, 354FG – 1. Fighter group losses:– 4FG – 1, 20FG – 2, 55FG – 2, 56FG – 1, 357FG – 2, 359FG – 1, 361FG – 1.

7PG despatched 23 F-5s and 6 Spitfires to France, Holland, Belgium and France.

24/25 FEBRUARY 1944

8AF 234 NIGHT LEAFLET OPERATION – FRANCE

	Despatched		Effective	Locality	No. of Leaflets	Losses
1BD				LORIENT, TOURS, NANTES, BREST, REIMS		
B-17	422BS	5	5	2208–2226 hrs	250 bundles	0

Like bubbling cauldrons, smoke and dust rise high above the two Messerschmitt assembly plants at Regensburg, Obertraubling (1) and Prüfening (2). Less than an hour before *Esky* and other 385BG Fortresses arrived, 15AF bombers from Italy had attacked. Considerable damage was inflicted on these aircraft plants in what were to be the final missions of Big Week.

INCIDENT

A flak battery at Augsburg had an unusual success in defending the works on 25 February 1944. A chance shell fragment sliced into the bomb-bay of the 381st Group lead aircraft and set off a smoke marker bomb. Faced with a fire and possible explosion the pilot had little option but to salvo the bomb load immediately. Whereupon about half the other group in the formation, misled by this misfortune, dropped their bombs, all short of the target.

The broken machines of vanquished enemies were always an attraction for children. An Me 109 despatched the 381BG's only loss on 25 February, the Fortress crashing at Willmandingen near Stuttgart. Six of the crew perished. (H. Grimminger)

25 FEBRUARY 1944

8AF 235

	Despatched		Effective	Target		Bombs Tonnage	E/A	Losses MIA	E	Dam	Casualties KIA	WIA	MIA
3BD	B-17	290	267	REGENSBURG A/I	(P) & (T/Os)	561.5HE 82.0IB	13–1– 7	12	1	82	4	12	110
1BD	B-17	268	196	AUGSBURG A/I	(P) & (T/O)	441.0HE	8–4– 4	13	0	172	0	12	130
			50	STUTTGART I/A	(P)	168.0IB							
2BD	B-24	196	172	FÜRTH A/I	(P) & (T/Os)	391.0HE 59.0IB	2–2– 2	6	2	44	0	2	61
TOTALS:		754	685			1702.5	23–7–13	31	3	298	4	26	301

REMARKS:– Groups participating: 3BD – 94BG, 95BG, 96BG, 100BG, 385BG, 388BG, 390BG, 447BG, 452BG. 1BD – 91BG, 92BG, 303BG, 305BG, 306BG, 351BG, 379BG, 381BG, 384BG, 401BG, 457BG, 482BG. 2BD – 44BG, 93BG, 389BG, 392BG, 445BG, 446BG, 448BG, 453BG. 1 3BD, 1 1BD and 11 2BD a/c attacked T/Os. Bomb types used:– 1000GP, 500GP, 100IB, 120Frag. 1BD also dropped 2,000,000 leaflets on Augsburg. Bomb group losses:– 92BG – 2, 93BG – 2, 96BG – 4, 100BG – 2, 305BG – 3, 306BG – 3, 379BG – 1, 381BG – 1, 384BG – 1, 385BG – 1, 389BG – 390BG – 2, 446BG – 1, 447BG – 2, 448BG – 1, 453BG – 1, 457BG – 2. 92BG B-17 interned in Switzerland. 1 3BD B-17 ditched near Hythe, 8 rescued. On return 447BG B-17 cr. near Tonbridge, pilot killed, rest of crew parachuted. 448BG B-24 c/l, through fuel shortage, at Chipping Ongar A/F. B/d 44BG B-24 c/l Lympne A/F.

VIII FC FO 251

Despatched		Groups	E/A	Losses MIA	E	Dam	Casualties KIA	WIA	MIA
P-38	73	20FG, 55FG	1–2– 0	0	1	0	0	0	0
P-47	687	4FG, 56FG, 78FG, 352FG, 353FG, 355FG, 356FG, 359FG, 361FG, 358FG (IX FC), 362FG (IX FC), 365FG (IX FC)	13–2–10	1	0	6	0	1	1
P-51	139	357FG, 354FG (IX FC), 363FG (IX FC)	12–0– 3	2	1	0	0	0	2
TOTALS:	899		26–4–13	3	2	6	0	1	3

REMARKS: Fighter support for 8AF 235. 361FG, 363FG, 365FG flew two missions. Fighter group e/a credits:– 4FG – 5, 55FG – 1, 56FG – 3, 78FG – 1, 353FG – 1, 357FG – 6, 361FG – 3, 354FG – 7, 362FG – 1. Fighter group losses:– 357FG – 2, 358FG – 1. 55FG P-38 crashed at Langford, pilot safe.

7PG despatched 16 F-5s and 2 Spitfires to Holland, France and Germany.

A hit in the wing has ignited something in the vicinity of the 'Tokyo tanks' and threatens imminent explosion. Lt Foster Perry's crew and B-17G 42-31820 did not come back to Chelveston this day, 25 February.

25/26 FEBRUARY 1944

8AF 236 NIGHT LEAFLET OPERATION – FRANCE

	Despatched		Effective	Locality	No. of Leaflets	Losses
1BD				GRENOBLE, TOULOUSE, CHARTRES, CAEN, RAISMES		
B-17	422BS	5	5	2129–2335 hrs	250 bundles	0

26 FEBRUARY 1944

7PG despatched 2 F-5s to Germany. 1 a/c intercepted by e/a.

28 FEBRUARY 1944

8AF 237

	Despatched		Effective	Target	Bombs Tonnage	E/A	Losses MIA	E	Dam	Casualties KIA	WIA	MIA
2BD				ECALLES SUR BUCHY(P)								
	B-24	81	49	V/S	131.0	0–0–0	0	0	1	0	0	0

REMARKS: Groups participating: 2BD – 93BG 446BG 448BG. Bomb types used: 500GP.

VIII FC FO 253

Despatched		Groups	E/A	Losses MIA	E	Dam	Casualties KIA	WIA	MIA
P-47	61	56FG	0	0	0	0	0	0	0

REMARKS: Fighter support, 8AF 237.

8AF 238

	Despatched		Effective	Target		Bombs Tonnage	E/A	Losses MIA	E	Dam	Casualties KIA	WIA	MIA
1BD	B-17	134	68	PAS DE CALAIS V/S	(P)			2	0	30	0	3	20
			10	ROAD JUNCTION E OF YERVILLE	(O)								
			7	RAIL SIDING SW OF ABBEVILLE	(O)								
3BD	B-17	124	41	PAS DE CALAIS V/S	(P)			5	0	45	0	2	43
			6	T/Os									
TOTALS:		258	132			379.5	0–0–0	7	0	75	0	5	63

REMARKS:Groups participating:– 1BD – 303BG, 305BG, 306BG, 379BG, 384BG. 3BD – 94BG, 95BG, 95BG, 100BG, 385BG, 390BG, 447BG. Bomb types used:– 500GP. Bomb group losses:– 303BG – 1, 384BG – 1, 385BG – 3, 447BG – 2. 385BG B-17 ditched off Dungeness, 9 rescued.

VIII FC FO 254

Despatched		Groups	E/A	Losses MIA	E	Dam	Casualties KIA	WIA	MIA
P-38	81	20FG, 55FG	0	0	1	0	0	0	0
P-47	94	355FG, 356FG	0	0	0	0	0	0	0
P-51	22	4FG	1–0–0 (G)	0	0	0	0	0	0
TOTALS:	197		1–0–0 (G)	0	1	0	0	0	0

REMARKS: Fighter support, 8AF 238. 4FG use P-51s for the first time. 1 20FG P-38 c/l, pilot safe.

7PG despatched 6 F-5s and 1 Spitfire to France and Germany.

28/29 FEBRUARY 1944

8AF 239 NIGHT LEAFLET OPERATION – FRANCE

	Despatched		Effective	Locality	No. of Leaflets	Losses
1BD				AMIENS, RENNES, PARIS, ROUEN, LE MANS		
B-17	422BS	5	5	2023–2055 hrs	250 bundles	0

Miss Donna Mae (centre) and other B-17s of 94BG at rest at Bury St.Edmunds after the group had returned from Brunswick on leap year's day. Looking west across runway 04 and No.1 hangar the sky is marked with numerous contrails, invariably the case on a clear day in East Anglia. Trees around aircraft dispersals were originally in farm hedgerows and left as an aid to camouflage when the airfield was constructed.

29 FEBRUARY 1944

8AF 240

	Despatched	Effective	Target	Bombs Tonnage	E/A	Losses MIA	E	Dam	Casualties KIA	WIA	MIA
3BD			BRUNSWICK								
	B-17 226	218	A/I (P) & T/O	457.2		1	0	54	0	4	10

REMARKS: Groups participating:– 3BD – 94BG, 95BG, 96BG, 100BG, 385BG, 388BG, 390BG, 447BG, 452BG. 3 a/c dropped on T/Os. Bomb types used:– 500GP, 100GP, 100IB. Bomb group losses:– 388BG – 1. MIA 388BG B-17 ditched off Holland, had 452BG crew:– POW.

VIII FC FO 255

Despatched		Groups	E/A	Losses MIA	E	Dam	Casualties KIA	WIA	MIA
P-38	61	20FG, 55FG	0–0–0	2	0	1	0	0	2
P-47	346	56FG, 352FG, 355FG, 356FG, 359FG, 361FG, 358FG (IX FC), 362FG (IX FC)	1–0–0	1	0	1	0	0	1
P-51	147	4FG, 357FG, 354FG (IX FC), 363FG (IX FC)	0–0–0	1	0	0	0	0	1
TOTALS:	554		1–0–0	4	0	2	0	0	4

REMARKS: Fighter support, 8AF 240. Fighter group e/a credits:– 56FG – 1. Fighter group losses:– 20FG – 2, 354FG – 1, 358FG – 1. 364FG pilot in 1 MIA 20FG a/c.

8AF 241

	Despatched	Effective	Target	Bombs Tonnage	E/A	Losses MIA	E	Dam	Casualties KIA	WIA	MIA
2BD	B-24 48	38	LOTTINGHAM V/S (P)	112.5	0	0	0	0			

REMARKS: Groups participating: 2BD – 93BG, 389BG, 392BG, 445BG. 1 group turned back over England as they were unable to locate the other groups. Bomb types used: 500GP.

VIII FC FO 256

Despatched		Groups	E/A	Losses MIA	E	Dam	Casualties KIA	WIA	MIA
P-47	79	78FG, 365FG (IX FC)	0	1	0	0		0	1

REMARKS: Fighter support, 8AF 241. Fighter group losses:– 78FG – 1, lost through engine failure, pilot parachuted.

7PG despatched 4 F-5 and 1 Spitfire to France and Germany.

29 FEBRUARY/1 MARCH 1944

8AF 242 NIGHT LEAFLET OPERATION – FRANCE

	Despatched	Effective	Locality	No. of Leaflets	Losses
1BD			ORLEANS, LILLE, REIMS, CAMBRAI, CHATEAUROUX		
B-17	422BS 5	5	2025–2121 hrs	250 bundles	0

801BG despatched 12 B-24s on *Carpetbagger* operations.

1 MARCH 1944

7PG despatched 2 Spitfires to Germany; 1 Spitfire MIA.

1/2 MARCH 1944

8AF 243 NIGHT LEAFLET OPERATION – FRANCE

	Despatched		Effective	Locality	No. of Leaflets	Losses
1BD				BREST, TOURS,		
B-17	422BS	5	5	LORIENT, NANTES,	250 bundles	0
				REIMS		
				2005–2115 hrs		

2 MARCH 1944

8AF 244

	Despatched		Effective	Target	Bombs Tonnage	E/A	Losses MIA	E	Dam	Casualties KIA	WIA	MIA
1BD				FRANKFURT AM	156.0HE		8	0		1	5	80
	B-17	327	101	MAIN M/Y (P)	67.0IB							
			103	FRANKFURT								
				OFFENBACH (O)	355.0HE							
			49	LUDWIGSHAFEN (O)	106.0IB							
			20	LIMBURG (O)								
			12	FISCHBACH (O)								
			8	T/Os								
2BD	B-24	154	36	FRANKFURT AM MAIN	92.0IB		1	3		16	4	11
				M/Y (P)	6.0HE							
			46	T/Os	107.0IB							
TOTALS:		481	375		889.0	2–0–2	9	3	175	17	9	91

REMARKS: Groups participating:– 1BD – 91BG, 92BG, 303BG, 305BG, 306BG, 351BG, 379BG, 381BG, 384BG, 401BG, 457BG, 482BG; 2BD – 44BG, 93BG, 392BG, 446BG, 448BG, 458BG. 1BD a/c that attacked a T/O did so because of navigational error. Only last CW of 2BD managed to bomb, through a break in the clouds; other formations had PFF failures. First mission for 458BG. Bomb types used:– 500GP 100IB. Bomb group losses:– 92BG – 2, 93BG – 1, 303BG – 1, 305BG – 1, 351BG – 1, 379BG – 1, 381BG – 1, 401BG – 1. 458BG B-24 crashed at Hellesdon, 7 k, 3 inj, house burnt out. 2 389BG B-24s collided during assembly and cr. at Swainsthorpe, 9 k, and Ilketshall St.Margaret, crew baled.

VIII FC FO 257

Despatched		Groups	E/A	Losses MIA	E	Dam	Casualties KIA	WIA	MIA
P-38	33	364FG	0–0–0	0	0	1	0	0	0
P-47	445	56FG, 352FG,	13–2–3	3	0	7	0	0	2
		353FG, 355FG,							
		356FG, 359FG,							
		361FG,							
		358FG (IX FC), 362FG(I XFC),							
		365FG (IX FC)							
P-51	111	4FG 357FG	4–0–1	1	0	2	0	0	1
TOTALS:	589		17–2–4	4	0	10	0	0	3

REMARKS: Fighter support, 8AF 244 (Frankfurt). First mission for 364FG. Fighter group e/a credits:– 4FG – 2, 56FG – 1, 355FG – 5, 357FG – 2, 358FG – 3. Fighter group losses:– 4FG – 1, 56FG – 1, 352FG – 1, 365FG – 1. Pilot of 352FG P-47 MIA, rescued.

	Despatched		Effective	Target	Bombs Tonnage	E/A	Losses MIA	E	Dam	Casualties KIA	WIA	MIA
3BD	B-17	106	84	CHARTRES A/D (P)	158.2	0–0–0	1	0	12	0	1	10

REMARKS: Groups participating:– 3BD – 95BG, 96BG, 100BG, 388BG, 390BG. 452BG late in taking off, because of bomb fusing problems, was recalled before leaving English coast. 390BG failed to bomb because of rack malfunction in leaders a/c. Bomb types used: 100IB. Bomb group losses:– 390BG – 1.

VIII FC FO 257

Despatched		Groups	E/A	Losses MIA	E	Dam	Casualties KIA	WIA	MIA
P-38	89	20FG, 55FG	0–0–0	0	1	0		0	0
P-47	145	78FG, 362FG (IX FC),	0–0–0	0	0	0		0	0
		365FG (IX FC)							
P-51	47	354FG (IX FC)	2–0–0(G)	0	0	0		0	0
TOTALS:	281		2–0–0(G)	0	1	0	0	0	0

REMARKS: Fighter support, 8AF 244. 55FG P-38 c/l on return.

7PG despatched 6 F-5 and 2 Spitfires to France and Germany.

2/3 MARCH 1944

8AF 245 NIGHT LEAFLET OPERATION – FRANCE

	Despatched		Effective	Locality	No. of Leaflets	Losses
1BD				CAEN, AMIENS,		
B-17	422BS	5	5	ROUEN, CHARTRES, RENNES 2015–2054 hrs	250 bundles	0

Carpetbagger operation. 1 B-24 MIA

One of the 100BG aircraft missing after the abortive raid on Berlin, 3 March, landed shot up on a Schleswig airfield, presenting the enemy with their first intact B-17G. Lt Gossage and crew thought they were safe in Sweden until surrounded by enemy troops. The aircraft later operated for the Luftwaffe in KG 200. (via J.G. Foreman)

3 MARCH 1944

8AF 246

	Despatched		Effective	Target	Bombs Tonnage	E/A	Losses MIA	E	Dam	Casualties KIA	WIA	MIA
1BD	B-17	260	61	WILHELMSHAVEN (O)			3	0		0	3	25
3BD	B-17	295	14	T/Os			6	0		2	0	58
2BD	B-24	193	4	T/Os			2	0		3	8	20
OTALS:		748	79		194.8	3–1–1	11	0	45	5	11	103

REMARKS: Groups participating:– 1BD – 91BG, 92BG, 303BG, 305BG, 306BG, 351BG, 379BG, 381BG, 384BG, 401BG, 457BG, 482BG; 3BD – 94BG, 95BG, 96BG, 100BG, 385BG, 388BG, 390BG, 447BG, 452BG; 2BD – 44BG, 93BG, 392BG, 445BG, 446BG, 448BG, 453BG, 458BG. Primaries were industrial areas and aviation industry plants at Berlin, Erkner and Oranienburg. Deteriorating weather and dense contrails forced the formations to turn back or seek T/Os. Bomb types used:– 500GP, 100IB. Upon recall the 1 CBW formation flew a reciprocal course through heavy contrails meeting the 4 CBW head on; a 94BG B-17 and 91BG B-17 were lost in a collision and another B-17 was reported as going down after being hit by debris. Bomb group losses:– 91BG – 1, 92BG – 1, 94BG – 1, 100BG – 3, 381BG – 1, 392BG – 1, 447BG – 2, 458BG – 1. 1 B-24 seen down in sea. 1 447BG B-17 ditched, 2 rescued. 93BG B-24 cr. on t/o, crew safe.

VIII FC FO 259

	Despatched		Groups	E/A	Losses MIA	E	Dam	Casualties KIA	WIA	MIA
	P-38	89	20FG, 55FG, 364FG	0–0–0	1	0	1		0	1
	P-47	484	56FG, 78FG, 352FG, 353FG, 355FG, 356FG, 359FG, 361FG, 358FG (IX FC), 362FG (IX FC)	0–0–0	0	1	13		1	0
	P-51	130	4FG, 357FG, 354FG (IX FC), 363FG (IX FC)	8–1–3	6	0			0	5
TOTALS:		730		8–1–3	7	1	14		1	6

REMARKS: Fighter support, 8AF 246. P-38s flew over Berlin, first 8AF a/c to do so. Fighter group e/a credits:– 4FG – 5, 354FG – 2, 363FG – 1. Fighter group losses:– 4FG – 4, 20FG – 1, 357FG – 1, 354FG – 1. 357FG P-51 ditched, pilot rescued. 20FG P-38 came down in sea off The Hague. 354FG P-51 abandoned near enemy coast. 362FG P-47 c/l – Cat E base.

7PG despatched 6 F-5 and 2 Spitfires to France, Belgium and Germany.

INCIDENT

The 65th Fighter Wing Air-Sea Rescue controllers were acutely aware that their efforts to save the lives of airmen forced to come down in the sea were sometimes frustrated by an individual's confusion. Lives had been lost because distress signals and location details were not given accurately, fully and clearly, or because survival procedures were not followed. Knowledge that a man could not hope to survive more than five to ten minutes exposure in the North Sea in winter was understandably a fearful prospect to a pilot in a single-engine fighter. ASR records made particular note of personal coolness displayed in an incident on 3 March 1944: 'Chambers 54 (363rd F. Sqdn., 357th Group) came through on a regular Mayday call at 1158 hours, stating that his engine had quit and was burning. The pilot retained his composure at all times. He gave excellent calls at intervals and at 1204, while at an altitude of 7,000 feet, the pilot gave his last call and baled out. Pectin 37 (4th Group), hearing the distress call, asked if he could be of assistance. A fix was obtained on 37 and it was determined that he was much closer than any other spotters. Hence he was given a steer to where 54 baled out, and when over the position the pilot asked to go down to the deck, where he would be able to make a thorough search. Shortly thereafter he discovered the pilot in his dinghy. He remained with the pilot for an hour, at which time he was relieved by other spotters. The position of the pilot was approximately 10 miles east of Deal. Two Spitfires and one Walrus of 277 Sqdn of Hawkinge were engaged in the search from 1213 to 1400 hours. At 1325 they saw boats pick up the pilot. The pilot, Lt Foy, was taken to Ramsgate Naval Sick Bay. He suffered only slight shock.' Robert Foy kept his head, got clear of his parachute and into his inflated dinghy as quickly as possible. Two months later in another Mustang he went through a repeat performance and again lived to fly another day. He became one of the three top air aces in his Group.

3/4 MARCH 1944

Carpetbagger operation, 2 B-24 MIA.

The bomb load explodes an hour after a 93BG B-24 crashed on take-off at Hardwick, 3 March. (H. Coleman)

4 MARCH 1944

8AF 247

	Despatched		Effective	Target		Bombs Tonnage	E/A	Losses MIA	E	Dam	Casualties KIA	WIA	MIA
1BD	B-17	264	100	BONN	(O)			4	0	89	1	7	40
			44	DÜSSELDORF	(O)	258.0HE							
			35	COLOGNE	(O)	170.3IB							
			7	FRANKFURT	(O)								
3BD	B-17	238	30	BERLIN/KLEIN MACHNOW	(P)	42.8HE 24.6IB		11	1	31	2	4	101
			33	T/Os		36.25HE 38.3IB							
TOTALS:		502	249			570.25	6–2–3	15	1	120	3	11	141

REMARKS: Groups participating:– 1BD – 91BG, 303BG, 305BG, 306BG, 351BG, 379BG, 381BG, 384BG, 401BG, 457BG, 482BG; 3BD – 94BG, 95BG, 96BG, 100BG, 385BG, 388BG, 390BG, 447BG, 452BG. Primaries were industrial areas in the suburbs of Berlin. 2BD also took off but abandoned mission because of severe weather during assembly. 3 B-17 groups turned back at the French coast due to inability to form up properly through the severe weather. All remaining formations except first CW of 3BD turned back in the vicinity of the Ruhr and sought T/Os. The 13CBW carried on to the primary and bombed, the first USAAF bombers to attack the German capital. 5 of the 3BD losses came from this force. Bomb types used:– 500GP, 500IB, 100IB. 1BD also dropped 1,072,000 leaflets on Cologne. Bomb group losses:– 94BG – 2, 95BG – 4, 96BG – 1, 100BG – 1, 381BG – 1, 384BG – 3, 385BG – 1, 447BG – 1, 452BG – 1. 1 3BD B-17 ditched, 10 rescued. 447BG B-17 c/l Friston forest, 1 of crew died of a heart attack.

VIII FC FO 260

Despatched		Groups	E/A	Losses MIA	E	Dam	Casualties KIA	WIA	MIA
P-38	86	20FG, 55FG, 364FG	0–0–0	4	2	1	1	0	4
P-47	563	4FG, 56FG, 78FG, 352FG, 353FG, 355FG, 356FG, 359FG, 361FG, 358FG (IX FC), 362FG (IX FC), 365FG (IX FC)	3–1–3 1–0–0(G)	4	1	5		0	3
P-51	121	4FG, 357FG, 354FG (IX FC), 363FG (IX FC)	5–2–1	16	1	1	1		16
TOTALS:	770		8–3–4 1–0–0(G)	24	4	7	2	0	23

REMARKS: Fighter support, 8AF 247. 362FG and 365FG flew 2 missions each. 4FG sent 2 sqdns of P-47s and 1 sqdn of P-51s. 363FG despatched 33 a/c but bad weather saw the formations scattered at the Dutch coast with 11 P-51s reported missing. Fighter group e/a credits:– 4FG – 2, 357FG – 2, 359FG – 2, 354FG – 1. Fighter group losses:– 4FG – 1, 20FG – 3, 55FG – 1, 56FG – 1, 78FG – 2, 353FG – 1, 357FG – 1, 354FG – 2, 363FG – 11. 55FG P-38 cr. on t/o, pilot k. On return 4FG P-51 cr. Framlingham, pilot k. 354FG P-51 down in sea 25 miles from Lowestoft. 20FG P-38 c/l Spanhoe, pilot safe. 365FG P-47 c/l base, pilot safe.

7PG despatched 4 F-5 and 2 Spitfires to France and Germany. (1 Spitfire was despatched to Berlin but was recalled due to weather.)

4/5 MARCH 1944 *Carpetbagger* operation.

INCIDENT

The problems of the P-38 were understandably a damper to morale in the three 8th Air Force groups flying them in the early spring of 1944. There was nothing more disheartening for a pilot than to fly to a rendezvous with bombers only to have an engine fail en route. Lightnings returning on one engine from deep in enemy territory were also easy prey for Luftwaffe fighters. During penetration for escort to Berlin on 4 March the 20th Group P-38Js flown by Lt Charles Hallberg and Lt Edgar Malchow both developed engine trouble. The formation leader, informed that the two aircraft were turning back, despatched 2/Lt Joe Ford to act as their escort. Ford, on his first combat operation, took up position above the two troubled Lightnings as they headed west. Forced to weave his P-38 to avoid over-running his slower charges, Ford realised his fuel was diminishing rapidly. Nearing the Dutch coast his worst fears were realised when he caught sight of six FW 190s low and to the rear, gaining fast upon him. Warning Hallberg and Malchow to be prepared to take cover in the clouds, Ford began to climb to keep his advantage. He then saw two of the enemy drop their auxiliary tanks and start to climb after him. Ford was now forced to drop his external tanks to gain speed but one of the Focke Wulfs was closing rapidly. Deciding he could not reach the safety of cloud cover in time, Ford turned his Lightning to meet the German, who evaded a head-on pass by breaking away and diving. The inexperienced American pilot – in his own words – 'began breathing normally again' when he found the other enemy aircraft had lost contact and were nowhere to be seen. He located the two Lightnings – which had not been attacked – only to run into heavy flak near the Dutch coast. The functioning (left) engine of Malchow's P-38 was hit and started to lose coolant and overheat. Ford radioed the suggestion of re-starting the right engine. By this time smoke had been drawn into the cockpit by the heating system and Malchow had been forced to jettison his canopy to clear the fumes. Unfeathering the right propeller, Malchow was relieved to see it run satisfactorily, allowing the labouring left motor, near to seizing, to be shut down. Both handicapped Lightnings appeared to have radio trouble and Ford had to fly close to maintain visual contact in the cloud and poor visibility over the sea. His request to Air-Sea Rescue for a homing was acknowledged and, given a course to the nearest airfield in England, he was able to lead his charges to a safe landing. Little fuel remained in his own aircraft's tanks. The Distinguished Flying Cross was the regular award for special achievement in air operations and many hundreds were presented to pilots of VIII Fighter Command. The 20th Group claimed Joe Ford was the first to receive his award for action on his first mission.

EVENT

Many improvements and modifications to aircraft and equipment adopted by 8th Air Force originated with personnel at combat bases. The inventive flair of mechanics, armourers and service specialists contributed considerably to the efficiency of operations. A typical example of this ingenuity was concerned with the bomb-bay doors of the Liberator. These were unconventional, in that instead of being hinged they were flexible in operation and rolled up the outside of the fuselage thus causing a minimum of drag when open. Locking pins secured them in the fully closed position and when engaged electrical and mechanical devices also locked the bomb release in the nose in the safe position, to ensure bombs were not dropped through closed doors. Unfortunately, when the doors were fully open, vibration sometimes caused the doors to creep an inch or two and the locking pins would engage, unknown to the bombardier, and prevent the immediate release of bombs and an accurate strike on the target. The accuracy of many drops was spoilt through the bomb door safety device coming into play.

On his own initiative, Sgt Aaron Schultz, a squadron armourer in 389th Group, worked on this problem and devised a modification that prevented the locking pins engaging unless the bomb door creep was more than between 12 and 18 inches – when the doors would be in danger of being struck by released bombs. It was a simple modification that took only an hour to complete on a Liberator and after satisfactory trials in March 1944 all 389th B-24s gradually received the modification. In August it was approved for all 8th Air Force B-24s and the following month Schultz was given the Bronze Star in acknowledgement of his work.

5 MARCH 1944

8AF 248

	Despatched		Effective	Target	Bombs Tonnage	E/A	Losses MIA	E	Dam	Casualties KIA	WIA	MIA
2BD	B-24	219	62	BERGERAC A/F (S) & (L)								
			60	COGNAC/CHATEAU-BERNARD A/F (L)	361.0HE 31.0IB							
			41	LANDES DE BUSSAC A/F (S) & (L)								
			1	LA ROCHE A/F (L)								
TOTALS:		219	164		392.0	14–2–5	4	1	23	0	1	35

REMARKS: Groups participating:–2BD – 44BG, 93BG, 389BG, 392BG, 445BG, 446BG, 448BG, 453BG, 458BG. Primaries were airfields at Mont De Marsan, Cayeux and Bordeaux/Merignac. Bomb types used:– 500GP, 100GP, 100IB. Bomb group losses:– 389BG – 1, 392BG – 1, 448BG – 2. 44BG B-24 crashed on t/o at Shipdham. 392BG B-24 ditched in Channel, 6 rescued.

VIII FC FO 261

Despatched		Groups	E/A	Losses MIA	E	Dam	Casualties KIA	WIA	MIA
P-38	34	364FG	0–0–0	2	1	0	1	0	1
P-47	185	78FG, 356FG, 361FG	0–0–0		1	0	1	0	0
P-51	88	4FG, 357FG, 363FG (IX FC)	14–0–6 0–0–6(G)	3	1	1	0	1	3
TOTALS:	307		14–0–6 0–0–6(G)	5	3	1	2	1	4

REMARKS: Fighter support, 8AF 248. Fighter group e/a credits:– 4FG – 9, 357FG – 7. Fighter group losses:– 4FG – 1, 357FG – 2, 364FG – 2. 361FG P-47 crashed after t/o, pilot killed. Pilot of 364FG P-38 rescued from sea. 357FG P-51 abandoned near Dungeness, pilot rescued. On return 4FG P-51 c/l near Warbleton, pilot injured.

7PG despatched 4 F-5 and 3 Spitfires to France, Belgium and Germany.

5/6 MARCH 1944

8AF 249 NIGHT LEAFLET OPERATION – FRANCE

	Despatched		Effective	Locality	No. of Leaflets	Losses
1BD B-17	422BS	5	5	LE MANS, PARIS, ORLEANS, REIMS 2132–2152 hrs	250 bundles	0

Carpetbagger operation.

Chopstick – G. George, the 482BG pathfinder lead of the 3BD force goes down over Berlin city on 6 March. Flak ignited the right main fuel tanks which exploded shortly after the second photograph was taken. On board were Brig.Gen Russ Wilson, 4th Combat Wing CO, three men of 385BG (Group bombardier, navigator and an officer flying as tail gunner) plus eight men of 482BG. Only three survived, one being pilot Capt 'Red' Morgan, the Medal of Honor winner, who managed to clip on his parachute as he fell. Note chin radome extended.

6 MARCH 1944

8AF 250

	Despatched		Effective	Target		Bombs Tonnage	E/A	Losses MIA	E	Dam	Casualties KIA	WIA	MIA
1BD	B-17	262	248	BERLIN	(S)	459.5HE		18	2	172	2	8	184
3BD	B-17	242	226	TEMPLIN	(O)	109.5IB		35	3	121	0	15	354
				VERDEN	(O)	371.0HE							
				KALKEBERGE	(O)	175.0IB							
				POTSDAM	(O)								
				ORANIENBURG	(O)								
				WITTENBERG	(O)								
2BD	B-24	226	198	GENSHAGEN I/A	(P)	368.0HE		16	1	54	15	8	148
				BERLIN	(S)	165.0IB							
				POTSDAM	(O)								
TOTALS:		730	672			1648.0	97–28–60	69	6	347	17	31	686

REMARKS: Groups participating:– 1BD – 91BG, 92BG, 303BG, 305BG, 306BG, 351BG, 379BG, 381BG, 384BG, 401BG, 457BG, 482BG; 3BD – 94BG, 95BG, 96BG, 100BG, 385BG, 388BG, 390BG, 447BG, 452BG; 2BD – 44BG, 93BG, 389BG, 392BG, 445BG, 446BG, 448BG, 453BG, 458BG. Primaries were industrial areas in the suburbs of Berlin. 1 B-17 group returned to base after it was unable to locate its CW. Bomb types used:– 500GP, 500IB, 100IB. 2,448,000 leaflets also released from bombers. Bomb group losses:– 91BG – 6, 92BG – 4, 93BG – 1, 94BG – 1, 95BG – 8, 100BG – 15, 306BG – 1, 379BG – 1, 381BG – 3, 388BG – 7, 389BG – 1, 390BG – 1, 392BG – 1, 401BG – 1, 445BG – 2, 446BG – 1, 448BG – 1, 452BG – 2, 453BG – 4, 457BG – 2, 458BG – 5, 482BG – 1. An Me 410 collided with a 457BG B-17 bringing down another 457BG as they spun down. 392BG B-24 cr. Gt.Dunham after t/o, all k. On return 2 B-17s down in sea off Norfolk coast, 1 crew rescued. 2 453BG B-24s ditched, 1 man saved from one, 5 from the other. 1 448BG B-24 and 3 B-17s (1 – 388BG, 1– 306BG, 1 – 100BG) interned in Sweden. B/d 452BG B-17 c/l on return. B/d 379BG B-17 Cat E at base. B/d 447BG B-17 Cat E. B/d 390BG B-17 Cat E base. B/d 305BG B-17 – Cat E base.

VIII FC FO 262

Despatched		Groups	E/A	Losses MIA	E	Dam	Casualties KIA	WIA	MIA
P-38	86	20FG, 55FG, 364FG	3–0– 1	1	0	0	0	0	1
P-47	615	56FG, 78FG, 352FG, 353FG, 355FG, 356FG, 359FG, 361FG, 358FG (IX FC), 362FG (IX FC), 365FG (IX FC)	36–7–12	5	3	4	0	2	5
P-51	100	4FG, 357FG, 354FG (IX FC)	43–1–20	5	0	2	0	0	5
TOTALS:	801		81–8–21 1–0–12(G)	11	3	6	0	2	11

REMARKS: Fighter support, 8AF 250. 359FG, 358FG, 362FG each flew two missions. 55FG P-38s were forced to turn back, due to an excessive number of engine failures. Fighter group e/a credits:– 4FG – 14, 20FG – 1, 56FG – 10, 78FG – 3, 353FG – 3, 355FG – 8, 365FG – 5, 357FG – 20, 359FG – 3, 361FG – 5, 364FG – 1, 354FG – 7. Fighter group losses:– 4FG – 4, 56FG – 1, 78FG – 2, 356FG – 1, 362FG – 1, 364FG – 1, 354FG – 1. On return 353FG P-47 c/l base, pilot injured. 361FG b/d P-47 c/l base, pilot safe; 359FG P-47 cr., pilot injured.

7PG despatched 9 F-5s and 2 Spitfires to France, Belgium, Holland and Germany.

6/7 MARCH 1944

8AF 251 NIGHT LEAFLET OPERATION – FRANCE

	Despatched		Effective	Locality	No. of Leaflets	Losses
1BD B-17	422BS	5	5	NANTES, CAMBRAI, LILLE, CHATEAUROUX, LORIENT 2029–2130 hrs	250 bundles	0

Carpetbagger operation.

8 MARCH 1944

8AF 252

	Despatched		Effective	Target		Bombs Tonnage	E/A	Losses MIA	E	Dam	Casualties KIA	WIA	MIA
3BD	B-17	179	98	BERLIN/ERKNER	(P)	47.5HE 139.0IB		23	1		2	5	234
			33	WILDAU (O) & T/Os		18.5HE 52.5IB							
1BD	B-17	235	222	BERLIN/ERKNER	(P)	123.5HE 244.0IB		5	0		1	2	40
			3	T/Os		2.0HE 4.0IB							
2BD	B-24	209	150	BERLIN/ERKNER	(P)	120.5HE 226.0IB		9	2		1	7	90
			33	BERLIN CITY (O) & T/Os		25.5HE 56.5IB							
TOTALS:		623	539			1059.5	63–17–19	37	3	228	4	14	364

REMARKS: Groups participating: 3BD – 94BG, 95BG, 96BG, 100BG, 385BG, 388BG, 390BG, 447BG, 452BG; 1BD – 91BG, 92BG, 303BG, 305BG, 306BG, 351BG, 379BG, 381BG, 384BG, 401BG, 457BG, 482BG; 2BD – 44BG, 93BG, 389BG, 392BG, 445BG, 446BG, 448BG, 453BG, 458BG. Lead a/c of first CW (45CBW) hit by e/a and turned back, deputy took over but turned short at the IP and to avoid a collision with the second CW; the 45CBW attacked Wildau. 1 group, plus 9 a/c of another group, from the 2BD were forced to attack Berlin City as T/O in order to avoid a B-17 unit approaching primary. Mass fighter attack on 45CBW groups. Bomb types used:– 500GP, 500IB, 100GP, 100IB. Bomb group losses:– 91BG – 1, 94BG – 2, 95BG – 1, 96BG – 6, 100BG – 1, 303BG – 1, 381BG – 1, 388BG – 5, 389BG – 2, 390BG – 3, 401BG – 1, 446BG – 3, 448BG – 2, 452BG – 5, 453BG – 1, 458BG – 1. 448BG B-24 ditched, 2 rescued. 44BG B-24 cr. at Shipdham. B/d 390BG B-17 force landed at Debach. 445BG B-24 cr. at Fressingfield.

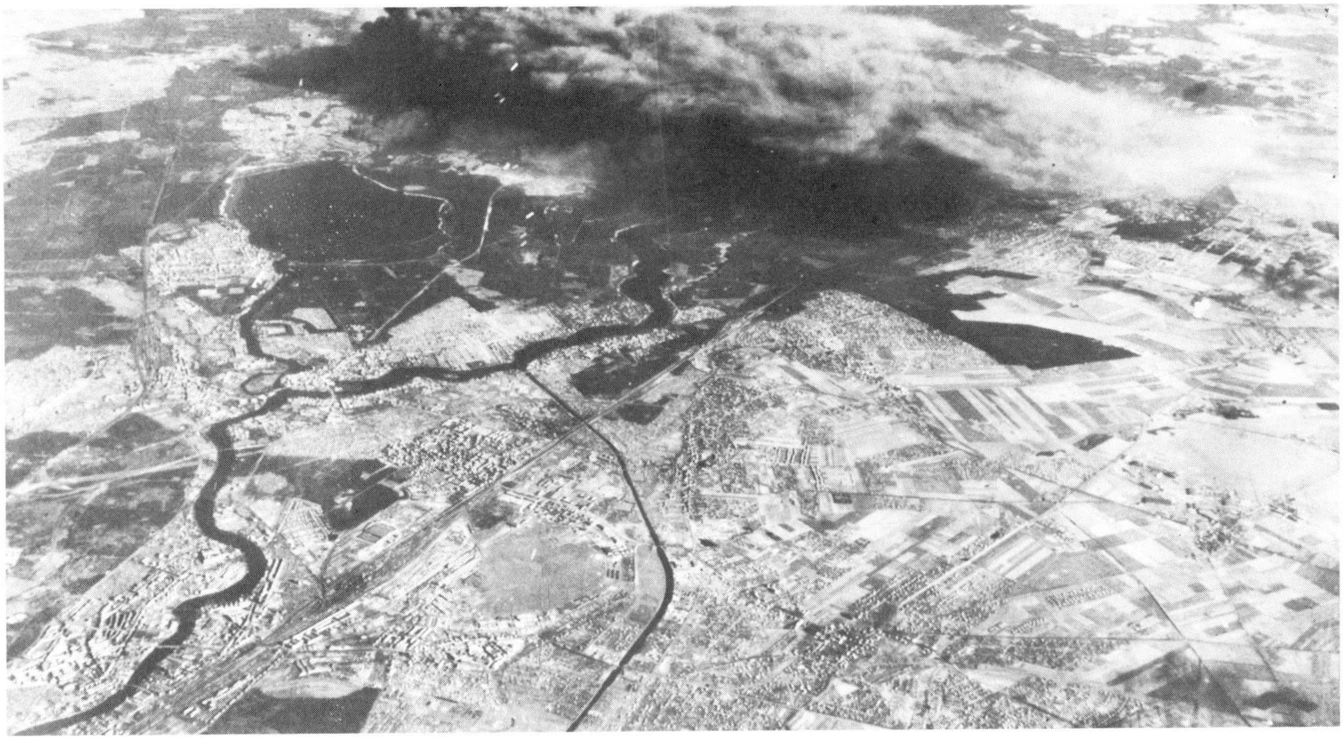

A view across Berlin's southern suburbs from a departing Liberator of the burning VKF bearing factory at Erkner on 8 March. The small specks highlighted against the smoke cloud are cable balloon defences. In the foreground an airport can be seen between the river Spree and an adjoining canal.

Berlin bound, 8 March. Lt John Godfrey (l) and Lt Nick Megura (r), 4FG pilots who in their recently received P-51 Mustangs shot their way into acehood this day. Both were credited with two enemy fighters destroyed, and Godfrey also had a 'probable', later re-assessed as a confirmed kill. Megura would take his ailing Mustang (shot up by a P-38 he claimed) to Sweden and internment in May while Godfrey (here developing a moustache) was destined to become one of the leading fighter aces of the Eighth. Both were former RCAF fliers.

Two other pilots scoring this day were Capt Clarence Anderson (l) who claimed his first victory and Lt Don Bochkay who got his fourth. Both were members of the Eighth's first P-51 group, 357FG, which on 11 March, when these pilots posed, could boast 59 'kills' in its first month of operations. Both Anderson and Bockhay would play a considerable part helping 357FG have the highest air claims of all Eighth P-51 groups by VE-Day.

VIII FC FO 263

Despatched		Groups	E/A	Losses MIA	E	Dam	Casualties KIA	WIA	MIA
P-38	104	20FG, 55FG, 364FG	9–2– 5	3	1	2	1	0	4
P-47	613	56FG, 78FG, 352FG, 353FG, 355FG, 356FG, 359FG, 361FG, 358FG (IX FC), 362FG (IX FC)	49–6–18	10	13	4	2	2	10
P-51	174	4FG, 352FG, 355FG, 357FG, 354FG (IX FC), 363FG (IX FC)	29–4– 9	5	2	1	0	0	4
TOTALS:	891		79–8–25 8–4– 7(G)	18	16	7	3	2	18

REMARKS: Fighter support, 8AF 252. 359FG, 361FG, 358FG, 362FG each flew two missions. 352FG and 355FG flew mixed formations of P-47s and P-51s. Fighter group e/a credits: 4FG – 16, 56FG – 28, 352FG – 2, 353FG – 5, 355FG – 1, 356FG – 2½, 357FG – 7, 361FG – 1½, 364FG – 9, 354FG – 4, 363FG – 2. Fighter group losses:– 4FG – 1, 55FG – 1, 56FG – 5, 353FG – 1, 355FG – 2 (1 P-47 & P-51), 356FG – 1, 357FG – 1, 364FG – 2, 354FG – 1, 358FG – 1, 362FG – 1, 363FG – 1. 2 separate collisions involving 352FG P-47s ascending in cloud: 1 cr. Bracon Ash, pilot k, 1 cr. Hapton, pilot safe, the 2 others force landed – Cat E. On return 78FG P-47 cr. at Barking, pilot k; 359FG P-47 c/l, South Elmham St.Peter, pilot safe; 3 353FG P-47s c/l; 55FG P-38 cr. Dovercourt, pilot k; 375FG P-51 c/l at Leiston; 56FG P-47 cr. Hollesley, pilot baled. 361FG c/l base on return. Two 362FG P-47s c/l – Cat E – Manston and base.

7PG despatched 3 F-5 and 2 Spitfires on PR over France and Germany.

9 MARCH 1944

8AF 253

	Despatched		Effective	Target		Bombs Tonnage	E/A	Losses MIA	E	Dam	Casualties KIA	WIA	MIA
1BD	B-17	224	208	BERLIN	(S)	364.0HE 128.0IB		3	0		10	3	30
3BD	B-17	137	131	BERLIN	(S)	189.5HE 114.0IB		3	1		0	3	13
2BD	B-24	165	150	HANNOVER BRUNSWICK NIENBURG	(S) (S) (S)	303.5HE 107.0IB		2	1		0	12	20
TOTALS:		526	490			1207.0	1–0–0	8	2	221	10	18	63

REMARKS: Groups participating:– 1BD – 91BG, 92BG, 303BG, 305BG, 306BG, 351BG, 379BG, 381BG, 384BG, 401BG, 457BG, 482BG; 3BD – 94BG, 95BG, 100BG, 385BG, 388BG, 390BG, 447BG, 452BG; 2BD – 44BG, 93BG, 389BG, 392BG, 445BG, 446BG, 448BG, 453BG, 458BG. 2BD dropped on anti-aircraft fire after their PFF a/c failed. Bomb types used:– 500GP, 100IB. 2,012,000 leaflets also dropped by bombers. Bomb group losses:– 92BG – 2, 384BG – 1, 388BG – 1, 445BG – 1, 447BG – 2, 448BG – 1. MIA 384BG B-17 had its tail knocked off by a bomb over Berlin. 448BG B-24 ditched, 3 men rescued. 447BG B-17 ditched, 10 men rescued. 92BG B-17 interned in Sweden. 388BG had one B-17 MIA with the 96BG. On return b/d 392BG B-24 c/l Beccles A/F, crew safe; 447BG B-17 c/l Honington A/F, crew safe.

T/Sgt Ansel Snook, a 447BG engineer gunner on the third Berlin raid, was at 46 believed to be the oldest gunner then flying with the 8AF. The top turret in the picture is the low profile Sperry type. The guns could not be depressed below the horizontal.

Home from the third major raid on Berlin, B-17s of 379BG break formation to circle for a landing approach. A left hand orbit was flown with left hand elements peeling off first.

VIII FC FO 264

Despatched		Groups	E/A	Losses MIA	E	Dam	Casualties KIA	WIA	MIA
P-38	83	20FG, 55FG, 364FG	0–0–0	1	2	0	0	1	1
P-47	572	56FG, 78FG, 352FG, 353FG, 356FG, 359FG, 361FG, 358FG (IX FC), 362FG (IX FC)	0–0–0	0	0	0	0	0	0
P-51	153	4FG, 352FG, 355FG, 357FG, 354FG (IX FC), 363FG (IX FC)	0–0–0	0	1	0	1	0	0
TOTALS:	808		0–0–0	1	3	0	1	1	1

REMARKS: Fighter support, 8AF 253. 352FG, 359FG and 361FG flew two missions each (352FG flew a mixed formation of P-47s and P-51s on each one). Fighter group losses:– 364FG – 1. 55FG P-38 cr. on t/o, pilot inj. 355FG P-51 c/l on t/o, pilot k. On return 55FG P-38 cr. nr. Tuddenham A/F, pilot baled.

7PG despatched 4 F-5 and 2 Spitfires on PR over France and Germany.

10/11 MARCH 1944

8AF 254 NIGHT LEAFLET OPERATION – BELGIUM

	Despatched		Effective	Locality	No. of Leaflets	Losses
1BD						
B-17	422BS	5	5	BRUSSELS, ANTWERP, GHENT, MONCEAU-SUR-SAMBRE 2127–2137 hrs	250 bundles	0

Over 150 heavy bombers were lost or salvaged during the week of raids on Berlin. Unlike the previous autumn, 8AF could absorb such losses through the veritable flood of men and aircraft now arriving from the USA. New replacement Liberators usually went to the Warton Base Air Depot for theatre modification where this line was awaiting delivery to 2AD bases on 10 March.

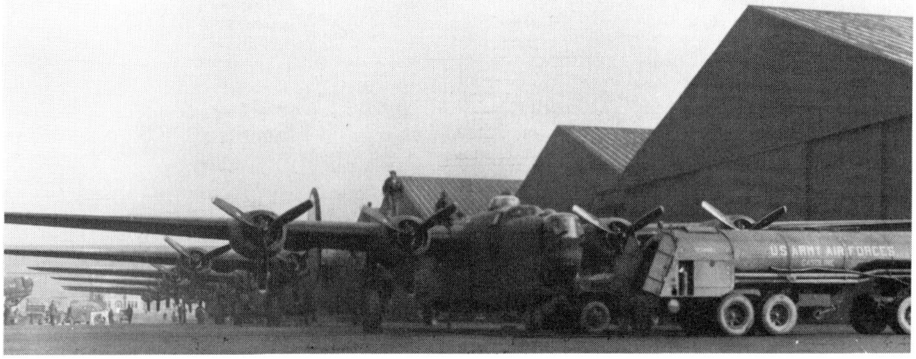

11 MARCH 1944

8AF 255

	Despatched		Effective	Target	Bombs Tonnage	E/A	Losses MIA	E	Dam	Casualties KIA	WIA	MIA
1BD	B-17	62	62	MÜNSTER M/Y (P)	78.0HE		0	0		0	0	0
3BD	B-17	62	62	& T/O	164.3IB		1	0		0	0	10
TOTALS:		124	124		242.3	0	1	0	24	0	0	10

REMARKS: Groups participating:– 1BD – 351BG, 401BG, 457BG; 3BD – 94BG, 385BG, 447BG. 1 1BD B-17 dropped on Bentheim as T/O and 2 3BD B-17s dropped on Burgsteinfurt accidentally. Bomb types used:– 500GP, 100GP, 100IB. Bomb group losses:– 447BG B-17 down in sea, crew lost.

VIII FC FO 265

Despatched		Groups	E/A	Losses MIA	E	Dam	Casualties KIA	WIA	MIA
P-47	90	356FG, 359FG	0–0–0	0	0	2	0	0	0
P-51	50	355FG	0–0–0	2	0	0	0	0	2
TOTALS:	140		0–0–0	2	0	2	0	0	2

REMARKS: Fighter support, 8AF 255 (Münster). Fighter group losses:– 355FG – 2.

8AF 255

	Despatched		Effective	Target	Bombs Tonnage	E/A	Losses MIA	E	Dam	Casualties KIA	WIA	MIA
2BD	B-24	51	34	WIZERNES V/S (P)	127.2	0–0–0	0	0	1	0	0	0

REMARKS: Groups participating:– 44BG, 93BG. Bomb types used:– 100GP, 1000GP.

VIII FC FO 265

Despatched		Groups	E/A	Losses MIA	E	Dam	Casualties KIA	WIA	MIA
P-38	40	364FG	0–0–0	0	0	0	0	0	0
P-47	213	352FG, 353FG	0–0–0	2	1	2	0	1	2
TOTALS:	253		0–0–0	2	1	2	0	1	2

REMARKS: Fighter support, 8AF 255 (WIZERNES). 364FG P-38s were intended to be escort to B-24s but this was amended to P-47s of 353FG. However, escort was abandoned due to weather. 352FG carried out low level sweeps. Fighter group losses:– 352FG – 2, 352FG P-47 abandoned 10 miles W of Somme estuary, pilot lost. On return 352FG P-47 c/l at Manston, pilot injured.

12 MARCH 1944

8AF 256

	Despatched		Effective	Target	Bombs Tonnage	E/A	Losses MIA	E	Dam	Casualties KIA	WIA	MIA
2BD	B-24	52	52	St.POL/SIRACOURT (P) & T/Os	202.5	0	0	1	26	0	1	0

REMARKS: Groups participating: 44BG, 93BG, 392BG. 6 a/c dropped on T/Os. A group of P-38s were assigned as escort, but was unable to t/o. Bomb types used:– 1000GP, 100IB. 44BG B-24 c/l Friston on return.

13 MARCH 1944

8AF 257

	Despatched		Effective	Target	Bombs Tonnage	E/A	Losses MIA	E	Dam	Casualties KIA	WIA	MIA
1BD	B-17	85	7	POIX (O)	21.0		2	0	24	0	1	20
3BD	B-17	42	0				0	0	37	0	0	0
2BD	B-24	144	0				0	1	13	6	0	0
TOTALS:		271	7		21.0	0	2	1	74	6	1	20

REMARKS: Groups participating: 1BD – 351BG, 379BG, 401BG, 457BG; 3BD – 95BG, 447BG; 2BD – 93BG, 389BG, 445BG, 446BG, 448BG, 453BG. Primaries were V-weapon sites in the Pas de Calais area, but weather prevented most from bombing. Bomb group losses:– 379BG – 1, 401BG – 1. During assembly 93BG B-24 exploded in mid-air and cr. at Benacre, 6 killed, 4 baled.

13 MARCH 1944 *(contd.)*

VIII FC FO 267

Despatched		Groups	E/A	Losses MIA	E	Dam	Casualties KIA	WIA	MIA
P-47	213	352FG, 353FG, 356FG, 359FG, 361FG	0–0–0	0	0	1	0	0	0

REMARKS: Fighter support, 8AF 257. All P-51Bs grounded for modifications.

Luck of the game. Lt.Col Joe Kruzel, Air Executive of 361FG (deputy CO) and Maj Roy Caviness, CO 376FS, led an escort mission from Bottisham on 13 March. Kruzel escaped from Java in 1942 where he shot down three Japanese aircraft and added four German fighters to his score while with the 361st. Caviness flew two tours with the Group, was twice acting CO and then last CO before hostilities ceased but never had a credit for destroying an enemy aircraft in air combat.

INCIDENT

The fifteen 100th Group B-17s missing on the first large scale raid on Berlin was the heaviest loss suffered by any 8th Air Force group up to that time. Replacements soon filled empty barracks and the Group kept on flying missions but the overall sense of shock was not easily dispelled. Mindful that this was the third occasion on which the 100th had been decimated, 8th Air Force Headquarters decided a visit to Thorpe Abbotts by the commanding generals would benefit morale. Exactly a week after the last debacle, Generals Spaatz, Doolittle, LeMay and Kissner arrived, ostensibly to present decorations and carry out a tour of inspection. Following the more official duties the party had dinner in the officers' mess and then mixed socially, signing short snorters (autographed bank notes) and discussing various topics. The 8th's commander was surrounded by a group of men who were asking about the spectacular Tokyo raid to where he had led a force of carrier-launched B-25s for which he received his country's highest decoration. Doolittle was one of the most accomplished pilots of his day so when someone asked: 'General, who flew your plane?', the initial response was: 'Well, I'll be goddamned!' During this informal get-together an incident occurred which Jimmy Doolittle would delight to recount in later years. He was approached by a red-haired young 2/Lt who appeared to be the worse for drink. The young man poked his finger in the general's chest and said: 'You think we don't know what you're here for?' Still prodding Doolittle he continued: 'Well, let me tell you we do; you're here to improve our morale and if there's anything goin' to ruin our morale it's havin' a bunch of generals around here trying to fix it.' General Spaatz, a stickler for military etiquette, was incensed, but General Doolittle restrained him from reprimanding their outspoken critic.

13/14 MARCH 1944

8AF 258 NIGHT LEAFLET OPERATION – FRANCE

	Despatched		Effective	Locality	No. of Leaflets	Losses
1BD				REIMS, ORLEANS,		
B-17	422BS	7	7	PARIS, AMIENS, ROUEN, CHARTRES 2104–2137 hrs	350 bundles	0

15 MARCH 1944

8AF 259

	Despatched		Effective	Target	Bombs Tonnage	E/A	Losses MIA	E	Dam	Casualties KIA	WIA	MIA
3BD	B-17	187	185	BRUNSWICK I/A (S)	562.0IB		1	0	31	1	1	10
2BD	B-24	157	145	& T/Os	183.0HE		2	0	15	0	3	20
TOTALS:		344	330		745.0	0–0–1	3	0	46	1	4	30

REMARKS: Groups participating: 3BD – 94BG, 95BG, 96BG, 100BG, 385BG, 388BG, 390BG, 447BG, 452BG; 2BD – 44BG, 389BG, 392BG, 445BG, 453BG, 458BG. 1 B-24 dropped on Wolfenbüttel as T/O. 1 B-24 released on Brunswick as (S) and Hildesheim as T/O. Bomb types used:– 500GP, 100GP, 100IB. Bomb group losses:– 44BG – 1, 100BG – 1, 392BG – 1.

VIII FC FO 269

Despatched		Groups	E/A	Losses MIA	E	Dam	Casualties KIA	WIA	MIA
P-38	121	20FG, 55FG, 364FG	0	4	1	0	0	0	4
P-47	467	56FG, 78FG, 352FG, 353FG, 355FG, 356FG, 359FG, 361FG, 358FG (IX FC), 362FG (IX FC)	39–3–13	1	0	5	0	0	1
TOTALS:	588		38–3–13 1–0– 0(G)	5	1	5	0	0	5

REMARKS: Fighter support, 8AF 259. 358FG flew two missions. Fighter group e/a credits: 56FG – 24, 78FG – 2, 352FG – 5, 356FG – 1, 359FG – 1, 364FG – 2. Fighter group losses:– 55FG – 1, 56FG – 1, 364FG – 3. 55FG P-38 lost ditched, pilot lost. 55FG P-38 cr., pilot safe.

7PG despatched 2 F-5 and 1 Spitfire to France and Germany (Heligoland).

8AF 260

Despatched		Groups	E/A	Losses MIA	E	Dam	Casualties KIA	WIA	MIA
P-47	8	353FG	0	0	0	0	0	0	0

REMARKS: 2 P-47s with 2 × 1000GP bombs, and 6 other P-47s as escort, sent to make a test drop on a barge in the Zuider Zee.

15/16 MARCH 1944

8AF 261 NIGHT LEAFLET OPERATION – FRANCE

	Despatched		Effective	Locality	No. of Leaflets	Losses
1BD						
B-17	422BS	7	7	RENNES, LILLE, REIMS, LE MANS, PARIS, CHARTRES 2115–2152 hrs	350 bundles	0

16 MARCH 1944

8AF 262

	Despatched		Effective	Target	Bombs Tonnage	E/A	Losses MIA	E	Dam	Casualties KIA	WIA	MIA
3BD	B-17	221	188	AUGSBURG (P)	317.0HE		13					
			18	ULM (O)	158.5IB			0		1	8	130
1BD	B-17	280	213	AUGSBURG (P)	424.0HE		5	0		0	2	41
			46	GESSERTSHAUSEN (O)	138.0IB							
2BD	B-24	239	197	FRIEDRICHSHAFEN (P)	275.5HE		5	1		6	7	46
			13	T/Os	266.0IB							
TOTALS:		740	675		1579.0	68–32–43	23	1	179	7	17	217

REMARKS: Groups participating:– 3BD – 94BG, 95BG, 96BG, 100BG, 385BG, 388BG, 390BG, 447BG, 452BG; 1BD – 91BG, 92BG, 303BG, 305BG, 306BG, 351BG, 379BG, 381BG, 384BG, 401BG, 457BG, 482BG; 2BD – 44BG, 93BG, 389BG, 392BG, 445BG, 446BG, 448BG, 453BG, 458BG. 1 sqdn of 1BD a/c turned back at the French coast as it was unable to locate the rest of its CW, 1 group attacked Ulm as T/O because it was unable to see the PFF markers at Augsburg. 1 CW mistook Gessertshausen for Augsburg on PFF screen. Bomb types used:– 1000GP, 500GP, 100IB, 120 Frag. 6,032,000 leaflets also dropped from bombers. Bomb group losses:– 91BG – 1, 92BG – 1, 93BG – 2, 94BG – 1, 95BG – 4, 96BG – 1, 384BG – 2, 385BG – 3, 389BG – 1, 390BG – 2, 445BG – 1, 447BG – 1, 452BG – 1, 457BG – 1, 458BG – 1. 2 B-17s (91BG, 95BG) and 2 B-24s (93BG, 389BG) interned and 2 B-17s (385BG) and 1 B-24 cr. in Switzerland, 1 457BG B-17 and 1 458BG B-24 came down in the sea, 13 crew members rescued. B/d 44BG B-24 cr. Friston A/F, burned.

As Capt Glendon Davis brought his P-51 in for a strafing pass to ensure destruction of this crash-landed Me 110, the gun camera recorded the escape of a crew member. The man can be seen running from the burning aircraft and throwing himself on the ground as the P-51 opens fire. Davis and another 357FG pilot had previously attacked the Me 110 while flying near Ulm.

Seven bombers damaged in the raids on southern Germany on 16 March limped into neutral Switzerland. 389BG's *Galloping Katie* exhibited a feathered prop' when Lt Snyder brought her skidding to a stop on Dübendorf's runway. (via H. Holmes)

VIII FC FO 270

Despatched		Groups	E/A	Losses MIA	E	Dam	Casualties KIA	WIA	MIA
P-38	125	20FG, 55FG, 364FG	0–0– 0	1	0	0	0	0	0
P-47	608	56FG, 78FG, 352FG, 353FG, 356FG, 359FG, 361FG, 358FG (IX FC), 362FG (IX FC)	25–3–17	3	0	5	0	0	3
P-51	135	4FG, 355FG, 357FG, 354FG (IX FC)	53–4–16	6	2	5	0	0	6
TOTALS:	868		77–7–20 1–0–13(G)	10	2	10	0	0	9

REMARKS: Fighter support, 8AF 262. 359FG, 361FG, 362FG each flew two missions. Lt Q. Brown, 78FG, claimed 4 e/a destroyed, 3 in the air and 1 on the ground plus two others damaged. Fighter group e/a credits:– 4FG – 13, 56FG – 11, 78FG – 7, 352FG – 2, 355FG – 16, 356FG – 1, 357FG – 10, 359FG – 3, 354FG – 14. Fighter group losses:– 4FG – 1, 20FG – 1, 78FG – 1, 353FG – 2, 355FG – 2, 357FG – 2, 354FG – 1. 20FG P-38 down in sea off Hove, pilot rescued. 355FG P-51 c/l on return. 357FG P-51 cr. on t/o, pilot safe.

7PG despatched 6 F-5s and 2 Spitfires to France and Germany.

REMARKS: 2 F-5s Cat E. 1 abandoned through instrument failure before being despatched, and 1 was abandoned through engine failure on return.

17 MARCH 1944

8AF 263

Despatched		Groups	E/A	Losses MIA	E	Dam	Casualties KIA	WIA	MIA
P-47	135	78FG, 353FG, 359FG, 361FG	3–2–8(G)	2	0	0	0	0	2

REMARKS: Low level strafing attacks against airfields in France. 15 a/c (353FG) bombed Soesterburg A/F. 25 a/c (361FG) attacked Chartres A/F. 78FG and 359FG unable to attack due to weather but carried out low level sweeps. Group losses:– 78FG – 2.

18 MARCH 1944

8AF 264

	Despatched		Effective	Target		Bombs Tonnage	E/A	Losses MIA	E	Dam	Casualties KIA	WIA	MIA
1BD	B-17	290	284	OBERPFAFFENHOFEN A/I	(P)	428.0HE 155.0IB		8	0	102	1	9	80
				LECHFELD A/D	(P)								
				LANDSBERG A/D	(P)								
				MEMMINGEN A/F	(O)								
				T/Os									
3BD	B-17	221	196	MUNICH CITY		301.0HE 152.0IB		7	1	80	3	4	70
				OBERPFAFFENHOFEN A/I	(O)								
				LECHFELD A/D	(O)								
				T/Os									
2BD	B-24	227	77	FRIEDRICHSHAFEN/ LÖWENTHAL A/I	(P)	246.0HE 264.0IB		28	3	60	6	9	286
			38	FRIEDRICHSHAFEN/ MANZELL A/I	(P)								
			52	FRIEDRICHSHAFEN (ZEPPELIN) A/I	(P)								
			22	FRIEDRICHSHAFEN CITY	(S)								
			9	T/Os									
TOTALS:		738	678			1546.0	45–10–17	43	4	242	10	22	436

REMARKS: Groups participating:– 1BD – 91BG, 92BG, 303BG, 305BG, 306BG, 351BG, 379BG, 381BG, 384BG, 401BG, 457BG; 3BD – 94BG, 95BG, 96BG, 100BG, 385BG, 388BG, 390BG, 447BG, 452BG, 482BG; 2BD – 44BG, 93BG, 389BG, 392BG, 445BG, 446BG, 448BG, 453BG, 458BG. Bomb types used:– 1000GP, 500GP, 100IB, 120Frag. 5,328,000 leaflets released from bombers. Bomb group losses:– 44BG – 8, 91BG – 1, 92BG – 1, 93BG – 1, 94BG – 2, 96BG – 1, 100BG – 3, 351BG – 4, 384BG – 2, 390BG – 1, 392BG – 14, 445BG – 2, 446BG – 1, 448BG – 1, 453BG – 1. 4 B-17s (92BG, 351BG and 2 384BG) and 12 B-24s (6 – 44BG, 3 – 392BG, 1 – 445BG, 1 – 446BG, 1 – 448BG) down in Switzerland. 2 392BG B-24s collided over France going to target. 1 3BD B-17 struck by bombs from above and lost. On return, 453BG B-24 cr. at Goudhurst, 4 k., b/d 392BG B-24 force landed at Gravesend, 1 k 2 WIA. B/d 44BG B-24 c/l Kingsnorth A/F. B/d 100BG B-17 Cat E Raydon.

VIII FC FO 273

Despatched		Groups	E/A	Losses MIA	E	Dam	Casualties KIA	WIA	MIA
P-38	113	20FG, 55FG, 364FG	11–2–1	5	0	1		0	4
P-47	598	56FG, 78FG, 352FG, 353FG, 356FG, 359FG, 361FG, 358FG (IX FC), 362FG (IX FC)	2–1–3	2	1	6		0	2
P-51	214	4FG, 355FG, 357FG, 354FG (IX FC), 363FG (IX FC)	26–2–6	6	2	3		1	6
TOTALS:	925		36–4–7 3–2–2(G)	13	3	10	0	1	12

REMARKS: Fighter support, 8AF 264, 352FG, 359FG, 361FG, 363FG each flew two sorties. 78FG despatched A, B & C formations for the first time – 96 a/c t/o Duxford. Fighter group e/a credits:– 4FG – 10, 20FG – 7, 55FG – 3, 56FG – 2, 355FG – 5, 357FG – 2, 354FG – 7. Fighter group losses:– 4FG – 2, 20FG – 4, 55FG – 1, 356FG – 1, 357FG – 2, 359FG – 1, 354FG – 1, 363FG – 1. 1 20FG P-38 down in sea, 5 miles E. of Bradwell, pilot rescued. 355FG P-51 cr. after t/o, pilot injured. B/d 361FG P-47 exploded after landing. 363FG P-51 Cat E.

7PG despatched 5 F-5s and 1 Spitfire to France and Germany.

Winter still held southern Germany in its grip when the Luftwaffe experimental base at Lechfeld received a pounding. Fortunately an extensive cloud bank to the east terminated just short of the target so that a visual attack could be made. Departing B-17G is 305BG's *Daley's Male*.

18/19 MARCH 1944

8AF 265 NIGHT LEAFLET OPERATION – FRANCE

	Despatched	Effective	Locality	No. of Leaflets	Losses
1BD B-17	422BS 6	6	CAMBRAI, LILLE, PARIS, AMIENS, ROUEN, CAEN 2115–2139 hrs	300 bundles	0

19 MARCH 1944

8AF 266

	Despatched		Effective	Target		Bombs Tonnage	E/A	Losses MIA	E	Dam	Casualties KIA	WIA	MIA
1BD	B-17	129	117	WIZERNES & WATTEN V/Ss	(P)			1		74	0	1	10
3BD	B-17	64	56	MARQUISE/ MIMOYECQUES V/S	(P)			0		14	0	1	0
TOTALS:		193	173			505.75	0	1	1	88	0	2	10

REMARKS: Groups participating:– 1BD – 303BG, 351BG, 379BG, 384BG, 401BG, 457BG; 3BD – 95BG, 100BG, 390BG. Bomb types used:– 1000GP, 500GP. Bomb group losses:– 384BG – 1.

VIII FC 274

Despatched		Groups	E/A	Losses MIA	E	Dam	Casualties KIA	WIA	MIA
P-47	82	359FG, 361FG	0	0	0	1	0	1	0

REMARKS: Fighter support, 8AF 266.

8AF 268/VIII FC 274

	Despatched		Groups	E/A	Losses MIA	E	Dam	Casualties KIA	WIA	MIA
	P-47	35	78FG	0	0	0	0	0	0	0
	P-51	39	4FG	0	0	0	0	0	0	0
TOTALS:		74		0	0	0	0	0	0	0

REMARKS: 4FG carried out sweep while 78FG P-47s bombed Gilze–Rijen A/F. 25 bomb-carrying P-47s despatched, 20 attacked with 20 × 500GP. 10 P-47s flew escort.

7PG despatched 1 F-5 and 1 Spitfire to France and Holland.

19/20 MARCH 1944

8AF 267 NIGHT LEAFLET OPERATION – HOLLAND

	Despatched		Effective	Locality	No. of Leaflets	Losses
1BD B-17	422BS	6	6	THE HAGUE, ROTTERDAM, LEEUWARDEN, UTRECHT, AMSTERDAM 2114–2140 HRS	300 bundles	0

20 MARCH 1944

8AF 269

	Despatched		Effective	Target		Bombs Tonnage	E/A	Losses MIA	E	Dam	Casualties KIA	WIA	MIA
3BD	B-17	122	9	FRANKFURT	(S)	90.0		2	1	44	1	8	10
			19	BINGEN	(O)								
			17	T/Os									
1BD	B-17	231	42	FRANKFURT	(S)	176.0		3	0	106	0	0	30
			54	MANNHEIM	(O)								
			5	T/Os									
2BD	B-24	92	1	BRETUIT A/F	(O)	2.5		2	0	15	0	3	21
TOTALS:		445	147			268.5	2–0–0	7	1	165	1	11	61

REMARKS: Groups participating: 3BD – 94BG, 96BG, 385BG, 388BG, 447BG, 452BG; 1BD – 91BG, 303BG, 305BG, 306BG, 351BG, 379BG, 381BG, 384BG, 401BG, 457BG; 2BD – 93BG, 389BG, 445BG, 446BG, 448BG, 453BG. High cloud caused most bombers to abandon the mission; some had penetrated 200 miles. Bomb types used:– 500GP, 500IB, 100IB, 100GP. 900,000 leaflets also released from bombers. Bomb group losses: 91BG – 1, 96BG – 1, 381BG – 1, 388BG – 1, 401BG – 1, 448BG – 2. 96BG B-17 abandoned over Seaton, Cornwall, a/c cr. into sea. B/d 452BG B-17 Cat E on return.

VIII FC FO 275

Despatched		Groups	E/A	Losses MIA	E	Dam	Casualties KIA	WIA	MIA
P-38	44	364FG	0	0	0	0	0	0	0
P-47	345	56FG, 78FG, 352FG, 353FG, 356FG, 359FG, 361FG	1–0–1(G)	6	0	9	0	0	6
P-51	205	4FG, 355FG, 357FG, 354FG (IX FC), 363FG (IX FC)	4–0–1	2	0	3	0	0	2
TOTALS:	594		4–0–1 1–0–1(G)	8	0	12	0	0	8

REMARKS: Fighter support, 8AF 269. 79 IX FC P-51s participating under VIII FC control. 56FG flew two missions. Fighter group e/a credits:– 56FG – 3, 356FG – 1. Fighter group losses:– 356FG – 6, 363FG – 2. 356FG losses mostly to ground fire while strafing airfield.

21 MARCH 1944

8AF 270

	Despatched		Effective	Target	Bombs Tonnage	E/A	Losses MIA	E	Dam	Casualties KIA	WIA	MIA
2BD	B-24	65	56	WATTEN V/S (P)	213.8	0	0	0	7	0	0	0

REMARKS: Groups participating: 2BD – 44BG, 93BG, 392BG, 458BG. Bomb types used:– 2000GP, 1000GP, 100GP.

VIII FC FO 276

Despatched		Groups	E/A	Losses MIA	E	Dam	Casualties KIA	WIA	MIA
P-47	48	78FG	0	0	0	0	0	0	0

REMARKS: Fighter support, 8AF 270.

8AF 271/VIII FC FO 276

Despatched		Groups	E/A	Losses MIA	E	Dam	Casualties KIA	WIA	MIA
P-51	41	4FG	12–0–0 9–0–4(G)	7	0	2	0	1	7

REMARKS: Carried out sweep of Bordeaux area. Fighter group e/a credits:– 4FG – 10. Fighter group losses:– 4FG – 7. Ground fire was cause of most losses.

7PG despatched 1 Spitfire to France (La Rochelle area).

21/22 MARCH 1944

8AF 272 NIGHT LEAFLET OPERATION – HOLLAND

	Despatched		Effective	Locality	No. of Leaflets	Losses
1BD B-17	422BS	6	6	THE HAGUE, AMSTERDAM, LEEUWARDEN, ROTTERDAM, UTRECHT 2102–2133 hrs	300 bundles	0

22 MARCH 1944

8AF 273

	Despatched		Effective	Target	Bombs Tonnage	E/A	Losses MIA	E	Dam	Casualties KIA	WIA	MIA
1BD	B-17	287	277	BERLIN (S)			4			0		
3BD	B-17	187	183	&T/Os	514.5HE		3			0		
2BD	B-24	214	197		956.75IB		5			0		
TOTALS:		688	657		1471.25	0–0–0	12	1	347	0	20	135

REMARKS: Groups participating:– 1BD – 91BG, 92BG, 303BG, 305BG, 306BG, 351BG, 379BG, 381BG, 401BG, 457BG; 2BD – 44BG, 93BG, 389BG, 445BG, 446BG, 448BG, 453BG, 458BG, 466BG; 3BD – 94BG, 95BG, 96BG, 100BG, 385BG, 388BG, 390BG, 447BG, 452BG. Primaries were aviation industry plants at Oranienburg and Basdorf where 8/10 to 10/10 cloud prevented attack. 1 B-24 in total dropped on Heide as a T/O. Totals include 9 PFF of 482BG – last regular mission for this group. 6,368,000 leaflets also released from bombers. No serious challenge to mission from e/a. Bomb types used:– 500GP, 100IB. First mission of 466BG. Bomb group losses:– 91BG – 1, 94BG – 1, 96BG – 1, 305BG – 2, 351BG – 1, 446BG – 2, 447BG – 1, 458BG – 1, 466BG – 2. 2 B-24s of 466BG collided over Holland. 1 466BG B-24 interned in Sweden. The missing 351BG B-17 not seen to join formation after t/o. MIA 96BG hit by bombs from own group. B/d B-17 c/l Horsey, 5 crew baled out over Germany, others safe.

Berlin again. B-17G 42-97136, one of the new 'silver' finish natural metal finish aircraft then coming into service, takes off from Grafton Underwood's runway 06 on 22 March. Lt Knapp was at the controls.

A strike camera in a 96BG Fortress unloading M-47 incendiaries at Oranienburg on 22 March caught a moment of impending disaster. *Ruth L*, Lt N.L. Young and crew, was in the way of the cascade and the left tail stabiliser was knocked off with possible other hits. The B-17 went down – some 'chutes were seen.

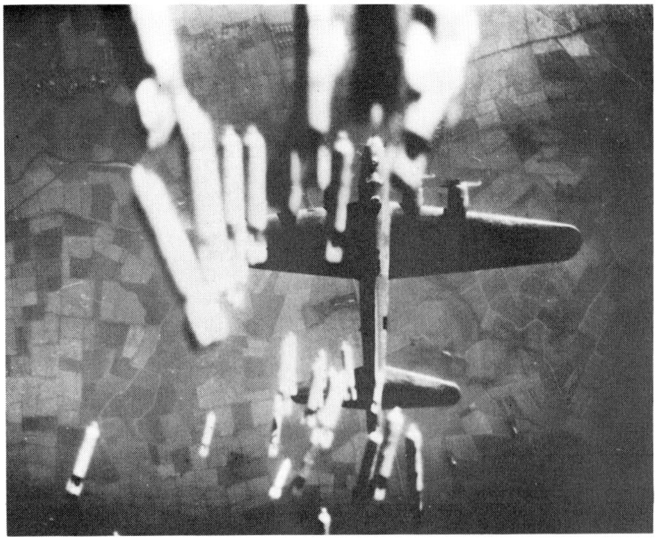

VIII FC FO 277

Despatched		Groups	E/A	Losses MIA	E	Dam	Casualties KIA	WIA	MIA
P-38	125	20FG, 55FG, 364FG	0	3	0	7		0	3
P-47	496	56FG, 78FG, 352FG, 353FG, 356FG, 359FG, 361FG, 358FG (IX FC), 362FG (IX FC), 368FG (IX FC)	1–0–0(G)	5	1	9		1	5
P-51	196	4FG, 355FG, 357FG, 354FG (IX FC), 363FG (IX FC)	0	4	2	0		0	4
TOTALS:	817		1–0–0(G)	12	1	16	0	1	12

REMARKS: Fighter support, 8AF 273. 221 IX FC a/c participated under VIII FC control. No fighter air combats. 56FG flew A, B & C formations. Fighter group losses:– 55FG – 1, 56FG – 4, 357FG – 1, 361FG – 1, 364FG – 2, 354FG – 3. 361FG P-47 cr. in sea 12 miles from Southwold, pilot missing. 1 78FG P-47 and 2 357FG P-51s written off in accidents, pilots safe.

7PG despatched 1 F-5 and 1 Spitfire to Holland and Germany.

22/23 MARCH 1944

8AF 274 NIGHT LEAFLET OPERATION – FRANCE & HOLLAND

	Despatched		Effective	Locality	No. of Leaflets	Losses
1BD				PARIS, THE HAGUE,		
B-17	422BS	6	6	AMSTERDAM, LEEUWARDEN 2135–2207 hrs	263 bundles	0

23 MARCH 1944

8AF 275

	Despatched		Effective	Target		Bombs Tonnage	E/A	Losses MIA	E	Dam	Casualties KIA	WIA	MIA
3BD	B-17	224	205	BRUNSWICK	(S)	476.9		16	1	221	3	6	158
			3	T/Os									
1BD	B-17	300	47	MÜNSTER	(S)	769.0		6	0	56	1	3	61
			249	T/Os									
2BD	B-24	244	68	HANDORF A/F	(P)	510.0		6	0	45	0	1	59
			36	ACHMER CITY									
			21	ACHMER A/F									
			12	MÜNSTER	(S)								
			52	OSNABRÜCK									
			14	T/Os									
TOTALS:		768	707			1755.0	33–8–11	28	1	322	4	10	278

REMARKS: Groups participating: 3BD – 94BG, 95BG, 96BG, 100BG, 385BG, 388BG, 390BG, 447BG, 452BG; 1BD – 91BG, 92BG, 303BG, 305BG, 306BG, 351BG, 379BG, 381BG, 384BG, 401BG, 457BG; 2BD – 44BG, 93BG, 389BG, 392BG, 445BG, 446BG, 448BG, 453BG, 458BG, 466BG. T/Os for 1BD include: Hamm (83 a/c), Ahlen (67 a/c) and Neubeckum (19 a/c). 45CBW formation early at target and met by e/a when no escort on hand; 388BG B-17 lost collided with e/a. Bomb types used:– 1000GP, 500GP, 100IB, 120 Frag. 1,440,000 leaflets also dropped from bombers. Bomb group losses:– 92BG – 5, 94BG – 2, 96BG – 2, 305BG – 1, 385BG – 3, 388BG – 5, 445BG – 1, 448BG – 1, 452BG – 4, 453BG – 1, 458BG – 1, 466BG – 2. 96BG B-17 in sea off Aldeburgh, crew rescued. 94BG B-17 ditched, crew lost. B/d 452BG B-17 c/l at A/F on return.

VIII FC FO 278

Despatched		Groups	E/A	Losses MIA	E	Dam	Casualties KIA	WIA	MIA
P-38	119	20FG, 55FG, 364FG	0	0	0	0	0	0	0
P-47	539	56FG, 78FG, 352FG, 353FG, 356FG, 359FG, 361FG, 358FG (IX FC), 362FG (IX FC)	4–0–10	0	1	1	0	0	0
P-51	183	4FG, 355FG, 357FG, 354FG (IX FC), 363FG (IX FC)	18–1– 6	4	0	1	0	0	4
TOTALS:	841		20–1– 6 2–0–10(G)	4	1	2	0	0	4

REMARKS: Fighter support, 8AF 275. 4 IX FC groups participated under VIII FC control. 56FG flew two missions. Fighter group e/a credits:– 4FG – 13, 354FG – 4, 358FG – 1. Fighter group losses: 357FG – 1, 354FG – 3. 362FG P-47 c/l base.

7PG despatched 3 F-5 and 4 Spitfires to Germany, Holland and France. 1 a/c was intercepted by e/a.

23/24 MARCH 1944

8AF 276 NIGHT LEAFLET OPERATION – FRANCE

	Despatched		Effective	Locality	No. of Leaflets	Losses
1BD				GRENOBLE, VICHY,		
B-17	422BS	5	5	LYON, TOULOUSE, LIMOGES 2227–2304 hrs	262 bundles	0

24 MARCH 1944

8AF 277

	Despatched		Effective	Target	Bombs Tonnage	E/A	Losses MIA	E	Dam	Casualties KIA	WIA	MIA
1BD	B-17	230	60	SCHWEINFURT (P)	130.2		3	3	68	14	1	30
			162	FRANKFURT (S)	382.0							
2BD	B-24	206	148	ST.DIZIER A/F	463.7		0	0	24	0	3	0
			33	NANCY/ESSEY A/F	105.0							
TOTALS:		436	403		1080.9	0–0–0	3	3	92	14	4	30

REMARKS: Groups participating:– 1BD – 91BG, 303BG, 305BG, 306BG, 351BG, 379BG, 381BG, 384BG, 401BG, 457BG; 2BD – 44BG, 389BG, 392BG, 445BG, 446BG, 448BG, 453BG, 458BG, 466BG. 6 1BD a/c unable to t/o due to a blocked perimeter track. Most 1BD a/c turned on Frankfurt after encountering heavy cloud and dense contrails. Bomb types used:– 1000GP, 500GP, 100IB, 20 frag. 496,000 leaflets also released from bombers. Bomb group losses:– 305BG – 1, 381BG – 2. 2 B-17s collided in Schweinfurt area. PFF 305BG B-17 cr. on t/o base when bound for another base to lead mission, 21 k (11 crew, 8 US servicemen in hut and 2 children in bungalow). 381BG B-17 cr. shortly after t/o from Ridgewell. 384BG B-17 c/l near Nuthampstead during assembly.

VIII FC FO 279

Despatched		Groups	E/A	Losses MIA	E	Dam	Casualties KIA	WIA	MIA
P-38	84	55FG, 364FG	0	2	0	0	0	0	2
P-47	301	56FG, 78FG, 356FG, 361FG, 362FG (IX FC)	1–0–0 2–0–4(G)	0	0	0	0	0	0
P-51	155	4FG, 355FG, 354FG (IX FC), 363FG (IX FC)	0	3	0	0	0	0	2
TOTALS:	540		1–0–0 2–0–4(G)	5	0	0	0	0	4

REMARKS: Fighter support, 8AF 277, 226 IX FC a/c participated under VIII FC control. 7 fighter groups unable to t/o due to poor weather conditions. 2 groups of P-47s in support of B-24s, all other groups in support of B-17s. Fighter group losses:– 55FG – 2, 354FG – 3. 2 55FG P-38s collided over Nancy. 2 354FG P-51s collided over the sea, 1 pilot rescued 5 miles E. of Clacton.

7PG despatched 6 F-5 and 1 Spitfire on PR over France.

24/25 MARCH 1944

8AF 278 NIGHT LEAFLET OPERATION – FRANCE & BELGIUM

	Despatched		Effective	Locality	No. of Leaflets	Losses
1BD				TOURS, LORIENT,		
B-17	422BS	5	5	BRUSSELS, CHARLEROI, ANTWERP 2133–2210 hrs	250 bundles	0

25 MARCH 1944

7PG despatched 2 F-5 and 3 Spitfires on PR over France, Holland and Germany.

25/26 MARCH 1944

8AF 279 NIGHT LEAFLET OPERATION – BELGIUM

	Despatched		Effective	Locality	No. of Leaflets	Losses
1BD				BRUSSELS, ANTWERP,		
B-17	422BS	6	6	CHARLEROI, AMSTERDAM 2129–2136 hrs	300 bundles	0

In late March 1944 a special 8AF detachment for experimenting with night intruder operations became operational under RAF 100 Group at Little Snoring. Two P-51Bs and two P-38Js were used but after a number of sorties it was clear the aircraft were unsuitable for this type of work and the unit was withdrawn. Maj Tom Gates was in command. The fighters' undersides were painted black and a yellow lightning stripe was the unofficial insignia. (via T. Cushing)

Bombing Pas de Calais V-weapon sites entailed only a short period of time in hostile airspace but the quality and quantity of the flak was equal to that at many important targets in Germany. This 448BG gunner was one of 31 flak casualties (four fatal) on 26 March. With no rear fuselage door the only speedy way to retrieve a stretcher patient was through a gun window. (R. Patterson)

26 MARCH 1944

8AF 280

	Despatched		Effective	Target	Bombs Tonnage	E/A	Losses MIA	E	Dam	Casualties KIA	WIA	MIA
1BD	B-17	243	234	9 V/S PAS DE CALAIS (P)			4	1	134	1	10	40
2BD	B-24	185	138				1	0	38	1	5	10
3BD	B-17	145	128	7 V/S CHERBOURG (P)			0	0	64	0	0	0
TOTALS:		573	500		1271.0		5	1	236	2	15	50

REMARKS: Groups participating: 1BD – 91BG, 303BG, 306BG, 351BG, 379BG, 381BG, 384BG, 401BG, 457BG; 2BD – 44BG, 389BG, 392BG, 445BG, 448BG, 453BG, 458BG; 3BD – 94BG, 95BG, 96BG, 388BG, 390BG, 447BG, 452BG. Bomb types used:– 1000GP, 500GP. Bomb group losses:– 303BG – 1, 306BG – 1, 379BG – 1, 392BG – 1, 401BG – 1. Aborting 401BG B-17 cr. landing base.

VIII FC FO 281

Despatched		Groups	E/A	Losses MIA	E	Dam	Casualties KIA	WIA	MIA
P-47	266	56FG, 78FG, 352FG, 353FG, 359FG, 361FG	1–1–4(G)	1	0	5	0	0	1

REMARKS: Fighter support for 8AF 280. 1 group of 50 P-47s of IX FC also flew under VIII FC control. Fighter group losses: 353FG – 1.

7PG despatched 18 F-5 and 4 Spitfires on PR over France, Belgium and Germany.

26/27 MARCH 1944

8AF 281 NIGHT LEAFLET OPERATION – FRANCE

	Despatched		Effective	Locality	No. of Leaflets	Losses
1BD				CAEN, RENNES,		
B-17	422BS	6	6	AMIENS, PARIS,	300 bundles	0
				ROUEN		
				2114–2206 hrs		

27 MARCH 1944

8AF 282

	Despatched		Effective	Target	Bombs Tonnage	E/A	Losses MIA	E	Dam	Casualties KIA	WIA	MIA
2BD	B-24	168	72	PAU/PONT LONG A/F	381.5HE		3	4	18	20	1	31
			49	BIARRITZ A/F	67.5IB							
			47	MONT DE MARSAN A/F								
3BD	B-17	256	123	BORDEAUX/MERIGNAC			2		51	11	2	20
				A/F	540.5HE							
			118	CAYEUX A/F (O)	42.0IB							
			7	CHARTRES A/F (O)								
1BD	B-17	290	55	ST.JEAN D/ANGELY			1		37	0	1	10
				A/F								
			59	LA ROCHELLE/								
				LA LEU A/F	743.0HE							
			2	T/Os	78.0IB							
			74	TOURS/PARCAY								
				MESLAY A/D								
			35	USINE LIOTARD A/D								
				Wks (TOURS A/F)								
			60	CHARTRES A/F								
TOTALS:		714	701		1852.5		6	5	106	31	4	61

REMARKS: Groups participating:– 2BD – 44BG, 389BG, 392BG, 445BG, 453BG, 458BG, 466BG; 3BD – 94BG, 95BG, 96BG, 100BG, 385BG, 388BG, 390BG, 447BG, 452BG; 1BD – 91BG, 303BG, 305BG, 306BG, 351BG, 379BG, 381BG, 384BG, 401BG, 457BG. 7 447BG B-17s failed to locate own group so joined 1BD force attacking Chartres. Bomb types used:– 500GP, 100GP, 100IB, 120 frag. Bomb group losses:– 44BG – 2, 306BG – 1, 388BG – 1, 447BG – 1, 453BG – 1. 2 466BG B-24s collided during assembly and cr. at Hoe and Gressenhall. On return b/d 466BG B-24 c/l base. B/d 44BG B-24 c/l Tangmere A/F.

Lead of 453BG on 27 March was *Cabin in the Sky* with Lt Lien's crew and the Group Operations Officer Maj Cofield as Air Commander. A photographer in a wing aircraft recorded the grinning waist gunner as the bomber was on its way. Flak at Pau was moderate but one shell made a direct hit on the lead B-24 – there were only three survivors. Maj James Stewart (of the movies) became the new Ops Officer at Old Buckenham.

A load of 500 pounders is salvoed over Bordeaux/Merignac airfield by a 452BG B-17G on 27 March. This, like all B-17Gs arriving since the end of 1943 had enclosed waist gun positions making life less icy for the gunners. Named *Dog Breath*, the bomber went missing on 19 June 1944, one of the few 8AF Fortresses interned in Spain.

The decision to convert all 8AF fighter groups to the P-51 Mustang involved a large re-training programme for pilots and ground crews. In order that servicing the liquid-cooled Merlin engine could be mastered by mechanics who currently worked on the P-47's air-cooled Double Wasp, a P-51B was sent to scheduled units well in advance of planned conversion date. Here 359FG men get their first look at the works of a Mustang at East Wretham, 27 March.

VIII FC FO 282

Despatched		Groups	E/A	Losses MIA	E	Dam	Casualties KIA	WIA	MIA
P-38	132	20FG, 55FG, 364FG	0	2	1	0		0	2
P-47	706	56FG, 78FG, 352FG, 353FG, 356FG, 359FG, 361FG, 362FG (IX FC), 365FG (IX FC), 366FG (IX FC), 368FG (IX FC)	6–0– 2	5	1	4		1	5
P-51	122	4FG, 355FG, 357FG, 354FG (IX FC)	2–0– 3 30–1–11 (G)	3	0	1		0	3
TOTALS:	960		8–0– 5 30–1–11(G)	10	2	5	0	1	10

REMARKS: Fighter support, 8AF 282. 243 IX FC a/c participated under VIII FC control. 3 IX FC P-47 groups flew two missions. Fighter group e/a credits:– 4FG – 3, 56FG – 4, 355FG – 2, 359FG – 2, 362FG – 1. Fighter group losses:– 4FG – 1, 56FG – 4, 355FG – 1, 357FG – 1, 359FG – 1, 364FG – 2. A 55FG P-38 c/l and a 56FG with b/d rated Cat E.

7PG despatched 12 F-5 and 1 Spitfire on PR over France.

28 MARCH 1944

8AF 283

	Despatched		Effective	Target	Bombs Tonnage	E/A	Losses MIA	E	Dam	Casualties KIA	WIA	MIA
2BD	B-24	77	0	IJMUIDEN E-BOAT PENS	0		0	0	0	0	0	0
1BD	B-17	182	117 59	DIJON/LONGVIC A/F (P) REIMS/CHAMPAGNE A/F (P)	400.5HE 86.0IB		0	1	60	3	1	0
3BD	B-17	191	127 61	CHATEAUDUN A/F (P) CHARTRES A/F (P)	362.0HE 88.0IB		2	0	59	0	1	28
TOTALS:		450	364		936.5	0–0–0	2	1	119	3	2	28

REMARKS: Groups participating:– 2BD – 93BG, 448BG; 1BD – 91BG, 303BG, 305BG, 306BG, 379BG, 381BG, 384BG; 3BD – 94BG, 95BG, 96BG, 100BG, 385BG, 388BG, 390BG, 447BG, 452BG. 2BD recalled due to excessive clouds and failure of escort to t/o. Bomb types used:– 500GP, 100IB. Bomb group losses: 452BG – 2. 96BG B-17 set on fire, 8 of crew baled over enemy territory, pilot and engineer brought a/c back and landed at Biggin Hill. 381BG B-17 abandoned over UK, a/c crashed in sea off Bawdsey.

VIII FC FO 283

Despatched		Groups	E/A	Losses MIA	E	Dam	Casualties KIA	WIA	MIA
P-38	46	20FG	0	0	0	0	0	0	0
P-47	284	56FG, 78FG, 352FG, 353FG, 359FG, 361FG	0–0– 1	0	0	0	0	0	0
P-51	123	4FG, 355FG, 357FG	30–1–32(G)	3	0	0	0	0	3
TOTALS:	453		30–1–33(G)	3	0	0	0	0	3

REMARKS: Fighter support, 8AF 283. Fighter group losses:– 4FG – 1, 357FG – 2. 355FG strafed Dijon/Longvic A/F after bombing.

7PG despatched 10 F-5 and 5 Spitfires on PR over France, Belgium, Holland and Germany.

The only bombers missing in action on 28 March were from 452BG. One had the right wing severed by Chateaudun flak and spun into the clouds. The knowledge that centrifugal force would hold the occupants, giving little hope of escape, was heartrending for spectators in other bombers.

Right. At first sight a Fortress over its target at Reims/Champagne. Closer examination shows that the bomber's tail is kinked to the right. A direct shell hit in the rear fuselage killed three men and ripped out the side and bottom of the fuselage. 1/Lt Dan Henry managed to fly *Who Dat* back to Ridgewell where it was decided a landing could not be risked. The crew baled out and the B-17 headed out to sea.

29 MARCH 1944

8AF 284

	Despatched		Effective	Target		Bombs Tonnage	E/A	Losses MIA	E	Dam	Casualties KIA	WIA	MIA
1BD	B-17	236	193	BRUNSWICK	(S)					66	2	5	90
			20	UNTERLÜSS	(O)	132.0HE							
			18	STEDORF	(O)	343.0IB							
			2	T/Os									
TOTALS:		236	233			475.0	8–3–6	9	1	66	2	7	90

REMARKS: Groups participating:– 1BD – 91BG, 92BG, 303BG, 305BG, 306BG, 351BG, 379BG, 381BG, 384BG, 401BG, 457BG. Bomb types used:– 100GP, 100IB. 4,060,000 leaflets also released from bombers. Bomb group losses:– 91BG – 2, 305BG – 3, 306BG – 3, 457BG – 1. 401BG B-17 salvaged though b/d.

VIII FC FO 284

Despatched		Groups	E/A	Losses MIA	E	Dam	Casualties KIA	WIA	MIA
P-38	50	364FG	2–0– 1	2	3	1	2	0	2
P-47	242	56FG, 352FG, 353FG, 356FG, 359FG		1	2	8	0	2	0
P-51	136	4FG, 355FG, 357FG 354FG (IX FC)		9	1	3	0	1	8
TOTALS:	428		44–4–13 13–7–14(G)	12	6	12	2	3	10

REMARKS: Fighter support, 8AF 284 (Brunswick). 353FG flew two missions. Col Duncan, 353FG, strafed a captured B-17 parked at Lingen. Fighter group e/a credits:– 4FG – 21, 56FG – 2, 353FG – 6, 355FG – 12, 356FG – 2, 357FG – 1, 364FG – 2, 354FG – 2. Fighter group losses: 4FG – 3, 353FG – 1, 355FG – 3, 357FG – 3, 364FG – 2. 2 357FG P-51s collided in cloud, shortly after t/o, and cr. in sea off Leiston. MIA 364FG P-38 & 355FG P-51 abandoned mid-channel, pilots lost. On return, 4FG pilot rescued 24 miles off Orfordness. 353FG P-47 abandoned over N.Sea, pilot rescued. 364FG P-38 cr. at Thorpe Abbotts, after pilot baled. 364FG P-38 cr. Knettishall, pilot k. 364FG P-38 cr. Tibenham, pilot k. 356FG P-47 c/l Leiston, pilot inj.

8AF 284

	Despatched		Effective	Target		Bombs Tonnage	E/A	Losses MIA	E	Dam	Casualties KIA	WIA	MIA
2BD	B-24	77	30	WATTEN V/S	(P)	115.0	0–0–0	0	2	6	18	1	0

REMARKS: Groups participating:– 2BD – 93BG, 446BG, 448BG. PFF failures prevented most from bombing. Bomb types used:– 2000GP, 1000GP. 2 93BG B-24s collided during assembly and cr. at Henham, 2 baled 18 killed; another 19 US personnel killed, 38 injured, plus 4 civilians, when bombs detonated during rescue attempts.

VIII FC FO 284

Despatched		Groups	E/A	Losses MIA	E	Dam	Casualties KIA	WIA	MIA
P-47	37	361FG	0	0	0	0	0	0	0

REMARKS: Fighter support, 8AF 284 (Watten).

30 MARCH 1944

8AF 285 FO 67FW 14

Despatched		Groups	E/A	Losses MIA	E	Dam	Casualties KIA	WIA	MIA
P-47	74	359FG, 361FG	0	0	0	0	0	0	0

REMARKS: 24 P-47 fighter-bombers, escorted by 50 other P-47s, sent to bomb Soesterburg A/F (359FG) and Eindhoven A/F (361FG). A locomotive and railway station damaged and 5.75 tons of bombs dropped.

8AF 285 FO 66FW 53

Despatched		Groups	E/A	Losses MIA	E	Dam	Casualties KIA	WIA	MIA
P-47	22	78FG	1–0–0 1–0–2(G)	1	0	3	0	0	1

REMARKS: Despatched to strafe Venlo, Twente/Enschede and Deelen A/Fs. Group losses:– 78FG – 1.

7PG despatched 2 Spitfires on PR over Germany.

30/31 MARCH 1944

8AF 286 NIGHT LEAFLET OPERATION – FRANCE

	Despatched		Effective	Locality	No. of Leaflets	Losses
1BD B-17	422BS	6	6	ROUEN, RENNES, REIMS, PARIS, AMIENS 2125–2155 hrs	300 bundles	0

31 MARCH 1944

7PG despatched 7 F-5 and 4 Spitfires on PR over France, Belgium and Germany.

1 APRIL 1944

8AF 287

	Despatched		Effective	Target		Bombs Tonnage	E/A	Losses MIA	E	Dam	Casualties KIA	WIA	MIA
3BD	B-17	245	0	LUDWIGSHAFEN		0		0	0	7	0	0	0
2BD	B-24	195	17	STRASBOURG	(O)	260.0HE							
			101	PFORZHEIM	(O)	225.0IB		12	3	42	9	12	113
			38	SCHAFFHAUSEN	(O)								
			9	GRAFENHAUSEN	(O)								
TOTALS:		440	165			485.0	1–1–0	12	3	49	9	12	113

REMARKS: Groups participating:– 3BD – 94BG, 95BG, 96BG, 100BG, 385BG, 388BG, 390BG, 447BG, 452BG. 2BD – 44BG, 93BG, 389BG, 392BG, 445BG, 446BG, 448BG, 453BG. 3BD turned back after encountering heavy cloud over France. PFF failure resulted in bad navigational errors; a/c were 100 miles S of intended course. Strasbourg, France and Schaffhausen, Switzerland were bombed in error. US later paid Swiss $1,000,000 as a formal apology. Bomb types used:– 1000GP, 500GP, 100GP, 100IB. Bomb group losses:– 93BG – 2, 389BG – 3, 445BG – 3, 448BG – 4. 448BG B-24 interned in Switzerland. 448BG B-24 ditched off Dunkirk, 8 rescued by fishing boat, two days later. 445BG B-24 cr. at Long Stratton after t/o, 9 k, 1 injured. B/d 93BG B-24 Cat E. Rochester A/F and B/d 93BG B-24 Cat E base.

VIII FC FO 286

Despatched		Groups	E/A	Losses MIA	E	Dam	Casualties KIA	WIA	MIA
P-47	280	56FG, 78FG, 352FG, 353FG, 356FG, 361FG	13–1–19	2	0	12	0	0	2
P-51	195	4FG, 352FG, 357FG, 354FG (IX FC), 363FG (IX FC)	5–2– 4	2	0	2	0	0	2
TOTALS:	475		5–2– 4 13–1–19 (G)	4	0	14	0	0	4

REMARKS: Fighter support, 8AF 287. Only 13 out of 17 groups assigned managed to t/o because of weather. A P-51 group which was scheduled to report on weather over Germany unable to t/o because of weather. 352FG flew a mixed formation of P-47s and P-51s. Fighter group e/a credits:– 4FG – 3, 354FG – 2. Fighter group losses:– 56FG – 1, 78FG – 1, 357FG – 2.

INCIDENT

Such was the urgency to provide a substantial force of Mustangs for long-range escort that when the first squadron of 352nd Group to convert from Thunderbolts, the 486th, went out on 1 April 1944 on a *Ramrod* to Ludwigshafen, the average flying time on the new fighter was less than five hours per pilot. This situation was undesirable and several accidents that occurred during the introductory period could be traced to inexperience with the new type.

5 APRIL 1944

8AF 288

	Despatched		Effective	Target	Bombs Tonnage	E/A	Losses MIA	E	Dam	Casualties KIA	WIA	MIA
2BD	B-24	50	21	ST.POL/ SIRACOURT V/S (P)	57.0	0–0–0	0	0		0	0	0

REMARKS: Groups participating:– 2BD – 93BG, 458BG, 466BG. Clouds hindered bombing. Bomb types used:– 500GP.

VIII FC FO 287

Despatched		Groups	E/A	Losses MIA	E	Dam	Casualties KIA	WIA	MIA
P-47	50	361FG	0–0–0	0	0	0	0	0	0

REMARKS: Fighter support, 8AF 288.

8AF 289/VIII FC FO 288

Despatched		Groups	E/A	Losses MIA	E	Dam	Casualties KIA	WIA	MIA
P-38	96	20FG, 364FG	0	1	0	4	0	0	1
P-47	236	56FG, 78FG, 352FG, 353FG, 356FG, 359FG, 361FG	2–0– 2	1	0	4	0	0	1
P-51	124	4FG, 352FG, 355FG	96–4–120	7	0	3	1	0	6
TOTALS:	456		10–1– 2 88–3–120(G)	9	0	11	1	0	8

REMARKS: Strafing attacks on A/Fs in Germany. Heavy cloud hindered most groups but the 4FG attacked 5 A/Fs claiming 45 e/a and 355FG 6 A/Fs claiming 51 e/a. 352FG flew a mixed formation of P-47s and P-51s. Fighter group e/a credits:– 4FG – 4, 355FG – 8. 78FG damaged a parked B-17 at one A/F it attacked. Fighter group losses:– 4FG – 4, 20FG – 1, 78FG – 1, 355FG – 3. 20FG P-38, hit by Flak, cr. deliberately into a parked Me 110. 4FG P-51 abandoned 20 miles from Clacton, pilot rescued but died later.

INCIDENT

The perils of ground strafing were brought home to the 4th Group in no uncertain terms on the 5 April 1944 attack on airfields in the Berlin area. Four Mustangs were lost to ground fire although the pilots of all escaped with their lives, including the great ace Duane Beeson. The most miraculous survival was that of Lt Franklin Bunte, who gave this account after release from POW camp:–

'I spotted a "drome with several aircraft on it and dove to attack it. Went across the field right on the deck indicating about 425 mph, firing at a Ju 52. About 10 to 15 seconds later I felt a hell of a lot of heat, looked down in the cockpit and saw flames coming back from the motor along the left side. My pants and boot were already on fire so I realised I wouldn't have time to get enough altitude to jump before burning to a crisp. At the same time I noticed I was directly over a lake, so I jammed the stick forward and passed out. I have no recollection of hitting the water. I came to under the surface and felt my aircraft settle on the bottom. At this point I guess I panicked, for I started trying to undo my 'chute harness, instead of the safety belt; thinking that if I could get out of that I would get out of the ship. It didn't take long for bells to start ringing and lights flashing. I finally went out completely and the last thing I remember was that I was still fighting my 'chute harness. I came to on the surface of the lake and managed to pull one side of my Mae West, but I didn't have enough strength to pull the other. After what seemed like an eternity of passing out and regaining consciousness, I made the shore. Dragged myself out of the water and started crawling towards a small shack. Was soon picked up by civilians and turned over to the Luftwaffe.'

5/6 APRIL 1944

801BG despatched 17 B-24s on *Carpetbagger* operations. 1 B-24 MIA.

6 APRIL 1944

8AF 290

	Despatched		Effective	Target	Bombs Tonnage	E/A	Losses MIA	E	Dam	Casualties KIA	WIA	MIA
2BD	B-24	12	12	WATTEN V/S (P)	44.0	0–0–0	0	0	0	0	0	0

REMARKS: Groups participating: 2BD – 44BG, 93BG, 392BG, 446BG, 448BG. Bomb types used: 2000GP, 1000GP. Weather prevented all but one box bombing.

continued on next page

6 APRIL 1944 *(contd.)*

VIII FC FO 289

Despatched		Groups	E/A	Losses MIA	E	Dam	Casualties KIA	WIA	MIA
P-47	27	352FG	0–0–0	0	0	0	0	0	0

REMARKS: Fighter support, 8AF 290.

8 APRIL 1944

8AF 291

	Despatched		Effective	Target		Bombs Tonnage	E/A	Losses MIA	E	Dam	Casualties KIA	WIA	MIA
2BD	B-24	350	190	BRUNSWICK A/I	(P)	622.7HE	58–9–32	30	2	87	8	23	300
			48	LANGENHAGEN A/F	(O)	160.7IB							
			59	ROSSLINGEN	(O)								
			6	T/Os									
1BD	B-17	59	59	OLDENBURG A/F	(P)	110.5HE	?	0		32	0	5	0
						37.5IB							
3BD	B-17	255	83	QUAKENBRÜCK A/F	(P)	457.0HE	?	4		128	1	3	40
			60	ACHMER A/F	(P)								
			41	RHEINE A/F	(P)								
			22	TWENTE ENSCHEDE	(O)								
			21	HESEPE	(O)								
			19	HANDORF	(O)								
			3	T/Os									
TOTALS:		664	611			1388.4	?	34	2	247	9	31	340

REMARKS: Groups participating:– 2BD – 44BG, 93BG, 389BG, 392BG, 445BG, 446BG, 448BG, 453BG, 458BG, 466BG. 1BD – 91BG, 381BG. 3BD – 94BG, 95BG, 96BG, 100BG, 385BG, 388BG, 390BG, 447BG, 452BG. Most of 1BD force was cancelled due to fog at bases. Bomb types used:– 500GP, 300GP, 200GP, 100GP, 100IB, 20 Frag. Heavy fighter attacks on B-24s. Bomb group losses– 44BG – 11, 93BG – 1, 94BG – 1, 96BG – 2, 392BG – 2, 446BG – 2, 447BG – 1, 453BG – 7, 458BG – 1, 466BG – 6. On return 392BG B-24 cr. Sidestrand, 5 k, 5 inj. Another b/d 392BG B-24 later salvaged base.

VIII FC FO 291

Despatched		Groups	E/A	Losses MIA	E	Dam	Casualties KIA	WIA	MIA
P-38	136	20FG, 55FG, 364FG		5	0	3	0	0	5
P-47	438	56FG, 78FG, 352FG, 353FG, 356FG, 359FG, 361FG, 358FG (IX FC), 362FG (IX FC)		4	2	12	0	0	4
P-51	206	4FG, 352FG, 355FG, 357FG, 354FG (IX FC), 363FG (IX FC)		14	0	3	0	0	14
TOTALS:	780		88–3–46 49–6–38 (G)	23	2	18	0	0	23

REMARKS: Fighter support, 8AF 291. 175 IX FC a/c flew under VIII FC control; 352FG flew on penetration and withdrawal with a mixed formation of P-47s and P-51s. 20FG unable to t/o for escort but was despatched on a lone strafing mission to Germany later in day. Fighter group e/a credits:– 4FG – 31, 20FG – 7, 55FG – 1, 355FG – 5, 357FG – 5, 361FG – 9, 354FG – 20, 362FG – 2, 363FG – 2. Fighter group losses:– 4FG – 4, 20FG – 4, 55FG – 1, 78FG – 1, 352FG – 1, 353FG – 2, 355FG – 3, 361FG – 1, 354FG – 4, 363FG – 2. On return b/d 78FG P-47 cr., pilot safe. 358FG P-47 Cat E. 353FG loss was 359FG pilot and a/c in strafing unit.

A 93BG B-24J, displaying recently applied squadron letters GO(328BS), heads for Bourges at 15,500 feet, 10 April. Revised equipment increased weight of new Liberators to a point where high altitude performance was impaired. To improve control, the ball turret was not lowered unless fighter attack was imminent. (2AD Memorial Library)

8/9 APRIL 1944

8AF 292 NIGHT LEAFLET OPERATION – BELGIUM

	Despatched		Effective	Locality	No. of Leaflets	Losses
1BD				LIEGE, BRUSSELS, GHENT, ANTWERP, MONT-SUR-SOMBRE		
B-17	422BS	5	5	2215–2227 hrs	1,000,000	0

9 APRIL 1944

8AF 293

	Despatched		Effective	Target		Bombs Tonnage	E/A	Losses MIA	E	Dam	Casualties KIA	WIA	MIA
1BD	B-17	145	41	RAHMEL A/I	(P)	263.5HE		6		44	8	9	60
			96	MARIENBURG A/I	(P)	59.0IB							
			3	T/Os									
2BD	B-24	246	106	TUTOW A/I	(P)	195.0HE		14		30	17	6	140
			14	PARCHIM	(S)	124.5IB							
			6	T/Os									
3BD	B-17	151	33	POSEN A/I	(P)	234.0HE		12		93	0	6	120
			85	WARNEMÜNDE A/I	(P)	81.5IB							
			18	ROSTOCK/ MARIENEHE A/F.	(O)								
TOTALS:		542	402			957.5	45–8–14	32	10	167	25	21	320

REMARKS: Groups participating:– 1BD – 91BG, 303BG, 351BG, 379BG, 384BG, 401BG, 457BG; 2BD – 44BG, 93BG, 389BG, 392BG, 445BG, 446BG, 448BG, 453BG, 458BG, 466BG; 3BD – 94BG, 96BG, 385BG, 388BG, 390BG, 447BG, 452BG. 40CW abandoned mission over England. Several other units abandoned the mission at various points along route, due to poor weather. Some 1BD a/c of Rahmel force released 2 seconds early, mistaking a crippled a/c which jettisoned for the leader's drop. 351BG placed 86% of bombs within 1000 ft of the AP and 35% within 500 ft. 96BG placed 28% within 1000ft and 71% within 2000ft. Bomb types used:– 500GP, 100GP, 100IB. Bomb group losses:– 44BG – 1, 94BG – 1, 96BG – 2, 384BG – 1, 388BG – 3, 389BG – 1, 392BG – 1, 401BG – 2, 445BG – 1, 448BG – 2, 452BG – 6, 453BG – 2, 457BG – 3, 458BG – 4, 466BG – 2. 7 B-24s (1 – 44BG, 1 – 445BG, 2 – 448BG, 2 – 453BG, 1 – 458BG) and 3 B-17s (1 – 96BG, 1 – 388BG, 1 – 401BG) interned in Sweden. 303BG B-17 cr. on t/o at Winwick, Hunts. 389BG and 392BG B-24s collided over Foulsham and cr. nr. Bintree, 17 k. On return, b/d 392BG B-24 c/l Beccles, crew safe; 95BG B-17 c/l at Beccles and burnt out; 457BG B-17 c/l at Trunch due to b/d. 448BG B-24 cr. base. 392BG B-24 Cat E base.

VIII FC FO 292

Despatched		Groups	E/A	Losses MIA	E	Dam	Casualties KIA	WIA	MIA
P-38	119	20FG, 55FG, 364FG		2	2	9	1	0	2
P-47	387	56FG, 78FG, 352FG, 353FG, 356FG, 359FG, 361FG, 358FG (IX FC), 362FG (IX FC)		4	1	2	2	2	3
P-51	213	4FG, 352FG 355FG, 357FG, 354FG (IX FC), 363FG (IX FC)		4	1	0	0	0	4
TOTALS:	719		20–1–6 19–0–8 (G)	10	4	11	3	2	9

REMARKS: Fighter support, 8AF 293. 171 IX FC a/c participated under VIII FC control. Bad weather prevented 1 P-47 group from t/o and delayed others. 352FG flew a mixed formation of P-47s and P-51s. Fighter group e/a credits:– 56FG – 8, 78FG – 1, 352FG – 2, 354FG – 10. Fighter group losses:– 4FG – 1, 20FG – 1, 56FG – 1, 352FG – 2, 353FG – 2, 364FG – 1, 363FG – 2. 353FG P-47 in sea off Felixstowe, pilot rescued. 56FG P-47 in sea 50 miles off Lowestoft, pilot rescued but died. 55FG P-38 cr. shortly after t/o, pilot killed. On return a 356FG P-47 cr. at Gissing, pilot killed. 364FG P-38 c/l – Cat E. 474FG pilot in MIA 20FG a/c. One 352FG loss was radio relay a/c.

9/10 APRIL 1944

8AF 294 NIGHT LEAFLET OPERATION – FRANCE

	Despatched		Effective	Locality	No. of Leaflets	Losses
1BD				ROUEN, PARIS, AMIENS, CAEN		
B-17	422BS	5	5	2224–2338 hrs	2,752,000	0

REMARKS: Two single engined e/a attacked one B-17 during withdrawal, one of which was claimed as destroyed, the first credited on a night mission.

801BG despatched 23 B-24s on *Carpetbagger* operations.

A parachute silk scarf was a favoured addition to flying clothes to keep out the cold. That worn by Lt Louis Norley, one of 4FG's most successful and enduring pilots, also served as a good luck token, having been part of a canopy that had carried a fellow pilot to safety. Debden; 10 April.

10 APRIL 1944

8AF 295

	Despatched		Effective	Target	Bombs Tonnage	E/A	Losses MIA	E	Dam	Casualties KIA	WIA	MIA
1BD	B-17	238	123	EVERE A/F & A/I (P)	330.5HE	0–0–0	1	0	99	0	4	10
			39	BRUSSELS A/I (P)	199.5IB							
			52	BRUSSELS/ MELSBROEK A/F (P)								
			20	BERGEN OP ZOOM (O)								
3BD	B-17	248	21	COURCELLES A/I (P)	310.0HE	0–2–1	1	2	19	0	0	10
			42	FLORENNES/JUZAINE A/F (S)	217.0IB							
			60	DIEST/SCHAFFEN A/F (S)								
			62	MALDAGEM A/F (S)								
			21	BEAUMONT SUR OISE A/F (O)								
2BD	B-24	243	151	BOURGES A/I & A/F (P)	490.5HE	6–0–0	1	0	3	0	1	10
			28	ORLEANS/BRICY A/F (S)	143.0IB							
			21	ROMARANTIN A/F (S)								
			15	MARQUISE/ MIMOYECQUES V/S (P)								
TOTALS:		729	655		1690.5	6–2–1	3	2	121	0	5	30

REMARKS: Groups participating:– 1BD – 91BG, 92BG, 303BG, 305BG, 306BG, 351BG, 379BG, 381BG, 384BG, 401BG, 457BG; 3BD – 94BG, 95BG, 96BG, 100BG, 385BG, 388BG, 390BG, 447BG, 452BG; 2BD – 93BG, 389BG, 392BG, 445BG, 446BG, 448BG, 453BG, 458BG, 466BG, 467BG. First mission for 467BG. Bomb types used:– 1000GP, 500GP, 100GP, 100IB. Bomb group losses:– 95BG – 1, 389BG – 1, 401BG – 1. 94BG B-17 cr. shortly after t/o trying to return to base.

VIII FC FO 293

	Despatched		Groups	E/A	Losses MIA	E	Dam	Casualties KIA	WIA	MIA
	P-38	51	364FG	0–0– 0	0	0	0	0	0	0
	P-47	295	56FG, 78FG, 352FG, 353FG, 356FG, 359FG, 361FG,	12–0– 7	1	0	4	0	0	1
	P-51	150	4FG, 352FG, 355FG, 357FG, 354FG (IX FC)	40–0–16	1	0	1	0	0	1
TOTALS:		496		8–0– 1 44–0–22 (G)	2	0	5	0	0	2

REMARKS: Fighter support, 8AF 295. 364FG flew continuous support for B-24s (93BG & 392BG) attacking Marquise/Mimoyecques V/S. 352FG flew mixed formation of P-47s and P-51s. Fighter group e/a credits:– 352FG – 6, 354FG – 6. Fighter group losses:– 4FG – 1, 356FG – 1.

8AF 296 VIII FC FO 294

Despatched		Groups	E/A	Losses MIA	E	Dam	Casualties KIA	WIA	MIA
P-38	39	20FG	0	0	0	0	0	0	0

REMARKS: Fighter-bomber mission. First *Droopsnoot* mission for 20FG. 29 P-38s as bombers, rest as escort to attack Florennes/Juzaine A/F, but clouds covered target so bombs were dropped in Channel. Fighter group e/a credits:– 20FG – 1.

	Despatched		Groups	E/A	Losses MIA	E	Dam	Casualties KIA	WIA	MIA
	P-38	51	55FG	0–0–0	2	0	1	0	0	2
	P-47	7	353FG	2–0–1 (G)	0	0	0	0	0	0
TOTALS:		58		2–0–1 (G)	2	0	1	0	0	2

REMARKS: Fighter-bomber mission. First *Droopsnoot* mission for 55FG. 34 P-38s as bombers. 16 a/c attacked Coulommiers A/F dropping 17.0 tons after primary at St.Dizier was found to be cloud covered. 353FG gave area support and then strafed Villaroche A/F. Fighter group losses:– 55FG – 2.

	Despatched		Groups	E/A	Losses MIA	E	Dam	Casualties KIA	WIA	MIA
	P-38	28	20FG	0	1	0	0	0	0	1
	P-47	46	359FG	0	0	0	0	0	0	0
TOTALS:		74		0–0–0	1	0	0	0	0	1

REMARKS: Fighter-bomber mission, using *Droopsnoot* method. 27 P-38s attacked Gütersloh dropping 13.0 tons. 359FG as escort. Fighter group losses:– 20FG – 1.

10/11 APRIL 1944

8AF 297 NIGHT LEAFLET OPERATION – FRANCE

	Despatched		Effective	Locality	No. of Leaflets	Losses
1BD				LILLE, LE MANS, CHARTRES, REIMS, ORLEANS		
B-17	422BS	5	5	2212–2258 hrs	2,000,000	0

801BG despatched 23 B-24s on *Carpetbagger* operations.

11 APRIL 1944

8AF 298

	Despatched		Effective	Target		Bombs Tonnage	E/A	Losses MIA	E	Dam	Casualties KIA	WIA	MIA
2BD	B-24	274	121	OSCHERSLEBEN A/I	(P)	494.7HE	27– 2– 1	12	1	63	5	9	122
			99	BERNBURG A/I	(P)	173.5IB							
			9	HALBERSTADT A/I	(S)								
			9	EISLEBEN	(O)								
			5	T/Os									
1BD	B-17	341	108	SORAU A/I	(P)	399.1HE	12– 2– 3	19	3	190	12	13	200
			17	COTTBUS A/I	(P)	345.7IB							
			16	DOBBERPHEL	(O)								
			127	STETTIN	(O)								
			20	TRECHEL	(O)								
			23	T/Os									
3BD	B-17	302	35	ARNIMSWALDE I/A	(S)	453.5HE	34–20–19	33	1	153	2	9	330
			52	PÖLITZ	(S)	180.4IB							
			172	ROSTOCK	(O)								
			15	T/Os									
TOTALS:		917	828			2046.9	73–24–23	64	5	406	19	31	652

REMARKS: Groups participating:– 2BD – 44BG, 93BG, 389BG, 392BG, 445BG, 446BG, 448BG, 453BG, 458BG, 466BG, 467BG; 1BD – 91BG, 92BG, 303BG, 305BG, 306BG, 351BG, 379BG, 381BG, 384BG, 401BG, 457BG; 3BD – 94BG, 95BG, 96BG, 100BG, 385BG, 388BG, 390BG, 447BG, 452BG. Bomb types used:– 1000GP, 500GP, 500IB, 100GP, 100IB, 120Frag. 2,400,000 leaflets also released from bombers. MOH awarded to 1/Lt Edward S. Michael for his actions this day. Well directed enemy fighter operations against bombers in Stettin and Hannover areas. Bomb group losses:– 44BG – 1, 91BG – 1, 92BG – 8, 94BG – 4, 95BG – 7, 96BG – 11, 305BG – 2, 306BG – 2, 381BG – 1, 384BG – 1, 385BG – 3, 388BG – 4, 389BG – 3, 392BG – 3, 401BG – 4, 446BG – 2, 447BG – 2, 452BG – 2, 466BG – 3. A 392BG B-24 lost hit by a frag bomb, released from an a/c above. 9 B-17s interned in Sweden (1 – 91BG, 2 – 92BG, 1 – 94BG, 1 – 96BG, 1 – 305BG, 1 – 388BG, 1 – 447BG). 379BG B-17 cr. at Stow Bardolph, during assembly, 9 killed, 1 injured. On return 303BG B-17 c/l at Mepal A/F. 446BG B-24 c/l base. B/d 305BG B-17 c/l Waltham A/F.

A Swedish J9 fighter (US Seversky EP-106) escorts 96BG's battle damaged 42-97212 with Lt Gillespie and crew to Malmö airfield on 11 April. The bomber – with fuselage door missing – was one of 11 96th B-17s missing this day after prolonged encounters with enemy fighters. During April and May 96BG had 55 B-17s MIA, the highest loss rate of any B-17 group for a two month period. Later in 1944 interned crews were usually repatriated through a US–Swedish agreement that the men would not participate in any further combat in Europe.

The Supreme Allied Commander Europe took a look at his heavy bombers on 11 April. Col Claude Putnam shows General 'Ike' a 4,000 lb bomb. For all its potential, this missile was impractical for use with B-17s and B-24s being too large for internal stowage. Eighth's CG, Jimmy Doolittle, is at right of picture.

11 APRIL 1944 *(contd.)*

VIII FC FO 295

Despatched		Groups	E/A	Losses MIA	E	Dam	Casualties KIA	WIA	MIA
P-38	124	20FG, 55FG, 364FG		0	0	0	0	0	0
P-47	454	56FG, 78FG, 352FG, 353FG, 356FG, 359FG, 361FG, 362FG (IX FC), 365FG (IX FC)		7	0	16	0	0	7
P-51	241	4FG, 352FG, 355FG, 357FG, 354FG (IX FC), 363FG (IX FC)		9	0	13	0	0	9
TOTALS:	819		51–5–25 65–0–67 (G)	16	0	29	0	0	16

REMARKS: Fighter support, 8AF 298. 90 IX FC a/c participated under VIII FC control. 352FG flew two missions P-47s and P-51s on penetration and P-47s on withdrawal. Fighter group e/a credits:– 4FG – 6, 78FG – 1, 352FG – 3, 355FG – 8, 357FG – 23, 359FG – 2, 354FG – 4, 363FG – 3. Fighter group losses:– 78FG – 1, 352FG – 1, 355FG – 2, 356FG – 2, 357FG – 3, 359FG – 3, 354FG – 2, 362FG – 1, 363FG – 1. 368FG pilot in one 359FG MIA a/c.

11/12 APRIL 1944

8AF 299 NIGHT LEAFLET OPERATION – FRANCE

	Despatched		Effective	Locality	No. of Leaflets	Losses
1BD				PARIS, ROUEN, LE MANS, RENNES, VICHY, LYON, LIMOGES, TOULOUSE		
B-17	422BS	5	5	2301–0055 hrs	2,000,000	0

801BG despatched 12 B-24s on *Carpetbagger* operations.

12 APRIL 1944

8AF 300

	Despatched		Effective	Target	Bombs Tonnage	E/A	Losses MIA	E	Dam	Casualties KIA	WIA	MIA
1BD	B-17	97	0	SCHWEINFURT		10–6–7	5	0	0	0	0	0
2BD	B-24	184	0	ZWICKAU & OSCHERSLEBEN			0	0	25	0	2	52
3BD	B-17	174	0	SCHKEUDITZ, HALLE & LEIPZIG			1	2	1	12	14	4
TOTALS:		455	0		0	10–6–7	6	2	26	12	16	56

REMARKS: Groups participating: 2BD – 93BG, 389BG, 392BG, 445BG, 448BG, 453BG, 458BG, 467BG; 3BD – 94BG, 95BG, 100BG, 390BG, 452BG. Clouds and dense contrails caused severe problems and eventual abandonment of mission. 1BD turned back before French coast. 3BD turned back shortly after French coast. 2BD penetrated to the German border before turning back. 2BD lost 5 a/c to e/a attacks. Bomb group losses:– 445BG – 5, 452BG – 1. MIA 452BG B-17 ditched 20 mls from Clacton, 4 of crew rescued. 447BG B-17 cr. at Thorpe Morieux after t/o, 7 killed, 3 inj. 452BG B-17 c/l Caister. Prior to mission a 96BG PFF B-17 was shot down by an intruder while on approach to 390BG base in darkness – a/c cr. Gt.Glemham.

VIII FC FO 296

Despatched		Groups	E/A	Losses MIA	E	Dam	Casualties KIA	WIA	MIA
P-38	124	20FG, 55FG, 364FG		3	0	3	0	0	3
P-47	449	56FG, 78FG 353FG, 356FG, 359FG, 361FG, 362FG (IX FC), 366FG (IX FC), 368FG (IX FC)		0	2	17	0	0	0
P-51	193	4FG, 352FG, 355FG, 357FG, 354FG (IX FC), 363FG (IX FC)		2	0	1	0	0	2
TOTALS:	766		18–1–3 1–0–8 (G)	5	2	21	0	0	5

REMARKS: Fighter support, 8AF 300. Fighter group e/a credits:– 4FG – 4, 78FG – 4, 354FG – 1, 366FG – 5. Fighter group losses:– 55FG – 1, 357FG – 1, 364FG – 2, 363FG – 1.

Despatched		Groups	E/A	Losses MIA	E	Dam	Casualties KIA	WIA	MIA
P-51	8	357FG	0	0	0	0	0	0	0

REMARKS: For escort of 2 photo-recce P-38s in Munich area, although only two managed to keep up with the P-38s during their runs.

13 APRIL 1944

8AF 301

	Despatched		Effective	Target		Bombs Tonnage	E/A	Losses MIA	E	Dam	Casualties KIA	WIA	MIA
1BD	B-17	172	154	SCHWEINFURT I/A	(P)	205.0HE		14	1	127	0	11	139
			1	T/O		141.3IB							
2BD	B-24	211	60	OBERPFAFFENHOFEN A/I		310.9HE 162.1IB		6	0	45	1	3	60
			93	LECHFELD A/F	(P)								
			29	LAUFFERN	(O)								
			2	T/Os									
3BD	B-17	243	207	AUGSBURG A/I	(P)	383.0HE		18	2	178	3	16	170
			20	AUGSBURG CITY	(O)	152.4IB							
TOTALS:		626	566			1354.7	22–13–24	38	3	350	4	30	369

REMARKS: Groups participating:– 1BD – 91BG, 303BG, 351BG, 379BG, 381BG, 384BG, 401BG, 457BG; 2BD – 44BG, 93BG, 389BG, 392BG, 445BG, 446BG, 448BG, 453BG, 458BG, 466BG, 467BG; 3BD – 94BG, 95BG, 96BG, 100BG, 385BG, 388BG, 390BG, 447BG, 452BG. 40CBW (92BG, 305BG, 306BG) abandoned mission during assembly. Bomb types used: 1000GP, 500GP, 100IB, 120Frag. 5,200,000 leaflets also released from bombers. Attacks by e/a on 1BD and 3BD heaviest since 11/1/44. Bomb group losses:– 44BG – 1, 94BG – 3, 95BG – 1, 96BG – 5, 303BG – 1, 351BG – 1, 381BG – 1, 384BG – 9, 385BG – 2, 388BG – 1, 390BG – 3, 401BG – 2, 445BG – 2, 447BG – 3, 453BG – 1, 466BG – 1, 467BG – 1. 10 B-17s (2 – 94BG, 1 – 95BG, 1 – 96BG, 2 – 385BG, 1 – 390BG, 3 – 447BG) and 3 B-24s (1 – 44BG, 1 – 453BG, 1 – 466BG) interned in Switzerland. 1 B-24 down in sea, crew lost. 94BG B-17 in sea, crew rescued. On return 401BG B-17 c/l at Manston; b/d 96BG B-17 c/l at Honington; b/d 447BG B-17 cr. Ham Street, pilot killed.

VIII FC FO 298

Despatched		Groups	E/A	Losses MIA	E	Dam	Casualties KIA	WIA	MIA
P-38	134	20FG, 55FG, 364FG		3	1		0	1	2
P-47	504	56FG, 78FG, 352FG, 353FG, 356FG, 359FG, 361FG, 362FG (IX FC), 365FG (IX FC)		2	0		0	0	2
P-51	233	4FG, 352FG, 355FG, 357FG 354FG (IX FC), 363FG (IX FC)		4	1		0	1	4
TOTALS:	871		42–8–10 35–0–21 (G)	9	2	11	0	2	8

REMARKS: Fighter support, 8AF 301. 204 IX FC a/c participated under VIII FC control. 352FG and 362FG flew two missions, 352FG providing P-51s for penetration and P-47s for withdrawal. Fighter group e/a credits:– 4FG – 5, 56FG – 4, 78FG – 2, 352FG – 1, 355FG – 6, 357FG – 7, 354FG – 13, 363FG – 2, 365FG – 1. Fighter group losses:– 4FG – 2, 20FG – 1, 55FG – 1, 78FG – 1, 359FG – 1, 354FG – 2, 363FG – 1. 55FG P-38 ditched, pilot rescued. 55FG P-38 cr. at base, pilot injured. 4FG P-51 c/l Debden on return – leading ace Capt Gentile celebrating completion of tour with low pass over A/F struck ground.

INCIDENT

Ramrods flown by the 56th and 78th Fighter Groups on 13 April marked the first anniversary of operations by these groups. Both celebrated the occasion by intercepting enemy aircraft and claiming victories, two by pilots who had participated in their group's initial operation a year before. One was the 56th's deputy commander, Lt.Col David Schilling, who gained his 14th confirmed victory, while 1/Lt Charles Peal of the 78th gained his second. Peal was flying his 99th sortie in a Thunderbolt.

Stingy, 96BG leadship on 13 April had its hydraulics shot up and on return to base the undercarriage would not lower. Diverted to crash-land at Honington air depot where repairs could more easily be effected, the ball turret was first jettisoned. Lt Litowitz then 'bellied' the B-17 without crushing the chin turret and apart from bent propellers the bomber sustained little damage. *Stingy* again had to belly-in at Honington in late June and was put back in the air for a second time. (S. Evans)

The crumpled result of Don Gentile's ill-judged daisy-cutting buzz job to celebrate the completion of his last operational flight on 13 April. Despite his standing as top scoring fighter pilot ace with 23 air victories (then) his superiors were decidedly unhappy about the destruction of a hard come by $60,000 (£15,000) fighter in full view of pressmen.

13/14 APRIL 1944

8AF 302 NIGHT LEAFLET OPERATION – HOLLAND

	Despatched		Effective	Locality	No. of Leaflets	Losses
1BD				AMSTERDAM, THE HAGUE, EINDHOVEN		
B-17	422BS	5	4	2235–2252 hrs	800,000	0

15 APRIL 1944

8AF 303/VIII FC FO 299

Despatched		Groups	E/A	Losses MIA	E	Dam	Casualties KIA	WIA	MIA
P-38	132	20FG, 55FG, 364FG	7–0– 2	11	0	16	0	0	11
P-47	262	56FG, 78FG, 352FG, 353FG, 356FG, 359FG, 361FG	20–1–23	7	1	13	0	0	7
P-51	222	4FG, 352FG, 355FG, 357FG, 354FG (IX FC), 363FG (IX FC)	31–0–10	15	1	5	0	0	12
TOTALS:	616		18–1– 6 40–0–29 (G)	33	2	34	0	0	30

REMARKS: Strafing sweeps of central and western Germany, primary objective, airfields. 86 IX FC a/c participated under VIII FC control. 20FG, 78FG and 353FG were forced to abandon mission due to weather. 352FG flew a mixed formation of P-47s and P-51s. Fighter group e/a credits:– 4FG – 1, 55FG – 5, 352FG – 7, 355FG – 1, 364FG – 1. Fighter group losses:– 4FG – 3, 55FG – 3, 56FG – 3, 78FG – 2, 352FG – 3 (1 P-47 & 2 P-51), 355FG – 4, 357FG – 1, 361FG – 1, 364FG – 8, 354FG – 3, 363FG – 2. 19 of fighters lost victims of weather conditions. 352FG a/c down in sea, pilot rescued 3 days later. 2 4FG P-51 collided off Hook of Holland on penetration, 1 pilot rescued, 1 died. 363FG P-51 down in sea, pilot rescued. 1 MIA P-38 down in sea, pilot lost. 363FG P-51 cr. on return. 361FG P-47 Cat E.

17 APRIL 1944

8AF 304

	Despatched		Effective	Target	Bombs Tonnage	E/A	Losses MIA	E	Dam	Casualties KIA	WIA	MIA
2BD	B-24	15	14	WIZERNES V/S (P)	51.0	0	0	0	0	0	0	0

REMARKS: Groups participating: 2BD – 93BG, 467BG. Bomb types used: 1000GP. Experimental mission with 5 PFF a/c.

VIII FC FO 301

Despatched		Groups	E/A	Losses MIA	E	Dam	Casualties KIA	WIA	MIA
P-47	33	353FG	0	0	0	0	0	0	0

REMARKS: Fighter support, 8AF 304. After escort had become established B-24s fired on them.

17/18 APRIL 1944

8AF 305 NIGHT LEAFLET OPERATION – FRANCE

	Despatched		Effective	Locality	No. of Leaflets	Losses
1BD				RENNES, BREST, NANTES, LORIENT, ST.NAZAIRE		
B-17	422BS	5	5	2248–2258 hrs	1,480,000	0

18 APRIL 1944

8AF 306

	Despatched		Effective	Target	Bombs Tonnage	E/A	Losses MIA	E	Dam	Casualties KIA	WIA	MIA
1BD	B-17	280	275	ORANIENBURG/	171.0HE		3	0	90	0	0	29
				GERMANDORF A/I (P)	350.0IB							
				ORANIENBURG/								
				ANNAHOF A/I (P)								
				PERLEBERG A/F (O)								
				WITTENBERGE (O)								
				T/Os								
2BD	B-24	275	38	BRANDENBURG A/I (P)	183.0HE		2	0	20	0	5	20
			121	RATHENOW A/I (P)	396.0IB							
			12	CUXHAVEN (O)								
			7	WITTENBERGE (O)								
			70	T/Os								
3BD	B-17	221		ORANIENBURG/	191.0HE		14	0	94	2	12	139
				ANNAHOF A/I (O)	354.0IB							
			210	BRANDENBURG (O)								
				LÜNEBURG A/F (O)								
				RATHENOW (O)								
				T/Os								
TOTALS:		776	733		1645.0	13–5–6	19	0	204	2	17	188

REMARKS: Due to poor weather several units bombed T/Os in Berlin area. Groups participating:– 1BD – 91BG, 92BG, 303BG, 305BG, 306BG, 351BG, 379BG, 381BG, 384BG, 401BG, 457BG; 2BD – 44BG, 93BG, 389BG, 392BG, 445BG, 446BG, 448BG, 453BG, 458BG, 466BG, 467BG; 3BD – 94BG, 95BG, 96BG, 100BG, 385BG, 388BG, 390BG, 447BG, 452BG. Bomb types used: 500IB, 100GP, 100IB. Bomb group losses:– 94BG – 8, 96BG – 3, 303BG – 1, 351BG – 1, 381BG – 1, 390BG – 3, 392BG – 1, 458BG – 1. 1 390BG B-17 interned in Switzerland. 96BG B-17s lost were PFF a/c leading 94BG and 447BG – 4CBW became isolated from main 3BD Force and came under heavy fighter attack.

VIII FC FO 304

Despatched		Groups	E/A	Losses MIA	E	Dam	Casualties KIA	WIA	MIA
P-38	119	20FG, 55FG, 364FG	0–0– 0	1	3	7	0	0	0
P-47	296	56FG, 78FG, 353FG, 356FG, 359FG, 361FG	2–0– 1	1	0	3	0	0	1
P-51	219	4FG, 352FG, 355FG, 357FG, 354FG (IX FC), 363FG (IX FC)	18–0–12	3	0	18	0	0	3
TOTALS:	634		4–0– 1 16–0–12 (G)	5	3	28	0	0	4

REMARKS: Fighter support, 8AF 306. 76 IX FC a/c participated under VIII FC control. Fighter group e/a credits:– 4FG – 4, 356FG – 1. Fighter group losses:– 4FG – 3, 20FG – 1, 361FG – 1. 20FG P-38 abandoned over sea when an engine caught fire, pilot rescued, 18 mls from Dutch coast. On return, 55FG P-38 c/l near base and at Southwold, pilots safe; 20FG P-38 c/l Frostenden, pilot safe.

8AF 306

	Despatched		Effective	Target	Bombs Tonnage	E/A	Losses MIA	E	Dam	Casualties KIA	WIA	MIA
2BD	B-24	12	12	WATTEN V/S (P)	43.5	0–0–0	0	0	1	0	0	0

REMARKS: Groups participating: 2BD – 93BG, 446BG, 448BG. Bomb types used: 1000GP. Experimental mission with pathfinders.

VIII FC FO 304

Despatched		Groups	E/A	Losses MIA	E	Dam	Casualties KIA	WIA	MIA
P-47	36	365FG (IX FC)	0–0–0	0	0	0	0	0	0

REMARKS: Fighter support, 8AF 306 (Watten). 365FG flew under VIII FC control.

18/19 APRIL 1944

8AF 307 NIGHT LEAFLET OPERATION – NORWAY

	Despatched		Effective	Locality	No. of Leaflets	Losses
1BD				STAVANGER, OSLO, BERGEN, TRONDHEIM		
B-17	422BS	5	5	2336–0041 hrs	2,560,000	0

REMARKS: Leaflet 'bombs' used for the first time.

19 APRIL 1944

8AF 308

	Despatched		Effective	Target		Bombs Tonnage	E/A	Losses MIA	E	Dam	Casualties KIA	WIA	MIA
1BD	B-17	277	107	KASSEL/WALDAU A/I	(P)	433.5HE	1–0–4	5	0	119	1	5	47
			52	KASSEL/ BETTENHAUSEN A/I	(P)	181.1IB							
			53	ESCHWEGE A/F	(P)								
			54	KASSEL/ ALTENBAUNA A/I	(S)								
			4	LIMBURG	(O)								
			1	T/O									
3BD	B-17	246	122	LIPPSTADT A/F	(P)	402.5HE		0	0	21	2	8	55
			120	WERL A/F	(P)	168.0IB							
			1	T/O									
2BD	B-24	249	117	PADERBORN A/F	(P)	184.5HE		0	1	10	1	3	8
			62	GÜTERSLOH A/F	(P)	305.0IB							
			5	SOEST	(S)								
			8	KOBLENZ	(S)								
			12	BÜREN	(O)								
			26	T/Os									
TOTALS:		772	744			1674.6	1–0–4	5	1	150	4	16	110

REMARKS: Groups participating:– 1BD – 91BG, 92BG, 303BG, 305BG, 306BG, 351BG, 379BG, 381BG, 384BG, 401BG, 457BG; 3BD – 94BG, 95BG, 96BG, 100BG, 385BG, 388BG, 390BG, 447BG, 452BG; 2BD – 44BG, 93BG, 389BG, 392BG, 445BG, 446BG, 453BG, 458BG, 466BG, 467BG. Bomb types used:– 500GP, 100GP, 100IB. Bomb group losses:– 91BG – 3, 381BG – 2. On return a b/d 466BG B-24 c/l at Attlebridge.

VIII FC FO 305 and 306

Despatched		Groups	E/A	Losses MIA	E	Dam	Casualties KIA	WIA	MIA
P-38	127	20FG, 55FG, 364FG	0–0–0	0	0	0		0	0
P-47	439	56FG, 78FG, 352FG, 353FG, 356FG, 359FG, 361FG, 365FG (IX FC), 368FG (IX FC)	0–0–0	0	0	4		0	0
P-51	131	4FG, 352FG, 355FG, 357FG, 363FG (IX FC)	16–1–2	2	0	5		0	2
TOTALS:	697		16–1–2	2	0	9	0	0	2

REMARKS: Fighter support, 8AF 308. 84 IX FC a/c participated under VIII FC control. 352FG despatched P-51s on continuous support and P-47s for withdrawal cover. Fighter group e/a credit:– 4FG – 5, 352FG – 3, 355FG – 4, 357FG – 4. Fighter group losses:– 4FG – 1, 355FG – 1. P-51 groups encountered approx. 100 e/a.

8AF 308

	Despatched		Effective	Target	Bombs Tonnage	E/A	Losses MIA	E	Dam	Casualties KIA	WIA	MIA
2BD	B-24	27	27	WATTEN V/S (P)	77.5	0	1	0	0	0	0	0

REMARKS: Special PFF mission. Groups participating:– 2BD – 93BG, 448BG. Bomb types used:– 500GP. Bomb group losses:– 448BG – 1. 448BG B-24 ditched, 3 rescued.

Despatched		Groups	E/A	Losses MIA	E	Dam	Casualties KIA	WIA	MIA
P-47	47	405FG (IX FC)	0	0	0	0	0	0	0

REMARKS: Fighter support, 8AF 308 (Watten). 405FG flew under VIII FG control.

20 APRIL 1944

8AF 309

	Despatched		Effective	Target	Bombs Tonnage	E/A	Losses MIA	E	Dam	Casualties KIA	WIA	MIA
1BD	B-17	348	264	V/Ss PAS DE CALAIS & CHERBOURG (P)	869.0HE		3	0	182	1	5	30
			12	T/Os.								
3BD	B-17	282	174	V/S PAS DE CALAIS & CHERBOURG (P)	604.0HE		4	1	127	1	20	39
			7	T/Os								
2BD	B-24	212	113	V/Ss PAS DE CALAIS (P)	419.0HE		2	2	36	10	9	20
TOTALS:		842	570		1892.0		9	3	345	12	34	89

REMARKS: Groups participating: 1BD – 91BG, 92BG, 303BG, 305BG, 306BG, 351BG, 379BG, 381BG, 384BG, 401BG, 457BG; 3BD – 94BG, 95BG, 96BG, 100BG, 385BG, 388BG, 390BG, 447BG, 452BG; 2BD – 44BG, 93BG, 389BG, 392BG, 445BG, 446BG, 448BG, 453BG, 458BG, 466BG, 467BG. 24 V-weapon sites attacked, out of 33 briefed. Bomb types used:– 1000GP, 500GP. 453BG B-24s had an 8,000 lb bomb load. Bomb group losses:– 94BG – 1, 96BG – 1, 390BG – 1, 401BG – 2, 445BG – 1, 448BG – 1, 452BG – 1, 457BG – 1. 448BG B-24 and 452BG B-17 ditched N of Calais: a total of 6 crew members rescued. 388BG B-17 c/l on t/o, crew safe. 93BG B-24 cr. near Hawkinge A/F, 6 killed. B/d 445BG B-24 c/l Horham A/F.

VIII FC FO 307

	Despatched		Groups	E/A	Losses MIA	E	Dam	Casualties KIA	WIA	MIA
	P-38	89	20FG, 364FG	0–0–0	0	0	0	0	0	0
	P-47	211	56FG, 353FG, 356FG, 359FG, 361FG	1–0–1	0	0	0	0	0	0
	P-51	88	4FG, 352FG, 355FG	7–0–1	2	0	1	0	0	2
TOTALS:		388		4–0–2 4–0–0 (G)	2	0	1	0	0	2

REMARKS: Fighter support, 8AF 309. Fighter group e/a credits:– 56FG – 1, 352FG – 3, 355FG – 1. Fighter group losses:– 355FG – 2.

VIII FC FO 307

	Despatched		Groups	E/A	Losses MIA	E	Dam	Casualties KIA	WIA	MIA
	P-47	31	78FG	0–0–0	0	0	0	0	0	0
	P-51	35	357FG	0–0–0	0	0	0	0	0	0
TOTALS:		66		0–0–0	0	0	0	0	0	0

REMARKS: First 8AF P-51 fighter-bomber mission. 35 P-51s to be escorted by 31 P-47s, but P-47s were unable to locate P-51s. 33 a/c attacked Cambrai/Epinoy A/F dropping 16.5 tons. 1 a/c dropped 0.5 tons on Vitry A/F.

VIII FC FO 307

	Despatched		Groups	E/A	Losses MIA	E	Dam	Casualties KIA	WIA	MIA
	P-38	56	55FG	0	0	0	0	0	0	0
	P-47	36	78FG	0	0	0	0	0	0	0
TOTALS:		92		0	0	0	0	0	0	0

REMARKS: Fighter-bomber mission. 56 P-38s as fighter bombers escorted by 36 P-47s unable to bomb St.Trond A/F due to weather conditions.

20/21 APRIL 1944

8AF 310 NIGHT LEAFLET OPERATION – FRANCE

	Despatched		Effective	Locality	No. of Leaflets	Losses
1BD				NANTES, ORLEANS, PARIS, TOURS		
B-17	422BS	5	5	2238–2246 hrs	1,920,000	0

To publicise the forthcoming opening of the movie and theatre world supported London Stage Door Canteen for Allied servicemen, a Ridgewell B-17 was 'christened' with the name of this establishment on 21 April. Walking away from the aircraft are show business personalities Alfred Lunt and the gorgeous Vivienne Leigh. Sharing a joke with Subaltern Mary Churchill (the PM's daughter) is Maj Gen Fred Anderson, head of 8AF Operations.

21/22 APRIL 1944

801BG despatched 6 B-24s on *Carpetbagger* operations.

22 APRIL 1944

8AF 311

	Despatched		Effective	Target		Bombs Tonnage	E/A	Losses MIA	E	Dam	Casualties KIA	WIA	MIA
3BD	B-17	248	219	HAMM M/Y	(P)	458.0HE		5	1	66	0	6	55
			19	SOEST	(O)	122.0IB							
			1	T/O									
1BD	B-17	278	240	HAMM M/Y	(P)	723.0HE	0–0–0	3	0	72	0	1	34
			15	HAMM CITY	(S)	39.0IB							
			20	BONN	(O)								
2BD	B-24	277	179	HAMM M/Y	(P)	347.5HE		7	14	59	46	28	64
			50	KOBLENZ	(O)	294.0IB							
			36	T/Os									
TOTALS:		803	779			1983.5	20–6–8	15	15	197	46	35	153

REMARKS: Groups participating:– 3BD – 94BG, 95BG, 96BG, 100BG, 385BG, 388BG, 390BG, 447BG, 452BG; 1BD – 91BG, 92BG, 303BG, 305BG, 306BG, 351BG, 379BG, 381BG, 384BG, 401BG, 457BG; 2BD – 44BG, 93BG, 389BG, 392BG, 445BG, 446BG, 448BG, 453BG, 458BG, 466BG, 467BG. Bomb types used: 500GP, 500IB, 100GP, 100IB. 1,280,000 leaflets also released from bombers. Bomb group losses:– 91BG – 1, 100BG – 1, 303BG – 2, 385BG – 2, 389BG – 1, 390BG – 1, 392BG – 1, 445BG – 2, 447BG – 1, 448BG – 1, 453BG – 1, 458BG – 1. Bombers returned after dark and enemy fighters infiltrated stream resulting in 14 a/c wrecked by being shot down by e/a, or in c/ls. B/d 467BG B-24 cr. near Barsham, 7 k, 3 baled. 467BG B-24 s/d at Rackheath by intruders which also dropped bombs on this base. S/d 448BG B-24 cr. Worlingham after crew baled. 453BG B-24 cr. near Southwold, 5 baled, 4 killed, 1 missing. 448BG B-24 shot down at Kessingland. 2 458BG B-24s shot down near Horsham St.Faith, 9 killed, 5 wounded. 389BG B-24 c/l at Hethel, hitting signals hut and killing men inside, crew safe. 389BG B-24 shot down Cantley. 448BG B-24 shot down in sea off Hopton. 448BG B-24 shot up by intruder c/l on Seething runway and two following B-24s ran into it, all 3 wrecked. B/d 453BG B-24 Cat E at Tibenham A/F. Going out 305BG B-17 caught fire, 3 baled out and lost, a/c landed Bungay A/F, Cat E.

VIII FC FO 309

Despatched		Groups	E/A	Losses MIA	E	Dam	Casualties KIA	WIA	MIA
P-38	132	20FG, 55FG, 364FG		2	1			0	2
P-47	485	56FG, 78FG, 352FG, 353FG, 356FG, 359FG, 361FG, 362FG (IX FC), 365FG (IX FC), 368FG (IX FC)		5	0			0	4
P-51	242	4FG, 352FG, 355FG, 357FG, 358FG (IX FC), 363FG (IX FC),		6	0		0	1	6
TOTALS:	859		34–2–9 6–0–7 (G)	13	1	22	0	1	12

REMARKS: Fighter support, 8AF 311. 314 IX FC participated under VIII FC control. 20FG also despatched 8 P-38s to escort RAF Warwicks looking for ditched aircrews, early in the morning. 352FG despatched P-47s on penetration and P-51s to carry out sweeps. 356FG P-47s carried out dive bombing attack after escort duties, dropping 80 × 100IB. Fighter group e/a credits: 4FG – 14, 55FG – 3, 352FG – 1, 353FG – 1, 357FG – 2, 359FG – 7, 368FG – 4. Fighter group losses:– 4FG – 1, 55FG – 2, 352FG – 1, 353FG – 1, 359FG – 1, 361FG – 1, 362FG – 1, 363FG – 4, 368FG – 1. 353FG P-47 abandoned over sea off Suffolk coast, pilot rescued next day. Aborting 364FG P-38 cr. near base, pilot baled.

The sinking sun throws long shadows as 446BG leaves the Ruhr smoke screens (left) on 22 April. The group and others of 2nd Division would arrive home after dark and find the Luftwaffe there too. (J. Archer)

In the resulting pandemonium of the Luftwaffe intruder operation a new 389BG B-24J, 44-40085 *Z* was hit in the hydraulics by cannon shells and crash landed on blacked-out Hethel demolishing the radar building in which two men were billeted. Lt Foley's crew escaped, some rescued by Capt John Driscoll, group Armaments Officer, seen here silhouetted against the flames.

22/23 APRIL 1944

8AF 312 NIGHT LEAFLET OPERATION – FRANCE

	Despatched	Effective	Locality	No. of Leaflets	Losses
1BD			ORLEANS, TOURS, PARIS, NANTES, LILLE, REIMS, CHARTRES, ROUEN		
B-17	422BS 5	5	2251–2344 hrs	1,440,000	0

23 APRIL 1944

8AF 313/VIII FC FO 311

Despatched		Groups	E/A	Losses MIA	E	Dam	Casualties KIA	WIA	MIA
P-38	136	20FG, 55FG, 364FG	1–0– 1	2	2	2	0	0	2
P-47	166	78FG, 353FG, 356FG, 359FG, 361FG	7–0–22	5	0	19	0	0	5
P-51	80	352FG, 357FG	3–0– 1	0	0	2	0	0	0
TOTALS:	382		11–0–24 (G)	7	2	23	0	0	7

REMARKS: Fighter-bomber, *Droopsnoot* and strafing attacks in France, Belgium and Germany. 55FG bombing Laon A/F with 48 P-38s using *Droopshoot*, with 78FG as escort. 20FG bombing Tours A/F and Châteaudun A/F on *Droopsnoot*, with 352FG as escort. 357FG made dive bombing attack on A/F thought to have been Leningen. 359FG carried out dive bombing attack with 17 a/c and a further 17 as escort on Le Culot A/F. 361FG dive bombed Chievres and Denain/Prouvy A/Fs with 24 a/c and a further 16 as escort. 356FG carried out glide bombing and strafing attacks on Hagenau A/F. 353FG made sweeps and strafing attacks in NW Germany. 364FG despatched 36 a/c as escort to 8 Recon Wing a/c but turned back 10 miles from French coast due to R/T failure. Fighter group losses:– 20FG – 2, 353FG – 2, 356FG – 3. 20FG P-38 c/l – Cat E. 364FG P-38 cr. near base after m/f, pilot baled.

23/24 APRIL 1944

8AF 314 NIGHT LEAFLET OPERATION – FRANCE

	Despatched	Effective	Locality	No. of Leaflets	Losses
1BD			RENNES, BREST, LORIENT, ST.NAZAIRE, NANTES		
B-17	422BS 5	5	2354–0012 hrs	1,780,000	0

801BG despatched 9 B-24s on *Carpetbagger* operations.

The 384BG fell foul of enemy fighters on 24 April. One B-17 that didn't return attempted to make Switzerland but had to belly near Füssen in the shadow of the Alps. Local people took a great deal of interest in the wreck of the 'American terror fliers'. (Herr Radinger)

24 APRIL 1944

8AF 315

	Despatched		Effective	Target	Bombs Tonnage	E/A	Losses MIA	E	Dam	Casualties KIA	WIA	MIA
1BD	B-17	281	57	LANDSBERG A/F (P)	443.0HE		27		112	4	22	260
			84	OBERPFAFFENHOFEN A/I								
			109	ERDING A/D (P)								
			18	T/Os								
3BD	B-17	243	58	FRIEDRICHSHAFEN/ MANZELL A/I (P)	423.0HE		9		119	7	4	71
			55	FRIEDRICHSHAFEN I/A (P)	163.0IB							
			98	FRIEDRICHSHAFEN/ LÖWENTHAL A/I (P)								
			15	NECKARSULM I/A (S)								
			3	T/Os								
2BD	B-24	230	120	GABLINGEN A/F (P)	303.0HE		4		26	0	1	40
			98	LEIPHEIM A/F (P)	232.0IB							
			1	T/Os								
TOTALS:		754	716		1739.0	20–1–36	40	1	257	11	27	371

REMARKS: Groups participating:– 1BD – 91BG, 92BG, 303BG, 305BG, 306BG, 351BG, 379BG, 381BG, 384BG, 401BG, 457BG; 3BD – 94BG, 95BG, 96BG, 100BG, 385BG, 388BG, 390BG, 447BG, 452BG; 2BD – 93BG, 389BG, 392BG, 445BG, 446BG, 448BG, 453BG, 458BG, 466BG, 467BG. 44BG grounded because of an outbreak of ptomaine poisoning. 1 3BD group attacked Neckarsulm (S) because primary was obscured by smoke. Bomb types used:– 500GP, 100GP, 100IB. 480,000 leaflets also released. Bomb group losses:– 92BG – 5, 94BG – 1, 95BG – 2, 96BG – 1, 303BG – 3, 305BG – 1, 306BG – 10, 351BG – 1, 384BG – 7, 385BG – 1, 388BG – 2, 390BG – 1, 392BG – 2, 445BG – 1, 448BG – 1. 448BG B-24 in sea after hit by a runaway turret in another B-24, 6 saved by ASR. 13 B-17s (3 – 92BG, 1 – 94BG, 2 – 95BG, 2 – 303BG, 3 – 306BG, 2 – 384BG – 1 cr. in lake) and a 392BG B-24 down in Switzerland. 351BG B-17 down in sea off Ramsgate, 10 rescued. 385BG B-17 in sea off Dungeness, 3 rescued.

VIII FC FO 312

Despatched		Groups	E/A	Losses MIA	E	Dam	Casualties KIA	WIA	MIA
P-38	131	20FG, 55FG, 364FG	4–1–0	0	1	7		0	0
P-47	490	56FG, 78FG, 353FG, 356FG, 359FG, 361FG, 358FG (IX FC), 362FG (IX FC), 365FG (IX FC), 368FG (IX FC)	2–1–0 36–0–16(G)	5	0	15		0	5
P-51	246	4FG, 352FG, 355FG, 357FG, 354FG (IX FC), 363FG (IX FC)	64–4–2 21–0–20(G)	12	0	8		0	12
TOTALS:	867		58–0–38 (G) 66–6–20	17	1	30	0	0	17

REMARKS: Fighter support, 8AF 315. 306 IX FC a/c participated under VIII FC control. Fighter group e/a credits: 4FG – 18, 20FG – 4, 55FG – 1, 352FG – 1, 355FG – 19, 357FG – 22, 354FG – 3, 362FG – 2. Fighter group losses:– 4FG – 3, 352FG – 1, 353FG – 1, 355FG – 4, 356FG – 1, 357FG – 4, 362FG – 2, 365FG – 1. 55FG P-38 c/l near Manston.

24/25 APRIL 1944

8AF 316 NIGHT LEAFLET OPERATION – HOLLAND & FRANCE

	Despatched		Effective	Locality	No. of Leaflets	Losses
1BD				AMSTERDAM, ROTTERDAM, THE HAGUE, UTRECHT, LILLE, REIMS		
B-17	422BS	5	5	2322–2344 hrs	1,120,000	0

801BG despatched 8 B-24s on *Carpetbagger* operations.

25 APRIL 1944

8AF 317

	Despatched		Effective	Target		Bombs Tonnage	E/A	Losses MIA	E	Dam	Casualties KIA	WIA	MIA
2BD	B-24	199	7	MANNHEIM M/Y	(P)	61.2HE		5	0	26	1	4	49
			16	LANDAU M/Y (O)		16.0IB							
			8	T/Os									
1BD	B-17	229	42	NANCY/ESSAY A/F	(P)	238.5HE		2	0	33	1	3	20
			98	METZ/FRASCATY A/F	(P)	112.7IB							
			2	T/Os									
3BD	B-17	126	121	DIJON/LONGVIC A/F	(P)	297.8HE		0	0	29	0	2	0
						40.2IB							
TOTALS:		554	294			766.4	0–0–0	7	0	88	2	9	69

REMARKS: Groups participating:– 2BD – 93BG, 389BG, 445BG, 446BG, 448BG, 453BG, 458BG, 466BG, 467BG; 1BD – 91BG, 92BG, 303BG, 305BG, 306BG, 351BG, 379BG, 381BG, 384BG, 401BG, 457BG; 3BD – 95BG, 96BG, 100BG, 388BG, 390BG, 452BG. Bomb types used:– 500GP, 100IB, 120 Frag. Bomb group losses:– 381BG – 1, 448BG – 2, 453BG – 2, 457BG – 1, 458BG – 1. 3 B-24s interned in Switzerland (2 – 448BG, 1 – 453BG).

VIII FC FO 313

	Despatched		Groups	E/A	Losses MIA	E	Dam	Casualties KIA	WIA	MIA
	P-38	177	20FG, 55FG, 364FG	5–0–9	0	1	2	0	0	0
	P-47	296	56FG, 78FG, 353FG, 356FG, 359FG, 361FG	5–0–8	0	0	3	1	0	0
	P-51	246	4FG, 352FG, 355FG, 357FG, 354FG (IX FC), 363FG (IX FC)	24–7–26	2	1	1	0	0	2
TOTALS:		719		5–0–1 29–7–42 (G)	2	2	6	1	0	2

REMARKS: Fighter support, 8AF 317. 88 IX FC a/c participated under VIII FC control. 55FG P-38s bombed Amiens/Glisy A/F, using *Droopsnoot* method, prior to rendezvous with bombers on withdrawal. Fighter group e/a credits:– 78FG – 2, 359FG – 1, 354FG – 1. Fighter group losses:– 354FG – 2. Aborting 364FG P-38 pilot baled near Risby after m/f.

8AF 317

	Despatched		Effective	Target		Bombs Tonnage	E/A	Losses MIA	E	Dam	Casualties KIA	WIA	MIA
2BD	B-24	28	27	WIZERNES V/S	(P)	88.0	0–0–0	0	0	0	0	0	0

REMARKS: Groups participating: 2BD – 93BG, 392BG. Bomb types used:– 1000GP. Special operation using GH.

VIII FC FO 313

Despatched		Groups	E/A	Losses MIA	E	Dam	Casualties KIA	WIA	MIA
P-47	40	359FG	0	0	0	0	0	0	0

REMARKS: Fighter support, 8AF 317 (Wizernes).

25/26 APRIL 1944

8AF 318 NIGHT LEAFLET OPERATION – FRANCE

	Despatched		Effective	Locality	No. of Leaflets	Losses
1BD				20 towns incl. CALAIS, METZ, BLAINVILLE, PARIS, MULHOUSE,		
B-17	422BS	6	6	REIMS	4,200,000	0

801BG despatched 6 B-24s on *Carpetbagger* operations.

26 APRIL 1944

8AF 319

	Despatched		Effective	Target		Bombs Tonnage	E/A	Losses MIA	E	Dam	Casualties KIA	WIA	MIA
3BD	B-17	183	127	BRUNSWICK I/A	(S)	345.0HE		0	1	56	0	1	0
			47	HILDESHEIM/ HANNOVER AREA		86.0IB							
			4	T/Os (O)									
1BD	B-17	168	165	BRUNSWICK I/A	(S)	269.5HE		0	1	65	9	2	0
			1	T/O		110.0IB							
2BD	B-24	238	0	PADERBORN		0		0	0	18	1	0	0
TOTALS:		589	344			810.5	0–0–0	0	2	139	10	3	0

REMARKS: Groups participating:– 3BD – 94BG, 95BG, 96BG, 100BG, 385BG, 388BG, 447BG, 452BG; 1BD – 91BG, 92BG, 305BG, 306BG, 351BG, 381BG, 401BG, 457BG; 2BD – 93BG, 389BG, 392BG, 445BG, 446BG, 448BG, 453BG, 458BG, 466BG, 467BG. Lead a/c of last CW 3BD had fire which caused PFF failure, so bombs released in Hildesheim – Hannover area as T/O. Heavy overcast prevented all a/c from attacking primaries. B-24s failed to bomb because there were no PFF a/c in their formations. Bomb types used:– 1000GP, 500GP, 100IB. 306BG B-17 cr. near Thurleigh after t/o. 452BG B-17 cr. t/o, crew safe.

VIII FC FO 315

Despatched		Groups	E/A	Losses MIA	E	Dam	Casualties KIA	WIA	MIA
P-38	90	20FG, 364FG	0	1	0		0	0	1
P-47	311	56FG, 78FG, 353FG, 356FG, 359FG, 362FG (IX FC), 365FG (IX FC)	0	0	1		1	0	0
P-51	153	4FG, 352FG, 355FG, 354FG (IX FC)	0	4	0		0	0	4
TOTALS:	554		0	5	1	10	1	0	5

REMARKS: Fighter support, 8AF 319. 116 IX FC a/c participated under VIII FC control. Fighter group losses:– 355FG – 1, 364FG – 1, 354FG – 3. 364FG P-38 down in sea, pilot lost. On return a 356FG P-47 cr. at Bromeswell, pilot killed – mid-air collision; other a/c landed safely.

8AF 319

	Despatched		Effective	Target	Bombs Tonnage	E/A	Losses MIA	E	Dam	Casualties KIA	WIA	MIA
1BD	B-17	62	0	COLOGNE	0	0	0	0	0	0	0	0

REMARKS: Groups participating: 1BD – 303BG, 379BG, 384BG. Recalled at mid-Channel because of weather. First attempt to use 2000 lb glide bombs (*Grapefruit*) on external racks.

VIII FC FO 315

Despatched		Groups	E/A	Losses MIA	E	Dam	Casualties KIA	WIA	MIA
P-47	43	361FG	2–0–0	0	0	0	0	0	0
P-51	47	357FG	0–0–0	0	0	0	0	0	0
TOTALS:	90		2–0–0 (G)	0	0	0	0	0	0

REMARKS: Fighter support for 8AF 319 (Cologne). After bombers were recalled, escort carried out sweeps.

VIII FC FO 315

Despatched		Groups	E/A	Losses MIA	E	Dam	Casualties KIA	WIA	MIA
P-38	51	55FG	0	0	0	0	0	0	0

REMARKS: Fighter-bomber mission using *Droopsnoot* method. 33 P-38s as bombers, 20 as escort and 1 as PR attacking Le Mans A/F dropping 17.0 tons of 500GP bombs.

8AF 321

Despatched		Groups	E/A	Losses MIA	E	Dam	Casualties KIA	WIA	MIA
P-51	28	352FG	0	0	0	0	0	0	0

REMARKS: Fighter-bomber mission. 4 P-51s as escort, 24 dive-bombed Cormeilles-en-Vexin A/F dropping 11.7 tons of 500GP bombs.

26/27 APRIL 1944

8AF 320 NIGHT LEAFLET OPERATION – BELGIUM

	Despatched		Effective	Locality	No. of Leaflets	Losses
1BD				GHENT, ANTWERP, BRUSSELS, LIEGE, GOSSELIES		
B-17	422BS	5	5	2330–2358 hrs	800,000	0

A 458BG crew arrive at *Rhapsody In Junk* for their second mission of the day on 28 April. More hours of daylight enabled 8AF to do this on a number of occasions during the following weeks. Tanks are being topped off – a B-24 took 2814 US gallons.

27 APRIL 1944

8AF 322

	Despatched		Effective	Target		Bombs Tonnage	E/A	Losses MIA	E	Dam	Casualties KIA	WIA	MIA
1BD	B-17	206	133	V/Ss PAS DE CALAIS & CHERBOURG (P)		596.8HE		2	0	116	0	1	20
			18	V/Ss PAS DE CALAIS & CHERBOURG	(O)								
3BD	B-17	187	156	V/Ss PAS DE CALAIS & CHERBOURG (P)		619.3HE		1	0	111	0	6	10
2BD	B-24	203	160	V/Ss PAS DE CALAIS (P)		631.0HE		1	2	25	3	9	10
			9	V/Ss PAS DE CALAIS (O)									
TOTALS:		596	476			1847.1	0–0–0	4	2	252	3	16	40

REMARKS: Groups participating:– 1BD – 91BG, 92BG, 303BG, 305BG, 306BG, 351BG, 379BG, 381BG, 384BG, 401BG, 457BG; 3BD – 94BG, 95BG, 96BG, 100BG, 385BG, 388BG, 390BG, 447BG, 452BG; 2BD – 44BG, 93BG, 389BG, 392BG, 445BG, 446BG, 448BG, 453BG, 458BG, 466BG, 467BG. 25 V-weapon sites briefed, of which 21 were attacked and 5 others were attacked as T/Os because some squadrons had problems in picking up primaries in haze. Bomb types used:– 2000GP, 1000GP, 500GP. Bomb group losses:– 44BG – 1, 91BG – 1, 384BG – 1, 447BG – 1. On return 446BG B-24 c/l Cliftonville, Kent. B/d 44BG B-24 c/l base.

VIII FC FO 316

Despatched		Groups	E/A	Losses MIA	E	Dam	Casualties KIA	WIA	MIA
P-38	47	364FG	0–0–0	0	0	0	0	0	0
P-47	262	56FG, 78FG, 353FG, 359FG, 361FG	0–0–2	1	0	0	0	0	1
P-51	48	357FG	0–0–0	1	0	0	0	0	1
TOTALS:	357		0–0–2 (G)	2	0	0	0	0	2

REMARKS: Fighter support, 8AF 322. Fighter group losses:– 357FG – 1, 361FG – 1. 357FG P-51 MIA through engine failure.

27 APRIL 1944 (*contd.*)

VIII FC FO 316

Despatched		Groups	E/A	Losses MIA	E	Dam	Casualties KIA	WIA	MIA
P-38	54	55FG	0	0	0	0	0	0	0

REMARKS: Fighter bomber mission, using *Droopsnoot* method. 53 bombers with 2 a/c as escort, 52 attacked Roye Amy A/F dropping 51.5 tons of 1000GP bombs.

VIII FC FO 316

Despatched		Groups	E/A	Losses MIA	E	Dam	Casualties KIA	WIA	MIA
P-38	48	20FG	0	0	0	6	0	0	0

REMARKS: Fighter-bomber mission, using *Droopsnoot* method. Primary was obscured so 36 a/c attacked Albert/Meaulte A/F dropping 35.5 tons of 1000GP bombs. 1 squadron bounced by P-47s and forced to jettison bombs.

VIII FC FO 67 FW 20

Despatched		Groups	E/A	Losses MIA	E	Dam	Casualties KIA	WIA	MIA
P-51	28	352FG	0	0	0	0	0	0	0

REMARKS: Fighter-bomber mission. 23 P-51s as bombers of which 17 dive bombed Cormeilles-en-Vexin A/F dropping 7.75 tons.

8AF 323

	Despatched		Effective	Target		Bombs Tonnage	E/A	Losses MIA	E	Dam	Casualties KIA	WIA	MIA
2BD	B-24	198	72	CHALONS SUR MARNE M/Y (P)		556.7HE		0	2	22	24	6	1
			118	BLAINVILLE SUR L'EAU M/Y (P)									
1BD	B-17	168	103	NANCY/ESSAY A/F	(P)	371.6HE		2		33	0	0	20
			60	TOUL/CROIX DE METZ LANDING GROUND (P)		74.8IB							
3BD	B-17	120	98	LE CULOT A/F	(O)	264.5HE/Frag		2		29	1	0	20
			20	OSTEND/ MIDDELKERKE A/F (O)									
TOTALS:		486	471			1303.3		4	4	84	25	6	41

REMARKS: Groups participating: 2BD – 392BG, 445BG, 446BG, 448BG, 453BG, 458BG, 466BG, 467BG; 1BD – 92BG, 305BG, 306BG, 351BG, 379BG, 384BG, 401BG, 457BG; 3BD – 94BG, 100BG, 385BG, 447BG. Clouds prevented 3BD attacking primary or secondary. Bomb types used: 1000GP, 500GP, 100IB, 120 Frag. Bomb group losses:– 100BG – 1, 305BG – 2, 447BG – 1. 446BG B-24 cr. Flixton after t/o, 10 killed. On return, b/d 392BG B-24 cr. on cliffs at Westgate-on-Sea, 8 killed.

VIII FC FO 317

Despatched		Groups	E/A	Losses MIA	E	Dam	Casualties KIA	WIA	MIA
P-38	106	20FG, 55FG, 364FG	0–0–0	0	0	0	0	0	0
P-47	283	56FG, 78FG, 353FG, 356FG, 359FG, 361FG	6–0–2	4	0	2	0	0	2
P-51	154	4FG, 352FG, 355FG, 357FG	1–0–4	0	0	1	0	0	1
TOTALS:	543		3–0–1 4–0–5 (G)	4	0	3	0	0	3

REMARKS: Fighter support, 8AF 323. 1 squadron of 353FG P-47s dive bombed Florennes A/F, dropping 30 × 100GP bombs, during withdrawal support. Fighter group e/a credits:– 356FG – 4. Fighter group losses:– 356FG – 3, 361FG – 1.

27/28 APRIL 1944

8AF 324 NIGHT LEAFLET OPERATION – FRANCE

	Despatched		Effective	Locality	No. of Leaflets	Losses
1BD				23 towns incl.		
B-17	422BS	5	5	CAMBRAI, ORLEANS, RENNES, NANTES, BREST, TOURS, LORIENT, CAEN, LE MANS, LIMOGES, CHATEAUROUX	3,360,000	0

801BG despatched 21 B-24s on *Carpetbagger* operations. 1 B-24 MIA.

The silk streamers attached to these bombs were a leadplane signal to other bombardiers to salvo release all bombs at once. A smoke marker can also be seen (lower right). This particular drop by 379BG at Metz/Frescaty airfield, 28 April, resulted in a near ideal concentrated strike right on the hangar line.

28 APRIL 1944 A.M.

8AF 325

	Despatched		Effective	Target		Bombs Tonnage	E/A	Losses MIA	E	Dam	Casualties KIA	WIA	MIA
1BD	B-17	117	116	AVORD A/F	(P)	310.7	0	2	0	38	0	0	20

REMARKS: Groups participating: 91BG, 306BG, 351BG, 379BG, 381BG. Bomb types used: 1000GP, 300GP, 100IB, 100Frag. Bomb group losses:– 91BG – 1, 381BG – 1.

VIII FC FO 318

	Despatched		Groups		E/A	Losses MIA	E	Dam	Casualties KIA	WIA	MIA
	P-47	118	56FG, 78FG		0–0–2	0	0	0	0	0	0
	P-51	87	352FG, 357FG	8–0–3		2	0	2	0	0	2
TOTALS:		205			8–0–5 (G)	2	0	2	0	0	2

REMARKS: Fighter support, 8AF 325 (Avord). Fighter group losses:– 352FG – 1, 357FG – 1. 357FG P-51 MIA through engine failure.

8AF 325

	Despatched		Effective	Target		Bombs Tonnage	E/A	Losses MIA	E	Dam	Casualties KIA	WIA	MIA
3BD				SOTTEVAST V/S	(P)								
	B-17	106	18	& T/Os		54.0	0	2	0	47	0	3	21

REMARKS: Groups participating:– 94BG, 95BG, 100BG, 385BG, 390BG. Clouds prevented most bombers from bombing. Bomb types used: 1000GP. Bomb group losses:– 100BG – 2. 3 a/c attacked T/Os.

VIII FC FO 318

Despatched		Groups	E/A	Losses MIA	E	Dam	Casualties KIA	WIA	MIA
P-47	46	356FG	0	0	0	0	0	0	0

REMARKS: Fighter support, 8AF 325 (Sottevast V/S).

VIII FC FO 318

Despatched		Groups	E/A	Losses MIA	E	Dam	Casualties KIA	WIA	MIA
P-38	45	20FG	0	1		1	0	0	1

REMARKS: Fighter-bomber mission, using *Droopsnoot* method. 34 P-38s as bombers, all of which attacked Tours A/F dropping 17.0 tons of 1000GP bombs. Fighter group losses:– 20FG – 1.

VIII FC FO 318

	Despatched		Groups	E/A	Losses MIA	E	Dam	Casualties KIA	WIA	MIA
	P-38	52	55FG	0–0–0	0	0	1	0	0	0
	P-47	36	353FG	1–0–1 (G)	0	0	0	0	0	0
TOTALS:		88		1–0–1 (G)	0	0	1	0	0	0

REMARKS: Fighter-bomber mission. 55FG with 49 a/c as bombers attacked Châteaudun A/F, using *Droopsnoot* method, dropping 24.5 tons of 1000GP bombs. 353FG with 32 P-47s dive bombed the same target dropping 15.8 tons of 500GP.

28 APRIL 1944 P.M.

8AF 325

	Despatched		Effective	Target	Bombs Tonnage	E/A	Losses MIA	E	Dam	Casualties KIA	WIA	MIA
2BD	B-24	47	47	MARQUISE/ MIMOYECQUES V/S (P)	183.0	0	0	1	6	0	9	0

REMARKS: Groups participating:– 2BD – 93BG, 389BG, 466BG. Bomb types used:– 2000GP, 1000GP.

VIII FC FO 318

Despatched		Groups	E/A	Losses MIA	E	Dam	Casualties KIA	WIA	MIA
P-47	50	361FG	0	0	0	0	0	0	0

REMARKS: Fighter support, 8AF 325 (Marquise).

VIII FC FO 65FW 97

Despatched		Groups	E/A	Losses MIA	E	Dam	Casualties KIA	WIA	MIA
P-47	24	56FG	0	0	0	0	0	0	0

REMARKS: Fighter-bomber mission. 16 a/c as bombers, attacked an unidentified A/F near Paris dropping 24.0 tons of 500 lb fragmentation bombs, after they found their primary cloud-covered.

28/29 APRIL 1944

8AF 326 NIGHT LEAFLET OPERATION – FRANCE, BELGIUM, HOLLAND

	Despatched		Effective	Locality	No. of Leaflets	Losses
1BD B-17	422BS	5	5	17 towns incl. ANTWERP, BRUSSELS, PARIS, TOURS, LORIENT, NANTES, ORLEANS, ZWOLLE, LEEUWARDEN, TURNHOUT, AMERSFOORT	1,640,000	0

801BG despatched 21 B-24s on *Carpetbagger* operations.

29 APRIL 1944

8AF 327

	Despatched		Effective	Target		Bombs Tonnage	E/A	Losses MIA	E	Dam	Casualties KIA	WIA	MIA
3BD	B-17	218	158	BERLIN	(P)	291.0HE		28	0	0	4	20	260
			24	MAGDEBURG	(O)	188.0IB							
			10	BRANDENBURG	(O)								
			4	T/Os									
1BD	B-17	228	210	BERLIN	(P)	316.0HE 155.0IB		10	0	311	1	7	100
2BD	B-24	233	212	BERLIN	(P)	158.0HE 390.0IB		25	2	121	13	11	246
TOTALS:		679	618			1498.0	73–26–34	63	2	432	18	38	606

REMARKS: Groups participating:– 3BD – 94BG, 95BG, 96BG, 100BG, 385BG, 388BG, 390BG, 447BG, 452BG; 1BD – 91BG, 92BG, 303BG, 305BG, 306BG, 351BG, 379BG, 381BG, 384BG, 401BG, 457BG; 2BD – 44BG, 93BG, 389BG, 392BG, 445BG, 446BG, 448BG, 453BG, 458BG, 466BG, 467BG. 4CBW off course, strongly opposed by e/a, attacked Magdeburg as T/O. Bomb types used:– 1000GP, 500GP, 500IB, 100GP, 100IB. Bomb group losses: 44BG – 2, 91BG – 1, 92BG – 2, 94BG – 2, 95BG – 2, 303BG – 2, 306BG – 1, 384BG – 1, 385BG – 7, 388BG – 2, 389BG – 2, 390BG – 1, 392BG – 6, 401BG – 3, 446BG – 1, 447BG – 11, 448BG – 6, 452BG – 3, 453BG – 2, 458BG – 1, 466BG – 2, 467BG – 3. A shot-down B-24 cr. with bomb load into the Volkswagen factory near Fallersleben. 2 392BG B-24s collided whilst under fighter attack. 458BG B-24 interned in Sweden. On return 447BG B-17 ditched, crew rescued. 1 389BG B-24 PFF a/c ditched 23 miles off Gt Yarmouth, 7 rescued. 453BG B-24 ditched 39 miles off Orfordness, 9 saved; 452BG B-17 ditched, crew rescued; 44BG B-24 ditched, 10 rescued; on return 392BG B-24 abandoned and cr. Walcot, pilot killed; 392BG B-24 cr. near base, all killed. MIA 389BG PFF B-24 with 44BG.

VIII FC FO 320

				Losses			Casualties		
Despatched		Groups	E/A	MIA	E	Dam	KIA	WIA	MIA
P-38	117	20FG, 55FG, 364FG		3	0	7	0	0	2
P-47	463	56FG, 78FG, 353FG, 356FG, 359FG, 361FG, 358FG (IX FC), 362FG (IX FC)		0	1	16	0	1	0
P-51	234	4FG, 352FG, 355FG, 357FG, 354FG (IX FC), 363FG (IX FC)		10	0	7	0	0	10
TOTALS:	814		16–6–9 6–1–5 (G)	13	1	30	0	1	12

REMARKS: Fighter support, 8AF 327. 173 IX FC a/c participated under VIII FC control. 56FG flew two missions. Fighter group e/a credits:– 352FG–2, 355FG–1, 361FG–2, 354FG–6. Fighter group losses:– 4FG–2, 355FG–1, 364FG–3, 354FG–3, 363FG–4. 359 FG P-47 Cat E.

EVENT

For many months it had been policy for groups to despatch one or two bombers additional to the planned mission force, to take the place of any aircraft that had to abandon the mission due to mechanical or other problems before the formation left the English coast. These 'spares', if not required, would then return to base. General Doolittle considered this wasteful effort and at a commanders' meeting at *Pinetree* on 29 April he announced that henceforth there would be no spares. All bombers taking off would go on the mission.

29/30 APRIL 1944

8AF 328 NIGHT LEAFLET OPERATION – FRANCE & HOLLAND

	Despatched		Effective	Locality	No. of Leaflets	Losses
1BD				21 towns in Northern France and the Low Countries		
B-17	422BS	4	4		1,060,000	0

801BG despatched 14 B-24s on *Carpetbagger* operations.

30 APRIL 1944

8AF 329

	Despatched		Effective	Target		Bombs Tonnage	E/A	Losses MIA	E	Dam	Casualties KIA	WIA	MIA
1BD	B-17	116	114	LYON/BRON A/F	(P)	277.5HE		1	0	8	0	0	10
3BD	B-17	124	118	CLERMONT-FERRAND/ AULNAT A/F	(P)	294.5HE		0	0	9	0	0	0
2BD	B-24	55	52	SIRACOURT V/S	(P)	203.0HE		0	0	3	0	1	0
TOTALS:		295	284			775.0	3–0–6	1	0	20	0	1	10

REMARKS: Groups participating:– 1BD – 91BG, 92BG, 303BG, 305BG, 306BG, 379BG, 381BG, 401BG, 457BG; 3BD – 94BG, 96BG, 385BG, 388BG, 447BG, 452BG; 2BD – 93BG, 389BG, 445BG, 453BG. Bomb types used:– 1000GP. Bomb group losses:– 92BG – 1.

1/Lt Alvin Juchheim shot down two FW 190s on the last day of April. His gun camera film recorded the escape of the pilot of one as the 78FG ace closed for another burst.

30 APRIL 1944 *(contd.)*

VIII FC FO 321

Despatched		Groups	E/A	Losses MIA	E	Dam	Casualties KIA	WIA	MIA
P-38	128	20FG, 55FG, 364FG	0–0– 0	1	0	1	0	0	1
P-47	268	56FG, 78FG, 353FG, 356FG, 359FG, 361FG	9–1– 5	0	0	4	0	0	0
P-51	248	4FG, 352FG, 355FG, 357FG, 354FG (IX FC), 363FG (IX FC)	20–0–17	4	1	6	0	1	3
TOTALS:	644		18–1– 5 11–0–17 (G)	5	1	11	0	1	4

REMARKS: Fighter support, 8AF 329 and fighter-bomber attacks. 97 IX FC a/c participated under VIII FC control. 1 squadron of 353FG P-47s dive bombed Romorantin A/F dropping 14 × 100GP bombs, whilst on withdrawal support. Two P-38 groups despatched to Tours A/F, 20FG as bombers, 55FG as escort: 44 P-38s attacked dropping 35 × 1000GP using *Droopsnoot* and 4 × 500GP from low-level. After the attack these two groups carried out sweeps in support of 1BD & 3BD. 364FG gave continuous escort to the 2BD, the only escort for this division. Fighter group e/a credits:– 4FG – 1, 78FG – 4, 352FG – 2, 357FG – 9, 363FG – 1. Fighter group losses:– 4FG – 1, 20FG – 1, 357FG – 2, 363FG – 1. 357FG P-51 lost to accident, a/c came down in Channel, pilot rescued. On return 4FG P-51 c/l Manston A/F.

8AF 331 FO 66FW 59 & FO 67FW 21

Despatched		Groups	E/A	Losses MIA	E	Dam	Casualties KIA	WIA	MIA
P-38	46	20FG, 364FG	0	0	0	2	0	0	0
P-47	31	353FG	0	0	0	3	0	0	0
P-51	51	339FG	0	0	0	0	0	0	0
TOTALS:	128		0	0	0	5	0	0	0

REMARKS: Fighter-bomber attacks. 20FG attacked Orleans/Bricy A/F, with 22 a/c using *Droopsnoot* method, dropping 6.9 tons of frag bombs. Escort for 20FG was provided by 364FG. 353FG dive bombed this same target, shortly after the P-38s with 21 a/c dropping 14.5 tons of GP and frag bombs. 5 further 353FG P-47s attacked a V-weapon site as T/O. 339FG, flying its first mission, swept the area prior to the fighter-bomber attacks. A 20FG P-38 damaged by dirt and debris from an exploding bomb dropped by a dive bombing P-47. Another 20FG P-38 struck by bomb dropped by a preceding a/c, which came through the propeller and hit the inside of the engine nacelle, a/c returned safely.

30 APRIL/1 MAY 1944

8AF 330 NIGHT LEAFLET OPERATION – FRANCE, BELGIUM & HOLLAND

	Despatched		Effective	Locality	No. of Leaflets	Losses
1BD B-17	422BS	4	4	21 towns incl. ZWOLLE, HALA, ALOST, LOUVAIN, LEEUWARDEN, REIMS, METZ, STRASBURG, EPINAL, TOURS. SAARGUEMINES MULHOUSE, TROYES, ORLEANS	2,230,000	0

801BG despatched 20 B-24s on *Carpetbagger* operations.

1 MAY 1944

8AF 332 CROSSBOW Targets

	Despatched		Effective	Target		Bombs Tonnage	E/A	Losses MIA	E	Dam	Casualties KIA	WIA	MIA
1BD	B-17	161	18	POIX A/F	(O)	47.5	0	0	0	20	0		0
			15	MONTDIDIER A/F	(O)	44.0	0	0	1	0	0		0
			18	ROYE/AMY A/F	(O)	54.0	0	0	0	0	0		0
2DB	B-24	183	57	PAS DE CALAIS	(P)	222.0	0	0	1	15	5		0
3BD	B-17	187	22	PAS DE CALAIS	(P)	61.75	0	0	1	19	0		9
TOTALS:		531	130			429.25HE	0–0–0	0	3	54	5	7	9

REMARKS: Weather frustrated all but three attacks on 23 V-sites briefed. Groups participating:– 1BD – 92BG, 303BG, 305BG, 306BG, 351BG, 379BG, 384BG, 401BG, 457BG; 2BD – 93BG, 389BG, 445BG, 446BG, 448BG, 453BG, 466BG, 467BG; 3BD – 94BG, 95BG, 96BG, 100BG, 385BG, 388BG, 390BG, 447BG, 452BG. A 92BG B-17 cr. Hawkinge on return. 93BG B-24 c/l on t/o, 5 killed. B/d 385BG B-17 c/l Mendlesham after all crew except pilot baled over France.

VIII FC FO 322

	Despatched		Groups	E/A	Losses MIA	E	Dam	Casualties KIA	WIA	MIA
	P-47	119	356FG, 359FG, 361FG	0–0–0	0	0	0	0	0	0
	P-51	90	352FG, 357FG	0–0–0	0	0	0	0	0	0
TOTALS:		209		0–0–0	0	0	0	0	0	0

REMARKS: Escort for 8AF 332. Additionally 36 P-51s of 339FG flew a sweep to the Belgian coast for orientation.

8AF 333

	Despatched		Effective	Target		Bombs Tonnage	E/A	Losses MIA	E	Dam	Casualties KIA	WIA	MIA
1BD	B-17	110	52	TROYES M/Y	(P)	158.0		1	0	52	0		10
			57	REIMS M/Y	(P)	168.0							
2BD	B-24	151	59	BRUSSELS M/Y	(P)	254.0		0	0	21	0		0
			40	LIEGE M/Y	(P)	157.0							
3BD	B-17	125	42	METZ M/Y	(P)	124.5		2	1	43	0		20
			13	BRUSSELS M/Y	(P)	39.0							
			64	SAARGUEMINES M/Y	(P)	192.0							
TOTALS:		386	328			1092.5HE	0	3	1	116	0	4	30

REMARKS: Visual bombing. Groups participating:– 1BD – 91BG, 92BG, 305BG, 306BG, 351BG, 379BG, 381BG, 384BG; 2BD – 44BG, 93BG, 389BG, 392BG, 445BG, 446BG, 448BG, 453BG, 458BG, 466BG, 467BG; 3BD – 95BG, 96BG, 100BG, 388BG, 390BG, 452BG. Bomb group losses:– 91BG – 1, 96BG – 1, 452BG – 1. B/d 452BG B-17 c/l base on return, crew safe.

VIII FC FO 323

	Despatched		Groups	E/A	Losses MIA	E	Dam	Casualties KIA	WIA	MIA
	P-38	120	20FG, 55FG, 364FG		2		0	0	0	0
	P-47	272	56FG, 78FG, 353FG, 356FG, 359, 361FG	1–0–1	0		4	0	0	4
	P-51	166	4FG, 352FG, 355FG, 357FG	5–0–2	1	0	1	0	0	0
TOTALS:		558		6–0–3	3	0	5	0	0	4

REMARKS: Fighter support 8AF 333. Total fighter sorties despatched on 1 May were 761 (118 P-38, 371 P-47 and 272 P-51) which included units of IX FC under VIII FC control. Fighter group e/a credits:– 4FG – 4, 355FG – 1, 361FG – 1. Fighter Groups losses:– 20FG – 2, 355FG – 1.

1/2 MAY 1944

8AF 334 NIGHT LEAFLET OPERATION

	Despatched		Effective	Country	No. of Leaflets	Losses	Dam
1BD	B-17	5	5	FRANCE & HOLLAND	1,550,000	0	

REMARKS: Leaflets dropped over 25 towns.

801BG despatched 25 B-24s on *Carpetbagger* operations.

2 MAY 1944

8AF 335

	Despatched		Effective	Target		Bombs Tonnage	E/A	Losses MIA	E	Dam	Casualties KIA	WIA	MIA
2BD	B-24	50	50	PAS DE CALAIS V/S	(P)	197.0	0	0	0	0	0	0	0

REMARKS: GH attack on *Crossbow* targets. Groups participating: 93BG, 389BG, 445BG, 453BG.

VIII FC FO 324

	Despatched		Groups	E/A	Losses MIA	E	Dam	Casualties KIA	WIA	MIA
	P-47	50	361FG	0	0	0	0	0	0	0
	P-51	52	339FG	0	0	0	0	0	0	0
TOTALS:		102		0	0	0	0	0	0	0

REMARKS: Escort for 8AF 335.

3 MAY 1944

8AF 336

	Despatched		Effective	Target		Bombs Tonnage	E/A	Losses MIA	E	Dam	Casualties KIA	WIA	MIA
2BD	B-24	51	47	PAS DE CALAIS V/S	(P)	173.0	0	0	0	33	0	3	0

REMARKS: GH attack on V-sites at Wizernes. Led by 6 93BG PFF a/c. Groups participating: 93BG, 44BG, 392BG.

VIII FC FO 325

Despatched		Groups	E/A	Losses MIA	E	Dam	Casualties KIA	WIA	MIA
P-47	48	78FG	0	0	0	0	0	0	0
P-51	53	339FG	0	0	0	0	0	0	0

REMARKS: Escort for 8AF 336.

3/4 MAY 1944

8AF 337 NIGHT LEAFLET OPERATION

	Despatched		Effective	Country	No. of Leaflets	Losses	Dam
NLS	B-17	5	5	FRANCE, BELGIUM and HOLLAND	960,000	0	1

REMARKS: Leaflets dropped over 26 localities. 1 B-17 intercepted by night fighter received slight damage.

801BG despatched 9 B-24s on *Carpetbagger* operation.

Leading ace Capt 'Bob' Johnson climbing into the cockpit of his personal P-47 on a 62FS dispersal pad at Boxted, 4 May. At this date he had 25 confirmed victories and four days later would claim two more. The contrast in size between pilot and P-47 shows well in this unusual view.

4 MAY 1944

8AF 338

	Despatched		Effective	Target		Bombs Tonnage	E/A	Losses MIA	E	Dam	Casualties KIA	WIA	MIA
1BD	B-17	360	40	BERGEN/ ALKMAAR A/F	(O)	116.0	0	0	1	15	2	1	0
2BD	B-24	231	0				0	0	0	0	0	0	0
TOTALS:		591	40			116.0	0	0	1	15	2	1	0

REMARKS: Mission to Berlin, Brunswick and targets in central Germany frustrated by cirrus clouds between 13,000 and 23,000 ft., mission recalled. Only 41 CBW attacked a T/O visible through break in clouds. Groups penetrating:– 1BD – 303BG, 305BG, 306BG, 351BG, 379BG, 384BG, 401BG, 457BG; 2BD – 392BG, 448BG, 458BG, 466BG, 467BG. B/d B-17 c/l on return.

VIII FC FO 326

Despatched		Groups		E/A	Losses MIA	E	Dam	Casualties KIA	WIA	MIA
P-38	50	20FG			0	0	1	0	0	0
P-47	179	56FG, 356FG, 359FG,	361FG	8–2–5	2	3	8	0	1	2
P-51	287	4FG, 339FG, 352FG, 355FG, 354FG (IX FC), 363FG (IX FC)		1–0–1	1	2	0	0	0	1
TOTALS:	516			9–2–6	3	5	9	0	1	3

REMARKS: Escort for 8AF 338. P-51 force included 95 a/c of IX FC under VIII FC control. Fighter group e/a credits:– 56FG – 3, 355FG – 1, 356FG – 6. Fighter group losses:– 355FG – 1, 356FG – 2. On return, A 357FG P-51 c/l, pilot safe. 363FG P-51 cr. near Manston, pilot baled. 56FG P-47s c/l Orford and Beaumont, out of fuel. 356FG P-47 c/l, pilot injured.

5 MAY 1944

8AF 339

	Despatched		Effective	Target		Bombs Tonnage	E/A	Losses MIA	E	Dam	Casualties KIA	WIA	MIA
2BD	B-24	46	33	SOTTEVAST	(P)	76.5	0	0	1	6	4	0	0

REMARKS: A GH lead attack on Sottevast V-site but bombed by visual means when PFF equipment failed. Groups participating: 93BG(PFF), 458BG, 466BG, 467BG. On return a b/d 458BG B-24 c/l Odiham, 4 killed.

VIII FC FO 327

Despatched		Groups	E/A	Losses MIA	E	Dam	Casualties KIA	WIA	MIA
P-51	52	339FG	0	0	0	0	0	0	0

REMARKS: Escort for 8AF 339.

5/6 MAY 1944

801BG despatched 21 B-24s on *Carpetbagger* operations. 1MIA.

6 MAY 1944

8AF 340

	Despatched		Effective	Target		Bombs Tonnage	E/A	Losses MIA	E	Dam	Casualties KIA	WIA	MIA
1BD	B-17	90	0	PAS DE CALAIS V/S		0	0	0	0	48	0	0	0
2BD	B-24	78	70	SIRACOURT V/S	(P)	261.5	0	0	0	0	0	0	0
TOTALS:		168	70			261.5	0	0	0	48	0	0	0

REMARKS: *Noball* targets. 1BD force returned with bombs due to cloud obscuring objectives – 2BD bombed on marker flares released by 93BG GH B-24s. Groups participating: 2BD – 93BG, 446BG, 448BG, 453BG. B-17 encountered Flak over Alderney. First mission of 398BG.

VIII FC FO 328

Despatched		Groups		E/A	Losses MIA	E	Dam	Casualties KIA	WIA	MIA
P-38	57	474FG (IX FC)		0	0	0	0	0	0	0
P-47	47	56FG	0	0	0	0	0	0	0	0
P-51	81	339FG, 359FG		0	0	0	0	0	0	0
TOTALS:	185		0	0	0	0	0	0	0	0

REMARKS: Escort and support 8AF 340. 57 IX FC P-38 participated under VIII FC control. 359FG flying first P-51 operation.

INCIDENT

Launching a bomber mission was a highly complex operation demanding precise planning and execution at every stage from receipt of the mission alert to the departure of the last aircraft. The battle experienced stations had developed a regular routine to ensure smooth functioning; something a new group often had difficulty in achieving during its initial fling. An example of how a seemingly minor lapse could escalate to a grand foul-up occurred on 6 May when the 398th Bomb Group entered combat. In the excitement of preparations the Duty Operations Officer in the operations room forgot to alert the kitchen staff. In consequence when briefing time arrived the crews hadn't been fed. From then on one problem followed another. Briefing was late and hurried. There was a traffic jam in the equipment room. Not all aircraft were loaded with bombs. The crews didn't have time to co-ordinate signals and other operational details before going out to their bombers. The truck transportation to the dispersals failed to materialise, leaving many crews to wander around the airfield on foot trying to locate their charges for the mission. In spite of everything, the 398th was determined to go to war. Some B-17s took off with incomplete bomb loads, others with makeshift crews. Several taking off too late to assemble on the group leader made their own formations and joined any group they could find. But they bombed *Noball* targets and all came back. Col Hunter, the CO, and his staff painstakingly sought the cause of each miscarriage and took steps to see that there was no repetition. Next day everything went smoothly, which was just as well as the 398th was pushed right in the deep end – Berlin. All came back.

The 3rd Strategic Air Depot was noted for some ingenious ideas. To strengthen the damaged fuselage of 44BG B-24H 42-50328 for a flight from Shipdham to Watton for repairs, a telegraph pole was placed along the bomb-bay catwalk and braced against the bulkhead with a jack (bottom of photo): 10 June. (W. Noble)

6/7 MAY 1944

8AF 341 NIGHT LEAFLET OPERATION

	Despatched		Effective	Country	No. of Leaflets	Losses	Dam
NLS	B-17	5	5	FRANCE & BELGIUM	3,220,000	0	1

REMARKS: Leaflets dropped in 19 locations. One B-17 b/d in action with night fighters. Claimed a probably destroyed e/a.

801BG despatched 22 B-24s on *Carpetbagger* operations.

7 MAY 1944

8AF 342

	Despatched		Effective	Target		Bombs Tonnage	E/A	Losses MIA	E	Dam	Casualties KIA	WIA	MIA
1BD	B-17	330	283	BERLIN	(P)	700.5	0	6	1	185	1	4	57
			31	T/O		82.5							
3BD	B-17	270	231	BERLIN	(P)	546.0	0	2	1	80	7	10	26
			8	T/O		15.5							
TOTALS:		600	553			1344.5	0	8	2	265	8	14	83

REMARKS: PFF attack on Berlin. Groups participating: 1BD – 91BG, 92BG, 303BG, 305BG, 306BG, 351BG, 379BG, 381BG, 384BG, 398BG, 401BG, 457BG; 3BD – 94BG, 95BG, 96BG, 100BG, 385BG, 388BG, 390BG, 447BG, 452BG. Bomb group losses:– 91BG – 1, 96BG – 1, 351BG – 1, 379BG – 2, 384BG – 1, 385BG – 1, 401BG – 1. B/d 303BG B-17 wrecked in c/l. During assembly 100BG B-17 cr. Herringfleet, 5 k.

	Despatched		Effective	Target		Bombs Tonnage	E/A	Losses MIA	E	Dam	Casualties KIA	WIA	MIA
2BD	B-24	322	147	MÜNSTER	(P)	412.0	0	0	1	22	1	2	6
			165	OSNABRÜCK	(P)	446.0	1	1					
TOTALS:		322	312			858.0	0	1	1	22	1	2	6

REMARKS: PFF/GH attacks. Groups participating: 2BD – 44BG, 93BG, 389BG, 392BG, 445BG, 446BG, 448BG, 453BG, 458BG, 466BG, 467BG. B/d 389BG B-24 ditched in sea on return, 2 rescued.

VIII FC FO 329

Despatched		Groups	E/A	Losses MIA	E	Dam	Casualties KIA	WIA	MIA
P-38	153	20FG, 55FG, 364FG		2	0	5	0	0	1
P-47	317	56FG, 78FG, 356FG, 361FG		1	0	3	0	0	1
P-51	284	4FG, 339FG, 352FG, 355FG, 357FG		1	1	1	0	0	1
TOTALS:	754		0	4	1	9	0	0	3

REMARKS: Escort and support for 8AF 342 morning missions to Germany. Additionally 82 P-51s of IX FC (354FG and 363FG) and 47 RAF Mustangs flew in support of this force. No encounters with e/a. Fighter group losses:– 55FG – 1, 339FG – 1, 356FG – 1, 364FG – 1. The 55FG P-38 lost ditched near Felixstowe, pilot rescued. A 339FG P-51 cr. near base, pilot safe.

VIII FC FO 329

	Despatched		Effective	Target		Bombs Tonnage	E/A	Losses MIA	E	Dam	Casualties KIA	WIA	MIA
3BD	B-24	67	29	LIEGE M/Y	(P)	84.5	0	0	0	0	0	0	0

REMARKS: First missions of 486BG and 487BG. Assembly abortive in morning and second attempt in afternoon. Cloud prevented part of force from bombing. Visual sighting by some squadrons but target missed. (7 May was the first day over 900 8AF bombers attacked targets and only the second time on which over 1000 were airborne for ops.)

VIII FC FO 330

Despatched		Groups	E/A	Losses MIA	E	Dam	Casualties KIA	WIA	MIA
P-47	24	56FG	0	0	0	0	0	0	0
P-51	51	339FG	0	0	0	0	0	0	0

REMARKS: Support for Liège Force.

7/8 MAY 1944

8AF 343 NIGHT LEAFLET OPERATION

Despatched	Effective	Country	No. of Leaflets	Losses	Dam
4	3	FRANCE	1,600,000	0	0

REMARKS: Leaflets dropped on 16 localities in central France.

801BG despatched 14 B-24s on *Carpetbagger* operations.

8 MAY 1944

8AF 344

	Despatched		Effective	Target		Bombs Tonnage	E/A	Losses MIA	E	Dam	Casualties KIA	WIA	MIA
1BD	B-17	500	386	BERLIN	(P)	892.0		25	1	169	1	7	261
&			36	BRUNSWICK	(L)	90.0							
3BD			8	MAGDEBURG–	(L)	18.5							
			6	BRUNSWICK		11.5							
			17	BRANDENBURG	(L)	42.0							
2BD	B-24	307	288	BRUNSWICK	(P)	794.5		11	7	28	7	8	112
			1	T/O		2.5							
TOTALS:		807	742			1851.0	76–16–16	36	8	197	8	15	373

REMARKS: PFF bombing. The 45CBW became separated from Berlin force and came under heavy attack from e/a, subsequently attacking Brunswick. 14 B-17s bombed T/Os in Brunswick area. Bomb types used:– 500GP, 1000GP, 100IB, 500IB. Leading B-24s (2CBW) came under heavy fighter attack. Groups participating:– 1BD – 91BG, 92BG, 303BG, 305BG, 306BG, 351BG, 379BG, 381BG, 384BG, 398BG, 401BG, 457BG; 2BD – 44BG, 93BG, 389BG, 392BG, 445BG, 446BG, 448BG, 453BG, 458BG, 466BG, 467BG; 3BD – 94BG, 95BG, 96BG, 100BG, 385BG, 388BG, 390BG, 447BG, 452BG. Bomb group losses:– 92BG – 1, 306BG – 5, 401BG – 1. 2BD – 445BG – 2, 453BG – 8, 467BG – 1. 3BD – 96BG – 10, 100BG – 1, 385BG – 1, 388BG – 2, 390BG – 3, 452BG – 1. The 92BG and 1 306BG B-17 cr. Sweden. 96BG B-17 lost in collision with FW 190. 448BG B-24 c/l Woodbridge A/F after explosion of Frag bomb in a/c. On return b/d 453BG B-24 cr. Morningthorpe, b/d 453BG B-24 c/l Watton A/F crew safe; 466BG B-24 c/l Rivenhall A/F, 2 men baled over Germany; b/d 44BG B-24 cr. Halvergate, 2 k; b/d 452BG B-17 cr. into truck at base, driver killed; b/d 467BG B-24 c/l Walton. 458BG B-24 cr. t/o Frettenham, 4 k.

VIII FC FO 331

Despatched		Groups	E/A	Losses MIA	E	Dam	Casualties KIA	WIA	MIA
P-38	152	20FG, 55FG, 364FG	6–0– 3	4	0	0	0	0	4
P-47	295	56FG, 78FG, 353FG, 356FG, 361FG	9–1– 5	4	1	3	0	1	4
P-51	282	4FG, 339FG, 352FG, 355FG, 357FG, 359FG	40–3–12	5	1	1	0	0	5
TOTALS:	729		55–4–20	13	2	4	0	1	13

REMARKS: Additional to above totals, IX FC provided 76 P-51s (354FG & 363FG) and 50 P-38s (474FG) with loss of 1 354FG P-51 and claims of 4–0–2. After escort some VIII FC units strafed T/Os. Fighter group e/a credits:– 56FG – 6, 353FG – 21, 357FG – 3, 359FG – 10, 361FG – 3, 364FG – 4, 354FG – 4. Fighter group losses:– 20FG – 1, 56FG – 1, 78FG – 1, 352FG – 1, 357FG – 2, 359FG – 2, 361FG – 2, 364FG – 3. 56FG P-47 and 355FG P-51 Cat E.

8AF 345

	Despatched		Effective	Target		Bombs Tonnage	E/A	Losses MIA	E	Dam	Casualties KIA	WIA	MIA
1BD	B-17	101	92	GLACERIE V/S	(P)	238.0	0	5	1	29	0	0	28
& 3BD				SOTTEVAST V/S	(P)								
3BD	B-24	63	57	BRUSSELS/ SCHAERBECK M/Y	(P)	163.5	0	0	0	29	2	2	19
TOTALS:		164	149			401.5	0	5	1	58	2	2	47

REMARKS: P.M. mission. B-17s bombed by GH and visual, B-24s visual. Groups participating:– 1BD – 303BG, 379BG, 384BG (Sottevast); 3BD – 95BG, 96BG, 100BG, 388BG, 390BG, 452 BG (Glacerie), 486BG, 487BG. Bomb group losses:– 384BG – 3, 388BG – 1, 390BG – 1. B/d 384BG B-17 ditched 60 miles from Thorney Island, 2 saved. On return a B-17 c/l.

VIII FC FO 332

Despatched		Groups	E/A	Losses MIA	E	Dam	Casualties KIA	WIA	MIA
P-47	97	78FG, 353FG	0	0	0	0	0	0	0

REMARKS: Escort and support for 8AF 345.

INCIDENT

The value of *Carpet*, the electronic device for jamming the Würzburg range-seeking radars of the German flak batteries, was well illustrated by the outcome of the two raids on Berlin early in May 1944. An identical approach course to the city was flown by B-17 formations on both days, but on the first *Carpet* was not used and on the following day it was. A subsequent survey showed that flak fragment hits were over twice as numerous on the 7 May raid than on the 8th, even though the B-17 formations had only taken 10 minutes to cross the target area on the 7th while taking 14 minutes on the 8th. *Carpet* equipment was being installed in a number of bombers in at least two groups of each combat wing. First used by the 8th Air Force in October 1943, the device was basically a powerful transmitter that operated on the same frequencies as the flak radar. It was found that its use offered some protection to formations flying as far as half a mile from the jamming aircraft.

Over Cherbourg, 8 May, a flak burst made a direct hit on the tail gun position of *Forbidden Fruit*, blasting it completely away and killing the gunner. Capt Edward Skurka put the 452BG cripple down on Rattlesden where it overran and came to rest in a meadow.

Over the Pas de Calais on 8 May 379BG's *Patches* shed a propeller which cartwheeled back and embedded itself in wing and fuselage. One blade penetrated the side of the radio room narrowly missing the radio operator's head. Back at base, crew chief M/Sgt James L. Smith surveys the damage.

8/9 MAY 1944

8AF 346 NIGHT LEAFLET OPERATION

Despatched	Effective	Country	No. of Leaflets	Losses	Dam
4	3	FRANCE	1,600,000	0	

REMARKS: Leaflets dropped at 10 locations.

801BG despatched 15 B-24s on *Carpetbagger* operations.

9 MAY 1944

8AF 347

	Despatched		Effective	Target		Bombs Tonnage	E/A	Losses MIA	E	Dam	Casualties KIA	WIA	MIA
1BD	B-17	220	37	THIONVILLE M/Y	(P)	91.0		0	0	38	0	0	0
			53	THIONVILLE A/F	(P)	93.0							
			75	ST.DIZIER A/F	(P)	140.0							
			53	LUXEMBOURG M/Y	(P)	133.0							
2BD	B-24	290	96	FLORENNES A/F	(P)	200.0		2	0	13	1	1	44
			101	ST.TROND A/F	(P)	227.0		2	0				
			63	LIEGE M/Y	(P)	224.0							
			10	NIVELLES A/F	(O)	26.0							
			6	HODY A/F	(O)	12.0							
3BD	B-17	242	71	JUVINCOURT A/F	(P)	151.0							
			113	LAON/ATHIES A/F	(P)	117.0		2	0	44	1	1	20
			43	LAON/COUVRON A/F	(P)	79.0							
			10	LILLE/VENDEVILLE A/F	(O)	19.0							
			1	CHIEVRES A/F	(O)	2.0							
3BD	B-24	71	68	LAON/COUVRON A/F	(P)	164.0		0	1	22	1	0	0
TOTALS:		823	802			1678.0	0	6	1	117	3	2	64

REMARKS: Visual attacks. Start of the pre-invasion bombing of enemy installations in France. Bomb types used:– 100GP, 500GP, 1000GP, 100IB. Groups participating:– 1BD – 91BG, 92BG, 303BG, 305BG, 306BG, 351BG, 379BG, 381BG, 384BG, 398BG, 401BG, 457BG; 2BD – 44BG, 93BG, 389BG, 392BG, 445BG, 446BG, 448BG, 453BG, 458BG, 466BG, 467BG; 3BD – 94BG, 95BG, 96BG, 100BG, 385BG, 388BG, 390BG, 447BG, 452BG, 486BG, 487BG. Bomb group losses:– 2BD – 389BG – 1, 448BG – 1, 453BG – 1, 466BG – 1. 3BD – 94BG – 1, 447BG – 1. B/d 389BG B-24 ditched 20 mls off Ramsgate, 2 saved. B/d 447BG B-17 ditched 22 mls SE Dungeness, 7 rescued. B/d 446BG B-24 c/l base on return.

VIII FC FO 333

	Despatched		Groups	E/A	Losses MIA	E	Dam	Casualties KIA	WIA	MIA
	P-38	144	20FG, 55FG, 364FG	0–0–0	1	1	0	0	0	1
	P-47	277	56FG, 78FG, 353FG, 356FG, 361FG	2–0–1 1–0–4(G)	0	0	0	0	0	0
	P-51	247	4FG, 339FG, 352FG, 355FG, 357FG, 359FG	1–0–0	6	0	1	0	0	6
TOTALS:		668		3–0–1(A) 1–0–4(G)	7	1	1	0	0	7

REMARKS: Additional to above totals, 100 P-51s (354FG & 363FG) and 102 P-38s (370FG & 474FG) of IX FC provided withdrawal cover, with claim of 2–0–0. Fighter group e/a credits:– 339FG – 2, 357FG – 1, 354FG – 2. Fighter group losses:– 4FG – 4, 20FG – 1, 357FG – 2. 55FG P-38 c/l, pilot safe.

9/10 MAY 1944

8AF 348 NIGHT LEAFLET OPERATION

	Despatched		Effective	Country	No. of Leaflets	Losses	Dam
1BD	B-17	3	3	HOLLAND & BELGIUM	1,340,000	0	

REMARKS: Leaflets dropped over 4 Dutch and 3 Belgian localities.

801BG despatched 13 B-24s on *Carpetbagger* operations.

On a fine spring day, 9 May, 389BG received a Distinguished Unit Citation streamer from Gen Spaatz for its part in the low-level Ploesti oilfields raid. Three of the surviving B-24Ds that took part were drawn up behind the General's saluting dais where they provided excellent vantage points for spectators. The far aircraft is *Miss Liberty* with 35 missions to its credit. The nearest, *Old Irish* with 50. There also happen to be over 50 men on top of *Old Irish*!

10 MAY 1944

Heavy bomber mission to Germany abandoned during early stages due to deteriorating weather. First 8AF ASR sorties flown over North Sea by 2 P-47s from Boxted.

10/11 MAY 1944

8AF 349 NIGHT LEAFLET OPERATION

	Despatched		Effective	Country	No. of Leaflets	Losses	Dam
1BD	B-17	3	3	BELGIUM	1,800,000	0	

REMARKS: Leaflets dropped over 11 localities.

801BG despatched 13 B-24s on *Carpetbagger* operations.

11 MAY 1944

8AF 350

	Despatched		Effective	Target		Bombs Tonnage	E/A	Losses MIA	E	Dam	Casualties KIA	WIA	MIA
2BD	B-24	144	94	MULHOUSE M/Y	(P)	337.0		1	0	17	1	7	40
			13	ORLEANS/BRICY A/F	(O)	39.0		0	0				
			19	BELFORT M/Y	(O)	57.0		0	2				
			2	MEZIDON/PITHIVIERS	(O)	6.0		0	0				
2BD	B-24	74	33	BELFORT M/Y	(P)	82.5		1	0				
			24	CHAUMONT M/Y	(O)	60.0		0	0				
2BD	B-24	76	68	EPINAL M/Y	(P)	168.0		3	0				
			1	CAEN A/F	(O)	2.5		0	0				
3BD	B-24	70	0	CHAUMONT M/Y	(P)	0		3	1	30	0	1	31
TOTALS:		364	254			752.0	0	8	3	47	1	8	71

REMARKS: Visual bombing. Groups participating:– 2BD – 44BG, 93BG, 389BG, 392BG, 445BG, 446BG, 447BG, 453BG, 458BG, 466BG, 467BG, 492BG, 486BG, 487BG. First mission of 492BG. 92CBW force failed due to faulty navigation taking lead formation into Flak area where lead plane shot down. Bomb group losses:– 44BG – 1, 389BG – 1, 458BG – 1, 466BG – 1, 467BG – 1, 487BG – 3. MIA B-24s of 458BG and 467BG interned Switzerland. On return, two 492BG B-24s c/l due to fuel shortage, one at Bury St.Edmunds A/F, 1 killed; one at West Wittering, Sussex. B/d 487BG B-24 abandoned over English coast reversed direction after crew baled and cr. in Chichester, 1 K.

11 MAY 1944 *(contd.)*

VIII FC FO 335

				Losses			Casualties		
Despatched		**Groups**	**E/A**	**MIA**	**E**	**Dam**	**KIA**	**WIA**	**MIA**
P-38	147	20FG, 55FG, 364FG	2-0-0(G)	0	0	2	0	0	0
P-47	188	56FG, 78FG, 353FG, 356FG	3-0-2 2-0-6(G)	2	0	6	0	0	2
P-51	201	339FG, 352FG, 357FG, 359FG	3-0-0(G)	3	1	2	0	0	3
TOTALS:	536		3-0-2 7-0-6(G)	5	1	10	0	0	5

REMARKS: Escort and support for 8AF 350. Fighter group losses:– 78FG – 2, 359FG – 3. Fighter group e/a credits:– 78FG – 3. On return, a 359FG P-51 cr. near Manston, pilot safe.

8AF 351

						Bombs		Losses			Casualties		
	Despatched		**Effective**	**Target**		**Tonnage**	**E/A**	**MIA**	**E**	**Dam**	**KIA**	**WIA**	**MIA**
1BD	B-17	609	58	SAARBRÜCKEN M/Y	(P)	166.0		5	1				
&			53	LUXEMBOURG M/Y	(P)	158.0		0					
3BD			60	EHRANG M/Y	(P)	161.0		1					
			55	KONS KARTHAUS M/Y	(P)	147.0		0					
			16	VOLKINGEN M/Y	(O)	47.0		0					
			12	THIONVILLE M/Y	(S)	36.0		0					
			19	BETTEMBOURG M/Y	(O)	57.0		0					
			49	BRUSSELS M/Y	(P)	136.0		0					
			55	BRUSSELS/MIDI M/Y	(P)	148.0		0					
			119	LIEGE M/Y	(P)	350.0		2					
			20	MALINES RR/J	(O)	60.0		0					
			31	T/O		93.0		0					
TOTALS:		609	547			1559.0	0	8	1	172	2	23	83

REMARKS: Groups participating: 1BD – 91BG, 92BG, 303BG, 305BG, 306BG, 351BG, 379BG, 381BG, 384BG, 398BG, 401BG, 457BG; 3BD – 94BG, 95BG, 96BG, 100BG, 385BG, 388BG, 390BG, 447BG, 452BG. Bomb group losses:– 100BG – 1, 303BG – 1, 305BG – 3, 306BG – 1, 379BG – 1, 390BG – 1. On return, b/d 303BG B-17 c/l Southend A/F.

VIII FC FO 336

				Losses			Casualties		
Despatched		**Groups**	**E/A**	**MIA**	**E**	**Dam**	**KIA**	**WIA**	**MIA**
P-38	99	IX FC	0	0	0	0	0	0	0
P-47	182	78FG, 353FG, 361FG & IX FC	0	0	0	0	0	0	0
P-51	190	4FG, 355FG, 361FG & IX FC	11-0-4	4	0	0	0	0	4
TOTALS:	471		11-0-4	4	0	0	0	0	4

REMARKS: 266 IX FC fighters participated and are included in totals. Only claims by 354FG of IX FC. Fighter group losses:–4FG – 1, 354FG – 1, 363FG – 2. MIA 4FG pilot lost in sea.

11/12 MAY 1944

8AF 352 NIGHT LEAFLET OPERATION

					No. of				Casualties		
	Despatched		**Effective**	**Country**	**Leaflets**	**Losses**	**E**	**Dam**	**KIA**	**WIA**	**MIA**
NLS	B-17	5	4	DENMARK	2,400,000	0	0	0	2	3	0

801BG despatched 4 B-24s on *Carpetbagger* operations.

12 MAY 1944

8AF 353

						Bombs		Losses			Casualties		
	Despatched		**Effective**	**Target**		**Tonnage**	**E/A**	**MIA**	**E**	**Dam**	**KIA**	**WIA**	**MIA**
1BD	B-17	326	224	MERSEBURG O/I	(P)	430.4		1	3	189	4	6	20
			87	LÜTZKENDORF O/I	(P)	168.5		1					
			2	HEDRONGEN	(O)	3.7							
			1	BULLSTADT	(O)	1.8							

continued on facing page

								Losses			Casualties		
		Despatched	Effective	Target		Bombs Tonnage	E/A	MIA	E	Dam	KIA	WIA	MIA
3BD	B-17	295	74	ZWICKAU O/I	(P)	153.0		41	1	162	3	8	377
			140	BRÜX O/I	(P)	309.0							
			11	CHEMNITZ	(O)	26.2							
			14	GERA M/Y	(O)	25.2							
			15	HOF	(O)	28.5							
			4	T/O		4.6							
2BD	B-24	265	116	ZEITZ O/I	(P)	256.4		2	1	61	0	7	33
			99	BÖHLEN O/I	(P)	220.0		1	4				
			14	MERSEBURG	(S)	29.0							
			1	OSTEND A/F	(O)	2.5							
			12	T/O		23.9							
TOTALS:		886	814			1687.7	0	46	9	412	7	21	430

REMARKS: First 8AF attack on oil production. Visual attack. Strong enemy fighter reaction against leading elements of 3BD. Groups participating:– 1BD – 91BG, 92BG, 303BG, 305BG, 306BG, 351BG, 379BG, 381BG, 384BG, 398BG, 401BG, 457BG; 2BD – 44BG, 93BG, 389BG, 392BG, 445BG, 446BG, 448BG, 453BG, 458BG, 466BG, 467BG, 492BG; 3BD – 94BG, 95BG, 96BG, 100BG, 385BG, 388BG, 390BG, 447BG, 452BG. Bomb group losses:– 44BG – 1, 92BG – 1, 93BG – 1, 94BG – 2, 95BG – 1, 96BG – 12, 100BG – 2, 385BG – 2, 388BG – 1, 389BG – 1, 447BG – 7, 452BG – 14, 457BG – 1. Two 96BG B-17 collided when under attack. 95BG & two 452BG B-17s ditched on return, 26 men rescued. On return b/d 93BG B-24 c/l Woodbridge A/F, crew safe; MIA 385BG B-17 abandoned over Thames, crew baled Southend. B/d 452BG B-17 Cat E. 2 96BG PFF a/c lost, one with 447BG.

VIII FC FO 337

Despatched		Groups	E/A	Losses MIA	E	Dam	Casualties KIA	WIA	MIA
P-38	153	20FG, 55FG, 364FG	2–0– 0	0	0	0	0	0	0
P-47	201	56FG, 78FG, 353FG, 356FG, 361FG	26–0– 8	4	0	4	0	0	4
P-51	381	4FG, 339FG, 352FG, 355FG, 357FG, 359FG, 361FG	33–0– 3 5–0– 2(G)	3	0	9	0	0	3
TOTALS:	735		61–0–11 5–0– 2(G)	7	0	13	0	0	7

REMARKS: Escort and support for 8AF 353. Not included in the above totals are 245 IX FC P-38s and P-51s which also participated with claims of 9–0–1 and 3 losses. Fighter group e/a credits:– 4FG – 10, 20FG – 1, 55FG – 1, 56FG – 18, 78FG – 6, 352FG – 6, 353FG – 2, 357FG – 14. Fighter group losses:– 56FG – 3, 78FG – 1, 352FG – 1, 357FG – 2.

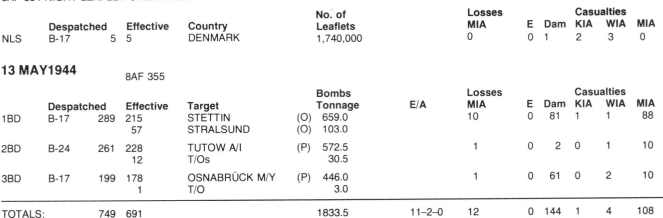

The crew were lucky that there was no fire when B-24H 42-94964 failed to rise on the morning of 13 May and crashed off the end of the runway. Only S/Sgt William Pletcher was trapped in the shattered nose and there were soon many willing hands to tug at the twisted metal and lift him out through the broken turret.

12/13 MAY 1944

8AF 354 NIGHT LEAFLET OPERATION

	Despatched		Effective	Country	No. of Leaflets	Losses MIA	E	Dam	Casualties KIA	WIA	MIA
NLS	B-17	5	5	DENMARK	1,740,000	0	0	1	2	3	0

13 MAY1944

8AF 355

	Despatched		Effective	Target		Bombs Tonnage	E/A	Losses MIA	E	Dam	Casualties KIA	WIA	MIA
1BD	B-17	289	215	STETTIN	(O)	659.0		10	0	81	1	1	88
			57	STRALSUND	(O)	103.0							
2BD	B-24	261	228	TUTOW A/I	(P)	572.5		1	0	2	0	1	10
			12	T/Os		30.5							
3BD	B-17	199	178	OSNABRÜCK M/Y	(P)	446.0		1	0	61	0	2	10
			1	T/O		3.0							
TOTALS:		749	691			1833.5	11–2–0	12	0	144	1	4	108

REMARKS: 1BD briefed for oil targets in western Poland but cloud forced attacks on T/Os along Baltic coast. Fighter attacks directed at this force. Groups participating:– 1BD – 91BG, 92BG, 303BG, 305BG, 306BG, 351BG, 379BG, 384BG, 398BG, 401BG, 457BG; 2BD – 44BG, 93BG, 389BG, 392BG, 445BG, 446BG, 448BG, 453BG, 458BG, 466BG, 467BG, 492BG; 3BD – 94BG, 95BG, 96BG, 100BG, 385BG, 388BG, 390BG, 447BG, 452BG. Bomb group losses:– 305BG – 3, 306BG – 1, 379BG – 3, 384BG – 2, 401BG – 1, 447BG – 1, 466BG – 1.

The 379BG back over Kimbolton after a 10 hour cloud frustrated mission to oil targets in Poland on 13 May. Three of their number did not return; one lay wrecked near a building at St.Heddinge, Denmark. (J. Helme)

VIII FC FO 338

	Despatched		Groups	E/A	Losses MIA	E	Dam	Casualties KIA	WIA	MIA
	P-38	153	20FG, 55FG, 364FG		1	0	5	0	0	1
	P-47	238	56FG, 78FG, 353FG, 356FG	14–2– 9	2	1	0	0	1	2
	P-51	346	4FG, 339FG, 352FG, 355FG, 357FG, 359FG, 361FG	33–1– 4	2	0	7	0	0	2
TOTALS		737		47–3–13	5	1	12	0	1	5

REMARKS: Escort and support for 8AF 355. Deepest penetration by P-51s to date – 1,470 miles to Posen. Not included in the above totals are 370 IX FC P-47s, P-38s and P-51s which also participated with claims of 11–1–3(A) and 15–0–27(G) and 4 losses. Fighter group e/a credits:– 56FG – 5, 339FG – 1, 352FG – 16, 355FG – 11, 356FG – 6, 357FG – 5. Fighter group losses:– 4FG – 1, 20FG – 1, 56FG – 1, 352FG – 1, 356FG – 1. B/d 356FG P-47 c/l Beccles, pilot injured. MIA 4FG a/c and pilot lost in sea on going out.

15 MAY 1944

8AF 356

	Despatched		Effective	Target		Bombs Tonnage	E/A	Losses MIA	E	Dam	Casualties KIA	WIA	MIA
1BD	B-17	58	38	MARQUISE/ MIMOYECQUES V/S	(P)	133.0	0	0	0	5	0	0	0
2BD	B-24	108	90	SIRACOURT V/S	(P)	352.0	0	0	0	8	0	0	0
TOTALS:		166	128			485.0	0	0	0	13	0	0	0

REMARKS: PFF attack (GH) on *Noball* targets. Bomb groups participating: 1BD – 303BG, 379BG, 384BG. 2BD – 44BG, 93BG, 389BG, 392BG, 445BG, 453BG, 492BG.

VIII FC FO 339

Despatched		Groups	E/A	Losses MIA	E	Dam	Casualties KIA	WIA	MIA
P-51	104	339FG, 357FG	0	1	0	0	0	0	1

REMARKS: Fighter group losses:– 339FG – 1 (engine failure).

15/16 MAY 1944

8AF 357 NIGHT LEAFLET OPERATION

	Despatched		Effective	Country	No. of Leaflets	Losses MIA	E	Dam
NLS	B-17	3	3	BELGIUM & FRANCE	1,100,000	0	1	0

REMARKS: Leaflets dropped at 10 locations. B/d B-17 c/l on return. 1 k, 3 inj.

801BG despatched 5 B-24s on *Carpetbagger* operations.

19 MAY 1944

8AF 358

	Despatched		Effective	Target		Bombs Tonnage	E/A	Losses MIA	E	Dam	Casualties KIA	WIA	MIA
1BD	B-17	413	321	BERLIN	(P)	683.0		7	0	210	0	9	76
			49	KIEL P/A	(S)	107.4							
3BD	B-17	175	174	BERLIN	(P)	392.5		9	2	79	3	7	61
			1	T/O		2.5							
2BD	B-24	300	272	BRUNSWICK A/I	(P)	701.5		12	0	64	1	8	119
			1	T/O		2.5							
TOTALS:		888	818			1889.4	0	28	2	353	4	24	256

REMARKS: Very heavy cloud forced use of PFF methods (H2X). Both forces opposed by fighters. Bomb groups participating:– 1BD – 91BG, 92BG, 303BG, 305BG, 306BG, 351BG, 379BG, 381BG, 384BG, 398BG, 401BG, 457BG; 2BD – 44BG, 93BG, 389BG, 445BG, 446BG, 448BG, 453BG, 458BG, 466BG, 467BG, 492BG; 3BD – 94BG, 95BG, 96BG, 100BG, 385BG, 388BG, 390BG, 447BG, 452BG. Bomb group losses:– 91BG – 1, 94BG – 1, 95BG – 1, 100BG – 3, 303BG – 1, 379BG – 1, 381BG – 2, 388BG – 1, 390BG – 1, 392BG – 3, 398BG – 1, 401BG – 1, 448BG – 1, 452BG – 2, 457BG – 1, 492BG – 8. The 95BG B-17 landed in Sweden. The 388BG B-17 ditched 30 miles N. of Yarmouth, 10 saved. A 100BG B-17 ditched, 10 saved on 21 May. Danes rescued crew of ditched B-17. 388BG B-17 c/l Walton A/F after collision during assembly with 452BG B-17 which cr. New Buckenham.

VIII FC FO 342

Despatched		Groups	E/A	Losses MIA	E	Dam	Casualties KIA	WIA	MIA
P-38	155	20FG, 55FG, 364FG	0–0– 2 1–0– 0(G)	4	2	5	0	0	4
P-47	182	56FG, 78FG, 353FG, 356FG	29–0–16 2–0– 0(G)	4	0	4	0	0	3
P-51	363	4FG, 339FG, 352FG, 355FG, 357FG, 359FG, 361FG	41–0– 5 4–0–10(G)	11	0	7	0	0	10
TOTALS:			70–0–23 7–0–10(G)	19	2	15	0	0	17

REMARKS: Escort and support 8AF 358. Not included in above totals are 264 IX FC fighters which also participated with claims of 4–0–6(A) and 13–0–5(G). Fighter group e/a credtis:– 4FG – 7, 55FG – 14, 56FG – 5, 78FG – 12, 339FG – 3, 352FG – 7½, 356FG – 11, 357FG – 10, 359FG – 10½. Fighter group losses:– 4FG – 1, 56FG – 1, 339FG – 2, 352FG – 1, 355FG – 2, 356FG – 3, 357FG – 1, 359FG – 3, 361FG – 1, 364FG – 4. A 339FG P-51 lost was engulfed by locomotive explosion while strafing. Two pilots baled into sea and were rescued – 56FG and 361FG. Two 364FG pilots baled into sea but lost. 2 20FG P-38s Cat E, pilots safe.

A 20 mm cannon shell from an FW 190 blew out a section of tail fin on *Sparky* during the Berlin raid of 19 May. 2/Lt John Keys and crew brought the aircraft safely back to Thorpe Abbotts.

20 MAY 1944

8AF 359

	Despatched		Effective	Target		Bombs Tonnage	E/A	Losses MIA	E	Dam	Casualties KIA	WIA	MIA
1BD	B-17	190	90	ORLY A/F	(P)	249.0		0	4	48	20	6	0
			73	VILLACOUBLAY A/D	(P)	192.0							
2BD	B-24	177	125	REIMS A/F & M/Y	(P)	333.1		0	0	5	0	0	0
3BD	B-17 & B-24	271	0	LIEGE & BRUSSELS M/Ys		0		2	4	41	17	16	17
TOTALS:		638	288			774.0	0	2	8	114	37	22	17

REMARKS: Visual attacks. Heavy cloud caused 3BD to abandon mission and part of 2BD to be recalled. Groups participating: 1BD – 91BG, 92BG, 303BG, 305BG, 306BG, 351BG, 379BG, 381BG, 384BG, 398BG, 401BG, 457BG; 2BD – 389BG, 445BG, 453BG, 458BG, 466BG, 467BG; 3BD – 94BG, 95BG, 96BG, 100BG, 385BG, 388BG, 390BG, 447BG, 452BG, 486BG, 487BG. Bomb group losses:– 447BG – 2, collision over sea after assembly. 2 rescued from one B-17. Due to heavy ground mists and poor visibility 8 B-17s and 3 B-24s destroyed in assembly and t/o accidents. 3 92BG B-17s collided on runway at base. Two 486BG and one 487BG B-24s cr. after t/o at Waldingfield, Preston St. Mary (10 k) and Long Melford (6 k), respectively. One 388BG B-17 exploded on t/o. 457BG B-17 c/l Snetterton A/F.

VIII FC FO 343A

Despatched		Groups	E/A	Losses MIA	E	Dam	Casualties KIA	WIA	MIA
P-38	146	20FG, 55FG, 364FG	2–0–1 1–0–1(G)	1	0	5	0	0	1
P-47	177	56FG, 78FG, 353FG, 356FG	0	1	0	0	0	0	1
P-51	334	4FG, 339FG, 352FG, 355FG, 357FG, 359FG, 361FG	0	2	0	0	0	0	2
TOTALS:	657		2–0–1 1–0–1(G)	4	0	5	0	0	4

REMARKS: Escort and support for 8AF 359. Not included in above totals are 296 IX FC fighters which participated. Fighter group e/a credits:– 55FG – 2. Fighter group losses:– 55FG – 1, 355FG – 2, 356FG – 1.

21 MAY 1944

8AF 360

	Despatched		Effective	Target		Bombs Tonnage	E/A	Losses MIA	E	Dam	Casualties KIA	WIA	MIA
1BD	B-17	40	25	MARQUISE/ MIMOYECQUES V/S	(P)	94.5	0	0	0	13	0	0	0
2BD	B-24	110	99	SIRACOURT V/S	(P)	365.0	0	0	0	1	0	0	0
TOTALS:		150	124			459.5	0	0	0	14	0	0	0

REMARKS: GH PFF attack on *Noball* targets. Groups participating: 1BD – 379BG, 384BG; 2BD – 44BG, 93BG, 392BG, 446BG, 448BG, 458BG, 466BG, 467BG, 492BG.

VIII FC FO 345

Despatched		Groups	E/A	Losses MIA	E	Dam	Casualties KIA	WIA	MIA
P-47	48	56FG	0	0	0	0	0	0	0

REMARKS: Escort for 8AF 360.

VIII FC FO 344

Despatched		Groups	E/A	Losses MIA	E	Dam	Casualties KIA	WIA	MIA
P-38	145	20FG, 55FG, 264FG	2–0– 0 6–0– 3(G)	8	2	12	1	0	8
P-47	139	78FG, 353FG, 356FG	1–0– 0	4	0	21	0	0	3
P-51	333	4FG, 352FG, 339FG, 355FG, 359FG, 361FG, 357FG	17–0– 2 77–0–64(G)	15	1	20	0	0	15
TOTALS:	617		20–0– 2 83–0–67(G)	27	3	53	1	0	26

REMARKS: First *Chattanooga* strafing mission to attack rail stock in Germany. 225 locomotives attacked and 91 credited as destroyed. Airfields and other ground targets also attacked, although the strategic value of one 352FG pilot's claim – 25 cows killed – was considered dubious. P-47s attacked rail bridges in Western Germany dropping 37 tons 500lb bombs. Fighter group e/a credits:– 4FG – 1, 55FG – 1, 339FG – 13, 355FG – 1, 356FG – 1, 359FG – 2, 364FG – 1. Fighter group losses:– 4FG – 1, 55FG – 6, 339FG – 4, 352FG – 1, 353FG – 2, 356FG – 2, 357FG – 3, 359FG – 4, 361FG – 2, 364FG – 2. A 353FG pilot saved after baling out over sea 20 miles from Felixstowe. On return 364FG P-38 c/l base, pilot safe. B/d 55FG P-38 cr. Old Buckenham, pilot K. 352FG P-51 c/l base.

22 MAY 1944

8AF 361

	Despatched		Effective	Target		Bombs Tonnage	E/A	Losses MIA	E	Dam	Casualties KIA	WIA	MIA
1BD	B-17	342	289	KIEL P/A	(P)	623.0		5	1	209	4	3	78
& 3BD			5	T/O		12.5							
2BD	B-24	96	94	SIRACOURT V/S	(P)	336.5		0	0	1	0	0	0
TOTALS:		438	388			972.0	0	5	1	210	4	3	78

REMARKS: PFF attacks. Groups participating:– 1BD – 91BG, 92BG, 303BG, 305BG, 306BG, 351BG, 379BG, 381BG, 384BG, 398BG, 401BG, 457BG; 2BD – 93BG, 445BG, 448BG, 453BG; 3BD – 94BG, 96BG, 385BG, 388BG, 447BG, 452BG. Bomb group losses:– 305BG – 2, 384BG – 1, 388BG – 2. On return 388BG B-17 c/l Catfield, 2 killed.

VIII FC FO 346

Despatched		Groups	E/A	Losses MIA	E	Dam	Casualties KIA	WIA	MIA
P-38	145	20FG, 55FG, 364FG	8–1–5	3	1	1		0	3
P-47	95	56FG, 356FG	12–1–2	3	2	2		0	2
P-51	328	4FG, 339FG, 352FG, 355FG, 357FG, 359FG, 361FG	2–2–1	1	0	1		0	1
TOTALS:	568		22–4–8	7	3	4		0	6

REMARKS: Escort and support for 8AF 342. Fighter group e/a credits:– 4FG – 2½, 20FG – 1, 55FG – 3, 56FG – 12, 364FG – 4. Fighter group losses:– 4FG – 1, 20FG – 1, 56FG – 3, 364FG – 2. One 56FG pilot rescued from sea. Two 56FG P-47s c/l on return. MIA 4FG P-51 c/l Sweden – shot up by P-38. 20FG P-38 Cat E.

8AF 362 VIII FC FO 347

Despatched		Groups	Target	Bombs Tonnage	E/A	Losses MIA	E	Dam
P-47	130	56FG, 78FG, 353FG, 356FG	HASSELT R/B (P)	25.3	0	1	0	1
			LIEGE T/O	19.5	0			

REMARKS: Fighter-bomber attack against Hasselt and Liège rail bridges. Fighter group losses:– 353FG – 1.

EVENT

At a ceremonial parade an RAF officer formally handed the safe-keeping of North Pickenham airfield to the Commanding Officer of the 492nd Group on 22 May 1944. This was the 77th and last installation in the United Kingdom to be transferred to the 8th Air Force; of this total, 66 were airfields and the rest depots or headquarters sites. These installations housed 82 major operational units. Additionally, 8th Air Force organisations had lodger units at several RAF stations.

22/23 MAY 1944

8AF 363 NIGHT LEAFLET OPERATION

	Despatched		Effective	Country	No. of Leaflets
NLS	B-17	4	4	HOLLAND	320,000

REMARKS: Hague, Haarlem, Rotterdam and Utrecht localities.

801BG despatched 12 B-24s on *Carpetbagger* operations.

Attempting to make an emergency landing at Ford airfield on 23 May, a 306BG Fortress crashed into the bomb dump with this result. Six of the crew were killed.

23 MAY 1944

8AF 364

	Despatched		Effective	Target		Bombs Tonnage	E/A	Losses MIA	E	Dam	Casualties KIA	WIA	MIA
1BD	B-17	580	34	METZ M/Y	(P)	102.0		2	2	50	12	4	0
&			139	SAARBRÜCKEN M/Y	(S)	357.0							
3BD			37	NEUNKIRCHEN	(S)	111.0							
			36	EPINAL M/Y	(P)	97.0							
			12	BAYON M/Y	(S)	31.0							
			17	ORLEANS/BRICY A/F	(P)	39.0							
			54	CHAUMONT M/Y	(P)	160.0							
			18	CHATEAUDUN A/F	(P)	49.0							
			18	CAEN/CARPIQUET A/F	(S)	54.0							
			12	T/O		26.0							
2BD	B-24	465	167	ORLEANS/BRICY A/F	(P)	474.0	0	1	1	33	10	0	10
&			84	BOURGES A/F	(P)	195.0							
3BD			88	AVORD A/F	(P)	295.0							
			97	ETAMPES/ MONDESIR A/F	(P)	290.0							
			1	T/O		3.0							
TOTALS:		1045	814			2283.0	0	3	3	83	22	4	10

REMARKS: Visual attacks on airfields and rail targets in France. First mission of 34BG flying with other 3BD B-24 units to Etampes. Bomb groups participating:– 1BD – 91BG, 92BG, 303BG, 305BG, 306BG, 351BG, 379BG, 381BG, 384BG, 398BG, 401BG, 457BG; 2BD – 44BG, 93BG, 389BG, 392BG, 445BG, 446BG, 448BG, 453BG, 458BG, 466BG, 467BG, 492BG; 3BD – 34BG, 94BG, 95BG, 96BG, 100BG, 385BG, 388BG, 390BG, 447BG, 452BG, 486BG, 487BG. Bomb group losses:– 96BG – 1, 305BG – 1, 446BG – 1. During assembly a 351BG B-17 and 458BG B-24 collided, cr. at Hoxne, 16 killed. The 96BG B-17 ditched 15 miles SW Shoreham, 9 saved. On return 306BG B-17 cr. landing at Ford A/F, 5 killed.

23 MAY 1944

VIII FC FO 348

Despatched		Groups	E/A	Losses MIA	E	Dam	Casualties KIA	WIA	MIA
P-38	96	20FG, 55FG, 364FG	0	0	0	0	0	0	0
P-47	142	56FG, 78FG, 353FG, 356FG	0	0	1	1	0	0	0
P-51	324	4FG, 339FG, 352FG, 355FG, 357FG, 359FG, 361FG	0	0	0	1	0	0	0
TOTALS:	562		0	0	1	2	0	0	0

REMARKS: Escort and support for 8AF 363. Not included in the above totals are 644 IX FC fighters which participated under VIII FC control and lost 2 P-47s and 2 P-38s. B/d 356FG P-47 Cat E after landing Hawkinge.

8AF 365

Despatched		Groups	Target	Bombs Tonnage	E/A	Losses MIA	E	Dam	Casualties KIA	WIA	MIA
P-51	103	359FG, 361FG	HASSELT R/B	17.5	0	1	0		0	0	1

REMARKS: First 8AF P-51 fighter-bomber mission. 75 attacked, 14 P-51s of total acted as escort. Bridge destroyed. Fighter group losses: 361FG – 1.

23/24 MAY 1944

8AF 366 NIGHT LEAFLET OPERATION

	Despatched		Effective	Country	No. of Leaflets	Losses	Dam
NLS	B-17	5	4	BELGIUM & HOLLAND	928,000	0	

801BG despatched 7 B-24s on *Carpetbagger* operations

24 MAY 1944

8AF 367

	Despatched		Effective	Target		Bombs Tonnage	E/A	Losses MIA	E	Dam	Casualties KIA	WIA	MIA
2BD	B-24	490	151	ORLY A/F	(P)	469.5		0	0	33	0	0	0
&			168	MELUN A/F	(P)	500.9							
3BD			58	POIX A/F	(S)	170.0							
			23	CREIL A/F	(S)	91.5							

continued on facing page

		Despatched	Effective	Target		Tonnage	E/A	MIA	E	Dam	KIA	WIA	MIA
1BD	B-17	616	464	BERLIN	(P)	1081.3		33	1	256	4	24	482
&			34	NAUEN	(O)	71.0							
3BD			13	RECHLIN	(O)	31.0							
			6	T/O		14.0							
TOTALS:		1106	917			2429.2	0	33	1	289	4	24	482

REMARKS: Visual attacks on airfields in the Paris areas and PFF and visual bombing of Berlin. Bomb groups participating:– 1BD – 91BG, 92BG, 303BG, 305BG, 306BG, 351BG, 379BG, 381BG, 384BG, 398BG, 401BG, 457BG; 2BD – 44BG, 93BG, 389BG, 392BG, 445BG, 446BG, 453BG, 458BG, 466BG, 467BG, 492BG; 3BD – 34BG, 94BG, 95BG, 96BG, 100BG, 385BG, 388BG, 390BG, 447BG, 452BG, 486BG, 487BG. Bomb group losses:– 91BG – 1, 92BG – 1, 94BG – 1, 95BG – 1, 100BG – 9, 303BG – 1, 305BG – 1, 306BG – 1, 351BG – 1, 379BG – 3, 381BG – 6, 384BG – 1, 385BG – 1, 398BG – 2, 401BG – 1, 447BG – 1, 457BG – 1. Opposed by some 200 e/a. 100BG became separated from bomber stream by weather and contrails and subjected to heavy attack. 94BG B-17 ditched in N. Sea, crew of 10 rescued. 2 MIA 379BG B-17s collided after a hit by Flak. During assembly 385BG B-17 c/l Fornham All Saints, crew safe.

VIII FC FO 349

	Despatched		Groups	E/A	Losses MIA	E	Dam	Casualties KIA	WIA	MIA
	P-38	144	20FG, 55FG, 364FG	6–0–2	1	0	1		0	1
	P-47	178	56FG, 78FG, 353FG, 356FG	0–0–0	1	0	1		0	1
	P-51	280	4FG, 339FG, 352FG, 355FG, 357FG, 359FG, 361FG	27–7–4	8	1	4		1	8
TOTALS:		602		33–7–6	10	1	6	0	1	10

REMARKS: Escort and support for 8AF 367. Not included in totals are 351 IX FC fighters under control of VIII FC, losing 6. Fighter group e/a credits:– 4FG – 8, 20FG – 2, 339FG – 10, 352FG – 4, 355FG – 2, 357FG – 1, 359FG – 1, 361FG – 2, 364FG – 2. Fighter group losses:– 4FG – 1, 20FG – 1, 78FG – 1, 339FG – 1, 352FG – 2, 355FG – 1, 361FG – 3. A 359FG P-51 cr. base, m/f pilot injured.

8AF 368 (65FW FO99 & 66FW FO61)

	Despatched		Effective	Target		Bombs Tonnage	E/A	Losses MIA	E	Dam	Casualties KIA	WIA	MIA
	P-51	124	59	BEAUMONT-SUR-OISE R/B	(P)	23.5	3–0–0 2–0–1(G)	3	0	6	0	1	3
			29	ST.LEGER/ ALBERT A/F	(O)	7.5							
			34	SOISSONS R/B	(P)	12.5							
	P-47	74	44	CREIL R/B	(P)	20.0		0	0	1	0	0	0
			28	VERBERIE R/B	(P)	8.0							
	P-51	24	U/known	Escort P-51 F/B				0	0	0	0	0	0
TOTALS:		222	194 plus			71.5	3–0–0 2–0–1(G)	3	0	7	0	1	3

REMARKS: Fighter-bomber attacks on rail bridges in France. Groups participating:– 4FG, 56FG, 78FG, 339FG, 355FG,357FG. Fighter group e/a credits: 339FG – 3. Fighter group losses:– 339FG – 1, 357FG – 2.

24/25 MAY 1944

8AF 369 NIGHT LEAFLET OPERATION

	Despatched		Effective	Country	No. of Leaflets	Losses	Dam
1BD	B-17	4	4	FRANCE & BELGIUM	2,540,000	0	0

801BG despatched 3 B-24s on *Carpetbagger* operations

25 MAY 1944

8AF 370

	Despatched		Effective	Target		Bombs Tonnage	E/A	Losses MIA	E	Dam	Casualties KIA	WIA	MIA
2BD	B-24	307	74	BELFORT M/Y	(P)	222.4		2	0	57	0	0	20
			134	MULHOUSE M/Y	(P)	348.0							
			12	TONNERE M/Y	(S)	30.0							
			37	BRETIGNY A/F	(S)	90.5							
			1	DIJON A/F	(S)	3.0							

continued on next page

25 MAY 1944 *(contd.)*

1BD	B-17	320	75	NANCY/ESSEY A/F	(P)	130.0		0	0	14	0	0	0
			69	METZ M/Y	(P)	161.3							
			56	THIONVILLE M/Y	(O)	137.3							
			36	SAARGUEMINES M/Y	(P)	90.0							
			36	BLAINVILLE M/Y	(P)	90.0							
			3	LIEGE A/F	(S)	7.5							
3BD	B-24	103	67	MONTIGNIES SUR SAMBRE M/Y	(P)	198.0		0	0	3	0	0	0
			9	ALOST M/Y	(S)	23.5							
3BD	B-17	247	52	BRUSSELS/ SCHAERBECK M/Y	(P)	127.5		2	1	71	1	6	28
			29	BRUSSELS/MIDI M/Y	(P)	71.0							
			18	BRUSSELS/ MELSBROEK M/Y	(S)	45.0							
			50	LIEGE/GUILLEMINES M/Y	(P)	125.0							
			50	LIEGE/RENORY M/Y	(S)	121.0							
2BD	B-24	18	18	FECAMP GUN BATTERY	(P)	51.8		0	0	0	0	0	0
3BD	B-17	38	18	FECAMP GUN BATTERY	(P)	50.0		0	0	0	0	0	0
1BD			15	ST.VALERY GUN BATTERY	(P)	45.0		0	0	0	0	0	0
TOTALS:		406	326			2166.3	0	4	1	145	1	6	48

REMARKS: Visual attacks on rail installations and airfields in France and Belgium. Although weather was clear small formations (389BG, 448BG, 92BG, 390BG) bombed coastal gun emplacements on PFF leaders in an experiment connected with the forthcoming invasion. Groups participating:– 1BD – 91BG, 92BG, 303BG, 305BG, 306BG, 351BG, 379BG, 381BG, 384BG, 401BG, 457BG; 2BD – 44BG, 93BG, 389BG, 392BG, 445BG, 446BG, 448BG, 453BG, 458BG, 466BG, 467BG, 492BG, 3BD – 34BG, 94BG, 95BG, 96BG, 100BG, 385BG, 388BG, 390BG, 447BG, 452BG, 486BG, 487BG. Bomb group losses:– 44BG – 1, 388BG – 2, 446BG – 1. Five men from b/d 388BG B-17 baled over e/t and 2 from a 385BG B-17 also baled out and missing. B/d 94BG B-17 Cat E on return.

VIII FC FO 350

Despatched		Groups	E/A	Losses MIA	E	Dam	Casualties KIA	WIA	MIA
P-38	136	20FG, 55FG, 364FG	3–1–0	9	0	8	0	0	9
P-47	181	56FG, 78FG, 353FG, 356FG	4–1–2 3–0–5(G)	0	0	6	0	0	0
P-51	287	4FG, 339FG, 352FG, 355FG, 357FG, 359FG, 361FG	6–0–1	3	0	1	0	0	3
TOTALS:	604		13–2–3 3–0–5(G)	12	0	15	0	0	12

REMARKS: Escort and support for 8AF 370. Not included in above totals are 207 IX FC fighters under VIII FC control. Fighter group e/a credits:– 4FG – 4, 78FG – 2, 339FG – 1, 356FG – 2, 364FG – 3. Fighter group losses:– 4FG – 2, 20FG – 3, 359FG – 1, 364FG – 6. Fighters detailed to strafe rail targets after escort.

OTHER OPERATIONS: 9 F-5s of 7PG despatched on PR to France. 3 B-17s on routine weather recon mission and 2 on special weather flights, and 1 Mosquito of 802RG on special weather flight.

25/26 MAY 1944

8AF 371 NIGHT LEAFLET OPERATION

NLS B-17s, 4 despatched, 4 effective: locations in France.

7PG's *Dot & Dash*, piloted by Col Paul Cullen, arrived at Poltava via Italy on 25 May – the first operational 'shuttle' using a Soviet base.

26 MAY 1944

FO 65 100 & FO 101

Despatched		Groups	E/A	Losses MIA	E	Dam	Casualties KIA	WIA	MIA
P-38	58 (30 & 28)	479FG	0	0	0	0	0	0	0

REMARKS: Two fighter sweeps of Dutch coast for familiarisation purposes. First operations of 479FG, last of the 15 8AF Fighter groups to enter combat.

OTHER OPERATIONS: 2 B-17 on routine maritime weather recon. 1 B-17 on special recon.

INCIDENT

An initiation period for units prior to operations enabled both pilots and executive staff to become familiar with standard procedures for the European war theatre, while the service personnel established base facilities and made ready the aircraft. This was followed by training missions to satisfy Command that the group functioned both smoothly and efficiently. When the 479th Fighter Group's P-38s set out to fly their introductory combat sweep on 26 May 1944, VIII Fighter Command finally attained their full planned complement of 15 operational fighter groups. The 479th had become operational quicker than any other group in the Command – 11 days – having only arrived at Wattisham on the 15th. Previously the record was the 356th Group's 14 days; next in standing were the 339th and 364th Groups which both took 21 days.

26/27 MAY 1944

8AF 372 NIGHT LEAFLET OPERATION

NLS B-17s, 4 despatched, 4 effective: locations in Holland.

27 MAY 1944

8AF 373

	Despatched		Effective	Target		Bombs Tonnage	E/A	Losses MIA	E	Dam	Casualties KIA	WIA	MIA
1BD	B-17	344	150	LUDWIGSHAFEN C/I	(P)	367.5		12	0	98	2	5	114
			125	MANNHEIM M/Y	(P)	295.5							
			18	LACHEN/APEYER-DORF	(O)	42.5							
			19	M/Y MANNHEIM AREA	(O)	46.0							
			6	T/O		15.0							
3BD	B-17	269	98	KARLSRUHE M/Y	(P)	239.0		7	1	89	1	3	70
			53	STRASBOURG/ MEINAU A/I	(P)	130.0							
			49	STRASBOURG M/Y	(P)	115.5							
3BD	B-24	86	69	WOIPPY A/I	(P)	140.0		0	0	0	0	1	0
			3	T/O		7.0							
2BD	B-24	369	145	SAARBRÜCKEN M/Y		364.0		5	1	18	3	4	50
			66	NEUNKIRCHEN M/Y	(P)	164.0							
			72	KONS/KARTHUS M/Y	(P)	216.0							
			3	T/O		7.0							
3BD	B-17	40	36	FECAMP GUN BATTERY	(P)	102.0		0	0	0	0	0	0
2BD	B-24	18	18	ST.VALERY	(P)	51.0		0	0	0	0	0	0
TOTALS:		1126	930			2302.0	0	24	2	205	6	13	234

REMARKS: Visual bombings, chiefly against rail targets. Groups participating:– 1BD – 91BG, 92BG, 303BG, 305BG, 306BG, 351BG, 379BG, 381BG, 384BG, 398BG, 401BG, 457BG; 2BD – 44BG, 93BG, 389BG, 392BG, 445BG, 446BG, 448BG, 453BG, 458BG, 466BG, 467BG, 492BG; 3BD – 34BG, 94BG, 95BG, 96BG, 100BG, 385BG, 388BG, 390BG, 447BG, 452BG, 486BG, 487BG. H2X attacks conducted again against coastal batteries in Pas de Calais (389BG, 392BG, 44BG, 96BG, 388BG, 452BG). Bomb group losses:– 91BG – 1, 94BG – 1, 96BG – 4, 305BG – 1, 351BG – 6, 381BG – 1, 389BG – 2, 390BG – 1, 452BG – 1, 457BG – 3, 458BG – 2, 492BG – 1. 5 bombers landed in Switzerland – one each from 91BG, 351BG, 385BG, 458BG and 492BG. During assembly two 458BG B-24s collided N. of Cromer, one cr. in sea, 2 men baled from the other which was able to land safely at base. 3 MIA 96BG B-17s were lost in two separate collisions over target. MIA 94BG PFF a/c had part 385BG crew.

VIII FC FO 351

Despatched		Groups	E/A	Losses MIA	E	Dam	Casualties KIA	WIA	MIA
P-38	170	20FG, 55FG, 364FG, 479FG	0–0–0	1	1	0	0	0	1
P-47	238	56FG, 78FG, 353FG, 356FG	1–0–1 2–0–0(G)	0	0	0	0	0	0
P-51	302	4FG, 339FG, 352FG, 355FG, 357FG, 359FG, 361FG	34½–1–4 7–0–2(G)	6	1	8	0	1	6
TOTALS:	710		35½–1–5 9–0–2(G)	7	2	8	0	1	7

REMARKS: Escort and support for 8AF 373. Not included in totals are 425 IX FC fighters under VIII FC control which claimed 4–0–0 for loss of 1. Fighter group e/a credits:– 78FG – 1, 352FG – 12½, 357FG – 23½, 361FG – 1. Fighter group losses:– 4FG – 1, 55FG – 1, 357FG – 4, 361FG – 1. (Only 357FG losses due to enemy action; 1 357FG P-51 landed in Switzerland.) B/d 55FG P-38 Cat E. Going out 361FG P-51 c/l 10 miles from base, pilot inj.

8AF 374 65 FW 102

Despatched		Effective	Target	Bombs Tonnage	E/A	Losses MIA	E	Dam	Casualties KIA	WIA	MIA
P-47	24	24	BARGE CONVOY		0	0	0	1	0	0	0

REMARKS: 56FG F/B attack on barges between Willenstadt and Meerije. Two barges destroyed.

OTHER OPERATIONS: 7 PG despatched 33 F-5s, 21 effective to France and Germany. 3 B-17s despatched on routine weather mission.

INCIDENT

Aborting – the general term for abandoning an operational flight because of mechanical or personnel failure – was something no crew wanted to be involved in. Once keyed up for a mission, the majority of combat crews wished to see it through as another to be struck off the statutory 30 in a tour. The authorities demanded a valid reason for a turn-back. However obvious the justification, there was always a slight stigma about having to abort; the thought that other airmen might be suspicious that the failure was engineered. There were few crews who did not have to abort a mission at one time or another for very good reasons and, while they occurred, the 'fixed' aborts were few. Early returns also meant fewer bombs on the target and a group with poor maintenance and a high record of number of abortives was soon under scrutiny by high command. So, for both personal and operational reasons, a decision to turn back was never lightly taken. The lengths that some men would go to avoid an abort is well illustrated by an incident on 27 May 1944 when the 100th Group was assembling for a raid on Strasbourg. While high over England the oxygen supply lines to the right waist and ball turret fractured on B-17 '007'. The waist gunner could be 'plugged in' to the other side of the fuselage and also make use of the emergency oxygen bottles, but these could not be taken into the ball turret. The situation was assessed and it was established there would be insufficient emergency oxygen to supply the two men all the way to the target and back. 1/Lt Carroll Woldt found he had no option but to abort and informed the crew. Ball gunner S/Sgt Edward Foulds then suggested he should bale out as this would ensure sufficient oxygen for the right waist gunner and any likely emergencies. After some discussion Woldt was persuaded to give permission. Two other gunners held open the fuselage door while Foulds jumped. A safe landing was made and Foulds returned to base while his comrades flew on to the target.

27/28 MAY 1944

8AF 375 NIGHT LEAFLET OPERATION

NLS B-17s, 4 despatched, 3 effective; locations in Belgium and France.

Also on night operations: 2 B-17s of 482BG taking H2X scope photos.

28 MAY 1944

8AF

	Despatched		Effective	Target		Bombs Tonnage	E/A	Losses MIA	E	Dam	Casualties KIA	WIA	MIA
1BD & 3BD	B-17	610	38	RUHLAND/SCHWARZ-HEIDE O/T	(P)	69.5	20–21–18	17	1	107	3	15	155
			12	DESSAU A/I	(P)	30.0							
			15	ZWICKAU A/I	(S)	25.7							
			28	LEIPZIG A/I	(S)	69.5							
			14	BÖHLEN	(O)	35.0							
			16	MEISSEN	(O)	32.4							
			19	BRANDIS/POLENZ	(O)	47.5							
			17	WÜSTEN-SACHSEN A/F	(O)	42.5							
			12	FRANKFURT M/Y	(O)	30.0							
			32	ÜBIGAU	(O)	53.3							
			20	DESSAU	(O)	43.5							
			4	FRANKFURT	(O)	8.3							
			5	CAMBURG	(O)	9.0							
			22	T/O		57.2							
3BD	B-17	255	105	KÖNIGSBURG/ MAGDEBURG O/D	(P)	240.5	16– 8– 6	9	0	64	3	2	90
			55	MAGDEBURG/ ROTHENSEE O/I	(P)	114.3							
			17	DESSAU	(S)	31.8							
			6	GERA M/Y	(O)	11.4							
3BD	B-24	106	66	LÜTZKENDORF/ HALLE	(P)	155.4		3	0	16	0	1	3
			10	WETZLAR	(O)	21.9							
			6	T/O		13.2							
2BD	B-24	311	63	MERSEBURG/LEUNA O/T	(P)	145.7	1– 0– 0	3	0	23	1	1	26
			187	ZEITZ–TROGLITZ O/I	(P)	447.3							
			10	LIMBURG	(O)	25.0							
			8	MEMMINGEN	(O)	21.3							
			9	SAALFELD	(O)	24.0							
			10	T/O		24.6							
1BD	B-17	59	58	COLOGNE/ EIFELTOR M/Y	(P)	109.0	0– 0– 0	0	0	0	0	0	0
TOTALS:		1341	864			1829.8	37–29–24	32	1	210	7	19	274

REMARKS: Major effort against oil targets. Some primaries cloud-shrouded but most bombing visual. Glide bombs used by 41CBW Force attacking Cologne M/Y but weapon proved unsuccessful. Luftwaffe fighters made concentrated attack on 94CBW Dessau Force, shooting down 12 B-17s. Groups participating:– 1BD – 91BG, 92BG, 303BG, 305BG, 306BG, 351BG, 379BG, 384BG, 398BG, 401BG, 457BG; 2BD – 44BG, 93BG, 389BG, 392BG, 445BG, 446BG, 448BG, 453BG, 458BG, 466BG, 467BG, 492BG; 3BD – 34BG, 94BG, 95BG, 96BG, 100BG, 385BG, 388BG, 390BG, 447BG, 452BG, 486BG, 487BG. Bomb group losses:– 44BG – 1, 100BG – 1, 303BG – 1, 305BG – 1, 351BG – 5, 385BG – 1, 388BG – 2, 389BG – 2, 390BG – 5, 401BG – 7, 457BG – 3, 486BG – 2, 487BG – 1. B/d 401BG B-17 ditched, 10 rescued. On return, b/d 401BG B-17 c/l base. MIA 389BG PFF a/c flying with 445BG and 453BG.

VIII FC FO 352

Despatched		Groups	E/A	Losses MIA	E	Dam	Casualties KIA	WIA	MIA
P-38	182	20FG, 55FG, 364FG, 479FG	0–0–0	0	0	0	0	0	0
P-47	208	56FG, 78FG, 353FG, 356FG	2–0–1 0–0–1(G)	4	2	3	0	0	4
P-51	307	4FG, 339FG, 352FG, 355FG, 357FG, 359FG, 361FG	25–1–5	5	1	8	0	1	5
TOTALS:	697		27–1–6 0–0–1(G)	9	3	11	0	1	9

REMARKS: Escort and support for 8AF 376. Not included in totals are 527 IX FC fighters despatched under VIII FC control which claimed 33–0–10(A) and 5–0–7(G) for loss of 5. Fighter group e/a credits:– 4FG – 7½, 78FG – 1, 352FG – 7½, 353FG – 1, 355FG – 2, 357FG – 7. Fighter group losses:– 4FG – 2, 78FG – 3, 352FG – 1, 353FG – 1, 355FG – 2. 361FG P-51 c/l Fowlmere A/F. B/d 78FG P-47 Cat E. 356FG P-47 cr. on t/o, pilot inj.

OTHER OPERATIONS: 30 F-5s and 5 Spitfires of 7FG despatched to France and Germany. 2 B-17s on routine maritime weather recon.

INCIDENT

Collision was an ever present risk in close fighter–fighter action, both with enemy aircraft and those from one's own formation. When several units became embroiled in an air battle the danger increased. On 28 May 1944, as the 78th Group's P-47s manoeuvred at 22,000 ft to engage an enemy formation, Cpt Alwin Juchheim, then leading ace of the Group, collided head-on with a 363FG P-51. The Mustang exploded in flames; the P-47, with a severed wing, went into a spin. A single parachute was seen to open and two 78th Group Thunderbolts circled as it descended to determine whether it was their comrade or the Mustang pilot. At about 12,000 ft they were suddenly aware that an Me 109 also appeared to be taking an interest and thus distracted the P-47 pilots lost track of parachute and its passenger. Some weeks later it was learned that only Juchheim survived the accident.

28/29 MAY 1944

8AF 377 NIGHT LEAFLET OPERATION

NLS B-17s, 5 despatched, 5 effective; locations in Belgium and Norway.

Also on night operations, 2 482BG B-17s taking H2X scope photos.

801BG despatched 22 B-24s on *Carpetbagger* operations. 1 B-24 MIA.

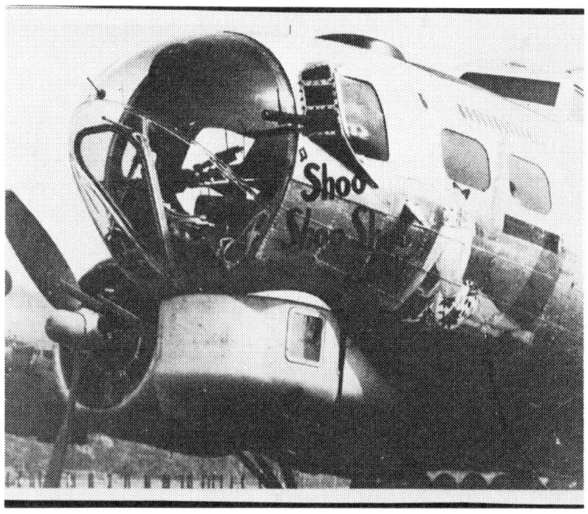

A 91BG Fortress that sought sanctuary in Sweden on 29 May. Later converted for transport use and operated in Scandinavia and France post-war, the aircraft was eventually secured by the USAF Museum, one of only three B-17s that saw combat with the 8AF still surviving 35 years after hostilities. The girl in the sarong was borrowed from a Vargas painting and appeared on several aircraft. (see 22/6/44)

29 MAY 1944

8AF 379

	Despatched		Effective	Target		Bombs Tonnage	E/A	Losses MIA	E	Dam	Casualties KIA	WIA	MIA
2BD	B-24	443	224	PÖLITZ O/T	(P)	546.5	29–15–10	17	3	150	2	10	161
&			167	TUTOW A/D	(P)	436.5							
3BD			14	RENDSBURG A/F	(O)	35.0							
			9	MISDROY	(O)	22.5							
			1	SCHWERIN	(O)	2.5							
3BD	B-17	251	149	LEIPZIG/MOCKAU A/I	(P)	349.2	11– 4– 5	9	0	80	0	3	90
			50	LEIPZIG/ HEITERBLICK A/I	(P)	113.9							
			4	T/O		9.6							
1BD	B-17	299	91	KRZESINKI A/I	(P)	202.3	22–18–14	8	0	97	0	5	67
			58	POSEN A/I	(P)	131.5							
			52	SORAU A/I	(P)	129.7							
			48	COTTBUS A/I	(P)	111.4							
			19	SCHNEIDEMÜHL A/F	(O)	39.5							
			2	T/O		4.4							
TOTALS:		993	888			2054.5	62–37–29	34	3	327	2	18	318

REMARKS: Visual attacks on aircraft plants and oil installations. For second day running strong enemy fighter formations opposed bombers. Groups participating:– 1BD – 91BG, 92BG, 303BG, 305BG, 306BG, 351BG, 379BG, 381BG, 384BG, 398BG, 401BG, 457BG; 2BD – 44BG, 93BG, 389BG, 392BG, 445BG, 446BG, 448BG, 453BG, 458BG, 466BG, 467BG, 492BG; 3BD – 34BG, 94BG, 95BG, 96BG, 100BG, 385BG, 388BG, 390BG, 447BG, 452BG, 486BG, 487BG. Bomb group losses:– 34BG – 3, 44BG – 2, 91BG – 1, 92BG – 2, 95BG – 1, 100BG – 1, 305BG – 3, 351BG – 1, 384BG – 1, 388BG – 1, 389BG – 1, 390BG – 2, 392BG – 4, 445BG – 1, 447BG – 1, 452BG – 3, 466BG – 1, 467BG – 1, 487BG – 1, 492BG – 3. Losses include 2 B-17s and 6 B-24s landing in Sweden (one each from 91BG, 92BG, 34BG, 389BG, 445BG, 492BG and 2 from 44BG). The 351BG B-17 ditched, crew of 9 saved. A 492BG B-24 ditched 43 miles from Cromer, 9 saved. On return b/d 392BG B-24 cr. Thorpe near Norwich after crew baled; b/d 392BG B-24 c/l Sporle, crew safe. B/d 34BG B-24 Cat E.

29 MAY 1944 *(contd.)*

VIII FC FO 353

Despatched		Groups	E/A	Losses MIA	E	Dam	Casualties KIA	WIA	MIA
P-38	184	20FG, 55FG, 364FG, 479FG	0–0– 0	0	0	0		0	0
P-47	187	56FG, 78FG, 353FG, 356FG	1–0– 1	4	0	3		0	3
P-51	302	4FG, 339FG, 352FG, 355FG, 357FG, 359FG, 361FG	38–1– 4 16–0–15(G)	6	0	6		0	5
TOTALS:	673		39–1– 5 16–0–15(G)	10	0	9		0	8

REMARKS: Escort and support for 8AF 379. Not included in totals are 592 IX FC fighters which claimed 1–0–0 and lost 2. Fighter groups e/a credits: 4FG – 5, 339FG – 5, 452FG – 4, 359FG – 12, 361FG – 14. Fighter group losses:– 4FG – 1, 339FG – 2, 353FG – 3, 356FG – 1, 359FG – 2, 361FG – 1. 353FG pilot baled out 16 miles E. of Orford, rescued. 361FG pilot baled over sea, rescued. Fighters detailed to strafe rail targets after escort.

OTHER OPERATIONS: 7PG despatched 24 F-5s and 4 Spitfires on photo recon to German targets. 2 B-17s on routine weather recon of British Isles.

29/30 MAY 1944

801BG despatched 23 B-24s on *Carpetbagger* operations. 1 B-24 MIA.

30 MAY 1944

8AF 380

	Despatched		Effective	Target		Bombs Tonnage	E/A	Losses MIA	E	Dam	Casualties KIA	WIA	MIA
1BD	B-17	268	83	DESSAU A/I	(P)	190.0	8–5–1	9	0	81	0	2	86
			107	HALBERSTADT A/I	(P)	145.0							
			51	OSCHERSLEBEN A/I	(P)	118.0							
			5	T/O		12.5							
2BD	B-24	369	135	OLDENBURG A/D	(P)	379.0		1	2	36	1	2	9
			147	ROTENBURG A/D	(P)	428.0							
			71	ZWISCHENAHN A/D	(P)	192.8							
			1	NORDHOLZ A/F	(O)	3.0							
3BD	B-24	91	46	MÜNSTER/HANDORF A/F	(P)	132.8		2	1	36	1	6	9
			36	DIEPHOLZ A/F	(P)	103.2							
3BD	B-17	126	62	REIMS M/Y	(P)	181.5		0	0	24	0	0	0
			60	TROYES M/Y	(P)	179.5							
3BD	B-17	40	39	BRUSSELS/ SCHAERBECK M/Y	(P)	115.0		0	0	12	0	0	0
3BD 104	B-17	84	76	PAS DE CALAIS V/S	(P)	320.0		0	0	12	3	2	10
TOTALS:		928	919			2500.2	8–5–1	12	3	201	5	12	114

REMARKS: Visual attacks against aircraft industry targets in Germany and marshalling yards in France and Belgium. First mission of 489BG. Groups participating:– 1BD – 91BG, 303BG, 351BG, 379BG, 381BG, 384BG, 398BG, 401BG, 457BG; 2BD – 44BG, 93BG, 389BG, 392BG, 445BG, 446BG, 448BG, 453BG, 458BG, 466BG, 467BG, 489BG, 492BG; 3BD – 34BG, 94BG, 95BG, 96BG, 100BG, 385BG, 388BG, 390BG, 447BG, 452BG, 486BG, 487BG. Bomb group losses:– 34BG – 1, 91BG – 1, 303BG – 1, 351BG – 1, 381BG – 3, 398BG – 1, 401BG – 2, 487BG – 1, 489BG – 1. 487BG B-24 ditched near Lowestoft, 8 saved. Two b/d 453BG B-24s c/l base.

VIII FC FO 354

Despatched		Groups	E/A	Losses MIA	E	Dam	Casualties KIA	WIA	MIA
P-38	186	20FG, 55FG, 364FG, 479FG	0–0–0	0	0	3	0	0	0
P-47	184	56FG, 78FG, 353FG, 356FG	2–0–0	1	0	0	0	0	1
P-51	302	4FG, 339FG, 352FG, 355FG, 357FG, 359FG, 361FG	48–3–2 7–0–3(G)	8	2	4	0	0	8
TOTALS:	672		50–3–2 7–0–3(G)	9	2	7	0	0	9

REMARKS: Escort and support for 8AF 380. Not included in totals are 637 IX FC Fighters which claimed 8–0–2(A) and 0–0–4(G) for loss of 3. Fighter group e/a credits:– 4FG – 2, 339FG – 5, 352FG – 14½, 353FG – 2, 355FG – 4½, 357FG – 18, 359FG – 3½. Fighter group losses: 4FG – 3, 339FG – 2, 353FG – 1, 357FG – 2, 359FG – 1. A 357FG pilot baled and rescued from sea. 361FG P-51 cr. near base, pilot safe. 359FG P-51 Cat E, pilot safe. MIA 4FG P-51s all involved in collisions.

8AF 381 FIGHTER BOMBER-MISSION

Despatched		Effective	Target		Bombs Tonnage	E/A	Losses MIA	E	Dam	Casualties KIA	WIA	MIA
P-47	100	37	LONGUEIL R/B	(P)	37.0	0–0–0	1			0	0	1
		26	BEAUMONT-SUR-OISE R/B (P)		12.0							
		23	CANLY-LE-JOUQUE R/B (P)		6.0							
P-38	1	12	CREIL R/B	(S)	16.0							

REMARKS: Under 65FW FO102 and 66FW FO62, 56FG, 353FG and 356FG briefed to bomb four rail bridges in NW France. 56FG employed a P-38 *Droopsnoot* to sight for high level P-47 formation drop. Other units dive bombed. Fighter group losses:– 353FG – 1.

OTHER OPERATIONS: 7PG despatched 22 F-5s and 3 Spitfires to Germany, France and the Low Countries. 3 B-17s and 2 Mosquitoes on routine weather missions.

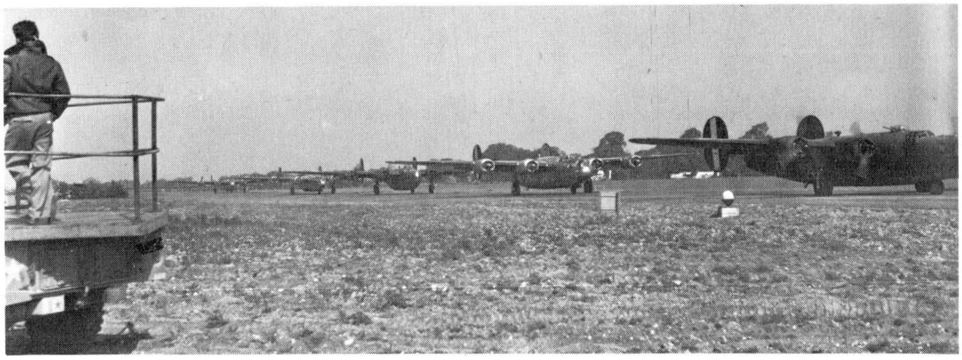

Rolling along the Hethel perimeter track, 389BG Liberators set out for Germany on the last day of May. The Liberators wear the new colour tail markings introduced at the beginning of the month as an aid to unit identification at long range.

31 MAY 1944

8AF 382

	Despatched		Effective	Target		Bombs Tonnage	E/A	Losses MIA	E	Dam	Casualties KIA	WIA	MIA
1BD	B-17	246	36	LUXEUIL M/Y	(P)	97.0		0	0	45	1	4	0
			30	FLORENNES/JUZAINE A/F (O)		90.0							
			23	GILZE–RIJEN A/F	(O)	69.0							
			12	ROOSENDAAL M/Y	(O)	35.0							
			4	NAMUR M/Y	(O)	12.0							
			3	T/O		9.0							
3BD	B-17	287	88	OSNABRÜCK M/Y	(P)	264.0		1	0	58	0	1	10
			54	SCHWERTE M/Y	(P)	156.0							
			52	OESKE M/Y	(O)	135.0							
			50	HAMM M/Y	(O)	148.0							
2BD & 3BD	B-24	491	0	FRANCE & BELGIUM RAIL TARGETS		0		0	1	7	0	0	0
2BD	B-24	5	4	BEAUMONT–SUR–OISE R/B	(P)	7.0		0	0	0	0	0	0
				MELUN BRIDGES	(O)								
TOTALS:		1029	356			1022.0	0	1	1	105	1	5	10

REMARKS: Marshalling yards and aircraft industry targets in Germany and rail targets in France and Belgium. Weather caused abandonment of attacks on some primaries. 2BD Force recalled due to cloud. Fronts up to 26,000ft in some areas. Visual attacks on primaries:– 1BD – 91BG, 92BG, 303BG, 305BG, 306BG, 351BG, 379BG, 381BG, 384BG, 398BG, 401BG, 457BG; 2BD – 44BG, 93BG, 389BG, 392BG, 445BG, 446BG, 448BG, 453BG, 458BG, 466BG, 467BG, 489BG, 492BG; 3BD – 34BG, 94BG, 95BG, 96BG, 100BG, 385BG, 388BG, 390BG, 447BG, 452BG, 486BG, 487BG, 490BG. First use of Azon radio-controlled bombs by 8AF – 458BG made unsuccessful attacks on bridges in France. First mission of 490BG – one a/c failed to receive recall signal and bombed a T/O which was not credited by 8AF. Bomb group losses:– 96BG – 1. 446BG B-24 cr. Hickling during assembly, 9 crewmen baled.

VIII FC FO 355

Despatched		Groups	E/A	Losses MIA	E	Dam	Casualties KIA	WIA	MIA
P-38	193	20FG, 55FG, 364FG, 479FG	1–0–0(G)	0	0	1	0	0	0
P-47	180	56FG, 78FG, 353FG, 356FG	0–0–0	1	0	3	0	0	1
P-51	309	4FG, 33FG, 352FG, 355FG, 357FG, 359FG, 361FG	3–0–1(G)	2	0	0	0	0	2
TOTALS:	682		4–0–1(G)	3	0	4	0	0	3

REMARKS: Escort and support for 8AF 382. Not included in totals are 647 IX FC fighters with no claims or losses. Fighter group e/a credits:– 56FG – 5. Fighter group losses:– 4FG – 2, 356FG – 1.

31 MAY 1944 *(contd.)*

8AF 383 FIGHTER-BOMBER MISSION

	Despatched		Effective	Target		Bombs Tonnage	E/A	Losses MIA	E	Dam	Casualties KIA	WIA	MIA
	P-47	45	43	GÜTERSLOH A/F	(P)	14.8	5–1–3	0	0	1	0	0	0
	P-47	36	35	GÜTERSLOH A/F	(P)	16.5	0–0–0	0	0	0	0	0	0
	P-38	35	?	RHEINE/HOPSTEN A/F	(S)	19.0	5–0–0(G)	0	0	0	0	0	0
TOTALS:		116				50.3	5–1–3 5–0–0(G)	0	0	1		0	0

REMARKS: Attacks on German airfields with 500lb and 100lb GP bombs. P-38s of 20FG used *Droopsnoot* lead. Fighter Group e/a credits:– 56FG – 5. Other unit involved, 353FG.

OTHER OPERATIONS: 23 F-5s and 4 Spitfires of 7PG on photo mapping and damage assessment sorties. 3 B-17s and 2 Mosquitoes on routine weather missions.

31 MAY/1 JUNE 1944

22 B-24s of 801BG on *Carpetbagger* sorties over France.

1 JUNE 1944

7PG despatched 2 F-5s and 2 Spitfires on PR to Antwerp and Bourges A/F. Routine weather recon by 2 B-17s. Mosquito of 802RG flew a weather recon sortie to Ruhr area.

EVENT

Since the 482nd Group was taken off combat operations on 23 March 1944 to act primarily as a Pathfinder School, the only sorties over enemy territory were night flights testing new equipment or to take H2X (or 'Mickey') scope pictures. Large K-24 cameras were installed to photograph the images produced on the cathode ray tubes (scopes). Radar operators could then be provided with prints showing typical images specific targets would produce on the scope. On the night of 1 June, B-17s 42-97692 *M-Mike* and 42-97623 *O-Oboe* were despatched from Alconbury to take scope photographs of the French coast from Cherbourg to Le Havre. The resultant prints from photographs taken by 2/Lt Michael Sperber, the 'Mickey' operator on *O-Oboe*, were excellent and used to brief combat group PFF crews for bombing the invasion coast on the morning of D-Day.

1/2 JUNE 1944

22 B-24s of 801BG on *Carpetbagger* operations.

2 JUNE 1944

8AF 384

	Despatched		Effective	Target		Bombs Tonnage	E/A	Losses MIA	E	Dam	Casualties KIA	WIA	MIA
1, 2 &	B-17	633	521	PAS DE CALAIS V/S	(P)	1514.5		0	0	11	1	1	1
3BD	B-24	293	284	PAS DE CALAIS V/S	(P)	992.0		0	0	0	0	0	0
		926	805			2506.5	0	0	0	11	1	1	1

ESCORT: 42 P-38s, 165 P-47s, 134 P-51s. No claims or losses.

REMARKS: All bomb groups operating. 64 *Noball* targets attacked visually and 49 by GH. 3BD B-24s recalled.

8AF 385

1 & 3BD	B-17	242	163	R/R TARGETS PARIS	(P)	462.0							
			49	CONCHES A/F	(O)	117.0							
			12	BEAUMONT-SUR-OISE A/F	(O)	36.0		2	0	90	0	0	18
			1	CAEN/CARPIQUET A/F	(O)	3.0							
2BD	B-24	77	13	BRETIGNY A/F	(P)	39.0		5	2	37	1	4	50
			47	CREIL A/F	(O)	140.0							
			14	VILLENEUVE A/F	(O)	44.0							
TOTALS:		319	299			841.0	0	7	2	127	1	4	68

ESCORT: 162 P-38s, 83 P-47s, 152 P-51s. No claims or losses.

REMARKS: Afternoon mission to airfields and rail targets in France. Cloud hindered attacks. All 3BD B-17 groups and 1BD less 94CBW groups participated. 2BD despatched 489BG and 491BG – first mission of latter. Bomb group losses:– 385BG – 1, 390BG – 1, 489BG – 4, 491BG – 1. Two b/d 489BG B-24 cr. Leiston A/F and Thames area, 1 k. All Fighter groups operating. No claims or losses.

FIGHTER-BOMBER MISSION

Despatched		Effective	Target		Bombs Tonnage	E/A	Losses MIA	E	Dam	Casualties KIA	WIA	MIA
P-38	7	3	OSTEND BRIDGE	(O)	3.0	0	0					0

OTHER OPERATIONS: 7PG despatched 3 F-5s on low-level PR of French bridges, F-5 was damaged. 3 B-17s and 1 Mosquito on routine weather recon. over Atlantic.

GENERAL: Start of Operation *Cover* with the object of deceiving the enemy into believing the invasion would be in the Pas de Calais.

2/3 JUNE 1944

8AF NIGHT LEAFLET OPERATION

NLS B-17, 5 despatched, 5 effective; to Belgium and France.

801BG despatched 18 B-24s on *Carpetbagger* operations.

3 JUNE 1944

8AF 388

Despatched		Effective	Target		Bombs Tonnage	E/A	Losses MIA	E	Dam	Casualties KIA	WIA	MIA
B-17	238	219	PAS DE CALAIS	(P)	634.0		0	0	21	0	0	0
B-24	124	120	PAS DE CALAIS	(P)	344.0		0	0	24	0	0	0
B-17	102	97	PAS DE CALAIS	(P)	275.0		0	0	2	0	0	0
B-24	104	98	PAS DE CALAIS	(P)	327.0		0	0	0	0	0	0
TOTALS:	568	534			1580.0	0	0	0	47	0	0	0
P-38	91		ESCORT									
P-47	129		FOR 1st RAID				0	0	0	0	0	0
P-38	102		ESCORT				0	0	1	0	0	0
P-47	34		FOR 2nd RAID				0	0	0	0	0	0
P-51	83						1	0	0	0	0	1
TOTALS:	439					0	1	0	1	0	0	1

REMARKS: Extensive cloud caused cancellations with mostly PFF bombing at 23 tactical targets – coastal defences, etc; in the Pas de Calais in the afternoon 16 of the same targets attacked by PFF. Bomb groups participating: 1BD – 91BG, 92BG, 303BG, 306BG, 351BG, 381BG, 384BG, 398BG, 401BG, 457BG; 2BD – 44BG, 93BG, 389BG, 445BG, 446BG, 448BG, 453BG, 466BG, 467BG; 3BD – 94BG, 96BG, 385BG, 388BG, 447BG, 452BG. No bomber losses. All Fighter groups operating except 4FG, 352FG and 359FG. No claims. A 355FG P-51 MIA due to mechanical failure.

OTHER OPERATIONS: 1 B-17 on RCM over Pas de Calais with 12 P-51 escort. 1 B-17 and 2 B-24s on combat camera sorties of French coast.

3/4 JUNE 1944

23 B-24s of 801BG on *Carpetbagger* operations; France.

4 JUNE 1944

8AF 389

Despatched		Effective	Target		Bombs Tonnage	E/A	Losses MIA	E	Dam	Casualties KIA	WIA	MIA
B-17	201	183	PAS DE CALAIS	(P)	524.0		0	0	10	0	0	0
B-24	56	51	PAS DE CALAIS	(P)	143.0		0	0	0	0	0	0
TOTALS:	257	234			667.0	0	0	0	10	0	0	0
P-47		130	ESCORT 8AF 389				0	0	0	0	0	0
P-51		42					2	0	0	0	0	0
TOTALS:		172					2	0	0	0	0	0

8AF 390

Despatched		Effective	Target		Bombs Tonnage	E/A	Losses MIA	E	Dam	Casualties KIA	WIA	MIA
B-17	246	222	PAS DE CALAIS	(P)	639.5		0	1	12	1	0	0
B-24	68	53	PAS DE CALAIS	(P)	165.0		0	0	6	0	0	0
TOTALS:	314	275			804.5	0	0	1	18	1	0	0

REMARKS: PFF attacks coastal defences in the Pas de Calais. 1BD groups of 1CBW, 40 CBW, 41 CBW; 2BD groups of 20 CBW and 3BD groups of 13 CBW and 45 CBW participated in these missions. 355FG and 359FG P-51 MIA.

4 JUNE 1944 *(contd.)*

8AF 391

	Despatched		Effective	Target		Bombs Tonnage	E/A	Losses MIA	E	Dam	Casualties KIA	WIA	MIA
1 & 3BD	B-17	263	48	MASSEY/ PALAISEAU R/B	(P)	138.0		0	1	34	0	0	0
			48	MASSEY/ PALAISEAU R/B	(P)	144.0							
			50	VERSAILLES/ METELOTS R/B	(P)	150.0							
			34	VILLENEUVE/ ST.GEORGE R/B	(P)	98.0							
2 & 3BD	B-24	185	23	BOURGES A/F	(P)	28.0		0	3	27	10	4	0
			72	ROMORANTIN/ PRUNIERES A/F	(P)	216.0							
			56	AVORD A/F	(P)	153.1							
			55	BRETIGNY A/F	(P)	150.0							
			8	MELUN BRIDGES	(P)	2.5							
TOTALS:		448	394			1079.6	0	0	4	61	10	4	0

8AF 391

Despatched		Effective	Target	Bombs Tonnage	E/A	Losses MIA	E	Dam	Casualties KIA	WIA	MIA
P-47	135		ESCORT 8AF 391		0	0	0	0	0	0	0
P-51	277				1–0–0	1	1	1	0	0	0
TOTALS:	412				1–0–0	1	1	1	0	0	0

REMARKS: B-17s attacked rail bridges and B-24s airfields in Paris area. *Azon* attack on Melun bridges by 458BG. Bomb groups participating:– 1BD – 351BG, 401BG, 457BG; 2BD – 389BG, 392BG, 445BG, 453BG, 458BG, 492BG; 3BD – 34BG, 94BG, 96BG, 385BG, 388BG, 447BG, 486BG, 487BG, 490BG. No bomber losses. During assembly 492BG B-24 cr. Graveston, 10 k; 390BG B-17 cr. in flames Easthorpe, crew baled, 1 k; 491BG B-24 cr. Sizewell, 9 k. B/d 392BG B-24 cr. Sleaford after crew baled over Norfolk. P-38 groups non-op and a/c being painted with black and white stripes for D-Day. 356FG also stood down. Fighter group e/a credits:– 361FG – 1. Fighter group losses:– 355FG – 1, 359FG – 1, 361FG – 1. 78FG P-47 c/l near base due to m/f.

OTHER OPERATIONS: 7PG despatched 15 F-5s to France (1 F-5 landed Sardinia). Weather recon by 2 B-17s over UK and Atlantic. 2 Mosquitoes on WR over Schelde and Paris areas.

5 JUNE 1944

8AF 392

	Despatched		Effective	Target		Bombs Tonnage	E/A	Losses MIA	E	Dam	Casualties KIA	WIA	MIA
1, 2 & 3BD	B-17	464	423	CHERBOURG PAS DE CALAIS C/D	(P)	1896.0		4	0	37	0	5	38
	B-24	206	203	CHERBOURG/ PAS DE CALAIS C/D	(P)			2	1	39	1	5	9
TOTALS:		670	626			1896.0	0	6	1	76	1	10	47
	P-47	127		ESCORT 8AF 392				1	1	0	0	0	0
	P-51	245						1	0	0	0	0	0
TOTALS:		372					0	2	1	0	0	0	0

8AF 393 FIGHTER-BOMBER MISSION

Despatched		Effective	Target		Bombs Tonnage	E/A	Losses MIA	E	Dam	Casualties KIA	WIA	MIA
P-51	8	7	LILLE MT CONVOY	(P)	3.0							
		1	LILLE/ VENDEVILLE A/F	(O)	1.0							
TOTALS:	8	8			4.0		0			0	0	0

REMARKS: Attacking on coastal defences in the Le Havre, Caen, Boulogne and Cherbourg areas. Bomb groups participating: 44BG, 91BG, 93BG, 94BG, 95BG, 96BG, 100BG, 303BG, 379BG, 384BG, 385BG, 388BG, 389BG, 390BG, 446BG, 447BG, 448BG, 452BG, 458BG, 467BG, 489BG, 491BG. Bomb group losses:– 44BG – 1, 100BG – 2, 390BG – 2, 491BG – 1. Ground rocket scored direct hit on 390BG B-17 causing it to collide with another, both lost. B/d 44BG PFF B-24 ditched after leading 489BG, part crew baled over England, Col Leon Vance rescued from Channel and later awarded Medal of Honor. P-38 groups, 356FG and 359FG stood down. No claims. Fighter group losses:– 78FG – 1, 352FG – 1. 56FG P-47 c/l Ardleigh, pilot safe. 8AF 393 was afternoon attack by 4FG P-51s on enemy road convoy spotted earlier in day.

OTHER OPERATIONS: 3 B-17s on routine WR over UK and Atlantic.

5/6 JUNE 1944

801BG despatched 11 B-24s on *Carpetbagger* operations. 1 B-24 MIA Belgium.

6 JUNE 1944

8AF 394

	Despatched		Effective	Target		Bombs Tonnage	E/A	Losses MIA	E	Dam	Casualties KIA	WIA	MIA
	B-17	882	659	ASSAULT ON BEACHES	(P)	3096.0		0	0	14	1	1	0
	B-24	543	418	ASSAULT ON BEACHES	(P)			1	1	1	11	1	13
	B-24	296	37	ARGENTAN	(O)	109.0		2	0	0	0	0	0
	B-17	84	0	ARGENTAN		0		0	0	1	0	0	0
TOTALS:		1805	1114			3205.0	0	3	1	16	12	2	13

8AF 395

2BD	B-24	73	58	CAEN	(P)	157.0		0	0	0	0	0	0
1, 2 & 3BD	B-24	300	125	BEACH-HEAD	(P)	1490.0		1	1	11	0	0	0
	B-17	409	325	BEACH-HEAD	(P)			0	0	5	10	0	0
TOTALS:		782	508			1647.0	0	1	1	16	10	0	0
	P-38	555		ESCORT & CONTINUOUS PATROL THROUGH-OUT THE DAY. VIII FC & IX FC			26-0-8	0	1	0	0	0	0
	P-47	414					4-0-9 (G)	5		3	0	0	4
	P-51	750						22	1	11	1	1	20
								21	1				
TOTALS:		1719					26-0-8 4-0-9 (G)	25	2	14	1	1	24

FIGHTER-BOMBER MISSIONS

	P-47	182	UN-REPORTED	VARIOUS TACTICAL TARGETS NORTHERN FRANCE		Unknown
	P-51	218				
	P-47	49		ESCORT		
	P-51	17				
TOTALS:		466				

REMARKS: Coastal targets in area of invasion beaches between Le Havre and Cherbourg. 8AF 394 carried out at first light – PFF. 8AF 395 later in day. All bomb groups operating. First mission of fortieth and the last 8AF regular bomb group – 493BG. First group over beach head – 446BG. Bomb group losses:– 487BG – 1, 490BG – 1, 493BG – 2. Two 493BG B-24s lost in collision. 487BG lost only bomber due to enemy action out of 2362 sent. 490BG B-24 cr. on Chesil beach, 7 saved. Going out 34BG B-24 cr. Corfe Castle, 10 k. 389BG B-24 exploded and cr. Northrepps prior to 8AF 395. Bomb rack failures caused 489BG and 491BG to drop bombs at various points in England on return. All fighter groups operated. Fighter group e/a credits:– 4FG – 4½, 56FG – 3, 78FG – 2, 339FG – 4, 352FG – 2, 355FG – 9. Fighter group losses:– 4FG – 10, 56FG – 1, 78FG – 1, 352FG – 2, 353FG – 1, 355FG – 2, 356FG – 2, 357FG – 3, 361FG – 3. The 78FG pilot baled over sea, rescued. 352FG P-51 cr. t/o base, pilot k. 20FG P-38 c/l landing base, pilot safe. 56FG flew 11 missions, other groups between 6 and 10 during day. One 4FG loss was 339FG pilot and a/c on detachment. B/d 355FG P-51 Cat E.

OTHER OPERATIONS: 7PG F-5 MIA.

To encourage the strafing of enemy airfields, VIII FC let it be known that aircraft destroyed on the ground stood equal to those shot down. While strafing was far more dangerous some pilots still considered air victories more indicative of personal prowess. At the end of May 'Goody' Goodson and 'Kid' Hofer were the top scoring 8AF pilots in ground victories, each with 15. Goodson's scoreboard makes no distinction between air and ground kills but Hofer's covers only those he has claimed in the air – although two sail ships and a train shot-up were represented. Within a month of posing for these photos (4 June) both pilots would be lost, Goodson a POW after strafing, Hofer downed in an air battle and killed. They were not flying the aircraft depicted, which both have the British Malcolm bubble hood for better visibility. The alsatian is a 334FS pet (known as Duke, or Mutt or by several ribald names) that frequently 'got into' photographs.

INCIDENT

The most detailed eye-witness report of the Normandy landings received by the Supreme Allied Commander on D-Day came from none other than the head of the 8th Air Force. Two P-38 Lightnings that took off from Bovingdon that morning were piloted by Lt.Gen Doolittle and Maj.Gen Earle Partridge, respectively Commander and Deputy Commander of the 8th; in all probability no other two-plane fighter element ever carried such high rank. The two generals intended to accompany the heavy bombers to observe the effects of their drop ahead of the invasion troops. An almost unbroken undercast hid the beaches and the bombers were guided by radar. Doolittle and Partridge flew back towards England to seek a break in the cloud and go in at a lower altitude. Doolittle spotted such a hole and went down; Partridge, whose attention was momentarily diverted to a problem in the cockpit, did not see his leader peel off and contact was lost between the two. Jimmy Doolittle came out of the clouds at about 1,500 ft and turned back towards the Normandy beaches where he flew back and forth for nearly an hour and a half before returning to Bovingdon. The Lightning's unmistakable twin-booms made the fighter easy to identify and none of the gunners on the hundreds of ships below loosed off rounds at the scouting General.

EVENT

The 6 June 1944 is marked in history as the date of the cross-Channel invasion of continental Europe – D-Day. It was also the occasion of another significant event: on the morning of the assault an estimated 11,000 aircraft were in the air over southern England boosting world-wide flights that day to a total higher than any other since the beginning of aviation.

Resplendent in D-Day dress of black and white stripes a 355FG P-51B sits on dispersal at Steeple Morden awaiting the great day. (Blair via Hunsberger)

Anxious mechanics watch as 361FG Mustangs return to base from a Mission to the D-Day beachhead.

6/7 JUNE 1944

8AF 396 NIGHT LEAFLET OPERATION

NLS B-17, 12 despatched, 12 effective; France and Low Countries.

7 JUNE 1944

8AF 397

	Despatched		Effective	Target		Bombs Tonnage	E/A	Losses MIA	E	Dam	Casualties KIA	WIA	MIA
1BD	B-17	182	58	CONDÉ SUR NOIREAU	(P)	171.0		0	0	17	0	0	0
			60	FLERS	(P)	177.0							
			54	FALAISE	(P)	155.0							
2BD	B-24	291	66	ARGENTAN	(P)	198.0							
			19	VASCOEUIL	(O)	57.0		0	1	0	8	3	0
			61	LAIGLE	(P)	167.0							
			83	LISIEUX	(P)	234.0							
TOTALS:		473	401			1159.0		0	1	17	8	3	0

8AF 398

	Despatched		Effective	Target		Bombs Tonnage	E/A	Losses MIA	E	Dam	Casualties KIA	WIA	MIA
1 & 3BD	B-17	487	23	NIORT	(O)	58.0							
			40	NANTES BRIDGE	(O)	68.0		1	1	78	1	4	0
			190	NANTES	(P)	490.0							
			132	KERLIN/BASTARD A/F	(P)	284.0							
	B-24	88	13	POUANCE	(O)	39.0		1	7	96	20	8	12
			13	BLAIN	(O)	39.0							
			13	CHATEAUBRIAND	(O)	39.0							
			25	LAVAL A/F	(O)	75.0							
			12	VITRÉ	(O)	36.0							
			12	TOURS/LA ROCHE	(P)	36.0							
			3	TOURS	(O)	8.0							
TOTALS:		575	476			1172.0	0	2	8	174	21	12	12

VIII FC FO 373, 374, 375, 376

	Despatched		Effective	Target	Bombs Tonnage	E/A	Losses MIA	E	Dam	Casualties KIA	WIA	MIA
	P-38	526		PATROLS BEACH-HEAD ETC.			0	0	0	0	0	0
	P-51	294		ESCORT N. FRANCE		2–0–1 0–0–2 (G)	8	0	0	0	0	0
TOTALS:		820				2–0–1 0–0–2(G)	8	0	0	1	0	7

FIGHTER BOMBER MISSIONS

P-47	505	GENERAL STRAFING OVER NORTHERN FRANCE	196.0	29–1–12	10	0	0	0	0	0
P-51	148			25–0–12 (G)	4	3	0	1	0	12
TOTALS:	653		196.0	29–1-12 25–0–12 (G)	14	3	0	1	0	12

REMARKS: Mission to tactical targets in NW France during morning by 2CBW, 20CBW, 41CBW, 92CBW, 94CBW groups and 392BG. In afternoon 1CBW groups and 305BG to Kerlin/Bastard A/F, all 3BD B-17 groups to Nantes and all 3BD B-24 groups to Angers – which was cloud covered. Bomb group losses:– 487BG – 1. 381BG – 1 – ditched 30 miles W of Jersey, 10 rescued. On return at dusk, enemy intruder a/c attacked 34BG while over its base. One 34BG shot down on base, another at Wetheringsett, and a third cr. Nedging, total 12 k. Two 490BG B-24s Cat E after a landing collision at Feltwell A/F. 34BG B-24 cr. landing Eye A/F. During assembly 446BG B-24 cr. Rumburgh, 8 k.

Continuous fighter support, some groups flying nine missions during day. Fighter group e/a credits:– 56FG – 12, 78FG – 3, 339FG – 2, 353FG – 9½, 361FG – 2. Fighter group losses:– 4FG – 1, 56FG – 5, 78FG – 2, 352FG – 2, 353FG – 3, 355FG – 6, 357FG – 1, 359FG – 1, 361FG – 1. 2 4FG P-51s collided after t/o, 1 cr. near base, pilot k., the other a/c landed – Cat E. B/d 4FG P-51 c/l Merston A/F.

OTHER OPERATIONS: 7PG despatched 8 F-5s and 6 Spitfires on PR to Germany, France and Holland. 2 B-17s, 2 B-24s and 1 Mosquito on PR cover of beach-head. 1 B-24 cr. in England on return. 2 B-17s on routine weather flights and 3 Mosquitoes on special weather flights.

INCIDENT

Airmen had something of the reputation of anglers when it came to exaggerated stories. Low flying was a favourite. The day after D-Day pilots did have to fly low as the cloud base was down to a few hundred feet over the Continental coast. High Command wanted the 7th Photo Group to obtain cover of activity on the rail network around Antwerp to provide information on possible troop movements. Lts Bateson and Moss, despatched in their unarmed F-5s to perform the mission, elected to fly very low to obtain the element of surprise and hopefully elude the defences. Skimming over the Belgian coast Moss was confronted with a flock of birds. In trying to avoid them he flew through the top of a large tree and emerged with small branches lodged in various places and a bird corpse in a radiator. Back at base the evidence was used to good effect in emphasising how low he had flown. When Bateson returned he insisted he was so low that in flying down the streets of Antwerp he 'could see the tears in a pretty girl's eyes' as he left. He very nearly didn't leave as some flak gunners managed to silence one of his aircraft's engines as he crossed the coast at Knokke.

7/8 JUNE 1944

8AF 399 NIGHT LEAFLET OPERATION

NLS B-17, 10 despatched, 10 effective, Holland, France & Belgium.

14 B-24s of 801BG despatched on *Carpetbagger* ops, France.

8 JUNE 1944

8AF 400

	Despatched		Effective	Target		Bombs Tonnage	E/A	Losses MIA	E	Dam	Casualties KIA	WIA	MIA
1 & 3BD	B-17	640	66	LA FRILLIERE	(P)	182.0		1	1	63	11	0	10
			36	ORLEANS	(P)	110.0							
			30	RENNES A/F	(P)	81.0							
			18	BRUZ	(O)	54.0							
			60	ORLEANS/LES AUBRAIS M/Y	(P)	202.0							
			25	NANTES	(P)	67.0							
			31	LA HUCHETIERE	(P)	61.0							
			61	TOURS/LA RICHE	(P)	120.0							
			57	CINQ MARS BRIDGE	(P)	123.0							
			2	RENNES	(O)	4.0							
			13	T/O		13.0							
2 & 3BD	B-24	538	5	DINON	(O)	15.0		2	3	73	17	4	20
			67	PONTAUBAULT	(P)	199.0							
			1	PRECEY	(O)	3.0							
			1	CINQ MARS BRIDGE	(O)	3.0							
			24	ANGERS (ST.LAUD)	(P)	72.0							
			19	ANGERS	(P)	55.0							
			14	LE MANS/ARNAGE A/F	(P)	35.0							
			30	GRANDVILLE HARBOUR	(O)	116.0							
			13	PONTAUBAULT	(P)	35.0							
			19	RENNES, BRIDGE NEAR	(O)	63.0							
			42	NANTES	(P)	94.0							
			9	PRECEY	(O)	21.0							
			55	CINQ MARS BRIDGE	(P)	122.0							
			26	T/O		26.0							
TOTALS:		1178	724			1876.0	0	3	4	136	28	4	30

8 JUNE 1944 *(contd.)*

VIII FC FO 377

	Despatched		Effective	Target	Bombs Tonnage	E/A	Losses MIA	E	Dam	Casualties KIA	WIA	MIA
	P-51		116	ESCORT FOR BOMBERS		3–0– 1	2	1				
	P-38	381		SWEEPS AND			0	1				
	P-47	24		PATROLS BEACH-		1–0– 0	0	0				
	P-51	89		HEAD AND CHANNEL AREAS			3	1				
	P-47	333		FIGHTER-BOMBER		27–2– 4	6	0				
	P-51	526		MISSIONS COMMUNI-CATIONS IN NW FRANCE	256.0	21–0–11 (G)	11	1				
TOTALS		1353			256.0	31–2– 5 21–0–11 (G)	22	4		1	0	21

REMARKS: Heavy bombers attacked rail targets and airfields in France. 2 attempts to attack Melun bridge by 458BG *Azon* unit foiled by cloud. All bomb groups operating except 34BG. Bomb group losses:– 390BG – 1, 446BG – 1, 493BG – 1. During assembly 486BG B-24 cr. at Gosfield, 7 k; 388 BG B-17 cr. Burnt Fen, 10 k; 448BG B-24 c/l Woodbridge A/F after Frag bomb exploded, crew safe. 491BG B-24 cr. t/o base, 9 k. All Fighter groups operated. Fighter group e/a credits:– 56FG – 7, 339FG – 11, 353FG – 5, 355FG – 1, 356FG – 3, 361FG – 3. Fighter group losses:– 4FG – 2, 339FG – 3, 352FG – 3, 355FG – 2, 356FG – 6, 357FG – 1, 359FG – 4, 361FG – 1. 357FG pilot baled over Channel and rescued. 356FG pilot baled off Orford, lost. MIA 4FG P-51 collided on return; 364FG P-38 cr. Funtington, pilot baled. B/d 355FG P-51 Cat E. 339FG P-51 abandoned over UK coast, pilot safe.

OTHER OPERATIONS: 7PG despatched 18 F-5s and 3 Spitfires on PR to France. 2 F-5s MIA 1 802RG Mosquito on beach-head area recon, cr. Wycombe Marsh on return, crew killed. 1 802RG Mosquito on WR to NW France. 2 B-17s on routine weather flights.

9 JUNE 1944

Bad weather prevented operations. P-38s attempted shipping cover off Normandy. 7PG despatched 5 a/c but all turned back. 2 B-17 performed routine weather flights over UK and Atlantic.

10 JUNE 1944

8AF 403

	Despatched		Effective	Target		Bombs Tonnage	E/A	Losses MIA	E	Dam	Casualties KIA	WIA	MIA
1 & 3BD	B-17	507	24	EQUIHEN	(P)	48.0		0	1	36	6	4	0
			23	HARDELOT	(P)	46.0							
			26	ST.GABRIEL	(P)	52.0							
			36	GAEL A/F	(P)	72.0							
			55	NANTES/ BOUGUENAIS A/F	(P)	109.0							
			59	VANNES A/F	(P)	117.0							
			26	BERCK	(P)	51.0							
			39	MERLIMONT PLAGE	(P)	75.0							
			10	TOUCQUET-PARIS-PLAGE	(P)	19.0							
2BD	B-24	257	23	WIMEREAU	(P)	67.0		1	2	28	0	0	10
			34	BOULOGNE	(P)	92.0							
			26	DREUX A/F	(P)	46.0							
			39	CONCHES A/F	(S)	101.0							
			65	EVREUX/FAUVILLE A/F	(P)	165.0							
			13	BOULOGNE	(P)	41.0							
	B-24	119	45	CHATEAUDUN A/F	(P)	124.0							
			66	ORLEANS/BRICY A/F	(P)	182.0		0	0	0	0	0	0
TOTALS:		883	609			1407.0		1	3	64	6	4	10

VIII FC FO 379, 380, 381

	Despatched		Effective	Target	Bombs Tonnage	E/A	Losses MIA	E	Dam	Casualties KIA	WIA	MIA
	P-38	405		SWEEPS AND ESCORT		5–2–1		0				
	P-47	3		BEACH-HEAD AND		0–0–1 (G)	7	0				
	P-51	364		N FRANCE FOR ABOVE BOMBERS								
	P-47	506		FIGHTER-BOMBER		8–0–2	15	3				
	P-51	213		MISSIONS COMMUNI-CATION TARGETS BEACH-HEAD AREA	254.2	1–0–1 (G)	2	1				
TOTALS:		1,491			254.2	13–2–3 1–0–2(G)	24	4		1	0	24

REMARKS: Heavy bombers to tactical targets in France, airfields and choke-points. Morning force consisted of groups of 1CBW, 2CBW, 20CBW, 41CBW, 45CBW, 92CBW, 95CBW, 96CBW and 492BG. Later groups of 14CBW and 96CBW attacked airfields (492BG flew 2 missions). Bomb group losses:– 448BG – 1. A 303BG B-17 cr. at Great Gidding 6 k. Two B-24s c/l on return. 446BG B-24 cr. Metfield, crew baled, 1 k. All Fighter groups operated, despatching between 2 and 9 missions each. Fighter group e/a credits:– 78FG – 9, 339FG – 2, 352FG – 3, 353FG – 1, 359FG – 1. Fighter group losses:– 4FG – 2, 56FG – 1, 78FG – 9, 339FG – 1, 352FG – 3, 353FG – 4, 356FG – 1, 357FG – 1, 359FG – 1, 361FG – 1. 'Going out' two 78FG P-47s collided in cloud and cr. Southminster, 1 pilot killed, 1 baled. Two P-51 pilots (339FG and 352FG) baled over sea and lost. B/d 353FG P-47 and 359FG P-51 cr. beach-head, pilots safe.

10/11 JUNE 1944

8AF 404 NIGHT LEAFLET OPERATION

NLS B-17, 11 despatched, 11 effective, Norway and France.

11 JUNE 1944

8AF 405

	Despatched		Effective	Target		Bombs Tonnage	E/A	Losses MIA	E	Dam	Casualties KIA	WIA	MIA
1 & 3BD	B-17	471	38	BEAUMONT-LE-ROGER A/F	(P)	83.0		2	1	5	0	0	20
			50	BERNAY/ST.MARTIN A/F	(P)	111.0							
			33	CONCHES A/F	(S)	80.0							
			37	DINARD/PLEURTUIT A/F	(P)	91.0							
			27	TOUCQUET-PARIS-PLAGE	(P)	68.0				6			
			34	MERLIMONT PLAGE	(P)	77.0							
			50	PONTAUBAULT BRIDGE	(P)	96.0							
			36	BERCK	(P)	81.0							
			4	T/O		9.0							
2BD	B-24	584	34	CORMEILLES-EN-VEXIN A/F	(P)	92.0		1	0	14	1	3	4
			27	BEAUVAIS/ NIVELLIERS A/F	(P)	79.0							
			12	BEAUVAIS/TILLE A/F	(O)	30.0							
			36	BEAUMONT-SUR-OISE A/F	(P)	98.0							
			7	POIX A/F	(O)	13.0							
			19	VICOMTE-SUR-RANCE	(P)	57.0							
			19	CREIL A/F	(P)	51.0							
			18	MONTFORD BRIDGE	(P)	70.0							
			41	BLOIS/ST.DENIS	(P)	123.0							
			32	MONTAUBAN M/Y	(O)	128.0							
			52	T/O		174.0							
TOTALS:		1055	606			1611.0	0	3	1	19	1	3	24

VIII FC FO 382

	Despatched		Target	Bombs Tonnage	E/A	Losses MIA	E	Dam	Casualties KIA	WIA	MIA
	P-38	143	PATROLS BEACH-HEAD		2–0–0	0	0		0	0	0
	P-47	87	AREA FOR BOMBER			0	0		0	0	0
	P-51	144	FORCE			0	0		0	0	0
	P-38	77	FIGHTER-BOMBER	214.0	3–2–5	3	0		0	0	3
	P-47	195	MISSIONS COMMUNI-		0–0–1(G)	1	0		0	0	1
	P-51	268	CATION TARGETS OVER NW FRANCE			4	0		0	0	3
TOTALS:		914		214.0	5–2–5 0–0–1 (G)	8	0		0	0	7

REMARKS: Tactical targets in support of invasion:– Airfields and rail targets in Paris area, Brittany and Loire valley. All B-17 groups of 4CBW, 13CBW, 45DBW and 94CBW plus 91BG, 92BG and 381BG. All B-24 groups except 448BG participated although the 3BD groups failed to bomb. Bomb group losses:– 96BG – 1, 390BG – 1, 491BG – 1. The 491BG B-24 ditched 6 miles E of Beachy Head, 5 rescued. One B-17 c/l in England.

All fighter groups operating – some flew 3 missions. Fighter group e/a credits:– 55FG – 8, 356FG – 2. Fighter group losses:– 4FG – 2, 55FG – 3, 78FG – 1, 355FG – 1, 359FG – 1. One 352FG pilot baled over sea 6 miles from Le Touquet and rescued.

11/12 JUNE 1944

8AF 406 NIGHT LEAFLET OPERATION

NLS B-17, 5 despatched, 5 effective; France and Low Countries. 1 B-17 with b/d.

12 JUNE 1944

8AF 407

	Despatched		Effective	Target	Bombs Tonnage	E/A	Losses MIA	E	Dam	Casualties KIA	WIA	MIA
1, 2 & 3BD	B-17	769	691	16 A/Fs iN NW FRANCE & 6 R/R BRIDGES IN RENNES & ST.NAZAIRE AREA	3,103.0	1–1–0	6	1	188	5	5	39
	B-24	673	586				2	2	52	2	9	19
TOTALS:		1,442	1277		3,103.0	1–1–0	8	3	240	7	14	58

VIII FC FO 383 & 384

Despatched		Effective	Target	Bombs Tonnage	E/A	Losses MIA	E	Dam	Casualties KIA	WIA	MIA
P-38	234		ESCORT, SWEEPS, PATROLS OVER CHANNEL NW OF PARIS & RENNES AREA		20–0– 8	3	1		0	0	
P-47	80				1–0– 0 (G)	1	0		0	0	
P-51	201					3	0		0	0	
P-38	93		FIGHTER-BOMBER 5 R/R TARGETS IN TOURS – PARIS AREA		5–0– 2	1	1		0	0	
P-47	183				1–0– 0 (G)	8	1		0	0	
P-38	45		ESCORT TO 9AF B-26 AND A-20		0	0	0		0	0	
P-51	152					0	0		0	0	
TOTALS:	988				25–0–10 2–0– 0 (G)	16	3		0	0	15

REMARKS: All bomb groups operated. Visual bombing. Luftwaffe operated in strength for first time since D-Day. Bomb group losses:– 100BG – 2, 303BG – 1, 306BG – 1, 351BG – 1, 385BG 1, 446BG – 1, 448BG – 1. The 351BG B-17 ditched 25 miles SE of Dungeness, all rescued. A 100BG B-17 ditched 5 miles N of Calais, 3 saved. Going out 93BG B-24 cr. Newport, Essex, crew baled. B/d 467BG B-24 became first heavy bomber to land on a Normandy airstrip. Bomb loading accident at Deenethorpe, 7 men killed. On return 388BG B-17 c/l Honington, m/f; b/d 445BG B-24 cr. landing Gt. Ashfield A/F.

All Fighter groups operated. Fighter group e/a credits:– 56FG – 5, 353FG – 8½, 352FG – 3. Fighter group losses:– 20FG – 4, 78FG – 1, 353FG – 8, 359FG – 3. Two pilots (364FG and 353FG) who baled out over Channel, rescued. 20FG P-38 cr. near base after t/o. B/d 20FG P-38 and 56FG P-47 c/l beach-head.

OTHER OPERATIONS: 7PG despatched 29 F-5 and Spitfires on PR to France and Germany. 3 Mosquitoes of 802BG scouted for the bombers. 1 Mosquito on WR and 2 B-17s on routine WR.

12/13 JUNE 1944

8AF 408 NIGHT LEAFLET OPERATION

NLS B-17, 7 despatched, 7 effective; France and Belgium.

16 B-24 of 801BG on *Carpetbagger* sorties.

13 JUNE 1944

8AF 409

	Despatched		Effective	Target	Bombs Tonnage	E/A	Losses MIA	E	Dam	Casualties KIA	WIA	MIA
1BD	B-17	139	37	EVREUX/ FAUVILLE A/F	(P) 89.0		0	0	30	0	0	0
			52	DREUX A/F	(P) 116.0							
			40	ST.ANDRE DE L'EURE	(S) 90.0							
TOTALS:		139	129		295.0	0	0	0	30	0	0	0

8AF 410

1BD	B-17	112	41	BEAUMONT-SUR-OISE A/F	(P) 94.0			0	15	0	0	0
			56	BEAUVAIS/ NIVELLIERS A/F	(P) 124.0							

continued on facing page

	Despatched		Effective	Target	Bombs Tonnage	E/A	Losses MIA	E	Dam	Casualties KIA	WIA	MIA
2BD	B-24	148	10	DINARD/PLEURTUIT (O) A/F	26.0		2	1	16	1	0	19
			26	PLOERMEL BRIDGE	67.0							
			19	VANNES BRIDGE	48.0							
			24	VICOMTE-SUR-RANCE BRIDGE	58.0							
			21	MONTFORT-SUR-MEU BRIDGE	52.0							
			12	PORCARO BRIDGE	27.0							
			3	T/O	7.0							
TOTALS:		260	212		503.0	0	2	1	31	1	0	19

VIII FC FO 386 & 387

Despatched		Effective	Target	Bombs Tonnage	E/A	Losses MIA	E	Dam	Casualties KIA	WIA	MIA
P-51	113	101	ESCORT FOR 8AF 409		4–0–0	0	0		0	0	1
P-38	12		ESCORT FOR 8AF 410			0	0				
P-47	47					0	0				
P-51	174					1	0				
P-38	97	58	FIGHTER-BOMBER MISSIONS	23.0		2	0		0	0	2
		17	LA POISSONNIERE MONTJEAN	8.5							
P-47s	199	43	LA PORT BOULET	15.0	2–0–0	1	1		0	0	2
		24	MONTLOUIS	15.0							
		33	TRANSPORT TARGETS	11.0							
		47	LA PORT BOULET	36.0							
		31	CHINON	15.5							
P-51	35		ESCORT FIGHTER-BOMBERS			0	0		0	0	0
P-38	12		ESCORT 9AF BOMBERS			0	0		0	0	0
P-47	35					0	0		0	0	0
P-38	64	62	CHANNEL PATROL			0	0		0	0	0
TOTALS:	675	416		124.0	6–0–0	4	1		0	0	5

REMARKS: 8AF 409 flown by 41CBW groups. Part of 8AF 410 Force frustrated by cloud: groups attacking were 91BG, 398BG, 93BG, 445BG, 453BG, 458BG and 489BG. Bomb group losses:– 93BG – 2. A 445BG B-24 exploded in a c/l at Manston A/F.

All fighter groups operating: Fighter group e/a credits:– 78FG – 2, 356FG – 1, 361FG – 3. Fighter group losses:– 20FG – 2, 56FG – 1, 339FG – 1. The 2 P-38s lost fell to heavy Flak over Guernsey. B/d 355FG P-47 c/l beach-head.

OTHER OPERATIONS: 16 F-5 and Spitfires on PR to France and Germany. 1 F-5 MIA. 1 Mosquito on WR Paris area and 3 B-17s on routine WR.

13/14 JUNE 1944

8AF 411 NIGHT LEAFLET OPERATION

NLS B-17, 8 despatched, 8 effective; France.

6 B-24s of 801BG on *Carpetbagger* operations France.

The top top brass. On a rare visit to Britain, Gen George Marshall, the overall boss of the US Army, visited Bassingbourn on 13 June for a look at the 8AF. Flanking the four-star General are two-star Fred Anderson (8AF Ops) and one-star Bob Williams (CG 1BD). Behind Anderson Gen Arnold with four stars chats with Col Henry Terry, CO 91BG and a very experienced bomber pilot.

14 JUNE 1944

8AF 412

	Despatched		Effective	Target		Bombs Tonnage	E/A	Losses MIA	E	Dam	Casualties KIA	WIA	MIA
1BD	B-17	502	134	LE BOURGET A/F	(P)	332.2	0–5–1	11	0	139	6	14	97
			24	COULOMMIERS A/F	(P)	45.5							
			25	CREIL A/F	(O)	45.7							
			69	BRETIGNY A/F	(P)	126.3							
			50	MELUN A/F	(P)	82.0							
			66	CREIL A/F	(P)	78.9							
			69	ETAMPES A/F	(P)	87.7							
2BD	B-24	466	103	CHATEAUDUN A/F	(P)	215.3		0	0	33	0	0	0
			97	ORLEANS/ BRICY A/F	(P)	182.0							
			61	EMMERICH O/R	(P)	175.6							
			63	EINDHOVEN A/F	(P)	82.2							
			50	BEAUVOIS	(P)	125.0							
			12	T/O		30.0							
			44	DOMLEGER	(P)	125.0							
			7	COXYDE A/F	(O)	17.5							
			4	BEACHES	(O)	10.0							
3BD	B-24	191	7	HAM-SUR-SOMME	(P)	3.5		2	2	56	10	2	4
			8	T/O		10.3							
			52	LILLE/VENDEVILLE	(P)	151.7							
			12	CALAS TRES	(O)	31.0							
			24	T/O		31.2							
			12	DENAIN DROUSEY	(O)	7.6							
			39	LAON/ATHIES	(P)	99.0							
			70	CHIEVRES	(O)	214.3							
3BD	B-17	351	35	ST.TROND A/F	(P)	70.3		1	2	73	0	0	1
			95	FLORENNES A/F	(P)	327.2							
			52	LE CULOT	(P)	43.5							
			61	BRUSSELS/ MELSBROEK	(P)	141.8							
2BD	B-24	15	7	HAM-SUR-SOMME BRIDGE	(P)	17.5		0	0	0	0	0	0
			5	T/O (AZON)		12.5							
TOTALS:		1525	1357			2922.3		14	4	301	16	16	102

VIII FC FO 388 & 389

Despatched		Effective	Target	Bombs Tonnage	E/A	Losses MIA	E	Dam	Casualties KIA	WIA	MIA
P-47	103		ESCORT FOR 1 & 2BD			2	0				2
P-47	176	168	FIGHTER-BOMBER MISSIONS LUFT-WAFFE HQ (CHANTILLY) & PANZER COLUMNS	42.8	0–0–1	0	0				0
P-38	242	234	BEACHHEAD PATROLS		4–1–7	3	1				3
P-47	190	178	& SWEEPS IN FRONT			1	0				1
P-51	197	171	OF BOMBER FORCE			1	0				1
TOTALS:	908	751		42.8	4–1–8	7	1		0	0	7

REMARKS: Visual attacks on airfields in France and the Low Countries, construction and supply sites in northern France and oil refinery in Holland. 1BD groups attacking were all of 40CBW, 41CBW and 94CBW and 381BG. All 2BD groups except 445BG participated. All 3BD groups despatched. 458BG *Azon* unit operated. Bomb group losses:– 92BG – 1, 95BG – 1, 351BG – 3, 384BG – 1, 401BG – 1, 457BG – 5, 493BG – 2. One 457BG B-17 ditched off Hastings, 5 saved. On return, a 94BG B-17 and 96BG B-17 cr. landing base. 493BG B-24 cr. Melton, 10 k. 34BG B-24 c/l Manston A/F.

All fighter groups except 4FG operating. Fighter group e/a credits:– 55FG – 3, 357FG – 2. Fighter group losses:– 20FG – 2, 55FG – 3, 356FG – 1, 357FG – 1. 4FG preparing for shuttle mission to the Soviet Union. 364FG P-38 c/l beach-head.

OTHER OPERATIONS: 7PG despatched 29 F-5s and 5 Spitfires on PR to France and Belgium. 3 Mosquitoes on WR (1 scouted 3BD targets) (1 at 2BD targets). 2 B-17s on routine weather flights.

14/15 JUNE 1944

8AF 413 NIGHT LEAFLET OPERATION

NLS B-17, 4 despatched, 3 effective; France.

20 B-24s of 801BG on *Carpetbagger* sorties.

A ground launched rocket missile caused this damage to 388BG's *Panhandle* during an attack on a V-weapon site, 15 June. The missile struck No.3 engine, ricocheted into the fuselage and exploded leaving Sgt Biggs, the top turret gunner, with nasty burns. Despite extensive damage to various control lines Lt McFarlene brought the bomber down safely at Manston.

Lt Harry White managed to crash-land B-24H 42-95025 at Eye after it was badly damaged by enemy fighters during a surprise attack over France on 15 June. The tail gunner was killed by enemy fire and after a cannon shell exploded in the fuselage the two waist gunners baled out. (via S. Evans)

15 JUNE 1944

8AF 414

	Despatched		Effective	Target	Bombs Tonnage	E/A	Losses MIA	E	Dam	Casualties KIA	WIA	MIA
1 & 3BD	B-17	747	71	NANTES R/B N	210.0		2	1	267	0	7	18
			46	NANTES R/B E	137.0							
			70	ANGOULEME M/Y	204.0							
			71	LA POISSONNIERE R/V	176.0							
			144	BORDEAUX/MERIGNAC A/F	343.0							
			12	GAEL A/F	35.0							
			10	VIADUCT N. OF NANTES	25.0							
			172	HANNOVER/MISBURG O/R	419.0							
			17	WILSTER	42.0							
			16	WESERMÜNDE	40.0							
			2	HANNOVER AREA	5.0							
			1	HELIGOLAND	2.0							
			59	BEAUVOIR V/S	176.0							
2 & 3BD	B-24	614	27	ST.CYR	81.0		0	2	109	0	5	0
			54	TOURS-LA RICHE R/B	174.0							
			12	TOURS-LA RICHE H/B	36.0							
			46	GUYANCOURT A/F	69.0							
			61	EVREUX/ FAUVILLE A/F	183.0							
			89	LE PORT BOULET R/B	267.0							
			44	CINQ MARS BRIDGE	141.0							
			12	ETAPLES R/B (*AZON*)	6.0							
			7	PECRONE R/B (*AZON*)	4.0							
			59	TOURS-LA FRILLERIE	199.0							
			12	LE MANS A/F	46.0							
			8	T/O	22.0							
			21	BUC A/F	63.0							
			45	ETAMPES/MODESIR A/F	118.0							
			12	ORLEANS/SARAN A/F	36.0							
TOTALS:		1361	1200		3259.0	0	2	3	376	0	12	18

15 JUNE 1944 *(contd.)*

VIII FC FO 390 & 391

	Despatched		Effective	Target	Bombs Tonnage	E/A	Losses MIA	E	Dam	Casualties KIA	WIA	MIA
	P-38	96		B-17 & B-24 ESCORT		5–0–5	2	0		0	0	2
	P-47	202					0	0		0	0	0
	P-51	211					1	1		0	0	1
	P-38	48	36	FIGHTER-BOMBER MISSION ETAPLES	34.5		1	0		0	0	1
	P-38	185	177	FIGHTER SWEEP IN FRONT OF BOMBER FORCE			0	0		0	0	0
TOTALS:		742			34.5	5–0–5	4	1		0	0	4

REMARKS: Airfields and rail targets in NW France. Oil targets in W.Germany. Visual bombing. Groups participating:– all 1BD except 379BG and 401BG, all 2BD except 458BG, all 3BD. Only *Azon* unit of 458BG operating. Bomb group losses:– 306BG – 1, 381BG – 1, 492BG – 1. B/d 388BG B-17 down Manston A/F, Cat E. B/d 392BG B-24 down Eye A/F, Cat E. 492BG crew baled over beach-head.

All Fighter groups except 301FG operating. Fighter group e/a credits:– 339FG – 4, 356FG – 1. Fighter group losses:– 20FG – 1, 55FG – 1, 339FG – 1, 364FG – 1. A 357FG P-51 cr. on t/o base.

OTHER OPERATIONS: 7PG despatched 20 F-5s and 6 Spitfires to France, Belgium, Holland and Germany. 1 Spitfire MIA. 2 802RG Mosquitoes weather scouting for bombers. 3 B-17 on routine Atlantic and UK weather flights.

16 JUNE 1944

8AF 416

	Despatched		Effective	Target	Bombs Tonnage	E/A	Losses MIA	E	Dam	Casualties KIA	WIA	MIA
1BD	B-17	146	38	LAON/ATHIES A/F	114.0		1	0	58	0	3	9
			38	JUVINCOURT A/F	114.0							
			17	LAON/COUVRON A/F	48.0							
			18	R/R T/O	54.0							
2BD	B-24	224	17	BEAUVAIS/TILLE A/F (O)	54.0		0	1	13	5	2	0
			12	ST.ANDRE DE L'EURE A/F	32.0							
			43	DOMLEGER V/S	126.0							
			44	SAUTRECOURT V/S	117.0							
			48	RENESCURE V/S	121.0							
			21	BEAUVOIR V/S	62.0							
			17	AUTHE A/F	51.0							
TOTALS:		370	313		893.0	0	1	1	71	5	5	9

VIII FC FO 393

	Despatched		Effective	Target	Bombs Tonnage	E/A	Losses MIA	E	Dam	Casualties KIA	WIA	MIA
	P-38	165		ESCORT FOR ABOVE		1–0–0	0	0		0	0	0
	P-47	88					0	0		0	0	0
	P-51	172					0	0		0	0	0
	P-51	70		SWEEP AGAINST STALLED TRAINS			0	0		0	0	0
	P-38	50		FIGHTER-BOMBER ATTACKS ON TROOPS IN ARRAS-ST.POL AREA	32.0		3	1		0	0	3
	P-47	75					0	0		0	0	0
TOTALS:		620			32.0	1–0–0	3	1		0	0	3

REMARKS: Airfields and *Noball* V-weapon sites in France. Poor weather restricted operations. Groups participating:– 1BD – 303BG, 379BG, 384BG; 2BD – 93BG, 446BG, 448BG, 489BG, 491BG. Bomb group losses:– 379BG – 1. B/d 93BG B-24 cr. Redenhall, 5 k, 4 inj. All fighter groups except 4FG operating. Extensive use of drop tanks as incendiaries in attacks on rail traffic. The four P-38 groups were of this date back on regular operations having been detailed to beach-head patrol from 6 June to 15 June. Fighter group e/a credits:– 56FG – 1. Fighter group losses:– 55FG – 3. A 20FG P-38 cr. Purleigh, pilot killed.

OTHER OPERATIONS: 3 B-17s on routine weather flights. 1 Mosquito on WR over France.

16/17 JUNE 1944

8AF 417 NIGHT LEAFLET OPERATION

NLS B-17, 10 despatched, 10 effective; France

17 JUNE 1944

8AF 418

	Despatched		Effective	Target		Bombs Tonnage	E/A	Losses MIA	E	Dam	Casualties KIA	WIA	MIA
1BD	B-17	174	52	MONCHY-BRETON A/F	(P)	118.4		2	0	22	0	0	20
			18	CHATEAUDUN A/F	(P)	33.8							
			18	VILLIERS/L'EVEQUE A/F	(O)	40.0							
			31	R/R BRIDGE AT NOYEN	(O)	67.5							
2BD	B-24	158	9	MELUN A/F	(P)	26.5		0	0	0	0	0	0
			12	BRUNNELLES	(O)	35.5							
			1	T/O		3.0							
			26	GUYANCOURT/ CAUDRON A/F	(P)	66.0							
			1	DREUX	(O)	2.5							
			1	ST.VALERY	(O)	2.5							
			17	BRETIGNY A/F	(P)	50.0							
			28	LAVAL A/F	(P)	83.0							
			18	LE MANS/ARNAGE A/F	(P)	52.9							
TOTALS: 10		332	232			581.6	0	2	0	22	0	0	20

VIII FC FO 394	Despatched	Target	Bombs Tonnage	E/A	Losses MIA	KIA	WIA	MIA
P-38	43	ESCORT 1BD B-17		1–0–0	0	0	0	0
P-47	39				0	0	0	0
P-51	90				1	0	0	1
P-47	87	ESCORT 2BD B-24		2–0–1	0	0	0	0
P-51	170			3–0–0 (G)	0	0	0	0
P-38	99	FIGHTER-BOMBER R/R BRIDGES AT CORBIE AND PERONNE	42.0		4	0	0	4
TOTALS:	528		42.0	3–0–1 3–0–0 (G)	5	0	0	5

REMARKS: Airfields in France, mostly PFF groups participating:– 1BD – all 40CBW and 94CBW; 2BD – all14CBW, 20CBW, 96CBW and 389CBW, 445BG. Bomb group losses:– 306BG – 2. Fighter group e/a credits:– 78FG – 2, 353FG – 1. Fighter group losses:– 20FG – 3, 55FG – 1, 339FG – 1.

8AF 419

	Despatched		Effective	Target		Bombs Tonnage	E/A	Losses MIA	E	Dam	Casualties KIA	WIA	MIA
2 & 3BD	B-24	312	80	ANGERS A/F	(P)	184.9		1	0	35	0	0	10
			55	TOURS A/F	(P)	134.7							
			1	LE MANS	(O)	2.0							
			75	LAVAL A/F	(P)	223.0							
			25	LONRAY A/S	(P)	60.8							
			38	ESSAY A/S	(P)	98.2							
TOTALS:		312	274			703.6	0	1	0	35	0	0	10

VIII FC FO 395	Despatched	Target	Bombs Tonnage	E/A	Losses MIA	KIA	WIA	MIA
P-47	122	ESCORT B-24s			0	0	0	0
P-51	148				1	0	0	1
P-38	49	FIGHTER-BOMBER CORBIE–PERRONNE R/R BRIDGES ETC	55.5		2	0	0	2
P-47	39				0	0	0	0
P-38	47	ESCORT FOR ABOVE			0	0	0	0
TOTALS:	405		55.5	0	3	0	0	3

REMARKS: Airfields in France – afternoon mission. Groups participating:– 2BD – all 95CBW and 96CBW, 392BG, 446BG, 492BG; 3BD – 34BG, 486BG, 493BG. Bomb group losses:– 458BG – 1. Fighter group losses:– 357FG – 1, 479FG – 2.

All fighter groups except 4FG operating on Mission 418 or 419.

OTHER OPERATIONS: 7PG despatched 18 F-5s and 5 Spitfires to France, Belgium and Holland. 2 Mosquitoes of 802RG over continent on WR. 4 B-17s despatched on WR UK and Atlantic.

17/18 JUNE 1944

8AF 420 NIGHT LEAFLET OPERATION

NLS B-17, 10 despatched, 9 effective; France.

18 JUNE 1944

8AF 421

	Despatched		Effective	Target		Bombs Tonnage	E/A	Losses MIA	E	Dam	Casualties KIA	WIA	MIA
1BD	B-17	522	18	HARBURG-EBANO O/R		48.0		4	2	172	1	7	39
			35	HAMBURG (CITY)	(S)	73.5							
			54	HAMBURG-EUROTANK O/R		146.5							
			35	HAMBURG (CITY)	(S)	90.5							
			36	HAMBURG-SCHINDLER O/R		80.0							
			20	HAMBURG (CITY)	(S)	44.0							
			38	HAMBURG-OSSAG O/R		97.0							
			22	HAMBURG (CITY)	(S)	48.5							
			209	HAMBURG (CITY)	(S)	533.0							
2BD	B-24	421	45	STADE A/F	(P)	108.0		4	0	47	0	8	39
			88	HAMBURG	(O)	229.0							
			80	HAMBURG	(O)	215.0							
			27	BREMERHAVEN	(O)	64.0							
			13	HUSUM A/F	(O)	33.0							
			8	HELIGOLAND A/F	(O)	24.0							
			1	WRIST M/Y	(O)	3.0							
			79	BREMERHAVEN	(O)	206.0							
			28	WESERMÜNDE	(O)	72.0							
			9	NORDENHAM	(O)	18.0							
			5	T/O		13.0							
3BD	B-17	368	88	HANNOVER-MISBURG O/R		210.0		3	0	112	0	3	31
			60	HANNOVER (CITY)		187.0							
			2	T/O		5.0							
			18	BREMEN-OSLEBSHAUSEN		43.0							
			85	BREMEN AREA	(O)	208.5							
			3	T/O		7.5							
2BD	B-24	67	54	BRUNSBÜTTEL		131.0		0	0	6	0	0	0
			58	WATTEN V/S		220.0							
TOTALS:		1378	1218			3158.0	0	11	1	337	1	18	109
VIII FC													
	P-38	47		ESCORT 1BD				0	0		0	0	0
	P-51	66						0	0		0	0	0
	P-38	48		ESCORT 2BD GERMANY				0	0		0	0	0
	P-51	84						0	1		0	0	0
	P-38	103		ESCORT 3BD				0	0		0	0	0
	P-47	124						0	0		0	0	0
	P-51	65						0	0		0	0	0
	P-47	48		ESCORT 2BD WATTEN				0	0		0	0	0
	P-38	98	94	FIGHTER-BOMBER R/R BRIDGES IN ST.QUENTIN AREA		13.9		0	0		0	0	0
	P-47	87	82					0	0		0	0	0
	P-51	47		SWEEP DOL DE BRETAGNE				3	0		0	0	3
TOTALS:		817				13.9		3	1		0	0	3

REMARKS: First major mission to strategic targets since D-Day. Oil refineries at Hamburg and Misburg briefed for 1BD and 3BD. Oil refineries at Bremen and Luftwaffe control centres at Fassberg and Stade briefed for 2BD. Weather deteriorated and attacks made by PFF. Groups participating:– all 1BD and 3BD B-17s, all 2BD B-24s less 95CBW. Bomb group losses:– 91BG – 1, 95BG – 1, 305BG – 1, 379BG – 1, 398BG – 1, 447BG – 2, 448BG – 1, 458BG – 1, 492BG – 2. B/d 492BG B-24 ditched off Gr. Yarmouth, 2 rescued, the other 492BG a/c landed Sweden. On return, a b/d B-17 c/l in England. In afternoon a small force of 2BD B-24s attacked *Noball* targets by GH. Groups involved were

93BG, 448BG, 458BG, 467BG, 489BG, 491BG. MIA 91BG PFF a/c had pact 398BG crew. All Fighter groups operating. No claims. Fighter group losses:– 4FG – 3. 4FG P-51 c/l base on return. Two groups of fighter-bombers did not bomb due to weather.

OTHER OPERATIONS: 7PG despatched 13 F-5s and 1 Spitfire on PR over France. 2 802RG Mosquitoes scouting for bombers over Germany. 4 802RG Mosquitoes on WR Hamburg and Paris areas. 2 B-17s on routine WR over UK and Atlantic.

18/19 JUNE 1944

8AF 422

9 B-24s of 801BG on *Carpetbagger* operations France. 1 B-24 MIA hit tree at drop zone.

482BG H2X Mosquito on scope photo mission.

19 JUNE 1944

8AF 423

	Despatched		Effective	Target	Bombs Tonnage	E/A	Losses MIA	E	Dam	Casualties KIA	WIA	MIA
1 &	B-17	464	84	BORDEAUX/ MERIGNAC A/F (P)	152.5		7	2	11	0	3	59
3BD			34	LANDES-DE-BUSSAC A/F (P)	64.5							
			39	CAZAUX A/F (P)	71.0							
			92	CORMES ECLUSE A/F (P)	235.0							
			12	CABANAC A/F (O)	22.5							
			3	T/O	7.5							
8AF 424												
1 &	B-17	267	96	PAS DE CALAIS V/S	540.0		0	0	50	0	0	0
2BD	B-24	156	144				1	1	9	0	2	10
3BD	B-17	124	120	PAS DE CALAIS V/S	582.0		0	0	15	0	0	0
	B-24	156	150				0	0	13	0	0	0
TOTALS:		1167	774		1675.0	0	8	3	98	0	5	69
VIII FC												
	P-38	88		ESCORT 8AF 423			4					4
	P-51	261					6					6

VII FC FO 400

Despatched		Effective	Target	Bombs Tonnage	E/A	Losses MIA	E	Dam	Casualties KIA	WIA	MIA
P-38	101		ESCORT FIRST			0	0				0
P-47	86		*NOBALL*			0	0				0
P-38	95		ESCORT SECOND			0	1				0
P-47	36		*NOBALL*			0	0				0
P-51	48					0	0				0
TOTALS:	715				0–0–0	16			0	0	16

REMARKS: Sent to 6 airfields in Bordeaux area for 8AF 423. Heavy cloud up 30,000 ft caused several formations to abandon mission. Groups attacking were 91BG, 100BG, 379BG, 381BG, 384BG, 390BG, 398BG, 401BG, 452BG, 457BG. Bomb group losses:– 381BG – 1, 379BG – 1, 401BG – 3, 447BG – 1, 452BG – 1. Going out 2 379BG B-17s collided, 1 cr. in Thames, 1 at Canvey, 11 k. On return, 452BG B-17 c/l Wattisham A/F, crew safe. 2 MIA B-17s (401BG & 452BG) interned in Spain. MIA 447BG B-17 was 94BG a/c with 447BG crew. 8AF 424 flown in afternoon to *Noball* targets but only that part of force with GH leaders able to bomb. All groups of 41CBW plus 305BG and 306BG from 1BD took part. All groups of 2CBW, 14CBW, 95CBW plus 458BG, 466BG from 2BD took part. 3BD force did not attack. Bomb group losses:– 93BG – 1. B/d B-24 c/l on return. Of VIII FC fighters, 56FG and 356FG not operating. Fighter group e/a claims: 361FG – 1. Fighter group losses:– 4FG – 1, 339FG – 3, 355FG – 2, 361FG – 6, 479FG – 4. A collision over Murau claimed 2 of 479BG P-38s MIA. 20FG P-38 c/l near base on return.

OTHER OPERATIONS: 7PG despatched 4 F-5s and 4 Spitfires to France and Germany. 2 B-17s and 2 B-24s on combat camera missions over France. Return flight to UK by 7PG F-5 from Soviet Union. 3 Mosquitoes on WR over continent. 3 B-17s on routine WR, UK and Atlantic.

20 JUNE 1944

8AF 425

	Despatched		Effective	Target		Bombs Tonnage	E/A	Losses MIA	E	Dam	Casualties KIA	WIA	MIA
2BD	B-24	146	126	PAS DE CALAIS V/S	(P)	312.0		1	1	83	4	8	24
3BD	B-17	341	95	MAGDEBURG/ ROTHENSEE	(P)	215.2	2–0–6	6	2	116	0	11	60
			137	FALLERSLEBEN	(P)	305.0							
			52	KÖNIGSBERG	(P)	115.3							
	B-24	191	169	HANNOVER/MISBURG	(P)	498.0		1	1	89	4	6	9
			3	T/O		7.9							
1BD	B-17	512	60	HARBURG/EBANO	(P)	178.5		7	0	349	1	13	63
			53	HARBURG/RHENANIA	(P)	155.2							
			107	HAMBURG/EURO-TANK	(P)	315.2							
			26	HAMBURG/ SCHINDLER	(P)	72.5							
			53	HAMBURG/ DEUT.PETR.AG	(P)	155.5							
			51	HAMBURG/ALBRECHT	(P)	147.6							
			54	HAMBURG/ SCHLIEMANNS	(P)	160.7							
			50	HAMBURG/ RHENANIA-OSSAG	(P)	144.5							
			12	BRUNSBÜTTEL CANAL LOCK	(O)	34.7							
			2	T/O		6.0							
2BD	B-24	358	245	PÖLITZ	(P)	278.4	10–3–2	34	0	205	3	6	343
			71	OSTERMOOR	(P)	214.0							
			12	T/O		24.6							
8AF 426													
	B-24	380	196	PAS DE CALAIS AREA V/S		575.4		1	0	96	0	0	0
	B-17	37	33										
TOTALS:		1965	1607			3916.2	12–3–8	50	4	938	12	44	499

VIII FC

	Despatched		Effective	Target		Bombs Tonnage	E/A	Losses MIA	E	Dam	Casualties KIA	WIA	MIA
	P-47	44		ESCORT *NOBALL* 8AF 425			3–0– 0	1			0	0	1
	P-38	98		ESCORT 3BD			10–1–10	1			0	0	1
	P-47	86					8–0– 3 (G)	1			0	0	0
	P-51	38						0			0	0	1
	P-38	96		ESCORT 1BD				0			0	0	0
	P-47	48						0			0	0	0
	P-38	50		ESCORT 2BD			28–1– 9	3			0	0	0
	P-51	221					5–0– 9 (G)	0			0	0	0
	P-47	72		ESCORT *NOBALL*				0			0	0	0
	P-51	40		8AF 426				0			0	0	0
	P-47	78		FIGHTER-BOMBER									
			8	MARLE M/Y	(P)	4.0	5–0– 6 (G)	0			0	0	0
			6	THIONVILLE M/Y	(P)	3.0							
			2	TERGNIER M/Y	(P)	1.0							
			4	VERSIGNY M/Y	(P)	2.0							
			12	PLANTLÜNNE A/F	(P)	11.0							
			12	ENSCHEDE A/F	(P)	13.0							
	P-47	38	20	PARIS-SOISSONS AREA		10.0		0			0	0	0
	P-47	40	24	PLANTLÜNNE/ ENSCHEDE		13.2		0			0	0	0
	P-51	162	162	STRAFING PARIS AREA				2			0	0	2
TOTALS:		1111				57.2	41–2–19 18–0–18 (G)	8	1		0	0	5

REMARKS: Visual attacks on oil and industrial targets in Germany and Poland and a small force to *Noball* targets. 8AF 426 was a further attack on *Noball* targets. Groups participating in first *Noball* were 93BG, 445BG, 448BG, 453BG, 466BG, 467BG, 489BG, 491BG. Bomb group losses:– 445BG – 1. B/d B-24 of 466BG c/l Ashford A/F on return. All 1BD and 3BD B-17 groups participated in Germany mission, also 3BD B-24 groups less 34BG and all 2BD groups apart from 489BG and 491BG. Bomb group losses:– 1BD – 91BG – 1, 92BG – 1, 303BG – 1, 306BG – 1, 379BG – 1, 381BG – 1, 457BG – 1; 2BD – 44BG – 1, 93BG – 2, 389BG – 6, 392BG – 4, 446BG – 3, 448BG – 3, 453BG – 1, 492BG – 14; 3BD – 96BG – 3, 385BG – 1, 388BG – 2, 487BG – 1. 20 of these MIA bombers landed or cr. in Sweden (44BG – 1, 93BG – 1, 389BG – 3, 392BG – 2, 446BG – 3, 448BG – 3, 453BG – 1, 492BG – 6). 379BG B-17 ditched 8 miles E. of Yarmouth, 9 saved. Going out 2 388BG B-17s collided, 1 returned base, 1 cr. in sea off Cromer after crew baled over land. B/d 388BG B-17 c/l base, crew safe. 490BG B-24 cr.t/o, 2 k. B/d 96BG B-17 Cat E. Second *Noball* mission flown by 457BG B-17s and 93BG, 389BG, 392BG, 446BG, 458BG, 466BG, 486BG, 489BG, 490BG, 491BG, 492BG, 493BG B-24s. Losses: 489BG – 1. B/d 491BG B-24 c/l on beach at Dungeness, 7 survived. All fighter groups active. Fighter group e/a credits:– 4FG – 9½, 78FG – 3, 352FG – 4, 355FG – 13, 357FG – 5, 359FG – 1. Fighter group losses:– 4FG – 2, 78FG – 1, 352FG – 2, 357FG – 1, 359FG – 1, 479FG – 1. 81 P-51s of IX FC supported Magdeburg mission and lost 1 a/c. On return 361FG P-51 c/l base, pilot safe.

OTHER OPERATIONS: 7PG despatched 24 F-5s and 6 Spitfires to Germany, Holland and France. 2 Mosquitoes of 802RG scouting ahead of bombers. 1 Mosquito on WR to Germany. 2 B-17 on routine UK/Atlantic WR.

20/21 JUNE 1944

8AF 427 NIGHT LEAFLET OPERATION

NLS B-17, 5 despatched, 5 effective; France.

25 B-24s of 801BG on *Carpetbagger* operations, France.

21 JUNE 1944

8AF 428

	Despatched		Effective	Target		Bombs Tonnage	E/A	Losses MIA	E	Dam	Casualties KIA	WIA	MIA
3BD	B-17	163	145	RUHLAND/ SCHWARZHEIDE O/I (FRANTIC MISSION)	(P)	Unknown		1	0	*	1	5	10
1BD	B-17	496	456	BERLIN	(P)	1081.0	16–20–19	16	0	216	1	10	148
			12	T/O		30.0							
2BD	B-24	368	69	GENSHAGEN	(P)	171.0	13– 3– 3	19	2	150	21	20	182
			40	POTSDAM	(O)	103.0							
			8	STENDAL	(O)	20.0							
			47	BERLIN	(S)	115.0							
			52	MARIENFELDE	(P)	118.0							
			23	GENSHAGEN	(O)	56.0							
			16	RANGSDORF	(O)	40.0							
			10	TREBBIN	(O)	25.0							
			8	SELVIG	(O)	20.0							
			28	NIEDERSCHÖNWEIDE	(P)	71.0							
			1	BEDERKESA	(O)	3.0							
			7	T/O BERLIN AREA		17.0							
3BD	B-17	207	80	BASDORF	(P)	181.0		9		142			
			103	BERLIN	(P)	254.0							
			5	T/O		10.0							
TOTALS:		1234	1110			2315.0	29–23–22	45	2	508	24	44	420
8AF 429													
2BD	B-24	75	70	PAS DE CALAIS V/S		200.0				5			
TOTALS:		1309	1180			2515.0	29–23–22	45	2	573	24	44	420

* Second force 3BD damage included with first force

	Despatched		Effective	Target	Bombs Tonnage	E/A	Losses MIA	E	Dam	Casualties KIA	WIA	MIA
VIII FC												
	P-38	72		ESCORT 3BD		3–0–1	2	0		0	0	0
	P-47	38		RUHLAND		0–0–2 (G)	2	0		0	0	0
	P-51	122										
	P-38	99		ESCORT 1BD		4–0–3	1	0		0	0	0
	P-47	95										
	P-51	73										
	P-38	148		ESCORT 2BD		13–0–6	0	1		0	0	0
	P-47	147					0	0		0	0	0
	P-51	116					1	0		0	0	1
	P-38	108		ESCORT 3BD BERLIN			1	0		0	0	1
	P-47	81					1	0		0	0	1
	P-51	91					1	1		0	0	1
	P-47	99		ESCORT 8AF 429			0	0		0	0	0
TOTALS:		1269				20–0–10 0–0– 2(G)	4	2		0	0	4

REMARKS: Major missions to Berlin and Ruhland. Ruhland force, 3BD groups of 13CBW and 45CBW, continued east to land in Soviet Union. All 1BD and 3BD B-17 groups participated in Berlin and Basdorf attacks. Visual bombing. All 2BD groups except those of 95CBW attacked targets in Berlin area. 8AF 429 was to *Noball* targets and involved groups of 20CBW and 95CBW plus 389BG and 466BG. Bomb group losses:– 44BG – 1, 91BG – 5, 93BG – 1, 94BG – 1, 303BG – 3, 351BG – 1, 381BG – 3, 384BG – 1, 385BG – 2, 389BG – 6, 390BG – 1, 392BG – 1, 401BG – 1, 445BG – 2, 446BG – 1, 447BG – 1, 448BG – 3, 452BG – 5, 453BG – 1, 457BG – 2, 466BG – 1, 467BG – 2. 13 MIA bombers landed or cr. in Sweden (93BG – 2, 351BG – 1, 381BG – 1, 384BG – 1, 385BG – 2, 389BG – 2, 448BG – 1, 457BG – 1, 466BG – 1, 467BG – 1). 390BG B-17 ditched, 9 saved. A 445BG B-24 ditched, 4 saved. Two B-17s of Basdorf mission collided over target and lost. 466BG B-24 cr. after t/o near base, 7 killed. On return a b/d 445BG B-24 cr. Gillingham, Norfolk, 5 killed. Prince Bernhard of the Netherlands flew with 489BG to *Noball* target. MIA 91BG PFF a/c had part 398BG crew. All fighter groups active. 4FG and squadron of 352FG accompanied 3BD B-17s to Soviet Union. Fighter group e/a credits:– 4FG – 2, 339FG – 3, 352FG – 8, 355FG – 3. Fighter group losses:– 4FG – 1, 55FG – 1, 56FG – 1, 359FG – 1. IX FC provided 441 fighters in support of 8AF, claiming 9–0–6 for loss of 7. A 20FG P-38 c/l near base on return, pilot safe. B/d P-51 c/l England.

OTHER OPERATIONS: 7PG despatched 16 F-5s and 8 Spitfires to Germany and France. 802RG despatched 1 Mosquito on WR Berlin, 1 Mosquito on WR Brussels, and 2 Mosquitoes to Soviet Union. 2 B-17s on routine WR Atlantic.

INCIDENT

For months S/Sgt Robert L. Gilbert spent his days – and sometimes nights – servicing and repairing fighters at an exposed corner of Debden airfield. His particular charge was the Mustang of Maj James Goodson, CO of 336 Fighter Squadron and a leading ace. Bob Gilbert's work was vital but his view of combat was secondhand from the pilots he served. When volunteers were required for temporary duty in another war zone Gilbert decided he would like to see more of the world and the war. He and 32 other service personnel from 4th Group were transported to B-17 bases where they learned that they would fly as waist gunners on the first 8th Air Force 'shuttle' mission to Russia for servicing the escorting P-51s from their own group. Early on 21 June Gilbert boarded a 452nd Group B-17 and was on his way. The Fortresses were attacking the synthetic oil plants at Ruhland en route to Russia giving Gilbert and the other mechanics a grandstand view of the proceedings. Near Warsaw enemy fighters made a pass at the bombers and Bob Gilbert suddenly became more than a spectator. With his Fortress on fire, he joined the bomber men in parachuting for their lives. His landing was hard but safe and the Poles who came to his aid were quick to hide him from the Germans. For the next five weeks he lived with Polish partisans who eventually passed him to the Russians. From a US base in Russia he was flown to North Africa and then back to Debden where he arrived in mid-August. The day before Gilbert went down in enemy territory, 'Goody' Goodson was forced to belly-in while strafing, but unlike his P-51 crew chief the ace was captured and spent the rest of the war in prison camp.

From the window of a Poltava building a US serviceman took this long exposure of the start of the Luftwaffe attack on the base. Tracers from Russian defences criss-cross above the parked B-17s and the first marker flares from the German bombers illuminate the scene.

21/22 JUNE 1944

8AF 430 NIGHT LEAFLET OPERATION

NLS B-17, 5 despatched, 5 effective; France.

21 B-24s of 801BG on *Carpetbagger* operations; France.

Luftwaffe night bombing attack on Poltava base of *Frantic* B-17s in Soviet Union destroyed 44 B-17s and damaged 26.

22 JUNE 1944

8AF 431

		Despatched	Effective	Target		Bombs Tonnage	E/A	Losses MIA	E	Dam	Casualties KIA	WIA	MIA
	B-17	108	85	PAS DE CALAIS AREA		594.0		1	0	64	0	0	10
	B-24	194	132					0	0	59	0	0	0
8AF 432													
1BD	B-17	319	13	TINGRY	(P)	36.5		3	1	81	2	5	29
			12	ABBEVILLE	(P)	35.5							
			11	MAZINGARBE	(P)	17.3							
			13	FURNES A/F	(O)	37.0							
			10	PONT A VENDIN	(P)	10.8							
			1	DOUAI RR YARD	(O)	3.0							
			13	LA VAUBALIERS	(P)	36.0							
			35	ROUEN OIL DEPOT	(P)	68.7							
			12	TANK AREA N OF ROUEN	(O)	24.5							
			69	GHENT/ MARITIME M/Y	(P)	205.7							
			76	LILLE/FIMES M/Y	(P)	226.5							
			12	DOUAI R/R NEAR	(O)	12.0							
2BD	B-24	149	43	ST.CYR A/F	(P)	126.0	1–0–0	0	0	67	1	0	3
			36	BUC A/F	(P)	107.8							
			46	GUYANCOURT/ CAUDRON A/F	(P)	135.0							
			5	TOURS/LA RICHE BR	(P)	5.5							
			13	T/O		38.7							
3BD	B-17	216	11	MELUN BR	(O)	27.5	1–0–0	4	1	187	2	0	30
			11	MELUN M/Y	(O)	26.5							
			70	NUCOURT V/S	(P)	207.5							
			38	BRIE-COMTE-ROBERT SUG									
			11	LIEUSANT R/R	(O)	21.9							
			33	ETAMPES A/F	(O)	62.9							
3BD	B-24	103	1	DREUX A/F		30.0		2	3	37	1	2	23
			101	O/D PARIS	(P)	240.0							
	B-24	10	9	SAMUR BR (AZON)	(P)	5.0		0	0	0	0	0	0
TOTALS:		1099	922			2441.1	2–0–0	10	6	478	6	7	95

8AF 431

Despatched		Effective	Target	Bombs Tonnage	E/A	Losses MIA	E	Dam	Casualties KIA	WIA	MIA
P-47	165		ESCORT 8AF 431 & FIGHTER-BOMBERS	12.5		0	2		1	0	1
P-51	97					1	0		0	0	0
P-47	108	108	ESCORT 1BD & FIGHTER-BOMBERS	5.0	1–0–0	0	0		0	0	0
P-38	200	187	ESCORT 2BD		1–0–0	5	1		0	0	5
P-47	46	36				0	0		0	0	0
P-51	86	78	ESCORT 3BD			3	0		0	0	3
P-51	43	41	ESCORT AZON								
TOTALS:	735	450		17.5	2–0–0	9	3		1	0	9

REMARKS: Visual attacks on industrial targets and airfields in NW France. Groups participating:– all 1BD and 3BD and those of 14CBW, 20CBW, 95CBW of 2BD. 8AF 431 was a *Noball* mission composed of small formations from all BD. Bomb group losses:– 96BG – 2, 303BG – 2, 351BG – 1, 381BG – 1, 390BG – 1, 447BG – 1, 490BG – 1, 493BG – 1. 303BG B-17 ditched 5 miles off Beachy Head, 6 saved. 447BG B-17 lost abandoned over beach-head, crew baled. B/d 489BG B-24 cr. Arundel on return, 3 k. B/d 490BG B-24 c/l near Dover. B/d 34BG B-24 c/l Dungeness beach, crew safe. B/d 447BG B-17 Cat E. B/d 34BG B-24 abandoned over English coast.

All Fighter groups except 4FG operating. 127 P-47s went on to bomb A/Fs and M/Ys after escort duty. Fighter group e/a credits:– 353FG – 1, 356FG – 1, 479FG – 1. Fighter group losses:– 20FG – 1, 339FG – 1, 355FG – 1, 359FG – 2, 479FG – 4. 20FG P-38 c/l Sudbury A/F. 56FG P-47 cr. on return, pilot k. 56FG P-47 c/l near base, pilot safe.

OTHER OPERATIONS: 7PG despatched 24 F-5s and 5 Spitfires on PR French A/Fs and V-1s in flight. 802RG despatched 1 Mosquito to scout for B-24s, 1 Mosquito on WR Paris area, 2 B-17 on routine WR. 8AF 433 was a daylight leaflet operation flown by a single 422BS B-17 to La Glacrie.

INCIDENT

The annals of the 8th Air Force contain innumerable instances of bravery and endeavour in returning a crippling aircraft to friendly territory. Few, however, can equal the perseverance displayed by T/Sgt Alvin Gibbons during a mission to bomb a marshalling yard at Tournan en Brie near Paris on 22 June 1944. The 34th Group formation ran into an accurate flak barrage as it approached the target area. Gibbons was in his top turret when a shell, making a direct hit on the Liberator's nose, exploded, forcing the bomber into a climbing attitude for a few seconds. Gibbons went forward to find that both pilot and co-pilot had been wounded by shell splinters; the former, F/O Marvin Hayes, severely. Thinking the bomber doomed, the shocked co-pilot and the navigator baled out. Going down into the nose Gibbons could see that the bombardier had been killed instantly and that the floor of his compartment had been blasted away leaving a gaping hole. On the far side Gibbons saw that the gunner was trapped in the nose turret, trying desperately to free himself. With the aid of another gunner the wounded pilot was lifted from his seat and Gibbons, who had a little experience in flying light aircraft, took over the controls. He found that the rudders were inoperative, that most of the instrumentation had been destroyed and an engine had stopped. The heavy Liberator was perilously near to stalling but Gibbons managed to regain the Channel and head for England, although this had to be accomplished in wide orbits when another engine failed and most directional control was lost. Gibbons directed a gunner to take a parachute and hand it across the gaping hole in the bombardier's compartment as soon as the nose gunner had freed the turret doors. After many anxious minutes when it was feared the B-24 might suddenly run out of flying speed, the English coast was crossed, by which time another engine was losing power. The wounded pilot was helped to the bomb-bay so that he could parachute, while the nose gunner and the rest of the crew also vacated the bomber successfully, before Gibbons put the aircraft on automatic pilot and quickly jumped through the open bomb-bay. He had hardly cleared the aircraft before it nosed up and then fell off in a spin. Gibbons' composure in this critical situation was primarily responsible for saving the lives of the five other airmen and his own.

22/23 JUNE 1944

8AF 434 NIGHT LEAFLET OPERATION

NLS B-17, 9 despatched, 9 effective; France and Low Countries

1 B-17 with b/d.

10 B-24s of 801BG on *Carpetbagger* operations France.

Off Limits, a 34BG B-24 that only just regained England on 22 June. No.1 engine was put out of action by flak and No.2 by an FW 190. Rapidly losing height the bomber was down to 400 ft when it reached Dungeness where Lt. Guy Gipson managed to avoid hitting electric cables before crash-landing on shingle. (via S. Evans)

23 JUNE 1944

8AF 435

	Despatched		Effective	Target		Bombs Tonnage	E/A	Losses MIA	E	Dam	Casualties KIA	WIA	MIA
1BD	B-17	134	110	PAS DE CALAIS		532.7		0	0	3	0	0	0
& 2BD	B-24	106	102	V/S AREA						2			
8AF 436													
3BD	B-17	109	13	NANTEUIL	(P)	25.0		1	0	2	0	1	10
			2	T/O		5.0							
2BD	B-24	219	113	JUVINCOURT A/F	(P)	261.2		6	2	81	1	3	58
& 3BD			46	LAON/ATHIES A/F	(P)	125.0							
			23	COULOMMIERS A/F	(P)	61.1							
			1	SOISSONS A/F	(P)	2.6							
TOTALS:		568	410			1012.6		7	2	88	1	4	68
VIII FC													
	P-51	165	141	ESCORT FOR *NOBALL*				1	0		0	0	1
	P-47	155		ESCORT FOR				0	0		0	0	0
	P-51	83		8AF 436				0	0		0	0	0
	P-38	195	169	FIGHTER-BOMBER PARIS AREA BR	(P)	90.8		2	0		0	0	2
TOTALS:		598	310			98.1		3	0		0	0	3

REMARKS: GH on *Noball* targets and visuals on airfields and rail targets eastern France. Bomb groups operating were those of 1CBW, 2CBW, 14CBW, 45CBW, 94CBW, 96CBW and 34BG, 93BG, 487BG, 493BG. Bomb group losses:– 95BG – 1, 392BG – 3, 453BG – 1, 487BG – 1, 492BG – 1. B/d 392BG B-24 c/l Manston. A/F 458BG B-24 c/l Swannington during assembly, crew safe. All fighter groups operating except 4FG. No claims. Fighter group losses:– 55FG – 2, 361FG – 1. P-51 lost was engulfed in explosion of ammunition train. After escort P-47s bombed Givet M/Y.

OTHER OPERATIONS: 7PG despatched 8 F-5s and 1 Spitfire on PR France. 802RG despatched 1 Mosquito to scout for 3BD, 3 Mosquitoes on WR North Sea and France, 3 B-17s on routine UK/Atlantic WR.

23/24 JUNE 1944

801BG despatched 21 B-24s *Carpetbagger* operations.

24 JUNE 1944

8AF 438

	Despatched		Effective	Target		Bombs Tonnage	E/A	Losses MIA	E	Dam	Casualties KIA	WIA	MIA
1BD	B-17	74	38	SAUMUR BR	(P)	197.5		0	0		0	0	0
			36	TOURS/LA RICHE A/F BR									
2BD & 3BD	B-24	407	34	TOUSSUS/LE NOBLE	(P)	84.4		2	0	81	0	0	20
			45	CHATEAUDUN A/F	(P)	111.8							
			45	ORLEANS/BRICY A/F	(P)	89.6							
			12	PONT AUDMER	(O)	31.1							
			78	CONCHES A/F	(O)	188.6							
			9	DREUX A/F	(O)	19.2							
			11	TOUSSUS/PARIS	(O)	27.9							
			31	FIGHTER STRIP	(O)	77.5							
1BD & 3BD	B-17	340	213	BREMEN O/I	(P)	526.3		1	0	105	0	2	9
			40	BREMEN (CITY)	(O)	114.0							
			53	WESTERMÜNDE A/I	(O)	127.0							
	B-17	86	11	ROUEN	(O)	27.5		1	0	13	0	0	9
	B-24	60	0					0	0	1	0	0	0
TOTALS:		967	656			1622.4		5	0	200	0	2	38

8AF 439

	Despatched		Effective	Target		Bombs Tonnage	E/A	Losses MIA	E	Dam	Casualties KIA	WIA	MIA
1BD	B-17	62	13	HOLQUE E/S	(P)	39.0		0	0	17	0	0	0
			12	ST.POL M/Y	(S)	17.0							
			32	PAS DE CALAIS V/S		80.0							
2BD	B-24	167	14	ABBEVILLE P/S	(P)	36.4		2	1	44	0	0	20
			12	PONT-A-VENDIN TRANSF.	(P)	36.0							
			12	TINGRY E/S	(P)	31.1							
			67	PAS DE CALAIS V/S		241.0							
TOTALS:		229	162			480.5	0	2	1	61	0	0	20

VIII FC

Despatched		Effective	Target	Bombs Tonnage	E/A	Losses MIA	E	Dam	Casualties KIA	WIA	MIA
P-51	135	121	ESCORT BRIDGE B-17s		4–0–2(G)	0			0	0	0
P-38	45	151a/c	ESCORT B-24s			1			0	0	1
P-47	36		2 & 3BD			0			0	0	0
P-47	36	35	ESCORT ROUEN BOMBERS			0			0	0	0
P-38	185	251	ESCORT		2–0–0(G)	0			0	0	0
P-47	85		BREMEN FORCE			0			0	0	0
P-47	71	118	ESCORT 8AF 439			0			0	0	0
P-51	50					0			0	0	0
P-51	25		SWEEP ANGERS/ LE MANS AREA (8AF 439)		25–0–6(G)	0			0	0	0
TOTALS: 750		726			31–0–8(G)	1			0	0	1

REMARKS: Oil target Bremen (PFF), bridges and airfields France and *Noball* targets. 91BG and 381BG operated against bridges. B-24s of 92CBW, 93CBW, 95CBW, 96CBW groups and 93BG, 446BG attacked airfields. The Bremen Force was 4CBW, 40CBW, 41CBW, 45CBW groups and 390BG. A third Force despatched to France encountered heavy cloud and only 100BG bombed. 8AF 439 involved groups of 2CBW, 20CBW, 94CBW, 95CBW, 96CBW. Bomb group losses:– 44BG – 1, 93BG – 1, 100BG – 1, 303BG – 1, 381BG – 1, 448BG – 1, 453BG – 1. B/d B-24 c/l on return near Battle.

All Fighter groups operating except 4FG. No claims. Fighter group losses: 55FG – 1.

In the spring of 1944 3BD added five B-24 groups to its nine B-17 groups. The problems of operating two different types were so great that 3BD immediately made plans to convert all the B-24 units to B-17s, a change not completed until October. There was an Officers' Club rumour that in order to expedite the change the Lib' groups were being sent to the 'flakiest' targets. Certainly these units suffered severely in this respect but principally due to the lower altitudes at which they operated. Two flak perforated B-24Hs that dropped in and await repairs are 487BG's 42-50373 at Woodbridge on 22 June and 493BG's 41-28865 at Raydon on 26 June.

24/25 JUNE 1944

8AF 440 NIGHT LEAFLET OPERATION

NLS B-17, 5 despatched, 5 effective; France.

25 JUNE 1944

8AF 441

	Despatched		Effective	Target		Bombs Tonnage	E/A	Losses MIA	E	Dam	Casualties KIA	WIA	MIA
2BD	B-24	258	18	MAZINGARBE	(P)	47.8		1	1	26	1	2	0
			23	BEUVRY	(P)	63.5							
			7	NUNQUE	(P)	13.4							
			8	HOLQUE	(P)	18.6							
			10	ST.OMER/ LONGUENESSE	(P)	26.5							
			7	PONT-A-VENDIN	(P)	13.5							
			2	CHOCQUES	(P)	3.8							
			12	DOULLENS	(P)	36.0							
			10	ABBEVILLE	(P)	26.4							
			11	AMIENS/ST.MAURICE	(P)	24.0							
			8	BOULOGNE	(P)	15.0							
			11	CALAIS	(P)	20.7							
			11	TINGRY	(P)	21.0							
			12	AUBE-SUR-RISLE	(P)	29.6							
			12	LA VAUPALIER	(P)	14.5							
			12	PERONNE A/F	(P)	25.8							
			43	T/O		105.7							
3BD	B-24	137	59	ST.AVORD A/F	(P)	132.8		1	0	0	0	0	10
			48	BOURGE A/F	(P)	118.6							
1BD	B-17	263	64	MONTBARTIER O/D	(P)	147.0		5	1	114	10	5	45
			104	TOULOUSE/ FRANCAZAL A/F	(P)	230.5							
			72	TOULOUSE/ BLANGNAC A/F	(P)	143.5							

8AF 442

	Despatched		Effective	Target		Bombs Tonnage	E/A	Losses MIA	E	Dam	Casualties KIA	WIA	MIA
3BD	B-17	189	70	SOIGNY BRIDGE	(P)	140.0		1	0	20	0	2	19
			21	AUXERRE BRIDGE	(P)	52.0							
			38	SENS BRIDGE	(P)	77.0							
			28	CLAMECY	(P)	65.0							
			20	NOGENT		34.2							
			21	NANTEUIL	(P)	63.0							
			12	FOLOUS	(P)	36.0							
			13	ROMILLY-SUR-SEINE	(O)	27.9							
			18	ORLY A/F	(O)	40.1							
			3	ORLY M/Y	(O)	6.0							
			12	ETAMPES/MONDESIR A/F	(O)	30.6							
2BD	B-24	274	35	BRETIGNY A/F	(P)	82.0		5	2	104	11	7	59
			11	BUC A/F	(P)	33.0							
			63	VILLACOUBLAY A/D	(P)	168.9							
TOTALS:		1121	929			2133.1	0	13	4	264	22	16	133

VIII FC

	Aircraft	Despatched	Effective	Target	Bombs Tonnage	E/A	Losses MIA	E	Dam	KIA	WIA	MIA
	P-47	68	90	ESCORT 2BD			0			0	0	0
	P-51	34					0			0	0	0
	P-38	102	134	ESCORT 3BD		8–0–4	0			0	0	0
	P-47	44					0			0	0	0
	P-38	46	206	ESCORT 1BD		10–0–1	0			0	0	0
	P-47	36					0			0	0	0
	P-51	146					1			0	0	1
	P-38	127		ESCORT 8AF 442		4–0–3	0			0	0	0
	P-47	35					0			0	0	0
	P-51	181					1			0	0	1
	P-47	43	41	FIGHTER-BOMBER EVREUX/FAUVILLE L/G	12.5		0			0	0	0
TOTALS:		862	471		12.5	22–0–8	2			0	0	2

REMARKS: Airfields, power and transformer stations and an oil dump in France were targets for first operation. Bridges and airfields in Paris area targets for afternoon mission. 3BD B-17s dropped supplies to French partisans during 8AF 442 and OSS agents also dropped to instruct in use of arms (Operation *Zebra*). All bomb groups operated during day. Bomb group losses:–34BG – 1, 91BG – 1, 100BG – 1, 379BG – 2, 381BG – 1, 398BG – 1, 401BG – 1, 466BG – 1, 489BG – 2, 491BG – 1, 493BG – 1. A 91BG and 379BG B-17s landed Spain. 100BG loss was 390BG a/c. MIA 34BG ditched off Shoreham, 3 saved. Two 489BG B-24s cr. and c/l on return to base, 10 k. B/d 91BG B-17 cr. Wincanton, 9 k. During assembly 389BG B-24 c/l Woodbridge A/F after fire.

All Fighter groups except 4FG operated. Fighter group e/a credits:– 20FG – 1, 55FG – 4, 352FG – 1, 361FG – 10, 364FG – 7½. Fighter group losses:– 352FG – 1, 361FG – 1.

25/26 JUNE 1944

801BG despatched 24 B-24s on *Carpetbagger* operations.

26 JUNE 1944

EASTERN COMMAND

Despatched		Effective	Target	Bombs Tonnage	E/A	Losses MIA	E	Dam	Casualties KIA	WIA	MIA
B-17	73	72	DROHOBYZ	104.0							
P-51	103		ESCORT FOR ABOVE								

REMARKS: *Frantic* force and escort attacked target in Hungary and landed in Italy.

27 JUNE 1944

8AF 443

	Despatched		Effective	Target	Bombs Tonnage	E/A	Losses MIA	E	Dam	Casualties KIA	WIA	MIA
1, 2	B-24	187	11	CREIL A/F (O)	29.0		5					
& 3BD			12	T/O	27.0			2	104	2	7	51
	B-17	64	195	PAS DE CALAIS	509.0		0	0	8	0	0	0
TOTALS:		251	218		565.0		5	2	112	2	7	51

VIII FC

	Aircraft	Despatched	Effective	Target	Bombs Tonnage	E/A	Losses MIA	E	Dam	KIA	WIA	MIA
	P-51	191	149	ESCORT & FIGHTER-BOMBERS	37.0	6–0–0	2	0	1	0	0	2
				FIGHTER-BOMBER								
	P-38	193	46	CONNANTRE A/F (P)	15.4		3	3	0	0	1	3
	P-47	158	36	VILLENEUVE/ZERTES (P) A/F	9.0	10–0–8	0	0	0	0	0	0
	P-51	49	32	COULOMMIERS A/F (O)	8.3	1–0–0(G)	0	0	0	0	0	0
			246	PARIS AREA-TRANSPORT	39.7							
TOTALS:		480	360		72.4	16–0–8 1–0–0(G)	5	3	1	0	1	5

REMARKS: *Noball* supply sites, Pas de Calais, Criel and Chantilly area. Weather prevented bombing of primaries. Groups participating:– 34BG, 93BG, 379BG, 384BG, 398BG, 445BG, 448BG, 486BG, 492BG. Bomb group losses:– 44BG – 1, 445BG – 1, 448BG – 3. Two B-24s c/l in England. 93BG B-24 c/l Kingsnorth A/F.

All Fighter groups except 4FG operating. Fighter group e/a credits:– 20FG – 1, 56FG – 6, 339FG – 5, 352FG – 4, 353FG – 2. Fighter group losses:– 352FG – 1, 355FG – 1, 364FG – 2, 479FG – 1. B/d 20FG P-38s c/l Wittering and base. 55FG P-38 c/l, pilot inj.

OTHER OPERATIONS: 7PG despatched 3 F-5s on D/A over France. 802RG despatched 3 Mosquitoes and 2 B-17s on routine WR.

Maj Alex Andrews (at co-pilot's window), an 8AF HQ special observer detailed to monitor combat morale, was flying in 379BG's *Lil Satan* on 25 June when an 88 mm shell hit its nose. The pilots were able to fly the B-17 back to England and land at Hunsden. The bombardier was mortally wounded.

INCIDENT

On 27th June, Brig.Gen A.W. Vanaman, recently appointed A-2 (Head of Intelligence) at 8th Air Force Hq., flew as an observer with 1/Lt Clarence Jamison's crew on 379th Group Fortress *Nightjar N-Nan*. The target was a V-weapon storage area at St.Martin L'Hortier where anti-aircraft fire was encountered on the bomb run. One shell burst near to No.4 engine and soon after the engineer reported a fire. The pilots saw flames coming from the oil filter plate on the nacelle and immediately alerted the crew for possible bale out. The burning engine was shut down but as the flames persisted, intermittently trailing from wing to tailplane, and an explosion appeared imminent, the pilot gave the bale out order. The navigator, bombardier, engineer, co-pilot and General complied, leaving by the nose hatch. Jamison had difficulty in getting the bomber to fly on automatic pilot and before he could leave his position he heard one of the crew in the rear of the aircraft report that the fire had gone out. Seeing this was the case Jamison countermanded his order and stayed at the controls. None of the four men in the rear had baled out although remaining on the alert in case the fire reappeared. After jettisoning the bomb load Jamison flew the Fortress safely back to base. Apparently a fuel line had been severed and escaping gasoline ignited by the engine exhaust. There was little damage and the aircraft was scheduled for operations again next day. General Vanaman spent the rest of the war in a POW camp. Because of the circumstances of his arrival it is said his captors were suspicious that he was a deliberate plant by counter-intelligence.

27/28 JUNE 1944

8AF 444 NIGHT LEAFLET OPERATION

NLS B-17, 4 despatched, 4 effective; France.

801BG despatched 16 B-24s on *Carpetbagger* operations, France. 1 801BG B-24 on training flight shot down by intruder at Eaton Socon.

28 JUNE 1944

8AF 445

	Despatched		Effective	Target		Bombs Tonnage	E/A	Losses MIA	E	Dam	Casualties KIA	WIA	MIA
1BD & 3BD	B-17	485	36	FISMES BR	(P)	72.0		1	1	99	0	2	9
			72	LAON/COUVRON A/F	(P)	91.1							
			60	LAON/ATHIES A/F	(P)	119.8							
			64	JUVINCOURT A/F	(P)	127.1							
			20	ANIZY LE CHATEAU BR	(P)	40.0							
			18	DUGNY O/D	(P)	40.0							
			28	DENAIN/PROUVY A/F	(O)	63.4							
			19	LE BOURGET A/F	(O)	41.0							
			24	T/O		39.1							

continued on facing page

2BD	B-24	378	331	SAARBRÜCKEN M/Y (P)	893.5		1	0	125	0	8	10
			11	FLORENNES/JUZAINE(O) A/F	26.0							
			1	GIVET BR (O)	3.0							
TOTALS:		992	684		1554.0	0	2	1	224	0	10	19
VIII FC												
	P-38	188	539	ESCORT & FIGHTER-BOMBER		1–0–0	0	0		0	0	0
	P-47	169					1	0		0	0	1
	P-51	231					1	2		0	0	1
	P-47	50	30	FIGHTER-BOMBER (P) LA PERTHE A/F	7.1		0	0		0	0	0
TOTALS:		638	569		7.1	1–0–0	2	2		0	0	2

REMARKS: Airfields, supply dumps, bridges, an oil depot in Paris area and Saarbrücken M/Y were primaries. Groups participating:– all 1BD except 398BG, all 2BD except 44BG and 93BG, and 4CBW groups. Bomb group losses:– 303BG – 1, 389BG – 1. 447BG B-17 cr. at Woolpit, crew baled safely.

All Fighter groups participated. Fighter group e/a credits:– 20FG – 1. Fighter group losses:– 352FG – 1, 356FG – 1. A 352FG P-51 cr. SW Manston, pilot baled.

OTHER OPERATIONS: 7PG despatched 6 F-5s, 2 Spitfires and 1 B-25 on PR to Germany and France. 1 F-5 cr. NW Oxford, pilot killed. 802RG despatched 3 Mosquitoes on WR Paris and Irish Sea, 2 Mosquitoes to scout for 2BD and 3BD, 2 B-17s on routine WR UK/Atlantic.

INCIDENT

There can be few survival stories to surpass that which involved two members of an 801 Group B-24 in the early hours of 28 June. On a *Carpetbagger* training flight the Liberator was at about 2,000 ft east of Bedford when the airframe shuddered violently. At first the pilots were at a loss to know what was happening; by the time they realised the bomber was under attack the fuselage was ablaze and it was too late to take evasive action. No one on board expected to encounter an enemy intruder in the night sky over this part of England. At the 'bale out' signal, bombardier Robert Sanders left his position in the nose, scrambling up to the flight deck to fetch his parachute lodged near the bomb bay bulkhead. To his horror he found that area a mass of flames and his parachute burning. He quickly returned to the nose where navigator Robert Callahan was about to jump through the hatch he had opened. Sanders explained his fearful situation. There was now only one way in which it might be possible to save the bombardier's life. Callahan sat down on the edge of the hatch and let Sanders straddle his back and wrap his arms round him. Then locked together both men dropped out into the slipstream, Sanders with a vice-like grip on Callahan's harness. The jolt when the parachute opened was the crucial moment but Sanders maintained his hold. He then worked his way round so that both men could lock their arms round each other to better their position for the inevitable heavy landing. Supporting a double load the parachute descended rapidly and seemingly moments after leaving the stricken bomber the two men thudded into the ground. Callahan sustained a fractured ankle, Sanders a sprain and both a few cuts and bruises, exceedingly minor injuries in view of their manner of arrival in a wheat field near Eaton Socon. The only other person of the crew of six to escape from the doomed B-24 was the badly burned tail gunner.

28/29 JUNE 1944

18 B-24s of 801BG on *Carpetbagger* operations; France.

When this 447BG B-17G ended up on its belly at a runway intersection on Rattlesden, 29 June, it presented a hazard to other aircraft. There was only one speedy way to remove the 30 ton obstruction, bombs, fuel and all; by brute force with a bulldozer and three Cletracs each pushing against an engine. (R. Zorn)

29 JUNE 1944

8AF 447

	Despatched		Effective	Target		Bombs Tonnage	E/A	Losses MIA	E	Dam	Casualties KIA	WIA	MIA
3BD	B-17	179	81	BÖHLEN O/I	(P)	177.0		4	0	111	2	5	30
			61	WITTENBERG	(S)	133.0							
1BD	B-17	380	41	LEIPZIG/ HEITERBLICK	(P)	95.0		2	1	76	0	2	21
			19	LEIPZIG	(P)	47.0							
			30	LEIPZIG/TAUCHA A/F	(P)	73.0							
			18	WITTENBERG	(O)	20.0							
			14	QUACKENBRÜCK	(O)	25.0							
			15	LIMBACH	(O)	35.0							
			2	T/O		5.0							
2BD & 3BD	B-24	591	54	BERNBURG	(P)	144.0		9	3	204	2	12	92
			47	ASCHERSLEBEN	(P)	148.0							
			81	MAGDEBURG	(P)	221.0							
			74	OSCHERSLEBEN	(P)	203.0							
			42	FALLERSLEBEN A/I	(P)	106.0							
			26	STENDAL A/F	(S)	66.0							
			46	BURG A/F	(S)	115.0							
			9	GARDELEGEN A/F	(S)	23.0							
			8	ZERBST A/F	(O)	21.0							
			8	OEBISFELDE/ KALTENDORF	(O)	21.0							
			4	LEOPOLDSHALL M/Y	(O)	11.0							
			35	T/O		86.0							
TOTALS:		1150	705			1775.0		15	4	391	4	19	143

VIII FC

Despatched		Effective	Target		Bombs Tonnage	E/A	Losses MIA	E	Dam	Casualties KIA	WIA	MIA
P-38	203	674	(8th & 9th FC)			34–0–9	0			0	0	0
P-47	216		ESCORT			16–0–8	0			0	0	0
P-51	352		ALL MISSIONS			(G)	3			0	0	3
P-38	8	4	FIGHTER-BOMBER IJMUIDEN SHIPPING	(P)	2.2		0			0	0	0
TOTALS:	779	678			2.2	34–0–9 16–0–8(G)	3	0		0	0	3

REMARKS: Major mission to strategic targets in Leipzig area. Synthetic oil plant at Böhlen, a bearing works and 11 small aircraft assembly and component plants in Leipzig area. At one time bomber stream stretched 200 miles across Germany. No major air opposition. Bomb groups participating: all 1BD and 3BD B-17s; all B-24 groups except 487BG, 490BG. Bomb group losses:– 44BG – 2, 95BG – 1, 303BG – 1, 390BG – 1, 447BG – 2, 448BG – 2, 457BG – 1, 458BG – 2, 467BG – 1, 489BG – 1, 493BG – 1. 390BG ditched 20 miles W of Alkmaar, RAF launch rescuing crew shot up by Ju 88. MIA 489BG B-24 collided with 491BG a/c which did not go down. On return, 401BG B-17 c/l and burned Greenham Common A/F; b/d 392 BG B-24 c/l at base; b/d 392BG B-24 c/l Frettenham, 1 k; 44BG B-24 c/l Covehithe.

All Fighter Groups except 359FG active. P-38s of 364FG made *Droopsnoot* bombing on shipping. Fighter group e/a credits: 339FG – 8, 357FG – 20½, 361FG – 3. Fighter group losses:– 339FG – 1, 357FG – 1. 38 IX FC P-51s also provided escort, claiming 1–0–0 for loss of 1.

OTHER OPERATIONS: 7PG despatched 9 F-5s and 1 Spitfire to France and Germany (2 F-5s were returning to UK from Italy). 802RG despatched 3 Mosquitoes to scout for bombers, 3 Mosquitoes on WR France and Germany, and 2 B-17 on routine WR UK/Atlantic.

30 JUNE 1944

8AF 448

	Despatched		Effective	Target		Bombs Tonnage	E/A	Losses MIA	E	Dam	Casualties KIA	WIA	MIA
1BD	B-17	75	39	MONTDIDIER A/F	(P)	74.1		0	0	27	0	0	0
			24	LE CULOT A/F	(P)	45.4							
			11	COXYDE/FURNES A/F	(O)	20.6							
3BD	B-24	78	26	EVREUX/FAUVILLE A/F	(P)	71.9		0	0	0	0	0	0
			35	CONCHES A/F	(P)	105.0							
TOTALS:		153	135			317.0		0	0	27	0	0	0

VIII FC													
	P-51	178	168	ESCORT & STRAFING		16.4		0	0		0	0	0
				FIGHTER-BOMBER									
	P-38	144	13	JOIGNY BRIDGE	(P)	1.3	3–3–4	1	0		0	0	1
	P-47	166	12	NOGENT-SUR-SEINE	(P)	6.0	1–0–0	0	1		1	0	0
	P-51	51	39	JOINVILLE/ CHEVILLON	(O)	9.8	(G)	0	0		0	0	0
			22	NEVERS M/Y	(O)	4.8							
			14	SULLY BRIDGES	(O)	3.5							
			15	R/R BRIDGE NEAR GIEN	(O)	3.8							
			9	CHENOISE BRIDGE	(O)	0.9							
			1	NEVERS BRIDGE	(O)	0.3							
			180	PARIS AREA	(P)	45.4							
TOTALS:		539	305			75.8	3–3–4 1–0–0(G)	1	1		1	0	1

REMARKS: GH attacks on airfields in France and Belgium by 41CBW and 92CBW groups and 493BG. No losses.

All Fighter groups operating except 4FG and 361FG. Fighter bomber attacks on M/Y, bridges and transportation targets in France. Fighter group e/a credits:– 20FG – 2, 56FG – 1. Fighter group losses:– 55FG – 1. On return, 353FG P-47 cr. Diss, pilot killed. ASR P-47 shoots down first V-1 claimed by 8AF.

OTHER OPERATIONS: 2 F-5 sorties abortive. 802RG despatched 6 WR sorties – UK/Atlantic and Calais areas. On this date all special activity units placed under one central control.

1 JULY 1944

8AF 449

	Despatched		Effective	Target	Bombs Tonnage	E/A	Losses MIA	E	Dam	Casualties KIA	WIA	MIA
2BD	B-17	78	0	MONT LOUIS FERME (P)	0		0	0	0	0	0	0
& 3BD	B-24	245	9		19.5		1	0	10	0	1	9
TOTALS:		323	9		19.5	0	1	0	10	0	1	9
VIII FC												
	P-51	166	124	ESCORT		5–0–5	1	1				
	P-38	97	82	FIGHTER-BOMBER		0–0–0	0					
	P-47	169		RAIL AND ROAD	8.75	3–0–3	1	2				
	P-51	99		TARGETS IN N FRANCE		0–0–0	0	0				
TOTALS:		531	206		8.75	8–0–8	2	3		2	0	2

REMARKS: Bombers recalled from *Noball* targets because of deteriorating weather, only 486BG continued and bombed. Bomb group losses:– 486BG – 1. Weather limited fighter missions to 20FG, 78FG, 352FG, 353FG, 357FG, 361FG, 364FG. Fighter group credits:– 78FG – 4, 352FG – 1, 357FG – 4. Fighter group losses:– 78FG – 1, 357FG – 1. 2 78FG P-47s collided on t/o base, pilots killed. 361FG P-51 cr. Southend, pilot baled.

OTHER OPERATIONS: 802RG despatched 1 Mosquito to scout for bombers, 2 Mosquitoes on WR, UK and Bay of Biscay, 3 B-17 (2 turned back) on routine Atlantic WR.

1/2 JULY 1944

801BG despatched 18 B-24s on *Carpetbagger* operation, France.

During June the Air/Sea/Rescue squadron flew 442 sorties with its 25 'war weary' P-47Ds. A maintenance hangar was erected for the unit at the N.W. corner of Boxted airfield and was in use before completion.

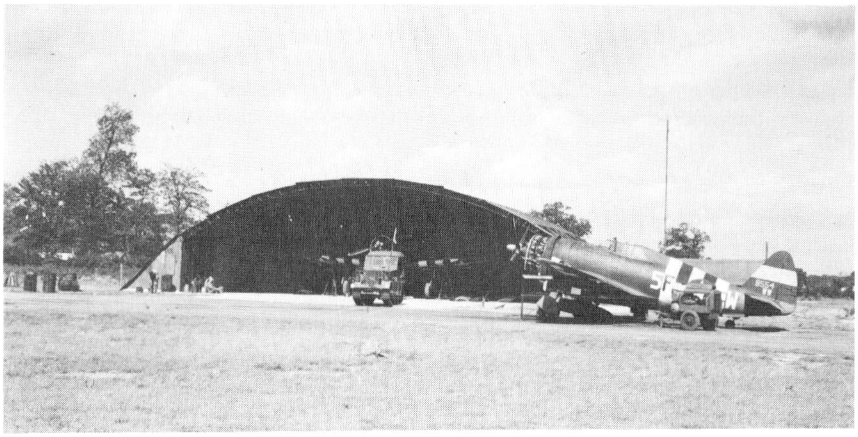

2 JULY 1944

8AF 450

	Despatched		Effective	Target	Bombs Tonnage	E/A	Losses MIA	E	Dam	Casualties KIA	WIA	MIA
1 & 3BD	B-17	78	24	FLEURY V/S	53.5		0	0	33	0	0	0
			24	FRESSIN V/S	53.5							
			21	BLENGERMONT V/S	54.8							
			1	T/O	2.3							
2 & 3BD	B-24	272	21	RENESCURE V/S	60.8		1	1	0	0	4	9
			13	SANTRECOURT V/S	37.9							
			36	CREPY V/S	102.5							
			35	FIEFS V/S	83.6							
			22	COURBRONNE V/S	60.4							
			23	BLANC PIGNON V/S	56.1							
			12	BELLOY-SUR-SOMME V/S	31.8							
			24	VIGNACOURT V/S	58.0							
			13	HAUTE COTE I V/S	23.8							
			13	MONT LOUIS FERME V/S	26.2							
TOTALS:		350	282		705.2	0	1	1	33	0	4	9

Despatched		Effective	Target	Bombs Tonnage	E/A	Losses MIA	E	Dam	Casualties KIA	WIA	MIA
P-51	171	166	ESCORT		0	0	0		0	0	0

REMARKS: PFF attacks on *Noball* targets in Pas de Calais. Groups participating: 2CBW, 20CBW, 40CBW, 92CBW groups and 34BG, 458BG, 467BG. Bomb group losses:– 487BG – 1. A 487BG B-24 cr. near Dunmow, crew baled.

Fighter escort provided by 339FG, 355FG, 359FG, 361FG. No claims. 4FG shuttle contingent operating from Italy credited with 7–0–0 and 352FG 2–0–0 for loss of 4 4FG and 2 352FG P-51s. B/d 4FG P-51 c/l Italy, pilot WIA.

OTHER OPERATIONS: 7PG despatched 3 F-5s on PR France. 802RG despatched 2 Mosquitoes on WR to France, 2 B-17s on routine Atlantic WR.

2/3 JULY 1944

37 B-24s of 801BG on *Carpetbagger* operations, France.

3 JULY 1944

	Despatched		Effective	Target		Bombs Tonnage	E/A	Losses MIA	E	Dam	Casualties KIA	WIA	MIA
3BD	B-17	57	55	ARAD M/Y	(P)	154.5		1	0	0	0	0	0
	P-51	42	42	ESCORT				0	0	0	0	0	0

REMARKS: Mission by 13CBW and 45CBW groups with 15AF from Italy. 4FG & 486FS as escort. Bomb group losses:– 390BG – 1.

OTHER OPERATIONS: 7PG despatched 9 F-5s and 1 Spitfire on PR Germany and France. (1 F-5 to proceed on to Italy and 1 to Poltava, Soviet Union after missions.) 802RG despatched 1 Mosquito on WR over channel and 2 B-17s over Atlantic.

3/4 JULY 1944

38 B-24s of 801BG on *Carpetbagger* operations.

4 JULY 1944

8AF 451

	Despatched		Effective	Target		Bombs Tonnage	E/A	Losses MIA	E	Dam	Casualties KIA	WIA	MIA
1BD	B-17	300	24	DREUX A/F	(P)	45.6		1	2	37	0	1	9
			24	ILLIERS L'EVEQUE A/F	(P)	42.1							
			13	CONCHES A/F	(O)	23.9							
			1	T/O		2.0							
2 & 3BD	B-24	258	49	EVREUX A/F	(P)	92.0		0	2	52	0	2	0
			56	CONCHES A/F	(P)	132.2							
			50	BEAUMONT LE ROGER A/F	(P)	110.2							
			12	CREIL A/F	(P)	27.0							
			25	BEAUMONT-SUR-OISE A/F	(P)	56.5							
TOTALS:		558	364			531.5	0	1	4	89	0	3	9

VIII FC													
	P-38	199	569	ESCORT				2	0				
	P-47	189						1	1				
	P-51	244						1	0				
	P-38	144		FIGHTER-BOMBER									
	P-47	176	29	NEVERS M/Y	(P)	7.3	17–0–10	1	1				
			25	JOINVILLE BRIDGE	(P)	5.5	1–0– 0 (G)	2	0				
			14	PERRIGNY M/Y	(P)	3.5							
			14	FRESNES BRIDGE	(P)	3.5							
			8	CERCY/LA TOURS M/Y	(P)	2.0							
			6	ST.FLORENTIN	(P)	1.5							
			16	CHARTRE-CHATEAUDUN M/Y	(P)	4.0							
			8	CAMBRAI M/Y	(P)	1.5							
			4	ROUEN BRIDGE	(P)	1.0							
			5	T/O		1.7							
TOTALS:		952	698			26.5	17–0–10 1–0– 0(G)	7	2	8	1	4	7

REMARKS: Airfields and bridges in France but weather again hampered operations and of 12 B-17 groups despatched only 379BG & 384BG attacked primaries. B-24 groups attacking were those of 14CBW, 92CBW, 95CBW and 490BG. Bomb group losses:– 381BG – 1. On return 389BG B-24 c/l Edburton, crew safe. 44BG B-24 cr. Shalford, crew baled. B/d 379BG B-17 c/l Felpham. B/d 398BG B-17 c/l Truleigh Sands, crew safe.

All Fighter groups except 359FG active. Fighter group e/a credits:– 56FG – 20. Fighter group losses:– 56FG – 1, 78FG – 1, 339FG – 1, 353FG – 1, 479FG – 3. On return, a 20FG P-38 cr. Lodsworth, pilot killed. B/d 78FG P-47 c/l on coastal A/F.

OTHER OPERATIONS: 7PG despatched 13 F-5s to France. 802RG despatched 2 Mosquitoes to NW France on WR, and 2 B-17s on routine Atlantic WR. Test of rocket bombs by B-17 of 8TO off Sheringham.

INCIDENT

The 20th Century Arrives at Miss Cheney's

When B-17G '2000' arrived at Kimbolton, the nickname *Mojo* was bestowed but the bomber was commonly referred to as *Twentieth Century*. This aircraft, a GH pathfinder, led a fairly untroubled life until 4 July 1944 when flak put two engines out of action over France. The ailing bomber was able to reach England, making landfall near Bognor Regis, but before an airfield could be located a third engine began to lose power. What happened thereafter is narrated by Miss Ethel Cheney of No.18 Downview Road, Felpham:–

'For the duration of the war I was working away from home as a WVS Welfare Officer for evacuees and 4 July 1944 was my first day back at home. I was due to have visitors on this day, and was standing at my kitchen sink washing up the breakfast things. The time was about twenty past nine. Looking out of the window I could see an aeroplane circling overhead and then saw that it was coming down to land. It touched down in the field behind my house and as I looked I was horrified to see the 'plane thundering towards me. As I stood there, riveted to the spot, I put my hands up to my face and offered up a quick prayer for protection. When I realised that I was still alive, I took my hands away from my face and was amazed at the sight which met my eyes. The aeroplane had come to rest in my garden and when it was only about 50 feet from my house it had turned through 90 degrees and stopped with its wing tip only six feet from my back door. All of the crew had jumped out and were dancing, shouting and cheering on my lawn. I went down the path towards them and said, "I'll make you some tea", to which they replied, "Coffee would be better." They all came into my kitchen where I gave them coffee. Only two were slightly hurt, one having had his shoulder dislocated and another had some shrapnel wounds around his waist, but none needed hospital treatment. As it was Independence Day the airmen decided to set off all the flares which they had, and this they did in a ditch opposite my house. Later in the day my visitors arrived – Dr and Mrs Lamour – and we all had tea together with the pilot, whose name was Mayo R. Adams Jnr. He came from Virginia and had been married for one year. This was almost the last of the missions which he had to do. Whilst we were talking Mrs Lamour said: "I expect your wife is very lovely", to which he replied: "She's *very* lovely Marm."

The view from Miss Cheney's back door. The local bobby and firemen are on hand while Lt Masoni, the navigator, romps with little Barbara Deane who has never had such an exciting day in her street.

That night a plane arrived at Tangmere to take the airmen back to their home base and next day an American dismantling crew started work. There were nine men and they were billeted locally and stayed for about three weeks. I think they stayed in a Bognor hotel and had a good time. They were all very keen on the girls, you know: they were the limit! The youngest member of the crew was 18 years old Joe Kendrick who came from Texas. The others called him "Baby". At 9.30 each morning they arrived at my house for coffee and then started work. I remember they were very keen to find a special type of bomb sight which was missing. I think they found it. One morning they arrived at 9 o'clock and I said, "Oh! You are early for your coffee." Sheepishly, they said they had come to say goodbye as they had finished the job and had to move on. As they went they said, "Joe would like you to adopt him!" I said, "Oh! That's nice." After they had all gone, Joe came back and said to me would I do him a favour and write to his folks back home. They were very worried about his well-being and would be pleased to know that he had such good friends in England. I said I would. As he went he looked at a photo I had of my niece who was very pretty and said that if she was here then he would stop and he would let me adopt him. They were the limit!'

On 4 July 1969, exactly 25 years to the day after *Twentieth Century* dropped in on Miss Cheney, Mayo Adams returned and took tea with her.

4/5 JULY 1944

36 B-24s of 801BG despatched on *Carpetbagger* operations; 3 MIA. B/d B-24 cr. on landing Ford, 4 baled over e/t.

802RG H2X Mosquito on mission – abortive. Despatched by 482BG – 802RG detachment at Alconbury until late July 1944.

5 JULY 1944

8AF 453

	Despatched		Effective	Target		Bombs Tonnage	E/A	Losses MIA	E	Dam	Casualties KIA	WIA	MIA
1BD	B-17	79	20	VOLKEL A/F	(P)	55.5		0	0	0	0	0	0
			38	GILZE-RIJEN A/F	(P)	105.0							
			19	NOLL	(O)	61.5							
2BD	B-24	221	36	LE COULET A/F	(P)	67.5		0	0	49	0	1	0
			13	EINDHOVEN A/F	(P)	37.7							
			43	BOIS DE CASSAN V/S	(P)	122.5							
			29	FORET DE L'ISLE ADAM V/S	(P)	106.0							
			29	MERY SUR OISE V/S		103.5							
			5	MELSBROEK A/F	(P)	9.0							
			2	TULEMONT A/F	(O)	2.0		0	0	13	0	0	0
3BD	B-17	71	70	BEZIERS M/Y	(P)	183.0							
TOTALS:		371	304			853.2		0	0	52	0	1	0
VIII FC													
	P-51	192	180	ESCORT 1 & 2BD			4–0–2 1–0–0 (G)	2					
	P-47	97	228a/c	ESCORT FOR 3BD			18–1–9	2	0		0	0	2
	P-51	156					1–0–0 (G)	1	0		0	0	1
				FIGHTER-BOMBER			3–0–0	2	0		0	0	2
	P-47	93	7	VEULETTES BR	(P)	1.7	1–0–0 (G)						
			7	PANTGOUIN	(P)	1.7							
			10	L'ARCHE BR	(P)	2.4							
			22	ROUEN	(P)	5.5							
			10	SEINE LOCKS	(P)	2.5							
			7	BOISSY LE BOIS	(P)	1.6							
			6	COMMUNICATION TARGETS		1.6							
	P-38	190	181	ESCORT				2	1		0	0	2
TOTALS:		728	668			17.0	25–1–11 3–0– 0 (G)	9	1		0	0	9

REMARKS: Airfields in Holland and Belgium, *Noball* targets and M/Ys in France. Visual and PFF attacks. Groups participating:– 1BD – 303BG, 379BG; 2BD – 93BG, 389BG, 445BG, 446BG, 459BG, 466BG, 467BG. 3BD force attacking Beziers comprised 13CBW and 45CBW shuttle groups returning from Italy.

All Fighter groups operating. 4FG and 352FG contingents on Soviet Union–Italy shuttle returned with Beziers bombers. Fighter group e/a credits:– 20FG – 1, 56FG – 12, 78FG – 2, 353FG – 1, 355FG – 1, 357FG – 4, 361FG – 4. Fighter group losses:– 55FG – 1, 56FG – 1, 78FG – 2, 353FG – 1, 355FG – 1, 361FG – 2, 479FG – 1. One 78FG P-47 lost shot down by Spitfires in error. Lt. Col Gabreski became 8AF leading ace with 28 victories. 479FG P-38 Cat E.

OTHER OPERATIONS: 7PG despatched 4 F-5s and 2 Spitfires on PR France. 802RG despatched 2 Mosquitoes to scout for bombers, 1 on WR Paris area, and 2 on WR UK/Atlantic. 2 B-17s on WR UK/Atlantic.

EVENT

As the realisation of the demise of the Third Reich became evident to many Germans, Allied propaganda became more effective. In addition to the special units such as the Night Leaflet Squadron, both RAF and USAAF heavy bombers dropped leaflets in the course of normal combat missions. In stepping up this activity, 8th Air Force selected two groups in each Division which, from 5 July, would often have some aircraft in regular bombing formations loaded only with leaflets. In fact, during July 1944, when the total of leaflets dispensed was more than twice the total by all US carriers during 1943, an average of eight aircraft on every heavy bomber mission carried only leaflets. The groups involved were the 91st, 306th, 445th, 447th, 487th and 491st. Leaflets were usually packed in a special T-2 leaflet bomb developed in the theatre. It was designed to burst open at between 2,000 and 2,500 ft from the ground and cover a 200 × 50 yard area with the contents. This device first came into use in June and replaced an improvised leaflet bomb adapted from an incendiary cluster casing.

5/6 JULY 1944

NLS B-17, 8 despatched, 8 effective; France. 1 B-17 MIA.

801BG despatched 8 B-24s on *Carpetbagger* operations.

802RG H2X Mosquito on scope photo mission.

On 6 July the King and Queen with 18-year-old Princess Elizabeth and escorted by General Doolittle visited several 8AF stations. At Thurleigh the Princess 'christened' a B-17 named *Rose of York* in her honour (originally labelled *Princess Elizabeth*, it was changed on consideration of the propaganda value it would give the Germans if the B-17 was brought down in their country). At Kimbolton the royal visitors met the men who looked after *Four Of A Kind* (so named because the last four digits of its serial number were 7777). In the picture the King and Doolittle chat while Lt Col James Du Bose (379BG Executive) explains for the ladies as the bomber sets out on its fifth mission to lead an afternoon attack on V-weapon sites.

6 JULY 1944

	Despatched		Effective	Target		Bombs Tonnage	E/A	Losses MIA	E	Dam	Casualties KIA	WIA	MIA
8AF 455													
	B-17	641	556	PAS DE CALAIS V/S		1785.5		0	1	161	2	2	0
	B-24	159	133	PAS DE CALAIS V/S					0	59	0	1	0
2BD	B-24	262	229	KIEL S/Y	(P)	658.7		3	1	105	0	8	22
			1	T/O		3.0							
8AF 456													
	B-17	104	73	PAS DE CALAIS V/S		654.5		0	0	23	0	0	0
	B-24	176	148	& BRIDGES S. OF PARIS				0	0	27	0	1	0
TOTALS:		1342	1140			3101.7	0	3	2	375	2	12	22
VIII FC													
	P-38	141	204	ESCORT 8AF 455			4–0–0	1	0		0	0	1
	P-51	83						0	0		0	0	0
	P-51	189	168	ESCORT KIEL				1	0		0	0	1
	P-38	49	212	RAIL & ROAD TRAFFIC PARIS AREA			11–1–2	0	0		0	0	0
	P-47	185						2	0		0	0	2
	P-38	134	443	ESCORT 8AF 456 & FIGHTER-BOMBER		5.0		0	0		0	0	0
	P-47	143						1	0		0	0	0
	P-51	214						0	0		0	0	0
TOTALS:		1138	1027			5.0	15–1–2	5	0		0	0	4

REMARKS: First missions were to *Noball* targets with all 1BD and 3BD groups participating plus those of 2BD, 2CBW and 20CBW. Kiel mission flown by 14CBW, 95CBW, 96CBW groups. Afternoon *Noball* mission flown by:– 1BD – 379BG, 384BG, 401BG, 457BG; 2BD – 389BG, 445BG; 3BD – 100BG, 385BG, 390BG, 388BG, 447BG, 452BG, 34BG, 490BG. T/Os attacked by Pas de Calais forces were Armentières M/Y, Denain Provy A/F, Vitry en Artois A/F, Moorseele A/F, Berck A/F, Gien bridge and Sully bridge. Bomb group losses:– 392BG – 1, 487BG – 1, 492BG – 2. One 492BG B-24 ditched, 7 rescued. B/d 398BG B-17 c/l Penshurst, crew safe. B/d 445BG B-24 c/l near Shipdham.

All Fighter groups operating. Fighter group e/a credits:– 55FG – 3, 56FG – 5, 78FG – 5, 353FG – 2, 356FG – 1, 357FG – 1, 479FG – 1. Fighter group losses:– 56FG – 1, 78FG – 1, 355FG – 1, 479FG – 1.

OTHER OPERATIONS: 7PG despatched 42 F-5s and 12 Spitfires on PR to France and Germany. 802RG despatched 1 Mosquito on PR, 3 Mosquitoes to scout for bombers, 4 Mosquitoes on WR over Continent, 1 Mosquito to Italy and 2 B-17s on routine Atlantic WR.

The prize exhibit among field-improvised bomber armament was the six-gun chin turret on 384BG's *West's End*. The fixed .50 battery was fired by the pilot and intended to meet Luftwaffe 'Company Front' tactics. A number of missions were flown with this armament but no record of success is known. *West's End* was salvaged after flak forced it to belly in at Manston on 6 July.

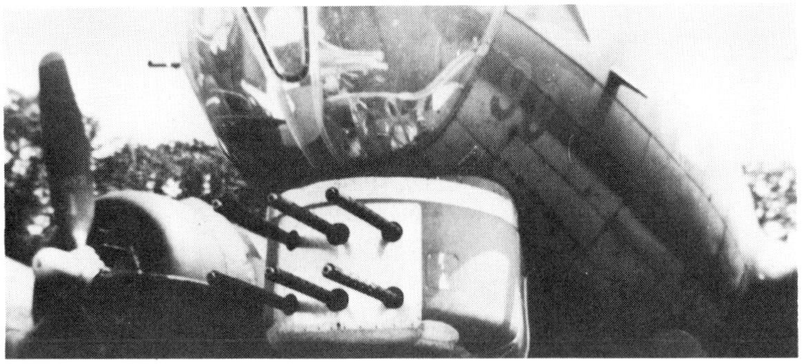

6/7 JULY 1944

8AF 457 NIGHT LEAFLET OPERATION

NLS B-17, 7 despatched, 7 effective; Belgium and France.

20 B-24s of 801BG on *Carpetbagger* operations; 801BG C-47 made first landing at secret A/S in Ain area. 801BG B-24 MIA Belgium.

2 H2X Mosquitoes of 802RG on mission – aborted.

7 JULY 1944

8AF 458

	Despatched		Effective	Target		Bombs Tonnage	E/A	Losses MIA	E	Dam	Casualties KIA	WIA	MIA
2BD	B-24	373	102	LÜTZKENDORF O/I	(P)	229.1	39–5–10	28	1	126	3	11	274
			64	HALLE O/I	(P)	156.1							
			73	ASCHERSLEBEN A/I	(P)	203.7							
			90	BERNBURG A/I	(P)	256.9							
			8	T/O		22.1							
3BD	B-17	303	64	BÖHLEN O/I	(P)	148.0		2	0	112	0	3	20
			51	MERSEBURG O/I	(P)	105.5							
			32	LÜTZKENDORF A/F	(S)	43.4							
			67	KOLLEDA A/F	(S)	138.7							
			16	GÖTTINGEN M/Y	(O)	39.2							
			22	T/O		42.2							
1 & 3BD	B-17	453	79	LEIPZIG/MOCKAU O/I	(P)	193.5							
			114	LEIPZIG/TAUCHA O/I	(P)	264.1		7	2	152	15	5	50
			15	LEIPZIG/ABTNA-UNDORF	(P)	37.0							
			46	LEIPZIG B/I	(P)	120.0							
			35	LEIPZIG/HEITERBLICK	(P)	86.8							
			35	KOLLEDA A/F	(O)	82.1							
			19	LEIPZIG STATION	(O)	46.2							
			7	NORDHAUSEN	(O)	17.5							
TOTALS:		1129	939			2232.1	39–5–10	37	3	390	18	19	344
VIII FC													
	P-38	100	224	ESCORT 2BD			46–1–16	1	0		0	0	1
	P-47	64						0	0		0	0	0
	P-51	91						3	0		0	0	3
	P-38	44	185	ESCORT 3BD			9–0–1	0	0		0	0	0
	P-47	49					3–0–1 (G)	1	0		0	0	1
	P-51	114						1	0		0	0	1
	P-47	111	247	ESCORT LEIPZIG			20–0–2	0	0		0	0	0
	P-51	183					1–0–0 (G)	0	1		0	1	0
TOTALS:		756	656				75–1–19 4–0–1 (G)	6	1		0	1	6

REMARKS: Major mission to strategic targets in central Germany: oil, bearing and aircraft plants. Groups participating:– all 2BD except 20CBW, all 1BD and 3BD B-17s. Bomb group losses:– 1BD – 379BG – 3, 398BG – 2, 401BG – 1, 457BG – 1. 2BD – 44BG – 3, 389BG – 5, 392BG – 5, 453BG – 1, 458BG – 1, 489BG – 1, 492BG – 12. 3BD – 390BG – 2. 14CBW suffered mass fighter attack on bomb run. 2 389BG B-24s collided going in at Dutch coast. MIA 457BG B-17 ditched 15 miles NE of Wash, 5 rescued. During assembly 2 384BG B-17s collided and cr. Withersfield 14 killed.

All Fighter groups active. Fighter group e/a claims: 4FG – 7, 20FG – 7, 55FG – 19½, 56FG – 10, 355FG – 2, 339FG – 6, 357FG – 3, 361FG – 9. Fighter group losses:– 4FG – 1, 20FG – 1, 353FG – 1, 355FG – 2, 357FG – 1. Col Duncan, CO 353FG and leading air ace, shot down and evaded. 339FG reported multiple collision near Leipzig – 3 B-17s and a fighter. MIA 4FG P-51 collided with Me 410. 361FG P-51 c/l t/o, pilot inj.

OTHER OPERATIONS: 7PG despatched 10 a/c to France and Germany. 802RG despatched 3 Mosquitoes to scout for bombers, 1 Mosquito on WR to Berlin, 2 Mosquitoes on UK/North Sea WR, and 2 B-17s on Atlantic WR. 1 Mosquito MIA.

7/8 JULY 1944

8AF 459 NIGHT LEAFLET OPERATION

NLS B-17, 6 despatched, 6 effective; France and Belgium.

19 B-24s of 801BG on *Carpetbagger* operations.

Engines crippled by flak 398BG's 42-97855 managed to get as far as the English coast where Capt Petersen set her neatly down on a sandbank between two minefields at Sandwich on 8 July.

8 JULY 1944

8AF 460

	Despatched		Effective	Target	Bombs Tonnage	E/A	Losses MIA	E	Dam	Casualties KIA	WIA	MIA
2BD	B-24	331	14	SCHORE BR	(O) 53.0		0	0	20	0	0	0
			9	WELLE BR	(O) 36.0							
			1	ORSEL A/F	(O) 4.0							
			1	T/O	2.0							
1BD	B-17	304	49	V-1 SITES	(P) 110.9		4	2	90	2	7	32
			37	ETAPLES BR	(P) 74.2							
			61	POIX A/F	(O) 148.6							
			11	ETAPLES C/P	(O) 24.0							
			12	ABBEVILLE A/F	(O) 26.2							
			13	ROAD JUNCTION	(O) 28.9		0	3	27	0	0	0
3BD	B-24	130	71	V-1 SITES	(P) 181.0							
			13	ST.VALERY EN CAUX A/F	(O) 32.0							
			11	ABBEVILLE R/R INTERS	(O) 25.3							
3BD	B-17	264	21	JAIGLE R/J	(O) 49.5		5	2	98	4	16	51
			10	CHANDAI R/J	(O) 20.0							
			11	NANTES/ GASSICOURT BR	(O) 31.5							
			11	NANTES R R BR	(O) 26.3							
			9	YVETOT R R TRACKS	(O) 24.0							
			11	NOGENT M/Y	(O) 22.0							
			6	ROUEN M/Y	(O) 18.0							
			20	BARENTON R/J	(O) 49.0							
			24	CONCHES A/F	(O) 70.0							
			11	ST.ANDRÉ DE L'EURE A/F	(O) 33.6							
			25	T/O	69.5							
TOTALS:		1029	462		1159.5	0	9	7	235	6	23	83

VIII FC

Despatched		Effective	Target	Bombs Tonnage	E/A	Losses MIA	E	Dam	Casualties KIA	WIA	MIA
P-38	142	266	ESCORT 2BD		20–0–19 (G)	0	0		0	0	0
P-51	138					1	0		0	0	1
P-47	39	36	ESCORT 1BD & FIGHTER-BOMBER	3.3		0	0		0	0	0
P-38	41	286	ESCORT 3BD		0–0– 1 (G)	0	0		0	0	0
P-47	142					0	0		0	0	0
P-51	121					0	0		0	0	0
P-47	91	86	FIGHTER-BOMBER ST.ANDRÉ DE L'EURE A/F	13.4		0	0		0	0	0
TOTALS:	714	674		16.7	20–0–20	1	0		0	0	1

REMARKS: Tactical missions:– bridges, tunnels, rail targets and *Noball* sites France. Mission encountered poor weather and many units recalled. Groups able to attack T/Os were 44BG, 91BG, 94BG, 303BG, 384BG, 385BG, 388BG, 390BG, 401BG, 447BG, 452BG, 457BG, 486BG. Bomb group losses:– 91BG – 1, 92BG – 1, 94BG – 1, 388BG – 2, 398BG – 2, 452BG – 2. The 94BG B-17 ditched 30 miles SE Dungeness, crew rescued. 385BG B-17 c/l base; 447BG B-17 c/l Sutton Bridge A/F. 2 B/d 398BG B-17s c/l southern England. 2 486BG and 1 487BG B-24s Cat E.

All Fighter groups except 4FG and 479FG operating. No claims. Fighter group losses:– 355FG – 1.

OTHER OPERATIONS: 7PG despatched 5 F-5s and 6 Spitfires to D/A and Germany A/Fs. 802RG despatched 3 Mosquitoes to scout for bombers, 2 Mosquitoes on WR France, and 2 B-17 on Atlantic WR.

8/9 JULY 1944

8AF 461 NIGHT LEAFLET OPERATION

NLS B-17, 5 despatched, 4 effective; France.

801BG despatched 17 B-24s on *Carpetbagger* operations.

9 JULY 1944

8AF 462

	Despatched		Effective	Target		Bombs Tonnage	E/A	Losses MIA	E	Dam	Casualties KIA	WIA	MIA
1BD	B-17	150	68	CHALONNES BR	(O)	135.0		1	0	10	0	0	9
			12	LE CREUSOT BR	(O)	24.0							
			12	BOUCHEMAINE BR	(O)	24.0							
			12	CHALONNES H/WAY BR	(O)	24.0							
			36	CHATEAUDUN A/F	(O)	68.0							
8AF 463													
3BD	B-24	104	37	LAUNCHING SITES	(P)	88.0		1	0	60	0	2	0
	B-17	77	12	ST.OMER/ LONGUENESSE A/F	(O)	26.8		0	0				
			3	T/O		7.0							
TOTALS:		331	192			396.8	0	2	0	70	0	2	9
VIII FC													
	P-47	46	155a/c	ESCORT 8AF 462				1	0		0	0	0
	P-51	130						1	0		0	0	1
	P-38	96	90	STRAFING MOULIN/ NEVERS/TOURS			1–0–1	1	0		0	0	1
	P-47	83	158a/c	ESCORT 8AF 463			5–0–3	0	0		0	0	0
	P-51	86						0			0	0	0
TOTALS:		441	403				6–0–4	3	0		0	0	2

REMARKS: First mission to bridges and airfields in France largely frustrated by cloud. 92BG, 305BG, 381BG, 398BG bombed T/Os. Second mission also encountered poor weather: 34BG bombed. Bomb group losses:– 34BG – 1, 379BG – 1. The 34BG B-24 ditched 45 miles S of Selsey Bill, 4 saved. Fighter groups not operating: 56FG, 357FG, 364FG, 479FG. Fighter group credits:– 20FG – 1, 353FG – 5. Fighter group losses:– 55FG – 1, 78FG – 1, 361FG – 1. The 78FG pilot baled 15 miles SE Worthing and was saved. MIA 379BG B-17 never seen after t/o.

OTHER OPERATIONS: 7PG despatched 2 F-5s on PR France. 802RG despatched 1 Mosquito to scout for bombers and 3 on WR England/France. 3 B-17s on Atlantic WR.

INCIDENT

Thunderbolts of the 353rd Group were sent to patrol the Argentan and Bernay area of France in support of heavy bombers bombing V-1 sites on 9 July. One squadron entered a fight between a number of Me 109s and Spitfires, claiming five of the enemy. During the mêlée 2/Lt Grover McLaughlin saw a Spitfire, turning with an Me 109, become separated from his own flight, so he decided to join the RAF fighter as a wingman. The Spitfire then disposed of the Messerschmitt, dipped wings in acknowledgement of the support and flew off. Apparently this was Wg.Cdr Bill Crawford-Crompton (21½ victories), one of the RAF's great aces, for when the 353rd returned to base the pilots were somewhat embarrassed to learn that the Wing Commander had reported that a Spitfire of the Free French squadrons he commanded had been shot down by a yellow and black checkerboard nosed P-47. The victim of this recognition error was Capt Michael Boudier (10 victories) who fortunately was able to bale out, although he spent the rest of the war in a prison camp.

9/10 JULY 1944

8AF 464 NIGHT LEAFLET OPERATION

NLS B-17, 6 despatched, 5 effective; France.

801BG despatched 37 B-24s on *Carpetbagger* operations.

10 JULY 1944

802RG despatched 2 Mosquitoes and 2 B-17s on routine WR.

10/11 JULY 1944

8AF 465 NIGHT LEAFLET OPERATION

NLS B-17 6 despatched, 6 effective; France and Holland.

801BG despatched 12 B-24s on *Carpetbagger* operations.

The 491BG's *Tubarao* heading for home at 22,000 ft over the Channel, 7 July. Beast face decorations were common on Liberators. (via S. Gotts)

11 JULY 1944

8AF 466

	Despatched		Effective	Target		Bombs Tonnage	E/A	Losses MIA	E	Dam	Casualties KIA	WIA	MIA
1BD	B-17	401	371	MUNICH M/Y	(P)	788.4		1	1	42	3	3	10
				PASSING E/S	(P)	6.9							
				TYRE WORKS	(P)								
			3	T/O									
3BD	B-17	340	183	MUNICH BMW WORKS	(P)	418.0		3	1	89	1	2	30
			106	MUNICH M/Y		242.5							
2BD	B-24	435	291	MUNICH CENTRE	(P)	681.8		16	2	0	8	14	149
			55	MUNICH/RIEM A/F	(P)	110.0							
			29	AUGSBURG	(O)	77.2							
			8	EPPINGEN	(O)	20.8							
			1	AUTOBAHN BR	(O)	2.6							
TOTALS:		1176	1047			2348.2	0	20	5	131	12	19	189

VIII FC

		Despatched	Effective	Target	E/A	Losses MIA	E	Dam	KIA	WIA	MIA
	P-38	52	209	ESCORT FOR 1BD		0	0		0	0	0
	P-47	97				0	0		0	0	0
	P-51	91				0	0		0	0	0
	P-38	47	166	ESCORT FOR 3BD		0	0		0	0	0
	P-47	48				0	0		0	0	0
	P-51	100				1	0		0	0	1
	P-38	98	324	ESCORT FOR 2BD	1–0–0 (G)	0	0		0	0	0
	P-47	122			1–0–0	1	0		0	0	1
	P-51	140			0–0–1	2	1		0	0	2
TOTALS:		795	699		1–0–1 (G) 1–0–0 (G)	4	1		0	0	4

REMARKS: Munich and Southern Germany. Visual conditions expected but H2X attacks had to be made. All 1BD and 3BD B-17 groups and all 2BD B-24 groups participated. Bomb group losses:– 1BD – 92BG – 1. 2BD – 44BG – 2, 389BG – 1, 392BG – 2, 445BG – 3, 446BG – 2, 453BG – 1, 458BG – 2, 467BG – 1, 492BG – 2; 3BD – 385BG – 1, 447BG – 2. Landing or cr. in Switzerland were 1 92BG and 2 447BG B-17s and 2 392BG, 1 445BG, 2 492BG B-24s. A 44BG B-24 ditched 15 miles off Beachy Head, 4 saved. A 389BG B-24 ditched 60 miles E of Clacton, 3 saved. During assembly 457BG B-17 caught fire and cr. Saham Toney, 3 k. On return, 100BG B-17 Lt Bentley, crew safe; 448BG B-24 cr. at Hoo, Kent, 1 k; 467BG B-24 cr. Hardwick A/F, 2 k.

All Fighter groups active. Fighter group e/a credits:– 339FG – 1 (a glider). Fighter group losses:– 4FG – 1, 78FG – 1, 339FG – 1, 359FG – 1. 355FG P-51 abandoned over UK, pilot baled.

OTHER OPERATIONS: 802RG despatched 3 Mosquitoes to scout for bombers, 2 Mosquitoes on WR over Continent, and 2 B-17 on Atlantic WR.

INCIDENT

Accidents with 'run-away guns' occurred on a number of occasions despite cautions and instructions to gunners on the matter. One of the most bizarre incidents happened at Thorpe Abbotts on the afternoon of 11 July 1944, shortly after the B-17s had returned from a fairly uneventful mission to Munich. Fortress '007' was parked on its dispersal near the control tower; the crew had vacated the aircraft but the ball turret gunner was underneath at his turret cleaning the guns. Suddenly one of the guns began to fire, sweeping the area as the turret swung from the recoil, causing all around to fling themselves flat on the ground for protection. The firing did not cease until the gun had consumed 207 rounds, killing the ball gunner, Sgt Homer Parish, as he tried to run to safety, and damaging three neighbouring B-17s. One B-17, hit by a tracer bullet in the wing, caught fire with the result that it was damaged beyond repair.

11/12 JULY 1944

8AF 467 NIGHT LEAFLET OPERATION

NLS B-17, 6 despatched, 6 effective; France.

801BG despatched 30 B-24s (1 aborted) on *Carpetbagger* operations.

802RG H2X Mosquito on scope photo mission.

12 JULY 1944

8AF 468

	Despatched		Effective	Target		Bombs Tonnage	E/A	Losses MIA	E	Dam	Casualties KIA	WIA	MIA
3BD	B-24	131	0	PAS DE CALAIS V/S		0		0	0	0	0	0	0

8AF 469

	Despatched		Effective	Target		Bombs Tonnage	E/A	Losses MIA	E	Dam	KIA	WIA	MIA
1, 2, & 3BD	B-17	759	1124	CITY OF MUNICH	(P)	2701.8		24	2	183	2	3	106
			16	ENSTINGEN	(O)	40.0							
	B-24	512	10	T/O		25.0			2	114	0	4	116
TOTALS:		1402	1150			2766.8		24	4	297	2	7	216

	144 RAF SPITFIRES			ESCORT 8AF 468								
VIII FC												
	P-38	193	717	ESCORT 8AF 469			0	1		0	1	0
	P-47	323					0	0		0	0	0
	P-51	287					0	0		0	0	0
TOTALS:		803	717			0	0	1		0	1	0

REMARKS: 8AF 468 was flown by the 5 3BD B-24 groups to *Noball* targets but adverse weather caused all a/c to return with bombs. 8AF 469 was another attempt at visual bombing in Munich area, again foiled by bad weather and a PFF attack was carried out. All 1BD and 2BD groups and 3BD B-17 groups participated. Bomb group losses: 1BD – 351BG – 1, 379BG – 1, 384BG – 1, 457BG – 3; 2BD – 389BG – 1, 446BG – 1, 448BG – 3, 453BG – 1, 458BG – 2, 467BG – 2, 491BG – 1, 492BG – 1; 3BD – 94BG – 2, 95BG – 1, 385BG – 2, 390BG – 1. Ten MIA a/c landed or cr. Switzerland (2 448BG and 457BG, 1 each 94BG, 390BG, 389BG, 458BG, 467BG, 491BG). 457BG B-17 ditched off Felixstowe, 9 rescued. Two bombers lost in collision over target. On return, 351BG B-17 c/l base; 448BG B-24 cr. near Hardwick A/F; 491BG B-24 c/l Chediston; 452BG B-17 c/l base.

All Fighter groups active. No claims or losses. A 20FG P-38 cr. t/o, pilot injured.

OTHER OPERATIONS: 7PG despatched 6 F-5s on PR to France.

802 despatched 3 Mosquitoes as weather scouts for bombers, 2 Mosquitoes on WR Channel and North Sea, and 1 B-17 on Atlantic WR.

12/13 JULY 1944

8AF 470 NIGHT LEAFLET OPERATION

NLS B-17, 6 despatched, 6 effective; France.

802RG H2X Mosquito on scope photo mission.

13 JULY 1944

8AF 471

	Despatched		Effective	Target	Bombs Tonnage	E/A	Losses MIA	E	Dam	Casualties KIA	WIA	MIA
1BD	B-17	399	356	MUNICH CITY (P)	830.4		4	1	156	8	7	36
			6	MUNICH R/R (O)	15.0							
			3	T/O	3.9							
3BD	B-17	278	100	MUNICH A/I (P)	244.3	11–4–8	5	2	129	0	9	50
			139	MUNICH CITY (O)	335.2							
			3	T/O	7.5							
2BD	B-24	366	298	SAARBRÜCKEN M/Y (P)	911.3		1	7	31	23	9	19
			3	T/O	9.0							
TOTALS:		1043	908		2356.6	11–4–8	10	10	316	31	25	105
VIII FC												
	P-38	87	292	ESCORT 1BD		2–1–2	1	0				
	P-47	98					1	0				
	P-51	144					0	0				
	P-38	98	170	ESCORT 3BD			0	1				
	P-47	51					0	0				
	P-51	46					1	0				
	P-51	85	81	ESCORT 2BD			1	1				
TOTALS:		609	543			2–1–2	5	1		0	0	3

REMARKS: Third mission to Munich area with resort to H2X attack due to cloud. Groups participating:– all 1BD and all 3BD B-17 groups except 95BG. All 2BD groups involved in Saarbrücken mission. Bomb group losses:– 1BD – 303BG – 1, 351BG – 1, 398BG – 1, 401BG – 1; 2BD – 448BG – 1; 3BD – 100BG – 2, 385BG – 1, 390BG – 1, 447BG – 1. Down in Switzerland: 1 303BG, 1 385BG, 2 100BG, 1 446BG. A 489BG B-24 cr. on t/o base, 9 k. During assembly 392BG B-24 cr. Wrangle Common, crew baled; 392BG B-24 c/l Whitchurch; 446BG B-24 cr. East Tunstall, crew killed. On return, 489BG B-24 cr. Sudbury, crew baled; a 491BG B-24 cr. Morningthorpe, 5 k. B/d 306BG B-17 c/l Gransden Lodge A/F. B/d 448BG B-24 c/l Cold Harbour, 5 inj. B/d 95BG B-17 and 388BG B-17 Cat E.

All Fighter groups active except 356FG and 357FG. Fighter group e/a credits:– 352FG – 1, 355FG – 1. Fighter group losses:– 4FG – 1, 20FG – 1, 55FG – 1, 56FG – 1, 359FG – 1. The 55FG and 56FG a/c collided nr Brussels. 20FG P-38 pilot baled over Thames estuary and rescued. The 359FG pilot baled 35 miles E of Clacton, pilot rescued. A P-51 c/l in England.

OTHER OPERATIONS: 7PG despatched 8 F-5s on PR France. 802RG Mosquito on H2X scope photo sortie Germany. 802RG despatched 1 Mosquito on WR UK and 1 on WR France.

13/14 JULY 1944

28 B-24s of 801BG on *Carpetbagger* operations.

14 JULY 1944

8AF 472

	Despatched		Effective	Target	Bombs Tonnage	E/A	Losses MIA	E	Dam	Casualties KIA	WIA	MIA
3BD	B-17	359		SPECIAL OPERATION OVER SOUTHERN FRANCE	3700 containers	5–2–2	0	0	15	0	0	0

8AF 473

2BD	B-24	131	39	PERONNE A/F	(P) 94.5	0	0	0	9	0	0	0
			54	MONTDIDIER A/F	(P) 122.5							
TOTALS:		131	93		217.0	0	0	0	9	0	0	0

VIII FC

	P-47	196	465	ESCORT 3BD		4–0–1						
	P-51	328		8AF 472								
	P-38	36	79	ESCORT B-24s			0	1		0	0	0
	P-51	52		8AF 473			0	0		0	0	0
	P-38	100	94	FIGHTER-BOMBER RAIL TARGETS E & SE PARIS	18.5	2–0–0	1	0		0	0	1
TOTALS:		712	638		18.5	6–0–1	1	1		0	0	1

REMARKS: 8AF 472 was Operation *Cadillac* – material and arms to French resistance fighters – seven dropping points in three regions – St.Lo, Vercorse and Limoges. Flown by all 3BD B-17 groups. Total 3,700 containers parachuted from low altitude. 2 B-17s landed beach-head after mission. 8AF 473 was an attack on airfields by 34BG, 486BG, 487BG, 493BG, B-24s. All Fighter groups except 479FG operating. Fighter group e/a credits:– 20FG – 2, 357FG – 4. Fighter group losses:– 20FG – 1. 20FG P-38 cr. Sibson on return, pilot safe. 361FG inadvertendly shot down RAF Spitfire.

OTHER OPERATIONS: 7PG despatched 2 F-5s on PR – 802RG despatched 3 Mosquitoes on WR.

Undercarriage lowered to restrict speed, 385BG Fortresses release parachute containers during Operation *Cadillac*. Of 3,780 released, 3,698 were recovered by the Maquis who radioed: 'Daylight raid very successful. Took place without hitch.'

14/15 JULY 1944

802RG despatched 2 Mosquitoes on H2X scope recon France.

15 JULY 1944

8AF 474

	Despatched		Effective	Target	Bombs Tonnage	E/A	Losses MIA	E	Dam	Casualties KIA	WIA	MIA
	P-38	94	169	ENEMY TRANSPORT	14.9		2	1	10	0	0	3
	P-47	84		SE OF PARIS			1	0	2	0	0	1
TOTALS:		178	169		14.9	0	3	1	12	0	0	4

REMARKS: Fighter-bomber attacks on road and rail transport in Paris area. Groups participating: 56FG, 356FG, 364FG, 479FG. Losses:– 56FG – 1, 364FG – 1, 479FG – 1. B/d 479FG P-38 c/l near Canterbury.

OTHER OPERATIONS: 802RG despatched 1 Mosquito on PR Continent, 4 Mosquitoes on routine UK/Continent WR and 2 B-17s on Atlantic WR.

With a 250 lb bomb under each wing and a 150 gallon belly tank, 62FS P-47Ds are marshalled on the west side of Boxted for a dive bombing mission on 15 July. The Thunderbolt's large nose restricted forward vision necessitating a weaving action while travelling along the perimeter track. The two stationary aircraft nearest the camera are angled across the track in order to get a good view of other aircraft. Extreme caution was required to avoid a collision in these circumstances. Only a few days before the propeller of a taxiing P-47 had amputated the tail of one ahead.

15/16 JULY 1944

8AF 475 NIGHT LEAFLET OPERATION

NLS B-17, 6 despatched, 6 effective; France.

27 B-24s of 801BG on *Carpetbagger* operations, France.

16 JULY 1944

8AF 476

	Despatched		Effective	Target		Bombs Tonnage	E/A	Losses MIA	E	Dam	Casualties KIA	WIA	MIA
1BD	B-17	407	213	MUNICH AERO ENG. WKS	(P)	492.1	2–3–2	10	2	112	2	7	81
			52	STUTTGART	(P)	119.8							
			54	AUGSBURG	(P)	157.9							
			50	TWO T/O		123.5							
3BD	B-17	238	206	STUTTGART	(S)	495.2		1	1	45	0	1	10
			2	T/O		5.0							
2BD	B-24	442	407	SAARBRÜCKEN M/Y	(P)	1143.3			2	45	1	3	0
TOTALS:		1087	984			2536.8	2–3–2	11	5	202	3	11	91

VIII FC

Despatched		Effective	Target	Bombs Tonnage	E/A	Losses MIA	E	Dam	Casualties KIA	WIA	MIA
P-38	48	240	ESCORT 1BD			0	0		0	0	0
P-47	47					0	0		0	0	0
P-51	192					1	0		0	0	1
P-38	43	214	ESCORT 3BD			0	0		0	0	0
P-47	50					0	0		0	0	0
P-51	146					1	0		0	0	1
P-38	85	169	ESCORT 2BD			1	1		0	0	0
P-38	85										
P-47	101					0	0		0	0	0
TOTALS:	712	623			0	3	1	5	0	0	2

REMARKS: Attacks on Munich area targets again frustrated by cloud. Unexpected front rose to 30,000 feet in places and many formations turned to attack secondary target. B-24s attacked Saarbrücken. Groups participating:- all 1BD, all 3BD B-17 except 100BG, all 2BD except 491BG. Bomb group losses:– 1BD – 91BG – 1, 92BG – 3, 306BG – 1, 381BG – 1, 384BG – 1, 398BG – 2, 401BG – 1; 3BD – 385BG – 1. The 385BG B-17 went to Switzerland. The 381BG B-17 ditched 40 miles E. of Clacton, 9 saved. On return, a 385BG B-17 cr. Capel St.Andrew, crew safe; 448BG B-24 c/l base. B/d 384BG B-17 c/l Woodbridge A/F. 305BG B-17 cr. landing base. B/d 445BG B-24 c/l Gt. Ashfield A/F, crew safe. First operation of P-51 scouting unit. All Fighter Groups active. Fighter group losses:– 20FG – 1, 339FG – 1, 352FG – 1. The 20FG pilot baled off Margate, rescued.

OTHER OPERATIONS: 7PG despatched 4 F-5 on PR France. 802RG despatched 7 a/c on routine WR and 2 Mosquitoes scouting for bombers.

16/17 JULY 1944

8AF 477 NIGHT LEAFLET OPERATION

NLS B-17, 5 despatched, 5 effective; France.

801BG despatched 24 B-24s on *Carpetbagger* operations.

802RG Mosquito on scope photo mission.

Although the Eighth's Mustang groups saw most of the air action with the Luftwaffe after D-Day, the most successful of all Thunderbolt groups, the 56FG still managed to enhance its record score. Lt Col Francis Gabreski made his 28th kill on 5 July, a total unsurpassed by any other American fighter pilot in Europe. Armourer Sgt Joe DiFranze does the honours on the 61FS commander's immaculate fighter, recently given a mottled green and grey camouflage. This dispersal point north of No.2 hangar always held Gabreski's P-47 at Boxted. Capt Fred Christensen, his ground crew and personal P-47D, *Rozzie Geth II*. Christensen had built up a score of 22 air victories over the past few months although further success was to elude him. His aircraft was unusual in that the victory scoreboard was carried on both sides. (As a side light, Crew Chief S/Sgt Conner, centre, once made the author's day by giving him a candy bar.) (Photos taken 15 July)

17 JULY 1944

8AF 478

	Despatched		Effective	Target		Bombs Tonnage	E/A	Losses MIA	E	Dam	Casualties KIA	WIA	MIA
1 & 3BD	B-17	331	25	FREVENT BR	(P)	75.0		1	1	64	0	3	9
			35	PERONNE BR	(P)	69.0							
			12	DOULLENS R/J	(P)	35.5							
			33	HAM-SUR-SOMME BR	(P)	97.5							
			32	ANIZY-LE-CHATEAU BR	(P)	92.5							
			36	JUSSY BR	(P)	106.0							
			35	AUXERRE BR	(P)	69.5							
			37	JOIGNY LA ROCHE BR	(P)	72.5							
			12	HESDIN F/D	(O)	35.0							
			11	LAON M/Y	(O)	33.0							
			12	TERGNIER BR	(O)	36.0							
			11	EU BR	(O)	33.0							
			12	FREVENT R/R & R/J	(O)	35.0							
			15	T/O		44.0							
2 & 3BD	B-24	339	52	BELFORT M/Y	(P)	149.0		0	3	54	2	7	0
			30	NANTEUIL BR	(P)	118.0							
			58	RILLY LA MONTAGNE DUMP	(P)	198.0							
			10	LES FOULONS BR	(P)	38.0							
			32	SULLY BR	(P)	79.5							
			36	GIEN BR	(P)	108.0							
			34	NEUVY-SUR-LOIRE BR	(P)	85.0							
			34	COULANGES BR	(P)	85.0							
			11	ST.DIZIER A/F	(O)	30.8							
			5	T/O		15.0							

8AF 479

	Despatched		Effective	Target		Bombs Tonnage	E/A	Losses MIA	E	Dam	Casualties KIA	WIA	MIA
	B-24	115	106	PAS DE CALAIS V/S		388.7		0	3	23	1	5	0
	B-17	69	34					0	0	28	0	0	0
TOTALS:		854	760			2129.0	0	1	7	169	3	15	9

17 JULY 1944 *(contd.)*

VIII FC

P-38	124	433	ESCORT 8AF 478		0	0	0	0	0	0
P-47	62				1	0	0	0	0	1
P-51	286				0	0	1	0	0	0
P-51	227	209	ESCORT 8AF 479		0	1	0	0	0	0
TOTALS:	699	642		0	1	1	1	0	0	1

REMARKS: First mission against tactical targets in France, second to *Noball* sites. Groups participating in 8AF 478 were 40CBW and 41CBW groups of 1BD, 94BG and 100BG of 3BD B-17, 2CBW, 92CBW, 93CBW groups and 93BG, 446BG, 489BG of 2BD and 3BD B-24. Groups participating in 8AF 479 were 96BG, 388BG, 448BG, 458BG, 466BG. Bomb group losses:– 379BG – 1. On return a 100BG B-17 c/l Friston Suffolk; a 493BG B-24, cr. Parkeston, crew baled. B/d 466BG B-24 c/l New Romney, 466BG B-24 c/l Woodchurch A/S Kent; 389BG B-24 c/l near Charing; 487BG B-24 cr. approach Lavenham A/F, 2 k; B/d 448BG B-24 Cat E base.

Four Fighter groups not operating: 55FG, 56FG, 353FG, 356FG. Fighter group losses:– 78FG – 1. 361FG P-51 Cat E.

OTHER OPERATIONS: 7PG despatched 41 F-5s and 8 Spitfires on PR, France and Germany. 802RG despatched 2 Mosquitoes to scout for bombers, 3 Mosquitoes on WR over Continent, and 2 B-17s on routine Atlantic WR.

S/Sgt John Miller in the Thorpe Abbotts combat library.

INCIDENT

When the B-17G *Lady Luck* landed at the 100th Group base on the afternoon of 17 July 1944 it brought back waist gunner S/Sgt John A. Miller from his 35th and last mission. Unknown to the rest of his crew and indeed the USAAF at large, Miller had made a little piece of history with a secret he kept to himself until he left the service after the war. While official records showed him as 19 he was, in fact, only 17 when he flew his combat tour, having falsified his age in order to join the Army Air Corps. Born 22 July 1926, Miller was a well developed lad when he confronted the recruiting sergeant in Kokomo, Indiana in October 1942. No birth certificate was demanded as John had persuaded his parents to sign the consent form. He was accepted and found himself on his way to basic training at 16 years three months. His intent of becoming an aerial gunner was nearly thwarted by his 180 pounds, but a few days of self-imposed starvation brought him down to an acceptable 175. After completion of gunnery training he was assigned to a B-24 crew, only to be taken at short notice to fill a vacancy in a B-17 bound for England. Miller resented the transfer but it probably saved his life as the B-24 crew later went to Italy and were lost when their bomber blew up over a target.

Soon after New Year's Day 1944, Miller's new crew arrived at Thorpe Abbotts with assignment to the most notorious of all Fortress groups. Their first mission was to Brunswick on 10 February. Antagonism between Miller and the co-pilot led to a shift to another crew that had a gunner in hospital. Again a change of crew probably saved Miller's life, for the one he had just left did not return from the disastrous Berlin mission on 6 March. Miller flew on that raid, his B-17 being one that returned safely; 15 other 100th Fortresses did not. He visited Berlin six times, five of these with Laurence Townsend's crew to which he was transferred when the gunner returned from hospital. During his 35 missions, which included the first Russia-Italy shuttle, seventeen-year-old Miller collected a DFC among other decorations and was credited with shooting down an Me 410. A week after his final combat flight, his last crew and bomber went down over St.Lo when flak hit their bomber. John Miller was almost certainly the youngest man to fly combat in 8th Air Force B-17s and undoubtedly the youngest bomber crewman to complete a tour of operations.

A 500 lb bomb smashed right through the nose of 305BG B-17 42-102555,KY:F, over the target on 18 July. The navigator, Lt L.J. Simpson, was killed. (via M. Gibson)

17/18 JULY 1944

8AF 480 NIGHT LEAFLET OPERATION

NLS B-17, 5 despatched, 5 effective: France and Holland.

801BG despatched 16 B-24s on *Carpetbagger* operations.

802RG Mosquito on scope photo mission.

18 JULY 1944

8AF 481

	Despatched		Effective	Target		Bombs Tonnage	E/A	Losses MIA	E	Dam	Casualties KIA	WIA	MIA
2 & 3BD	B-24	644	139	TROARNS	(P)	325.4		1	2	182			
			249	SOLIER	(P)	609.5							
			146	FRENOUVILLE	(P)	406.0							
			24	HUBERT LA FOLIE	(O)	56.9							
			12	MEZIDON M/Y	(O)	28.7							
3BD	B-17	291	107	KIEL	(P)	255.2		0	0	21			
			55	HEMMINSTEDT O/R	(P)	133.2							
			54	CUXHAVEN	(O)	122.7							
1BD	B-17	459	377	PEENEMÜNDE	(P)	995.0		3	0	64			
			37	ZINNOWITZ	(P)	92.0							
			20	STRALSUND M/Y	(O)	50.0							
TOTALS:		1394	1220			3074.0	0	4	2	267			
VIII FC													
	P-38	48	122	ESCORT 3BD B-17				0	0		0	0	0
	P-51	84						0	0		0	0	0
	P-38	93	297	ESCORT 1BD			21–0–12	0	0		0	0	0
	P-51	251						3	1		0	0	2
TOTALS:		476	419				21–0–12	3	1	5	0	0	2

REMARKS: B-24 groups – all except 491BG – attacked tactical targets in direct support of ground troops, Normandy. All 3BD B-17 groups except 385BG sent to Kiel where a PFF bombing of oil targets was made. All 1BD groups attacked Luftwaffe experimental stations at Peenemünde and Zinnowitz – visually. Bomb group losses:– 1BD – 91BG – 1, 306BG – 1, 381BG – 1; 2BD – 446BG – 1. The 3 B-17s MIA landed in Sweden. B/d 492BG B-24 c/l Normandy A/S. B/d 492BG B-24 abandoned over beach-head, crew safe.

Fighter groups not operating: 55FG, 56FG, 78FG, 353FG. 90RAF Spitfires escorted B-24s. Fighter group e/a credits:– 352FG – 20. Fighter group losses:– 352FG – 2, 355FG – 1. The 355FG pilot baled 40 miles E of Gt. Yarmouth, rescued. 352FG P-51 Cat E–pilot safe.

OTHER OPERATIONS: 7PG despatched 22 F-5s and 8 Spitfires to Germany, Belgium and France on PR.

802BG despatched 2 Mosquitoes scouting for bombers, 7 Mosquitoes on WR North Sea/Continent and 2 B-17s on Atlantic WR.

In support of the invasion forces 8AF fighters were directed to strafe military road transport behind the battle area. The 56FG's Capt Christensen caught this lorry and trailer and 'walks' his fire across an adjacent field towards his victim: 19 July.

Robert Riemensnider and the men who cared for *Bobby*. 20FG P-38s had elaborate record displays. Top hat symbols are for escort missions, umbrellas for top cover, brooms for sweeps, bombs for fighter-bomber work. (J. Hudgens via D. Morris)

INCIDENT

In July 1944 VIII Fighter Command converted three of its four P-38 equipped groups to the P-51 Mustang. High altitude performance limitation was the major reason for dispensing with the Lightning, the Allison engines having given considerable trouble when operated above 25,000 ft. Despite a near 50 per cent mechanical failure rate during one period of operations, some P-38Js endured with exceptionally good records. When the 55th Fighter Squadron flew its last Lightning mission on 19 July 1944 it had one veteran fighter, *Bobby*, with 96 sorties and 454 combat hours to its credit. A total of 395 of these hours were on the same engines and during its operational life only two turnbacks for mechanical reasons occurred. Much of this record was due to the careful maintenance of S/Sgt Herbert C. Macrow and his ground crew team plus the considerate pilotage of Lt Robert H. Riemensnider who flew 64 sorties in *Bobby*.

18/19 JULY 1944

25 B-24s of 801BG on *Carpetbagger* operations; France. 1 B-24 MIA collided with RAF a/c over France.

19 JULY 1944

8AF 482

Despatched		Effective	Target		Bombs Tonnage	E/A	Losses MIA	E	Dam	Casualties KIA	WIA	MIA
		106	HOLLSRIEGEL-SKREUTH	(P)	269.3							
		98	LECHFELD A/F	(P)	214.6							
B-17	378	123	AUSGBURG	(P)	274.7							
(1BD)		11	DAUN	(O)	27.5	6–4–4	11	0	121	2	12	100
		12	ULM M/Y	(O)	13.6							
		3	T/O		3.2							
		62	KEMPSTON	(P)	152.8							
		71	STRASBOURG	(P)	207.5							
		49	LEIPHEIM A/F	(P)	107.0							
B-24	333	45	LAUPHEIM A/F	(P)	114.9		1	0	37	0	1	10
(2BD)		1	KOBLENZ	(O)	2.6							
		9	BADEN-BADEN	(O)	22.5							
		54	BÖBLINGEN A/F	(O)	137.4							
		2	T/O		5.2							
B-17	291	52	EBELSBACH	(P)	128.0	0	3	0	140	8	2	30
3BD		173	SCHWEINFURT	(P)								
		15	DARMSTADT	(O)	30.9							
		16	DÜREN	(O)	39.0							
		2	T/O		2.0							
B-24	240	51	SAARBRÜCKEN	(P)	270.0	0	2	3	69	1	0	24
3BD		90	KOBLENZ	(O)	233.0							
		12	GERMÜNDEN	(O)	33.6							
		11	KARTHAUS	(O)	31.5							
		11	NEUNKIRCHEN	(O)	31.5							
		21	T/O		61.9							
TOTALS:	1242	1082			2780.4	6–4–4	17	4	347	11	15	164

VIII FC

Despatched		Effective	Target	E/A	Losses MIA	E	Dam	KIA	WIA	MIA
P-38	48				0			0	0	0
P-47	70	153	ESCORT 3BD B-17	20–0–9 (G)	1			0	0	1
P-51	46				0			0	0	0
P-47	48	44	ESCORT 2BD KOBLENZ		0			0	0	0
P-51	34	32	ESCORT 3BD B-24		0			0	0	0
P-47	73				1			0	0	1
P-51	198	224	ESCORT 1BD	17–0–4	4			0	0	4
P-38	96		ESCORT 2BD		1			0	0	1
P-47	48	217	STRASSBOURG	18–0–5 (G)	0			0	0	0
P-51	100				0			0	0	0
TOTALS:	761	670		17–0– 4 38–0–14 (G)	7	1	7	0	0	7

REMARKS: Industrial targets in Western and South-Western Germany. Mostly visual bombing. Groups participating:– all 3BD B-17 except 94BG; 2BD Koblenz Force, 14CBW and 448BG; all 3BD B-24; all 1BD; 2BD Strasbourg, 2CBW and 93BG, 446BG, 489BG. Bomb group losses:– 1BD – 91BG – 2, 303BG – 1, 351BG – 3, 384BG – 3, 398BG – 1, 401BG – 1; 2BD – 389BG – 1; 3BD – 34BG – 2, 95BG – 1, 96BG – 1, 390BG – 1. Three B-17s landed in Switzerland (91BG, 351BG, 384BG). A 388BG B-17 cr. after colliding near Bury St.Edmunds during assembly. 7 killed. 3 B-24s of 3BD cr. in UK. B/d 34BG B-24 abandoned by crew near Lympne A/F after heading a/c out to sea. MIA 351BG PFF B-17 with 457BG crew. All Fighter groups operating. First mission of 55FG after conversion to P-51. Fighter group e/a credits:– 4FG – 2, 352FG – 8, 355FG – 4. Fighter group losses:– 4FG – 2, 20FG – 1, 56FG – 1, 78FG – 1, 352FG – 1, 355FG – 1. MIA 4FG P-51 cr. Switzerland, pilot safe. B/d 356FG P-47 Cat E.

OTHER OPERATIONS: 7PG despatched 12 F-5s and 7 Spitfires to France, Belgium and Germany. 802RG despatched 2 Mosquitoes to scout for bombers, 2 Mosquitoes on WR Atlantic and France, and 2 B-17s on Atlantic WR.

INCIDENT

Francis 'Lefty' Grove was responsible for bringing down one enemy aircraft during twelve months of flying with the 4th Fighter Group and it happened without a shot being fired. During an escort mission on 19 July 1944 his flight observed three Me 109s at 32,000 ft. Grove described what happened next as follows:– 'One of the Jerries decided to make a run for it and dived for the deck. I went after him, and we went down at a terrific speed. All the time I couldn't get a shot at him. After diving 24,000 ft, the Jerry went into a spin. I guess he lost control because he baled out when we were only 7,000 feet from the ground.'

INCIDENT

Unauthorised 'buzzing' – a display of ultra-low or ultra-close flying to arrest attention – was officially prohibited. However, officialdom usually turned a blind eye. Very low flying was exhilarating for aircrew and either exciting or frightening for those on the ground, subjected to the thundering pass of several tons of machinery a few feet above their heads. 'Buzz jobs' were usually performed over home base on special occasions; the more daring would indulge in a lightning pass over some neighbouring airfield and hope they were not reported. If apprehended the culprits could face fines, various forms of confinement and even loss of promotion. It could be dangerous and several fighter pilots killed themselves by flying just a little too low. On 19 July 1944 a B-17 from the 95th Group visited the 78th Fighter Group base at Duxford where the pilot had once been assigned. In the late afternoon the Fortress took off on a joy ride with its own crew of three, two 78th pilots who were friends of the B-17 pilot, and 14 enlisted men from Duxford. The pilot decided to buzz the control tower, heading towards it and the technical site from the east only a few feet above the flying field. He judged his pull up over the tower accurately, but evidently did not see the warning blinker light mast on top of a hangar. The impact sheared off part of the left wing and tailplane. As the stricken bomber passed over the public road separating the airfield from the living sites it inverted before crashing into a barracks building. In addition to those in the B-17, one man in the barracks was killed and another two injured. As a result of this accident General Doolittle issued orders that unauthorised low flying was strictly prohibited and that intentional buzzing of airfields or hospitals would bring the strongest action against the perpetrators. Boys being boys, this did not put an end to illicit buzzing, as it was always difficult to prove what was intentional and what was unintentional.

On the approach to Lechfeld, 19 July, Flak battery 6/Schw. 443 with six Flak 37 88 mm guns at Scheuring opened fire. The second salvo put one shell into the fuselage of 398BG's B-17 42-102511, blasting it apart. The blazing front portion spun into the ground near Althegnenburg, the bombs detonating. The rear fuselage and tail floated down (top left second picture) and landed not far away. The tail gunner was alive but so badly injured he died within 30 minutes. The rest of the crew never had a chance to escape and perished. (H. Grimminger)

19/20 JULY 1944

8AF 483 NIGHT LEAFLET OPERATION

NLS B-17, 5 despatched, 5 effective: France and Belgium.

801BG despatched 5 B-24s on *Carpetbagger* operations.

482BG despatched 2 B-17s on night mission.

20 JULY 1944

8AF 484

	Despatched		Effective	Target		Bombs Tonnage	E/A	Losses MIA	E	Dam	Casualties KIA	WIA	MIA
1BD	B-17	417	107	DESSAU	(P)	253.0	11–9–7	15	0	188	1	10	129
			56	LEIPZIG/MOCKAU	(P)	124.7							
			45	LEIPZIG B/I	(P)	97.7							
			69	KÖTHEN	(P)	164.5							
			36	NORDHAUSEN A/F	(O)	90.0							
			12	GIESSEN A/F	(O)	21.7							
			23	KOLLEDA A/F	(O)	57.5							
			12	RUDOLSTADT	(O)	23.1							
			12	BITTERFELD	(O)	26.9							
			20	T/O		42.6							
3BD	B-17	295	53	LÜTZKENDORF	(P)	129.5		2	0	153	0	2	21
			155	MERSEBURG	(P)	374.0							
			47	WETZLAR	(O)	117.0							
			7	T/O		17.5							
3BD	B-24			RÜSSELHEIM	(P)			1	1		1	6	0

continued on next page

20 JULY 1944 *(contd.)*

2BD	B-24	460	123	ERFURT NORD A/F	(p)	312.3		1	0	31	0	2	9
			72	GOTHA	(P)	197.3							
			80	SCHMALKALDEN	(O)	245.9							
			12	BAD NAUHEIM	(O)	31.2							
			18	FULDA M/Y	(O)	50.0							
			7	KOBLENZ	(O)	17.0							
			12	IDSTEIN M/Y	(O)	35.5							
			9	HOMBURG M/Y	(O)	27.0							
			10	BAD SALZUNGEN M/Y	(O)	29.5							
			10	WERNHAUSEN M/Y	(O)	28.0							
			21	BERKA	(O)	27.0							
			11	ERFURT/ BINDERSLEBEN A/F	(O)	29.0							
			24	FREIBURG M/Y	(O)	62.0							
			6	BOPPARD	(O)	18.0							
			6	T/O		18.0							
TOTALS:		1172	1077			2667.4	11–9–7	19	1	372	2	20	159
VIII FC													
	P-38	51	253	ESCORT FOR 1BD			5–0–3	0	0		0	0	0
	P-47	49					2–0–0 (G)	2	0		0	0	2
	P-51	185						4	1		0	1	3
	P-38	50	178	ESCORT FOR 3BD			1–1–1	0	0		0	0	0
	P-47	60					1–0–4 (G)	0	0		0	0	0
	P-51	100						1	1		0	0	1
	P-47	47	45	ESCORT FOR 2BD			6–0–3 (G)	1	0		0	0	1
TOTALS:		542	476				6–1–4 9–0–7 (G)	8	2	12	0	1	7

REMARKS: Oil and industrial targets Western Germany. Groups participating: all 1BD B-17, all 3BD B-17 except 96BG, all 2BD, all 3BD B-24. Bomb group losses:– 1BD – 91BG – 8, 92BG – 1, 306BG – 2, 379BG – 1, 384BG – 1, 401BG – 2; 2BD – 458BG – 1; 3BD – 95BG – 1, 447BG – 1, 493BG – 1. The 306BG B-17 ditched 20 miles N. of Dunkirk, 9 saved. The 493BG B-24 ditched off Bawdsey, 9 saved. The 379BG B-17 landed Switzerland. A 486BG B-24 c/l Boreham. MIA 95BG a/c was PFF with part 100BG crew.

All Fighter groups active. First mission of P-51 by 20FG (one sqdn). Fighter group credits:– 355FG – 5, 359FG – 1, 361FG – 5. Fighter group losses:– 4FG – 1, 55FG – 1, 56FG – 1, 355FG – 2, 356FG – 2, 359FG – 1. A 355FG pilot baled 35 miles NE Margate, rescued. Lt.Col Gabreski, 56FG, highest scoring ace, lost strafing. 357FG P-51 c/l, pilot inj. 55FG P-38 Cat E.

OTHER OPERATIONS: 7PG despatched 8 F-5s and 8 Spitfires on PR to France, Belgium and Germany. 1 F-5 cr. England. 802RG despatched 3 Mosquitoes to scout for bombers, 3 Mosquitoes on WR Germany and France and 2 B-17s on routine WR UK/Atlantic.

A beautiful but lethal scene. *Star Duster* ploughs through a flak salvo while bound for Leipzig, 20 July. Seventeen days after this picture was taken both the subject aircraft and that from which it was taken, *Hubba Hubba*, were lost. (351BG Assoc.)

20/21 JULY 1944

8AF 485 NIGHT LEAFLET OPERATION

NLS B-17, 6 despatched, 6 effective; France.

801BG despatched 12 B-24s on *Carpetbagger* operation.

482BG despatched 2 B-17s and 1 860RG Mosquito on operations.

21 JULY 1944

	Despatched		Effective	Target		Bombs Tonnage	E/A	Losses MIA	E	Dam	Casualties KIA	WIA	MIA
2BD	B-24	433	54	OBERPFEFFEN-HOFEN PFF	(P)	139.0	10–2–0	22	3	181	1	7	205
			33	NEUAUBING	(P)	82.5							
			93	SAARBRÜCKEN M/Y	(O)	224.7							
			106	MUNICH	(O)	254.5							
			9	SCHORNDORF	(O)	23.0							
			13	BULLAY BRIDGE	(O)	45.0							
			78	T/O		206.3							
8AF 486													
3BD	B-24	96	17	DÜREN	(O)	41.0		2	0	12	0	0	20
			9	INDENBODEN	(O)	23.4							
			12	WALLDRUN M/Y	(O)	30.5							
			48	T/O		123.1							
3BD	B-17	241	90	REGENSBURG/ OBERTRAUBLING	(P)	233.5		4	0	88	2	1	38
			44	REGENSBURG/ PRÜFENING	(P)	106.0							
			40	STUTTGART	(O)	97.0							
			18	T/O		49.5							
1BD	B-17	340	70	EBELSBACH	(P)	159.7		3	0	81	1	3	25
			99	SCHWEINFURT	(P)	230.9							
			59	LUDWIGSHAFEN	(O)	147.0							
			12	LACHEN	(O)	30.0							
			12	BAD MÜNSTER	(O)	25.7							
			13	BAD KREUZNACH	(O)	26.1							
			12	SIMMERN M/S	(O)	23.4							
			13	EBELSBACH	(O)	32.5							
			8	WÜRZBURG	(O)	20.0							
			5	NECKARGEMÜND	(O)	9.5							
			13	T/O		31.9							
TOTALS:		1110	980			2415.7	10–2–0	31	3	362	4	11	288
ESCORT													
	P-47	63	262	ESCORT 2BD			2–0– 1	0					
	P-51	249					3–0–10 (G)	5					
	P-47	40	109	ESCORT 3BD B-24			1–0– 0	0					
	P-51	76						0					
	P-47	73	148	ESCORT 3BD B-17			3–0– 0	0					
	P-51	97						2					
	P-38	115	187a/c	ESCORT 1BD				1					
	P-47	48						0					
	P-51	34						0					
TOTALS:		795	706				6–0– 1 3–0–10 (G)	8	3	5	0	0	5

REMARKS: German aircraft industry, ball-bearing works and airfields in SW Germany. Visual attacks on primaries. Groups participating:– all 2BD, all 3BD B-24, all 3BD B-17 except 388BG, all 1BD except 91BG and 398BG. Last operation of 486BG and 487BG with B-24s. Bomb group losses:– 1BD – 305BG – 2, 457BG – 1; 2BD – 44BG – 4, 93BG – 1, 389BG – 1, 392BG – 3, 446BG – 3, 448BG – 1, 453BG – 2, 489BG – 1, 491BG – 4, 492BG – 2; 3BD – 34BG – 1, 94BG – 1, 95BG – 1, 96BG – 2, 490BG – 1. The 453BG a/c MIA collided over target. A 94BG B-17 and 448BG B-24 with damage flew to Italy. Eight B-24s went to Switzerland (1 each 389BG, 448BG, 490BG, 491BG, 2 492BG and 2 44BG – 1 cr).

The 305BG B-17 ditched 35 miles NE of North Foreland, 1 rescued. B/d 491BG B-24 cr. in sea after crew baled in Manston area. On return, b/d 392BG B-24 c/l Manston A/F and another b/d 392BG B-24 cr. Old Buckenham after crew baled. 93BG B-24 cr. landing Bolthead A/F.

All Fighter groups operating. Last use of P-38 by 20FG. Fighter group e/a claims: 55FG – 3, 352FG – 3, 359FG – 1. Fighter group losses:– 55FG – 1, 352FG – 3, 359FG – 2, 361FG – 1, 479FG – 1. Two 352FG pilots baled 20 miles NE Cromer, both rescued. Two 352FG P-51s Cat E, out of fuel, 1 cr. and 1 c/l. 359FG P-51 abandoned over England.

OTHER OPERATIONS: 7PG despatched 6 F-5s and 7 Spitfires to Belgium and Germany. 1 Mosquito despatched on H2X scope photography. 802RG despatched 2 Mosquitoes to scout for bombers, 3 Mosquitoes on WR Continent and 2 B-17 on WR UK/Atlantic.

INCIDENT

The 94th Group Fortress *Morgan's Raiders* was hit by flak over Regensburg on 21 July 1944. One engine was stopped and there were fears for another. Lt Kirnes and crew discussed their predicament; the 400 mile haul back to England was a long way. Finally they elected to go south over the Alps to the Allied held part of Italy which was nearer and less flak spiked. Late in the day they landed safely at Foggia. A similar decision was made by 1/Lt Melvin Alspaugh and crew in the damaged 448th Group Liberator *Dead End Kids*. They too flew to a 15th Air Force base. Both crews and aircraft eventually returned to Britain.

21/22 JULY 1944

8AF 487 NIGHT LEAFLET OPERATION

NLS B-17, 8 despatched, 8 effective: France. 1 B-17 damaged.

22 JULY 1944

8AF 488

Despatched		Effective	Target	Bombs Tonnage	E/A	Losses MIA	E	Dam	Casualties KIA	WIA	MIA
B-17	7	7	LEAFLETS TO BREMEN, HAMBURG & KIEL			0	0	1	0	0	0
P-51	34	27	ESCORT FOR ABOVE		0	0	2		1	0	0

REMARKS: Bad weather restricted operations. 3 305BG PFF B-17s and 4 306BG B-17s dropped leaflets over NW Germany. 4FG escorted. 4FG P-51 cr. after t/o Audley End, pilot killed. A 4FG P-51 c/l on return Carlton Hawthorne, pilot safe.

OTHER OPERATIONS: 802RG despatched 5 B-17s (2 aborted) on WR Atlantic/Azores and 1 Mosquito on WR central France.

22/23 JULY 1944

8AF 489 NIGHT LEAFLET OPERATION

NLS B-17, 7 despatched, 7 effective: France & Holland.

44 B-24s of 801BG despatched on *Carpetbagger* operations.

23 JULY 1944

8AF 490

	Despatched		Effective	Target		Bombs Tonnage	E/A	Losses MIA	E	Dam	Casualties KIA	WIA	MIA
1BD	B-17	82	78	CREIL A/F	(P)	147.4		1	1	2	2	1	0
2BD	B-24	198	57	LAON/ATHIES A/F	(P)	112.2		0	0	3	1	2	0
			61	LAON/COUVRON A/F	(P)	119.8							
			48	JUVINCOURT A/F	(P)	149.6							
TOTALS:		280	244			529.0	0	1	1	5	3	3	0
	P-38	49	177	ESCORT 8AF 490									
	P-51	144											

REMARKS: GH attacks on airfields in France. Groups participating:– 1BD – 303BG, 379BG; 2BD – 93BG, 389BG, 445BG, 448BG, 489BG, 491BG. Bomb group losses:– 303BG – 1. Lost a/c ditched 16 miles SE Selsey Bill, 9 saved. B/d 303BG B-17 c/l Greenham Common A/F.

Fighter groups supporting bombers: 352FG, 359FG, 361FG, 364FG.

OTHER OPERATIONS: 7PG despatched 1 Spitfire and 2 F-5s to Continent. 802RG despatched 2 Mosquitoes to scout for bombers, 4 Mosquitoes and 3 B-17s (1 aborted) on WR UK/Atlantic.

23/24 JULY 1944

8AF 491 NIGHT LEAFLET OPERATION

NLS B-17, 6 despatched, 6 effective; France.

801BG despatched 25 B-24s (4 aborted) on *Carpetbagger* ops.

482BG despatched 4 B-17s on night mission.

24 JULY 1944

8AF 492

	Despatched		Effective	Target	Bombs Tonnage	E/A	Losses MIA	E	Dam	Casualties KIA	WIA	MIA
1, 2 & 3BD	B-17	909	343	PERIERS/ST.LO AREA(P)	661.6		1	0	70	1	1	1
			35	GRANVILLE R/R JUNCTION (O)	68.4							
	B-24	677	106	T/O	205.5		2	0	74	1	1	20
			3	T/O	9.0							
TOTALS:		1586	487		944.5	0	3	0	144	2	2	21

VIII FC

	P-38	97	478	ESCORT FOR BOMBERS		1–0–1	3	0	0	0	0	3
	P-47	198				1–0–1 (G)	0	1	1	0	0	0
	P-51	207					0	0	0	0	0	0
	P-51	169	143	SWEEP LECHFELD & LEIPHEIM A/F		3–0–0 12–0–16	2	1	6	0	0	2
TOTALS:		671	621			4–0–0 13–0–17 (G)	5	2	7	0	0	5

REMARKS: Bombing in support of US 1st Army Offensive; Periers St.Lo. Ground haze prevented several formations bombing and others were recalled. All bomb groups despatched except 486BG and 487BG. Accidental release of bombs over Allied lines caused death of 20 US personnel and 60 plus wounded. Bomb group losses:– 34BG – 1, 401BG – 1, 489BG – 1. 401BG B-17 ditched, 8 saved.

All fighter groups except 361FG active. Fighter group e/a credits:– 352FG – 3, 479FG – 1. Losses:– 355FG – 2, 479FG – 3. Two 479FG P-38s collided. On return a 78FG P-47 c/l base.

OTHER OPERATIONS: 7PG despatched 22 F-5s on PR France. 1 F-5 MIA. 802RG despatched 1 Mosquito to scout for bombers, 2 Mosquitoes on WR France and North Sea, 2 B-17s on Atlantic WR.

24/25 JULY 1944

8AF 493 NIGHT LEAFLET OPERATION

NLS B-17, 7 despatched, 7 effective; France.

801BG despatched 6 B-24s on *Carpetbagger* operations.

802RG Mosquito on H2X mission.

25 JULY 1944

8AF 494

	Despatched		Effective	Target	Bombs Tonnage	E/A	Losses MIA	E	Dam	Casualties KIA	WIA	MIA
1, 2 & 3BD	B-17	917	843	PERIERS/ST.LO (P)	1723.1		1	0	41	0	0	9
			13	T/O	24.6							
	B-24	664	647	PERIERS/ST.LO AREA (P)	1647.6		4	2	132	0	9	37
8AF 495												
3BD	B-17	106	0	BRUSSELS/ MELSBROEK A/F	0		0	0		0	0	0
TOTALS:		1687	1503		3395.3	0	5	2	173	0	9	46

VIII FC

	P-38	97	483	ESCORT 8AF 494		12–1–3	0	0	0	0	0	0
	P-47	199				2–0–0 (G)	0	0	0	0	0	0
	P-51	204					2	0	5	0	0	2
	P-38	1	78	FIGHTER-BOMBER FOURNIVAL/BOIS DE MONT FUEL DUMP	15.0	0–0–1	0	0	1	0	0	0
	P-47	83					0	0	4	0	0	0
	P-38	26	0	ESCORT 8AF 495			0	0	0	0	0	0
	P-51	110					0	0	0	0	0	0
TOTALS:		720	561		15.0	12–1–4 2–0–0 (G)	2	0	10	0	0	2

REMARKS: Bombing in direct support of US 1st Army; Periers-St.Lo area. Despite every precaution to ensure there was no short bombing, two incidents resulted in death of 102 US troops and 380 being wounded. All bomb groups except 486BG and 487BG participated. Bomb group losses:– 100 BG – 1, 389BG – 2, 445BG – 1, 489BG – 1. 389BG B-24 c/l Manston A/F on return. 466BG B-24 c/l Swanton Morley A/F. Mission 495 to Brussels A/F was recalled due to cloud up to 29,000ft.

All fighter groups except 352FG and 359FG active. Fighter group e/a credits:– 55FG – 2, 339FG – 4, 357FG – 4. Fighter group losses:– 55FG – 1, 361FG – 1. 56FG operated P-38 Droopsnoot.

OTHER OPERATIONS: 7PG despatched 46 F-5 (10 aborted) and 1 Spitfire to France and Denmark. 1 F-5 MIA. 802RG despatched 1 Mosquito and 1 B-24 to weather scout for bombers, and 2 B-17s on WR UK/French coast.

25/26 JULY 1944

17 B-24s of 801BG on *Carpetbagger* operations.

26 JULY 1944

8AF 496

	Despatched		Effective	Target		Bombs Tonnage	E/A	Losses MIA	E	Dam	Casualties KIA	WIA	MIA
VIII FC													
	P-47	192	40	GIVET F/D	(P)	14.5	0	1	0	10	0	0	1
			93	ST.JUST M/Y	(O)								

REMARKS: Fighter-bomber mission to attack fuel dumps at Fournival/Bois de Mont and Givet. Groups participating: 56FG, 78FG, 353FG, 356FG. Fighter group losses: 78FG – 1.

OTHER OPERATIONS: 7PG despatched 5 F-5s to France and Germany. 802RG despatched 2 Mosquitoes on WR France and 2 B-17s on WR UK/Atlantic.

26/27 JULY 1944

8AF 497 NIGHT LEAFLET OPERATION

NLS B-17, 7 despatched, 7 effective; France.

801BG despatched 9 B-24s on *Carpetbagger* operations.

27 JULY 1944

8AF 498

	Despatched		Effective	Target		Bombs Tonnage	E/A	Losses MIA	E	Dam	Casualties KIA	WIA	MIA
	B-17	26	0	COASTAL BATTERIES		0		0	0	0	0	0	0
3BD	B-24	120	34	BRUSSELS/VILVORDE	(P)	96.9		0	1	32	0	0	0
			20	GRAVELINES C/B	(P)	62.5							
			11	GHENT/TERNEUZEN	(O)	33.0							
			1	T/O									
TOTALS:		146	66			192.4	0	0	1	32	0	0	0
VIII FC													
	P-38	35	154	ESCORT BOMBERS			1–0–0 (G)	0	0	0	0	0	0
	P-47	97						0	0	0	0	0	0
	P-51	32						1	0	0	0	0	1
8AF 499													
	P-38	51	193	FIGHTER-BOMBER		28.7	0–0–1 (G)	2	0	0	0	0	2
	P-47	100		RAIL TRAFFIC				0	0	2	0	0	0
	P-51	53		SOUTH OF ROUEN				1	1	0	0	0	1
				AND AMIENS									
TOTALS:		368	347			28.7	1–0–1 (G)	3	1	2	0	0	4

REMARKS: Coastal batteries at Ostend and Cap Gris Nez/Calais area were target for 447BG but weather prevented bombing. The 3 groups of 93CBW bombed a signal depot at Brussels and batteries at Gravelines. On return a 34BG B-24 exploded and cr. Hadlow.

Fighter groups operating: 20FG, 56FG, 78FG, 353FG, 356FG, 364FG, 479FG. Fighter group losses:– 364FG – 1, 479FG – 2. First use of P-51 by 364FG – flew 2 sqnds P-51, 1 sqdn P-38. Going out 20FG P-51 destroyed by lightning near Bedford, pilot baled.

OTHER OPERATIONS: 7PG despatched 3 F-5s on PR France. 802RG despatched 3 Mosquitoes on WR France, Germany and Belgium and 2 B-17s on Atlantic WR.

EVENT

A combat tour of 25 missions for bomber crewmen was originally introduced by 8th Air Force in the early spring of 1943. Then it was deemed necessary to bolster morale among airmen who, aware of the attrition amongst their kind, had hitherto the bleak prospects of flying until they were killed, made prisoner or removed from operations due to wounds or for medical reasons. A year later losses, as a percentage of sorties flown, had almost halved, theoretically doubling an individual's chances of completing a tour. At the same time the strength of the 8th Air Force had increased ten-fold and its commanders were faced with the prospect of more crews finishing 25 missions than there were new arrivals to replace them. Early in April 1944 the decision was taken to increase a tour to 30 missions but for those men who had at this time completed 15 or more, there would be a sliding scale – the nearer to 25 the fewer extra missions required. However, it was soon evident that with the increased rate of operations and the comparatively safer tactical missions in support of the forthcoming cross-Channel invasion, it would be necessary to extend a bomber crew's tour to 35 missions and a fighter pilot's tour from 200 to 300 combat hours flying. A directive to this effect was issued in late May. It was difficult for the crews of the B-17s and B-24s to accept that their sorties were any less dangerous and a definite drop in morale was quickly evident. Matters were not helped when, a month later, USAAF HQ in Washington directed 8th Air Force that it required no relief of combat duty determined by missions or hours flown. Only after evidence of positive combat fatigue was a man to be taken off operational flying. Mindful of the current morale problem 8th Air Force complied and at the same time circumnavigated the Pentagon's insensitive directive by hastily issuing one of their own which stated that examination of airmen for flying or combat fatigue was to be conducted at the discretion of unit flight surgeons but under no condition would this be postponed beyond a fixed specific maximum of 35 heavy bomber missions, 300 operational hours for fighters, 200 hours for photo reconnaissance and 500 hours for weather reconnaissance men. In practice these remained the maximum for tours with the respective types and airmen were still encouraged to think of them as points of relief.

27/28 JULY 1944

8AF 500 NIGHT LEAFLET OPERATION

NLS B-17, 7 despatched, 7 effective; Holland and France.

28 JULY 1944

8AF 501

	Despatched		Effective	Target		Bombs Tonnage	E/A	Losses MIA	E	Dam	Casualties KIA	WIA	MIA
2BD	B-24	180	0	NW FRANCE V/S, F/D & R/B	(P)	0		0	1	8	10	0	0
3BD	B-24	111	0	BRUSSELS & VILVORDE F/D & S/D	(P)	0		0	0	8	0	0	0
1 & 3BD	B-17	766	652	MERSEBURG/LEUNA O/I	(P)	1601.5	1–2–1	7	0	217	1	7	67
			36	LEIPZIG/TAUCHA O/I	(O)	90.0							
			18	WIESBADEN	(O)	43.0							
			8	T/O		20.0							
TOTALS:		1057	714			1754.5	1–2–1	7	1	233	11	7	67
VIII FC													
	P-47	183	235	ESCORT 2BD				0	0	1	0	0	1
	P-51	63						0	0	2	0	0	2
	P-51	53	40	ESCORT 3BD B-24				0	0	0	0	0	0
	P-38	62	386	ESCORT FOR B-17s			4–1–1	0	0	0	0	0	0
	P-51	392						2	0	3	0	0	3
TOTALS:		753	661				4–1–1	2	0	6	0	0	6

REMARKS: Signal depots, fuel dumps and V-weapon supply sites and a bridge in France and Belgium were targets for B-24s. 2BD despatched 93BG, 389BG, 445BG, 446BG, 453BG, 466BG. 3BD despatched 34BG, 490BG, 493BG. Bad weather prevented bombing. All 1BD groups and all 3BD B-17 except 447BG sent to Merseburg. Bomb group losses:– 95BG – 1, 96BG – 2, 100BG – 2, 351BG – 1, 398BG – 1. 2 100BG B-17s collided 26 miles from Lowestoft, 1 rescued. 96BG B-17, lost were PFF leaders for 452BG which collided near target; both had part 452BG crews. A 466BG B-24 cr. on t/o, 10 k.

All Fighter groups active. Fighter group e/a credits:– 339 FG – 1, 355FG – 3. Fighter group losses:– 55FG – 1, 359FG – 1. First reports of Me 163 rocket fighters in action. 364FG using P-51s and P-38s.

28/29 JULY 1944

8AF 502 NIGHT LEAFLET OPERATION

NLS B-17, 6 despatched, 6 effective; France.

482BG despatched 5 B-17s on night mission.

Making a landing approach to Eye airfield after the early morning mission on 29 July, 490BG B-24H *My Mama Done Told Me* struck a tree top and crashed just beside the main Ipswich–Norwich road right in front of the Swan Inn at Brome. All the crew escaped although two were so seriously injured they died. The bomber had engine trouble. (W. Whitlow)

29 JULY 1944

8AF 503

	Despatched		Effective	Target	Bombs Tonnage	E/A	Losses MIA	E	Dam	Casualties KIA	WIA	MIA
1 & 3BD	B-17	657	569	MERSEBURG/LEUNA O/I (P)	1410.0	15–8–3	15	1	349	1	17	138
			11	HILDESHEIM M/Y (O)	24.5							
			13	GÖTTINGEN (O)	32.5							
			10	T/O	24.4							
2BD	B-24	473	442	BREMEN/ OSLEBSHAUSEN O/R (P)	1249.4		2	0	96	3	2	15
			1	CUXHAVEN (O)	2.5							
			2	T/O	6.0							
3BD	B-24	98	38	JUVINCOURT A/F (P)	104.5		0	2	0	5	7	0
			36	LAON/COUVRON A/F (P)	103.3							
TOTALS:		1228	1122		2957.1	15–8–3	17	3	445	9	26	153
VIII FC												
	P-38	62	429	ESCORT B-17s		21–2–3	0	0	0	0	0	0
	P-47	47				3–0–2 (G)	0	0	1	0	0	0
	P-51	387					7	0	6	0	0	7
	P-51	109	106	ESCORT 2BD			0	0	0	0	0	0
	P-51	150	142	ESCORT 3BD B-24			0	0	0	0	0	0
TOTALS:		755	677			21–2–3 3–0–2 (G)	7	0	7	0	0	7

REMARKS: Oil targets. Merseburg attacked visually, Bremen by H2X means due to smoke and cloud. All 1BD groups except those of 40CBW, all 3BD B-17 groups except 95BG and 447BG, went to Merseburg. All 2BD groups except 458BG on Bremen mission. All 93CBW groups. Bomb group losses:– 44BG – 2, 96BG – 1, 100BG – 8, 351BG – 1, 384BG – 1, 385BG – 1, 388BG – 1, 390BG – 2. The 2 44BG B-24s collided during assembly and cr. in sea off Cromer, crews baled out, 1 rescued. A 490BG B-24 cr. t/o at Yaxley, 2 killed and another 490BG B-24 cr. on approach to land at base, 2 k, 7 inj. B/d 351BG c/l base.

All Fighter groups active. Fighter group e/a credits:– 20FG – 3, 339FG – 5, 352FG – 8, 357FG – 6, 479FG – 1. Fighter group losses:– 339FG – 3, 352FG – 1, 357FG – 3. 364FG flew P-38s and P-51s.

OTHER OPERATIONS: 7PG despatched 1 F-5 and 1 Spitfire and PR Germany. 802RG despatched 1 Mosquito for PR, 2 Mosquitoes to scout for bombers, 5 Mosquitoes on WR France and Germany and 2 B-17 on Atlantic WR.

29/30 JULY 1944

8AF 504 NIGHT LEAFLET OPERATION

NLS B-17, 6 despatched, 6 effective: France.

801BG despatched 44 B-24s (12 aborted) on *Carpetbagger* operations.

30 JULY 1944

8AF 505

	Despatched		Effective	Target	Bombs Tonnage	E/A	Losses MIA	Losses E	Losses Dam	Casualties KIA	Casualties WIA	Casualties MIA
VIII FC												
	P-47	101	237	SWEEPS OF EVREUX,		3–0–1	0	0	3	0	0	0
	P-51	154		ST.QUENTIN, PARIS, ORLEANS		9–0–0 (G)	1	0	2	0	0	1
TOTALS:		255	237			3–0–1 9–0–0 (G)	1	0	5	0	0	1

REMARKS: Fighter groups operating: 55FG, 78FG, 339FG, 353FG, 357FG. Fighter group e/a credits:– 357FG – 3. Losses:– 55FG – 1.

OTHER OPERATIONS: 7PG despatched 5 F-5s (2 aborted) on PR France. 802RG despatched 1 Mosquito or WR North Sea and 2 B-17s on WR Atlantic.

30/31 JULY 1944

8AF 506 NIGHT LEAFLET OPERATION

NLS B-17, 1 despatched but recalled.

801BG despatched 31 B-24s on *Carpetbagger* operations.

482BG despatched 2 B-17s on night mission.

31 JULY 1944

8AF 507

	Despatched		Effective	Target	Bombs Tonnage	E/A	Losses MIA	Losses E	Losses Dam	Casualties KIA	Casualties WIA	Casualties MIA
1 & 3BD	B-17	705	567	MUNICH	(P) 1499.3		10	0	331	2	6	82
			36	ALLACH	(P) 90.0							
			43	SCHLEISSHEIM	(P) 77.5							
			4	T/O	10.3							
2BD	B-24	486	447	LUDWIGSHAFEN C/I	(P) 1230.3		6	0	186	1	7	62
3BD	B-24	104	47	LAON/ATHIES A/F	(P) 106.5		0	0	4	0	0	0
			36	CREIL A/F	(P) 81.0							
			1	POIX A/F	(O) 1.5							
TOTALS:		1295	1181		3096.4	0	16	0	521	3	13	144
VIII FC												
	P-47	98	439	ESCORT FOR B-17s		0–1– 0	1	0	5	0	0	1
	P-51	411				18–0–12 (G)	2	0	3	0	0	2
	P-38	47	135	ESCORT 2BD			0	0	1	0	0	0
	P-51	97		ESCORT FOR 3BD			0	1	2	1	0	0
	P-47	48	38	B-24			0	0	0	0	0	0
TOTALS:		701	612			0–1– 0 18–0–12 (G)	3	1	11	1	0	3

REMARKS: PFF attacks on industrial targets at Munich; chemical works at Ludwigshafen; and visual on French airfields. All 1BD B-17 groups; all 3BD B-17 groups except 385BG and 447BG; all 2BD and 3BD B-24 groups (93CBW) participated. Bomb group losses:– 1BD – 91BG – 1, 381BG – 1, 401BG – 1, 457BG – 1; 2BD – 389BG – 1, 446BG – 1, 458BG – 1, 489BG – 3; 3BD – 94BG – 3, 388BG – 2, 452BG – 1. A 94BG and 401BG B-17 landed Switzerland. A 94BG B-17 ditched 25 miles off Aldeburgh, 9 saved. Two 489BG B-24s MIA collided. 389BG PFF a/c lost was leading 453BG.

All Fighter groups except 55FG on operations. Fighter group losses:– 78FG – 1, 352FG – 2. 12 P-51s of 1SF scouting for 1BD. 364FG all P-51s. 361FG P-51 cr. Cowlinge, pilot k.

OTHER OPERATIONS: 7PG despatched 29 F-5s and 6 Spitfires on PR to Western France and Brest area. 802RG despatched 2 Mosquitoes scouting for 2BD & 3BD, 2 Mosquitoes on WR France and 2 B-17 on WR Atlantic. ASR P-47 MIA.

31 JULY/1 AUGUST 1944

801BG despatched 13 B-24s on *Carpetbagger* operations.

1 AUGUST 1944

8AF 508

	Despatched		Effective	Target		Bombs Tonnage	E/A	Losses MIA	E	Dam	Casualties KIA	WIA	MIA
1BD	B-17	416	36	CHARTRES BRIDGE	(P)	72.0		3	2	32	9	0	27
			59	MELUN A/F	(P)	147.5							
			108	CHATEAUDUN A/F	(P)	268.8							
			58	CHARTRES A/F	(P)	126.6							
			112	ORLEANS/BRICY A/F	(P)	280.0							
			12	ETAMPES/MONDESIR A/F	(O)	30.0							
			15	T/O		27.7							
2BD	B-24	389	66	ROUEN	(P)	160.7		1	3	85	0	0	20
			44	NOGENT BRIDGE	(P)	152.0							
			47	MELUN A/F	(O)	133.5							
			29	ORLEANS/BRICY A/F	(O)	87.0							
			12	VILLEROCHE A/F	(O)	36.0							
			6	CHARTRES A/F	(O)	18.0							
			24	MONTEREAU BRIDGE	(O)	96.0							
			11	COULOMMIERS BRIDGE	(O)	44.0							
			12	NANTEUIL BRIDGE	(O)	48.0							
			33	T/O		131.5							
3BD	B-17	195	193	OPERATION BUICK SOUTH EAST FRANCE				0	0	5	0	0	0
3BD	B-17	100	76	TOURS A/F	(P)	169.5		1	1	55	0	6	10
3BD	B-24	191	61	PAS DE CALAIS V/S	(P)	151.0		0	0	5	0	0	0
TOTALS:		1291	1014			2179.8	0	5	6	182	9	6	57

VIII FC

	P-38	49	138	ESCORT 1BD		0	0	0	0	
	P-51	101				0	3	0	1	
	P-47	48	127	ESCORT 2BD	3–0–0(G)	2	0	3	0	
	P-51	97				0	1	0	0	
	P-51	53	51	ESCORT 3BD TOURS		2	2	0	0	
	P-47	84	81	ESCORT 3BD B-24		0	0	0	0	
TOTALS:		432	397		3–0–0(G)	4	7	3	1	6

REMARKS: Airfields, bridges and tactical targets in France attacked by all 1BD groups except 306BG and all 2BD groups. Tours A/F attacked by 486BG and 487BG with 390BG – First operation of 92CBW with B-17s. 3BD B-17 groups (less 100BG) flew operation *Buick*, dropping supplies to French Resistance fighters at four localities – Châlon-Sur-Saône, Savoie area, Haute-Savoie and west of Geneva. 2, 281 containers dropped. 3BD B-24 groups (93CBW) attacked *Noball* targets. Bomb group losses:– 1BD – 91BG – 1, 401BG – 2; 2BD – 453BG – 1; 3BD – 390BG – 1. The 2 401BG B-17s MIA collided over target. During assembly 384BG B-17s cr. Weldon, 9 k. On return a 390BG B-17 c/l Woodbridge A/F; a b/d 93BG B-24 cr. Sheerness, a 398BG B-17 c/l Merton A/F; 489BG B-24 c/l Halesworth A/F. 489BG B-24 cr. France.

All Fighter groups except 78FG on operations. Fighter group losses:– 353FG – 2, 355FG – 2. Two 339FG P-51s collided over battle lines, 1 c/l Manston, other pilot baled, near Ford. A 359FG P-51 cr. near Hunsdon on return, pilot baled. 4FG P-51 abandoned after t/o, pilot safe. 2 364FG P-51s collided after t/o and cr. Tuddenham, 1 killed, other pilot baled. B/d 353FG P-47 Cat E.

OTHER OPERATIONS: 7PG despatched 2 F-5s to Denmark, 38 F-5s and 6 Spitfires to Brest peninsula. 802RG despatched 4 Mosquitoes to scout for 2BD and 3BD, 2 Mosquitoes on WR France and 3 B-17s on WR Atlantic. 1SF despatched 8 P-51s to scout for 1BD – claimed 1–0–0.

HANG THE EXPENSE

Exaggerated hearsay has been the foundation of many a legend. The 100th Bomb Group's notoriety as the 'hard luck' group of the 8th Air Force began that way. Similarly the 100th's Frank Valesh became legend as the 8th's 'hard luck' pilot. This tag – which, understandably, Valesh strongly resented – arose through his frequent involvement in emergency situations during nine months of combat flying. It was almost as if fate had taken him to task over the nickname he bestowed on each of the seven B-17s he 'used up' – *Hang the Expense*.

Sent to England as replacements, he and his crew brought a new B-17 across the North Atlantic in September 1943. Upon arrival the Fortress was taken for modification while Valesh and his men went to a replacement centre for theatre indoctrination. They soon received a combat assignment, to the 100th Group. Valesh noted that people seemed to avoid talking about the 100th. He soon learned why, for on arrival at Thorpe Abbotts, 14 October, he discovered that his crew was one of several sent to fill out the Group following its loss of 12 over Münster four days earlier. Given a new B-17G, the nonchalant expression *Hang the Expense* was painted on. 'It seemed like a good idea at the time', was Frank's later, rueful, comment.

The first mission was never completed. Despatched as a spare, *Hang The Expense* took up position in the formation when another B-17 turned back with mechanical trouble. Halfway

Posing with their new B-17G on hardstand No.7 shortly after arrival at Thorpe Abbotts are: l to r: Kneeling, 2/Lts Frank Valesh (pilot), Maurice Zetlan (bombardier), John Booth (co-pilot) and Richard Johnson (navigator). Standing, John Mytko (engineer), Roy Urich (tail gunner), Louis Black (ball gunner), Paul Carbone and Herschel Broyles (waist gunner) and Ernest Jordan (radio). Johnson became the 'Mickey' operator when the crew went to PFF school and a new navigator, Al Franklin, was assigned.

Hang The Expense burns in Lodge Farm yard, quite close to the dispersal where the bomber was normally parked. (J. Archer)

Probably the most well-publicised photograph of a battle damaged 8AF bomber, this view of an RAF guard and a US serviceman looking at the gaping wound in the fourth *Hang The Expense*, was published in most wartime British and US newspapers. At the time it was assumed the gunner had been killed.

across the North Sea the pilots saw oil streaming back from the engines. Believing something was radically wrong, Valesh decided to abort. On landing it was discovered that too much oil had been put in the tank and expansion at high altitude had caused the release of the fluid. Valesh felt he had been over cautious and was apprehensive lest other pilots thought he was being cowardly in turning back. The next time there were no hitches and the crew could cross off their first successfully completed mission.

Due to bad weather the rate of operations was slow and air crews often had time on their hands. During these early weeks at Thorpe Abbotts, Frank Valesh became friendly with the American Red Cross girls who dispensed doughnuts and coffee to flight crews. Two of the girls, Mary Jane Cook and June Yaeger, expressed an interest in flying and on 26 November, when not scheduled for the day's mission, Valesh arranged to smuggle them aboard his B-17 for a local flight, ostensibly to slow-time a new engine. Flying unauthorised civilian passengers was not permitted but nevertheless occurred from time to time at most bases. Such trips were comparatively easy to arrange as the only men likely to see the passengers board were the ground crew and they would not carry tales. Valesh needed a co-pilot and navigator for the venture and, as his own were not on hand, he solicited two friends from another crew, 2nd Lts Russell 'Pinky' Flack and Andrew Campion to act as co-pilot and navigator respectively. With the girls standing behind the pilots' seats *Hang the Expense* was taxied out of hardstand No.7 and to the end of runway 28. At 1633 hrs, following the pre-take off check, the pilots advanced throttles and released brakes. *Hang The Expense* had covered the first third of the runway and was nearing flying speed when a locking pin in the tail wheel assembly broke causing the wheel to oscillate violently. Unaware of the cause of the severe vibration in the tail, Valesh decided to abandon take-off, cutting engine power. To his horror he found he could not keep the Fortress from veering off the runway to the right. Heavy braking failed to arrest the bomber's uncontrolled progress towards the airfield boundary and the farm beyond. Shearing through some trees *Hang the Expense* smashed into a timbered cart lodge which immediately took fire. The impact pitched Mary Jane Cook from behind the pilot down into the passage to the nose, while the other girl banged her head on the co-pilot's seat. Shocked and bruised, neither suffered serious injury and were quickly hustled out of the burning aircraft by the pilots. Fire fighters and ambulances were soon on the scene and conveyed the occupants of the bomber to the base hospital. Although Frank Valesh feared Campion – riding in the nose – had been killed, he too survived, cut and bruised. One of farmer Billy Draper's employees also had a narrow escape having walked away from the cart lodge a minute or two before the crash. Unbeknown to the authorities, an adjoining building to that demolished contained an illicit store of B-17 parts, secreted there 'by arrangement' for an enterprising crew chief who wished to make sure his bomber was not grounded for lack of a scarce spare.

The accident was officially attributed to equipment failure, but the presence of the two Red Cross girls could not be overlooked resulting in Valesh and his two compatriots being put on a court martial charge for the unauthorised flying of civilians. On 20 January 1944 the three officers were tried, found guilty of the

Hang The Expense bogged down at Eastchurch. A new tail turret was installed and after repair the bomber was returned to operations with the 100BG.

The PFF *Hang The Expense* that overrun runway 04 at Thorpe Abbotts on 19 May at 0347 hrs. The undercarriage was ripped off in a ditch and damage to the undersurfaces was substantial enough to make repair uneconomical.

charges and fined $100 each. The demands of military order had been met but sympathies at Thorpe Abbotts were mostly with the guilty who were just unlucky in being caught out. However, before the hearing, Frank Valesh was to fly seven more combat missions, receive promotion to 1st Lt and 'use up' two more Fortresses tagged *Hang The Expense*. One was so badly damaged after a raid on Kiel it had to be abandoned at an RAF airfield and the other, with two engines 'shot out', was bellied-in at Lympne. Despite the station commander's anger at the damage Valesh's sliding Fortress had done to the runway turf, the crew were accorded RAF hospitality, the officers being quartered in a commandeered stately home. Here they were delighted to discover that a continuous supply of drinks – scotch – could be had by simply ringing for the orderly who required only a signature as recompense. Who actually met the bill for their considerable indulgence, Valesh never discovered.

Four days after the court martial, Valesh and crew set out on their 13th mission – to Frankfurt. Lt Maurice Zetland, the regular bombardier, was assigned to another crew this day. Shortly after take-off the B-17 in which Zetland was flying took evasive action to avoid colliding with another aircraft and struck the ground, Zetland being the only man killed in the crash. Valesh was unaware of this tragedy when he took off over the burning wreck a few minutes later. The mission to Frankfurt passed without notable incident until the return to the Channel coast where flak from Ostend blossomed near by. 'Then there was the worst noise I ever heard in my life', Frank Valesh later recalled. 'The plane reared up out of control and started climbing steeply. The tail controls wouldn't respond. So I reached down and snapped on the auto-pilot and gradually the plane came back to level flight.'

In the rear of the current *Hang The Expense*, right hand waist gunner Herschel Broyles picked himself up an estimated seven feet from where he had been standing before the explosion. He felt, he said, 'As if someone had just hit me in the stomach with a plank.' Looking back towards the tail he was amazed to see a gaping hole where the rear gunner's compartment should have been and no sign of the occupant, Sgt Roy Urich. Using the interphone the other waist gunner, Sgt Paul Carbone, reported the situation to Valesh who then sent a *Mayday* signal. Within minutes two P-47s appeared alongside and shepherded the crippled Fortress back to England where the small grass airfield at Eastchurch on the Thames estuary was seen. Because of the damaged tail surface only gentle aileron turns could be made, but eventually Valesh was able to put the bomber down safely on what turned out to be a very waterlogged surface. Vacating the bomber the crew walked round to survey the damage. The complete gunner's compartment had been blasted away by an 88 mm shell that exploded in the fuselage opposite the escape door. The left elevator was shattered, the right damaged and a large part of the rudder was missing. This was the Valesh crew's third emergency landing in three weeks and engendered his pained comment, 'I'm getting damned tired of this business.' It was assumed the tail gunner had been killed instantly yet, at the end of hostilities, Roy Urich was found in a POW camp. His miraculous escape was due to wearing a parachute at the time, and having previously placed a number of flak vests on the floor around the gunner's seat. Although severely wounded by the blast, he was able to pull the release on his parachute.

They gave Frank Valesh a new Fortress but before it could become another *Hang The Expense* the crew were sent to Pathfinder School: one of two crews selected from the 100th Group. As it happened the new B-17G was eventually named *Our Gal Sal* by crew chief Harold Wildrick, and endured through 135 missions to become the most venerable Fortress in the Group.

Leaving Thorpe Abbotts at the beginning of February 1944, the Valesh crew went to Alconbury along with 13 other crews drawn from every group in the 3rd Division. They were to be trained in pathfinder techniques and formed into a special squadron to operate 'Mickey' (H2X radar) equipped B-17s; this was the 413th Bomb Squadron of the 96th Group. When training was completed in mid-March, the unit took up residence at the 96th's base – Snetterton Heath. Frank Valesh was given one of the 12 'Mickey' aircraft which soon sported the familiar tag *Hang The Expense*. Operations began at the end of March. The usual procedure involved despatching one or two pathfinder aircraft to bases where the resident group was scheduled to lead a combat wing. Here a Command Pilot – and often an additional navigator – would be taken aboard and the bomber take off again to head the formation from that base. On 29 April the Valesh crew went to Great Ashfield where a 385th Group senior officer took over the co-pilot's seat as Command Pilot. The 385th was flying its 100th mission that day, in the van of a combat wing formation headed for Berlin across an unbroken undercast. Over enemy territory the radar failed in both Valesh's and another pathfinder B-17's in the formation and the lead navigators were forced to resort to Dead Reckoning to find the course above the clouds. Unfortunately the bombers veered some 40 miles from the planned route, and being away from the escort were subjected to a mass assault by Luftwaffe fighters. In a few minutes a dozen B-17s had gone down and a few others were too badly crippled to get home. Although attacked, Valesh's bomber survived to deposit the Command Pilot back at his base where seven crews were found missing. It was a depressing situation and the Valesh crew were glad to get back to Snetterton Heath. They had certainly had their share of tricky situations, but the run was not yet over.

In the dark hours of 19 May they were despatched to their old base to fly pathfinder. Orbiting the airfield the pilots had difficulty in picking out the outer circle lights leading to the runway in use. Valesh was high when he brought *Hang The Expense* across the threshold and two warning flares were fired from the control van at the head of the runway. The flares ignited just ahead of the cockpit and momentarily blinded Valesh who, on making touch down, wasn't certain where he was on the runway. A boundary road ditch and hedge soon gave the answer and *Hang The Expense* ended up on its belly in a farmer's field. Four of the crew received minor injuries, but the precious radar B-17 was only fit for salvage. Frank was beginning to have doubts about that nickname.

Following this crash operations were conducted without any untoward incidents for a few weeks until once again a badly damaged aircraft was brought in for an emergency landing.

As more 'Mickey' aircraft and crews became available a pathfinder squadron was formed in each combat wing of 3rd Division. In early July one was set up at Horham for the 13th Wing – to which the 100th Group was assigned – and the Valesh crew moved to that base. At this time they were near the end of their required number of missions but flew additional sorties until new pathfinder crews were available. On finishing his detachment and returning to Thorpe Abbotts in late July, Frank Valesh had completed 29 combat missions. The strain of combat left its mark on most men who successfully completed an operational tour and Frank Valesh was no exception. When he arrived back in the United States almost a year after he had gone overseas his medical report stated he was tense, restless, apprehensive and 17 pounds lighter. After a few weeks' recuperation he went through transition training on B-29 Superfortresses but the war was over before he received a further assignment. This period of his service was devoid of any flying emergencies. It was not that he was superstitious, only that he thought it prudent not to make use of a certain nickname on aircraft he regularly flew.

An electrical fault started a fire in this 56FG Thunderbolt as it was being serviced on a Boxted hardstand. Once fire took hold it was extremely difficult to extinguish. The fighter, *Pengie III*, was personal aircraft of F/Lt Mike Gladych, a flamboyant Polish flier who had managed to attach himself to the 56FG.

1/2 AUGUST 1944

8AF 509 NIGHT LEAFLET OPERATION

NLS B-17, 6 despatched and effective; France and Belgium.

2 AUGUST 1944

8AF 510

	Despatched		Effective	Target		Bombs Tonnage	E/A	Losses MIA	E	Dam	Casualties KIA	WIA	MIA
3BD	B-17	156	37	MERY-SUR-OISE	(P)	107.5		2	0	47	1	2	18
			51	PARIS/ GENNEVILLIERS	(P)	124.7							
			38	PARIS/DUGNY	(P)	93.6							
			7	COURTALAIN R/J	(O)	20.0							
			12	BERNAY M/Y	(O)	35.0							
			4	T/O		12.0							
2BD	B-24	163	31	NOGENT-SUR-SEINE BR	(P)	105.5		0	1	23	0	2	0
			26	SENS O/D	(P)	78.0							
			36	NEUVY-SUR-LOIRE BR	(P)	124.0							
			10	PACY-SUR-ARMANCON	(P)	30.0							
			28	MANTEREAU R/B	(O)	111.5							
			12	ST.DIZIER A/F	(O)	36.0							
			3	CRETON A/F	(O)	9.0							
8AF													
	B-17	195	31	JUSSY R/B	(P)	93.0		3	0	45	3	1	28
			21	BEAUTOR R/B	(P)	62.5							
			22	AULNOYE R/B	(O)	65.5							
			11	CROCAL DE ST.QUENTIN BR	(O)	33.0							
			77	FLYING BOMB SITES	(P)	188.4							
2BD & 3BD	B-24	322	12	PERONNE R/B	(P)	47.0		0	5	78	2	0	0
			22	THENNES BR	(O)	88.0							
			11	ACHIET A/F	(O)	42.5							
			8	T/O		27.9							
			182	PAS DE CALAIS V/S	(P)	457.9							
TOTALS:		836	692			1992.5	0	5	6	193	6	5	46

2 AUGUST 1944 *(contd.)*

VIII FC

Despatched		Effective	Target	Bombs Tonnage	E/A	Losses MIA	E	Dam	Casualties KIA	WIA	MIA
P-51	158	132	ESCORT FOR 8AF 510			2	1	0	1	0	2
P-51	249	236	ESCORT FOR 8AF 511			5	1	0	0	0	5
			FIGHTER-BOMBER								
P-38	49		RAIL & ROAD	58.8	1–0–0	0	1	0	0	0	0
P-47	183		TRANSPORT PARIS–			1	0	6	0	0	1
P-51	51		AMIENS–BRUSSELS–			1	0	2	0	0	1
			ST. QUENTIN								
TOTALS:	690	368		58.8	1–0–0	9	3	8	1	0	9

REMARKS: Tactical targets France. Morning mission (510) was to attack oil and supply dumps and bridges in Paris area. Afternoon mission (511) to *Noball* target and bridges. 3BD force for 510 consisted of 94BG, 385BG, 388BG, 447BG, 452BG; the 2BD force consisted of 2CBW groups and 93BG, 448BG. Mission 511 flown by B-17s of 92CBW and 13CBW groups B-24s of 93CBW, 95CBW, 96CBW groups and 44BG, 392BG, 446BG. Bomb group losses:– 95BG – 1, 385BG – 1, 388BG – 1, 390BG – 2. A 448BG B-24 abandoned over Hardwick by crew. On return a 446BG B-24 c/l Knettishall A/F; b/d 392BG B-24 cr. Lymbridge Green, crew baled; b/d 392BG B-24 c/l Manston, 2 killed – 5 baled out.

All Fighter groups operating except 55FG. Fighter group e/a credits:– 353FG – 1. Fighter group losses:– 4FG – 1, 78FG – 1, 339FG – 1, 355FG – 3, 359FG – 1, 364FG – 1, 479FG – 1. 20FG P-51 cr. Werrington, pilot killed. Exploding train brought down 364FG P-51. 479FG P-38 c/l Debden A/F, pilot safe. 355FG P-51 Cat E, pilot safe.

OTHER OPERATIONS: 7PG despatched 10 F-5s and 4 Spitfires on PR to Germany and France. 802RG despatched 4 Mosquitoes to scout for bombers, 2 Mosquitoes on WR France and 2 B-17s on WR Atlantic.

INCIDENT

The frequency of operations by 8th Air Force bombers in the summer of 1944 was evident from the number of crewmen who completed a tour of 30 missions in under three months. This was in sharp contrast to the previous year where the average was more than double that period for 25 missions and with many crews taking nine months. When B-24 pilot Lt Charles C. Griffin returned from his 30th combat mission to the 491st Group base at Metfield on 2 August he had probably established a record. Having flown his first on 2 June he had taken just 62 days to complete this tour, averaging a mission nearly every two days.

2/3 AUGUST 1944

801BG despatched 42 B-24s on *Carpetbagger* operations.

3 AUGUST 1944

8AF 512

	Despatched		Effective	Target		Bombs Tonnage	E/A	Losses MIA	E	Dam	Casualties KIA	WIA	MIA
1BD	B-17	345	54	MULHOUSE M/Y	(P)	161.8	4–1–1	6	1	98	9	9	54
			62	SAARBRÜCKEN M/Y	(P)	184.7							
			106	MERKWILLE OIL REF	(P)	260.7							
			68	STRASBOURG M/Y	(P)	203.8							
			16	TOUL/CROIX DE METZ A/F	(O)	50.2							
			11	RR NEAR SAARBRÜCKEN	(O)	25.2							
			6	T/O		18.0							
3BD	B-17	155	36	JOIGNY/LA ROCHE BR	(P)	71.0		0	0	11	0	0	0
			38	TROYES BRIDGE	(P)	93.5							
2BD	B-24	172	27	CONCHES A/F	(O)	81.0		0	0	51	0	0	0
			11	ETAMPES MONDESIR A/F	(O)	33.0							
			12	MELUN M/Y	(O)	36.0							
			3	T/O		6.9							
8AF 513													
1BD	B-17	126	112	PAS DE CALAIS V/S		336.0		0	0	6	0	0	0
& 2BD	B-24	121	117			351.0		1	0	20	0	0	0
3BD	B-24	76	62	BRUSSELS/VIVORDE	(P)	143.5		0	1	49	2	0	0
			10	GHENT/TERNEUZEN	(P)	32.4							
			1	T/O		3.0							
2BD	B-24	159	22	PAS DE CALAIS V/S	(P)	62.6		1	3	38	4	4	10
			10	LILLE/MARQUETTE	(P)	28.6							
			10	LILLE/SEQUEDIN	(P)	28.0							
			28	COURCHELETTES	(P)	84.0							
			49	HARNES	(P)	147.0							
			8	GHENT M/Y	(O)	24.0							
TOTALS:		1154	879			2465.9	4–1–1	8	5	273	15	13	64

VIII FC

	Despatched		Effective	Target	Bombs Tonnage	E/A	Losses MIA	E	Dam	Casualties KIA	WIA	MIA
	P-51	200	175	ESCORT 1BD 8AF 512		6–0–0 5–0–1(G)	6			0	0	6
	P-51	103	96	ESCORT 3BD 8AF 512			0			0	0	0
	P-47	49	87	ESCORT 2BD 8AF 512			0			0	0	0
				FIGHTER-BOMBER 8AF 512			0			0	0	0
	P-38	47	133	RAIL TRAFFIC –	15.7	1–0–0	0					
	P-47	97		METZ – STRASBOURG – SAARBRÜCKEN		1–0–0(G)	1					
	P-51	46	43	ESCORT 8AF 513 *NOBALL*			0			0	0	0
	P-47	36	33	ESCORT 3BD B-24 8AF 513	2.8		0			0	0	0
	P-51	96	90	ESCORT 2BD 8AF 513			0			0	0	0
TOTALS:		726	657		18.5	7–0–0 6–0–1(G)	7	1	6	0	0	6

REMARKS: 8AF 512: rail and other targets in the French/German border area; oil dumps and bridges SE of Paris. 1BD Force consisted of 1CBW, 40CBW and 94CBW groups. 3BD sent 100BG and 487BG to Troyes and Joigny bridges, respectively. 2BD mission to bridges foiled by cloud – 2CBW groups attacked T/Os. Bomb group losses:– 92BG – 2, 305BG – 2, 351BG – 1, 381BG – 1. On return a 305BG B-17 cr. Wymington, 5 k.

Mission 513 was to oil installations and dumps in Brussels, Paris and Lille areas; *Noball* targets in the Pas de Calais. 1BD despatched the 41CBW groups; 2BD despatched all groups except those of 2CBW; 3BD despatched 93CBW groups. Bomb group losses:– 392BG – 1, 491BG – 1. On return a 392BG B-24 was abandoned over Wendling and cr. in sea. B/d 491BG B-24 cr. landing Grantham Common. B/d B-24 cr. burned Manston A/F. B/d 467BG B-24 cr. east of Norwich, 4 k.

All Fighter groups operating. Fighter group e/a credits:– 56FG – 1, 355FG – 6. Fighter group losses:– 4FG – 1, 56FG – 1, 355FG – 5. Ground claim by fighters was for a B-24 seen on airfield near Mulhouse. 359FG P-51 Cat E.

OTHER OPERATIONS: 7PG despatched 13 F-5s and 4 Spitfires on PR French and German targets. 802RG despatched 3 Mosquitoes to scout for bombers, 2 Mosquitoes on WR France and Atlantic and 2 B-17s on WR Atlantic.

4 AUGUST 1944

8AF 514

	Despatched		Effective	Target		Bombs Tonnage	E/A	Losses MIA	E	Dam	Casualties KIA	WIA	MIA
3BD	B-17	358	181	HAMBURG O/R	(P)	464.1	0–4–2	8	8	196	2	8	63
			50	BREMEN O/R	(P)	130.8							
			23	NORDHOF A/F	(O)	65.5							
			14	EINSWARDEN	(O)	31.1							
			7	T/O		14.0							
			22	OSTEND C/D	(P)	65.0							
1BD	B-17	425	221	PEENEMÜNDE	(P)	522.0	1–0–0	3	1	94	2	2	40
			110	ANKLAM A/F	(P)	255.5							
			70	ANKLAM A/I	(P)	173.8							
2BD	B-24	446	89	KIEL	(P)	252.3		4	0	114	2	2	40
			71	WISMAR A/I	(P)	179.3							
			88	SCHWERIN A/I	(P)	212.1							
			148	ROSTOCK A/I	(P)	370.3							
			12	SCHLUTUP	(O)	31.2							
			11	WARIEN	(O)	27.5							
			1	T/O		3.0							
3BD	B-24	78	29	HEMMINGSTEDT/ HEIDE O/R	(P)	115.8		0	0	0	0	0	0
			39	HUSUM A/F	(O)	110.8							
TOTALS:		1307	1186			3024.1	1–4–2	15	15	404	6	12	120

8AF 515 APHRODITE

		Target	Bombs Tonnage
B-17 4 R/c	2	MIMOYECQUES V/S	
6 control a/c	6	SIRACOURT V/S	20.0
		WATTEN V/S	
		WIZERNES V/S	

4 AUGUST 1944 *(contd.)*

8AF 516

	Despatched		Effective	Target	Bombs Tonnage	E/A	Losses MIA	E	Dam	Casualties KIA	WIA	MIA
2BD	B-24	95	24	PAS DE CALAIS V/S (P)	64.0		0	0	17	0	0	0
			11	MIDDELKERKE C/B (P)	32.5							
			11	GRAVELINES C/B (P)	33.0							
			12	ACHIET A/F (O)	34.3							
			6	VILLY/MONTIGNE M/Y (O)	17.8							
			6	LENS M/Y (O)	16.5							
1BD	B-17	59	12	LILLE/VENDEVILLE A/F (O)	27.0		0	0	12	0	0	0
			11	GRAVELINES BR (O)	27.5							
			13	T/O	32.5							
TOTALS:		154	106		285.1	0	0	0	29	0	0	0
8AF 525 MICRO H TEST												
482BG	B-17	4	3	BOIS DE LA HOUSSIÈRE F/D	3.0		0	0	0	0	0	0
VIII FC												
	P-47	200	234	ESCORT 3BD B-17		38–1–5	2	0	2	0		2
	P-51	50				9–0–1(G)	3	0	2	0		3
	P-51	250	223	ESCORT 1BD		4–0–4(G)	9	1	0	1		9
	P-38	48	209	ESCORT 2BD KIEL			0	1	0	1		0
	P-51	198					1	0	0	0		0
	P-47	69	67	FIGHTER-BOMBER PLANTLÜNNE A/F	12.3	30–0–5	1	1	8	0		1
	P-47	9	35	ESCORT 8AF 516			0	0	0	0		0
	P-51	27					0	0	0	0		0
	P-47	16	16	ESCORT APHRODITE			0	0	0		0	
	P-51	16	16				0	0	0	0		0
TOTALS:		883	800		12.3	68–1–10 13–0–5(G)	16	3	12	2	1	16

REMARKS: Mission 514 involved attacks on strategic targets: oil refineries, aircraft factories and a torpedo plant at Kiel. Visual bombing was carried out at Peenemünde experimental station and Kiel, most other primaries by PFF means. All bomb groups participated but 447BG briefed for targets at Ostend. Bomb group losses:– 1BD – 305BG – 1, 398BG – 2; 2BD – 446BG – 1, 448BG – 1, 492BG – 2; 3BD – 95BG – 1, 96BG – 1, 385BG – 1, 452BG – 1, 486BG – 3. Two 486BG lost in collision over Hamburg. A 381BG B-17 cr. near Wethersfield during assembly, crew killed. B/d 447BG B-17 c/l Woodbridge. The 95BG B-17 MIA ditched, crew rescued. MIA 448BG and one 492BG a/c in Sweden.

Mission 515 was the first *Aphrodite* operation using war-weary B-17s as radio-controlled flying bombs. Targets for the 4 drone B-17s were large *Noball* sites but were not hit – one drone B-17 cr. Sudbourne, 1 killed. Mission 516 was a GH attack on *Noball* targets and coastal batteries in the Pas de Calais by 379BG and 384BG B-17s and B-24s of 93BG, 392BG, 445BG, 453BG, 458BG, 492BG & 44BG GH.

All Fighter groups operated. Fighter group e/a credits:– 339FG – 8, 353FG – 13, 356FG – 15, 359FG – 1. Fighter group losses:– 20FG – 1, 339FG – 3, 353FG – 2, 356FG – 1, 357FG – 1, 359FG – 3, 361FG – 3, 364FG – 2. 20FG P-51 cr. t/o Sibson, pilot k. 479FG P-38 cr. t/o, pilot k. MIA 359FG P-51s landed Sweden. 353FG P-47 c/l Wattisham, pilot safe.

OTHER OPERATIONS: 7PG despatched 27 F-5s and 3 Spitfires on PR Continent. 802RG despatched 3 Mosquitoes on PR, 6 Mosquitoes scouting for bombers, 2 Mosquitoes on WR Brest area and 1 B-17 on WR Atlantic. 1SF despatched 11 P-51s to scout for 1BD.

INCIDENT

The 356th Group, generally less fortunate than most in meeting enemy fighters when at an advantage, had one of its most successful fights while flying P-47 Thunderbolts during an escort mission on 4 August. East of Bremen enemy formations were spotted and the Group climbed to 38,000 ft before launching an attack. The German fighters – Me 109s – immediately dived from 36,000 ft to 'the deck' with the P-47s in hot pursuit, an ill-chosen evasive tactic in view of the P-47s' superior diving speed. A total of 15 enemy fighters were credited destroyed as a result of this action, which ended with P-47s chasing Me 109s over the tree tops. For 1/Lt Westwood Fletcher it was his big day as a fighter pilot. He had previously undertaken 86 trips without a successful combat and on this occasion brought down two without firing a shot! Fletcher, followed by his wingman, was in hot pursuit of two Me 109s attempting to escape by extremely low flying in the hope of evading their pursuers. One German pilot misjudged a turn and collided with a large oak; a little further on the second Messerschmitt skidded across a meadow, crashed and exploded. Several pilots in the German aircraft encountered were obviously very inexperienced – but not all. 2/Lt Robert Gleason also destroyed his first and only enemy aircraft this day, only to find an Me 109 on his tail. Four 20 mm cannon shells hit the P-47 before violent evasive action got Gleason out of danger. One shell shattered the canopy and sprinkled the cockpit with fragments, a second detonated in a wing ammunition bay and exploded the remaining rounds, and the other two hit the tailplane and rudder. After landing his Thunderbolt Gleason counted 77 holes in the airframe.

5 AUGUST 1944

8AF 519

	Despatched		Effective	Target		Bombs Tonnage	E/A	Losses MIA	E	Dam	Casualties KIA	WIA	MIA
3BD	B-17	215	87	MAGDEBURG/KRUPP	(P)	205.0	3–1–3	3	0	189	2	8	28
			93	MAGDEBURG/ NEUSTADT	(P)	226.9							
			14	HELMSTEDT A/F	(S)	36.0							
			6	T/O		18.0							
3BD	B-24	78	70	HALBERSTADT A/F	(P)	196.1		1	0	7	0	0	9
			1	T/O		3.3							
2BD	B-24	452	98	BRUNSWICK AERO-ENG	(P)	266.4		7	2	147	13	5	55
			30	BRUNSWICK A/C COMP	(P)	82.9							
			44	BRUNSWICK/ BÜSSING	(P)	129.0							
			85	FALLERSLABEN	(P)	270.5							
			69	BRUNSWICK/ WILHELMITOR	(P)	180.5							
			65	BRUNSWICK/Me 110 ASSMBY	(P)	183.1							
			9	GOSLAR A/F	(S)	23.0							
			8	T/O		23.3							
1BD	B-17	426	143	HANNOVER/ LANGENHAGEN A/F	(P)	375.0		2	1	130	2	5	15
			72	DOLLBERGEN	(P)	274.5							
			176	NIENBURG	(P)	665.0							
			3	T/O		8.0							
8AF 520													
1BD	B-17	39	38	PAS DE CALAIS V/S	(P)	52.6		0	0	19	0	0	0
8AF MICRO H TEST													
482BG	B-17	2	2	BEUVRY P/S		1.5		0	0	0	0	0	0
TOTALS:		1212	583			3220.6	3–1–3	13	3	492	15	10	79
VIII FC													
	P-38	50	174	ESCORT 3BD B-17			19–1–7	1	0	1	0	0	1
	P-51	164					1–0–2(G)	3	0	5	1	1	3
	P-47	47	41	ESCORT 3BD B-24			4–0–1	0	0	0	0	0	0
	P-51	188	172	ESCORT 2BD			5–0–1 3–0–3(G)	0	0	1	0	0	0
	P-47	197	186	ESCORT 1BD			1–0–0	2	1	6	0	0	2
	P-51	12	10	ESCORT 8AF 520			0–0–1(G)	0	0	0	0	0	0
TOTALS:		658	583				29–1–9 4–0–6(G)	6	3	13	1	1	6

REMARKS: Mission 519; visual attacks on strategic targets in north and central Germany: oil refineries and tank and a/c production. Groups participating: all 1BD, all 2BD, all 3BD except 95BG and 390BG. Last mission of 490BG with B-24; group non-op until 27 August. Bomb group losses:–1BD – 381BG – 1, 457BG – 1; 2BD – 389BG – 1, 446BG – 1, 448BG – 1, 458BG – 1, 467BG – 2, 489BG – 1; 3BD – 34BG – 1, 100BG – 2, 487BG – 1.

From 448BG, 458FG and 489BG B-24s that ditched in the North Sea, 3, 9 and 10 men respectively were rescued. A 392BG B-24 cr. after t/o at Gressenhall, 10 killed. On return a 466BG B-24 cr. Happisburgh, crew baled. B/d 379BG B-17 Cat E. Mission 520 was on GH attack by 303BG on V-1 sites. Mission 521 was an abortive attempt to attack a thermal power station at Beuvry, France (2 B-17s & 8 P-51s).

All Fighter groups except 357FG operating. Fighter group e/a credits: 4FG – 2, 20FG – 4, 339FG – 3, 352FG – 6, 359FG – 4, 361FG – 5, 479FG – 4. Fighter group losses:– 20FG – 1, 78FG – 1, 352FG – 2, 353FG – 1, 479FG – 1. 339FG P-51 lost in collision with another 339FG a/c, cr. Thriplow, pilot k, other c/l base. 78FG P-47 Cat E.

OTHER OPERATIONS: 7PG despatched 34 F-5s, 3 Spitfires and 1 B-25 on PR and other duties, France, Belgium and Germany. 802RG despatched 2 Mosquitoes for PR and special duties France, 2 Mosquitoes on WR for 2BD and 3BD, 4 B-17s on routine WR. 1SF despatched 8 P-51s to scout for 1BD.

5/6 AUGUST 1944

8AF 522 NIGHT LEAFLET OPERATION

NLS B-17, 6 despatched, 6 effective; Holland and France.

801BG despatched 19 B-24s on *Carpetbagger* operations.

482BG despatched 2 B-17s on scope photo sorties.

With 1/Lt Harvey Mace at the controls and clutching two 108 US gallon drop tanks beneath the wings, *Sweet Helen II* waits turn to take off from Leiston on the second 8AF shuttle to Russia. The paper-plastic composition tanks, being light to handle and corrosion free, became preferred to metal types for use on Mustangs. They were manufactured in England. (M. Olmsted)

6 AUGUST 1944

8AF 524

	Despatched		Effective	Target	Bombs Tonnage	E/A	Losses MIA	E	Dam	Casualties KIA	WIA	MIA
1BD	B-17	414	126	BRANDENBURG ASS. PLANTS (P)	302.2	0–0–3	11	0	106	1	4	105
			69	BRANDENBURG M/I (P)	159.8							
			74	GENSHAGEN (P)	402.3							
			12	STENDAL A/F (S)	30.0							
			8	T/O	20.0							
3BD	B-17	154	45	BERLIN/DIESEL WKS (P)	106.3	0–2–3	5	1	103	1	6	45
			83	BERLIN/A/C ENG WKS (P)	197.8							
			4	NORDHOLZ A/F (S)	10.0							
			7	T/O	17.0							
3BD	B-17	78	75	GDYNIA/RAHMEL A/I	105.0	0–2–2	0	0	23	0	0	0
2BD	B-24	445	62	HAMBURG/ RHENANIA–OSSAG O/R (P)	162.5		8	3	290	13	16	83
			33	HAMBURG/EBAND O/R (P)	88.5							
			61	HAMBURG/RHENANIA O/R (P)	171.8							
			32	HAMBURG/SCHLIEMAN O/R (P)	90.5							
			72	HAMBURG/SCHULAU O/R (P)	203.4							
			54	HAMBURG/DEUTSCHE O/R								
			58	KIEL N/I (P)	170.0							
			23	HEMMINGSTEDT (S)	63.5							
			4	T/O	12.0							
3BD	B-24	91	24	PAS DE CALAIS V/S	58.0		0		9	0	0	0
TOTALS:		1186	929		2373.6	0–4–5	24	4	531	15	26	233
VIII FC												
	P-51	195	168	ESCORT 1BD		19–0–2	2	1	0	1	0	2
	P-51	144	107	ESCORT 3BD BERLIN		4–0–0 2–0–4(G)	1	0	3	0	1	1
	P-51	160	154	ESCORT *FRANTIC* FORCE		7–2–3	4	1	0	1	0	5
	P-38	44	196	ESCORT 2BD		1–0–2	0	0	0	0	0	0
	P-47	173					1	0	0	0	0	1
	P-47	24	24	ESCORT 3BD B-24			0	0	0	0	0	0
TOTALS:		740	713			31–2–7 2–0–4(G)	8	2	3	2	1	9

REMARKS: Very successful visual attacks on oil refineries, aircraft, ordnance and other factories in Germany; *Noball* targets in France. Groups participating:– all 1BD except 384BG, all 3BD except 447BG, all 2BD. 95BG and 390BG composed force bombing Gdynia and going to Soviet Union for second shuttle. Bomb group losses:– 1BD – 305BG – 1, 351BG – 6, 381BG – 1, 398BG – 1, 401BG – 1, 457BG – 1; 2BD – 44BG – 1, 392BG – 1, 448BG – 2, 458BG – 1, 467BG – 2, 489BG – 1; 3BD – 94BG – 2, 388BG – 1, 452BG – 1, 487BG – 1. MIA 452BG B-17 and a 448BG B-24 went to Sweden. On return 2 492BG B-24s cr. on landing approach base after colliding, 10 killed. Another 2BD B-24 c/l on return. B/d 385BG B-17 cr. Gt. Thelnetham, crew baled.

388BG despatched 2 *Aphrodite* B-17s with 2 B-17s and 1 B-24 control a/c but with drone B-17s lost in sea.

All Fighter groups operating. Fighter group e/a credits:– 4FG – 1, 20FG – 7, 78FG – 1, 339FG – 7, 352FG – 12, 355FG – 3, 357FG – 2. Fighter group losses:– 20FG – 1, 55FG – 2, 78FG – 1, 339FG – 2, 352FG – 1, 355FG – 1. The 357FG with 64 P-51s escorted 3BD B-17s to Soviet Union. 339FG and 55FG escorted this force to target, flying longest fighter mission from UK and return to date – 1,592 miles (6hrs 35min). One 339FG P-51 MIA landed in Sweden. On return a 352FG P-51 cr. Thetford, pilot killed and a 339FG P-51 cr. near Cambridge, pilot killed. Maj George Preddy, 352FG, claimed 6 e/a this day.

OTHER OPERATIONS: 7PG despatched 25 F-5s and 2 Spitfires on PR France and Germany and a B-25 on WR Channel. 802RG despatched 7 Mosquitoes on WR scouting operations and 2 B-17s on WR. 1SF despatched 8 P-51s to scout for bombers. ASR despatched 12 P-47s on patrol.

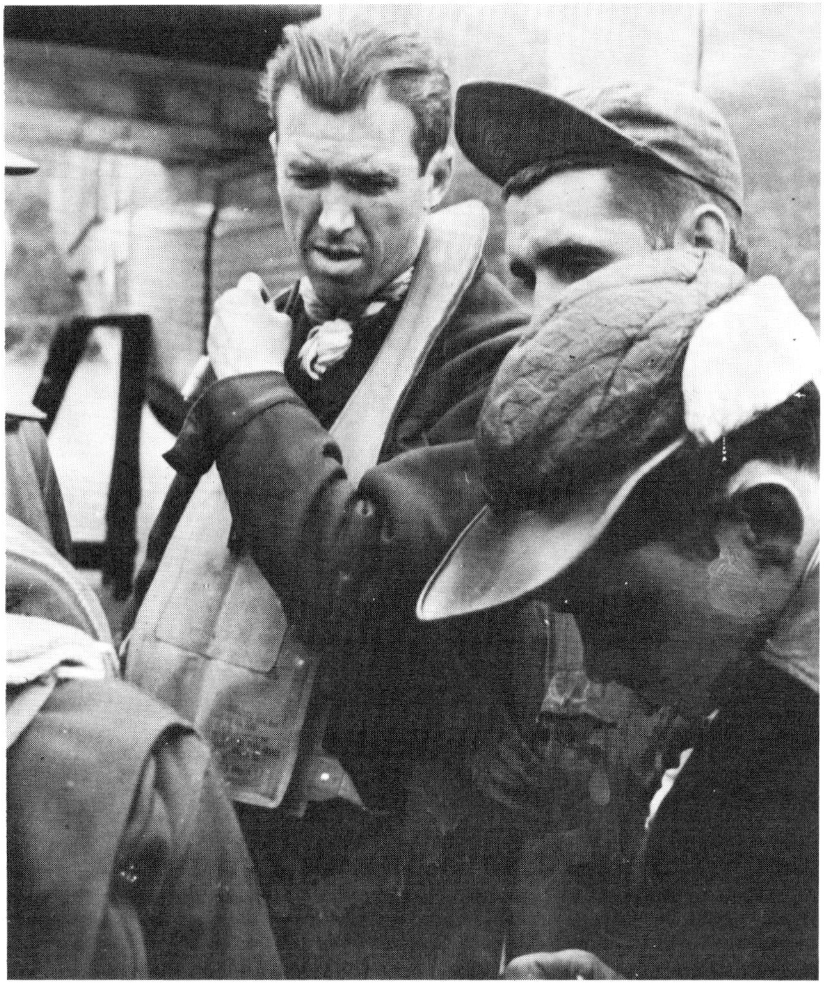

Major James Stewart, Operations Officer 453BG, gives details for Form 1 after a flight. Walter Matthau, a post-war Hollywood film star of note was also a member of the 453BG. (J. Archer)

Hamburg, 6 August. Another success in the oil campaign photographed from a B-24 of the 'hard luck' 492BG on its penultimate mission.

An 88 mm shell, which detonated against the fin top of this 457BG Fortress over Genshagen on 6 August did not stop the bomber getting home safely.

6/7 AUGUST 1944

8AF 526 NIGHT LEAFLET OPERATION

NLS B-17, 7 despatched, 7 effective; France.

801BG despatched 36 B-24s on *Carpetbagger* operations; France. 1 B-24 MIA.

482BG despatched 4 B-17s (1 aborted) on scope photo sorties.

7 AUGUST 1944

8AF 527

	Despatched		Effective	Target		Bombs Tonnage	E/A	Losses MIA	E	Dam	Casualties KIA	WIA	MIA
1BD	B-17	112	34	ST.LOUBES	(P)	84.3		0	1	26	0	2	0
			71	MONTBARTIER	(P)	177.5							
1BD	B-17	224	24	DUENY	(P)	72.0		0	1	80	0	0	0
			12	PARIS–ST.QUEN	(P)	22.8							
			23	BOURRON MARLOTTE	(P)	56.6							
			26	SENS	(P)	64.0							
			25	ST.FLORENTIN	(P)	62.2							
			36	NANTEUIL BRIDGE	(P)	106.5							
			23	MAINTENON BRIDGE	(O)	65.7							
			14	HOUDEN M/Y	(O)	22.8							
			1	ROUGLAF	(O)	2.7							
			23	CHARTRES A/F	(O)	62.3							
			11	CHATEAUDUN A/F	(O)	33.0							
3BD	B-17	182	1	MONTDIDIER A/F	(O)	3.0		0	0	35	0	1	0

continued on next page

7 AUGUST 1944 *(contd.)*

3BD	B-24	51	9	SEMUSE	(O)	22.5		1	0	19	0	0	11
			10	ANDENNE BR	(O)	24.9							
			8	T/O		20.6							
2BD	B-24	333	24	SALEUX	(P)	75.5		0	1	45	8	1	0
			23	RECQUES-SUR-COURSE	(P)	69.0							
			9	LANGERBRUGGE	(P)	25.3							
			11	RIEME/ERTVELD	(P)	26.0							
			37	DOULLENS BR	(P)	147.5							
			15	FREVENT BR	(P)	60.0							
			12	FACTORY NR. WENDELGHEM	(O)	28.8							
			1	T/O		2.0							
8AF 528 MICRO H TEST													
482BG	B-17	3	1	SEQUEX M/Y		.5		0	0	0	0	0	0
TOTALS:		905	484			1338.0	0	1	3	205	8	4	11
VIII FC													
	P-51	139	123	ESCORT 40CBW			1–0–3 0–0–1(G)	0	0	0	0	0	0
	P-51	97	96	ESCORT 1BD				0	0	0	0	0	0
	P-38	48	90	ESCORT 3 BD B-17				0	0	0	0	0	0
	P-51	52						0	0	0	0	0	0
	P-47	35	34	ESCORT 3BD B-24				0	0	0	0	0	0
	P-51	100	94	ESCORT 2BD				0	0	0	0	0	0
8AF 529													
	P-47	194	271	FIGHTER-BOMBER M/Y & R/R NORTH & EAST OF PARIS		52.5	4–0–1(G)	3	0	11	0	0	3
	P-51	85						2	0	0	0	0	2
TOTALS:		750	708			52.5	1–0–3	5	0	11	0	0	5

EASTERN COMMAND

	Despatched		Effective	Target		Bombs Tonnage	E/A	Losses MIA	E	Dam	Casualties KIA	WIA	MIA
3BD	B-17	55	55	TRZEBINIA O/R	(P)	133.8		0	0	0	0	0	0
	P-51	29		ESCORT *FRANTIC* B-17s				0	0	0	0	0	0
8AF 529													
	B-17	5	5	LEAFLET OPERATION FRANCE				0	0	3	0	0	0
TOTALS:		89	60			133.8	0	0	0	3	0	0	0

REMARKS: Fuel dumps and bridges in France with visual attacks on some primaries but heavy cloud forced many aircraft to return with bombs and other formations to be recalled. Groups participating:– 40CBW groups flew first 1BD mission; all 1BD groups of second force except 351BG, 398BG, 401BG crossed enemy coast; all 2BD groups except 392BG; 34BG and 493BG of 3BD B-24 force (third group, 490BG non-operational and converting to B-17); all 3BD B-17 groups except 95BG. *Frantic* Force 95BG, 390BG in Soviet Union attacked target in Poland and returned to Soviet Union. Bomb group losses:– 3BD – 34BG – 1. B/d 305BG B-17 c/l in Allied France. On return a 467BG B-24 cr. Rackheath, 8 killed. B/d 384BG B-17 c/l Ford A/F. Last mission of original 492BG – disbanded.

All Fighter groups operating. 357FG *Frantic* Force escorted B-17s. Fighter group e/a credits:– 357FG – 3 (UK based), 361FG – 1. Fighter group losses:– 4FG – 2, 56FG – 2, 353FG – 1. The 56FG losses due to collision.

OTHER OPERATIONS: 7PG despatched 32 F-5s and 6 Spitfires on PR France and Germany. 802RG despatched 7 Mosquitoes on WR and 2 Mosquitoes to scout for bombers, 2 B-17 on routine WR Atlantic/UK. 1 Mosquito MIA. 1SF despatched 10 P-51s. ASR despatched 14 P-47s for patrol. 1 B-17 and 4 P-51s on radio-relay. 11 P-51s escort for RAF Warwicks. 2 P-38s on radio-relay. 8AF 529 was a daylight operation by NLS over France. 482BG despatched 3 B-17s on night sorties, 2 aborted.

EVENT

The first-line life of a fighter aircraft in the 8th Air Force averaged about 120 days during 1944, with a chance of being written off in an accident or due to damage equal to that of going down through enemy action. Few individual fighters remained on combat operations for more than seven or eight months. However, there were exceptions. The 356th Group had a P-47D, number 222517, assigned when the Group arrived at Goxhill in September 1943, that flew missions for nine months. Nicknamed *Eager Eagle*, this Thunderbolt had over 400 hours' operational flying time with its original engine when relegated to training in August 1944. This entailed flying some 100,000 miles over western Europe, usually with Capt Harold Ogden at the controls, while S/Sgt Frank J. Williamson, its crew chief, was responsible for maintaining *Eager Eagle*.

No, not James Stewart the film star but Maj Edwin Millson, Group Bombardier of 379BG back from the mission of 8 August. He was frequently mistaken for the famous film star which he found had both advantages and disadvantages. Millson was one of the team responsible for the excellent bombing record of the 379BG.

8 AUGUST 1944

8AF 530

	Despatched		Effective	Target		Bombs Tonnage	E/A	Losses MIA	E	Dam	Casualties KIA	WIA	MIA
2BD & 3BD	B-24	414	115	PAS DE CALAIS V/S	(P)	297.2		1	1	139	11	9	9
			91	CLASTRES A/F	(P)	235.5							
			53	ROMILLY A/D	(P)	126.0							
			50	LA PERTHE A/F	(P)	136.0							
			12	LAON/ATHIES A/F	(P)	33.0							
			13	T/O		31.0							
			13	R/B	(O)	32.0							
			1	R/B	(O)	2.5							
			11	BRETIGNY A/F	(O)	31.5							
8AF 531													
1BD & 3BD	B-17	681	231	CAUVINCOURT	(P)	618.5	1-0-0	7	4	294	8	15	35
			99	BRETTEVILLE-SUR-LAISE S/P	(P)	324.8							
			99	ST.SYLVAIN S/P	(P)	327.0							
			1	GOUVIX S/P	(P)	4.5							
			67	T/O		213.0							
TOTALS:		1095	856			2412.5	1-0-0	8	5	433	19	24	44
VIII FC													
	P-51	50	41	ESCORT RAF – NORWAY				3	0	3	0	1	3
	P-47	96	265	ESCORT B-24s				0	0	0	0	0	0
	P-51	196						2	0	0	0	0	2
	P-51	100	91	ESCORT B-17			4-1-6	3	0	0	0	0	3
				FIGHTER-BOMBER									
	P-38	50	175	RR N & W					0	1	0	0	1
	P-47	88		OF DIJON				2	0	1	0	0	2
	P-51	52						2	0	1	0	0	2
TOTALS:		632	572				4-1-6	13	0	6	0	0	13

EASTERN COMMAND

	Despatched		Effective	Target		Bombs Tonnage	E/A	Losses MIA	E	Dam	Casualties KIA	WIA	MIA
3BD	B-17	78	38	BIZAU A/F	(P)	65.7		0	0	0	0	0	0
			35	ZILISTEA A/F	(P)	70.0							
TOTALS:		78	73			135.7	0	0	0	0	0	0	0
	P-51	55		ESCORT FOR ABOVE									

REMARKS: Mission 530 flown by all 2BD and 3BD B-24 groups to attack airfields and *Noball* targets in France. Mission 531 flown by all 1BD and 3BD B-17 groups except 95BG and 457BG to bomb enemy troop concentration and strongpoints S of Caen. 25 Canadian soldiers killed and 131 wounded by short bombing – part of 351BG made accidental release when lead a/c hit by flak. Bomb group losses:– 1BD – 91BG – 1, 306BG – 1, 379BG – 1, 398BG – 2, 401BG – 1; 2BD – 44BG – 1; 3BD – 100BG – 1. Abortive 44BG B-24 cr. Yaxham, 10 k. On return 351BG B-17 c/l base (401BG crew). B/d 398BG B-17 c/l liberated France. *Frantic* B-17s (95BG, 390BG) attacked Romanian airfields from Russian bases and flew to Italy. 452BG B-17 cr. landing base. 381BG B-17 abandoned near Caen, crew safe.

All Fighter groups except 20FG and 357FG (UK) operated. Fighter group e/a credits: 356FG – 2, 359FG – 1, 357FG – 1 (*Frantic*), 361FG – 1. Fighter group losses: 4FG – 3, 78FG – 1, 339FG – 1, 353FG – 1, 355FG – 2, 359FG – 2, 361FG – 1, 364FG – 1, 479FG – 1. MIA 4FG a/c down in Norway after escort to RAF CC Beaufighters on convoy strike.

OTHER OPERATIONS: 7PG despatched 22 F-5s and 5 Spitfires on PR France and Germany. 802RG despatched 5 Mosquitoes on PR and H2X scope photo sorties, 3 Mosquitoes on WR scouting for bombers, 3 Mosquitoes on WR France, and 2 B-17 on routine Atlantic WR. 1 Mosquito MIA. 1SF despatched 8 P-51s. ASR despatched 6 P-47s on patrol. 6 P-51s despatched to escort RAF Warwicks on ASR.

8/9 AUGUST 1944

8AF 532 NIGHT LEAFLET OPERATION

NLS B-17, 5 despatched, 5 effective; France.

9 AUGUST 1944

8AF 533

		Despatched	Effective	Target		Bombs Tonnage	E/A	Losses MIA	E	Dam	Casualties KIA	WIA	MIA
1BD	B-17	359	30	ULM	(S)	71.3	1–1–1	11	1	157	1	5	96
			103	PIRMASENS	(O)	259.5							
			34	SAARBRÜCKEN M/Y	(O)	84.0							
			56	ELSENBORN	(O)	140.0							
			41	KARLSRUHE	(O)	125.5							
			8	SPREICHER	(O)	20.0							
			29	LUXEMBOURG M/Y	(O)	67.5							
3BD	B-17	218	12	ST.VITH M/Y	(O)	31.8		3	1	94	0	5	18
			12	EINDHOVEN	(O)	28.0							
			16	AACHEN	(O)	38.5							
			7	T/O		14.5							
2BD	B-24	247	25	SINDELFINGEN	(P)	71.0		4	2	126	1	10	39
			147	SAARBRÜCKEN M/Y	(S)	352.5							
8AF 535 MICRO H TEST													
482BG	B-17	4	3	AUBIGNY A/S		6.0		0	0	0	0	0	0
TOTALS:		828	523			1310.1	1–1–1	18	4	377	2	20	153
VIII FC													
				FIGHTER-BOMBER				0					
	P-47	116	149	COMMUNICATIONS – FRANCE		24.4		0	0		0	0	0
	P-51	40		ESCORT FOR ABOVE									
	P-47	99	243	ESCORT 1BD			33–0–10	1	2		0	0	1
	P-51	193					24–0–15 (G)	1	5		0	0	1
	P-38	50	165	ESCORT 2BD			6–0–4	1	0		0	0	1
	P-47	48						0	0		0	0	0
	P-51	89						0	0		0	0	0
	P-47	41	162	ESCORT 3BD				0	0		0	0	0
	P-51	155						0	0		0	0	0
	P-38	16	16	ESCORT 8AF 535				0	0		0	0	0
TOTALS:		847	735				39–0–14 24–0–15(G)	3	7		0	0	3

REMARKS: Mission 533 despatched to strategic targets in SE Germany; aircraft and tank works, airfields and fuel depots. Weather deteriorated en route and 2BD and 3BD Force recalled when confronted with front rising to 28,000 ft. T/O attacked by most units. Groups participating: all 1BD; 2CBW, 14CBW, 96CBW, groups of 2BD; 4CBW, 45CBW, 92CBW, groups of 3BD. Bomb group losses:– 1BD – 92BG – 1, 305BG – 6, 351BG – 2, 379BG – 2; 2BD – 445BG – 1, 458BG – 1, 466BG – 2; 3BD – 385BG – 1, 452BG – 2. B/d 452BG B-17 ditched off Gt. Yarmouth, 9 saved. B/d 351BG B-17 ditched 5 miles off Bradwell Bay, 7 rescued. 445BG B-24 abandoned off Dungeness, 1 rescued. Abortive 458BG B-24 c/l base. B/d 445BG B-24 c/l Theberton, all safe. B/d 384BG and b/d 447BG B-17s Cat E.

All Fighter groups active. Fighter group e/a credits:– 20FG – 16, 359FG – 5, 364FG – 10. Fighter group losses:– 356FG – 1, 364FG – 1, 479FG – 1. Most successful day for both 20FG and 364FG since starting operations. 56FG s/d abandoned 458BG B-24 found orbiting Malmedy.

OTHER OPERATIONS: 7PG despatched 9 F-5s and 3 Spitfires on PR, France and Germany. 1 F-5 MIA. 25BG despatched 3 Mosquitoes on PR and 3 Mosquitoes on WR, France and Germany, 2 B-17s on WR Atlantic. 802RG provisional re-designated as 25BG. 1SF despatched 8 P-51s. 20 P-51s for RAF ASR Warwicks. 2 P-47, 2 P-51, 2 P-38 on radio-relay.

9/10 AUGUST 1944

8AF 536 NIGHT LEAFLET OPERATION

NLS B-17, 6 despatched, 6 effective; France and Holland.

25BG Mosquito on PR, Letreport area. 2 Mosquitoes on H2X PR Germany.

482BG despatched 4 B-17s on scope photo sorties.

Major Joe Thury clad in new Berger 'G-suit' pants that incorporated inflatable pads to counter pilot black-out in violent manoeuvres. At this date, 10 August, 339FG pilots were seeing how they liked the new aid. The benefits were such that it was soon adopted by all 8AF fighter units. Thury, who commanded 505FS, was to become one of the two most successful ground strafers with 25 enemy aircraft destroyed.

10 AUGUST 1944

8AF 537

	Despatched		Effective	Target		Bombs Tonnage	E/A	Losses MIA	E	Dam	Casualties KIA	WIA	MIA
2 & 3BD	B-24	175	31	JOIGNY	(P)	120.5		1	1	19	0	1	1
			31	PACY-SUR-ARMENCON	(P)	78.5							
			38	CLAMECY BRIDGE	(P)	140.5							
			23	ST.FLORENTIN	(P)	56.5							
			26	SENS	(P)	75.0							
			13	T/O		31.5							
TOTALS:		175	162			502.5	0	1	0	19	0	1	1
VIII FC													
	P-51	249	238	ESCORT B-24s			8–0–0	3					
	P-38	49	17	MASBARAUD-MERIGNAT	(P)	4.1		2					
	P-47	134	15	ST.MAURICE LA SOUTERRAINE	(P)	3.7		0					
	P-51	151	15	CONFLANS M/Y	(P)	3.8	19–0–8	4					
			15	GIVET M/Y	(P)	3.8							
			16	FURNAUX M/Y	(P)	4.0							
			25	BOLOGNE M/Y	(P)	6.3							
			9	RIMAUCOURT M/Y	(P)	2.3							
			47	TROYES, BAR-SUR-AUBE	(P)	11.7							
8AF 538 FIGHTER-BOMBER													
	P-47	107	36	BATRY	(P)	3.0	0–0–0	5					
	P-51	31		SOMMESOUS	(P)	3.0							
				VITRY M/Y	(P)	3.0							
				CHALIENS	(P)	1.0							
			4	CHATEAU-THIERRY M/Y	(P)	1.0							
			3	EPERNAY M/Y	(P)	1.0							
			4	CHANTILLY BR	(P)	1.0							
			7	COMPIEGNE AREA	(P)	1.2							
			11	ST.FIACRE M/Y	(P)	2.2							
			11	REIMS	(P)	2.2							
			11	MUIZON	(P)	2.2							
			12	ST.THOMAS EN AGRONNE M/Y	(P)	1.0							
			3	BEUY M/Y	(P)	.7							
			3	VALMY M/Y	(P)	.7							
			25	CHALONS–VITRY AREA	(P)	5.4							
TOTALS:		721	527			68.3	27–0–8	14	0	14	0	0	14

8AF 539 LEAFLET OPERATION

Despatched		Effective	Target	E/A	Losses MIA	E	Dam	Casualties KIA	WIA	MIA
B-17	1	1	BREST	0	0	0	0	0	0	0

REMARKS: Limited operations against fuel dumps and bridges SE of Paris by B-24s of 34BG, 446BG, 448BG, 491BG, 493BG. 489BG provided PFF lead a/c. Bomb group losses:– 448BG – 1. Two large forces of fighter-bombers also despatched during day to attack rail targets in central and eastern France. All fighter groups except 339FG and 353FG operating. Fighter group e/a credits:– 55FG – 4, 364FG – 4. Fighter group losses:– 20FG – 2, 55FG – 4, 78FG – 1, 357FG – 2, 359FG – 2, 364FG – 1, 479FG – 2. 357FG a/c lost in collision. Heavy loss to ground fire. 20FG destroyed 37 locomotives bringing total to 264 – record for VIII FC.

OTHER OPERATIONS: 7PG despatched 7 F-5s and 4 Spitfires to France and Germany. 25BG despatched 3 Mosquitoes to scout for bombers, 3 Mosquitoes on WR UK/France, and 2 B-17s on WR Atlantic/UK. ASR despatched 8 P-47s on routine patrol. 6 P-51s, 6 P-47s and a B-17 (with 4 P-47s as escort) on radio-relay.

10/11 AUGUST 1944

8AF 540 NIGHT LEAFLET OPERATION

NLS B-17, 4 despatched, 4 effective; France and Norway.

25BG despatched a B-25 and B-26 on PR *Noball* sites.

11 AUGUST 1944

8AF 541

	Despatched		Effective	Target		Bombs Tonnage	E/A	Losses MIA	E	Dam	Casualties KIA	WIA	MIA
3BD	B-17	157	76	MULHOUSE M/Y	(P)	185.7		0	0	16	0	0	0
			76	BELFORT M/Y	(P)	185.7							
			1	T/O		2.5							
2BD	B-24	141	36	PACY-SUR-ARMANCON	(P)	104.0		0	0	5	0	0	0
			34	ST.FLORENTIN	(P)	83.0							
			47	COULOMMIERS A/F	(P)	100.8							
3BD	B-17	77	76	VILLACOUBLAY A/D	(P)	136.3		1	0	17	0	1	9
3BD	B-24	65	45	TOUSSUS LE NOBLE A/F	(P)	110.0		0	1	0	0	0	0
			9	ORLEANS/SARAN A/F	(S)	22.3							
2BD	B-24	220	66	STRASBOURG FUEL DUMP	(P)	188.0		3	0	112	7	7	19
			65	STRASBOURG M/Y	(P)	177.5							
			60	SAARBRÜCKEN M/Y	(P)	172.5							
			10	NIVELLES A/F	(O)	30.0							
			1	T/O		3.0							
8AF 542													
1BD	B-17	294	275	BREST AREA		868.5		1	0	37	0	0	0
8AF 543 MICRO H TEST													
482BG	B-17	2	1	LA CHENAIE R/B		2.0			0	0	0	0	
TOTALS:		956	878			2371.8	0	5	1	187	7	8	28

VIII FC

		Despatched	Effective	Target	E/A	Losses MIA	E	Dam	KIA	WIA	MIA
	P-38	49	356	COVER 8AF		0	0	0	0	0	0
	P-51	341		541 & 542	0	1	1	0	0	1	1
	P-47	180	165	FIGHTER SWEEP PARIS AREA	3–0–0 2–0–0(G)	0	0	0	0	0	0
	P-47	8	7	ESCORT 8AF 543		0	0	0	0	0	0
TOTALS:		578	528		3–0–0 2–0–0(G)	1	1	0	0	1	1

REMARKS: Visual attacks on rail targets, fuel dumps and troop concentrations in the Brest peninsula. Four task forces made up Mission 541. Groups participating: 4CBW and 45CBW less 94BG composed B-17 force against M/Ys; 93BG, 392BG, 448BG were 2BD groups against fuel dumps and airfields; 100BG, 390BG, 486BG, 487BG, 34BG, 493BG made up 3BD Force against airfields; 2CBW, 95CBW, 96CBW groups went to Strasbourg area M/Ys. Mission 542 flown by groups of 1CBW, 41CBW and 94CBW. Bomb group losses:– 1BD – 457BG – 1; 2BD – 453BG – 1, 489BG – 1, 491BG – 1. 3BD–100BG – 1. The 489BG a/c landed Switzerland. The 453BG B-24 ditched 10 miles from North Foreland, 3 saved. Crew of MIA 457BG a/c baled over Allied lines France. 34BG B-24 cr. t/o base, crew safe.

All Fighter groups active except 359FG, 364FG. Fighter group e/a credits:– 78FG – 2, 353FG – 1. Fighter group losses:– 355FG – 1. 339FG P-51 c/l Luton A/F, m/f, pilot inj.

OTHER OPERATIONS: 7PG despatched 10 F-5s and 9 Spitfires on PR Germany and France. 25BG despatched, 5 Mosquitoes WR scouting for 2BD and 3BD bombers, 2 Mosquitoes on WR France and 3 B-17s on WR Atlantic/UK. ASR despatched 11 P-47s on patrols. 10 P-51s and 2 P-38s on radio-relays.

11/12 AUGUST 1944

8AF 544 NIGHT LEAFLET OPERATION

NLS B-17, 6 despatched, 6 effective; France.

801BG despatched 31 B-24s (3 abortive) on *Carpetbagger* operations; France.

482BG despatched 2 B-17s on scope photo-operations.

25BG despatched a Mosquito, B-25 and B-26 on PR France, and 1 Mosquito on H2X PR Pölitz.

Assembly collision was an ever present hazard in a clouded crowded morning sky. A 398BG B-17 and 392BG B-24 are believed to have touched on 12 August, although exactly what occurred is unknown as both crews perished. Apart from the undercarriage leg there is little left to identify this scene of desolation just outside Cheshunt with a Liberator.

Mosquito aircraft acquired from the British were popular for surveillance work. On 12 August NS569 was acting as camera ship for an Aphrodite mission involving a US Navy PBY Liberator piloted by Lt Joe Kennedy (brother of the post-war President). Near Walberswick the explosive filled drone suddenly blew up, the blast lifting the Mosquito and peppering it with fragments. The left engine was put out of action and pilot, Lt Robert Tunnel (left), managed to make an emergency landing at Halesworth. Navigator, Lt David McCarthy, holds pieces of Liberator retrieved from the Mosquito.

12 AUGUST 1944

8AF 545

	Despatched		Effective	Target	Bombs Tonnage	E/A	Losses MIA	E	Dam	Casualties KIA	WIA	MIA
2BD	B-24	276	61	LAON/COUVRON A/F (P)	156.5		3	1	46	10	7	32
			52	JUVINCOURT A/F (P)	131.2							
			63	LAON/ATHIES A/F (P)	158.1							
			75	MOURMELON A/F (P)	208.7							
1BD	B-17	301	69	METZ M/Y (P)	207.0		0	1	28	9	1	0
			72	CHAUMONT A/F (P)	136.2							
			67	BUC A/F	148.2							
			58	LA PERTHE A/F (P)	95.7							
			12	ETAMPES/MONDESIR (S) A/F	33.0							
3BD	B-17	73	69	TOULOUSE/ FRANCAZAL A/F (p)	158.8		0	0	0	0	0	0
TOTALS:		650	598		1433.4		3	2	74	19	8	32
VIII FC												
	P-47	24	386	ESCORT BOMBERS		1–0–0	0	0		0	0	0
	P-51	412					3	0		0	0	3
				FIGHTER-BOMBERS								
	P-38	95		TRANSPORTATION		5–0–0	1	0		0	0	1
	P-47	324	486	TARGETS	182.0	13–0–0	5	0		0	0	5
	P-51	170		PARIS – BRUSSELS AREA		(G)	7	0		0	0	7
				FIGHTER-BOMBER								
	P-47	20	220	TRANSPORTATION	98.6		0	0		0	0	0
	P-51	285		TARGETS NE FRANCE			2	3		0	0	2
TOTALS:		1330	109		280.6	6–0–0 13–0–0(G)	18	3	4	0	1	18

REMARKS: Visual attacks by bombers on Metz M/Y and airfields in central and eastern France. Fighters strafed and bombed enemy road transport in NE France. Bomb groups participating:– 2BD – all except 2CBW groups; 1BD – all 40CBW, 41CBW groups and 91BG, 398BG; 3BD – 95BG, 390BG (*Frantic* Force returning from Italy). Bomb group losses:– 1BD – 381BG – 1; 2BD – 44BG – 1, 466BG – 2. A 466BG B-24 ditched 50 miles from Lowestoft, 7 rescued. A 398BG B-17 cr. Loudwater, crew killed, during assembly, believed collided with 392BG B-24 which cr. Cheshunt, crew killed.

All Fighter groups operating. Fighter group e/a credits:– 56FG – 2, 356FG – 2, 479FG – 1. Fighter group losses:– 20FG – 2, 55FG – 3, 56FG – 1, 352FG – 2, 353FG – 2, 355FG – 1, 356FG – 2, 361FG – 4, 479FG – 1. Heavy loss to ground fire. Burning 4FG P-51 abandoned over Latchingdon going out. On return 364FG P-51 c/l near Eastbourne, pilot injured. 355FG P-51 Cat E, pilot safe.

OTHER OPERATIONS: 7PG despatched 19 F-5s and 8 Spitfires on PR France and Germany, 1 F-S MIA. 25BG despatched 4 Mosquitoes to scout for bombers, 3 Mosquitoes and 1 B-26 on WR Continent, and 2 B-17s on WR UK/Atlantic. 1 Mosquito MIA. 1SF despatched 10 P-51s to scout for 1BD. ASR despatched 14 P-47s. Abortive *Aphrodite* mission involved 2 B-17s, 2 PVY, 2 Mosquitoes, 2 P-38s and 4 P-51s (US Navy drone Liberator exploded in air near Blythburgh, 2 killed). 26 P-51s and 9 P-47s as radio-relays.

12/13 AUGUST 1944

8AF 546 NIGHT LEAFLET OPERATION

NLS B-17, 6 despatched, 6 effective; France.

25BG despatched a Mosquito, B-25 and B-26 on PR France, and 1 Mosquito on H2X PR Germany.

13 AUGUST 1944

8AF 548

	Despatched		Effective	Target		Bombs Tonnage	E/A	Losses MIA	E	Dam	Casualties KIA	WIA	MIA
1, 2 & 3BD	B-17	798	634	BATTLE AREA SUPPORT	(P)	1980.0		7	1	484	2	8	63
			69	LE MANOIR BRIDGE	(P)	207.5							
			54	T/O		102.9							
	B-24	466	347	BATTLE AREA SUPPORT	(P)	660.0		5	0	0	1	4	50
			34	ST.MALO	(P)	136.0							
			69	ILE DE CEZEMBRE	(P)	275.0							
8AF 549 BATTY No. 1													
388BG	B-17	1	1	LE HAVRE P/A		0		0	0	0	0	0	0
8AF 550 MICRO H TEST													
482BG	B-17	4	2	LA CHENAIE R/J		4.0		0	0	0	0	0	0
TOTALS:		1269	1209			3265.4	0	12	1	484	3	12	113
VIII FC													
P-51		136	131	ESCORT BOMBERS									
	P-38	96	844	FIGHTER-BOMBER		347.5	0–0–1(G)	0	0		0	1	0
	P-47	388		TRANSPORTATION				4	4		1	1	4
	P-51	445		SEINE AREA				9	0		0	0	9
TOTALS:		1065	975			347.5	0–0–1(G)	13	4	17	1	2	13

REMARKS Visual attacks in support of ground forces on coastal batteries and transportation choke points between Le Havre and Paris. Bomb groups participating: all 1BD; all 2BD except 44BG; all 3BD except 390BG. Bomb group losses:– 1BD – 91BG – 1, 92BG – 1, 305BG – 1, 379BG – 2, 398BG – 1; 2BD – 44BG – 1, 93BG – 1, 466BG – 1, 467BG – 1, 491BG – 1; 3BD – 94BG – 1. 388BG B-17 cr. on t/o. Mission 549 to Le Havre flown by 388BG *Aphrodite* unit involved first use of the TV guided 2000 lb bombs carried by B-17 with B-17, P-38 and Mosquito support a/c. Target missed and Mosquito destroyed by exploding bomb.

All Fighter groups except 20FG and 357FG active. Operations against ground targets in battle area by fighter bombers again brought heavy losses. No e/a claims. Fighter group losses:– 4FG – 1, 55FG – 2, 339FG – 2, 352FG – 2, 353FG – 3, 356FG – 1, 361FG – 2. Fighters claimed destruction of 776 enemy vehicles and guns, damage to 1,281. B/d 78FG P-47 cr. near base, pilot k.

OTHER OPERATIONS: 7PG despatched 9 F-5s and 5 Spitfires and a B-25 to France and Germany. 25BG despatched 2 Mosquitoes to scout for bombers, 2 Mosquitoes on WR Brest area, 5 Mosquitoes on PR France, and 2 B-17s on WR Atlantic/UK. 2 B-17s, 1 P-38 and 1 Mosquito on special operations. 1 Mosquito MIA. ASR despatched 20 P-47s on patrols.

INCIDENT

The 100th Bomb Group lost its most famous Fortress during the second week of August 1944, two old B-17Fs that had survived through the period of heavy loss when the average life of a bomber in the Group was about 11 missions. On 11 August *Royal Flush*, the aircraft in which Lt Rosenthal and his men from *Rosie's Riveters* were the only crew to return to base after the disastrous Münster mission in October 1943, went down over France. Hit by flak between No.3 engine and the fuselage shortly after dropping its bombs, the Fortresses was seen spiralling down with No.3 smoking. It crashed in a harvest field within sight of the target airfield, Villacoublay. Six men baled out, one allegedly being killed by machine gun fire from the ground. Lt Alfred Aske and his crew were on their fifth mission; *Royal Flush* was on its 75th.

Three days later *Hard Luck*, the Fortress associated with the number 13, was hit by flak from batteries near Ludwigshafen. Just before reaching the IP the aircraft dropped out of formation and jettisoned the bomb load. Carrying Lt J. David and crew, *Hard Luck* was last seen with an engine smoking trailing the formation towards the target. This Fortress had set a maintenance record for a B-17F by flying 50 missions, involving 630 hours flight time on the original Studebaker-made engines, without ever 'losing' a supercharger. High altitude flight was not conducive to long engine life and the hydraulically-actuated supercharger regulators gave frequent trouble. Pilotage had a great influence on the matter and the Crew Chief, M/Sgt 'Zip' Myers, rightly proud of *Hard Luck's* record, would not tolerate inexperienced crews taking the bomber out if it could possibly be avoided. It was said that one young pilot, fresh from the training fields, complained to his squadron superiors about the Sergeant's attitude: 'Hell, you gotta show him your blood chit before he'll even let you touch the fuselage!' In May 1944, after 50 missions. the engines were changed although one was so good it was re-installed after modification. Back on operations *Hard Luck* completed 11 more missions before going down on her 62nd. The patched and worn B-17F had delivered 249,810 lbs of bombs in a year and a day with the 'Bloody Hundredth'. She was the last of her kind from Thorpe Abbotts to fall.

13/14 AUGUST 1944

8AF 551 NIGHT LEAFLET OPERATION

NLS B-17, 6 despatched, 6 effective; France, Holland and Belgium.

492BG despatched 36 B-24 on *Carpetbagger* operations.

482BG despatched 4 B-17s on radar scope photo operations.

25BG despatched a Mosquito, B-25 and B-26 on PR France, and 2 Mosquitoes on H2X PR Berlin area.

14 AUGUST 1944

8AF 552

	Despatched		Effective	Target		Bombs Tonnage	E/A	Losses MIA	E	Dam	Casualties KIA	WIA	MIA
2BD	B-24	376	108	LYON/BRON A/F	(P)	274.8		0	1	32	0	2	0
			70	DOLE/EVAUX A/F	(P)	152.1							
			83	DIJON/LONGVIC A/F	(P)	211.8							
			46	ANIZY BR	(P)	180.6							
			34	FISMES BR	(P)	129.0							
			12	LIART R/J	(O)	48.0							
			1	T/O		2.6							
3BD	B-24	77	38	SAINTES R/J	(P)	114.0		0	0	0	0	0	0
			38	ANGOULEME R/J	(P)	109.5							
3BD	B-17	349	110	MANNHEIM	(P)	268.0		2	0	232	0	8	18
			144	LUDWIGSHAFEN	(P)	307.8							
			72	MANNHEIM/ SANDHOFEN A/F	(P)	187.3							
			4	T/O		11.4							
1BD	B-17	381	12	SINDELFINGEN	(P)	30.0		0	0	20	0	0	0
			74	STUTTGART/ ECHTERDINGEN	(P)	182.0							
			92	HAGENAU A/F	(S)	227.0							
			72	METZ/FRASCATY A/F	(P)	162.7							
			46	KAISERSLAUTERN	(O)	115.0							
			24	FLORENNES A/F	(O)	60.0							
			10	TRIER	(O)	25.0							
			9	CHIEVRES A/F	(O)	21.5							
			16	T/O		38.0							
TOTALS:		1183	1115			2858.1	0	2	1	284	0	10	18
VIII FC													
	P-47	24	92	ESCORT 2BD				0	0	0	0	0	0
	P-51	71						0	0	0	0	0	0
	P-51	42	40	ESCORT 3BD B-24				0	0	0	0	0	0
	P-51	99	88	ESCORT 3BD B-17				0	0	0	0	0	0
	P-51	193	168	ESCORT 1BD			10–0–11	1	0	0	0	0	1
				FIGHTER-BOMBER									
	P-38	34	136	TRANSPORTATION		39.8	3–0– 0	1	0	0	0	0	1
	P-47	121		PARIS AREA				2	1	2	0	0	2
TOTALS:		584	524			39.8	13–0–11	4	1	2	0	0	4

REMARKS: Visual attacks by B-24s on airfields and rail targets in France and B-17s on aero-engine and oil plants in SW Germany. Bomb groups participating:– All 1BD except 379BG and 398BG; all 2BD (95CBW disbanded this date and groups to other wings); all 3BD except 95BG. Bomb group losses:– 100BG – 1, 452BG – 1. 489BG B-24 c/l England.

All Fighter groups active. Fighter group e/a credits:– 353FG – 1. Fighter group losses:– 78FG – 1, 355FG – 1, 356FG – 1, 479FG – 1. From this date the strafing of all ground personnel within the borders of France forbidden. 78FG P-47 c/l on t/o, pilot safe.

OTHER OPERATIONS: 7PG despatched 50 F-5s, 6 Spitfires on PR, Belgium, France and Germany. 2 F-5s MIA. 25BG despatched 3 Mosquitoes on PR France, 4 Mosquitoes to scout for bombers, 1 Mosquito on WR France/Germany, and 3 B-17s on Atlantic/UK WR. 1SF despatched 8 P-51 to scout for 1BD. ASR despatched 16 P-47s on patrols. 36BS despatched 4 B-24s on RCM. 9 P-51s, 6 P-47s and 2 B-17s (with 4 P-38s escort) on radio-relay.

14/15 AUGUST 1944

8AF 553 NIGHT LEAFLET OPERATION

NLS B-17, 6 despatched, 6 effective; France. Claimed 1–0–0.

492BG despatched 37 B-24s on *Carpetbagger* operations; France. 1 B-24 MIA.

25BG despatched 2 B-26s and 2 Mosquitoes on PR France.

15 AUGUST 1944

8AF 554

	Despatched		Effective	Target	Bombs Tonnage	E/A	Losses MIA	E	Dam	Casualties KIA	WIA	MIA
1BD	B-17	219	38	WIESBADEN A/F	(P) 108.0	4–2–0	9	2	86	7	8	81
			65	FRANKFURT/ ESCHBORN A/F	(P) 187.5							
			108	COLOGNE/ OSTHEIM A/F	(P) 274.0							
			3	T/O								
2BD	B-24	350	90	ZWISCHENAHN A/F	(P) 233.6	9–1–2	4	0	6	0	1	40
			54	PLANTLÜNNE A/F	(P) 132.2							
			91	WITTMUNDHAFEN A/F	(P) 204.7							
			67	VECHTA A/F	(P) 190.7							
			10	HOPSTEIN A/F	(O) 28.5							
3BD	B-17	298	104	VENLO A/F	(P) 207.0		2	0	6	0	0	19
			109	HANDORF A/F	(P) 274.2							
			75	TWENTE/ ENSCHEDE A/F	(P) 177.2							
			3	T/O	7.5							
3BD	B-24	65	59	FLORENNES/ JUZAINE A/F	(P) 146.3		1	0	3			
			1	T/O	2.5							
TOTALS:		932	877		2171.4	13–3–2	16	2	156	7	9	149
VIII FC												
	P-51	141	112	ESCORT 1BD		10–0–1	1	0	2	0	0	1
	P-38	49	163a/c	ESCORT 2BD		4–0–0	2	0	0	0	0	2
	P-51	129				7–0–9(G)	2	0	3	0	1	2
	P-51	124	118	ESCORT 3BD			0	0	0	0	0	0
	P-47	35	33	FIGHTER-BOMBER BRAINE-LE-COMTES			1	0	4	0	0	4
TOTALS:		478	426		13.8	14–0–1 7–0–9(G)	6	0	9	0	1	9

REMARKS: Visual attacks on airfields in western Germany and the Low Countries. Groups participating:– 1CBW groups and 92BG, 303BG, 306BG of 1BD; all 2BD except 491BG, which was moving to a new base; all 3BD except 45CBW. Bomb group losses:– 1BD – 303BG – 9; 2BD – 466BG – 4; 3BD – 385BG – 2, 493BG – 1. 1 BD and 2BD losses to concentrated fighter attacks. 306BG B-17 cr. on t/o base, 5 k. B/d 303BG B-17 Cat E.

All Fighter groups active. Fighter group e/a credits:– 355FG – 1, 364FG – 10. Fighter group losses:– 4FG – 1, 56FG – 1, 355FG – 1, 359FG – 1, 479FG – 2.

OTHER OPERATIONS: 7PG despatched 29 F-5s, 7 Spitfires on PR France, Belgium, Holland and Germany. 25BG despatched 4 Mosquitoes on PR France and Low Countries, 3 Mosquitoes to scout for bombers, 2 Mosquitoes on WR UK/Germany, and 2 B-17s on UK/Atlantic WR. 1SF despatched 8 P-51s to scout for 1BD. ASR despatched 28 P-47s on patrol. 4 P-51 and 2 B-17s (with 4 P-51 escort) on radio-relays.

15/16 AUGUST 1944

492BG despatched 12 B-24s on *Carpetbagger* operations.

25BG despatched a B-25 and Mosquito on PR France, and 1 Mosquito on H2X PR SE Germany.

16 AUGUST 1944

8AF 556

	Despatched		Effective	Target	Bombs Tonnage	E/A	Losses MIA	E	Dam	Casualties KIA	WIA	MIA
1BD	B-17	425	102	DELITZSCH A/D	(P) 259.8	6–4–6	10	1	234	4	9	93
			60	HALLE A/I	(P) 148.3							
			88	BÖHLEN O/I	(P) 206.7							
			92	SCHKEUDITZ A/I	(P) 217.4							
			15	NAUMBURG	(O) 28.9							
			13	HALBERSTADT A/F	(O) 27.5							
			9	T/O	20.1							
3BD	B-17	234	101	ZEITZ O/I	(P) 226.1		6		88	0	3	56
			105	ROSITZ O/I	(P) 250.8							
			3	T/O	7.5							

continued on facing page

	Despatched		Effective	Target		Bombs Tonnage	E/A	Losses MIA	E	Dam	Casualties KIA	WIA	MIA
3BD	B-24	65	51	HALBERSTADT A/F	(P)	117.0		0	1	8	0	0	0
			10	QUEDLINBURG A/F	(O)	30.0							
			1	T/O		2.6							
2BD	B-24	366	99	DESSAU A/I	(P)	233.4		7	0	173	0	5	66
			71	KÖTHEN A/I	(P)	188.5							
			87	MAGDEBURG/ ROTHENSEE O/I	(P)	225.0							
			67	MAGDEBURG/ NEUSTADT A/I	(P)	189.1							
			2	T/O		3.0							
TOTALS:		1090	976			1473.0	0	23	2	269	0	8	122
VIII FC													
	P-47	48	246	ESCORT 1BD			15–1–3	0	0		0	0	0
	P-51	241					0–0–3(G)	0	1		0	1	0
	P-47	42	166	ESCORT 3BD B-17			5–0–1	2	0		0	0	2
	P-51	147						0	0		0	0	0
	P-38	46	42	ESCORT 3BD B-24				0	0		0	0	0
	P-47	41	158	ESCORT 2BD			12–0–0	0	0		0	0	0
	P-51	127						1	0		0	0	1
TOTALS:		692	612				32–1–4 0–0–3(G)	3	1	11	0	1	3

REMARKS: Visual attacks on oil refineries and aircraft plants in central Germany. Groups participating:– all 1BD except 303BG; all 2BD except 491BG; all 3BD except 96BG, 100BG and 452BG. Bomb group losses:– 1BD – 91BG – 6, 305BG – 1, 306BG – 2, 351BG – 1; 2BD – 389BG – 1, 445BG – 2, 448BG – 1, 453BG – 1, 467BG – 1, 489BG – 1; 3BD – 95BG – 4, 388BG – 1, 390BG – 1. The 489BG B-24 MIA was struck by a bomb. B/d 91BG B-17 c/l Halesworth A/F. MIA 388BG B-17 lost through collision near target.

All Fighter groups active. Fighter group e/a credits:– 4FG – 1, 20FG – 8, 339FG – 5, 352FG – 3, 355FG – 11, 356FG – 1, 359FG – 3. Fighter group losses:– 55FG – 1, 339FG – 1, 355FG – 1. 364FG P-51 cr. after t/o, pilot injured.

OTHER OPERATIONS: 7PG despatched 14 F-5s to France and Germany. 25BG despatched 4 Mosquitoes on PR, 3 Mosquitoes to scout for bombers and 2 Mosquitoes on WR France and Germany, 1 Mosquito and 2 B-17s on WR UK/Atlantic. ASR despatched 18 P-47s. 9 P-51s and 6 P-47s on radio-relays.

16/17 AUGUST 1944

8AF 557 NIGHT LEAFLET OPERATION

NLS B-17, 8 despatched, 8 effective; France.

36BS despatched 4 B-24s on RCM.

25BG despatched a B-25 and B-26 on PR France, and 2 Mosquitoes on H2X PR Germany.

17 AUGUST 1944

8AF 558 *AZON*

	Despatched		Effective	Target	Bombs Tonnage	E/A	Losses MIA	E	Dam	Casualties KIA	WIA	MIA
2BD	B-24	10	0	LES FOULOUS R/B	0	0	0	0	0	0	0	0
8AF 559 BATTY No.2												
3BD	B-17	1	1	LA PALLICE P/A	2.0	0	0	0	0	0	0	0
VIII FC												
	P-38	47	397	FIGHTER-BOMBER	172.0	3–0–3	0	0	0	0	0	0
	P-47	139		PARIS/BRUSSELS AREA			0	0	1	0	0	0
	P-51	318		COMMUNICATION TARGETS			7	0	4	0	1	7
TOTALS:		504	397		172.0	3–0–3	7	0	5	0	1	7

REMARKS: Only operation by bombers was abandoned because of deteriorating weather. Fighters bombed and strafed rail and road targets behind battle lines. All Fighter groups active except 20FG and 361FG. No e/a claims air. Fighter group losses:– 55FG – 1, 339FG – 1, 352FG – 2, 357FG – 1, 359FG – 1, 364FG – 1. Mission 559 was *Batty* TV bomb attack on La Pallice by 1 B-17 with support of a B-17, P-38 and 11 P-51s of 339FG.

OTHER OPERATIONS: 25FG despatched 1 Mosquito on PR Germany, and 1 Mosquito PR Brest area, 1 Mosquito which abandoned mission, 2 Mosquitoes on WR Continent, 1 Mosquito scouting for 2BD and 2 B-17 on WR Atlantic/UK. ASR despatched 4 P-47s on patrol. 2 P-51, 2 P-38 and 1 B-17 on radio-relays.

17/18 AUGUST 1944

8AF 560 NIGHT LEAFLET OPERATION

NLS B-17, 7 despatched, 7 effective; France.

492BG despatched 33 B-24s on *Carpetbagger* operations.

36BS despatched 2 B-24s on RCM.

25BG despatched a Mosquito, B-25 and B-26 on PR *Noball* sites, and 2 Mosquitoes on H2X PR Germany.

18 AUGUST 1944

8AF 561

	Despatched		Effective	Target		Bombs Tonnage	E/A	Losses MIA	E	Dam	Casualties KIA	WIA	MIA
3BD	B-24	52	43	ROYE/AMY A/F	(P)	76.3		2	1	37	2	1	21
			10	T/O		26.0							

8AF 562

	Despatched		Effective	Target		Bombs Tonnage	E/A	Losses MIA	E	Dam	Casualties KIA	WIA	MIA
1BD	B-17	269	36	LIEGE/BENOIT BR	(P)	103.0		0	0	57	0	5	0
			24	MAASTRICHT BR	(P)	72.0							
			35	YVOIR BR	(P)	105.0							
			37	NAMUR BR	(P)	109.5							
			26	LIEGE/SERAING BR	(P)	76.0							
			35	HUY BR	(P)	102.5							
			12	EINDHOVEN A/F	(O)	36.0							
			25	VISE BR	(P)	73.3							
			13	TONGRES M/Y	(O)	39.0							
			12	T/O		36.0							
2BD	B-24	256	78	METZ A/F	(P)	241.5		0	1	0	4	2	0
			60	WOIPPY	(P)	162.2							
			35	LANEUREVILLE	(P)	86.8							
			70	NANCY/ESSEY A/F	(P)	196.0							
3BD	B-17	195	116	ST.DIZIER A/F	(P)	215.6		0	0	7	0	0	0
			39	PACY-SUR-ARMANCON	(P)	98.4							
			38	BOURRAN	(P)	94.5							
			1	T/O		2.5							
TOTALS:		772	745			1952.1	0	2	2	101	6	8	21

Milestones were always good for a celebration and such an occasion was completion of 100 missions. The 466BG arranged its 100th Mission Party for 18 August, 10 days after reaching the century. Entertainments were many and included a baseball match played near the control tower between Attlebridge and Martlesham teams. Free beer was available and consumed by many of the spectators. In the background the big bombers stand as a reminder of the war that men should try to forget for a few hours. *Black Cat* is the nearest.

VIII FC

Despatched		Effective	Target	Bombs Tonnage	E/A	Losses MIA	E	Dam	Casualties KIA	WIA	MIA
P-51	99	96	ESCORT 8AF 561			0	0	0	0	0	0
P-51	103	99	ESCORT 1BD		46–0–15	0	1	0	0	0	0
P-38	50					1	0	1	0	0	1
P-51	43	88	ESCORT 2BD			1	0	0	0	0	1
P-51	96	93	ESCORT 3BD		2–0– 3(G)	2	0	0	0	0	2
			FIGHTER-BOMBER								
P-47	246	323	SEINE/BRUSSELS	146.7	10–1– 5	3	1	3	1	0	4
			AREA –								
P-51	271		TRANSPORTATION			10	1	3	0	0	10
TOTALS:	858	611		146.7	56–1–20 2–0– 3(G)	17	3	7	1	0	18

REMARKS: Mission 561 was an attack on Roye/Amy A/F by the two 3BD B-24 groups. Bomb group losses:– 34BG – 1, 493BG – 1. Mission 562 involved the three BD against bridges, airfields, fuel dumps and an aero-engine plant in France and Belgium. Groups participating:– 41CBW, 94CBW groups and 92BG, 305BG of 1BD; all 2BD except 93BG, 446BG, 489BG; all 3BD B-17 groups. A 467BG B-24 cr. Kirby Bedon on return, 4 killed. 2 458BG B-24s collided on route to target causing 1 a/c to land in France. MIA 34BG PFF a/c with 493BG.

All Fighter groups active. Fighter group e/a credits:– 4FG – 7, 356FG – 4, 357FG – 2. Fighter group losses:– 4FG – 9, 353FG – 2, 355FG – 2, 356FG – 1, 359FG – 2, 479FG – 1. B/d 352FG P-51 c/l Manston. 78FG P-47 and 361FG P-51 collided over Bottisham, 78FG pilot killed.

OTHER OPERATIONS: 7PG despatched 25 F-5s and 6 Spitfires on PR, France and Germany. 25BG despatched 2 Mosquitoes scouting for bomber, 4 Mosquitoes on WR France and Germany, 1 B-24, 2 B-17 on WR UK/Atlantic. ASR despatched 12 P-47s on patrols. 2 F-5s escorted by 16 P-51s flew special PR to Peenemünde. 2 P-38s and 2 P-51s on radio-relay.

18/19 AUGUST 1944

8AF 564 NIGHT LEAFLET OPERATION

NLS B-17, 7 despatched, 7 effective; France.

482BG despatched 3 B-17s on test operation MICRO H Beacon. 2 a/c effective.

36BS despatched 6 B-24s on RCM.

25BG despatched 2 B-26s and a Mosquito on PR Paris area, and 2 Mosquitoes (1 aborted) on H2X PR NW Germany.

Glenn Miller and the American Band of the AEF he conducted played at USAAF installations in England between July and October 1944. On the occasion of 466BG's 100th Mission Party he was at Attlebridge. After the show Capt John Woolnough, a lead B-24 pilot, spotted Miller talking to the Chaplain in the Officers' Club and summoned courage to ask if he would pose for a photograph that Woolnough could send to a brother who was an avid fan of the great musician. Miller agreed provided it was taken in some private place to avoid a deluge of similar requests. All the doors to adjacent rooms were found to be locked with the exception of the latrine. Miller was apparently much amused at the makeshift studio which undoubtedly provided the most extraordinary location for any photograph of this much photographed man. The tops of the urinals can be seen behind Major Miller (l) and Capt Woolnough (r). (J. Woolnough)

19 AUGUST 1944

Weather prevented offensive operations. 7PG despatched 8 F-5s and 4 Spitfires (4 a/c aborted) on PR Germany and France. 25BG despatched 2 Mosquitoes to Germany, 2 to Brest area, 1 to Baltic, 1 to Italy; and 2 B-17s UK/Atlantic; all on WR.

19/20AUGUST 1944

25BG despatched 1 H2X Mosquito to Bremen, MIA.

20 AUGUST 1944

25BG despatched 1 Mosquito to France/Belgium on WR; and 1 B-17 in WR UK/Atlantic. 1 Mosquito MIA.

21 AUGUST 1944

25BG despatched 1 Mosquito on WR France/Belgium and 1 B-17 on WR UK/Atlantic. A 7PG F-5 returned from Soviet Union.

Each of the Strategic Air Depots serving the Bomb Divisions had manufacturers' representatives to deal with tricky technical problems and monitor their company's product in service. At Honington Boeing's man was Bob Sturges (right) here inspecting the wing tip vents introduced on B-17s to dispel the dangerous fumes from the Tokyo Tanks: 22 August.

The most disastrous crash involving an 8AF aircraft occurred on 23 August when B-24H 42-50291 trying to land at the big air depot at Warton during a storm overshot and hit the village school and an adjacent café at Freckleton. A total of 58 people were killed or died of injuries including 35 children in the school. Men worked into the night shifting rubble in the hope of finding survivors. The bomber had been on a test flight.

22 AUGUST 1944

25BG despatched 3 Mosquitoes on WR France, Germany and UK, and 2 B-17 on WR UK/Atlantic.

23 AUGUST 1944

Despatched		Effective	Target	Bombs Tonnage	E/A	Losses MIA	E	Dam	Casualties KIA	WIA	MIA
			FIGHTER-BOMBER								
P-47	163	142	ST.OMER TO REIMS	21.0	0	0	0	2	0	0	0

REMARKS: Weather continued to prevent bomber operations. The four P-47 groups – 56FG, 78FG, 353FG, 356FG – carried out attacks on rail transportation in northern France without loss.

OTHER OPERATIONS: 7PG despatched 6 F-5s (1 aborted) on PR France and Germany, 1 F-5 MIA Germany. 25BG despatched 3 Mosquitoes (aborted) to France and Germany; and 3 B-17s on Atlantic WR. ASR despatched 6 P-47s on patrols. 2 P-47s on radio-relay. 1 F-5 MIA Germany.

23/24 AUGUST 1944

8AF 567 NIGHT LEAFLET OPERATION

NLS B-17, 6 despatched, 6 effective; France and Belgium.

25BG despatched B-26 and a Mosquito on flash photo sorties; France, and 1 Mosquito on abortive H2X PR sortie.

24 AUGUST 1944

8AF 568

	Despatched		Effective	Target		Bombs Tonnage	E/A	Losses MIA	E	Dam	Casualties KIA	WIA	MIA
2BD	B-24	433	99	BRUNSWICK/ QUERUM A/I	(P)	280.5	0–0–1	5	1	183	0	1	54
			125	BRUNSWICK/ WAGGUM A/I	(P)	313.7	0–0–1						
			72	HANNOVER/ LANGENHAGEN A/I	(P)	211.2							
			88	MISBURG O/I	(P)	218.0		5	1	183			
			5	T/O		14.0							
1BD	B-17	451	30	KOLLEDA A/F	(P)	75.0	10–3–3	16	2	189	3	39	148
			129	WEIMAR	(P)	303.1							
			185	MERSEBURG O/I	(P)	436.8							
			11	NORDHAUSEN A/F	(O)	27.5							
			11	VORDEN A/F	(O)	27.5							
			10	LEIPZIG	(O)	25.0							
			2	STADE A/F	(O)	5.0							
			37	GOSLAR A/F	(O)	92.0							
			7	T/O		16.9							

continued on facing page

	Despatched		Effective	Target		Bombs Tonnage	E/A	Losses MIA	E	Dam	Casualties KIA	WIA	MIA
3BD	B-17	383	139	BRÜX O/I	(P)	310.9							
			135	RUHLAND O/I	(P)	293.4							
			65	FREITAL O/I	(P)	161.5		3	1	143	1	5	18
			65	FREITAL O/I	(P)	161.5							
			15	T/O		32.8							
	B-24	52	43	KIEL/WALTHER	(P)	124.0		2	1	32	0	0	27
			3	HEMMINGSTEDT A/F	(O)	9.0							
			2	T/O		5.0							
TOTALS:		1319	1213			2982.8	10–3–4	26	5	547	4	45	247
VIII FC													
	P-38	48	248	ESCORT 2BD			2–0–0	0		0	0	0	0
	P-47	148					8–0–0	0		0	0	0	0
	P-51	90					(G)	2		2	0	0	1
	P-51	152	121	ESCORT 1BD			4–0–1	0		0	0	0	0
	P-47	48	240	ESCORT 3BD B-17			4–0–0	0		0	0	0	0
	P-51	236					6–0–0(G)	2		1	0	0	2
	P-51	17	17	ESCORT 3BD B-24				0		0	0	0	0
TOTALS:		739	626				10–0–1 14–0–0(G)	4		3	0	0	3

REMARKS: Visual attacks on strategic targets in Germany with some PFF on T/Os. Oil and aircraft industries and an armaments factory were primaries. All bomb groups participated. Bomb group losses:– 1BD – 92BG – 1, 303BG – 2, 305BG – 6, 379BG – 2, 401BG – 3, 457BG – 2; 2BD – 44BG – 1, 389BG – 1, 446BG – 1, 448BG – 1, 491BG – 1; 3BD – 34BG – 2, 95BG – 1, 96BG – 1, 388BG – 1. The 389BG B-24 and a 34BG B-24 landed Sweden. B/d 96BG B-17 ditched 15 miles off Lowestoft, 9 saved. On return b/d 34BG B-24 abandoned and cr. on house at Holt, crew safe. 448BG B-24 hit by bomb from another a/c c/l base on return. Last mission of 3BD B-24s. 3 B/d B-17s Cat E – 92BG, 95BG and 305BG.

All Fighter groups operating. Fighter group e/a credits:– 4FG – 2, 353FG – 2, 357FG – 2, 364FG – 4. Fighter group losses:– 4FG – 2, 55FG – 1, 339FG – 1. A 4FG pilot MIA, baled 60 miles E off Gt Yarmouth and rescued next day.

OTHER OPERATIONS: 7PG despatched 6 F-5s and 4 Spitfires on PR France and Germany. 25BG despatched 45 Mosquitoes on WR Germany, France and Belgium, 4 Mosquitoes to scout for bombers, and 2 B-17s on Atlantic/UK WR. 1SF despatched 8 P-51 to scout for 1BD. ASR despatched 22 P-47s on patrol.

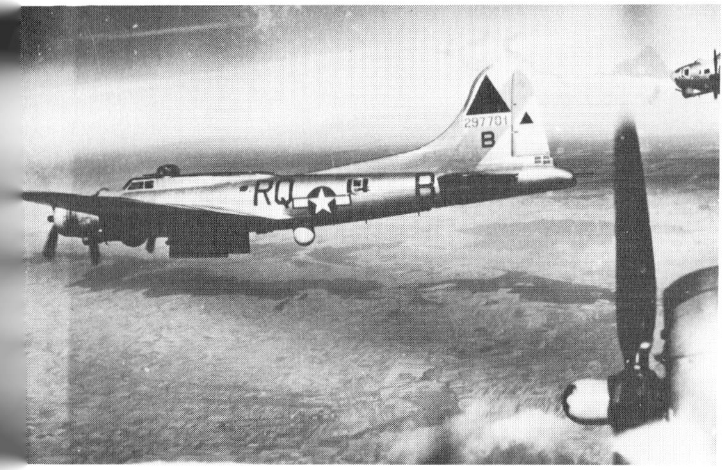

Bomb doors open, 'Honey Bucket' down, *Nadine* approaches Weimar on 24 August. Although the bombing was visual it was practice for the 'mickey ship' to have its radar working in case cloud intervened during the bomb run. There were sufficient H2X B-17s available in August for most groups to have their own pathfinders and not depend solely on the PFF unit set up in each combat wing. 351BG supplied PFF aircraft for the whole 94th Combat Wing, hence the absence of the group letter J. The small triangle on the rudder was an unofficial squadron marking.

The fire hazard in aircraft is well illustrated by the remains of this new Fortress, 44-6485, just received by 401BG, undergoing an acceptance check, 23 August. Mechanics working in the bomb bay caused an electrical spark which ignited escaping oxygen. Fire fighting foam could not extinguish the blaze before irreparable damage was done.

24/25 AUGUST 1944

8AF 569 NIGHT LEAFLET OPERATION

NLS B-17, 1 despatched, 1 effective; Brest.

25 AUGUST 1944

	Despatched		Effective	Target		Bombs Tonnage	E/A	Losses MIA	E	Dam	Casualties KIA	WIA	MIA
2BD	B-24	435	116	ROSTOCK A/I	(P)	311.5		5	2	55	0	5	64
			81	LÜBECK A/I	(P)	196.5							
			106	SCHWERIN A/I	(P)	256.2							
			11	GROSSENBRODE A/F	(O)	27.5							
			91	WISMAR A/I	(P)	219.2							
			4	T/O		11.0							
3BD	B-17	380	179	RECHLIN EXP STA	(P)	436.3		8	1	182	0	10	64
			169	PÖLITZ O/I	(P)	384.5							
			6	T/O		14.0							
1BD	B-17	376	146	PEENEMÜNDE EXP STA	(P)	365.5		5		75	1	9	45
			73	ANKLAM A/F	(p)	181.0							
			108	NEUBRANDENBURG A/F	(P)	177.5							
			21	PAROW A/F	(O)	52.5							
			5	T/O		12.5							
8AF 571 AZON													
2BD	B-24	10	10	MOERDIJK BK		20.0		0	0	0	0	0	0
8AF 572													
1BD	B-17	38	31	HENIN LITTARD C/P	(P)	89.0			0	0	0	0	0
2BD	B-24	69	17	TERTRE C/P		41.5							
			10	LA LOUVIERE C/P	(P)	30.0			0	24	0	4	0
			18	WILLERBROECK C/P	(P)	54.0							
			12	TILLER/LIEGE C/P	(P)	36.0							
			4	ST.TROND A/F	(O)	12.0							
			1	T/O		3.0							
TOTALS:		1308	1219			2911.2	0	18	3	336	1	28	159

VIII FC

Despatched		Effective	Target	Bombs Tonnage	E/A	Losses MIA	E	Dam	Casualties KIA	WIA	MIA
P-47	98	243	ESCORT 2BD 8AF 570		11–2– 3	0					
P-51	168					1					
P-47	49	215	ESCORT 3BD		4–0– 2	0					
P-51	193				(G)	4					
P-47	46	171	ESCORT 1BD 8AF 570		36–0–28	0					
P-51	154				(G)	2					
P-47	36	36	ESCORT *AZON* 8AF 571			0					
P-38	44	152	ESCORT 8AF 572			0					
P-51	128					0					
TOTALS:	916	817			11–2–3 40–0–30(G)	7	0	7	0	0	6

REMARKS: Mission 570 was a major operation against aircraft component plants, Luftwaffe experimental stations, and the synthetic oil industry. Visual bombing at primaries. All bomb groups except 93BG participated. (34BG and 493BG now stood down to convert to B-17.) Bomb group losses:– 1BD – 92BG – 4, 457BG – 1; 2BD – 446BG – 2, 453BG – 1, 458BG – 1, 489BG – 1; 3BD – 95BG – 4, 96BG – 1, 388BG – 1, 447BG – 1, 487BG – 1. MIA a/c in Sweden – 92BG – 2, 95BG – 1, 453BG – 1, 457BG – 1, 489BG – 1. B/d 447BG B-17 ditched 60 miles W of Haarlem, 9 saved. B/d 467BG B-24 c/l Belton on return. 452BG B-17 and 446BG B-24 Cat E bases. Mission 571 was flown by 458BG *Azon* force but target missed. Mission 572, visual attacks on liquid oxygen and ammonia plants in Belgium and northern France flown by B-17 groups of 94CBW with 303BG leads and B-24s of 93BG, 389BG, 458BG.

All Fighter groups active. Fighter group e/a credits:– 4FG – 3, 355FG – 2, 361FG – 3, 479FG – 7. Fighter group losses:– 4FG – 1, 20FG – 1, 352FG – 1, 357FG – 2, 364FG – 2. The MIA 357FG a/c down in Sweden. The 352FG pilot baled 100 miles NE off Gt Yarmouth, rescued.

OTHER OPERATIONS: 7PG despatched 12 F-5s and 5 Spitfires on PR Germany and France. 25BG despatched 4 Mosquitoes to scout for bombers, 5 Mosquitoes on WR Continent, and 2 B-17s on WR Atlantic/UK. 1SF despatched 7 P-51s to scout for 1BD. ASR despatched 34 P-47s on patrols and 15 P-51s also on sea search. 36BS despatched 6 B-24s on RCM. 6 P-47s, 4 P-51s, 3 B-17s on radio-relay.

25/26 AUGUST 1944

8AF 573 NIGHT LEAFLET OPERATION

NLS B-17, 6 despatched, 6 effective; France and Belgium.

492BG despatched 1 C-47 on *Carpetbagger* operations.

8AF 574 482BG despatched 3 B-17s on radar test. Also dropped leaflets.

6 B-24s on night RCM mission. 25BG despatched 1 Mosquito and 3 B-26s on night PR over France and 1 Mosquito on H2X scope sortie Germany.

26 AUGUST 1944

8AF 575

	Despatched		Effective	Target		Bombs Tonnage	E/A	Losses MIA	E	Dam	Casualties KIA	WIA	MIA
3BD	B-17	359	27	KERANDIEU C/B	(P)	68.3		0	3	4	18	0	0
			35	BREST/PTE DE ST.MATHIEU	(P)	106.0							
			20	BREST/ILE LONGUE C/B	(P)	38.0							
			7	BREST/PONSCORF C/B	(P)	13.1							
			9	BREST/KERVINIOV C/B	(P)	16.7							
			21	CORNOVAILLES C/B	(P)	38.8							
			18	BREST/PTE DES ESPAGNOLES III		31.8							
			21	BREST/PTE DES ESPAGNOLES II		39.9							
8AF 576													
2BD	B-24	109	41	LUDWIGSHAFEN C/I	(P)	105.5		7	0	53	2	3	70
			33	EHRANG M/Y	(S)	93.7							
			8	KONS/KARTHAUS M/Y	(S)	24.0							
			11	ALZEY	(O)	23.5							
			2	T/O		5.2							
1BD	B-17	259	89	GELSENKIRCHEN/ BUER O/R	(P)	158.8		3	0	89	0	5	26
			85	GELSENKIRCHEN/ NORDSTERN O/R	(P)	94.2							
			19	DEELEN A/F	(S)	36.0							
			11	T/O		2.2							
2BD	B-24	220	71	SALZBERGEN O/R	(P)	216.5		0	0	2	0	0	0
			36	EMMERICH O/R	(P)	102.5							
			73	DÜLMEN F/D	(P)	219.2							
			36	EINDHOVEN A/F	(S)	106.0							
8AF 577 *AZON*													
	B-24	10	9	MOERDIJK R/B	(P)	0		0	0	0	0	0	0
8AF 578													
1BD	B-17	37	0	BELGIUM C/I	(P)	0		0	0	0	0	0	0
8AF 579 MICRO H TEST													
	B-17	3	3	SPECIAL BOMB TEST MEAULTE A/I	(P)	6.0		0	0	0	0	0	0
TOTALS:		997	685			1545.9	0	10	3	148	20	8	96
VIII FC													
	P-51	49	48	ESCORT 3BD				1					
	P-51	81	77	ESCORT 20CBW			1–0–0(G)	0					
	P-47	48	159	ESCORT 1BD				0					
	P-51	141											
	P-38	50	129	ESCORT 2BD MAIN				1	0	0	0	0	1
	P-47	36						0	0	0	0	0	0
	P-51	46						1	1	0	0	0	1

continued on next page

26 AUGUST 1944 *(contd.)*

Type	Despatched	Effective	Target	Bombs Tonnage	E/A	Losses MIA	E	Dam	Casualties KIA	WIA	MIA
P-47	183		FIGHTER-BOMBER TRANSPORT TARGETS	54.0	1–0–0	2		9	0	1	1
P-51	206		BELGIUM, E FRANCE & W GERMANY			7	0	6	0	0	7
P-51	32	32	ESCORT *AZON*			0	0	0	0	0	0
P-47	7	7	ESCORT *BATTY*			0	0	0	0	0	0
P-51	18	18	ESCORT 8AF 579			0	0	0	0	0	0
TOTALS:	897	833		54.0	1–0–0 1–0–0(G)	12	1	15	0	1	10

REMARKS: Mission 575 was an attack on gun batteries in Brest area by all 3BD B-17 groups. Mission 576 was the main operation of the day with oil refineries, fuel stores and chemical works as primaries. Ludwigshafen Force composed of 20CBW groups; all 1BD less 351BG, 457BG, 303BG went to Gelsenkirchen and bombed visually; the other 2BD B-24 groups attacked oil refineries. Bomb group losses:– 2BD – 446BG – 3, 448BG – 4; 1BD – 306BG – 1, 379BG – 1, 384BG – 1. MIA 379BG B-17 ditched 60 miles W. off Haarlem, 2 rescued. Two 390BG B-17s collided during assembly and cr. Weston, Herts killing 14 crewmen, and 2 civilians in a house struck by wreckage. B/d 388BG B-17 c/l Ermington, 4 k. Mission 577 was flown by 458BG to attack a bridge with *Azon* bombs but cloud prevented attack. Mission 578 was also cover for *Batty* No 3 with 1 B-17 with TV bombs (plus a support team of 1 B-17, 1 P-38 and 7 P-47s) being frustrated by cloud over selected targets in Holland. 94CBW groups flew 578 but weather prevented attacks on liquid oxygen plants at La Louviere, Torte and Willebroeck.

All Fighter groups operated. Fighter group e/a credits:– 353FG – 1. Fighter group losses:– 55FG – 5, 78FG – 1, 339FG – 1, 353FG – 1, 355FG – 1, 361FG – 2, 479FG – 1. The 339FG and 353FG pilots both baled and were rescued from North Sea. 364FG P-51 cr. on t/o base, pilot safe. Exploding ammo train destroyed 1 361FG P-51.

OTHER OPERATIONS: 7PG despatched 30 F-5s and 9 Spitfires to France and Germany. 35BG despatched 4 Mosquitoes to scout for bombers, 3 Mosquitoes on WR Continent, and 1 B-17 and 1 B-24 WR Atlantic/UK. 37 P-38s and P-51s on ASR searches. 1 P-51 MIA. 1SF despatched 5 P-51s to scout for 1BD. 1 B-17, 2 P-47s and 6 P-51s on radio-relays.

26/27 AUGUST 1944

8AF 582 NIGHT LEAFLET OPERATION

NLS B-17, 6 despatched, 6 effective; France and Belgium.

8AF 581 RCM

36BS B-24, 7 despatched, 7 effective; jamming in aid of RAF. BC.

25BG despatched 2 B-26s and 1 Mosquito on night PR France.

8AF 580 MICRO H TEST

482BG despatched 3 B-17s on test operations. Leaflets also dropped by the 2 a/c effective.

27 AUGUST 1944

8AF 583 & 584

	Type	Despatched	Effective	Target		Bombs Tonnage	E/A	Losses MIA	E	Dam	Casualties KIA	WIA	MIA
3BD	B-17	426	5	AUSUM A/F	(O)	11.5		2	0	16	0	0	9
			1	FLENSBURG M/Y	(O)	2.5							
			4	T/O		10.0							
1BD	B-17	371	60	ESBJERG A/F	(O)	147.5		1	2	54	1	5	10
			37	EMDEN M/Y & DOCKS	(O)	92.5							
			34	WILHELMSHAVEN	(O)	78.5							
			11	HELIGOLAND	(O)	27.5							
			1	ISLAND OF SYLT	(O)	2.5							
			1	ISLAND OF FANØ	(O)	2.5							
2BD	B-24	406	34	HELIGOLAND	(O)	98.0		0	0	3	0	0	0
TOTALS:		1203	188			473.0	0	3	2	73	1	5	19
VIII FC													
	P-51	194	180	ESCORT 3BD				3	1	2	1	0	3
	P-51	167	156	ESCORT 1BD			1–0–0		1	9	0	0	7
							1–0–0(G)	7	0	1	0	0	0
	P-38	50	169	ESCORT 2BD				0	0	0	0	0	0
	P-51	134						0	0	7	0	0	0
	P-47	326	316	FIGHTER-BOMBER TRANSPORT E. FRANCE		95.0	14–0–4(G)	1			0	0	1
TOTALS		871	821			95.0	1–0–0 15–0–4(G)	11	2	19	1	0	11

REMARKS: Major operation against Berlin and strategic targets in north and central Germany involving all operational bomber groups except 384BG. First mission of 490BG with B-17s. Very high cloud was encountered over Denmark and north Germany and bombers were recalled. Some attacked T/Os. Bomb group losses:– 1BD – 303BG – 1; 3BD – 385BG – 1, 447BG – 1. MIA 385BG a/c ditched, 9 saved. A 379BG cr. Slipton during assembly, crew baled. B/d 303BG cr. Badingham, crew baled (tail gunner over e/t).

All Fighter groups active. Fighter group e/a claims:– 359FG – 1. Fighter group losses:– 20FG – 4, 352FG – 2, 359FG – 1, 56FG – 1, 339FG – 1, 364FG – 2. A 55FG P-51 cr. base, pilot killed. CO 20FG baled over sea at Danish coast, picked up by fishing boat and made POW. On return, 364FG P-51 cr. landing base, pilot safe.

OTHER OPERATIONS: 7PG despatched 15 F-5s on PR France, Holland and Germany. 25RG despatched 3 Mosquitoes to scout for bombers 2 Mosquitoes on WR Germany/UK and 2 B-17s on Atlantic/UK WR. ASR despatched 42 P-47s on patrols with 18 P-51s as escorts. 2 P-38s, 6 P-47s, 4 P-51s and 2 B-17s (with 4 P-51s as escort) on radio-relays. 1SF despatched 9 P-51s to scout for 1BD.

27/28 AUGUST 1944

8AF 585 NIGHT LEAFLET OPERATION

NLS B-17, 6 despatched, 6 effective; France and Holland.

482BG despatched 2 B-17s on scope photo operation.

36BS despatched 6 B-24s on RCM.

28 AUGUST 1944

Despatched		Effective	Target	Bombs Tonnage	E/A	Losses MIA	E	Dam	Casualties KIA	WIA	MIA
			FIGHTER-BOMBER TRANSPORTATION								
P-38	49	174	TARGETS	81.1	12–1–0	1	3	1	0	0	1
P-47	165		GERMAN/FRENCH		3–0–4(G)	0	0	1	0	0	0
P-51	46		BORDER			0	0	0	0	0	0
			TRANSPORTATION								
P-38	46	143	TARGETS	83.9	4–0–0	0	0	0	0	0	0
P-47	149		FRANCE, BELGIUM, HOLLAND		3–0–2(G)	3	0	2	0	0	3
P-51	380	un-reported	TRANS. STRAFING – FRENCH/GERMAN BORDER		3–0–0 5–0–2(G)	16	0	12	0	0	15
TOTALS:	835	317 plus		165.0	19–1–0 11–0–8(G)	20	3	16	0	0	19

REMARKS: Fighter-bomber and strafing attacks on rail targets in Holland, Belgium, France and Germany. All groups except 361FG. Heavy loss to ground fire. Fighter group e/a credits: 55FG – 2, 56FG – 6, 78FG – 1, 353FG – 9, 355FG – 1, 479FG – 2. Fighter group losses:– 4FG – 5, 20FG – 1, 78FG – 2, 339FG – 1, 355FG – 8, 356FG – 1, 359FG – 1, 479FG – 1. The 339FG pilot baled over sea near Margate, rescued. A 479FG P-38 c/l Friston, pilot safe. Two 479FG P-38s c/l Allied airstrips, France, pilots safe.

OTHER OPERATIONS: 7PG despatched, 1 F-5 on PR Brest area. 25BG despatched 1 Mosquito on WR Brest and 1 B-17 WR Atlantic/UK. ASR despatched 21 P-47 on patrols. 2 P-38s, 2 P-47s, 2 P-51s and 1 B-17 on radio-relays.

28/29 AUGUST 1944

8AF 588 NIGHT LEAFLET OPERATION

NLS B-17, 6 despatched, 6 effective; France and Holland.

29 AUGUST 1944

Despatched		Effective	Target	Bombs Tonnage	E/A	Losses MIA	E	Dam	Casualties KIA	WIA	MIA
			FIGHTER-BOMBER TRANS. TARGETS								
P-38	44	104	FRANCE, BELGIUM,	53.3	20–0–7(G)	0	0	0	0	0	0
P-47	158		GERMANY			3	0	8	0	0	3
TOTALS:	202	104		53.3	20–0–7(G)	3	0	8	0	0	3

REMARKS: Continuing bad weather restricted operations. Fighter-bomber attacks against rail targets in France and Belgium conducted by the four P-47 and single P-38 groups of VIII FC. Fighter group losses:– 353FG – 2, 356FG – 1. One P-47 of 353FG lost when e/a it was strafing exploded.

OTHER OPERATIONS: 25BG despatched 2 B-17s on Atlantic/UK WR. ASR despatched 11 P-47s on patrols. 2 P-47s on radio-relays.

29/30 AUGUST 1944

36BS despatched 4 B-24s on RCM.

30 AUGUST 1944

8AF 590

	Despatched		Effective	Target		Bombs Tonnage	E/A	Losses MIA	E	Dam	Casualties KIA	WIA	MIA
	B-17	159	107	PAS DE CALAIS V/S		556.7		0	0	22	0	0	0
	B-24	145	108	PAS DE CALAIS V/S									
8AF 591													
1 & 3BD	B-17	637	282	KIEL	(P)	690.0		0	1	136	0	0	0
			327	BREMEN	(P)	753.0							
			4	T/O		9.0							
TOTALS:		941	823			2008.7	0	0	1	158	0	0	0

30 AUGUST 1944

VIII FC

	Despatched		Effective	Target	Bombs Tonnage	E/A	Losses MIA	E	Dam	Casualties KIA	WIA	MIA
	P-51	16	16	ESCORT *NOBALL*			0	0	0	0	0	0
	P-51	294	258	ESCORT 8AF 591			0	0	0	0	0	0
TOTALS:		310	274			0	0	0	0	0	0	0

REMARKS: Mission 590 was an attack on V-1 launching sites using GH and H2X methods by 41CBW groups and 401BG of 1BD and 2CBW, 14CBW groups and 93BG, 466BG of 2BD. Mission 591 was a PFF attack on the ports of Kiel and Bremen by 1CBW, 40CBW groups and 351BG, 457BG of 1BD and all 3BD B-17 groups. 486BG B-17 Cat E.

Fighter escort for 8AF 590 provided by 4FG and for 8AF 591 by 20FG, 55FG, 339FG, 352FG, 357FG, 359FG. No claims or losses by bombers and fighters.

OTHER OPERATIONS: 25BG despatched 2 Mosquitoes to scout for bombers, 2 Mosquitoes on WR Brest area and 1 on WR Bremen, and 2 B-17s on WR Atlantic/UK. ASR despatched 8 P-47s on routine patrols. 2 B-17s with 8 P-51s were sent on special operation to Italy but 5 landed in liberated France. 2 P-51s and 2 B-17s on radio-relay.

30/31 AUGUST 1944

8AF 592 NIGHT LEAFLET OPERATION

NLS B-17, 6 despatched, 6 effective; France and Belgium.

36 despatched 6 B-24s on RCM. 2 P-38s on intruder ops.

At the beginning of September, 96CBW groups began flying fuel and supplies from England to US forces in France, using mostly war weary B-24s. War trophies and wine filled many an aircraft on the return journey.

31 AUGUST 1944

No operations by bombers or fighters. 7PG despatched 1 F-5 on PR and 1 F-5 on WR to NW France. 25BG despatched 2 Mosquitoes on PR Brest, 2 Mosquitoes on WR France and Germany and 1 B-24 on Atlantic WR.

31 AUGUST/1 SEPTEMBER 1944

8AF 594 NIGHT LEAFLET OPERATION

NLS B-17, 6 despatched, 6 effective; France.

482BG despatched 3 B-17s on scope photo operations.

492BG despatched 37 C-47s and B-24s on *Carpetbagger* operations.

1 SEPTEMBER 1944

8AF 595

Despatched		Effective	Target		Bombs Tonnage	E/A	Losses MIA	E	Dam	Casualties KIA	WIA	MIA
B-17	679	1	HALLACH	(O)	3.0		0	2	5	17	2	0
B-24	294	0			0		0	1	0	13	0	0

8AF 597 *AZON*

B-24	12	12	RAVENSTEIN R/B	(P)	24.0		0	0	0	0	0	0

8AF 599 MICRO H TEST

482BG B-17	3	3	NIVELLES FUEL DUMP	(P)	3.0		0	0	0	0	0	0
TOTALS:	988	16			30.0	0	0	3	5	30	2	0

VIII FC

P-38	47	508	ESCORT BOMBERS			0	0	0	0	0	0
P-51	496					3	1	1	0	0	2
P-47	273	265	FIGHTER-BOMBERS R/R N & NE FRANCE	70.0	5–0–2 5–0–2 (G)	3	1	28	0	0	3
P-47	33	33	SWEEP BRUSSELS/ ANTWERP AREA	0	0	0	0	0	0	0	0
P-51	15	15	ESCORT *AZON*			0	0	0	0	0	0
P-51	2	2	ESCORT 8AF 599			0	0	0	0	0	0
TOTALS:	866	823		70.0	5–0–2 5–0–2(G)	6	2	29	0	0	5

REMARKS: Mission 595 was despatched to targets at Ludwigshafen, Forêt de Haguenan, Gustavsburg, Mainz and Hallach. Mission recalled as leading 3BD bombers encountered high cloud over France. Groups claiming credit sorties:– 94BG, 95BG, 96BG, 100BG, 390BG, 490BG. Two 490BG B-17s collided and crashed in liberated France. PFF 466BG B-24 cr. t/o Horsham St. Faith A/F, 12 k. Mission 597 was an attack on a bridge in Holland by 458BG using *Azon* bombs. Mission 599 was a Micro H mission to attack a fuel dump in Bois de la Haussiere, Belgium.

All Fighter groups operating. The four P-47 groups each despatched two forces to bomb and strafe ground targets behind the enemy battle front. Fighter group e/a credits: 78FG – 5, Fighter group losses:– 55FG – 1, 78FG – 2, 356FG – 1, 359FG – 1, 364FG – 1. 3 352FG P-51s f/l in liberated France. Pilot of 364FG P-51 MIA baled over North Sea, rescued. Pilot of 359FG P-51 baled over sea but lost. B/d 56FG P-47 Cat E base.

OTHER OPERATIONS: 7PG despatched 20 F-5s on PR Belgium coast, France and Germany. 25BG despatched 1 Mosquito on PR Brest area, 3 Mosquitoes on WR Belgium, Holland and N France, 2 Mosquitoes to scout for bombers and 1 B-24 on WR UK/Atlantic. ASR despatched 20 P-47s on patrols, 2 P-51s also on ASR. 2 P-38s, 6 P-47s, 6 P-51s and 1 B-17 on radio-relays. 2BD B-24s began flying fuel from UK to France for US Army.

1/2 SEPTEMBER 1944

492BG despatched 44 B-24s (13 aborted) on *Carpetbagger* ops.

25BG despatched 2 Mosquitoes on H2X PR Germany, 1 aborted.

36BS despatched 4 B-24s on RCM.

482BG despatched 3 B-17s on scope photo mission.

2 SEPTEMBER 1944

8AF 596

Despatched		Effective	Target	Bombs Tonnage	E/A	Losses MIA	E	Dam	Casualties KIA	WIA	MIA
P-47	36	34	STRAFING BELGIUM		0	0	2	7	0	0	0

REMARKS: Only offensive activity was a fighter sweep by 56FG. Two b/d 56FG P-47s c/l on return, one at Manston A/F – hit pole and tree while strafing.

OTHER OPERATIONS: 25BG despatched 2 Mosquitoes to the Continent on WR (one aborted) and 1 B-24 and 1 B-17 on Atlantic/UK WR. ASR despatched 8 P-47s on patrols. 2 P-47s on radio-relay.

2/3 SEPTEMBER 1944

801BG despatched 2 C-47s on *Carpetbagger* to France.

3 SEPTEMBER 1944

8AF 601

	Despatched		Effective	Target		Bombs Tonnage	E/A	Losses MIA	E	Dam	Casualties KIA	WIA	MIA
3BD	B-17	404	393	G/B, BREST AREA	(P)	1037.9		2	0	13	0	0	16
8AF 602													
1BD	B-17	345	325	LUDWIGSHAFEN/ OPAU O/I	(P)	969.0		1	0	103	0	0	9
			1	T/O		3.0							
			5	LEAFLETS									
TOTALS:		749	724			2009.9	0	3	0	126	0	0	25

VIII FC

		Despatched	Effective	Target	Bombs Tonnage	E/A	Losses MIA	E	Dam	KIA	WIA	MIA
	P-51	16	15	ESCORT 3BD			0	0	0	0	0	0
	P-38	50	49	FIGHTER-BOMBER BREST AREA – 8AF 601			0	0	0	0	0	0
	P-51	254	233	ESCORT 1BD		7–0–1	1	0	2	0	0	1
	P-47	127	125	STRAFING T/T BELGIUM		0–0–1 (G) 0	1	1	18	0	1	1
TOTALS:		447	422		0	7–0–1 0–0–1(G)	2	1	20	0	1	1

REMARKS: Mission 601 was a visual attack by B-17s on gun emplacements in the Brest area. All 3BD Groups participated. Bomb group losses:– 100BG – 1, 452BG – 1. The 452BG a/c lost to flak over Channel Islands. Mission 602 was a PFF bombing of Ludwigshafen involving 1BD. Groups participating: all 1BD except 351BG. Bomb group losses:– 305BG – 1.

Fighter groups operating: 20FG, 55FG, 78FG, 352FG, 353FG, 356FG, 357FG, 359FG, 364FG, 479FG. Fighter group e/a credits: 55FG – 7. Fighter group losses:– 78FG – 1, 359FG – 1. Pilot of b/d 78FG P-47 baled over Manston. P-38 mission abandoned due to weather.

OTHER OPERATIONS: 7PG despatched 1 F-5 to Brest. 25BG despatched 4 Mosquitoes on WR France, Belgium and S. Germany and 2 B-17s on WR UK/Atlantic. 1SF despatched 9 P-51s to scout, 1 P-51 c/l France. ASR despatched 14 P-47s on patrols. 2 B-17s and 10 P-51s on radio-relay. 8AF 603 was *Aphrodite* using B-24 drone with US Navy crew drone and 9 support a/c and 15 P-51s for escort. 16 B-17s were despatched on a special operation. 61 B-24s delivered 183.0 tons freight to Orleans/Bricy A)F.

4 SEPTEMBER 1944

REMARKS: Bad weather prevented offensive operations. 25BG despatched 3 Mosquitoes on WR Brest/Paris/Atlantic, and 2 B-24s UK/Atlantic. 4 B-24s on *Truckin'* operation to Orleans/Bricy with 12 tons freight.

4/5 SEPTEMBER 1944

492BG despatched 40 B-24s and 4 C-47s on *Carpetbagger* operations.

5 SEPTEMBER 1944

8AF 605

	Despatched		Effective	Target		Bombs Tonnage	E/A	Losses MIA	E	Dam	Casualties KIA	WIA	MIA
3BD	B-17	218	203	STUTTGART A/I	(P)	464.0		2	0	109	1	5	18
			4	T/O		9.5							
1BD	B-17	303	277	LUDWIGSHAFEN O/I	(P)	723.9		2	0	163	2	11	18
			1	T/O		3.0							
2BD	B-24	218	183	KARLSRUHE M/Y	(P)	463.5		2	4	78	0	0	22
			2	T/O		4.0							
8AF 606													
3BD	B-17	143	143	BREST AREA	(P)	449.9		2	0	1	0	0	18
TOTALS:		882	813			2117.8	0	8	4	351	3	16	54

At Stuttgart on 5 September the 452BG dropped bombs on an intervalometer setting to obtain a long pattern strike on the Daimler-Benz aero-engine factory. The Fortress is *Lady Janet* in which two pilots would earn posthumous Medals of Honor on 9 November. (J. Archer)

Number 1 feathered, turbo on No.2 out and a flak punctured main tyre, 388BG's *Little Joe Jr.* comes to rest safely off Knettishall's runway 15. Relieved from noise and anxiety, a crew member unbuckles his harness in the afternoon sunshine, 5 September. (W. Duane)

VIII FC

Despatched		Effective	Target	Bombs Tonnage	E/A	Losses MIA	E	Dam	Casualties KIA	WIA	MIA
P-51	160	147	ESCORT STUTTGART		19–0– 0 14–0–27 (G)	2	1	4	0	0	2
P-51	155		ESCORT 1BD			1	0	2	0	0	1
P-38	48	48	STRAFING – T/T		0–0– 2	0	0	1	0	0	0
P-47	167	167	W. GERMANY		62–0–30 (G)	4	2	10	0	0	4
			FIGHTER-BOMBER								
P-38	40	67	HANAU/GIESSEN	5.0	2–0– 0	1	0	1	0	1	1
P-47	29		AREA		66–0–28 (G)	3	1	3	0	0	3
P-51	22	21	ESCORT 8AF 606			0	0	0	0	0	0
TOTALS:	621	450		5.0	21–0– 2 192–0–85(G)	11	4	21	0	1	11

REMARKS: Mission 605 went to SE Germany with attacks on an aero-engine plant, oil refinery and rail yards. Groups participating: 3BD, all 13CBW and 45CBW groups; 1BD – 91BG, 92BG, 303BG, 306BG, 351BG, 384BG, 398BG, 401BG; 2BD, all 2CBW, 14CBW and 96CBW groups. 1BD made PFF attack, 2BD and 3BD visual. Bomb group losses:– 1BD – 91BG – 1, 351BG – 1; 2BD – 389BG – 2; 3BD – 388BG – 1. 390BG – 1. One 389BG B-24 and the 390BG B-17 landed Switzerland. B/d 392BG B-24 c/l Le Bourget and 2 466BG B-24s also c/l France, crews safe apart from 2 men who baled. On return a 458BG B-24 c/l West Malling A/F. Mission 606, a visual attack on enemy positions around Brest was carried out by B-17s of 4CBW groups with 486BG, 490BG. Bomb group losses:– 486BG – 2 (collided over target). 458BG despatched 12 B-24s on *Azon* mission but recalled over UK.

All Fighter groups operating. Fighter group e/a credits:– 55FG – 15, 56FG – 8, 339FG – 2, 353FG – 1, 356FG – 1. Fighter group losses:– 55FG – 1, 56FG – 3, 78FG – 2, 339FG – 1, 353FG – 1, 356FG – 1, 364FG – 1, 479FG – 1. 4FG P-51 pilot baled over liberated France, safe. A Swiss Me 109 was shot down by P-51s near Dübendorf. 3 b/d 56FG P-47s c/l France, pilots safe.

OTHER OPERATIONS: 7PG despatched 1 F-5 to Holland, 1 Spitfire to Stuttgart on PR. 1 Spitfire MIA (shot down by Me 262 jet). 25BG despatched 3 Mosquitoes to scout for bombers, 4 Mosquitoes on WR UK/Continet, and 1 B-17 WR UK/Atlantic. 1SF despatched 7 P-51s to scout for 1BD. ASR despatched 18 P-47s on patrols. 2 B-17s, 2 P-38s, 4 P-47s, 12 P-51s on radio-relays. 88 B-24s on *Truckin'* mission carried 264 tons freight to France. 11 B-24s were scheduled for an *Azon* mission but were recalled after t/o.

INCIDENT

One of the many local modifications tried out was a gun switch for withholding fire from the two outer guns in each wing of a P-47, restricting fire to four machine guns when the pilot operated the stick trigger. The device was fitted to Col Gray's Thunderbolt when he led the 78th Group down to a strafe on 5 September 1944 after an escort to south-west Germany. His verdict on this combat test of the device was, 'I found it excellent against locos and other ground targets . . . and that four guns do the job and by saving ammo approximately twice as many targets can be attacked. If necessary all eight guns can be turned on.'

5/6 SEPTEMBER 1944

8AF 608 NIGHT LEAFLET OPERATION

NLS B-17, 8 despatched, 7 effective; Belgium, Holland, Germany.

492BG despatched 46 B-24s and 2 C-47s on *Carpetbagger* operations. 1 a/c MIA.

36 BS despatched 4 B-24s on RCM in support of RAF bombers.

25BG despatched 1 B-26 on PR France, and 2 Mosquitoes on H2X PR C and SE Germany.

6 SEPTEMBER 1944

8AF 607

Despatched		Effective	Target	Bombs Tonnage	E/A	Losses MIA	E	Dam	Casualties KIA	WIA	MIA
P-38	49	49	STRAFING TRANSPORTATION		0	1	0	5	0	0	1
P-47	165	165	TARGETS HOLLAND & W. GERMANY			3	0	7	0	0	3
TOTALS:	214	214		0	0	4	0	12	0	0	4

REMARKS: Only offensive operations by fighters. Sweeps in Rotterdam, Aachen and Koblenz areas. The four P-47s and single P-38 group participated. Fighter group losses:– 78FG – 3, 479FG – 1.

OTHER OPERATIONS: 7PG despatched 7 F-5s on PR France and Germany. 25BG despatched 3 Mosquitoes on WR France/Atlantic, 1 Mosquito WR Germany and 2 B-17s WR UK/Atlantic. ASR despatched 6 P-47s on patrols. 1 B-17, 2 P-38s and 4 P-47s on radio-relays. 70 B-24s on *Truckin'* operation; 210 tons freight to France. A 489BG B-24 cr. on t/o Orleans/Bricy, crew safe.

Quince Brown in the first of two P-47s named *Okie* used during his original tour. (via R. Vincent)

With crew chief Jensen, prior to a mission near the end of his first tour. (via R. Vincent)

THE OKLAHOMA ACE

One of the pilots missing from the fighter sweeps on 6 September 1944 was the man who started it all for the 8th Air Force – Quince L. Brown Jr. Back in July 1943 he had been involved in an air battle during which evasive action took him down to an altitude where the Thunderbolt was at a performance disadvantage. In such circumstances the favoured method of evading interception was to apply maximum power and speed home over the tree tops. This Brown did and being over the enemy's territory decided to shoot at anything he saw that constituted a military target. He shot up a gun emplacement and freight train, bringing home to Duxford evidence of the damage the eight 50s could inflict. This was the first time that the Thunderbolt had been used for strafing, albeit by chance, a task at which it would later excel.

Quince Brown didn't always have to run; it was usually his adversaries. As he learned his trade in the cockpit of a Thunderbolt he exhibited those qualities that were the mark of a good fighter pilot – decisive, alert, cool and aggressive. He became the top-scoring ace in his group, the 78th, which was rarely in an advantageous situation when it met the enemy. Good fortune played an undeniable part in positioning combatants in one piece of sky at the same time. However, when the enemy was on hand, Quince Brown acquitted himself well. In the 97 combat sorties of his first tour he took his 'kills' into double figures – most achieved while flying his personal P-47D named *Okie*. He shot down four enemy aircraft on 16 March 1944, the first occasion that an 8th Air Force pilot had been credited with such a score on a single mission. He was a superb pilot and much of his expertise could be attributed to a long period as an instructor at Randolph Field, Texas and Enid Field, Oklahoma. Commissioned in April 1941, Quince was celebrating his 24th birthday when the Japanese attacked Pearl Harbor on 7 December 1941, but he had to spend 19 months teaching other men to fly before going overseas to a combat theatre. Even then he was assigned to the training base at Atcham and three months were to pass before he finally reached a combat squadron.

On completion of his tour Quince Brown left Duxford for 30 days' leave back home in Bristow, Oklahoma. He had the opportunity to return to instructing, but volunteered to go back to the 78th Group for a second tour. He received a new P-47 which he nicknamed *Okie II* and promotion from Captain to Major. Further combats took his score of enemy aircraft to 13 air victories – he was the only man in the Group with a score in double figures at the time.

On the day of his loss, his 136th sortie, the 78th Group was briefed to strafe enemy installations in the Gemünd area. The weather was poor with only about three-quarters of a mile visibility although a solid overcast at some 2,000 ft offered a refuge if enemy defences were encountered. Brown was leading his squadron in the assigned target area when at approximately 1455 hrs he spotted Vogelsand airfield and radioed his intention of going to investigate. As the flight approached in line astern they met heavy ground fire. *Okie II* was seen to be hit by tracers and after crossing the airfield and climbing sharply to about 1,200 ft, Brown jettisoned the canopy and baled out. He was seen to land safely in a field at Schleiden near the town of Weirmuehle, and to run and hide in some long grass.

Apparently apprehended by a German civilian with a gun, Brown was taken prisoner. But before the military arrived he was shot in the back of the head at close range and killed. The civilian informed the German authorities that the US pilot had tried to escape, but in 1946 a War Crimes court found him guilty of murder and ordered an execution. In those final months of hostilities Quince Brown was one of many Allied fliers killed out of hand by irate civilians. Personal loss or the general devastation and casualties resulting from air attack generated intense hatred.

6/7 SEPTEMBER 1944

8AF 610

25BG despatched 1 Mosquito on H2X PR Hannover area.

482BG despatched 2 B-17s (1 aborted) on scope photo sorties.

36BS despatched 4 B-24s on RCM in support of RAF.

7 SEPTEMBER 1944

25BG despatched 2 Mosquitoes on WR France, and 2 B-24s on UK/Atlantic WR.

7/8 SEPTEMBER 1944

492BG despatched 40 B-24s on *Carpetbagger* ops.

8 SEPTEMBER 1944

8AF 611

	Despatched		Effective	Target		Bombs Tonnage	E/A	Losses MIA	E	Dam	Casualties KIA	WIA	MIA
1BD	B-17	384	348	LUDWIGSHAFEN/ OPAU O/I	(P)	1008.0		5	2	185	11	15	45
2BD	B-24	300	247	KARLSRUHE M/Y	(P)	664.7		4	0	92	7	9	29
			1	LUDWIGSHAFEN	(S)	3.0							
3BD	B-17	386	167	GUSTAVSBURG AV/I	(P)	543.2		1	1	132	0	3	9
			166	KASSEL O/D	(P)	380.8							
			23	T/O		48.2							
TOTALS:		1070	952			2647.9	0	10	3	409	18	18	83
VIII FC													
	P-51	95	88	ESCORT 1BD				0	0	0	0	0	0
	P-51	93	82	ESCORT 2BD				0	1	0	0	0	0
	P-51	161	144	ESCORT 3BD				0	0	0	0	0	0
	P-38	48	160	FIGHTER-BOMBER EAST OF RHINE – T/T		7.1	7–0–1 (G)	0	0	0	0	0	0
	P-47	157		STRAFING				1	0	9	0	1	1
	P-51	99	94	W. GERMANY			3–0–1 (G)	1	0	4	0	0	1
TOTALS:		653	568			7.1	10–0–2 (G)	2	1	13	0	1	2

REMARKS: Industrial targets in the Mainz and Ludwigshafen area. Attacks were mostly visual at primaries with some use of PFF at all. Bomb groups participating: 1BD – all groups except 385BG and 486BG (493BG first mission with B-17). Bomb group losses:– 1BD – 91BG – 1, 351BG – 1, 379BG – 2, 398BG – 1; 2BD – 389BG – 1, 392BG – 1, 453BG – 1, 466BG – 1; 3BD – 390BG – 1. The 453BG B-24 ditched, 4 saved. During assembly a 351BG cr. Langtoft Common, 8 k. Several damaged a/c landed on Continent. B/d 92BG B-17 c/l in France. 388BG B-17 cr. liberated France due to m/f, crew baled.

All Fighter groups except 364FG active. Fighter group losses:– 352FG – 1, 353FG – 1. Several fighters landed at Continental A/Fs On return, 361FG P-51 cr., pilot baled.

OTHER OPERATIONS: 7PG despatched 15 F-5s and 7 Spitfires on PR Brest and W. Germany. 1 F-5 and 1 Spitfire MIA. 25BG despatched 3 Mosquitoes to scout for bombers, 2 Mosquitoes on WR S and W France and 2 B-24s on WR Atlantic. 1SF despatched 7 P-51s to scout for 1BD. ASR despatched 8 P-47s on patrols. 12 P-51s, 4 P-47s and 2 P-38s on radio-relay. 110 B-24s on *Truckin'* missions Orleans/Bricy A/F with 330 tons freight.

8/9 SEPTEMBER 1944

8AF 615 NIGHT LEAFLET OPERATION

NLS B-17, 8 despatched, 7 effective: Low Countries, France and Germany.

36 BS despatched 4 B-24s on RCM.

492BG C-47 on *Carpetbagger* operation France.

25BG despatched 1 Mosquito on H2X PR Leipzig area.

9 SEPTEMBER 1944

8AF 613

	Despatched		Effective	Target		Bombs Tonnage	E/A	Losses MIA	E	Dam	Casualties KIA	WIA	MIA
3BD	B-17	72	68	OPERATION GRASSY 25 MILES S. OF BESANCON				0	0	0	0	0	0

8AF 614

	Despatched		Effective	Target		Bombs Tonnage	E/A	Losses MIA	E	Dam	Casualties KIA	WIA	MIA
1BD	B-17	419	387	MANNHEIM M/Y	(P)	1149.2		5	0	197	0	10	54
			2	T/O		3.0							
2BD	B-24	337	265	MAINZ M/Y	(P)	648.8		3	3	104	5	0	33
			24	WORMS M/Y	(O)	58.3							
			6	KOBLENZ	(O)	13.0							
3BD	B-17	384	251	DÜSSELDORF M/I	(P)	698.2		6	2	148	2	3	63
			11	LEVERKUSEN	(O)	27.5							
			12	BONN	(O)	30.0							
			16	T/O		40.0							
TOTALS:		1212	1042			2668.0	0	14	5	449	7	13	150
VIII FC													
	P-51	32	30	ESCORT 8AF 613				0	0	0	0	0	0
	P-51	152	140	ESCORT 1BD				0	0	0	0	0	0
	P-51	128	125	ESCORT 2BD				0	0	0	0	0	0
	P-51	155	142	ESCORT 3BD 8AF 614				1	0	0	0	0	0
	P-47	44	44	SWEEP UNGEN/MÜNSTER/ HALTERN AREAS			1–0–0 0–1–0 (G)	0					
	P-47	126	196	FIGHTER-BOMBER DUTCH ISLANDS/ BELGIUM AREAS		37.8	8–0–3	7	1	14	0	1	7
	P-51	77					5–0–2 (G)	1	1	3	0	0	0
TOTALS:		714	677			37.8	9–0–3 5–1–2(G)	9	2	17	0	1	7

REMARKS: Mission 613, operation *Grassy* was flown by 94BG and 447BG B-17s to drop 180 containers to French Resistance Fighters in Southern France. Mission 614 was against targets in Western Germany with primaries attacked by both visual and PFF means. Groups participating: all 1BD except 306BG; all 2BD except 93BG, 446BG; all 3BD except 4CBW groups. Bomb group losses:– 1BD – 91BG – 1, 303BG – 1, 305BG – 1, 379BG – 1, 401BG – 1; 2BD – 392BG – 1, 458BG – 1, 489BG – 1; 3BD – 390BG – 5, 490BG – 1. B/d 486BG B-17 cr. France. A 458BG B-24 cr. Crowland, crew baled. 491BG B-24 cr. after t/o, Stanford Battle area, 5 k. Some b/d a/c landed in liberated France. 2 445BG B-24s collided, 1 c/l Woodbridge A/F. Aborting 95BG B-17 cr. base, crew safe.

All Fighter groups except 355FG, 479FG operated. Fighter group e/a credits: 78FG – 8, 353FG – 1. Fighter group losses:– 4FG – 1, 55FG – 1, 56FG – 3, 78FG – 1, 356FG – 3. Pilot of 4FG P-51 MIA baled over sea, rescued. 361FG P-51 c/l near Liege. B/d 356FG P-47 Cat E.

OTHER OPERATIONS: 7PG despatched 24 F-5s and 3 Spitfires on PR Germany. 1 Spitfire MIA. 25BG despatched 2 Mosquitoes on WR Germany, 3 Mosquitoes scouting for bombers and 2 B-24s on WR UK/Atlantic. 1SF despatched 7 P-51 to scout for bombers. ASR despatched 28 P-47s on patrols. 1 B-17, 2 P-51s, 2 P-47s on radio-relays.

9/10 SEPTEMBER 1944

8AF 618 NIGHT LEAFLET OPERATION

NLS B-17. 7 despatched, 7 effective: Belgium, France, Germany.

492BG despatched 40 B-24s and C-47s on *Carpetbagger* operations.

36BS despatched 4 B-24s on RCM.

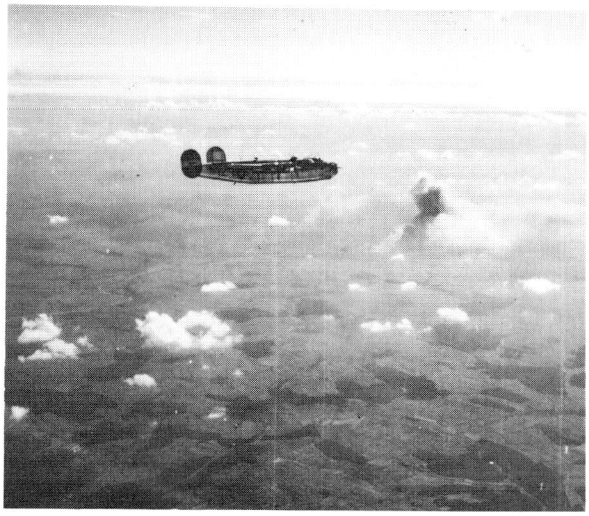

Dust and smoke funnel up from Ulm rail yards as 491BG leaves for home; 10 September.

Sunday afternoon sight-seeing for the French. Flak bursts sent 457BG's *You Never Know* out of control over Gaggenau on 10 September and two gunners, thinking the bomber doomed, jumped from the still open bomb bay. The pilot, Lt Hampton, managed to regain control and bring the damaged B-17 down in liberated France near Joigny without injury to the rest of the crew. Premature bale outs were a frequent occurrence and understandable when a crewman had seen a bomber spin down before any men could leave it. (via S. Blandin)

Smoke billows a mile high from a tank factory at Nürnberg, 10 September, as a 487BG Fortress makes for England.

10 SEPTEMBER 1944

8AF 619

	Despatched		Effective	Target		Bombs Tonnage	E/A	Losses MIA	E	Dam	Casualties KIA	WIA	MIA
2BD	B-24	388	247	ULM M/Y	(S)	630.8		1	1	65	1	2	10
			100	HEILBRONN M/Y	(S)	254.2							
			2	T/O		6.0							
3BD	B-17	385	60	FÜRTH A/C COMP. FAC.	(P)	145.5		3	0	147	0	7	28
			173	NÜRNBERG TANK FAC.	(P)	414.9							
			112	GIEBELSTADT A/F	(P)	279.7							
			13	DARMSTADT	(O)	31.7							
			8	T/O		20.0							
1BD	B-17	372	140	GAGGENAU M.T. FAC.	(P)	412.0		3	5	169	0	9	27
			73	SINDELFINGEN ENG FAC	(P)	211.3							
			116	ZUFFENHAUSEN JET FAC	(P)	343.3							
			19	T/O		54.0		0	0	0	0	0	0
8AF 620 GB-4 No 1													
3BD	B-17	1	1	DÜREN		1.0		0	0	0	0	0	0
TOTALS:		1145	1063			2803.4	0	7	6	381	1	18	65

		Despatched	Effective	Target	E/A	Losses MIA	E	Dam	KIA	WIA	MIA
VIII FC											
	P-38	31	153	ESCORT 2BD		0	0	1	0	0	0
	P-51	145				2	3	3	1	0	2
	P-47	35	221	ESCORT 3BD	1–0– 0	0	0	0	0	0	0
	P-51	206			38–0–44 (G)	3	0	2	0	0	3
	P-51	153	135	ESCORT 1BD	1–1– 0 29–0– 1 (G)	0	0	0	0	0	0
	P-47	135	121	STRAFING COLOGNE/FRANKFURT/ KASSEL AREAS	10–0–21 (G)	8	1	4	0	0	8
TOTALS:		705	630		1–0–0 77–0–66(G)	13	4	10	1	0	13

REMARKS: Attacks on targets in the Stuttgart area. PFF bombing by 2BD, PFF and visual by 3BD and visual by 1BD. Bomb Groups participating:– all 1BD; all 2DB except 448BG; all 3BD except 95BG and 385BG. Bomb group losses:– 1BD – 381BG – 1, 398BG – 1, 401BG – 1, 2BD – 446BG – 1; 3BD – 96BG – 1, 390BG – 2. B/d 457BG B-17 c/l France and b/d 457BG abandoned over France. 2 457BG B-17s collided over France, 1 cr. near St.Quentin, 7 k., other a/c returned to base. B/d 384BG B-17 c/l France. B/d 92BG B-17 cr. near Netz, crew baled. B/d 445BG B-24 c/l Manston A/F. Mission 620 was first trial of GB-4 radio/visual control bomb by 388BG *Aphrodite* unit. P-38 photo a/c and 9 P-51 escorts accompanied B-17.

All Fighter groups operating. Fighter group e/a credits:– 4FG – 4, 55FG – 1, 359FG – 1. Fighter group losses:– 55FG – 1, 56FG – 2, 78FG – 6, 339FG – 2, 359FG – 1, 361FG – 1. 78FG P-47 c/l Belgium pilot safe. A 355FG P-51 c/l Liege, pilot safe. The 55FG P-51 lost cr. into hangar while strafing Herzogenaurach A/F. On return 4FG P-51 cr. Boxted A/F, pilot killed. 361FG P-51 c/l Montdidier A/F.

OTHER OPERATIONS: 7PG despatched 10 F-5s on PR Brest and Germany, and 3 Spitfires on PR Belgium and France. 25BG despatched 2 Mosquitoes to scout for bombers, 4 Mosquitoes on WR France and North Sea and 1 B-17 and 2 B-24s on Atlantic/UK WR. ASR despatched 16 P-47s on patrols. 1SF despatched 6 P-51s to scout for 1BD. 1 B-17, 20 P-51s, 5 P-47s and 2 P-38s as radio-relays.

Mission 620 was a special *Azon* test involving 1 B-17, 1 P-38 and 9 P-51s to Düren.

10/11 SEPTEMBER 1944

8AF 621 RADAR AND PHOTO RECONNAISSANCE OPERATION

482BG B-17, 3 despatched, 3 effective: Germany. Leaflets also dropped.

8AF 622 NIGHT LEAFLET OPERATION

NLS B-17, 7 despatched, 6 effective: France, Holland, Germany.

492BG despatched 35 B-24s and C-47s on *Carpetbagger* operations.

36BS despatched 3 B-24s on RCM.

11 SEPTEMBER 1944

8AF 623

	Despatched		Effective	Target		Bombs Tonnage	E/A	Losses MIA	E	Dam	Casualties KIA	WIA	MIA
3BD	B-17	384	22	RUHLAND O/I	(P)	53.0	12–16–1	16	3	94	2	4	153
			75	BÖHLEN O/I	(P)	173.0							
			39	BRÜX O/I	(P)	95.3							
			75	CHEMNITZ O/I	(P)	146.4							
			66	FULDA TYRE PLANT	(O)	159.7							
			40	FULDA M/Y	(O)	95.1							
			16	T/O		38.5							
1BD	B-17	351	111	MERSEBURG O/I	(P)	278.6	1– 1–2	13	2	106	2	21	120
			96	LÜTZKENDORF O/I	(P)	233.7							
			12	LABEJUM	(O)	30.0							
			71	EISENACH	(O)	177.5							
			6	ROSSLA	(O)	15.0							
			25	T/O		62.5							
2BD	B-24	396	87	MISBURG O/I	(P)	243.2	4– 8–1	10	2	179	1	13	102
			33	MAGDEBURG O/I	(P)	78.5							
			27	MAGDEBURG ORD. DEPOT	(P)	64.7							
			88	HANNOVER ENG WKS	(P)	298.7							
			70	CITY OF MAGDEBURG	(O)	157.2							
			45	STENDAL	(O)	107.5							
			9	DIEPHOLZ	(O)	22.5							
			3	T/O		8.2							
TOTALS:		1131	1016			2438.8	17–25–4	40	7	379	5	38	375
VIII FC													
	P-51	275	252	ESCORT 3BD			57–2–12						
							26–0–25 (G)	4	2	5	0	0	4
	P-47	165	247	ESCORT 2BD			13–0– 1	0	0	2	0	0	0
	P-51	97					4–0– 2 (G)	3	2	4	0	0	3
	P-38	33	164	ESCORT 1BD			45–5–10	0	0	0	0	0	0
	P-51	145					12–0–16 (G)	10	4	7	0	0	14
TOTALS:		440	411			0	115–7–23 42–0–43 (G)	17	8	18	0	0	21

REMARKS: Major attack on synthetic oil plants and refineries. All 2BD bombing PFF; Merseburg visual but rest of 1BD targets PFF; all 3BD targets PFF except Chemnitz and Böhlen. For the first time since 28 May the Luftwaffe contested the bombers in force – over 500 fighters. Bomb groups participating: all 1BD except 398BG and 457BG; all 2BD except 446BG; all 3BD except 385BG and 388BG. Bomb group losses:– 1BD – 92BG – 8, 305BG – 1, 306BG – 1, 379BG – 1, 384BG – 1, 401BG – 1; 2BD – 93BG – 3, 392BG – 4, 448BG – 2, 458BG – 1; 3BD – 94BG – 2, 95BG – 1, 100BG – 11, 447BG – 2. The 2 94BG B-17s MIA collided over target. MIA 392BG B-24 ditched 40 miles E. off Gt. Yarmouth, 8 saved. B/d 401BG B-17 cr. Kings Norton on return. B/d 453BG B-24 c/l in liberated France. B/d 491BG B-24 c/l Romilly, France B/d 100BG B-17 cr. near Eastchurch. B/d 100BG B-17 cr. France, crews baled. The Chemnitz force (96BG, 452BG) continued on to Soviet Union (the third *Frantic* mission). Heavy fighter attacks on 92BG and 100BG. B/d 493BG B-17 Cat E. B/d 92BG B-17 c/l near Paris.

All Fighter groups operating. Fighter group e/a credits:– 4FG – 4, 55FG – 13, 339FG – 14, 352FG – 27, 355FG – 12, 359FG – 26, 361FG – 1, 364FG – 13. Fighter group losses:– 4FG – 2, 55FG – 4, 339FG – 2, 352FG – 2, 355FG – 3, 359FG – 5, 361FG – 1, 364FG – 2. 3 4FG P-51s cr. or c/l France and Belgium. (2 4FG pilots baled Liege and Paris) 1 361FG P-51 c/l RAF A/F pilot safe. Highest fighter claims and losses to date. 20FG escorted *Frantic* mission to Soviet Union. MIA 361FG P-51 lost in collision with HB. 355FG P-51 c/l France. 364FG P-51 c/l base. A 20FG P-51 s/d over Soviet battle lines and another c/l out of fuel, pilots safe.

OTHER OPERATIONS: 7PG despatched 32 F-5s and Spitfires on PR Germany. 25BG despatched 3 Mosquitoes to scout for bombers, 3 Mosquitoes on WR Germany and Frisian Islands, and 1 B-24 on WR Atlantic/UK. 1SF despatched 8 P-51s to scout for bombers. ASR despatched 16 P-47s on patrols. 3 B-17s, 10 P-51s, 2 P-38s on radio-relays Mission 624 was *Aphrodite* operation, involving a *Castor* B-17 drone, with control B-17 and 16 P-51s. Pilot killed baling out of drone.

11/12 SEPTEMBER 1944

8AF 625 NIGHT LEAFLET OPERATION

NLS B-17, 6 despatched, 6 effective: France and Germany.

35BS despatched 5 B-24s on RCM for RAF bombers.

492BG despatched 38 B-24s on *Carpetbagger* operations.

INCIDENT

If 2/Lt John Becht was apprehensive about the eleventh day of the month, it was quite understandable after his experiences on 11 September 1944. Returning from Merseburg the 92nd Group B-17 in which he was flying was set on fire and over France Becht and the rest of the crew had to take to their parachutes. Two months before, on 11 July, Becht had been aboard the *Berlin Special* making assembly over Essex when it caught fire and he was ordered to bale out. Two months to the day before that, 11 May, when he was still training in the US, the bomber in which he was flying caught fire and Becht had to 'hit the silk'. After such a series of 'incidents' the young bombardier couldn't decide whether the 11th was a lucky or unlucky day!

12 SEPTEMBER 1944

8AF 626

	Despatched		Effective	Target		Bombs Tonnage	E/A	Losses MIA	E	Dam	Casualties KIA	WIA	MIA
1BD	B-17	299	59	RUHLAND O/I	(P)	142.5	14–9–7	19	4	94	6	11	171
			79	BRÜX O/I	(P)	189.7							
			30	PLAUEN	(O)	82.5							
			48	LAUTA	(O)	119.5							
			12	ETTERWINDEN	(O)	22.5							
			11	KITZINGEN	(O)	27.5							
			11	KARLSBAD	(O)	27.5							
			21	T/O		52.5							
3BD	B-17	348	144	MAGDEBURG/ ROTHENSEE	(P)	329.5	13–5–5	12	1	161	1	9	109
			73	MAGDEBURG/ FRIEDRICHSTADT	(P)	167.9							
			35	BÖHLEN	(P)	82.7							
			46	FULDA	(O)	111.0							
			11	MOLBIS	(O)	26.0							
			8	T/O		18.1							
2BD	B-24	241	66	HEMMINGSTEDT	(P)	165.0		4	0	49	3	1	37
			58	KIEL	(P)	149.5							
			34	MISBURG	(P)	89.5							
			38	LAHARTE	(O)	106.7							
			12	NORTHEIM M/Y	(O)	36.0							
			11	HANNOVER	(O)	29.0							
			3	HEMMINGSTEDT	(O)	8.5							
			3	T/O		6.7							
TOTALS:		888	813			1990.3	27–14–12	35	5	304	10	22	307
VIII FC													
	P-47	48	238	ESCORT 1BD			29–2– 4	0	0		0	0	0
	P-51	229					21–0–16 (G)	10	2		0	0	10
	P-47	80	236	ESCORT 3BD			25–0– 4	0	0		0	0	0
	P-51	191					5–0–15(G)	2	0		0	0	2
	P-38	31	105	ESCORT 2BD				0	0		0	0	0
	P-47	51						0	0		0	0	0
	P-51	32						0	0		0	0	0
TOTALS:		662	579			0	54–2– 8 26–0–31(G)	12	2	10	0	0	12

REMARKS: For the second day running a major assault on the German oil industry, again contested by a strong force of enemy fighters. 3BD was able to bomb visually at all targets but 1BD and 2BD had to use PFF at some. Bomb groups participating:– all 1BD except 91BG, 92BG and 401BG; all 2BD except 389BG, 453BG and the groups of 96CBW; all 3BD groups except 452BG. Bomb group losses:– 1BD – 303BG – 2, 306BG – 8, 351BG – 6, 384BG – 1, 398BG – 1, 457BG – 1; 2BD – 392BG – 1, 445BG – 1, 491BG – 2; 3BD – 385BG – 1, 388BG – 1, 487BG – 1, 493BG – 9. On return a b/d 306BG B-17 cr. Manston, 2 killed. MIA 379BG a/c collided. 2 B/d 351BG B-17s c/l Belgium, 379BG and 493BG B-17s Cat E.

All Fighter groups operating:– except 20FG. E/a credits:– 4FG – 7, 55FG – 5, 56FG – 3, 339FG – 3, 352FG – 13, 355FG – 4, 359FG – 10, 361FG – 13, 364FG – 2. Fighter group losses:– 4FG – 2, 55FG – 1, 352FG – 1, 355FG – 3, 359FG – 4, 361FG – 1. On return, 2 359FG P-51s c/l Abbeville and Woodbridge A/F.

OTHER OPERATIONS: 7PG despatched 25 F-5s and 10 Spitfires on PR to Germany (4 P-51s to escort for 2 a/c going to Leipzig area). 25BG despatched 3 Mosquitoes to scout for bombers, 3 Mosquitoes on WR France and Germany, and 1 B-17 and 1 B-24 on WR Atlantic/UK. 1SF despatched 8 P-51s for 1BD. ASR despatched 14 P-47s on patrols. 3 B-17s, 2 P-38s, 2 P-47s, 4 P-51s on radio-relays. 36 96CBW B-24s despatched on *Truckin'* mission to France.

12/13 SEPTEMBER 1944

8AF 627 NIGHT LEAFLET OPERATION

NLS B-17, 7 despatched, 7 effective; France, Holland, Germany.

36BS despatched 6 B-24s on RCM.

492BG despatched 36 B-24s and C-47s (7 aborted) on *Carpetbagger* operations.

13 SEPTEMBER 1944

8AF 628

	Despatched		Effective	Target		Bombs Tonnage	E/A	Losses MIA	E	Dam	Casualties KIA	WIA	MIA
3BD	B-17	376	109	STUTTGART/ SINDELFINGEN O/I	(P)	296.7		4	2	134	1	2	37
			74	LUDWIGSHAFEN O/I	(P)	211.5							
			95	DARMSTADT	(S)	270.8							
			8	WIESBADEN	(S)	24.0							
			22	MAINZ	(O)	64.8							
			12	M/Y NEAR WIESBADEN	(O)	36.0							
			3	T/O		9.0							
2BD	B-24	342	65	SCHWABISH HALL A/F	(P)	169.5		4	2	127	0	3	39
			65	ULM M/D	(P)	161.0							
			45	WEISSENHORN	(P)	108.3							
			1	REICHELSHEIM	(O)	3.0							
			77	LÜTZKENDORF O/I	(P)	188.2	1–0–0	7	3	145	4	8	67
			141	MERSEBURG O/I	(P)	334.5							
			12	EISENACH	(O)	28.4							
			17	GIESSEN	(O)	40.0							
1BD		297	7	GERA	(O)	27.5							
			7	ALTENBURG	(O)	17.0							
			19	T/O		46.5							
8AF 629 *AZON*													
2BD	B-24	11	6	HEMMINSTEDT O/R	(P)	12.5							
			5	KROPP AMMO DUMP	(S)	14.0		0	0	0	0	0	0
TOTALS:		1026	790			2063.2	1–0–0	15	7	406	5	13	143
EASTERN COMMAND													
	B-17	74	73	*FRANTIC* DIOSGYÖR	(P)	263.0		0	0	0	0	0	0
VIII FC													
	P-47	98	92	ESCORT 3BD			6–0–2 (G)	0					
	P-38	31	99	ESCORT 2BD			14–0–5 (G)	0					
	P-51	74						2					
	P-47	36	233	ESCORT 1BD			33–0–4	0					
	P-51	238						6					
	P-51	48	40	STRAFING MUNICH AREA			5–0–0 (G)	2					
	P-51	15	15	ESCORT FOR *AZON*				0					
	P-51	63	63	ESCORT *FRANTIC*				0					
TOTALS:		603	542			0	33–0–4 25–0–7(G)	10	1	9	0	0	9

REMARKS: Oil and industrial targets in South Germany attacked by visual means. Bomb groups participating:– all 1BD except 351BG, 381BG; all 2BD except 96CBW groups and 93BG; all 3BD. Bomb group losses:– 1BD – 92BG – 4, 303BG – 1, 306BG – 1, 384BG – 1; 2BD – 392BG – 1, 453BG – 1, 491BG – 2; 3BD – 96BG – 1, 490BG – 2, 493BG – 1. On return b/d 447BG B-17 landed Woodbridge – Cat E. B/d 401BG B-17 c/l Belgium. 453BG B-24 c/l Prouvy, France. One 92BG B-17 MIA landed Switzerland. *Frantic* force (96BG, 452BG with 20FG) flew from Soviet Union to Italy attacking target in Hungary and returned to Soviet Union – B-17 aborted. B/d 379BG B-17 cr. Continent, crew safe. On return, 385BG B-17 cr. Kentford, crew baled, 1 k. 491BG B-24 c/l Bentwaters A/F. B/d 92BG B-17 cr. Woodbridge A/F, 3 k.

All Fighter groups operated except 355FG. First use of P-51s by 479FG (1 sqdn.). Fighter group e/a credits:– 55FG – 16, 357FG – 15, 364FG – 2. Fighter group losses:– 4FG – 1, 55FG – 2, 339FG – 2, 357FG – 4, 361FG – 1. A 357FG pilot baled 55 miles off Clacton, saved. 357FG P-51 with m/f abandoned near Brussels, pilot safe.

OTHER OPERATIONS: 7PG despatched 10 F-5s and 7 Spitfires on PR Germany. 25BG despatched 4 Mosquitoes to scout for bombers, 3 Mosquitoes on WR France and 2 B-24s on WR Atlantic/UK. 1SF despatched 8 P-51 to scout for 1BD. 7 P-51s despatched as escort for PR F-5s. ASR despatched 20 P-47s on patrols. 4 P-51s, 6 P-47s, 3 B-17s on radio-relays. Mission 630 was a special bombing test carried out by 1 B-17 with a Mosquito and 16 P-51s escorting.

INCIDENT

Even the advent of weather scouts preceding bomber formations did not completely eliminate doubt about conditions ahead. An instance occurred on 13 September 1944 when the 401st Group went to Merseburg. In the vicinity of Aachen at around 25,000 ft wisps of cirro-stratus were encountered. To the leaders it looked as if the formation was approaching 'solid weather' so they began to climb in order to go over the threatening front ahead. The high box was briefed to bomb from 28,700 ft, an unusually high level for attack occasioned by the flak defences at this target. Now the high box pilots found they were having to go to 30,700 ft and apply maximum power to stay there – engines were averaging 2,400 rpm with 42 inch manifold pressure (supercharger boost), an overstrain that caused some to fail. But the weather front did not materialise and turned out to be nothing more than cirrus haze. The effort of operating at the extra 2,000 ft in rarefied air dispersed the formation. Even so the visual drop averaged 20 per cent of bombs within 1,000 ft of the aiming point nearly six miles below.

13/14 SEPTEMBER 1944

8AF 631 NIGHT LEAFLET OPERATION

NLS B-17, 8 despatched, 8 effective; Holland, Belgium, Germany.

36BS despatched 6 B-24s on RCM.

14 SEPTEMBER 1944

8AF 632 *APHRODITE*

388BG despatched 2 B-17 *Castor* drones, 2 B-17 control a/c, 1 Mosquito observation a/c and 31 353FG and 78FG P-47s as escort to Hemmingstedt oil refinery. Target missed.

15 SEPTEMBER 1944

8AF 633 *FRANTIC VI*

3BD despatched 110 B-17s to drop supplies to Warsaw patriots but a weather front encountered over North Sea forced a recall. 156 P-51 of 4FG, 355FG, 357FG despatched as escort 149 crossed into enemy air space. 2 P-51s MIA – 357FG, believed to have collided in cloud.

OTHER OPERATIONS: 7PG despatched 2 F-5s on PR Germany, and 2 F-5s on special WR. 25BG despatched 2 Mosquitoes on WR Germany and 1 Mosquito WR Brest, and 2 B-24s on WR Atlantic/UK. ASR despatched 2 P-47s on patrols. 2 P-51s on radio-relays.

16 SEPTEMBER 1944

8AF 635

Despatched		Effective	Target		Bombs Tonnage	E/A	Losses MIA	E	Dam	Casualties KIA	WIA	MIA
P-47	178		FIGHTER-BOMBER MANNHEIM KAISERSLAUTERN AREA. AHLHORN A/F				0	0	6	0	0	0
P-51	149	295		P)	12.6	6–0–1(G)	1	0	10	0	0	1
TOTALS:	327	295			12.6	6–0–1(G)	1	0	16	0	0	1

REMARKS: Bad weather restricted operations. Fighter groups operating:– 20FG, 56FG, 78FG, 352FG, 353FG, 355FG, 356FG, 459FG, 361FG, 364FG, 479FG. Fighter group losses:– 364FG – 1.

OTHER OPERATIONS: 7PG despatched 15 F-5s and 3 Spitfires on PR Germany and Eastern France (8 P-51s flew escort for some PR a/c). 25BG despatched 4 Mosquitoes on WR Belgium, France and Germany and 2 B-24s on WR Atlantic/UK. ASR despatched 12 P-47s on patrols and 4 P-51s also on ASR search. 1 B-17 and 2 P-47s on radio-relays.

16/17 SEPTEMBER 1944

8AF 636 NIGHT LEAFLET OPERATION

NLS B-17, 9 despatched, 7 effective: France, Holland, Germany.

492BG despatched 32 B-24s and C-47s on *Carpetbagger* ops. 1 B-24 MIA.

36BS despatched 5 B-24s on RCM.

17 SEPTEMBER 1944

8AF 637

Despatched		Effective	Target	Bombs Tonnage	E/A	Losses MIA	E	Dam	Casualties KIA	WIA	MIA
B-17	875	815	FLAK BATTERIES	3115.6		2	1	119	9	6	15
		6	ETC. HOLLAND (P) EISENACH	23.4		0	0	0	0	0	0
TOTALS:	875	821		3139.0	0	2	1	119	9	6	15

VIII FC

Despatched		Effective	Target	Bombs Tonnage	E/A	Losses MIA	E	Dam	Casualties KIA	WIA	MIA
P-51	153	141	ESCORT B-17			1	0	0	0	0	1
			FIGHTER-BOMBER								
P-38	36	503	HOLLAND-FLAK	44.5	7–0–0	0	0	0	0	0	0
P-47	201		POSITIONS GROUND		1–0–0 (G)	6	4	41	0	2	5
P-51	313		TARGETS: ESCORT TO 1ST ALLIED AIRBORNE ARMY			7	2	6	0	0	6
TOTALS:	703	644		44.5	7–0–0 1–0–0(G)	14	6	47	0	2	12

REMARKS: Operations in support of airborne landings in Holland. Bomb groups participating:– all 1BD except 91BG; all 3BD except 13CBW groups. First mission of 34BG with B-17. Bomb group losses:– 384BG – 1, 457BG – 1. 401BG B-17 cr. after t/o at Weldon, 9 killed.

All Fighter groups operating. Fighter group e/a credits:– 4FG – 6, 356FG – 1, 361FG – 1. Fighter group losses:– 4FG – 2, 55FG – 1, 56FG – 1, 78FG – 1, 353FG – 1, 356FG – 3, 359FG – 1, 361FG – 1, 364FG – 2, 479FG – 1(P-51). A 55FG and 78FG pilots that baled were rescued from North Sea. B/d 56FG P-47 c/l near Southwold, pilot safe. 2 other b/d 56FG P-47s and 1 b/d 356FG P-47 Cat E, 357FG P-51 c/l t/o, all pilots safe. B/d 352FG P-51 c/l near Brussels, pilot safe. Non-operational 20FG P-51 ex-Italy c/l at Pohay (SW of Paris) due to m/f, pilot safe.

OTHER OPERATIONS: 7PG despatched 11 F-5s on PR Holland, France and Germany. 25BG despatched 10 Mosquitoes on WR Continent, 1 Mosquito to scout for *Frantic* bombers and 2 B-24s WR Atlantic/UK. ASR despatched 20 P-47s on patrols and 2 P-51s also on ASR Search. 1 B-17, 8 P-51s, 4 P-47s on radio-relays. *Frantic* force 72 B-17s and 59 P-51s (96BG, 452BG and 20FG) returned to UK from Italy but were not briefed to bomb on route. 101 B-24s on *Truckin'* mission with fuel to France.

17/18 SEPTEMBER 1944

36BS despatched 6 B-24s on RCM.

The low-level supply drop to advance Allied airborne forces in Holland exposed many B-24s to murderous ground fire. The way to lessen the chance of being hit was to fly as low as possible. Chasing shadows and grazing horses show these two 392BG Liberators were very close to the flat Dutch countryside.

18 SEPTEMBER 1944

8AF 639

	Despatched		Effective	Target	Bombs Tonnage	E/A	Losses MIA	E	Dam	Casualties KIA	WIA	MIA
2BD	B-24	252	248	SUPPLY DROP – AIRBORNE ARMY HOLLAND	782.0 FREIGHT		7	6	154	1	26	61
8AF 640												
	B-17	110	107	*FRANTIC VII* WARSAW SUPPLIES	1248 CONTAINERS	0	1	0	7	0	0	0
TOTALS		362	355			0	8	6	161	1	26	61
VIII FC	P-51	374	UN-	ESCORT B-24s &	10.5	29–0–1	20	1	16	0	0	20
	P-47	185	KNOWN	GROUND ATTACK IN				8	30	1	0	0
	P-38	16		SUPPORT OF ALLIED FORCES HOLLAND				0	0	0	0	0
	P-51	150	137	ESCORT *FRANTIC VII*		4–0–0 3–0–6 (G)	2	0	0	0	0	2
TOTALS:		725	137 plus		10.5	33–0–1 3–0–6(G)	22	9	46	1	0	22

REMARKS: Mission 639, the re-supply of US airborne Forces in the Nijmegen-Eindhoven areas by B-24s flying at very low altitude; each a/c carried 20 bundles of supplies. Groups participating:– all 14CBW and 20CBW. Bomb group losses:– 93BG – 2, 392BG – 2, 489BG – 2, 491BG – 1. One 93BG a/c MIA ditched 37 miles off Orfordness, 3 rescued. B/d 392BG B-24 c/l Brussels A/F. 2 b/d 491BG B-24s c/l Woodbridge A/F and 1 each at Watton A/F, Hawkinge A/F and Brussels A/F. Mission 640 was flown by all 13CBW groups to drop supplies to Poles in the Warsaw rising and continue on to Soviet Union. Bomb group losses:– 390BG –1. This proved to be the last *Frantic* shuttle mission.

All Fighter groups operating. 355FG with 64 P-51s escorted *Frantic* shuttle mission force to Soviet Union. Fighter group e/a credits:– 355FG – 4, 357FG – 26, 359FG – 3, 361FG – 4. Fighter group losses:– 56FG – 8, 78FG – 5, 353FG – 1, 355FG –2, 356FG – 1, 357FG – 2, 359FG – 2, 361FG –1. 56FG had another 8 P-47 cr. or c/l with b/d, 7 behind Allied lines, pilots safe, and 1 at Southminster, pilot killed. All losses in support of airborne forces due to Flak. 359FG P-51 Cat E.

OTHER OPERATIONS: 7PG despatched 7 F-5s on PR Germany and Holland, and 1 F-5 on WR Scheldt area. 25BG despatched 1 Mosquito on PR Holland, 5 Mosquito to scout for bombers on supply drops, 2 Mosquitoes on WR Atlantic. 1 Mosquito MIA. 2 B-17s, 8 P-51s and P-47s on radio-relays – 96CBW B-24s on *Truckin'* mission to France with fuel supplies.

Parachute containers being released from a low flying B-24 over Son, NNE of Eindhoven. Jeeps carrying US airborne troops are passing through the village where national flags have been hung out. The 466BG aircraft was apparently on loan to the 491BG.

Parachutes with containers go down, 18 September. Another leaves the 'Joe Hole' (opening where ball turret once situated) of B-24J 44-40164 as the 491BG sweeps at 300 ft over gliders near Eindhoven.

A 95BG Fortress lands at Poltava after the final shuttle mission into Russia. Soviet obstruction and suspicions made further operations untenable.

18/19 SEPTEMBER 1944

8AF 641 NIGHT LEAFLET OPERATION

NLS B-17, 8 despatched, 8 effective; France, Holland, Germany.

36BS despatched 7 B-24s on RCM.

19 SEPTEMBER 1944

8AF 642

	Despatched		Effective	Target	Bombs Tonnage	E/A	Losses MIA	E	Dam	Casualties KIA	WIA	MIA
3BD	B-17	380	87	KOBLENZ M/Y	(O) 244.5		4		159	0	3	37
			37	LIMBURG M/Y	(O) 101.5							
			35	LIMBURG BR	(O) 82.0							
			25	KOBLENZ BR	(O) 75.0							
			38	WIESBADEN	(O) 109.5							
			12	WIESBADEN A/F	(O) 82.5							
			39	DILLENBURG M/Y	(O) 97.5							
			14	WETZLAR	(O) 40.5							
			24	DARMSTADT M/Y	(O) 60.2							
			13	KOBLENZ R/R LINE	(O) 39.0							
			13	KOBLENZ RHINE BR	(O) 36.0							
1BD	B-17	416	186	HAMM M/Y (P)	460.1				120			
			32	SOEST M/Y	(P) 95.2		3	2		0	3	18
			64	DORTMUND/UNNA DEPOT	(P) 180.3							
			6	RHEINE M/Y	(O) 18.0							
			3	MÜNSTER M/Y	(O) 8.8							
			2	OSNABRÜCK	(O) 5.8							
			5	HAMM	(O) 15.0							
			11	DILLENBURG	(O) 32.0							
			11	RAESFELD M/Y	(O) 33.0							
			9	WESEL M/Y	(O) 26.2							
			7	EMMERICH	(O) 20.5							
			6	T/O	18.0							
EASTERN COMMAND												
3BD	B-17	100	Unknown	SZOLNOK M/Y	(P) Unknown		0	0	0	0	0	0
TOTALS:		896	679 plus		1881.1 plus	0	7	4	345	0	6	55
VIII FC												
	P-47	45	131	ESCORT 3BD		3–0–1	1	0	0	0	0	1
	P-51	100					0	0	0	0	0	0
	P-47	32	109	ESCORT 1BD			0	0	0	0	0	0
	P-51	109					0	0	0	0	0	0
	P-51	182	172	PATROLS HOLLAND		23–4–14	6	1	2	1	0	6
	P-51	61		ESCORT *FRANTIC* B-17s			0	0	0	0	0	0
TOTALS:		528	412			26–4–15	7	1	2	1	0	7

REMARKS: All 1BD and 3BD groups except those of 13CBW despatched against marshalling yards in western Germany, ordnance depots at Bielefeld and Unna, and an oil refinery at Rheine. Cloud prevented some 1BD and all 3BD Formations from attacking primaries. Visual bombing. Bomb group losses:– 1BD – 351BG – 1, 379BG – 1, 384BG – 1; 3BD – 96BG – 1, 486BG – 1, 493BG – 2. The 351BG B-17 ditched, crew saved. *Frantic* B-17s bombed target in Hungary on way to Italy. B/d 305BG B-17 c/l on Continent on return.

All Fighter groups operating except 20FG, 78FG, 353FG, 355FG, 479FG. Fighter group e/a credits:– 55FG – 3, 357FG – 25, 364FG – 4. Fighter group losses:– 356FG – 1, 357FG – 5, 364FG – 1. 361FG P-51 cr. landing base, pilot k.

OTHER OPERATIONS: 7PG despatched 16 F-5s and 6 Spitfires on PR Germany and Holland. 2 F-5s and 1 Spitfire MIA. 25BG despatched 1 Mosquito on PR Holland – a/c MIA, 6 Mosquitoes on WR Continent, and 4 B-24s on WR Atlantic/UK. 1SF despatched 8 P-51s to scout for bombers. 3 B-17s, 14 P-51 escort, 2 P-51s, 2 P-47s on radio-relays. 2BD B-24 flying fuel to France.

20 SEPTEMBER 1944

	Despatched		Effective	Target	Bombs Tonnage	E/A	Losses MIA	E	Dam	Casualties KIA	WIA	MIA
	P-38	26	644	PATROLS OVER	4.1		0	1	0	0	0	0
	P-47	183		AIRBORNE LANDINGS			0	1	3	0	0	0
	P-51	470		IN HOLLAND			1	1	4	0	0	0
TOTALS:		679	644		4.1	0	1	3	7	0	0	0

REMARKS: Weather restricted operations. All Fighter groups except 355FG operating. Fighter group losses:– 359FG – 1. The 359FG pilot baled 40 miles off Gt. Yarmouth, rescued. B/d 56FG P-47 c/l Continent. 479FG P-38 cr. t/o. 361FG P-51 c/l.

OTHER OPERATIONS: 7PG despatched 6 F-5s to Holland. 25BG despatched 6 Mosquitoes on WR Continent and 2 B-24s WR Atlantic/UK. 2 B-17s, 4 P-51s, 2 P-47s and 2 P-38s on radio-relays. 40 B-24s of 2BD on *Truckin'* mission; gasoline to Lille, France. A 458BG B-24 cr. Hellesdon on t/o, crew killed.

21 SEPTEMBER 1944

8AF 644

	Despatched		Effective	Target		Bombs Tonnage	E/A	Losses MIA	E	Dam	Casualties KIA	WIA	MIA
3BD	B-17	154	147	LUDWIGSHAFEN/ OPAU O/I		412.3	0	0	0	54	0	0	0
			2	T/O		6.0							
1BD	B-17	153	141	MAINZ M/Y	(P)	405.5		0	0	52	0	2	0
2BD	B-24	179	144	KOBLENZ M/Y	(P)	374.7		2	3	83	15	3	18
			12	T/O		31.5							
TOTALS:		486	446			1230.0	0	2	3	189	15	5	18

VIII FC

	Despatched		Effective	Target	Bombs Tonnage	E/A	Losses MIA	E	Dam	Casualties KIA	WIA	MIA
	P-38	27	39	ESCORT 3BD			1					
	P-51	18										
VIII FC												
	P-51	35	34	ESCORT 1BD			0	0	0	0	0	0
	P-51	46	44	ESCORT 2BD			1	0	0	0	0	1
	P-47	71	90	HOLLAND PATROLS		20–0–2	3	1	2	0	0	3
	P-51	24										
TOTALS:		221	207		0	20–0–2	4	1	2	0	0	4

REMARKS: Attacks on targets in western Germany by PFF with some units at Mainz M/Y able to bomb visually. Bomb groups participating:– 1BD – 41CBW groups and 91BG, 381BG; 2BD – 20CBW groups and 392BG, 445BG, 453BG; 3BD – 45CBW groups and 486BG, 490BG. Bomb group losses:– 2BD – 93BG – 1, 392BG – 1. B/d 446BG B-24 cr. Bredfield, 10 k. 93BG B-24 cr., 5 k.

Fighter groups operating: 55FG, 56FG, 353FG, 357FG, 359FG, 479FG. Fighter group e/a credits:– 56FG – 15, 353FG – 4. Fighter group losses:– 56FG – 2, 353FG – 1, 479FG – 1. 56FG P-47 c/l Continent.

OTHER OPERATIONS: 7PG despatched 3 F-5s on PR, Germany and Holland. 25BG despatched 1 Mosquito to scout for bombers, 2 Mosquitoes on WR Belgium and France, and 2 B-17s, 2 P-51s, 2 P-47s on radio-relays. 84 2BD B-24s on *Truckin'* mission, 403 tons fuel to France.

22 SEPTEMBER 1944

8AF 645

	Despatched		Effective	Target		Bombs Tonnage	E/A	Losses MIA	E	Dam	Casualties KIA	WIA	MIA
1 & 3BD	B-17	453	410	KASSEL/HENSCHEL	(P)	1035.5		3	0	104	0	7	27
			10	WETZLAR		29.5							
			7	T/O		18.6							
2BD	B-24	208	208	KASSEL/HENSCHEL		624.0		0	0	3	0	0	0
TOTALS:		661	635			1707.6	0	3	0	107	0	7	27

VIII FC

	Despatched		Effective	Target	Bombs Tonnage	E/A	Losses MIA	E	Dam	Casualties KIA	WIA	MIA
	P-51	286	268	ESCORT FOR BOMBERS			1	1		0	0	1
	P-47	79	77	PATROL ARNHEM AREA			1	1		0	0	0
TOTALS:		365	345		0	0	2	2		0	0	1

REMARKS: Armoured vehicle and motor vehicle factories at Kassel bombed by PFF. Groups participating:– 1BD – all except 41CBW groups and 91BG, 457BG; 2BD – 14CBW and 20CBW groups and 445BG, 453BG; 3BD – 4CBW and 93CBW groups and 487BG. Bomb group losses:– 1BD – 92BG – 1; 3BD – 34BG – 1, 487BG – 1. *Frantic* force (84 B-17s and 51 P-51s) returned from Italy.

Fighter groups operating: 56FG, 339FG, 353FG, 357FG, 359FG, 361FG, 364FG. Fighter group losses:– 78FG – 1, 357FG – 1. 355FG – 2 during return from Italy. 364FG P-51 cr. near Liège, pilot safe. 352FG P-51 c/l Luxemburg, m/f.

OTHER OPERATIONS: 7PG despatched 6 F-5s and 3 Spitfires on PR Germany and Holland. 25BG despatched 3 Mosquitoes to scout for bombers, 4 Mosquitoes on WR Low Countries and Brest, 2 B-24s on WR Atlantic/UK. Scout Forces despatched 18 P-51s on WR for bombers. 1 P-51 MIA. ASR despatched 2 P-47s for patrol (aborted). 108 B-24s flying fuel to France. 2 B-17s, 8 P-51s, 2 P-47s on radio-relays.

22/23 SEPTEMBER 1944

36BS despatched 4 B-24s on RCM.

23 SEPTEMBER 1944

FIGHTER ESCORT

	Despatched		Effective	Target	Bombs Tonnage	E/A	Losses MIA	E	Dam	Casualties KIA	WIA	MIA
	P-38	40	559	SUPPORT OF TWO	10.4	27–2–6	0	0	0	0	0	0
	P-47	136		LANDINGS IN			4	1	25	0	1	4
	P-51	410		NIJMEGEN AREA			10	1	10	0	0	10
TOTALS:		586	559		10.4	27–2–6	14	2	35	0	1	14

REMARKS: Weather again restricted operations. Support for ground operations in Holland includes 9AF 370FG P-38 operating with 8AF. All Fighter groups operating except 56FG, 355FG, 359FG, 479FG. Fighter group e/a credits:– 339FG – 7, 353FG – 15, 364FG – 2. Fighter group losses:– 78FG – 1, 339FG – 3, 352FG – 5, 353FG – 3, 364FG – 2. MIA 364FG P-51 down in Sweden. B/d 339FG P-51 c/l Brussels. B/d 356FG P-47 cr. Continent.

OTHER OPERATIONS: 7PG despatched 2 F-5 to Holland on PR. 25BG despatched 5 Mosquitoes on WR North Sea, Low Countries, France and 4 B-24s on WR Atlantic/UK. 1 B-24 c/l at base. ASR despatched 11 P-47s on patrols. 10 P-51s, 2 P-38s, 2 P-47s and 1 B-17 on radio-relays. 162 B-24s flying fuel to France. A 458BG B-24 missing. B/d 466BG B-24 cr. Woodbridge A/F, crew baled (a/c had accidentally flown over enemy lines).

23/24 SEPTEMBER 1944

36BS despatched 6 B-24s on RCM.

24 SEPTEMBER 1944

Bad weather prevented bomber and fighter operations. 7PG despatched 2 F-5s on low level PR Arnhem and Nijmegen, both a/c MIA. 25BG despatched 2 B-24s on WR UK. 1 B-24 WR for *Truckin'* mission, and 1 Mosquito to WR Holland to N France. 47 B-24s (6 aborted) on *Truckin'*; fuel to France. 1 458BG B-24 MIA.

24/25 SEPTEMBER 1944

36BS despatched 3 B-24s on RCM.

25 SEPTEMBER 1944

8AF 647

	Despatched		Effective	Target	Bombs Tonnage	E/A	Losses MIA	E	Dam	Casualties KIA	WIA	MIA
3BD	B-17	534	400	LUDWIGSHAFEN/ OPAU (P) LUDWIGSHAFEN M/Y (P)	1133.5		3	1	86	0	9	0
			46	T/O	128.0							
1BD	B-17	444	410	FRANKFURT IND AREA (S)	1149.8		2	0	41	0	0	18
			2	T/O	6.0							
2BD	B-24	328	257	KOBLENZ/MOSEL M/Y(P) KOBLENZ/RHEIN M/Y (P)	673.5		0	0	14	0	0	0
TOTALS:		1306	1115		3090.8		2	1	141	0	9	18
VIII FC												
	P-51	216	200	ESCORT 3BD			0	0	0	0	0	0
	P-38	35	210	ESCORT 1BD			2	0	1	0	0	2
	P-51	192										
	P-38	39	157	ESCORT 2BD		0–0–2 (G)	0	0	0	0	0	0
	P-47	48					0	0	0	0	0	0
	P-51	92					1	0	2	0	0	1
TOTALS:		622	567		0	0–0–2(G)	3	0	3	0	0	3

REMARKS: Marshalling yards in western Germany and the synthetic oil plant at Ludwigshafen bombed by PFF. Only a T/O attacked by visual means. Bomb groups participating:– all 3BD except 95BG; all 1BD except 303BG; all 2BD except 96CBW groups. Bomb group losses:– 1BD – 381BG – 1, 384BG – 1. B/d 452BG B-17 abandoned over Luxemburg, crew safe.

All Fighter groups except 56FG, 78FG, 353FG operating. Totals include 55 9AF fighters operating under 8AF control. Fighter group losses:– 4FG – 1, 352FG – 1, 359FG – 1. SAAF exchange pilot in lost 4FG P-51.

OTHER OPERATIONS: 7PG despatched 2 F-5 on PR Nijmegen. 2 F-5 MIA. 25BG despatched 4 Mosquitoes on WR UK/Continent, 4 B-24s on WR Atlantic/Azores/UK. 1 Mosquito MIA. ASR despatched 8 P-47s on patrols. 2 P-38s, 1 B-17, 2 P-47s, 18 P-51s on radio-relays. 10 P-51s to scout for bombers. 176 B-24s on *Truckin'*, fuel to France. A 466BG B-24 missing.

25/26 SEPTEMBER 1944

36BS despatched 3 B-24s on RCM.

26 SEPTEMBER 1944

8AF 648

	Despatched		Effective	Target		Bombs Tonnage	E/A	Losses MIA	E	Dam	Casualties KIA	WIA	MIA
1BD	B-17	422	383	OSNABRÜCK M/Y & S/I		948.5		2	0	101	2	2	18
			10	RHEINE A/F	(O)	25.0							
			3	HESEPE A/F	(O)	7.5							
			4	T/O		8.5							
2BD	B-24	317	274	HAMM M/Y(P)		821.8		3	0	53	0	0	31
			1	LIESBORN	(O)	3.0							
3BD	B-17	420	381	BREMEN MT/I	(P)	1026.5		4	0	208	0	10	21
			13	BREMERHAVEN	(O)	30.0							
			1	T/O		1.5							
TOTALS:		1159	1070			2872.3	0	9	0	362	2	12	70
VIII FC													
	P-51	144	134	ESCORT 1BD			2–0–3 (G)	0	1	0	0	0	0
	P-51	146	138	ESCORT 2BD				1	0	0	0	0	1
	P-51	142	133	ESCORT 3BD				1	2	0	0	0	1
	P-38	67	320	HOLLAND – SUPPORT			32–1–8	1	0	0	0	0	1
	P-47	173		FOR 1ST ALLIED				0	1	5	0	0	0
	P-51	96		AIRBORNE ARMY				0	0	4	0	0	0
TOTALS:		768	725				32–1–8 2–0–3(G)	3	4	9	0	0	3

REMARKS: Rail targets and armoured vehicle factories in western Germany. 1BD attacked visually; 2BD and 3BD both visually and PFF. Bomb groups participating:– all 1BD except 306BG; all 2BD except 96CBW groups; all 3BD except 452BG, 490BG. Bomb group losses:– 1BD: 303BG – 1, 457BG – 1; 2BD – 446BG – 2, 491BG – 1; 3BD – 385BG – 2, 388BG – 1, 447BG – 1. A 385BG B-17 ditched, 7 rescued. MIA 388BG B-17 ditched off Calais, crew rescued.

All Fighter groups operating. Fighter group e/a credits:– 497FG – 27. Fighter group losses:– 339FG – 1, 361FG – 1, 479FG – 1. B/d 353FG P-51 cr. Ranworth Broad, pilot baled. Totals include 67 P-38s of 9AF operating under VIII FC control (claims 4–0–0). 1 352FG, a 357FG, a 361FG P-51s Cat E.

OTHER OPERATIONS: 7PG despatched 9 F-5s on PR Holland and Germany. 25BG despatched 3 Mosquitoes on WR UK/North Sea, and 5 B-24s on WR north and central Atlantic. Scouting Forces despatched 28 P-51s on WR for bombers. First mission of 2nd Scouting Force. ASR despatched 8 P-47s on patrols. 2 B-17s, 12 P-51s and 2 P-47s on radio-relays. 96CBW and 302ATW despatched 165 B-24s on *Truckin'* mission to France with fuel.

INCIDENT

The appearance of the German jet and rocket powered fighters with their considerable speed advantage over the P-51 in level flight was more a cause of frustration than concern to the Mustang pilots. To shoot down one of these elusive adversaries was a particularly inviting challenge and many pilots went to great lengths to achieve this aim. An illuminating example of an attempt to destroy an Me 262 is found in the encounter report of 361st Groups 1/Lt Urban Drew for 26 September 1944.

'I was leading Cadet Blue Flight in Cadet Squadron. We had just sighted the bombers and the marker flares in the vicinity of the target at Hamm. We were flying about 20,000 ft. I saw this unidentified aircraft cross under me about 10,000 ft below. He was flying on a course 90 degrees to ours. I could see it was a twin engine ship of some sort. I called the squadron leader and got permission to go down on a bounce. I started down in about a 60 degree dive with my wing tanks still on. As I got lower I could see I wasn't gaining any on the aircraft so I dropped my tanks. I was hitting about 500 mph and didn't seem to be closing on the aircraft at all. He actually was pulling further away from me. Just about that time, I saw the spurts of smoke that usually come out of a jet-propelled aircraft. He was still diving in about a 30 degree dive. I called out to the Group that I was chasing a jet-propelled aircraft and wasn't having too much luck. By this time we were right on the deck. I could see I wasn't gaining on the jet-job and was about to give up the chase when he started a shallow turn to the left. I immediately started a sharper turn to cut him off. As I was cutting him off he started tightening his turn. When we finally passed each other all I could get was about a 90 degree deflection shot, which didn't do me any good at all. I racked my ship around and started after him again, thinking that his speed would have been cut down some in his turn. As we straightened out I could see he wasn't pulling away from me but I couldn't gain on him either. I had everything wide open and was indicating about 410 mph straight and level on the deck. I chased him on this leg of the hunt about 30 seconds when I observed this airfield directly ahead of me. I could see the jet pilot intended to drag me across the field behind him. I called my flight and told them to hug the deck as closely as they could and I started a sharp right turn to skirt the edge of the airdrome. The flak was terrific and one of my wingmen was hit and had to bale out. There was a small marshalling yard directly ahead of me and I was going too fast to miss it. They opened up with another heavy flak barrage from all over the marshalling yard. The jet-job was still ahead of me and flying on a fairly straight course. I had been firing on the ship in his turns and every time I thought I was anywhere near being in range so I had used up quite a bit of my ammunition. Just then another jet-propelled aircraft dropped out of the lower cloud layer, which was about 4,000 ft, and headed for my flight. My wingman started a sharp turn into him but the jet pilot kept right on going and made no attempt to stay around and mix it up. The first jet-job started another shallow turn and I started firing from about 1,000 yds. I was too far out of range and couldn't get any hits on him at all. The jet-propelled ship then headed back for the airfield. I had fired all my ammunition except a couple hundred rounds and my wingman had been separated when he turned into the other jet so I decided it was just about time I left. I climbed up, after pin-pointing myself for the rest of the Group, and headed home.'

Drew expended 1,376 rounds during his fruitless pursuit – which also happened to be the only air firing conducted by any of the escort fighters that day. He had better luck a week later, making an air fighting first by shooting down two Me 262s shortly after their take-off.

It says much for the sound construction of the Fortress that 351BG's Capt Geiger was able to land 42-98004 at base with this damage. Over Cologne, 27 September, an 88 mm shell exploded in the fuselage blasting a special radio operator and the ball gunner in his turret out of the aircraft.

26/27 SEPTEMBER 1944

8AF 649 NIGHT LEAFLET OPERATION

NLS despatched 3 B-24s and 6 B-17s; France, Holland and Germany.

36BS despatched 4 B-24s on RCM.

25BG despatched 1 Mosquito on PR Holland.

27 SEPTEMBER 1944

8AF 650

	Despatched		Effective	Target		Bombs Tonnage	E/A	Losses MIA	E	Dam	Casualties KIA	WIA	MIA
1BD	B-17	462	421	COLOGNE	(S)	1246.7		0	1	165	3	7	1
			10	BLATZHEIM	(O)	29.7							
3BD	B-17	415	214	LUDWIGSHAFEN/ OPAU	(P)	585.7		2	0	142	3	9	19
			171	MAINZ	(P)	398.0							
			4	T/O		12.0							
2BD	B-24	315	248	KASSEL/HENSCHEL	(P)	707.5	5–3–0	26	6	41	20	2	245
			35	GÖTTINGEN	(O)	92.5							
TOTALS:		1192	1103			3072.1	5–3–0	28	7	348	26	18	265
VIII FC													
	P-47	45	221	ESCORT 1BD			5–0–0	0	0	3	0	0	0
	P-51	191						0	0	0	0	0	0
	P-47	95	212	ESCORT 3BD			1–0–0	0	0	1	0	0	0
	P-51	129						0	0	0	0	0	0
	P-38	25	207	ESCORT 2BD			25–0–6	0	0	2	0	0	0
	P-47	35					5–0–1 (G)	0	0	2	0	0	0
	P-51	58						2	1	0	0	0	2
TOTALS:		678	640				31–0–6 5–0–1(G)	2	1	6	0	0	2

REMARKS: Industrial and transportation targets in western Germany were all attacked by PFF methods. All bomb groups participating except the three 96CBW groups which were still assigned to the *Truckin'* operation. Bomb group losses:– 2BD – 445BG – 25, 491BG – 1; 3BD – 34BG – 1, 486BG – 1. The 486BG B-17 in sea after assembly collision Claydon, crew baled. 2 489BG B-24s collided on return and cr. Walberswick, 20 killed. 2 b/d 445BG B-24s c/l France, and 1 c/l Old Buckenham. B/d 351BG B-17 Cat E at base. 445BG loss of 28 a/c out of 37 despatched to fighter attack was largest loss for a group on any mission. B/d 453BG B-24 c/l France.

All Fighter groups operating. Totals include 23 9AF P-38s under 8AF control. Fighter group e/a credits:– 4FG – 5, 352FG – 4, 353FG – 1, 355FG – 3, 361FG – 18. Fighter group losses:– 361FG – 1, 479FG – 1. A 479FG P-51 c/l Kirton on return, pilot safe.

OTHER OPERATIONS: 25BG despatched 1 Mosquito on PR Holland, 4 Mosquitoes on WR Holland and Belgium, and 6 B-24s WR Atlantic/UK. 1SF and 2SF despatched 18 P-51s on WR for bombers. ASR despatched 8 P-47s. 4 P-38s also on ASR. 1 B-17, 4 P-47s, 16 P-51s on radio-relays. 163 B-24s on *Truckin'* mission, fuel to France.

INCIDENT

The so-called 'Company Front' tactics employed by the Luftwaffe's special bomber assault units, the *Sturmgruppen*, proved highly effective against B-17 and B-24 formations on several occasions during the summer and autumn of 1944. But for the presence of fighter escort it was evident that the 8th Air Force bombers would have been decimated by these mass attacks. As many as 48 heavily armed and armoured FW 190s, in close following wedges of 8 to 16, saturated the bombers' defensive fire and frequently disrupted their formation in a first pass. The most successful day for the *Sturmgruppen* was their 27th September slaughter of the wandering 445th Group; in three minutes they littered the countryside near Kassel with the burning wrecks of a score of Liberators. One of the surviving B-24 pilots, 1/Lt Don Smith, gave a graphic description: 'In one glance I saw four German fighters and five of our bombers going down. It was indescribable. Hollywood couldn't think of anything to match it.' Next day, despite the presence of American fighters, IV/JG 3, another *Sturmgruppe*, assailed the B-17s of 41st Combat Wing as they turned at their IP for Magdeburg. Eighteen B-17s went down before P-38s and P-51s could intervene, 11 from the veteran 303rd Group whose lead bomber pilot, 1/Lt Bernard Montana, later described the attack with implied outrage: 'When we turned on our bomb run we were attacked by about 50 Nazi fighters en masse, coming at us in a solid bunch. On their first pass they knocked down some of our planes. Then they swung out, came in again and again from all directions until our entire formation was shot up. Those guys were like mad men – with but one idea – to knock us down in a suicidal attack.'

27/28 SEPTEMBER 1944

8AF 651 NIGHT LEAFLET OPERATION

NLS B-17, 10 despatched, 8 effective; France, Holland, Germany.

36BS despatched 4 B-24s on RCM.

25BG despatched 2 Mosquitoes on PR Holland.

INCIDENT

The 27 September 1944 was a day of disaster for the 445th Group; when straying from the bomber stream it lost 25 B-24s, the highest loss for a single group in any 8th Air Force operation. The occasion of this disaster proved to be the most successful day for one Mustang squadron that heard the bombers' call for help and was soon on the scene. Led by 1/Lt Victor Bocquin, the 361st Group's 376th Fighter Squadron was able to intercept several of the heavily armoured FW 190s of *Sturmgruppe* II/JG 4 and the Me 109 escort. In combats that ranged from 24,000 ft to 'the deck' 376th pilots in their yellow-nosed P-51s accounted for 18 of the enemy and probably prevented complete elimination of the 445th Group force. One pilot, 1/Lt William Beyer, alone shot down five of the FW 190s and Bocquin destroyed three enemy fighters. At this date the 18 victories credited to the 376th stood as a record total for any 8th Air Force squadron in a single day's operations.

28 SEPTEMBER 1944

8AF 652

	Despatched		Effective	Target		Bombs Tonnage	E/A	Losses MIA	E	Dam	Casualties KIA	WIA	MIA
1BD	B-17	445	23	MAGDEBURG/ ROTHENSEE O/I	(P)	57.5	10–7– 5	23	2	126	0	8	208
			359	MAGDEBURG	(S)	918.2							
			35	T/O		85.8							
3BD	B-17	342	301	MERSEBURG/LEUNA O/I	(P)	772.8		10	4	251	4	15	92
			10	T/O		21.0							
2BD	B-24	262	243	KASSEL/HENSCHEL MT/I	(P)	700.8		1	0	86	0	0	10
			1	T/O		4.0							
TOTALS:		1049	972			2560.1	10–7–5	34	6	463	4	23	309
VIII FC													
	P-38	23	263	ESCORT 1BD			24–0–13	0	0	0	0	0	0
	P-51	275					1–0– 0(G)	5	1	4	0	0	5
	P-51	231	212	ESCORT 3BD			2–1– 0	1	0	0	0	0	1
	P-47	195	171	ESCORT 2BD				1	0	3	0	0	1
TOTALS:		724	646				26–1–13 1–0– 0(G)	7	1	7	0	0	7

REMARKS: Oil and military vehicle plants in central Germany attacked by PFF means. Bomb groups participating:– all 1BD; all 2BD except 96CBW groups; all 3BD except 96BG and 493BG. Bomb group losses:– 1 BD – 303BG – 11, 379BG – 2, 384BG – 2, 398BG – 1, 401BG – 1, 457BG – 6; 2BD – 389BG – 1; 3BD – 34BG – 1, 95BG – 1, 100BG – 1, 388BG – 5, 486BG – 1, 487BG – 1. Two 388BG a/c collided over target. B/d 401BG B-17 c/l Belgium, crew safe. B/d 398BG B-17 c/l Brussels, crew safe. B/d 388BG B-17 c/l near Liège, crew safe. B/d 490BG B-17 Cat E. B/d 95BG B-17 cr. Continent, 3 k. Bombers encountered heavy fighter attacks.

All Fighter groups operating. Fighter group e/a credits:– 4FG – 1, 20FG – 7, 339FG – 2, 364FG – 3, 479FG – 13. Fighter group losses:– 20FG – 1, 56FG – 1, 357FG – 1, 359FG – 1, 361FG – 1, 364FG – 2. 364FG P-51 c/l Brussels A/F, pilot safe.

OTHER OPERATIONS: 7PG despatched 10 F-5s and 3 Spitfires on PR Germany. 25BG despatched 6 Mosquitoes on WR UK/Continent, and 4 B-24s on WR Atlantic/UK. 1SF and 2SF despatched 28 P-51s on WR for bombers. ASR despatched 10 P-47s on patrols. 1 B-17, 5 P-47s and 23 P-51s on radio-relays. 194 B-24s were despatched on *Truckin'* mission with fuel to France. 1SF P-51 c/l near Liège, pilot safe.

INCIDENT

The general consensus of opinion among bomber crewmen was that the worst part of any mission was the tense post-briefing pre-take-off period of waiting when the 'knot of apprehension tightened in your gut'. Imagine the added stress to the nervous system for Lt Budd and crew when a groundman walked into an invisible propeller arc of their Fortress *Budd's Dudds* as the bomber waited to leave Deenethorpe for Magdeburg on 28 September 1944. The man had made the fatal error of trying to dodge between the bombers' 'cab-rank' on the perimeter track. Death was instantaneous, the blades severing an arm and slashing through the body cavity. Lt Budd, alarm in his voice, radiod the control tower for an ambulance. There followed an exchange of messages. Finally the deputy commander of 401st Group instructed Lt Budd to 'Continue on your mission, taxi and take-off immediately.'

28/29 SEPTEMBER 1944

8AF 653 NIGHT LEAFLET OPERATION

NLS despatched 4 B-24s and 6 B-17s to France, Holland, Germany.

36BS despatched 5 B-24s on RCM.

29 SEPTEMBER 1944

Weather restricted operations. 7PG despatched 3 F-5s and 3 Spitfires on PR Germany. 25BG despatched 2 Mosquitoes on WR North Sea and France, and 4 B-24s on WR Atlantic/UK. 190 B-24s (3 aborted) on *Truckin'* operation; fuel to France.

INCIDENT

The advent of scouting fighter aircraft for providing target weather information to the commanders of bomber task forces proved to be of considerable value in ensuring the fulfilment of a mission. In fact, Brig.Gen Leon Johnson, Commander of the 14th Combat Wing and one of the longest serving and most experienced bomber leaders in the 8th, was of the opinion that nothing had done more to increase the efficiency of bomber operations than the introduction of weather scouts. The second such unit, the 2nd Scouting Force serving the 2nd Division, commenced operations on 26 September 1944 under Lt.Col John Brooks, a veteran B-24 pilot. Two days later the Division's bomber leaders were quick to appreciate the value of these few Mustangs preceding their bombers to the target area. The Scouts radioed information about changes in wind direction and velocity, assisting the Division Commander in making subsequent decisions. Upon reaching the target at Kassel which was overcast, the Scouting Force leader, using the call sign 'Shamrock Red', made a sound recommendation for bombing by pathfinder means. Throughout the flow of bomber boxes over the target the Scouting Force remained in the vicinity reporting results of bombing and offering advice for effecting the rally of the last two wings over the target, which the Scout Leader considered should slow down slightly in order to close up their rather spread formations. Throughout the route home the scouts again reported weather conditions well in advance of the returning bombers assisting the Division Commander in selecting the best altitudes for return to base.

29/30 SEPTEMBER 1944

8 AF 654 NIGHT LEAFLET OPERATION

NLS despatched 5 B-24s and 5 B-17s to Holland, France and Germany.

30 SEPTEMBER 1944

8AF 655

	Despatched		Effective	Target		Bombs Tonnage	E/A	Losses MIA	E	Dam	Casualties KIA	WIA	MIA
3BD	B-17	266	257	BIELEFELD M/Y	(P)	596.0		4	1	24	0	3	28
2BD	B-24	255	206	HAMM M/Y	(P)	560.7		1	0	32	0	0	10
			12	MÜNSTER	(O)	38.5							
			1	T/O		3.0							
1BD	B-17	313	14	MÜNSTER/ HANDORF A(F	(P)	41.5		3	0	85	1	2	36
			35	MÜNSTER M/Y	(P)	104.0							
			239	MÜNSTER	(O)	699.8							
			1	T/O		3.0							
TOTALS:		834	765			2046.5	0	8	1	141	1	5	74
VIII FC													
	P-47	102	240	ESCORT 3BD					0	0	0	0	0
	P-51	150											
	P-38	18	170	ESCORT 2BD					0	0	0	0	0
	P-47	36											
	P-51	129											
	P-47	48	177	ESCORT 1BD					0	0	0	0	0
	P-51	146							1	0	0	0	0
	P-51	97	86	SWEEP NW GERMANY					1	0	0	0	0
TOTALS:		726	673				0	0	2	0	0	0	0

REMARKS: PFF attacks on M/Ys and A/Fs in western Germany. Bomb groups participating:– all 1BD groups except 303BG, 351BG, 381BG; all 2BD except 96CBW groups; all 3BD except 4CBW groups and 34BG, 388BG, 486BG. Bomb group losses:– 1BD – 401BG – 2, 457BG – 1; 2BD – 44BG – 1; 3BD – 487BG – 2, 493BG – 2. Two B-17s collided over sea on penetration. 452BG B-17 cr. UK.

All Fighter groups operating: No losses or claims. 364FG P-51 c/l base on return, pilot safe. 359FG P-51 c/l – Cat E, pilot safe.

30 SEPTEMBER 1944

OTHER OPERATIONS: 7PG despatched 4 F-5s and 1 Spitfire on PR Germany. 25BG despatched 3 Mosquitoes on WR Continent/UK, 3 B-24s on WR Azores/Atlantic/UK. Scouting Forces despatched 28 P-51s on WR for bombers. ASR despatched 9 P-47s on patrols. 2 B-17s, 18 P-51s, 4 P-47s, 4 P-38s on radio-relays. 116 B-24s *Truckin'* mission with fuel to France.

1 OCTOBER 1944

Weather prevented combat operations. 25BG despatched 2 Mosquitoes on WR UK/North Sea and 4 B-24s on WR Azores/Atlantic/UK. Mission 656 was a daylight leaflet operation by 4 B-17s and 6 B-24s to France, Holland and western Germany (1 B-24 aborted). 1 P-38 despatched on special test mission.

1/2 OCTOBER 1944

8AF 657 NIGHT LEAFLET OPERATION

NLS despatched 10a/c, 9 effective; France, Holland, Belgium.

25BG despatched 2 Mosquitoes on PR Low Countries.

2 OCTOBER 1944

8AF 658

	Despatched		Effective	Target		Bombs Tonnage	E/A	Losses MIA	E	Dam	Casualties KIA	WIA	MIA
1BD	B-17	305	129	KASSEL/ BETTENHAUSEN	(P)	319.4		0	1	89	0	5	0
			143	KASSEL	(O)	271.8							
			12	FRITZLAR A/F	(O)	30.0							
			1	T/O		2.5							
3BD	B-17	458	384	KASSEL/HENSCHEL MT/I	(P)	970.6		2	2	144	16	1	20
			31	WIESBADEN	(O)	75.3							
			9	GESECKE		21.5							
			17	T/O		40.3							
1BD	B-17	124	110	COLOGNE/FORD MT/I	(P)	272.5			1	36	0	0	0
8AF 659													
2BD	B-24	308	266	HAMM M/Y	(P)	684.7		2	2	144	1	0	18
			29	HANDORF A/F	(O)	69.5							
			1	MÜNSTER	(O)	2.5							
TOTALS:		1195	1132			2760.6	0	4	6	413	17	6	38
VIII FC													
	P-47	98	228	ESCORT 1BD				0	0		0	0	0
	P-51	153						0	0		0	0	0
	P-47	40	219	ESCORT 3BD				0	0		0	0	0
	P-51	200						0	0		0	0	0
	P-47	42	53	ESCORT 41CBW				0	0		0	0	0
	P-51	16						0	0		0	0	0
	P-38	12	212	ESCORT 2BD				0	0		0	0	0
	P-47	8						0	0		0	0	0
	P-51	203						1	2		1	0	1
TOTALS:		772	712				0	1	2	7	1	0	1

REMARKS: Mission 658; PFF attacks on industrial targets at Cologne and Kassel. Mission 659; PFF attack on Hamm M/Y. Bomb groups participating:– all 1BD except 381BG and 457BG; all 2BD (first combat mission for 96CBW groups since *Truckin'* operation began on 12 Bomb group losses:– 2BD – 453BG – 1, 491BG – 1; 3BD – 34BG – 1, 452BG – 1. A 92BG B-17 cr. Wellesbourne Mountford after assembly collision, crew baled. Two 447BG B-17s collided and cr. Kettlebaston and Hitcham, 16 k. B/d 447BG and 457BG B-17s c/l Belgium, crew safe. On return, a 489BG B-24 c/l Beccles, 1 k.

All Fighter groups operated. 353FG using P-51s for the first time. Fighter group losses:– 4FG – 1. A 479FG P-51 cr. on t/o, pilot killed. 361FG P-51 cr. after t/o, pilot baled.

OTHER OPERATIONS: 7PG despatched 4 F-5s and 1 Spitfire on PR Germany. 25BG despatched 3 Mosquitoes on WR NE France and C. Germany, and 4 B-24s on WR Atlantic/UK. Scouting Forces despatched 27 P-51s (3-aborted) on WR for bombers. ASR despatched 13 P-47s on patrols. 2 B-17s, 6 P-47s, 13 P-51s on radio-relays. Mission 660 involved 2 B-17s with 15 P-51s as escort on day leaflet mission to Dutch Islands.

2/3 OCTOBER 1944

NLS despatched 5 B-24s and 3 B-17s to Holland, France and Germany.

25BG despatched 2 Mosquitoes on PR Low Countries.

Hangover Haven appeared to live up to its name while landing at base, 3 October. Leaving the runway on an erratic course due to the collapse of the left undercarriage leg it managed to mutilate a civilian car before coming to rest on a GI truck. Nobody was hurt but there was an expensive heap of mangled machinery.

Bombers Moon is caught in the strike photo of a higher 489BG Liberator as the second wave of bombers aim for the fuel storage area on Speyerdorf airfield, 3 October. First strikes fall slightly short of aiming point.

3 OCTOBER 1944

8AF 662

	Despatched		Effective	Target		Bombs Tonnage	E/A	Losses MIA	E	Dam	Casualties KIA	WIA	MIA
3BD	B-17	380	49	GIEBELSTADT A/F	(P)	115.0		0	0	130	0	2	0
			256	NÜRNBERG	(O)	619.0							
			11	ULM	(O)	26.0							
			13	LUDWIGSHAFEN	(O)	32.5							
			24	T/O		58.0							
1BD	B-17	228	198	NÜRNBERG MT/I	(P)	483.0		3	1	63	2	4	28
			10	ÖTTINGEN A/F	(O)	25.0							
1BD	B-17	119	87	WESSELING O/R	(P)	217.5		0	1	51	0	0	0
			26	COLOGNE	(O)	65.0							
			1	T/O		2.5							
2BD	B-24	338	139	GAGGENAU	(P)	402.5		0	1	38	0	2	0
			111	LACHEN/ SPEYERDORF	(P)	294.0							
			19	PFORZHEIM A/F	(S)	52.5							
			19	OFFENBURG M/Y	(S)	55.0							
			30	SPEYER A/F	(O)	70.7							
			2	LACHEN	(O)	5.0							
TOTALS:		1065	995			2522.7	0	3	3	282	2	8	28
	P-47	49	260	ESCORT 3BD			2–0–0	0	0				
	P-51	243					(G)	4	1				
	P-47	48	227	ESCORT 1BD				0	0				
	P-51	188						0	1				
	P-47	24	24	ESCORT 41CBW				0	0				
	P-38	13	188	ESCORT 2BD				0	0				
	P-47	48											
0	0												
TOTALS:		753	699					4	2	10	0	1	4

REMARKS: 1BD and 3BD attacked airfields and industrial targets in Germany by PFF means. 2BD was able to bomb visually. Bomb groups participating:– all 3BD except 381BG and 457BG; all 2BD (first combat mission for 96CBW groups since *Truckin'* operation began on 12 Sep); all 3BD except 490BG. 41CBW groups attacked Wesseling by GH. Bomb group losses:– 1BD – 92BG – 2, 351BG – 1. On return a 448BG B-24 c/l near Calais, crew safe; b/d 401BG B-17 c/l base, crew safe; b/d 384BG B-17 f/l Belgium – Cat E.

All Fighter groups operating. 479FG flew its last mission with P-38s, which was also last use of this type as a fighter by 8AF. Fighter group losses:– 55FG – 1, 353FG – 1, 355FG – 2. B/d 353FG P-51 cr. France, pilot baled. 359FG P-51 c/l Continent.

OTHER OPERATIONS: 7PG despatched 4 F-5s on PR Germany. 25BG despatched 2 Mosquitoes on PR Germany, 2 Mosquitoes on WR Continent, 3 B-24s on WR Atlantic/UK. Scouting Forces despatched 29 P-51s on WR for bombers. ASR despatched 23 P-47s on patrols. 10 a/c despatched on radio-relay.

3/4 OCTOBER 1944

8AF 663 NIGHT LEAFLET OPERATION

NLS despatched 6 B-24s and 4 B-17s; France, Germany, Holland, Belgium.

25BG despatched 2 Mosquitoes on PR Low Countries.

4 OCTOBER 1944

Bad weather – 25BG despatched 2 Mosquitoes (1 aborted) on PR Holland, and 3 Mosquitoes on WR North Sea, and 4 B-24s on WR Azores/Atlantic/UK.

4/5 OCTOBER 1944

8AF 664 NIGHT LEAFLET OPERATION

NLS despatched 5 B-24s and 4 B-17s (1a/c aborted); Low Countries, France, Germany.

36BS despatched 5 B-24s on RCM.

25BG despatched 1 Mosquito on night photography; Low Countries.

5 OCTOBER 1944

8AF 665

	Despatched		Effective	Target		Bombs Tonnage	E/A	Losses MIA	E	Dam	Casualties KIA	WIA	MIA
1BD	B-17	348	248	COLOGNE	(O)	726.7		3	2	156	1	0	16
			11	COBLENZ	(O)	33.0							
			27	BRECHTEN	(O)	79.8							
			14	DORTMUND	(O)	41.5							
2BD	B-24	360	107	RHEINE M/Y	(P)	168.1		0	1	7	0	0	0
			175	LIPPSTADT A/F	(P)	491.0							
			28	PADERBORN A/F	(P)	81.3							
			8	HERFORD M/Y	(O)	21.0							
			2	LIPPERODE A/F	(O)	4.0							
3BD	B-17	382	235	MÜNSTER/ LODDENHEIDE A/F	(P)	644.7		6	1	190	0	6	55
			68	MÜNSTER/HANDORF A/F	(P)	122.3							
			10	RHEINE M/Y	(O)	27.5							
			2	T/O		5.7							
TOTALS:		1090	935			2446.6		9	4	353	1	6	71
VIII FC													
	P-51	193	181	ESCORT 1BD				3	0	0	0	0	3
	P-47	96	260	ESCORT 2BD			1–0–0	0	0	3	0	0	0
	P-51	195					15–0–7(G)	1	0	1	0	0	1
	P-47	49	234	ESCORT 3BD				0	0	0	0	0	0
	P-51	200											
TOTALS:		733	675				1–0–0 15–0–7(G)	5	0	4	0	0	4

REMARKS: Industrial targets, airfields and railways in western Germany. 1BD used GH and H2X; 2BD bombed visually; 3BD used PFF means. Bomb groups participating: all 1BD except 91BG and 401BG; all 2BD except 448BG; all 3BD except 388BG and 487BG. Bomb group losses:– 1BD – 92BG – 1, 379BG – 1, 384BG – 1; 3BD – 94BG – 1, 96BG – 1, 385BG – 1, 452BG – 1, 486BG – 1, 493BG – 1. Three B-17s ditched; 94BG crew lost; 92BG, 2 rescued; 379BG all rescued. B/d 398BG, 457BG and 486BG B-17s down on Continent, Cat E.

All Fighter groups operating. Fighter group losses:– 339FG – 1, 352FG – 1, 355FG – 1, 359FG – 1, 364FG – 1. The 339FG pilot baled, 40 miles from Aldeburgh, rescued.

OTHER OPERATIONS: 7PG despatched 7 F-5s on PR Germany. 25BG despatched 7 Mosquitoes on WR North Sea/France, and 5 B-24s on WR Atlantic/UK. Scouting Forces despatched 28 P-51s on WR for bombers. ASR despatched 18 P-47s on patrols. 4 P-38s were despatched on a special operation. 2 B-27s, 4 P-47s, 10 P-51s on radio-relays.

5/6 OCTOBER 1944

8AF 666 NIGHT LEAFLET OPERATION

NLS despatched 10 a/c, 8 a/c effective; France, Holland, Germany.

36BS despatched 7 B-24 on RCM.

25BG despatched 1 Mosquito on night photography; Low Countries.

6 OCTOBER 1944

8AF 667

	Despatched		Effective	Target		Bombs Tonnage	E/A	Losses MIA	E	Dam	Casualties KIA	WIA	MIA
1BD	B-17	447	199	STARGARD A/F	(P)	493.0		1	0	34	0	0	9
			12	STETTIN	(P)	30.0							
			73	NEUBRANDEN-BURG A/I	(P)	177.5							
			110	STRALSUND	(O)	367.3							
			36	KAPPELN	(O)	3.5							
			1	FREIENWALDE	(O)	0.5							
			1	T/O	(O)	2.5							
3BD	B-17	418	68	BERLIN/SPANDAU M/D	(P)	167.4	3–9–5	17	1	234	3	4	154
			138	BERLIN/SPANDAU A/I	(P)	309.9							
			76	BERLIN/SPANDAU M/D	(P)	156.8							
			100	BERLIN/TEGEL AFV/I	(P)	265.0							
			10	T/O		22.6							
2BD	B-24	406	121	HARBURG RHENANIA EBANO O/I	(P)	319.7		1	0	127	1	2	10
			89	HAMBURG/GLINDE M/D	(P)	238.9							
			79	HAMBURG/ KLOCKNER A/I	(P)	220.1							
			46	WENZENDORF A/I	(P)	134.0							
			29	STADE A/F	(O)	79.3							
			8	HAMBURG AREA	(O)	24.0							
			2	NORDHOLZ A/F	(O)	6.0							
			1	OTTERSBERG	(O)	3.0							
			1	BREMERVORDE	(O)	3.0							
TOTALS:		1271	1200			3024.5	3–9–5	19	1	395	4	6	173
VIII FC													
	P-51	202	180	ESCORT 1BD			3–1– 3 30–0–14(G)	3	2	4	0	0	3
	P-51	414	363	ESCORT 3BD			15–0– 5	1	0	3	0	0	4
	P-47	168	156	ESCORT 2BD			1–0– 0	0	0	6	0	0	0
TOTALS:		784	699				19–1–8 30–0–14(G)	4	2	13	0	0	7

REMARKS: Industrial targets in northern Germany. Weather caused 1BD attack on Pölitz to be abandoned. All visual bombing except the 2BD attack on Harburg which was PFF. Bomb groups participating:– all 1BD and 2BD, all 3BD except 493BG. Bomb group losses:– 1BD – 379BG – 1, 2BD – 489BG – 1; 3BD – 94BG – 4, 100BG – 1, 385BG – 10, 447BG – 1, 490BG – 1. Mass fighter attack on 4CBW brought down 14 B-17s. B/d 94BG B-17 ditched 1 mile off Lowestoft, 2 rescued. On return m/f 34BG B-17 cr. Brampton, Suffolk, crew baled. MIA PFF 94BG B-17 with pact 385BG crew.

All Fighter groups operating. Fighter group e/a credits:– 4FG – 3, 355FG – 3, 357FG – 7, 359FG – 4, 361FG – 1, 479FG – 2. Fighter group losses:– 55FG – 1, 352FG – 1, 361FG – 2. The ground claims total includes 30–0–12 seaplanes destroyed by 20FG at five bases from Stettin to Lübeck. On return 364FG P-51 c/l Halvergate, pilot safe. 352FG P-51 Cat E.

OTHER OPERATIONS: 7PG despatched 8 F-5s and 4 Spitfires to Germany and Holland on PR. 1 F-5 MIA (shot down Me 262). 25BG despatched 1 Mosquito on WR Germany, and 3 B-24s on WR Atlantic/UK. ASR despatched 16 P-47s on patrols. 1 B-17, 6 P-47s and 20 P-51s on radio-relays. Scouting Forces despatched 29 P-51s (4 aborted) on WR for bombers.

6/7 OCTOBER 1944

8AF 668 NIGHT LEAFLET OPERATION

NLS despatched 6 B-24s and 4 B-17s; Germany, Holland, France.

36BS despatched 7 B-24s on RCM.

25BG despatched 2 Mosquitoes on night PR Holland.

EVENT

By the autumn of 1944 the 379th Bomb Group had emerged as the 8th Air Force's overall leader in bombing and engineering efficiency through persistently showing low losses, few mechanical abortives, more bombers over and more bombs on targets than any other group. Indeed, the commander of 41st Combat Wing – of which 379th Group was part – went on record as saying the 379th stood No.1 in the whole USAAF at this time. Some of this success can be traced to the Group's participation in the short range missions where GH bombing aids were employed, but the major factor was the high level of efficiency in all departments established by the original CO, Col Maurice Preston, and his staff. At the same time it appears some men at Kimbolton did not proceed with as much care at play as they did at work for the 379th also had, as the Group historian noted, 'A record of which we are not proud', the highest VD rate in the Division. As a result all personnel had to attend a VD lecture each month before being allowed 'on pass'. Despite this cautioning the 379th retained this embarrassing position as well as that of combat supremacy into the winter of 1944–45.

7 OCTOBER 1944

8AF 669

	Despatched		Effective	Target		Bombs Tonnage	E/A	Losses MIA	E	Dam	Casualties KIA	WIA	MIA
1BD	B-17	149	142	PÖLITZ O/I	(P)	347.8		17	0	106	2	17	171
1BD	B-17	333	59	RUHLAND O/I	(P)	147.5		3	0	172	0	0	0
			60	ZWICKAU A/F	(O)	150.0							
			58	ZWICKAU MT/I	(O)	141.7							
			30	DRESDEN	(O)	72.5							
			24	FREIBURG	(O)	60.0							
			87	T/O		217.5							
3BD	B-17	451	86	BÖHLEN O/I	(P)	205.0	11–13–10	16	2	240	2	15	149
			88	LÜTZKENDORF O/I	(P)	205.5							
			129	MERSEBURG/LEUNA O/I	(P)	309.3							
			24	NORDHAUSEN A/F	(O)	57.0							
			51	BIELEFELD	(O)	123.0							
			27	T/O HAMELN		63.0							
2BD	B-24	489	25	MAGDEBURG/	(P)	65.0							
				ROTHENSEE O/I	(P)	65.0		4	1	183	2	6	38
			62	MAGDEBURG/ BÜCKAU O/I	(P)	180.0							
			88	KASSEL/ ALTENBAUNA	(P)	142.5							
			122	KASSEL/HENSCHEL MT/I	(P)	326.0							
			129	CLAUSTHAL	(O)	384.4							
			4	HENGELO M/Y	(O)	15.0							
			10	BERGEN/STEINFORT	(O)	24.0							
			6	T/O		17.0							
TOTALS:		1422	1401			3188.2	11–13–10	40	3	701	6	38	358
VIII FC													
	P-51	108	93	ESCORT 94CBW			7–0–3	1	0	0	0	0	1
	P-51	256	214	ESCORT 1BD			12–0–0 1–0–1(G)	4	1	1	0	1	4
	P-47	70		ESCORT 3BD			10–0–1	1	0	2	0	0	1
	P-51	216						1	1	1	0	0	1
	P-38	41	214	ESCORT 2BD			8–0–0(G)	0	0	0	0	0	0
	P-47	113						1	0	1	0	0	1
	P-51	96						3	0	1	0	0	2
TOTALS:		900	521				29–0–4 9–0–1(G)	11	2	7	0	1	10

REMARKS: Oil installations at Pölitz, Brüx, Ruhland, Böhlen, Lützkendorf, Merseburg and Magdeburg, and armoured vehicle plants at Kassel. Visual bombing except at some 3BD targets. Major operation with all bomb groups operating. 94CBW groups composed Pölitz Force. Bomb group losses:– 1BD – 92BG – 1, 305BG – 1, 351BG – 7, 384BG – 1, 401BG – 5, 457BG – 5; 2BD – 44BG – 2, 392BG – 1, 489BG – 1; 3BD – 34BG – 2, 94BG – 8, 95BG – 3, 96BG – 1, 100BG – 1, 447BG – 1. MIA a/c landing or cr. in Sweden – 351BG – 5, 401BG – 2, 457BG – 1. 388BG c/l Walpole during assembly. MIA 457BG B-17 ditched, crew rescued.

All Fighter groups operating. Fighter group e/a credits:– 55FG – 2, 78FG – 3, 355FG – 1, 356FG – 1, 357FG – 4, 361FG – 8, 364FG – 1, 479FG – 2. Fighter group losses:– 4FG – 1, 20FG – 3, 55FG – 1, 78FG – 1, 356FG – 1, 359FG – 1, 361FG – 1, 479FG – 2. 479FG pilots baled and rescued from MIA a/c. Two 20FG P-51s MIA collided. 354FG and 474FG of 9AF operating under 8AF control from Debden and Honington respectively – 40 P-51s and 41 P-38s despatched and included in totals. 4FG pilot baled over sea, saved. B/d 359FG P-51 Cat E. 361FG P-51 Cat E, pilot inj.

OTHER OPERATIONS: 7PG despatched 29 F-5s and 7 Spitfires on PR Germany. 25BG despatched 3 Mosquitoes on WR Belgium, France, Germany, Denmark, and 4 B-24s on WR Atlantic/UK. 1SF and 2SF despatched 31 P-51s on WR for bombers. ASR despatched 20 P-47s on patrols and 8 P-51s also on ASR search. 1 B-17, 2 P-47s, 14 P-51s on radio-relays.

EVENT

While the liberation of France meant that flight time over hostile territory to many targets in Germany had been halved, the anti-aircraft guns withdrawn as the Allies advanced added to the already formidable concentrations in the Reich. Defences at the vital synthetic oil plants were bolstered and frequently took a heavy toll of the B-17s and B-24s. Just how effective these defences could be was evinced at Pölitz, near Stettin, on 7 October 1944. On a day of attacks on the German oil industry the 94th Wing alone had been assigned this important target, ordered to mount a maximum effort. 149 B-17s were despatched in four group boxes, the last a composite. Aware of an estimated 270 105 mm and 88 mm guns in place at Pölitz, the route planned allowed an eight minute bomb run and exit out over the bay of Stettin. En route to the target the composite group overran the 401st Group and the 351st Group went wide at the IP. Manoeuvres to rectify the situation resulted in two groups bombing within 30 seconds of one another. Even though the whole force was in range for less time than originally planned, 17 B-17s were shot down or so badly crippled that they did not return to England, 30 received major damage and 76 minor damage; only 19 of the B-17s reaching the target went unscathed. Perhaps the most worrying aspect to 8th Air Force was the fact that four of the bombers lost were leadships and five deputies, indicating that the flak batteries aimed for the van of a formation. What was not known at the time was that the H2X emissions from these aircraft were tracked by German ground radar and aided range computations.

INCIDENT

By the late summer of 1944 few B-17F model Fortresses remained in service for normal bombing operations. Since the last of this type, without the chin turret, had been assigned to combat groups in the previous autumn, combat attrition so thinned their numbers that within nine months they had become a comparative rarity in a formation. Most of the remainder were retired to training duties, chiefly because the B-17F had hydraulically actuated turbo-supercharger regulators that were sluggish in operation, liable to failure in extreme temperatures and thus they became thoroughly unpopular with pilots. A few had new type electronic controls fitted, but this refinement was not considered worthwhile for the majority of these ageing battle veterans. The last 8th Air Force B-17F on regular bombing operations was *Blind Date*, the pride of the 388th Group. This Fortress was also the last surviving 'original' bomber of those the Group received in the United States before flying to England in June 1943.

Blind Date had flown on most of the famous 8th Air Force missions and, as the repair patches to her skin indicated, had attracted quite a bit of attention from the enemy. Her gunners were credited with five enemy fighters in beating off attacks. Two successive crews had been assigned this bomber for combat tours and another had charge of her when, on 7 October, *Blind Date* took off from Knettishall bound for Böhlen on her 67th operation and the crew's second. Evidently age was beginning to tell, for as the bomber climbed No.1 engine suddenly burst into flames. Fearing that the fire would get out of control before he could reach the safety of an airfield 2/Lt Harold Resch, deciding to make a crash-landing, selected a ploughed field at Walpole. After coming to rest the crew vacated the blazing Fortress at great speed and ran to warn the occupants of nearby houses and a school that ten 500 lb bombs might soon explode. In fact it was nearly two hours later that the explosion occurred and distributed what little remained of the famous bomber. No one was injured and only minor damage was done to houses.

7/8 OCTOBER 1944

36BS despatched 6 B-24s on RCM in support RAF operations.

8 OCTOBER 1944

7PG despatched 1 F-5 to Walcheren. 25BG despatched 2 Mosquitoes on WR Belgium, France, UK, and 3 B-24s on WR Atlantic ASR despatched 6 P-47s and 6 P-51s and 6 B-17s also on ASR search. 25BG despatched first *Skywave* LORAN navigational equipment calibration mission, flown by Mosquito to land at San Severo, Italy.

8/9 OCTOBER 1944

36BS despatched 7 B-24s (1 aborted) on RCM.

9 OCTOBER 1944

8AF 670

	Despatched		Effective	Target		Bombs Tonnage	E/A	Losses MIA	E	Dam	Casualties KIA	WIA	MIA
1BD	B-17	345	329	SCHWEINFURT B/I	(S)	817.2		0		15	0	0	0
			1	T/O		2.5							
3BD	B-17	381	210	MAINZ M/Y	(P)	493.7		0	0	84	0	0	0
			148	GUSTAVSBURG A/I	(P)	353.5							
2BD	B-24	384	360	KOBLENZ M/Y	(S)	972.6		1	3	17	1	0	10
			1	T/O		3.0							
TOTALS:		1110	1049			2642.5		1	3	116	1	0	10
VIII FC													
	P-51	364	338	ESCORT 1BD				0	3	0	0	1	0
	P-38	38	202	ESCORT 3BD				0	0	2	0	0	0
	P-47	181						0	0	0	0	0	0
	P-51	295	271	ESCORT 2BD			1–0–0						
							1–0–0(G)	0	0	0	0	0	0
TOTALS:		878	811				1–0–0 1–0–0(G)	0	3	2	0	1	0

REMARKS: PFF attacks on industrial targets in south and central Germany. Only two primaries hit. Bomb groups participating: all 1BD except 94CBW groups; all 2BD; all 3BD except 390BG. Bomb group losses:– 93BG – 1. B/d 392BG B-24 c/l West Bradenham, 1 killed. 445BG B-24 c/l Manston A/F on return. B/d 491BG B-24 c/l Continent.

All Fighter groups operating. A 20FG P-51 cr. on t/o. 354FG despatched 42 P-51s and 474FG 38 P-38s under 8AF control. Last mission of 9AF groups under VIII FC control. 55FG P-51 Cat E.

OTHER OPERATIONS: 7PG despatched 4 F-5s to Germany on PR. 25BG despatched 2 Mosquitoes on WR Continent, 1 Mosquito to Italy, 5 B-24s on WR Atlantic/UK. Scouting Forces despatched 18 P-51s on WR for bombers. ASR despatched 32 P-47s on patrols and 12 P-51s and 8 B-24s also on ASR search. 2 B-17s, 2 P-47s and 12 P-51s on radio-relays.

INCIDENT

When Capt Ken L. Gilbert brought the 93rd Bomb Group B-24 *Missouri Sue* back from Koblenz on 9 October 1944 he had established a record believed unsurpassed for an 8th Air Force B-24 crewman. The occasion was his 75th combat mission, the result of flying two consecutive combat tours in a six-month period. Gilbert began combat missions with that to Oschersleben on 12 April 1944 and completed his first tour exactly three months to the day on 12 July.

10 OCTOBER 1944

36BS despatched 7 B-24s (6 effective) on RCM bad weather spoof sorties in conjunction with 8AF 671, a leaflet operation by 2 B-24s over Holland.

25BG despatched 4 Mosquitoes on WR Continent and 4 B-24s on WR Atlantic/UK. ASR despatched 16 P-47s on patrols, and 8 P-51s also on ASR search.

11 OCTOBER 1944

8AF 672

	Despatched		Effective	Target		Bombs Tonnage	E/A	Losses MIA	E	Dam	Casualties KIA	WIA	MIA
1BD	B-17	135	57	WESSELING O/I	(P)	169.0	0	4	0	61	3	6	38
			73	KOBLENZ M/Y	(S)	211.5							
	P-47	139	135	ESCORT B-17s			0	1	0	0	0	0	0

REMARKS: GH attack by 41CBW groups although primary was clear for visual bombing. Bomb group losses:– 303BG – 2, 384BG – 2.

Fighter escort provided by 56FG, 78FG, 356FG. Fighter group losses:– 56FG – 1.

OTHER OPERATIONS: 25BG despatched 2 Mosquitoes on PR France and Belgium, 3 Mosquitoes (1 aborted) on WR Atlantic/UK. ASR despatched 17 P-47s on patrols and 8 P-51s also on ASR search. (4FG: also strafed barges.) 6 P-47s on radio-relays.

11/12 OCTOBER 1944

8AF 673 NIGHT LEAFLET OPERATION

NLS despatched 9 a/c to France, Holland, Germany.

1 P-38 despatched on special radar monitoring sortie.

12 OCTOBER 1944

8AF 674

	Despatched		Effective	Target		Bombs Tonnage	E/A	Losses MIA	E	Dam	Casualties KIA	WIA	MIA
2BD	B-24	290	267	OSNABRÜCK M/Y	(S)	692.6		2	0	67	0	0	19
			5	DIEPHOLZ A/F	(O)	12.8							
3BD	B-17	262	238	BREMEN A/I	(P)	625.0		1	1	59	7	1	9
			1	T/O		3.0							
TOTALS:		552	511			1333.4		3	1	126	7	1	28
	P-47	36	210	ESCORT 2BD			1–1–0	0					
	P-51	183						0					
	P-47	49	273	ESCORT 3BD			17–2–1	0					
	P-51	246						5					
TOTALS:		514	483				18–3–1	5	0		0	0	5

REMARKS: Weather prevented attacks on primaries at Vechta, Achmer, Rheine and Varrelbusch by 2BD which used PFF on secondary and T/O. 3BD bombed visually. Bomb groups participating: all 2BD except 448BG; all 3BD except 92CBW and 93CBW groups and 388BG. Bomb group losses:– 2BD – 93BG – 1, 466BG – 1; 3BD – 447BG – 1. 452BG B-17 cr. after assembly collision at Coates, 7 k.

All Fighter groups operating except 20FG, 356FG, 359FG. Fighter group e/a credits:– 56FG – 1, 78FG – 2, 357FG – 8, 364FG – 8. Fighter group losses:– 357FG – 1, 364FG – 4.

OTHER OPERATIONS: 7PG despatched 2 F-5s and 1 Spitfire on PR Germany. 25BG despatched 5 Mosquitoes on WR Continent, 3 B-24s on WR Azores/Atlantic/UK. 2SF and 3SF despatched 19 P-51s on WR for bombers. ASR despatched 4 P-47s on patrols. 1 B-17, 4 P-47s, 10 P-51s on radio-relays.

12/13 OCTOBER 1944

8AF 675 NIGHT LEAFLET OPERATION

NLS despatched 8 a/c to Holland, France, Germany. 2 B-24s MIA.

13 OCTOBER 1944

7PG despatched 1 F-5 and 3 Spitfires on PR Germany, France and Belgium. 25BG despatched 5 Mosquitoes on WR France, Belgium, Germany, and 3 B-24s on WR Azores/Atlantic/UK.

14 OCTOBER 1944

8AF 676

	Despatched		Effective	Target		Bombs Tonnage	E/A	Losses MIA	E	Dam	Casualties KIA	WIA	MIA
1BD	B-17	94	90	SAARBRÜCKEN M/Y	(P)	240.8		0	0	8	0	0	0
2BD	B-24	117	117	KAISERSLAUTERN	(P)	330.8		0	0	8	0	0	0
8AF 677													
1BD	B-17	343	326	COLOGNE/ GEREON M/Y	(P)	913.4		2		93	0	3	20
			1	T/O		3.0							
2BD	B-24	318	121	COLOGNE/EIFELTER	(P)	321.2		3	1	137	1	2	20
			127	COLOGNE/ (P) GREMBERG		350.5							
			9	EUSKIRCHEN	(O)	25.0							
3BD	B-17	379	314	COLOGNE/ GEREON M/Y	(S)	826.8		0	2	123	1	3	0
			1	T/O		2.6							
TOTALS:		1251	1106			3014.1	0	5	3	369	2	8	40
	P-51	107	105	ESCORT 1BD 8AF 676				0	1				
	P-51	151	148	ESCORT 2BD 8AF 676				1	0				
	P-51	153	141	ESCORT 1BD 8AF 677				0	1				
	P-47	66	177	ESCORT 2BD 8AF 677				0	0				
	P-51	118						0	0				
	P-47	52	151	ESCORT 3BD 8AF 677				0	0				
	P-51	102						0	0				
TOTALS:		749	732				0	1	2		1	0	1

REMARKS: Mission 676:– GH attacks on two targets. Groups participating:– 41CBW groups of 1BD and 44BG, 93BG, 389BG, 453BG, 466BG of 2BD. Mission 677:– PFF attacks on Cologne. Bomb groups participating:– all 1BD except 41CBW groups; all 2BD except those engaged in 8AF 676; all 3BD except 13CBW groups. Bomb group losses:– 305BG – 2, 392BG – 1, 458BG – 1, 467BG – 1. MIA 305BG a/c collided. B/d 392BG B-24 c/l Belgium. B/d 486BG B-17 cr. Lille. Another 486BG B-17 c/l Continent.

All Fighter groups operating: Fighter group e/a credits:– 4FG – 2. Fighter group losses:– 361FG – 1. A 479FG P-51 c/l Charleroi, Belgium, pilot safe. B/d 4FG P-51 cr. Eurville, France, pilot k.

OTHER OPERATIONS: 7PG despatched 1 F-5 on PR to Germany. 25BG despatched 1 Mosquito on PR Germany, 3 Mosquitoes on WR Continent/UK, and 4 B-24s on WR Atlantic/Azores/UK. 1SF, 2SF, 3SF despatched 29 B-51s on WR for bombers. ASR despatched 14 P-47s on patrols. 3 B-17s, 2 P-47s, 16 P-51s on radio-relays.

14/15 OCTOBER 1944

36BS despatched 7 B-24s on RCM.

15 OCTOBER 1944

8AF 678

	Despatched		Effective	Target		Bombs Tonnage	E/A	Losses MIA	E	Dam	Casualties KIA	WIA	MIA
1BD	B-17	454	127	COLOGNE/ NIPPES M/Y		345.5		4	3	293	14	15	40
			111	COLOGNE/KALK M/Y	(P)	315.5							
			141	COLOGNE/GERON M/Y	(P)	394.1							
			11	KOBLENZ/LÜTZEL M/Y	(O)	30.5							
8AF 678													
3BD	B-17	385	148	COLOGNE/EIFELTOR M/Y	(P)	400.2		2	3	230	10	19	18
			24	COLOGNE/IMBERT	(P)	71.5							
			50	COLOGNE/ GEREON M/Y	(S)	146.5							
			117	COLOGNE/KALK M/Y	(S)	312.0							
			11	WESTER M/Y	(O)	30.2							
			1	T/O		2.8							

continued on facing page

2BD	B-24	369	61	REISHOLZ O/R	(P)	160.2		1	0	106	3	7	10
			64	MONHEIM/RHENANIA O/I	(P)	155.5							
			185	COLOGNE/ GEREON M/Y	(S)	513.9							
			13	DORMIGEON	(S)	35.0							
			5	LIMBURG M/Y	(O)	15.9							
			12	WORRINGEN	(O)	33.5							
			6	COLOGNE-A/F NEAR	(O)	18.0							
8AF 678A *APHRODITE* AND COVER MISSION													
	B-17	24	23	HELIGOLAND N/I	(P)	78.5		0	0	0	0	0	0
	B-17	9	2	HELIGOLAND N/I	(P)	10.0							
TOTALS:		787	722			1983.8	0	7	6	639	27	41	68
	P-51	151	146	ESCORT 1BD				0	1		0	0	0
	P-51	154	150	ESCORT 3BD				2	1		0	0	2
	P-51	141	131	ESCORT 2BD				1	1		0	0	1
	P-51	18	18	ESCORT B-17 HELIGOLAND				0	0		0	0	0
	P-51	16	15	ESCORT *APHRODITE*				0	0		0	0	0
	P-38	2	2	APHRODITE				0	0		0	0	0
TOTALS:		482	462				0	3	3		0	0	3

REMARKS: Industrial, oil and rail targets in the Cologne area. PFF bombing except at Reisholz and Monheim where 2BD was able to attack visually. All bomb groups participated:– Bomb group losses:– 1BD – 303BG – 1, 306BG – 2, 457BG – 1; 2BD – 389BG – 1; 3BG – 486BG – 1, 487BG – 1. 398BG B-17 cr. after t/o Anstey, 10 killed. 34BG B-17 cr. t/o base, crew injured. 486BG cr. t/o base, 8 killed. A 351BG B-17 c/l Belgium. 91BG B-17 Cat E. B/d 390BG B-17 Belgium, 1 k.

All Fighter groups except 356FG operating. Fighter group e/a credits:– 78FG – 7. Fighter group losses:– 55FG – 1, 78FG – 1, 361FG – 1. 55FG P-51 c/l Belgium. 364FG P-51 c/l SE Liège, pilot safe. 355FG P-51 cr., pilot safe.

OTHER OPERATIONS: 7PG despatched 5 F-5s and 1 Spitfire on PR Germany. 1 F-5 MIA. 25BG despatched 6 Mosquitoes on WR North Sea/France, and 3 B-24s on WR Atlantic/UK. Scouting Forces despatched 26 P-51s on WR for bombers. ASR despatched 12 P-47s on patrols. 3 B-17s, 4 P-47s and 10 P-51s on radio-relays. Mission 678A was an *Aphrodite* operation with 2 *Castor* drone B-17s, 7 B-17s and 2 P-38s for control and observation and 16 P-51s for escort.

15/16 OCTOBER 1944

8AF 679 NIGHT LEAFLET OPERATION

NLS despatched 5 B-17s and 4 B-24s (1 a/c aborted). Holland, France, Germany.

25BG despatched 4 Mosquitoes on night PR Continent.

16 OCTOBER 1944

25BG despatched 1 Mosquito on WR Western France, 2 Mosquitoes on WR UK and 3 B-24s on WR Atlantic/UK. ASR despatched 2 P-47s on patrol and 4 B-24s and 8 P-51s also on ASR Search.

16/17 OCTOBER 1944

8AF 680 NIGHT LEAFLET OPERATION

NLS despatched 2 B-17s and 7 B-24s; France, Holland, Germany.

October was a comparatively quiet month for air fights with the Luftwaffe but 357FG managed to reach the 400 destroyed mark to underline its position as the fastest scoring group in 8AF. The pilot who brought the 357th to this mark was 1/Lt Charles Yeager when on 12 October he led his squadron to 'bounce' a score of Me 109s – most evidently flown by ill-trained pilots. 'Chuck' Yeager alone despatched five for an individual record in his group. This short, tenacious man would earn greater fame in post-war years as pilot of the first aircraft to break the sound barrier. His personal P-51D on which he posed for the photographers, 16 October, was named for his wife.

An Aphrodite mission with radio-controlled explosive filled bombers was launched on 15 October. Photos from an accompanying Lightning show (1) Two 'mother ships' flanking the B-17 'baby' drone approaching the sea across Hickling Broad and the parachute of a crew member who baled out (white spot) descending near Ludham airfield: (2) Another B-17 flying above chrome yellow painted drone, 42-30039, retired by 384BG; (3) Operation of the smoke tank under the 'baby' so that 'mother' can keep it in sight as it nears its target: (4) Hit by flak, the moment of the impact as the baby explodes in the sea short of the target, Heligoland naval installation seen beyond the smoke pall in the final picture (5).

When MGM heard that a B-17 crew in England had named their bomber for the delectable Lana Turner they arranged for the 'world premiere' of the star's latest film, *Marriage Is A Private Affair*, to be staged at the base concerned – Debach. It was popular enough to draw this early queue at the hangar serving as cinema. *Tempest Turner* was drawn up outside and her crew photographed in flight gear. They are, left to right: Sgt Mann, Lt Caporgno, Lt Koch, Lt Long, Lt Lewis, Sgt Adickes, Sgt Cross, Sgt Roberts and Sgt Elder. The two men without flight clothes are Capt Bill Hector, 862BS Ops Officer, and Maj Pete Sianis, its CO.

17 OCTOBER 1944

8 AF 681

	Despatched		Effective	Target		Bombs Tonnage	E/A	Losses MIA	E	Dam	Casualties KIA	WIA	MIA
1BD	B-17	455	34	COLOGNE/ GREMBERG M/Y	(P)	70.1		1	2	263	1	6	9
			216	COLOGNE/EIFELTOR M/Y	(P)	459.0							
			151	COLOGNE/KALK M/Y	(O)	301.3							
			2	T/O		4.4							
3BD	B-17	453	295	COLOGNE/ GEREON M/Y	(P)	639.0		3	1	150	2	10	37
			142	COLOGNE/KALK M/Y	(P)	302.7							
2BD	B-24	430	179	COLOGNE/KALK M/Y	(O)	501.4		0	1	73	0	0	0
			231	COLOGNE/ GEREON M/Y	(O)	640.3							
TOTALS:		1338	1250			2917.2	0	4	4	486	3	16	46
	P-47	68	274	ESCORT 1BD				0					
	P-51	222						0					
	P-47	65	271	ESCORT 3BD				0					
	P-51	216						1					
	P-47	48	229	ESCORT 2BD				0					
	P-51	192						0					
TOTALS:		811	774				0	1	0		0	0	1

REMARKS: PFF attacks on targets in the Cologne area. The 2BD primary, a chemical plant at Leverkusen, was not attacked due to weather. All bomb groups participated: Bomb group losses:– 1BD – 305BG – 1; 3BD – 34BG – 1, 95BG – 1, 388BG – 1. B/d 453BG B-24 abandoned over France, crew safe. 2 b/d 398BG B-17s c/l France. B/d 388BG B-17 c/l Honington.

All Fighter groups operating. Fighter group losses:– 364FG – 1.

OTHER OPERATIONS: 25BG despatched 1 Mosquito on PR Continent, 4 Mosquitoes on WR Atlantic/Continent and 4 B-24s on WR Atlantic/UK. ASR despatched 12 P-47s on patrols. 2 B-17s, 2 P-47s and 10 P-51s on radio-relays. Scouting Forces despatched 33 P-51s on WR for bombers (1 P-51 c/l base).

18 OCTOBER 1944

8AF 682

	Despatched		Effective	Target		Bombs Tonnage	E/A	Losses MIA	E	Dam	Casualties KIA	WIA	MIA
3BD	B-17	337	300	KASSEL/MITTEFELD	(P)	819.6		2	0		0	1	18
			1	COLOGNE	(O)	2.7							
			2	T/O		5.4							
1BD	B-17	118	79	COLOGNE-FORD PLANT	(P)	232.2		0	0	22	1	2	0
			30	COLOGNE/NIPPES M/Y	(O)	88.5							
2BD	B-24	112	39	LEVERKUSEN I/C	(P)	111.0		3	0	26	0	0	27
			30	COLOGNE/NIPPES M/Y	(O)	67.0							
TOTALS:		567	481			1326.4	0	5	0	48	1	3	45

18 OCTOBER 1944 *(contd.)*

		Despatched	Effective	Target	E/A	Losses MIA
	P-47	102	388	ESCORT 3BD		4
	P-51	311				
	P-47	45	38	ESCORT 1BD		0
	P-51	146	139	ESCORT 2BD		1
TOTALS:		604	565			5

REMARKS: PFF attacks on Kassel; GH attacks on Cologne and Leverkusen targets. Some operations cancelled. Bomb groups participating: 41CBW groups and 351BG of 1BD; 2CBW and 44BG, 466BG of 2BD; all 3BD except 34BG. Bomb group losses:– 2BD – 44BG – 3; 3BD – 96BG – 1, 390BG – 1.

All Fighter groups except 20FG and 359FG operating. Fighter group losses:– 339FG – 2, 353FG – 1, 355FG – 1, 357FG – 1.

OTHER OPERATIONS: 25BG despatched 3 Mosquitoes on WR Continent/UK, and 3 B-24s on WR Atlantic/UK. Scouting Forces despatched 25 P-51s on WR for bombers. ASR despatched 10 P-47s on patrols. 4 P-47s, 8 P-51s and 3 B-17s (with 4 P-51s as escort) and radio-relays.

19 OCTOBER 1944

8AF 683

	Despatched		Effective	Target		Bombs Tonnage	E/A	Losses MIA	E	Dam	Casualties KIA	WIA	MIA
2BD	B-24	381	50	GUSTAVSBURG AFV/I	(P)	172.0		5	1	148	0	3	49
			280	MAINZ M/Y	(S)	968.8							
3BD	B-17	267	217	MANNHEIM	(S)	638.5		1	0	97	2	1	10
			34	T/O		80.0							
1BD	B-17	374	25	MANNHEIM AFV/I	(P)	74.5		0	0	182	2	4	0
			257	MANNHEIM	(S)	757.7							
			9	RÜDESHEIM	(O)	22.2							
			8	BAD KREUZNACH	(O)	24.0							
			32	KARLSRUHE	(O)	79.0							
			2	STEYER	(O)	6.0							
			10	KREUZNACH	(O)	18.1							
			21	T/O		56.1							
TOTALS:		1022	945			2896.9	0	6	1	427	4	8	59
	P-47	50	195	ESCORT 3BD				1	1				
	P-51	153											
	P-47	50	286	ESCORT 1BD				0	0				
	P-51	260						1	0				
	P-47	47	226	ESCORT 2BD				0	0				
	P-51	193						0	1				
TOTALS:		753	707				0	2	3		1	0	2

REMARKS: Mission despatched to industrial targets at Mannheim, Ludwigshafen, Gustavsburg and Mainz but only two primaries bombed. Bomb groups participating:– all 1BD; all 2BD; all 3BD except 385BG and 490BG. All PFF or GH bombing. Bomb group losses:– 2BD – 389BG – 1, 446BG – 1, 453BG – 1, 489BG – 2; 3BD – 34BG – 1. MIA 489BG a/c collided near target. B/d 489BG B-24 c/l Henstead, crew safe.

All Fighter groups operating: Fighter group losses:– 20FG – 1, 357FG – 1. 78FG P-47 c/l base. 479FG P-51 shot down Allied AA at Calais, pilot baled. 339FG P-51 cr. near Ghent, pilot k.

OTHER OPERATIONS: 7PG despatched 1 F-5 on PR Holland/Germany. 25BG despatched 2 Mosquitoes on PR Continent, 2 Mosquitoes on WR Continent and 4 B-24s on WR Azores/Atlantic/UK. Scouting Forces despatched 30 P-51s (4 aborted) on WR for bombers. ASR despatched 8 P-47s on patrols. 4 P-47s, 16 P-51s and 2 B-17s (with 2 P-51s for escort) on radio-relays.

19/20 OCTOBER 1944

8AF 684 NIGHT LEAFLET OPERATION

NLS despatched 5 B-17s and 5 B-24s; France, Holland, Germany.

36BS despatched 7 B-24s on RCM.

20 OCTOBER 1944

25BG despatched 1 Mosquito on WR Continent and 3 B-24s on WR Atlantic/UK.

After flying missions with 91BG, *Duke of Paducah* was assigned to the 67FW as a radio-relay aircraft for its fighter units. The old bomber was fitted with special radio equipment (note the array of additional aerial masts) and its usual duty was to orbit over the North Sea during a long-range mission to pick up radio messages from fighters and relay them to the Fighter Wing control room. When this picture was taken at Lavenham on 20 October the *Duke* had recently suffered the collapse of the right main landing gear. (via S. Evans)

21 OCTOBER 1944

7PG despatched 1 F-5 on PR Holland and Germany.

25BG despatched 5 Mosquitoes on WR Continent, and 5 B-24s on WR Azores/Atlantic/UK.

21/22 OCTOBER 1944

36BS despatched 8 B-24s (1 aborted) on RCM.

22 OCTOBER 1944

8AF 685

	Despatched		Effective	Target		Bombs Tonnage	E/A	Losses MIA	E	Dam	Casualties KIA	WIA	MIA
1BD	B-17	379	148	BRUNSWICK/ BÜSSING	(P)	434.7		2	2	15	20	3	16
			171	HANNOVER/ HANOMAG	(P)	501.7							
			35	BIELEFELD		105.0							
			6	T/O		18.0							
2BD	B-24	373	353	HAMM M/Y	(P)	975.5		0	0	29	0	0	0
3BD	B-17	379	352	MÜNSTER M/Y	(P)	868.4		0	0	13	0	0	0
			8	T/O		25.5							
TOTALS:		1131	1073			2928.8	0	2		57	20	3	16
	P-47	147	379	ESCORT 1BD				0	0		0	0	0
	P-51	269						1	1		0	0	1
	P-51	212	196	ESCORT 2BD				0	1		0	0	0
	P-51	157	147	ESCORT 3BD				0	0		0	0	0
TOTALS:		785	722					1	2		0	0	1

REMARKS: PFF attacks on targets in Western Germany. Bomb groups participating:– all 1BD except 381BG, 384BG; all 2BD except 44BG, 453BG; all 3BD except 94BG, 452BG. Bomb group losses:– 306BG – 2. MIA 306BG B-17s collided 25 miles NE Gt. Yarmouth, 1 rescued. On return 2 305BG B-17s collided and cr. Thurleigh, 19 k.

All Fighter groups operated. Fighter group losses:– 364FG – 1. On return, a 357FG P-51 c/l base and 355FG P-51 cr. Continent.

OTHER OPERATIONS: 25BG despatched 2 Mosquitoes on WR Belgium and Germany and 4 B-24s on WR Atlantic/UK. ASR despatched 12 P-47s on patrols. Scouting Forces despatched 33 P-51s (4 aborted) on WR for bombers. One SF P-51 c/l Holland. 1 B-17, 2 P-47s and 12 P-51s on radio-relays.

23 OCTOBER 1944

25BG despatched 2 Mosquitoes on WR Low Countries and 3 B-24s on WR Atlantic/UK.

23/24 OCTOBER 1944

8AF 686 NIGHT LEAFLET OPERATION

NLS despatched 6 B-24s and 3 B-17s; France and Holland.

36BS despatched 6 B-24s (5 effective) on RCM for RAF bombers.

24 OCTOBER 1944

	Despatched		Effective	Target	Bombs Tonnage	E/A	Losses MIA	E	Dam	Casualties KIA	WIA	MIA
				FIGHTER-BOMBER								
	P-47	174	379	ELBURG & FACTORY	24.0	1–0–0	2	0		0	0	2
	P-51	241		NIENBURG		4–0–3(G)	5	2		0	0	5
TOTALS:		415	379		24.0	1–0–0 4–0–3(G)	7	2		0	0	7

REMARKS: Fighter-bomber operation in Hannover/Kassel area. Groups operating: 20FG, 56FG, 339FG, 352FG, 353FG, 356FG, 357FG, 359FG, 364FG. Fighter group e/a credits: 359FG – 2. Fighter group losses:– 56FG – 2, 352FG – 1, 353FG – 2, 364FG – 2. (9AF fighters in totals.)

OTHER OPERATIONS: 25FG despatched 1 Mosquito on WR Belgium and Germany and 4 B-24s Azores/Atlantic. ASR despatched 6 P-47s on patrols. 1 B-17, 6 P47s and 4 P-51s on radio-relays.

24/25 OCTOBER 1944

36BS despatched 6 B-24s on RCM.

25BG despatched 5 Mosquitoes on night PR Continent. (1 on H2X sortie) 1 Mosquito cr. near Ypres, 1 killed.

25 OCTOBER 1944

8AF 688

	Despatched		Effective	Target		Bombs Tonnage	E/A	Losses MIA	E	Dam	Casualties KIA	WIA	MIA
3BD	B-17	455	214	HAMBURG/RHENANIA O/R	(P)	494.9		1	0	94	0	0	9
			221	HAMBURG/HARBURG	(P)	527.0							
			1	T/O		2.4							
2BD	B-24	225	216	NEUMÜNSTER A/F	(P)	590.6		0	0	0	0	0	0
			3	MÜNSTER	(O)	6.2							
			1	UTERSUM	(O)	1.5							
1BD	B-17	297	179	HAMBURG/HARBURG O/R	(S)	261.0		1	0	16	0	1	9
			106	HAMBURG/RHENANIA O/R	(S)	306.5							
			1	T/O		1.5							
1BD	B-17	131	27	GELSENKIRCHEN/ NORDSTERN	(P)	60.0		0	0	49	0	0	0
			100	HAMM M/Y	(S)	221.9							
2BD	B-24	142	91	SCHOLVEN/BUER	(P)	246.1		0	0	39	0	0	0
			34	MÜNSTER	(S)	96.0							
			1	GRONAU	(O)	2.9							
TOTALS:		1250	1195			1195.9	0	2	0	198	0	1	18

					Losses MIA	E	Dam	KIA	WIA	MIA
	P-51	139	129	ESCORT 3BD	1	1		0	0	0
	P-51	42	41	ESCORT 2BD	0	0		0	0	0
	P-51	255	221	ESCORT 1BD	0	1		0	0	0
	P-47	50	50	ESCORT 1BD HAMM	0	0		0	0	0
	P-47	36	34	ESCORT 2BD MÜNSTER	0	0		0	0	0
TOTALS:		522	475		1	2	0	0	0	0

REMARKS: Oil and industrial targets in Western Germany attacked by PFF means. Main Forces used H2X, the forth and fifth Forces used GH. Bomb groups participating· all 1BD except 398BG; all 2BD except 458BG; all 3BD except 100BG and 487BG. Bomb group losses:– 390BG – 1, 457BG – 1.

All Fighter groups except 78FG, 339FG, 355FG, 361FG operating. Fighter group losses:– 353FG – 1. MIA 353FG P-51 shot down into sea by B-24 gunner, pilot baled, saved. 364FG P-51 cr. t/o, pilot safe.

OTHER OPERATIONS: 7PG despatched 1 F-5 to Germany, 4 F-5s were recalled. 25BG despatched 5 Mosquitoes on WR Continent and 4 B-24s on WR Azores/Atlantic/UK. Scouting Forces despatched 35 P-51s on WR for bombers. ASR despatched 12 P-47s on patrols. 1 B-17, 6 P-38s, 4 P-51s, P-47s on radio-relays.

INCIDENT

Within the vast daily effort of the 8th Air Force there were sometimes human tragedies unrelated to the course of operations. One such occurred on 25 October 1944 when shortly after take-off from Sudbury the pilot of the 486th Group Fortress *Deepseat-Baker* was informed that a ground man, a Corporal, had stowed away on board. The pilot radioed the Air Leader for advice and was told to continue the mission as there was flight clothing and an oxygen mask in the bomber which the extra man could use. The Corporal was originally in a distressed state but appeared to settle down in the rear fuselage. When the bomber had reached 19,000 ft on its way to the target, and while the waist gunner was looking out of his window, the stowaway suddenly released the side door and jumped out. He was not wearing a parachute.

26 OCTOBER 1944

8AF 689

	Despatched		Effective	Target		Bombs Tonnage	E/A	Losses MIA	E	Dam	Casualties KIA	WIA	MIA
1BD	B-17	430	155	BIELEFELD	(P)	458.2		0	0	10	0	0	0
			108	MÜNSTER/LUDWIG	(P)	313.2							
			24	GÜTERSLOH	(O)	72.0							
			87	MÜNSTER	(O)	193.5							
			1	T/O		2.0							
3BD	B-17	432	155	HANNOVER/ HANOMAG	(P)	466.2		0	2	14	16	1	0
			221	HANNOVER	(O)	522.4							
			36	BIELEFELD	(O)	93.0							
			1	T/O		3.5							
2BD	B-24	246	242	MINDEN/ MITTELLAND CANAL	(P)	851.0		0	0	5	0	0	0
2BD	B-24	117	65	BOTTROP/WELHEIM	(P)	180.6		0	0	37	0	1	0
			33	MÜNSTER	(O)	97.5							
TOTALS:		1225	1104			3253.1	0	0	2	66	16	2	0
	P-51	215	204	ESCORT 1BD				1	0		0	0	1
	P-47	49	235	ESCORT 3BD				0	1		0	0	0
	P-51	205						0	0		0	0	0
	P-47	36	128	ESCORT 2BD MINDEN			2–0–0	0	0		0	0	0
	P-51	103						0	0		0	0	0
	P-51	66	59	ESCORT 2BD BOTTROP									
TOTALS:		674	626				2–0–0	1	1	0	0	0	1

REMARKS: PFF attacks on industrial and communications targets in Western Germany. Bomb groups participating:– all 1BD except 384BG; all 2BD; all 3BD except 493BG. No losses. Two 452BG B-17s collided during assembly and cr. Rockland and Caston, 16 killed.

All Fighter groups except 354FG and 479FG. Fighter group losses:– 20FG – 1. On return a 78FG P-47 c/l base, pilot safe.

OTHER OPERATIONS: 25BG despatched 3 Mosquitoes on WR Continent/UK and 4 B-24s on WR Azores/Atlantic/UK. Scouting Forces despatched 22 P-51s on WR for bombers. 1 B-17, 6 P-47s, 14 P-51s on radio-relays.

INCIDENT

Tragedy marked the end of a unique aircraft in the inventory of 8th Air Force combat units. The 7th Photo Group operated the Force's only B-25 Mitchell, used for courier flights with photographic material to various bases in the UK and liberated Europe. On 26 October *Miss Nashville* (as it was nicknamed) was sent to Chalon-sur-Seine in France, but near that airfield some American anti-aircraft gunners failed to recognise the aircraft as friendly and blasted it into flames. In the ensuing crash two of the crew were killed and a third member very badly burned. The Mitchell, a B-25C, had originally been acquired by the 3rd Bomb Wing back in the winter of 1942–43 when plans were for this organisation to receive both B-25 and B-26 medium bomber groups. The B-25s never materialised and this lone example of the type on hand had been passed to the 7th Photo Group in summer 1943 for use, initially, as a dual trainer for Lightning pilots, and later on night photographic sorties.

26/27 OCTOBER 1944

25BG despatched 1 Mosquito on H2X PR Augsburg area.

36BS despatched 6 B-24s on RCM.

27 OCTOBER 1944

7PG despatched 1 Spitfire on PR NW Germany.

25BS despatched 5 Mosquitoes on WR Germany, France and Low Countries and 5 B-24s on WR Azores/Atlantic/UK.

27/28 OCTOBER 1944

8AF 690 NIGHT LEAFLET OPERATION

NLS despatched 2 B-17s and 7 B-24s (8 a/c effective) to 38 locations in Holland, France, Germany.

25BG despatched 1 Mosquito on night PR Cologne/Bonn area.

28 OCTOBER 1944

8AF 691

	Despatched		Effective	Target	Bombs Tonnage	E/A	Losses MIA	E	Dam	Casualties KIA	WIA	MIA
3BD	B-17	192	184	HAMM M/Y	(P) 456.3		0	1	42	0	0	0
			1	T/O	1.4							
1BD	B-17	190	178	MÜNSTER M/Y	(P) 497.4		3	1	96	0	12	29
TOTALS:		382	363		955.1	0	3	2	138	0	12	29
	P-51	105	93	ESCORT 3BD			0			0	0	0
	P-51	112	106	ESCORT 1BD			2			0	0	2
TOTALS:		217	199			0	2	0		0	0	2

REMARKS: PFF attacks on marshalling yards at Hamm and Münster with some visual bombing at Münster. Bomb groups participating: 1BD – 351BG, 381BG, 398BG, 401BG, 457BG; 3BD – 34BG, 95BG, 390BG, 487BG, 490BG. Bomb group losses:– 398BG – 3. 487BG B-17 cr. Continent. 401BG B-17 c/l base.

Fighter escort provided by 20FG, 339FG, 357FG, 364FG. Fighter group losses:– 364FG – 2.

OTHER OPERATIONS: 7PG despatched 1 F-5 on PR Holland and W. Germany. 25BG despatched 4 Mosquitoes on WR Continent/UK, 1 Mosquito on experimental nav. flight and 3 B-24s on WR Azores/Atlantic/UK. Scouting Forces despatched 14 P-51s (6 effective) on WR for bombers. ASR despatched 10 P-47s on patrols. 1 B-17 on radio-relay.

28/29 OCTOBER 1944

8AF 692 NIGHT LEAFLET OPERATION

NLS despatched 3 B-17s and 6 B-24s to France, Holland, Germany.

25BG despatched 6 Mosquitoes on night PR; Ruhr.

29 OCTOBER 1944

7PG despatched 14 F-5s and 2 Spitfires on PR Germany and Holland. 1 F-5 MIA.

25BG despatched 1 Mosquito on PR Holland, 2 Mosquitoes on WR C.Germany and 5 B-24s on WR Azores/Atlantic/UK.

29/30 OCTOBER 1944

25BG despatched 1 Mosquito on H2X scope mission Chemnitz and 4 Mosquitoes on PR Germany.

EVENT

Col Don Blakeslee, the 'Chief Cook' of 4th Fighter Group, flew his last combat sortie on 30 October 1944, a *Ramrod* to Hamburg. He had been in action since 1941 and flown over 350 sorties, amassing some 900 hours' flying time, half as much again as any other American fighter pilot in Europe. Exactly how many hours was a subject Blakeslee avoided. In his determination not to be retired he interpreted the headings for his operational log literally and only recorded times to coast out and coast in, which totalled considerably less than the full flight period for each mission. He could not, however, hide the fact that he had been around Debden for a long time and his superiors decided that his captaincy of 4th Group should end. Blakeslee was persuaded to take a well earned month's leave in the US in September 1944 and during his absence Lt.Col Claiborne Kinnard – from nearby Steeple Morden – was put in charge. The controlling 65th Fighter Wing Headquarters felt the 4th needed a shake-up as most of the old hands had either been lost or gone home and the experience level of remaining pilots was generally low – the Group had a large number of recently assigned pilots due to heavy losses during the summer months. Kinnard made changes but he had a difficult time. Even pilots fresh from training schools were quick to adopt the superior attitude which characterised the Group at that time; the 4th was *the elite* American fighter outfit; its heritage was the RAF Eagle Squadrons. It seemed to many observers that pilots of the 4th were less cautious in the cause of justifying this position: 'They were proud to be thought the raunchiest bunch of pilots on the scene.' Blakeslee's return to his old command did not help matters although Kinnard remained as deputy. Gen Jesse Auton, the Wing CO, finally put a date on combat retirement for both his famous fighter leaders, Blakeslee and Zemke; the end of October. A violent storm retired Zemke and Blakeslee went to a desk job. He was not happy, soon returning to the States – and life at Debden was never quite the same without his presence.

30 OCTOBER 1944

8AF 693

	Despatched		Effective	Target		Bombs Tonnage	E/A	Losses MIA	E	Dam	Casualties KIA	WIA	MIA
2BD	B-24	357	72	HAMBURG/HARBURG O/R	(P)	197.4		2	0	30	0	0	19
			67	HAMBURG/RHENANIA O/R	(P)	192.6							
			28	HAMBURG	(O)	81.6							
			25	CUXHAVEN		64.0							
			9	UETERSEN	(O)	27.0							
			21	WESERMÜNDE	(O)	57.0							
			1	BREMEN	(O)	3.0							
			1	T/O		3.6							
1BD	B-17	463	209	HAMM M/Y	(S)	486.6				17	0	1	2
			192	MÜNSTER M/Y	(S)	444.5							
			12	OSNABRÜCK	(O)	26.9							
			2	ENSCHEDE	(O)	4.5							
			4	T/O		7.5							
3BD	B-17	459	Abandoned	MERSEBURG/ LEUNA O/I						2	0	0	0
8AF 693A *APHRODITE*													
3BD	B-17	27	26	HELIGOLAND N/B	(P)	90.0		0	0		0	0	0
	B-17	5	2	HELIGOLAND	(P)	10.0		0	0		0	0	0
TOTALS:		1311	671			1696.2	0	2	0	49	0		
	P-47	56	293	ESCORT 2BD				0			0	0	0
	P-51	264						4			0	0	4
	P-47	135	123	ESCORT 1BD				1			0	0	1
	P-51	508	482	ESCORT 3BD				0			0	0	0
	P-47	8	8	ESCORT HELIGO-LAND B-17				0			0	0	0
	P-47	7	7	ESCORT *APHRODITE* B-17				0			0	0	0
											0	0	0
TOTALS:		978	913					5	0	0	0	0	5

REMARKS: Deteriorating weather caused the recall of 3BD and 1BD to seek secondaries in a major mission against German oil production. All bombing by PFF. Bomb groups participating:– all 1BD; all 2BD except 445BG and 489BG; all 3BD except 487BG. Bomb group losses:– 44BG – 1, 458BG – 1.

All Fighter groups except 20FG operating. Fighter group losses:– 359FG – 1, 361FG – 1, 479FG – 3.

OTHER OPERATIONS: 7PG despatched 2 F-5s on PR Germany. 25BG despatched 1 Mosquito on PR Germany, 4 Mosquitoes on WR Holland, Belgium, Germany and 3 B-24s on WR Azores/UK. Scouting Forces despatched 34 P-51s (32 effective) on WR for bombers. ASR despatched 14 P-47s on patrols. 1 B-17, 6 P-47s, 15 P-51s on radio-relays. Mission 693A was an *Aphrodite* and cover attack on Heligoland. 2 *Castor* drones were accompanied by 3 control B-17s with 7 P-47s as escort. 1 drone failed to respond to control and crashed in Sweden.

INCIDENT

The Berger G2 pressure suit – basically a series of inflatable pads strapped round torso and legs – introduced during the summer of 1944 as an aid to maintaining consciousness during sharp manoeuvres, proved highly advantageous to fighter pilots in combat; all groups were using it by October. Although primarily intended to enhance combat performance it also had an additional life-saving value not initially appreciated. Many fighters had been lost through getting into spins in bad weather and crashing because the pilots had blacked-out while trying to regain control. Now the G-suit (as it was soon named) frequently proved a life-saver in such situations. A notable example occurred on the last day of October, when the forecast of clear weather proved false. The legendary Hubert Zemke, flying his 155th and last planned mission, was leading 479th Group 'A' formation on a bomber escort. Increasing amounts of cloud were encountered as the Mustangs pressed deeper into Germany. South-east of Hamburg, where the bombers disappeared into a towering cloud front, Zemke elected to lead his force over it. At 24,000 ft the leading flight penetrated the murk and encountered severe turbulence. Zemke immediately called an about turn and banked left, but before he could complete the manoeuvre his Mustang was thrown violently on its back and sent hurtling downwards. His wingman, Lt Dick Creighton, had followed the turn and suddenly found the control stick wrenched from his hand and flailing his knees, while the rudder pedals vibrated under his feet. Realising he was in a vicious spin, and unable to bring the juddering P-51 under control, he tried to bale out but the canopy would not open. In desperation he again tried to get the aircraft out of the spin – it had now plummeted 14,000 ft – and to his relief the nose gradually began to come up. On pulling out of the dive the airspeed was indicating 550 mph and the accelerometer – the instrument recording the pull against gravity – 8 G. The pull out was not a moment too soon for Creighton had to manoeuvre violently to avoid hitting tree tops. Somewhat shaken he began a long straight climb to regain altitude.

Lt Walter Drake, leader of the second element in Zemke's flight, also tried to follow his leader and ended up in a vicious spin that ripped off both drop tanks. He recovered at 3,000 ft with the accelerometer reading 9 G. Lt Doug Holmes, his wingman, disappeared completely at this time. The following flight, led by 434th Fighter Sqdn. CO. Lt.Col Jim Herren, attempted to climb out of the overcast. At 25,000 ft Herren's Mustang stalled out and spun. His pull out coming at 3,000 ft was even more extreme and registered 9.6 G. Fortunately the Mustang stayed in one piece although the wings, tailplane and fin were badly warped.

Zemke and Holmes were not so lucky as their aircraft broke up, both men baling out. Herren was killed. None of the three pilots who recovered from spins had experienced even the beginning of a grey-out thanks to the G-suit. In Creighton's case it was instrumental in saving his life.

30/31 OCTOBER 1944

8AF 694 NIGHT LEAFLET OPERATION

NLS despatched 2 B-17s and 7 B-24s; Holland and Germany.

36BS despatched 7 B-24s on RCM.

25BG despatched 2 Mosquitoes (1 aborted) to SE Germany on H2X scope recon.

31 OCTOBER 1944

25BG despatched 6 Mosquitoes on WR Germany, Denmark, Czechoslovakia and 4 B-24s on WR Azores/Atlantic/UK.

31 OCTOBER/1 NOVEMBER 1944

8AF 695 NIGHT LEAFLET OPERATION

NLS despatched 3 B-17s and 5 B-24s; Holland, France, Germany.

36BS despatched 7 B-24s on RCM in support of RAF.

25BG despatched 1 Mosquito on H2X PR Schweinfurt.

On 1 November 379BG's *Swamp Fire* became the first 8AF Fortress to complete 100 bombing sorties without ever having to abandon an operation due to mechanical difficulties. The occasion was marred by the failure of No.2 engine forcing an attack on a T/O. Back at base crew chief M/Sgt De Salvo paints on the hundredth symbol. *Swamp Fire* collected plenty of battle damage in its travels – 10 flak splinter patches can be seen on the nose. (M. Olmsted)

1 NOVEMBER 1944

8AF 696

	Despatched		Effective	Target		Bombs Tonnage	E/A	Losses MIA	E	Dam	Casualties KIA	WIA	MIA
1BD	B-17	142	113	GELSENKIRCHEN/ NORDSTERN O/I	(P)	277.3		0	0	24	1	0	0
			23	HAMM M/Y	(S)	57.0							
			1	T/O		2.5							
2BD	B-24	144	143	GELSENKIRCHEN/ BUER O/I	(P)	406.6		0	0	25	0	0	0
3BD	B-17	38	13	RÜDESHEIM R/B	(P)	30.5			0	7	0	0	0
			24	KOBLENZ	(S)	69.0		0					
TOTALS:		324	317			842.9	0	0	0	56	1	0	0
	P-47	25	140	ESCORT 1BD			1–0–0	0	0				
	P-51	146						1	0				
	P-47	24	109	ESCORT 2BD			1–0–0	0	0				
	P-51	88						0	1				
	P-51	38	37	ESCORT 3BD				0	0				
TOTALS:		321	286				2–0–0	1	1		1	0	1

REMARKS: PFF bombing of two synthetic oil installations and a rail bridge. 1BD Force was 41CBW making GH attack; 2BD groups participating were all except 445BG, 446BG, 448BG, 467BG. 3BD Force consisted of 94BG and 447BG using the new Micro-H blind bombing technique.

Fighter groups operating as escort: 4FG, 20FG, 56FG, 355FG, 356FG, 357FG, 352FG, 359FG, 361FG. Fighter group losses: 20FG – 1. Fighter group e/a credits:– 56FG – ½, 352FG – ½ (shared Me 262). 361FG P-51 cr. on return Beechamwell, pilot k. 361FG P-51 strafed C-47 on 9AF A/S in error.

OTHER OPERATIONS: 7PG despatched 2 F-5s Germany. 25BG despatched 1 Mosquito to Italy on PR, 5 Mosquitoes on WR Denmark, Germany, Low Countries and 5 B-24s on WR Azores/UK. Scouting Forces despatched 23 P-51s on WR for bombers. 1 Mosquito MIA. ASR despatched 10 P-47s on patrols. 4 P-47s and 14 P-51s on radio-relays.

1/2 NOVEMBER 1944

8AF 697 NIGHT LEAFLET OPERATION

NLS despatched 3 B-17s and 5 B-24s: Holland.

36BS despatched 7 B-24s on RCM.

25BG despatched 2 Mosquitoes on H2X PR C. and SE Germany. 1 a/c MIA.

This spectacular photograph of a B-17 disintegrating in flames appeared in many publications during and after World War II but without identity or mention of the full significance of the event. The Fortress was 486BG's *Blue Streak*, the first combat loss of 834BS in the 78 missions flown since entering combat. 2/Lt David Paris and crew perished. Navigator 1/Lt William Beeson was on his 32nd and last scheduled mission, the rest of the crew on number five or six. An 88 mm shell exploded the left main fuel tank over Merseburg, 2 November. The propeller from No.2 engine can be seen falling away.

2 NOVEMBER 1944

8AF 698

	Despatched		Effective	Target		Bombs Tonnage	E/A	Losses MIA	E	Dam	Casualties KIA	WIA	MIA
3BD	B-17	460	383	MERSEBURG/LEUNA O/I	(P)	901.7	6– 2– 2	12	1	339	3	13	101
			13	WOLFENBÜTTEL	(O)	29.0							
			23	HALLE	(O)	56.5							
			17	T/O		42.5							
1BD	B-17	223	210	MERSEBURG/LEUNA	(P)	469.5	30–33–25	26	1	152	0	11	420
			5	T/O		9.0							
2BD	B-24	208	172	BIELEFELD BR	(P)	390.3		0	0	17	0	0	0
			10	BIELEFELD M/Y	(S)	26.0							
			9	BIELEFELD	(O)	22.0		0					
2BD	B-24	146	131	CASTROP/RAUXEL O/I	(P)	403.0		1	0	23	1	2	10
1BD	B-17	137	107	STERKRADE O/I	(P)	250.5		1	0	52	0	0	9
			20	RHEINE M/Y	(S)	48.1							
TOTALS:		1174	1100			2648.1	36–35–27	40	2	583	4	26	540
	P-38	34	31	(9AF) ESCORT 3BD			46–3–10	0			0	0	0
	P-51	483	433				25–0– 0(G)	8			0	0	8
	P-51	245	209	ESCORT 1BD LEUNA			56–2–15	6			0	0	5
	P-47	146	143	ESCORT 2BD BIELEFELD				2			0	0	2
	P-47	40	37	ESCORT 2BD CASTROP				0			0	0	0
	P-47	20	20	ESCORT 1BD STERKRADE				0			0	0	0
TOTALS:		968	873				102–5–25 25–0–0(G)	16	0	0	0	0	15

REMARKS: Synthetic oil installations in central Germany and rail targets at Bielefeld. Merseburg force attacked on PFF guidance. Bomb groups participating:– all 3BD except 34BG, 490BG; all 1BD except 351BG, 381BG and 41CBW groups. 41CBW attacked Sterkrade using GH and some visual bombing. All 2BD groups except 445BG, 458BG operated; Bielefeld Force made GH and visual attacks and comprised 93BG, 448BG, 467BG, 489BG, 491BG: Castrop Force attacked with GH and comprised 44BG, 93BG, 389BG, 392BG, 446BG, 453BG, 466BG. Bomb group losses:– 1BD – 91BG – 13, 303BG – 1, 398BG – 3, 401BG – 1, 457BG – 9; 2BD – 453BG – 1; 3BD – 34BG – 1, 94BG – 1, 95BG – 1, 385BG – 1, 447BG – 5, 486BG – 2, 493BG – 1. 91BG and 457BG attacked by e/a when no escort on hand. B/d 447BG, B-17 ditched, crew saved. Two 447a/c collided on route to target, one cr. the other c/l Belgium. B/d 92BG B-17 c/l Woodbridge A/F. Lt R.E. Femoyer, 447BG awarded Medal of Honor for action this day.

All Fighter groups operating. Fighter group credits: 4FG – 4, 20FG – 28, 55FG – 17½, 339FG – 2, 352FG – 39, 353FG – 4, 355FG – 8, 357FG – 4, 359FG – 5½, 361FG – 8, 364FG – 13, 479FG – 2. Fighter group losses:– 20FG – 3, 55FG – 1, 352FG – 2, 353FG – 1, 355FG – 2, 357FG – 1, 361FG – 2, 364FG – 1, 479FG – 3. One MIA 20FG P-51 pilot baled over sea, lost. MIA 353FG P-51 pilot baled, rescued. First major effort by Luftwaffe to oppose 8AF mission since early September with 400 e/a in action. Total includes 9AF P-38s.

OTHER OPERATIONS: 25BG despatched 2 Mosquitoes on experimental navigation sorties, 5 Mosquitoes on WR Continent and 4 B-24s on WR Azores/Atlantic/UK. Scouting Forces despatched; 33 P-51s on WR for bombers. 12 B-17s provided *Chaff* screen for bombers – first use of separate force. 2 P-47s, 8 P-15s on radio-relays.

2/3 NOVEMBER 1944

8AF 699 NIGHT LEAFLET OPERATION

NLS despatched 3 B-17s and 5 B-24s: Holland and Germany.

36BS despatched 7 B-24s on RCM.

3 NOVEMBER 1944

25BG despatched 1 Mosquito on *Skywave* navigation flight to Italy (a/c cr. Italy, crew baled), 3 Mosquitoes on WR Continent and 4 B-24s on WR Azores/Atlantic/UK.

4 NOVEMBER 1944

8AF 700

	Despatched		Effective	Target		Bombs Tonnage	E/A	Losses MIA	E	Dam	Casualties KIA	WIA	MIA
3BD	B-17	228	151	NEUNKIRCHEN O/I	(P)	426.5		0	0	5	0	0	0
			35	SAARBRÜCKEN M/Y	(S)	96.0							
			13	NEUNKIRCHEN M/Y	(S)	31.5							
2BD	B-24	222	210	HANNOVER/MISBURG O/I	(P)	591.3		3	0	93	1	0	28
1BD	B-17	257	238	HAMBURG/HARBURG O/I	(P)	701.1		0	0	9	0	0	0
			9	NORDHOLZ A/I	(O)	26.8							
			2	T/O		5.7							
3BD	B-17	193	186	HAMBURG/RHENANIA O/I	(P)	450.0		2	0	61	0	1	18
			2	T/O		5.0							
1BD	B-17	119	91	BOTTROP/WELHUN O/I	(P)	220.0		0	0	24	0	0	0
			26	HAMM M/Y	(S)	64.5							
	B-24	141	133	GELSENKIRCHEN/ NORDSTERN		368.1							
TOTALS:		1160	1096			2986.5	0	5	0	192	1	1	46
	P-47	77	76	ESCORT NEUNKIRCHEN				0	0		0	0	0
	P-51	50		(9AF P-51s)				0	0		0	0	0
	P-47	48	371	ESCORT MISBURG			0–0–1 (G)	0	0		0	0	0
	P-51	372						0	1		0	0	1
	P-51	139	124	ESCORT HARBURG			0–0–1 (G)	1	1		0	0	1
	P-51	110	110	ESCORT 3BD HAMBURG					0		0	0	0
	P-51	40	37	ESCORT BOTTROP			0–0–1	1	0		0	0	0
	P-47	54	50	ESCORT NORDSTERN					0		0	0	0
TOTALS:		890	768				0–0–1 0–0–2(G)	2	2	0	0	0	2

REMARKS: PFF attacks on the oil industry in Western Germany. Bomb groups participating:– all 1BD except 91BG 457BG; all 2BD except 445BG; all 3BD except 100BG. Neukirchen attacked by 13CBW, 45CBW, 92CBW using Micro H; Bottrop attacked by 41CBW using GH; Misburg attacked by 93BG, 392BG, 446BG, 458BG, 467BG, 489BG using GH and H2X – Nordstern, 2BD Force used same technique. Bomb group losses:– 2BD – 93BG – 1, 392BG – 1, 446BG – 1; 3BD – 94BG – 1, 447BG – 1. MIA 94BG B-17 ditched, crew lost.

All Fighter groups operating. Fighter group losses:– 356FG – 1, 359FG – 1. A group of 9AF P-51s escorted first Force and lost 1 P-51 shot down by 9AF a/c. On return a 339FG P-51 c/l near Kessingland, pilot safe.

OTHER OPERATIONS: 25BG despatched 1 Mosquito on PR France, 5 Mosquitoes on WR UK/Continent and 4 B-24s and 1 B-17 on WR Atlantic/UK. 1 Mosquito MIA. Scouting Forces despatched 36 P-51s on WR for bombers. ASR despatched 17 P-47s on patrols and 6 P-51s also on ASR search. 305BG despatched 12 B-17s as screening Force for 1BD bombers. 1 B-17, 7 P-47s, 18 P-51s as radio-relays.

4/5 NOVEMBER 1944

8AF 701 NIGHT LEAFLET OPERATION

NLS despatched 3 B-17s and 6 B-24s; France, Holland, Germany.

36BS despatched 6 B-24s on RCM.

INCIDENT

When the bombers returned from Frankfurt on 5 November 1944, deteriorating weather caused some formations to be diverted to coastal airfields in England. Part of the 351st Group put down at RAF Beccles in high winds, blowing rain and an overcast. When conditions improved the B-17s prepared to take off but the pilots could not understand the instructions from the control tower given by an RAF man with a very pronounced accent. Confusion reigned until the formation leader, Maj John Gorham, decided the only thing to be done was to go to the tower himself and handle the radio 'American' fashion. It was yet another case of two nations divided by a common language.

Caught in a massive flak barrage over Ludwigshafen on 5 November, 447BG had seven B-17s sustain major damage and ten minor, but no men were wounded or aircraft lost. Gunner Sgt Francis Schuster thought an engine had been blown off his Fortress when cowlings and large pieces of metal sailed past his right waist window. No.2 engine was still there, if battered. Inspection after the mission revealed one cylinder detached from the crankcase.

5 NOVEMBER 1944

8AF 702

	Despatched		Effective	Target		Bombs Tonnage	E/A	Losses MIA	E	Dam	Casualties KIA	WIA	MIA
1BD	B-17	452	396	FRANKFURT M/Y	(P)	1612.5		1	2	126	1	3	9
			36	HANAU M/Y	(O)	107.5							
			4	T/O		13.5							
3BD	B-17	454	219	LUDWIGSHAFEN M/Y	(P)	640.5		11	0	298	1	5	103
			177	LUDWIGSHAFEN I/O	(P)	507.0							
			33	KAISERSLAUTERN M/Y	(O)	99.0							
			4	T/O		10.5							
2BD	B-24	366	333	KARLSRUHE M/Y	(S)	1036.3		0	3	28	6	8	112
			12	LANDAU	(O)	44.0							
TOTALS:		1272	1214			4070.8	0	12	5	452	8	16	112
	P-47	48	206	ESCORT 1BD				0			0	0	2
	P-51	172						2			0	0	2
	P-47	34	192	ESCORT 3BD				0			0	0	0
	P-51	174						1			0	0	1
	P-47	48	228a/c	ESCORT 2BD				2			0	0	2
	P-51	190						1			0	0	1
TOTALS:		666	626				0	6	0		0	0	6

REMARKS: Marshalling yards in Western Germany. H2X used by all forces but some 2BD and 3BD Formations able to attack visually. Bomb groups participating:– all 1BD except 92BG; all 2BD except 445BG; all 3BD except 390BG. Bomb group losses:– 1BD – 379BG – 1; 3BD – 34BG – 1, 94BG – 1, 100BG – 1, 388BG – 2, 452BG – 1, 487BG – 1, 490BG – 2, 493BG – 2. On return 401BG B-17 c/l Flambridge, crew safe; b/d 401BG B-17 f/l Gt. Dunmow A/F – Cat E; b/d 467BG B-24 c/l Bungay A/F, crew safe; 466BG B-24 c/l Lenwade, 3 k; b/d B-24 c/l Manston A/F; 93BG B-24 cr Shipmeadow, 2 k.

All Fighter groups operating. Fighter group losses:– 4FG – 1, 20FG – 1, 55FG – 1, 56FG – 2, 359FG – 1. One 56FG pilot baled North Sea, lost.

OTHER OPERATIONS: 7PG despatched 3 F-5s and 1 Spitfire on PR Germany. 25BG despatched 4 Mosquitoes on WR Continent/UK, and 2 B-24s and 1 B-17 on WR Azores/Atlantic/UK. Scouting Force despatched 28 P-51s (27 effective) on WR for bombers. ASR despatched 15 P-47s on patrols, 1 B-17, 4 P-47s and 18 P-51s on radio-relays.

5/6 NOVEMBER 1944

8AF 703 NIGHT LEAFLET OPERATION

NLS despatched 3 B-17s and 7 B-24s; France, Holland, Germany.

6 NOVEMBER 1944

8AF 704

	Despatched		Effective	Target		Bombs Tonnage	E/A	Losses MIA	E	Dam	Casualties KIA	WIA	MIA
1BD	B-17	291	142	HAMBURG/HARBURG O/R	(P)	423.5		4	0	103	2	2	36
			138	HAMBURG/RHENANIA O/R	(P)	413.0							
			3	HAMBURG/LÜBECK	(O)	9.0							
3BD	B-17	262	23	NEUMÜNSTER A/I	(P)	54.9		0	0	10	1	0	0
			231	NEUMÜNSTER M/Y	(S)	556.7							
			3	T/O		7.5							
2BD	B-24	215	204	MINDEN/ MITTELLAND CANAL	(P)	651.5		1	0	31	0	0	10
			2	T/O		6.0							
1BD	B-17	101	87	BOTTROP O/I	(P)	198.1		0	0	39	0	0	0
			12	HAMM M/Y	(S)	27.0							
2BD	B-24	143	134	STERKRADE O/I	(P)	434.5		0	0	27	0	0	0
			1	VREDEN	(O)	4.0							
3BD		119	65	DUISBURG/BENZOL O/I	(P)	134.9		0	0	18	0	0	0
			43	RHEYDT M/Y	(O)	104.9							
TOTALS:		1131	1088			3025.5		5	0	228	3	2	46

6 NOVEMBER 1944 *(contd.)*

Despatched		Effective	Target	Bombs Tonnage	E/A	Losses MIA	E	Casualties Dam	KIA	WIA
P-51	258	238	ESCORT HARBURG			1	1	0	0	1
P-51	102	93	ESCORT NEUMÜNSTER			1	0	0	0	1
P-47	44	43	ESCORT BOTTROP			0	0	0	0	0
P-51	271	257	ESCORT MITTELLAND			0	0	0	0	0
P-51	43	40	ESCORT STERKRADE		0–0–1	3	0	0	0	3
P-47	54	51	ESCORT DUISBURG			0	0	0	0	0
P-51	30		SCOUTING FORCES			0	0	0	0	0
TOTALS:	802	722			0–0–1	5	1 ?	0	0	5

REMARKS: PFF attacks on the oil industry in Western Germany. All bomb groups operating except 398BG and 445BG. Duisburg Force (45CBW and 94BG) used Micro H. Bottrop Force (41CBW) used GH. Sterkrade Force (44BG, 389BG, 446BG, 466BG, 489BG) used GH. Other Forces used H2X. Bomb group losses:– 1BD – 381BG – 2, 401BG – 1, 457BG – 1; 2BD – 448BG – 1. B/d 486BG B-17 c/l near Ghent and b/d 388BG B-17 c/l Gosselies, Belgium.

All Fighter groups operating: Fighter group e/a credits:– 4FG – 2, 357FG – 1, 361FG – 1. Fighter group losses:– 4FG – 2, 55FG – 1, 364FG – 1, 479FG – 1. MIA 55FG and 479FG P-51 pilots baled North Sea, lost.

OTHER OPERATIONS: 7PG despatched 8 F-5s and 4 Spitfires on PR Germany. 2 F-5s MIA. 25BG despatched 7 Mosquitoes on WR Continent and 1 B-17 and 4 B-24s on WR Azores/Atlantic/UK. Mosquito c/l S. Pickenham, 1 killed. ASR despatched 25 P-47s on patrols and 4 P-51s also on ASR search. 12 B-17s despatched as screening force for bombers. 1 B-17, 4 P-47s and 18 P-51s on radio-relays.

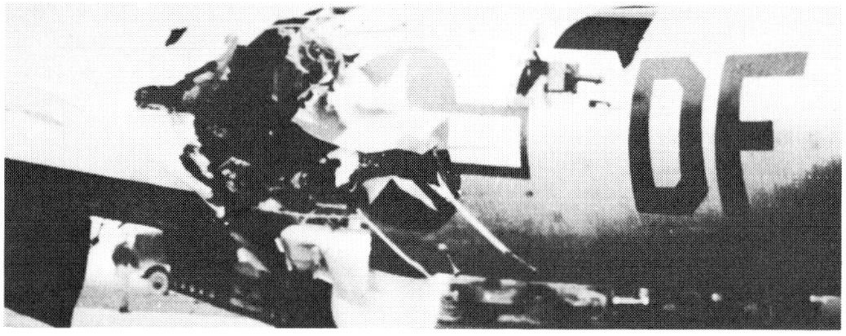

German flak batteries always set their aim on the lead aircraft of a formation and often hit them. A shell struck this 91BG lead while bomb doors were open and radome extended. Despite the gaping wound the bomber was brought back for a safe landing at Rackheath, 6 November.

6/7 NOVEMBER 1944

36BS despatched 8 B-24s on RCM.

25BG despatched 4 Mosquitoes on PR Germany; 1 a/c cr. near base on return, 1 k, 1 inj.

7 NOVEMBER 1944

25BG despatched 1 Mosquito on PR to Duisburg area, 4 Mosquitoes on WR Continent/UK and 2 B-17s and 1 B-24 Azores/Atlantic/UK. ASR despatched 5 P-47s on patrols. 225 B-17s (3BD) and 310 B-24s (2BD) with 148 P-51s despatched on a practice mission to simulate attack against tactical targets. A 100BG B-17 caught fire and cr. Felixstowe, 2 killed.

8 NOVEMBER 1944

8AF 705

	Despatched		Effective	Target		Bombs Tonnage	E/A	Losses MIA	E	Dam	Casualties KIA	WIA	MIA
1BD	B-17	267	193	MERSEBURG/LEUNA O/I	(P)	477.5		3	0	85	0	1	27
			2	T/O		5.0							
	B-17	12	9	SCREENING FORCE									
2BD	B-24	145	77	RHEINE M/Y	(P)	158.0		0	0	15		0	0
			8	NORDHORN CANAL	(O)	20.0							
			8	ENSCHEDE	(O)	23.0							
			1	T/O		2.5							
3BD	B-17	266	RECALLED	MERSEBURG/LEUNA O/I		0		0	0		0	0	0
TOTALS:		690	298			686.0		3	0	100	0	1	27
	P-47	146	752	ESCORT 1BD & 3BD			2–0–1	2	0		0	0	2
	P-51	693					0–0–1 (G)	9	2		0	0	9
	P-47	37	36	ESCORT 2BD				0	0		0	0	0
	P-51	14	11	SCOUTING FORCES				0	0		0	0	0
TOTALS:		890	799				2–0–1 0–0–1(G)	11	2	?	0	2	11

REMARKS: PFF attack on Merseburg oil by B-17s and Rheine marshalling yard by B-24s. Bomb groups participating:– 1BD – 92BG, 306BG, 379BG, 384BG, 398BG, 401BG, 457BG; 2BD – 44BG, 93BG, 392BG, 448BG, 453BG, 458BG, 491BG. Bomb group losses:– 379BG – 1, 384BG – 1, 457BG – 1. B/d 401BG B-17 landed France, salvaged. 3BD B-17s recalled due to weather.

All Fighter groups operating. 3BD escort joined 1BD escort. Fighter group e/a credits:– 20FG – 1, 357FG – 1½, 361FG – 1, 364FG – 1. Fighter group losses:– 4FG – 1, 20FG – 1, 55FG – 2, 353FG – 1, 356FG – 2, 357FG – 1, 359FG – 1, 479FG – 2. MIA 479FG a/c collided near Minden. On return 364FG P-51 c/l near Manston, pilot inj. 357FG P-51 cr. Belgium, pilot inj.

OTHER OPERATIONS: 25BG despatched 5 Mosquitoes on WR Continent/UK, and 2 B-24s and 2 B-17s on WR Azores/Atlantic/UK. ASR despatched 20 P-47s on patrols and 2 P-51s also on ASR search. 3 B-17s, 2 P-47s, 18 P-51s on radio-relays. 2 P-51s on radio-relay MIA.

8/9 NOVEMBER 1944

8AF 706 NIGHT LEAFLET OPERATION

NLS despatched 5 B-17s and 12 B-24s (2 a/c aborted): France, Holland, Germany.

9 NOVEMBER 1944

8AF 707

	Despatched		Effective	Target		Bombs Tonnage	E/A	Losses MIA	E	Dam	Casualties KIA	WIA	MIA
3BD	B-17	460	47	THIONVILLE T/T	(P)	105.0		4	4	96	8	6	27
			276	SAARBRÜCKEN M/Y	(S)	847.7							
			34	SAARLAUTERN	(O)	115.0							
			3	T/O		7.0							
1BD	B-17	437	217	METZ T/T	(P)	806.5		0	3	13	19	0	0
			128	METZ T/T	(P)	490.5							
			41	SAARBRÜCKEN M/Y	(S)	162.5							
			28	KOBLENZ	(O)	107.5							
2BD	B-24	402	92	METZ T/T	(P)	249.5		0	1	5	0	0	0
			90	METZ T/T	(P)	333.5							
			116	METZ T/T	(P)	345.5							
			87	METZ T/T	(P)	126.5							
			15	SAARBRÜCKEN M/Y	(S)	54.5							
	B-17	10	10	SCREENING FORCE									
TOTALS:		1309	1184			3751.2	0	4	8	114	27	6	27
	P-51	192	187	ESCORT 3BD				0	0		0	0	0
	P-51	184	176	ESCORT 1BD				0	0		0	0	0
	P-51	119	113	ESCORT 2BD				0	3		0	0	0
				FIGHTER-BOMBER									
	P-47	149	139	FRANKFURT		20.2	0	1	0		0	0	1
	P-51	62		LANNHEIM AREA				4	0		0	0	3
	P-51	32	30	SCOUTING FORCES				0	0		0	0	0
TOTALS:		738	645			20.2	0	5	3	0	0	1	4

REMARKS: Front line strong points and tactical targets in the Metz and Thionville areas. 1BD and 2BD bombed visually and with GH aid; 3BD bombed visually and with some resort to H2X. All Bomb groups except 493BG participated. Bomb group losses:– 388BG – 1, 452BG – 2, 487BG – 1. B/d 452BG B-17 cr. France, 3 killed – Lts Gott and Metzger posthumously awarded Medal of Honor for action leading to this incident. 91BG B-17 c/l France: 452BG B-17 cr in sea during assembly, crew lost. B/d 467BG B-24 c/l and burned Woodbridge A/F. Two 303BG B-17s collided during assembly, 17 killed. A 388BG B-17 accidentally dropped a 1,000lb bomb at Langham, Suffolk; houses damaged. On return 388BG B-17 cr. Luxembourg, 2 k, 7 safe. B/d 390BG B-17 c/l Continent.

All Fighter groups operating. Fighter group losses:– 20FG – 2, 78FG – 1, 352FG – 1, 355FG – 1. B/d 339FG P-51 c/l Charleville, France. 364FG P-51 Cat E after landing accident base.

OTHER OPERATIONS: 7PG despatched 3 F-5s and 1 Spitfire to Germany. 25BG despatched 3 Mosquitoes on WR Continent/UK and 3 B-24s and 1 B-17 on WR Azores/Atlantic. ASR despatched 18 P-47s on patrol. 6 P-47s, 22 P-51s on radio-relays.

9/10 NOVEMBER 1944

8AF 708 NIGHT LEAFLET OPERATION

NLS despatched 5 B-17s and 12 B-24s; France, Holland, Germany.

36BS despatched 7 B-24s (6 effective) on RCM. 1 B-24 cr. France.

A 486BG Fortress lifts from the release of its load. With the coming of another winter, more often than not bombing was through cloud by PFF means. At Wiesbaden airfield on 10 November the new Micro-H system was used, promising much greater accuracy.

10 NOVEMBER 1944

8AF 709

	Despatched		Effective	Target		Bombs Tonnage	E/A	Losses MIA	E	Dam	Casualties KIA	WIA	MIA
2BD	B-24	302	229	HANAU/ LANGENDIEBACH A/F	(P)	413.5		1	1	46	1	2	9
			61	HANAU M/Y	(S)	112.5							
3BD	B-17	235	105	WIESBADEN A/F	(P)	177.6		2	4	90	0	7	20
			73	WIESBADEN/HALLE	(S)	125.0							
			4	T/O		7.1							
1BD	B-17	203	96	COLOGNE BUTZWEILERHOF A/F	(P)	177.5		1	0	95	2	5	9
			97	COLOGNE/OSTHEIM A/F	(P)	180.7							
	B-17	12	12	SCREENING FORCE									
TOTALS:		752	677			1193.9	0	4	5	231	3	14	38
	P-47	45	261	ESCORT 2BD			4–0–0						
	P-51	236											
	P-51	154	142	ESCORT 3BD									
	P-51	191	182	ESCORT 1BD			2–0–0						
	P-47	87	79	FIGHTER-BOMBER COMMUNICACTIONS N & C. GERMANY			1–0–0 (G)						
	P-51	35	35	SCOUTING FORCES									
	P-51	60	58	STRAFING AND D/A PHOTOS									
TOTALS:		808	757				6–0–0 1–0–0(G)	0	0	0	0	0	0

REMARKS: PFF attacks on airfields in Western Germany. All 2BD groups participated and bombed by GH and H2X. 3BD Force consisted of 45CBW groups and 94BG, 100BG, 390BG, 486BG. 3BD used Micro H and H2X. 1BD Force consisted of 41CBW groups and 381BG, 398BG. 1BD used GH. Bomb group losses:– 1BD – 303BG – 1; 2BD – 467BG – 1; 3BD – 96BG – 1, 100BG – 1. B/d 94BG B-17 c/l near Brussels. On return 491BG B-24 cr. near North Pickenham A/F, 1 k. 1 B/d 452BG B-17 and 2 b/d 486BG B-17s c/l on Continent. Last mission of 489BG.

All Fighter groups operating. No credits.

OTHER OPERATIONS: 25BG despatched 5 Mosquitoes on WR Continent/UK and 2 B-24s and 1 B-17 on WR Azores/Atlantic/UK. ASR despatched 10 P-47s on patrols. 6 P-47s and 20 P-51s on radio-relays.

10/11 NOVEMBER 1944

8AF 711 NIGHT LEAFLET OPERATION

NLS despatched 6 B-17s and 9 B-24s (1 aborted). Holland and Germany.

36BS despatched 8 B-24s (7 effective) on RCM.

Viewed from the high group (93BG) the lead group (446BG) manoeuvres for the run on Bottrop oil refineries, 11 November. 446BG lead is a GH equipped 93BG aircraft with an H2X 446BG as deputy lead on the right wing (note special tail marking that identifies this a/c as a PFF). Although a visual sighting was made the PFF run was continued as a back-up. (J. Archer)

11 NOVEMBER 1944

8AF 712

	Despatched		Effective	Target	Bombs Tonnage	E/A	Losses MIA	E	Dam	Casualties KIA	WIA	MIA
3BD	B-17	197	146	OBERLAHNSTEIN M/Y (P)	396.0		0	1	31	1	0	0
			24	KOBLENZ M/Y (S)	68.5							
			2	TRIER (O)	6.0							
1BD	B-17	129	100	GELSENKIRCHEN/ BUER O/R (P)	236.8		0	1	1	7	0	0
			23	RHEINE M/Y (S)	56.5							
2BD	B-24	143	124	BOTTROP O/R (P)	344.2		1	0	39	0	0	10
			1	RECKLINGHAUSEN (O)	3.0							
	B-17	13	12	SCREENING FORCES			0		0	0	0	0
TOTALS:		482	432		1111.0	0	1	2	71	8	0	10
	P-47	41	179	ESCORT 3BD			0					
	P-51	138					0					
	P-51	52		ESCORT 1BD			1					
	P-47	36	98	ESCORT 2BD			0					
	P-51	69					0					
	P-51	31	31	SCOUTING FORCES			0					
TOTALS:		367	308			0	1	0	0	0	0	0

REMARKS: PFF attacks on oil refineries and marshalling yards in Western Germany. 3BD used Micro H and H2X, 1BD used GH and H2X, 2BD used GH. 2BD Force consisted of 45CBW groups and 95BG, 385BG, 447BG, 487BG, 493BG. 1BD Force consisted of 41CBW groups and 305BG. 2BD Force consisted of 93BG, 392BG, 446BG, 466BG, 467BG. Bomb group losses:– 453BG – 1. During assembly, a 303BG B-17 cr. near Much Wenlock, 7 killed; 385BG B-17 exploded and cr. Easton, 1 killed.

All Fighter groups except 20FG, 356FG, 359FG operating. Fighter Group losses:– 364FG – 1.

OTHER OPERATIONS: 48 a/c despatched on special operations including WR. ASR despatched 8 P-47 on patrols. 10 P-51s and 2 P-47s on radio relays.

11/12 NOVEMBER 1944

36BS despatched 7 B-24s on RCM in support of RAF bombers.

12 NOVEMBER 1944

Period of extremely bad weather with low extensive cloud set in.

25BG despatched 5 Mosquitoes on WR Continent/UK and 2 B-24s on WR Azores/Atlantic. ASR despatched 5 P-47s on patrols and 2 P-51s also on ASR search. 36BS despatched 1 B-24 on flight to test SCS51 for precision bombing in overcast from 25,000ft.

13 NOVEMBER 1944

25BG despatched 4 Mosquitoes on WR Continent/UK and 3 B-24s and 1 B-17 on WR Azores/Atlantic/UK.

13/14 NOVEMBER 1944

8AF 713 NIGHT LEAFLET OPERATION

NLS despatched 4 B-17s and 8 B-24s (10 a/c effective); Holland, France, Germany.

14 NOVEMBER 1944

7PG despatched 2 Spitfires on PR to Böhlen area Germany. 8 P-51s of 55FG provided escort. 25BG despatched 6 Mosquitoes on WR Continent/UK, and 2 B-24s and 2 B-17s on WR Azores/Atlantic/UK.

Combat operations rarely allowed opportunities for such close-in beautifully echeloned flying. *Precocious Pat* and green nosed friends snapped by the section leader were on a training flight, 15 November. The 359FG pilots, front to rear, were: Lts Ralston, Klem and Burtner. In common with other 8AF fighter squadrons these aircraft had recently acquired coloured rudders as an extra form of squadron identification.

15 NOVEMBER 1944

25BG despatched 5 Mosquitoes on WR France, Germany, Low Countries and 1 Mosquito on special sortie over Holland (first *Red Stocking* night mission to receive radio messages from agents and 3 B-24s and 1 B-17 on WR Azores/Atlantic/UK. 31 B-17s and 16 P-51s in a fighter-bomber affiliation practice mission.

15/16 NOVEMBER 1944

8AF 714 NIGHT LEAFLET OPERATION

NLS despatched 6 B-17s and 6 B-24s: Holland, France, Germany.

36BG despatched 5 B-24s (4 effective) on RCM. 1 B-24 cr. on t/o.

16 NOVEMBER 1944

8AF 715

	Despatched		Effective	Target		Bombs Tonnage	E/A	Losses MIA	E	Dam	Casualties KIA	WIA	MIA
3BD	B-17	495	486	DÜREN AREA T/T	(P)	1688.3		0	1	8	0	1	0
1BD	B-17	501	490	ESCHWEILER AREA T/T	(P)	1776.3		0	2	8	1	2	6
2BD	B-24	243	228	ESCHWEILER AREA T/T	(P)	655.8		0	0	0	1	0	
	B-17	4	4	SCREENING FORCE				0	0	0	0	0	0
TOTALS:		1243	1208			4120.4	0	0	3	16	1	4	6
	P-51	159	151	ESCORT 3BD				0	1				
	P-51	107	98	ESCORT 2BD				1	3				
	P-51	16	16					0	0				
TOTALS:		282	265				0	1	4	0	1	1	1

REMARKS: PFF attacks on gun positions east of Aachen as prelude to Allied ground offensive. Bomb groups participating:– all 3BD except 96BG; all 1BD except 398BG; 14CBW and 96CBW groups and 93BG, 448BG of 2BD. 3BD Force used Micro H and H2X, 1BD used GH and H2X, 2BD used GH. 384BG B-17 cr. Belgium. B/d 486BG B-17 f/l Continent – Cat E. On return poor visibility forced 1BD B-17s to land at A/Fs in West of England – Tilstock, Sleap, Gaydon, Chatford, Ossington etc.

All Fighter groups except 4FG, 352FG, 356FG, 359FG, 364FG, 479FG operated. Groups for 1BD escort grounded by weather. Fighter group losses:– 355FG – 1. A 339FG P-51 c/l France. 361FG P-51 cr. after t/o near Baldock, pilot k.

OTHER OPERATIONS: 7PG despatched 10 F-5s and 4 Spitfires on PR Germany. 25BG despatched 1 Mosquito on *Red Stocking* sortie over Holland, 5 Mosquitoes on WR Continent/UK, and 3 B-24s Azores/Atlantic/UK. ASR despatched 16 P-47s on patrols. 2 P-47s and 11 P-51s on radio relays.

17 NOVEMBER 1944

25BG despatched 6 Mosquitoes on WR Continent/UK and 2 B-17s and 1 B-24 on WR Azores/Atlantic/UK.

18 NOVEMBER 1944

8AF 716

	Despatched		Effective	Target	Bombs Tonnage	E/A	Losses MIA	E	Dam	Casualties KIA	WIA	MIA
				SWEEPS								
	P-47	47	374	LANGENSEEBOLD,		26–2– 6	2	0		0	0	2
	P-51	355		WEISSENBORN, FREIHAM & NEUBURG & A/Fs		69–0–41 (G)	5	2		0	0	5
TOTALS:		402	374			26–2– 6 69–0–41(G)	7	2	0	0	0	7

REMARKS: Fighter strafing sweep flown by 4FG, 56FG, 339FG, 353FG, 355FG, 357FG, 361FG, 479FG. Fighter group e/a credits:– 4FG – 1, 56FG – 12, 339FG – 8, 353FG – 1, 357FG – 4. Fighter group losses:– 4FG – 1, 56FG – 2, 339FG – 3, 357FG – 1. B/d 339FG P-51 cr France, pilot safe. B/d 479FG cr. near Grave, France, pilot safe.

OTHER OPERATIONS: 7PG despatched 2 F-5s and 1 Spitfire on PR Germany. 25BG despatched 2 Mosquitoes on WR Continent/UK, and 25 B-17s and 1 B-24 (B-24 aborted) on WR Azores/Atlantic/UK. ASR despatched 12 P-47s (11 effective) on patrols. 2 P-47s and 16 P-51s on radio-relays. 36BS despatched 1 B-24 on RCM with *Mandrel* and *Dina* in jamming test of enemy VHF in connection with 8AF Fighter sweeps.

18/19 NOVEMBER 1944

8AF 717 NIGHT LEAFLET OPERATION

NLS despatched 4 B-24s and 6 B-17s (8 a/c effective): Belgium, Holland, France.

36BS despatched 5 B-24s on RCM in support of RAF.

19 NOVEMBER 1944

7PG despatched 15 F-5s and 4 Spitfires (15 a/c effective) on PR Germany. 24 P-51s of 4FG and 20FG provided escort to PR a/c. 25BG despatched 2 Mosquitoes on WR France and Germany, and 1 B-24 and 3 B-17s on WR Azores/Atlantic/UK.

20 NOVEMBER 1944

8AF 718

	Despatched		Effective	Target		Bombs Tonnage	E/A	Losses MIA	E	Dam	Casualties KIA	WIA	MIA
1BD	B-17	160	61	GELSENKIRCHEN/ SCHOWEN O/I	(P)	141.0		0	0	25	0	0	0
			93	MÜNSTER M/Y	(S)	231.0							
	B-17	12	12	SCREENING FORCE				0	0	0	0	0	0
TOTALS:		172	166			372.0	0	0	0	25	0	0	0
	P-47	56	214	ESCORT 1BD				0	0		0	0	0
	P-51	171											
				FIGHTER-BOMBER									
	P-47	48	310	WESTERN GERMANY		6.0	0	1	0		0	0	1
	P-51	271		MISC. TARGETS				7	1		0	0	7
	P-51	12	12	SCOUTING FORCES				0	0		0	0	0
TOTALS:		558	322			6.0	0	8	1	0	0	0	8

REMARKS: GH attack on Gelsenkirchen oil industry by 41CBW groups. No losses.

All Fighter groups participating except 78FG, 352FG, 364FG. Fighter group losses: 4FG – 2, 55FG – 2, 56FG – 1, 355FG – 1, 356FG – 1, 359FG – 1. First operation of 356FG with P-51. Pilot of 359FG P-51 baled 22 miles E Clacton, lost.

OTHER OPERATIONS: 7PG despatched 4 F-5s and 2 Spitfires Germany. 25BG despatched 5 Mosquitoes on WR Continet and 2 B-24s and 2 B-17s (1 B-24 aborted) on WR Azores/Atlantic/UK. ASR despatched 10 P-47s on patrols. 2 B-17s, 4 P-47s, 16 P-51s on radio-relays.

The name game. A surprising number of ground crew men came to develop a liking for the tea dispensed by the YMCA van that regularly toured bomber airfields. At Wendling appreciation was shown by naming a B-24H for the service and inviting 17-year-old Maureen Mayne of Norwich, one of the girls who worked on the 'tea wagon', to perform the christening, 20 November. Maureen officiates with a cup of tea.

20/21 NOVEMBER 1944

8AF 719 NIGHT LEAFLET OPERATION

NLS despatched 6 B-17s and 7 B-24s; Holland, France, Germany.

36BS despatched 5 B-24s on RCM for RAF.

21 NOVEMBER 1944

8AF 720

	Despatched		Effective	Target		Bombs Tonnage	E/A	Losses MIA	E	Dam	Casualties KIA	WIA	MIA
1BD	B-17	421	200	MERSEBURG/LEUNA	(P)	475.8	1–0–1	14	3	205	1	16	129
			12	MERSEBURG FLAK G/B	(O)	22.3							
			24	MEPPEN	(O)	60.0							
			11	LEEUWARDEN A/F	(O)	25.0							
			10	QUAKENBRÜCK	(O)	25.0							
			12	HUNFELD M/Y	(O)	30.0							
			12	HERSFELD M/Y	(O)	30.0							
			10	HERSFELD AUTO-BAHN	(O)	25.0							
			21	FRIEDBURG	(O)	57.2							
			10	APOLDA	(O)	24.8							
			69	T/O		172.5							
3BD	B-17	492	166	OSNABRÜCK M/Y	(S)	451.5		7	3	142	2	6	65
			77	GIESSEN M/Y	(L)	200.0							
			24	LINGEN	(L)	71.5							
			9	BIELEFELD M/Y	(L)	22.5							
			62	WETZLAR	(L)	162.1							
			23	KOBLENZ M/Y	(L)	87.0							
			35	T/O		66.8							
2BD	B-24	366	171	HAMBURG/ RHENANIA	(P)	474.6		4	2	220	19	8	89
			178	HAMBURG/DPAG	(P)	479.6							
			1	T/O		3.0							
	B-17	12	12	SCREENING FORCE									
TOTALS:		1291	1149			2966.2	1–0–1	25	8	567	22	30	283
	P-51	310	268	ESCORT 1BD			63–7–20	9			0	0	9
							3–0– 2 (G)				0	0	0
	P-51	420	382	ESCORT 3BD				4			0	0	4
	P-47	140	177	ESCORT 2BD			5–0– 2	1			0	0	1
	P-51	51					2–0– 1 (G)	1			0	0	1
	P-51	33	31	SCOUTING FORCES				0			0	0	0
TOTALS:		954	858				68–7–22	15	?	?	0	0	15
							5–0– 3(G)						

REMARKS: PFF attacks (H2X) on oil targets in Germany. 3BD Force unable to attack primaries at Sterkrade, Lendorf and Hamburg. Bomb groups participating:– all 1BD except 384BG; all 2BD; all 3BD except 388BG. Bomb group losses:–1BD – 91BG – 1, 303BG – 4, 306BG – 1, 351BG – 1, 398BG – 5, 401BG – 2; 2BD – 445BG – 1, 446BG – 1, 448BG – 1, 453BG – 1; 3BD – 95BG – 1, 96BG – 3, 385BG – 1, 486BG – 1, 493BG – 1. 96BG B-17 c/l on t/o on railway line, crew safe. During assembly 2 389BG B-24s collided and cr. at Carleton Rode, 17 killed. B/d 398BG and 2 91BG B-17s c/l Belgium. 96BG abandoned by crew over liberated Holland. B/d 401BG B-17 and 390BG B-17 c/l on Continent. MIA 453BG B-24 landed in Sweden. 486BG and 487BG now under control of 4CBW.

All Fighter groups operating. Fighter group e/a credits:– 4FG – 6, 20FG – 1, 78FG – 5, 339FG – 2, 352FG – 19½, 359FG – 17, 361FG – 1, 364FG – 18. Fighter group losses:– 4FG – 2, 20FG – 1, 78FG – 1, 339FG – 3, 353FG – 1, 355FG – 1, 359FG – 3, 364FG – 3.

OTHER OPERATIONS: 7PG despatched 1 Spitfire and 1 F-5 on PR Venlo Bridge. 25BG despatched 5 Mosquitoes WR Continent/UK and 2 B-24s and 1 B-17 Azores/Atlantic/UK. ASR despatched 17 P-47s on patrols. 1 B-17, 1 B-24, 6 P-47s, 16 P-51s on radio-relays.

INCIDENT

An unnamed B-17G, 43-38545, of the 324th Bomb Sqdn, 91st Bomb Group, flak damaged over Merseburg on its third mission, 21 November 1944, was abandoned over Belgium by Lt DeBolt and his crew. Two engines were 'out' and it appeared a third was about to fail. The undercarriage had been lowered and the bomber was set out on automatic pilot to facilitate baling out. After the crew had jumped the Fortress continued a stable descent and landed itself in a ploughed field, sustaining damage to a wing tip and propeller when one main wheel became bogged down and spun the bomber round. A nearby British Army anti-aircraft crew left their gun to offer assistance and were understandably amazed to find no-one aboard!

21/22 NOVEMBER 1944

8AF 721 NIGHT LEAFLET OPERATION

NLS despatched 7 B-17s and 5 B-24s: France, Holland, Germany.

36BS despatched 6 B-24s on RCM.

25BG despatched 3 Mosquitoes on night PR Venlo.

482BG despatched 3 B-17s on radar scope sorties. 1 B-17 f/l Belgium.

One of the many ideas that originated with combat units was this parachute location strap. Parachute packs were usually placed on the fuselage floor as duties and flak jackets made it impractical to wear them. In an emergency packs were often dislodged by violent movement of the aircraft and crew members had difficulty in locating them; precious seconds could be lost, often being the difference between life and death. 401BG personnel devised this simple strap with clips to keep parachute and man together without impeding duties.

22 NOVEMBER 1944

7PG despatched 4 F-5s on PR Germany. 1 F-5 MIA (landed Sweden).

25BG despatched 1 Mosquito on *Red Stocking* sortie, 5 Mosquitoes on WR Continent/UK, and 1 B-24 and 2 B-17s on WR Atlantic/UK. 2 Mosquitoes cr., 1 after t/o at Saham Toney, 1 while trying to land at Thompson A/F; both crews k.

23 NOVEMBER 1944

8AF 722

	Despatched		Effective	Target		Bombs Tonnage	E/A	Losses MIA	E	Dam	Casualties KIA	WIA	MIA
1BD	B-17	155	134	GELSENKIRCHEN/ NORDSTERN O/I	(P)	315.9		0	0	0	0	0	0
				DUISBURG M/Y	(S)	31.6							
	B-17	13	13	SCREENING FORCE				0	0	0	0	0	0
TOTALS:		188	147			347.5	0	0	0	0	0	0	0
	P-51	78	73	ESCORT 1BD				1	1	0	0	0	1
	P-51	12	10	SCOUTING FORCES				0	0	0	0	0	0
TOTALS:		90	83				0	1	1	0	0	0	1

REMARKS: GH attack on oil plant at Gelsenkirchen by 41CBW groups and 457BG.

Escort by 20FG and 352FG. Fighter group losses:– 20FG – 1.

OTHER OPERATIONS: 25BG despatched 4 Mosquitoes on WR Continent/UK and 2 B-17s and 2 B-24s on WR Azores/Atlantic/UK. ASR despatched 18 P-47s on patrols, 4 P-51s on raid relays. B-17 screening forces provided by 351BG.

23/24 NOVEMBER 1944

36BS despatched 6 B-24s (5 effective) on RCM.

24 NOVEMBER 1944

25BG despatched 2 Mosquitoes on WR Continent/UK and 2 B-17s and 2 B-24s on WR Atlantic/UK.

25 NOVEMBER 1944

8AF 723

	Despatched		Effective	Target		Bombs Tonnage	E/A	Losses MIA	E	Dam	Casualties KIA	WIA	MIA
3BD	B-17	388	315	MERSEBURG/LEUNA	(P)	908.3		8	2	147	3	4	64
			5	T/O		13.3							
1BD	B-17	378	356	MERSEBURG/LEUNA	(P)	482.8		0	2	50	4	1	0
			4	T/O		10.0							
2BD	B-24	271	254	BINGEN M/Y	(P)	742.3		0	0	43	0	1	0
	B-17	6	6	SCREENING FORCES				0	0	0	0	0	0
TOTALS:		1043	940			2156.7	0	8	4	240	7	6	64
	P-51	370	336	ESCORT 3BD			2–0–0 (G)	4	0	0	0	0	4
	P-51	430	380	ESCORT 1BD			7–0–8 (G)	2	1	0	0	0	2
	P-47	130	129	ESCORT 2BD				0	0	0	0	0	0
	P-51	35	28	SCOUTING FORCES				0	0	0	0	0	0
TOTALS:		965	873				9–0–8(G)	6	1	0	0	0	6

REMARKS: The synthetic oil plant at Merseburg was attacked by a strong force of B-17s using H2X while B-24s bombed Bingen M/Y using GH. Intense flak at Merseburg damaged many 3BD B-17s and first reports indicated 57 as missing. Some 30 of these were later located at Allied airfields on the Continent. Bomb groups participating:– all 1BD except 303BG, 306BG; all 2BD; all 3BD except 13CBW groups. Bomb group losses:– 3BD – 96BG – 1, 388BG – 1, 447BG – 2, 452BG – 1, 487BG – 1, 490BG – 1, 493BG – 1. On return 96BG B-17 c/l Westleton; 398BG B-17 cr. Barkway; b/d 487BG cr. Framlingham, 1 k. B/d 457BG B-17 c/l Marck, France.

All Fighter groups operating. Fighter group losses: 353FG – 4, 355FG – 1, 356FG – 1. Totals include 137 9AF Fighters.

OTHER OPERATIONS: 7PG despatched 3 F-5s on PR Louent and St.Nazaire. 25BG despatched 5 Mosquitoes on WR Continent/UK and 3 B-17s and 1 B-24 on WR Azores/Atlantic/UK. ASR despatched 8 P-47s on patrols. 1 B-17, 4 P-47s, 18 P-51s on radio-relays. 36BS despatched 6 B-24s on first of regular operations to provide VHF jamming screen for 8AF bombers.

25/26 NOVEMBER 1944

8AF 724 NIGHT LEAFLET OPERATION

NLS despatched 7 B-17s and 6 B-24s (12 a/c effective): France, Holland, Germany.

36BS despatched 3 B-24s on RCM for RAF operations.

482BG despatched 3 B-17s on radar scope sorties.

26 NOVEMBER 1944

8AF 725

	Despatched		Effective	Target		Bombs Tonnage	E/A	Losses MIA	E	Dam	Casualties KIA	WIA	MIA
1BD	B-17	406	118	ALTENBEKEN	(P)	346.5	4–6– 7	10	4	160	4	6	93
			243	MISBURG O/I	(P)	710.0							
			19	OSNABRÜCK M/Y	(S)	52.0							
			3	T/O		9.0							
2BD	B-24	350	240	BIELEFELD/ SCHILDESCHE R/V	(P)	799.5	12–5– 4	21	3	53	15	6	196
			57	MISBURG O/I	(P)	152.5							
			26	HANNOVER M/Y	(O)	69.5							
			1	T/O		4.0							
3BD	B-17	381	266	HAMM M/Y	(P)	763.3		3	1	86	0	1	27
			37	GÜTERSLOH M/Y	(O)	99.8							
			36	BIELEFELD M/Y	(O)	103.3							
			24	HERFORD M/Y	(O)	71.5							
			3	T/O		8.5							
TOTALS:		1137	1073			3189.4	16–11–11	34	8	299	19	13	316
	P-47	64	292	ESCORT 1BD			67–2– 11	0	0	0	0	0	0
	P-51	249						3	2	0	0	0	3
	P-47	48	208	ESCORT 2BD			42–0–18	2	0	0	0	0	2
	P-51	197						3	0	0	0	0	3
	P-51	138	132	ESCORT 3BD			3–0– 1(G)	1	0	0	0	0	1
	P-51	36	36	SCOUTING FORCES			5–1– 2	0	0	0	0	0	0
TOTALS:		132	668				114–3–31 3–0– 1(G)	9	2	0	0	0	9

REMARKS: Attacks on rail viaducts, marshalling yards and oil installations in Western Germany. 1BD used GH at Altenbeken and H2X on other targets. 2BD used GH on primaries with some visual bombing. Apart from a visual attack on Gütersloh, 3BD used H2X. Bomb groups participating: all 1BD except 379BG; all 2BD except 467BG; all 3BD except 486BG. Bomb group losses:– 1BD – 91BG – 3, 303BG – 1, 305BG – 1, 351BG – 1, 381BG – 1, 398BG – 3. 2BD – 389BG – 1, 445BG – 5, 491BG - 15; 3BD – 388BG – 1, 390BG – 1, 487BG – 1. 453BG B-24 cr. Kenninghall after t/o, all killed. B/d 491BG B-24 abandoned over Belgium, 91BG B-17 c/l Denain A/F. B/d 445BG c/l base. B/d 351BG B-17 c/l Belgium. B/d 303BG, B-17 f/l Belgium, Cat E – 3 men blown out by flak burst. B/d 91BG B-17 Halesworth A/F and burned, crew safe. 490BG B-17 c/l Continent. More than 500 enemy fighters airborne – the 15 B-24s lost by 491BG near Hannover were to fighters.

All Fighter groups operating. Fighter group e/a credits:– 78FG – 9, 339FG – 29, 353FG – 3, 355FG – 21, 356FG – 21, 361FG – 23, 364FG – 8, 479FG – 1. Fighter group losses:– 55FG – 2, 78FG – 2, 339FG – 2, 353FG – 1, 355FG – 1, 364FG – 1.

OTHER OPERATIONS: 7PG despatched 7 F-5s and 2 Spitfires on PR Germany, 1 F-5 MIA. 25BG despatched 2 Mosquitoes on WR Germany and 1 Mosquito WR Ireland/UK and 2 B-24s and 1 B-17 on WR Azores/Atlantic/UK. ASR despatched 11 P-47s on patrols. 1 Mosquito sent on special operation Holland. 4 P-51s sent on special photo mission to Altenbeken. 36BS despatched 6 B-24s on RCM for 8AF bombers. 2 B-17s, 4 P-47s, 8 P-51s on radio-relays.

26/27 NOVEMBER 1944

8AF 726 NIGHT LEAFLET OPERATION

NLS despatched 8 B-17s and 6 B-24s (12 a/c effective): France, Holland, Germany.

36BS despatched 3 B-24s on RCM for RAF bombers.

27 NOVEMBER 1944

8AF 727

	Despatched		Effective	Target		Bombs Tonnage	E/A	Losses MIA	E	Dam	Casualties KIA	WIA	MIA
3BD	B-17	190	148	BINGEN M/Y	(P)	309.5		0	0	46	0	2	0
			2	T/O		4.4							
1BD	B-17	186	181	OFFENBURG M/Y	(P)	525.6		0	0	14	0	1	0
			1	FREIBURG	(O)	2.0							
2BD	B-24	154	144	OFFENBURG M/Y	(P)	343.6		0	0	9	0	0	0
			7	T/O		16.0							
TOTALS:		530	483			1201.1	0	0	0	69	0	3	0
	P-51	95	91	ESCORT 3BD				1	0	0	0	0	1
	P-51	107	105	ESCORT 1BD				2	1	0	0	0	2
	P-51	48	45	ESCORT 2BD				0	0	0	0	0	0
	P-47	95	460	FIGHTER-BOMBER 4 OIL CENTRES			98-4-11	2	0	0	0	0	2
	P-51	398		N & C GERMANY			4-0- 1(G)	10	0	0	0	0	10
	P-51	27	26	SCOUTING FORCES				0	0	0	0	0	0
TOTALS:		770	727				98-4-11 4-0- 1(G)	15	1	0	1	2	15

REMARKS: PFF attacks on marshalling yards in Germany. 3BD used H2X; 1BD and 2BD used GH with some visual bombing. Bomb groups participating: 1BD – 41CBW groups and 91BG, 398BG; 2BD – 44BG, 93BG, 389BG, 445BG, 448BG, 466BG, 467BG; 3BD – 4CBW's five groups and 96BG, 452BG.

All Fighter groups operating. Fighter group e/a credits: 56FG – 3, 352FG – 18, 353FG – 18, 355FG – 1, 356FG – 2, 357FG – 30, 359FG – 12, 361FG – 5, 479FG – 2. Fighter group losses:– 55FG – 1, 56FG – 1, 78FG – 1, 339FG – 2, 352FG – 3, 353FG – 2, 357FG – 1, 359FG – 1, 361FG – 1, 364FG – 2. MIA 55FG P-51 cr. in sea. 364FG P-51 cr. near St.Dizier, pilot k. The 361FG pilot evaded.

OTHER OPERATIONS: 7PG despatched 1 F-5 on PR St.Nazaire. 25BG despatched 4 Mosquitoes on WR Continent/UK and 5 B-17s and 1 B-24 on WR Azores/Atlantic/UK. ASR despatched 24 P-47s on patrols. 36BS despatched 5 B-24s on RCM for 8AF operations. 1 Mosquito on special mission over Belgium and Germany.

27/28 NOVEMBER 1944

36BS despatched 3 B-24s on RCM for RAF bombers.

28 NOVEMBER 1944

25BG despatched 3 Mosquitoes on WR France/Atlantic/UK and 2 B-17s and 1 B-24 (1 B-17 recalled) on WR Azores/Atlantic/UK. 1 Mosquito despatched on *Red Stocking* operation. 36BS despatched 5 B-24s on RCM jamming and 3 B-24s on 'Spoof' RCM.

28/29 NOVEMBER 1944

8AF 728 NIGHT LEAFLET OPERATION

NLS despatched 6 B-17s and 6 B-24s (10 a/c effective): Holland, Germany.

36BS despatched 2 B-24s on RCM in support of RAF.

29 NOVEMBER 1944

8AF 729

		Despatched	Effective	Target		Bombs Tonnage	E/A	Losses MIA	E	Dam	Casualties KIA	WIA	MIA
1BD	B-17	445	391	MISBURG O/I		1152.0		0	0	6	0	0	0
			36	OSNABRÜCK	(O)	96.0							
			5	T/O		15.0							
2BD	B-24	307	144	ALTENBEKEN R/V	(P)	440.5		1	0	9	0	0	10
			152	BIELEFELD/ SCHILDESCHE R/V	(P)	512.0							
			2	T/O		7.0							
3BD	B-17	312	294	HAMM M/Y	(P)	524.0		0	1	87	0	3	0
			4	T/O		12.0							
	B-17	13	12	SCREENING FORCE – T/O		3.0		0	0	0	0	0	0
TOTALS:		1077	1040			2761.5	0	1	1	102	0	3	10
	P-47	35	419	ESCORT 1BD									
	P-51	428											
	P-47	50	261	ESCORT 2BD									
	P-51	247											
	P-51	120	112	ESCORT 3BD									
	P-47	32	26	ESCORT SCREENING FORCE									
	P-51	34	31	SCOUTING FORCES									
TOTALS:		946	849				0	0	0	0	0	0	0

REMARKS: PFF attacks on viaducts rail targets and oil refineries in Germany. 1BD and 3BD used H2X, 2BD used GH. Bomb Groups participating: all 1BD; all 2BD except 458BG; all 3BD except the five 4 BW groups. Bomb Group losses:– 445BG – 1.

All Fighter groups operating. 112 P-38 of 9AF supported mission.

OTHER OPERATIONS: 7PG despatched 4 F-5s and 3 Spitfires on PR Germany. 25BG despatched 2 Mosquitoes on WR Germany, 1 Mosquito WR Irish Sea and 3 B-17 and 1 B-24 on WR Azores/Atlantic/UK. ASR despatched 15 P-47s on patrols. 1 Mosquito on special operation Holland and W. Germany. 36BS despatched 7 B-24s (6 effective) on RCM for 8AF operations. 1 B-17, 6 P-47s, 20 P-51s on radio-relays.

A Sturm FW 190 dives away through falling bombs at Misburg after attacking 491BG.

29/30 NOVEMBER 1944

8AF 730 NIGHT LEAFLET OPERATION

NLS despatched 6 B-17s and 7 B-24s; Holland, Germany.

36BS despatched 2 B-24s on RCM for RAF operations.

30 NOVEMBER 1944

8AF 212

		Despatched	Effective	Target		Bombs Tonnage	E/A	Losses MIA	E	Dam	Casualties KIA	WIA	MIA
1BD	B-17	451	68	BÖHLEN O/I	(P)	166.3		11	4	287	8	16	100
			132	ZEITZ O/I	(P)	320.4							
			116	MERSEBURG/ LEUNA O/I	(S)	289.8							
			22	GOTHA	(O)	52.5							
			17	RUDOLSTADT	(O)	42.0							
			21	GERA	(O)	52.0							
			10	OHRDRUF	(O)	22.5							
			12	FULDA	(O)	30.0							
			12	SAALFELD	(O)	30.0							
			6	MEERANE	(O)	15.0							
			9	T/O		22.5							
3BD	B-17	539	301	MERSEBURG/ LEUNA O/I	(P)	726.1		17	6	325	17	42	295
			169	LÜTZKENDORF O/I	(P)	413.1							
			9	WEISSENFELS	(O)	22.5							
			19	ZEITZ O/I	(O)	47.2							
			12	T/O		30.6							
2BD	B-24	291	180	NEUNKIRCHEN M/Y	(P)	436.5		1	2	4	0	0	9
			104	HOMBURG M/Y	(P)	252.0							
TOTALS:		1281	1219			2971.0	0	29	12	616	24	58	304

Despatched		Effective	Target	Bombs Tonnage	E/A	Losses MIA	Casualties E	Dam	KIA	WIA	MIA
P-51	384	357	ESCORT 1BD		4–0–0	2	0	0	0	0	2
P-47	64	452	ESCORT 3BD			0	0	0	0	0	0
P-51	434					0	2	0	0	0	0
P-47	60	56	ESCORT 2BD			1	0	0	0	0	1
P-51	33	30	SCOUTING FORCES			0	0	0	0	0	0
TOTALS:	972	895			4–0–0	3	2	0	0	1	3

REMARKS: Major operation by B-17 forces against oil plants in SE Germany while B-24s attacked rail targets. 1BD bombed visually; 3BD bombed visually with some use of H2X at Leuna; 2BD bombed with GH aid. All bomb groups except 467BG participated. Bomb group losses; 1BD – 91BG – 1, 92BG – 1, 379BG – 6, 384BG – 2, 398BG – 1; 2BD – 446BG – 1; 3BD – 34BG – 1, 95BG – 2, 96BG – 2, 100BG – 1, 390BG – 7, 447BG – 1, 486BG – 2, 487BG – 1. B/d 490BG, 493BG and 91BG B-17s c/l Belgium. On return 2 94BG B-17s collided over base, 1 cr. 8 killed; 1 c/l, crew safe. B/d 384BG B-17 abandoned over Continent, 4 k; 2 b/d 390BG B-17s f/l France – Cat E; 2 b/d 457BG B-17s c/l France; b/d 445BG and 446BG B-24s cr. Continent.

All Fighter groups operating. 98 P-38s and 18 P-51s of 9AF also participated. Fighter group e/a credits: 352FG – 3, 364FG – 1. Fighter group losses:– 56FG – 1, 364FG – 2. 357FG P-51 c/l base, pilot injured; another 357FG P-51 c/l Boreham, pilot safe.

OTHER OPERATIONS: 25BG despatched 1 Mosquito on PR Germany, 1 Mosquito on special operations Belgium and Germany, 6 Mosquitoes on WR Continent/UK and 2 B-24s and 1 B-17 (1 B-24 aborted) on WR Azores/Atlantic/UK. ASR despatched 13 P-47s on patrols. 36BS despatched 6 B-24s on RCM for 8AF operations. 1 B-17, 1 B-24, 4 P-47, 18 P-51 on radio-relays.

30 NOVEMBER/1 DECEMBER 1944

8AF 732 NIGHT LEAFLET OPERATION

NLS despatched 7 B-17s and 6 B-24s; Holland, Germany.

482BG despatched 3 B-17s on radar scope photo sorties; Gladbeck area.

36BG despatched 2 B-24s on RCM in support of RAF ops.

1 DECEMBER 1944

7PG despatched 2 F-5s to Germany – recalled. 25BG despatched 5 Mosquitoes on WR Continent/UK, and 2 B-17s and 1 B-24 on WR Azores/UK. 36BS despatched 4 B-24s on RCM jamming and 3 B-24s on RCM 'Spoof' mission. 1 Mosquito on *Red Stocking* mission over Holland and Germany.

1/2 DECEMBER 1944

8AF 733 NIGHT LEAFLET OPERATION

NLS despatched 7 B-17s and 7 B-24s; Holland, France, Germany.

36BS despatched 1 B-24 on RCM for RAF operations.

2 DECEMBER 1944

8AF 734

	Despatched		Effective	Target	Bombs Tonnage	E/A	Losses MIA	E	Dam	Casualties KIA	WIA	MIA
2BD	B-24	143	135	BINGEN M/Y (P)	359.0	2–1–1	11	0	4	0	2	102
			2	T/O	6.0							
1BD	B-17	152	125	OBERLAHNSTEIN M/Y(P)	465.5		0	0	0	0	0	0
			9	KOBLENZ/LUTZEL M/Y (P)	26.3							
			6	T/O	17.5							
3BD	B-17	160	Abandoned	– WEATHER			0	0	0	0	0	0
TOTALS:		455	277		874.3	2–1–1	11	0	4	0	2	102
	P-51	104	97	ESCORT 2BD		4–1–2	0	0		0	0	0
	P-51	169	158	ESCORT 1BD		6–0–0	0	0		0	0	0
	P-51	156	153	ESCORT 3BD		7–0–0	0	0		0	0	0
	P-47	44	133	SWEEP COLOGNE, KASSEL,		15–1–4	3	0		0	0	3
	P-51	101		MEININGEN, MANNHEIM, FRANKFURT AREA			1	2		0	0	1
	P-51	30	28	SCOUTING FORCES			0	0		0	0	0
TOTALS:		604	569		0	32–2–6	4	2		0	1	4

2 DECEMBER 1944 *(contd.)*

REMARKS: GH attacks on marshalling yards by 1BD and 2BD. 3BD despatched to Koblenz but mission abandoned due to weather. Bomb groups participating:– 1BD – 41CBW groups and 301BG; 2BD – 44BG, 93BG, 389BG, 392BG, 446BG, 466BG; 3BG – 13CBW groups and 94BG, 487BG. Bomb group losses:– 44BG – 2, 389BG – 1, 392BG – 6, 446BG – 2. B-24s attacked by fighters west of the Rhine.

All Fighter groups except 78FG, 339FG, 356FG, 479FG operating. Fighter group e/a credits:– 4FG – 2, 20FG – 6, 56FG – 11, 355FG – 1, 357FG – 6, 361FG – 3, 364FG – 2. Fighter group losses:– 20FG – 1, 56FG – 3. 20FG P-51 cr. near Brussels, pilot injured. 364FG P-51 c/l Bawdsey on return, pilot safe.

OTHER OPERATIONS: 25BG despatched 3 Mosquitoes on WR Germany, 1 Mosquito WR Atlantic and 1 B-24 and 2 B-17s on WR Azores/Atlantic/UK. 36BS despatched 6 B-24s on RCM in support of 8AF operations. ASR despatched 16 P-47s on patrols. 1 B-17, 1 B-24, 2 P-47s, 12 P-51s on radio-relays.

2/3 DECEMBER 1944

8AF 735 NIGHT LEAFLET OPERATION

NLS despatched 7 B-17s and 6 B-24s; France, Holland, Germany.

36BS despatched 2 B-24s on RCM in support of RAF ops.

3 DECEMBER 1944

25BG despatched 2 Mosquitoes on WR Germany, 2 Mosquitoes WR Irish Sea/UK, and 4 B-17s on WR Azores/Atlantic/UK. ASR despatched 4 P-47s on patrols. 36BS despatched 7 B-24s on RCM.

4 DECEMBER 1944

8AF 736

	Despatched		Effective	Target		Bombs Tonnage	E/A	Losses MIA	E	Dam	Casualties KIA	WIA	MIA
1BD	B-17	419		KASSEL M/Y	(P)	613.8		0	4	3	0	0	0
			188	SOEST M/Y	(P)	553.6							
			2	T/O		6.0							
2BD	B-24	315	199	BEBRA M/Y	(P)	554.8		1	0	15	0	0	10
			78	KOBLENZ M/Y	(O)	212.3							
			21	GIESSEN M/Y	(O)	59.5							
			1	T/O		2.8							
3BD	B-17	457	62	GIESSEN M/Y	(P)	183.3		2	1	106	0	1	18
			221	MAINZ M/Y	(P)	638.8							
			119	FRIEDBURG M/Y	(O)	336.3							
			24	FULDA	(O)	67.5							
			11	BARGES ON RHINE	(O)	31.5							
			6	T/O		16.0							
TOTALS:		1191	1144			3276.2	0	3	5	124	0	1	28
	P-47	75	375	ESCORT 1BD				0			0	0	0
	P-51	318						1			0	0	1
	P-47	49	290	ESCORT 2BD			6–0–11	0			0	0	0
	P-51	254					(G)	0			0	0	0
	P-51	244	238	ESCORT 3BD				2			0	0	2
	P-51	37	36	SCOUTING FORCES				0			0	0	0
TOTALS:		977	939				6–0–11(G)	3	1	?	0	0	3

REMARKS: PFF attacks on rail targets in Germany. 1BD used GH at Soest and H2X at Kassel; 2BD used GH at Bebra and H2X on other targets; 3BD used Micro H at Giessen, visual at Friedburg and H2X on others. All bomb groups participated except 306BG. Bomb group losses:– 2BD – 44BG – 1; 3BD – 390BG – 1, 452BG – 1. B/d 398BG B-17 f/l Belgium – Cat E. B/d 91BG B-17 f/l Continent. 384BG B-17 c/l after t/o near Deenethorpe. B/d 452BG and 457BG B-17s c/l Continent.

All Fighter groups operating. Fighter group losses:– 20FG – 1, 339FG – 1, 353FG – 1. 72 P-38s of 9AF participated.

OTHER OPERATIONS: 7PG despatched 2 F-5s on PR Cologne/Koblenz. 25BG despatched 4 Mosquitoes on WR Continent and 2 B-17s and 2 B-24s on WR Azores/Atlantic/UK. 36BS despatched 8 B-24s on RCM in support of 8AF operations. ASR despatched 16 P-47s on patrols. 12 B-17s and 2 Mosquitoes carried out screening operation for bombers. 1 B-17, 1 B-24, 6 P-47s, 14 P-51s on radio-relays.

4/5 DECEMBER 1944

8AF 737 NIGHT LEAFLET OPERATION

NLS despatched 11 B-17s and B-24s (10 a/c effective); Holland, France, Germany.

36BS despatched 2 B-24s on RCM in support of RAF.

25BG despatched 1 Mosquito on night PR Bonn/Koblenz.

5 DECEMBER 1944

8AF 738

	Despatched		Effective	Target		Bombs Tonnage	E/A	Losses MIA	E	Dam	Casualties KIA	WIA	MIA
3BD	B-17	229	217	BERLIN/TEGEL	(P)	517.9		3	0	105	0	3	30
			2	NIENBURG	(O)	5.0							
			4	T/O		8.8							
1BD	B-17	222	187	BERLIN/TEGEL	(P)	442.3		9	0	64	1	5	85
			17	T/O		43.3							
2BD	B-24	129	114	MÜNSTER M/Y	(P)	288.5		0	0	10	0	0	0
	B-24	6	6	SCREENING FORCES									
8AF 739 *APHRODITE*													
	B-17	5	2					0		0	0	0	0
TOTALS:		591	549			1305.8	0	12	0	179	1	8	115
	P-51	345	301	ESCORT 3BD			65–4–17 0–0– 2(G)	6	1		0	0	6
	P-51	366	329	ESCORT 1BD			25–3– 6	9	0		1	0	9
	P-47	103	141	ESCORT 2BD				0	1		0	0	0
	P-51	45						2	0		0	0	2
	P-51	25	23					0	0		0	0	0
	P-51	17	17	ESCORT *APHRODITE*			1–0– 0	0	0		0	0	0
TOTALS:		901	811				91–7–28 0–0– 2(G)	17	2	?	1	0	17

REMARKS: PFF attacks by B-17s on munitions and tank works at Berlin and by B-24s on Münster rail yards. H2X used at all B-17 targets and to supplement the GH technique at Münster. Bomb groups participating:– 1BD – 91BG, 305BG, 306BG, 351BG, 398BG, 401BG; 2BD – 14CBW groups and 93BG, 389BG, 445BG, 446BG; 3BD – 45CBW groups and 34BG, 95BG, 100BG, 490BG. Bomb group losses:– 1BD – 91BG – 3, 305BG – 3, 306BG – 2, 351BG – 1; 3BD – 34BG – 1, 96BG – 1, 452BG – 1.

All Fighter groups operating. Fighter group e/a credits:– 4FG – 1, 55FG – 6, 353FG – 9, 355FG – 13, 356FG – 11, 357FG – 22, 364FG – 11, 479FG – 14. Fighter group losses:– 339FG – 2, 353FG – 2, 355FG – 1, 356FG – 5, 357FG – 2, 361FG – 1, 479FG – 4. One 479FG P-51 MIA down in Channel. B/d 364FG P-51 cr. near Liège, pilot k. 56FG P-47 c/l, pilot inj.

OTHER OPERATIONS: 7PG despatched 15 F-5s and 4 Spitfires (15 a/c effective) on PR Holland and Germany. 25BG despatched 5 Mosquitoes on WR Continent/UK, and 3 B-17s and 1 B-24 on WR Azores/Atlantic/UK. ASR despatched 22 P-47s on patrols and 8 P-51s also on ASR search. 1 B-17, 1 B-24, 4 P-47s, 16 P-51s on radio-relays. 36BS despatched 9 B-24s (8 effective) on RCM in support of 8AF operations. Mission 739 was *Aphrodite* involving 2 B-17 *Castor* drones, 3 B-17 control and observation a/c, P-38 observation and photo a/c and 17 P-51 escort.

5/6 DECEMBER 1944

8AF 740 NIGHT LEAFLET OPERATION

NLS despatched 4 B-17s and 8 B-24s (11 a/c effective); Holland, France, Germany.

482BG despatched 3 B-17s on scope photo sorties of battle lines.

25BG despatched 1 Mosquito on night PR Bonn area.

6 DECEMBER 1944

8AF 741

	Despatched		Effective	Target		Bombs Tonnage	E/A	Losses MIA	E	Dam	Casualties KIA	WIA	MIA
1BD	B-17	264	244	MERSEBURG/ LEUNA I/O	(P)	584.7		0	1	81	0	4	0
			4	T/O		9.9							
	B-17	12	12	SCREENING FORCE									
3BD	B-17	269	202	MERSEBURG/ LEUNA I/O	(P)	491.8		4	0	91	0	0	37
			14	MERSEBURG	(O)	35.0							
			16	HANNOVER	(O)	39.4							
			20	T/O		48.5							
2BD	B-24	119	112	BIELEFELD M/Y	(P)	378.0		0	0	52	0	0	0
			1	T/O		3.5							
2BD	B-24	154	140	MINDEN AQUEDUCT	(P)	411.0		0	0	26	0	0	0
			9	LOCKUM R/J	(O)	25.0							
TOTALS:		818	774			2026.8	0	4	1	250	0	4	37
	P-51	285	256	ESCORT 1BD				1	1		1	0	1
	P-47	22	278	ESCORT 3BD				0	0		0	0	0
	P-51	288						0	0		0	0	0
	P-51	104	94	ESCORT BIELEFELD				0	0		0	0	0
	P-47	47	91	ESCORT MINDEN				0	0		0	0	0
	P-51	52						0	0		0	0	0
	P-51	32	28	SCOUTING FORCES				0	0		0	0	0
TOTALS:		830	747				0	1	1	?	1	0	1

REMARKS: B-17s attacked the German oil industry and B-24s bombed rail targets. All Forces employed H2X apart from 9 B-24s which were visual on Lockum. Bomb groups participating: 1BD – 40CBW groups and 303BG, 384BG, 401BG, 457BG; 2BD – 14CBW and 96CBW groups at Bielefeld and 389BG, 446BG, 448BG, 453BG at Minden; 3BD – 4CBW and 93CBW groups. Bomb group losses:– 385BG – 1, 447BG – 1, 486BG – 2. A 91BG B-17 c/l.

All Fighter groups except 56FG operating. Fighter group losses:– 364FG – 1. 20FG P-51 cr. Wix, pilot killed.

OTHER OPERATIONS: 7PG despatched 4 F-5s on PR Germany. 25BG despatched 4 Mosquitoes (3 effective) on WR Continent/UK, and 3 B-17s on WR Azores/Atlantic/UK. 36BS despatched 8 B-24s on RCM in support of 8AF operations 1 B-24, 21 P-51s on radio-relays.

6/7 DECEMBER 1944

8AF 742 NIGHT LEAFLET OPERATION

NLS despatched 4 B-17s and 11 B-24s (11 a/c effective); Holland, France, Germany.

36BS despatched 2 B-24s on RCM for RAF.

7 DECEMBER 1944

25BG despatched 5 Mosquitoes on WR Continent/UK, and 3 B-17s and 1 B-24 on WR Azores/Atlantic/UK. 36BS despatched 8 B-24s on RCM for RAF.

8 DECEMBER 1944

25BG despatched 3 B-17s on WR Azores/Atlantic/UK.

36BS despatched 8 B-24s on RCM and 'Spoof' operations.

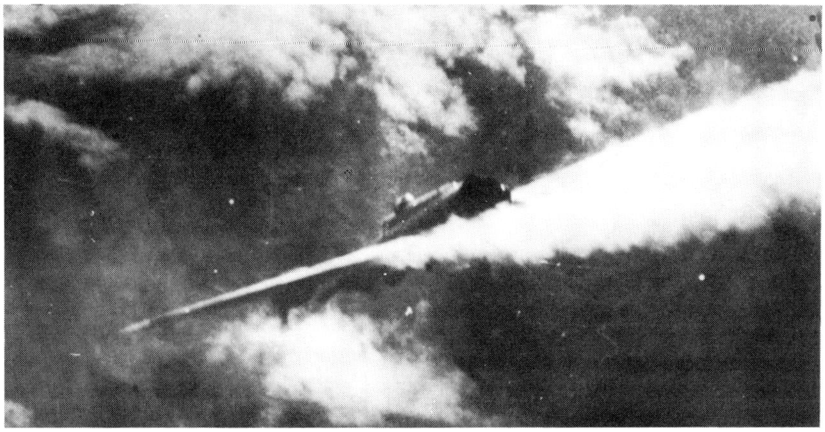

Fuselage completely severed aft of the wing, the 379BG leadship (B-17G 42-97170), plunges earthward following a collision on 9 December. (IWM)

9 DECEMBER 1944

8AF 743

	Despatched		Effective	Target		Bombs	E/A	Losses			Casualties		
						Tonnage		MIA	E	Dam	KIA	WIA	MIA
1BD	B-17	413	94	STUTTGART/ BÖBLINGEN A/F	(P)	174.8		1	4	63	0	3	9
			25	STUTTGART/ ECHTERDINGEN A/F	(P)	46.6							
			262	STUTTGART/ UNTERTURKHEIM M/Y	(P)	594.7							
			10	HALINGEN	(O)	18.9							
			4	T/O		9.4							
TOTALS:		413	395			844.4	0	1	4	63	0	3	9
	P-51	231	247	ESCORT 1BD			1–0–0						
	P-47	36											
	P-51	7	6	SCOUTING FORCE									
TOTALS:		274	253				1–0–0	0	0	?	0	0	0

REMARKS: Airfields and rail targets in the Stuttgart area. GH used by all Formations with opportunities for visual sighting at Böblingen A/F and the M/Y. Bomb groups participating:– all 1BD except 401BG. Bomb group losses:– 306BG – 1. B/d 457BG B-17 f/l Continent – Cat E. 2 379BG B-17s collided over France on return, 1 cr. Romilly, 7 k. B/d 306BG B-17 c/l Continent.

Fighter groups operating: 4FG, 20FG, 78FG, 339FG, 352FG, 355FG, 361FG. Fighter groups e/a credits:– 352FG – 1.

OTHER OPERATIONS: 25BG despatched 6 Mosquitoes on WR Continent/UK, and 3 B-17 on WR Azores/Atlantic/UK. ASR despatched 9 P-47s on patrols. 36BS despatched 12 B-24s on RCM for 8AF operations with 12 P-51s as escort. 1 B-24, 2 P-47s and 12 P-51s on radio-relays. 1 Mosquito on special operation to Stuttgart.

9/10 DECEMBER 1944

8AF 744 NIGHT LEAFLET OPERATION

NLS despatched 4 B-17s and 7 B-24s; Holland, France, Germany.

36BS despatched 1 B-24 on RCM in support RAF.

25BG despatched 5 Mosquitoes (3 effective) on night PR Germany. (2 H2X sorties).

482BG despatched 3 B-17s on radar scope sorties.

10 DECEMBER 1944

8AF 745

	Despatched		Effective	Target		Bombs	E/A	Losses			Casualties		
						Tonnage		MIA	E	Dam	KIA	WIA	MIA
2BD	B-24	225	173	BINGEN M/Y	(P)	755.1		0	0	4	0	0	0
			3	T/O		14.7							
3BD	B-17	309	277	KOBLENZ/ LÜTZEL M/Y	(P)	586.0							
			13	T/O		30.3		0	2	27	2	0	0
TOTALS:		534	466			1386.1	0	0	2	31	2	0	0
	P-47	42	287	ESCORT 2BD				1	1		0	0	0
	P-51	275						1	1		0	0	0
	P-47	62	226	ESCORT 3BD				0	0		0	0	0
	P-51	178						0	0		0	0	0
	P-51	111	96	FIGHTER SWEEP EAST OF BOMBERS TARGETS			0–0–1	1	1		0	0	1
	P-51	22	22	SCOUTING FORCES				0	0		0	0	0
TOTALS:		690	631				0–0–1	2	2		0	0	2

REMARKS: PFF attacks on rail targets in Germany. Bomb groups participating:– all 2BD except 392BG, 448BG; all 3BD except 93CBW groups and 96BG, 100BG, 487BG.

All Fighter groups except 356FG, 361FG, 364FG operating. Fighter group losses:– 20FG – 1, 355FG – 1. On return a 20FG P-51 c/l near March. 4FG P-51 c/l Hatfield Broad Oak.

OTHER OPERATIONS: 25BG despatched 5 Mosquitoes on WR Continent/UK, and 4 B-17s on WR Azores/Atlantic/UK. ASR despatched 10 P-47s on patrols. 36BS despatched 8 B-24s (1 aborted) on RCM with 12 P-51s as escort. 1 B-17, 1 B-24, 2 P-47s, 12 P-51s on radio-relays. 1 Mosquito on *Red Stocking* sortie to Holland and 1 Mosquito on special sortie for 3BD.

11 DECEMBER 1944

8AF 746

	Despatched		Effective	Target		Bombs Tonnage	E/A	Losses MIA	E	Dam	Casualties KIA	WIA	MIA
1BD	B-17	334	319	FRANKFURT M/Y	(P)	918.3		0	2	9	0	0	0
			2	T/O		6.0							
2BD	B-24	353	297	HANAU M/Y	(P)	771.5		4	0	7	0	0	36
			5	KARLSRUHE	(S)	20.5							
			2	T/O		6.0							
3BD	B-17	540	353	GIESSEN M/Y	(P)	847.7		0	1	9	0	2	0
			135	KOBLENZ M/Y	(S)	403.2							
			12	EUSKIRCHEN		26.0							
			11	T/O		30.6							
1BD	B-17	182	171	MANNHEIM BRS	(P)	506.0		1	0	18	0	0	9
2BD	B-24	177	154	MAXIMILIANSAU BR	(P)	396.0		0	0	8	0	0	2
			6	HANAU M/Y	(S)	16.0							
TOTALS:		1586	1467			3947.8	0	5	3	51	0	2	47
	P-51	181	167	ESCORT 1BD				0	0		0	0	0
	P-51	159	143	ESCORT 2BD				1	1		0	0	1
	P-47	49	349	ESCORT 3BD			0–0–1	0	0		0	0	0
	P-51	326					(G)	1	1		0	0	1
	P-51	59	54	ESCORT 1BD MANNHEIM				0	0		0	0	0
	P-47	37	34	ESCORT 2BD HANAU				0	0		0	0	0
	P-51	30	30	SCOUTING FORCES				0	0		0	0	0
TOTALS:		841	777				0–0–1(G)	2	2	?	0	0	2

REMARKS: Largest forces of bombers so far despatched by 8AF on one operation. Rail targets and bridges in western Germany attacked by PFF means. All bomb groups operating. 3BD Force used Micro H and H2X; main 1BD and 2BD Forces used H2X; 1BD Force against bridges (41CBW groups and 381BG) used GH and H2X; 2BD Force against bridges (93BG, 389BG, 446BG, 466BG) used GH. Bomb group losses:– 1BD – 381BG – 1; 2BD – 445BG – 2, 491BG – 2. B/d 92BG cr. France. 401BG f/l Continent – Cat E. 94BG B-17 abandoned over Belgium, crew baled.

All Fighter groups operating. Fighter group losses:– 4FG – 1, 55FG – 1. On return, a 339FG P-51 caught fire and pilot baled over Frinton, safe. 4FG P-51 abandoned over France.

OTHER OPERATIONS: 7PG despatched 2 F-5s on PR Germany. 25BG despatched 5 Mosquitoes on WR Continent/UK and 4 B-17s on WR Azores/Atlantic/UK. ASR despatched 15 P-47s on patrols. 4 Mosquitoes despatched on special operations. 36BS despatched 9 B-24s on RCM for 8AF operations. 2 B-17s, 1 B-24, 2 P-47s, 10 P-51s on radio-relays.

11/12 DECEMBER 1944

8AF 747 NIGHT LEAFLET OPERATION

NLS despatched 3 B-17s and 8 B-24s; France, Holland, Germany. 1 B-24 MIA.

12 DECEMBER 1944

8AF 748

	Despatched		Effective	Target		Bombs Tonnage	E/A	Losses MIA	E	Dam	Casualties KIA	WIA	MIA
1BD	B-17	380	337	MERSEBURG/LEUNA	(P)	988.4		1	0	25	1	0	10
			10	NORDHAUSEN	(S)	30.0							
			12	T/O		35.8							
2BD	B-24	378	270	HANAU M/Y	(P)	712.7		3	0	45	11	0	20
			69	ASCHAFFENBURG M/Y	(P)	166.2							
			17	GELNHAUSEN	(S)	40.6							
			8	FRIEDBURG M/Y	(L)	19.4							
3BD	B-17	497	461	DARMSTADT M/Y	(P)	333.2		0	2	7	0	0	0
			9	DIEBURG	(L)	26.7							
			4	T/O		12.0							
	B-17	15	15	SCREENING FORCES				0	0	0	0	0	0
	B-24	5											
TOTALS:		895	858			1310.8	0	4	2	77	12	0	30

	P-51	447	392	ESCORT 1BD			0–0–1(G)	7	2				
	P-47	39	193	ESCORT 2BD				0	1				
	P-51	177						0	0				
	P-47	53	214	ESCORT 3BD							0	0	
	P-51	180											
	P-51	32	32	SCOUTING FORCES				0	0				
TOTALS:		928	831					7	3	?	2	0	6

REMARKS: PFF (H2X) attack on Merseburg and visual attacks on rail targets in Germany. Bomb groups participating:– all 1BD except 379BG; all 2BD; all 3BD except 94BG. Bomb group losses:– 1BD – 457BG – 1; 2BD – 389BG – 1, 445BG – 1, 446BG – 1. B/d 351BG B-17 c/l St.Trond, Belgium. MIA 446BG B-24 ditched going out, 7 miles off Southwold, 3 rescued. Aborting 493BG B-17 c/l and exploded base. B/d 384BG B-17 c/l Continent – Cat E. On return 2 490BG B-17s collided after landing base – Cat E.

All Fighter groups operating. Fighter group losses:– 339FG – 1, 356FG – 2, 364FG – 4. 20FG P-51 c/l near Antwerp. 479FG P-51 abandoned over Belgium, pilot killed in parachute descent by collision with B-26. 479BG P-51 c/l Belgium, pilot killed. Pilot of MIA 356FG P-51 baled over sea 30 miles from Margate, saved.

OTHER OPERATIONS: 7PG despatched 5 F-5s and 2 Spitfires on PR enemy-held positions French Atlantic coast. 25BG despatched 3 Mosquitoes on WR in support of 1BD, 2 Mosquitoes on WR Belgium, Holland, Germany. 1 Mosquito on H2X operation Augsburg – Lechfeld A/F, and 4 B-17s on WR Azores/Atlantic/UK. ASR despatched 15 P-47s on patrols. 36BS despatched 7 B-24s on RCM for 8AF operations. 1 B-24, 4 P-47s, 14 P-51s on radio-relays.

12/13 DECEMBER 1944

8AF 749 NIGHT LEAFLET OPERATION

NLS despatched 7 B-24s and 4 B-17s; France, Holland, Germany.

36BS despatched 1 B-24 on RCM for RAF.

482BG despatched 1 B-17 on operations – recalled.

13 DECEMBER 1944

7PG despatched 7 a/c but they were recalled due to bad weather. 25BG despatched 4 B-17s (2 effective) on WR to and from the Azores. 36BS despatched 3 B-24s on RCM. 1 Mosquito on *Red Stocking* mission over Holland.

14 DECEMBER 1944

25BG despatched 2 Mosquitoes on WR Continent/UK, and 3 B-17s to and from the Azores. ASR despatched 2 P-47s on patrols.

14/15 DECEMBER 1944

25BG despatched 1 Mosquito on H2X PR Ulm area – last H2X by 25BG at night.

15 DECEMBER 1944

8AF 750

	Despatched		Effective	Target		Bombs Tonnage	E/A	Losses MIA	E	Dam	Casualties KIA	WIA	MIA
1BD	B-17	334	318	KASSEL M/Y TANK FAC	(P)	933.0		0	6	11	25	1	0
			5	T/O		15.0							
3BD	B-17	340	327	HANNOVER M/Y	(P)	939.3		1	0	7	0	0	0
			6	T/O		18.0							
TOTALS:		674	656			1905.3	0	1	6	18	25	1	0
	P-51	296	268	ESCORT 1BD				2	1		0	0	2
	P-47	99	241	ESCORT 3BD				0	0		0	0	0
	P-51	157						0	0		0	0	0
	P-51	24	19					0	0		0	0	0
TOTALS:		434	528				0	2	1	?	0	0	2

REMARKS: H2X bombing of rail targets and an armoured vehicle factory by B-17s. Bomb groups participating:– all 1BD except 41CBW groups; 93CBW groups and 94BG, 96BG, 385BG, 388BG, 447BG, 486BG of 3BD. Bomb group losses:– 487BG – 1. B/d 91BG and 401BG B-17s f/l Continent – Cat E. MIA 487BG B-17 ditched 18 miles off Southwold, crew rescued. A 92BG B-17 cr. after t/o and exploded, crew safe. On return a 305BG B-17 cr. Norton, Northants, after flying into radio mast in poor visibility, crew killed. 2 306BG B-17s collided over Greenham Common, 16 k.

Fighter groups not operating: 20FG, 352FG, 361FG, 479FG. Fighter group losses:– 355FG – 1, 364FG – 1. MIA 364FG P-51 in sea 45 miles E of Clacton, pilot baled and lost.

OTHER OPERATIONS: 7PG despatched 2 F-5s on PR Germany. 25BG despatched 4 Mosquitoes on WR Continent/UK and 4 B-17s on WR Azores/Atlantic/UK. ASR despatched 16 P-47s on patrols, 1 c/l Westleton on return. 1 B-24 and 4 P-51s on radio-relays. 3 Mosquitoes flew a *Chaff* screening operation for bombers; 1 Mosquito on *Red Stocking* sortie Holland. 36BS despatched 6 B-24s (5 effective) on RCM for 8AF operations.

An idea to combat mass fighter attacks from the rear was the installation of an M-10 rocket launcher under the rear fuselage of a Liberator. A trial installation was made at Hethel on a B-24H inherited from 489BG, depicted here after completion of installation on 15 December. Later an air firing trial was conducted over the Wash range. White square on rudder is special 'keep clear' identification marking. (J. Archer & Official)

15/16 DECEMBER 1944

8AF 751 NIGHT LEAFLET OPERATION

NLS despatched 3 B-17s (2 effective); France and Germany.

16 DECEMBER 1944

8AF 752

	Despatched		Effective	Target		Bombs Tonnage	E/A	Losses MIA	E	Dam	Casualties KIA	WIA	MIA
3BD	B-17	236	81	STUTTGART M/Y	(P)	225.3		1	1	9	3	0	9
			33	BIETINGHEIM	(P)	100.8							
			1	T/O		3.0							
TOTALS:		236	115			329.1	0	1	1	9	3	0	9
	P-51	114	106	ESCORT 3BD									
	P-51	10	10	SCOUTING FORCE									
TOTALS:		124	116				0	0	1		0	0	0

REMARKS: Extremely poor weather conditions resulted in only the 95BG, 486BG and 490BG attack rail target at Stuttgart from the 3BD Force despatched. 1BD abandoned the mission over England. Bomb group losses:– 95BG – 1. During attempted assembly; 379BG B-17 cr. Bozeat, 9 baled, 1 k. in a/c; 303BG B-17 cr. Alnwick, all killed. On return, 95BG B-17 cr. landing base, crew safe.

Fighter groups operating were 55FG, 339FG and 353FG. A P-51 cr. near Needham Market, pilot baled.

OTHER OPERATIONS: 25BG despatched 4 Mosquitoes on WR Continent/UK, and 4 B-17s on WR Azores/Atlantic/UK. 2 Mosquitoes on special mission to Holland. 36BS despatched 5 B-24s on RCM for 8AF operations. ASR despatched 2 P-47s on patrols. 6 P-51s on radio-relays.

17 DECEMBER 1944

25BG despatched 2 Mosquitoes on WR Continent, and 4 B-17s on WR Azores/Atlantic/UK. The B-17 at the Azores cr. while taxiing – Cat E.

17/18 DECEMBER 1944

8AF 753 NIGHT LEAFLET OPERATION

NLS despatched 3 B-17s and 7 B-24s (8 a/c effective); France, Holland, Germany.

36BS despatched 1 B-24 on RCM in support of RAF.

18 DECEMBER 1944

8AF 754

	Despatched		Effective	Target		Bombs Tonnage	E/A	Losses MIA	E	Dam	Casualties KIA	WIA	MIA
2BD	B-24	358	0	RECALLED MISSION		0		0	0	0	0	0	0
1BD	B-17	385	32	COLOGNE/KALK M/Y	(P)	90.8		0	0	1	0	0	0
			102	KOBLENZ/LÜTZEL	(S)	295.7							
			74	KAISERSLAUTERN	(S)	199.2							
			11	BONN	(L)	32.5							
3BD	B-17	220	157	MAINZ M/Y	(P)	433.4		0	1	2	0	0	1
			13	T/O		35.3							
	B-17	22	22	SCREENING FORCE									
TOTALS:		985	411			1086.9		0	1	3	0	0	1
	P-51	110	103	ESCORT 2BD				0			0	0	0
	P-51	116	110	ESCORT 1BD				2			0	0	2
	P-51	162	150	ESCORT 3BD				0			0	0	0
	P-47	49	255	FIGHTER SWEEP			3–0–0	1			0	0	1
	P-51	305		WESTERN GERMANY				1			0	0	1
	P-51	31	29	SCOUTING FORCES				0			0	0	0
TOTALS:		773	647				3–0–0	4	1	?	0	0	4

REMARKS: Communication and tactical targets in western Germany. 1BD used H2X; 3BD Micro H. Extensive cloud forced the recall of 2BD and part of the other forces. Groups attacking were: 1CBW, 41CBW groups and 306BG of 1BD; 94BG, 100BG, 390BG, 447BG, 452BG, 487BG of 3BD. A 94BG B-17 abandoned over France, crew baled, 1 missing.

All Fighter groups except 78FG on operations. Fighter group e/a credits:– 4FG – 5, 356FG – 1, 359FG – 1. Fighter group losses:– 4FG – 1, 56FG – 1, 356FG – 1, 359FG – 1. M/f 359FG P-51 cr. Continent.

OTHER OPERATIONS: 7PG despatched 13 F-5s and 2 Spitfires Germany. 25BG despatched 5 Mosquitoes (2 aborted); Germany/France/UK, and 4 B-17s Azores/Atlantic/UK. ASR despatched 14 P-47s on patrols. 36BS despatched 9 B-24s (8 effective) on RCM for 8AF operations. 4 Mosquitoes on special duties with bombers. 1 B-17, 1 B-24, 2 P-47s, 15 P-51s on radio-relays.

18/19 DECEMBER 1944

8AF 755 NIGHT LEAFLET OPERATION

NLS despatched 4 B-17s and 9 B-24s (12 a/c effective); France, Germany, Holland.

36BS despatched 1 B-24 on RCM in support of RAF.

19 DECEMBER 1944

8AF 756

	Despatched		Effective	Target		Bombs Tonnage	E/A	Losses MIA	E	Dam	Casualties KIA	WIA	MIA
1BD	B-17	172	144	SIX TAC/T	(P)	424.2		0	0	0	0	0	0
			24	KOBLENZ M-Y	(S)	66.0							
2BD	B-24	156	62	TWO TAC/T	(P)	183.5		0	2	0	11	0	0
			82	EHRANG M/Y	(S)	258.5							
TOTALS:		328	312			932.5	0	0	2	0	11	0	0
	P-47	41	37	ESCORT			7–0–1		3		0	1	3
	P-51	4	4	SCOUTING FORCES									
TOTALS:		45	41			0	7–0–1	0	3		0	1	3

REMARKS: Tactical targets in the Luxembourg, Ehrang and Koblenz area with the purpose of impeding the German counter offence launched in the Ardennes on 16 December. GH used at 8 tactical targets and H2X elsewhere. Bad weather limited effort and caused diversion of returning bombers to west England. During assembly a 93BG B-24 cr. Alburgh, Norfolk, 9 killed. A 446BG B-24 abandoned near Brussels.

Only Fighter group operating was 78FG. Fighter group e/a credits:– 78FG – 7. A 78FG c/l on t/o, pilot safe and 3 78FG P-47s c/l Continent, pilots safe.

20 DECEMBER 1944

25BG despatched 4 B-17s on WR Azores/Atlantic/UK.

21 DECEMBER 1944

25BG despatched 2 B-17s on WR Atlantic/UK.

22 DECEMBER 1944

25BG despatched 1 B-17 to Azores, and 1 Mosquito on WR English Channel.

23 DECEMBER 1944

8AF 757

	Despatched		Effective	Target	Bombs Tonnage	E/A	Losses MIA	E	Dam	Casualties KIA	WIA	MIA
1BD	B-17	152	148	EHRANG M/Y (P)	392.1		0	0	45	1	1	0
2BD	B-24	113	31	JUNKERATH C/C (P)	73.8		0	0	74	0	3	0
			48	AHRWEILER C/C (P)	124.0							
			27	DAHLEM C/C (P)	71.8							
3BD	B-17	152	40	KAISERSLAUTERN M/Y (P)	186.8	6–4–5			77	0	1	7
			29	HOMBURG R/J (P)	87.0							
			68	HOMBURG M/Y (P)	179.3							
			6	T/O	16.5							
	B-17	6	6	SCREENING FORCE			0	0	0	0	0	0
TOTALS:		423	403		1131.3	6–4–5	1	0	196	1	5	7
	P-51	62	54	ESCORT 1BD		20–0–3	0	0		0	0	0
	P-51	254	243	ESCORT 2BD		1–0–0	1	1		0	0	1
	P-51	117	112	ESCORT 3BD		2–0–0	0	0		0	0	0
	P-47	56	163	FIGHTER SWEEP		46–1–15	3	0		0	0	3
	P-51	127		BONN AREA			3	0		0	0	3
	P-51	20	20				0	0		0	0	0
TOTALS:		636	592			69–1–18	7	1	?	0	0	7

REMARKS: Marshalling yards, communication centres and a rail junction in the rear of the battle area were targets for small forces despatched in poor weather. 1BD was able to bomb visually; 2BD on GH with some visual sightings; 3BD used Micro H at Homburg M/Y, was visual on the R/J and visual and H2X at Kaiserslautern. Bomb groups participating:– 1BD – 92BG, 303BG, 305BG, 384BG; 2BD – 2CBW and 14CBW groups and 466BG; 3BD – 94BG, 486BG, 490BG, 493BG. Bomb group losses:– 94BG – 1.

All Fighter groups except 20FG, 78FG, 339FG operating. 352FG moves to Belgium. Fighter group e/a credits:– 56FG – 32, 352FG – 2, 357FG – 4, 359FG – 2, 361FG – 3, 364FG – 20, 479FG – 12. Fighter group losses:– 55FG – 1, 56FG – 3, 357FG – 1, 361FG – 1, 479FG – 1.

OTHER OPERATIONS: 7PG despatched 10 F-5s and 7 Spitfires on PR Germany. 1 F-5 MIA. 25BG despatched 1 Mosquito on PR to Pölitz area, 2 Mosquitoes on WR Continent/UK, and 1 B-17 on WR Atlantic/UK. 1 Mosquito despatched on special operation. 36BS despatched 2 B-24s on RCM in support of 8AF operations. ASR despatched 11 P-47s on patrols.

23/24 DECEMBER 1944

8AF 758 NIGHT LEAFLET OPERATION

NLS despatched 5 B-17 and 7 B-24s (10 a/c effective); France, Holland, Germany.

25BG despatched 5 Mosquitoes on PR Western Germany.

24 DECEMBER 1944

8AF 760

	Despatched		Effective	Target	Bombs Tonnage	E/A	Losses MIA	E	Dam	Casualties KIA	WIA	MIA
3BD	B-17	858	96	BABENHAUSEN A/F (P)	325.3	18–5–1	8	11	337	15	21	76
			60	GROSS OSTHEIM A/F (P)	223.8							
			85	ZELLHAUSEN A/F (P)	313.1							
			100	BILBIS A/F (P)	325.8							
			189	DARMSTADT A/F (P)	234.2							
			143	FRANKFURT–RHEINE A/F (P)	494.2							

Everything that will fly was the order and the groups compiled. 467BG put up 62 for the Christmas Eve maximum effort, including the gaily coloured assembly ship (trailing aircraft of nearest box). 453BG despatched 64 sorties on this raid, highest number of B-24s by a single group.

			37	PFORZHEIM M/Y	(S)	101.6						
			24	KAISERSLAUSTERN M/Y	(S)	87.4						
			6	HAILDRAUM	(S)	18.0						
			37	T/O (26)		127.5						
1BD	B-17	542	53	NIDDA A/F	(P)	132.5		2	9	109	21	23	18
			198	MERZHAUSEN A/D	(P)	495.0						
			43	ETTINGHAUSEN A/F	(P)	107.5						
			54	KIRCHGONS A/F	(P)	135.0						
			74	GIESSEN A/F	(P)	185.0						
			42	KOBLENZ	(S)	105.0						
			4	BABENHAUSEN	(S)	10.0						
			7	DARMSTADT	(S)	17.5						
			5	KAISERSLAUTERN	(S)	12.5						
			20	T/O		56.0						
2BD	B-24	634	27	RUWER	(P)	71.3		2	3	150	1	5	20
			28	PFAZEL	(P)	25.3						
			62	WITTLICH	(P)	168.1						
			32	ELLER	(P)	89.0						
			11	COCHEM	(P)	28.0						
			35	BITBURG	(P)	87.0						
			59	MAYEN	(P)	152.5						
			54	AHRWEILLER	(P)	144.3						
			25	RHEINBACH	(P)	71.0						
			62	EUSKIRCHEN	(P)	174.4						
			24	DAUN	(P)	58.1						
			59	GEROLSTEIN	(P)	174.4						
			18	WETTELDORF	(P)	47.0						
			26	SCHÖNECKEN	(P)	53.5						
			75	T/O (18)		179.3						
8AF 759												
	B-24	12	10	LA PALLICE C/B	(P)	22.0		0	0	0	0	0	0
TOTALS:		2046	1884			5052.1	18–5–1	12	23	487	37	49	114

Despatched		Effective	Target	Bombs Tonnage	E/A	Losses MIA	E	Dam	Casualties KIA	WIA	MIA
P-51	358	343	ESCORT 3BD		53–0– 6	7	1				7
P-51	368	350	ESCORT 1BD		13–1–13	3	1				3
P-47	50	87	ESCORT 2BD		4–0– 0	0	0				0
P-51	42						0				0
P-51	24	24	SCOUTING FORCES		3–0– 1	0	0				0
P-51	11	9	ESCORT PR		1–0– 0	0	0				0
TOTALS:	853	813				10	2		0	0	10

REMARKS: A high pressure area extending across western Europe brought clear skies and allowed 8AF to launch a maximum effort against airfields and communication centres in western Germany. Mission 760 proved to be the largest air strike operation of the war. All bombing was visual and all bomb groups operated, including 482BG (12 B-17s). Bomb group losses:– 1BD – 92BG – 1, 303BG – 1, 2BD – 448BG – 1, 458BG – 1; 3BD – 385BG – 1, 390BG – 2, 447BG – 1, 452BG – 1, 487BG – 3. 487BG attacked by e/a while still over Allied Belgium and 3 of the 9 B-17s shot down fell behind enemy lines as MIA. Freezing conditions and ground fog caused many t/o accidents: 91BG B-17 cr. after t/o Foxton, crew safe; 92BG B-17 cr. t/o base, 6 k; 2 398BG B-17s cr. t/o base, 2 k; 457BG B-17 cr. t/o Holme, 1 k. On return 445BG B-24 cr. landing Chivenor A/F; b/d 303BG B-17 c/l Snetterton A/F; 92BG B-17 c/l Bury St. Edmunds, 7 k; 3 34BG B-17s Cat E after landing collision, crews safe; b/d 452BG B-17 c/l Continent; b/d 388BG B-17 cr. Liège, Belgium, crew baled; 3 92BG B-17 c/l Belgium, 3 k. Bad weather over home bases caused most 1BD groups to be diverted to airfields in eastern East Anglia.

All Fighter groups operated except 78FG and 339FG (both fogged in). Fighter group e/a credits:– 4FG – 1, 55FG – 15, 353FG – 8, 355FG – 1, 357FG – 30, 359FG – 10, 361FG – 4, 479FG – 1. Fighter group losses:– 55FG – 3, 353FG – 1, 356FG – 1, 357FG – 3, 359FG – 1, 361FG – 1. A 55FG and 357FG P-51 collided over enemy territory. 479FG P-51 c/l near Bruges, pilot safe. 357FG P-51 c/l Continent.

OTHER OPERATIONS: 7PG despatched 9 Spitfires and 8 F-5s (1 F-5 aborted) on PR Germany with 11 P-51s as escort. 1 F-5 c/l base. 25BG despatched 10 Mosquitoes on PR Germany, 2 Mosquitoes on WR France, Holland, Germany, and 3 B-17s on Wr Azores/Atlantic/UK. 36BS despatched 5 B-24s on RCM for bombers. 3 Mosquitoes flew a screening operation. ASR despatched 18 P-47s on patrols. Mission 759 was special bombing operation by 492BG B-24s on coastal batteries.

Back from Oschersleben. Col Castle (nearest door), 'Pappy' Colby (next to his CO) and crew pose beside *Sugar Puss II*. (F Colby)

Fred Castle exchange opinions with a co-pilot after a mission. Gordon Thorup, his Air Executive at 94BG and a distinguished combat pilot himself, remembered his commander as: 'A man of high intelligence, resolute in character, indomitable in spirit, and unwavering moral strength. He was quick to sense weakness, steadfast in his determination to improve the operational capability of his Command, and was indefatigable in the application of his personal efforts in accomplishment of his goals.'

THE GENTLE HERO

Of the forty-seven thousand 8th Air Force dead and missing, none gave his life in such exalted circumstances as Brigadier General Frederick Castle. Air leader of the largest force of bombers ever despatched on combat operations, he took over the controls of a stricken Fortress to give the crew a chance to parachute to safety. This action brought the posthumous award of his country's highest honour for bravery, an award which Castle would have seen as a tribute to all who died with that bomber rather than to him personally. For here was a man of unusual humility whose quiet ways seemed to belie involvement in heroics.

With the 8th Air Force from its earliest days, Fred Castle's story is traced back to 1907 when two cadets at the US Military Academy, No. 4586, Benjamin F. Castle and 4596, Henry H. Arnold, struck up a friendship. When Lt Ben Castle's wife gave birth to their first child in Manila the following year Lt Arnold, who had also been posted to the Philippines, became along with 235 other graduates of the Class of '07 the boy's godfather. It is a West Point tradition that the first boy born to a Class member after graduation automatically becomes the Class Godson. The friendship between the two men endured, both eventually moving into military aviation. Ben Castle was Aviation Attaché in Paris following World War I, but he resigned from the Army in 1919 to enter business; 'Hap' Arnold continued his service to become 'the father' of the Army Air Forces.

Moulded in the traditional Army atmosphere, it was to be expected that young Frederick Walter Castle would follow his father in a military career. Enlisting in the New Jersey National Guard in 1924 he later came top in a competition for a place at West Point, which he entered in July 1926. A brilliant all-rounder, he ranked No.7 in his Class of 241 cadets. Commissioned, he served with the Engineers before being accepted for pilot training in the Air Corps. After gaining his wings he flew pursuit biplanes with a squadron at Selfridge Field, but flying opportunities were limited in the then small Corps and after this assignment Fred Castle was sent to supervise a large group of jobless young men in forestry work. This was a Civilian Conservation Corps post in a governmental scheme to help widespread unemployment. With no immediate prospects of returning to regular flying or having a more challenging assignment, Fred Castle decided to resign from the Army. In 1934 he joined a company of the Allied Chemical and Dye Corporation, working initially as a statistician and assistant sales manager, later moving to another branch of the Corporation. His business acumen and reputation were such that in September 1938 he was asked to join the Sperry Gyroscope Company, becoming assistant to the president. Sperry were heavily involved in producing equipment for the US forces, notably the secret Norden bombsight and aircraft gun turrets, projects which brought the young executive into contact with Arnold, who was apparently impressed by his godson's industry and administrative ability. Fred had not completely relinquished the military, having remained on the Reserve, receiving promotion to 1/Lt in 1940. When the United States entered World War II he was anxious to return to active duty, but at the same time careful to wait until he could see an opportunity of doing the kind of work suited to his ability and liking. However, his talents had not gone unnoticed in high places.

Brig.Gen Ira Eaker, Arnold's old friend and colleague, was to head a bomber force the USAAF was preparing to establish in the United Kingdom to engate in the strategic bombing of Germany. He was shortly leaving for England to lay the groundwork for operations and to aid in this task assembled a small staff of officers to accompany him. One selected was Lt Harris Hull who once served with Eaker on manoeuvres and, when a civilian, had worked for Sperry Gyroscope. From Hull General Eaker learned that Fred Castle was so highly regarded by Sperry he was being considered as their future President despite his youth. A brief investigation left Eaker in no doubt that Castle – whose father he knew – would be particularly suited to tackling the difficult logistical problems expected in the UK. Eaker asked General Arnold to have Fred Castle called to active duty and when the need of his skills to organise bases and depot facilities in England was put to Castle it proved a challenge much to his liking.

Eaker's seven-man party, arriving in England on 20 February 1942, were the first personnel of the 8th Air Force although they were not then identified as such. Castle's efficiency in his assigned task, and extraordinary appetite for work, quickly earned him promotion. A Captain prior to reaching England, he was elevated to Major a month later and in less than a year of his return to active duty he became a full Colonel – a rank qualifying the post of A-4, Air Chief of Staff for Supply.

Planning the vast network of installations and organising the supply facilities was not only an exacting job but often frustrating in the face of local shortages and delays in shipments from the United States. Castle conscientiously persevered by working exceedingly long hours causing fellow officers, such as Bierne Lay, to be concerned for his health. But Castle was not easily prevailed upon to take life easier. He possessed such dedication that he could not rest while matters remained outstanding. This dedication to duty was reflected in his personal conduct. His speech was guarded, his dress correct, and behaviour always that becoming of an officer, following the code of conduct taught at West Point. However, Castle's propriety tended to be viewed as stuffiness by some fellow officers.

While Fred Castle excelled in planning and organisation, like many other staff officers at 8th Air Force Headquarters he desired a combat command. There was no more challenging and demanding job in the USAAF than that of Group Commander. Not only was the commander responsible for the administration of two to three thousand men on his station, but he was expected to fly as a combat leader. If the group faltered in any way, the displeasure of high command usually fell on the Group CO. On the other hand the boss of the Air Force's basic tactical formation had a considerable degree of freedom to run the Group as he saw fit. It was very much a make or break situation. Occasionally Castle would broach the subject of command with General Eaker, in an almost apologetic way, hoping he could soon be spared from his job and allowed to join a combat group. The General had intimated that those aspiring to be combat leaders would eventually be returned to the United States to train and bring over new groups. But in the early summer of 1943 a situation developed that gave Castle and another Headquarters officer their opportunities.

Godfather and Godson at Bury St.Edmunds. With Le May, Williams and Anderson they look at a damaged B-17.

A new B-17 wing had become operational in May 1943 and the performance of its three groups was causing concern; bombing results were generally poor and losses high. In two groups, the 94th and 95th, attrition was so bad that some squadrons were no longer viable operational units. High Command found air discipline wanting and a lack of confidence. Changes were called for. Provisional Combat Wings were then being set up to afford tactical control of formations and the original commanders of the 94th and 95th were put in command of these while their battered groups were taken over by the officers from *Pinetree*. Castle was given the 94th. It was a similar situation to that confronting his colleague Frank Armstrong earlier in the year, with notable differences. The 94th men were not so demoralised as the 306th Group had been. Despite losses – nine of their B-17s failed to return from the last mission – a comparatively brief spell of combat had not dissolved the general brashness that characterised the flush of new groups received by the 8th Air Force in the spring of 1943. Frank Armstrong and Fred Castle were also very different personalities.

When Castle, the new CO of the 94th, arrived at Rougham (Bury St.Edmunds) air base on 20 June, personnel of his headquarters were apparently unsure if his status was temporary or permanent. In any event the change in command was resented.

A star pinning ceremony at Bury to mark his promotion to Brigadier General. In the background are (l to r): Lt.Col Birdsall, Col Perkins and Col. Dougher. The date, 4 December.

The following morning officers were ordered to assemble in the briefing room, where the newcomer addressed them. It was generally accepted that on a combat station military protocol was more relaxed, but the assorted attire of the assembled combat fliers was hardly in keeping with the standard set by the slight, trim, correctly uniformed Colonel who addressed them. Having quietly outlined what he expected of his new command in operations he concluded with the request that in future they conduct themselves like officers and gentlemen, which included attiring themselves like officers. This introduction endeared few to the new CO, indeed many were dismayed that high command could inflict such a seemingly hidebound leader upon them. It was noted that at no time during his address did Castle use invective, in marked contrast to general conversation on the base where descriptive adjectives were often colourful, to put it mildly. When it was learned he had previously been a staff officer in supply, and a 'West Pointer' to boot, opinion bordered on contempt.

Next day the Group was despatched on a mission to Hüls and Castle went with them, sitting on a camp stool positioned behind the pilots in the leading bomber of the high squadron. He chose to fly with Capt Franklin Colby who, at 41, was the oldest combat pilot in the 8th Air Force. Pilots of that age were usually assigned to training or transport duties in the States. Whether Colby's assignment to a combat group was due to some clerical error was never resolved, but Castle quickly recognised him as one of the most competent pilots in the 94th. 'Pappy' Colby – the inevitable nickname of anyone twice the age of most fliers – observed that Castle remained 'as cool as a cucumber' making notes throughout attacks on the formation by enemy aircraft.

During post-mission interrogation a former colleague of Castle's from 8th Air Force Headquarters was present and was overheard to make remarks that indicated Castle had been on a number of combat flights, which came as a surprise to the 94th crews who thought they had a novice at the helm. There were suspicions in some quarters that this incident had been stage managed. Castle's standing with his younger officers was further strained when, at the first station party attended, he quietly invited individuals who had become a little more than merry to return to quarters. It had become customary to work off the tensions of combat at parties: for the CO to check this revelry by reprimanding those imbibing too heavily, was strongly resented. The gulf between Castle and some of his officers widened. He tended to keep himself to himself and that was the way they liked it. A few found confirmation of this supposed aloofness in Castle's delegation of duties to his Air Executive. As these sometimes included the censure of wayward personnel the CO's detractors saw this as a weakness – by taking refuge in a surrogate. On the contrary it was part of a deliberate policy to involve the more senior of his officers in tightening the reins and steering the 94th in the direction required.

There is no doubt that Castle relished his command as a letter to his family, dated three days after taking over, clearly reveals: 'I've been trying for several days to write you the wonderful news of my new job, you have probably already guessed it. I am commanding a Bomb Group! I don't believe there could be a tougher job in the world, but I love it. The first raid on which I led my outfit will always be the high water mark of all my experiences. This job is the one I've worked for ever since I've been here, and I'm happy. But it keeps me working morning, noon and night, so for a while my letters will be brief.' His appetite for work was indeed prodigious. He did not confine himself solely to operations but took an interest in all sections on the base, asking questions, solving problems and striving for maximum efficiency. To this end he used what he called his Command Book. Pre-war business experience had taught him the value of statistics, by the information that could be derived from them and acted upon. He had his staff provide regular records on all aspects of operations, maintenance and supply for entry in the Command Book. His systematic approach impressed his seniors and influenced similar projects in the USAAF.

For men with several combat missions under their belts practice flights were an unpopular and, many thought, an unnecessary chore. But Castle's determination to improve the performance of his Group brought frequent training missions for all crews. Castle flew on most practices himself, giving instructions over the radio. On one occasion some pilots vented their displeasure by broadcasting sarcastic remarks. Voice distortion over the radio made it impossible to tell from whom the comments emanated. At first it appeared that the Group Captain had chosen to ignore them, for no reprimand came over the air. However, at the end of the post-mission critique, as Castle prepared to leave the briefing room, he coolly observed: 'By the way, gentlemen, I consider the remarks made over the air to me today as beneath the dignity of the officers under my command.' It had the desired effect; there was no more radio heckling.

Although the younger officers could not easily accept this quiet, reserved man, he began to gain their respect for his leadership of any missions that looked to be particularly difficult. In a period of good weather in late July the 8th Air Force made several long-range strikes into Germany. On the 28th the 94th and other 4th Wing groups were briefed for the deepest penetration so far, to attack the Focke Wulf fighter factory at Oschersleben. The weather over the North Sea was far from clear and the Fortress formations became separated while flying between layers of stratus. Enemy fighters added to the disruption and by the time the German coast was reached only the 94th joined by elements of four other groups was left. Colonel Castle was again flying with 'Pappy' Colby and aware of this depleted force elected to go on. The formation reached the target without further hindrance from fighters and although extensive cloud made bombing difficult the factory was severely damaged.

The 94th returned to base with no losses but Castle was taken to task by 4th Wing for continuing with only a small formation on this deep penetration. Subsequently he was awarded the Silver Star for his leadership of the raid, an award mentioned in a letter to his family with typical modesty: 'Did you hear I had been awarded the Silver Star? It was for the trip where we went close to Berlin to hit a plane factory. I am naturally very proud, but feel that it should be considered more an award to my outfit than to me. They're a swell bunch of lads.'

Castle enjoyed a growing popularity among the enlisted men through his frequent appearances at their place of work. Occasionally, following a mission and while still in flying clothes that made rank less obvious, he would eat in their mess. By the time he had taken the group on the African shuttle mission he had won the respect of most of his former critics. Initially this came from his leadership of any mission that looked 'tough'. Even those officers to whom West Pointers were anathema, or found his continual quest for excellence irritating, recognised that they had a fighter at the helm. The more perceptive realised they had an unusually intelligent and dedicated commander and came to admire him greatly, if still finding him rather aloof. Castle, in fact, had his own standards, and involvement in the boisterous activities of his younger fliers was not for him. His friends were among the more thoughtful and intellectual members of the Group. And while he drove himself at work he did know how to enjoy his recreation – he played tennis and squash, liked the theatre and dancing, and was not averse to a late night session of poker. Visits to historical places and walks in the beautiful wooded countryside around the base were his chosen relaxations when time allowed.

He was also a great Anglophile and had a number of British friends and acquaintances with whom he would spend short leaves. They found him a warm personality and noted how popular he was with children, with whom he easily established a rapport. One English lady concluded he was a great man . . . 'but so much *nicer* than most great men'. Another friend was 'Robby' Robbins, landlord of the imposing timbered Swan Inn, a well known hostelry in the picturesque village of Lavenham a few miles south of Bury St.Edmunds. Here Castle would go to have a drink and relax; he liked the genial folk at the Swan. The walls of one bar room were covered with the signatures of Allied servicement and Fred Castle was persuaded to add his.

He enjoyed intellectual company and impressed many British academics. The historian George Trevelyan, then Master of Trinity College, Cambridge, commented that he had never met such a fine young man – and then added 'among my American friends', a qualification that much amused Fred, although he still considered it quite a recommendation. The commander of the 94th Bomb Group was an idealist and thought much about the future, expressing his views in conversations and letters. Some of his writings were published and it was rumoured that he had also penned verse.

Most of these off-duty activities were unknown to the men at Rougham airfield. Few knew where Castle went when he left the base. Perhaps there was a deliberate effort on his part to escape from the camaraderie of a combat organisation, lest he fall into the trap that had beset many a commander of identifying himself too closely with his men.

The old problem of over-work was ever present. He flew too much and spent too much time at his desk, seeking to improve the performance of his Group. Several of his ideas were put into practice. Aware of the confusion that often arose when bombers from various groups were trying to get into formation in the half-light of dawn, he thought out and experimented with a succession of techniques using smoke canisters and flares to facilitate assembly, eventually devising a system which became standard in the 8th Air Force. He also tried to improve on instrument climb-out procedures in bad weather.

In April 1944 Castle was given command of the 4th Combat Bombardment Wing, a well deserved promotion. Those at Division Headquarters also hoped that in the new assignment he would not feel it was his duty to fly so much. As the Wing embraced the 94th with two other groups at nearby stations, and also had its headquarters at Rougham airfield, Castle remained in familiar haunts. An organisational experiment during November 1944, involving the 4th Wing absorbing the units of another B-17 combat wing, made it the largest in the 8th Air Force with five groups. This merited the commander's promotion to Brigadier General and, as if under obligation to justify his new rank, Castle again worked himself close to physical exhaustion – at a time when operations were about to reach a critical stage.

In mid-December the Germans launched their largest offensive since the Normandy landings against US Army positions in the Ardennes with the intention of racing to Antwerp to deny the port to the Allies and cutting their forces in two. A period of particularly bad weather was chosen so that the superior Allied air power would be prevented from having its usual disruptive influence. For several days low cloud and fog were so persistent that flying was out of the question. The weather began to lift on 23 December and by Christmas Eve it was at last possible for the Allied air forces to launch a maximum effort against communications targets backing the German offensive. The 8th Air Force put every bomber into the sky that was in condition, including several that had long been retired from combat. More than 2,000 Fortresses and Liberators were scheduled plus a thousand fighters; it was to be the biggest raid of the war.

On the 23rd Castle had been out visiting other stations under his command – his idea of resting, his doctor having insisted that he take things easy. Colonel Nicholas Perkins, Chief of Staff at 4th Wing, in the operations room that evening, recalled: 'Lt. Colonel MacDonald (Deputy C of S Operations) was due to lead the Wing and I was to be in the second group. The orders kept coming down . . . . we were put on maximum effort . . . . everything that could fly, training aircraft as well, whether or not they had guns . . . . then we were assigned to lead the 3rd Division. I realised then if General Castle knew this he would take the lead himself, so I told the people in the ops room that if he came in to keep busy and not volunteer information about the mission unless they got a direct question. We all knew what he would do if he heard about the mission and we all knew Mac was a fine leader and wanted to go. Then we got word that the 3rd Division was to lead the entire 8th Air Force! Shortly afterwards General Castle walked in, looking very tired, and said his chauffeur had just let him out at the ops room and he only wanted to say he was back and was on his way to bed. He asked if we were "stood down" again and I said no . . . . we might be able to get off. He said, "Fine, it's about time because we have to stop that breakthrough. I'll see them off in the morning, but I've got to get to bed." To our relief he walked on out after saying goodnight. But he didn't walk far, because within less than a minute he stuck his head in the door and asked who was leading the Division . . . . I had to say 4th Wing. He came all the way in and asked who was leading the 8th Air Force, and I had to say the 3rd Division. He thought a minute and said as I recall, "I'm sorry Mac, I'm going to have to take your place tomorrow. This is the kind of thing they pay me for, and this is what they would expect me to lead." He almost didn't fly next day.'

Before dawn on Christmas Eve, Castle was driven down the winding road that led to Lavenham airfield, home of the 487th Bomb Group whose formation was to be in the van. He was conveyed to the bleak, frost speckled hardstand where the Fortress and crew assigned to lead were ready. The aircraft was equipped with H2X radar and other specialised equipment. Her crew chief, Sgt James Ackerman, reckoned she was one of the sweetest Flying Forts on the field, 'she would fly off hands without trimming and the auto-pilot was perfect'. The B-17 had no nickname and was simply known by the last three digits of its serial number, 'Treble Four'. For this flight a nine-man crew was aboard, including two navigators – one the Group navigator – and a radar navigator. The General took the co-pilot's seat – the usual occupant flying in the tail turret – and at 0900 hrs 'Treble Four' was on her way down the runway on the start of her seventh mission. It was Castle's 30th and his first since promotion.

Although the weather was fine some elements of the Wing did not appear at the various rendezvous points on time; in consequence the leading formations were some 15 minutes behind schedule on the climb across the Channel and over Belgium. The 487th tried to make up lost minutes in order to meet the fighter escort prior to crossing the battle lines. When still some 20 miles away the No.4 engine of 'Treble Four' started to falter. As Lt Harriman, the pilot, was still able to keep position at 22,000 ft the Fortress retained the lead. But nearing the vicinity of the front line a flight of Me 109s made a sudden and unexpected attack out of the sun.

It was unusual for enemy fighters to intercept over friendly territory and there were no Allied fighters on hand to meet them.

In this frontal pass the bomber may have been hit in the troubled engine for it started to vibrate and lose power. No longer able to keep up, Castle radioed the deputy leader, Capt Mayfield Shilling, to take over and told Lt Harriman to let 'Treble Four' drop back and fly at the rear of the formation. Control of the aircraft proved difficult and the Fortress drifted some distance to the left of the other bombers where it was again attacked by enemy fighters. Castle gave directions to the pilot for evasive action, but a cannon shell shattered the nose plexiglass and wounded a navigator. As 'Treble Four' pulled back towards the formation it was subjected to a third attack by enemy fighters, this time from the rear with many strikes all over the bomber. The radar-operator and the co-pilot in the tail were wounded. Both Nos.3 and 4 engines were set on fire. Castle's voice came calmly over the interphone: 'Okay men, we've been hit – get out.' The Fortress then fell into a dive but was quickly levelled out, whether by Castle or Lt Harriman or both is not known, but at some point Castle took over the controls, ordering Harriman forward to get his parachute. Castle then lowered the undercarriage to cut flying speed to facilitate the crew's bale out. The engineer, bombardier and navigators left via the nose hatch and the pilot was seen to enter the nose looking for his parachute. The wounded radar man and the co-pilot managed to parachute from the rear of the Fortress as did the waist gunner. As they left, oxygen bottles were blazing in the fuselage. Before the pilot could make his escape the right wing tank exploded, sending the blazing bomber into a spin from 12,000 ft. It crashed near a château at Hods in Belgium, killing Castle and Harriman instantly. Of those who baled out, the co-pilot died of wounds and the body of the radio-operator was found in an open field without a parachute.

Obviously Castle deliberately took control of the stricken aircraft in order to give the pilot a chance to parachute. It was also apparent that he did not order the jettisoning of the bomb load when the aircraft was first in trouble for fear of killing Allied troops or Belgian civilians, probably hoping to drop them beyond enemy lines or when a sparsely populated area could be found. It was typical of the man, of his humility and integrity, to risk his own life for those of others.

Frederick Walker Castle seemed to many to be a strange man because he did not conform to the general pattern of social behaviour amongst fighting men. He was the antithesis of the tough, hard talking leader that tended to dominate the combat commands in the 8th Air Force. Yet he gave his life to leadership and had a combat record few other men of his rank could equal. As a man to whom duty was paramount he would have wanted nothing better than to be remembered as the only General in his country's history to die in a direct act to try and save the lives of his subordinates.

25 DECEMBER 1944

8AF 761

	Despatched		Effective	Target		Bombs Tonnage	E/A	Losses MIA	E	Dam	Casualties KIA	WIA	MIA
2BD	B-24	248	12	WAHLEN C/C	(P)	35.8	3–1–3	4	3	92	2	4	40
			37	PELM C/C	(P)	81.2							
			40	PRÜM c/C	(P)	106.3							
			41	HALLSCHLAG C/C	(P)	121.5							
			33	MURLENBACH C/C	(P)	99.5							
			16	PRONSFELD C/C	(P)	42.0							
			12	HILLESHEIM C/C	(O)	2.5							
			11	MARMEGEN C/C	(O)	29.5							
			10	NETTERSHEIM C/C	(O)	27.5							
			21	BUDESHEIM C/C	(O)	58.3							
			9	MECHERNICH C/C	(O)	21.5							
3BD	B-17	174	38	KAISERSLAUTERN R/R	(P)	113.2	0–0–1	1	1	36	0	0	9
			9	BAD MÜNSTER R/B	(P)	27.0							
			36	HERMESKEIL	(P)	108.0							
				SIMMERN C/C									
				MARSCHEID R/B									
			44	AHRWEILER R/B	(P)	131.0							
			17	BAD KREUZNACH R/B	(O)	51.0							
			11	ELLER R/B	(O)	32.5							
			1	T/O		2.5							
TOTALS:		422	388			1090.8	3–1–4	5	4	128	2	4	49
	P-51	156	144	ESCORT 2BD			6–0–1	3	2				
	P-51	294	278	ESCORT 3BD			40–6–7	6	1		0	0	6
	P-51	10	10	SCOUTING FORCE				0	0		0	0	0
TOTALS:		460	432				46–6–8	9	3	?	1	0	9

REMARKS: Communication centres and rail bridges west of the Rhine attacked visually with GH also used by 2BD. Bomb group participating: 2BD – 20CBW, 96CBW groups and 389BG, 445BG; 3BD – 13CBW groups and 490BG, 493BG. Bomb group losses:– 2BD – 389BG – 3, 467BG – 1; 3BD – 390BG – 1. B/d 467BG B-24 cr. Vowchurch, UK, after crew baled over Belgium. B/d 445BG and 467BG B-24s c/l Continent.

All Fighter groups except 78FG, 339FG, 359FG operating. Fighter group e/a credits:– 4FG – 9, 55FG – 5, 56FG – 8, 352FG – 11, 353FG – 1, 355FG – 4, 356FG – 6, 479FG – 14. Fighter group losses:– 4FG – 1, 55FG – 1, 355FG – 1, 356FG – 2, 479FG – 4. A 352FG P-51 and 479FG P-51 shot down by US AA Belgium, 1 killed. 4FG P-51 shot down ground fire and cr. liberated Belgium, pilot k. 361FG moved to Belgium base.

OTHER OPERATIONS: 7PG despatched 4 Spitfires and 2 F-5s on PR Germany. 25BG despatched 1 Mosquito on WR Belgium, and 5 B-17s on WR Azores/Atlantic/North Sea/UK. 36BS despatched 8 B-24s on RCM for 8AF operations. ASR despatched 18 P-47s on patrols.

EVENT

The unusually prolonged period of fog that settled on western Europe in mid-December 1944 gave Field Marshal von Rundstedt just the weather he wanted to launch the major German land offensive against US positions in the Ardennes, was commented upon by one of the 8th Air Force's most dedicated diarists, S/Sgt Edgar Matlock of the 351st Group at Polebrook. On Christmas Day this crew chief wrote: 'It was cold this morning, the ground was frozen and the fog which moved into our vicinity in the morning of the 19th continued throughout the day in undiminished intensity – aside from Christmas services conducted by the chaplains there was little activity at our base. During the afternoon some combat personnel came back to the base in trucks from the bases at which they landed yesterday, skeleton crews were left with the airplanes to return to the base if this infernal fog ever lifts – Christmas dinner was served in all of the Mess Halls at the evening meal. There was turkey, dressing, cranberry sauce, and most of the usual fixings. Our second Xmas in England – Low temperatures today, 17 degrees F.'

INCIDENT

The youngest fighter group in the Eighth, the 479th, had good reason to remember Christmas Day 1944. While supporting B-24s bound for the marshalling yards at Kassel, its Mustangs became involved in their largest action of the war as Luftwaffe fighters attempted to intercept the bombers. The result was the 479th biggest 'bag' in the air, 17 destroyed credits for the loss of four Mustangs and pilots. During one mêlée Lt Jim Bouchier became separated from the rest of his squadron and at lower altitude joined up with two blue-nosed Mustangs heading towards friendly territory at about 1,500 ft.

The trio, in vee formation, were just west of the River Roer between Julich and Düren when the leader went down to investigate. Bouchier, lagging slightly behind, did not observe what had attracted attention, but followed. They were down to 500 ft, flying norht-west over snow covered terrain, when Bouchier saw the leading Mustang break left in a climbing turn and trail coolant. Realisation came that they were under fire from the ground, but before Bouchier could take evasive action his Mustang juddered under the impact of a 40 mm shell hitting the radiator. As he climbed away he glimpsed the leader's Mustang diving into a field. His cockpit filling with smoke caused him to shed the canopy, roll the fighter over and bale out when he reached 1,000 ft. He landed safely but heavily on the frozen ground. As he picked himself up he saw soldiers approaching and was relieved to see they were GIs – he was down behind Allied lines. During the emergency of the preceding few seconds his concern had been extricate himself from the stricken P-51; now he concluded that 'friendly' anti-aircraft fire had caused his downfall.

Bouchier was taken to a field artillery command post at Langweiler where the commander of a US Army battery telephoned his regrets that two of three P-51s thought to have been Me 109s had been shot down and a pilot killed. The dead man's identity tags showed him to be George E. Preddy. Faulty aircraft recognition had cost the United States one of her most accomplished fighter aces in this tragic accident.

26 DECEMBER 1944

8Af 762

	Despatched		Effective	Target		Bombs Tonnage	E/A	Losses MIA	E	Dam	Casualties KIA	WIA	MIA
3BD	B-17	74	9	ANDERNACH M/Y	(P)	27.0	0–0–1	0	0	30	0	0	0
			23	NEUWIED R/B	(P)	67.5							
			12	NEUWIED M/Y	(S)	35.1							
			12	SINZIG C/C	(S)	36.0							
			1	MAYEN C/C	(O)	3.0							
2BD	B-24	77	35	SINZIG R/B	(P)	97.0		0	0	0	0	0	0
			36	NIEDERLAHNSTEIN M/Y	(P)	86.3							
TOTALS:		151	128			351.9	0–0–1	0	0	30	0	0	0
	P-47	48	249	ESCORT BOMBERS			8–0–0	0	0		0	0	0
	P-51	213						0	0		0	0	0
	P-51	73	70	SWEEP – SUPPORT BOMBERS			3–0–0	2	1		0	0	2
	P-51	2	2	SCOUTING FORCE				0	0		0	0	0
TOTALS:		336	321				11–0–0	2	1	?	0	0	2

REMARKS: Poor weather restricted operations. Only a small force of B-17s and B-24s struck rail targets behind the battle area. Visual and PFF methods used by both Formations. Bomb groups participating: 2BD – 93BG, 446BG, 466BG, 467BG; 3BD – 452BG, 486BG.

Fighter groups not operating were: 4FG, 20FG, 78FG, 339FG, 353FG, 355FG. Fighter group e/a credits:– 56FG – 3, 352FG – 13½, 356FG – 4, 361FG – 6. Fighter group losses:– 356FG – 2. 352FG and 361FG temporarily operating under 9AF. 352FG P-51 c/l Belgium.

OTHER OPERATIONS: 7PG despatched 2 F-5s and 2 Spitfires on PR Germany. 25BG despatched 2 Mosquitoes (1 aborted) on H2X scope photo mission Ulm, and 1 Mosquito on WR N Ireland/Atlantic, and 1 B-17 on WR from Azores to UK. ASR despatched 9 P-47s on patrols.

INCIDENT

At Koblenz on 26 December 1944 the lead Fortress of 486th Group was bracketed by flak, sustaining severe damage to two engines, hydraulics and other vital components. Losing height the bomber left formation and made it back alone to Sudbury on the remaining good engines. A crash-landing was successfully accomplished, which was not surprising as one of the pilots had more experience of this method of coming back to earth than any other in the whole USAAF. Captain Dick Grace was more than a celebrity, who before the war had earned a living crashing aeroplanes for the Hollywood movie cameras; he was at this date the oldest combat pilot in the 8th Air Force. Grace had also flown combat in World War I, nearly being shot down in his Spad on the Western Front and later flying bombing raids from Italy. He earned fame, however, for his exploits in movies such as *Wings* and *Hell's Angels*, where he deliberately engineered spectacular crash scenes and flew aeroplanes to destruction. This dangerous occupation cost him a broken neck and many other injuries in more than a score of crashes. At the beginning of World War II he volunteered for flying duties with the Army Air Forces who were uncertain about taking a pilot in his forties who had suffered crushing and dislocation of the cervical vertebrae, however well it had mended. He was accepted, but with the proviso of Limited Service. His experience gained him a position as test pilot but Grace was continually agitating to get into a combat unit. Eventually he managed to become a ferry pilot and while delivering a B-24 to England gained an appointment to see an old acquaintance, Jimmy Doolittle. The General said that if Grace was ever available for re-assignment he could find him a place in the 8th Air Force. On return to America Dick Grace quickly arranged to make himself available and eventually received orders to join the Combat Crew Replacement Centre at Bovingdon. If the authorities thought the ageing and battered former stunt pilot best suited to instructional duties, Grace had other ideas. It was not long before he had made friends at some of the combat bases he visited and persuaded commanders to let him fly as an observer. He put in four missions this way – and added another broken rib to his history of injuries when a shell fragment walloped into his flak jacket. Finally, by using his influence with friends in the right places he managed to get himself on combat status with a posting to the 486th Group as a Squadron Operations officer. For Grace this was as good as a licence to fly whenever he wanted. A three-quarter inch long flak fragment, one of 167 that hit the B-17 in which Grace was flying on the Koblenz raid, also penetrated the distinguished flier's side just above the hip. Hospitalised for a few days he was back flying combat again on 10 January 1945, his 47th birthday! Dick Grace was a small man, and like many small men tenacious in his endeavours and seemingly fearless. Having completed a tour of combat experience with the 486th in February 1945, before other orders could reach him he promptly got himself posted to the 448th Group at Seething as Assistant Group Operations Officer to fly in B-24s. He managed to stay until the Group's penultimate mission of the war, 21 April, but by that date orders to return to the USA had caught up with him. Grace was truly a born survivor.

26/27 DECEMBER 1944

8AF 763 NIGHT LEAFLET OPERATION

NLS despatched 3 B-17s and 6 B-24s; Holland, Germany.

27 DECEMBER 1944

8AF 764

	Despatched		Effective	Target		Bombs Tonnage	E/A	Losses MIA	E	Dam	Casualties KIA	WIA	MIA
3BD	B-17	227	118	FULDA M/Y	(P)	349.0		0	1	45	9	0	0
			63	ANDERNACH M/Y	(P)	168.3							
			7	NEUWIED R/B	(P)	21.0							
			13	T/O		38.0							
2BD	B-24	182	19	KAISERSLAUTERN R/B	(P)	53.0		1	5	60	18	11	6
			33	KAISERSLAUTERN M/Y	(P)	93.5							
			46	HOMBURG M/Y	(P)	106.1							
			57	NEUNKIRCHEN M/Y	(P)	146.5							
			8	ENKENBACH R/J	(O)	24.0							
			9	ST.WENDEL M/Y	(O)	22.0							
1BD	B-17	232	72	EUSKIRCHEN M/Y	(P)	192.0		1	1	83	9	6	9
			58	GEROLSTEIN R/J	(P)	152.6							
			34	BULLAY R/B	(P)	101.5							
			25	ALTENAHR R/B	(P)	75.0							
			12	HILLESHEIM	(O)	30.0							
			1	ECKFELD	(O)	3.0							
TOTALS:		641	575			1578.2		2	7	188	36	17	15
	P-51	46	44	ESCORT 3BD				1			0	0	1
	P-51	96	88	ESCORT 2BD				2			0	0	2
	P-51	48	46	ESCORT 1BD				0			0	0	0
	P-47	17	163	FIGHTER-SWEEP			29½–1–9	0			0	0	0
	P-51	168						2			0	0	2
	P-51	15	15	SCOUTING FORCE				0			0	0	0
TOTALS:		390	356				29½–1–9	5		?	0	0	5

REMARKS: Freezing fog at bases again restricted operations. Rail targets in western Germany supporting the battle front were attacked visually with 3BD using Micro H on a rail bridge and 1BD using H2X on Koblenz M/Y. Bomb groups participating:– 1BD – 40CBW and 41CBW groups; 2BD – 14CBW and 96CBW groups and 93BG, 446BG, 389BG; 3BD – 13CBW groups and 34BG, 94BG, 385BG, 493BG. Bomb group losses:– 1BD – 384BG – 1; 2BD – 446BG – 1. MIA 446BG B-24 ditched off Kent coast, 3 rescued. A 390BG B-17 cr. after t/o Parham village, 9 killed. 453BG B-24 cr. on t/o, 6 killed – Mission then cancelled for group. 384BG B-17 cr. attempting landing at Manston, 9 k. B/d 466BG B-24 c/l France. 446BG B-24 cr. t/o, 9 k.

All Fighter groups except 55FG, 78FG, 339FG, 355FG. Fighter group e/a credits:– 352FG – 22½, 364FG – 29½. Fighter group losses:– 352FG – 2, 359FG – 2, 364FG – 1.

OTHER OPERATIONS: 25BG despatched 1 Mosquito on H2X photo sortie to Regensburg, 2 Mosquitoes on chaff screening operation (1 Mosquito cr. on t/o), 1 Mosquito on WR UK, and 5 B-17 on WR Azores/Atlantic/UK. ASR despatched 2 P-47s on patrols.

A 96BG pathfinder framed in a winter scene. Two days after Christmas freezing fog had decorated every East Anglian tree with rime ice to a degree not seen for a great many years before or after. Beautiful to behold, it was a forerunner of a period of bitter weather.

27/28 DECEMBER 1944

8AF 765 NIGHT LEAFLET OPERATION

NLS despatched Germany.

28 DECEMBER 1944

8AF 766

	Despatched		Effective	Target		Bombs Tonnage	E/A	Losses MIA	E	Dam	Casualties KIA	WIA	MIA
2BD	B-24	361	28	HOMBURG M/Y	(P)	103.2		2	1	121	10	2	22
			20	BULLAY BR	(P)	52.0							
			31	KAISERSLAUTERN R/B	(P)	84.0							
			123	KAISERSLAUTERN M/Y	(P)	339.5							
			18	NEUNKIRCHEN M/Y	(P)	71.2							
			20	ZWEIBRÜCKEN	(S)	55.0							
			32	BIERBACH	(S)	63.4							
			12	T/O		33.0							
3BD	B-17	535	109	IRLICH R/B	(P)	324.5		0	0	4	1	0	0
			399	KOBLENZ/MOSEL M/Y	(S)	1019.6							
			2	T/O		5.0							
1BD	B-17	379	36	SIEBURG M/Y	(P)	98.0		0	2	2	1	2	0
			11	TROISDORF M/Y	(P)	28.3							
			75	BRÜHL M/Y	(P)	204.4							
			71	REMAGEN BR	(P)	209.5							
			131	KOBLENZ/LÜTZEL M/Y	(P)	366.2							
			1	SINZIG	(S)	3.5							
			5	T/O		13.6							
TOTALS:		1275	1158			3171.9	0	2	3	127	12	4	22
	P-51	161	147	ESCORT 2BD									
	P-51	247	236	ESCORT 3BD									
	P-51	168	158	ESCORT 1BD									
	P-51	30	27	SCOUTING FORCES									
TOTALS:		606	568				0	0	1		0	0	0

REMARKS: Continued pounding of rail and road bridges and centres in western Germany. 1BD and 2BD used 9H and H2X; 3BD used Micro H and H2X. Bomb groups participating: all 1BD except 303BG and 457BG; all 2BD; all 3BD. Bomb group losses:– 44BG – 1, 392BG – 1. 44BG B-24 cr. after t/o and burned. 351BG B-17 c/l Belgium. On return 306BG B-17 cr. St. Albans, crew baled, 1 k.

All Fighter groups operating. No claims or losses. 364FG P-51 abandoned over base due to m/f, pilot safe.

OTHER OPERATIONS: 25BG despatched 2 Mosquitoes for 1BD scouts, 2 Mosquitoes on H2X sorties Pölitz (with 3 P-51s as escort), 2 Mosquitoes on Wr Continent, and 2 B-17s on WR Azores/Atlantic/UK. 36BS despatched 10 B-24s on RCM sorties for 8AF operations. ASR despatched 17 P-47s on patrols.

28/29 DECEMBER 1944

8AF 767

	Despatched		Effective	Target	Bombs Tonnage	E/A	Losses MIA	E	Dam	Casualties KIA	WIA	MIA
492BG	B-24	16	7	DE LA COLIBRE	18.0		0	0	0	0	0	0

8AF 768 NIGHT LEAFLET OPERATION

NLS despatched 2 B-24s; Belgium.

29 DECEMBER 1944

8AF 769

	Despatched		Effective	Target		Bombs Tonnage	E/A	Losses MIA	E	Dam	Casualties KIA	WIA	MIA
3BD	B-17	219	124	FRANKFURT M/Y	(P)	300.0		1	2	101	0	5	12
			67	ASCHAFFENBURG M/Y	(P)	167.5							
			10	FRANKFURT STH M/Y	(S)	24.4							
			9	T/O		22.4							
1BD	B-17	304	144	BINGEN M/Y	(P)	367.4		2	0	132	0	11	15
			74	BULLAY R/B	(P)	216.0							
			50	WITTLICH C/C	(P)	108.5							
			12	GROSSLITTGEN	(O)	27.0							
			13	T/O NEAR DIEKIRCH		29.3							
2BD	B-24	262	9	SCHLEIDEN C/C	(P)	24.5		1	3	95	17	5	0
			31	ZÜLPICH C/C	(P)	81.5							
			51	IRLICH R/B	(P)	154.5							
			32	STADTKYLL C/C	(P)	93.0							
			26	GEROLSTEIN M/Y	(P)	67.5							
			30	REMAGEN BRIDGE	(P)	103.5							
			10	PRÜM C/C	(P)	17.0							
			8	DUPPACH	(O)	21.5							
			19	FENSBACH	(O)	49.5							
			11	ST.VITH	(O)	30.5							
			14	T/O(10)		39.8							
3BD	B-17	38	35	LUNEBACH C/C	(P)	87.5		0	0	23	0	0	0
			1	TELM M/Y	(O)	2.5							
	B-17	4	4	SCREENING FORCE									
TOTALS:		827	784			2035.3		4	5	351	17	21	17

Despatched		Effective	Target	Bombs Tonnage	E/A	Losses MIA	E	Dam	Casualties KIA	WIA	MIA
P-51	282	267	ESCORT 3BD			2	1				
P-51	64	61	ESCORT 1BD			1	0				
P-51	119	106	ESCORT 2BD			0	0				
P-51	104	101	ESCORT 452BG			0	2				
P-47	107	81	FIGHTER SWEEP			0	0				
P-51	47					0	0				
P-51	27	26	SCOUTING FORCE			0	0				
TOTALS:	724	668				3	3	?	0	0	2

REMARKS: Communications targets in western Germany. 1BD bombed visually at Bingen and by GH at other targets; 2BD used GH on primaries and attacked T/Os visually; 3BD bombing was all visual. Bomb groups participating:– 1BD – 91BG, 303BG, 305BG, 306BG, 379BG, 398BG, 401BG, 457BG; 2BD – all groups except 448BG, 458BG, 491BG; 3BD – 13CBW groups and 452BG, 486BG, 487BG, 493BG. The attack on Lunebach was carried out by 452BG. Bomb group losses:– 1BD – 306BG – 1, 398BG – 1; 2BD – 467BG – 1; 3BD – 487BG – 1. B/d 467BG B-24, abandoned over Suffolk, and cr. in sea. 2 467BG B-24s cr. Wroxham after t/o, 12 killed. 1 467BG B-24 damaged on t/o c/l Attlebridge. B/d 398BG B-17 c/l, 6 k. B/d 91BG B-17 f/l Continent – Cat E.

All Fighter groups except 356FG and 359FG operating. 78FG using P-51s for first time. Fighter group losses:– 78FG – 1 (P-51), 339FG – 1, 364FG – 1. Two 479FG P-51 wrecked when landing base on return, pilots safe. 78FG P-51 wrecked when landing base on return, pilots safe. 78FG P-51 MIA down in sea 3 miles off Orfordness, pilot baled and saved.

OTHER OPERATIONS: 25BG despatched 2 Mosquitoes on PR to Ulm area, 3 Mosquitoes as screening Force for bombers, 3 Mosquitoes on WR Continent, and 2 B-17s on WR to and from the Azores. ASR despatched 8 P-47s on patrols.

EVENT

When the Wehrmacht launched its offensive through the Ardennes one of the tasks given the Allied air forces was destruction of bridges over the Rhine to stem the flow of supplies and reinforcements. A bridge was a small target for a bomber at 20,000 ft and difficult to hit in ideal conditions. Given inclement weather when visual opportunities were few and bombing was performed on Gee-H or Micro-H radar aids success was much less likely. A record of one crew's experiences on the first 8th Air Force heavy bomber mission to the Rhine bridges, 29 December 1944, was made by 1/Lt Soloman Greenberg, navigator on Lt Allen Bryson's B-24 in 453rd Bomb Group, as follows.

'It is a dismal morning, bitter cold and driving rain. We make our way up the walk a hundred yards or so to the officers' mess. Mission breakfasts are usually a time of some joviality, but not today. There is a general feeling of depression. We thought we had the war won, and suddenly the enemy has launched an offensive and Antwerp is threatened. It is easy to think that the worst might happen, and that we will be thrown off the continent. There is no reassuring rumour to blunt this feeling. We are in trouble, no doubt about it.

The ride to the briefing room is quiet in the big trucks. The enlisted men join us at our seats and they too are sombre. We have been into the "Bulge" twice in the past few days, and so far have not been effective. Now the usual guessing game, what will the target be for today? My bombardier Albert Gehrt next to me as usual is eating a chocolate bar. He had an addiction for them and I sometimes see him on the honey bucket in the toilet, eating his chocolate.

After ten or twelve minutes the crew from G-2 arrives to begin the briefing. The red curtain across the map of Europe is drawn and we see the mission route, right to the Rhine, a shallow penetration at best, so that we will still be working as tactical support. Up until today, the bridges across the Rhine were not to be bombed. Now, that is about to change, increasing our apprehension. Things must be worse than we surmised. Our target, the Ludendorff Bridge at Remagen. This will be a radar bomb run, with cloud cover expected all the way from departure to return.

We draw our heavy flight clothes and parachutes, climb into the trucks and go out to the hardstand. As the officer in charge of oxygen supplies, I check the pressure at each station. They are all full. I drop my maps and 'chute into the nose compartment and stretch out in the waist area right behind the bomb bay, hoping to catch a few more winks. These do not come, the rain is pelting the plane with a rhythm that prevents sleep. I am about as miserable physically as I can be. Al Gehrt comes by, kicks me in the foot and advises me that the birds are walking so how can we possibly fly. I assume this is one of his bad jokes but Al is from Kansas and knows a lot about birds.

I wander up to the flight deck and watch Bryson and Watson check their lists, a sight I had watched many times before. The ceiling appears to be three or four hundred feet high, and this is the kind of day where the cloud tops are indicated as being at "twenty". Always a guess since there is no better data available. The fact is, they are often much higher. I keep hoping for a yellow flare, or perhaps even a red one cancelling the mission. This will not develop. The flare is green. We go through the engine "start up", and begin to taxi, a long line of aircraft moving slowly in patches of fog. It is finally our turn at the threshold. I stand behind Bryson and call out the airspeed. We are a long time getting up to eighty, and then it seems like there will be no more. The runway is running out and then we are at ninety, one hundred, one hundred five, which is critical and then one hundred ten at which time Bryson pulls the plane off the ground as we all pray for sufficient airspeed. I think I see us barely clear the power lines at the end of the runway, but one cannot be certain. There is not enough visibility. The wheels are tucked away and we begin our turn to climbing course. At about eight hundred feet altitude our tail gunner Bob Atkins sees a plane burning, or whatever it is that is burning so fiercely on the ground below. Within the next two minutes the other gunners spot two additional fires. There is a brief discussion about carburettor icing over the intercom and then Bryson asks for some quiet. The conversation stops until the gunners spot another burning plane.

We spend fifteen uneventful minutes climbing on course for Buncher 6, our group formating beacon. There is little to do and then suddenly we are out of the clouds and looking for other planes from our group. We have a black painted tail with a white diagonal stripe, easy enough to spot. Five minutes later we are part of the formation, not in our assigned spot, but at least in the right area. The others come in slowly, and this will not be a formation Col Larry Thomas would be proud of. He delights in nice tight formation, but not today.

We depart the Buncher a few minutes late and head out to the I.P. The weather is as forecast. Absolutely terrible. We are between two layers of clouds at 20,000 ft. Bombing altitude will be twenty-one five. We are carrying six 1000 pound bombs and while the chances of a direct hit are slim, any one of these bombs could do the job nicely.

We cross the coast of the continent on time, near Ostend. The route is across Belgium, down into France, and then into Germany over Aachen. I advise the gunners when we cross enemy territory and they test fire their guns. We also have an oxygen check every ten minutes, as much to relieve the monotony as a safety exercise. I am uncomfortable about being in a sandwich of clouds. Too easy for enemy fighters to come through, make their attacks, and then disappear in a dive.

We will approach the target from the south on a northerly heading. This will give the radar bombing operator a continuous view of the Rhine to set up his drop. At the initial point we open our bomb bay doors, and the gunners begin to throw out the chaff, an exercise not particularly significant. There will be meagre flak on this mission. I am watching my clock and the compass and we have about two minutes to the estimated drop time. Suddenly from nowhere, my compass spins to the right as the entire formation appears to side-step in a flank right exercise. A leap to the window at the right hand side of my compartment and there, for the first time that day, there is a hole in the clouds, and the bridge beneath. The lead plane drops its bombs and the smoke markers attached signal for me to jettison our own. I grip the red handle, depress the plunger at the top and at the same time swing the handle to a horizontal position. A brief second later I hear our radioman, Dave Mitchnick, call "bombs away". It appears to have been a second too late. Whoever it was that spotted the hole had little time to make the last-second change. The clouds close up again, and home we go. Nature has tempted us with that opening, but couldn't work. We know we have missed.

The return home, routine and uneventful, with lots of conjecture as to what might have been had someone called for a dry run, and then come around again, but it just didn't happen that way. It all happened too quickly.'

During the next few weeks there were other attempts to demolish the Remagen bridge by bombing but these too were unsuccessful. Later the enemy also failed to destroy the bridge before it had given the Allies their first foothold across the Rhine.

30 DECEMBER 1944

8AF 770

	Despatched		Effective	Target		Bombs Tonnage	E/A	Losses MIA	E	Dam	Casualties KIA	WIA	MIA
3BD	B-17	526	314	KASSEL M/Y	(P)	859.6		3	0	37	0	0	24
			181	MANNHEIM M/Y	(P)	486.8							
			9	T/O		30.9							
1BD	B-17	414	35	BISCHOFFSHEIM M/Y	(P)	75.5		1	1	24	12	0	6
			72	BULLAY R/B	(P)	216.0							
			72	KAISERSLAUTERN R/B	(P)	214.5							
			144	KAISERSLAUTERN M/Y	(S)	414.3							
			45	MAINZ M/Y	(S)	109.3							
			25	KASSEL (CITY)	(O)	55.8							

continued on next page

30 DECEMBER 1944 *(contd.)*

		Despatched	Effective	Target		Bombs Tonnage	E/A	Losses MIA	E	Dam	KIA	WIA	MIA
2BD	B-24	369	61	ALTENAHR R/B	(P)	184.0		0	0	1	0	0	0
			91	AUSKIRCHEN R/B	(P)	243.0							
			58	IRLICH R/B	(P)	162.3							
			57	REMAGEN BRIDGE	(P)	173.0							
			87	MECHERNICH M/Y	(P)	240.3							
	B-17	6	6	SCREENING FORCE									
TOTALS:		1315	1257			3465.3		4	1	62	12	0	30
	P-51	325	301	ESCORT 3BD				2			0	0	2
	P-51	154	144	ESCORT 1BD				0			0	0	0
	P-47	72	63	ESCORT 2BD				0			0	0	0
	P-51	21	20	SCOUTING FORCES				0			0	0	0
TOTALS:		572	528					2	0	?	0	0	2

REMARKS: All bomb groups participated in attacks on rail and communications targets in western Germany. 1BD used GH on primaries and H2X on others; 2BD used GH; 3BD used H2X. Bomb group losses:– 1BD – 398BG – 1; 3BD – 390BG – 1, 447BG – 2. MIA 447BG B-17s collided in target area. On return 5 men baled over sea from b/d 493BG B-17 which f/l Woodbridge A/F. 92BG B-17 cr. on approach to East Kirkby A/F, 9 k.

All Fighter groups except 356FG and 364FG operating. Fighter group losses: 55FG – 1, 357FG – 1.

OTHER OPERATIONS: 25BG despatched 1 Mosquito on special operation, 2 Mosquitoes on H2X photo sorties Regensburg and Augsburg, 4 Mosquitoes on WR North Sea/Continent, and 4 B-24s on WR Azores/Atlantic/UK. 36BS despatched 5 B-24s on RCM for 8AF operations. 2 P-51s on radio-relays. ASR despatched 13 P-47s on patrols.

30/31 DECEMBER 1944

8AF 771 NIGHT LEAFLET OPERATION

NLS despatched 8 B-24s and 3 B-17s; Holland, Luxembourg, Germany.

36BS despatched 1 B-24 on RCM for RAF.

482BG despatched 1 B-17 on scope photo recon of battle area.

31 DECEMBER 1944

8AF 772

	Despatched		Effective	Target		Bombs Tonnage	E/A	Losses MIA	E	Dam	Casualties KIA	WIA	MIA
3BD	B-17	526	62	WENZENDORF I/A	(P)	181.5	26–8–16	27	1	288	5	29	248
			68	HAMBURG O/I	(P)	206.0							
			24	HAMBURG/ WILHELMSBURG O/I	(P)	57.5							
			68	HAMBURG WILHELMSBURG O/I	(P)	172.0							
			71	HAMBURG/ GRASSBRUK O/I	(P)	205.0							
			72	HAMBURG I/A	(P)	236.7							
			96	MISBURG O/I	(P)	233.0							
			13	STADE A/F	(O)	38.5							
			9	NORDHOLZ A/F	(O)	22.0							
			1	HELIGOLAND	(O)	1.5							
			17	T/O		42.4							
1BD	B-17	418	109	NEUSS M/Y	(P)	292.8		0	2	29	0	1	0
			83	KREFELD-URDINGEN M/Y	(P)	224.3							
			69	EHRANG/ KORDEL R/R	(P)	172.0							
			34	BUZBURG C/C	(P)	86.8							
			37	PRÜM C/C	(P)	90.8							
			34	BLUMENTHAL C/C	(P)	83.0							
			22	MÖNCHEN-GLADBACH	(S)	60.0							
			2	T/O		5.3							
			54	REMAGEN BR	(P)	138.5							
			48	KOBLENZ/ LUTZWEILER BR	(P)	173.5							

continued on facing page

2BD	B-24	371	60	ENGERS BR	(P)	195.0	0 -1- 0	0	3	49	0	1	0
			56	IRLICH BR	(P)	156.5							
			62	KOBLENZ/GUS R/B	(P)	224.5							
			30	EUSKIRCHEN R/J & R/B	(P)	84.7							
			10	BINGEN M/Y	(S)	35.5							
			36	T/O		100.0							
	B-17	12	12	SCREENING FORCE									
TOTALS:		1327	1259			3524.3	26–9–16	27	6	366	5	31	248
	P-47	61	316	ESCORT 3BD			59½–2– 5	2	0		0	0	2
	P-51	293					1 –0–0(G)	7	0		0	0	7
	P-51	171	162	ESCORT 2BD			1– –0–0	0	0		0	0	0
	P-51	211	198	ESCORT 1BD				1	1		0	0	1
	P-51	16	13	ESCORT PR				0	0		0	0	0
	P-51	33	32	SCOUTING FORCES			1 –0–0	0					
TOTALS:		785	721				61½–2–5 1 –0–0(G)	10	1	?	0	0	10

REMARKS: For the first time for two weeks strategic targets were attacked in addition to communications along the German army supply routes. 3BD attacked visually; 1BD and 2BD used GH. All bomb groups except 306BG participated. Bomb group losses:– 3BD – 34BG – 1, 94BG – 1, 95BG – 2, 100BG – 12, 388BG – 2, 390BG – 2, 452BG – 5, 487BG – 1, 493BG – 1. On return, 453BG B-24 f/l Florennes A/F – Cat E. B/d 392BG B-24 c/l Beetley A/F. B/d 351BG B-17 c/l base. 486BG B-17 cr. t/o Lt. Cornard, crew safe. B/d 398BG B-17 and 445BG B-24 c/l Continent.

All Fighter groups operating. Fighter group e/a credits:– 56FG – 5, 78FG – 1, 339FG – 6, 352FG – 1, 353FG – 1, 359FG – 11½, 364FG – 25. Fighter group losses:– 56FG – 2, 339FG – 2, 352FG – 1, 359FG – 4, 364FG – 1. 357FG P-51 c/l base.

OTHER OPERATIONS: 7PG despatched 7 F-5s and 2 Spitfires on PR Berlin area (with 16 P-51 escort). 25BG despatched 4 Mosquitoes on special operation, 6 Mosquitoes on WR Continent, and 4 B-17s on WR Azores/Atlantic/UK. 36BS despatched 8 B-24s on RCM in support of 8AF. 13 P-51s and 4 P-47s on radio-relays. ASR despatched 16 P-47s on patrols.

31 DECEMBER/1 JANUARY 1945

8AF 773 NIGHT LEAFLET OPERATION

NLS despatched 8 B-24s and 2 B-17s; France, Germany, Belgium.

Although Martin Marauder bomber units had been transferred to the 9AF in October 1943, the type was still to be found at some 8AF bases serving in other roles. (1) *El Diablo*, a small tail B-26B, saw combat with 322BG in 1943 and was still soldiering on in January 1945 as a trainer with 3CCRC. (2) There was a special target towing version, the AT-23B; this snow-bound example operated with the 4th G & TT Flight. (3) A few were modified, like B-26G 43-34205, for photo reconnaissance with 25BG(R). Twelve photo-flash sorties are indicated by symbols on the black camouflage finish. (H. Holmes and USAAF)

The scene of desolation at Steeple Morden on the morning of 1 January after 91BG's B-17G *Heats On* crashed into a Mustang dispersal point. The bomber had just taken off from Bassingbourn on its 92nd mission when engine trouble forced the pilot to try and make an emergency landing at the 355FG base. The B-17 crew were killed in the ensuing explosion and a number of P-51 mechanics seriously injured.

1 JANUARY 1945

8AF 774

	Despatched		Effective	Target		Bombs Tonnage	E/A	Losses MIA	E	Dam	Casualties KIA	WIA	MIA
1AD	B-17	451	11	MAGDEBURG O/I	(P)	23.6		2	3	71	10	8	18
			292	KASSEL/HENSCHEL M/Y	(S)	687.8							
			26	GÖTTINGEN M/Y	(S)	60.5							
			12	HADAMAR	(O)	26.9							
			12	WETZLAR	(O)	30.0							
			15	DILLENBURG	(O)	35.2							
			11	KOBLENZ	(O)	23.4							
			12	WETTER	(O)	26.1							
			8	LIMBURG	(O)	18.3							
			7	KIRCHBUNDEN	(O)	15.7							
			22	T/O		48.3							
3AD	B-17	109	54	DOLLBERGEN O/I	(P)	127.6		0	3	43	10	0	0
			24	EHMEN O/I	(P)	42.9							
			12	KOBLENZ M/Y	(O)	23.3							
			4	LIMBURG	(O)	9.0							
			5	T/O		12.4							
2AD	B-24	273	56	KOBLENZ/LUTZEL R/B	(P)	179.0		1	4	63	20	8	10
			57	IRLICH R/B	(P)	195.5							
			30	KOBLENZ/GULS R/B	(P)	98.1							
			6	REMAGEN R/B	(P)	15.0							
			9	ENGERS R/B	(O)	31.0							
			1	TRIER	(O)	4.0							
			26	ANDERNACH	(O)	69.0							
			6	T/O		18.0							
	B-17	12	12	SCREENING FORCE			6–0–2	5	1	0	0	0	45
8AF 774 APHRODITE													
	B-17	5	2	OLDENBURG									
TOTALS:		850	732			1820.6	6–0–2	8	11	177	40	16	73
	P-51	374	327	ESCORT 1AD			17–1–1	2	1		0	0	2
	P-47	48	199	ESCORT 3AD				0	0		0	0	0
	P-51	159						0	0		0	0	0
	P-51	70	66	ESCORT 2AD				0	0		0	0	0
	P-51	26	23	SCOUTING FORCES				0	0		0	0	0
	P-51	11	11	PR ESCORTS				0	0		0	0	0
	P-51	33	25	ESCORT SPECIAL OPS				0	0		0	0	0
	P-47	4											
TOTALS:		725	651				17–1–1	2	1	?	0	0	2

On New Year's Day the Luftwaffe undertook a major strafing raid against Allied airfields. At Brussels/Melsbroek they found many 8AF aircraft that had put down because of weather or difficulties and in a few minutes had set fire to a dozen and left others badly damaged. These photos, taken soon after the Me 109s and FW 190s had left, show (1) smoke from burning bombers billowing into the hazy atmosphere: (2) 34BG B-17 43-38406 with the left wing tanks ablaze – next to it is a fire-gutted 467BG aircraft: (3) a foam-drenched 1st Scouting Force P-51D where the fire fighters had some success. (R. Zorn)

REMARKS: Bomb Divisions redesignated Air Divisions from this date. Oil installations and rail bridges and junctions in western Germany attacked visually and by PFF as conditions allowed at individual targets. Bomb groups participating:– all 1AD; all 2AD except 448BG; 4BW groups of 3AD. Bomb group losses:– 1AD – 92BG – 1, 305BG – 4, 306BG – 1, 398BG – 1; 2AD – 467BG – 1. 398BG B-17 cr. in sea, 6 saved. 445BG cr. t/o base, 1 killed. 453BG B-24 cr. on t/o (hit parked B-24), 7 k. 91BG B-17 cr. after t/o Steeple Morden A/F, 9 k. On return, b/d 92BG B-17 c/l France; b/d 392BG B-24 c/l France; 388BG and 401BG B-17 f/l France – Cat E; 446BG B-24 cr. t/o Bungay A/F, 9 k. Screening Force provided by 92BG, 305BG were 8 minutes late for escort and attacked by FW 190s when 50 miles ahead of bombers. 2 447BG B-17s cr. t/o, one at Brettenham, one at base, crews safe. B/d 384BG B-17 c/l Detling A/F.

All Fighter groups operating. Fighter group e/a credits:– 4FG – 5, 352FG – 23, 359FG – 4, 364FG – 8, 479FG – ½. Fighter group losses:– 359FG – 2, 364FG – 2. 55FG fired on by bombers they were escorting.

OTHER OPERATIONS: 7PG despatched 9 F-5s and 1 Spitfire on PR Germany. 25BG despatched 2 Mosquitoes on PR Germany, 5 Mosquitoes on WR Continent/UK, and 4 B-17s Azores/Atlantic/UK. 36BS despatched 7 B-24s on RCM for 8AF 774. 4 Mosquitoes (3 effective) on special operations. 1 B-17, 4 P-51s on radio-relays. ASR despatched 22 P-47s on patrols and 4 P-51s also on ASR search.

1/2 JANUARY 1945

8AF 775 NIGHT LEAFLET OPERATION

NLS despatched 5 B-24s and 3 B-17s; Belgium, Germany.

36BS despatched 1 B-24 on RCM for RAF.

2 JANUARY

8AF 776

	Despatched		Effective	Target		Bombs Tonnage	E/A	Losses MIA	E	Dam	Casualties KIA	WIA	MIA
1AD	B-17	299	74	GEROLSTEIN M/Y	(P)	210.5		0	0	70	0	0	0
			68	MAYEN C/C	(P)	198.5							
			34	PRÜM C/C	(P)	96.3							
			34	DAUN C/C	(P)	99.5							
			37	KYLLBURG C/C	(P)	108.5							
			36	BITBURG C/C	(P)	83.4							
			3	T/O		9.3							
2AD	B-24	296	59	IRLICH R/B	(P)	162.0		0	1	26	0	0	0
			56	REMAGEN R/B	(P)	142.5							
			65	KOBLENZ/LUTZEL R/B	(P)	176.5							
			59	KOBLENZ/GULS R/B	(P)	185.0							
			43	ENGERS R/B	(P)	114.9							
			3	T/O		8.5							
3AD	B-17	410	73	BAD KREUZNACH M/Y	(P)	212.5		4	2	36	10	2	37
			67	BAD KREUZNACH R/J	(P)	198.5							
			34	KAISERSLAUTERN R/B	(P)	100.0							
			66	EHRANG M/Y	(P)	187.1							
			70	LEBACH TANK CONCS	(P)	252.0							
			58	LEBACH TANK CONCS	(P)	201.0							
			3	TRIER M/Y	(O)	10.3							
			11	ST.WENDEL M/Y	(O)	37.0							
			3	T/O		9.0							
	B-17	6	6	SCREENING FORCES				0	0	0	0	0	0
TOTALS:		1011	962			2802.8	0	4	3	132	10	2	37
	P-51	130	128	ESCORT 1AD									
	P-47	53	215	ESCORT 2AD				1	1		0	0	1
	P-51	169						0	0		0	0	0
	P-51	127	125	ESCORT 3AD				2	1		0	0	2
	P-51	24	24	PR ESCORT				0	0		0	0	0
TOTALS:		503	492				0	3	2	0	0	0	3

REMARKS: Communications and tactical targets in western Germany. 3AD bombed visually; 1AD also visual except for Prüm which was GH; 2AD all GH. Bomb groups participating:– all 1AD except 303BG, 305BG, 398BG, 401BG; all 2AD except 44BG, 446BG; all 3AD. Bomb group losses:– 34BG – 1, 390BG – 1, 452BG – 2. During assembly 96BG exploded and cr. Barton Bendish, 9 killed. B/d 390BG B-17 cr. Continent.

All Fighter groups operating. Fighter group e/a credits:– 4FG – 2, 361FG – 5. Fighter group losses:– 4FG – 1, 78FG – 1, 357FG – 1. On return, a 353FG P-51 c/l near Antwerp and a 479FG P-51 pilot baled over Merville.

OTHER OPERATIONS: 7PG despatched 6 F-5s and 1 Spitfire on PR Germany (with 30 P-51 escort). 25BG despatched 4 Mosquitoes for support of 1 and 3ADs, 4 Mosquitoes on WR Continent/UK and 4 B-17s on WR Azores/Atlantic/UK. 36BS despatched 6 B-24s on RCM for 8AF 776. ASR despatched 14 P-47s on patrols.

2/3 JANUARY 1945

8AF 777 NIGHT LEAFLET OPERATION

NLS despatched 2 B-17s and 6 B-24s (7 a/c effective); France and Germany.

36BS despatched 1 B-24 on RCM for RAF.

25BG despatched 1 A-26 on *Red Stocking* mission Holland.

3 JANUARY 1945

8AF 778

	Despatched		Effective	Target		Bombs Tonnage	E/A	Losses MIA	E	Dam	Casualties KIA	WIA	MIA
3AD	B-17	417	141	FULDA M/Y	(P)	402.8		0	0	1	0	2	0
			124	ASCHAFFENBURG M/Y	(P)	336.2							
			38	GEMÜND C/C	(P)	108.8							
			36	SCHLEIDEN C/C	(P)	106.7							
			36	KOBLENZ/MOSEL M/Y	(S)	102.8							
			25	PFORZHEIM M/Y	(O)	71.2							
			3	T/O		8.4							

continued on facing page

2AD	B-24	325	31	ALTSTADT M/Y	(P)	89.1		0	2	1	0	0	0
			41	HOMBURG M/Y	(P)	106.6							
			55	ZWEIBRÜCKEN M/Y	(P)	142.2							
			84	NEUNKIRCHEN M/Y	(P)	228.7							
			59	LANDAU M/Y	(P)	159.9							
			41	PIRMASENS RAILHEAD	(P)	107.0							
1AD	B-17	421	72	HERMULHEIM WEST M/Y	(P)	210.0		0	0	11	0	0	0
			36	HERMULHEIM EAST M/Y	(P)	106.8							
			98	ST.VITH C/C	(P)	246.8							
			36	MONDRATH R/J	(P)	90.0							
			1	HORREM R/J	(P)	3.0							
			129	COLOGNE	(S)	379.6							
			10	RHEYDT	(O)	29.8							
			3	T/O		8.0							
TOTALS:		1168	1099			3044.4		0	2	14	0	2	0
	P-51	227	219	ESCORT 3AD			4–0–0	1	4		0	0	1
	P-51	148	143	ESCORT 2AD				0	0		0	0	0
	P-51	150	145	ESCORT 1AD				3	0		0	0	3
	P-51	32	32	SCOUTING FORCES				0	0		0	0	0
	P-51	32	32	PR ESCORT				0	0		0	0	0
TOTALS:		589	571				4–0–0	4	4	?	1	0	4

REMARKS: Rail and communications targets in western Germany. All PFF attacks, H2X supplemented by GH in 1AD and 2AD and Micro H in 3AD. Bomb groups participating:– all 1AD except 92BG; all 2AD; all 3AD except 388BG 493BG. B/d 453BG B-24 abandoned by crew near Saarbrücken. Another B-24 also cr. France.

All Fighter groups except 56FG, 352FG, 361FG operating. Fighter group e/a credits:– 55FG – 4. Fighter group losses:– 20FG – 1, 55FG – 1, 359FG – 1, 364FG – 1. Pilot of 20FG P-51 MIA baled 18 miles NW Ostend, lost. 353FG P-51 cr. Capel St.Mary after t/o, pilot killed. 479FG P-51 c/l near Ipswich A/F, pilot safe.

OTHER OPERATIONS: 7PG despatched 5 F-5s (1 recalled) on PR Germany (with 31 P-51 escort). 25BG despatched 2 Mosquitoes on PR Kassel area, 2 Mosquitoes scouting for bombers, 1 Mosquito on *Red Stocking* mission to Holland, 5 Mosquitoes on WR Continent/UK, and 4 B-17s on WR Azores/Atlantic/UK. 36BS despatched 4 B-24s on RCM for 8AF 778. 3 B-17s, 6 P-51s, 2 Mosquitoes (11 a/c effective) as screening force for bombers. ASR despatched 16 P-47s on patrols and 4 P-51 also on ASR search. 2 P-51s on radio-relays.

4 JANUARY 1945

25BG despatched 3 Mosquitoes on WR Continent, and 4 B-17s on WR Azores/Atlantic/UK. ASR despatched 8 P-47s on patrols.

Reinforced tents and home made shacks that served as accommodation 'out on the line' did not look to provide adequate protection against winter's chill but could be surprisingly comfortable. These are on bleak Nuthamstead – highest of all 8AF operational bases. Note man dislodging snow from tent. (M. Osborn)

4/5 JANUARY 1945

8AF 779 NIGHT LEAFLET OPERATION

NLS despatched 1 B-17 and 8 B-24s; Holland, Belgium, Germany. 1 B-24 MIA.

8AF 780 NIGHT BOMBING OPERATION

492BG despatched 12 B-24s, 10 effective, to Coubre Point Coastal battery (near Bordeaux), 16.8 tons HE dropped by H2X.

5 JANUARY 1945

8AF 781

	Despatched		Effective	Target		Bombs Tonnage	E/A	Losses MIA	E	Dam	Casualties KIA	WIA	MIA
2AD	B-24	259	32	NEUSTADT M/Y	(P)	73.0		0	3	51	6	1	0
			42	SOBERNHEIM M/Y	(P)	94.0							
			31	COCHEM M/Y & R/B	(P)	72.8							
			18	KIRM M/Y	(P)	43.3							
			39	PIRMASENS R/R	(P)	103.7							
			3	ST.INGBERT M/Y	(P)	9.0							
			51	NEUNKIRCHEN M/Y	(S)	137.7							
			8	RHEINKIRCHEN C/C	(O)	21.4							
			7	NEUBRÜCKE C/C	(O)	18.6							
			1	PRÜM C/C	(O)	3.0							
			1	BURG C/C	(O)	3.0							
3AD	B-17	370	57	HANAU M/Y	(P)	154.3		1	6	89	13	9	1
			81	FRANKFURT M/Y	(P)	201.8							
			32	WAXWEILER C/C	(P)	92.5							
			27	WETTELDORF C/C	(P)	76.0							
			33	PRONSFELD C/C	(P)	101.0							
			29	KAISERSLAUTERN	(S)	78.1							
			29	HEILBRONN	(O)	59.5							
			11	T/O		29.0							
1AD	B-17	379	70	NIEDERBREISIG A/F	(P)	129.9		0	1	20	0	0	0
			54	NIEDERMENDIG A/F	(P)	100.7							
			37	DUMPELFELD C/C	(P)	105.9							
			35	KALL C/C	(P)	101.9							
			37	HEIMBACH RR	(P)	107.9							
			1	MECHERNICH C/C	(P)	3.0							
			96	KOBLENZ M/Y	(S)	217.5							
			2	PRONSFELD C/C	(O)	3.9							
			1	WAXWEILER C/C	(O)	1.9							
			4	T/O		8.9							
	B-17	24	24	SCREENING FORCE				0	0	0	0	0	0
TOTALS:		1032	893			2153.2	0	1	10	160	19	10	1
	P-51	177	164	ESCORT 2AD				0	0		0	0	0
	P-51	213	194	ESCORT 3AD			1–0–0 4–0–0(G)	0	0		0	0	0
	P-51	117	109	ESCORT 1AD				1	1		0	0	1
	P-51	44	44	ESCORT PR				0	0		0	0	0
	P-51	33	26	SCOUTING FORCES				0	0		0	0	0
TOTALS:		584	537				1–0–0 4–0–0(G)	1	1	?	0	0	1

REMARKS: Rail targets and airfields in central Germany. 2AD bombed visually and with GH; 3AD visually and PFF; 1AD used GH and H2X. Bomb groups participating:– all 1AD except 379BG, 457BG; all 2AD except 458BG, 491BG; all 3AD except 93CBW groups and 487BG. Bomb group losses:– 3AD – 388BG – 1. 491BG abandoned mission when two B-24s cr. near Swaffham, after t/o in snow storm. On return, 2 96BG B-17s c/l Belgium, crews safe; a 398BG B-17 c/l on Continent; 466BG B-24 c/l Attlebridge A/F. 388BG B-17 cr. landing at Hawkinge A/F, 4 killed. MIA 388BG B-17 down near front line, 6 crewmen evaded. B/d 100BG B-17 cr. France, crew killed. B/d 452BG B-17 cr. near Saarbrücken, crew safe.

All Fighter groups except 56FG and 364FG operating. Fighter group e/a credits:– 357FG –1. Fighter group losses:– 352FG – 1. 20 FG P-51 c/l Leiston A/F.

OTHER OPERATIONS: 7PG despatched 7 F-5s and 2 Spitfires on PR France and Germany (escorted by 44 P-51s). 25BG despatched 3 Mosquitoes (2 effective) on PR Berlin, 3 Mosquitoes 'chaff' screening for bombers, 4 Mosquitoes (3 effective) on WR Continent/UK, and 4 B-17s on WR Azores/Atlantic. 36BS despatched 10 B-24s (7 effective) on RCM for 8AF 781. ASR despatched 12 P-47s on patrols. 2 P-47s on radio-relays.

INCIDENT

The precise assessment of losses by units could take hours after the general return as there was always a possibility that a missing aircraft and crew had landed safely elsewhere. Most of France and Belgium was in Allied hands by late 1944 and if an aircraft came down in a remote area it could be a day or two before word was received. The fate of 2/Lt Clem Schaller's crew and the

452nd Group's B-17 *Panting Stork II* was a mystery for a week due to unusual circumstances. Over Hanau, on 5 January, the bomber was blasted by flak and nursed back through clouds and snow storms to France. A break in the clouds enabled the crew to see an airfield on the fringe of a town and *Panting Stork II* was brought in for a successful force-landing. A US infantry officer and some MPs drove up in a jeep and informed the crew that German paratroops were believed in the area, and as there was no safe accommodation near by it would be best if the airmen stayed in the Fortress until transport could be arranged to take them to Paris. The waist gunner, Sgt Robert Gray, was taken by jeep to collect K-rations and returned bringing three rifles. After eating the crew settled down for the night as best they could, although no one got much sleep as it was so cold. A blizzard developed and was still raging in the morning. At times the Fortress crew could not even see the engines of the aircraft, conditions were so bad. The storms did not abate and the men became really concerned when they were forced to spend another four nights in their snowbound refuge. Visibility continued to be bad, hiding all landmarks and it appeared folly to attempt to venture out in such weather. Although mindful of the warning about the presence of enemy troops, they realised that the soldiers that arrived after the crashlanding had forgotten them. On the sixth day conditions improved and four of the men set out to get food, successfully reaching the nearby town and making contact with US troops. This time they arranged for the whole crew to be 'liberated' and they were put on a truck going west.

5/6 JANUARY 1945

8AF 782 NIGHT LEAFLET OPERATION

NLS despatched 4 B-24s and 1 B-17; SE Belgium.

6 JANUARY 1945

8AF 783

	Despatched		Effective	Target		Bombs Tonnage	E/A	Losses MIA	E	Dam	Casualties KIA	WIA	MIA
3AD	B-17	258	62	WORMS M/Y	(P)	155.5		0	2	55	5	2	0
			34	KAISERSLAUTERN M/Y	(P)	97.5							
			64	LUDWIGSHAFEN M/Y	(S)	205.0							
			31	ANNWEILER	(O)	89.0							
			22	KUSEL M/Y	(O)	63.5							
			29	T/O		84.0							
1AD	B-17	422	71	COLOGNE SOUTH R/B	(P)	210.0		1	1	17	0	1	10
			35	COLOGNE DEUTZ H/B	(P)	105.0							
			72	KEMPERNICH C/C	(P)	212.2							
			38	BONN RHINE H/B	(S)	112.8							
			183	COLOGNE/KALK M/Y	(S)	539.0							
			3	T/O		9.0							
2AD	B-24	130	31	BONN RHINE H/B	(P)	82.5		0	1	17	0	0	0
			95	KOBLENZ/MOSEL M/Y	(S)	255.2							
			1	T/O		3.0							
	B-17	6	6	SCREENING FORCE						0	0	0	0
TOTALS:		816	778			2223.2	0	1	4	89	5	3	10
	P-51	121	109	ESCORT 3AD			14–0–1(G)	1	2		1	0	1
	P-51	229	219	ESCORT 1AD				1	2		1	0	1
	P-51	181	172	ESCORT 2AD				0	0		0	0	0
	P-47	60	36	FIGHTER-BOMBERS SIEGEN M/Y	(P)	7.3		0	0		0	0	0
	P-51	23	23	SCOUTING FORCES				0	0		0	0	0
	P-51	8	8	ESCORT PR				0	0		0	0	0
TOTALS:		622	567			7.3	14–0–1(G)	2	4	?	2	0	2

REMARKS: Communications and rail targets in western Germany. GH and H2X attacks by all Divisions but 3AD able to make some visual drops. Bomb groups participating:– all 1AD except 384BG; 93BG, 389BG, 445BG, 448BG of 2AD; all 3AD except 93CBW groups and 452BG, 486BG. Bomb group losses:– 1AD – 379BG – 1. 487BG B-17 c/l Alpheton after t/o. 94BG B-17 cr. after t/o, 5 killed, 3 civilians injured. Going out 448BG B-24 with m/f cr. Horsey Island, crew baled. On return a 398BG B-17 f/l Continent – Cat E. MIA 379BG GH a/c had 91BG crew plus 379BG GH man.

All Fighter groups except 339FG, 352FG, 357FG, 361FG operating. Fighter group losses:– 55FG – 1, 359FG – 1. A 359FG P-51 cr. t/o base, pilot k. 78FG P-51 cr. near Halstead, pilot k. 78FG and 359FG P-51s c/l on Continent, pilot safe.

OTHER OPERATIONS: 7PG despatched 4 F-5s on PR W Germany. 25BG despatched 2 Mosquitoes on H2X scope photo mission Brüx area (with 8 P-51s escort), 2 Mosquitoes 'chaff' screening for 1AD, 1 Mosquito on *Red Stocking* sortie Holland and W Germany, 4 Mosquitoes on WR Continent, and 4 B-17s on WR Azores/Atlantic/UK. ASR despatched 14 P-47s on patrols and 4 B-17s on ASR search. 1 B-24, 1 P-51 on radio-relays Lille area. 36BS despatched 5 B-24s on RCM for 8AF 783.

6/7 JANUARY 1945

8AF 784 NIGHT LEAFLET OPERATION

NLS despatched 6 B-17s; Belgium, Holland.

7 JANUARY 1945

8AF 785

	Despatched		Effective	Target		Bombs Tonnage	E/A	Losses MIA	E	Dam	Casualties KIA	WIA	MIA
3AD	B-17	265	109	HAMM M/Y	(S)	325.0		0	0	5	0	0	0
			74	PADERBORN M/Y	(S)	220.5							
			74	BIELEFELD M/Y	(S)	218.0							
			2	T/O		6.0							
1AD	B-17	351	39	BLANKENHEIM C/C	(P)	115.0		0	0	3	0	2	0
			39	KALL C/C	(P)	110.8							
			110	BITBURG C/C	(P)	321.7							
			75	EUSKIRCHEN C/C	(P)	221.5							
			35	COLOGNE/LUTZEL BR	(O)	105.0							
3AD	B-17	147	14	HOHENZOLLERN BR	(P)	60.0		2	0	10	1	0	19
			22	RODENKIRCHEN H/B	(P)	63.0							
			80	COLOGNE/KALK M/Y	(S)	218.0							
			11	LIMBURG	(O)	32.0							
			11	KOBLENZ	(O)	31.5							
			1	T/O		3.0							
2AD	B-24	304	54	LANDAU M/Y	(P)	208.1		1	0	10	0	1	9
			31	ACHERN RAIL & C/C	(P)	115.3							
			26	KAISERSLAUTERN RR/I	(P)	70.5							
			64	ZWEIBRÜCKEN M/Y	(P)	164.5							
			99	RASTATT M/Y	(P)	271.8							
			8	DURRMENZ	(O)	23.0							
			1	KARLSRUHE	(O)	3.0							
	B-17	6	6	SCREENING FORCE				0	0	0	0	0	0
TOTALS:		1073	985			2907.2	0	3	0	28	1	3	28
	P-51	204	197	ESCORT 3AD 1st FORCE				1					
	P-51	160	159	ESCORT 1AD				0					
	P-51	95	91	ESCORT 3AD 2nd FORCE				0					
	P-51	102	94	ESCORT 2AD				0					
	P-47	40	88	FIGHTER SWEEP									
	P-51	54						0					
	P-51	12	12	ESCORT PR				0					
	P-51	33	33	SCOUTING FORCES				0					
TOTALS:		700	674				0	1	0	?	0	0	1

REMARKS: Communications centres, rail targets, bridges and an oil storage depot in western Germany. All PFF attacks except T/Os of 2AD which were visual. All bomb groups except 1CBW groups participated. First Force 3AD (4BW and 93CBW) used H2X; Second Force 3AD used Micro H and H2X; 1AD used GH and H2X and 2AD GH. Bomb group losses:– 2AD – 448BG – 1; 3AD – 95BG – 1, 96BG – 1. MIA 3AD B-17s lost collided.

All Fighter groups operating except 352FG, 361FG. Fighter group losses:– 55FG – 1.

OTHER OPERATIONS: 7PG despatched 2 F-5s on PR Germany. 25BG despatched 2 Mosquitoes (with 4 P-51 escort) on PR Holland and N Germany (1 Mosquito aborted), 5 Mosquitoes on WR Continent (with P-51 escort), and 3 B-17s on WR Azores/Atlantic/UK. 1 Mosquito and 1 A-26 despatched on *Red Stocking* operation, A-26 c/l base. 36BS despatched 7 B-24s on RCM for 8AF 785. ASR despatched 12 P-47s on patrols and 4 B-17s, 4 P-51s also on ASR search.

7/8 JANUARY 1945

8AF 786 NIGHT LEAFLET OPERATION

NLS despatched 2 B-17s and 5 B-24s; SE Belgium, France.

25BG despatched 1 Mosquito on long-range *Skywave* navigation sortie Czechoslovakia.

8 JANUARY 1945

8AF 787

	Despatched		Effective	Target		Bombs Tonnage	E/A	Losses MIA	E	Dam	Casualties KIA	WIA	MIA
1AD	B-17	151	36	WISSEMBOURG C/C	(P)	106.3		0	2				
			36	ALZEY H & R/B	(P)	105.5							
			65	SPEYER M/Y	(S)	198.0							
			4	T/O		11.5							
1AD	B-17	117	37	KYLLBURG C/C	(P)	108.5		1	1	24	1	7	9
			24	SCHWEICH C/C	(P)	69.0							
			37	SPEICHER C/C	(P)	107.5							
			12	KOBLENZ M/Y	(S)	35.7							
2AD	B-24	30	24	STADTKYLL C/C	(P)	67.3		0	0	0	0	0	0
			2	T/O		6.0							
2AD	B-24	204	14	WITTLICH C/C	(P)	37.5		0	2	0	0	1	0
			29	OUDLER C/C	(P)	77.8							
			18	CLERF C/C	(P)	48.3							
			31	BURGH REULAND C/C	(P)	82.5							
			30	DASBURG C/C	(P)	72.3							
			2	T/O		6.0							
3AD	B-17	225	33	WAXWEILLER C/C	(P)	82.5		1	1	47	0	0	0
			29	LUNEBACH C/C	(P)	72.5							
			131	FRANKFURT M/Y	(S)	257.0							
			1	T/O		2.0							
	B-17	9	9	SCREENING FORCE				0	0	0			
TOTALS:		736	604			1553.7	0	2	6	71	1	8	9
	P-51	229	219	FREELANCE TO ALL BOMBER FORCES									
	P-51	8	8	ESCORT PRU									
	P-51	32	29	SCOUTING FORCES									
TOTALS:		269	256				0	0			0	0	0

REMARKS: PFF attacks on communication centres, rail targets and bridges in Germany. 1AD used GH and H2X; 2AD used HG; 3AD used Micro H and H2X. Bomb groups participating:– 92BG, 306BG, 381BG, 398BG in first 1AD Force; 41CBW groups in second 1AD Force; 458BG as first 2AD Force; 14CBW groups and 93BG, 446BG, 466BG in second 2AD Force; 45CBW and 4BW groups except 94BG in 3AD Force. 12 B-17s of 45CBW dropped on US troops at Waxweiler. Bomb group losses:– 1AD – 384BG – 1; 3AD – 447BG – 1. B/d 92BG B-17 abandoned and cr. Rheims. 306BG B-17 cr. Rochester A/F, 1 killed. On return, 453BG B-24 abandoned and cr. East Wretham, crew safe; 466BG B-24 c/l Shipdham, crew safe; 303BG B-17 cr. landing base – Cat E; 487BG B-17 c/l St. Margarets, Kent, crew safe.

Fighter groups operating: 4FG, 20FG, 78FG, 339FG, 355FG, 479FG.

OTHER OPERATIONS: 7PG despatched 3 F-5s on PR Germany. 25BG despatched 2 Mosquitoes on PR Germany (with 8 P-51 escort), 3 Mosquitoes screening for bombers, and B-17s on WR Azores/Atlantic/UK. 36BS despatched 13 B-24s (10 effective) on RCM for 8AF 787. ASR despatched 8 P-47s on patrols.

A yellow tailed 487BG B-17 (43-39068) reposes on its belly beside wheat ricks at St.Margarets, Kent. The stranger arrived on the farm on its way home from Germany, 8 January.

8/9 JANUARY 1945

8AF 788 NIGHT LEAFLET OPERATION

NLS despatched 1 B-17 and 4 B-24s (2 a/c effective); St.Hubert.

9 JANUARY 1945

25BG despatched 5 Mosquitoes on WR Continent/UK, and 4 B-17s Atlantic/UK. 36BS despatched 5 B-24s on RCM operations.

Touching down at Leiston from the 10 January escort, Lt Rocco Lepore's *Pretty Pat* suddenly skidded off the runway, careered across the airfield and smashed into a revetment bank. Ice and pilot fatigue were 357FG's findings on cause. This was one of many similar accidents in the freezing conditions of January 1945. (M. Olmsted)

10 JANUARY 1945

8AF 789

	Despatched		Effective	Target		Bombs Tonnage	E/A	Losses MIA	E	Dam	Casualties KIA	WIA	MIA
3AD	B-17	428	31	COLOGNE–RODENKIRCHEN H/B	(P)	91.5		5	5	199	10	6	48
			34	COLOGNE–SOUTH R/B	(P)	102.0							
			10	COLOGNE–DEUTZ H/B	(P)	27.0							
			52	COLOGNE–HOHENZOLLERN R/B	(P)	149.0							
			105	KARLSRUHE M/Y	(P)	308.0							
			20	COLOGNE–GEREON M/Y	(S)	54.5							
			11	DUISBURG BRIDGE	(O)	33.0							
			21	OBERKASSEL BRIDGE	(O)	63.0							
			28	DÜSSELDORF	(O)	83.5							
			17	T/O		49.5							
			16	T/O	(10)	46.5							
2AD	B-24	233	23	STEINBRÜCK H/B	(P)	61.0		0	2	7	0	3	0
			70	SCHÖNBERG H/B	(P)	186.0							
			60	WEWELER H/B	(P)	166.0							
			20	DASBURG H/B	(P)	53.0							
			1	PRÜM	(O)	3.0							
1AD	B-17	458	63	BONN/HANGELAR A/F	(P)	117.7		5	11	140	5	15	52
			98	EUSKIRCHEN/ ODENDORF A/F	(P)	182.1							
			83	COLOGNE/OSTHEIM A/F	(P)	152.4							
			52	GYMNICH A/F	(P)	94.1							
			43	COLOGNE M/Y	(S)	81.5							
			8	EUSKIRCHEN M/Y	(O)	13.3							
			8	BELECKE M/Y	(O)	14.2							
			12	DÜREN M/Y	(O)	22.8							
			26	T/O		44.9							
TOTALS:		1119	912			2196.5	0	10	18	346	15	24	100
	P-51	152	137	COVER ALL BOMBERS				6	1		0	0	0
	P-47	54	123	SWEEP-FREELANCE			1–0–0	1	0		0	0	0
	P-51	101		SUPPORT BOMBERS			2–0–0(G)	1	4		0	0	1
	P-51	15	13	DIVE BOMB NEUSTADT M/Y				0	0		0	0	0
	P-51	8	6	ESCORT PR				0	0		0	0	0
	P-51	32	28	SCOUTING FORCES				0	0		0	0	0
TOTALS:		362	307				1–0–0 2–0–0(G)	2	5	?	1	0	2

REMARKS: Airfields, rail targets and bridges in Germany. 3AD attacked some targets visually but most by PFF; 2AD bombed by GH; 1AD bombed by GH with some visual sightings. Bomb groups participating:– all 1AD; all 2AD except 44BG, 446BG; all 3AD except 487BG. Bomb group losses:– 1AD – 305BG – 1, 306BG – 1, 379BG – 2, 384BG – 1, 3AD – 95BG – 1, 100BG – 1, 390BG – 1, 452BG – 1, 490BG – 1. MIA 379BG B-17s collided. 493BG B-17 cr. Monewden after t/o, 4 killed. On return 392BG B-24 c/l Seething A/F, crew safe. 1 303BG and 1 401BG B-17 c/l France. 91BG B-17 cr. landing Brussels/Evere A/F and hit hangar, crew killed. B/d 100BG B-17 c/l Belgium. 2 b/d 92BG and 2 b/d 305BG B-17 c/l nr. Liège, Belgium. 388BG B-17 c/l near Abbeville, crew safe. During assembly 452BG B-17 cr. on Thorpe Abbotts bomb dump, crew baled. 384BG B-17 c/l after t/o, crew safe. 453BG B-24 cr. Rushford, crew baled. B/d 384BG B-17 c/l Manston A/F. B/d 457BG B-17 abandoned over Belgium, 1 k. B/d 306BG B-17 c/l Hombeck, Belgium. B/d 490BG B-17 cr. Continent, 3 k.

Fighter groups operating: 20FG, 56FG, 78FG, 339FG, 352FG, 353FG, 357FG, 361FG, 364FG. Fighter groups e/a credits:– 357FG – 1. Fighter group losses:– 357FG – 1, 364FG – 1. 78FG P-51 c/l on t/o, pilot safe. 2 353FG P-51s collided on t/o, Cat E. 357FG P-51 cr. landing, pilot safe. On return 356FG P-51 cr. Biggleswade, pilot k. Aborting 56FG P-47 cr. Clacton, pilot safe.

OTHER OPERATIONS: 25FG despatched 2 Mosquitoes on PR Brux area (6 P-51 escort), 4 Mosquitoes on WR Continent, and B-17s on WR Azores/Atlantic/UK. 1 Mosquito on *Red Stocking* operation Holland. 36BS despatched 4 B-24s on RCM. ASR despatched 12 P-47s on patrols.

INCIDENT

The winter weather of 1944–45 was exceptionally bad in England. The frequent rains of the autumn were followed by many days of persistent fog – some of the worst this century – which gave way to freezing conditions and several weeks of snow, thaw and snow again during the New Year. The lot of the ground crews was miserable and the whole effort to sustain operations made exceedingly difficult. An insight on the problems that could arise in launching a mission in appalling weather conditions can be found in the following extract from the records of 493rd Group then based at Debach, Suffolk.

'It is sincerely hoped that no future mission will be as difficult to get airborne as was this Group's hundredth mission on 10 January. To say business was *unusual* that day would certainly be a case of gross understatement. It had snowed immediately before take-off, making taxiing in the darkness even more tricky than usual, with the result that several aircraft got stuck off hardstands. After the first few planes were airborne, Lt Butler's plane crashed and exploded two miles north of the field. Not long thereafter, the perimeter collapsed beneath an aircraft just arriving at the take-off position on the only runway that could be used. Plans were immediately changed to taxi aircraft downwind on the runway in use, so that they could execute a 180 degree turn just before reaching the plane blocking the take-off position and start their take-off roll from there. Shortly after this plan was put into operation, another plane had a tyre blow out on the runway in use. Regardless of all the difficulties encountered that morning, 30 aircraft were despatched on their mission.'

INCIDENT

With the large scale operations conducted by 8th Air Force, accident and error were inevitable through human fallibility, the limitations of aircraft and equipment and the hostile environment. Good bombing and the destruction of targets became commonplace; it was the occasional lapses that tended to attract undue attention among bomber men. The 305th Bomb Group, a 'pioneer' organisation with a very distinguished record, suffered one of its most humiliating maulings on 10 January 1945, while engaged in a mission that should not have been particularly difficult. The 1st Division was attacking enemy airfields and the 305th primary target was Gymnich with nearby Cologne marshalling yards as secondary, both some 30 miles beyond the Allied front line. As cloud might obscure the targets a 305th lead crew collected a special GH pathfinder from the 379th Group – which specialised in this technique using the radio signals beamed by ground stations to help establish a bomb release point. Upon reaching the Cologne area persistent contrails marred visibility and a run was started on the secondary. The lead bomber then saw that Gymnich was clear and turned for a visual attack on the briefed approach from the south-east. Unfortunately the 13-plane formation was battling against a 100 mph headwind which severely reduced speed, and so allowed the anti-aircraft defences a better opportunity to obtain accurate range and altitude data. The lead 305th Fortress passed over Gymnich airfield without releasing its bombs and thus the rest of the formation also held their loads. A left turn was made and the squadron manoeuvred for another attempt. Flak had caused damage to a few aircraft – one so badly that it had to head for friendly territory. On the second run, to the amazement of crews in following aircraft, the lead plane again failed to drop. By now the flak gunners had really got the measure of the bombers five miles above, putting a very accurate barrage amongst them and bringing down one of the B-17s and damaging most of the others. Six were so badly hit that, coming off target, they jettisoned bombs and headed west. The squadron leader was still determined to bomb the target and prepared to make a third run but by now only three Fortresses remained and so this attempt was finally abandoned. Why the lead bombardier's bombs had twice failed to drop was a mystery, until the discovery that the bomb rack electrical switches were in the 'off' position. Standing operating procedure in the 305th Group called for these to be set to 'on' after the bay had been loaded; in the 379th Group the procedure was to leave the switches 'off' until the bomb fuse pins were removed during assembly. These conflicting practices precipitated this abortive attack which cost eleven men killed, two wounded, plus one B-17 shot down, another abandoned over Belgium, one wrecked in a crash-landing at Le Culot and the rest damaged to varying degrees. The lead bombardier later had to appear before a court martial but was exonerated. Conflicting group practices were adjudged the major cause. Nevertheless, for some, tragic failures of this kind always left the worrying thought, so hard to come to terms with, that they might inadvertently have contributed to the circumstances in which their comrades met their deaths.

11 JANUARY 1945

7PG despatched 9 F-5s on PR Germany. 1 F-5 damaged. 25BG despatched 2 Mosquitoes on WR Germany, and 3 B-17s on WR Azores/Atlantic/UK. 4FG provided 8 P-51s (2 effective) for PR escort.

11/12 JANUARY 1945

8AF 790 NIGHT LEAFLET OPERATION

NLS despatched 2 B-17s and 6 B-24s (4 a/c effective); Belgium.

12 JANUARY 1945

25BG despatched 4 Mosquitoes on WR Low Countries, Germany, and 5 B-17s on WR Azores/Atlantic/UK.

Flying conditions were atrocious on 13 January and led to several accidents. One of these 355FG pilots being briefed for the escort to southern Germany was to be killed in a crash, believed due to icing, soon after take-off. Tail colours of B-24 units usually escorted by the Group are exhibited on map. Blackboard gives times and places on mission route. (355FG Assoc)

13 JANUARY 1945

8AF 791

	Despatched		Effective	Target		Bombs Tonnage	E/A	Losses MIA	E	Dam	Casualties KIA	WIA	MIA
3AD	B-17	367	31	MAINZ R/B	(P)	61.0		2	1	126	1	4	19
			95	MAINZ/ GUSTAVSBURG R/B	(P)	238.5							
			119	BISCHOFSHEIM M/Y	(P)	294.5							
			74	MAINZ M/Y	(S)	160.5							
			13	EUSKIRCHEN	(O)	29.5							
			7	T/O		17.0							
2AD	B-24	276	86	WORMS R/B	(P)	235.0		1	1	39	0	2	10
			87	KAISERSLAUTERN M/Y	(P)	248.7							
			89	RÜDESHEIM R/B	(P)	231.5							
			1	T/O		3.0							
1AD	B-17	315	71	GERMERSHEIM R/B	(P)	212.0		5	4	9	3	7	42
			76	MANNHEIM H/R & R/B	(P)	228.0							
			159	MAXIMILIANSAU R/B	(P)	477.0							
			1	T/O		3.0							
TOTALS:		958	909			2439.2	0	8	6	174	4	13	71
	P-51	80	79	ESCORT 3AD				0	3				
	P-51	118	114	ESCORT 2AD				1	1				
	P-51	82	77	ESCORT 1AD				0	2				
	P-47	37	102	SWEEP–FREELANCE			3–0–0	0					
	P-51	75		SUPPORT BOMBERS			3–0–1(G)	1	1				
	P-51	4	4	ESCORT PR				0	0				
	P-51	45	45	FIGHTER-BOMBER MANNHEIM–TRIER ETC		11.5		0	0				
	P-51	28	20	SCOUTING FORCES				0	0				
TOTALS:		469	441			11.5	3–0–0 3–0–0(G)	2	7	?	8	1	1

REMARKS: Marshalling yards and Rhine rail bridges. 3AD used Micro H and 2AD GH but some formations in both Forces able to bomb visually. 1AD used GH at Germersheim and attacked other targets visually. Bomb groups participating:– all 1AD except 91BG, 306BG, 351BG, 384BG; all 2AD; all 3AD except 490BG. Bomb group losses:– 1AD – 303BG – 3, 457BG – 1; 2AD – 448BG – 1; 3AD – 96BG – 1, 493BG – 1. B/d 398BG B-17 c/l base. 2 398BG B-17s f/l France – Cat E. B/d 448BG B-24 abandoned over Stowmarket, a/c cr. Sarrat.

All Fighter groups except 20FG, 78FG, 364FG operating. Fighter group e/a credits:– 55FG – 3. Fighter group losses:– 55FG – 1, 479FG – 1. MIA 479FG P-51 ditched off Clacton, pilot rescued but died. 78FG P-51 cr. t/o base, pilot killed. 353FG P-51 cr. t/o base, pilot killed. 359FG P-51 cr. Ashill after t/o, pilot killed. 357FG P-51 cr. Butley after t/o, pilot killed. 356FG P-51 cr. Grundisburgh after t/o, pilot killed. 357FG P-51 cr. Laxfield after t/o, pilot k. 355FG P-51 cr. Melbourn, pilot k. Weather bad – icing and extensive cloud.

OTHER OPERATIONS: 7PG despatched 6 F-5s and 1 Spitfire (1 F-5 aborted) on PR Germany (1 F-5 had 4 P-51 escort). 25BG despatched 3 Mosquitoes 'chaff' screening for bombers, 4 Mosquitoes on WR Continent, and 4 B-17s on WR Azores/Atlantic/UK. 2 Mosquitoes on a special operation aborted. 36BS despatched 5 B-24s on RCM. ASR despatched 8 P-47s on patrols. B/d 34BG B-17 c/l Manston A/F. B/d 303BG B-17 cr. Continent.

14 JANUARY 1945

8AF 792

	Despatched		Effective	Target		Bombs Tonnage	E/A	Losses MIA	E	Dam	Casualties KIA	WIA	MIA
3AD	B-17	370	186	DERBEN O/I	(P)	550.8	31–9–7	6	1	121	0	4	149
			90	MAGDEBURG O/I	(P)	222.5							
			36	HALLENDORF	(S)	87.8							
			8	OSNABRÜCK M/Y	(O)	24.0							
			19	T/O		51.8							
2AD	B-24	348	91	HEMMINGSTEDT O/I	(P)	250.5		0	1	80	8	1	0
			89	EHMEN P.O.L. DEPOT	(P)	237.0							
			145	HALLENDORF O/I	(P)	386.8							
			1	WANGEROOGE ISLAND	(O)	3.0							
1AD	B-17	187	36	COLOGNE/ RODENKIRCHEN H/B	(P)	106.5		1	3	92	0	4	10
			71	COLOGNE/DEUTZ H/B	(P)	210.0							
			67	COLOGNE/ HOHENZOLLERN H/B	(P)	190.0							
			1	BERG	(O)	3.0							
			1	COLOGNE	(O)	3.0							
	B-17	6	6	SCREENING FORCE				0	0	0			
TOTALS:		911	847			2326.7	31–9–7	7	5	293	8	9	159
	P-51	331	295	ESCORT 3AD			89½–0–14 3 –0– 5(G)	5	3		0	0	5
	P-51	295	261	ESCORT 2AD			14½–0– 0	1	1		0	0	1
	P-51	42	40	ESCORT 1AD			9 –0– 5	2	0		0	1	2
	P-47	62	116	SWEEP N GERMANY			42 –0– 6	2	1		0	0	2
	P-51	76						1	0		0	0	1
	P-51	22	19	ESCORTING PR				0	0		0	0	0
	P-51	32	30	SCOUTING FORCES				0	0		0	0	0
TOTALS:		860	761				155 –0–25 3 –0– 5(G)	11	5		0	1	11

REMARKS: Oil refineries and plants in central Germany and highway bridges at Cologne. Clear skies allowed all bombers to attack visually. Bomb groups participating:– all 3AD except 388BG and 452BG; all 2AD; all 1AD except 41CBW groups and 305BG. Bomb group losses:– 1AD – 91BG – 1, 3AD – 34BG – 2, 390BG – 9, 487BG – 4, 493BG – 1. 2 B-17s MIA collided over Holland. B/d 351BG B-17 cr. Belgium. 91BG B-17 c/l Denain A/F – Cat E. On return, 458BG B-24 cr. on landing approach to base at Mile Cross, Norwich; 8 k. 381BG B-17 cr. Continent. MIA 493BG B-17 in Sweden.

All Fighter groups operating. Strong Luftwaffe fighter reaction. Fighter group e/a credits:– 20FG – 21, 55FG – 2, 56FG – 19, 78FG – 14, 382FG – 5½, 353FG – 9, 355FG – 18, 356FG – 13, 357FG – 48½, 359FG – 7, 479FG – 1. 357FG claim of 56½ aerial victories was the largest number ever shot down by a group on one mission. Fighter group losses:– 55FG – 1, 56FG – 2, 78FG – 1, 339FG – 1, 356FG – 1, 357FG – 3, 359FG – 1, 361FG – 1. MIA 339FG P-51 hit electric cables while strafing. 339FG P-51 cr. after t/o, pilot injured. One 56FG P-47 MIA cr. in sea 25 miles off Clacton, pilot baled but lost. 364FG P-51 cr. after t/o, pilot safe. 56FG P-47 cr. t/o – Cat E.

OTHER OPERATIONS: 7PG despatched 12 F-5s and 4 Spitfires (15 a/c effective) on PR Germany (19 P-51 escort). 25BG despatched 2 Mosquitoes on H2X sortie Brüx, 4 Mosquitoes on WR Continent, and 3 B-17s on WR Azores/Atlantic/UK. ASR despatched 24 P-47s on patrols. 1 B-17, 1 B-24, 10 P-51s on radio-relays.

INCIDENT

2/Lt Emery Taylor considered he was more than lucky to be alive after what occurred on a bomber escort on 14 January. His 352nd Group Mustang developed engine trouble, stalled and lost 10,000 ft before he could right it and regain power. The P-51 was now flying low in the vicinity of the ground fighting and was promptly greeted with some accurate flak which put three holes through the cockpit hood, wrecked the rudder controls and set the engine on fire. Taylor climbed to 6,000 ft, jettisoned the hood, released his safety straps and tried to go over the side but the slipstream was so strong it toppled him back into the cockpit. He again pulled himself up to escape and although successful the slipstream hurled him back against the armour plate projection behind the seat. About 30 minutes later the 21-year-old pilot regained consciousness to find he was suspended some 10 feet above the ground. Looking up he saw that his open parachute and lines had wrapped round the branch of a tree through which he had evidently plunged. His clothing was torn, he had bruises and scratches and a sore head. Then, to his amazement, he noticed the rip cord of his parachute was still in place. Evidently when he had been knocked out in striking the armour plate his parachute pack had snagged some projection causing the canopy to blossom out as he fell to earth.

14/15 JANUARY 1945

8AF 793 NIGHT LEAFLET OPERATION

NLS despatched 2 B-17s and 5 B-24s; SE Belgium, Germany.

15 JANUARY 1945

8AF 794

	Despatched		Effective	Target		Bombs Tonnage	E/A	Losses MIA	E	Dam	Casualties KIA	WIA	MIA
1AD	B-17	223	111	INGOLSTADT M/Y	(P)	266.4		0	0	5	0	0	0
			107	FREIBURG M/Y	(P)	269.0							
			1	REUDENSTADT M/Y	(O)	2.5							
2AD	B-24	120	75	REUTLINGEN M/Y	(S)	156.5			1				
			19	TÜBINGEN	(O)	51.0							
			10	URICH	(O)	21.0							
			7	TÜBINGEN M/Y	(O)	13.5							
			1	MAHLBERG	(O)	2.5							
			1	T/O		2.5							
3AD	B-17	297	253	AUGSBURG M/Y	(S)	681.5		0	0	16	1	0	0
			29	BOBINGEN	(O)	66.8							
			5	T/O		13.5							
TOTALS:		640	619			1546.7	0	0	1	21	1	0	0
	P-47	53	183	ESCORT 1AD				0	0		0	0	0
	P-51	139						0	1		0	0	0
	P-51	117	109	ESCORT 1AD			1–0–0	0	0		0	0	0
	P-51	204	184	ESCORT 3AD				2	0		0	0	2
	P-51	167	156	SWEEP–GERMANY			1–0– 0 12–0–19	0	0		0	0	0
	P-51	63	62	FIGHTER-BOMBER GENSINGEN M/Y ETC	(P)	31.0		0	0		0	0	0
	P-51	7	6	ESCORT PR				0	0		0	0	0
	P-51	32	29	SCOUTING FORCES				0	0		0	0	0
TOTALS:		782	729			31.0	14–0–19	2	1	?	0	0	2

REMARKS: Marshalling yards in Germany. 1AD used H2X; 2AD was able to attack visually; 3AD attacked Augsburg using H2X and T/Os visually. Bomb groups participating:– 40CBW, 41CBW groups and 91BG of 1AD; 445BG, 446BG, 448BG, 453BG of 2AD; 45CBW and 93CBW groups and 94BG, 447BG, 487BG of 3AD. A 303BG B-17 f/l France – Cat E. B/d 448BG B-24 c/l on beach near Ostend.

All Fighter groups except 352FG operating. Fighter group e/a credits:– 55FG – 1, 357FG – 1. Fighter group losses:– 55FG – 1, 78FG – 1. 364FG P-51 cr. landing base.

OTHER OPERATIONS: 7PG despatched 2 F-5s and 2 Spitfires (6 P-51s escort for 1 Spitfire) on PR Germany. 1 Spitfire aborted and cr. landing at French base. 25BG despatched 1 Mosquito on PR Germany, 5 Mosquitoes on WR Continent/UK, and 4 B-17s on WR Azores/Atlantic/UK. 36BS despatched 6 B-24s on RCM. ASR despatched 10 P-47s on patrols. 1 B-17, 1 B-24, 2 P-47s, 8 P-51s on radio-relays.

15/16 JANUARY 1945

8AF 795 NIGHT LEAFLET OPERATION

NLS despatched 2 B-17s and 7 B-24s; Holland, Germany.

16 JANUARY 1945

8AF 796

	Despatched		Effective	Target		Bombs Tonnage	E/A	Losses MIA	E	Dam	Casualties KIA	WIA	MIA
2AD	B-24	364	61	MAGDEBURG/ ROTHENSEE O/I	(P)	112.7		2	8	?	3	20	22
			67	RUHLAND O/I	(P)	149.5							
			138	DRESDEN M/Y	(S)	341.8							
			61	MAGDEBURG M/I	(S)	123.7							
			5	T/O		12.2							
3AD	B-17	263	146	DESSAU M/Y	(S)	430.0		0	2	?	1	3	0
			96	BITTERFELD C/I	(S)	273.0							
			4	T/O		12.0							
TOTALS:		627	578			1454.9	0	2	10	?	4	23	22

P-51	392	368	ESCORT 2AD			1	7				
P-51	203	194	ESCORT 3AD			0	0				
P-47	56	68	SWEEP			0	1				
P-51	15					0	0				
P-51	7	5	ARMED PHOTO MISSION			0	0				
P-51	20	19	SCOUTING-FORCES			0	0				
TOTALS:	693	654			0	1	8	?	3	1	1

REMARKS: Planned major strike at oil and industrial targets in Germany frustrated by weather with recalls and cancellations for B-17 Forces. 2AD made visual and H2X attacks and 3AD all H2X. Bomb groups participating: all 2AD; 4CBW and 93CBW groups of 3AD. Bomb group losses:– 93BG – 1, 448BG – 1. During assembly 34BG B-17 cr. Ampton, 1 k. On return, 2 b/d 392BG B-24s abandoned over France; 2 392BG B-24s c/l France, 1 392BG B-24 cr. Tuddenham A/F. 458BG B-24 c/l Dijon. 95BG B-17 cr. France. Because of heavy ground fog over English bases 70 B-24s landed on Continent and several B-17s groups at airfields in West of England. 44BG B-24 cr. France, crew baled; 44BG B-24 abandoned over UK, crew baled.

All Fighter groups except 20FG and 78FG operating. Fighter group losses:– 4FG – 1. Bad weather caused 273 P-51s of first Force and 89 of second to land on Continent. 9 fighters cr. or c/l in England – 3 pilots killed. 359FG P-51 cr. t/o base, pilot killed; 357FG P-51 cr. Earl Soham, pilot killed. On return, 4FG P-51 cr. near Lympne A/F, pilot k.; 4FG P-51 cr. near Folkestone, pilot baled. 56FG P-47 cr. Clacton, pilot baled; another 56FG P-47 cr. near base, pilot baled.

OTHER OPERATIONS: 7PG despatched 1 Spitfire on PR Berlin and Misburg. 25BG despatched 2 Mosquitoes on H2X sorties W. Germany, 3 Mosquitoes on WR Low Countries/Germany and 5 B-17s on WR Azores/Atlantic/UK. 36BS despatched 5 B-24s on RCM. ASR despatched 10 P-47s on patrols. 1 B-17, 2 P-47s, 12 P-51s on radio-relays.

16/17 JANUARY 1945

8AF 797 NIGHT LEAFLET OPERATION

NLS despatched 1 B-24; Belgium.

The 491BG pathfinder leading 14CBW on 17 January took a direct hit in the wing.

17 JANUARY 1945

8AF 798

	Despatched		Effective	Target	Bombs Tonnage	E/A	Losses MIA	E	Dam	Casualties KiA	WIA	MIA
3AD	B-17	158	40	HAMBURG/RHENANIA (P) O/I	106.2		4	0	88	0	1	39
			34	HAMBURG/ALBRECHT (P) O/I	100.0							
			73	HAMBURG U/B (P)	224.0							
			1	T/O	3.0							
2AD	B-24	84	78	HARBURG/RHENANIA (P) O/I	187.0		4	1	57	0	7	44
			1	BORKUM A/F (O)	3.0							
1AD	B-17	458	397	PADERBORN M/Y (P)	1154.0		1	0	6	0	0	9
			37	BIELEFELD/ SCHILDESCHE R/V (P)	105.0							
			4	T/O	11.5							
TOTALS:		700	665		1893.7	0	9	1	151	0	8	72
	P-47	49	61	ESCORT 3AD			0	1		0	0	0
	P-51	25					3	0		0	0	3
	P-51	55	46	ESCORT 2AD			2	0		0	0	2
	P-51	118	108	ESCORT 1AD			1	0		0	0	1
	P-51	87	80	SWEEP			0	0		0	0	0
	P-51	28	25	SCOUTING FORCES			1	0		0	0	1
TOTALS:		362	320			0	7	1	?	0	0	7

REMARKS: Visual attacks on oil refineries at Hamburg and Harburg. GH and H2X attacks on rail targets. Bomb groups participating:– 3AD – 13CBW groups and 96BG, 452BG; 2AD – 44BG, 93BG, 389BG, 445BG, 458BG, 467BG, 491BG; 1AD – all groups. Bomb group losses:– 1AD – 351BG – 1; 2AD – 93BG – 2, 458BG – 1, 491BG – 1; 3AD – 452BG – 4. MIA a/c landing in Sweden: 1 – 93BG, 1 – 458BG, 2 – 452BG.

All Fighter groups except 55FG, 352FG, 359FG, 361FG operating. Fighter group losses:– 4FG – 1, 20FG – 1, 78FG – 2, 339FG – 2, 355FG – 1. 78FG P-51 cr. on t/o base. 78FG P-51 MIA in sea 55 miles E. Gt.Yarmouth, pilot baled, lost. 4FG P-51 pilot baled going out 20 miles E. Lowestoft, lost.

OTHER OPERATIONS: 25FG despatched 1 Mosquito on H2X PR, 4 Mosquitoes on WR Continent/UK, and 2 B-17s Azores/Atlantic/UK. 36BS despatched 7 B-24s on RCM. ASR despatched 20 P-47s on patrols. 1 B-24, 4 P-51s on radio-relays. 4 a/c on special operation.

18 JANUARY 1945

8AF 799

		Despatched	Effective	Target	Bombs Tonnage	E/A	Losses MIA	E	Dam	Casualties KIA	WIA	MIA
3AD	B-17	114	114	KAISERSLAUTERN B/R(P)	322.3							
	B-17	6	6	SCREENING FORCE								
TOTALS:		120	120		322.3	0	0	0	0	0	0	0
	P-51	113	105	ESCORT			3	0		0	0	3
	P-51	4	4	SCOUTING FORCES			0	0		0	0	0
TOTALS:		117	109			0	3	0	?	0	0	3

REMARKS: Bad weather limited operations. Only 4CBW groups (less 447BG) attacked rail targets, using H2X. Escort provided by 55FG, 353FG, 355FG, 356FG. Fighter group losses:– 55FG – 1, 353FG – 1, 356FG – 1. MIA 356FG P-51 spun into sea off Clacton.

OTHER OPERATIONS: 25BG despatched 4 Mosquitoes on WR Continent/UK and 4 B-17s on WR Azores/Atlantic/UK. 36BS despatched 7 B-24s on RCM. ASR despatched 10 P-47s on patrols.

19 JANUARY 1945

7PG despatched 2 F-5s on PR Lorient area. 25BG despatched 2 Mosquitoes on H2X sorties Rastatt and Germersheim areas, 2 Mosquitoes on WR Continent and 4 B-17s on WR Azores/Atlantic/UK.

19/20 JANUARY 1945

8AF 800 NIGHT LEAFLET OPERATION

NLS despatched 2 B-17s and 9 B-24s; Holland, Belgium, Germany.

482BG despatched 3 B-17s on H2X scope photo sorties; Frankfurt, Mannheim, Kaiserslautern.

20 JANUARY 1945

8AF 801

		Despatched	Effective	Target	Bombs Tonnage	E/A	Losses MIA	E	Dam	Casualties KIA	WIA	MIA
3AD	B-17	154	12	STERKRADE/HOLTEN O/I (P)	33.0		1	1	39	5	16	52
			115	RHEINE M/Y (S)	306.2							
1AD	B-17	155	24	STERKRADE/HOLTEN O/I (P)	60.0		0	1	29	3	17	9
			110	RHEINE M/Y (S)	263.0							
3AD	B-17	223	187	HEILBRONN M/Y (P)	545.3		2	1	18			
			8	PFORZHEIM M/Y (S)	22.7							
			2	T/O	6.0							
1AD	B-17	230	170	MANNHEIM N & R/B (P)	418.5		1	4	29			
			21	MANNHEIM (O)	52.5							
			24	STUTTGART (O)	60.0							
			1	T/O	2.5							
	B-17	10	10	SCREENING FORCE								
TOTALS:		772	684		1769.7	0	4	7	115	8	33	61
	P-51	103	95	ESCORT 3AD 1st FORCE			1			0	0	1
	P-51	96	94	ESCORT 1AD 1st FORCE			0			0	0	0
	P-51	48	39	ESCORT 3AD 2nd FORCE			0			0	0	0
	P-51	137	130	ESCORT 1AD 2nd FORCE		1–0–0	1			0	0	1
	P-51	39	36	FRANKFURT – SWEEP			1			0	0	1
	P-51	16	16	ST. VITH/DÜREN – SWEEP			0			0	0	0
	P-51	16	16	SCOUTING FORCES			0			0	0	0
TOTALS:		455	426			1–0–0	3	0	?	0	0	3

REMARKS: Synthetic oil industry at Sterkrade. Rail targets and bridges in Western Germany. All Forces used H2X. 1AD T/Os attacked visually. Bomb groups participating:– 3AD first force comprised 34BG, 388BG, 452BG, 490BG; 1AD first force comprised 305BG, 306BG, 351BG, 457BG; 3AD second force consisted of 13CBW and 4BW groups less 94BG; 1AD second force consisted of 1CBW and 41CBW groups. Bomb group losses:– 1AD – 398BG – 1; 3AD – 95BG – 1, 390BG – 1, 452BG – 1. 34BG B-17 cr. Gipping after t/o, 2 killed. Aborting 91BG c/l base. On return a 384BG B-17 cr. Clopton and another 384BG B-17 cr. Tur Langton after crew baled in a severe snowstorm. B/d 379BG B-17 c/l on return. B/d 390BG B-17 c/l Steinbourg.

Fighter groups operating: 4FG, 78FG, 339FG, 353FG, 355FG, 357FG, 359FG, 364FG. Fighter group e/a credits:– 357FG – 2. Fighter group losses:– 78FG – 1, 355FG – 1, 357FG – 1.

OTHER OPERATIONS: 7PG despatched 3 F-5s on PR Germany. 25BG despatched 4 Mosquitoes (1 aborted) screening bombers, 5 Mosquitoes on WR Continent/UK and 3 B-17s on WR Azores/Atlantic/UK. 36BS despatched 8 B-24s on RCM. ASR despatched 10 P-47s on patrols.

INCIDENT

Mustangs of 357th Group accounted for two Me 262 jets during an escort to the Munich area on 20 January. One fell to the guns of 1/Lt Dale Karger when the Luftwaffe pilot, unwisely executing a sharp turn, lost speed and allowed his pursuers to come within firing range. This was Karger's fifth victory, according him the accolade of acehood – the fortieth such in his group. Only 19 years old, Karger was probably the youngest man in the 8th Air Force to become an ace. Although many of his fellow fighter pilots at Leiston were only a few months his senior, they were not above teasing Karger with the nickname 'Bobby Socks'.

20/21 JANUARY 1945

482BG despatched 2 B-17s (1 aborted) on H2X scope sorties.

21 JANUARY 1945

8AF 803

	Despatched		Effective	Target		Bombs Tonnage	E/A	Losses MIA	E	Dam	Casualties KIA	WIA	MIA
1AD	B-17	379	257	ASCHAFFENBURG M/Y	(P)	735.8		2	2	4	18	0	2
			66	ASCHAFFENBURG O/I	(P)	195.0							
			24	PFORZHEIM M/Y	(O)	72.0							
			3	MANNHEIM/LANZ AFV	(O)	9.0							
3AD	B-17	382	254	MANNHEIM M/Y	(P)	709.5		6	3	53	3	12	55
			21	MANNHEIM/LANZ AFV	(P)	51.8							
			16	MANNHEIM H & R/B	(P)	47.5							
			10	PFORZHEIM M/Y	(O)	30.0							
			4	SPEYER	(O)	12.0							
			3	T/O		8.6							
2AD	B-24	152	68	HEILBRONN M/Y	(P)	155.1		0	4	2	0	3	0
			11	PFORZHEIM M/Y	(O)	30.2							
			14	ARNBACH C/C	(O)	31.0							
			1	MANNHEIM C/C	(O)	3.0							
			1	REUTLINGEN	(O)	1.5							
TOTALS:		912	753			2092.0	0	8	9	59	21	15	57
	P-51	139	112	ESCORT 1AD									
	P-51	150	138	ESCORT 3AD			2–0–0(G)						
	P-47 P-51	32 98	120	ESCORT 2AD			6–0–1(G)						
	P-51	48	45	FIGHTER SWEEP									
	P-51	26	26	SCOUTING FORCES									
	P-51	7	6	ARMED PHOTO – PÖLITZ									
	P-51	23	22	ESCORT PR									
TOTALS:		523	469				8–0–1(G)	0			0	0	0

REMARKS: Industrial and rail targets in central Germany. 1AD used GH and H2X; 3AD used Micro H and H2X; 2AD used H2X and primary and attacked other targets visually. Bomb groups participating:– all 1AD except 92BG; all 3AD except 34BG, 94BG; 14CBW groups and 446BG, 453BG, 458BG, 466BG of 2AD. Bomb group losses:– 1AD – 303BG – 2; 3AD – 96BG – 1, 385BG – 1, 388BG – 1, 390BG – 1, 486BG – 1, 493BG – 1. 385BG cr. Bradwell near Coggeshall during assembly. On return a 390BG B-17 cr. into sea off Southwold; 2 381BG B-17s collided on return base, 18 k. Yeldham, 458BG c/l Woodbridge A/F. 458BG B-24 c/l near Rheims. 453BG B-24 abandoned over France, crew baled. 447BG B-17 abandoned over France, crew baled, 2 killed. 44BG B-24 cr. Continent. 490BG B-17 cr. Continent.

All Fighter groups except 353BG, 359FG, 361FG, 364FG operating. No loss or claims.

OTHER OPERATIONS: 7PG despatched 4 F-5s on PR Germany. 25BG despatched 2 Mosquitoes on PR Germany, 2 Mosquitoes (1 aborted) on H2X sortie Germany, 5 Mosquitoes on WR Continent/UK, and 4 B-17s on WR Azores/Atlantic/UK. 1 Mosquito MIA. 36BS despatched 5 B-24s on RCM. ASR despatched 14 P-47s on patrols.

INCIDENT

Following experiments in the autumn of 1944, selected aircraft in P-51 fighter groups were fitted with a camera fixed to the rear of the pilot's armoured seat to take oblique angle photographs. This enabled additional photographic intelligence to be gathered about targets attacked or other installations in enemy territory. An example of the useful part these K-25 cameras could play was well illustrated by the mission of 21 January when a flight from 355th Group's 358th Fighter Squadron was briefed to photograph the Pölitz oil refineries near Stettin soon after the heavy bombers had attacked them. Led by Capt Noble Peterson, three camera-equipped Mustangs made runs through the heavy but inaccurate Pölitz flak at 20,000 and 15,000 ft. On the way home two Me 262s attempted interception but were driven off – being armed the P-51s had an advantage over normal photo reconnaissance aircraft. Photographs obtained produced prints of such clarity that it was possible for interpreters to assess the damage to production to such an extent that another proposed mission to the Pölitz plant was cancelled.

21/22 JANUARY 1945

8AF 804 NIGHT LEAFLET OPERATION

NLS despatched 2 B-17s and 9 B-24s; Holland, France, Germany.

482BG despatched 2 B-17s on H2X scope sorties.

25BG despatched 3 Mosquitoes on night PR Holland, 1 Mosquito aborted and cr. landing, base.

22 JANUARY 1945

8AF 805

	Despatched		Effective	Target	Bombs Tonnage	E/A	Losses MIA	E	Dam	Casualties KIA	WIA	MIA
1AD	B-17	206	167	STERKRADE/HOLTEN(P) O/I	402.0		5	3	144	0	13	45
			1	RHEINE M/Y (S)	2.5							
			12	DINSLAKEN (O)	28.8							
			5	OSNABRÜCK (O)	10.0							
			8	HEIDEN (O)	20.0							
			4	T/O	10.0							
TOTALS:		206	197		473.3	0	5	3	144	0	13	45
	P-47	36	85	ESCORT 1AD		3–0–1(G)	0	0		0	0	0
	P-51	75					0	0		0	0	0
	P-51	136	128	SWEEP – ST.VITH/ KARLSRUHE DARMSTADT/KOBLENZ AREAS			1	0		0	0	1
	P-51	11	10	SCOUTING FORCE			0	0		0	0	0
TOTALS:		258	223			3–0–1(G)	1	0	?	0	0	1

REMARKS: Visual attack on synthetic oil plant at Sterkrade and T/Os by 41CBW and 96CBW groups and 91BG, 398BG. Bomb group losses:– 303BG – 1, 351BG – 1, 384BG – 2, 457BG – 1. During assembly a 401BG B-17 cr. Saltby. On return a 398BG B-17 f/l Continent – Cat E. B/d 91BG B-17 c/l Metfield A/F.

Fighter groups operating: 56FG, 78FG, 352FG, 356FG, 361FG. Fighter group losses:– 361FG – 1.

OTHER OPERATIONS: 7PG despatched 2 F-5s PR Germany, 1 F-5 PR French Atlantic coast. 1 F-5 cr. after refuelling stop Manston. 25BG despatched 2 Mosquitoes on H2X special operation, 3 Mosquitoes 'chaff' screening, 5 Mosquitoes on WR Continent/UK, and 4 B-17s on WR Azores/Atlantic/UK. 1 WR Mosquito MIA. ASR despatched 4 P-47s on patrols. 36BS despatched 7 B-24s on RCM.

22/23 JANUARY 1945

8AF 806 NIGHT LEAFLET OPERATION

NLS despatched 1 B-17 and 8 B-24s; Holland, France,

25BG despatched 3 Mosquitoes (2 effective) on night PR Holland. Aborting a/c c/l Foulsham A/F, crew inj.

492BG despatched 1 B-24 on special operations.

Thick black smoke from burning fuel fills the afternoon sky at Old Catton, and marks the spot of yet another crash. All the crew were killed in this 467BG B-24. The cause, loss of engine power on one side during a turn. Non-operational, 22 January.

23 JANUARY 1945

8AF 807

	Despatched		Effective	Target		Bombs Tonnage	E/A	Losses MIA	E	Dam	Casualties KIA	WIA	MIA
1AD	B-17	99	88	NEUSS M/Y	(P)	252.0		1	3	41	4	4	10
3AD	B-17	110	81	NEUSS M/Y	(P)	24.2		0	0	54	1	2	0
			12	NEUSS BRIDGE	(O)	36.0							
TOTALS:		209	181			312.2	0	1	3	95	5	6	10
	P-51	79	74	ESCORT BOMBERS				0	1				
	P-51	75	68	SWEEP – TACTICAL AREA			1–0–0	0	0				
	P-51	17	16	SCOUTING FORCE				0	0				
TOTALS:		171	158				1–0–0	0	1	?	0	0	0

REMARKS: The attack on Neuss M/Y carried out with GH by 1AD Force and Micro H by 3AD Force, both supplemented by H2X. Bomb groups participating:– 41CBW groups and 398BG of 1AD; 34BG, 95BG, 390BG, 493BG of 3AD. Bomb group losses:– 91BG – 1. MIA 91BG B-17 was PFF a/c leading 398BG and with that group's CO on board. 379BG B-17 cr. after t/o into base quarters, 4 crew and 5 e/m k. B-17 cr. landing Wendling A/F. B/d 398BG B-17 c/l Continent.

Fighter groups operating: 352FG, 353FG, 355FG. 353FG P-51 c/l north of Antwerp, pilot safe. 355FG P-51 c/l base.

23 JANUARY 1945

OTHER OPERATIONS: 25BG despatched 2 Mosquitoes and 1 P-38 on H2X sorties Germany, 1 Mosquito 'chaff' screening for 1AD, 4 Mosquitoes on WR Continent and 5 B-17s on WR Azores/Atlantic/UK. 36BS despatched 5 B-24s on RCM. ASR despatched 6 P-47s on patrols.

23/24 JANUARY 1945

8AF 808 NIGHT LEAFLET OPERATION

NLS despatched 5 B-24s; Holland.

24 JANUARY 1945

No offensive operations from UK. 352FG and 361FG flew patrols and sweeps from bases in Belgium, 70 a/c despatched and 67 effective on four separate flights. Fighter group e/a credits:– 352FG – 3. Fighter group losses:– 352FG – 1. 25BG despatched 1 Mosquito on *Red Stocking* operation Holland, 2 Mosquitoes on WR Continent and 3 B-17s Azores/Atlantic/UK. 36BS despatched 5 B-24s on RCM.

25 JANUARY 1945

No offensive operations from UK. 352FG and 361FG flew sweeps in the tactical area; 122 P-51s despatched 111 P-51s effective. Fighter group e/a credits:– 361FG – 2. Fighter group losses:– 361FG – 1.

7PG despatched 2 F-5s on PR W. Germany. 25BG despatched 3 B-17s on WR Azores/Atlantic/UK.

26 JANUARY 1945

361FG despatched 32 P-51s (1 aborted) on patrol of battle front area. 7PG despatched 3 F-5s on PR St.Nazaire – Lorient areas. 25BG despatched 2 Mosquitoes on H2X PR Germersheim and Rastatt, 3 Mosquitoes on WR Continent. 36BS despatched 3 B-24s on RCM.

27 JANUARY 1945

25BG despatched 3 Mosquitoes on WR Atlantic/France/Low countries/Germany/North Sea, and 4 B-17s WR Azores/Atlantic/UK.

28 JANUARY 1945

8AF 809

	Despatched		Effective	Target		Bombs Tonnage	E/A	Losses MIA	E	Dam	Casualties KIA	WIA	MIA
2AD	B-24	225	115	KAISERSTUHL O/I	(P)	300.5		7	2	97	2	7	71
			58	GNEISENAU I/O	(P)	154.3							
			5	NEHEIM	(O)	15.0							
			9	LIPPSTADT	(O)	24.3							
			11	T/O		28.0							

continued on next page

28 JANUARY 1945 *(contd.)*

1AD	B-17	421	273	COLOGNE/ GREMBERG M/Y	(P)	659.8		3	0	172			
			69	COLOGNE/ HOHENZOLLERN BR	(P)	170.5							
			7	BIELEFELD	(S)	17.2							
			31	GÜTERSLOH	(S)	76.3							
			3	T/O		7.3							
3AD	B-17	360	169	HOHENBUDBERG M/Y	(P)	447.5		0	2	195	14	20	0
			80	DUISBURG/ RHEINHAUSEN BR	(P)	224.5							
			10	DUISBURG HIGHWAY BR	(S)	29.0							
			13	FRIEMERSHEIM	(O)	39.0							
			2	T/O		8.0							
TOTALS:		1006	855			2201.2	0	10	4	464	16	31	106
	P-51	77	68	ESCORT 2AD									
	P-51	76	69	ESCORT 1AD									
	P-51	38	35	ESCORT 3AD									
	P-51	40	40	TACTICAL AREA SWEEP									
	P-51	18	13	SCOUTING FORCES									
TOTALS:		249	225				0	0	?	0		0	0

REMARKS: With the prospect of improved weather over Germany, a large force of bombers were despatched to attack marshalling yards, bridges and benzol plants at Dortmund. 2AD bombers GH and visual; 1AD, GH and H2X; 3AD Micro H and visual. Bomb groups participating:– all 1AD, all 2AD except 446BG and 467BG; all 3AD except 447BG. Bomb group losses:– 1AD – 92BG – 1, 384BG – 1, 457BG – 1; 2AD – 44BG – 1, 93BG – 3, 389BG – 1, 392BG – 2. 94BG B-17 cr. t/o base, 7 k. MIA 392BG B-24s collided when one hit by flak. On return, b/d 379BG B-17 with only pilot aboard f/l Woodbridge A/F – rest crew baled e/t – Cat E. 486BG B-17 c/l Woodbridge A/F. B/d 44BG B-24 c/l Belgium.

Fighter groups operating: 20FG, 78FG, 355FG, 359FG, 361FG, 479FG.

OTHER OPERATIONS: 7PG despatched 1 F-5 on PR St.Nazaire – Lorient, 1 F-5 on PR Germany. 25BG despatched 3 Mosquitoes (1 aborted) on PR Rastatt and Germersheim, 3 Mosquitoes on 'chaff' for 1AD (1 cr. after t/o) and 1 P-38 on H2X sortie Freiburg. 5 Mosquitoes on WR Continent/UK and 2 B-17s Azores/Atlantic/UK. 36BS despatched 5 B-24s (4 effective) on RCM. ASR despatched 8 P-47s on patrols.

28/29 JANUARY 1945

8AF 810 NIGHT LEAFLET OPERATION

NLS despatched 2 B-17s and 6 B-24s; Holland, Luxemburg, Germany.

482BG despatched 3 B-17s (1 aborted) on H2X scope sorties.

29 JANUARY 1945

8AF 811

	Despatched		Effective	Target		Bombs Tonnage	E/A	Losses MIA	E	Dam	Casualties KIA	WIA	MIA
1AD	B-17	415	144	SIEGEN R/O	(P)	420.3		0	4	7	0	0	0
			110	NIEDERLAHNSTEIN R/C	(P)	326.0							
			104	KOBLENZ/MOSEL M/Y	(S)	304.5							
			37	BAD KREUZNACH M/Y	(O)	107.7							
3AD	B-17	386	93	KASSEL HENSCHEL O/I	(P)	258.2		0	2	28	18	1	0
			154	KASSEL M/Y	(S)	44.3							
			76	BIELEFELD M/Y	(O)	224.0							
			35	KOBLENZ	(O)	100.7							
			2	T/O		6.0							
2AD	B-24	357	124	HAMM M/Y	(S)	329.5		1	0	18	0	0	9
			206	MÜNSTER M/Y	(S)	568.0							
			9	SOEST M/Y	(O)	24.5							
TOTALS:		1158	1094			3113.7	0	1	6	53	18	1	9

	P-51	254	235	ESCORT 1AD	1–0–1	1	1	1	0	5
	P-51	224	207	ESCORT 3AD	4–0–1	0	1	0	0	0
	P-47	37	173	ESCORT 2AD	1–0–0(G)	0	0	0	0	0
	P-51	158				1	0	0	0	1
	P-51	27	23	SCOUTING FORCE		0	0	0	0	0
TOTALS:		700	638		5–0–2 1–0–0(G)	2	2 ?	1	0	6

REMARKS: Industrial plants at Kassel and rail targets in Central Germany were attacked by H2X. All bomb groups except 95BG participated. Bomb group losses:– 389BG – 1. On return 2 96BG B-17s collided and cr. N. Lopham; b/d 398BG B-17 f/l Continent – Cat E. 398BG B-17 cr. landing base. B/d 379BG B-17 c/l on Continent. B/d 384BG B-17 c/l Molesworth A/F.

All Fighter groups except 352FG operating. Fighter group e/a credits:– 55FG – 4. Fighter group losses:– 355FG – 1, 359FG – 1. One P-51 MIA believed shot down in error by 339FG P-51. A 353FG P-51 c/l on t/o, pilot safe. 359FG P-51 cr., pilot k.

OTHER OPERATIONS: 7PG despatched 3 F-5s on PR Germany. 25BG despatched 2 Mosquitoes on PR Rastatt and Germersheim 1 P-38 on H2X sortie, Freiburg. 4 Mosquitoes on WR Continent and 3 B-17s on WR Atlantic/UK. 1 Mosquito flew *Red Stocking* sortie Germany. 36BS despatched 5 B-24s on RCM. 5ERS despatched 10 P-47s on ASR sorties. (The ASR unit given official squadron status from 28/1/45.)

29/30 JANUARY 1945

8AF 812 NIGHT LEAFLET OPERATION

NLS despatched 1 B-17 and 8 B-24s (8 effective) Germany, Holland.

25BG despatched 3 Mosquitoes on night PR Belgium and Germany.

30 JANUARY 1945

7PG despatched 2 F-5s on PR Germany. 25BG despatched 4 B-17s on WR Azores/Atlantic/UK.

31 JANUARY 1945

8AF 813

	Despatched		Effective	Target	Bombs Tonnage	E/A	Losses MIA	E	Dam	Casualties KIA	WIA	MIA
2AD	B-24	291	0	BRUNSWICK, HALLENDORF	0	0	0	3		6	3	0
	B-17	112	0		0	0	0	1		0	5	0
TOTALS:		403	0		0	0	0	4		6	8	0
	P-51	10		SCOUTING FORCE								
	P-51	176	0	ESCORT 2AD								
TOTALS:		186	0			0	0			0	0	0

REMARKS: Doubtful weather conditions for return to bases necessitated re-call of mission. 2AD (2CBW, 20CBW and 96CBW groups) were approaching Dummer Lake when told to return. 3AD was approaching Dutch coast. 453BG B-24 cr. t/o at base, crew safe. On return a 446BG B-24 cr. Tunstall after crew baled near Cambridge. Aborting 100BG B-17 cr. at base. 389BG B-24 cr. Scarborough, 6 k.

OTHER OPERATIONS: 25BG despatched 2 Mosquitoes on WR Continent/UK, and 3 B-17s Azores/Atlantic/UK. 36BS despatched 7 B-24s on RCM.

1 FEBRUARY 1945

8AF 814

	Despatched		Effective	Target		Bombs Tonnage	E/A	Losses MIA	E	Dam	Casualties KIA	WIA	MIA
1AD	B-17	463	74	MANNHEIM M/Y	(P)	217.3		0	2	24	0	3	0
			70	LUDWIGSHAFEN M/Y	(P)	205.4							
			270	MANNHEIM H & R/B	(S)	791.6							
			11	PFORZHEIM	(O)	32.7							
			3	T/O		8.8							
3AD	B-17	236	26	WESEL R/B	(P)	66.0		0	0	2	0	0	0
			113	WESEL R/B	(P)	315.0							
			36	KREFELD M/Y	(S)	103.0							
			13	BARTH	(O)	38.5							
TOTALS:		699	616			1778.3	0	0	2	26	0	3	0

1 FEBRUARY 1945 *(contd.)*

		Despatched	Effective	Target					
	P-51	151	142	ESCORT 1AD					
	P-51	53	49	ESCORT 3AD					
	P-51	22	20	SCOUTING FORCES					
	P-51	102	87	SWEEP–FREELANCE SUPPORT					
TOTALS:		328	298		0	0	0	0	0

REMARKS: Rail targets and bridges in Western Germany. Both B-17 forces used Micro - H and H2X. Bomb groups participating:– all 1AD; 4BW groups and 95BG, 390BG of 3AD. On return b/d 398BG B-17 cr. Hollesley, 3 injured. No bombers or fighters MIA.

Fighter groups operating: 4FG, 20FG, 55FG, 353FG, 357FG, 359FG, 379FG. A 20FG P-51 cr. Luxembourg after pilot forced to bale.

OTHER OPERATIONS: 7PG despatched 2 F-5s on PR St.Nazaire. 25BG despatched 3 Mosquitoes screening for bombers, 4 Mosquitoes on WR Continent/UK, 3 B-17s on WR Azores/Atlantic/UK; 2 Mosquitoes and 1 P-38 on H2X PR Freiburg, Speyer and Germersheim. 36BS despatched 7 B-24s on RCM. 5ERS despatched 13 P-47s on ASR patrols. 4 P-51s as escort for special operation.

1/2 FEBRUARY 1945

8AF 815 NIGHT LEAFLET OPERATION

NLS despatched 9 B-24s (6 effective); Holland, France, Germany.

25BG despatched 2 Mosquitoes on PR Germany.

2 FEBRUARY 1945

352FG despatched 24 P-51s (22 effective) on sweep over Koblenz area. No offensive operations from UK.

25BG despatched 5 Mosquitoes on WR Continent/UK, 2 B-17s on WR Atlantic/UK and 1 P-38 on H2X Germany. 36BS despatched 6 B-24s on RCM. 1 aircraft undertook special mission.

2/3 FEBRUARY 1945

8AF 816 NIGHT LEAFLET OPERATION

NLS despatched 1 B-17 and 8 B-24s; W.Germany.

25BG despatched 2 Mosquitoes on night PR North Germany and 1 Mosquito.

3 FEBRUARY 1945

8AF 817

	Despatched		Effective	Target		Bombs Tonnage	E/A	Losses MIA	E	Dam	Casualties KIA	WIA	MIA
1AD	B-17	467	443	BERLIN/TEMPELHOF M/Y	(P)	1061.0		14	2	184	12	7	110
			1	BROMSCHE	(O)	2.5							
			1	BAD ZWISCHENAHN	(O)	1.5							
			1	SOGEL	(O)	2.5							
3AD	B-17	536	494	BERLIN/TEMPELHOF M/Y	(P)	1205.7		9	4	155	6	4	79
			13	GATOW	(O)	32.0							
			2	LÜNEBURG	(O)	4.5							
			10	T/O		25.0							
2AD	B-24	434	116	MAGDEBURG/ ROTHENSEE O/I	(P)	269.0							
			246	MAGDEBURG M/Y	(L)	572.5							
			17	WESERMÜNDE	(O)	40.0							
			12	MÖCKERN	(O)	30.0		2	1	58	0	0	19
			9	CUXHAVEN	(O)	20.5							
			2	YECHTA A/F	(O)	5.0							
			3	T/O		7.5							
TOTALS:		1437	1370			3279.2	0	25	7	397	18	11	208
	P-51	280	262	ESCORT 1AD			12–1– 0	2	2		0	0	2
	P-51	333	313	ESCORT 3AD			17–0–11 (G)	5	0		0	0	5
	P-51	232	210	ESCORT 2AD				0	0		0	0	0
	P-47	44	41	SWEEP – FRIEDERSDORF A/F			9–0– 6	1	0		0	0	1
	P-51	24	24	ESCORT PR A/C			0–0– 1	0	0		0	0	0
	P-51	35	35	SCOUTING FORCES				0	0		0	0	0
TOTALS:		948	885				21–1– 7 17–0–11(G)	8	2	?	0	0	8

REMARKS: A major attack on Berlin by B-17s while B-24s struck the synthetic oil plant at Magdeburg involved all bomb groups. 1AD bombed visually; 3AD was visual with some use of H2X; 2AD was visual except for Magdeburg M/Y which was an H2X last resort for nearly two thirds of the force when cloud obscured the primary. Bomb group losses:– 1AD – 91BG – 2, 92BG – 1, 305BG – 1, 306BG – 3, 379BG – 1, 381BG – 2, 384BG – 2, 398BG – 2; 2AD – 93BG – 1, 389BG – 1; 3AD – 95BG – 2, 96BG – 1, 100BG – 3, 452BG – 1, 487BG – 1, 493BG – 1. B/d 486BG B-17 c/l behind Soviet lines Poland; b/d 384BG B-17, b/d 401BG B-17 and b/d 490BG B-17 f/l Poland. (384BG and 401BG a/c returned later in month) Berlin Flak brought down 24 B-17s. Two B-17s ditched and 17 men rescued. On return, b/d 398BG c/l Woodbridge A/F, crew safe; 486BG B-17 cr. flames Reydon, 5 k. B/d 306BG B-17 cr. Continent, 7 k. B/d 446BG B-24 cr. Continent. 34BG B-17 Cat E in landing accident. MIA a/c in Sweden: 1 – 306BG, 1 – 452BG.

All Fighter groups operating. Fighter group e/a credits:– 55FG – 12, 56FG – 9. Fighter group losses:– 56FG – 1, 78FG – 3, 352FG – 1, 353FG – 1, 357FG – 1, 364FG – 1. Two 352FG P-51s c/l Continent.

OTHER OPERATIONS: 7PG despatched 9 F-5s and 7 Spitfires (with escorts) on PR Germany. 25BG despatched 3 Mosquitoes on H2X PR Germany, 3 Mosquitoes on 'chaff' screening for bombers, 5 Mosquitoes on WR Continent/UK and 4 B-17s on WR Azores/Atlantic/UK.

5ERS despatched 15 P-47s on ASR search. 36BS despatched 7 B-24s on RCM. 1 B-17, 1 B-24, 4 P-51s on radio-relays.

Contrails streaming, a 381BG Fortress crosses the Tempelhof area. One of the thousand-strong force that attacked the German capital on 3 February.

Taxiing in from the 3 February Berlin raid *La Rhonda* and other Molesworth Fortresses viewed from the control tower. This was 303rd's 311th mission from England, a total unsurpassed by any other group. P-47 in background is 303BG's formation monitoring aircraft.

INCIDENT

Bomber men came to accept losses amongst their number although the hope remained with every mission that their group would escape flak and fighters. When a crew neared the end of a tour the goodwill of every other flier went with them; a boost to faith in each individual's own chances of survival. But nothing shattered that lift to morale more than the loss of a crew near or on their last assigned mission. On 3 February 1945 the Eighth went to Berlin, always a tough one and probably causing some apprehension for 1/Lt Lewis Kloud and crew, although it was not apparent to other men at Sudbury that morning. The 486th Group made the mission without loss and Kloud and crew seemed all but headed for the USA. When the Group's formation let down over the North Sea on return the gunners in the rear of the B-17 went forward to celebrate with the rest of the crew up front. To the horror of men in other 486th B-17s flames suddenly appeared at the waist windows of *Blue Grass Girl* and soon the whole of the rear fuselage was engulfed. The Fortress dropped away from the formation and four parachutes appeared; a fifth man jumped but too late before the flaming mass smashed into a field at Church Farm, Reydon not far from Southwold. Later it was learned that as the gunners could not get back to the rear of the aircraft to get their parachutes, Kloud and the co-pilot had given them theirs. This incident probably did more to dampen morale at Sudbury than any other during the 486th's 188 missions.

INCIDENT

During previous attacks on Berlin and targets in north-east Germany badly damaged bombers had often sought sanctuary in neutral Sweden. With the rapid westwards advance of Soviet forces an alternative was presented when the 8th Air Force attacked the enemy capital on 3 February and was taken by at least six Fortress crews. One was B-17 43-37913, piloted by 1/Lt Arthur Ogle with Maj John Rex as Command Pilot, leading a 486th Group formation. The tremendous flak barrages encountered over Berlin that day disabled an engine on the bomb run and another as the bomber turned for home. A strong head wind was too much for the remaining over-taxed engines and one of these also failed. Rex directed Ogle to try and reach Poland beyond the Soviet battle lines. The Fortress lost height rapidly and was down to about 8,000 ft when passing over an artillery duel which indicated the battle lines. Inevitably the remaining engine under full power began to show signs of serious strain and a successful belly-landing was accomplished in a large field. Before the crew could emerge from the bomber it was surrounded by armed men, Polish partisans who, after satisfying themselves as to the airmen's identity, escorted them to a farmhouse, from where they were later collected by Soviet troops and conveyed to an infantry brigade headquarters. Here food and vodka were provided and toasts drunk to the Allied cause. Russian hospitality was considerable, in the circumstances. General Ceckmosaf, commander of a Soviet tank unit, had the Americans as dinner guests and gave them small items of Soviet and German equipment as souvenirs. Eventually the Fortress men were transported to Kiev and then, from a USAAF base in the Ukraine, flown back to the UK via Tehran, Cairo, Naples, Marseilles and Paris. Understandably the unexpected adventures and travels of the Ogle crew made them celebrities on their return to Sudbury.

3/4 FEBRUARY 1945

8AF 818 NIGHT LEAFLET OPERATION

NLS despatched 1 B-17 and 10 B-24s; Holland, W.Germany.

4 FEBRUARY 1945

7PG despatched 3 F-5s on PR Germany (1 F-5 had 2 P-51 escort). 25BG despatched 3 Mosquitoes on WR UK/Atlantic and 3 B-17s on WR Atlantic. 5ERS despatched 4 P-47s on ASR search and 12 B-17s and 8 P-51s also on ASR search. 1 Mosquito on *Red Stocking* operation SW Germany.

4/5 FEBRUARY 1945

8AF 819 NIGHT LEAFLET OPERATION

NLS despatched 9 B-24s (7 effective); Holland and Germany.

5 FEBRUARY 1945

25BG despatched 5 Mosquitoes on WR Continent/UK and 3 B-17s on WR Azores/Atlantic/UK. 5ERS despatched 8 P-47s on ASR patrols. 25BG despatched 2 Mosquitoes (1 aborted) on H2X PR Kassel. 36BS despatched 7 B-24s on RCM – 1 B-24 MIA. 20FG and 78FG provided a total of 7 P-51s for escort of 2 abortive Mosquito H2X sorties.

5/6 FEBRUARY 1945

8AF 820 NIGHT LEAFLET OPERATION

NLS despatched 2 B-17s and 8 B-24s; Holland, Germany.

And still they come back. Lt Gay brought this badly battle damaged 452BG B-17G Fortress, 44-8527, back to Woodbridge emergency airfield on 6 February. The nose had also been blasted. (S. Evans)

6 FEBRUARY 1945

8AF 821

	Despatched		Effective	Target		Bombs Tonnage	E/A	Losses MIA	E	Dam	Casualties KIA	WIA	MIA
3AD	B-17	535	437	CHEMNITZ M/Y	(S)	824.5		3	10	83	22	7	24
			22	GREIZ	(O)	55.0							
			13	SAALFELD	(O)	32.5							
			22	ZWICKAU	(O)	52.2							
			1	REICHENBACH	(O)	2.5							
			1	SCHMALKALDEN	(O)	2.5							
1AD	B-17	414	37	CHEMNITZ M/Y	(S)	92.3		0	3	32	19	0	0
			88	GOTHA M/Y	(O)	216.5							
			68	GIESSEN	(O)	167.5							
			36	SAALFELD	(O)	90.0							
			35	OHRDRUF	(O)	91.0							
			34	EISFELD	(O)	85.0							
			32	SCHMALKALDEN	(O)	74.5							
			13	EISENACH	(O)	30.0							
			12	WALTERSHAUSEN	(O)	30.0							
			12	DIRLOS	(O)	30.0							
			12	OSTHEIM	(O)	30.0							
			11	FRIEDRICHRODA	(O)	27.5							
			2	STEINBACH	(O)	6.7							
			1	MEPPEN	(O)	2.5							
			1	T/O		1.5							
2AD	B-24	434	418	MAGDEBURG M/Y	(S)	727.2		2	1	61	0	0	18
			1	MEPPEN BRIDGE	(O)	1.0							
			1	QUACKENBRÜCK	(O)	2.5							
TOTALS:		1383	1310			2674.9	0	5	14	176	41	7	42

	P-51	295	272	ESCORT 3AD		3–0–0 (G)	2	6		0	0	2
	P-51	293	273	ESCORT 1AD		1–0–1	2	1		0	0	2
	P-51	262	235	ESCORT 2AD			0	0		0	0	0
	P-51	38	33	SCOUTING FORCE			0	0		0	0	0
	P-51	8	8	ESCORT PR			0	0		0	0	0
	P-51	8	8	ESCORT ASR			0	0		0	0	0
TOTALS:		904	829			1–0–1 3–0–0(G)	4	7	?	0	0	4

REMARKS: All bomb groups except 384BG were despatched to attack oil targets at Lützkendorf, Magdeburg and Böhlen. The expected conditions for visual attack did not materialise and extensive cloud forced attacks on t/o or secondaries by H2X. 1AD was able to carry out some visual bombing. Bomb group losses:– 2AD – 93BG – 1, 466BG – 1; 3AD – 452BG – 1, 487BG – 2. During assembly, 490BG cr. Darsham, crew baled; 453BG B-24 cr. Deopham, 10 k. 490BG and 388BG B-17s collided and cr. Prickwillow and Wicken, crews baled, 1 k and 2 civilians. On return, 486BG B-17 cr. Upper Beeding, Sussex, 10 k. 2 351BG B-17s collided on landing approach and cr. base, 19 killed. 2 b/d 490BG B-17s cr. France, 12 k in one; b/d 493BG B-17 c/l Poland; b/d 452BG B-17 f/l Woodbridge A/F, b/d 100BG B-17 cr. Rochester A/F, 1 inj; b/d 487BG B-17 abandoned over UK, cr. in sea; 487BG B-17 cr. landing base.

All Fighter groups operating. Fighter group losses:– 4FG – 2, 55FG – 1, 339FG – 1. On return 4 55FG P-51s c/l on Continent, pilots safe. A 339FG P-51 cr. Isle of Wight, pilot killed. 364FG P-51 cr. after pilot baled near Ford A/F. MIA 4FG P-51 pilot baled 55 miles from Southwold, lost. 339FG P-51 cr. Continent.

OTHER OPERATIONS: 25BG despatched 1 Mosquito and 1 P-38 on H2X PR Kassel area, 3 Mosquitoes on 'chaff' screening, 3 Mosquitoes on WR Continent/UK and 5 B-17s on WR Atlantic/UK. 36BS despatched 8 B-24s on RCM. 5ERS despatched 22 P-47s and 1 OA-10 on patrols. First planned operation of OA-10 amphibian. 4 B-17s also on ASR search. 1 B-17, 1 B-24 6 P-51s on radio-relays.

7 FEBRUARY 1945

8AF 822

	Despatched		Effective	Target	Bombs Tonnage	E/A	Losses MIA	E	Dam	Casualties KIA	WIA	MIA
1AD	B-17	295	1	ESSEN	(O) 3.0	0	0	0	0	0	0	0
	P-51	80	41	ESCORT 1AD								
	P-51	36	36	PATROL SIEGEN								
TOTALS:		116	77			0	0	0		0	0	0

REMARKS: 1AD bombers encountered a weather front rising to 30,000ft over the North Sea and were recalled. One trailing B-17 did not receive recall signal and continued to drop its load on Gee fix over Essen. Fighter groups also turned back or were recalled. 364FG flew a fighter sweep without incident.

OTHER OPERATIONS: 25BG despatched 3 Mosquitoes on 'chaff' screening, 1 Mosquito on a *Red Stocking* operation, 3 Mosquitoes on WR Continent/UK and 3 B-17s on WR Azores/Atlantic/UK. 4ERS despatched 2 P-47s on ASR patrol. 36BS despatched 6 B-24s on RCM.

7/8 FEBRUARY 1945

8AF 823 NIGHT LEAFLET OPERATION

NLS despatched 10 B-24s: Holland, Germany.

25BG despatched 4 Mosquitoes on night PR Misburg–Hamburg area. 1 Mosquito MIA.

8 FEBRUARY 1945

	Despatched		Effective	Target	Bombs Tonnage	E/A	Losses MIA	E	Dam	Casualties KIA	WIA	MIA
1, 2 &	B-17	150	0	ALL RECALLED								
3AD	B-24	264	0	BEFORE LEAVING ENGLISH COAST								
TOTALS:		414	0			0	0	0	0	0	0	0
	P-51	99	98	SWEEP–STRAFING RAIL TRAFFIC		1–0–0						
	P-51	13	11	ESCORT PR								
TOTALS:		112	109			1–0–0	0	0		0	0	0

REMARKS: Bombers assembled for mission but weather forced abandonment before a/c despatched from England. Continental based 352FG and 361FG operated. Fighter group e/a credits:– 361FG – 1. 20FG, 55FG, 78FG, 479FG provided a flight each for PRU escorts.

OTHER OPERATIONS: 7PG despatched 18 F-5s, 7 Spitfires and 1 P-38 on PR Germany. 25BG despatched 3 Mosquitoes on 'chaff' dispensing (all abandoned mission), 4 Mosquitoes on WR Atlantic/Continent/UK and 4 B-17s on WR Azores/Atlantic/UK. 1 Mosquito MIA. 5ERS despatched 11 P-47s on ASR search. 36BS despatched 6 B-24s on RCM.

9 FEBRUARY 1945

8AF 824

		Despatched	Effective	Target		Bombs Tonnage	E/A	Losses MIA	E	Dam	Casualties KIA	WIA	MIA
2AD	B-24	313	10	MAGDEBURG/ ROTHENSEE O/I	(P)	23.0	0–0– 1	3	1	51	14	5	20
			268	MAGDEBURG M/Y	(S)	614.7							
			9	TARCHEN	(O)	25.0							
			1	QUACKENBRÜCK A/F	(O)	1.0							
3AD	B-17	311	198	WEIMAR M/I	(S)	417.5	0–1– 1	3	1	7	0	1	28
			11	JENA	(O)	27.5							
			25	GIESSEN M/Y	(O)	60.0							
			15	GÖTTINGEN M/Y	(O)	24.0							
			24	FULDA	(O)	58.7							
			11	EISENACH M/I	(O)	26.2							
			4	T/O		10.0							
1AD	B-17	304	233	LÜTZKENDORF O/I	(P)	577.8		1	2	64	6	3	26
			12	ERFURT	(S)	32.5							
			13	EISENACH	(O)	32.5							
			13	EISLEBEN	(O)	30.0							
			11	MONTESADA	(O)	27.5							
			3	T/O		7.5							
2AD	B-24	65	64	BIELEFELD/ SCHILDESCHE R/V	(P)	142.5		0	0	0	0	0	0
1AD	B-17	151	72	PADERBORN/ ALTENBEKEN R/V	(P)	215.5		1	0	1	(casualties incl. in Divisional totals above)		
			75	ARNSBERG R/V	(P)	233.5							
3AD	B-17	152	107	DÜLMEN O/I	(S)	315.5							
			21	MÜNSTER M/Y	(O)	63.0		0	0	10			
TOTALS:		1296	1200			2965.4	0–1–2	8	4	133	20	9	74
	P-51	173	151	ESCORT 2AD MAIN			9–0– 5 1–0– 0 (G)	1	0				
	P-51	274	271	ESCORT 3AD MAIN			8–1– 3 2–0– 9 (G)	1	1				
	P-51	215	193	ESCORT 1AD MAIN			2–1– 0 34–0– 3 (G)	3	1				
	P-47	40	39	ESCORT 2AD SECOND				0	0		0	0	0
	P-51	53	47	ESCORT 1AD SECOND				0	0		0	0	0
	P-51	60	55	ESCORT 3AD SECOND				0	0		0	0	0
	P-51	35	33	SCOUTING FORCES			5–1– 0	0	0		0	0	0
	P-51	21	20	ESCORT PR				0	0		0	0	0
TOTALS:		871	809				24–3– 8 37–0–12(G)	5	2	?	0	0	5

REMARKS: Major operational effort with all bomb groups participating. Oil targets were primaries for main Forces. All B-24 groups except 389BG and 445BG sent to Magdeburg and bombed with H2X. 4BW, 13CBW, 45CBW groups made up main 3AD Force but weather forced H2X and visual attacks on secondaries and T/Os.

1AD main Force, consisting of 40CBW groups and 303BG, 384BG, was able to attack visually at Lützkendorf and other targets except Eisenach where H2X was used. Bielefeld viaduct was attacked by 389BG and 445BG using GH. 379BG led 1CBW groups in attack on two viaducts by GH. 93CBW groups attacked Dülmen using Micro H and Münster with H2X. 385BG now operating with 93CBW although not officially transferred from 4CBW until 17 February. Bomb group losses:– 1AD – 303BG – 1, 379BG – 1; 2AD – 392BG – 1, 453BG – 1, 491BG – 1; 3AD – 447BG – 2, 487BG – 1. A 457BG B-17 c/l t/o, crew safe. 2 303BG B-17s lost in collision Allied territory, 5 k. MIA 453BG B-24 ditched on return, 6 rescued. On return, 2 453BG B-24 collided over base; 1 cr. Old Buckenham, 11 k.

All Fighter groups operating. Fighter groups e/a credits:– 20FG – 2, 339FG – 1, 355FG – 3, 357FG – 2, 479FG – 10. Fighter group losses:– 78FG – 1, 355FG – 1, 357FG – 1, 359FG – 1, 364FG – 1, 479FG – 1. MIA 364FG P-51 in sea off Ostend, pilot baled over land and safe. On return 355FG P-51 c/l Birch A/F. 4FG P-51 cr. t/o, pilot safe.

OTHER OPERATIONS: 7PG despatched 11 F-5s and 2 Spitfires on PR Germany. 25BG despatched 2 Mosquitoes and 1 P-38 on H2X PR Germany, 2 Mosquitoes 'chaff' dispensing for 1AD, 1 Mosquito on *Red Stocking* ops, 5 Mosquitoes on WR Continent and 4 B-17s on WR Azores/Atlantic/UK. 5ERS despatched 17 P-47s on ASR patrols. 36BS despatched 6 B-24s on RCM. 1 B-17, 1 B-24, 10 P-51s on radio-relays.

Orbiting the field after return from the 9 February escort one 357FG Mustang ran out of fuel. Lt Noel Breen managed to crash-land, ending up in a farmyard with the tail of his broken fighter resting against the house. (M. Olmsted)

INCIDENT

From early 1943, when it was known that the enemy had captured some US aircraft, there were suspicions that these were being used to monitor and interfere with 8th Air Force operations. Aircrew reports of friendly types acting suspiciously became a frequent feature of post-mission interrogations in the summer and autumn of 1943 and continued intermittently until the end of hostilities. Despite reports of suspected enemy operated American fighters, there was no organised action by the Luftwaffe involving the use of the few captured examples they had. Thus these reports must be attributed to faulty aircraft recognition of which a typical example took place on 9 February 1945.

The 356th Group P-51s were flying east to a rendezvous with bombers. When about 20 miles north-east of Meiningen at 27,000 ft the flight, led by Lt Louis Switzer, observed three Mustangs headed in the opposite direction. They were assumed to be on their way home from escort. These three fighters were flying slightly higher and to one side of the 356th, affording their pilots a clear view for 'friendly' identification to be made. Wisely, Switzer had kept an eye on the passers-by and he saw their leader turn and begin to come in behind his flight. Switzer immediately started a gentle turn to the left to expose the Mustang's distinctive wing form and national markings to the approaching trio. The strangers, however, continued their attack and Switzer had no option but to order his flight to 'break' and drop wing tanks. The two flights of Mustangs passed head-on with no firing by the attackers who, evidently at last realising their mistake, raced away south. The 356th Group flight, devoid of drop tanks, had to abandon their mission and report the encounter as one with suspected enemy-operated P-51s. No doubt embarrassed by their error, the other P-51 pilots were loath to make much of this incident in their reports and thus it has remained a mystery.

10 FEBRUARY 1945

8AF 825

	Despatched		Effective	Target		Bombs Tonnage	E/A	Losses MIA	E	Dam	Casualties KIA	WIA	MIA
1AD	B-17	164	140	DÜLMEN O/I	(S)	413.5		0	0	5	0	0	0
			9	IJMUIDEN U/B	(P)	40.5							
			1	LINGEN	(O)	3.0							
			6	SCREENING FORCE									
TOTALS:		164	156			457.0	0	0	0	5	0	0	0
	P-51	106	102	ESCORT 1AD				0					
	P-51	21	20	ESCORT PR				0					
	P-51	6	3	SCOUTING FORCE				0					
	P-51	104	102	STRAFING - STEINHUDER LAKE AREA				2					
TOTALS:		237	227				0	2	1	?	1	0	1

REMARKS: 94CBW groups and 306BG attacked Dülmen oil storage depot by Micro H – 1 a/c of this force attacked a T/O using H2X. The 92BG carried out the first *Disney* mission (Royal Navy rocket bombs) against U-boat pens – visual attack.

Fighter groups operating: 20FG, 55FG, 78FG, 352FG, 355FG, 356FG, 361FG. Fighter group losses:– 355FG – 1, 356FG – 1. MIA 355FG a/c cr. in sea after pilot baled 35 miles NE Gt. Yarmouth, pilot found dead. On return, 355FG P-51 c/l Northrepps, pilot safe.

OTHER OPERATIONS: 7PG despatched 5 F-5s and 1 Spitfire on PR Holland and Germany. 25BG despatched 2 Mosquitoes and 1 P-38 on H2X Germany, 1 Mosquito on *Red Stocking*, 2 Mosquitoes on WR Continent/UK and 4 B-17s on WR Azores/Atlantic/UK. 36BS despatched 6 B-24s on RCM. 5ERS despatched 10 P-47s on ASR patrols.

Luckily Mrs Frankie, the occupant of 240 Norbury Avenue, Norbury, was not in her kitchen when an F-5 Lightning smashed into her backyard on 11 February. The 7PG pilot returning from a mission had to bale out over London when the fuel tanks ran dry.

10/11 FEBRUARY 1945

8AF 826 NIGHT LEAFLET OPERATION

NLS despatched 1 B-17 and 12 B-24s (11 a/c effective): Holland, Germany. 1 man KIA.

482BG despatched 4 B-17s on H2X scope photos Giessen, Marburg, Frankfurt, Mannheim.

11 FEBRUARY 1945

8AF 827

	Despatched		Effective	Target		Bombs Tonnage	E/A	Losses MIA	E	Dam	Casualties KIA	WIA	MIA
2AD	B-24	127	124	DÜLMEN O/I	(S)	335.8		0	0	0			
			1	LOCHERN ROAD JUNC	(O)	3.0		0	0	0			
TOTALS:		127	125			335.8	0	0	0	0	0	0	0
	P-51	54	50	ESCORT 2AD				0			0	0	0
	P-51	51	48	FIGHTER-BOMBER CELLE/UELZEN R/R	(O)	12.0		0			0	0	0
	P-51	192	183	SWEEP NW GERMANY				1			0	0	1
	P-51	11	7	ESCORT PR a/c				0			0	0	0
	P-51	8	8	SCOUTING FORCE				0			0	0	0
TOTALS:		316	296			12.0	0	1		?	0	0	1

REMARKS: 392BG, 445BG, 448BG, 453BG and 96CBW groups attacked Dülmen oil depot using Micro H. One B-24 attacked a T/O by H2X.

Fighter groups operating: 4FG, 352FG, 357FG, 359FG, 361FG. Fighter group losses:– 4FG – 1. A P-51 on PR escort suffered engine failure and pilot baled over Luxembourg.

OTHER OPERATIONS: 7PG despatched 3 F-5s and 2 Spitfires. 1 F-5 cr. London when fuel exhausted on return, pilot baled. 25BG despatched 3 Mosquitoes on WR Continent/UK, and 4 B-17s on WR Azores/Atlantic/UK. 5ERS despatched 4 P-47s on ASR patrols. 36BG despatched 6 B-24s on RCM.

12 FEBRUARY 1945

25BG despatched 1 P-38 on H2X sortie Kassel, 2 Mosquitoes on WR Atlantic/UK and 3 B-17s on WR Azores/Atlantic/UK. Continental based 361FG flew uneventful patrol battle area.

12/13 FEBRUARY 1945

8AF 828 NIGHT LEAFLET OPERATION

NLS despatched 7 B-24s (6 effective); Holland, Germany.

13 FEBRUARY 1945

7PG despatched 2 F-5s on PR Minden/Hannover area with 3 P-51s as escort. 25BG despatched 7 Mosquitoes (6 effective) on WR Atlantic/Continent/UK and 4 B-17s Azores/Atlantic/UK. 36BS despatched 8 B-24s on RCM. 4 P-51s of 352FG conducted WR Brunswick/Hannover area. 1 25BG Mosquito on *Red Stocking* sortie Germany.

13/14 FEBRUARY 1945

8AF 829 NIGHT LEAFLET OPERATION

NLS despatched 9 B-24s; Holland, Germany.

25BG despatched 3 Mosquitoes on night PR Germany, and 1 Mosquito on *Skywave* sortie Germany.

14 FEBRUARY 1945

8AF 830

	Despatched		Effective	Target		Bombs Tonnage	E/A	Losses MIA	Losses E	Losses Dam	Casualties KIA	Casualties WIA	Casualties MIA
1AD	B-17	461	311	DRESDEN M/Y	(P)	771.0	1–0–0	5	3	54	4	15	49
			62	PRAGUE	(O)	152.5							
			25	BRÜX	(O)	62.8							
			12	PILSEN	(O)	27.5							
			25	T/O		62.5							
3AD	B-17	457	294	CHEMNITZ M/Y	(P)	718.5		1	3	103	2	4	14
			38	EGER A/F	(O)	94.2							
			33	BAMBERG	(O)	87.3							
			23	SONNEBERG	(O)	57.5							
			24	TACHAU	(O)	60.0							
			12	HOF M/Y	(O)	27.5							
			17	T/O		42.5							
2AD	B-24	375	340	MAGDEBURG M/Y	(S)	811.1		1	2	16	0	0	9
			1	EMLICHEIM	(O)	2.5							
			1	MEPPEN	(O)	2.5							
			1	BODENTEICH	(O)	3.0							
			1	T/O		2.5							
3AD	B-17	84	37	WESEL H/B	(P)	110.0		0	0	15	0	0	0
			35	DÜLMEN OIL DEPOT	(S)	103.5							
			1	AHAUS	(O)	3.0							
TOTALS:		1377	1293			3201.9	1–0–0	7	8	188	6	19	72
	P-51	316	281	ESCORT 1AD				3	1				
	P-51	238	224	ESCORT 3AD				2	1				
	P-51	273	253	ESCORT 2AD			10–0–3	2	0				
	P-51	30	26	ESCORT WESEL FORCE				0	0				
	P-47	49	44	SWEEP–MAGDEBURG AREA				0	0				
	P-51	24	24	ESCORT PR a/c				0	0				
	P-51	32	29	SCOUTING									
TOTALS:		962	881					7	2	?	1	0	7

REMARKS: All bomb groups participated in missions to oil and rail targets in Germany. 2AD was unable to attack its primary – an oil refinery at Magdeburg. H2X was used by all main Forces with some visual sighting by 1AD and 3AD Formations. Wesel road bridge was the target for 447BG and 487BG (which did not take part in main 3AD mission): 447BG made visual attack and 487BG used Micro H on secondary. Bomb group losses:– 1AD – 92BG – 1, 306BG – 2, 351BG – 1, 379BG – 1; 2AD – 389BG – 1; 3AD – 390BG – 1. 2 490BG B-17s collided and cr. France. B/d 398BG B-17 c/l St.Trond. B/d 392BG B-24 c/l near East Dereham, crew safe. 95BG B-17 cr. Continent. 379BG B-17 cr. landing Liège A/F, 3 k, 4 inj. 381BG B-17 cr. Luxembourg, 4 k.

All Fighter groups participating. Fighter group e/a credits:– 356FG – 7, 364FG – 1, 479FG – 9. Fighter group losses:– 20FG – 1, 55FG – 1, 78FG – 1, 359FG – 2, 361FG – 1, 479FG – 1. 2 78FG P-51 f/l in Poland, pilot safe. 364FG P-51 cr. landing Horham A/F, pilot safe.

OTHER OPERATIONS: 7PG despatched 15 F-5s and 7 Spitfires (with escorts) on PR Germany. 1 Spitfire MIA. 25BG despatched 1 Mosquito and 1 P-38 on H2X PR Germany, 3 Mosquitoes screening for bombers, 1 Mosquito on *Red Stocking* operation, 5 Mosquitoes (1 aborted) on WR Continent/UK and 3 B-17s on WR Azores/Atlantic/UK. 36BS despatched 7 B-24s on RCM. 5ERS despatched 16 P-47s on ASR patrols. 1 B-17, 1 B-24, 3 P-51s on radio-relays.

14/15 FEBRUARY 1945

8AF 831 NIGHT LEAFLET OPERATION

NLS despatched 10 B-24s; Holland, Germany.

25BG despatched 4 Mosquitoes on night PR Holland, and 1 Mosquito on *Skywave* navigation sortie Germany.

482BG despatched 2 B-17s on H2X scope sorties Hannover.

15 FEBRUARY 1945

8AF 832

	Despatched		Effective	Target		Bombs Tonnage	E/A	Losses MIA	E	Dam	Casualties KIA	WIA	MIA
3AD	B-17	459	435	COTTBUS M/Y	(S)	1064.5		1	1	34	0	3	9
			1	DRESDEN	(O)	2.5							
			1	QUACKENBRÜCK	(O)	2.5							
			2	T/O		5.0							
1AD	B-17	224	210	DRESDEN	(S)	461.9		0	4	8	7	8	0
			1	LINGEN	(O)	2.2							
			1	EMS–WESER CANAL	(O)	2.2							
2AD	B-24	372	353	MAGDEBURG O/I	(P)	898.5		1	3	32	2	0	3
3AD	B-17	76	58	RHEINE M/Y	(L)	174.0							
			13	MÜNSTER	(O)	39.0		0	0	0	0	0	0
TOTALS:		1131	1075			2652.3	0	2	8	74	9	11	12
	P-51	173	153	ESCORT 3AD			2–0–0	0	3		0	0	0
	P-51	158	141	ESCORT 1AD				1	0		0	0	1
	P-51	120	110	ESCORT 2AD				0	0		0	0	0
	P-47	27	27	ESCORT 3AD SECOND TF				0	0		0	0	0
	P-51	4	4	ESCORT PR				0	0		0	0	0
	P-51	28	25	SCOUTING FORCES				0	0		0	0	0
TOTALS:		510	460				2–0–0	1	3	?	0	0	1

REMARKS: All bomb groups except 92BG and 306BG participated. Only 2AD was able to attack its primary at Magdeburg, as weather conditions prevented 3AD and 1AD bombing oil targets at Böhlen and Ruhland. Apart from some visual sightings by 3AD all bombing was by H2X. 3AD secondary force that attacked Rheine M/Y comprised 385BG. Bomb group losses:– 2AD – 392BG – 1; 3AD – 95BG – 1. A 303BG B-17 cr. on t/o base, crew safe. 2 305BG B-17 cr. after t/o near base and at Rushden, 7 killed. 448BG B-24 cr. Elsing during assembly, 2 killed. On return, 303BG B-17 c/l Lakenheath A/F; 389BG B-24 c/l East Carleton. B/d 446BG B-24 cr. landing Beccles A/F. B/d 95BG B-17 c/l Continent.

All Fighter groups except 4FG, 78FG, 339FG, 352FG, 355FG, 361FG operating. Fighter group e/a credits: 55FG – 2. Fighter group losses:– 364FG – 1. Three 353FG P-51s c/l Continent, pilots safe.

OTHER OPERATIONS: 7PG despatched 16 F-5s and 5 Spitfires on PR Germany. 1 F-5 MIA. 25BG despatched 5 Mosquitoes (3 effective) 'chaff' dispensing for bombers, 5 Mosquitoes on WR Continent/UK and 4 B-17s on WR Azores/Atlantic/UK. 5ERS despatched 22 P-47s on ASR patrols. 36BS despatched 7 B-24s on RCM. 1 B-24, 2 P-51s on radio-relays.

16 FEBRUARY 1945

8AF 833

	Despatched		Effective	Target		Bombs Tonnage	E/A	Losses MIA	E	Dam	Casualties KIA	WIA	MIA
3AD	B-17	223	208	HAMM M/Y	(P)	598.0		2	1	95	0	7	11
			1	OSNABRÜCK	(O)	3.0							
			1	MEPPEN	(O)	1.5							
			1	RHEINE	(O)	3.0							
1AD	B-17	375	104	NORDSTERN O/I	(P)	308.3		5	1	170	0	8	46
			112	MINSTER STEIN O/I	(P)	330.5							
			78	DORTMUND/ HARPENERWEG O/I	(P)	188.0							
			30	MÜNSTER M/Y	(S)	74.4							
			23	LANGENDREER	(O)	55.5							
			2	T/O		6.0							
2AD	B-24	362	174	OSNABRÜCK M/Y	(P)	445.3		1	0	26	0	0	10
			94	RHEINE M/Y	(P)	278.5							
			46	SALZBERGEN O/I	(P)	126.5							
			31	BURGSTEINFURT	(O)	88.0							
3AD	B-17	76	63	WESEL R/B	(P)	189.0		0	0	0	0	0	0
			13	RHEINE M/Y	(O)	39.0							
	B-24	6	6	SCREENING FORCE				0	0	0	0	0	0
TOTALS:		1042	987			2734.5	0	8	2	291	0	15	67

	P-51	45	44	ESCORT 3AD								
	P-51	39	38	ESCORT 1AD								
	P-51	50	50	ESCORT 2AD								
	P-51	51	45	ESCORT 3AD WESEL								
	P-51	4	4	SCOUTING FORCE								
	P-51	4	4	ESCORT PR								
	P-51	4	4	ESCORT SPECIAL OP								
TOTALS:		197	189			0	0	1	?	0	0	0

REMARKS: Benzol plants, oil refineries and marshalling yards in Central Germany. 3AD main force used H2X, Micro H and some visual aims; 1AD used GH and some visual; 2AD used GH and H2X. 3AD Force sent to Wesel rail bridge (385BG and 447BG) bombed visually and with H2X on a T/O. Bomb groups participating: 45CBW groups and 94BG, 486BG, 487BG, 490BG attacked Hamm; all 1AD groups except 384BG; all 2AD groups except 44BG. Bomb group losses:– 1AD – 303BG – 1, 401BG – 3, 457BG – 1; 2AD – 467BG – 1. 3BD – 388BG – 1, 452BG – 1. MIA 388BG B-17 cr. in sea after assembly, crew baled over Suffolk coast, safe. On return b/d 401BG abandoned over Bardney; b/d 392BG B-24 abandoned and cr. Pudding Norton; 379BG B-17 abandoned and cr. Carleton Rode. Extremely poor visibility forced returning bombers to be diverted to Continental or West England A/Fs. B/d 452BG B-17 Cat E base.

Fighter groups operating: 339FG, 352FG, 361FG. On return a 339FG P-51 c/l Coltishall A/F, pilot safe.

OTHER OPERATIONS: 7PG despatched 4 F-5s and 2 Spitfires on PR Germany. 25BG despatched 1 P-38 on H2X sortie Freiburg. 1 Mosquito on H2X sortie Speyer; 3 Mosquitoes 'chaff' screening for bombers, 1 Mosquito on WR North Sea/UK, and 4 B-17s on WR Azores/Atlantic/UK. 36BS despatched 7 B-24s on RCM. 1 B-17 on special sortie with 4 361FG P-51s as escort.

17 FEBRUARY 1945

8AF 834

	Despatched		Effective	Target	Bombs Tonnage	E/A	Losses MIA	E	Dam	Casualties KIA	WIA	MIA
3AD	B-17	346	260	FRANKFURT M/Y	(P) 641.6		3	1	106	6	2	28
			45	GIESSEN M/Y	(O) 109.1							
			12	ASCHAFFENBURG	29.9							
			10	HANAU	22.4							
			4	T/O	8.8							
1AD	B-17	261		RECALLED			0	0	0	0	0	0
2AD	B-24	288		RECALLED			2	1	0	11	0	10
TOTALS:		895	331		811.8	0	5	2	106	17	2	38
	P-51	167	151	ESCORT 3AD			1	1		0	0	1
	P-51	4	4	ESCORT PR			0	0		0	0	0
	P-51	12	12	SCOUTING FORCE			0	0		0	0	0
TOTALS:		183	167			0	1	1	?	0	0	1

REMARKS: Synthetic oil plants were main primaries. All 3AD groups except 447BG despatched. Deteriorating weather forced recall of 1AD and 2AD forces before reaching enemy airspace. Weather was so bad that some a/c controls froze and several had to jettison bombs during assembly. Bomb group losses:– 2AD – 453BG – 1, 467BG – 1; 3AD – 388BG – 2, 390BG – 1. MIA 390BG B-17 exploded 20 miles NW Ostend, 1 rescued. MIA 453BG B-24 ditched near Cromer, 4 rescued. MIA 467BG B-24 cr. in sea off Yarmouth, crew lost. 466BG B-24 cr. Field Dalling, 3 killed plus Italian POW working in field. During assembly a 452BG B-17 cr. Tibenham, 6 k.

Fighter groups operating: 55FG, 353FG, 357FG. Fighter group losses:– 55FG – 1. A 353FG P-51 cr. after t/o base, pilot killed.

OTHER OPERATIONS: 7PG despatched 5 F-5s and 1 Spitfire on PR Germany (with 3 P-51 escort). 25BG despatched 6 Mosquitoes on WR Continent/UK and 3 B-17s on WR Azores/Atlantic/UK. 5ERS despatched 4 P-47s on ASR search. 36BS despatched 6 B-24s on RCM. 4 P-51s on radio-relays.

18 FEBRUARY 1945

7PG despatched 4 G-5s on PR Nürnberg area. 8 P-51s (6 effective) despatched as escort. 25BG despatched 1 Mosquito on special operation, 3 Mosquitoes on WR Continent/Atlantic/UK and 2 B-17s Atlantic/UK. 5ERS despatched 6 P-47s and 1 OA-10 on ASR search.

In the early months of 1945 Maj Gen Earle Partridge, CG 3rd Division, carried out a series of inspections at stations in his Command with the object of maintaining military standards. On 19 February it was Knettishall's turn, the 388BG having stood down from operations that day. The only thing really marring an otherwise satisfactory inspection was the number of uncontrolled pet dogs which thought the runway parade great fun, barked at the marchers and did certain acts unbecoming to the occasion. Here the General and his aides leave the parade ground, with canine escort.

19 FEBRUARY 1945

8AF 835

	Despatched		Effective	Target		Bombs Tonnage	E/A	Losses MIA	E	Dam	Casualties KIA	WIA	MIA
3AD	B-17	196	155	OSNABRÜCK M/Y	(P)	428.0		0	1	21	0	1	0
			24	MÜNSTER M/Y	(S)	68.0							
			10	HASELUNNE	(O)	29.0							
2AD	B-24	291	97	MESCHEDE-HENSCHEL	(P)	265.7		1		8			
			86	JUNGENTHAL M/I	(P)	227.5							
			94	SIEGEN M/Y	(P)	251.5							
1AD	B-17	422	74	DORTMUND/ HOESCH O/I	(P)	217.2		0	1	59	1	0	0
			99	BOCHUM/ CAROLINEGLUCH O/I	(P)	293.5							
			37	ALM/PLUTO O/I	(P)	106.5							
			36	GELSENKIRCHEN/ BUER O/I	(P)	104.0							
			162	MÜNSTER M/Y	(S)	478.1							
3AD	B-17	144	131	RHEINE M/Y	(P)	431.5							
3AD	B-17	82	68	WESEL R/B		184.0		0	0	25	0	0	0
TOTALS:		1135	1073			3084.5	0	1	2	113	1	1	9
	P-51	42	38	ESCORT 3AD FIRST				0			0	0	0
	P-47 P-51	32 98	122	ESCORT 2AD				0			0	0	0
	P-51	96	91	ESCORT 1AD				1			0	0	1
	P-51	48	48	ESCORT 3AD RHENE				0			0	0	0
	P-51	37	32	ESCORT 3AD WESEL				0			0	0	0
	P-51	179	163	SWEEP – HANNOVER, MAGDEBURG, BRUNSWICK AREAS			2–0–0 1–0–0 (G)	5			0	0	5
	P-51	28	27	SCOUTING FORCES				1			0	0	1
TOTALS:		560	521				2–0–0 1–0–0(G)	7		?	0	0	7

REMARKS: Oil, industrial and rail targets. 13CBW groups and 96BG, 452BG made up first task Force which used Micro H at primary with some H2X and on other targets. 2AD despatched all groups except 44BG, 392BG, 467BG for a GH attack on primaries. 1AD despatched all groups except 401BG for GH attack on primaries with H2X and visual at Münster. 3AD second Force – 34BG, 385BG, 486BG, 493BG – attacked Rheine using Micro H and H2X. 3AD third Force – 94BG, 447BG attacked Wesel bridge using Micro H. Bomb group losses:– 2AD – 389BG – 1; During assembly burning 92BG B-17 abandoned and cr. Temple Grafton. Aborting 95BG B-17 cr. landing base.

All Fighter groups except 352FG, 361FG operating. Fighter group e/a credits:– 55FG – 2. Fighter group losses:– 20FG – 1, 55FG – 1, 359FG – 1, 364FG – 4. B/d 78FG P-51 s/d Allied AA fire near Rhine, pilot baled, safe.

OTHER OPERATIONS: 25BG despatched 3 Mosquitoes 'chaff' screening for 1AD, 1 Mosquito on bomber monitor sortie, 2 Mosquitoes on WR Continent/UK, and 4 B-17 on WR Azores/Atlantic/UK. 5ERS despatched 12 P-47s on ASR patrols, 1 P-47 c/l. 36BS despatched 2 B-24s on RCM, 1 effective – 1 B-24 cr. on t/o base.

20 FEBRUARY 1945

8AF 836

	Despatched		Effective	Target	Bombs Tonnage	E/A	Losses MIA	E	Dam	Casualties KIA	WIA	MIA
2AD	B-24	360	1	STEIG CITY (O)	2.5		0	1	0	3	2	0
3AD	B-17	450	403	NÜRNBERG STN & M/Y(P)	989.2		3	2	162	9	7	29
			16	SCHILTACH (O)	40.0							
			9	T/O	22.5							
1AD	B-17	454	428	NÜRNBERG STN & M/Y(P)	1114.5		2	0	79	0	3	18
			3	T/O	8.2							
TOTALS:		1264	860		2176.9	0	5	3	241	12	12	47
	P-51	141	123	ESCORT 2AD		2–0– 0	1					
	P-51	170	163	ESCORT 3AD		8–0–2 (G)	5					
	P-51	167	152	ESCORT 1AD			0					
	P-47	32	194	SWEEP – RAIL &		12–0– 1	7					
	P-51	177		ROAD TRAFFIC		35–1–20 (G)						
	P-51	29	28	SCOUTING FORCES			0					
	P-51	10	10	ESCORT PR A/C			0					
TOTALS:		726	670			14–0– 1 35–1–20 (G)	13	2	?	1	0	12

REMARKS: All three divisions despatched to Nürnberg but 2AD abandoned mission over Belgium due to weather conditions. Only a single B-24 of 389BG that did not receive signal continued and made a visual attack on a T/O. Other bomb groups participating:– all 1AD and all 3AD except 385BG and 486BG. Visual and H2X bombing at Nürnberg. Bomb group losses:– 1AD – 91BG – 1, 379BG – 1; 3AD – 388BG – 2, 487BG – 1. A 493BG B-17 cr. river Deben, Ramsholt after t/o, 8 killed. B/d 466BG B-24 cr. Belgium, 3 killed.

All Fighter groups except 352FG and 361FG operating. Fighter group e/a credits:– 4FG – 2, 20FG – 7, 55FG – 1, 356FG – 1. Fighter group losses:– 4FG – 1, 20FG – 3, 55FG – 4, 78FG – 1, 339FG – 2, 356FG – 2. MIA 339FG P-51s collided Germany. One MIA 55FG P-51 in Channel, pilot baled, rescued. On route out a 339FG P-51 spun in near Valenciennes, pilot killed.

OTHER OPERATIONS: 7PG despatched 5 F-5s and 1 Spitfire on PR (F-5s had 10 P-51 escort). 25BG despatched 4 Mosquitoes 'chaff' dispensing for 1AD and 2AD (1 aborted), 2 Mosquitoes on WR Germany, and 3 B-17s on WR Azores/Atlantic/UK. 5ERS despatched 18 P-47s and 1 OA-10 on ASR search. 36BS despatched 7 B-24s on RCM. 1 B-17, 1 B-24, 2 P-51s on radio-relays.

By early spring it was practice in most groups for the pathfinder (H2X) aircraft to be concentrated in one of the four squadrons together with lead crews. At Lavenham 838BS was the 'lead squadron'; one of its B-17G's exhibiting an H2X radome rests on a Lavenham hardstand, 20 February. (R. Zorn)

INCIDENT

The 20th Group's Joe Ford, who had distinguished himself on his first combat mission by shepherding two ailing Lightnings back to England, was shot down while strafing on 20 February 1945. By then a veteran, Capt Ford bellied his Mustang into a large field near Nürnberg after its engine was hit. A member of his flight, Lt McGee, no doubt mindful of the successful retrieval made by a P-51 pilot who landed close to a shot down buddy and flew him out, lowered his undercarriage to try and land near Ford's P-51. He overshot on his first pass but made a successful touch-down at the second try. Unfortunately the surface of the field was so wet that McGee's Mustang nosed up briefly before coming to a stop, bending a propellor blade. Ford ran out of an adjoining wood where he was hiding and together the men discarded pieces of equipment and McGee's parachute before squeezing into the cockpit. The take-off attempt was not to be successful for the ground was so waterlogged that when McGee attempted to taxi the tail lifted and the propeller churned up mud. Other orbiting 20th P-51 pilots finally saw the two men abandon the venture and the bogged Mustang and run into the woods. Both eventually ended up in the nearby POW camp.

20/21 FEBRUARY 1945

8AF 837 NIGHT LEAFLET OPERATION

NLS despatched 11 B-24s (10 effective); Holland, Germany.

8AF 838 NIGHT BOMBING OPERATION

492BG despatched 30 B-24s to Neustadt M/Y dropping 58.5 tons by PFF. No casualties.

492BG despatched 7 B-24s (6 effective) on *Carpetbagger* operations.

25BG despatched 2 Mosquitoes on night PR Holland, and 1 Mosquito on *Skywave* sortie Holland and Denmark.

21 FEBRUARY 1945

8AF 839

	Despatched		Effective	Target		Bombs Tonnage	E/A	Losses MIA	E	Dam	Casualties KIA	WIA	MIA
3AD	B-17	416	396	NÜRNBERG M/Y	(P)	965.2		0	1	195	0	3	0
			9	T/O		21.6							
1AD	B-17	451	434	NÜRNBERG M/Y	(S)	1069.0		0	0	103	1	3	0
			2	T/O		5.0							
2AD	B-24	395	375	NÜRNBERG STN & M/Y	(P)	825.7		0	0	63	1	3	0
			1	SPEYER	(O)	1.0							
			2	T/O		3.4							
TOTALS:		1262	1219			2890.9	0	0	1	361	2	9	0
	P-51	200	189	ESCORT 3AD				2			0	0	2
	P-51	191	184	ESCORT 1AD			2–0–0 (G)	0			0	0	0
	P-47	37	175	ESCORT 2AD			2–0–0 (G)	0			0	0	0
	P-51	156						3			0	0	3
	P-51	46	45	SWEEP–MEININGEN COBURG NÜRNBERG AREAS				1			0	0	1
	P-51	101	98	SUPPORT 9AF BOMBER			0–0–1 (G)	0			0	0	0
	P-51	31	23	SCOUTING FORCES				1			0	0	1
	P-51	30	29	ESCORT PR				0			0	0	0
TOTALS:		792	743				4–0–1 (G)	7		?	0	0	7

REMARKS: Further attacks on the important rail centre at Nürnberg. H2X used apart from some visual sighting by 3AD Formations. Bomb groups participating:– all 1AD except 92BG; all 2AD except 491BG; all 3AD except 96BG, 390BG, 447BG. On way to target burning 388BG B-17 abandoned over Belgium. During morning pre-flighting, a 447BG B-17 exploded at base, destroying 2 others and injuring 6 men.

All Fighter groups operating. 352FG and 361FG supported 9AF operations. Fighter group e/a credits: 356FG – 1. Fighter group losses:– 4FG – 2, 55FG – 1, 78FG – 1, 353FG – 1, 355FG – 1, 3SF – 1.

OTHER OPERATIONS: 7PG despatched 10 F-5s and 7 Spitfires on PR Germany (with escort). 1 F-5 MIA. 25BG despatched 1 Mosquito on PR N France, 3 Mosquitoes on WR Continent/UK, and 5 B-17s on WR Azores/Atlantic/UK. 36BS despatched 7 B-24s on RCM. 5ERS despatched 15 P-47s and 3 OA-10s on ASR patrols. 1 B-24 and 14 P-51s on radio-relays. 1 25BG Mosquito on *Red Stocking* sortie SW Germany.

21/22 FEBRUARY 1945

8AF 840 NIGHT BOMBING OPERATION

492BG despatched 29 B-24s (25 effective) to Duisburg power and gas stations where 57.5 tons dropped by PFF. 1 B-24 MIA; 1 B-24 abandoned over Continent.

25BG despatched 3 Mosquitoes on night PR Kamen.

As part of an exercise to make 8AF personnel appreciate the RAF Bomber Command's contribution to their joint campaign, veteran Lancaster *S for Sugar* visited nearly every base during February. On the 21st it was at North Pickenham where personnel were allowed aboard. The 125 mission scoreboard also caused great interest.

Lead squadron of 401BG makes a direct hit on a bridge over rail lines at Ludwigslust on the first day of *Clarion*. Bombing was from 12,000 feet, about half the normal height.

The 457BG heads out across an undercast bound for Salzwedel marshalling yards. Although the lead aircraft has its H2X radome extended the cloud disappeared and visual attack was possible. Nearest B-17 is *Maguire's Chop House*.

22 FEBRUARY 1945

8AF 841

	Despatched		Effective	Target		Bombs Tonnage	E/A	Losses MIA	E	Dam	Casualties KIA	WIA	MIA
3AD	B-17	522	1	KITZINGEN M/Y	(P)	3.0	0–0– 1	2	0	29	0	2	19
			2	ZWICKAU M/Y	(P)	6.0							
			64	BAMBERG M/Y	(P)	187.0							
			143	ANSBACH	(O)	420.0							
			24	AALEN M/Y	(O)	71.5							
			26	NEUSTADT M/Y	(O)	78.0							
			24	DONAUESCHINGEN	(O)	70.5							
			25	REUTLINGEN	(O)	74.5							
			77	ULM	(O)	232.5							
			21	FREIBURG	(O)	63.0							
			8	SINGEN M/Y	(O)	23.0							
			22	SCHWENNINGEN M/Y	(O)	64.0							
			11	VILLINGEN M/Y	(O)	32.0							
			10	HAFINGEN	(O)	28.5							
			42	T/O		125.0							
2AD	B-24	452	51	HALBERSTADT M/Y	(P)	113.5							
			11	SÄNGERHAUSEN	(P)	23.5							
			30	NORDHAUSEN M/Y	(P)	74.0		4	0	68	0	2	38
			23	VIENENBURG	(P)	51.5							
			52	PEINE M/Y	(P)	142.2							
			55	HILDESHEIM M/Y	(P)	148.2							
			48	KREIENSEN M/Y	(P)	131.3							
			48	NORTHEIM M/Y	(P)	124.5							
			19	WALLHAUSEN M/Y	(O)	41.5							
			8	OKER M/Y	(O)	16.0							
			11	NORDHAUSEN	(O)	31.0							
			30	ESCHWEGE M/Y	(O)	70.0							
			29	GÖTTINGEN M/Y	(O)	83.0							
			1	LINDERN R/B & H/B	(O)	3.0							
			8	CELLE M/Y	(O)	23.5							
			10	OTTBERGEN	(O)	28.0							
			1	T/O		1.5							
1AD	B-17	454	72	WITTENBERG	(P)	216.0		1	0	0	0	1	9
			73	STENDAL	(P)	214.2							
			59	SALZWEDEL	(P)	197.5							
			73	UELZEN	(P)	214.3							
			11	WITTSTOCK	(P)	33.0							
			39	LÜNEBURG	(P)	115.5							
			48	LUDWIGSLUST	(P)	136.2							
			13	GRABOW	(O)	39.0							
			24	KOBBELITZ	(O)	70.5							
			12	DANNENBERG	(O)	35.7							
			13	KLOTZE	(O)	38.5							
TOTALS:		1428	1372			3895.1	0–0–1	7	0	97	0	5	66
	P-51	168	163	ESCORT 3AD				3			0	0	3
	P-47	33	246	ESCORT 2AD			19–0–16 (G)	0			0	0	0
	P-51	233						4			0	0	4
	P-51	280	268	ESCORT 1AD			4–2–18	5			0	0	5
							3–0– 5 (G)						
	P-51	103	99	FREELANCE			2–0– 0	1			0	0	1
				SUPPORT									
				BOMBERS									
	P-51	32	28	SCOUTING FORCES			2–0– 3 (G)	0			0	0	0
	P-51	13	13	ESCORT PR				0			0	0	0
TOTALS:		862	817				4–2–18	13	1	?	0	0	13
							24–0–24 (G)						

REMARKS: Operation *Clarion*, a major assault on German rail and road communications by Allied air forces. All bomb groups participated in visual attacks. Some 3AD units also resorted to H2X. Bombing conducted from an optimum 10,000 ft to achieve accuracy at targets without flak defences. Bomb group losses:– 1AD – 398BG – 1; 2AD – 392BG – 1, 458BG – 2, 491BG – 1; 3AD – 452BG – 1, 486BG – 1.

All Fighter groups operating. Fighter group e/a credits: 20FG – 1, 352FG – 1, 353FG – 2, 364FG – 2. Fighter group losses:– 78FG – 1, 339FG – 2, 353FG – 1, 355FG – 1, 356FG – 1, 359FG – 2, 361FG – 1, 364FG – 2, 479FG – 2. One MIA 359FG pilot baled 40 miles E. Hook, lost. MIA 479FG P-51 accidentally shot down by strafing 4FG P-51. On return 364FG P-51 cr. landing – Cat E.

OTHER OPERATIONS: 7PG despatched 10 F-5s and 5 Spitfires on PR Germany (with escort). 25BG despatched 6 Mosquitoes on WR Continent/Atlantic/UK, and 4 B-17s Azores/Atlantic/UK. 36BS despatched 7 B-24s on RCM. 5ERS despatched 18 P-47s and 2 OA-10s on ASR patrols and 4 P-51s also on ASR search. 12 P-51s on radio-relays.

INCIDENT

One of the most tragic ironies of the air war concerned those Allied fliers who escaped unhurt from aircraft shot down in enemy territory, only to be killed later by the bombs or bullets of their own side. Occasionally there was an even more depressing twist to this situation of friend inadvertently killing friend. An instance was that involving Lt J.R. Walker's crew following a mission to Northeim marshalling yards on 22 February 1945. For their group, the 392nd, the bombing altitude of 6,000 ft was the lowest ever briefed, the aim being to increase accuracy in attacking a small area target. Flak at Northeim was not effective but near Amsterdam the 392nd formation did encounter accurate salvoes. Walker's B-24 had No.3 engine disabled but, more worrying, was a diminishing fuel supply. At the Dutch coast Walker realised he would not be able to cross the North Sea and elected to fly south along the coast until reaching liberated territory. The Liberator was losing height rapidly and had to be 'bellied-in' near Zoeterwoude where it came to rest beside the house and buildings of farmer Tinus Janson. Apart from the tail the aircraft was not badly damaged and the crew emerged little hurt. The farmer and other Dutch people befriended the young Americans and arranged for them to be sheltered by the Resistance movement. Four days later an RAF reconnaissance Spitfire returned to base with photographs of the coastal area west of the Hague. On some frames of the film the image of a fairly intact Liberator was clearly visible. A long standing directive required the destruction of all Allied aircraft observed to have come down in enemy territory with battle damage, to prevent the enemy obtaining intelligence on new equipment and modifications. Later the same day RAF fighter bombers strafed and ignited the Liberator but sadly the benefactor of the crew, farmer Janson, who unwisely came out to watch the show, was killed by their gunfire.

The reconnaissance photograph taken by a 542 Squadron Spitfire that revealed the little damaged B-24.

INCIDENT

The tail compartment in a B-17 was a lonely perch, remote from other crew positions. Just how remote was never better illustrated than by what befell 19-year-old S/Sgt Charles Sibray on the 22 February 1945 raid on Ansbach marshalling yard. Manning the tail guns in a 486th Group Fortress, Sibray heard the pilots say No.1 engine was being shut down. Turning his head to look through a side window Sibray could see smoke and flame trailing from under the left wing and this information he immediately reported over the interphone. A moment later the pilot ordered all crew members to be prepared for the bale-out signal. Clipping on his chest pack parachute, the tail gunner disconnected his main oxygen and interphone lines and moved behind his seat to where he could release and kick out the emergency door. He then returned to his seat, reconnected oxygen and interphone and awaited further instructions. None came. He called up the pilots but receiving no reply assumed they were too busy coping with the situation to respond. Smoke was still issuing from the wing, although not so heavily and as the bomber continued smoothly on its way Sibray thought the emergency had passed and the pilots were going to try to get the B-17 to friendly territory. Obeying the rule of crew discipline, Sibray stuck to his post. Some 30 minutes later more flak appeared near the bomber's tail and Sibray called out the position of bursts so the pilots could take evasive action. His calls were not acknowledged and the aircraft continued without change of course. The gunner was now apprehensive that all was not right. Even if the interphone was faulty the pilots would surely have manouevred the bomber out of range of the flak. Perhaps the crew in the nose had been injured. Taking a walk-around oxygen bottle he crawled out of the tail position and past the retracted tail wheel to find no gunner in the waist. The radio room was also empty. He negotiated the bomb-bay catwalk and opened the door onto the flight deck. To his fearful amazement the cockpit was deserted; the blinking light of the automatic pilot indicated what controlling force held the Fortress in level flight. Realising he was alone, Sibray's first reaction was to offer a silent prayer. During the few seconds when he had disconnected his interphone lines to leave his position and release the escape door the pilot had apparently given the bale-out order to the crew. For over an hour the tail gunner had unknowingly been alone in the Fortress which had flown 150 miles over hostile territory on automatic pilot. Seeing that the fire in the wing still persisted Sibray decided it was time he too departed. After his parachute descent and safe landing he found he was in France from where he was returned to his base. The rest of the crew had been made prisoner in Germany, believing their bomber (44-6599; 4N:R) was a victim of flak. In fact, the 486th Group formation did not encounter any enemy fire at Ansbach and the damage done to the lost bomber was through the accidental discharge of a .50 gun in another Fortress.

22/23 FEBRUARY 1945

8AF 842 NIGHT LEAFLET OPERATION

NLS despatched 12 B-24s; Holland and Germany.

492BG despatched 7 B-24s (5 effective) on *Carpetbagger* operations.

25BG despatched 3 Mosquitoes on night PR Frankfurt and Hanau, and 1 Mosquito on *Skywave* sortie Holland and Denmark.

23 FEBRUARY 1945

8AF 843

	Despatched		Effective	Target	Bombs Tonnage	E/A	Losses MIA	E	Dam	Casualties KIA	WIA	MIA
3AD	B-17	446	61	TREUCHTLINGEN M/Y (P)	175.0		0	1	34	0	1	0
			52	CRAILSHEIM M/Y (P)	114.0							
			74	NEUMARKT M/Y (P)	210.7							
			109	ANSBACH M/Y (P)	297.0							
			95	KITZINGEN M/Y (P)	284.8							
			2	NÖRDLINGEN (O)	5.0							
			24	SCHWABISCH HALL (O)	70.0							
			7	WINTERHAUSEN (O)	21.0							
			2	T/O	6.0							
1AD	B-17	460	110	PLAUEN M/Y (P)	325.0		0	1	16	0	3	0
			49	MEININGEN (O)	145.5							
			12	ADELSBERG (O)	35.0							
			12	HILDBURGHAUSEN (O)	33.0							
			88	KITZINGEN (O)	263.5							
			13	LICHTENFELS (O)	38.7							
			12	SCHWEINFURT (O)	35.5							
			25	ELLINGEN (O)	70.0							
			48	ÖTTINGEN (O)	140.5							
			37	WÜRZBURG (O)	111.0							
			38	CRAILSHEIM (O)	112.5							
			1	ZWOLLE (O)	3.0							
2AD	B-24	368	57	WEIMAR M/Y (P)	135.7		1	4	6	21	4	0
			10	FULDA M/Y (P)	24.0							
			46	GERA M/Y (P)	107.8							
			104	PADERBORN (O)	231.0							
			50	OSNABRÜCK (O)	136.5							
			25	JENA (O)	59.5							
			20	SCHLUCHTERN (O)	56.5							
			9	FRITZLAR (O)	21.5							
			9	REICHENBACH (O)	20.5							
			9	STEINAU (O)	23.5							
			1	T/O	3.0							
TOTALS:		1274	1211		3316.7	0	1	6	56	21	8	0
	P-51	203	194	ESCORT 3AD		5–0– 2 (G)	2			0	0	2
	P-51	208	193	ESCORT 1AD		1–0– 0	3			1	0	3
	P-51	110	105	ESCORT 2AD			0			0	0	0
	P-47	33	141	SWEEP–NEUBURG		9–0–14 (G)	0			0	0	0
	P-51	117		LANDSBERG & LEIPHEIM A/Fs			1			0	0	1
	P-51	4	4	ESCORT PR A/C			0			0	0	0
	P-51	30	30	SCOUTING FORCES			0			0	0	0
TOTALS:		705	667			1–0– 0 14–0–16 (G)	6	1	?	1	0	6

REMARKS: Second day of the *Clarion* operation. All bomb groups except 34BG and 95BG operating. Bomb group losses:– 2AD – 446BG – 1. MIA 446BG B-24 ditched, 3 rescued. On return, 2 458BG B-24s collided in cloud and cr. Skeyton and Felmingham, 15 killed; 453BG B-24 c/l Carleton Rode, crew injured; 388BG B-17 c/l Knettishall A/F. 379BG B-17 f/l Continent – Cat E. B/d 93BG B-24 f/l Continent.

All Fighter groups except 352FG and 361FG operating. Fighter group e/a credits:– 364FG – 7. Fighter group losses:– 78FG – 1, 355FG – 1, 357FG – 1, 359FG – 3. Ground claim made by 479FG was for B-17 on enemy A/F. 359FG P-51 cr. Continent, pilot k.

OTHER OPERATIONS: 7PG despatched 10 F-5s (with escort) on PR Germany. 25BG despatched 7 Mosquitoes on WR Continent/UK, and 3 B-17s on WR Azores/Atlantic/UK. 5ERS despatched 17 P-47s and 2 OA-10s on ASR patrols. 36BS despatched 7 B-24s on RCM. 1 B-24, 2 P-47s, 16 P-51s on radio-relays. 1 25BG Mosquito on *Red Stocking* sortie SW Germany.

23/24 FEBRUARY 1945

8AF 844 NIGHT BOMBING OPERATION

492BG despatched 27 B-24s (24 effective) for a PFF attack on Neuss M/Y where 59.2 tons bombs dropped.

24 FEBRUARY 1945

8AF 845

	Despatched		Effective	Target		Bombs Tonnage	E/A	Losses MIA	E	Dam	Casualties KIA	WIA	MIA
1AD	B-17	362	70	HAMBURG/ HARBURG O/I	(P)	204.5		0	0	26	0	2	0
			278	HAMBURG ALBRECHT O/I	(P)	809.5							
			6	T/O		18.0							
2AD	B-24	280	104	MISBURG O/I	(P)	279.5		1	1	16	4	3	12
			61	LEHRTE M/Y	(P)	141.0							
			76	BIELEFELD M/Y	(S)	207.8							
			11	HANNOVER	(O)	30.5							
			2	LINGEN	(O)	5.0							
			5	T/O		15.0							
3AD	B-17	383	200	BREMEN DESCHIMAG U/Y	(P)	585.9		1	1	162	0	7	9
			134	BREMEN W R/B	(P)	391.0							
			12	MINDEN	(O)	36.0							
			8	OSNABRÜCK	(O)	12.0							
			5	QUACKENBRÜCK	(O)	15.0							
			1	BRINKUM	(O)	1.5							
3AD	B-17	76	70	WESEL R/B	(P)	23.0		0	0	22	0	0	0
	B-17	13	12	SCREENING FORCE				0	0	0	0	0	
TOTALS:		1114	1055			2775.2		2	2	226	4	12	21
	P-51	195	181	ESCORT 1AD				4			0	0	4
	P-51	179	166	ESCORT 2AD				5			0	0	5
	P-51	98	93	ESCORT 3AD BREMEN			1–0–3 (G)	2			0	0	2
	P-51	29	29	ESCORT 3AD WESEL				0			0	0	0
	P-51	46	43	FREELANCE FOR BOMBERS				0			0	0	0
	P-51	28	28	SCOUTING FORCES				0			0	0	0
	P-51	17	17	ESCORT PR A/C				0			0	0	0
TOTALS:		592	557				1–0–3 (G)	11		?	0	0	11

REMARKS: Oil refineries and rail targets attacked by H2X. A further attempt by a 3AD Force to destroy the Wesel bridge employed Micro H. Bomb groups participating:– all 1AD except 398BG; all 2AD; all 3AD except 452BG and 493BG. 351BG acted as 'chaff' screening force for 1AD. Wesel Force comprised 385BG, 390BG, 490BG. Bomb group losses:– 2AD – 93BG – 1, 3AD – 94BG – 1. 388BG B-17 cr. on t/o, crew safe. 445BG B-24 cr. t/o Gissing, 4 k.

All Fighter groups except 56FG, 356FG, 364FG, 479FG. Fighter group losses:– 4FG – 1, 20FG – 1, 55FG – 2, 78FG – 4, 352FG – 2, 353FG – 1.

OTHER OPERATIONS: 7PG despatched 19 F-5s and 4 Spitfires on PR Germany (with escort). 25BG despatched 3 Mosquitoes 'chaff' dispensing for bombers, 1 Mosquito as monitor for 2AD, 6 Mosquitoes as WR Continent/UK, and 4 B-17s on WR Azores/Atlantic/UK. 5ERS despatched 18 P-47s and 2 OA-10s on ASR patrols. 36BS despatched 7 B-24s on RCM. 1 B-24, 6 P-51s on radio-relays.

A mechanic, his ear tuned to the engine sound, watches as a 30 ton Liberator forces its way into the morning sky from Wendling's main runway, 24 February. The B-24H is the second *YMCA Flying Service* named for the local tea waggon.

EVENT

When Allied heavy bombers began their campaign against the German oil industry in May 1944 there were 81 identified targets, 58 refineries and 23 synthetic plants. At the time of the 8th Air Force missions to oil targets on 24 February, all the refineries were believed no longer functioning and only four of the synthetic plants appeared to be still in production. In any case, by this date only 45 of these oil installations were still in German hands, the Soviet armies having overrun those in the Balkans. It was estimated that production had fallen from 1,250,000 tons at the start of the campaign to less than 300,000 tons in nine months. The 8th Air Force heavies had concentrated their effort on the synthetic industry based on the brown coal of south-east Germany, while the RAF attacked the plants in the Ruhr fed with the hard coal of that district. The 15th Air Force bombers concentrated on installations in the Balkans and Austria.

The name game. 381BG Fortress *Stage Door Canteen*, which had been adopted by the movie world, completed 100 missions in February 1945 and on the 25th actresses Anna Neagle, Jean Kent and Phyllis Calvert arrived with a large celebration cake to dispense among crew and ground crew. By this time the worthy B-17G had reached 105 missions so extra candles were added. Here Anna Neagle cuts the first slice. Onlookers appear more interested in the glamorous film star than in the cake.

24/25 FEBRUARY 1945

8AF 846 NIGHT LEAFLET OPERATION

NLS despatched 12 B-24s; Holland, Germany.

25 FEBRUARY 1945

8AF 847

	Despatched		Effective	Target		Bombs Tonnage	E/A	Losses MIA	E	Dam	Casualties KIA	WIA	MIA
1AD	B-17	377	63	FRIEDRICHSHAFEN/ MAYBACH AFV/I	(P)	187.5		2	1	135	1	2	18
			73	MUNICH STN & M/Y	(P)	215.7							
			174	MUNICH OST M/Y	(P)	512.8							
			51	ULM M/Y	(S)	152.2							
			1	KENZINGEN	(O)	3.0							
3AD	B-17	452	315	MUNICH M/Y	(P)	989.6		3	1	197	1	3	27
			88	NEUBURG	(P)	261.0							
			13	KAUFBEUREN	(O)	36.0							
			12	LUDWIGSFELDT M/Y	(O)	35.5							
			1	KEMPTEN	(O)	3.0							
			2	DURLADINGEN	(O)	6.0							
			1	RORTWELL	(O)	3.0							
			5	T/O		15.0							
2AD	B-24	368	115	ASCHAFFENBURG M/Y	(P)	259.9		0	1	31	3	6	0
			54	ASCHAFFENBURG AFV/I	(P)	125.8							
			93	SCHWABISCH HALL A/F	(P)	249.0							
			96	GIEBELSTADT A/F	(P)	216.5							
TOTALS:		1197	1157			3180.5	0	5	3	363	5	11	45
	P-51	149	136	ESCORT 1AD			1–0– 2 (G)	2	0		0	0	2
	P-51	145	140	ESCORT 3AD			2–0– 3 (G)	0	0		0	0	0
	P-51	135	126	ESCORT 2AD				0			0	0	0
	P-47	21	262	SWEEP – N &			21–0– 4	0	1		0	0	0
	P-51	263		CENTRAL GERMANY			10–0–12 (G)	6	0		0	0	6
	P-51	8	8	ESCORT PR A/C				0	0		0	0	0
	P-51	34	32	SCOUTING FORCES				0	0		0	0	0
TOTALS:		755	704				21–0– 4 13–0–17 (G)	8	1	?	0	0	8

REMARKS: Tank factories, airfields associated with jet a/c, oil depots and rail targets were attacked visually – with the exception of Maybach factory which was bombed by GH. Bomb groups participating:– all 1AD except 91BG and 306BG; all 2AD except 389BG; all 3AD except 94BG and 390BG. Bomb group losses:– 1AD – 92BG – 1, 351BG – 1; 3AD – 95BG – 1, 388BG – 1, 486BG – 1. MIA 95BG, 96BG and 351BG B-17s cr. landed Switzerland. During assembly 446BG B-24 cr. Capel St.Mary, crew baled. On return 398BG B-17 cr. landing base. 96BG B-17 cr. Continent.

All Fighter groups operating. Fighter group e/a credits: 4FG – 2, 20FG – 7, 55FG – 7, 78FG – 2, 355FG – 1, 364FG – 2. Fighter group losses:– 4FG – 1, 20FG – 3, 356FG – 3, 364FG – 1. 55FG claimed to have shot down 7 Me 262 jets.

OTHER OPERATIONS: 7PG despatched 4 F-5s on PR Germany (with escort). 1 F-5 MIA. 25BG despatched 3 Mosquitoes 'chaff' dispensing for 1AD, 1 Mosquito on monitor sortie for 2AD, 6 Mosquitoes on WR Continent/UK. 36BS despatched 7 B-24s on RCM. 5ERS despatched 24 P-47s and 2 OA-10s on ASR search, 12 P-51s on radio-relays.

25/26 FEBRUARY 1945

8AF 848 NIGHT LEAFLET OPERATION

NLS despatched 12 B-24s; France, Holland, Germany.

25BG despatched 1 Mosquito on *Skywave* sortie SE Germany.

Dawn chorus at Horsham St.Faith as 458BG prepares to set out on its 200th mission. Waiting turn to move onto the main runway, most aircraft still have bomb bay doors rolled up to let fuel fumes escape. Second B-24 in line, *Table Stuff* appears to have trouble as both left motors have been stopped.

26 FEBRUARY 1945

8AF 849

	Despatched		Effective	Target		Bombs Tonnage	E/A	Losses MIA	E	Dam	Casualties KIA	WIA	MIA
1AD	B-17	377	363	BERLIN/ SCHLESISCHER R/S	(P)	895.5		2	0	21	0	1	18
			1	OSNABRÜCK	(O)	2.5							
3AD	B-17	446	418	BERLIN/ ALEXANDERPLATZ	(P)	1250.7		1	1	43	8	2	9
			4	R/S T/O		11.0							
2AD	B-24	361	285	BERLIN NORTH R/S	(P)	650.3		0	2	26	0	3	3
			37	EBERSWALDE	(S)	68.7							
			4	T/O		7.5							
	B-17	17	17	SCREENING FORCES				0	0	0	0	0	0
	B-24	6	6					0	0	0	0	0	0
TOTALS:		1207	1135			2886.2	0	3	3	90	8	6	30
	P-51	244	214	ESCORT 1AD			4–0–0	0					
	P-51	240	232	ESCORT 3AD			2–0–0 (G)	3					
	P-47	20	20	ESCORT 2AD				0					
	P-51	190	190					0					
	P-51	32	31	SCOUTING FORCES				0					
TOTALS:		726	687				4–0–0 2–0–0 (G)	3	1	?	0	0	2

REMARKS: PFF (H2X) attacks on Berlin targets. Bomb groups participating: all 1AD except 398BG; all 2AD; all 3AD except 490BG. Bomb group losses:– 1AD – 92BG – 1, 384BG – 1; 3AD – 452BG – 1. Aborting 388BG B-17 cr. Rt range, France, 8 k. 93BG B-24 c/l and 491BG B-24 abandoned Soviet-held territory; crew baled, safe.

All Fighter groups operating. Fighter group losses:– 78FG – 1, 357FG – 1. MIA 357FG pilot baled over sea, rescued. 479FG made ground claim for enemy B-17 at Steenwizk. 20FG P-51 cr. Continent.

OTHER OPERATIONS: 25BG despatched 3 Mosquitoes 'chaff' screening for bombers, 3 Mosquitoes on special operation, 4 Mosquitoes on WR Continent/Atlantic/UK, and 5 B-17s on WR Azores/Atlantic/UK. 5ERS despatched 18 P-47s and 1 OA-10s on ASR patrols. 36BS despatched 6 B-24s on RCM.

26/27 FEBRUARY 1945

8AF 850 NIGHT LEAFLET OPERATION

NLS despatched 12 B-24s; Holland, Germany.

492BG despatched 5 B-24s on *Carpetbagger* operation.

27 FEBRUARY 1945

8AF 851

	Despatched		Effective	Target		Bombs Tonnage	E/A	Losses MIA	E	Dam	Casualties KIA	WIA	MIA
2AD	B-24	351	314	HALLE M/Y	(P)	723.8		2	0	4	1	0	18
			21	BITTERFELD (O)		51.0							
			3	T/O		5.7							
3AD	B-17	378	355	LEIPZIG C/C	(P)	1013.6		0	1	3	1	0	0
			3	T/O		8.6							
1AD	B-17	378	362	LEIPZIG C/C	(S)	916.0							
			4	T/O		10.0		0	0	0	1	0	0
TOTALS:		1107	1062			2728.7	0	2	1	7	3	0	18

P-47	18	196	ESCORT 2AD	1–0– 0	0	0		0	0	0
P-51	197			45–0– 3 (G)	2	1		0	0	2
P-51	243	235	ESCORT 3AD	1–0– 0 36–0–16 (G)	0	0		0	0	0
P-51	246	218	ESCORT 1AD		0	0		0	0	0
P-51	28	28	SCOUTING FORCES		0	0		0	0	0
P-51	13	13	ESCORT PR A/C		0	0		0	0	0
TOTALS:	745	690		2–0– 0 81–0–19 (G)	2	1	?	0	0	2

REMARKS: Road and rail communications at Halle and Leipzig attacked using H2X. Bomb groups participating:– all 1AD except 305BG; all 2AD; all 3AD except 96BG, 100BG, 385BG, 487BG. Bomb group losses:– 2AD – 445BG – 2. B/d 486BG B-17 c/l Continent.

All Fighter groups operated. Fighter group e/a credits: 55FG – 1, 355FG – 1. Fighter group losses:– 4FG – 2. 479FG P-51 c/l near Detling A/F.

OTHER OPERATIONS: 7PG despatched 2 F-5s and 2 Spitfires on PR central and E Germany (with escort). 25BG despatched 3 Mosquitoes dispensing 'chaff' for 1AD, 1 Mosquito as monitor for 2AD, 1 Mosquito on *Red Stocking* operation, 4 Mosquitoes on WR Germany/UK, and 4 B-17s on WR Azores/Atlantic/UK. 36BS despatched 6 B-24s on RCM. 5ERS despatched 18 P-47s and 1 OA-10 on ASR patrols. 2 P-51s and 1 B-24 on radio-relays.

27/28 FEBRUARY 1945

8AF 852 NIGHT BOMBING OPERATION

492BG despatched 26 B-24s (23 effective) to Wilhelmshafen oil storage where 58.7 tons bombs dropped by PFF.

8AF 852 NIGHT LEAFLET OPERATION

NLS despatched 1 B-17 and 11 B-24s; Holland, Germany.

Load 'em up again. Ordnance man operates the electric hoist on the narrow catwalk of a B-24 while another steadies the 500 lb bomb being taken into the bay of a 44BG Liberator at Shipdham, 28 February.

28 FEBRUARY 1945

8AF 854

		Despatched	Effective	Target	Bombs Tonnage	E/A	Losses MIA	E	Dam	Casualties KIA	WIA	MIA
1AD	B-17	378	143	SOEST M/Y (P)	390.1		1	0	0	0	0	3
			151	HAGEN M/Y (P)	429.5							
			74	SCHWERTE M/Y (P)	209.2							
			1	T/O	2.9							
2AD	B-24	346	95	ARNSBERG VIADUCT (P)	253.0		0	0	0	0	0	0
			77	SIEGEN M/Y (P)	213.3							
			79	MESCHEDE HENSCHEL M/I (P)	210.5							
			81	BIELEFELD VIADUCT (P)	227.5							
			1	NEUSTADT RD JUNC (O)	3.0							
3AD	B-17	380	364	KASSEL M/Y (S)	922.0		0	0	0	0	0	0
			6	T/O (6)	20.5							
TOTALS:		1104	1072		2881.5	0	1	0	0	0	0	3
	P-51	112	106	ESCORT 1AD			0			0	0	0
	P-51	123	117	ESCORT 2AD			1			0	0	1
	P-51	118	113	ESCORT 3AD		0–0–1 10–0–4 (G)	1			0	0	1
	P-51	318	308	STRAFING WÜRZBURG – MUNICH AREA		8–0–6 (G)	3			0	0	3
	P-47	20	18	FIGHTER-BOMBER ABLAR/OFFENBACH/ WERDORF	2.3		0			0	0	0
	P-51	30	29				0			0	0	0
	P-51	16	16	ESCORT PF A/C								
TOTALS:		737	707		2.3	0–0– 1 18–0–10 (G)	5	?		0	0	5

REMARKS: PFF attacks on rail targets in Germany. 1AD and 2AD used GH; 3AD used H2X. Bomb groups participating: all 1AD except 92BG and 381BG; all 2AD; all 3AD except 34BG, 95BG, 388BG, 447BG. Bomb group losses:– 1AD – 457BG – 1. MIA 457BG B-17 ditched 10 miles from North Foreland, 6 rescued.

All Fighter groups operating. Fighter group losses:– 55FG – 1, 78FG – 1, 359FG – 2, 479FG – 1.

OTHER OPERATIONS: 7PG despatched 4 F-5s and 1 Spitfire on PR Germany (with escort). 25BG despatched 5 Mosquitoes on special operation in support of 1AD and 2AD, 4 Mosquitoes on WR Ireland/Holland/Germany, and 3 B-17s on WR Azores/Atlantic/UK. 36BS despatched 6 B-24s (5 effective) on RCM. 5ERS despatched 16 P-47s and 1 OA-10 on ASR search and patrols. 8 P-51s on radio-relays.

28 FEBRUARY/1 MARCH 1945

8AF 855 NIGHT LEAFLET OPERATION

NLS despatched 11 B-24s; Holland & Germany.

25BG despatched 1 Mosquito on *Skywave* sortie SE Germany.

8AF 856 NIGHT BOMBING OPERATION

492BG despatched 24 B-24s (22 effective) to Freiburg rail depot where 63 tons bombs dropped by PFF.

EVENT

Problems with high octane aviation fuels in fighter engines came to a head in March 1945 when groups were instructed to return to the use of 130 grade which, as it was in short supply, would initially only be used in the fuselage tank in the P-51. The previous year 'Superfuel' 150 grade was introduced in an operational test, approved and became generally available during the summer. Opinions quickly changed as it was soon found that there was a marked increase in the lead fouling of spark plugs from use of this fuel. In September 1944, when all groups were using 150 grade, there were several take-off crashes as a direct result of loss of ignition under full power due to fouled plugs. Carburettor adjustments helped but did not banish the problems with 'Purple Peril Gas' as pilots referred to it. An anti-lead additive was then introduced, the resulting mixture identified as PEP fuel. The 355th Group tried it operationally and confirmed that PEP solved the spark plug problem, and early in 1945 this fuel superseded straight 150 grade. Hardly were the stations supplied when another problem began – a dramatic reduction in engine life due to valve seat damage. In an effort to combat this latest problem pilots were advised to cruise at low power settings on long range but this simply re-introduced the plug fouling problem. By March most groups were clamouring to go back to the trusty old 130 grade!

1 MARCH 1945

8AF 857

	Despatched		Effective	Target		Bombs Tonnage	E/A	Losses MIA	E	Dam	Casualties KIA	WIA	MIA
1AD	B-17	452	115	BRUCHSAL M/Y	(P)	338.8		0	0	27	0	0	0
			69	REUTLINGEN M/Y	(P)	207.0							
			85	NECKARSULM M/Y	(P)	250.0							
			107	HEILBRONN M/Y	(P)	316.8							
			36	GÖTTINGEN M/Y	(P)	104.0							
			25	HEIDELBERG	(S)	74.5							
2AD	B-24	321	253	INGOLSTADT M/Y	(P)	606.3		0	1	0	0	0	0
			62	AUGSBURG	(S)	126.0							
3AD	B-17	449	449	ULM M/Y	(P)	1324.3		0	2	3	16	2	0
			2	T/O		6.4							
	B-24	6	6	SCREENING FORCE				0	0	0	0	0	0
TOTALS:		1228	1209			3354.1	0	0	3	30	16	2	0
	P-51	100	92	ESCORT 1AD				2	2		0	0	2
	P-51	194	181	ESCORT 2AD			1–0–0	1			0	0	1
	P-51	152	147	ESCORT 3AD			1–0–0 9–0–7 (G)	3			0	0	3
	P-51	32	31	SCOUTING FORCES			1–0–1	1			0	0	1
	P-51	10	9	ESCORT PR A/C				0			0	0	0
TOTALS:		488	460				3–0–1 9–0–7 (G)	7	2	?	0	0	7

REMARKS: Marshalling yards in central and southern Germany. Three plants suspected of making Me 262 jet parts could not be attacked owing to cloud. 1AD and 3AD units able to make some visual attacks but most bombing by H2X. Bomb groups participating:– all 1AD; all 2AD; all 3AD except 100BG and 486BG. Two 385BG B-17s lost in a collision over Belgium, 16 killed. On return 392BG B-24 c/l Hollesley, crew safe.

All Fighter groups except 20FG, 55FG, 56FG, 352FG, 357FG, 359FG operating. Fighter group e/a credits:– 353FG – 1, 355 – 1. Fighter group losses:– 78FG – 3, 355FG – 1, 356FG – 1, 364FG – 1, 479FG – 1. 356FG P-51 cr. Monewden, pilot safe. 4FG P-51 cr. near Brussels, pilot safe.

OTHER OPERATIONS: 7PG despatched 8 F-5s on PR Germany (with escort). 25BG despatched 2 Mosquitoes on radio test and scout sorties Germany, 4 Mosquitoes on WR Continent/UK, and 4 B-17s on WR Azores/Atlantic/UK. 36BS despatched 6 B-24s on RCM. 5ERS despatched 14 P-47s and 1 OA-10 on ASR patrols. 1 B-24 on radio-relays. 1 25BG Mosquito on *Red Stocking* sortie Holland.

Everyone comes to look as 1/Lt Earl Stier brings a badly damaged Mustang back to Duxford on 1 March. No one was more amazed than Stier after he climbed out of the cockpit and went back to look at the gaping hole made by a direct flak hit. Nearly half the vertical tail had been blasted away.

INCIDENT

Mr. Lucky, a veteran B-17G of the 385th Group, lived up to its name for more than a year until 1 March 1945 when it flew in the low element of a formation bound for Ulm. Over Belgium cloud banks rose to more than 13,000 ft and to Sgt Joe F. Jones in the tail gun compartment of *Mr. Lucky* it appeared that the B-17s alongside were near the tops. Suddenly they were immersed in the mist and just as quickly out of it. At that moment Jones was aware of violent movement, a loud noise following which he realised that the continual thunder of the engines and accompanying vibration felt in the tail had ceased. Pressure in his ears told him the Fortress was descending rapidly. Alarmed, he called the pilot on the interphone but there was no response. Convinced the aircraft was out of control, he grabbed his parachute and made for the gunner's escape door just behind him. The door would not open so he pulled the hinge pins and tried to kick it out, bracing himself against the other side of the narrow fuselage to get leverage, but the door stuck fast. He then tried to go forward into the waist only to find the fuselage distorted with twisted metal and loose cables barring his way. Just what had occurred – a flak hit, collision or structural failure – Jones did not know but he could tell the bomber was still descending rapidly. In desperation he even thought of releasing his parachute and feeding it out over the tail guns to act as an air brake. Then, realising this was futile, he again braced himself across the fuselage, took out a cigarette, lit it, took one draw . . . and then oblivion. Three days passed before Jones regained consciousness to learn he was in a British Army hospital at Ostend. A Belgian, Gilbert Deschepper, came to visit him daily and from him and the nursing staff Joe Jones learned that he alone of the crew was 'Mr. Lucky'. His Fortress had, through some unknown cause, collided with another and been severed aft of the wing. The tail half had fallen to earth with Joe trapped in it, its speed of descent slowed by the planing actions of the elevators. Despite this the impact in a field at Slijpe was violent and when Deschepper and some other Belgians arrived on the scene they at first thought that the man in the crumpled tail was dead. After tearing away metal they extracted him and were surprised to find him alive and with little obvious hurt except a badly cut tongue. In hospital injury to the lower abdomen was found and the medical men fully expected Jones to die in his coma from shock to his system and internal bleeding. But Joe Jones did recover, having no major injuries, and was back at his base at Great Ashfield in April. No one was more amazed at his incredible escape than Joe himself. As an outcome, an enduring bond of friendship arose between him and his Belgian rescuers.

1/2 MARCH 1945

8AF 858 NIGHT LEAFLET OPERATION

NLS despatched 11 B-24s; Holland and Germany.

25BG despatched 4 Mosquitoes on night PR Germany and 1 A-26 on *Red Stocking* operation.

2 MARCH 1945

8AF 859

	Despatched		Effective	Target		Bombs Tonnage	E/A	Losses MIA	E	Dam	Casualties KIA	WIA	MIA
1AD	B-17	450	60	BÖHLEN O/I	(P)	138.0	2–0– 1	3	1	52	1	4	29
			36	ROSITZ O/R	(P)	80.6							
			36	BÖHLEN G/B	(P)	90.0							
			255	CHEMNITZ	(S)	594.2							
			12	PENIG	(O)	25.9							
			13	SAALFELD	(O)	29.3							
			12	JOCKETA	(O)	24.6							
			12	T/O		26.6							
			1	COLOGNE	(O)	2.3							
2AD	B-24	321	38	MAGDEBURG/ ROTHENSEE O/I	(P)	85.0		3	0	61	1	0	28
			257	MAGDEBURG/ BUCKAU AFV/I	(P)	360.7							
			4	T/O		11.0							

continued on next page

3AD	B-17	455	24	RUHLAND O/I	(P)	57.9	6–3–10	8	0	53	1	2	72
			406	DRESDEN	(S)	1080.6							
			1	T/O		2.5							
	B-24	6											
TOTALS:		1232	1167			2589.2	8–3–11	14	1	166	3	6	129
	P-51	272	254	ESCORT 1AD			7½–1– 4	0	0		0	0	0
							0 –0– 6 (G)						
	P-47	22	187	ESCORT 2AD			5 –2– 0	0	0		0	0	0
	P-51	180						0	2		0	0	0
	P-51	249	225	ESCORT 3AD			54 –3–16	13	0		0	0	13
							36 –0–23 (G)						
	P-51	28	25	SCOUTING FORCE				0	0		0	0	0
	P-51	23	22	ESCORT PR A/C				0	0		0	0	0
TOTALS:		774	713				66½–6–20	13	2	?	0	0	13
							36 –0–29 (G)						

REMARKS: Synthetic oil plants at Böhlen, Magdeburg and Ruhland and a tank works at Magdeburg were primaries. 1AD and 2AD made visual and H2X attacks, 3AD only H2X. 305BG sent to attack flak batteries at Böhlen prior to main attack. All bomb groups except 452BG and 493BG participated. Bomb group losses:– 1AD – 305BG – 2, 398BG – 1; 2AD – 392BG – 1, 466BG – 1, 467BG – 1; 3AD – 96BG – 3, 385BG – 4, 390BG – 1. MIA 392BG B-24 accidentally shot down by another B-24 in gun test over e/t. Two 96BG B-17s lost collided over sea.

All Fighter groups operating. Fighter group e/a credits:– 78FG – 14, 339FG – 14, 352FG – 6, 353FG – 15, 357FG – 14. Fighter group losses:– 55FG – 1, 78FG – 1, 339FG – 3, 353FG – 3, 357FG – 5. On return a 479FG P-51cr. while landing base.

OTHER OPERATIONS: 7PG despatched 14 F-5s and 4 Spitfires on PR Germany (with escort) and 2 F-5s and 1 Spitfire on PR St.Nazaire. 25BG despatched 2 Mosquitoes on screening operations with bombers, 6 Mosquitoes on WR Continent/North Sea, and 4 B-17s on WR Azores/Atlantic/UK. 5ERS despatched 20 P-47s and 2 OA-10s on ASR patrols. 36BS despatched 6 B-24s (5 effective) on RCM. 1 B-24 on radio-relay. 1 25BG Mosquito and 1 A-26 on *Red Stocking* sortie Germany.

2/3 MARCH 1945

8AF 860 NIGHT LEAFLET OPERATION

NLS despatched 12 B-24s, 11 effective; Holland, Germany.

482BG despatched 6 B-17s on radar scope sorties Nürnberg, Augsburg, Stuttgart.

492BG despatched 4 B-24s on *Carpetbagger* operations.

3 MARCH 1945

8AF 861

	Despatched		Effective	Target		Bombs Tonnage	E/A	Losses MIA	E	Dam	Casualties KIA	WIA	MIA
1AD	B-17	114	23	MISBURG O/R	(P)	68.5		0	0	11	9	5	0
			82	HANNOVER/ HANOMAG AFV/I	(S)	204.7							
			2	LEMFORD	(O)	3.6							
1AD	B-17	222	24	RUHLAND O/I	(P)	60.0		0	2	63			
			166	CHEMNITZ M/Y	(S)	399.5							
			11	PLAUEN	(O)	27.5							
			16	T/O		40.0							
2AD	B-24	94	41	NIENBURG BR	(P)	117.0		0	0	3	0	0	0
			48	BIELEFELD M/Y	(S)	131.5							
			1	T/O		3.0							
2AD	B-24	219	219	MAGDEBURG/ ROTHENSEE O/R	(P)	479.2	1–0–0	4	0	77	0	3	39
3AD	B-17	453	77	BRUNSWICK/ BÜSSING	(P)	235.2							
			53	BRUNSWICK/ WILKE O/I	(P)	165.5							
			61	BRUNSWICK/MIAG M/I	(P)	188.1							
			37	DOLLBERGEN O/R	(P)	126.2							
			53	DEDENHAUSEN O/R	(P)	159.9	1–2–4	5	0	53	0	1	41
			56	NIENHAGEN O/R	(P)	195.2							
			38	HILDESHEIM VDM	(S)	101.5							
			36	BIELEFELD M/Y	(O)	110.7							
			23	HERFORD	(O)	73.5							
			2	T/O		5.0							
TOTALS:		1102	1069			2895.3	2–2–4	9	2	207	9	9	80

	P-51	46	44	ESCORT MISBURG		0–0– 1	1	0		0	0	1
	P-51	214	193	ESCORT RUHLAND		3–0– 0 10–0–23 (G)	2	0		0	0	2
	P-51	144	129	ESCORT MAGDEBURG		0–0– 2	2	0		0	0	2
	P-51	21	19	ESCORT NIENBURG			0	0		0	0	0
	P-51	180	169	ESCORT 3AD		0–0– 4 9–0– 2 (G)	2	1		0	0	2
	P-51	107	100	SWEEP–LEIPZIG/ MAGDEBURG AREA		1–0– 3	1	0		0	0	1
	P-51	31	30	SCOUTING FORCES			0					
TOTALS:		743	684			4–0–8 19–0–25 (G)	8	1	?	0	0	8

REMARKS: 1AD Misburg Force (41CBW groups) bombed by H2X. 1AD Ruhland Force (91BG, 92BG, 305BG, 398BG, 401BG, 457BG) attacked the primary visually and secondary by H2X. 2AD Nienburg Force (96CBW groups) attacked the primary visually and secondary by H2X. 2AD Magdeburg Force (all other 2AD groups) attacked visually. 3AD groups (all except 94BG and 385BG) attacked visually. Bomb group losses: 2AD – 445BG – 2, 448BG – 2; 3AD – 95BG – 1, 100BG – 1, 487BG – 1, 493BG – 2. MIA 448BG B-24s collided near target. 2 b/d 92BG B-17s collided and cr. near Brussels, 9 k.

All Fighter groups operating. Fighter group e/a credits:– 352FG – 1. Fighter group losses:– 4FG – 1, 55FG – 2, 339FG – 3, 359FG – 1, 479FG – 1. MIA 55FG P-51 piloted by Lt Liles c/l on Prague/Letnany A/F while strafing. Lt Howes landed to pick Liles up but was unable to get his P-51 airborne. Aborting P-51 c/l base.

OTHER OPERATIONS: 7PG despatched 16 F-5s and 8 Spitfires on PR France and Germany. 25BG despatched 1 Mosquito on PR Enschede, 3 Mosquitoes on special sorties, 5 Mosquitoes on WR Continent/UK, and 4 B-17s on WR Azores/Atlantic/UK. 5ERS despatched 18 P-47s and 1 OA-10 on ASR patrols. 36BS despatched 4 B-24s on RCM. 1 25BG Mosquito on *Red Stocking* sortie Germany.

3/4 MARCH 1945

8AF 862 NIGHT BOMBING OPERATION

492BG despatched 24 B-24s, 18 effective, dropping 65.0 tons on Emden M/Y using PFF.

482BG despatched 4 B-17s on radar scope sorties.

4 MARCH 1945

8AF 863

	Despatched		Effective	Target	Bombs Tonnage	E/A	Losses MIA	E	Dam	Casualties KIA	WIA	MIA
1AD	B-17	373	69	SCHWABMÜNCHEN A/I (P)	169.3		0	2	9	0	3	0
			223	ULM M/D (P)	657.3							
			59	ULM M/Y (S)	173.5							
			12	REUTLINGEN (O)	36.0							
			1	T/O	3.0							
2AD	B-24	274	18	ASCHAFFENBURG (O)	41.0		1	0	19	8	0	0
			11	TUTTLINGEN (O)	27.2							
			10	ASTADTAACH (O)	24.5							
			8	PFORZHEIM (O)	18.5							
			11	STUTTGART M/Y (O)	26.5							
			10	DONAUESCHINGEN R/R (O)	23.5							
			50	STUTTGART (O)	116.7							
			36	T/O	84.0							
3AD	B-17	376	69	INGOLSTADT R/I (S)	175.7		0	2	7	17	0	0
			75	ULM M/Y (S)	123.5							
			1	AUSBUCH (O)	3.0							
			3	T/O	9.0							
	B-17	5	5	SCOUTING FORCES			0	0	0	0	0	0
TOTALS:		1028	671		1712.2	0	1	4	35	25	3	0
	P-51	156	150	ESCORT 1AD			0	1		0	0	0
	P-47	41	139	ESCORT 2AD			0	0		0	0	0
	P-51	117					0	0		0	0	0
	P-51	186	172	ESCORT 3AD			1	1		0	0	1
	P-51	22	21	SCOUTING FORCES			0	0		0	0	0
TOTALS:		522	482			0	1	2	?	0	0	1

REMARKS: Weather prevented both 2AD and 3AD attacking primaries; airfields associated with jet a/c use and industrial targets at Baumenheim, Nürnberg, Fürth and Ingolstadt. 1AD Force (all groups except 92BG and 457BG) bombed by GH; 2AD Force (all groups) bombed by H2X with some visual but some groups were recalled over e/t. Only leading elements of 3AD bombed using H2X. 3AD not participating or being recalled over friendly territory: 34BG, 390BG, 447BG, 487BG, 490BG, 493BG. Bomb group losses:– 467BG – 1. MIA 467BG B-24 ditched on return 10 miles off Cromer, 2 saved. Cloud caused all 2AD units to seek T/Os. 9 466BG B-24s bombed Basel and 6 392BG B-24s bombed Zürich, both units believing they were over Freiburg. Swiss casualties were 5 killed and 19 injured. After t/o a burning 401BG B-17 abandoned and cr. Bitteswell, crew safe. Bombers assembled over beacons in France. 34BG B-17 cr. France.

All Fighter groups operating. Fighter group losses:– 78FG – 1. A 339FG P-51 cr. on t/o and a 339FG P-51 cr. landing.

OTHER OPERATIONS: 7PG despatched 2 F-5s and 1 Spitfire to La Pallice and La Rochelle. 25BG despatched 4 Mosquitoes 'chaff' screening for 1AD, 1 Mosquito monitor for 2AD, 5 Mosquitoes (1 aborted) on WR UK/North Sea/Atlantic, 1 Mosquito on WR Germany, and 4 B-17s on WR Azores/Atlantic/UK. 5ERS despatched 15 P-47s and 1 OA-10 on ASR patrols. 3SF using B-17s for weather scouting for first time.

4/5 MARCH 1945

8AF 864 NIGHT LEAFLET OPERATION

NLS despatched 1 B-17 and 11 B-24s; Holland, Germany. 1 B-17 MIA shot down into Stour estuary by AA during intruder raid.

5 MARCH 1945

8AF 865

	Despatched		Effective	Target		Bombs Tonnage	E/A	Losses MIA	E	Dam	Casualties KIA	WIA	MIA
1AD	B-17	151	128	CHEMNITZ	(S)	306.1		0	0	15	0	0	0
			10	PLAUEN C/I	(O)	23.4							
3AD	B-17	152	105	CHEMNITZ	(S)	257.4		1	0	0	0	0	9
			24	PLAUEN C/I	(O)	59.0							
			9	FULDA C/I		22.5							
2AD	B-24	126	120	HAMBURG HARBURG I/O	(P)	323.5		0	0	0	0	0	0
TOTALS:		429	396			991.9	0	1	0	15	0	0	9
	P-51	232	197	ESCORT 1AD				0	1		1	0	0
	P-51	188	172	ESCORT 3AD				0	2		0	0	0
	P-47	51	186	ESCORT 2AD				0	0		0	0	0
	P-51	149						0	0		0	0	0
	P-51	27	27	KREUZTAL M/Y/ GIRKEN ROTH		13.5		0	1		0	0	0
	P-51	28	28	SCOUTING FORCES				0	0		0	0	0
	P-51	14	14	ESCORT PR A/C				0	0		0	0	0
TOTALS:		689	624			13.5	0	0	4	?	1	0	0

REMARKS: B-17 Forces were prevented from attacking the synthetic oil plant at Ruhland by weather. All targets bombed using H2X. 1AD Force consisted of 351BG, 381BG, 398BG, 457BG. 2AD Force consisted of all groups except 93BG, 466BG, 467BG. 3AD Force consisted of 385BG, 388BG, 452BG, 490BG. Bomb group losses:– 388BG – 1.

All Fighter groups operating. 361FG conducted fighter-bomber mission. A 78FG P-51 cr. t/o, pilot killed. On return, 339FG P-51 c/l Continent, pilot safe. 361FG P-51 cr. Continent. 364FG P-51 pilot baled near Tonges, safe.

OTHER OPERATIONS: 7PG despatched 4 F-5s on PR Germany (with escort). 25BG despatched 3 Mosquitoes 'chaff' dispensing for bombers, 1 Mosquito as 2AD monitor (aborted) 5 Mosquitoes on WR Continent/UK, and 4 B-17s on WR Azores/Atlantic/UK. 36BS despatched 2 B-24s on RCM. 5ERS despatched 12 P-47s and 1 OA-10 on ASR patrols. 20 P-51s on radio-relays.

5/6 MARCH 1945

8AF 866 NIGHT BOMBING OPERATION

492BG despatched 24 B-24s, 21 effective, dropping 52.5 tons on Wiesbaden rail station by PFF markers.

8AF 867 NIGHT LEAFLET OPERATION

NLS despatched 11 B-24s, 9 effective; Holland, France, Germany.

6 MARCH 1945

Only Fighter groups operating were 352FG and 361FG which despatched 63 P-51s on 9AF support missions. 7PG despatched 1 F-5 with 3 P-51s escorting on PR to Hamburg area. 25BG despatched 3 Mosquitoes on WR Continent/UK and 3 B-17s on WR Azores/Atlantic/UK. 36BS despatched 2 B-24s on RCM.

6/7 MARCH 1945

8AF 868 NIGHT LEAFLET OPERATION

NLS despatched 12 B-24s; Holland, Germany.

482BG despatched 6 B-17s, 5 effective, on radar scope PR Germany.

492BG despatched 5 B-24s on *Carpetbagger* operations.

25BG despatched 1 Mosquito on *Skywave* sortie Italy.

7 MARCH 1945

8AF 869

	Despatched		Effective	Target		Bombs Tonnage	E/A	Losses MIA	E	Dam	Casualties KIA	WIA	MIA
2AD	B-24	246	144	SOEST M/Y	(P)	380.9		0	1	3	10	0	0
			80	BIELEFELD/ SCHILDESCHE W/V	(P)	236.5							
1AD	B-17	344	11	PADERBORN M/Y	(S)	34.5		0	1	20	1	0	0
			24	DORTMUND-HORDER VEREIN O/I	(P)	69.0							
			62	DORTMUND-HARPENERWEG O/I	(P)	188.2							
			113	SIEGEN M/Y	(S)	329.2							
			87	GIESSEN M/Y	(S)	281.5							
3AD	B-17	340	100	DATTELN-EMSCHER LIPPE O/I	(P)	340.0		0	0	56	0	0	0
			73	DATTELN-EMSCHER LIPPE O/I	(P)	243.5							
			77	CASTROP RAUXEL O/I	(P)	267.8							
			43	SIEGEN M/Y	(S)	146.0							
			28	GIESSEN M/Y	(S)	93.2							
			1	T/O		.2							
	B-24	6	6	SCREENING FORCE				0	0	0	0	0	0
	B-17	6	6					0	0	0	0	0	0
	B-17	4	4	SCOUTING FORCE				0	0	0	0	0	0
TOTALS:		946	859			2610.5	0	0	2	79	11	0	0
	P-47	39	77	ESCORT 2AD				0			0	0	0
	P-51	38											
	P-51	85	74	ESCORT 1AD				0			0	0	0
	P-51	75	76	ESCORT 3AD				0			0	0	0
	P-51	38	37	SWEEP–DÜMMER LAKE, KASSEL KOBLENZ				0			0	0	0
	P-51	23	23	ESCORT PR A/C				1			0	0	1
	P-51	24	24	SCOUTING FORCE				0			0	0	0
TOTALS:		322	311				0	1		1	0	0	1

REMARKS: Oil and communication targets attacked with PFF aids. 1AD and 2AD used GH and H2X; 3AD used Micro H and H2X. Bomb groups participating:– all 1AD except 305BG, 351BG, 381BG; all 2AD except 44BG and 448BG; all 3AD except 45CBW groups and 490BG. A 389BG B-24 cr. after t/o at Old Costessey, crew killed. On return 303BG c/l Hedenham, crew injured.

Fighter groups operating: 55FG, 56FG, 78FG, 356FG, 357FG, 364FG, 479FG. On return a 359FG P-51 pilot baled and landed near Wix.

OTHER OPERATIONS: 7PG despatched 5 F-5s and 1 Spitfire on PR W and C Germany (with escort). 1 7PG P-51 MIA. 25BG despatched 3 Mosquitoes screening for bombers, 1 Mosquito on special sorties, 5 Mosquitoes on WR Continent/North Sea, and 3 B-17 on WR Azores/Atlantic/UK. 36BS despatched 5 B-24s on RCM. 5ERS despatched 8 P-47s and 1 OA-10 on ASR patrols.

7/8 MARCH 1945

8AF 870 NIGHT LEAFLET OPERATION

NLS despatched 12 B-24s, 11 effective; Germany, Holland.

8AF 871 NIGHT BOMBING OEPRATION

492BG despatched 20 B-24s, 19 effective, dropping 150.0 tons on Dortmund by PFF. 1 B-24 MIA.

25BG despatched 1 Mosquito on *Red Stocking* operation, and 1 Mosquito on *Skywave* sortie Germany, a/c c/l base on return.

8th MARCH 1945

8AF 872

		Despatched	Effective	Target		Bombs Tonnage	E/A	Losses MIA	E	Dam	Casualties KIA	WIA	MIA
2AD	B-24	360	70	BETZDORF M/Y	(P)	189.0		0	0	3	0	0	0
			114	SIEGEN M/Y	(P)	298.9							
			73	DILLENBURG M/Y	(P)	194.3							
			10	LIMBURG	(O)	22.4							
			10	FRANKFURT	(O)	29.0							
3AD	B-17	526	99	LANGENDREER ROBERT MUSER O/I	(P)	334.7		0	0	26	0	0	0
			63	LANGENDREER BRUCHSTRASSE O/I	(P)	204.0							
			110	DORTMUND GNEISENAU O/I	(P)	380.8							
			122	FRANKFURT HEDDERNHEIM C/F	(P)	444.4							
			69	GIESSEN M/Y	(S)	240.4							
			18	FRANKFURT M/Y	(S)	63.0							
			13	WETZLAR	(O)	45.5							
1AD	B-17	458	114	ESSEN EMIL O/I	(P)	338.9		0	1	0	0	0	0
			37	BOTTROP MATHIES STINNES O/I	(P)	112.2							
			75	BUER SCHOLREN O/I	(P)	223.5							
			111	HÜLS AUGUST VIKTORIA O/I	(P)	327.6							
			109	ESSEN M/Y	(O)	321.5							
	B-17	9	9	SCREENING FORCE				0	0	0	0	0	0
TOTALS:		1353	1226			3770.1	0	0	1	29	0	0	0
	P-51	102	99	ESCORT 2AD									
	P-51	99	95	ESCORT 3AD									
	P-51	98	93	ESCORT 1AD									
	P-51	27	27	SCOUTING FORCES									
TOTALS:		326	314					0	1		0	0	0

REMARKS: Benzol plants at Langendreer, Dortmund, Essen, Bottrop and Hüls, an oil plant at Gelsenkirchen, and rail targets were primaries for Forces involving all bomb groups. 1AD and 2AD attacked primaries using GH; 3AD attacked with Micro H. All other bombing by H2X.

Fighter groups participating: 4FG, 20FG, 339FG, 353FG, 355FG, 359FG. A 339FG P-51 cr. landing on return.

OTHER OPERATIONS: 7PG despatched 2 F-5s on PR Germany. 25BG despatched 3 Mosquitoes on special operations, 5 Mosquitoes on WR Continent/Norway/UK, and 4 B-17s on WR Azores/Atlantic/UK. 5ERS despatched 10 P-47s on ASR patrols. 36BS despatched 5 B-24s on RCM.

1 25BG Mosquito on *Red Stocking* sortie Germany.

8/9 MARCH 1945

8AF 873 NIGHT LEAFLET OPERATION

NLS despatched 11 B-24s, 11 effective; France, Holland, Germany.

8AF 874 NIGHT BOMBING OPERATION

492BG despatched 15 B-24s, 15 effective, dropping 37.5 tons on Dortmund M/Y.

482BG despatched 6 B-17s on H2X scope photo operation, Regensburg, Brunswick, Kassel.

492BG despatched 7 B-24s, 4 effective on *Carpetbagger* operations.

9 MARCH 1945

8AF 875

		Despatched	Effective	Target		Bombs Tonnage	E/A	Losses MIA	E	Dam	Casualties KIA	WIA	MIA
3AD	B-17	423	150	FRANKFURT/OST M/Y	(P)	371.9		3	1	182	0	7	28
			222	FRANKFURT/MAIN M/Y	(P)	596.6							
			38	FRANKFURT C/F	(P)	121.8							
			6	SCREENING FORCE									

Pride of 446BG, *Ronnie*, in the process of unloading forty 100 lb demolition bombs and two incendiary clusters on Rheine marshalling yards, 9 March. An original aircraft of the Group, *Ronnie* was claimed as the first 8AF B-24 to complete 100 missions. It needed a special plea by 446BG Command to prevent the bomber being salvaged after a heavy landing on the Continent in January. Repairs took several weeks.

1AD	B-17	336	318	KASSEL M/Y & M/I	(P)	675.0		3	2	118	0	4	28
			6	SCREENING FORCE									
2AD	B-24	282	97	MÜNSTER M/Y	(P)	234.8		1	0	52	0	1	12
			93	RHEINE M/Y	(P)	230.8							
			87	OSNABRÜCK M/Y	(P)	196.9							
	B-17	4	4	3AD SCOUTING FORCE				0	0	0	0	0	0
TOTALS:		1045	1021			2427.8	0	7	3	352	0	12	68
	P-51	101	94	ESCORT 3AD			0–0–1		0				
	P-51	99	97	ESCORT 1AD					1				
	P-51	51	47	ESCORT 2AD					0				
	P-47	47	141	SWEEP–FREELANCE					1				
	P-51	103		SUPPORT BOMBER					0				
	P-51	27	27	SCOUTING FORCES					0				
	P-51	15	15	ESCORT PR A/C			0–0–1		0				
TOTALS:		443	421				0–0–2	0	2	?	0	0	0

REMARKS: Marshalling yards and industrial plants. 3AD used visual, Micro H, H2X and smoke markers to attack primaries; 1AD was able to attack visually; 2AD used GH and H2X. 12 B-24s in 2AD totals released 'chaff'. Bomb group losses:– 1AD – 92BG – 1, 381BG – 1, 398BG – 1; 2AD – 389BG – 1; 3AD – 95BG – 1, 96BG – 1, 490BG – 1. 2 rescued. On return, a 398BG B-17 cr. landing base. 306BG B-17 Cat E on Continent. B/d 96BG B-17 c/l Continent.

Fighter groups operating: 55FG, 56FG, 78FG, 352FG, 356FG, 357FG, 359FG, 361FG, 364FG, 479FG. Continental based groups supported 9AF with 103 sorties. Fighter group e/a credits:– 361FG – 1. Two 361FG P-51 c/l on Continent, pilots safe.

OTHER OPERATIONS: 7PG despatched 1 F-5 on PR Lorient, 12 F-5s (1 aborted) and 3 Spitfires on PR Germany (with escort). 25BG despatched 1 Mosquito on PR N France, 1 Mosquito on *Skywave* ex Italy, 3 Mosquitoes 'chaff' screening for 1AD, 3 Mosquitoes on WR Continent/North Sea, and 3 B-17s Azores/Atlantic/UK. 5ERS despatched 12 P-47s and 1 OA-10 on ASR patrols. 36BS despatched 4 B-24s on RCM.

9/10 MARCH 1945

8AF 876 NIGHT LEAFLET OPERATION

NLS despatched 11 B-24s, 11 effective; Holland, France, Germany.

492BG despatched 9 B-24s, 2 effective, on *Carpetbagger* operations.

482BG despatched 5 B-17s on H2X scope photo sorties.

10 MARCH 1945

8AF 877

	Despatched		Effective	Target		Bombs Tonnage	E/A	Losses MIA	E	Dam	Casualties KIA	WIA	MIA
2AD	B-24	376	115	ARNSBERG R/V	(P)	320.7		0	0	1	0	0	0
			129	PADERBORN M/Y	(P)	319.4							
			114	BIELEFELD R/V	(P)	310.0							
			10	BIELEFELD M/Y	(S)	27.5							
3AD	B-17	526	138	SOEST M/Y	(P)	351.3		0	1	44	0	2	0
			109	DORTMUND/SÜD M/Y	(P)	262.1							
			111	DORTMUNDERFELD M/Y	(P)	270.3							
			153	DORTMUND/EVING M/Y	(P)	372.3							
1AD	B-17	457	89	SINSEN R/C	(P)	184.6		0	0	26	0	1	0
			38	COESFELD R/C	(P)	83.2							
			116	SCHWERTE M/Y	(P)	249.4							
			41	HAGEN M/Y	(P)	89.7							
			136	DORTMUND M/Y	(S)	295.6							
			33	HAMM	(O)	71.3							
3AD	B-17	12	12	SCREENING FORCE				0	0	0	0	0	0
	B-17	3	3	3AD SCOUTING FORCE				0	0	0	0	0	0
TOTALS:		1374	1347			2958.0	0	0	1	71	0	3	0
	P-51	155	146	ESCORT 2AD				0	0		0	0	0
	P-51	158	152	ESCORT 3AD				0	1		0	0	0
	P-51	100	98	ESCORT 1AD				2	0		0	0	2
	P-47	23	144	FREELANCE SUPPORT			2–0–1	0			0	0	0
	P-51	127		BOMBERS									
	P-51	74	72	SUPPORT 9AF				0	0		0	0	0
	P-51	28	27	SCOUTING FORCES				0	0		0	0	0
	P-51	5	5	ESCORT PR A/C				0	0		0	0	0
TOTALS:		670	644				2–0–1	2	1	?	0	0	2

REMARKS: Rail targets all attacked by PFF methods. All bomb groups except those of 93CBW participated.

All Fighter groups except 78FG operating with 352FG and 361FG supporting 9AF operations with 72 sorties. Fighter group e/a credits:– 56FG – 2. Fighter group losses:– 359FG – 2. Both 359 a/c MIA were shot down by US AA over Remagen. A 339FG P-51 abandoned by pilot over Belgium after being shot up by B-17.

OTHER OPERATIONS: 7PG despatched, 7 F-5s and 4 Spitfires on PR French Atlantic coast and Ruhr (with escorts). 25BG despatched 4 Mosquitoes 'chaff' screening for bombers, 3 Mosquitoes on special operations, 4 Mosquitoes on WR Continent/North Sea, and 4 B-17s on WR Azores/Atlantic/UK. 5ERS despatched 13 P-47s and 2 OA-10s on ASR patrols. 36BS despatched 5 B-24s on RCM. 1 25BG Mosquito on *Red Stocking* sortie.

INCIDENT

Detailed to escort a combat wing of Fortresses attacking in the Dortmund area on 10 March 1945, a section leader of 339th Group was checking on the position of the various bomber formations as they withdrew from the target. Below and to the left of his Mustangs was a B 17 group that could not be identified so he directed a member of his flight, Lt Jerome Sainlar, to 'go in' and observe the markings on the bombers. The B-17s were about 2,000 ft below and Sainlar dived to a position where he could see the bombers had red tail tips. Looking for the usual group identity letter Sainlar descended further by putting his Mustang into a broadside skid towards the B-17s. A series of thuds and the alarming realisation that his fighter was being shot at brought an abrupt change in direction as he endeavoured to get out of range. The P-51 had taken an estimated 10 hits, two bullets having gone through the canopy behind his head. The engine or coolant system had also been damaged and while Sainlar was able to nurse the crippled machine back past Allied lines, near St.Trond the engine burst into flames necessitating a hasty exit and parachute descent. It was recorded in Group records that Sainlar 'took a very dim view of this anything but cordial treatment'. Two days later he was returned to base in a 'friendly' bomber, thoroughly convinced of the truth of the adage that anything that flies and hasn't got four engines is an enemy 'plane to a bomber gunner.

10/11 MARCH 1945

8AF 879 NIGHT BOMBING OPERATION

492BG despatched 13 B-24s, 13 effective, dropping 31.5 tons on Münster M/Y by PFF.

8AF 880 NIGHT LEAFLET OPERATION

NLS despatched 12 B-24s, 12 effective; France, Holland, Germany.

11 MARCH 1945

8AF 881

		Despatched	Effective	Target		Bombs Tonnage	E/A	Losses MIA	E	Dam	Casualties KIA	WIA	MIA
2AD	B-24	352	344	KIEL/KRUPP GERMANIA U/Y	(P)	882.6		0	0	2	0	0	0
3AD	B-17	485	469	HAMBURG/ WILHELMSBURG O/R	(P)	1123.8		1	0	41	0	3	10
			1	T/O		2.5							
1AD	B-17	413	406	BREMEN/ DESCHIMAG U/Y	(P)	1012.4		0	0	9	0	0	0
	B-17	6	6	SCREENING FORCE				0	0	0	0	0	0
TOTALS:		1256	1226			3021.3	0	1	0	52	0	3	10
	P-47	49	232	ESCORT 2AD				0					
	P-51	198						1					
	P-51	265	252	ESCORT 3AD				2					
	P-51	255	237	ESCORT 1AD				1					
	P-51	18	18	ESCORT PR A/C				0					
	P-51	29	27	SCOUTING FORCES				0					
TOTALS:		814	766				0	4		?	1	0	3

REMARKS: H2X attacks on U-boat yards and an oil refinery in north Germany. Bomb groups participating:– all 1AD except 91BG; all 2AD except 458BG; all 3AD except 95BG. Bomb group losses:– 487BG – 1.

All Fighter groups operating. Fighter group losses:– 78FG – 1, 353FG – 1, 359FG – 1, 479FG – 1. MIA 353FG P-51 cr. in sea going out, pilot lost. MIA 479FG P-51 pilot baled 20 miles E Lowestoft, found dead.

OTHER OPERATIONS: 7PG despatched 6 F-5s and 1 Spitfire on PR French Atlantic coast and Germany (with escort). 25BG despatched 8 Mosquitoes 'chaff' screening for bombers, 1 Mosquito as monitor for 2AD, 1 Mosquito on special radio sortie, 3 Mosquitoes on WR Continent/North Sea, and 3 B-17s on WR Azores/Atlantic/UK. 36BS despatched 5 B-24s on RCM. 5ERS despatched 11 P-47s and 1 OA-10 on ASR patrols. 1 B-17, 1 B-24 (with 2 P-51 escort), 10 P-51s on radio-relays.

11/12 MARCH 1945

8AF 882 NIGHT LEAFLET OPERATION

NLS despatched 12 B-24s, 11 effective; Holland, Germany.

482BG despatched 5 B-17s, 4 effective, on H2X scope PR Germany.

12 MARCH 1945

8AF 883

		Despatched	Effective	Target		Bombs Tonnage	E/A	Losses MIA	E	Dam	Casualties KIA	WIA	MIA
2AD	B-24	227	220	SWINEMÜNDE M/Y	(P)	521.5		0	0	0	0	0	0
3AD	B-17	230	223	SWINEMÜNDE M/Y	(P)	547.5		0	0	2	0	0	0
			1	HUSUM M/Y	(O)	2.5							
1AD	B-17	220	218	SWINEMÜNDE M/Y	(P)	539.5		1	0	4	1	0	10
2AD	B-24	154	74	WETZLAR M/Y	(P)	186.2		0	0	0	0	2	0
			75	FRIEDBERG M/Y	(P)	176.6							
3AD	B-17	298	113	MARBURG M/Y	(P)	245.2		0	0	4	0	0	0
			141	SIEGEN M/Y	(P)	243.6							
			24	FRANKFURT M/Y	(S)	40.5							
1AD	B-17	226	116	BETZDORF M/Y	(P)	261.9		0	0	0	0	0	0
			110	DILLENBURG M/Y	(P)	238.0							
TOTALS:		1355	1315			3003.0		1	0	10	1	2	10

continued on next page

12 MARCH 1945 *(contd.)*

	P-51	150	129	ESCORT 2AD SWINEMÜNDE		1					
	P-51	150	139	ESCORT 3AD SWINEMÜNDE	4–0–1	3					
	P-51	152	144	ESCORT 1AD SWINEMÜNDE		0					
	P-47 P-51	51 152	192	ESCORT 4th, 5th 6th TASK FORCES		0					
	P-51	108	97	SWEEP-BOMBER SUPPORT		0					
	P-51	10	10	ESCORT PR A/C		0					
	P-51	24	23	SCOUTING FORCES		0					
TOTALS:		797	734		4–0–1	4	1		0	0	3

REMARKS: Marshalling yards attacked by PFF, all bomb groups participating. Swinemünde bombed by H2X with each Division sending a task Force. 1AD sent 40CBW and 94CBW groups; 2AD sent 20CBW groups and 389BG, 392BG, 445BG, 467BG; 3AD sent 34BG, 95BG, 100BG, 385BG, 452BG, 486BG. 2AD second Force consisted of 44BG, 453BG, 458BG, 466BG, 491BG and used GH. 3AD second Force consisted of 94BG, 96BG, 388BG, 390BG, 447BG, 487BG, 490BG, 493BG and used Micro H. 1AD second Force consisted of 1CBW and 41CBW groups and used GH. Bomb group losses:– 92BG – 1. MIA 92BG B-17 landed Sweden.

All Fighter groups except 356FG operating. Fighter group e/a credits:– 339FG – 4. Fighter group losses:– 4FG – 1, 55FG – 1, 78FG – 2. One MIA 78FG P-51 in sea 45 miles W Ijmuiden, pilot baled and rescued by OA-10 (this P-51 was on radio-relay). 339FG P-51 c/l Soviet held territory.

OTHER OPERATIONS: 7PG despatched 5 F-5s and 2 Spitfires on PR Germany (with escort). 25BG despatched 4 Mosquitoes 'chaff' screening for 2AD, 1 Mosquito as monitor for 2AD, 5 Mosquitoes on WR Continent/Baltic/UK, and 4 B-17s on WR Azores/Atlantic/UK. 5ERS despatched 10 P-47s and 2 OA-10s on ASR patrols. 36BS despatched 5 B-24s on RCM. 1 B-17, 1 B-24, 16 P-51s on radio-relay. 1 P-51 MIA (see above).

12/13 MARCH 1945

8AF 884 NIGHT LEAFLET OPERATION

NLS despatched 12 B-24s, 11 effective; Holland, Germany.

492BG despatched 10 B-24s, 4 effective on *Carpetbagger* operations.

13 MARCH 1945

Weather restricted operations. Continental based 361FG despatched 16 P-51s on uneventful sweep of Remagen/Koblenz area. 7PG despatched 17 F-5s on PR Germany. 25BG despatched 1 Mosquito on *Red Stocking* operation, 4 Mosquitoes on WR Continent/North Sea, and 4 B-17s on WR Azores/Atlantic/UK.

13/14 MARCH 1945

8AF 885 NIGHT LEAFLET OPERATION

NLS despatched 10 B-24s, 9 effective; Germany, Holland.

482BG despatched 5 B-17s (1 a/c aborted) on H2X PR Plauen, Ulm, Heilbronn.

14 MARCH 1945

8AF 886

	Despatched		Effective	Target		Bombs Tonnage	E/A	Losses MIA	E	Dam	Casualties KIA	WIA	MIA
3AD	B-17	526	58	NIENHAGEN O/R	(P)	197.0		2	1	188	3	6	19
			75	HANNOVER/ GEBRÜDER M/I	(P)	264.0							
			61	HANNOVERSCHE MASCHNBAU	(P)	207.8							
			74	HANNOVER EISENWERKE	(P)	221.0							
			56	MISBURG O/R	(P)	192.5							
			80	SEELZE M/Y	(P)	176.8							
			29	OSNABRUCK	(S)	132.0							
			61	HANNOVER M/Y	(S)	192.8							

continued on facing page

A gaping flak wound in the radio room, Lt Edward Aubuchon brings his Fortress into Thorpe Abbotts on the afternoon of 14 March.

1AD	B-17	449	72	VLOTHO R/RB	(P)	214.5		1	0	56	0	1	9
			114	BAD OSTEN-HAUSEN R/B	(P)	338.5							
			144	LÖHNE M/Y & R/J	(P)	313.8							
			60	HILDESHEIM VDM WKS	(P)	205.2							
			39	OSNABRÜCK	(S)	113.2							
			12	HAMELN M/Y	(O)	41.7							
			1	DIEMONDE	(O)	1.0							
			1	WETZLAR M/Y	(O)	2.2							
2AD	B-24	272	31	HOLZWICKEDE M/Y	(P)	73.0		0	0	4	1	5	0
			126	GÜTERSLOH M/Y	(P)	317.4							
			110	GIESSEN M/Y	(S)	255.3							
	B-17	6	6	SCREENING FORCE				0	0	0	0	0	0
8AF 887 DISNEY													
1BD	B-17	9	9	IJMUIDEN E/P		39.1		0	0	0	0	0	0
TOTALS:		1262	1219			3498.8	0	3	1	248	4	12	28
	P-51	204	192	ESCORT 3AD				0	2		0	0	0
	P-51	194	182	ESCORT 1AD			1–0–1	0	0		0	0	0
	P-47	54	185	ESCORT 2AD			3–0–0	1	0		0	0	1
	P-51	140						0	0		0	0	0
	P-51	33	29	SUPPORT 9AF BOMBERS			1–0–0	0	0		0	0	0
	P-51	50	50	SWEEP–STEIN-HUDER-KASSEL			11–0–0	0	0		0	0	0
	P-51	82	82	SWEEP–REMAGEN BRIEDGEHEAD				1	1		0	0	1
	P-51	20	20	ESCORT PR A/C				0	0		0	0	0
	P-51	27	26	SCOUTING FORCES			1–0–0	0	0		0	0	0
TOTALS:		804	766				17–0–1	2	3	?	0	0	2

REMARKS: Oil, rail and industrial targets. All bomb groups except 2CBW groups participated. 3AD attacked visually and with H2X; 1AD was visual at all targets except Osnabrück which was attacked using GH; 2AD was visual and H2X. Bomb group losses:– 1AD – 398BG – 1; 3AD – 390BG – 2. Prior to t/o a 458BG B-24 caught fire and exploded at base, no casualties. Abortive 487BG B-17 cr. Carlton Colville, crew baled, 2 killed. Mission 887 was first use of *Disney* rocket bombs by 92BG.

All Fighter groups operating. Fighter group e/a credits: 56FG – 3, 352FG – 1, 353FG – 11, 356FG – 1. Fighter group losses:– 56FG – 1, 361FG – 1. On return 2 78FG P-51 c/l base, pilots safe. MIA 56FG P-47 in sea off Ostend, pilot lost. 361FG P-51 c/l Continent.

OTHER OPERATIONS: 7PG despatched 33 F-5s and 3 Spitfires on PR Germany and Czechoslovakia (with escorts). 25BG despatched 4 Mosquitoes 'chaff' screening for 2AD, 1 Mosquito monitor for 2AD, 4 Mosquitoes on WR Holland, Germany, Eire, and 4 B-17s on WR Azores/Atlantic/UK. 5ERS despatched 18 P-47s and 4 OA-10s on ASR patrols and search – a German pilot rescued by OA-10. 36BS despatched 4 B-24s on RCM.

14/15 MARCH 1945

8AF 888 NIGHT BOMBING OPERATION

492BG despatched 7 B-24s which dropped 13.5 tons on Wiesbaden M/Y by PFF.

482BG despatched 3 B-17s on H2X PR Grafenwöhr and also dropped leaflets on Fulda.

25BG despatched 2 Mosquitoes on night PR Altenbeken, 1 abort.

15 MARCH 1945

8AF 889

	Despatched			Effective	Target		Bombs Tonnage	E/A	Losses MIA	E	Dam	Casualties KIA	WIA	MIA
2AD	B-24	372		308	ZOSSEN ARMY HQ	(P)	666.8		1	1	32	3	4	5
				31	GARDLINGEN R/C	(O)	71.0							
				11	PAREY R/B	(O)	25.7							
				3	T/O		4.8							
1AD	B-17	300		276	ZOSSEN ARMY HQ	(P)	706.4		0	0	20	1	4	16
				13	STENDAL M/Y	(O)	32.5							
				3	T/O		8.5							
1AD	B-17	149		145	ORANIENBURG M/Y	(P)	367.0		1	1	55	0	8	66
3AD	B-17	526		467	ORANIENBURG M/Y	(P)	1327.5		7	0	233			
				31	WITTENBERG	(O)	91.0							
				12	HAVELBERG	(O)	35.0							
				1	DURSTADT M/Y	(O)	3.0							
				1	MELLENDORF M/Y	(O)	3.0							
				1	SCHMARSAU	(O)	3.0							
				1	DEDELSTORF A/F	(O)	3.0							
	B-17	6		6	SCREENING FORCE				0	0	0	0	0	0
TOTALS:		1353		1310			3348.0	0	9	2	340	4	16	87
	P-47	54		255	ESCORT 2AD				0					
	P-51	220							2					
	P-51	156		142	ESCORT 1AD 1st FORCE			1–0–0	1					
	P-51	98		82	ESCORT 1AD 2nd FORCE				1					
	P-51	254		238	ESCORT 3AD				0					
	P-51	30		29	SCOUTING FORCES				0					
	P-51	9		9	SWEEP–BONN/ KOBLENZ				0					
	P-51	12		9	ESCORT PR				0					
TOTALS:		833		764				1–0–0	4	6		1	0	3

REMARKS: All bomb groups operating. 2AD and 1AD first Force attacked a German Army HQ near Berlin and T/Os visually. 1AD second Force consisting of 1CBW groups and 351BG also attacked visually at Oranienburg. 3AD attacked visually but some units had to resort to H2X on T/Os. Bomb group losses:– 1AD – 398BG – 1; 2AD – 392BG – 1; 3AD – 94BG – 1, 388BG – 1, 447BG – 4. 487BG – 1. B/d 303BG B-17, 2 b/d 487BG B-17s and 1 b/d 445BG B-24 c/l liberated Poland. MIA 392BG B-24 ditched 30 miles NE Gt. Yarmouth, 6 rescued. B/d 381BG c/l Woodbridge A/F. B/d 453BG B-24 c/l Continent, 3 k.

All Fighter groups operating. 361FG flew a sweep. Fighter group e/a credits:– 359FG – 1. Fighter group losses:– 20FG – 1, 55FG – 1, 356FG – 1, 364FG – 1. 355FG P-51 c/l Poland. 2 56FG P-47s collided on t/o, 1 pilot killed. 2 353FG P-51s Cat E after t/o collision, pilots safe. MIA 55FG P-51 in sea, pilot saved by OA-10. 20FG P-51 c/l near Peterborough, pilot safe.

OTHER OPERATIONS: 7PG despatched 24 F-5s and 4 Spitfires on PR Germany (with escorts). 25BG despatched 8 Mosquitoes 'chaff' screening for 2AD, 4 Mosquitoes on WR Continent/UK, and 3 B-17s on WR Azores/Atlantic/UK. 5ERS despatched 10 P-47s and 2 OA-10s on ASR patrols and search. 36BS despatched 5 B-24s on RCM. 1 B-17, 1 B-24, 8 P-51s on radio-relays.

15/16 MARCH 1945

8AF 890 NIGHT BOMBING OPERATION

492BG despatched 16 B-24s, 14 effective, dropping 35.7 tons on Münster rail station by PFF.

25BG despatched 3 Mosquitoes on night PR Altenbeken area.

16 MARCH 1945

No offensive operations. 7PG despatched 41 a/c on PR Germany (including escort). 25BG despatched 4 Mosquitoes on WR Continent/UK and 4 B-17s on WR Azores/Atlantic/UK. 5ERS despatched 5 P-47s on patrols. 13 a/c were despatched on special operations.

EVENT

The value of some defensive gun positions on Fortresses had long been in question, particularly when considered against the performance advantages that removal would provide. The tail guns had always been the most useful defence point and became more so with the introduction of jet fighters whose high speed demanded an attack approach on the rear of the bombers to better the chance of hits. In March 1945 1st CBW instructed its three groups to experiment with the following deletions: 91st

Group to fly one squadron without waist guns and gunners, 381st Group to fly one squadron with ball turrets removed, and the 398th Group to fly a squadron without chin turrets. On the 16th of the month the 3rd Division instructed 94th Group to remove from all its B-17s the chin and ball turrets, with a hand-held 'tunnel' gun substituted for the latter. Sixty-five 94th B-17s had been modified by the end of the month. The benefits derived were: an average saving of 35 US gallons per hour in fuel consumed, five inches less manifold pressure for average performance giving a saving in engine wear, an improvement in take-off and general flying characteristics, 2,200 lb saving in weight, crew reduced from nine to eight men, and less maintenance for ground personnel.

16/17 MARCH 1945

8AF 891 NIGHT LEAFLET OPERATION

NLS despatched 12 B-24s, 12 effective; Germany, Holland.

482BG despatched 5 B-17s, 4 effective, on H2X PR Augsburg, Munich and Stuttgart.

492BG despatched 22 B-24s, 20 effective, on *Carpetbagger* operations.

17 MARCH 1945

8AF 892

	Despatched		Effective	Target		Bombs Tonnage	E/A	Losses MIA	E	Dam	Casualties KIA	WIA	MIA
3AD	B-17	527	214	RUHLAND O/I	(P)	594.3		4	1	46	1	1	35
			138	BITTERFELD O/I	(S)	381.0							
			125	PLAUEN/VOMAG M/I	(L)	350.9							
			19	FULDA	(O)	46.5							
			11	COTTBUS	(O)	33.0							
			3	T/O		9.0							
1AD	B-17	449	152	BÖHLEN O/I	(P)	378.4		1	2	15	0	0	9
			127	MOLBIS O/I & P/S	(P)	350.8							
			71	JENA, ZEISS WORKS	(S)	220.1							
			51	ERFURT M/Y	(S)	150.9							
			36	ALTENBURG		107.5							
			3	T/O		8.8							
2AD	B-24	346	170	MÜNSTER M/Y	(P)	420.3		0	0	3	0	0	0
			146	HANNOVER-HANOMAG AFV/P	(P)	387.2							
			9	HERFORD	(O)	25.5							
	B-24	6	6	SCREENING FORCE				0	0	0	0	0	0
TOTALS:		1328	1281			3464.2		5	3	64	1	1	44
	P-51	280	252	ESCORT 3AD				1	0		0	0	1
	P-51	283	266	ESCORT 1AD				1	0		0	0	1
	P-51	128	122	ESCORT 2AD				0	0		0	0	0
	P-51	86	79	FREELANCE SWEEP				0	1		0	0	0
	P-51	32	28	SCOUTING FORCES				0	0		0	0	0
	P-51	11	9	ESCORT PR				0	0		0	0	0
TOTALS:		820	756				0	2	1		0	0	2

REMARKS: Cloud extended from 15,000 ft down to 1,000 ft and 9/10 to 10/10. All bomb groups operating against oil, industrial and rail targets. Bombing by PFF:– 1AD and 3AD used H2X; 2AD used GH and H2X. Bomb group losses:– 1AD – 384BG – 1; 3AD – 95BG – 1, 388BG – 1, 487BG – 1, 490BG – 1. B/d 305BG, 398BG and 487BG B-17s c/l Poland.

All Fighter Groups except 56FG operating. Fighter group losses:– 353FG – 1, 364FG – 1. 78FG P-51 c/l Poland, pilot safe.

OTHER OPERATIONS: 7PG despatched 2 F-5s and 1 Spitfire on PR Germany (with escort). 25BG despatched 2 Mosquitoes as monitors for 2AD, 8 Mosquitoes 'chaff' screening for 1AD, 5 Mosquitoes on WR Continent/Atlantic and 5 B-17s on WR Azores/Atlantic/UK 25BG B-17 MIA over Atlantic. 5ERS despatched 16 P-47s and 2 OA-10s on ASR patrols. 36BS despatched 13 B-24s and 1 P-38 on RCM. 2 B-17s, 1 B-24 on radio-relays.

17/18 MARCH 1945

8AF 893 NIGHT LEAFLET OPERATION

NLS despatched 9 B-24s, 9 effective; Germany, Holland, France.

482BG despatched 6 B-17s on H2X PR Brunswick, Kassel, Dessau.

25BG despatched 1 Mosquito on *Skywave* sortie SW Germany.

Skymarkers and 1000 pounders can be seen below this 467BG B-24 dropping towards the Tegel armoured vehicle factory (on far shore of lake) during 8AF's last major mission to Berlin.

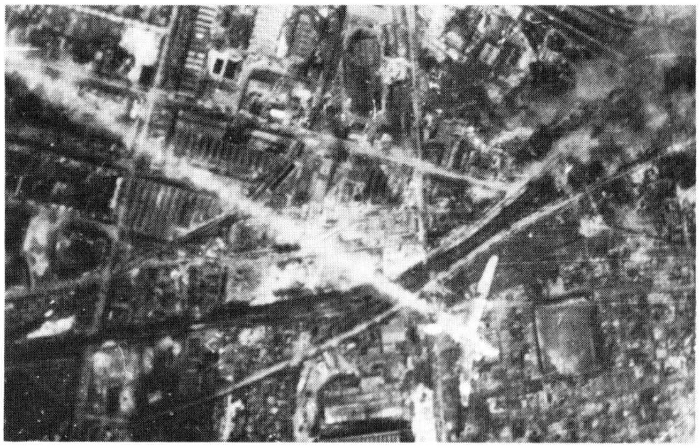

A victim of Berlin flak, 467BG B-24 42-52546 goes down, bomb bay aflame on 18 March.

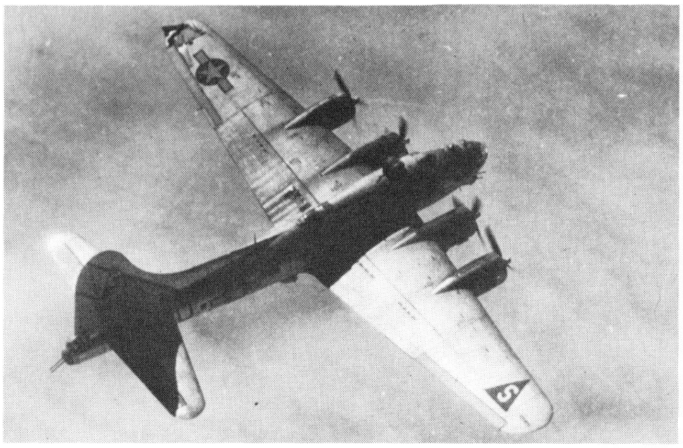

Winged. 401 BG's *Net Result* piloted by 2/Lt Cameron leaves Berlin. Fortunately the direct hit blasted up and out otherwise it might have fired the fuel tanks only a few inches away.

Back at Glatton a crowd gathers to see what 30 mm fire from an Me 262 jet has done to the trailing edge of 457BG B-17 *Lady Be Good*. Everyone is impressed.

18 MARCH 1945

8AF 894

	Despatched		Effective	Target		Bombs Tonnage	E/A	Losses MIA	E	Dam	Casualties KIA	WIA	MIA
1AD	B-17	450	421	BERLIN/ SCHLESISCHER R/S	(P)	1067.4	6–0–0	5	8	268	1	18	49
			13	ZEHDNUK	(S)	33.3							
			1	VECHTA	(O)	2.6							
3AD	B-17	530	495	BERLIN/NORD	(P)	1419.3	1–1–1	7	6	319	1	12	79
			3	LUDWIGSLUST	(O)	8.4							
			3	T/O		7.2							
2AD	B-24	347	80	BERLIN/	(P)	184.5		1	1	127	1	1	11
				HENNINGSDORF AFV/I	(P)	184.5							
			225	BERLIN/TEGEL AFV/I	(P)	420.9							
			9	ORANIENBURG	(O)	21.0							
			9	UELZEN	(O)	19.5							
			3	T/O		5.2							
	B-17	2	2	SCOUTING FORCE				0	0	0	0	0	0
TOTALS:		1329	1184			3373.8	7–1–1	13	15	714	3	31	139
	P-51	199	179	ESCORT 1AD			4–0–2	2					
	P-51	238	219	ESCORT 3AD			7–0–1	2					
	P-51	254		ESCORT 2AD			3–0–1	2					
	P-51	30	27	SCOUTING FORCES				0					
	P-51	12	1	ESCORT PR a/c				0					
TOTALS:		733	426 plus				14–0–4	6	1	4	0	0	5

REMARKS: Railway stations and tank plants in the Berlin area were attacked visually or by H2X as weather permitted. All bomb groups participated. Bomb group losses:– 1AD – 92BG – 1, 305BG – 1, 379BG – 1, 401BG – 1, 457BG – 1; 2AD – 467BG – 1; 3AD – 100BG – 3, 385BG – 1, 390BG – 2, 452BG – 1. B/d bombers c/l or f/l in Soviet controlled territory were 1 34BG, 1 92BG, 1 100BG, 2 303BG, 1 305BG, 1 385BG, 1 390BG, 1 398BG, 1 487BG B-17 and 1 467BG B-24. Most concentrated and successful attacks by Me 262 jets on bombers. Poor visibility enabled e/a to avoid escorts. 8 B-17s lost to flak. MIA 452BG B-17 collided 50 miles from Ijmuiden, 11 men lost. B/d 305BG, 379BG and 452BG a/c cr. Continent, Cat E. On return 398BG B-17 cr. landing base.

All Fighter groups except 56FG operating. Fighter group e/a credits:– 55FG – 4, 339FG – 4, 352FG – 3, 359FG – 2, 364FG – 2. Fighter group losses:– 4FG – 1, 55FG – 1, 352FG – 1, 353FG – 1, 361FG – 1, 364FG – 1. P-51s c/l or f/l behind Soviet lines were 1 352FG and 1 353FG. 353FG P-51 c/l after being shot at by Soviet fighter. 352FG, 353FG, 357FG, 359FG all reported contact with Soviet Yak-9 and La-5 fighters in Berlin area. MIA 4FG P-51 pilot rescued by another 4FG pilot who landed and picked him up. 339FG P-51 c/l St. Trond A/F, pilot safe.

OTHER OPERATIONS: 7PG despatched 5 F-5s on PR Germany (with escort). 25BG despatched 10 Mosquitoes 'chaff' screening and monitoring for 1AD and 2AD, 5 Mosquitoes (1 aborted) on WR Continent and 4 B-17s on WR Atlantic/UK. 5ERS despatched 10 P-47s and 2 OA-10s on ASR search. 36BG despatched 13 B-24s, 12 effective, on RCM. 1 B-17, 1 B-24, 8 P-51s on radio-relays.

18/19 MARCH 1945

8AF 895 NIGHT LEAFLET OPERATION

NLS despatched 10 B-24s, 10 effective; France, Holland, Germany.

482BG despatched 6 B-17s, 6 effective on H2X PR Dessau, Kassel, Brunswick.

25BG despatched 1 Mosquito on *Skywave* sortie France and Italy.

19 MARCH 1945

8AF 896

	Despatched		Effective	Target		Bombs Tonnage	E/A	Losses MIA	E	Dam	Casualties KIA	WIA	MIA
3AD	B-17	496	177	ZWICKAU MT/I	(S)	493.8	1–1– 2	4	4	121	9	5	49
			197	JENA OPTICAL WKS.	(S)	563.1							
			32	PLAUEN	(O)	96.0							
			44	FULDA M/Y	(O)	127.3							
			10	SAALFELD M/Y	(O)	30.0							
			4	T/O		11.5							
1AD	B-17	436	404	PLAUEN	(S)	1007.4		1	2	4	9	3	9
			20	FULDA M/Y	(O)	48.8							
			1	PRISSIG	(O)	2.5							
2AD	B-24	341	125	NEUBURG A/F	(P)	284.3		1	0	0	0	0	11
			84	LEIPHEIM A/F	(P)	189.5							
			126	BAUMENHEIM AV/I	(P)	289.2							
TOTALS:		1273	1224			3143.4	1–1–2	6	6	125	18	8	69
	P-51	198	183	ESCORT 3AD			2–0– 3	4					
	P-51	153	141	ESCORT 1AD				0					
	P-51	194	175	ESCORT 2AD			5–0– 0	0					
	P-51	98	95	FREELANCE FOR			33–2–14	6					
	P-51	28	27	BOMBERS SCOUTING FORCE				0					
	P-51	4	2	ESCORT PR a/c				0					
TOTALS:		675	623				40–2–17	10	0	?	0	0	9

REMARKS: Only 2AD was able to attack primaries visually. Cloud forced 3AD to use H2X with some visual sightings on secondaries and T/Os. 1AD attacked a secondary by H2X and was visual at T/Os. All bomb groups participated. Bomb group losses:– 1AD – 384BG – 1; 2AD – 44BG – 1; 3AD – 96BG – 1, 385BG – 1, 452BG – 2. One MIA B-17 in sea off Clacton. On return 2 487BG B-17s collided over Allied territory and cr. 384BG B-17 cr. Reigate 9 k. B/d 305BG B-17 Cat E base. 2 b/d 452BG B-17s c/l Poland, crews safe.

All Fighter groups except 20FG and 56FG operating. Fighter group e/a credits:– 4FG – 1, 78FG – 32, 355FG – 2, 357FG – 1, 359FG – 3. Fighter group losses:– 55FG – 1, 78FG – 5, 353FG – 3, 359FG – 1. MIA 353FG P-51 lost in sea 40 miles off Orfordness. MIA 55FG P-51 pilot baled near Walcheren, rescued.

OTHER OPERATIONS: 7PG despatched 15 F-5s and 2 Spitfires on PR Germany (with escorts). 25BG despatched 9 Mosquitoes screening and monitoring for 1, 2 and 3AD, 5 Mosquitoes on WR UK/Atlantic/Continent and 2 B-17 on WR Azores/Atlantic. 5ERS despatched 19 P-47s (11 effective) and 3 OA-10s on ASR patrols. 36BS despatched 13 B-24s and 2 P-38s on RCM, 1 a/c aborted. 1 B-17, 1 B-24, 10 P-51s on radio-relays.

19/20 MARCH 1945

8AF 897 NIGHT LEAFLET OPERATION

NLS despatched 12 B-24s, 11 effective; Holland, Germany.

482BG despatched 5 B-17s, 4 effective, on H2X PR Germany.

492BG despatched its first *Red Stocking* mission using 1 Mosquito.

20 MARCH 1945

8AF 898

	Despatched		Effective	Target		Bombs Tonnage	E/A	Losses MIA	E	Dam	Casualties KIA	WIA	MIA
3AD	B-17	152	13	HAMBURG/BLOHM & VOSS U/Y	(P)	39.0	1–0– 3	0	0	0	1	2	0
			133	HAMBURG PORT	(S)	388.7							
1AD	B-17	162	149	HAMBURG PORT	(S)	439.7	5–3– 2	3	1	54	0	0	27
			1	NORDHOLZ A/F	(O)	.5							
2AD	B-24	129	114	HEMMINGSTEDT O/I	(P)	308.0		1	0	9	0	0	12
	B-17	6	6	SCREENING FORCE				0	0	0	0	0	0
	B-17	2	2	SCOUTING FORCE				0	0	0	0	0	0
TOTALS:		451	418			1175.9	6–3–5	4	1	63	1	2	39
	P-51	79	70	ESCORT 3AD			0–0– 2	0					
	P-51	75	72	ESCORT 1AD			0–0– 2	0			0	0	0
	P-51	75	75	ESCORT 2AD			2–0– 1 1–0– 2 (G)	1			0	0	1
	P-51	82	78	STRAFING – BREMEN, HANNOVER AREA			2–0– 3 3–0– 2 (G)	1			0	0	1
	P-51	27	26	SCOUTING FORCES				0			0	0	0
	P-51	17	17	ESCORT PR a/c				0			0	0	0
TOTALS:		355	338				4–0–8 4–0–4 (G)	2	0	?	0	0	2

REMARKS: A small formation in 3AD force was able to bomb the primary at Hamburg visually, all other 3AD and 1AD units bombed secondaries or T/Os using H2X. 2AD was able to attack its primary visually. Bomb groups participating:– 1AD – 92BG, 303BG, 305BG, 384BG; 2AD – all groups; 3AD – 45CBW groups and 34BG, 95BG, 385BG, 447BG. Bomb group losses:– 1AD – 303BG – 2, 384BG – 1; 2AD – 445BG – 1. B/d 34BG B-17 c/l Eye A/F.

All fighter groups except 56FG, 352FG, 353FG, 361FG, 364FG operating. Fighter group e/a credits: 339FG – 2, 357FG – 2. Fighter group losses:– 55FG – 1, 339FG – 1.

OTHER OPERATIONS: 7PG despatched 11 F-5s and 2 Spitfires on PR Germany (with escort). 25BG despatched 9 Mosquitoes 'chaff' screening for bombers (1 Mosquito MIA), 1 Mosquito on special operation, 5 Mosquitoes on WR Germany and 5 B-17s on WR Azores/Atlantic/UK. 5ERS despatched 12 P-47s and 2 OA-10s on ASR patrols. 36BS despatched 10 B-24s on RCM. 1 B-24 cr. t/o base. 8 P-51s on radio-relays.

8AF 899 SPECIAL BOMBING OPERATION

482BG despatched 1 B-17 which dropped 2.0 tons on Oberursel at 1650 hrs from 25,000 ft. First operational test of Micro H Mk II. Escorted by 4 P-51s.

20/21 MARCH 1945

8AF 900 NIGHT LEAFLET OPERATION

NLS despatched 12 B-24s; Holland and Germany.

492BG despatched 1 Mosquito on *Red Stocking* and 2 A-26 on *Carpetbagger* operations. 1 A-26 MIA.

Lt.Col Vincent Masters commanded the only combat squadron in 8AF to operate both bomber and fighter types. In February 1945 the 3rd Scouting Force was given squadron status as 862BS and a few B-17s to supplement the P-51s in weather scout missions for 3rd Division. Masters, like the other Scout Force commanders, was a former bomber leader having come from 385BG. Note the panel bearing *Master's Mistress* has been transferred from his previous personal P-51.

21 MARCH 1945

8AF 901

	Despatched		Effective	Target		Bombs Tonnage	E/A	Losses MIA	E	Dam	Casualties KIA	WIA	MIA
3AD	B-17	152	107	PLAUEN AV/I	(S)	312.3	3–3–3	5	0	48	0	7	56
			34	REICHENBACH	(O)	95.0					(totals for all 3AD raids)		
			1	T/O		3.0							
3AD	B-17	151	129	HARDORF A/F	(P)	321.0		1	1	71			
			14	VORDEN A/F	(O)	42.8							
3AD	B-17	214	57	ZWISCHENAHN A/F	(P)	180.6		0	0	0			
			77	MARX A/F	(P)	238.7							
			74	WITTMUNDHAFEN A/F	(P)	178.4							
2AD	B-24	518	61	AHLHORN A/F	(P)	151.0		0	0	21	0	0	0
			165	HESEPE A/F	(P)	352.6							
			180	ACHMER A/F	(P)	415.1							
			90	ESSEN/MÜLHEIM A/F	(P)	90.0							
1AD	B-17	373	159	HOPSTEN A/F	(P)	325.0		1	0	49	1	3	9
			180	RHEINE A/F	(P)	362.0							
			13	HESEPE A/F	(O)	24.7							
			12	ACHMER A/F	(O)	22.7							
8AF 904													
2AD	B-24	92	90	ESSEN/MÜLHEIM A/F		194.6		0	0	60	0	1	0
TOTALS:		1408	1353			3114.9	3–3–3	7	1	189	1	11	65
	P-51	314	273	ESCORT 3AD 1st TF			9–0– 0 3–0– 0 (G)	3	1		0	0	3
	P-51	98	94	ESCORT 3AD 2nd TF			0–0– 2	0	0		0	0	0
	P-51	109	108	ESCORT 3AD 3rd TF			2–0– 8 (G)	1	0		0	0	1
	P-51	99	95	ESCORT 2AD			35–0–30 (G)	3	0		0	0	3
	P-51	102	97	ESCORT 1AD			6–0– 0 (G)	2	0		0	0	2
	P-51	36	36	SWEEP–GIEBELSTADT A/F			0–0– 6 (G)	0	0		0	0	0
	P-51	13	13	ESCORT PR a/c				0	0		0	0	0
	P-51	35	35	SCOUTING FORCES				0	1		0	0	0
TOTALS:		806	751				9–0– 2 46–0–44 (G)	9	2	?	0	0	9

REMARKS: Mission directed primarily against jet fighter bases. Visual bombing by all forces with GH and at Hopsten A/F. All bomb groups except 384BG participated. First 3AD task force consisted of 94BG, 100BG, 388BG, 490BG. Second 3AD task force consisted of 95BG, 390BG, 452BG. Third 3AD task force consisted of 34BG, 385BG, 447BG, 486BG, 487BG, 493BG. Bomb group losses:– 1AD – 457BG – 1, 3AD – 94BG – 1, 100BG – 1, 452BG – 1, 490BG 3. B/d 452BG B-17 burned after landing base.

All fighter groups except 56FG operating. Fighter group e/a credits 55FG – 1, 78FG – 5, 339FG – 1, 361FG – 2. Fighter group losses:– 4FG – 2, 55FG – 2, 353FG – 3, 355FG – 1, 364FG – 1. 78FG P-51 c/l in Soviet held territory, pilot safe. 4FG P-51 c/l Belgium.

OTHER OPERATIONS: 7PG despatched 9 F-5s, 1 P-38 and 1 Spitfire on PR Germany (with escort). 25BG despatched 4 Mosquitoes 'chaff' screening for 1AD, 2 Mosquitoes as monitors for 2AD and 3AD, 6 Mosquitoes on WR Continent/UK and 4 B-17s on WR Azores/Atlantic/UK. 5ERS despatched 16 P-47s and 3 OA-10s on ASR patrols and 4 P-51s also on ASR search. 36BS despatched 11 B-24s on RCM.

8AF 902 *DISNEY* OPERATION

305BG despatched 3 B-17s, 3 effective, to attack Ijmuiden E/P with 10.6 tons rocket-bombs. 6 P-51s flew as escort.

8AF 903 TEST OPERATION

482BG despatched 1 B-17 to Oberursel dropping 2.0 tons as Micro H Mk II test, 4 P-51s escorted.

21/22 MARCH 1945

8AF 905 NIGHT LEAFLET OPERATION

NLS despatched 9 B-24s, 8 effective; Holland, Germany.

482BG despatched 4 B-17s on H2X PR: Wiesbaden and Paderborn.

22 MARCH 1945

8AF 906

	Despatched		Effective	Target		Bombs Tonnage	E/A	Losses MIA	E	Dam	Casualties KIA	WIA	MIA
3AD	B-17	114	99	AHLHORN A/F	(P)	186.7		1	0	0	0	0	9
			13	OLDENBURG M/Y	(O)	24.0							
1AD	B-17	457	36	BOTTROP M/C	(P)	76.1		0	3	111	2	8	0
			111	BARNINGHOLTEN M/C	(P)	235.7							
			74	DORSTEN M/C	(P)	194.4							
			116	WESTERHOLT M/C	(P)	253.9							
			74	FELDHAUSEN N M/C	(P)	183.7							
			39	FELDHAUSEN S M/C	(P)	80.4							
3AD	B-17	297	67	HINSBECK M/C	(P)	193.7		0	0	114	0	3	0
			73	GERESHEIM M/C	(P)	209.6							
			75	RATINGEN M/C	(P)	215.7							
			74	MÜLHEIM M/C	(P)	181.6							
2AD	B-24	342	168	KITZINGEN A/F	(P)	378.5		0	1	1	8	0	0
			75	GIEBELSTADT A/F	(P)	175.1							
			82	SCHWAB. HALL A/F	(P)	186.3							
			8	WÜRZBURG	(S)	19.2							
3AD	B-17	113	109	FRANKFURT/ RHEIN-MAIN A/F	(P)	274.4		0	0	31	0	0	0
	B-17	6	6	SCREENING FORCE				0	0	0	0	0	0
	B-17	2	2	3AD SCOUTING FORCE				0	0	0	0	0	0
TOTALS:		1331	1301			3069.0	0	1	4	257	10	11	9
	P-51	99	95	ESCORT 3AD 1st TF				0			0	0	0
	P-51	99	95	ESCORT 1AD				0			0	0	0
	P-51	48	48	ESCORT 3AD 2nd TF			0–0–1 (G)	0			0	0	0
	P-51	153	138	ESCORT 2AD			3–0–1 13–0–7 (G)	2			0	0	2
	P-51	56	56	ESCORT 3AD 3rd TF				0			0	0	0
	P-51	22	19	ESCORT PR a/c			11–1–3	1			0	0	1
	P-51	153	150	ESCORT 15AF BOMBERS									
	P-51	32	31	SCOUTING FORCES				0			0	0	0
TOTALS:		662	632				14–1–4 13–0–8 (G)	3	1	?	0	0	3

REMARKS: Attacks on barracks, military encampments and airfields. All bombing visual and all bomb groups participating. 3AD first task force consisted of 13CBW groups; 3AD second task force consisted of 4CBW groups; 3AD third task force consisted of 45CBW groups. Bomb group losses:– 3AD – 390BG – 1. B/d 91BG B-17 c/l B-58 Belgium. On return 392BG B-24 caught fire and cr. Horstead, Norfolk, 4 baled, 8 killed. B/d 384BG B 17 f/l Continent – Cat E. B/d 381BG B-17 cr. Continent. 44BG B-24 cr. t/o.

All fighter groups except 56FG operating. Fighter group e/a credits:– 4FG – 11, 55FG – 1, 78FG – 2. Fighter group losses:– 55FG – 2, 355FG – 1. A 339FG P-51 cr. on t/o base, pilot safe. 4FG, 355FG, 479FG supported 15AF bombers from Italy – a first occasion. 352FG and 361FG supported RAF bombers.

OTHER OPERATIONS: 7PG despatched 22 a/c, 19 effective on PR Germant (with escort). 25BG despatched 9 Mosquitoes chaff screening for bombers, 1 Mosquito as monitor for 2AD, 5 Mosquitoes on WR Continent/UK and 5 B-17s on WR Azores/Atlantic/UK. 5ERS despatched P-47s and 2 OA-10s on ASR patrols (OA-10 rescued RAF pilot). 36BS despatched 4 B-24s on RCM. 482BG despatched 1 B-17 on Micro-H Mk II bombing test Gelnhausen A/F, 4 P-51s as escort.

22/23 MARCH 1945

8AF 907 NIGHT LEAFLET OPERATION

NLS despatched 10 B-24s, 9 effective; Holland, Germany.

482BG despatched 2 B-17s on H2X PR Koblenz area and leaflets dropped Essen.

25BG despatched 3 Mosquitoes, 2 effective, on night PR Altenbeken. 1 a/c cr. t/o base, crew safe.

492BG despatched 2 Mosquitoes on *Red Stocking* operation.

The togglier, Lt L.J. Clements, was killed by the 88 mm shell that took the nose piece off 96BG's 43-39107 over Hengesty, 23 March. The bomber was force-landed on Woensdrecht airfield.

23 MARCH 1945

8AF 908

	Despatched		Effective	Target		Bombs Tonnage	E/A	Losses MIA	E	Dam	Casualties KIA	WIA	MIA
2AD	B-24	319	79	RHEINE BRIDGE	(P)	216.3		3	1	95	1	3	35
			80	OSNABRÜCK M/Y	(P)	246.0							
			142	MÜNSTER M/Y & R/T	(P)	441.0							
			2	HOYA A/F	(O)	6.0							
3AD	B-17	519	113	HENGSTEY M/Y	(P)	281.4							
			91	GIESECKE M/Y	(P)	232.4		3	2	178	6	4	27
			184	HOLZWICKEDE M/Y	(P)	395.0							
			38	DORTMUND/ UNNA M/Y	(P)	89.5							
			31	SIEGEN M/Y	(S)	78.1							
			19	MESCHEDE	(S)	56.0							
			10	MARBURG M/Y	(S)	20.8							
			13	HERDECKE	(O)	39.0							
			1	HALIGER	(O)	3.1							
			10	SCHWERTE	(O)	20.2							
1AD	B-17	438	145	COESFELD M/Y	(P)	148.0		1	0	0	0	3	10
			120	RECKLINGHAUSEN M/Y	(P)	356.6							
			141	GLADBECK M/Y	(P)	436.0							
			13	WESTERHOLT M/Y	(O)	38.8							
			12	HECHFELDT	(O)	36.3							
TOTALS:		1276	1244			3140.5	0	7	3	273	7	10	72
	P-51	80	79	ESCORT 2AD									
	P-51	82	82	ESCORT 3AD									
	P-51	79	71	ESCORT 1AD									
	P-51	131	125	SWEEP – BREMEN, KASSEL AREA			1–0–0 0–0–1 (G)						
	P-51	84	71	SWEEP–SUPPORT 9AF									
	P-51	16	16	ESCORT PR a/c									
	P-51	27	25	WEATHER RECONN									
TOTALS:		499	469				1–0–0 0–0–1 (G)	0			0	0	0

REMARKS: All bomb groups operating against rail targets in west and central Germany. All bombing visual. Bomb group losses:– 1AD – 384BG – 1; 2AD – 93BG – 1, 389BG – 1, 445BG – 1; 3AD – 34BG – 1, 100BG – 1, 388BG – 1. Aborting 466BG B-24 cr. landing base and hit another B-24, crew safe. On return 95BG B-17 cr. Campsea Ash after collision, crew baled but 1 killed and 1 lost in sea. 447BG B-17 c/l Continent.

All fighter groups except 56FG operating. Fighter group e/a credits: 359FG – 1. 352FG and 361FG flew sweep in support of 9AF.

OTHER OPERATIONS: 7PG despatched 15 F-5s and 4 Spitfires on PR Germany (with escort). 25BG despatched 8 Mosquitoes 'chaff' screening for bombers, 2 Mosquitoes as monitors for 2AD and 3AD, 1 Mosquito on WR France/UK and 3 B-17s on WR Azores/Atlantic/UK. 5ERS despatched 14 P-47s and 3 OA-10s on ASR patrols (6 RAF men rescued by OA-10). 36BS despatched 1 P-38 on radar search and 12 B-24s, 11 effective on RCM.

8AF 909 TEST OPERATION

482BG despatched 1 B-17 which dropped 2.0 tons bombs on Ettinghausen A/F in Micro H Mk II test. 4 P-51s escorted.

23/24 MARCH 1945

8AF 910 NIGHT LEAFLET OPERATION

NLS despatched 10 B-24s, 9 effective; Holland, Germany.

25BG despatched 2 Mosquitoes on night PR Altenbeken.

492BG despatched 19 B-24s on *Carpetbagger* operation Denmark.

24 MARCH 1945

8AF 911

	Despatched		Effective	Target		Bombs Tonnage	E/A	Losses MIA	E	Dam	Casualties KIA	WIA	MIA
1AD	B-17	179	175	VECHTA A/F	(P)	582.6		1	0	0	0	1	9
			1	RHEINE A/F	(O)	3.5							
3AD	B-17	527	114	STEENWIJK A/F	(P)	303.4		1	0	2	1	0	9
			74	ZWISCHENAHN A/F	(P)	253.1							
			88	VAREL A/F	(P)	397.5							
			113	VARRELBUSCH A/F	(P)	339.2							
			111	PLANTLÜNNE A/F	(P)	382.5							
			13	WITTMUNDHAFEN A/F	(O)	39.0							
			2	T/O		6.3							
1AD	B-17	294	36	RHEINE A/F		108.0	1–0–0	3	1	100	8	5	28
			62	HOPSTEN A/F		114.5							
			72	FÜRSTENAU/ VECHTEL A/F	(P)	133.5							
			73	ACHMER A/F		227.9							
			36	HESEPE A/F		69.0							
			1	T/O		2.0							
2AD	B-24	58	58	NORDHORN A/F	(P)	121.7							
2AD	B-24	240	122	AMERICAN ASSAULT AREA SUPPLIES		312.0		14	4	103	5	30	116
			118	BRITISH ASSAULT AREA SUPPLIES		270.3							
2AD	B-24	182	96	STORMEDE A/F	(P)	229.0		0	0	16			
			65	KIRTORF A/F	(P)	144.0							
			11	TREYSA M/Y	(O)	23.8							
			9	ZIEGENHAIN A/F	(S)	19.4							
3AD	B-17	114	104	ZIEGENHAIN A/F	(P)	327.6		0	0	2	0	0	0
			6	SIEGEN M/Y	(S)	16.1							
1AD	B-17	153	152	TWENTE/ENSCHEDE A/F	(P)	348.7		0	0	20	0	0	0
	B-17	2	2	SCOUTING FORCE				0	0	0	0	0	0
TOTALS:		1749	1714			4774.6	1–0–0	19	5	243	14	36	162
	P-47	24	1158	AREA SUPPORT			53–0–2	0			0	0	0
	P-51	1203		BOMBERS			0–0–4 (G)	9			0	0	8
	P-47	35	95	ESCORT LAST 3 TFs				0			0	0	0
	P-51	68											
	P-51	20	19	SCOUTING FORCES				0			1	0	0
	P-51	8	8	ESCORT MOSQUITO				0			0	0	0
	P-51	17	17	ESCORT PR				0			0	0	0
TOTALS:		1375	1297				53–0–2 0–0–4 (G)	9	1	?	1	0	8

REMARKS: Operations in support of Operation *Varsity*, American and British forces crossing the Rhine. Airfields in west and north-west Germany were all attacked visually with most groups flying morning and afternoon missions. First task force consisted of 91BG, 306BG, 351BG, 381BG, 384BG. Second task force consisted of all 3AD groups. Third task force consisted of 92BG, 303BG, 305BG, 306BG, 379BG, 398BG, 401BG, 457BG. Fourth task force consisted of 96CBW groups. Fifth task force was a supply drop by 2CBW, 14CBW and 20CBW groups flying at between 300–400ft. This force suffered all B-24 losses for day mostly to small arms fire. Sixth task force consisted of all 2AD groups. Seventh task force consisted of 13CBW groups. Eighth task force consisted of all 1AD groups. Bomb group losses:– 1AD – 379BG – 2, 381BG – 1, 457BG – 1; 2AD – 44BG – 2, 389BG – 2, 392BG – 1, 445BG – 2, 446BG – 2, 448BG – 2, 491BG – 3; 3AD – 96BG – 1. B/d 392BG B-24 c/l France. B/d 448BG B-24 abandoned over Manston, crew safe. B/d 401BG B-17 cr. Westhall, 6 killed. B/d 389BG B-24 cr. Continent.

All fighter groups operating. Escort for first five forces was in the nature of area support and patrol. Fighter group e/a credits: 55FG – 2, 353FG – 23, 355FG – 2, 357FG – 14, 359FG – 13. Fighter group losses:– 20FG – 1, 55FG – 1, 353FG – 5, 356FG – 1, 361FG – 1. On return, 357FG P-51 cr. base, pilot killed. MIA 356FG P-51 pilot baled over sea, rescued.

OTHER OPERATIONS: 7PG despatched 19 a/c on PR Germany (with escorts), 25BG despatched 4 Mosquitoes on monitor operations for bombers, 1 Mosquito special recon (with P-51 escort); this a/c MIA, 3 Mosquitoes on WR Atlantic/Continent/UK and 4 B-17s on WR Azores/Atlantic/UK. 5ERS despatched 23 P-47s and 4 OA-10s on ASR patrols (OA-10 rescued P-51 pilot). 36BG despatched 12 B-24s on RCM.

A stricken B-24 – believed from 392BG – just before a crash-landing near Hamminkeln during the re-supply drop on 24 March.

Loading parachute containers at Seething for the following day's crossing of the Rheine operation. Each B-24 had a 2½ ton load, part of which was carried in the rear fuselage, to be pushed out through the ball turret well.

INCIDENT

There were many instances of friend attacking friend in the air during World War II. The overriding cause was faulty aircraft recognition and despite regular instruction fighter pilots in both Allied and Axis air forces continued to exhibit their deficiencies in this skill, often with tragic consequences. An aircraft type that was frequently involved as a target was the De Havilland Mosquito, invariably mistaken for an Me 410 despite its distinctive recognition features. Such was the frequency of 'bounces' by US fighters on reconnaissance Mosquitoes of the 25th Group during daylight sorties over Germany, that their tail surfaces were painted bright red as an identity feature. Even this aid failed to provide complete immunity and when it was decided to provide an escort for Mosquito sorties to guard against interception, the enemy was not the only reason. But even that did not deter some trigger-happy pilots looking for twin-engined Messerschmitts. On the day the Allies launched the offensive to cross the Rhine, 25th Group Mosquito NS711, with Lt Stubblefield as pilot and Lt Richmond as navigator, was despatched to reconnoitre an area where enemy reinforcements might be on the move. Two flights of four Mustangs from 479th Group were provided as shepherds taking up position about 500 yards behind and 500 feet above their charge. The course took them via Antwerp, Aachen and the Remagen bridgehead to Siegen and then north-east towards Kassel. At 1700 hours the Mustang pilots saw other aircraft heading west below them at about 17,000 ft. These were identified as 9th Air Force Thunderbolts with yellow tails, four of which suddenly changed course and appeared to be joining the P-51s. The Mosquito crew had also seen the Thunderbolts and made a slow diving turn to the left to expose the aircraft and markings for identification, following which it completed 360 degrees and continued on course. Lt William Barsky, leading the P-51s, was then alarmed to see that two of the P-47s were lining up on the Mosquito's tail. Shouting a warning to the reconnaissance pilot over the radio, he jettisoned drop tanks and put his Mustang into a dive to try and ward off the P-47s. The leading Thunderbolt had already opened fire and the Mosquito pilot was heard calling, 'Get 'em off my tail!' At that moment its left engine burst into flames followed by the disintegration of the aircraft which broke into three main pieces. As they fell a single parachute blossomed. Enraged at this action the Mustang pilots 'chased P-47s all over the sky', 'sitting' on their tails and provoking a great deal of violent wing rocking – 'don't shoot, we're friendly' sign. Barsky followed the offending aircraft back to their base at Le Culot where he landed and reported the folly of his pilots to Lt.Col Slayden, CO of the 36th Fighter Group.

24/25 MARCH 1945

8AF 912 NIGHT LEAFLET OPERATION

NLS despatched 12 B-24s, 10 effective; Germany, Holland.

482BG despatched 3 B-17s on H2X PR of battle lines.

492BG despatched 1 Mosquito on *Red Stocking* and 24 B-24s on *Carpetbagger* Scandinavia.

25BG despatched 2 Mosquitoes on PR Altenbeken.

25 MARCH 1945

8AF 913

	Despatched		Effective	Target		Bombs Tonnage	E/A	Losses MIA	E	Dam	Casualties KIA	WIA	MIA
2AD	B-24	272	59	EHMEN O/D	(P)	156.9	2–4–9	4	2	19	16	2	39
			127	HITZACKER O/D	(P)	327.2							
			57	BÜCKEN O/D	(P)								
	B-17	737	0	OIL PLANTS				0	3	0	9	0	0
TOTALS:		1009	243			484.1	2–4–9	4	5	19	25	2	39
	P-47	38	223	ESCORT 2AD			4–0–3	0			0	0	0
	P-51	204						0			0	0	0
	P-51	48	47	SUPPORT B-26s 9AF				0			0	0	0
	P-51	24	24	FIGHTER-BOMBER – SCHMALGE AMMO DUMP		6.0		1			0	0	1
	P-51	11	11	2 SCOUTING FORCE			0–0–1	0			0	0	0
	P-51	16	16	ESCORT PR a/c				0			0	0	0
TOTALS:		341	321			6.0	4–0–4	1		?	0	0	1

REMARKS: 1009 bombers of all three divisions t/o for attacks on seven oil plants and a tank factory. Bad weather during assembly and the increasing possibility of adverse conditions on return caused 1AD and 3AD to be recalled. 2AD had by then been despatched. All 2AD bomb groups except 446BG participated. Bomb group losses:– 448BG – 4. Losses to isolated squadron of 448BG attacked by jets. One b/d a/c reached Sweden but was shot down by e/a near coast, 8 rescued. Upon t/o a 34BG B-17 cr. near base, 9 k. During assembly 2 392BG B-24s collided and cr. Skeyton, 16 killed, 4 baled. 351BG B-17 cr. and exploded on t/o base. 401BG B-17 abandoned by crew over Saltby A/F. B/d 448BG B-24 f/l Manston – Cat E.

Fighter groups operating: 56FG, 339FG, 352FG, 361FG, 479FG continental based groups dive-bombed and supported 9AF. Fighter group e/a credits:– 56FG – 2, 352FG – 1, 479FG – 1. Fighter group losses:– 352FG – 1.

OTHER OPERATIONS: 7PG despatched 8 F-5s and 3 Spitfires on PR Germany (with escorts). 25BG despatched 1 Mosquito as monitor for 2AD, 2 Mosquitoes on PR Germany, 6 Mosquitoes on WR Continent/UK and 4 B-17s on WR Azores/Atlantic/UK. 1 WR Mosquito MIA. 5ERS despatched 6 P-47s and 2 OA-10s on ASR patrols. 36BS despatched 3 B-24s on RCM and 2 P-38s on radar search.

25/26 MARCH 1945

8AF 914 NIGHT LEAFLET OPERATION

NLS despatched 10 B-24s, 10 effective; Germany, Holland.

25BG despatched 1 Mosquito on *Skywave* sortie Berlin.

26 MARCH 1945

8AF 915

	Despatched		Effective	Target		Bombs Tonnage	E/A	Losses MIA	E	Dam	Casualties KIA	WIA	MIA
1AD	B-17	185	12	ZEITZ O/I	(P)	29.5		0	1	25	1	5	0
			130	PLAUEN VOMAG AFV/I	(S)	320.7							
			25	MEININGEN	(O)	62.5							
			11	WÜRZBURG	(O)	27.5							
3AD	B-17	152	139	PLAUEN VOMAG AFV/I	(P)	413.5		0	3	1	18	0	0
			12	OELSNITZ	(O)	36.0							
			1	MARKT ERLBACH	(O)	3.0							
TOTALS:		337	330			892.7	0	0	4	26	19	5	0
	P-51	238	194	ESCORT 1AD				0					
	P-51	121	98	ESCORT 3AD				0					
	P-51	118	110	FREELANCE FOR BOMBERS				0					
	P-51	27	26	ESCORT PR a/c				0					
	P-51	23	22	SCOUTING FORCES				0					
TOTALS:		527	450				0	0	4		2	0	0

REMARKS: Poor weather restricted operations, but visual attacks made. 1AD – 351BG, 379BG, 381BG, 384BG, 457BG; 3AD – 34BG, 96BG, 385BG, 452BG. During assembly 34BG and 452BG B-17s collided and cr. Framsden and Crettingham, all k. On return 384BG B-17 c/l Cranbrook, 1 k.

All Fighter groups except 56FG, 356FG, 357FG, 359FG, 479FG operating. 353FG P-51 pilot baled Braintree when a/c iced up. 20FG P-51 c/l near Ipswich, pilot killed. 78FG P-51 abandoned over France, pilot safe. On return 4FG P-51 cr. Sutton, pilot killed. 2 339FG P-51s collided but landed safely at base.

OTHER OPERATIONS: 7PG despatched 12 F-5s and 1 Spitfire on PR Germany and Austria (with escorts). 25BG despatched 6 Mosquitoes 'chaff' screening for bombers, 4 Mosquitoes on WR Germany and France and 3 B-17s onWR Azores/Atlantic/UK. 36BS despatched 3 B-24s on RCM and 1 P-38 on radar search. 1 B-24, 6 P-51s on radio-relays.

26/27 MARCH 1945

482BG despatched 6 B-17s on H2X PR S.W. Germany, leaflets dropped.

492BG despatched 1 Mosquito on *Red Stocking* operation.

27 MARCH 1945

No operations by 8AF bombers. 37 P-47s and 78 P-51s of 56FG, 356FG, 357FG despatched to escort 262 RAF Lancasters bombing Paderborn. 110 P-47s and P-51s sorties. No claims or losses.

OTHER OPERATIONS: 7PG despatched 2 F-5s on PR Brunswick and Paderborn with 4 P-51s as escort. 25BG despatched 6 Mosquitoes on WR Continent/North Sea/UK and 4 B-17s on WR Azores/Atlantic/UK. 5ERS despatched 4 P-47s and 1 OA-10 on ASR patrols. 36BS despatched 12 B-24s on RCM and 2 B-24s on radar search.

27/28 MARCH 1945

8AF 916 NIGHT LEAFLET OPERATION

NLS despatched 10 B-24s, 9 effective; Holland, Germany.

482BG despatched 7 B-17s on H2X PR battle area and Schweinfurt. Leaflets also dropped.

492BG despatched 1 Mosquito on *Red Stocking* operation.

28 MARCH 1945

8AF 917

	Despatched		Effective	Target		Bombs Tonnage	E/A	Losses MIA	E	Dam	Casualties KIA	WIA	MIA
1AD	B-17	446	318	BERLIN/SPANDAU M/I	(P)	876.5		2	5	133	1	8	19
			65	BERLIN/FALKENSEE	(P)	161.5							
			6	STENDAL	(S)	20.0							
			1	HANNOVER	(O)	3.0							
			21	T/O		55.5							
3AD	B-17	519	34	HANNOVER HANOMAG AFV/I	(P)	100.8		0	0	66	0	3	0
			431	HANNOVER M/Y	(S)	1258.3							
			10	MINDEN	(O)	30.0							
			5	T/O		15.0							
TOTALS:		965	891			2520.6	0	2	5	199	1	11	19
	P-51	272	245	ESCORT 1AD				0	2				
	P-51	99	86	ESCORT 3AD				0	0				
	P-51	9	8	ESCORT PR a/c				0	0				
	P-51	10	6	SCOUTING FORCES				0	0				
TOTALS:		390	345				0	0	2		0	0	0

REMARKS: A 10/10 undercast forced B-17s to bomb on H2X at tank and armament factories. All B-17 groups participated. Bomb group losses:– 303BG – 1, 401BG – 1. B/d 401BG B-17 abandoned over Belgium, crew safe. MIA 303BG B-17 c/l foreshore at Rye. Fighter groups operating were 4FG, 20FG, 78FG, 339FG, 352FG, 355FG, 361FG, 364FG. 339FG P-51 cr. on t/o, pilot safe. 339FG P-51 c/l near Colchester, pilot safe.

OTHER OPERATIONS: 7PG despatched 3 F-5s on PR Germany (with escorts). 25BG despatched 7 Mosquitoes 'chaff' screening for bombers, 4 Mosquitoes on WR Continent/UK and 4 B-17s on WR Azores/Atlantic/UK. 5ERS despatched 1 OA-10 on ASR patrol. 9 P-51s on radio-relays.

29 MARCH 1945

No offensive operations. 7PF despatched 1 F-5 on PR Germany. 25BG despatched 4 Mosquitoes on WR Continent/North Sea/UK and 5 B-17s on WR Azores/Atlantic/UK.

29/30 MARCH 1945

492BG despatched 2 Mosquitoes on *Red Stocking* operations.

30 MARCH 1945

8AF 918

	Despatched		Effective	Target		Bombs Tonnage	E/A	Losses MIA	E	Dam	Casualties KIA	WIA	MIA
3AD	B-17	530	26	HAMBURG U/Y	(P)	78.0	0–1–3	3	2	252	14	10	28
			169	HAMBURG O/D	(P)	467.4							
			38	HAMBURG U/Y	(P)	109.0							
			263	HAMBURG P/A	(S)	744.1							
			1	BREMEN	(O)	3.0							
1AD	B-17	448	318	BREMEN U/Y	(P)	831.0		1	1	225	1	6	11
			109	BREMEN R/B	(P)	323.0							
2AD	B-24	382	273	WILHELMSHAFEN U/Y	(P)	785.4		1	0	56	8	1	0
			85	WILHELMSHAFEN/ BAUHABEN P/A	(P)	239.3							
	B-17	36	32	FARGE U/Y	(P)	140.0		0	0	14	0	0	0
	B-17	6	6	SCREENING FORCE				0	0	0	0	0	0
TOTALS:		1402	1320			3720.2	0–1–3	5	3	547	23	17	39
	P-51	304	289	ESCORT 3AD			4–0–7 1–0–1 (G)	3					
	P-51	287	268	ESCORT 1AD			2–0–1	1					
	P-47 P-51	53 54	105	ESCORT 2AD				0					
	P-51	159	153	FREELANCE FOR BOMBERS			1–0–0	0					
	P-51	11	11	ESCORT PR a/c				0					
	P-51	31	26	SCOUTING FORCES				0					
TOTALS:		899	852				7–0–8 1–0–1 (G)	4		?	1	0	2

REMARKS: Attacks on targets connected with U-boat construction or operation. All bomb groups except 100BG operating. 3AD attacked primaries visually and other targets using H2X. 1AD and 2AD were both visual and H2X on primaries. 40CBW groups flew a *Disney* mission to Farge. Bomb group losses:– 1AD – 381BG – 1; 2AD – 491BG – 1; 3AD – 486BG – 1, 493BG – 2. MIA 491BG B-24 ditched, 2 rescued. Abortive 452BG B-17 cr. Hilgay, 7 killed. B/d 351BG B-17 f/l Continent – Cat E. 493BG B-17 cr. Bartlow, 6 k.

All Fighter groups operating. Fighter group e/a credits:– 55FG – 1, 78FG – 2, 339FG – 2, 352FG – 1, 361FG – 1, 364FG – 1. Fighter group losses:– 339FG – 1, 352FG – 1, 353FG – 1, 357FG – 1. MIA 357FG P-51 pilot baled over sea, rescued. MIA 353FG P-51 pilot baled over sea but killed when striking tail of a/c.

OTHER OPERATIONS: 7PG despatched 5 F-5s on PR Germany (with escorts). 25BG despatched 9 Mosquitoes 'chaff' screening for bombers, 3 Mosquitoes as monitors for 2AD and 3AD, 4 Mosquitoes on WR Atlantic/Continent/UK and 3 B-17s on WR Azores/Atlantic/UK. 5ERS despatched 12 P-47s and 3 OA-10s. 1 OA-10 lost when unable to t/o after rescue of bomber crewmen, taken in tow by launch and later sank. 36BS despatched 13 B-24s on RCM. 1 B-17, 1 B-24, 8 P-51s on radio-relays.

30/31 MARCH 1945

8AF 919 NIGHT LEAFLET OPERATION

NLS despatched 13 B-24s, 13 effective; Holland, Germany.

492BG despatched 19 B-24s on *Carpetbagger* operation to Norway, 1 B-24 MIA. 1 B-24 cr. Orkneys.

31 MARCH 1945

8AF920

	Despatched		Effective	Target		Bombs Tonnage	E/A	Losses MIA	E	Dam	Casualties KIA	WIA	MIA
3AD	B-17	229	137	ZEITZ O/I	(P)	399.2		3	1	108	1	2	30
			29	BAD BERKA O/I	(S)	81.2							
			20	GOTHA	(S)	55.0							
			25	ERFURT	(O)	70.3							
			8	T/O		23.7							
3AD	B-17	294	265	BRANDENBURG	(P)	718.7	0–1–0	0	0	1	0	0	0
			9	STENDAL	(O)	27.0							
			9	SALZWEDEL	(O)	27.0							
2AD	B-24	385	371	BRUNSWICK M/Y	(S)	989.2	3–2–1	2	3	3	10	1	29

continued on facing page

1AD	B-17	432	369	HALLE M/Y	(S)	1069.3		0	0	37	0	0	0
			8	LEIPZIG	(O)	22.5							
			36	WEIMAR	(O)	108.0							
			7	ASCHERSLEBEN	(O)	23.8							
			1	T/O		3.0							
	B-17	8	8	SCREENING FORCE				0	0	0	0	0	0
TOTALS:		1348	1302			3617.9	3–3–1	5	4	149	11	3	59
	P-51	120	117	ESCORT 3AD 1ST TF				1			0	0	1
	P-51	221	207	ESCORT 3AD 2ND TF			5–0–0	1			0	0	1
	P-47	53	253	ESCORT 2AD			0–0–7	0			0	0	0
	P-51	213						2			0	0	2
	P-51	233	225	ESCORT 1AD				0			0	0	0
	P-51	30	26	SCOUTING FORCES			1–0–1	0			0	0	0
	P-51	19	19	ESCORT PR a/c				0			0	0	0
TOTALS:		889	847				6–0–8	4		?	0	0	4

REMARKS: Synthetic oil plants at Zeitz, Lützkendorf and Merseburg, a refinery and munitions plant at Hannover and tank factory at Brunswick were primaries. Only two primaries attacked with some visual bombing and H2X at Zeitz by 3AD. H2X used by 1AD and 2AD at all targets. All bomb groups operating. First 3AD task force consisted of 13CBW and 45CBW groups; second 3AD task force was 4CBW and 93CBW. Bomb group losses:– 2AD – 389BG – 1, 453BG – 1; 3AD – 96BG – 1, 100BG – 1, 452BG – 1. During assembly a 93BG B-24 cr. South Cove, nr. Southwold, 9 k. B/d 466BG B-24 c/l liberated Holland. B/d 96BG B-17 Cat E Fulda A/F, Germany. 453BG B-24 cr. Tunern, Gr., 2 k.

All fighter groups operating. Fighter group e/a credits:– 78FG – 1, 353FG – 2, 361FG – 1. Fighter group losses:– 4FG – 1, 78FG – 1, 339FG – 1. 361FG – 1 MIA 78FG P-51 pilot baled 40 miles E Lowestoft, lost. 4FG intercepted by Soviet a/c. 1 SF P-51 abandoned near Ostend, pilot baled, safe.

OTHER OPERATIONS: 7PG despatched 10 F-5s, 8 effective, on PR Germany (with escorts). 25BG despatched 9 Mosquitoes 'chaff' screening, 1 Mosquito special operation, 4 Mosquitoes on WR Continent/Atlantic/UK and 4 B-17s on WR Atlantic/UK. 5ERS despatched 25 P-47s, 2 OA-10 and 1 B-17 on ASR patrols, search and rescue. OA-10 strafed by Me 262 while on sea and eventually sank. First successful lifeboat drop by ASR B-17. 26 P-51s also on ASR search and assistance – fought off Me 262 with 0–0–2 claims. 36BS despatched 3 B-24s on RCM. 1 B-17, 2 P-47s, 12 P-51s on radio-relays.

INCIDENT

Combat Bombardment Wing Headquarters each had a half dozen or so aircraft assigned for use by the staff. These included light liaison types such as UC-64s, UC-45s or C-78s for trips to combat bases, or a war-weary B-17 or B-24 for flights of long duration at higher altitudes, and a P-47 or P-51 fighter for monitoring formations. In the final weeks of the war when the Luftwaffe had all but been driven from the sky, Wing Headquarters aircraft sometimes accompanied bomber formations to shallow penetration targets to observe results.

In April 1st CBW received a brand new B-17 for use as a Command Scout. The ball and forward turrets were removed plus some bombing equipment with the result that the aircraft, lighter and with a more streamlined airframe, would fly at 180 to 190 mph indicated, 'pulling' only 29 inches of manifold pressure. It could also easily make sustained flight at 200 mph IAS – which was nearly 300 mph true air speed at 25,000 ft. This staff aircraft was first used to accompany the Wing's regular B-17 force to the isolated Gironde river sites at the French Atlantic coast on 15 April. Two days later Brig.Gen Gross, the Wing CO, became more adventurous and decided to take it all the way to Dresden with the bombers. He planned to fly with the first box to cross the target, circle away and come in with the second and repeat the procedure for subsequent boxes. While circling from the first to the second box, an Me 262 appeared and made a firing pass at the Command Scout before the tail gunner could shoot. Fortunately the German pilot's aim was not too good for the only substantial damage was done by a cannon shell that exploded in the bomb bay, mangling a bulkhead and some wiring. The Fortress promptly made track for the nearest formation and stayed there all the way home. The 1st CBW Command Scout was later named *Our Bridget* in honour of an English secretary at Headquarters, Ella Prentice – who for some obscure reason was known as Bridget O'Prentice.

1 APRIL 1945

No offensive operations. 25BG despatched 5 B-17s on WR Azores/Atlantic/UK and 4 Mosquitoes on WR Atlantic/Continent/North Sea. 5ERS despatched 6 P-47s on ASR search and 24 P-51s (8 each from 355FG, 356FG, 357FG) on ASR search for reported lifeboat.

1/2 APRIL 1945

8AF 921 NIGHT LEAFLET OPERATION

NLS despatched 12 B-24s, 12 effective; Holland, Germany.

492BG despatched 1 Mosquito on *Red Stocking* operation.

2 APRIL 1945

8AF 922

	Despatched		Effective	Target	Bombs Tonnage	E/A	Losses MIA	E	Dam	Casualties KIA	WIA	MIA
1, 2 &	B-17	447	0	DENMARK A/Fs	0		1	0	0			
3AD	B-24	261					0	0	0			
TOTALS:		708	0		0	0	1	0	0	0	0	0
	P-47	52	572	ESCORT BOMBERS			1	1		0	0	1
	P-51	566					0	0		0	0	0
	P-51	27	26	SCOUTING FORCES			0	0		0	0	0
	P-51	15	15	ESCORT PR a/c			0	0		0	0	0
TOTALS:		712	613		0		1	1	0	0	0	1

REMARKS: Mission recalled due to bad weather when leading bombers were approaching Danish coast. Bomb group losses:– 466BG – 1. MIA B-24 suffered engine trouble and flew to Sweden where it cr.

All fighter groups except 352FG, 357FG, 361FG operating. Fighter group losses:– 364FG – 1. MIA P-51 pilot baled over sea, lost. On return 479FG P-51 cr. Sproughton, pilot safe.

OTHER OPERATIONS: 7PG despatched 7 F-5s on PR Germany (with escorts). 25BG despatched 1 Mosquito for 2AD, 1 Mosquito on WR North Sea/Atlantic and 1 B-17 on WR Atlantic. 5ERS despatched 13 P-47s and 1 OA-10 on ASR search and 4 B-24s and 11 P-51s also on ASR search. 36BS despatched 4 B-24s on RCM. 10 P-51s, 1 B-17 on radio-relays.

2/3 APRIL 1945

8AF 923 NIGHT LEAFLET OPERATION

NLS despatched 10 B-24s, 9 effective; Holland, France, Germany.

482BG despatched 3 B-17s (1 *Eagle*, 2 H2X) on radar scope PR Wilhelmshafen and Ulm.

492BG despatched 1 Mosquito on *Red Stocking* and 10 B-24s on *Carpetbagger* Denmark.

25BG despatched 1 Mosquito on *Skywave* sortie Continent – abortive.

3 APRIL 1945

8AF 924

	Despatched		Effective	Target	Bombs Tonnage	E/A	Losses MIA	E	Dam	Casualties KIA	WIA	MIA
1AD	B-17	224	218	KIEL/DEUTSCHE U/Y (P)	651.5		0	0	2	0	1	0
			2	FLENSBURG A/F (O)	6.0							
3AD	B-17	528	24	KIEL/HOWARDTS U/Y (P)	72.0		2	0	119	0	0	20
			475	KIEL/DEUTSCHE U/Y (P)	1500.0							
TOTALS:		752	719		2229.5	0	2	0	121	0	1	20
	P-51	175	157	ESCORT 1AD		1–0–0	1	0				
	P-51	394	360	ESCORT 3AD			1	2				
	P-51	100	98	SWEEP – KIEL AREA			0	1				
	P-51	4	44	ESCORT PR a/c			0	0				
	P-51	18	17	SCOUTING FORCES			2	0				
TOTALS:		691	636			1–0–0	4	3		0	0	3

REMARKS: All 3AD groups and 40CBW and 41CBW groups of 1AD were despatched to attack U-boat yards at Kiel. Bombing was by H2X. Bomb group losses:– 96BG – 1, 100BG – 1. MIA 96BG B-17 landed Sweden.

All fighter groups except 56FG, 479FG operating. 352FG and 361FG flew a sweep. 4FG flew ASR support. Fighter group losses:– 357FG – 1, 359FG – 1. 1SF and 3SF each had 1 P-51 MIA. MIA 359FG P-51 cr. in sea 60 miles off Lowestoft, pilot lost. 55FG P-51 baled off Belgian coast, safe. 55FG P-51 cr. t/o. 339FG P-51 cr. t/o. 357FG P-51 c/l base on return.

OTHER OPERATIONS: 7PG despatched 1 F-5 (with escort) on PR Germany. 25BG despatched 6 Mosquitoes 'chaff' screening for bombers, 5 Mosquitoes on support for 3AD (1 aborted), 7 Mosquitoes on WR Atlantic/Continent/North Sea and 4 B-17s on WR Azores/Atlantic/UK. 5ERS despatched 16 P-47s, 1 OA-10 and 1 B-17 on ASR patrol and 15 P-51s (4FG) also on ASR search. 36BS despatched 9 B-24s on RCM. 10 P-51s, 1 B-17, 1 B-24 on radio-relays. 1 Mosquito in Sweden m/f.

3/4 APRIL 1945

8AF 925 NIGHT LEAFLET OPERATION

NLS despatched 1 B-17 and 10 B-24s, 10 a/c effective; Holland, France, Germany.

482BG despatched 1 B-17 on *Eagle* scope photo sortie.

492BG despatched 1 Mosquito and 2 A-26s on special operations. On return, 1 A-26 c/l Rackheath A/F.

25BG despatched 1 Mosquito on *Skywave* sortie France and Germany – MIA (shot down by Me 262 jet).

EVENT

The first US serviceman travelling east to link up with Soviet ground forces moving west was not an infantryman, as might be supposed, but an 8th Air Force engineer! This claim to fame rested on 2/Lt John R. Campbell, CO of the 1st Mobile Reclamation and Repair Squadron who, looking for wrecked 8th Air Force aircraft, drove his jeep into Soviet-held territory a week before the US and Russian infantry met at the Elbe. Campbell was also unusual in having received a direct commission. It was made in recognition of his part in investigating the possibilities of the repair and salvage of aircraft that came down in liberated territory in the early days of the Allied cross-Channel invasion of Normandy. M/Sgt Campbell – as he was then – landed at Omaha Beach ten days after the initial landings and on his report and recommendations a small team was despatched which laid the foundations for an air service establishment which developed into the 5th Strategic Air Depot at Merville, France.

With the assignment of a score of P-51s the 7PG was able to provide its own escorts for many photo missions. One of these P-51s, on dispersal at Chalgrove, carries the Group identification marking, a broad red band under the exhaust stacks. Dark green rudder identifies 14PS.

4 APRIL 1945

8AF 926

	Despatched		Effective	Target		Bombs Tonnage	E/A	Losses MIA	E	Dam	Casualties KIA	WIA	MIA
2AD	B-24	438	33	PARCHIM A/F	(P)	87.0	6–4–6	6	1	76	1	0	59
			29	PERLEBERG A/F	(P)	65.3							
			97	WESENDORF A/F	(S)	219.0							
1AD	B-17	443	149	FASSBERG A/F	(P)	383.7		1	2	58	1	6	4
			37	HOYA A/F	(S)	105.0							
			13	DEDELSDORF A/F	(S)	39.0							
			39	UNTERLÜSS	(O)	104.0							
			24	T/O		80.5							
3AD	B-17	526	505	KIEL/DEUTSCHE S/Y	(P)	1497.5		3	0	50	0	0	27
			2	EGGEBECK A/F	(O)	6.0							
1AD	B-17	24	22	HAMBURG/ FINKENWARDER U/Y	(P)	99.0		0	0	0	0	0	0
TOTALS:		1431	950			2686.0	6–4–6	10	3	184	2	6	90
	P-47	58	324	ESCORT 2AD			14–0–20	1					
	P-51	293					9–0– 3	3					
	P-51	232	220	ESCORT 1AD				1					
	P-51	223	208	ESCORT 3AD				0					
	P-51	19	19	SCOUTING FORCES			0–0– 1	0					
	P-51	25	25	ESCORT PR a/c			1–0– 0	0					
	P-51	16	16	ESCORT ASR a/c				0					
TOTALS:		866	812				24–0–24	4		?	0	0	3

REMARKS: All bomb groups except 445BG operated. 1AD and 2AD attacked visually and those formations that could not were instructed to return with bombs. 3AD used H2X with some visual assistance. 305BG & 92BG flew a Disney mission to Hamburg. Bomb group losses:– 1AD – 92BG – 1; 2AD – 389BG – 1, 445BG – 2, 448BG – 3; 3AD – 95BG – 1, 385BG – 2. MIA 95BG B-17 landed Sweden. MIA 385BG B-17s collided over sea. Abortive 91BG B-17 c/l base during assembly. 305BG cr. during assembly (hit tree on t/o), crew baled. On return 446BG B-24 cr. Raveningham, crew baled.

All fighter groups operating. Fighter group e/a credits:– 4FG – 2, 339FG – 5, 355FG – 5, 364FG – 2. Fighter group losses:– 20FG – 1, 355FG – 3. MIA 20FG P-51 pilot baled 12 miles off Gt. Yarmouth, rescued.

OTHER OPERATIONS: 7PG despatched 8 F-5s on PR Germany (with escorts) and 2 P-38s on radar PR Berlin and Hamburg (with escort). 25BG despatched 9 Mosquitoes 'chaff' screening for 1AD and 3AD, 2 Mosquitoes as monitors for 2AD and 3AD, 3 Mosquitoes on WR North Sea/Continent and 4 B-17s on WR Azores/Atlantic/UK. 5ERS despatched 22 P-47s, 1 OA-10 and 2 B-17s on ASR patrols with 16 P-51s escorting (6 men from OA-10 lost 30/3/45 picked up from lifeboat). 36BS despatched 4 B-24s on RCM. 10 P-51s, 1 B-17, 1 B-24 (with 4 P-51s escort) on radio-relays.

4/5 APRIL 1945

8AF 927 NIGHT LEAFLET OPERATION

NLS despatched 12 B-24s, 11 effective; France, Germany.

492BG despatched 11 B-24s, 9 effective on *Carpetbagger* operations. Denmark.

25BG despatched 1 Mosquito on *Skywave* sortie W. Germany.

EVENT

Most combatants, if honest, would acknowledge that the safe completion of their combat tour was a point of great relief. But there were individuals who seemingly thrived on chancing their lives in action and would fly until the authorities ordered them to stop. To get their fill of action such men would seek combat in other theatres of war and several men who had flown in the Pacific areas moved on to the 8th Air Force. Outstanding was Capt Durward Fesmire, lead bombardier in 401st Group, with 98 missions in the South-West Pacific Area and 35 in Europe, totalling 133. He finished operations on the 401st's 200th mission, 28 January 1945. In the same group, T/Sgt James W. Cannon, a B-17 top turret gunner, flew 68 missions from New Guinea and Australia in B-25s, B-26s and B-17s before flying 34 in Europe between May and October 1944. 1/Lt Maurice Londer, a co-pilot in 95th Group, ran up a total of 85 of which 50 were in the Pacific flying as a non-commissioned engineer. Another B-17 veteran was 27-year-old T/Sgt Joseph D. Lillis, a radio operator in the 303rd Group, who put in 76 in the Pacific (where he was awarded the DSC) and 30 over Europe. S/Sgt Edsel Werner, a 23-year-old gunner in the 466th Group, was probably unique in having begun his combat with the 8th Air Force, transferred to the Mediterranean, before returning to England via the USA to fly a tour in Liberators. Werner first arrived in England in July 1942 with the armament section of 97th Bomb Group. He managed to make four unofficial trips over occupied Europe as a stand-in gunner before being accepted on permanent flying status. Following one more mission from England he went with the 97th to North Africa where he participated in another 51 combat flights, before being shipped back to the USA in June 1943 for rest and recuperation. A gunnery instructor post followed, but he soon tired of teaching others his trade and obtained an assignment to a B-24 replacement crew. In the autumn of 1944 he was crossing the Atlantic again to England. From Attlebridge, Werner added 36 more missions to his previous 56 for a grand total of 92. Even so, Werner was talking of going to the Pacific for further action.

5 APRIL 1945

8AF 928

	Despatched		Effective	Target		Bombs Tonnage	E/A	Losses MIA	E	Dam	Casualties KIA	WIA	MIA
1AD	B-17	436	211	INGOLSTADT M/D	(P)	618.9		1	2	2	11	2	0
			94	GRAFENWÖHR M/D	(P)	206.3							
			73	BAYREUTH M/Y	(P)	197.0							
			30	WEIDEN	(O)	94.3							
			1	NÜRNBERG	(O)	3.1							
2AD	B-24	397	151	PLAUEN M/Y	(P)	348.4		5	0	5	0	1	44
			39	BAYREUTH M/D	(P)	85.5							
			1	GRAFENWÖHR M/D	(O)	2.4							
			1	INGOLSTADT M/I	(O)	2.5							
3AD	B-17	521	59	UNTERSCHLAUERS-BACH A/F	(P)	162.2		4	2	112	8	7	39
			13	FÜRTH E/I	(P)	31.3							
			54	FÜRTH M/D	(P)	158.8							
			37	NÜRNBERG S. M/Y	(P)	109.6							
			271	NÜRNBERG STN M/Y	(S)	788.7							
	B-17	4	4	SCOUTING FORCE				0	0	0	0	0	0
TOTALS:		1358	1039			2815.3		10	4	119	19	10	83
	P-51	201	182	ESCORT 1AD			0–0–1 7–0–3(G)	0			0	0	0
	P-47	53	280	ESCORT 2AD			1–0–2	0			0	0	0
	P-51	251						1			0	0	1
	P-51	104	91	ESCORT 3AD				0			0	0	0
	P-51	18	18	ESCORT PR a/c				0			0	0	0
	P-51	35	35	SCOUTING FORCES				0			0	0	0
TOTALS:		662	606				1–0–3 7–0–3 (G)	1	0	?	0	0	1

REMARKS: Ordnance depots, marshalling yards and airfields were primaries. 1AD and 3AD bombed visually and with H2X; 2AD used H2X except for a T/O. All bomb groups except 381BG and 445BG operating. Bomb group losses:– 1AD – 379BG – 1; 2AD – 44BG – 1, 93BG – 1, 389BG – 1, 446BG – 1, 466BG – 1; 3AD – 34BG – 1, 94BG – 1, 100BG – 1, 490BG – 1. MIA 94BG B-17 disappeared during assembly. MIA 34BG B-17 shot down by flak in Dunkirk pocket – 6 rescued from sea. 457BG cr. t/o base, 11 k. MIA 379BG B-17 cr. Bellheim, later taken by Allied troops. 2 b/d 490BG B-17s cr. Continent. Collision damaged 384BG B-17 f/l Continent – Cat E.

All fighter groups except 350FG, 357FG. 359FG operating. Fighter group e/a credits:– 56FG – 1, Me 262. 20FG P-51 pilot baled over France, injured. Fighter group losses: 355FG – 1.

OTHER OPERATIONS: 7PG despatched 5 F-5s on PR Germany (with escort). 1 F-5 Cat E. 25BG despatched 8 Mosquitoes, 1 aborted on 'chaff' screening for 1AD and 3AD, 4 Mosquitoes on WR Germany/France/UK and 4 B-17s on WR Atlantic/UK. 5ERS despatched 20 P-47s, 1 OA-10 and 1 B-17 on ASR patrols. 36BS despatched 4 B-24s on RCM. 8 P-51s, 1 B-17, 1 B-24 and radio-relays.

5/6 APRIL 1945

8AF 929 NIGHT LEAFLET OPERATION

NLS despatched 12 B-24s, 12 effective; France, Holland, Germany.

492BG despatched 1 Mosquito on *Red Stocking* operation.

Crew chief Mike Giorgis (r) and his assistant Henry Hendricks have good reason to look pleased. Their charge, *Million Dollar Baby* (name painted on other side of nose), sports 125 mission symbols. As with all 94BG B-17s during the last weeks of the war, the ball and chin turrets have been removed. (94BG Assoc.)

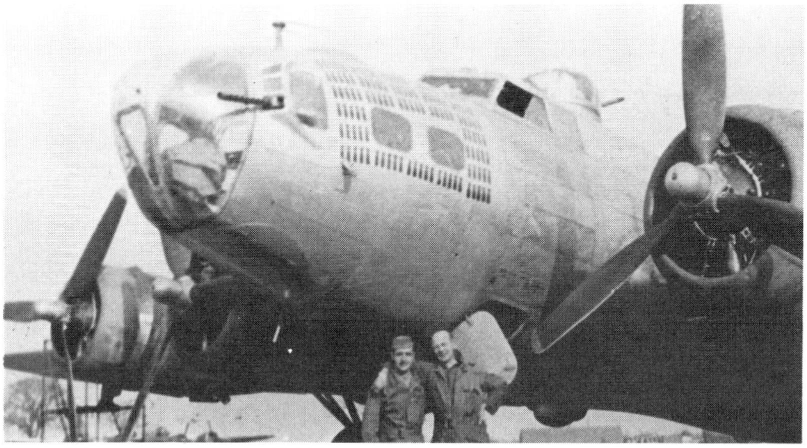

6 APRIL 1945

	Despatched		Effective	Target		Bombs Tonnage	E/A	Losses MIA	E	Dam	Casualties KIA	WIA	MIA
2AD	B-24	207	183	HALLE M/Y	(P)	401.7		0	0	3	0	0	0
			22	EISLEBEN	(O)	50.5							
1AD	B-17	230	215	LEIPZIG MAIN STN & M/Y	(S)	539.6		4	1	0	8	1	33
			11	HALLE M/Y	(O)	36.8							
3AD	B-17	222	106	LEIPZIG MAIN STN & M/Y	(S)	288.7		0	1	0	9	0	0
			109	GERA	(S)	311.4							
TOTALS:		659	646			1628.7	0	4	2	3	17	1	33
	P-47	39	201	ESCORT 2AD				0			0	0	0
	P-51	179											
	P-51	211	202	ESCORT 1AD				1			0	0	1
	P-51	199	190	ESCORT 3AD				0			0	0	0
	P-51	27	26	SCOUTING FORCES				0			0	0	0
	P-51	11	11	ESCORT PR a/c				0			0	0	0
TOTALS:		666	630				0	1		?	0	0	1

REMARKS: Targets in the Leipzig area all attacked by H2X. Weather attacks on an Army HQ at Halle and an oil depot at Stassfurt. Bomb groups participating:– all 2AD groups except 445BG; 40CBW and 41CBW groups of 1AD; 13CBW and 45CBW groups of 3AD. Bomb group losses:– 1AD – 303BG – 2, 384BG – 2. Losses due to two collisions. 384BG B-17 cr. Walgrave after t/o.

All fighter groups operating. Fighter group losses: 356FG – 1. 55FG c/l base on return, pilot safe. 4FG P-51 f/l near Aachen, pilot safe.

OTHER OPERATIONS: 7PG despatched 5 F-5s (1 aborted) on PR Germany (with escort). 25BG despatched 9 Mosquitoes, 7 effective, 'chaff' screening for bombers, 1 Mosquito on *Skywave* navigation flight – aborted, 6 Mosquitoes on WR Continent/UK and 4 B-17s on WR Azores/Atlantic/UK. 5ERS despatched 12 P-47s on ASR patrols. 36BS despatched 4 B-24s on RCM. 12 P-51s, 1 B-24, 2 P-47s on radio-relays.

6/7 APRIL 1945

492BG despatched 3 B-24s on *Carpetbagger* operations and 1 Mosquito on *Red Stocking* operation. 1 B-24 MIA.

Spring has come again. Ground men relax in a Duxford revetment near the CO's plane – Col John Landers with 36 air and ground kill symbols displayed.

EVENT

On 7 April 1945, 24-year-old M/Sgt Ralph Montavon of the 351st Group was decorated with the Legion of Merit by Brig.Gen Lacy, Commander, 94th Combat Wing. This was in recognition of Montavon's supervision of repair and maintenance of two B-17s that together completed 132 consecutive combat operations without having to return early due to mechanical failure. This sequence was broken on 25 November 1944 when one of the pair, *Devil's Mistress*, aborted through supercharger trouble. The other Fortress, *April Girl II*, continued an unblemished record and by the date of her crew chief's decoration had flown 111 missions, and added two more before hostilities ceased. *Devil's Mistress* also endured, to reach 92 missions by VE Day. Another crew chief in the same 510th Bomb Squadron, M/Sgt Seaborn Jones, had three B-17s under his supervision fly 158 missions without aborting. The first was shot down on its 56th, the other two had reached 40 and 63 respectively without turnbacks by the time that the Fortress with the higher total broke the sequence by aborting. Originally there was one crew chief to each heavy bomber, but with a build-up in squadron complements during 1944 many crew chiefs looked after two bombers each. Abortives reduced the effectiveness of a bombing force and to encourage good maintenance there was a general policy of giving publicity only to bombers with high numbers of missions which also had unblemished mechanical records. Several ground crews attained an abortive-free record with their charges for more than 100 missions. This was quite an achievement as high altitude flying put considerable strain on aircraft, particularly engines, while performing maintenance in the open during the frequent inclement weather was exceptionally trying.

7 APRIL 1945

8AF 931

	Despatched		Effective	Target		Bombs Tonnage	E/A	Losses MIA	E	Dam	Casualties KIA	WIA	MIA
3AD	B-17	529	143	KALTENKIRCHEN A/F	(P)	410.0	26–10–10	14	0	117	1	5	117
			36	BUCHEN O/D	(P)	108.0							
			104	GÜSTROW M/D	(P)	300.0							
			134	PARCHIM A/F	(P)	390.7							
			37	NEUMÜNSTER M/Y	(S)	111.0							
			48	SCHWERIN M/Y	(S)	117.9							
			1	SALZWEDEL A/F	(O)	5.0							
2AD	B-24	340	128	KRÜMMEL X/I	(P)	350.0	14– 2– 6	3	1	44	6	7	25
			168	DÜNEBURG X/I	(P)	452.8							
			26	NEUMÜNSTER M/Y	(S)	70.0							
1AD	B-17	442	115	HITZACKER O/D	(P)	284.0	0– 0– 1	0	0	27	1	3	0
			93	KOHLENBISSEN A/F	(P)	261.4							
			107	WESENDORF A/F	(P)	248.0							
			92	LÜNEBURG M/Y	(S)	266.9							
			13	UELZEN M/Y	(O)	41.6							
			12	FASSBERG A/F	(O)	33.9							
	B-17	3	4	SCOUTING FORCE				0	0	0			
TOTALS:		1314	1261			3451.2	40–12–17	17	1	188	8	15	142
	P-51	338	317	ESCORT 3AD			34–1– 8	3	1		0	0	3
	P-47	55	252	ESCORT 2AD			30–0– 7	2	1		0	0	2
	P-51	229											
	P-51	222	209	ESCORT 1AD				0	0		0	0	0
	P-51	29	29	SCOUTING FORCES				0	0		0	0	0
	P-51	25	23	ESCORT PR a/c				0	0		0	0	0
TOTALS:		898	830				64–1–15	5	2	?	0	0	5

REMARKS: Visual bombing at all primaries. Some use of H2X at secondaries and T/Os. All bomb groups participating except 491BG. The last major effort by Luftwaffe fighters against 8AF bombers. The only known occasion organised ramming was performed with 5 3AD B-17s lost to this tactic. Bomb group losses:– 2AD – 389BG – 2, 445BG – 1; 3AD – 100BG – 2, 385BG – 1, 388BG – 2, 390BG – 1, 452BG – 4, 486BG – 2, 490BG – 1, 493BG – 1. B/d 467BG B-24 abandoned over Continent, crew baled, safe.

All fighter groups operating. Fighter group e/a credits:– 4FG – 5, 55FG – 6, 56FG – 4, 78FG – 5, 339FG – 10, 353FG – 8, 355FG – 4, 356FG – 3, 357FG – 2, 479FG – 11. Fighter group losses:– 55FG – 1, 78FG – 1, 339FG – 1, 355FG – 2. 339FG P-51 c/l on return. 65FW P-51 cr. t/o, pilot safe. One MIA P-51 was shot down by 'friendly' a/c.

OTHER OPERATIONS: 7PG despatched 12 F-5s on PR Germany (with escorts). 25BG despatched 5 Mosquitoes on WR Continent/UK and 4 B-17s on WR Atlantic/UK. 5ERS despatched 14 P-47s and 1 OA-10 on ASR patrols. 36BS despatched 4 B-24s, 3 effective, on RCM. 16 P-51s, 1 B-17, 1 B-24 on radio-relays.

INCIDENT

Sonderkommando Elbe, the Luftwaffe unit specially formed to ram enemy bombers, flew its only known operation against the 8th Air Force on 7 April 1945. At least eight of the B-17s and B-24s lost that day were known or suspected lost through ramming tactics and in at least two other instances the rammer succumbed rather than the rammed. The volunteer German pilots were instructed to make a diving firing attack on the selected victim and if this failed to send the bomber down, it was to be rammed. Striking the bomber's fuselage forward of the tail with the wing of the fighter was the advised method. It was believed that the bomber's fuselage would break in two and at the same time the ram pilot would have an opportunity to bale out safely. One of the attacks that did not go according to plan was made against B-17 43-38058 of 490th Group captained by 1/Lt Carrol Cagle. An Me 109 was seen to make a diving attack from 8 o'clock and went on to smash its right wing into the Fortress against the waist gun position. The impact knocked the waist gunner over although he was not hurt. It was the Messerschmitt's wing that disintegrated, twisting the fighter down and under the B-17's fuselage, leaving a six foot gash and mangling the ball turret before cartwheeling across the lower surface of the right wing, knocking the supercharger off the inboard engine and part of the propeller from the outer, before finally disintegrating. S/Sgt Colby LeNeve, the ball gunner, was helped out of his wrecked turret by other gunners and given first aid – he suffered a broken arm. With two disabled engines the Fortress was later put down safely on an airfield in liberated territory.

8 APRIL 1945

8AF 932

	Despatched		Effective	Target		Bombs Tonnage	E/A	Losses MIA	E	Dam	Casualties KIA	WIA	MIA
1AD	B-17	339	31	DERBEN O/D	(P)	77.5		4	1	55	1	5	35
			73	SCHAFSTÄDT A/F	(P)	171.9							
			73	STENDAL M/Y WORKSHOPS	(S)	178.5							
			218	HALBERSTADT M/Y	(S)	594.7							
3AD	B-17	522	86	PLAUEN M/Y	(P)	258.3		5	0	58	1	1	43
			101	HOF M/Y	(P)	281.3							
			203	GRAFENWÖHR M/I	(P)	606.0							
			111	EGER M/Y	(P)	328.5							
2AD	B-24	302	51	BAYREUTH M/D	(P)	130.3		0	0	39	0	0	0
			89	FÜRTH/BLUMENTHAL JET A/I	(P)	208.6							
			57	UNTERSCHLAUERS-BACH A/F	(P)	127.6							
			91	ROTH A/F	(P)	216.2							
	B-17	10	10	SCREENING FORCE				0	0	0	0	0	0
TOTALS:		1173	1103			3179.4	0	9	1	152	2	6	78
	P-51	252	239	ESCORT 1AD				0	0		0	0	0
	P-51	246	235	ESCORT 3AD				0	0		0	0	0
	P-47	52	245	ESCORT 2AD				1	0		0	0	1
	P-51	200						0	0		0	0	0
	P-51	28	28	SCOUTING FORCES				0	1		0	0	0
	P-51	16	16	ESCORT PR a/c				0	0		0	0	0
TOTALS:		794	763				0	1	1	?	0	0	1

REMARKS: All bomb groups except 44BG and 384BG participated. 1AD attacked Derben visually and other targets visual and H2X; 3AD attacked visually and with H2X; 2AD was visual at all targets. Bomb group losses:– 1AD – 91BG – 2, 381BG – 1, 398BG – 1; 3AD – 94BG – 1, 486BG – 3, 487BG – 1. B/d 398BG B-17 Cat E.

All fighter groups except 357FG operating. Fighter group e/a credits:– 355FG – 3. Fighter group losses:– 355FG – 1. 3SF P-51 cr. landing base.

OTHER OPERATIONS: 7PG despatched 19 F-5s on PR Germany (with escorts). 25BG despatched 4 Mosquitoes 'chaff' screening for bombers, 4 Mosquitoes on WR Continent/UK and 4 B-17s on WR Azores/Atlantic/UK. 5ERS despatched 10 P-47s, 8 effective on ASR patrols – 2 ASR P-47s collided and cr. Fritton Lake, pilots killed. 36BS despatched 4 B-24s on RCM. 10 P-51s, 1 B-17, 1 B-24 on radio-relays.

8/9 APRIL 1945

8AF 933 NIGHT LEAFLET OPERATION

NLS despatched 11 B-24s, 11 effective; France, Holland, Germany.

25BG despatched 3 Mosquitoes on *Skywave* sorties (2 to Germany, 1 Italy).

8/9 APRIL 1945

8AF 934 NIGHT BOMBING OPERATION

492BG despatched 12 B-24s, 12 effective, dropping 29.3 tons Travemünde P/A by PFF. 1 Mosquito on *Red Stocking* operation.

482BG despatched 1 B-17 on *Eagle* scope PR Zeitz.

25BG despatched 3 Mosquitoes on night PR Germany.

9 APRIL 1945

8AF 935

	Despatched		Effective	Target		Bombs Tonnage	E/A	Losses MIA	E	Dam	Casualties KIA	WIA	MIA
1AD	B-17	333	107	OBERPFAFFEN-HOFEN A/F	(P)	297.4		0	2	12	0	1	0
			76	WOLFRATSHAUSEN M/I	(P)	225.3							
			139	FÜRSTENFELDBRUCK A/F	(P)	334.3							
3AD	B-17	289	128	SCHLEISSHEIM A/F	(P)	358.8		3	0	42	2	5	56
			66	NEUBURG A/F	(P)	179.2					(both 3AD raids)		
			89	NEUBURG O/D	(P)	242.0							
3AD	B-17	228	212	MUNICH/RIEM A/F	(P)	550.3		3	0	0			
			10	INGOLSTADT M/Y	(S)	29.0							
2AD	B-24	402	109	LECHFELD A/F	(P)	243.8		1	1	7	2	1	9
			96	MEMMINGEN A/F	(P)	211.3							
			88	LEIPHEIM A/F	(P)	217.9							
			62	LANDSBERG A/F	(P)	147.0							
			33	LANDSBERG EAST L/G	(P)	72.6							
TOTALS:		1252	1215			3108.9	0	7	3	61	4	7	65
	P-51	146	137	ESCORT 1AD			4–0–10(G)	0					
	P-51	203	193	ESCORT 2nd TF 3AD			1–0– 3 70–0–37(G)	3					
	P-51	151	149	ESCORT 3rd TF 3AD			6–0– 4(G)	1					
	P-51	205	193	ESCORT 2AD			4–0– 5(G)	0					
	P-47	58	58	FREELANCE BOMBER SUPPORT				0					
	P-51	58	58	ESCORT PR a/c			0–1– 1	0					
	P-51	25	24	SCOUTING FORCES				1					
TOTALS:		846	812				1–1– 4 84–0–56(G)	5	2	2	0	0	5

REMARKS: Visual bombing of underground oil storage at Neuburg, an ammunition plant at Wolfratshausen and jet airfields. All bomb groups except those of 40CBW participated. 4CBW and 93BCW made up the Neuburg Force; 13CBW and 45CBW the Munich Force. Bomb group losses:– 2AD – 458BG – 1; 3AD – 385BG – 1, 388BG – 2, 390BG – 1, 490BG – 1, 493BG – 1. MIA 390BG B-17 ditched, crew rescued. B/d 458BG B-24 c/l base, 2 killed. 2 b/d 351BG B-17s f/l Continent, Cat E. B/d 452BG B-17 cr. near Darmstadt, crew safe.

All fighter groups operating. 361FG flying from UK again. Fighter group e/a credits:– 55FG – 1, 361FG – 1. Fighter group losses:– 4FG – 2, 55FG – 1, 357FG – 1. 862BS (3SF) also had 1 P-51 MIA – in sea 35 miles E of Bradwell Bay, pilot lost. One MIA P-51 lost in collision. 20FG P-51 cr. on t/o. 357FG P-51 c/l on return, pilot safe.

OTHER OPERATIONS: 7PG despatched 32 F-5s on PR Germany (with escorts). 25BG despatched 4 Mosquitoes 'chaff' screening for 1AD, 4 Mosquitoes on WR Continent/UK (1 aborted and cr. Shepherds Grove A/F, 2 k.), and 4 B-17s on WR Azores/Atlantic/UK. 5ERS despatched 12 P-47s and 1 OA-10 on ASR patrols. 2 B-17s, 1 B-24 on radio-relays.

The Eighth's youngest bomb group, the 493rd, in close fomation at 27,900 feet approaching Schleissheim, 9 April. B-17Gs nearest camera are *Lil Wampus* (lower) and *Flak Flirter* (above). (via S. Evans)

9/10 APRIL 1945

8AF 936 NIGHT LEAFLET OPERATION

NLS despatched 11 B-24s, 10 effective; Holland, France,

8AF 937 NIGHT BOMBING OPERATION

492BG despatched 14 B-24s, 14 effective, dropping 33.1 tons on Stade A/F by PFF. 5 Mosquitoes escorted this force. (8AF 937)

492BG despatched 2 A-26s on *Carpetbagger* operations and 1 Mosquito on *Red Stocking*.

Flame springs out behind No.3 engine of 487BG Fortress 44-8702, a victim of Brandenburg flak on 10 April.

10 APRIL 1945

8AF 938

		Despatched	Effective	Target		Bombs Tonnage	E/A	Losses MIA	E	Dam	Casualties KIA	WIA	MIA
1AD	B-17	442	278	ORANIENBURG ARMY HQ M/D	(P)	797.3	7 –1– 8	9	2	50	1	0	84
			139	ORANIENBURG A/F & A/I	(P)	413.6							
			11	RECHLIN A/F	(S)	33.0							
3AD	B-17	144	132	NEURUPPIN A/F	(P)	392.3		1	0	44	1	7	80
			9	STENDAL M/Y	(S)	27.0							
3AD	B-17	372	138	BRANDENBURG/ BRIEST A/F	(P)	384.7	10 –3– 4	8	2	160			
			75	ZERBST A/F	(P)	222.0							
			147	BURG-BEI-MAGDEBURG A/F	(P)	438.8							
2AD	B-24	357	159	RECHLIN A/F	(P)	366.2		1	0	0	0	4	11
			103	RECHLIN/LÄRZ A/F	(P)	232.5							
			32	PARCHIM A/F	(P)	74.0							
			9	WITTENBERGE M/Y	(O)	21.0							
TOTALS:		1315	1232			3402.4	17–4–12	19	4	254	2	11	175
	P-51	289	273	ESCORT 1AD			11½–0– 8 56 –0–32 (G)	4			0		4
	P-51	117	112	ESCORT 2nd TF 3AD			128 –0–94 (G)	1			0		1
	P-51	175	172	ESCORT 3rd TF 3AD			6 –0– 2 84 –0–43 (G)	2			0		2
	P-51	220	207	ESCORT 2AD			1 –0– 1 20 –0–21	0			0		0
	P-47	62	59	FREELANCE SUPPORT FOR BOMBERS			2 –0– 2 41 –0–66 (G)	0			0		0
	P-51	15	15	ESCORT PR a/c				0			0		0
	P-51	30	30	SCOUTING FORCES				1			0		1
TOTALS:		905	868				2 –0– 2 309 –0–235 (G)	8		?	0	2	8

REMARKS: Visual bombing at all primaries and secondaries which were airfields known or suspected used by jet e/a and army base. All bomb groups except 392BG participated. 3AD flew two task forces, the first comprised 93CBW groups. Bomb group losses:– 1AD – 303BG – 1, 305BG – 2, 379BG – 2, 398BG – 1, 401BG – 1, 457BG – 2; 2AD – 453BG – 1; 3AD – 34BG – 1, 100BG – 1, 486BG – 2, 487BG – 4. MIA 305BG B-17s collided. B/d 100BG B-17 c/l Westleton, crew safe. B/d 401BG B-17 c/l Fassberg, Gr., crew safe. B/d 306BG B-17 cr. NE Hannover, 2 k. B/d 100BG B-17 cr. Continent.

All fighter groups except 361FG operating. Fighter group e/a credits: 4FG – 1, 20FG – 5, 55FG – 3, 56FG – 1, 352FG – 3, 353FG – 3, 356FG – 1, 359FG – 2, 364FG – 1. Fighter group losses:– 20FG – 3, 55FG – 1, 78FG – 2, 364FG – 1, 857BS (1SF) had 1 P-51 MIA. 78FG P-51 c/l. B/d 56FG P-47 cr. Belgium, pilot died of inj. 56FG P-47 c/l B-70 Belgium, pilot safe.

OTHER OPERATIONS: 7PG despatched 21 F-5s (1 aborted) on PR Germany (with escorts). 25BG despatched 4 Mosquitoes (1 aborted) 'chaff' screening for 1AD, 5 Mosquitoes on WR Continent/North Sea and 4 B-17 on WR Azores/Atlantic/UK. 5ERS despatched 14 P-47s, 3 OA-10s and 1 B-17 (with 4 P-51 escort) on ASR patrols. 36BS despatched 4 B-24s on RCM. 1 B-24 on radio-relays.

10/11 APRIL 1945

8AF 939 NIGHT LEAFLET OPERATION

NLS despatched 12 B-24s, 12 effective; Holland, France, Germany.

8AF 940 NIGHT BOMBING OPERATION

492BG despatched 14 B-24s, 13 effective, dropping 31.7 tons on Dessau rail depot by PFF. 1 Mosquito on *Red Stocking* operation.

25BG despatched 2 Mosquitoes on night PR Ijmuiden.

11 APRIL 1945

8AF 941

		Despatched	Effective	Target		Bombs Tonnage	E/A	Losses MIA	E	Dam	Casualties KIA	WIA	MIA
1AD	B-17	445	133	KRAIBURG M/I	(P)	381.0		1	1	15	0	1	10
			300	FREIHAM O/D	(P)	716.5							
			1	LANDSHUT M/D	(S)	2.5							
			1	TREUCHTLINGEN M/Y	(S)	1.3							
3AD	B-17	509	28	LANDSHUT M/D	(P)	75.8		0	0	0	0	0	0
			82	LANDSHUT M/Y	(P)	239.5							
			131	INGOLSTADT A/F	(P)	369.3							
			79	INGOLSTADT M/Y	(P)	237.0							
			70	TREUCHTLINGEN M/Y	(P)	207.0							
			108	DONAUWORTH M/Y	(P)	321.0							
2AD	B-24	346	80	REGENSBURG O/D	(P)	204.9		0	2	5	22	0	0
			79	REGENSBURG/ OBERTRAUBLING A/F	(P)	180.5							
			31	REGENSBURG M/D	(P)	85.0							
			71	NEUMARKT M/Y	(P)	175.0							
			73	AMBERG M/Y	(P)	167.5							
	B-17	3	3	SCOUTING FORCE				0	0	0	0	0	0
TOTALS:		1303	1270			3363.8	0	1	3	20	22	1	10
	P-51	294	273	ESCORT 1AD									
	P-51	294	281	ESCORT 3AD									
	P-47	55	211	ESCORT 2AD									
	P-51	163											
	P-51	52	52	FREELANCE REGENSBURG									
	P-51	29	28	SCOUTING FORCES									
	P-51	26	26	ESCORT PR									
TOTALS:		913	871				0	0	1		0	0	0

REMARKS: All bomb groups participated in visual attacks on a variety of targets. Last mission of 453BG. Bomb group losses:– 398BG – 1. 92BG B-17 cr. t/o base, crew safe. On return 2 446BG B-24s collided and cr. Wortwell and Redenhall, 22 killed.

All fighter groups except 356FG and 361FG operative. 55FG P-51 c/l on return, pilot safe. Strafing prohibited.

OTHER OPERATIONS: 7PG despatched 11 F-5s (1 aborted) on PR Germany (with escort). 25BG despatched 4 Mosquitoes 'chaff' screening for 1AD, 2 Mosquitoes on *Skywave* flights to and from Italy 5 Mosquitoes on WR North Sea/Continent and 4 B-17s on WR Azores/Atlantic/UK. 5ERS despatched 16 P-47s, 2 OA-10s and 1 B-17 on ASR patrols. 2 P-51s, 1 B-17, 1 B-24 on radio-relays.

11/12 APRIL 1945

8AF 942 NIGHT LEAFLET OPERATION

NLS despatched 9 B-24s, 9 effective; Germany.

492BG despatched 1 Mosquito on *Red Stocking* Germany, and 11 B-24s on *Carpetbagger* operation Denmark.

25BG despatched 1 Mosquito on *Skywave* sortie Italy.

Walking out to their white nosed Mustangs at Steeple Morden, 2nd Scout Force's 1/Lt Wilkins and Capt Lamers discuss their mission. Although Scout pilots were ordered to avoid combat unless attacked, Wilkins had an opportunity to dispatch an Me 262 jet on 1 March and took it.

12 APRIL 1945

No offensive operations from UK. 352FG and 361FG flew in support of 9AF B-26s. No loss or claims. 99 P-51s despatched, 95 effective.

OTHER OPERATIONS: 7PG despatched 2 F-5s on PR Germany with 4 P-51s as escort, 2 P-51s effective. 25BG despatched 6 Mosquitoes on WR Continent/UK and 4 B-17s on WR Azores/Atlantic/UK. 36BS despatched 4 B-24s on RCM, 2 P-51s on radio-relays.

12/13 APRIL 1945

8AF 944 NIGHT LEAFLET OPERATION

NLS despatched 10 B-24s, 9 effective; Holland, Germany.

482BG despatched 1 B-17 and 1 B-24 to take *Eagle* scope photos of Zeitz.

492BG despatched 2 Mosquitoes on *Red Stocking* operation and 6 B-24s on *Carpetbagger* operations, Denmark.

25BG *Skywave* Mosquito returns from Italy.

INCIDENT

An unusual accident occured on 13 April 1945 as the lead squadron of the 398th Bomb Group crossed the target. One B-17 apparently failed to release bombs for reasons unknown, but some two and a half minutes later it suddenly salvoed the whole load. The ten RDX explosive filled 500 pounders fell about 400 ft when two touched and detonated. The blast crippled the bomber from which the bombs had come and it went down. Most of the other Fortresses in the lead squadron were peppered with bomb fragments, five so badly that they had to make emergency landings at continental airfields, most to be later classified as only fit for salvage. Eight men were killed and several injured in these and other surviving bombers.

13 APRIL 1945

8AF 945

	Despatched		Effective	Target	Bombs Tonnage	E/A	Losses MIA	E	Dam	Casualties KIA	WIA	MIA
1AD	B-17	212	212	NEUMÜNSTER M/Y (S)	577.3	0	2	1	3	8	3	17
	P-51	278	256	ESCORT 1AD		137–0– 83	6			0	0	6
	P-47	49	97	FREELANCE BOMBER		147–0–137 (G)	1			0	0	1
	P-51	51		SUPPORT			1			0	0	1
	P-51	8	8	SCOUTING FORCES			0			0	0	0
	P-51	13	11	ESCORT PR a/c			0			0	0	0
TOTALS:		399	372			137–0– 83 147–0–137 (G)	8	3	?	0	0	8

REMARKS: Visual attack by 1CBW and 40CBW groups on Neumünster M/Y. Bomb group losses:– 398BG – 2. MIA 398BG B-17s lost to bomb explosion which caused extensive damage to 4 other 398BG a/c which were able to f/l on Continent and another which cr., 8 k.

Fighter groups operating: 4FG, 20FG, 56FG, 355FG, 356FG, 359FG, 361FG, 479FG. Fighter group losses:– 56FG – 1, 355FG – 1, 359FG – 1, 364FG – 2, 479FG – 3. Strafing of airfields ban lifted.

OTHER OPERATIONS: 7PG despatched 10 F-5s on PR Germany (with escorts). 25BG despatched 4 Mosquitoes on WR Continent/UK and 4 B-17s on WR Azores/Atlantic/UK. 5ERS despatched 10 P-47s, 1 OA-10 and 1 B-17 on ASR patrols. 36BS despatched 4 B-24s on RCM and 1 P-38 on radar search (with 4 P-51 escorts). 1 B-17, 1 B-24, 4 P-51s on radio-relays.

INCIDENT

The 56th Fighter Group, last remaining Thunderbolt group in the 8th, had been selected to combat test the new T-48 .50-calibre ammunition in February but the test was delayed until the troubles with the P-47M models were finally corrected. The T-48 rounds had a muzzle velocity of 3,400 ft per second and contained more incendiary compound to ensure greater effectiveness against the low-grade fuels believed to be used in German jet aircraft. The 56th had an opportunity to see the benefits of the new ammunition when they strafed Eggebeck airfield on 13 April 1945 and initially claimed 95 Luftwaffe aircraft destroyed. All told the 49 P-47Ms involved made 339 individual passes and expended 78,073 rounds of assorted .50-calibre. Lt Randel Murphy, who made a personal claim of 10, was using T-48 in his guns. Later in the month T-48 ammunition was issued to other groups but the opportunity to use it against enemy targets had then gone.

13/14 APRIL 1945

8AF 946 NIGHT BOMBING OPERATION

492BG despatched 12 B-24s, 10 effective; Beizenburg R/J dropping 22.5 tons by PFF.

8AF 947 NIGHT LEAFLET OPERATION

NLS despatched 11 B-24s, 10 effective; France, Germany.

492BG despatched 4 B-24s, 1 effective on *Carpetbagger* operations Denmark.

492BG despatched 1 Mosquito on *Red Stocking* operation.

14 APRIL 1945

8AF 948

	Despatched		Effective	Target	Bombs Tonnage	E/A	Losses MIA	E	Dam	Casualties KIA	WIA	MIA
3AD	B-17	490	480	BORDEAUX/ROYAN, POINTE COUBRE AND POINTE GRAVE: 15 ENEMY STRONG POINTS AND FLAK BATTERIES	1246.0		0	1	1	0	1	0
2AD	B-24	336	315	BORDEAUX/ROYAN, POINTE COUBRE AND POINTE GRAVE: 12 ENEMY STRONG POINTS AND FLAK BATTERIES	1017.5		2	3	1	18	8	12

continued on next page

1AD	B-17	341	338	BORDEAUX/ROYAN AREA FOUR ENEMY STRONG POINTS AND FLAK BATTERIES	1054.9		0	0	0	0	0	0
TOTALS:		1167	1133		3318.4	0	2	4	2	18	9	12
	B-17 P-51	5 24	31	SCOUTING FORCES								
	P-51	11	9	ESCORT PR a/c								
TOTALS:		40	40			0	0		?	0	0	0

REMARKS: Visual bombing of enemy pockets on French Atlantic coast. Bomb groups participating:– all 1AD except 1CBW groups; all 2AD; all 3AD except 95BG. Bomb group losses: 389BG – 2. MIA B-24s collided. 2 458BG B-24s cr. after t/o Horsham St.Faith, crew safe and Spixworth, 6 killed. 392BG B-24 cr. after t/o Gressenhall, 6 killed. Burning 388BG B-17 abandoned by crew over Lyon, France on way to target.

No operations by fighter groups.

OTHER OPERATIONS: 7PG despatched 8 F-5s on PR Royan and Germany (with escorts). 25BG despatched 9 Mosquitoes 'chaff' screening for bombers, 1 Mosquito on *Skywave* flight to Italy, 5 Mosquitoes on WR Continent and 3 B-17s on WR Azores/Atlantic/UK. 5ERS despatched 2 P-47s and 1 OA-10 on ASR patrols.

14/15 APRIL 1945

8AF 949 NIGHT LEAFLET OPERATION

NLS despatched 11 B-24s, 10 effective; Germany, Holland, France.

8AF 950 was an experimental bombing operation by 1 492BG Mosquito and B-24s against Neuruppin A/F, unsuccessful.

492BG despatched 4 B-24s, 1 effective, on *Carpetbagger* operations, Denmark and 1 Mosquito on *Red Stocking*.

15 APRIL 1945

8AF 951

	Despatched		Effective	Target	Bombs Tonnage	E/A	Losses MIA	E	Dam	Casualties KIA	WIA	MIA
3AD	B-17	529	492	ROYAN AREA: FOUR ENEMY STRONG POINTS & FLAK BATTERIES	822.9		0	0	5	0	0	0
2AD	B-24	359	341	ROYAN AREA: SIX ENEMY STRONG POINTS & FLAK BATTERIES	729.5		0	1	3	2	0	0
1AD	B-17	457	442	BORDEAUX/ROYAN, POINTE GRAVE & POINTE COUBRE: NINE ENEMY STRONG POINTS & FLAK BATTERIES	1303.0		0	0	0	0	0	0
	B-17	3	3	SCOUTING FORCE			0	0	0	0	0	0
TOTALS:		1348	1278		2855.4	0	0	1	8	2	0	0
	P-51	109	107	SUPPORTING 9AF B-26s			1			0	0	1
	P-51	20	20	SCOUTING FORCES			0			0	0	0
	P-51	7	6	ESCORT PR a/c			0			0	0	0
TOTALS:		136	133			0	1	?	?	0	0	1

REMARKS: Visual bombing on strong points on French Atlantic coast. All bomb groups participated. 2AD and 3AD tonnage included 500lb Napalm tanks, first and only use by heavy bombers as ballistics poor. 466BG B-24 cr. after t/o Mattishall, 2 killed.

No Fighter escort for heavy bombers. 4FG and 339FG provided escort for 9AF B-26s. Fighter group losses:– 339FG – 1.

OTHER OPERATIONS: 7PG despatched 6 F-5s on PR Royan and Germany (with escorts). 1 7PG P-51 cr. t/o. 25BG despatched 4 Mosquitoes 'chaff' screening for 1AD, 3 Mosquitoes as monitors for 2AD and 3AD, 3 Mosquitoes on WR Azores/Atlantic/UK. 5ERS despatched 6 P-47s and 2 OA-10s on ASR patrols. 4 P-51s on radio-relays, 1 4FG P-51 c/l Watten, near Dunkirk, pilot inj.

25BG despatched 1 Mosquito for *Skywave* operations from Italy and 2 Mosquitoes returned from Italy.

The death of Franklin Roosevelt, one of the most popular US Presidents of the century, brought genuine mourning at 8AF bases. This memorial service was conducted at Leiston on 15 April. (The corner posts are old drop tanks filled with concrete and designed to keep vehicles on the hard.) (A. Swanson)

A close formation gave a good bomb pattern on the target. The 500 pounders just released from these 467BG B-24s are aimed at Landshut, 16 April. Lead plane (hidden behind X7:F) has dropped a smoke marker bomb (centre) that has failed to ignite; that from deputy lead (far top) has fired. 467BG was to produce the best overall bombing record of any B-24 group. All B-24s in picture have *Carpet* blinker radar jammers – antenna housings are the small bumps under forward fuselage.

15/16 APRIL 1945

8AF 952 was an abortive operation by a 492BG Mosquito and 9 B-24s against Lechfeld A/F.

8AF 953 NIGHT LEAFLET OPERATION

NLS despatched 11 B-24s, 10 effective; France, Holland, Germany.

492BG despatched 1 Mosquito on *Red Stocking*.

16 APRIL 1945

8AF 954	Despatched		Effective	Target	Bombs Tonnage	E/A	Losses MIA	E	Dam	Casualties KIA	WIA	MIA
2AD	B-24	306	273	LANDSHUT M/Y (P)	679.8		1	2	8	0	0	7
1AD	B-17	454	74	REGENSBURG WEST (P) R/B	217.5		0	0	2	0	0	0
			72	REGENSBURG EAST (P) R/B	210.0							
			148	REGENSBURG M/Y (P)	391.1							
			77	PLATTING M/Y (P)	264.0							
			76	STRAUBING R/B (P)	241.8							
8AF 955												
3AD	B-17	489	485	ANTI-TANK DITCH AND DEFENCE LINE IN BORDEAUX AREA	1444.7		0	0	14	0	0	0
	B-17	3	3	SCOUTING FORCE			0	0	0	0	0	0
TOTALS:		1252	1208		3448.9	0	1	2	24	0	0	7
	P-47	55	299	ESCORT 2AD		228–0–109 (G)	1			0	0	1
	P-51	260					16			0	0	16
	P-51	262	240	ESCORT 1AD		2–0– 0 86–0– 66 (G)	3			0	0	3
	P-51	298	286	FREELANCE SUPPORT BOMBERS–66FW		1–0– 1 410–0–198 (G)	9				0	9
	P-51	22	19	SCOUTING FORCES			0			0	0	0
	P-51	16	16	ESCORT PR a/c			2			0	0	2
TOTALS:		913	860			3–0– 0 724–0–373 (G)	31	5	?	0	5	31

REMARKS: All 1AD and 2AD groups attacked rail and communication centres in Germany. All 3AD except 96BG and 390BG attacked targets in enemy strongholds on French Atlantic coast. All bombing visual except at Landshut which was by H2X. Bomb group losses:– 448BG – 1. 448BG B-24 cr. t/o base, 4 killed. 466BG B-24 abandoned over Belgium following collision, crew safe – other 466BG a/c involved landed safely at base.

All fighter groups operating. Fighter group e/a credits:– 55FG – 1, 361FG – 1, 364FG – 2. Fighter group losses:– 4FG – 8, 55FG – 4, 56FG – 1, 78FG – 2, 352FG – 2, 353FG – 3, 355FG – 4, 361FG – 2, 364FG – 1, 479FG – 4. Large scale strafing of enemy airfields brought huge claims and heavy losses to ground fire. B/d 4FG P-51 c/l Otterburg, Germany, pilot inj. (Allied area). 364FG P-51 cr. near Frankfurt, pilot safe. B/d 361FG P-51 Cat E. 357FG P-51 c/l Continent, pilot safe.

OTHER OPERATIONS: 7PG despatched 10 F-5s on PR France and Germany (with escorts). 2 7PG P-51 MIA. 25BG despatched 5 Mosquitoes 'chaff' screening for 1AD, 1 Mosquito on *Skywave* navigation flight from Italy, 4 Mosquitoes on WR Atlantic/UK/Germany, and 4 B-17s on WR Azores/Atlantic/UK. 5ERS despatched 13 P-47s, 2 B-17s and 2 OA-10s on ASR patrols. 36BS despatched 4 B-24s on RCM. 2 B-17s, 1 B-24 on radio-relays.

16/17 APRIL 1945

8AF 956 NIGHT LEAFLET OPERATION

NLS despatched 12 B-24s, 11 effective; France, Holland, Germany.

482BG despatched 1 B-17 and 1 B-24 on *Eagle* scope Düneburg.

492BG despatched 1 Mosquito on *Red Stocking*.

17 APRIL 1945

8AF 957

	Despatched		Effective	Target		Bombs Tonnage	E/A	Losses MIA	E	Dam	Casualties KIA	WIA	MIA
1AD	B-17	450	152	DRESDEN R/C	(P)	430.4	1–0–1	6	1	130	0	6	50
			276	DRESDEN M/Y	(P)	845.9							
3AD	B-17	410	76	DRESDEN-NEUSTADT	(P)	211.2		2	0	47	0	1	18
			87	AUSSIG R/J & R/S	(P)	255.6							
			115	ROUNDNICE O/D & M/Y	(P)	315.8							
			86	DRESDEN M/Y	(S)	245.3							
2AD	B-24	194	55	FISCHERN R/C & R/J	(P)	121.5		0	0	0	0	0	0
			36	KLADNO R/J & R/I	(P)	81.0							
			37	FALKENAU R/J & R/B	(P)	79.0							
			61	BEROUN R/R, M/Y & R/I	(P)	138.5							
TOTALS:		1054	981			2724.2	1–0–1	8	1	177	0	7	68
	P-51	257	230	ESCORT 1AD			2–0– 3 91–0–37 (G)	2			0	0	2
	P-51	276	265	ESCORT 2AD			11–0– 2 142–0–47 (G)	14			0	2	14
	P-47	56	228	ESCORT 2AD			53–0–29	0			0	0	0
	P-51	193						1			0	0	1
	P-51	25	24	SCOUTING FORCES				0			0	0	0
	P-51	9	9	ESCORT PR A/C				0			0	0	0
TOTALS:		816	756				13–0– 5 286–0–113 (G)	17	?	?	0	2	17

REMARKS: Rail targets in SE Germany and Czechoslovakia. All 1AD and 3AD groups participated bombing visually and with use of H2X at all targets. All 2AD groups excepting 44BG, 448BG and 458BG participated and bombed visually. Bomb group losses:– 1AD – 91BG – 1, 92BG – 2, 305BG – 1, 303BG – 2; 3AD – 486BG – 2. MIA 92BG B-17s collided.

All fighter groups operating. Fighter group e/a credits:– 55FG – 9, 339FG – 1, 357FG – 1, 364FG – 2. Fighter group losses:– 4FG – 1, 55FG – 5, 78FG – 2, 339FG – 2, 352FG – 1, 353FG – 2, 357FG – 3, 364FG – 1. On return, 4FG P-51 c/l French A/F; 364FG P-51 c/l Beccles A/F.

OTHER OPERATIONS: 7PG despatched 10 F-5s to Germany (with escorts). 25BG despatched 10 Mosquitoes 'chaff' screening for bombers, 3 Mosquitoes on WR Atlantic/Continent/UK, and 4 B-17s on WR Azores/Atlantic/UK. 5ERS despatched 8 P-47s, 1 B-17 and 2 OA-10s on ASR patrols. 36BS despatched 4 B-24s on RCM. 1 B-17, 1 B-24, 2 P-51s on radio-relays.

EAGER EL

Up to the late summer of 1944 the record of the 55th Fighter Group was, to quote one of the Headquarters officers, 'at best mediocre'. In the previous autumn the Group had been the first to take the P-38 Lightning into action from England, sustaining heavy losses, chiefly through the inadequacies of that aircraft. Although ably led, morale had not been of the highest order. Then came conversion to the P-51 Mustang and an up-turn in operational performance. But although the 55th occasionally starred, in the league standing of 8th Air Force fighter groups it remained something of an 'also-ran outfit'.

In October 1944 Headquarters received word from the controlling 66th Fighter Wing that they were sending the Group a Lieutenant Colonel, fresh from instructing in the States, who wanted to see some action. Unwelcome news, for a high rank novice could be a liability rather than an asset in a combat unit. There was also a suspicion that there might be more to this

Righetti beside his first Mustang: an autographed photo sent to a sister.

With other pilots at Wormingford. (C. Henry)

assignment than was revealed. Was the newcomer to be groomed for a command, an implant with a new broom mandate? Any change in command that did not involve advancement of a unit's own long-time officers engendered resentment; experienced men from other groups would be grudgingly accepted but men drawn from some Stateside organisation were met with disdain.

Lt.Col Elwyn Guido Righetti arrived at Wormingford airfield on 22 October 1944 where initial plans to assign him to a squadron were changed as he would have outranked everyone. Instead he joined Group Headquarters while flying with 338th Fighter Squadron to gain experience. Righetti was tall with a swarthy complexion and mop of dark locks that bore witness to his Franco-Latin forebears. A personable nature made him easy to get along with, but in view of his background the veterans did not rate his suitability as a fighter pilot very high. They learned that he had previously headed the advanced instructors' training unit at Randolph Field, Texas, where most of his wartime service had been spent since enlisting in the Air Corps in November 1939. There were too, a wife and baby daughter back in San Antonio; men with dependants were often concerned with staying alive and lacked the aggressiveness so necessary to the successful fighter pilot. It was then generally accepted that the occupant of a Mustang cockpit should ideally be about 20 years old, benefiting from the faster reactions with which youth is endowed. The newcomer was past 29, which made him one of the oldest pilots on the base.

Righetti acquired a Mustang for his personal use in the 338th Fighter Squadron and had the name *Katydid* plus a grasshopper insignia painted under the exhaust stacks. The aircraft's nickname was derived from Righetti's wife Cathryn who was known as Katy. After a week's familiarisation with operational procedures he took part in a combat mission. The date, 2 November, was an occasion when Luftwaffe fighters chose to rise in strength and the 55th's Mustangs encountered several. Righetti was flying as wingman to Capt Darrell Cramer leading 338th Squadron. As there seemed to be more Mustangs than German aircraft in the vicinity, Cramer took his flight down below the clouds to pick off any enemy fighters diving away from the battle above. As none could be found in the air Cramer led his flight to look for strafing targets. While following a railway track an Me 109 appeared slightly above, flying towards the Mustangs. Cramer pulled up to attack. As he opened fire the enemy aircraft banked right. Righetti, having overrun his leader, turned left and found himself in position to shoot at the Messerschmitt. After two short bursts the enemy hit the ground, the victory being shared with Cramer. It was a good start and during the next few missions the combat initiate revealed a surprising aggressiveness and enthusiasm for the job. On 21 November he led 338th Squadron for the first time and five days later was assigned as its commander. He appeared to have no qualms about the dangerous business of ground strafing railways and airfields where light flak defences were often formidable causing high losses. A bullet hit in a coolant pipe could bring down a Mustang; a shell burst could spin it into the ground.

Righetti's eagerness was becoming an inspiration. Some of the old hands still resented his presence but others acknowledged that he was a natural leader. On an escort to Bingen marshalling yards early in December, Righetti led a Group formation for the first time and thereafter with increasing frequency. On Christmas Eve 1944, when the 8th Air Force put its largest ever force into the sky, the 338th Squadron became embroiled with Focke Wulfs near Münster and their leader shot down two of the eight claimed. Enemy fighters were then rarely encountered in the air and Righetti's aggression was directed mainly at the German rail network, by following tracks until a train was seen and then shattering the locomotive's boiler with gun fire. At the turn of the year he had accounted for 21 locomotives destroyed in this way.

While determined in the air, on the ground Righetti exhibited most of the characteristics that distinguish a good commander. Firm and decisive, he was also receptive and considerate towards his men, with whom he regularly socialised.

The operational performance of the 55th improved during the last two months of 1944; in the first of 1945 it excelled, producing the best all-round record in the 66th Wing by destroying 55 enemy aircraft and 157 locomotives. Righetti's personal contribution was five of the former and ten more locos. On the 22nd he moved back to Group Headquarters and took the post of Air Executive. The CO, Col George Crowell, had only a few flying hours left to complete his second combat tour and it appeared likely Righetti would take his place at the head of the 55th; this proved to be the case exactly a month later.

In February 1945 the 55th established itself as the foremost scourge of the German rail network, for on two days alone, the 19th and 20th, they claimed 170 locomotives wrecked and their total for the month was assessed as 354. Thereafter, little moved by day on the permanent way in the Third Reich. Such havoc was not wrought without cost, for during the month 12 of the Group's Mustangs were lost while strafing. Despite this, a fresh spirit seemed to pervade the Wormingford base, a new *esprit de corps*. It would be wrong to attribute this solely to Righetti's influence for many of the Group's officers made major contributions, but there is no doubt he had become the catalyst. Strafing successes let the pilots see the contribution they were making towards victory; with a new confidence they pursued their dangerous work, now proclaiming themselves the 55th Fightin' Group. The combat exuberance of their leader led them to dub him 'Eager El'. As one of the younger pilots later asserted, 'We believed he was the best fighter leader in the Air Force and we were now the best fighter group.' To a staff officer who could take a more detached view Righetti 'personified what a Group Commander should be. You could tell by looking at him, or by listening to him, that he was the leader, that the Group was there to shoot down or up Germans . . . everything else was secondary to that purpose. He literally implied aggressiveness in everything he did'.

If leadership demanded exemplification, then few could have faulted Righetti on that score for he did not hesitate to undertake the most dangerous tasks himself. This was evident in shooting up enemy airfields where it was usual procedure for a formation commander to call in one of his elements to make a low pass across the target to test the strength of the flak defences, while the rest of the formation orbited at a safe altitude. If the defences were weak then the group would go down to the strafe: if formidable they would keep clear. Experienced leaders were valuable and were supposed not to expose themselves to unnecessary dangers, but Righetti frequently undertook to make the test pass. Such an occasion was the 21 March attack on Hopsten, suspected base of Me 262 jets. First a B-17 formation was to bomb the airfield following which the 55th, with each P-51 carrying one 500 lb fragmentation bomb, would attempt to silence remaining ground gun defences before strafing aircraft dispersals. After the heavies departed Righetti followed by his wingman descended to make two low-level orbits of Hopstein, specifically to draw enemy fire and identify the locations of the emplacements so other Mustangs could attack them. Despite the bombing, ground fire was intense and the tail of Righetti's Mustang was blasted by fragments from an exploding 37 mm shell: his wingman took a direct hit and crashed. Rightetti radioed the position of gun emplacements and then shot up and ignited the only two intact enemy aircraft he could see, one by firing through a wooden shed in his line of sight. Seeing no other worthwhile targets, and in view of the intense flak, he ordered the rest of the 55th away and rejoined them.

By early April the score of locomotives claimed by the 55th stood at 940 of which 575 had been attacked during the first three months of 1945. The Allied armies were now sweeping into Germany and restrictions were put on strafing road and rail traffic where it might hinder and endanger friendly forces. Reconnaissance showed that on some airfields the Luftwaffe had massed large numbers of aircraft. Perhaps there was no fuel left to fly them, but the 8th Air Force took no chances and the long range fighter groups were given the go-ahead to destroy as many as they could. The 66th Fighter Wing groups predominated in this work, each group vying for the biggest daily 'bag'. On 9 April the 55th had a success in the area between Munich and Salzburg, claiming 54 enemy planes on the ground and one in the air. Righetti got six, three being Me 262s. During the next few days other groups excelled with scores of over a hundred in a few cases. A week passed before the 55th was able to turn in another large score. Returning to the area south-east of Munich they found a great many aircraft at Bad Aibling, Neubiberg, and the Brunnthal landing ground on the *Autobahn*, destroying 52; Righetti's contribution being another six. The opposition was fierce and four Mustangs were lost to ground fire.

The following day the Group was alerted to escort B-17s to Dresden and its commander again elected to lead. At briefing his scheduled wingman was indisposed and Lt Carroll Henry, an effervescent Kentuckian eager to fly the mission, took his place. Apparently unknown to the staff at Wormingford it was Righetti's thirtieth birthday, part of which he had chosen to spend on a six-hour sortie in a Mustang. Shortly after noon he led 54 other P-51s into the air for the 400 mile flight across Europe. Two hours later the force rendesvoused with the bombers near Freiburg, accompanying them through the target area. After passing escort to another Mustang group, they turned back towards Dresden to search for strafing targets. Righetti led his flight down through a break in the clouds, but only he and Lt Henry were together when they emerged from the overcast where visibility was restricted by haze. They were flying at about 1,800 ft north of Dresden when an airfield came into view. They circled the field once and observed several parked aircraft, mainly single-engine types. Typically, Righetti chose to make a test pass and radioed his intention to Henry and for any others of his flight that might be in the vicinity. Henry asked for and received permission to accompany the leader. The two Mustangs dropped down east of the airfield to make their approach. As they neared their objective an FW 190 loomed out of the haze, undercarriage down. Righetti called to Henry to take it while he continued his strafing pass. Positioning his Mustang behind the unsuspecting Focke Wulf, Henry gave it a long burst when about 50 feet above the ground. Over-running his quarry, Henry turned for a second attack and saw the fighter had crashed and was burning. He then looked round for Righetti and noticed three Me 109s on fire. The defences appeared to be putting up little flak so he then made a strafing run from north to south, his shooting igniting an aircraft on the north-western side of the airfield. As Henry pulled up from this run he caught sight of Righetti's Mustang making another pass and at least seven enemy planes burning on the ground. Turning behind his leader he saw Righetti's Mustang was streaming a white trail, implying coolant. Before Henry could warn him, Righetti called over the radio: 'Windsor here gang, hit bad, oil pressure dropping fast, can't make it out of enemy territory, just enough ammo' left for one more pass.' Dismayed, Henry watched as Righetti turned to make that pass, giving him cover. The Colonel obtained good hits on two more parked aircraft, then pulled up slightly, levelled off and took a 270 degree course for friendly territory. About a minute and a half later Henry heard Righetti call: 'I've got to set it down.' In the haze, Henry above passed over his leader, slowed and tried to locate him by rocking his aircraft from side to side while calling over the radio. Eventually there was a response. 'I'm OK, broke my nose in landing. Got nine today. It's been a hell of a lot of fun working with you gang. Be seeing you a little later.' Henry tried to locate the Mustang which had evidently 'bellied in' as he flew over. Unsuccessful, he eventually had to turn for home.

On Carroll Henry's observations Elwyn Righetti was credited with nine strafing victories at Riesa/Canitz airfield. This brought his total of ground aircraft claims to 27, more than any other 8th Air Force fighter pilot. With over 30 locomotives and numerous other ground targets destroyed to his credit, he was surely the king of the American ground strafers, that most dangerous of fighter activities. Four other Wormingford Mustangs failed to return on 17 April, but three of these were accounted for in Allied territory on the continent and the pilot of the fourth was known to have parachuted safely. The knowledge that Righetti had survived the crash landing and was probably a prisoner helped to dispel the 55th's despondency over his loss; the fulfilment of his last message to 'be seeing you a little later' was expected. Not until the end of the hostilities was there apprehension as to his safety. Even then in the confusion following the collapse of Nazi Germany POWs often arrived in the Allied camp before word of their whereabouts was received. By June, Righetti's family having still had no news, there was grave concern. He was known to have crash landed some 20 miles north-west of Dresden, an area that now lay within the Soviet zone of occupation. Efforts to get US officers to the scene were frustrated by the Soviet authorities and from the limited enquiries that were conducted it was assumed that Righetti had been killed by German civilians. Because of the casualties sustained through air attack civilians had a strong animosity toward Allied fliers. Unlike most other pilots in his Group, Righetti often carried a revolver and his fellow fliers believed that he would not hesitate to use it if threatened. However, his fate must remain speculative. No grave was ever located.

In 1947 Elwyn Righetti's family, who lived at San Luis Obispo, California, attended a ceremony where his five-year-old daughter received a number of posthumous decorations, including the DSC, second highest standing decoration for bravery. Also in attendance were some of the men who had served with Righetti at Wormingford and held him in high esteem. Glowing tributes were paid. But the best appreciation of Elwyn Righetti can be found in the normally dull official operations reports of the 8th Air Force. On the evening of 17 April 1945, when Righetti was believed safe, Tom Welch, Jr, the senior intelligence officer at Wormingford and a long time member of the 55th Group, was moved to append the following to the day's operational report. There is probably no finer epitaph to an 8th Air Force pilot:– 'We're going to miss you, Colonel, all twenty-nine years of your bursting energy and vitality, your eagerness and courage, your initiative and leadership that moulded us into a deadly fightin' machine, whipping the Hun at every turn. We're going to miss your cheerfulness, your decisiveness, and your understanding of human nature. You spelled aggressiveness whenever and wherever you flew, and made us into one of the eagerest gangs of eager beavers. Your record speaks for itself – 34½ destroyed Heinies to your credit – 27 on the ground – 7½ in the air, and enemy ground installations too numerous to add up. All of us of Ole Five and Five salute you, "Eager El", a great leader, and a Fightin' Fighter.'

17/18 APRIL 1945

8AF 958 NIGHT LEAFLET OPERATION

NLS despatched 10 B-24s, 10 effective; France, Holland, Germany.

492BG despatched 20 B-24s, 19 effective on *Carpetbagger* operations, and 2 Mosquitoes on *Red Stocking*.

482BG despatched 1 B-17 and 1 B-24 on *Eagle* radar scope PR Ruhland.

25BG despatched 2 Mosquitoes on night PR Ijmuiden, and 1 Mosquito on and PR flight landing in Italy.

18 APRIL 1945

8AF 959

	Despatched		Effective	Target		Bombs Tonnage	E/A	Losses MIA	E	Dam	Casualties KIA	WIA	MIA
3AD	B-17	174	174	STRAUBING M/Y	(S)	524.6		0	0	0	0	0	0
3AD	B-17	121	97	KOLLIN M/Y	(P)	287.3		0	1	17	0	0	10
			21	PILSEN M/Y	(S)	61.8							
2AD	B-24	196	166	PASSAU M/Y	(P)	372.3		0	0	0	0	0	0
			28	PASSAU R/B & R/I	(P)	62.0							
1AD	B-17	276	9	TRAUNSTEIN E/T	(P)	20.0		2	0	25	0	0	10
			56	TRAUNSTEIN M/Y	(P)	179.7							
			148	ROSENHEIM M/Y & E/T	(P)	431.2							
			61	FREISING M/Y	(S)	149.5							
TOTALS:		767	760			2088.4	0	2	1	42	0	0	20
	P-51	99	99	ESCORT 1st TF 3AD							0	0	0
	P-51	160	157	ESCORT 2nd TF 3AD			3–0–4	1			0	0	1
	P-47	54	240	ESCORT 2AD			12–0–8(G)	0			0	0	1
	P-51	198						1					
	P-51	150	139	ESCORT 1AD				0			0	0	0
	P-51	103	101	SUPPORT 9AF B-26			1–0–2	0			0	0	0
	P-51	27	27	SCOUTING FORCES				0			0	0	0
	P-51	17	15	ESCORT PR a/c				0			0	0	0
TOTALS:		808	778				4–0–6 12–0–8(G)	2	?	?	0	0	2

REMARKS: Rail targets were attacked visually with some cases of resort to H2X by first and fourth task forces. Bomb groups participating:– 13CBW and 45CBW groups made up first 3AD task force; 93CBW groups made up second 3AD task force; 20CBW groups and 44BG, 445BG, 458BG, 466BG, 491BG made up 2AD force; 40CBW and 94CBW groups and 91BG, 398BG made up 1AD force. Bomb group losses:– 401BG – 1, 457BG – 1.

All fighter groups operating. Fighter group e/a credits:– 339FG – 1, 356FG – 1, 357FG – 2. Fighter group losses:– 357FG – 1, 479FG – 1.

OTHER OPERATIONS: 7PG despatched 13 F-5s, 11 effective, on PR Germany (with escorts). 25BG despatched 2 Mosquitoes as monitors for 1AD and 3AD, 3 Mosquitoes on WR Continent/Atlantic/UK, and 4 B-17s on WR Azores/Atlantic/UK. 5ERS despatched 12 P-47s, 4 OA-10s and 1 B-17 on ASR patrols and 4 P-51s also on ASR search. 36BS despatched 4 B-24s on RCM. 6 P-51s, 2 B-17s, 1 B-24 on radio-relays.

18/19 APRIL 1945

8AF 960 NIGHT LEAFLET OPERATION

NLS despatched 11 B-24s, 11 effective; France, Holland, Germany.

492BG despatched 18 B-24s, 17 effective, on *Carpetbagger* operations, Denmark and Norway.

492BG despatched 1 Mosquito on *Skywave* flight to Italy.

25BG despatched 1 Mosquito on PR Ijmuiden.

19 APRIL 1945

8AF 961

	Despatched		Effective	Target		Bombs Tonnage	E/A	Losses MIA	E	Dam	Casualties KIA	WIA	MIA
1AD	B-17	284	135	ELSTERWERDA M/Y	(P)	304.8		0	0	27	0	0	0
			143	FALKENBERG M/Y	(P)	331.1							
3AD	B-17	321	115	PIRNA R/R/I & R/B	(P)	337.3	6–1–2	5	0	13	0	0	46
			109	AUSSIG M/Y	(P)	307.3							
			87	KARLSBAD R/R/I & R/J	(P)	243.3							
TOTALS:		605	589			1523.8	6–1–2	5	0	40	0	0	46
	P-51	204	191	ESCORT 1AD			5–0–0	1			0	0	1
	P-51	206	197	ESCORT 3AD			7–0–3	0			0	0	0
	P-51	154	138	FREELANCE SUPPORT BOMBERS				0			0	0	0
	P-51	14	14	WEATHER RECONN				0			0	0	0
	P-51	6	6	ESCORT PR A/C				1			0	0	1
TOTALS:		584	546				12–0–3	2	3	?	0	0	2

REMARKS: Visual attacks on rail targets. Bomb groups participating:– all 1AD except 91BG, 92BG, 303BG, 351BG; all 3AD except 13CBW groups. Bomb group losses:– 447BG – 1, 490BG – 4. All losses to jet e/a.

Fighter groups not operating were: 4FG, 56FG, 355FG, 361FG. Fighter group e/a credits:– 55FG – 1, 357FG – 6, 364FG – 5. Fighter group losses:– 364FG – 1. 359FG P-51 c/l Croxton after t/o, pilot injured. MIA 364FG P-51 abandoned by pilot after being shot up by Soviet fighters. 364FG P-51 c/l liberated territory.

OTHER OPERATIONS: 7PG despatched 7 F-5s on PR Germany (with escorts). 1 7PG P-51 MIA. 25BG despatched 1 Mosquito on experimental navigation flight for night PR, 5 Mosquitoes 'chaff' screening for 1AD, 1 Mosquito as monitor for 1AD, 6 Mosquitoes on WR Continent/UK, and 4 B-17s on WR Azores/Atlantic/UK. 5ERS despatched 10 P-47s and 2 OA-10s on ASR patrols. 36BS despatched 4 B-24s on RCM. 4 P-51s, 2 B-17s on radio-relays.

19/20 APRIL 1945

25BG despatched 3 Mosquitoes on night PR Heligoland and Guernsey.

492BG despatched 16 B-24s, 11 effective on *Carpetbagger* operations. Norway; 2 a/c MIA. 2 Mosquitoes on *Red Stocking* Germany.

482BG despatched 3 H2X B-17s and 1 *Eagle* B-24 on radar scope PR Salzburg and Ingolstadt. Leaflets also dropped.

20 APRIL 1945

8AF 962

	Despatched		Effective	Target		Bombs Tonnage	E/A	Losses MIA	E	Dam	Casualties KIA	WIA	MIA
3AD	B-17	319	82	NAUEN R/I	(P)	202.5		0	0	15	0	1	0
			77	WUSTERMARK M/Y	(P)	192.5							
			57	NEURUPPIN M/Y	(P)	136.3							
			82	ORANIENBURG M/Y	(P)	227.5							
			1	NEURUPPIN A/F	(O)	2.5							
1AD	B-17	289	137	BRANDENBURG M/Y	(P)	339.3		1	0	10	0	0	10
			66	SEDDIN M/Y	(P)	161.8							
			82	TREUENBRIETZEN M/Y	(P)	201.7							
2AD	B-24	223	56	ZWIESEL R/B & R/J	(P)	123.5		0	0	0	0	0	0
			53	MÜHLDORF M/Y & R/J	(P)	115.8							
			55	IRRENLOHE R/R & R/J	(P)	125.5							
			54	KLATOVY R/R & R/J	(P)	124.3							
			1	STRAUBING M/Y	(S)	.5							
	B-17	6	6	SCREENING FORCE				0	0	0	0	0	0
TOTALS:		837	809			1953.7	0	1	0	25	0	1	10

continued on facing page

	P-51	271	258	ESCORT 3AD				1				
	P-51	241	227	ESCORT 1AD				0				
	P-47 P-51	57 177	228	ESCORT 2AD				0				
	P-51	108	100	FREELANCE SUPPORT 2nd & 3rd TF			7–0–4	0				
	P-51	25	22	SCOUTING FORCES				0				
	P-51	11	11	ESCORT PR A/C				0				
TOTALS:		890	846				7–0–4	0			0	0	0

REMARKS: Attacks on rail targets in the Berlin area and Czechoslovakia. All bombing visual except at Brandenburg where combination of visual and GH techniques used. Bomb groups participating:– 1AD – 41CBW and 94CBW groups and 91BG, 381BG; 2AD – 2CBW and 20CBW groups and 44BG, 392BG, 458BG, 467BG; 3AD – 4CBW, 13CBW and 93CBW groups. Bomb group losses:– 401BG – 1.

All fighter groups operating. Fighter group e/a credits:– 355FG – 4.

OTHER OPERATIONS: 7PG despatched 11 F-5s on PR Germany (with escorts). 1 F-5 MIA. 25BG despatched 9 Mosquitoes 'chaff' screening for bombers, 1 Mosquito return *Skywave* flight from Italy. 1 Mosquito as monitor for 2AD, 3 Mosquitoes on WR North Sea/Norway/UK, and 4 B-17s Azores/Atlantic/UK. 5ERS despatched 8 P-47s and 2 OA-10s on ASR patrols. 36BS despatched 4 B-24s, 3 effective, on RCM. 2 P-51s, 1 B-17, 1 B-24 on radio-relays.

20/21 APRIL 1945

492BG despatched 12 B-24s, 12 effective, on *Carpetbagger* operations. Norway 2 B-24s MIA.

482BG despatched 3 B-17s on H2X PR Regensburg and Ingolstadt, and 1 B-17 on *Eagle* PR Ingolstadt. Leaflets dropped.

492BG despatched 2 Mosquitoes on special operation (*Red Stocking*).

21 APRIL 1945

8AF 963

	Despatched		Effective	Target		Bombs Tonnage	E/A	Losses MIA	E	Dam	Casualties KIA	WIA	MIA
1AD	B-17	113	111	MUNICH M/Y	(L)	290.8		0	1	5	0	0	0
2AD	B-24	186	0	SALZBURG M/Y & R/B		0		1	0	4	0	1	12
3AD	B-17	232	6	LANDSBERG/ AMLECH A/F	(S)	18.0		1	1	1	8	0	7
			212	INGOLSTADT TOWN	(L)	519.0							
	B-17	1	1	SCOUTING FORCE				0	0	0	0	0	0
TOTALS:		532	330			827.8	0	2	2	10	8	1	19
	P-51	90	90	ESCORT 1AD				0	1		0	0	0
	P-51	109	99	ESCORT 2AD				0	0		0	0	0
	P-51	160	144	ESCORT 3AD				2	0		0	0	2
	P-47	57	48	SWEEP–SUPPORT 2AD				0	0		0	0	0
	P-51	5	4	ESCORT PR A/C				0	0		0	0	0
	P-51	23	23	SCOUTING FORCES				0	0		0	0	0
TOTALS:		444	408				0	2	1	?	0	0	2

REMARKS: Airfields associated with jet fighter use and rail targets in SE Germany. 1AD force bombed using H2X; 2AD abandoned mission due to 10/10 cloud over assigned targets; 3AD bombed Landsberg A/F visually and Ingolstadt using H2X. Bomb groups participating:– 1CBW groups of 1AD; 20CBW groups and 389BG, 466BG, 467BG of 2AD; 4CBW and 45CBW groups of 3AD. Bomb group losses:– 2AD – 466BG – 1; 3AD – 94BG – 1. On return 398BG B-17 cr. landing base. B/d 452BG B-17 cr. Continent, 8 k.

Fighter groups operating: 4FG, 20FG, 55FG, 56FG, 78FG, 355FG, 357FG. Fighter group losses:– 78FG – 2.

OTHER OPERATIONS: 7PG despatched 3 F-5s on PR Germany (with escorts). 25BG despatched 5 Mosquitoes 'chaff' screening for 1AD, 1 Mosquito to Italy for *Skywave* operations. 3 Mosquitoes on WR Czechoslovakia/Germany/Cherbourg, and 4 B-17s on WR Azores/Atlantic/UK. 5ERS despatched 8 P-47s and 2 OA-10s on ASR patrols. 2 B-17s and 1 B-24 on radio-relays.

21/22 APRIL 1945

8AF 964 NGHT LEAFLET OPERATION

NLS despatched 11 B-24s, 10 effective; France, Holland, Germany.

492BG despatched 2 Mosquitoes on *Red Stocking* operation Germany.

22 APRIL 1945

25BG despatched 2 Mosquitoes on WR Denmark and North Sea, and 3 B-17s Azores/Atlantic/UK.

25BG *Skywave* Mosquito to UK from Italy.

22/23 APRIL 1945

8AF 965 NIGHT LEAFLET OPERATION

NLS despatched 10 B-24s, 10 effective; France, Holland, Germany.

492BG despatched 12 B-24s, 4 effective, on *Carpetbagger* operations Norway.

482BG despatched 1 B-17 and 1 B-24 on *Eagle* scope PR Regensburg, 1 B-17 on *Eagle* scope PR Mannheim and 2 B-17s on H2X scope PR Munich, leaflets dropped.

23 APRIL 1945

25BG despatched 3 Mosquitoes on WR Norway/Denmark/North Sea, and 4 B-17s on WR Azores/Atlantic/UK. 1 B-17 flew a PR mission over the Continent. 36BS despatched 4 B-24s on RCM.

23/24 APRIL 1945

8AF 966 NIGHT LEAFLET OPERATION

NLS despatched 1 B-17 and 12 B-24s; France, Holland, Germany.

492BG despatched 14 B-24s on *Carpetbagger* operations Denmark.

482BG despatched 1 B-17 and 1 B-24 on *Eagle* PR and 2 B-17s on H2X PR Ingolstadt and Regensburg. Leaflets dropped.

492BG despatched 2 Mosquitoes, 1 effective, on *Red Stocking* operation.

24 APRIL 1945

25BG despatched 2 Mosquitoes on WR Continent/North Sea/Atlantic, and 4 B-17s on WR Azores/Atlantic/UK. 5ERS despatched 4 P-47s and 1 OA-10 on ASR patrols.

24/25 APRIL 1945

8AF 967 NIGHT LEAFLET OPERATION

NLS despatched 11 B-24s, 11 effective; France, Holland, Germany.

482BG despatched 2 B-17s and 1 B-24 on Eagle scope PR Munich and Augsburg.

25BG despatched 2 Mosquitoes on navigational flights – Italy and S. Germany.
492BG despatched 1 Mosquito on *Red Stocking* – cr. Winchfield on return.

25 APRIL 1945

8AF 968

	Despatched		Effective	Target		Bombs Tonnage	E/A	Losses MIA	E	Dam	Casualties KIA	WIA	MIA
1AD	B-17	307	78	PILSEN A/F	(P)	189.0		6	4	180	0	8	42
			198	PILSEN SKODA M/I	(P)	526.0							
2AD	B-24	282	109	SALZBURG M/Y	(P)	250.9		0	0	20	0	1	0
			56	BAD REICHENHALL M/Y	(P)	140.1							
			57	HALLEIN M/Y	(P)	147.5							
			56	TRAUNSTEIN E/T	(P)	132.3							
TOTALS:		589	554			1385.8	0	6	4	200	0	9	42
	P-51	206	188	ESCORT 1AD				0					
	P-51	216	203	ESCORT 2AD			1–0–0	0					
	P-51	19	17	SWEEP PRAGUE LINZ AREA			0–1–0	1					
	P-51	98	88	SUPPORT-RAF BOMBERS				0					
	P-51	19	17	SCOUTING FORCES				0					
	P-51	4	4	ESCORT ASR				0					
	P-51	22	22	ESCORT PR A/C				0					
TOTALS:		584	539				1–1–0	1	0	?	0	0	0

REMARKS: Final 8AF heavy bomber mission of war – airfields and rail targets in Czechoslovakia and SE Germany. All bombing visual with H2X assists at Pilsen A/F. Bomb groups participating:– 1CBW and 41CBW groups and 92BG and 305BG of 1AD; all 2AD groups. Bomb group losses:– 92BG – 1, 303BG – 1, 305BG – 1, 384BG – 1, 398BG – 2. All losses to flak. B/d 305BG B-17 c/l France. B/d 91BG B-17 f/l Illesheim A/F – Cat E. 2 379BG B-17s collided due to b/d and cr. Allied held territory, 9 k.

Fighter groups not operating were 55FG, 56FG, 339FG, 359FG. Fighter group e/a credits:– 479FG – 1. Last e/a – an Ar 234 jet – credited to an 8AF Fighter pilot (1/Lt Hilton O. Thompson). 20FG P-51 pilot baled near Düsseldorf into area taken by US troops. Fighter group losses:– 4FG – 1, pilot evaded capture – last 8AF fighter MIA.

OTHER OPERATIONS: 7PG despatched 5 F-5s on PR Germany and Czechoslovakia (with escorts). 25BG despatched 5 Mosquitoes 'chaff' screening for 1AD, 8 Mosquitoes on WR Continent/North Sea/Atlantic/UK, and 4 B-17s on WR Azores/Atlantic/UK. 5ERS despatched 9 P-47s and 2 OA-10s on ASR patrols. 36BS despatched 3 B-24s on RCM. 2 B-17s, 1 B-24, 6 P-51s on radio-relays.

THE MAN WHO WOULDN'T QUIT

When, on the pleasant spring afternoon of 25 April, Pathfinder B-17 '588' touched down safely at Bassingbourn following an attack on Pilsen, the young man in the Aircraft Commander's seat was unaware that this had been the last combat mission he, or the 8th Air Force heavy bombers, would fly. For Lt.Col Immanuel J. Klette it was his 91st sortie over *Festung Europa* in the cockpit of a B-17, a total unsurpassed by any other US heavy bomber pilot. 'Manny' Klette had long been something of a living legend, a man pointed out as a symbol of confidence to recently arrived replacement crews who after a few rough missions considered their future bleak. On the other hand there were many veterans at Bassingbourn who thought Klette was chancing his luck too far in the dangerous sky over Europe; the law of averages, it was thought, would eventually work against him. But Klette kept on flying combat missions. He knew the odds well enough, having started back in 1943 when only one man in three had a chance of coming through a 25-mission tour. His faith in his own ability to master dangerous situations was a major factor in his persistence. He would quote a Latin motto: *Nam et ipsa scientia potestas est* – Knowledge itself is Power. In furtherance of this belief Klette had learned to know the B-17 inside out, what was likely to happen to control when particular systems failed or were damaged, and how to overcome the difficulties. He developed a practice of studying all operational material, not only pilot's but navigator's and bombardier's as well. His logic in being well informed was that it both improved the success of a mission and the survival of combatants. 'Manny' Klette's story is a justification of that belief.

US servicemen examine the wreckage of B-17F 42-3449, WW:X in an oak wood near Wing. The fuselage broke in two aft of the radio room. (I. Klette)

Son of a Lutheran minister who emigrated from Germany to the Middle West, this first generation American's Christian name was taken from the Bible, its meaning being 'God with us'. Academically brilliant, having completed one university degree and working towards another, patriotism came to the fore when the US entered the war, his father having instilled in him an understanding of the totalitarian nature of Nazism.

In February 1943 he was despatched to the UK as co-pilot on 2/Lt Keith Conley's crew and subsequently assigned to the oldest combat B-17 group in the theatre, the 306th at Thurleigh. At that time morale was generally low at this station as a tour of operations had yet to be officially established. Completion of combat was by failure to return from a mission, death, serious wounds, transfer to a ground job or other physical barriers to continue flying. However, the 369th Bomb Squadron, in which Conley and his men were placed, had incurred no losses in recent weeks. The crew was immediately split up to fill vacancies in experienced crews, Klette joining 1/Lt Ed Maliszewski, whose original co-pilot had been given his own bomber.

Klette got off to a rough start when at Vegesack on 18 March the 306th was engaged by fighters and FW 190s blasted through the formation so close to Klette's Fortress that he could clearly see the pilots in their oxygen masks. The 369th's run of luck continued and during the first four months of Klette's service with the squadron – when he flew on nearly every operation – it lost no bombers over enemy territory. A tour of 25 missions was introduced during this period and Capt Maliszewski became one of the first pilots in the group to reach this figure and return home. Klette, with 10 missions under his belt, then re-joined his old pilot, Keith Conley, and went on to fly another 11 missions from the right seat. While he had seen plenty of action and harrowing sights, for him the most disturbing incident occurred on the 28 June mission to St.Nazaire. Persistent fighter attacks were directed at the rear of the formation but without any known hits on their bomber. Once out over the Bay of Biscay, Klette made the usual co-pilot's check of each crew member by calling over the interphone. No response was received from tail gunner Sgt Daley, who was on his 25th and last sortie. Klette went back to investigate where he could see Daley sitting over his guns. He put a hand on the gunner's shoulders and was about to say something to him when the upper part of Daley's body fell back into Klette's arms. With the help of a waist gunner he got Dailey out of the turret and back into the radio room but the gunner was dead, a bullet through his heart.

Late in July Klette was made a first pilot and given his own crew and a B-17F which he named *Connecticut Yankee*. He was sorry to leave the old crew and on his first mission with his own command, he was grieved that Conley's B-17 was one of two lost by the 369th Bomb Squadron that day – its first loss for 42 consecutive missions.

Having previously flown the Schweinfurt raid, Villacoublay airfield in France seemed by comparison a 'milk run' for Klette's 25th and final mission for the required tour. The reverse was to be the case. As the group entered its bombing run, accurate flak

Gen Gross, Manny Klette and Charlie Hudson pose beneath the 324BS leadplane after the highly successful mission of 14 March 1945. Maj Hudson, 91BG Group Bombardier, also had a considerable number of missions to his credit and earned a DSC over Anklam in October 1943. (I. Klette)

burst around damaging all but one of the 18 aircraft in formation. A shell exploded close to *Connecticut Yankee*'s No.4 engine which had to be feathered as they continued across the target. The same burst also put fragments into No.3 engine and this faltered and had to be shut down. Another shell had sent splinters into the nose and ball turrets causing more damage and wounding the ball gunner in the hand. With both engines stilled one side control was difficult, as Klette struggled to keep close to the formation knowing the fate of stragglers. The increase in power necessary to keep pace brought the right wing up and *Connecticut Yankee* continued on her way with a 45 degree list. The waist gunners were ordered into the radio room to keep weight forward and over the Channel ammunition and all other movable items were thrown out. If Klette could get the aircraft back to England he reasoned he would have a better chance by landing at Thurleigh rather than make an approach to a strange field. *Connecticut Yankee* was down to about 2,500 ft when Thurleigh finally came into view. Other B-17s were in the pattern so Klette did a gentle right hand orbit and line-up for the runway. At this crucial moment No.1 engine burst intc flames – probably through overstrain. As the co-pilot shut down No.1 a voice was heard over the radio from the control tower: 'Bale out, Klette, bale out.' The warning came from Col George Robinson, the Group CO. Undaunted, 'Manny' Klette still believed his best course of action was to try to land and with a superb display of skill succeeded, despite a flat tyre and the remaining engine losing power just after touch-down.

Prior to this mission Klette had applied to his Squadron and thence Group Commander for permission to fly another tour. This rare request was engendered by Klette's love of flying, his absorbing interest in the work of the 8th Air Force bombers, and his burning desire to help successfully to terminate the war in Europe. After a week's leave in Scotland he returned to Thurleigh to learn that Col Robinson had granted him permission to fly another five missions with the 306th. Klette was fated to fly only three of the five.

On 23 September 1943 the Group went to Nantes. The raid was despatched late in the day and bombing was carried out near sunset. As *Connecticut Yankee* was still under repair the Klette crew were in a borrowed Fortress. They were leading the high squadron when flak burst below the aircraft and a fragment hit Klette in the left shin bone. Damage was also done to the bomb bay doors which would not close, causing considerable drag. After leaving the target Klette noticed that one of the fuel tanks was quite low, having been holed and failing to self-seal. As the English coast was neared it became evident that there was insufficient fuel to reach home base and that both Nos.3 and 4 engines would have to be shut down. Leaving formation at dusk, a homing was called for and given – to the RAF airfield at Wing. The fuel situation became critical and the crew took up crash-landing positions in the radio room. Shortly afterwards Klette was forced to feather No.1 engine. No longer able to maintain altitude a rapid descent began from 2,000 ft and with landing lights turned on. Low cloud was encountered and Klette had to fly on instruments until they emerged. He could then see they were down to about 100 feet and flying into a series of valleys. Checking his descent momentarily, he observed directly ahead a large wooded area. There was now little in the way of options but to stall out in the tree tops. Unfortunately the initial impact involved a large oak which severed the left wing and brought the fuselage smashing down through other oaks onto the ground. The cockpit area was severely smashed and Klette knew he was badly injured but managed to drag himself out of the aircraft. Unknown to Klette, the navigator, Lt Madden, anxious to help locate an airfield, had remained in the nose and was trapped there in the crash. RAF personnel from Wing, half a mile away, were soon on the scene and extricated him; he had eight fractures; Klette had five. The rest of the crew escaped with only bruises and scratches.

The injured men were removed to the RAF Halton Hospital at Aylesbury where it was found Klette had fractures to pelvis and upper leg bones in addition to several cuts and bruises and his flak wound. His ability to walk properly again was in question: as far as the medical authorities were concerned, Klette's war was over. But 'Manny' had other ideas. In November 1943 after transfer to the US 2nd General Hospital in Oxford, he indicated to doctors that whatever the outcome of his treatment he preferred to remain in England rather than be returned to the US. Recuperation took time, but he was soon hobbling around the ward.

One of his wardmates at Oxford was 2/Lt Ted Shultz, whose stepfather was Ambassador Anthony Drexel Biddle. In the later stages of convalescence Shultz invited Klette to go with him to meet his mother and stepfather in London. Here Klette was introduced to Col Allen, Deputy Intelligence Officer at the recently formed USSTAF Headquarters. Klette mentioned his intention of remaining in England and that while he hoped he might eventually return to flying duties he expressed a desire to be involved in operational planning. Arising from this conversation, Col Allen arranged for Klette to join the Operations Section at USSTAF on release from the hospital. The day arrived in February 1944 and moving to Bushey Park Klette became actively engaged in the preparation of briefing for General Spaatz and senior staff. Later he became a briefing officer. During his time with USSTAF he absorbed a great deal of information on enemy capabilities, tactics and equipment, which helped to give him a much better appreciation of the problems confronting the heavy bomber offensive. He also worked on air matters for the 'Overlord Plan' – the cross-channel invasion. As his strength increased and he regained full use of his legs, Klette was reinstated on flying status and thereafter his thoughts turned towards a return to combat missions. An opportunity arose when he learned that his old squadron CO and former Group Executive at Thurleigh, Col Henry Terry, who had taken command of the 91st Group at Bassingbourn, was looking for a combat experienced officer to command one of his units. A transfer could not be permitted until approximately two months after D-Day, because of Klette's association with the plan and the risk to security should he be shot down and captured.

It was late July 1944 before his release came through and he was assigned – on the 30th – to command the 324th 'Wild Hare' Bomb Squadron at Bassingbourn. The 324th was a pathfinder unit operating H2X equipped B-17s and it now had a commander who was probably the most knowledgeable combat pilot in the whole 8th Air Force.

Lt.Col Klette in a familiar perch, July 1945. Last 91BG pilot to leave Bassingbourn he commanded the air echelon until disbanded at Drew Field. (I. Klette)

Capt Klette's first mission with his new command was to Brandenburg on 6 August, when he discovered that the B-17G was a heavier aircraft than the F models he had flown the previous year and so requiring higher power setting. He also found that the electronic supercharger controls were an advance on the oil regulated type of the old model Fortresses, giving faster reponse to power changes. The 324th CO had his own theories about several aspects of mission procedure, developed as a result of his observation at USSTAF. He held that a key tactic to good bombing was to plan the approach to the Initial Point in such a manner that when the formation passed over this landmark it was already on the briefed heading to bomb. The advantage lay in placing the bombardier, navigator and radar operator in a position to more easily monitor check points along the bomb run and thus pinpoint the target, than if turning in towards the target from a different heading. The disadvantage, of course, was that a lengthy straight and level bomb run would result, giving German anti-aircraft gunners more time and better opportunity to put an accurate barrage into the formation. At Ludwigshaven on 8 September Klette put this into practice for the 54 mile run to the target with need for only 2 degrees correction culminating in an excellent strike on target from 25,000 ft. Unfortunately a strong headwind arrested speed, an opportunity, coupled with the straight bomb run, which flak gunners did not miss, resulting in extensive flak damage to 29 of the 37 91st B-17s with one man killed and nine wounded.

The German oil industry was protected by formidable flak installations of which the most notorious was Merseburg/Leuna. On 21 November Klette led the entire 8th Air Force to this target through deteriorating weather in almost constant radio contact with his friend, Lt.Col Allison Brooks, Commander and leader that day of the 1st Scouting Force. Klette made a coded request that Brooks check the weather over the target area below the assigned bombing altitude. The ensuing coded conversation between the two combat veterans resulted in Klette's election to take his formation down from the assigned 27,000 ft to 17,000 ft to attack. The results were considered the most destructive ever achieved by the 8th Air Force at this much repaired target.

In Klette's opinion the prime factor in the creation of a good lead crew was combat experience; the best formation control, route discipline and accurate bombing was achieved by men with a score or more missions behind them. Few of his current command had run theirs into double figures. When the squadron bombed the wrong target and on another occasion led a formation into a fighter ambush by wandering off course, he felt a deep responsibility even though not directly involved. While he obviously had to delegate he nevertheless flew every mission he could, particularly those to difficult targets, believing in his ability to do the job accurately while incurring the minimum losses. Although he was already well versed on enemy defences from his studies at USSTAF, other members of his squadron noticed that he always studied the current intelligence reports and briefing data longer and far more thoroughly than any other pilot on the base. In fact 'Manny' Klette always had a mental picture of the current flak and fighter situation on the map of Germany. He varied the routes when he led to avoid obvious and suspected flak traps. He also developed a procedure for evading the radar-controlled barrages by timing 7 seconds after bomb release and then turning slowly left or right into a very steep bank. This and other tactics certainly paid off for in the 30 missions where he flew the lead group pathfinder only two B-17s were lost from that formation.

This personal concern to see the job performed with expertise was given added impetus by what occurred on a Berlin mission early in February 1945. Lt.Col Marvin Lord, 91st Group Operations Officer, had never been to Berlin and asked if he might take Klette's place in the lead plane. Despite Lord's higher rank Maj Klette was loath to let any pilot, however skilled, lead his most experienced crew so the matter was dropped. Because of deteriorating conditions the mission was cancelled before take-off and with the weather man predicting no improvement over the next 24 hours, Klette decided to leave for London to keep a dinner engagement that evening. In the unlikely event of the cloud dispersing and the mission being reinstated on the morrow he arranged that Marvin Lord could serve as Aircraft Commander with the lead crew. The forecasters were wrong and next day, 3 February, the Berlin mission was flown. The lead 91st aircraft took a direct flak hit in the waist shortly after bombs away and spun down in two parts. Of the 11 man crew the radio operator was on his 79th mission, the engineer on his 81st and the ball turret gunner – who had previously flown in the Pacific war – on his 108th. Klette took this to heart, not only due to the loss of friends and men he had built into one of the best lead teams in the Eighth, but because he felt that had he been in the Aircraft Commander's seat and made the usual sharp turn off target the flak barrage might have been avoided. From then on Klette was more determined than ever to fly on missions to difficult or important targets. This personal conviction in his ability to do the job better than those around might have been seen as conceit in some other situation but in these dangerous circumstances it instilled confidence in those other crews who followed his lead: if 'Manny Klette was 'up front' the right action would be taken whatever contingencies arose. This was cogently proven at Vlotho where a rail bridge spanning the Weser sped supplies to the Wehrmacht. On 14 March 1st Combat Wing was sent to smash it with the 91st Group in the lead. Brig.Gen William Gross rode as Aircraft Commander in the Pathfinder, with Klette as pilot. Visibility was poor and there was a profusion of Fortresses in the Vlotho area as groups, heading for another target, missed their timing. These formations obstructed the 91st bomb run causing Maj Hudson, the Group Bombardier, and Klette to decide on a 360-degree turn and another run. Photo reconnaissance the following day confirmed that the bridge was put out of use by the strikes obtained and Klette received his third DFC for the tricky task of manoeuvring the combat wing formations for this second and successful pass at the target.

His friend and boss, Col Terry, became concerned about Klette's appetite for combat: 'We had a rotation policy wherein the squadron commander would fly when that particular squadron was leading the group as combat wing or division lead. "Manny" would take his prescribed turns at leading the group but would also go on missions whenever his squadron flew. He did this so consistently I felt he wasn't paying enough attention to the administration of his squadron or attending enough staff meetings. I asked him to stay on the ground more but he still continued to go. I got my dander up and *ordered* him only to go when his turn to lead came up. He still went. What the hell are you going to do with a man like that? He'd give me that ready smile and all I could do was chew him out and let him go.' Col Terry was, of course, an ardent admirer of Klette and long aware of his abilities, knowledge and courage. He also knew him as a man who played hard too, a great practical joker and one – as Terry put it – 'who participated in all the extra-curricular activities that combat personnel seem so adept at practising'.

People would ask 'Manny' Klette when he was going to quit chancing his luck with Hitler's flak and fighters. 'When the war's over, I guess', he would reply. And when hostilities did cease it was hard to believe that this serious, cheerful 27-year-old was someone extraordinary. He bore no visible signs of having faced possible death 91 times or of shouldering the responsibility of leadership on 73 of these occasions. 'Manny' Klette had long ago learned to live with fear, to sublimate it with his conviction that he was needed to help win the war. There was no bravado, no seeking after records, just this intangible desire to get the job done. There were other distinguished veterans who felt the same way.

In addition to completing 91 combat missions, 'Manny' Klette also flew seven missions that were recalled before the enemy coast. His total combat flying time was 689 hours, 25 minutes. A formidable record by any standard.

25/26 APRIL 1945

8AF 969 NIGHT LEAFLET OPERATION

NLS despatched 11 B-24s, 11 effective; France, Holland, Germany.

492BG despatched 12 B-24s and 1 A-26 (7 a/c effective) on *Carpetbagger* operations Norway and 1 Mosquito on *Red Stocking* operation Germany.

482BG despatched 1 B-17 on *Eagle* scope PR Munich.

26 APRIL 1945

7PG despatched 3 F-5s on PR Germany and Czechoslovakia with 9 P-51s (1 aborted) as escorts. 25BG despatched 1 Mosquito on *Skywave* flight from Italy. 8 Mosquitoes on WR Continent/North Sea, and 4 B-17s on WR Azores/Atlantic/UK. 5ERS despatched 3 P-47s and 1 OA-10 on ASR patrols – OA-10 rescued crew of German 2-man submarine off The Hague. 4 P-51s also on ASR search for RAF personnel with 2 P-47s as radio-relays.

26/27 APRIL 1945

8AF 970 NIGHT LEAFLET OPERATION

NLS despatched 8 B-24s, 6 effective; France, Holland, Germany. 1 B-24 cr. after t/o near Leamington Spa.

492BG despatched 2 B-24s on *Carpetbagger* operations.

27 APRIL 1945

25BG despatched 2 Mosquitoes on WR Continent, and 4 B-17s on WR Azores/Atlantic/UK.

27/28 APRIL 1945

492BG despatched 1 Mosquito on *Red Stocking* operation.

28 APRIL 1945

25BG despatched 1 Mosquito on WR North Sea/UK, and 4 B-17s on WR Azores/Atlantic/UK.

28/29 APRIL 1945

492BG despatched 1 Mosquito on *Red Stocking* operation.

29 APRIL 1945

8AF 971 LEAFLET OPERATION

8 B-17s despatched to France, Holland, Germany.

25BG despatched 1 Mosquito on WR North Sea, and 4 B-17s on WR Azores/Atlantic/UK. 5ERS despatched 1 OA-10 on ASR patrol.

EVENT

The last 8th Air Force bomber sorties despatched to a target in Germany were those of the 482nd Bomb Group on the night of 29 April 1945. A single B-17 and B-24 were involved, both equipped with the new AN/APQ-7 Eagle radar, which featured a transverse sweeping scanner housed in an aerofoil shaped cover under the forward fuselage. The mission was to obtain radarscope photographs of Kiel harbour which only the B-17, '990', succeeded in obtaining, the B-24 '283' being forced to turn back when the radar was found not to be functioning properly.

29/30 APRIL 1945

482BG despatched 1 B-17 and 1 B-24 on *Eagle* scope PR Kiel, the B-24 aborted.

492BG despatched 1 Mosquito on *Red Stocking* operation.

30 APRIL 1945

8AF 972 LEAFLET OPERATION

7B-17s despatched, 6 effective; Holland, France.

25BG despatched 2 Mosquitoes (1 aborted) on experimental navigation flights, and 4 B-17s on WR Azores/Atlantic/UK.

1 MAY 1945

8AF 973 SUPPLY MISSION

	Despatched		Effective	Target	Food Tonnage
3AD	B-17	396	77	VOLKENBURG/ THE HAGUE	149.3
			79	HAGUE RACE TRACK	153.1
			81	YPENBURG/THE HAGUE	161.0
			155	ROTTERDAM	313.7

REMARKS: Food dropping mission to The Hague and Rotterdam flown by 13CBW, 45CBW and 93CBW groups of 3AD.

OTHER OPERATIONS: 3SF despatched 4 B-17s and 1 P-51 as weather scouts for B-17 force. 25BG despatched 1 Mosquito to Italy for *Skywave* operations. 2 Mosquitoes on WR Continent/UK and 4 B-17s on WR Azores/Atlantic/UK. 5ERS despatched 1 B-17 and 1 OA-10 on ASR patrols.

1/2 MAY 1945

8AF 974 NIGHT LEAFLET OPERATION

NLS despatched 5 B-24s, 4 effective; Germany.

25BG Mosquito on *Skywave* sortie Germany.

2 MAY 1945

8AF 975 SUPPLY MISSION

	Despatched		Effective	Target	Food Tonnage
3AD	B-17	401	250	SCHIPOL A/F	491.7
			40	VOGELENZANG	79.0
			20	ALKMAAR A/F	33.5
			20	HILVERSUM	40.5
			59	UTRECHT	115.4
			4	T/O	7.0

REMARKS: Food dropping mission to Holland flown by 13CBW, 45CBW and 93CBW groups of 3AD. 4 B-17s of 385BG damaged by 20 mm fire which ceased immediately green flare fired.

OTHER OPERATIONS: 25BG despatched 25BG *Skywave* Mosquito to UK from Italy. 4 Mosquitoes on WR Continent/UK, and 4 B-17s on WR Azores/Atlantic/UK. 5ERS despatched 2 P-47s and 1 B-17 on ASR patrols.

8AF 976 LEAFLET OPERATION

8 B-17s despatched; France, Holland, Germany. 9 P-51s despatched as escort.

2/3 MAY 1945

492BG despatched 1 Mosquito on *Red Stocking* operation.

25BG Mosquito on *Skywave* sortie W. Germany.

3 MAY 1945

8AF 977

	Despatched		Effective	Target	Food Tonnage
3AD	B-17	399	251	SCHIPOL A/F	472.5
			42	VOGELENZANG (OPEN SPACE)	76.7
			20	ALKMAAR A/F	37.7
			21	HILVERSUM (OPEN SPACE)	37.7
			58	UTRECHT (W EDGE OF)	108.8
			3	T/O	5.7

REMARKS: Food dropping mission Holland flown by 13CBW, 45CBW and 93CBW groups of 3AD.

OTHER OPERATIONS: 3SF despatched 2 B-17s and 1 P-51 as weather scouts for 3AD mission. 25BG despatched 2 Mosquitoes on *Red Stocking* operations Holland and Germany, 6 Mosquitoes on WR Continent/North Sea/Atlantic/UK, and 3 B-17s on WR Azores/Atlantic/UK. 5ERS despatched 3 OA-10s on ASR patrols.

8AF 978 LEAFLET OPERATION

14 B-17s despatched, 14 effective; Germany.

47P-51s despatcned, 43 effective as escort.

4 MAY 1945

25BG despatched 1 Mosquito on *Skywave* flight Holland and Germany, 3 Mosquitoes on WR Continent/UK, and 3 B-17s on WR Azores/Atlantic/UK.

4/5 MAY 1945

8AF 978 NIGHT LEAFLET OPERATION

NLS despatched 1 B-17 and 8 B-24s (7 a/c effective); France, Holland, Germany.

5 MAY 1945

8AF 980

	Despatched		Effective	Target	Food Tonnage
3AD	B-17	403	261	SCHIPOL A/F	480.6
			40	VOGELENZANG	75.4
			60	UTRECHT (W EDGE OF)	113.1
			16	N. OF HILVERSUM	30.2
			21	ALKMAAR	37.7
			4	OTHER TARGETS	7.5

REMARKS: Food dropping mission to Holland flown by 13CBW, 45CB, and 93CBW groups of 3AD.

OTHER OPERATIONS: 3SF despatched 5 B-17 and 1 P-51 as weather scouts for 3AD mission. 25BG despatched 1 Mosquito on *Skywave* flight Continent, 3 Mosquitoes on WR Continent/UK, and 4 B-17s on WR Azores/Atlantic/UK. 5ERS despatched 2 OA-10s on ASR patrols and 4 P-51s also on ASR patrols. 5 P-47s on radio-relays off Den Helder.

6 MAY 1945

8AF 981

	Despatched		Effective	Target	Food Tonnage
3AD	B-17	383	249	SCHIPOL A/F	454.3
			37	VOGELENZANG (E OF)	61.8
			59	UTRECHT (W OF)	111.2
			18	HILVERSUM (N OF)	32.1
			18	ALKMAAR A/F	33.9

REMARKS: Food dropping mission to Holland flown by 13CBW, 45CBW and 93CBW groups of 3AD.

OTHER OPERATIONS: 3SF despatched 3 B-17s and 1 P-51 as weather scouts for 3AD mission. 25BG despatched 1 Mosquito on WR UK, and 3 B-17s on WR Azores/Atlantic/UK. 5ERS despatched 1 B-17 on ASR patrol.

8AF 982 LEAFLET OPERATION

15 B-17s despatched France and Germany with 26 364FG P-51s despatched, 8 effective, as escort (18 P-51s could not locate B-17s).

6/7 MAY 1945

8AF 983 NIGHT LEAFLET OPERATION

NLS despatched 10 B-24s, 10 effective; France, Holland, Channel Islands.

452BG's *Virginia* unloads food boxes at Schipol airfield on 6 May.

7 MAY 1945

8AF 984

	Despatched		Effective	Target	Food Tonnage
3AD	B-17	231	154	SCHIPOL A/F	285.6
			25	VOGELENZANG	46.2
			28	UTRECHT (W OF)	52.8
			12	HILVERSUM (N OF)	22.6
			10	ALKMAAR A/F	18.8

REMARKS: Food dropping mission to Holland flown by 34BG, 96BG, 100BG, 385BG, 390BG, 493BG. 1 B-17 shot at by German troops and damaged. 95BG B-17 ditched after engine fire, 2 rescued.

OTHER OPERATIONS: 7 PG despatched 7 F-5s on PR Germany. 25BG despatched 4 B-17s on WR Azores/Atlantic/UK. 3SF despatched 2 B-17s as weather scouts for 3AD mission to Holland. 5ERS despatched 5 OA-10s on ASR patrols. 1 B-17 despatched on special operation over Holland. 1 B-17 despatched on radio-relays.

8AF 985 LEAFLET OPERATION

15 B-17s despatched, 15 effective; Germany. 32 P-51s despatched, 30 P-51s effective as escort.

At the end of hostilities *Eagle* radar B-17s were transferred from 482BG to 96BG which remained in Europe for some months. The distinctive scanner aerofoil is displayed by the latter unit's *Rugged But Right*. Object on ground is a covered auxiliary motor. (via G. Ward)

The US armoured division that captured Schweinfurt presented the Nazi flag flying at the bearing works to the 8AF group that suffered the highest losses at this target. Men of the 305BG were certainly appreciative.

8 MAY 1945

8AF 986 LEAFLET OPERATION

306BG 12 B-17s despatched, 12 effective; Germany.

OTHER OPERATIONS: 7PG despatched 11 F-5s on damage assessment PR Germany. 25BG despatched 5 B-17s on WR Azores/Atlantic/UK.

With peace aircraft could be parked in convenient locations and not spread far and wide round an airfield perimeter. 434FS at Wattisham managed to get over half its Mustangs on this hard standing cluster at Wattisham.

On 1 August the remaining 8AF bases were opened to the public. At Thorpe Abbotts small boys were in their element inspecting Capt Tower's P-51D adorned with 20 victories. (J. Archer)

INDEX

Index of Continental place names (wartime spelling)

United Kingdom Place Names with county locations (abbreviated)

8th Air Force Personnel

Other Persons, Military and Civilian